THE
BOER WAR

Front Endpaper:
Invading the Orange Free State. The Guards Brigade – part of Lord
Roberts's invasion force of 43,000 men with 117 guns – ford the Zand
River, 10 May 1900.

Back Endpaper:
'The Camp for Undesirables.' One of the British concentration camps in
which 20,000 Boers and 12,000 Africans, mainly women and children,
died of epidemics caused by neglect.

THE
BOER WAR

Thomas Pakenham

WEIDENFELD AND NICOLSON
LONDON

First published in Great Britain by
Weidenfeld and Nicolson Limited
91 Clapham High Street, London SW4

ISBN 0 297 77395 X

Set, printed and bound in Great Britain by
Cox and Wyman Ltd,
London, Fakenham and Reading

For Val, in gratitude once again.

And to the memory of the war veterans who told me what it was like to be there

'Look back over the pages of history; consider the feelings with which we now regard wars that our forefathers in their time supported ... see how powerful and deadly are the fascinations of passion and of pride.'

W. E. Gladstone, 26 November 1879, condemning the first annexation of the Transvaal

Contents

PART II BULLER'S REVERSE

Illustrations

Cartoons

Maps

Introduction

The war declared by the Boers on 11 October 1899 gave the British, in Kipling's famous phrase, 'no end of a lesson'. The British public expected it to be over by Christmas. It proved to be the longest (two and three-quarter years), the costliest (over £200 million), the bloodiest (at least twenty-two thousand British, twenty-five thousand Boer and twelve thousand African lives) and the most humiliating war for Britain between 1815 and 1914.

I decided to try to tell the story of this last great (or infamous) imperial war, taking as my raw material the first-hand, and largely unpublished, accounts provided by contemporaries.

It was an ambitious idea, to base the book largely on manuscript (and oral) sources. No one had made the attempt for seventy years. In the decade after 1902, the public suffered a barrage of Boer War books. This culminated in a bombardment from the Long Toms, as it were: the seven-volume *Times History of the War in South Africa* (1900–1909), edited by Leo Amery, and the eight-volume (Official) *History of the War in South Africa* (1906–1910), edited by General Maurice and others. These two massive works have dominated Boer War studies, and will remain indispensable to the historian. They incorporate, often anonymously, a vast mass of original material.

Understandably, as they were completed seventy years ago, both have their limitations.

In due course I began to read the confidential War Office files – those that survived a bizarre decision to 'weed' them in the 1950s – the files on which much of Amery's and Maurice's work had been based. I was also fortunate enough to be able to dig up, often in odd places, the private papers of most of the generals and politicians on the British side. So there was no shortage of new raw material. I stumbled on the lost archives of Sir Redvers Buller, the British Commander-in-Chief in 1899 – battle letters of Buller's which had remained hidden under the billiard table at Downes, his house in Devon, and in Lord Lansdowne's muniment room at Bowood; I sifted through the trunk-loads of Lord Roberts's papers rescued by the National Army Museum from the care of his most recent biographer, David James (who claims to have burnt every scrap of paper Lord Roberts ever wrote to his wife); I discovered a *Secret Journal* of the war, written by the War Office Intelligence Department, running to nearly a million words; I saw the private papers of the War Minister, Lord Lansdowne, and other members of Lord Salisbury's Cabinet. And I traced over a hundred unseen sets of letters and diaries, written by British officers and men who served in the war; these were generously lent to me by their descendants.

I was also privileged to capture on my tape-recorder the memories of fifty-two men who had actually fought in the war, the youngest of whom was eighty-six when I tracked him down.

These forays into the past were exciting and rewarding in themselves. And through them I came to see what I believe to be the main limitations of Amery's *Times History* and Maurice's *Official History*.

The *Times History* says too much. An eloquent narrative of the war, Amery's volumes (especially the first three, of which he wrote a large part himself) also represent what he calls an 'argument' – many sided but always partisan. Amery was a disciple of Milner, the man chiefly responsible for making the war. Amery was also caught up in the movement for Army Reform, and committed to one side in the struggle between the two factions in the British Army (the Roberts Ring and the Wolseley Ring) which fought the Boers in the intervals between fighting each other.

The *Official History* says too little. All its political chapters were eliminated in draft by the Colonial Secretary, Alfred Lyttelton, for fear of offending the ex-enemy, the Boers – that is, for fear of 'impeding the process of reconciliation', as he recorded in a confidential minute. And, for fear of offending their friends, the War Office staff found it equally impossible to write frankly about many of the 'regrettable incidents' which occurred in the war.

Moreover both the *Times History* and the *Official History* share one central weakness. Few sources from the Boer side of the hill, official or private, were available to their authors.

I have been extremely fortunate in the help I have received from modern South African historians. I owe a great debt to Godfrey Le May's incisive study *British Supremacy in South Africa, 1899–1907*. I have also borrowed freely from the work in Afrikaans of the Transvaal State Archivist, Dr J. H. Breytenbach, who has already completed four volumes of his monumental history of the war, based on the state archives, *Die Geskiedenis van die Tweede Vryheidsoorlog*. I have plundered many other works in Afrikaans, especially Dr J. A. Mouton's study of Joubert, and Professor Johann Barnard's seminal work on Botha, *Botha op die Natalse Front, 1899–1900*.

Among the new themes in this story I should like to emphasize four in particular.

First, there is a thin, golden thread running through the narrative, a thread woven by the 'gold bugs': the Rand millionaires who controlled the richest gold mines in the world. It has been hitherto assumed by historians that none of the gold bugs was directly concerned in making the war. But directly concerned they were. Owing to the great generosity of Sir Alfred Beit, and the directors of the Johannesburg firm of Barlow-Rand, I have had free access to the political papers of Ecksteins, the Rand subsidiary controlled, at the time of the Boer War, by Alfred Beit and Julius Wernher. I have found evidence here of an informal alliance between Sir Alfred Milner, the British High

Commissioner, and the firm of Wernher-Beit, the dominant Rand mining house. It was this secret alliance, I believe, that gave Milner the strength to precipitate the war.

Second, there is a broader strand in the story involving Sir Redvers Buller, who has passed into folklore as the symbol of all that was most fatuous in the late-Victorian British army. 'Nobody in their senses,' a distinguished modern historian, Julian Symons, has written, 'could possibly try to justify Buller's military actions during the Natal campaign.' I have made the attempt. At any rate I believe that Buller's mishaps – and mistakes – must be seen in the context of the feud between the Roberts Ring and the Wolseley/Buller Ring. St John Brodrick, who became British War Minister in 1900, later compared the wrangles between Lord Roberts and Sir Redvers Buller to those between Lord Lucan and Lord Cardigan which precipitated the Charge of the Light Brigade. Certainly this astonishing War Office feud at the end of the nineteenth century explains much that would otherwise be inexplicable in Britain's bungled preparations for war and her reverses during it. And in the end it was Buller, to his credit, who successfully hammered out the new tactics needed when a nineteenth-century army had to fight a twentieth-century war.

A third strand to the story involves the invisible majority of South Africans: the blacks. Contemporaries talked of the Boer War as a 'gentleman's war' and a 'white man's war'. No generalization could be more misleading. From digging in the War Office files, and talking to war veterans, one comes to realize what an important part in the war was played by Africans. Officially absent from the armies of both sides, perhaps as many as a hundred thousand were enrolled to serve British and Boers as labourers, drivers, guides and so on. By the end of the war, nearly ten thousand Africans were serving under arms in the British forces. Many non-combatants were flogged by the Boers or shot. In Mafeking alone, more than two thousand of the African garrison under the orders of Baden-Powell, were shot by the Boers or left by Baden-Powell to die of starvation. In general it was the Africans who had to pay the heaviest price in the war and its aftermath.

A fourth strand involves the plight of the Boer civilians, women and children caught up in the guerrilla war. To deny the guerrillas food and intelligence, Lord Kitchener ordered the British army to sweep the veld clean. The farms were burnt, the stock looted, the women and children concentrated in camps along the railway lines. Between twenty thousand and twenty-eight thousand Boer civilians died of epidemics in these 'concentration camps'. I have found much new evidence that Kitchener's methods of warfare, like the ruthless methods adopted by many modern armies against guerrillas, were self-defeating. The removal of civilians added to the bitterness of the guerrillas. It also freed them from trying to feed and protect their families. But whether or not Kitchener's methods succeeded as a military policy, they proved a gigantic political blunder. The conscience of Britain was stirred by the holocaust in the camps, just as the conscience of America was stirred by the holocaust in Vietnam. And if the guerrillas in South Africa lost the war, they won the peace.

It is a pleasure, after eight years of vicarious warfare, to be able to acknowledge the generosity of numerous people in Britain and South Africa who have helped me reach the peace.

I am deeply grateful to the following owners of important family papers (listed in the references at the back of this book) who have allowed me to quote from copyright and unpublished material in their care: the Marquess of Lansdowne, the Marquess of Salisbury, the Earl Haig, Lord Allenby, Lady Lucas, Lord Methuen, the late Captain Michael Buller, the late Miss Daisy Bigge, Brigadier Shamus Hickie, Myles Hildyard, Owen Keane, Major Trotter, Harry Oppenheimer, Mrs Rosemary Parker, Mrs Frances Pym (née Gough), Mrs Mackeson-Sandbach and Mrs Mackie Niven (née Fitzpatrick).

I am also most grateful to more than a hundred others who allowed me to use – and to borrow for unforgivably long periods – precious family records. Some of their names will be found at the back of this book. I remain very conscious of their generosity and forbearance.

Fifty-two veterans of the war, three of them South African (including one black South African) allowed me to record their war memories. I should like to record my own deep debt of gratitude to them – posthumously, alas, in most cases.

I have been most fortunate in the encouragement I have received in public libraries, museums, record offices and other archives in Britain, and in South Africa (where I collected material in 1972 and 1977). I should like to thank the staff and trustees of the following institutions who have allowed me to quote manuscript material listed at the back of this book. In Britain: the Army Museums Ogilby Trust (Spenser Wilkinson), Bodleian Library, Birmingham University (Chamberlain), British Museum (Balfour, Campbell-Bannerman and others), Christ Church (Lord Salisbury), Devon and Dorset Regimental Museum, Household Brigade Museum, Hove Central Library (Wolseley), India Office Library (White), King's College, London (Hamilton etc.), Liverpool Museum (Steavenson), Manchester Public Library, New College (Milner), National Army Museum (Baden-Powell and others), National Library of Scotland (Haldane and others), North Lancs. Regimental Museum, Sherwood Foresters Regimental Museum (Smith Dorrien), Public Record Office (Ardagh and others), Rhodes House (Rhodes), John Rylands Library (Bromley Davenport), Scottish Record Office (Dundonald), Society for the Propagation of the Gospel in Foreign Parts, University of St Andrews (Alford), Ministry of Defence Library, Westfield College (Lyttelton). In Southern Africa: the Africana Museum, Cape Archives, Natal Archives, Orange Free State Archives, Rhodesian National Archives, Transvaal Archives, De Beers Archives, Killie Campbell Museum, University of Witwatersrand. In Australia: the National Library of Australia.

I should also like to acknowledge the generosity of the following people who read all or part of my text, and made invaluable suggestions, many of which were adopted: my parents, Fiona Barbour, Professor Johann Barnard, Brian Bond, Janet Carleton, Laurence and Linda Kelly, Dr Shula Marks, Godfrey Le

May, Richard Mendelsohn, Kevin Nowlan, Julian Symons, Anthony Sampson and Dennis Kiley.

I owe an especially deep debt to the latter for helping to teach me Dutch and Afrikaans and raising the standard of my translations. I must also thank Dr Zak De Beer, Donald and Anita Fabian, Tertius Myburgh and all the Camerer family. They helped me in a hundred ways while I was in South Africa.

I must also acknowledge the skill and patience of four research assistants: Jane Hirst and Anna Collins in Britain, Enid de Waal and Elaine Katz in South Africa. And I must record the amazing good humour of Alexa Wilson and Maria Ellis who turned a writer's scrawl into a printer's typescript.

To Mary Cresswell-Turner, Sibylla Jane Flower and Dorothy Girouard, and to Kevin MacDonnell I owe the splendid photographs in this book, the majority of which will be new to historians of photography.

I am also greatly in the debt of my copy-editor, Michael Graham-Dixon, who displayed unflinching gallantry under fire.*

I am only too conscious of how much I owe all my friends at Weidenfeld's – especially Gila and Christopher Falkus and George Weidenfeld – and Joe Fox of Random House.

On Anne and Robin Denniston has fallen the heaviest burden of all. The book was planned and written under their roof.

Finally, I should like to thank my wife, Valerie, who has read all the words I have written and skilfully edited them. By eliminating my 'most interesting paragraphs', she has claimed (as Lord Salisbury said to Lord Curzon, after cutting to ribbons his book, *Persia*) 'a negative share in a great work'.

---

* In spelling South African place-names I have used the contemporary forms adopted by the *Official History*, not the modern Afrikaans forms.

Historical Note

The crisis in the Transvaal at the end of the nineteenth century was the culmination of two and a half centuries of Afrikaner expansion and conflict with Africans and British.

In 1652 the Dutch East India Company founded a shipping station at the Cape of Good Hope. At first the colony remained poor. After fifty years there were fewer than two thousand white settlers. And from the beginning these were outnumbered by their coloured servants (including imported slaves) on whom the Europeans depended for their manual labour. The settlers were mainly Dutch Calvinists, with a leavening of German Protestants and French Huguenot refugees. To Africa these Pilgrim Fathers brought a tradition of dissent and a legacy of resentment against Europe. The called themselves 'Afrikaners' or 'Afrikanders' (the people of Africa) and spoke a common language, a variant of Dutch that came to be called 'Afrikaans'. The poorest and most independent of them were the *trekboers* (alias Boers), the wandering farmers whose search for new grazing lands brought them progressively deeper into African territory.

In 1806, during the Napoleonic Wars, the British government took permanent possession of the colony. Britain's aim was strategic. The Cape was a naval base on the sea-route to India and the East. But the colony was too arid to tempt many British immigrants. The Afrikaners remained the majority – of the whites. Most of them were prepared to submit to British Crown rule, but a republican-minded minority, the Boers of the frontier, resented imperial interference, especially over their ill-treatment of the Africans. In 1834 Britain ordered slaves to be emancipated in every part of the Empire. This precipitated the Great Trek: the exodus in 1835–7 of about 5,000 Boers (with about 5,000 Coloured servants) across the Orange and Vaal rivers beyond the north-east frontiers of the colony. The *voortrekkers* (pioneers) quarrelled among themselves, but shared one article of faith: to deny political rights to Africans and Coloured people of mixed race.

For the next sixty years the British government blew hot and cold in its dealings with the Boers. In 1843 Britain created a second colony by annexing Natal, one of the areas in which the voortrekkers had concentrated. But in 1852 and 1854 Britain recognized the independence of the two new Boer republics, the Transvaal and the Orange Free State. Then in 1877 Britain annexed the Transvaal as the first step in an attempt to federate South Africa. This annexation was reversed in 1881, after Paul Kruger had led a rebellion (the First Boer War)

culminating in the defeat of the British at Majuba. The Transvaal's independence was restored, subject to conditions, including British supervision of its
foreign policy.

In 1895 two multi-millionaires, Cecil Rhodes and Alfred Beit, conspired to
take over the Transvaal for themselves and the Empire. The outcome of their
conspiracy provides the Prologue of this book. By now two great mineral
discoveries had turned the political map upside down. In 1870 began the
diamond-rush to Kimberley, on the borders of Cape Colony. It was diamonds
that smoothed Cape Colony's path to successful self-government within the
Empire. They also made Rhodes's and Beit's fortunes. Rhodes became Prime
Minister at the Cape. And together Rhodes and Beit founded a new British
colony, in African territory to the north of the Transvaal, re-named Rhodesia. In
1886 began the gold-rush to the Witwatersrand in the Transvaal. But this did not
smooth the Transvaal's path. Gold made it the richest and militarily the most
powerful nation in southern Africa. But gold also made, for the second time, the
fortunes of Rhodes and Beit – especially Beit. And it precipitated a collision
between the Boers and Uitlanders: the new immigrants, mainly British, swept
along in the gold-rush. The situation of the Uitlanders was unique. They were
believed to outnumber the Boers. Yet by means of a new franchise law, much
more restrictive than those of Britain or America, the Boers kept them starved of
political rights. In 1895 it was the political hunger of the Uitlanders – backed by
Rhodes's and Beit's millions – that seemed to offer the British a chance of taking
over the Transvaal once again from the Boers.

Rhodes's 'Big Idea'

Pitsani Camp (Bechuanaland border),
Mafeking (Cape Colony border) and Transvaal,
29 December 1895 – 2 January 1896

'Johannesburg is ready ... [this is] the big idea which
makes England dominant in Africa, in fact gives England
the African continent.'

> Secret letter from Cecil Rhodes to
> Alfred Beit in August 1895, when they
> hatched the plot to create a revolution
> at Johannesburg supported by a raid
> from Pitsani and Mafeking led by Dr
> Jameson

Johannesburg was not ready. That was the message of the last six code telegrams
to Dr Jameson. They confirmed his fears. So did a verbal report from Major
Heany, the special messenger sent by the Johannesburg 'Reform Committee',
the leaders of Rhodes's and Beit's revolutionary movement in the Transvaal.
The 'flotation', as they called the rising in which they proposed to seize Johannesburg, was going to be a flop. The revolutionaries were in a funk. 'Dead
against it ... fiasco ... you must not move ... too awful ... very sorry ...
Ichabod.'[1]

Jameson left Heany in the white bell-tent at Pitsani, his camp in Bechuanaland
within a few miles of the borders of both Cape Colony and the Transvaal. Heany
himself had never doubted Jameson's reaction. He had warned the committee,
'He'll come in sure as fate.' For twenty minutes on that hot Sunday afternoon, 29
December 1895, Jameson paced up and down in the sand outside the tent. Then
he called to Heany.

He was going in, despite everything, damn them. He'd 'lick the burghers all
round the Transvaal'. If the fellows at Johannesburg wouldn't start the rising as
agreed, their hands would have to be forced. It was a chance of a lifetime. At any
rate he wasn't spending another day at Pitsani Potlucko.[2]

'Boot and saddle!' Dust swirled across the parade ground, as the grey-suited,
slouch-hatted Rhodesian police paraded in a hollow square. 'Dress by the left!
Bugler!' Defiantly the bugle calls echoed off the tin walls of the single store at
Pitsani, and floated across the three miles of empty white veld between Pitsani

and the invisible Transvaal frontier. Silence, except for the shuffling of the troopers' horses – branded 'C.C.' on their rumps – and the hum of the wind in the single telegraph wire.[3]

Jameson had nearly four hundred Rhodesian mounted police at Pitsani, belonging to the Chartered Company. It was this company, created by Cecil Rhodes and Alfred Beit, that administered the new British colony of Rhodesia under Crown charter. Many of the police looked like colonials. They had that swagger, the loose seat in the saddle, and the easy lift and fall of the carbine on their hips.[4] Jameson had collected another one hundred and twenty volunteers twenty-five miles away at Mafeking – just within the borders of Cape Colony. That brought the total of the Chartered Company force up to about six hundred if one counted the Cape Coloured 'boys' who led the spare horses.[5] Jameson had originally planned to invade the Transvaal with fifteen hundred.[6] With six hundred it did seem a bit of a tall order: one regiment against the whole Boer army. But Jameson and the Rhodesian troopers had faced hopeless odds before. They had crushed Lobengula, King of the Matabele, in 1892: six hundred against six thousand Matabeles. This new expedition, according to Cecil Rhodes, would be 'easier than Matabeleland'.[7]

At Pitsani, after six months' work, Jameson had scraped together six Maxim machine-guns, two 7-pounder mountain guns and a 12½-pounder field piece.[8] Some other refinements were stacked on the wagons beside the black tin trunks of Sir John Willoughby and the staff: a cask of Cape brandy for the men, and crates of champagne for the officers.[9] Otherwise, they had cut the baggage train to the bone. The plan was to make a three-day dash for Johannesburg, before the Boer commandos could mobilize. Unfortunately, rumours about the rising – 'blabbing' was Jameson's word – had already reached the local papers. So it was now or never.[10]

'Eyes front!' On the burnished sand of the square, the lines of troopers saw Dr Jameson step into the sunlight. This was the great Dr Jim, pioneer Administrator of the Chartered Company in Rhodesia, and Cecil Rhodes's right-hand man. He was dressed in a fawn-coloured coat, a short, slight figure, with a pale face, nervous brown eyes, and a boyish grin. But his voice was a magnet.[11] He began something like this: 'Some of you lads may think we're going to attack Linchwe and his niggers.' Linchwe was the local Bechuana chieftain who had had the cheek to go all the way to Whitehall to protest against the take-over of his strip of land by the Chartered Company. 'Well, that's all bosh about Linchwe. We're going into the Transvaal in support of the Uitlanders.'[12]

Jameson took a crumpled piece of paper out of his pocket and began to read aloud in his nervous voice. It was a letter of invitation from the committee of Uitlanders in Johannesburg organized by Rhodes and Beit – the mine-executives, miners and others who comprised the British and foreign business community of the Transvaal. 'All the elements necessary for armed conflict. . . . The one desire of the people here is for fair play. . . . Thousands of unarmed men, women and children of our race will be at the mercy of well armed Boers. . . .'[13] Some of Jameson's officers may have felt a trifle embarrassed. It was stirring stuff about the women and children, but not the precise truth, they knew. The letter, written a month before and left undated, was supposed to be kept for the moment *after* the Johannesburg rising had begun.[14] Still, it was a wise precaution of Jameson's to take the letter as a kind of passport. It would cover them with both the Chartered Company and the Imperial government in case there were awkward questions. Without it, they might have looked like pirates. As it was, the three senior officers – Colonels Johnny Willoughby, Raleigh Grey and Bobby White – were worried about the risk of losing their dormant commissions in the British army. Jameson had reassured them with a wave of the hand; and they took it that Joseph Chamberlain (the Colonial Secretary) and the British government must be in the know.[15]

One last precaution: they must cut off communication with the Cape. Not that Jameson had shown any great regard for orders by telegram while the lines had been open. Working for Rhodes in these last years in Rhodesia had taught Jameson and Willoughby when to turn a blind eye to instructions: a Nelson eye to the telegram. Provided, that is, the orders were not personally signed by Rhodes. And one thing must have struck Jameson about the fiasco of the last few days. Each stage of the collapse of the movement in Johannesburg had been reported to him by way of Rhodes's office, but not one telegram was signed 'Rhodes'.[16] He had left the final decision to Jameson. Well, there would be no more orders to anyone at Pitsani for some time. Some troopers smashed down the telegraph poles and sliced off a long length from the single copper cable, burying it in the sand beside the poles. Jameson's other contingent were doing the same near Mafeking. To prevent the Boers being warned, the Boer line to Pretoria would be cut at Malmani, thirty miles beyond the frontier.[17]

Of course it was a wild gamble, this dash for Johannesburg. But then so was much of the work of Rhodes's Chartered Company, and in fact much of the history of the British Empire. 'Clive would have done it,' Jameson told a friend. He was sure of that.[18] If Jameson gambled and won – if they could rush Johannesburg into a rising and forcibly take over the Transvaal – they would be forgiven the illegality.[19] If they gambled and lost – well, the usual penalty was death. Death but not necessarily defeat. It was one of the lessons of history that it needed a disaster to make the British interested in their Empire. They seemed to prefer dead generals to living generals; they avenged them by completing their work. At least half the Empire had been conquered by dead men. People could see the process happening in the Sudan. Any day now the English would avenge Gordon by taking over the whole of the Mahdi's country. Already the same process was happening in the Transvaal – ever since the Battle of Majuba, where General Colley and four hundred men had been cut up by the Boers fourteen years before.[20]

Jameson knew what his staff officers felt about Majuba. They all came from decent regiments: Johnny Willoughby from the Horse Guards, Grey from the Inniskillings, Bobby White from the Welch Fusiliers.[21] It was British officers like this who took Majuba personally. Not just the thought of those brave fellows who died: also the shame of the others who had raised the white flag.

Majuba was 'unfinished business' for the British army, something to wipe off the slate.

In the gathering dusk the bugle sounded. Captain Lindsell and a dozen scouts clattered off down the rutted wagon road, then turned east towards the darkness. There could be no going back now. Jameson mounted a black stallion. He took off his felt hat, and there were three ringing cheers for the Queen. Then they trotted out of Pitsani, followed by the African servants and the mule-carts. The moon had risen, flashing on the tin walls of the village and the brass-and-steel mountings of the Maxims, before the column was engulfed in dust.[22]

Across the border and into the Transvaal rode the six hundred.

Four days had passed, and the morning of 2 January found Jameson's column halted close to a small whitewashed farm south of a kopje called Doornkop, in the brown, grassy hills of the Rand. They had ridden 170 miles into the Transvaal, with hardly a halt for sleep; the troopers were slipping from side to side in their saddles; and the officers were mixed with the men.[23] Ahead was their goal, Johannesburg, the Golden City, only a couple of hours' ride. As dawn broke, they could see the endless lines of tall iron chimneys, the gigantic wheels above the mine-shafts and the gleam of the mine-tailings, the golden slag in that lunar landscape. And their goal might indeed have been the moon, for all their chance of getting there.

Betrayal, that was the only word for it. Johannesburg had not risen. Their friends had made their peace with President Kruger and his Boers. The news had been brought to Jameson by two bicyclists. Not one armed volunteer had ridden out to join the column.[24] Now Jameson's path was barred by a relentless and invisible enemy.

For two days Jameson had carried on a running fight against the commandos. The Boers had got wind of them from the first. Jameson's men had cut the Boer telegraph wire at Malmani, but too late. (People said afterwards it was the fault of some troopers who got drunk and cut the fence wire instead.) At first the Boers had hung on their tail, picking off stragglers. Jameson's men had fought back as they had learnt to fight the Zulu impis: with the rattle of Maxims, the crash of shrapnel from the field-gun and the charge to the death. But the only dead were British. How could they fight mere puffs of smoke? That last night they had huddled together in a rough square formed by the ammunition carts, the ambulance wagons and the horses. The troopers fired into the darkness across their saddles.[25] At dawn Jameson sent a last laconic message to the men in Johannesburg. Though they had had two 'scrimmages', they were all right; but they would like a little help if it could be spared.[26]

If help didn't come, Jameson and his officers well knew what England expected of them. This was the moment they had been trained for ever since boyhood. It was the picture of the Last Stand above the fireplace in the school-room and the mess and the rectory. The Gatling has jammed; the colonel, eyes uplifted, grasps his sword; the little band sings 'God Save the Queen'; and, one by one, they fall.[27]

By eight o'clock Jameson's little band had suffered sixty-five killed and wounded. Inspector Cazalet was hit in the chest, Major Coventry in the spine, Captain Barry was dying.[28] And then reality at last broke in to Jameson's world of make-believe. Someone lifted a white flag – not a very good white flag, but the best they could do in the circumstances. It was made from the white apron of an African servant girl.[29] The firing ceased. From all around them, the Boers rose up out of the ground, 'like ants', as one officer put it.[30] Most of the Boers were dressed in ordinary brown working clothes, but a few had come straight from New Year festivities and had slung their rifles and bandoliers over their black Sunday best. The Boers disarmed the British, assisted the wounded and seized the baggage. In Bobby White's black tin box were found the code telegrams from Rhodes in the Cape and from the other plotters in Johannesburg. There was a spare copy of the 'women-and-children' letter, and the code book to go with the code telegrams.[31] It lay among the empty champagne bottles.[32]

The humiliation was complete when the dead were counted before burial. The British had lost sixteen, the Boers one man – one less than they had lost at Majuba.

Weeping, Jameson was led away in a cart to the gaol at Pretoria.[33]

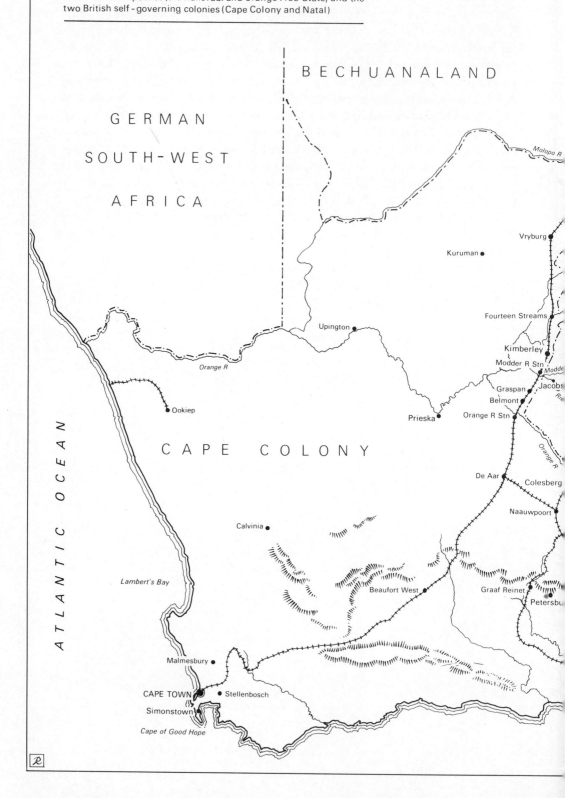

South Africa, 1899

The two Boer republics (the Transvaal and Orange Free State) and the
two British self-governing colonies (Cape Colony and Natal)

BECHUANALAND

GERMAN

SOUTH-WEST

AFRICA

Molopo R

Vryburg

Kuruman

Fourteen Streams

Upington

Kimberley

Modder R Stn

Modde

Orange R

Jacobs

Graspan

Rie

Belmont

Ookiep

Prieska

Orange R Stn

CAPE COLONY

Orange R

De Aar

Colesberg

Naauwpoort

Calvinia

Beaufort West

Graaf Reinet

Petersbu

ATLANTIC OCEAN

Lambert's Bay

Malmesbury

CAPE TOWN

Stellenbosch

Simonstown

Cape of Good Hope

PART I

Milner's War

'The Jameson Raid was the real declaration of war in the Great Anglo–Boer conflict.... And that is so in spite of the four years truce that followed ... [the] aggressors consolidated their alliance ... the defenders on the other hand silently and grimly prepared for the inevitable.'

Jan Smuts, 1906

"Won't be happy till he gets it."

CHAPTER 1
Out of the Abyss

SS *Scot* and South Africa,

18 November 1898 and before

As he spoke his eyelids seemed to tremble and to fall a
little over his keen grey eyes. In a flash the phrase of
Scudder's came back to me, when he had described the
man he most dreaded in the world. He had said that he
'could hood his eyes like a hawk'. Then I saw that I had
walked straight into the enemy's headquarters.

> John Buchan (Sir Alfred Milner's
> Private Secretary in South Africa,
> 1901–3), *The Thirty-Nine Steps*

In the small hours, Sir Alfred Milner, High Commissioner for South Africa and
Lieutenant-Governor of Cape Colony, was woken by a bright light in his eyes.
He had a stateroom on the starboard side of the upper deck. It was 4.00 a.m., he
noted in his diary (the small red diary which was the only companion and
confidant of his travels). That must be the Ushant lighthouse, the first land they
had sighted since Madeira. The wind was still blowing hard, but a big ship like
the 7,000-ton *Scot* took it in her stride.[1] Making $18\frac{1}{2}$ knots, she was the holder of
the record for the Cape Town run.[2] If she kept this up, Milner would be in time
to see Chamberlain at the Colonial Office on the 22nd. And tonight he might be
able to dine with his friends at Brooks's. How very jolly it would be to see the
blessed old boys again!

Milner slept once more and when he next awoke it was morning: a fine
morning, though cold. They were now about 120 miles from the Needles.
Grand. After eighteen gruelling months at the Cape, he felt he had earned a
holiday in England, even if it was to be a working holiday. His friend, Philip
Gell, his closest friend since schooldays at King's College, knew what he meant
when he wrote to say how he was longing to be back at 'Headquarters'.[3] Cape
society he had not enjoyed, to put it mildly; as Ozzy Walrond, his Private
Secretary (and a treasure), remarked, Cape Town was a fourth-rate provincial
town full of 'the most awful cads'.[4]

His own feelings for the dark continent were, understandably, more complicated, though he once admitted to Philip that Cape Town '*was* a rather beastly
hole'; in fact, when Milner compared his life at the Cape with his life in Egypt six

years before, as Baring's financial secretary, he could find nothing whatever in favour of the Cape. The people – the whites, that is – were much more congenial in Egypt. It was nearer England. Besides, Egypt, run by the British, was a place where it was easy to get things done.[5]

Of course, he had not arrived at the Cape at the best moment to enjoy its amenities. It was 1897. He had been sent out to pick up the pieces after Jameson's Raid.

The Raid: that had been the most extraordinary business. Despite the choppy seas and the cold wind, Milner spent most of the day pacing the port side of the deck, as one by one those delightful landmarks of the English coast swung into view: the Dorset Downs, the Purbeck hills, and the heady curves of Portland Bill.

His thoughts returned to South Africa. The 'Higher Powers' (as he put it in his donnish way) seemed to have achieved a miracle for the Afrikaners twice in the past. First at Majuba, then at Doornkop. How to avoid their winning a third time? He had views about that – increasingly strong views, although these had to remain, for the time being, a private heresy of his own.[6]

By now, Milner was a familiar sight to his fellow-passengers – fellow-prisoners, he would have called them – on the interminable voyage from the Cape. He hated the trip, tired as he was, for he hated being cooped up for nearly three weeks in a tub of a liner. He had always tried to play his part in the jollities on board ship, including (and this proved an appalling experience) some amateur theatricals. But for most of the voyage home he paced the deck, read the annual report of the Inland Revenue, or worked at his black box full of papers.[7]

The other passengers probably thought him a shy, austere, melancholy man. People generally did. With his long, thin face and downcast grey-brown eyes, he looked older than his forty-four years, and sadder than a brilliantly successful diplomatist should be. In fact, nothing surprised people, on first meeting him, more than his appearance. Was this really Sir Alfred Milner, the High Commissioner and Lieutenant-Governor of the Cape? Was this the man chosen by Joe Chamberlain to cut President Kruger down to size? He looked so gentle and detached. There was a whiff of All Souls or the British Museum about him.

People who knew him intimately received quite a different impression. When he began to talk his expression was as mobile as a kaleidoscope, and his smile was a sunburst. Suddenly that cold, thin face, the colour of ivory browned by age, became extraordinarily sweet and gentle.[8] Of course, few people ever did get to know him intimately. To these friends he showed a side of his nature that was both ardent and affectionate. As for his enemies, they hardly existed at this time, though soon enough he was to have his share.

To what did Milner owe his meteoric rise in the public service? It was a question he sometimes asked himself. Certainly not to his family connections – though in a different sense he felt he owed everything to his family. His parentage was unusual. If you listened hard when he pronounced his 'ths' there was a trace of a German accent. He was born in Giessen, near Frankfurt-on-Main, the son of a half-German medical student and an English gentlewoman who had come to Germany in straitened circumstances. His upbringing was divided between Germany and England, and marred by the fecklessness of his father and the ill-health of his mother. When he was fifteen his mother died, and he was sent to school in England. All these experiences left their stamp on him.[9] His heart was still to some extent divided between the two countries; his schoolboy heroes included Bismarck and Frederick the Great, as well as Cromwell and the younger Pitt; in the hurly-burly of London and South Africa he often longed for the solitude of the Bavarian woods.

But it was his English mother who was the driving force behind his life. At eighteen he won a senior scholarship to Oxford, an unheard-of feat for a boy from a London day school. He carried off the Craven, the Hertford – a whole litany of university prizes. He became the most brilliant son of Balliol, the Oxford college where Dr Jowett held court among a golden generation of undergraduates. As he progressed from prize to prize and triumph to triumph he had only one regret: if only she had lived to see it all.[10]

Against his father he was in complete reaction, so it appeared, though not at all disloyal or unfilial. That relentless capacity for work, that single-minded devotion to a cause – it was almost as though young Alfred was doing penance for the sins of his father.

Yet behind the upright young man, the paragon of English Victorian virtues, private and public, people occasionally detected something different. There was a frighteningly strained air to his self-control, as though most of his life was lived against the grain of his nature. He had strange eyes: keen grey eyes which he could hood like a hawk's. Inside Milner, repressed but not altogether extinguished, was something of the spirit of his father – romantic, Bohemian, restless, and perhaps even reckless as well.[11]

Of course, this dualism in his nature was well concealed from all but his closest friends. Milner's rise to fame could, as he reckoned himself, be attributed to one thing above all: he was absolutely sound and reliable. This was the reason, not merely his flair for writing or his financial expertise, for his having proved so useful to the leading men in both political parties: first as private secretary to Goschen, the Conservative Chancellor of the Exchequer; next, as financial secretary to Sir Evelyn Baring (later Lord Cromer), the British ruler of Egypt; then, as Chairman of the Inland Revenue, right-hand man to Sir William Harcourt, the Liberal Chancellor.

In due course, he was promoted by Joe Chamberlain to his job as High Commissioner – the man responsible for British colonies in South Africa. Milner was not told exactly why he had been chosen. But no doubt he had been given a shrewd idea by Joe and his Cabinet colleagues. They had had enough of men like Jameson and Rhodes – of schoolboy heroes and bungling empire-builders. Milner had a solid reputation in imperial questions. His best-selling book, *England in Egypt*, sounded a trumpet call for the Empire. But he was also an expert on death duties – not a bad preparation, perhaps, for the deadly grind of modern diplomacy. At all events, Milner was selected for his strength of character and his patience.[12] It was *im*patience, as the current Chancellor, Sir

Michael Hicks Beach, observed to Milner, that lay at the root of all Britain's mistakes in the past – from before Majuba to the Raid.[13]

Milner undoubtedly agreed. His own comment on his appointment to the Cape was characteristically modest. His only fear was that the job might fall through because no one at the Cape had ever heard of him. 'It would be rather awkward,' as he had told Philip Gell, if they jibbed, taking him to be 'the nephew of some great man who had to be provided for, or an inconvenient official who had to be got rid of'.[14]

In fact, few colonial viceroys had ever had a more splendid send-off than Milner's, when his friends gathered at the Café Monico to honour him before he left England. Numerous Balliol contemporaries attended – fellow-disciples of the great Dr Jowett: not only Philip Gell but Gell's brother-in-law, St John Brodrick, and Henry Asquith and George Curzon, the rising stars of the Liberal and Tory parties. 'Hurrah for the meek and the humble men of Balliol,' someone remarked, 'for they shall inherit the earth.' Leaders of the main political parties were there too: Joe Chamberlain shared with Asquith the honour of proposing Milner's health, and made a rousing imperialist speech – too rousing, some thought. In reply, Milner struck a more sympathetic note. He was cursed with the 'cross-bench mind'. He tended to see too many sides to every question. Though he added, disarmingly, that there was 'one question' on which he had 'never been able to see the other side', and that was imperial unity, the consolidation of the British Empire.[15]

And so he set off for the Cape, fêted on all sides, so charming and tactful and clever, so *sound*, above all, as everyone said at that dinner – the perfect emissary to restore British supremacy in South Africa and consolidate the far-flung Empire.

Two years at the Cape had taught him that his patience had a limit. It was not merely the endless wrangling with the Transvaal over minor issues, and the wrestling with the Afrikaners at the Cape. It was the legacy of the past that so appalled him – not merely the Raid but the chain of mistakes that preceded it. 'I hope South Africa is not going to be our one point of failure, but I feel very uneasy,' he wrote to Gell in April 1898. 'Somehow or other the more I know about it, the more profound is the abyss of our blunders in the past.'[16]

What did men like Milner mean when they talked in that mystical voice of 'imperial unity' and 'consolidating the Empire'? Was it all rhetoric, just a mood and an enthusiasm?[17] One must look back into South African history, into that 'abyss of blunders'.

Milner, he himself confessed, could not see two sides to the imperial question. In his eyes the nineteenth century in South Africa was a century of struggle for supremacy between Britain and Boer – and of abysmal blunders from the imperial standpoint.

During most of the century British policy was weak and vacillating, like British imperial policy in general.[18] On three occasions a positive attempt was made to solve the Boer question by adopting an active 'forward' (that is, expansionist) policy. On each occasion, and for various reasons – including impatience and the see-saw of party politics – the forward policy ended in disaster.

Yet the alternatives proved a set of still bigger blunders: years of drift and compromise. All the time their Boer adversaries, expanding their strongholds in the interior, squeezing the natives into the poorest land, yet still leaving an Afrikaner (Afrikaans-speaking) majority at the Cape, grew richer and more numerous, more dangerous to Britain and her Empire.

The first to seize the South African nettle was Sir Benjamin D'Urban, appointed Governor of eastern Cape Colony in 1833. It was by then forty years since Britain had first annexed the Cape, seizing the colony from Holland, for reasons of strategy, during the Revolutionary and Napoleonic Wars. The strategic motive was compelling for England – as it was to remain. Hold the Cape and she could protect the sea lanes to the East. This was the main reason why the Dutch had originally founded Cape Colony in the seventeenth century; it was a stepping-stone on the way to the Dutch East Indies. Now for the British it could be the Gibraltar of the South, the chief link in the chain of imperial defence between England and her most important overseas possession – India.

But how to ensure that the Cape remained under British control? This was the political puzzle that haunted Sir Benjamin D'Urban, and was to haunt all his successors. For the Cape was more than a base; it was a colony; and a colony whose Afrikaner inhabitants' loyalty was (to put it mildly) not beyond dispute. In this respect there was soon no parallel with the problem of the French in British Canada or any other British colonial problem. For the flood of British immigrants that would have provided a pro-British majority never materialized at the Cape. The country was too poor and arid to attract British immigration on any scale, and only for a period during the 1820s did the British government subsidize immigration. As a result, the Afrikaans-speaking South Africans remained a majority, and a stubborn one at that.[19]

When D'Urban arrived in 1833 he found the place in turmoil. With their seventeenth-century Dutch Protestant tradition – fundamentalist and egalitarian – the scattered Dutch colonists had always proved awkward to govern. In the days of Dutch rule there was frequent friction with the colonial government, and occasional bloodshed. After the British take-over, there were risings in 1795, 1799 and 1815. The 1815 affair resulted in the hanging at Slachter's Nek of five men who came to be regarded as the first political martyrs of the Afrikaner nation, though in fact they were condemned by Dutch-speaking judge and jurymen; moreover, they had forfeited the sympathy of most of their countrymen by a reckless alliance with some Xhosas, the local African tribe who greatly outnumbered both white communities combined.[20]

It is at this point – when one touches on the native side of the problem – that the difficulties of policy-making in South Africa, for both a colonial governor and his home government, become apparent. For it was not only the British who remained a minority among the population as a whole. The whites were a minority among the Africans. Any humanitarian attempt to reconcile the interests of the black majority with the colonists was certain to compound the other two problems: to reconcile two rival colonial communities with each other, and their interests, in turn, with those of the imperial power. In short, history presented South Africa with a triple formula for conflict – black against white, white against white, white against the mother country – and only a miracle could spare South Africa from an endless war.[21]

In the event, Sir Benjamin D'Urban was no miracle-worker. He was a heavy-handed veteran of the Peninsular War. He sacrificed the black Africans' interests, and bowed to white political pressures, in just the same way as so many rulers of South Africa were to do in the future. To conciliate the Boers – the frontier farmers – and unite the colony in loyalty to the Crown, he adopted a tough 'forward' policy towards the Xhosa. He supported the Boers who were in a state of endemic feud with the Xhosa over the frontier lands. He sent English red-coats to help locally commandeered troops – the Boer commandos. Together, D'Urban and the Boers sliced off a hundred-mile strip of new territory to add to the Cape. But, meanwhile, vacillations at Downing Street had hardened into a determination not to increase the size of the colony at the expense of the natives. Under pressure from British missionaries, the Colonial Secretary of the day repudiated D'Urban's annexation. Worse than this, from his own point of view, D'Urban was, in 1834, now instructed to put into effect a humanitarian new edict outlawing slavery from the British Empire, which he did with characteristic heavy-handedness.

This was the last straw for the Boers on the frontier. Away they trekked, beyond the Orange River and the Vaal, into new, seemingly empty territory where they could govern themselves – and handle the natives – as they thought fit. By 1837 these pioneers numbered five thousand, although the great majority of Afrikaans-speaking colonists remained at the Cape. The voortrekkers, as the pioneers became known, were organized on military lines, and included one young boy who would become famous, Paul Kruger. They took everything they needed with them, as they set off in their covered wagons across the endless brown veld: their sheep and their cattle, enough guns and gunpowder to subdue the natives, and enough resentment against England to last a century. So began the great exodus – a kind of inverted rebellion – that passed into folklore as the Great Trek, and created the two voortrekker republics, the Orange Free State and the Transvaal, as a national home for the Boers.[22]

D'Urban had blundered, that was clear; and D'Urban was recalled. But the blunder was shared by the Colonial Secretary, who failed to support the 'forward' policy in the Cabinet. This, at any rate, was the moral to be drawn by later imperialists like Milner.[23]

The same mistake, as Milner must have seen it, was made on the next occasion when the forward policy was tried – by another Peninsular general-turned-governor, Sir Harry Smith. At first, after D'Urban's recall, it was decided to let the voortrekkers stew in their own juice. No steps were taken to stop them crossing the fords of the Orange River, which would have been easy, nor was

trade with them forbidden. Instead, the Cape government issued a fiery proclamation reasserting authority over the erring Boers – and took good care not to
enforce it.[24]

But by 1847, when Smith took over, events had prodded Britain once more
into facing the Boer problem. In their progress north, the voortrekkers had
stirred up a hornet's nest in Natal, till then the preserve of the Zulus. The Boers
crushed Dingaan and his Zulu warriors at the Battle of Blood River on 16
December 1838. But their handling of African tribes elsewhere threatened to be
a source of permanent unrest. Reluctantly, Whitehall was persuaded that a
British colony of Natal, expensive as it might prove for the Crown, was at least a
lesser evil than another Boer republic. For Natal was not in the middle of
nowhere like the other Boer territories. It was plumb on the trade route to India.
In 1843 it was annexed by Britain and the chief port was renamed after
D'Urban.[25] (In contrast, the main town in the Zulu country to the north of the
Tugela River was called after Lady Smith, the Spanish bride whom dashing Sir
Harry had carried off from the Peninsula.)

As a British general, Sir Harry had seized Natal for the Crown. As a British
governor, he now proceeded to outplay the Boer expansionists at their own
game. He doubled the size of the Cape Colony, pushing out the frontier to the
Atlantic on the north-west, and across the Kei River to the east. A still greater
coup was to annex the voortrekkers' territory across the Orange and the Vaal
Rivers. When their neighbours in the Transvaal, led by Pretorius, marched
against him, Sir Harry dealt them a resounding defeat at the Battle of Boomplaatz. The result was political chaos in the Transvaal. Its annexation seemed
certain to follow.

But just then the Westminster see-saw came down with a bump, unseating Sir
Harry and miraculously restoring the power of the voortrekkers. New British
governments, successively led by Lord John Russell and Lord Derby, decided to
take a firm stand against colonial adventures. Sir Harry was recalled and his
conquests were repudiated. By the Sand (Zand) River Convention of 1852 and
the Bloemfontein Convention of 1854, the internal independence of the two
Boer republics of the Transvaal and the Orange Free State was guaranteed by
Britain.[26]

Why the sudden reversion to a policy of compromise? This time the forward
policy was not repudiated for humanitarian reasons, as at the time of D'Urban's
débâcle. The pressure came not from the missionaries of Exeter Hall but from
the Lords of the Treasury whose aim was financial retrenchment. The new
government was determined to economize as much as possible on the Empire.
For this was the heyday of Lord Palmerston and Free Trade. Britain had grown
rich by exploiting markets in regions, like Europe and the United States, where
she had no political control. Why pay for an empire, when Britain had free access
to the markets of the world? In 1872 Cape Colony followed Canada, New
Zealand and the Australian colonies in being granted 'responsible government' –
in other words, internal autonomy. And at the same time a discovery was made
that seemed to set the seal on the success of this policy: the discovery of the

world's largest pipe of diamonds at Kimberley in the Free State, close to the
Cape frontier.

The ensuing diamond boom in the Cape (which had, by some smart map-
reading, hastily incorporated Kimberley in its territory) transformed the
economy of the region. Trade flourished. Railways spread across the veld. At
last Britain's Cinderella colony had goods to sell to the mother country and the
money to buy her goods.[27] For her part, the mother country responded by
returning once more to the attack on the problem of the Boers.

The aim this time was a good deal more sophisticated than the fumblings of
D'Urban or the buccaneering of Sir Harry Smith. It had long struck British
statesmen that the central problem of South Africa – to impose British control,
despite the Afrikaners at the Cape and the Boers of the Transvaal – had analogies
with the problem of the French in Canada. In Canada, it was true, the British
settlers had soon swamped the French, whereas the Afrikaners would remain in
the majority at the Cape for the foreseeable future. But a federal constitution had
worked wonders in the French Canadian provinces. What about a federal
constitution for all four South African states, the two British colonies and the
two Boer republics? This was the plan of the new High Commissioner in 1877,
Sir Bartle Frere.

Strange to say, it was not the Boer republics that seemed the chief obstacles to
this scheme. The Boers in the Transvaal were in such a desperate state at this
time – hemmed in by the Zulus, their treasury bankrupt – that they seemed
prepared to acquiesce in becoming a British colony. The real obstacle was the
degree of colonial nationalism at the Cape that had been stimulated both by
responsible government and the diamond boom. In a reckless fit of impatience,
the British tried to force the hand of the Cape government by annexing the
Transvaal *before* federation was agreed. It was back to a forward policy with a
vengeance.[28]

Hence the third great blunder, which culminated in Majuba. At least Frere did
not begin by making the mistake committed by his predecessors, of acting
without authority from home. Together, he and the Tory Colonial Secretary,
Lord Carnarvon, concerted their scheme. The first step was to woo the Boers
with the same tactic as D'Urban had used: letting loose the British army on the
Boers' African adversaries.

Accordingly, the British precipitated the Zulu War of 1879, which, despite
some initial success for the Zulus, resulted in their extinction as a military nation
(and a peerage for the British commander, Sir Garnet Wolseley). Meanwhile,
without firing a shot, the British army had marched north to Pretoria. By 1877
the Union Jack was flying over the government buildings of the new British
colony of the Transvaal.[29]

For a moment it looked like a triumph of the forward policy. Pretoria
occupied, its loyalty secure, the Free State sure to follow, soon the great
federation of British South Africa. But the verge of triumph was the verge of the
abyss. The Conservatives had not managed to secure full Liberal support for the
annexation, and now Gladstone thundered at Midlothian: he would repudiate

the take-over. His arguments were based as much on financial orthodoxy (that is, economy) as on political radicalism. It became clear that the Liberals were as deeply divided on South Africa as they were on Ireland. The British annexation was left in the air. Sir Bartle Frere was recalled under a cloud. No money was invested in the colony, there were no improvements in business or administration to offset the loss of political independence for the Boers. Accordingly, the Boers' powerful tradition of nationalism, temporarily paralysed by an empty treasury and the Zulu menace, was suddenly given new life.

In 1880 the Boers under Paul Kruger rose in revolt against their new government, and within a few weeks inflicted three small, but shattering, reverses on the British army, culminating in the Battle of Majuba in British territory just inside the frontiers of Natal.[30]

By this time, Gladstone, Grand Old Man, was back in the seat for his third term. He was quick to seize on a compromise. He agreed to withdraw the large British force now hurrying to the rescue, led by Sir Fred Roberts, the hero of the march to Kandahar. He agreed to restore complete internal self-government to the Boers. There was one major qualification: Britain would reserve for herself ultimate control over the Transvaal's foreign affairs. Constitutionally it was an unusual, though not unique, arrangement. Britain was continuing to claim her status as paramount power in South Africa, although she did not claim the Transvaal as a colony or even as a member of her Empire.

Under pressure from well-wishers in Cape Colony and the Free State, Kruger consented to this arrangement, which was given the form of an international treaty in the Convention of Pretoria of 1881 and the Convention of London of 1884. But Kruger, who became President of the restored Transvaal Republic, did not conceal the fact that he was signing under protest, and would do his best to negotiate a third convention which would remove the shadow of British paramountcy from the Transvaal's independence. On their part, many British soldiers under Roberts felt deeply humiliated by the settlement. Moreover, it served to quicken, as soon emerged, the rising spirit of Jingoism.[31]

Such was the Abyss of Blunders.

To Milner the talk of avenging Majuba seemed distastefully crude. The battle itself was a conventional enough disaster: a poor tactical position, a diminutive force, a half-baked general. It was the whole annexation that had been hopelessly bungled. Frere had fumbled. Westminster had undermined him. The Treasury had ensured his failure. As for Gladstone's settlement, Milner could only wince at the thought. By settling for 'peace-under-defeat' before the main British army could arrive, Gladstone had taken one more step in confirming the Transvaal as that dangerous anachronism, a quasi-independent nation in Africa.[32]

What was to be done? It was here that the 'great game' for South Africa emerged as part of a much greater game – the struggle for world supremacy.

The phrases used – 'imperial unity' and 'consolidating the Empire' – were vague, conveniently vague. Milner himself knew what he meant by them. He prided himself on his realism – on the fact that he had no illusions about the true state of the British Empire. He was not misled, like the cruder kind of jingos, by the flag-waving and the drum-beating.[33] He shrank from these theatricals – 'walking on stilts', he called his job as viceroy.[34] He ridiculed the philosophy of the Gatling gun and the Last Stand. What he was interested in was power. Not merely for himself, but for England and the English race. This was the love of his life – English 'race patriotism', as he called it – pursued with the passion that he denied himself in most other ways.[35] But the power of the English race was not, as he saw it, at its climax. It was already in decline.

The years of drift and compromise in South Africa were part of this general decline. Indeed, in the other settler colonies, for half a century there had not even been an *attempt* at a forward policy; *all* policy had been weak and negative. And gradually British power was eroded as, one by one, these white colonies were granted internal self-government. It was true that the colonies themselves had grown richer and more powerful. It was also true that Britain had made vast new tropical conquests – especially during the recent scramble for Africa.

But were these new black colonies to be a source of either wealth or power? Until they were developed, no one could say. In Milner's eyes, as indeed in the eyes of all the more sophisticated imperialists, Britain's main concern was not with adding to or even developing the black Empire. It was with reasserting her power in the white Empire. Could the Empire now be made into a reality as a federal Greater Britain? Could it become the supreme world-state, with defence and trade controlled by a single grand imperial parliament? Or was the white Empire doomed to dissolve into a medley of nation-states, no closer to Britain than the first great ex-colony, America?

It was in South Africa, Milner believed, that the answer to this question would be found, one way or the other.[36] He thought he knew the dangers. In his personal philosophy of aiming for the 'Big Things of life', risks were unavoidable – and big risks, too.[37] Perhaps it was already too late. Perhaps the Empire, not the Transvaal, was the anachronism. Perhaps he was one himself. Time would show.[38] Of one thing Milner was certain. The present policy of compromise in South Africa – the backward policy – offered no chance of restoring Britain's power. In 1886 gold had been discovered in the Transvaal hills called Witwatersrand – the Rand. It was gold that had lured Rhodes and Beit in 1895 to try to re-annex the Transvaal to the British Empire – a scheme in which Chamberlain and the imperial government (so they claimed) had played no part. To the folly of Majuba had now been added the fiasco of the Raid.

Milner's own feelings towards the Raid and its political results were understandably more complicated than towards the earlier blunders.[39] In a sense he owed everything to the disaster. But for Jameson, he might have still been sitting in his office at Somerset House hiding his yawns as Chairman of the Inland Revenue. And there were aspects of the Raid, total fiasco though it had been, which offered, Milner thought, hopeful lessons for the future.

What no one, least of all Kruger, could have foreseen when the London Convention had been signed in 1884 was that the Rand would be discovered two years later. The resulting explosion in the wealth of the Transvaal had an explosive political result. Quite suddenly the Cape and Transvaal seemed to be exchanging roles, as political leadership of the sub-continent passed to the Transvaal. There was now a double anomaly about the two states. The Cape was a British colony, though the majority of the white inhabitants were Afrikaners; the Transvaal was still a Boer republic, though it appeared that the majority of its inhabitants were, by the mid-1890s, British, for the gold-rush had sucked in so many British immigrants. Who, then, was to control the Transvaal, richest state in Africa?[40] This was the question which Jameson tried to answer with his madcap ride across the veld.

When the Raid was imminent the old President declared, 'I shall wait until the tortoise puts out its head, then I shall cut it off.'[41] In the event he was far too clever to do anything of the sort. He had the tortoise wrapped up, so to speak, and sent to London as a gift for the Queen. It was to London that he sent Dr Jameson and the Raiders; to be sentenced by a Crown court, to the great embarrassment of all concerned, to terms ranging from fifteen months in gaol. Worse, Rhodes was revealed as the arch-plotter and arch-bungler of the whole affair. This was proved by two official enquiries and two public trials, in London and South Africa. It could not be denied, once Kruger had published to the world the amazing collection of code telegrams and other secret documents found on the battlefield of Doornkop.[42]

It was at the enquiry held by the Cape government that there emerged the answer to the central puzzle: why had the Johannesburg rising, organized by Rhodes, collapsed so ignominiously? As the man who had then been Prime Minister at the Cape, as well as Chairman of the Chartered Company, Rhodes himself was forced to testify – and a wretched figure he cut during the two days he was in the witness box. It turned out that he and his multi-millionaire backer, Alfred Beit, had hopelessly overestimated the strength of the opposition to Kruger among the Uitlanders. A large minority were not British at all, but were Afrikaners from the Cape, Germans, Frenchmen, even Americans. Of course, they had their grievances, including their lack of political rights. But they were earning good money in the gold mines, and were in no great hurry to overthrow the government. The same applied to many of the independent capitalists who had stakes in the Rand gold-fields. And even the Johannesburg 'Reformers' (the cardboard revolutionaries) had not been able to agree on the crucial question: once they had toppled Kruger's republic of the Transvaal, what would they put in its place? An Uitlander republic? Or, as Rhodes and Beit wanted, a British colony under the British flag?[43].

While the Reformers had pleaded for time to patch up their differences, Rhodes and Beit had kept their heads well buried in the sand. In Beit's case this was almost literally the case; he took a seaside holiday at Muizenberg during the crucial weekend when Jameson was due to set off. Rhodes had remained hovering about Groote Schuur, his palace in the pine woods above Cape Town, postponing the decision to recall Jameson, although the invasion was immediately repudiated by both the British and Cape governments.[44] William Schreiner, the Cape's Attorney-General, gave the Cape enquiry an account of an

interview with Rhodes during that period: Rhodes utterly broken down by the
fiasco of the rising; Rhodes blurting out that Jameson 'had upset his applecart';
Rhodes refusing to try to stop him with the abject excuse 'poor Jameson, we've
been friends for twenty years, how can I ruin him now?' Yet it also emerged that
Rhodes did try to ruin Jameson a few days later. He had sent a message to him in
Pretoria gaol instructing him to take the whole blame.[45]

This was the unsavoury story of the Raid as it emerged from the trials and
official enquiries. And absurd as were the illusions of the conspirators, the
political effects were real enough, as Milner knew to his cost. The Raid had
disastrously weakened the imperial position in South Africa. In 1898 Kruger was
re-elected as the President of the Transvaal for a fourth term, routing his more
progressive Boer opponents, and he was now the hero not only of the Boers in
the Transvaal, but of their fellow Afrikaners at the Cape. The bonds of a new
kind of Cape colonial nationalism, which Rhodes had inspired, were now
broken, and the Cape Afrikaners were forced back into the laager mentality they
had abandoned for a decade. Of course, this would not necessarily have been a
bad thing for imperialists, if the Cape had not had self-government. But it had,
and the Afrikaners remained in the majority.[46]

As for Rhodes, he was severely censured at both the Cape enquiry and the
parliamentary enquiry in London. He had been forced to resign both as Chairman of the Chartered Company and as Cape Prime Minister. He then
announced that he would abandon Cape politics and in future devote himself to
the country that bore his name. It was about time. Rhodes's gamble in sending
off most of the Rhodesian police with Jameson had helped precipitate native
risings by the Matabele and Mashona, which were only stamped out at heavy
financial cost to the Chartered Company.[47]

When Milner had been sent to the Cape in 1897 it was his job to restore the
world destroyed by Jameson. The first problem was how to deal with the
ex-colossus and his partners, including Alfred Beit. As Governor and High
Commissioner, it was Milner's job to be on good terms with all the pro-British
party, especially these ex-German, naturalized British millionaire 'gold-bugs'
like Alfred Beit. And on good terms he was. Yet he could not conceal from his
close friends his private feelings. Rhodes's and Beit's plan for invading the
Transvaal had been not only 'idiotic'; it was 'unscrupulous'.[48] He did not now
trust Rhodes and his associates an inch. 'They would give me away or anyone
else for the *least* of their own ends,' he declared in an outburst to Philip Gell.
They were 'money grubbers' and 'potential rebels'. Yet he could not help liking
Rhodes. It needed a 'moral and intellectual structure as complex' as his own to
realize that 'Rhodes is thoroughly untrustworthy yet cordially to admire him'.[49]

This was, of course, for the ears of only his closest friends. Indeed, Milner
once called the truth about Rhodes one of the *arcana imperii* (imperial secrets)
that could never be divulged except to the 'fully initiated augur'. 'For goodness
sake,' he added, 'do not let Grey' – Lord Grey was the new chairman of the
Chartered Company – 'ever know what I think ... Grey, excellent, simple-

minded fellow, would not be one-tenth of the use he undoubtedly is, if he did not take Rhodes at his own valuation.'[50] Milner had his own motives for telling this to Philip Gell. He wanted to install him, his most intimate and reliable friend, in a crucial position at 'Headquarters' – among the London gold-bugs. He hoped Gell could get a job at the London office of Wernher-Beit, the richest and most powerful of all the Rand mining houses.[51] (The personal assets of Wernher and Beit were valued in 1895 at £17 million, compared with Rhodes's £5 million.)[52] 'I had rather it were Wernher, Beit and Transvaal things', he told Philip, explaining this scheme, 'than Grey, Rhodes and Rhodesian things.' In fact, Philip had to settle for a seat with Grey on the board of the Chartered Company. But as Beit, too, was a director of Chartered, it would serve as a useful link with the Rand. If Milner had his way, it was Wernher and Beit, richer and less erratic than Rhodes, who had the most important part to play in the 'Great Game' in South Africa.[53]

It was for this – to concert a long-term strategy to deal with the Boers – that Milner had now come to see Chamberlain.

He had no doubt of the lessons of the past. The Raid was Rhodes's private attempt at a short cut to solve the Transvaal problem. It had failed as abjectly as the forward policy of the imperial government. But that did not prove that intervention was the wrong policy. If Milner was to intervene, his policy must be based on three principles: agreement with loyalists at the Cape, agreement with the Colonial Office at home, and the support of British public opinion on both sides of the political fence.

He knew what they would reply at the Colonial Office. Why attempt a forward policy at all? Time was on their side: only be patient and the Transvaal would fall into their lap. But time, Milner was sure, was *not* on their side, now that the Raid had strengthened Kruger's grip on his own people. So they simply could not afford to go on 'muddling through' and letting the Boers 'stew in their own juice'.[54] In fact, earlier that year, Milner had written to London to ask for permission to 'work up to crisis', to force a show-down with Kruger. Not to put too fine a point on it, he wanted to pick a quarrel over some issue or issues, and then let events force the crisis.[55]

At the time Chamberlain (embarrassed by the enquiry into the Raid) had told a friend that he wished 'everyone would forget the existence of the place [South Africa] for the next year or two'.[56] To Milner he had replied, politely but firmly, 'For the present at any rate our greatest interest in South Africa is peace . . . all our policy must be directed to this object.'[57] This had been the position in early 1898, when Britain had her hands full in dealing with French claims to the Upper Nile. What was Chamberlain's policy in December – after the British triumph in expelling the French from Fashoda?

Milner now had a doubly delicate diplomatic mission during his working holiday in England. First, he must expose the 'rose-coloured illusions' of Chamberlain and the Colonial Office: time, he would prove to them, was not on their side. Second, he must soften up the Press and politicians in general. He had no wish to end up, like Sir Bartle Frere, sacrificed on the altar of public opinion.[58]

This in its turn involved attendance at the dinner tables and country house parties of the great political hostesses of the day – a task not uncongenial to Milner.

High society provided an emollient conspicuously lacking in his official life as an administrator. Eight years before, as a thirty-seven-year-old financial secretary in Egypt, he had fallen in love for the first time. The girl was Margot Tennant and Milner asked her to marry him.[59] She had chosen his Balliol friend instead – Henry Asquith, the future Prime Minister. Milner had tried to shrug off the unrequited affair. 'Dear Blessed Old Boy,' he had told Philip, 'Don't "take on" about it. There are no bones broken. I have not been eaten by an ogress....'[60] But the rebuff intensified the struggle against the romantic yearnings of his father's temperament. Where could he now give them a better (and safer) outlet than in the towered and castellated homes of the great hostesses, in bicycling with Lady Alice Portal and punting with Ettie Grenfell? And even if he was hopeless at bridge, his welcome was assured. Alfred not only talked brilliantly about his imperial mission. He was a brilliant listener.[61]

That evening, 18 November, at eight, the special saloon coach carrying Milner steamed into Vauxhall Station. He took a cab to his bachelor chambers at 47 Duke Street. He had his 'old cave': the big red room on the ground floor. He was too tired to dine at Brooks'. A stack of letters awaited him, a deluge of invitations. Everyone wanted to hear about South Africa.[62]

Four days later Milner crossed the palatial courtyard of the Colonial Office in Whitehall on his way to see Chamberlain. He had every reason to feel depressed. It was not only that row of deceased proconsuls sculpted on the east façade, whose numbers included (like a kind of Bluebeard's gallery) the heads of D'Urban, Smith and Frere. He had also just heard the news from some friends in the CO: the Master – Chamberlain – was sticking to the 'no-war policy'.[63]

His own mind was made up. There were only two ways out of the abyss in South Africa. Either Kruger must make political reforms in his ramshackle republic or there must be a 'row'. To put it bluntly, the choice was between reform or war. And of the two, he believed 'war was more likely'.[64]

CHAPTER 2

Nods and Winks

London,
22 November – December 1898

'A war in South Africa would be one of the most serious
wars that could possibly be waged. It would be in the
nature of a Civil War. It would be a long war, a bitter war
and a costly war . . . it would leave behind it the embers of
a strife which I believe generations would hardly be long
enough to extinguish . . . to go to war with President
Kruger, to force upon him reforms in the internal affairs
of his state, with which [we] have repudiated all right of
interference – that would have been a course of action as
immoral as it would have been unwise.'

Joseph Chamberlain, speaking as
Colonial Secretary in the House of
Commons, May 1896

Earlier that day, 22 November, the Colonial Secretary, Joseph Chamberlain,
had briefed himself for Milner's visit. He worked, we are told, smoothly and
efficiently in his office like an imperious machine.

His biographer has described with awe the Chamberlain of this period.
Every day he arrived by cab from his home in Princes Gardens. In the Private
Secretary's room – a sort of ante-chamber between the main corridor and the
blue baize door of Chamberlain's room – three or four distinguished-looking
men in frock-coats are awaiting his arrival. These are the hierarchy, the high
priests of the Colonial Office. They warm their hands at the coal fire; one of
them goes to the brass rack on the mahogany table and picks up a file; it is tied up
in the proverbial red-tape, and the spidery sequence of minutes culminates in the
welcome initials, 'J.C.'. Now there is the ring of the table bell and the blue baize
door opens. The Master has arrived. 'The machine is ready to take some more,'
he says to the Private Secretary, who shuffles in with the files. He is only half in
jest. 'The sleeping city wakened at his touch,' as one of his admirers put it.[1]

From his desk Chamberlain eyed the world through his eye-glass, and it was
no wonder if the world trembled. Queen Victoria was the symbol of the mother
country, the Empire made flesh; Chamberlain seemed to epitomize its other
side, the dreadnought spirit. There he sat, the self-made man from Birmingham,

with a home-grown orchid in his button-hole and a diamond pin in his stock, his face as cool and handsome as a piece of his own Birmingham steel. His right hand rested on the huge brown globe, traced with the spider's web of cable routes and steamer lanes. It was this strong right hand that would pull the Empire together.[2]

Such was the impression Chamberlain liked, no doubt, to convey, and he conveyed it brilliantly. Yet there was another Joe Chamberlain, better known to his political colleagues than to his office staff or the public: emotional and impulsive, moody and sometimes despondent. For the frustrations of the last two and a half years at the CO had left their inner mark on him, not to speak of the wrangles in the Cabinet – and, of course, the searing experience of the Raid.

Yet the central trauma of Chamberlain's life was none of these. It had occurred twelve years earlier, and it haunted him still.

In 1886 Chamberlain was President of the Board of Trade in Gladstone's cabinet, and his prospects were dazzling. He had risen from the bed-rock of the British middle-class by way of a successful industrial career to the commanding heights of politics.[3] Head and shoulders above his fellow radicals, he could expect, when Gladstone retired, to be the next Liberal Prime Minister: perhaps one of the greatest of Britain's Prime Ministers. Then, in 1886, the Irish Home Rule ulcer burst and engulfed the Liberal Party, and he discovered he was that strange hybrid, both a radical and an imperialist. With Lord Hartington (later Duke of Devonshire), he founded the Liberal Unionists, and for nine long years he was in the wilderness.[4]

To Chamberlain the sacrifice seemed devastating. As he later blurted out to Lord Selborne, the son-in-law of Lord Salisbury, the 'dream of his life' had been to be Prime Minister; for the sake of principle he had sacrificed 'all his ambitions, all his hopes, all his dreams ... they had gone for ever into limbo'. Now he was exposed to the attacks of both parties, there were 'venomous and malignant attacks' from the right of the Tory party, while from his old friends among the radicals he had been abused as 'no public man before him ever had been'.

In April 1895 he had seriously considered resigning from politics. In the event, of course, he thought better of it; he had been impulsive; besides, the Tories were anxious to smooth his ruffled feathers.[5] A couple of months later the working agreement between Liberal Unionists and Conservatives took shape as a formal coalition. And one afternoon in June, the Parliamentary majority of the Liberal rump, now led by Lord Rosebery, vanished in a puff of smoke (it was actually during a debate on the supply of cordite). Chamberlain had come in from the cold. Lord Salisbury, the Tory Prime Minister, then offered him virtually any office he cared to name: the Treasury, Foreign Affairs, the War Office. The whole field was open to him. He chose the Colonies. The appointment was welcomed.[6] Yet it surprised those who, like Salisbury, had imagined he was only a 'theoretic imperialist', or thought him too ambitious to choose what had hitherto been a minor Cabinet post.[7]

The ensuing partnership had borne fruit much as might have been predicted: a measure of success, and a good deal of frustration for everyone.

On taking over, Chamberlain found the Colonial Office was almost a parody of a Whitehall department. Behind the glittering Roman façade, commissioned by Lord Palmerston, the place was unbelievably drab: miles of brown dado and lead-lined staircase. 'We must have all this smartened up,' Chamberlain told his Private Secretary, peering through his eye-glass at the worn carpet and the broken-down mahogany furniture in his room. Some fresh paint was eventually extorted from the Office of Works and electric light was installed to replace the candles and supplement the gaslights.[8] Yet the office remained bleak enough for a romantic like Chamberlain, whose own house at Highbury, in a Birmingham suburb, was filled with the gleam of Morris glass and the glow of Burne-Jones tapestries.[9]

Still more negative than the atmosphere of the building, Chamberlain found, was the spirit of its occupants. Like Milner, Chamberlain believed the new imperialism demanded of Britain a double task: to make a Greater Britain out of the white Empire, and to develop the black one. But how to achieve anything with an office staff of ninety-nine men (including the messengers) dedicated to the Treasury virtues of thrift and prudence?[10] The truth was that the Treasury allocation for the Empire (excluding India and Egypt) was a shoe-string – a mere £130,000 when Chamberlain took over the Colonies.[11] No wonder that the CO staff tended to look on their job with a certain cynicism, and any talk of the 'great estates' overseas had a hollow ring.[12]

His Cabinet colleagues were delighted for him to make speeches about imperial unity.[13] They seemed less anxious to take any practical steps to achieve his objects – especially if they cost money. And the second part of the imperial task – developing the black Empire – would hardly be cheap. In due course, Chamberlain had succeeded in persuading his cabinet colleagues to raise the Colonial Office budget to £600,000, but this was largely spent on the pacification of Uganda and a project in Cyprus.[14] It was a shocking fact, as Chamberlain admitted in public, that the great majority of the black colonies for which Britain was directly responsible had still, after a century, received no real benefit from imperial membership.[15]

Still, one must not exaggerate Chamberlain's own frustrations at this period. He had to admit that he found both Lord Salisbury and Arthur Balfour, his nephew and deputy, the soul of politeness. They recognized that his imperial ideas were a substitute for the lost dream of being a great radical Prime Minister. They flattered him in their languid, aristocratic way by reminding him of how he was indispensable to the party alliance – though this was only partly flattery. They supported him, to some extent, against the penny-pinching spirit of the Chancellor of the Exchequer, Sir Michael Hicks Beach. Above all, they saved him when his career seemed likely to be brought to an untimely end by that tornado from South Africa – the Jameson Raid.

The Raid. Chamberlain, too, had found this an extraordinary business. And if Milner felt baffled about the part Chamberlain had played, it was nothing to what Chamberlain sometimes felt himself. After one and a half years of public enquiries and private heart-searching he confessed to an admirer, 'The fact is that I can hardly say what I knew and what I did not.'[16]

Yet the evidence *was* there, whether Chamberlain liked it or not, locked away in those ministerial red boxes in his office. And, eighty years later, we can see that, if published, this evidence would have been the end of Chamberlain and might well have changed the course of history.[17]

The dilemma that faced Chamberlain when he took over the Colonies in 1895 was a delicate one. He shared Milner's view of South African policy in the past: that it had been one long blunder from the imperial standpoint. He recalled ruefully that he had served in Gladstone's cabinet, which made the culminating blunders of Majuba, the Pretoria and London Conventions and 'peace-under-defeat'. He shared Milner's distaste for Rhodes and the buccaneering of the Chartered Company.[18] But he had inherited from Lord Ripon, the outgoing Liberal Secretary of State, a passive leave-it-to-Rhodes policy for South Africa, which was supposed to result in federation. Soon after Chamberlain took up the seals of office, Rhodes pressed for new negotiations. And here was the dilemma. Chamberlain learned that an Uitlander *coup* was expected in Johannesburg, organized by Rhodes and Beit. Could the British government safely leave it all to these two men to handle? What if the *coup* resulted in an Uitlander republic under its own flag? Paradoxically, this would be even worse for Britain than the Boer republic. For it could postpone for ever the chance of creating a British federation of South Africa, built up on the gold of the Transvaal.[19]

Chamberlain's response to the dilemma was to adopt a course not unknown to political opportunists: he would take care 'not to know too much'. If the plot failed he could plead official ignorance; if it succeeded he could share (privately) the credit with Rhodes and Beit.[20] But this was not merely a policy of opportunism; it was extremely dangerous. To have knowledge, without complicity in the plot, was to tread a moral and political tightrope. Who but a brave man (or a lunatic) would share a tightrope with Cecil Rhodes?

On that fateful day when Jameson set out on his ride, Chamberlain was at home in Birmingham, waiting anxiously for news of the *coup*.[21] Characteristically, he had kept the Prime Minister and Balfour almost completely in the dark. The first the Prime Minister knew about the plot, it appears, was when he was told by Chamberlain, a week earlier, that a rising was imminent and they must 'watch the event' as it might 'turn out to their advantage'.[22] A few days later Chamberlain informed him that the rising was going to 'fizzle out' – partly because of the tiresome way in which the Uitlanders would not agree to exchange the Boer republic for a British colony.[23] Two days later, Chamberlain received the astonishing news that, despite everything, Jameson was going in. It was the night of the servants' ball at Highbury, and he was dressing for dinner when the special messenger arrived. He rose to the occasion. 'If this succeeds, it will ruin me,' he is supposed to have told his family, clenching his hands. 'I am going up to London to crush it.'[24] He dashed off in a cab from the servants' ball at midnight like the hero of a novel by Ouida.

In fact, when Rhodes fell from the tightrope, he nearly brought Chamberlain down with him. The policy of official deafness proved unworkable. At both ends of operations – in London and the Cape – members of Chamberlain's staff had been fully briefed by Rhodes and the plotters, and had taken action to help Rhodes which amounted to complicity. Chamberlain himself had become caught up in the web of half-knowledge and half-truth. Not only would it be most discreditable if those nods and winks ever came to light.[25] He had also personally intervened at one crucial moment in the plot – this was the time of a crisis over Venezuela – to remind Rhodes of the international situation, and a cable had been sent to 'hurry things along'.[26] And soon, after the opening of Bobby White's trunk, the whole world was buzzing with stories of the British government's complicity.[27]

Chamberlain's part in the great cover-up that followed Jameson's Raid – Jameson's break-in, so to speak – was not, one would imagine, an episode on which he looked back with any great pride. To Lord Salisbury he wrote a long memorandum in tones of injured innocence.[28] In Parliament he was his usual bland and masterful self, the Pushful Joe of the cartoonists. He gave as good as he got. Yet to his inner circle of friends, he made no secret of the fact that he had his back to the wall. 'I don't care a twopenny damn,' he said, 'for the whole lot of them.'[29] But how to suppress, or neutralize, the evidence that would come before the Parliamentary Committee of Enquiry? In the event, Lord Salisbury showed his confidence in his Colonial Secretary by insisting that he should himself serve on the Committee.[30] And in addition, certain other arrangements were made which effectively saved his bacon.

First, Chamberlain came to a sensible arrangement with Rhodes, Beit and their men. Jameson was secretly visited in prison by Chamberlain; and Jameson kept his mouth shut.[31] On their part, Rhodes and Beit agreed not to produce in court the so-called 'missing telegrams'. These were the cables from Rhodes's London office to Cape Town and the most damning evidence against Chamberlain outside his own red boxes. They detailed the course of his dealings with the Colonial Office and included the 'hurry-up' telegram, which especially implicated Chamberlain.[32] In return for Rhodes's and Jameson's good sense, Chamberlain agreed not to tamper with the charter of the Chartered Company, which could have been revoked as a result of the revelations about Rhodes's part in the Raid.[33]

Second, Chamberlain found someone on the Colonial Office staff who was prepared to offer himself as a scapegoat. This was Sir Graham Bower, the Imperial Secretary at the Cape, who had personally handled negotiations with the plotters. Out of patriotism – 'naval standards', he called it – he agreed to pretend he had not told his chiefs about the Jameson plan. His reward was swift: censure by the Committee and the ruin of his career.[34] Another possible scapegoat was also considered by Chamberlain: Bower's counterpart, Edward Fairfield, who had handled the London end of the negotiations, including the 'hurry-up' telegram. But Fairfield apparently did not feel like being sacrificed. It was fortunate for everyone that, shortly after he was told what was expected of him, he had a stroke and died.[35]

And so Chamberlain was able to appear at the London enquiry, and say with his hand on his heart, 'I had not then and . . . never had, any knowledge, or, until I think it was the day before the actual raid took place, the slightest suspicion of anything in the nature of a hostile or armed invasion of the Transvaal.' And he went on to pay eloquent tribute to poor Fairfield; how sad it was, he could say, somehow keeping a straight face, that Fairfield had misunderstood his orders, being so unusually deaf.[36]

In fact, it needed more than Chamberlain's eloquence, Fairfield's stroke, Bower's quixotic self-sacrifice and the deal with Rhodes and Beit to save the Colonial Secretary. He was saved by his enemies.

A few days after the Raid the Kaiser committed a blunder almost as colossal as Rhodes's, Beit's and Jameson's. He sent a telegram to congratulate Kruger on his escape. This immediately invested the Raid with the status of an international incident. In England, it provoked a storm of anti-German feeling. What infernal cheek, people said, for the Kaiser (Wilhelm II) to meddle in our sphere of influence. Queen Victoria wagged her finger at her impertinent grandson Willy. And everyone swung back behind the government. The fleet was mobilized before the sudden squall subsided. As for Jameson, instead of having to endure the expected jibes about the White Flag, he was the hero of the hour. From his prison cell he learnt that his ride had been set to music. 'Then, over the Transvaal border,/And gallop for life or death,' sang Alfred Austin, the Poet Laureate.[37] Jameson's statue was cast in Staffordshire clay. Grim-faced on his black stallion, he rode across a thousand mantelpieces.

Some of the admiration for Jameson did not fail to rub off on Chamberlain. Certainly it compounded the problems of Chamberlain's chief political enemies – the radical wing of the Liberal Party. How far could they go in pressing the charge of complicity against Chamberlain? With public opinion in this mood, they would be on dangerous ground. Moreover, there were all sorts of other reasons why Liberals were squeamish about pressing the charges. The leading Liberal imperialist, Lord Rosebery, was believed to have heard about the Raid from Rhodes's own lips much too early for Rosebery's own good. The leading radical, Sir William Harcourt, was a personal friend of Joe's and, apart from this, there was the call of patriotism. Who wanted to wash their dirty linen in front of the world?[38]

So Joseph Chamberlain appeared at the parliamentary enquiry and was met by a barrage of silence. The enquiry itself passed into folk-lore as the Lying-in-State at Westminster.[39]

What were the effects on Chamberlain of this two-year ordeal? His discomfiture certainly made him no more conciliatory to Kruger. He now had a personal score to settle with the old man – 'an ignorant, dirty, cunning and obstinate man who had known how to feather his own nest and to enrich all his family and dependants'. But nor had his sympathy for Kruger's opponents – the Uitlanders – increased with the Raid. He found them 'a lot of cowardly, blatant, selfish speculators who would sell their souls to have the power of rigging the market'. As for their leader, Cecil Rhodes, whom he had always privately distrusted, he now regarded him not only as a 'blunderer' who had alienated the Cape Afrikaners, but as a 'blackmailer' who had threatened to publish the missing telegrams if the Charter was revoked. 'What is there in South Africa,' he burst out, 'that makes blackguards of all who get involved in its politics?' Yet these were the men who, since the Raid, were Britain's only allies in South Africa.[40]

One can well imagine Chamberlain's feelings of frustration. The Raid had made him keener than ever to have a go at the Transvaal. By alienating the Cape Afrikaners, however, it had also deprived him of the means. In short, the effects of the Raid were not unlike the effects of drink, as described by the Porter in *Macbeth*: 'It provokes and unprovokes; it increases the desire and takes away the performance.'[41]

At 2.30 p.m. on 22 November Chamberlain received Milner in his room beyond the blue baize door, and Milner put the case for 'working up to a crisis'.[42] There is no record on the Colonial Office files of the interview, but we know the two men's lines of argument. The gap between them was still as wide as ever.

Time fought on the side of the enemy, Milner claimed. Kruger had returned after his re-election as President 'more autocratic and more reactionary than ever'. Now he was arming for the coming struggle with Britain. 'He has immense resources in money and any amount of ammunition of war, to which he is constantly adding.' No doubt he 'suffered from megalomania'. But either his government – a 'race-oligarchy' – or the Uitlanders must rule in the Transvaal, and Milner saw no sign of Kruger's government removing itself. Indeed, if Britain went to war with its European rivals, Kruger might seize the chance to attack the Cape.[43]

To this, Chamberlain repeated his conviction: the only policy now available was the policy of patience. First, because there were the political effects of that 'accursed Raid'. It had placed the country in a 'false position'; the Afrikaners at the Cape had been alienated; he must wait until they resumed their confidence in him. Second, there were positive advantages in playing the waiting game. British influence was increasing all the time; internal opposition to Kruger must develop by reaction and Kruger himself was not getting any younger.

Third and fourth, there were arguments against war. Chamberlain believed that military victories would be self-defeating: their ultimate aim was a union, in every sense, in South Africa. War would only arouse hatred and leave a legacy of bitterness. If war had to come, Kruger must be the aggressor and the Afrikaners at the Cape – or at least a large part of them – on the side of the Empire. War would be 'extremely unpopular' in Britain unless Kruger's behaviour was 'outrageous' and he put himself blatantly in the wrong. To do this he would have to make a 'serious breach' of the London Convention.[44]

Give Kruger enough rope, Chamberlain seemed to be saying.[45] To which Milner's reply was in effect that the old President had proved himself far too cunning to hang anyone, least of all himself.

*   *   *   *   *

Milner returned to his chambers in Duke Street with the result of his mission to see Chamberlain an apparent anti-climax. Yet Milner was not depressed. He had taken a hint from Joe – from one of those nods and winks – that London's 'no-war policy' did not tie Cape Town's or Johannesburg's hands. To 'get things "forrarder" by my own actions,' was how he described his policy after the interview.[46] It was in South Africa that a way of working up to the crisis must be found.

Meanwhile, he threw himself into the task of softening up public opinion at home, by stamping 'on rose-coloured illusions about South Africa'. It proved an awful rush. It was delicate work, too, for he had to catch up 'with *all* the leading politicians and pressmen – without seeming to run after them'.[47]

Fortunately, Milner could rely on his network of friendships – that finely spun web that stretched from Balliol to the Cabinet room by way of *The Times* in Printing House Square, Brooks' Club and Panshanger. At his first political house party that month, a weekend with Lord and Lady Cowper at Panshanger, he bumped into Arthur Balfour, the Deputy Prime Minister, George Curzon (it was a fortnight before Curzon left England to be Viceroy in India) and St John Brodrick, Under-Secretary at the Foreign Office. Curzon and Brodrick were Milner's own Balliol contemporaries, together with a third, Willie Selborne, and Austen Chamberlain; these were the 'Arthurians' (as young Winston Churchill was to call them), the men who would soon come to dominate the Tory Party under Balfour's leadership.[48] Already they were a hard, bright centre within the party. No wonder Milner enjoyed the weekend at Panshanger, even if he preferred the long political talks over the port to the party games, like 'the truth game', that were such a 'dangerous' feature of the Panshanger Friday-to-Monday.[49]

The guests that weekend also included Margot and Henry Asquith. It was now nine years since Margot had rejected Milner's proposal of marriage, and the scars had long healed. The Margot he had wooed beside the Pyramids (with what 'grace and poetry' she had danced the *pas seul* at Lady Baring's Christmas party)[50] was now Margot the political hostess, the Margot who shocked everyone by smoking cigarettes on the steps of the House of Commons, the Margot whose 'colossal indiscretions' made her such a delightful companion.[51] In fact, she had again become one of his most intimate friends. She would drop in to his chambers in Duke Street when he was in London and stay gossiping for hours. It was all absolutely innocent, of course, but not idle gossip by any means on Milner's part. Henry Asquith was now the leading Liberal in the party after Campbell-Bannerman and it was essential, if Milner were to woo the Liberals, that he should keep in with Henry Asquith. And not only with Henry and the Liberals. For Milner's aim was to spread the word about South Africa as widely as possible. And if you wanted something shouted from the house-tops, you had only to tell it in strictest confidence to Margot.

It was a 'delightful' excursion, Milner confessed, that weekend at Panshanger. It had set the pattern for the rest of Milner's trip. He saw George Buckle of *The Times,* and Spenser Wilkinson of *The Morning Post.*[52] (He found the 'wobbly

Liberals' of *The Manchester Guardian* 'very rotten' by contrast.')[53] He was invited everywhere: by the Roseberys of Mentmore, the Rothschilds of Tring, not to mention the Queen, the Prime Minister and the Prince of Wales. He found these visits, too, 'delightful'.[54]

He would apologize to his friends for troubling them with his 'boring screed'. 'You may think me a bore,' he told Lord Rosebery, the leading Liberal Imperialist, 'but I should like to tell you some things about that little corner of the imperial chess-board I am especially concerned with. It does not attract much attention at present. Heaven be praised!' And then he would go on to explain, for the hundredth time, the dangers of 'Krugerism'; how he wondered if the British government's 'policy-of-patience' would ever heal the South African ulcer, and yet how he himself would exhaust every effort in his search for peace.[55]

Of course, Milner's real policy – of 'working up to a crisis' – was kept secret from Margot and the Liberals.[56] Only a few intimates, like Philip Gell, knew these *arcana imperii*. And there was another secret of Milner's character that has remained locked till today in his private papers.

Incongruous as Milner's figure might seem in High Society, this shy, donnish figure in the boisterous world of drawing-rooms and gun-rooms, these jollities were an accepted by-product of Victorian official life. Still more incongruous – and a great deal less safe – was Milner's friendship with a girl called Cécile, whose lodgings in Brixton were paid for by him. The story of this strange affair has never been told – or even hinted at. But a careful scrutiny of Milner's unpublished diary shows that Milner had set up Cécile in a house near, but not too near, his bachelor chambers at Duke Street. It was an ardent friendship that had lasted at least nine years already, and cost Milner about a quarter (at an average of £450 a year) of his free income.[57] Together they bicycled over the South Downs; they went punting on the Thames, staying Friday to Monday at a hotel in Marlow; they played piquet and whist when he came to stay in her lodgings. One obvious rule had to be kept: Cécile never came to his chambers, let alone met him in public. Apparently she never met one of his friends.[58] Perhaps even Philip Gell never knew of Cécile's existence.

Milner's diary makes it clear that his friendship with Cécile was one of the dominant themes of his life, even during that working holiday in England. In the first week of December – the busiest phase of his English tour, when he was only able to snatch a few hours successively with Chamberlain at Birmingham, with Salisbury at Hatfield, and with Queen Victoria at Windsor – Milner vanished into the blue on a six-day bicycling trip with Cécile.[59]

The idea may seem a little absurd today: a middle-aged Viceroy, his mistress, and two bicycles vanishing on a mid-winter's tour of the South Downs and letting the South African crisis go hang for a week. But then there was nothing absurd about a bicycle in those days. Indeed, the bicycle was the sports car of the nineties, the sporting symbol of the age. (It added spice not only to love, but to politics. Cabinet ministers like Balfour – the 'divine Arthur' of the Panshanger set – went dashing down to Hatfield on their bikes to see the Prime Minister. It was on his bike that 'Pom' McDonnell, Salisbury's urbane Private Secretary, had sped from Hatfield to Osterley one sunny weekend in 1895 with the glorious news for Arthur: the Liberal government had fallen.)[60]

On their own wintry excursion, Milner and Cécile stayed in a Hampshire hotel. Although they had a private sitting-room where they 'played piquet till bed-time' (as Milner primly recorded in his diary)[61] the risk of exposure must have been considerable. A scandal might have ruined Milner. True, Victorian society winked at men-about-town who kept mistresses. But Viceroys had to avoid any hint of scandal. And the special moral and intellectual position that Milner had built up for himself – the austere 'civilian soldier of the Empire',[62] the dedicated philosopher-king – would have vanished like a puff of smoke. His enemies, who now thought him a prig, would have written him off as a humbug. His friends would have had a dangerous insight into his character – into that Bohemian side of him that he struggled so hard to control.

Perhaps the risk of discovery, the brinkmanship, added spice to the adventure. Certainly one of the features of the week that Milner must have felt most was its dream-like incongruity. What other great Victorian proconsul could vanish from the side of his Queen at Windsor and re-emerge at the side of his mistress in a seedy back-street of Brixton?

Indeed, there was an extraordinary episode on the fourth day when Milner had to return to the official world for a few hours to celebrate a great 'hooroosh': a send-off for George Curzon. He deposited his bike at Vauxhall Station, and took a cab to his chambers in Duke Street. He dealt hastily with the backlog of official letters. He dressed in his white tie; an hour later he was sitting in the Hotel Cecil between the Hon. Mrs Maguire and Lady Ulrica Duncombe at the table of the Duke of Marlborough. 'It was a most brilliant function and I greatly enjoyed it,' he recorded.[63] At eleven o'clock the party began to break up, and his companions drove off westwards to Mayfair. Milner walked alone across Waterloo Bridge, and then, when the coast was clear, hailed a cab and drove back to the other world south of the river.

It was all recorded in his diary – in the style of a maiden aunt describing a picnic. 'In most beautiful weather,' he wrote on 8 December, 'we rode by the Devil's Punch Bowl from Milford to Liphook, taking a late lunch at the Royal Hants Hotel and reaching Liphook just at sunset. It was really a wonderful day, more like mild autumn than winter, and the view from the top of Hind Head splendid.'[64]

Yet there were other splendid views from the top Milner had to consider – and they included the view from Government House. Perhaps Milner already knew in his heart that this was the last adventure with Cécile. On 23 January, two days before leaving for South Africa, he was to write in his diary in his meticulous italic hand, 'To Brixton ... to see C.' Then he added three words, curiously emotional words in that prim, dry record of facts, crossed them out and then scrawled them again in the margin of the page: 'to say goodbye'.[65]

Meanwhile, a new political strategy had taken shape in Milner's mind after the interview with Chamberlain. The 'no-war policy' did not tie his hands. Everything depended on the British subjects in the Transvaal. If they could be 'bucked up' and given competent leadership; if Wernher, Beit and the other 'gold-bugs' could be brought into line, too; if both their grievances could be presented to the British public in the correct light, in short, if the Uitlanders could be manoeuvred into the right, and Kruger into the wrong, then they could still 'screw Kruger'.[66] In other words, if Milner supplied the plan and the horse, that 'idiot' Jameson could ride again.

To arrange this himself he would have to wait till he reached the Cape. In the meantime he must pray to the Higher Powers that General Sir William Butler, the acting governor, acted with discretion, and that a premature crisis did not blow up in his absence.

CHAPTER 3

Champagne for the Volk

Pretoria,
23–29 December 1898

Geologist to Kruger in 1886: 'Mr President, the conglomerate
gold-beds and enclosing sandstones and quartzites were sea-shore
deposits formed during the subsidence of a coast line in ...'
Kruger to his wife: 'Mama, meet the gentleman who was there
when God made the earth.'

A fortnight after Milner had attended the great 'hooroosh' for George Curzon in
London, another kind of celebration took place in Pretoria, six thousand miles
away: a victory banquet for burghers and government. The conquering hero
was the Transvaal Commander-in-Chief, Commandant-General Piet Joubert,
and they were not giving him a send-off, like Curzon's; they were celebrating
his safe return. Joubert and his commandos had just marched back to Pretoria
after subduing, with the help of their Creusot artillery, a troublesome African
chief called Mpefu.[1]

For the battle-hardened commandos, it was the triumphant end to half a
dozen native wars in nearly as many years. No wonder that in the Grand Hotel,
Pretoria, that evening the candlelight playing on the blue-and-gold uniforms of
the state artillery and the green sash of the President reflected a certain swagger –
a kind of imperial glow, Afrikaner-style – that would not have been out of place
in the Hotel Cecil, London. The champagne, too, was excellent in Pretoria.
Since they had grown rich on the profits of the Rand, the Boers had come to
recognize how imported French wine, like imported French artillery, could add
to the success of most occasions.[2]

Oom Paul ('Uncle Paul', as the burghers affectionately called Kruger) spoke
briefly at the banquet. For the last few years he had been visibly failing in health,
plagued by eye trouble and other infirmities. Still, he remained a prodigy. At
seventy-three he was a national monument in his own lifetime, a heroic survival
from the Great Trek.[3] It was those days he recalled in his speech. He told the
story, as he loved to tell it on every possible occasion, of his own part in crushing
Dingaan and the Zulus at the Battle of Blood River.

'I do not say what I have heard,' he said, speaking the taal (Afrikaans) in his
gruff, jerky voice, 'but what I have seen with my own eyes.' He went on to

describe the battle in his homely way: the circle of covered wagons chained together in the laager; the gaps between the wagons closed by bundles of mimosa thorn; the attack of the Zulus, the air thick with assegais; the children melting down lead for bullets; the women hacking off the arms of the Zulus who tried to break through the thorn bushes. And the Lord, praise the Lord; He had given His people a great victory.

Kruger's extraordinary life had spanned the whole life of the State from the Battle of Blood River to Jameson's defeat at the Battle of Doornkop. It was now nearly the third anniversary of that victory. Kruger, under doctor's orders, retired early from the banquet, after receiving an ovation, to his small, whitewashed house in Church Street.[4]

It was in this same modest house that the news of the Raid had reached Kruger three years before, when Jameson was riding to Johannesburg. It was ten o'clock; his friends had found him asleep; a single sentry on duty at the gate; the house in darkness, apart from one electric bulb. On hearing the news, Kruger reluctantly agreed to have a horse saddled ready in case he had to leave Pretoria in a hurry. But had he already guessed what was afoot? He showed no sign of excitement. After agreeing to call out the commandos, he went back to sleep as if nothing had happened.[5]

To mark the anniversary of the Raid, people had now suggested that the government set up a monument. There was even talk of celebrating Jameson Day, equivalent to the Englishman's Guy Fawkes.[6] Kruger let it be known that he frowned on the latter idea. They had already one day of national rejoicing, Dingaan's Day (16 December) to celebrate the destruction of the Zulus. Perhaps Kruger added with characteristically heavy humour that it was not the moment – not yet, at any rate – to celebrate the destruction of the British.

The chief speech at that night's banquet was given by General Joubert. He rose to his feet, his Majuba medal agleam on his scarlet uniform, tall, bearded, suave, the leading Boer of his generation after President Kruger, and the runner-up in three presidential contests. Although he, too, had witnessed the Great Trek, as a child, Joubert presented a striking contrast to Kruger. If Kruger was the archetypal Boer of the backveld, Joubert typified the Boer of the towns. Not for him the baggy black suits of the old President, the clouds of smoke puffed from an enormous pipe, and the habit of underlining his words by spitting on the ground.[7] Joubert dressed like a gentleman, and was known for his progressive ideas. He had taught himself to read and write English as well as Dutch. His business acumen had earned him the name of 'Slim (Clever) Piet' as well as investments in land and gold shares that totalled, after his death, £230,000 – a tidy sum even by the standards of the Rand.

If Joubert had a weakness it was, the Boers said, his lack of moral courage. As a general, he hated imposing unpopular duties on the burghers; as a politician, he shrank from standing up to Kruger in the Raad (the Volksraad, alias the Transvaal Parliament). Not that he could be accused of being soft towards Africans, any more than any other 'Progressive' politicians. On the contrary, in both the

Raad and on the battlefield he had proved himself a firm advocate of keeping the Kaffirs in their place.[8]

Tonight Joubert was almost apologetic as he explained why there had been so little fighting in the campaign against Mpefu. There was no need to kill many Kaffirs. They fled into their caves. Mpefu fled across the Limpopo. Yet the war was just and necessary. Mpefu, the so-called 'Lion of the North', had the impertinence to call himself the King of Zoutpansberg, and claim some white settlers as his subjects. So the government sent the burghers and stopped the Lion's roar for ever.

There was cheering in the hall as Joubert reached his peroration: the usual patriotic appeal for unity. They must stand shoulder to shoulder against all opposition in the struggle for the 'land'. They must shed the last drop of blood for the 'volk'. Before midnight, the banquet concluded with the customary cheers, three times three, for the guest of honour and his wife. The Boer national anthem, the 'Volkslied', was played by the hotel band, the state artillerymen presented arms, and the guests trooped out into the city, where a picturesque contrast presented itself: the backveld Boers, in Pretoria for their Christmas pilgrimage, camped there in their covered wagons;[9] while high above the wooded valleys, throwing monstrous shadows in the moonlight, were three enormous forts, the pride of the Transvaal army, equipped with searchlights and the latest European artillery.[10]

It had been a triumphant evening for Joubert, the conquering hero, and Oom Paul, the father of the republic.

Of course, political realities are never so simple, least of all in a country like the Transvaal, which had leapt two centuries in the space of a decade. Kruger was neither so unyielding nor so secure as he appeared. Joubert, the picture of the loyal general, deeply resented Kruger's idiosyncratic methods of government and opposed much of his policy. Behind Joubert there had gathered the 'Progressives' (the young Turks) mustering about a third of the Raad. They were determined to modernize the ramshackle republic before it was too late.

Hence it was not true to say, as Milner had told Chamberlain, that there was no sign of the Transvaal reforming itself. Change was in the air, radical change, and supported (if reluctantly) by Kruger himself.

Chamberlain had called Kruger an 'ignorant, dirty, cunning' old man (borrowing the words, incidentally, from a private letter of that unusual Foreign Office official, Roger Casement).[11] Foreigners consistently underrated Kruger. It was partly a matter of style. The massive frame, the puffy features, half-covered by a mat of grey hair, had their counterpart in the gruff voice and the strange syntax.[12] Here was the epitome of the peasant; one of Brueghel's rustics escaped from the sixteenth century; an 'ugly customer' indeed (as Disraeli once called him in private) at the helm of government.[13]

It is true that in some ways Kruger appeared extremely crude. Joubert, who was also self-educated, adopted the European conventions of public speaking; he had mastered the art of saying nothing in a great many words. Kruger often said too much before he had spoken a sentence. And not only that, he actually seemed to believe much of what he said: that the earth was as flat as the Bible said,[14] that the Boers were the people of the Book, chosen by the Lord, and (as a kind of corollary) that the *rooineks* (English) deserved to be damned. Yet to people who knew Kruger well, it was clear that the old man's mind, like the Rand gold-mines, had its deep levels; that he was complex as well as crude.

He had been born in 1825 somewhere inside the borders of Cape Colony, the third child of an obscure trekboer (a migrant farmer) whose ancestors had come from Germany a century before. When he was ten, the family joined a pioneer column led by Andries Potgieter and set out on the Great Trek. His education was left to the Good Book and the rifle: the Bible read aloud by his father at the supper table, the rifle used to such effect that before long he had shot half a dozen lions. At seventeen he was deputy field cornet, and he did not disappoint his admirers. To his tally of lion, he added a list of African chiefs whom he subdued: Secheli, the Bechuana chieftain, Mapela of Waterberg and Monsioia. And at twenty-six he served on the Boer council of war which negotiated with Britain the Sand River Convention, recognizing Transvaal independence. At thirty-six he was Commandant-General.[15]

After 1877, when Britain had annexed the Transvaal and Sir Bartle Frere controlled it, Kruger emerged as the national champion. Twice he was sent to London to try to persuade the British to cancel the annexation. He failed, of course. But the First Boer War that followed (regarded by the Boers as the First War of Independence) brought him a double triumph: in the battles that culminated in Majuba, and in the diplomatic victories that followed. It was Kruger who helped persuade Gladstone to settle for peace, subject to the Convention. He was then elected for the first of four terms as President.[16]

The veld had bred in him the unusual qualities that made a man a successful leader in hunting lions or black men: the mixture of animal strength and human cunning, of self-reliance and faith in the Lord, and the steely will, strong but flexible, equally serviceable in advance and retreat.

But the veld had also bred in Kruger serious defects which emerged in time of peace. He was headstrong and autocratic and tactless.[17] One of his political opponents once described the extraordinary methods he used to woo the opposition: 'First he argues with me and, if that is no good, he gets into a rage and jumps round the room roaring at me like a wild beast . . . and if I do not give in then he fetches out the Bible and . . . he even quotes that to help him out. And if all that fails he takes me by the hand and cries like a child and begs and prays me to give in. . . . Say, old friend, who can resist a man like that?'[18] But many Boers, quite apart from the British, did not find these methods irresistible at all.

Among the Progressives, Kruger's reputation had suffered in the years of peace after Majuba. His diplomatic policies were dealt a near-fatal blow by British success in encircling the country during the scramble for Africa. Many Boers, including Joubert, believed in the 1880s that the Transvaal should expand northwards across the Limpopo; Rhodes trekked there first. The Boers also had their eyes on Tongaland as an outlet to the sea; the British took

Tonga-land. Kruger had to be content with a railway link to Lourenço Marques in Portuguese territory, which took years to build.[19]

By 1893 – two years before this railway was opened – Kruger's stock in the Transvaal had fallen so low that he almost lost the presidency to Joubert. Joubert's supporters in the Progressive Party maintained that he had won a majority of the votes, but the poll had been rigged. Joubert failed, characteristically, to insist on new elections.[20]

Joubert's party continued to harry Kruger inside and outside the Raad throughout the next three years. In their party newspaper *Land en Volk* they hammered home the message: 'Krugerism' was corrupt, inefficient and a ridiculous anachronism; high time Kruger was put in a museum. They baited Kruger for giving his country away to foreigners: the plum jobs were given to the Hollanders (Dutch immigrants) who acted as the administrators and technicians of the young state; the railway monopoly given to a foreign company, the Netherlands Railway Company; and the dynamite monopoly given to foreign speculators, the German and French shareholders of two foreign arms-manufacturing companies. In a country where the mines had such an insatiable appetite for dynamite, this monopoly was to make nearly £2 million profit, almost a licence to print money. Even some of Kruger's staunchest supporters thought this monopoly indefensible.[21]

By 1895 Kruger seemed to be coming to the end of his tether.[22] And then rescue came – from Dr Jameson.

The first great debt that Kruger owed Dr Jameson was that Jameson united the volk behind the Transvaal government. At a stroke, the fumbling old President became the hero of the Raid. The sneers of the Progressives were forgotten for the moment, and when the backveld burghers were cheerfully planning to hang Jameson and the Reformers (on the famous beam from Slachter's Nek) it was Kruger who showed studied moderation.[23]

The second great debt that Kruger owed Jameson was that the Raid rallied the volk *outside* the borders of the Transvaal – especially in the Orange Free State. The Free State was the sister republic of the Transvaal, the first of the twin homelands founded by the voortrekkers. And how enviable was its history in comparison with the Transvaal's. The British had long regarded it as a model republic: a show-piece of tolerance and good sense. For half a century – ever since the Bloemfontein Convention of 1854 – they had recognized it as a fully independent nation. On their part, the Free State Boers welcomed foreign immigrants and treated them well when they came. The Uitlanders in the Free State had all the political rights denied their counterparts in the Transvaal. But then how easy it was for everybody to behave impeccably in the Free State. Not an ounce of gold had been found – in those days – under its rolling veld. Only a trickle of immigrants came: no threat to its independence or national character.[24]

Now, since the Raid, a subtle change had come over the arcadian state. The President elected in 1896 was Marthinus Steyn, dedicated to closer union with the Transvaal. In 1897 a military pact had been concluded between the two republics, and Steyn had set the seal on this pact by visiting Pretoria in November 1898. In diplomacy, President Steyn could be expected to exert a moderating influence. But, if all failed, blood was thicker than water.[25] No wonder Kruger fêted President Steyn in Pretoria with a brass band and a State banquet; and in his official speech, Kruger brought the house down. It was his favourite kind of clowning: 'I'm just an old *simpleton*,' compared to those 'brilliant educated gentlemen from the Free State'. Kruger had every reason to celebrate. With the new military pact, he had pulled off a diplomatic *coup*. If it came to the crunch, the Free State could add fifteen thousand burghers to the Transvaal army of twenty-five thousand.[26]

These were two of the political effects of the Raid: uniting the volk inside and outside the Transvaal. But Dr Jameson's crowning achievement was to teach Kruger how deplorable was the state of his own burgher army.

True, when the call came, the burghers had answered it in their fashion. As Joubert reported: 'When the telegram was received that Jameson had crossed the border I would not believe it possible, but I sent round the country calling the men to arms. Each man jumps on his pony and rides off. He does not wait... but goes as he is.' Of course, it was easy for the six thousand burghers who had mobilized to round up Jameson's six hundred. But what if a real army had invaded the country? What if the British government had supported Jameson? The facts that the Raid brought to light were a scandal. By law, every burgher had to provide himself with a rifle and ammunition. Of the 24,238 burghers liable to be commandeered, 9,996 were found to have no rifle; the rest had old rifles or new rifles of an old pattern. There was only enough ammunition to make war for a fortnight. The country, concluded Kruger, was 'practically defenceless' at the time of the Raid; 'the burghers had neglected their sacred duty to arm themselves'.[27]

Now it was Kruger who proceeded to re-equip the Transvaal army at a cost of over £1 million. Joubert had stupidly ordered thirty-six thousand British Martini-Henry single shot rifles and six thousand Austrian Guedes rifles.[28] These had been superseded nearly ten years before by the new small-bore magazine rifles, the Lee Metford in Britain and the Mauser in Germany. Kruger told Joubert to buy a second rifle for each burgher, and made him import thirty-seven thousand Mausers from Krupp's factory in Germany.[29]

The best that could be said for Joubert was that he was building up an excellent artillery corps. He was to order twenty-two of the most modern pieces of artillery from Europe: from Creusot in France, four of the latest 155-mm heavy guns (later to be known as 'Long Toms') and six of the 75-mm field guns; from Krupp's, four of their 120-mm howitzers and eight of the 75-mm field guns. He was also buying from Maxim-Nordenfeld in Britain twenty of the experimental 1-pounders ('Pom-Poms') that were not yet in service with the British army.[30] But the State Artillery Corps was still a midget by European standards. Joubert was told they needed another eight of the 75-mm Creusots. He procrastinated till it was too late. 'What can I do with more guns?' he asked when pressed in the Raad, 'Have we not already more than we can use?'[31]

Kruger on his part had made some equally strange decisions. He commissioned those four elephantine fortresses, Despoort, Klapperkop, Schanzkop and Wonderboompoort, commanding Pretoria and the Rand. They cost over £300,000 – £1½ million according to one estimate.[32] What were they for? Militarily, it was hard to imagine. They offended the first principle of Boer tactics: mobility above all. Kruger's object seems to have been political: to overawe the Uitlanders. But the fortresses at Johannesburg had become the symbol of 'Krugerism', and the lesson the Uitlanders drew was the one Kruger least of all wished them to draw. They were too weak to beat Kruger alone, they must summon the help of the imperial government.[33]

Despite this blunder, and despite Joubert's bungling, Kruger had transformed the Transvaal's army since the Raid – just as Milner had warned Chamberlain. The burghers could mobilize in a week: twenty-odd commandos armed with the most modern guns and rifles, an effective force of over twenty-five thousand fighting men – forty thousand including their allies from the Free State. The combined army was four times the size of the British garrisons in the two colonies and the largest modern army in the entire sub-continent.[34]

These, then, were the main results of the Raid, as it affected Kruger: to strengthen his grip on the Transvaal, to rally the Free State to his side, to make his country a real military power. Yet the future was still ominous. The Raid had given him a breathing space, but the basic dilemmas remained. He must modernize the republic without alienating his deeply conservative burghers. He must make concessions to the Uitlanders without risking his country's independence. Above all, he needed a new convention with the British government in order to realize the voortrekkers' dream of fully independent nationhood.

His first task was to try to sweep clean what Milner described (and many Progressive Boers would have echoed him) as the 'Augean Stables' of the Transvaal administration.[35] Jan Smuts was the man on whom Kruger now relied to help with the task. That year, 1898, Kruger had displaced one of the Hollander immigrants and Smuts was appointed State Attorney, chief legal adviser to the government. It was a bold appointment; Smuts was only twenty-seven and totally inexperienced. But he had a reputation for academic brilliance combined with tact; though a stranger to both qualities, Kruger held no prejudice against them.[36] Smuts would now have to work fast if he was to pre-empt the attack of the Progressives, the Uitlanders and the imperial government. In fact, nothing would have astonished Milner and delighted Chamberlain more, had they known that Kruger, like Chamberlain, believed time fought on the side of the British.

Kruger's choice of Smuts showed all the old President's shrewdness. Yet how incongruous the partnership appeared. Smuts was an Afrikaner from the Cape; his first language, for the purpose of writing, was English, his favourite poets were Shelley, Shakespeare and Walt Whitman. He was tall and slight and absurdly young-looking, with his curly flaxen hair and a complexion that was always ready to flush like a girl's. His introduction to Kruger had been chilling.

Smuts had just married his childhood sweetheart, Isie, and brought her to the President's house to meet him. 'Whatever were you doing to marry such an ugly woman?' asked Kruger. A moment passed before Smuts realized this was a sample of the old man's elephantine humour. It was impossible to imagine Smuts himself playing the fool. There was a frightening intensity about him; the grey-blue eyes were strained and hard.[37]

As for his intellectual qualities, he had a record as dazzling as Milner's. Like other clever colonials, he had gone to Cambridge; there he earned a string of prizes, and took a double First in Law. These were golden years for Cambridge. It was the Cambridge of the philosophers Bertrand Russell and G. E. Moore. But little of this gold had rubbed off on Smuts, and he had lived for nothing but work. When he came home at last, he embarked on a legal career, writing political articles in his spare time. The keystone of his political faith, like that of other Afrikaners at the Cape, had been the idea of South African unity under the British flag.[38] Here was the 'great Temple of Peace and Unity' in which both white races would assemble, 'joyfully' accepting their differences, until they finally coalesced into a single great white nation spanning South Africa from the Zambezi to the Cape. And Rhodes was the man, Smuts had fondly imagined, who would help build the foundations of the temple.[39]

When it turned out that Rhodes was after all what his enemies claimed – a plotter and a traitor – Smuts's feelings can well be imagined. 'The man we had followed, who was to lead us to victory, had not only deserted us; he had ... betrayed us.'[40] Overnight Smuts transferred his hero-worship to Kruger. He shook the dust of the Cape off his feet and headed north to the Transvaal, where he practised at the Johannesburg Bar.[41]

By December 1898 Smuts had been State Attorney for six months. He flung himself into the work with his usual single-mindedness. As chief legal adviser to the government, he had to attend all the meetings of the Volksraad and most of those of the Executive Council, as well as to advise all the government departments. In fact, he had become the general factotum, not merely the legal adviser, to the government. But his main task, as Smuts saw it, was reform, and the first priority was to try to tackle the shortcomings in the administration – to 'clean up' the place, as he put it bluntly in a letter to a friend.[42]

How far and how fast could Smuts go in cleaning up corruption? The trouble was that, at the root of most of the corruption and inefficiency, was the system of monopolies and concessions. This system was, in Kruger's eyes, not a means of feathering his own nest, or his supporters'; it was, as he said, a 'cornerstone of his country's independence'. There was a purpose in allowing most of the £2 million profits of the dynamite monopoly to pass to German and French dynamite rings. By this means Kruger had built up one of the largest explosive factories in the world at Johannesburg. And apart from the military potential of this industry, Kruger could point to the useful political friends he had bought with that £2 million: German and French Uitlanders, foreign financiers and their governments. Kruger had in fact played off one set of Uitlanders, and one set of governments, against another.[43] Smuts decided to try to arrange for the question of monopolies to be settled as part of a great deal with the capitalists of the Rand.[44]

In another field Smuts *could* act swiftly: towards the regular Transvaal police. 'The new State Attorney,' one government-sponsored newspaper cautiously announced that autumn, 'is clearly bent on checking the indiscriminate reckless firing by foolish constables.'[45] In fact, there had been several recent instances when the 'Zarps', as the police were called ('Zuid Afrika Republik' was written on their shoulder flashes), had shot unarmed men when making arrests, and their victims were not confined to Kaffirs. Part of the trouble was that the six hundred Zarps were recruited almost exclusively from the poorest of urban poor whites. Obviously raw Boers of this particular minority – the six thousand-odd landless Boers in Johannesburg – would need tight discipline if they were to serve as police in a city whose other population numbered over forty thousand Uitlanders and fifty thousand black and coloured workers. In general, as one would expect, the Zarps reserved the worst of their treatment for the latter. That autumn the Zarps were alleged to have raided and beaten up a number of Cape Coloureds in Johannesburg. Smuts immediately suspended the official responsible. In the government enquiry that followed unpleasant facts came to light: forty coloured people had been dragged from their homes in the middle of the night, accused of breaking the pass law; some of them had been ill-treated; a sick girl had died, possibly as a result of the raid. The enquiry conceded that certain 'irregularities' had been committed. But no action was taken against the official responsible.[46]

Smuts now had a new political problem. The cause of the coloured people, who were British subjects, had been taken up by the acting British Agent in Pretoria, Edmund Fraser. Smuts decided to go and see Fraser about the matter and try to settle it man to man. He could hardly have guessed the extraordinary course the interview would take.

The two men met in Pretoria on 23 December 1898, the same day as the great victory banquet given for General Joubert.[47] Smuts must have been in a friendly mood, as there was a report in the Pretoria newspapers about a most conciliatory speech delivered in Grahamstown by General Sir William Butler, who was holding the fort while Milner was away on leave in London. Butler was quoted as saying, 'Unity is strength, but it should be a union of hearts, not a union forced by outside pressure.... To my mind South Africa needs no surgical operations, it needs rest and peace....'[48] The sentiments would have been unexceptional in most countries. But it was strange to hear such conciliatory talk from a British High Commissioner – and the not-so-veiled reference to the Raid. Smuts was all the more unprepared for his interview with Fraser.

After the two men had discussed the affair of the Cape Coloureds amicably enough, Fraser suddenly launched into an extraordinary outburst. The course of the dialogue, according to Smuts's notes, went something like this:

Fraser: 'We have now sat still for two years because our own officials put us in a false position in the Raid. The time has now come to take action.'
Smuts: 'Action? Could you explain what you mean?'

Fraser: 'Well, you see. Gladstone made a great mistake in handing you back the Transvaal after Majuba and before [instead of] defeating your army. It encouraged your idea of a great Afrikaner republic throughout South Africa. If you ask my opinion the time has come for us to end this nonsense by striking a blow. We've got to show who's the boss in South Africa....'

Smuts: 'But, whatever would give you occasion for this?'

Fraser: 'England's fed up with the maladministration in this country, and especially with the ill-treatment of British subjects. This is the point on which England will take action. I know perfectly well that England won't go to war over abstract subjects like suzerainty – that means nothing to the man in the street. She'll go to war about things that everyone can understand.'[49]

Go to war.... Smuts was left gasping by the interview. What was the meaning of these threats? Had Fraser gone mad, or was this a hint of the opening of a new and extremely dangerous phase in the endless wrangle between the two governments? Were the British looking for a *casus belli*? If so, this could not be the ill-treatment of coloured British subjects, whose plight would hardly wring the heart of everyone in England, let alone of their allies in South Africa.[50]

Smuts had not long to wait to learn the meaning of the puzzle. Already reports were reaching his desk of a great protest meeting arranged to take place next day in Johannesburg. The British Uitlanders were in uproar. A young Englishman called Edgar had been shot by a trigger-happy Zarp.[51] But that was not all. The Uitlanders intended to petition the British government to intervene on their behalf.

It was little in itself, but it was the pebble that starts the avalanche.

CHAPTER 4

'Voetsak'

'He has lost all confidence in Kruger. . . . He said we must
at first present our case to the world in a dignified &
strong manner & that if no attention is paid to it, the only
way to work on is a kind of revolution . . .'

> Georges Rouliot to Julius Wernher,
> 21 January 1899, describing a talk that
> week with J. B. Robinson, one of the
> Uitlander millionaires who had
> previously sided with Kruger

The news of the shooting of Tom Edgar had reached the leading Uitlanders a
few hours before it came to Smuts. This was the weekend before Christmas and
a party had gathered at Hohenheim, the suburban villa of Percy Fitzpatrick, a
Cape-born Uitlander who worked for the great mining house of Wernher-Beit.
There was a heatwave that weekend – it was almost too hot for tennis. The
guests played croquet, or they sat in the shade of the jacaranda trees. Perhaps
they discussed that strangely conciliatory speech by Milner's stand-in as High
Commissioner at the Cape, General Sir William Butler; Butler, an Irishman,
must be a 'Krugerite'. The burning topic was the great demonstration to be held
that afternoon to protest at the killing of Edgar.[1]

Hohenheim might have belonged to a Surrey stockbroker. Built in 'Randlords Gothic', it commanded the hillside on which lay Johannesburg. In the old
days no one had bothered about this brown, windy hillside. The place was not
even close to the stage-coach route from the Cape to Pretoria. There was no
village, just a couple of whitewashed farmhouses and a kraal for the Kaffirs. And
there was nothing much to see from the ridge – a splash of mealies, perhaps, and
an occasional clump of eucalyptus. Otherwise there was just the veld, the great
inland sea, quiet, poetic, melancholy.[2]

That was before the discovery of the gold-fields. Today, people who came to
Hohenheim saw one of the sights of Africa: an archipelago of townships, of
red-brick slums and green suburbs; a line of mine-wheels, mine-batteries
and mine-chimneys spouting smoke and steam across thirty miles of the
Rand.[3]

It was a geological phenomenon – too good to be true, it seemed at first. The other great gold-fields so far discovered – in the Klondyke, in California, and in Australia – were notoriously fickle. The ore of the Rand conglomerate (nick-named 'bankét' after a local sweet, a kind of almond rock) was not of a high grade, but its quality was uniquely uniform. And the sheer size of the ore body beggared belief. The main reefs stretched for thirty miles along the Rand; the outliers would be traced for 130 miles. But what was most extraordinary about the reefs was their depth. After a short interruption, the gold-bearing beds continued again downwards, 1,500 feet, 2,000 feet – and the mines followed them down.

The Rand seemed, almost literally, to be a bottomless pit. Although it was the outcrop mines that accounted for most of the marvellous increase in output (and the equally marvellous increase in dividends; from £2·5 million in 1897 to £4·8 million in 1898), it was becoming clear that the future lay with the deep-level mines. Already the gold mines of the Transvaal, producing £15 million worth in the current year, 1898, had left the diamond mines of the Cape far behind. Internationally, too, the Transvaal had broken every record at a time when monetary policies had transformed the world's demand for gold. By 1898, the Transvaal had overtaken Russia, Australia and even America. Now it was the greatest gold power in the world, expected to produce over £20 million in 1899, with reserves conservatively estimated at £700 million – of which £200 million would be clear profit for someone.[4] It was, said a British minister, accurately enough, the 'richest spot on earth.'[5]

And nature, so prodigal with her gold in the Transvaal, had added other largesse: a vast coalfield around Johannesburg, a vast pool of black and brown labourers all over South Africa.

If the Rand was a prodigy, so was Johannesburg – an infant prodigy of a city. After fifteen years its population exceeded fifty-thousand Europeans, and there were perhaps as many again living in the townships scattered over the Rand. It was the greatest concentration of Europeans in the whole sub-continent. The place had begun as a mining camp, a kind of Dodge City on the veld. White tents sprang up beside the diggings. The diggers looked as diggers should – big men in riding-boots and shirt-sleeves with wide-awake hats and revolvers in their belts. There were cheap hotels with pretty wooden balconies, and even prettier hostesses. But all that was soon changed once the mines became organized. The gold-rush died – to be replaced by an orderly stream of emigrants, pale-faced clerks and artisans from the depressed industrial towns of Britain, and Jewish shopkeepers from the ghettoes of Eastern Europe. Almost overnight the mining camp became an industrial centre, Dodge City became Salford.

Streets were laid out – broad, dusty, colonial streets with sober British names like Anderson Street and Commissioner Street. The centre of the city became solid and respectable, a place of stone-faced commercial buildings in the classical style, and broad pavements lit by gaslights. Beautiful it was not. The Golden City was still too raw and drab and dirty for that. But it was a real city, no one could deny it, and a homely place in its fashion.[6]

There was, however, another Johannesburg, a city in itself – the African

location where the 'mine boys' lived. The mines had an unquenchable appetite
for cheap labour; eighty-eight thousand Africans were employed on the Rand
during that year, 1898. This other Johannesburg was, by all accounts, an appalling place: full of typhoid, pneumonia and, what was nearly as bad, illegal
Johannesburg-made liquor. Hundreds of miners would be found dead drunk
every Monday morning and some would be actually dead, killed in drunken
weekend rioting.

Nearby, in more comfortable circumstances, lived the mixed-race community, the Cape Coloured people, who straddled the social scale between the
African labourers and the Europeans. They were the carpenters and the tram-car
drivers, the carters and the craftsmen; their wives worked as servants and
washerwomen. Finally, there were a couple of hundred Indians from Natal.
They ran cheap shops and stalls in the market, and the poor whites depended on
them.[7]

Yet, under these cosmopolitan layers, Boer and Jewish, black and brown,
Johannesburg still felt British – more British than either Cape Town or Natal. In
short, it felt like a British colonial city. It was this feeling that lay close to the
heart of the grievances of the Uitlanders.

It was Fitzpatrick ('Fitz'), the owner of Hohenheim, who constituted the leading
political mind among the Uitlanders. Years later he was to be famous as the
author of a sentimental children's book, *Jock of the Bushveld*. At this time he was a
fair-haired, thirty-six-year-old Irish Catholic from the Cape – a charmer. He had
headed north during the gold rush and had knocked about the gold-fields,
making and losing fortunes like other diggers, until he attracted the attention of
Alfred Beit's firm. Since then he had come to play a role for Wernher-Beit
something like the one Jameson had originally played in Rhodesia. He became,
here on the Rand, the firm's political watchdog. He had the better half of
Jameson's gifts – that contagious enthusiasm and the political ambition – without the schoolboy heroics.

At present, however, he had one crippling (if temporary) disadvantage. Like
other leading 'Reformers' – the Johannesburg revolutionaries – he had been
gaoled for a couple of months after the Raid, and only released on condition that
he kept out of politics for three years. The other leaders had chosen to leave the
country. Fitzpatrick was back with Wernher-Beit, but under parole: no politics,
not a whisper against the government until May 1899. That was the promise,
but you could no more keep Fitzpatrick from politics than his dog, Jock, from a
rat.[8]

All the grievances that had inspired the Raid remained; some had intensified.
The overwhelming anxiety of Fitzpatrick's employers, Wernher-Beit (acting
through their South African subsidiary, Eckstein's, which in turn controlled
Rand Mines), was the high cost of mining. It was a paradox that this should be
the concern of the men who had captured the richest slice of the Rand; their
company, Rand Mines, had roughly a third of the total output (compared with
the tenth that belonged to Rhodes's company, Consolidated Goldfields). But

Alfred Beit and Julius Wernher were the first financiers to recognize that the Rand's future lay with the deep levels.

The first of these deeps, Geldenhuis Deep, had come into production a few months before the raid; others had swiftly followed; they were profitable. But the deeps were especially vulnerable to increases of mining costs. Their ore was of low grade, like the ore of the upper-level mines. In addition, disproportionately more time and money were needed to bring them into production. It could take up to five years and millions of pounds before a mine produced a penny in return for the investment. Once in production, the deeps were more sensitive to increases in mining costs, as they needed disproportionately more dynamite and African labour. Both these vital commodities, according to Wernher-Beit and the Chamber of Mines which the firm dominated, were ruinously expensive in the Transvaal. Already the profit margin on good mines was slim enough: the Boers were now adding a five per cent profits tax.[9] Hence Wernher-Beit's instructions to Percy Fitzpatrick: try to make a deal with liberal Afrikaners in the government, men like Jan Smuts.

Fitzpatrick's response was complicated by the fact that he had his own political ambitions to reconcile with his work for Wernher-Beit. However, he believed there was no conflict of interest. His plan was to rebuild the old Reform Movement, to recreate that odd-looking alliance between international financiers and the British industrial proletariat on the Rand, by which Rhodes and Beit had planned to take over the Transvaal at the time of the Raid. In fact, the alliance was not so incongruous. Both mine owners and their white employees had a common interest in lowering the cost of living on the Rand. At present 'cruelly high' custom duties made it one of the most expensive countries in the world; 'outrageous' monopolies raised the costs still further. The price of lowering the cost of mining would be paid largely by Africans. For it was the 'ridiculously' high cost of African mining wages (though a fraction of white wages, man for man) that was the mine owners' constant source of complaint. The direct cause was that Africans did not want to work underground, because of the dangerous conditions. According to a newspaper report, there was a twenty per cent. *annual* death rate, mainly due to disease, among black miners. But the employers blamed the Boers for their incompetent method of recruiting labour, and the corrupt way they let the niggers drink themselves to death on illicit liquor.[10]

The political grievance which added to the bitterness was the fact that very few British Uitlanders had even now, in 1898, been given the vote. Under the original Transvaal franchise law, they would have had this option after five years' residence. By now the majority of the estimated sixty thousand male Uitlanders would have been able to exercise it, if they chose. This would have given them individual political equality with the thirty thousand Boer voters; and collectively they could have controlled the state. For obvious reasons, Kruger had changed the franchise law in 1888, raising the residence qualification from five to fourteen years.

Hence Fitzpatrick now, like the Reformers in 1895, decided to put 'franchise first'. It was the key to everything. But how could they force Kruger to disgorge the vote, and so let the control of the Transvaal pass to the British?[11]

Put your faith in the imperial government, was Fitzpatrick's answer. The idea of an 'Uitlander republic' had died with the collapse of the Reform Movement at the time of the Raid. In fact, its collapse had proved how right were Rhodes and Beit to insist on the Union Jack and the imperial connection. Since then, that £1–2 million spent on Boer rearmament excluded any chance of an internal revolt. The Uitlanders must appeal to Caesar, in the shape of the British government, to intervene on their behalf, the 'oppressed' British subjects of the Rand.

But how was Fitzpatrick to start the Uitlander ball rolling, so to speak? As the croquet balls sped across the lawn at Hohenheim, a new strategy was taking shape in Fitzpatrick's mind, that coincided with Sir Alfred Milner's (though neither man was then aware of this). The South African League – a new pro-imperialist pressure group, started by British professional men – had recently been protesting about harassment of coloured British subjects on the Rand. The case against the Zarps for persecuting the Cape Coloureds was in fact legally (and morally) a strong one, and topical, too. Only that week, on 20 December, the Zarps had launched a new wave of raids on Coloured cab-drivers, in which not only Cape men, but a dozen from St Helena, not subject to the pass laws, had been thrown in the *tronk* (gaol).[12] Later they had been fined, in clear breach of the law. Hence the visit of Jan Smuts that day to talk things over with Fraser, the acting British Agent. Fitzpatrick, however, was unimpressed by the League's tactics. The League would provide a convenient front behind which he could reconstitute the old Reform Movement. But the League must play down the grievances of coloured British subjects against the Zarps.[13] Britain will intervene, Fraser warned Smuts that day (presumably Fraser had been talking to Fitzpatrick) 'about things that everyone can understand'. So they must play up the Uitlander's own grievances for all they were worth – and more.

Five days earlier the chance had come.[14]

The shooting of Tom Edgar, a boiler-maker from Bootle, Lancashire, might seem an odd choice to work into an international incident. In fact, he had been shot by a Zarp as a result of a drunken brawl between two Uitlanders. The brawl would not have been out of place in Bootle. But the real circumstances of Edgar's life (like those of Jenkins's ear in the eighteenth century) were hardly relevant. What mattered was the effect on the British community. To many Uitlanders his shooting seemed like murder after they heard the first reports. The real story, as it emerged later, was less clear-cut.

It was after midnight, said his widow, Bessie Edgar, when she had heard her husband coming back up the alley-way. He had been out for a drink with his mates. He seems to have been a typical British Uitlander, except for his size; he was six foot six in his boots. He worked at Tarry's, the big engineering works in Harrison Street. Bessie said he was a quiet, respectable working man. He earned £26 a week, four times what he would get in good old England. They lived at

Florrie's Chambers: a collection of tin-roofed bungalows down a little alley-way near the Salisbury Mine.

As Edgar walked home there was the flump-flump from the mine battery and the crash of stones being unloaded from a skip. When he reached the end of the alley-way, he met two of his neighbours, one of them stripped to his underclothes because of the unusual heat. 'Voetsak,' said Foster, a little grasshopper of a man. 'Who did you say Voetsak to?' asked Edgar. 'Voetsak' is a rude word in Afrikaans which you use if you want to drive away a dog.

It was too dark to see very much, but if Edgar had himself had less to drink he might have noticed that Foster was tipsily talking to his dog, while relieving himself against the wall of his house. Edgar did not enquire further. With a single blow, he knocked Foster to the ground. The other neighbour, thinking Foster dead, ran off to get help. His cries of 'Police! Police!' echoed down Harrison Street.[15]

Edgar sat on his bed in his shirt-sleeves, waiting for the police to arrive. 'Impudent' was what he called Foster.[16] Perhaps he also gave Bessie his views on the Zarps. In that English-looking town they stuck out like a sore thumb. It was one of his workmates' main grievances. That and the high cost of living caused by the high taxes. 'Vampires' was the only word to describe the Boers.[17]

At that moment, Bessie heard shouts: 'Oopen op, police.' Someone rattled on the lock. Outside the door, in the darkness, stood four Boer policemen. To add to the Englishness – and incongruity – one of them was called Jones. Jones was distinguished by a moustache and a black macintosh. He drew his revolver, then threw himself against the door, which burst open.

According to Jones, Edgar then struck at him twice with an iron-shod stick. This was probably true, as a stick of this sort was later found in the doorway. But Jones was hardly grazed by the blows, if touched at all. He made no attempt to arrest Edgar, not an impossible job for four stout policemen. Instead, he raised his revolver at point-blank range. A bystander saw the flash of the gun and heard a woman scream. For a moment Edgar stood silhouetted against the lighted doorway. He reeled backwards and forwards. Then, his blood pouring on to the black macintosh of PC Jones, Edgar pitched forward into the arms of the second policeman.[18]

Such was the lurid story of the shooting of Edgar that was to emerge from evidence at court hearings. It differed in several ways from the account that had so far reached Fitzpatrick and his friends at Hohenheim. They did not yet know these mitigating facts: that Jones had been led to believe that Edgar had killed Foster, and that Edgar had probably struck Jones with a stick. To Fitzpatrick it seemed a clear-cut case of murder – and a chance not to be missed. The morning after the shooting, his friend William Hoskens, a close colleague from the old Reform Movement, took statements from Bessie Edgar and her friends. (Fitzpatrick himself could not play a direct part.) The statements were printed in *The Star*, the Rand newspaper subsidized by Wernher-Beit. An 'Edgar Relief Committee' was formed with the help of the League.[19]

And now luck sent the croquet ball rolling straight through Fitzpatrick's hoop. Jones was at first sent to gaol on a murder charge. The public prosecutor, a German immigrant called Dr Krause, then reduced the charge to manslaughter and released Jones on bail of only £200, less than the figure often levied on Uitlanders for trifling offences. The news reached Smuts too late. He ordered his colleagues to rearrest Jones.[20] But Fitzpatrick's friends had stirred to fever pitch the feelings of the British community. The shooting touched on a specially raw nerve, the belief that an Englishman's home was his castle – even in Johannesburg. Since Jones's release from gaol, it seemed to expose the rottenness of the whole Transvaal legal system.

By 3.30 p.m. that same afternoon, Christmas Eve, a crowd of nearly five thousand Uitlanders packed into the upper end of Market Square, the chequered straw hats of the artisans standing out among the bowler hats of the professional men. They had come to assert their rights as British subjects; they had been treated 'like helots' long enough.

Half an hour later, the procession reached the Standard Buildings in the heart of the city's business quarter, where the British vice-consul had his office. It was a large, grey stucco pile in the classical manner, flanked by a barber's shop and a billiard saloon. On the balcony, the members of the Edgar Relief Committee, Reformers and Leaguers, stood bare-headed to hear the reading of the petition. Below, the streets were sealed off by the immense throng of straw-hatted demonstrators.

The secretary of the South African League, an engineer called Dodd, began to read from the crumpled piece of paper on which someone had scribbled the Humble Petition to Her Britannic Majesty, Queen Victoria, from her loyal subjects resident on the Witwatersrand Goldfields. It begged her to instruct her representative to secure a 'full and impartial trial' of PC Jones, to extend her protection to their own lives and liberties and to take such other steps 'as might be necessary' to terminate the present 'intolerable state of affairs....'[21]

It was a melodramatic new beginning, this appeal to Caesar from the British subjects in the Transvaal. But at first it seemed to have ended in farce. Caesar, in the shape of Milner's stand-in, General Sir William Butler, sympathized with the Boers. He flatly refused to accept the petition. Privately he informed Chamberlain that it was 'all a prepared business' worked up by the South African League, who were the 'direct descendants' of the Reformers. He warned his chief, equally correctly, that the Raiders were once again on the warpath. What he had not grasped was that it was Beit's man, Fitzpatrick, who was the moving spirit behind the Reformers reformed. He blamed Rhodes. At any rate, despite the efforts of Fraser, the acting British Agent, to help the Leaguers, Butler refused to transmit the petition to London.[22]

Characteristically, it was the Transvaal authorities who now saved the situation for Fitzpatrick. First, they arrested his friends who had organized the Edgar demonstration on Christmas Eve on a technical charge, and assessed their bail at £1,000, five times that of PC Jones. The case against them fizzled out. But the Uitlanders were furious. They poured out for a second protest demonstration.

This time they took care to get permission from the authorities. The demonstration took place on 14 January in an amphitheatre outside the city – a large wood-and-iron building normally used for circuses. Once again Fitzpatrick could only be grateful for the reaction of the Boer authorities. Six or seven hundred Boers from a road-mending gang at the Main Reef – described even by a pro-Boer newspaper as 'whipped up' for the occasion – broke up the peaceful meeting, and beat up the Uitlanders with chair legs. The Zarps simply stood by. People claimed later that two Zarp lieutenants had been carried in triumph by the Boer mob and these two commended them for 'doing their duty'.[23]

Finally, when the trial of PC Jones at last took place in Johannesburg, the Boer judge had gone out of his way to help the League. He was a callow youth of twenty-five called Judge Kock; his father was a member of Kruger's Executive. He virtually directed the jury to acquit, after a long, rambling summary of the case. He added a phrase that was uncannily like the words the Zarps were said to have used at the amphitheatre meeting. After thanking the jury, he commended the police; he hoped that 'under difficult circumstances, they would always know how to do their duty'.

This was enough to keep the Uitlanders in uproar. By the end of February Fitzpatrick judged it time to circulate, privately, a second petition for imperial intervention. But Jan Smuts, the State Attorney, chose this moment for a dramatic strike. To forestall imperial intervention, Smuts made a dazzling offer, with Kruger's authority behind him: a general settlement with the mining companies that came to be called the 'Great Deal'. To show his personal confidence in Fitzpatrick, he was prepared to waive Fitzpatrick's parole and let him act as principal negotiator. It was a difficult stroke to counter. For three weeks Fitzpatrick played a double game in every sense, trying to get a deal for both mining companies and the Uitlanders, and determined to fail. On 28 March he leaked the confidential terms of the Great Deal to *The Star* and negotiations collapsed. Then Fitzpatrick took a train to Cape Town. In the same train travelled a large cardboard box containing the petition, signed by twenty-one thousand British subjects of the Rand, calling on the British government to intervene. Milner, now back in Cape Town, was being asked to forward this second petition to London.[24]

As the train clanked over the Orange River Bridge into British territory next day, Fitzpatrick crossed his Rubicon. The Raiders and Reformers had failed because they were divided and isolated. What Fitzpatrick could offer Milner was a powerful triple alliance: Britain, the mass of the Uitlanders and Wernher-Beit, the giant of the Rand.

CHAPTER 5
'Working up Steam'
Cape Town,
31 March – 9 May 1899

'If only the Uitlanders stand firm on the formula "no rest
without reform", we shall do the trick, my boy ... And
by the soul of St Jingo they get a fair amount of bucking
up from us all one way and another ...'

Milner to his colleague, the Imperial
Secretary George Fiddes, 3 January 1899

Milner had returned from England in buoyant spirits, despite General Butler's
astounding decision, while Milner was away, to reject the first Uitlander
petition.[1] (Butler 'is really superb' was Milner's comment. To have him 'out-
Krugering Kruger' was just 'too Gilbertian'.)[2] Fortunately, the Uitlanders had
paid no attention to Butler. And Milner was *well pleased*, he told his friends,
with the results of his own trip to England, even if he had 'hardly a moment's'
holiday[3] (no mention, of course, of the five days' bicycling with Cécile). He had
got a wink, so to speak, from Chamberlain. And he had managed, in his quiet
way, to tell a number of influential people about his 'little corner of the imperial
chess-board'.[4] Now he heard the latest developments on the Rand from Percy
Fitzpatrick's own lips.

That evening, 31 March, Fitzpatrick had arrived in Cape Town hot-foot from
the Johannesburg train. He was exhausted, so he said, by the strain of keeping
the negotiations with Smuts 'on the right lines' – making sure they failed. But
there in Milner's bleak, grey, gaslit study in Government House the two men
talked far into the night, as Fitzpatrick poured out the story of the Great Deal.[5]

First, Kruger was offering direct inducements to the mining houses, concerned with preferential mining rights and more acceptable mining taxes.
Second, he was offering a major concession to the Uitlanders in general. He
promised to recommend to the Raad that they should restore to the Uitlanders
their right to vote after five years' residence in the Transvaal – although this was
only to date from the time they applied for Boer citizenship.

In exchange, the Rand firms were required to make some concessions to
Kruger: most important, they must acquiesce in the continuation of the hated
dynamite monopoly (Kruger's source of Transvaal-made explosives). They
were also being asked for pledges on three political matters: to back the

Transvaal's stand against the claims of the Cape Coloured and 'Coolie' (Indian) traders, to damp down the agitation of the anti-Boer Press, and to repudiate those 'political mischief-makers', the South African League.[6]

It was 'astonishing', Kruger's offer, everyone agreed. But could the old fox be trusted? In London, Chamberlain gave him the benefit of the doubt. 'My own opinion is that the Government of the SAR [South African Republic; that is, Transvaal] *are* anxious to settle ... their financial difficulties, the strength of the South African League, their position with regard to the Dynamite Monopoly, the loss of support from Germany, the altered position of England since Fashoda – all make in favour of a settlement....'[7] Milner instinctively took the opposite view.[8] Now it turned out that Fitzpatrick, without any prompting from Milner (and only a few encouraging messages passed by way of Greene, the British agent in Pretoria), had taken precisely the same line as Milner.

The Great Deal, said Fitzpatrick, might be genuine as far as the Boer civil servants, like Smuts, were concerned. But Kruger himself had no intention of giving a fair deal to the Uitlanders. And, anyway, the Volksraad would never agree to the concession, whatever Kruger said. In short, the offer was a 'spoof', as Fitzpatrick had explained in a speech to a private meeting of all the Rand leaders.[9]

His own first step had been to sound the views of his principals, Alfred Beit and Julius Wernher, and here there was no disagreement. Early in March, Wernher went to see Lord Selborne, Under-Secretary at the Colonial Office, and Wernher's view coincided with Fitzpatrick's: he was puzzled by the terms of the offer, he said; he thought part of the explanation was that Dr Leyds, the Transvaal's Foreign Secretary, had been rebuffed on his recent travels in Holland, France and Germany with the words 'why don't you settle with these people?' But for precisely the same reason as Fitzpatrick, Wernher believed that 'nothing would come of the overture'.[10]

The next step was to get agreement with the other great firms on the Rand, especially Rhodes's firm, Consolidated Goldfields, whose head office, like Wernher-Beit's, was in London. It was Rhodes's firm, as Milner expected, that gave Fitzpatrick the greatest headache. The firm had sacked their engineer, Wybergh, for the part he had played in the Edgar affair as President of the South African League. And in London, when the chairman of the firm, Lord Harris, came to see Chamberlain a few days after Wernher had seen Selborne, the atmosphere was chilly. Earlier that year Rhodes had flirted with the idea of giving Kruger a loan. Now Lord Harris told Chamberlain that on their part they were inclined to accept the terms of the Great Deal. Chamberlain's reply was blunt: they could go ahead, of course; it was their own business; but he ought to know what the British public would say – 'the Financiers had sold their cause and their compatriots, and sold them cheap....'[11]

Meanwhile, Fitzpatrick had broadened the base of his campaign. To unite the mass of the Uitlanders behind the capitalists, he addressed a meeting of twenty-four Rand men, including the leaders of the South African League, at a private dinner on the Rand, and explained the course of the negotiations.[12]

Perhaps the political support that he had thus demonstrated tipped the balance in Fitzpatrick's favour when he came to deal with the other capitalists' representatives in the Rand, including ex-supporters of Kruger like J. B. Robinson. At any rate, by 27 March they had agreed on a joint resolution. The keystone of this was the demand for the restoration of the original five-year franchise; this must be retrospective – be offered at once to all Uitlanders who could prove five or more years of residence. Despite opposition from Rhodes's local manager, the new 'Declaration of Rights' was handed over to the Boer authorities by the three firms negotiating on behalf of the Rand, before Fitzpatrick gracefully caused the negotiations to collapse.

Such was the inside story of the rise and fall of Kruger's Great Deal. To Milner these details came as a revelation: not only that Fitzpatrick was working along precisely the same lines as himself, but that Beit and Wernher had backed him at every stage. In reply, Milner was perfectly frank with Fitzpatrick. He told him, according to a note Fitzpatrick wrote to Wernher that week, 'that in you and Mr Beit he has found quite a new and astonishing kind of millionaire – men with some higher conception than the piling up of money'. He congratulated him on the 'consummate statesmanship' with which he had handled – and broken off – the negotiations. And he admitted that, even in his 'most hopeful moments', he had not considered it possible that they should have been able to present a unanimous front 'in such a strong attitude'.[13]

Milner then opened his heart to Fitzpatrick in a way that both astonished and dazzled the Uitlander. Milner explained that the next phase of their campaign would lie with the Press in Britain. The rejection of the first petition by Butler had been a 'terrible mistake', which Fitzpatrick and his friends had, by 'an effort which is beyond all praise, turned to the best possible account. Now *all* hinges upon the treatment accorded to the [second] petition and that depends on the Press.' He begged Fitzpatrick to back him up there. And then he repeated to Fitzpatrick what he had told only his most intimate friends: 'The biggest real danger I have is that Chamberlain might get the idea I want to rush him.' If Milner himself tried to 'touch up' the Press, Joe might get this idea, and he would 'see me damned before he moved a finger'. So it was left to Fitzpatrick to 'do the Press'; he must try to 'get before the House and the public the mass of damning evidence that was in the petitions. . . . You must *not* allow the petition to fizzle.'[14]

Next, Milner discussed the possible replies of the imperial government. If the new petition was rejected, he would resign at once; but, fortunately, this possibility need not be considered. At the opposite extreme was the chance that the imperial government would choose to send an ultimatum threatening war; but this would only be done if publication of the petition 'should so fire public opinion as to make it imperative'. The third possibility was the most likely. Chamberlain would accept the petition, but postpone an ultimatum till Kruger had had more time to consider a climb-down.[15]

Milner begged Fitzpatrick to make a 'heroic effort' to hold together his new Reform Movement until they were ready for the 'great day of reckoning'. It might take time to get the imperial government 'up to the mark in principle'; and then they must be ready to strike 'within 24 hours – swift and instant'. Whatever the Uitlanders did – by holding protest meetings or anything else – they must keep within the law.

Milner concluded with one last, disarming indiscretion: 'Remember, it is the chance of a lifetime. You have got something now which you may never have again – a man here who is with you heart and soul – as keen as the keenest of you. I have just got letters from Fiddes and Greene [the Imperial Secretary and the British agent in Pretoria] – very excited. . . . I have to pour cold water on them and it breaks their hearts. They think I am not keen enough, but it is not that – *I am not going to let Joe think I want to rush him.*'[16]

The next five weeks were a nerve-racking period for Milner. As he had predicted, British public opinion did not lash itself into a frenzy over the Uitlanders. The British Press, it is true, took a broadly anti-Kruger line – even the Liberal *Daily Chronicle*, well known for its anti-imperialist views. But South African affairs did not long command the headlines in any party's newspapers. And every Tuesday, when the mailbag reached Cape Town with the London papers of three weeks earlier, Milner was forced to admit that what to himself and his staff was an 'all over-shadowing nightmare' – the threat to British supremacy in South Africa – was in England still a 'matter of faint interest exciting only a very small degree of attention'. How odd, he told Selborne, that this should be so. After all, people should think of the 'enormous material value of the thing involved' (presumably the importance of South Africa's £700 million gold industry for the British economy) and also the 'plainness of the moral issues'.[17] But there it was. No doubt Chamberlain would eventually publish a Blue Book with all the damning evidence against the Boers – including his own public despatches.

All Milner could do in the meantime was to keep the Uitlanders 'pegging away'. 'The game has been played admirably so far,' he told Greene, 'and with steady persistence' the Uitlanders could expect to win 'almost universal support' in Great Britain.[18] In effect, this meant that Greene had to keep the pot boiling on the Rand and keep it well publicized. Hence Greene encouraged Fitzpatrick to channel the Uitlanders' grievances into public protest – and Fitzpatrick needed no encouragement. From mid-April there were mass meetings at mines all along the Rand to demand restoration of the old five-year franchise, and Fitzpatrick planned to organize delegates for an 'Uitlander Parliament', not to negotiate a settlement, but to attract still more publicity for their plight.[19]

Once again, the most dangerous threat to this massive exercise in public relations came from Cecil Rhodes and his firm, Consolidated Goldfields. Despite their agreement to remain neutral, expressed in their having combined with Wernher-Beit in rejecting Kruger's 'Great Deal', the local directors passed a resolution censuring the meeting held by the miners in the recreation hall at the Village Main Reef Mine. They made no secret of their opposition to Fitzpatrick's policy of feeding the unrest; and they wrote to the directors of the Jubilee

Mine to persuade them to censure their own business manager for taking the platform at one of the miners' meetings. 'Nice little beast,' retorted Fitzpatrick in private to Wernher and Beit in London.[20] Meanwhile, also from London, there were new tales of Rhodes's personal antics; at a dinner party attended by Arthur Balfour, he had spent the evening singing Kruger's praises, according to one of Milner's old colleagues in Whitehall, saying that Kruger was a splendid old man, who had 'defended his wicket against all comers'.[21]

As tell as 'getting things "forrarder" locally', Milner had to work up the pressure on the British Cabinet to persuade them to accept the second petition. Hence the box-loads of secret despatches to Joe Chamberlain that the Wednesday mail-boat carried back to Whitehall. They were masterly documents – the first set at any rate. No one could have guessed the intensity of Milner's commitment to British intervention, when they read these urbane and detached despatches. For example, in his despatch welcoming the second Uitlander petition, and the consequent 'revival of the Reform Movement' temporarily extinguished by the Raid, he expressed surprise that this revival had taken place so soon, and declared it was still 'too early to say whether it is a passing and more or less fictitious agitation, or the expression of a deep and widespread popular sentiment'. He praised the 'statesmanship of the mining' magnates', yet modestly declared that he did not know who was their leader, but felt that there was 'some wise head or heads directing their action'. He asked no more than that the Reform movement should not be discouraged by Britain's ruling out interference at any time in the future under her moral right as a Paramount Power.[22]

In his next secret despatch, he took up the slogan 'franchise first' as the point on which all Reformers were united. Privately, Milner well knew that to take up the franchise was to place a time-bomb under Kruger, as it would in due course mean the end of the Boer majority in the Transvaal.[23] But in putting his case officially to Chamberlain, Milner affected to believe that this reform might only result in the election to the Raad of 'Boer members of a more liberal type', that might be 'equally and perhaps even more useful' than the election of Uitlanders. The Uitlanders' franchise was, however, he added, a 'stirring battle cry' which would excite sympathy all over the Empire – as opposed to the grievances of Cape boy cab-drivers, Indian traders and so on, about which it would be 'impossible to get the world generally to take any interest'.[24]

By mid-April, as the British public continued to take no interest in *any* South African issue – even the franchise – Milner's despatches became less urbane. He drew attention to the public meetings of working-class Uitlanders then taking place up and down the Rand. He warned Chamberlain that it could be a 'serious, perhaps irretrievable mistake if we did not take the present opportunity of definitely ranging ourselves on the side of the Reformers'. He conceded that there was a risk of war. But then the Boers would yield to 'nothing less than the threat of war, perhaps not even to that. . . . [But] If we succeed we shall get rid of this nightmare for ever.' And he threw down a challenge to Chamberlain (with a hint of blackmail): 'What has become of the intervention of the High Commissioner . . . which was certainly contemplated, if not absolutely promised' at the time of the Raid, and which my predecessor was allowed to postpone but never instructed to abandon?'[25]

Fortunately for Milner, these taunts brought no response from Joe, for the despatch took a fortnight to reach London, and by this time a new phase of the struggle was about to open. By then even Chamberlain himself had become disturbed by the lack of public interest in his South African policy, and an urgent request was sent to Milner for a despatch publication in Chamberlain's forthcoming Blue Book.[26]

It was the chance that Milner had been waiting for. Not for nothing had he once been the Assistant Editor of The Pall Mall Gazette. A few days later he cabled back one of the most flamboyant despatches ever sent by a Viceroy, one that came to be known as the 'Helot Despatch'. 'The case for intervention is overwhelming.... The spectacle of thousands of British subjects kept permanently in the position of helots ... calling vainly to Her Majesty's Government for redress ... a ceaseless stream of malignant lies about the intentions of the British government.'[27]

For months Milner had been longing to rub 'some vitriol' into one of his public despatches;[28] but the part he had been forced to play had precluded it. Now, it was his job to 'break the crockery', as he told Philip Gell, even if it would seem a strange metamorphosis for the 'calm and conciliatory diplomatist' to be the 'firebrand' spurring the British public to action. He saw no choice. Everything depended on arousing the public – on 'stiffening the wobblers', as he put it.[29] He alone could do the job. By nailing his own colours to the mast, he would also nail the government to his own policy.

It was 9 May when the British Cabinet was expected to decide whether to commit themselves to intervention. Milner's staff at Government House had been on tenterhooks for days. It so happened that the drains at Government House had chosen this moment to give trouble. What with that, and the endless cold downpours of rain – for winter had now come to the Cape – it proved a difficult time.

Milner could hardly snatch a moment away from the endless slog at the official boxes. The sheer quantity of work was 'really too awful for words', declared the faithful Ozzy, his Private Secretary.[30] The Chief would have to sell the race-horse he'd bought in a moment of euphoria, and later christened 'Chamberlain' (you couldn't rush him); no hope of having time to go racing.[31] And the bicycle Milner had shipped out from England (chosen for him by Cécile) had been put away, sad relic, in Government House.[32]

Milner himself admitted to being 'rather knocked up' by the strain of these last few days, according to his diary. He could not sleep properly; his heart seemed to be playing up. Still, he had bravely taken up a new sport – archery. He was given a few lessons by Mrs Hanbury Williams, the wife of his Military Secretary; she fancied herself as a toxophilite. He did not show any particular promise. But he got a breath of air, as the arrows hummed across the lawn of Government House and plumped into the red, white and blue concentric rings of the straw

target. It was the long hours he was cooped up at this desk that 'really killed
him'.[33]

What if Chamberlain failed to persuade the Cabinet to accept the call for
intervention on the side of the Uitlanders? 'I will take risks – big risks – but not
silly ones,' Milner had confided to Fitzpatrick a month before. 'If I go smash ... I
can go back to something else.'[34] Perhaps his mind was already turning to what
he would do if he was recalled, like those earlier advocates of a forward policy in
South Africa. He might give up politics altogether – by now he had saved
enough to live on – and live a life of 'contemplative obscurity'. That was one of
the great ambitions of his life, as he had decided years before, when he had
stopped in Athens (it was after being rejected by Margot Asquith) and wandered
alone at the foot of the Parthenon.[35]

The morning that Milner expected to hear the Cabinet's decision, he took his
ADC, charming, pink-cheeked Bendor Belgrave, for a ride up the path that led
from Cecil Rhodes's eyrie, Groote Schuur, towards the heights of Table Mountain. The dismal weather of the last few days had suddenly evaporated.[36] A cold
south-easter scraped bare the grey flanks of the mountain. At their feet lay the
whole Cape peninsula. It was one of Rhodes's favourite haunts, the kind of place
where a man can mistake himself for a colossus.

When they returned, the cypher cable from Chamberlain had arrived: 'The
despatch is approved. We have adopted your suggestion.'[37] It was as brief and as
blunt as that.

So he had won that round after all. The Cabinet had agreed to intervene –
peacefully at present – on the side of the Uitlanders. But Milner was allowed no
respite. A fortnight later he heard of another peaceful intervention: by Kruger's
allies. Hofmeyr and Schreiner, leaders of the Cape Afrikaners, proposed that
Milner should go and meet Kruger and try to settle matters face to face;
President Steyn offered Bloemfontein, the Free State capital, as the meeting-
place. Milner regarded the conference as premature. He was waiting eagerly for
the publication of the Blue Book containing Chamberlain's official reply to the
Uitlanders' second petition – and to his own 'Helot Despatch'. He would have
liked to postpone negotiations till after this Blue Book was published – and both
the British public and Kruger were properly briefed about the seriousness of the
situation. Now it was the Blue Book that would have to be postponed. If they
had rejected Steyn's invitation, 'it would have been too likely to lead to an outcry
both here and in England that we *wanted war*'.

Milner promised Chamberlain to be 'studiously moderate' at Bloemfontein.
But he wrote to Philip Gell with a hint of triumph. When the 'Helot Despatch'
was published, 'never again would people reproach him with discretion.'[38]

CHAPTER 6

'It is Our Country You Want'

The Orange Free State,
30 May – 6 June 1899

'The conference goes on its rather weary way ...
meanwhile our Uitlanders will lose patience, and upset
the game. We preach them the doctrine of faith in my
chief, and of patience for some time after the conference is
over ...'

> Major Hanbury Williams (Milner's
> Military Secretary) to British Military
> Intelligence from Bloemfontein
> 31 May 1899

The special train left the siding in Kroonstad a couple of hours before dawn on Tuesday 30 May. Then it resumed its journey steaming south down the single-track railway into the heart of the Free State. Before it reached the Zand River, the sun rose out of the mist, painting the mealie patches a rusty yellow and wiping the hoar frost off the metal sleepers.

It was a winter dawn, the hour when the veld shivered like a Canadian prairie. A silent landscape, except for the hiss and rattle of the steel wheels and the honk of the engine. An empty landscape, too, except for the inevitable African children watching the train go by: two wooden carriages and a ribbon of dun-coloured vapour trailing from the tall smoke-stack and cow-catcher back to the horizon.[1]

You could see this was no ordinary special. The engine was flying three flags: green stripes each side of the cow-catcher, orange on the boiler. They were the stripes of the Transvaal *vierkleur* and the Free State flag respectively. The same flags saluted the train at each station it passed, even the smallest wayside halt.[2]

In the first saloon carriage, dressed in his usual baggy black suit and hidden behind drawn blinds, sat President Kruger with his staff, including the State Attorney, Jan Smuts. Kruger's eyes blinked painfully behind his small gold spectacles. He would need a carriage closed against the cold wind when they reached Bloemfontein.[3]

At Vereeniging, the frontier post, they had received on the previous evening a parting address from members of the Transvaal Executive. Kruger replied with one of his homely parables. The present franchise law, he said, was like one of those farmers' dams that only let through the clean water: 'The clean water is the trusty Uitlanders and through our laws they shall come to join us, and the dirty water is the untrustworthy Uitlanders; they shall stay outside.' Kruger firmly repeated that he desired 'peace not war' and he 'yearned from his heart that the Conference, now planned to secure peace, should not fail'.[4]

The President had always been able to respond to a crisis. Now he was like an old war-horse scenting battle. Although he had accepted President Steyn's invitation to come to Bloemfontein for the conference, he was pessimistic about the outcome. Not that the truth about Milner was yet guessed by the Boers or other Afrikaners. The fiery 'Helot Despatch' was still locked away in Chamberlain's red box at the Colonial Office. But Kruger was intensely suspicious of Chamberlain, and Milner was one of Chamberlain's men. Kruger remembered the occasion in 1877, when he had met Sir Bartle Frere, then British High Commissioner. Kruger had then discovered, he said, that there were two separate men called Frere: one Frere, the charming diplomat with whom he spoke; the other Frere, the man who was planning to subdue the Transvaal. Now, in 1899, as Smuts put it, the same question could be asked of Milner as of Sir Bartle Frere: 'Which Milner do you mean?'[5]

In the current crisis, Kruger leant heavily on the support of his young State Attorney. As far as Smuts could judge, Kruger now believed 'war is unavoidable or will soon become so – not because there is any cause, but because the enemy is brazen enough not to wait for a cause'. Smuts, by contrast, thought the English would probably not be so stupid as to launch an 'unmotivated' war. 'If England,' he wrote to his old friend and political patron at the Cape, Jan Hofmeyr, 'should venture into the ring with Afrikanerdom without a formally good excuse, her cause in South Africa would be finished.'[6]

He did not believe that the Uitlanders' franchise could possibly give England a *casus belli*. He imagined England was 'stoking up' unrest on the Rand in order to 'make us lose our heads and so make a wrong move'. He thought that Chamberlain was understandably terrified of the current of Afrikaner solidarity sweeping the whole sub-continent. Still, he found the general situation very 'obscure and puzzling'.[7] He implored his Afrikaner allies in the Cape to try to persuade the British government to stop harassing the Transvaal.

In the event it was Smuts, not Milner, whom the Cape Afrikaners had tried to persuade. For weeks they had begged Smuts to placate the British government by making concessions to the Uitlanders. 'Do endeavour, my dear brother,' wrote William Schreiner, the Cape Prime Minister since the defeat of Rhodes's party in 1898, 'to secure reasonable concessions. If you have done that it will be an immense service to South Africa. Imagine the joy with which Rhodes and Co. would welcome the fact, if the President and Raad should be stung into an attitude of refusing to do what is reasonable. . . .'[8] From Jan Hofmeyr, Smuts received a shower of cabled advice: 'time for pouring oil on stormy waters and not on fire. Do not delay . . . situation is serious and time precious.' Hofmeyr also sent Smuts a warning: he must 'cherish no illusion about Colony'. Hofmeyr meant that if hostilities did break out Smuts must not expect the Cape Afrikaners to 'rush *en masse* to arms', especially as 'most of them know nothing about the bearing of arms'.[9]

As Smuts oscillated between the conciliatory mood of his friends at the Cape and the pessimism of his own venerable chief, the two Cape statesmen stepped up their peace offensive. Schreiner begged Smuts to use 'infinite patience' at the conference. He must peruade Kruger to improve his offer; recently Kruger had promised the Uitlanders the franchise after nine instead of fourteen years.[10] Smuts agreed to try. But doubts about Chamberlain's real motives still haunted him.

Suppose the whole conference were to be a sham, a piece of political theatre arranged by Chamberlain for the benefit of audiences at home and in the colonies? If that was the case, why humiliate themselves by making concessions? Indeed, they had already humiliated themselves. By the London Convention, England had specifically bound herself not to meddle in the internal affairs of the State. Now Chamberlain was sending Milner to Bloemfontein to wag his finger at Kruger for his supposed ill-treatment of the Uitlanders.

Smuts returned again to the overwhelming question: did Chamberlain really intend to try to reannex the Transvaal, quite regardless of public opinion? Was it to be war? Then the 'sooner the better'. His feelings boiled over. 'Our volk throughout South Africa must be baptized with the baptism of blood and fire before they can be admitted among the great peoples of the world.' And they would win. 'Either we shall be exterminated or we shall fight our way out ... and when I think of the great fighting qualities that our people possess, I cannot see why we should be exterminated.'[11]

Yet war seemed a world away as the special steamed into the station at Bloemfontein. It arrived punctually at ten o'clock. The whole town was *en fête*, as though the crisis was over. A triumphal arch spanned the main street. A great white banner draped the station: *'God leide uwe beraadslagingen'* – 'God direct your counsels'. In the place of honour beside the Transvaal's *vierkleur* was the Union Jack.[12]

Kruger shuffled from the train, peered through his gold spectacles, and began his reply to the address of welcome. I shall give 'everything, everything, everything' for peace, he said, grimly repeating the Dutch word *alles*. But if 'they touch my independence, I shall resist'.[13]

The same dawn that found Kruger's special train steaming south to Bloemfontein found a second special, flying two Union Jacks beside the cow-catcher, steaming north to the same destination.[14]

Sir Alfred Milner had woken half an hour earlier after a shaky night in the front carriage of the train. He looked at his watch. It was only six; the sky was still hardly distinguishable from the veld, but the train was already approaching De Aar Junction. At De Aar he was to meet, secretly, Percy Fitzpatrick's closest political ally from the Rand, H. C. Hull, an Uitlander solicitor. He would reassure Hull. HMG really did mean business this time.[15]

In fact, what were Chamberlain's *own* aims in the coming crisis? It was a question that preoccupied Milner and his Uitlander allies quite as much as Kruger and Smuts – and is puzzling even today. Milner knew the official (if private) answer. Since that crucial cabinet meeting on 9 May, both Chamberlain and the government were committed to Milner's policy of imperial intervention on behalf of the Uitlanders[16] – of 'turning the screw' on the old President till a 'climb-down' was achieved.[17]

But what did Chamberlain mean by a 'climb-down'? British demands – restoration of the five-year franchise, with a larger minority of seats in the Raad allocated to the Rand – might give the British Uitlanders individual political equality. It would not give them immediate collective supremacy. No one knew how many British Uitlanders there were in the Transvaal, nor how many of them would opt for Transvaal citizenship.[18] So the peaceful take-over of Kruger's state, on behalf of the Empire, might not be accomplished for years – not till after Milner's term as High Commissioner had expired. Would Chamberlain allow Milner to stiffen his demands? Not if Kruger conceded the five-year franchise, Milner had reason to believe. Chamberlain aimed at a diplomatic *coup* for himself, but only a limited settlement for the Uitlanders. It was all British public opinion would accept.[19]

It was Chamberlain's dependence on public opinion that filled Milner with a frustration bordering on despair. Of course, it was not Chamberlain's fault, he knew that. Joe was 'magnificent', he assured one of the Cabinet – a real 'imperial statesman'.[20] But British party politics, as he confessed to other, still closer friends, were 'rotten'.[21] He explained that 'for really big and crucial things, the weakness and the compromise, which it [party politics] involves, even with the strongest government, *must ruin any settlement.*'[22] Milner himself had no intention of compromising with Kruger. He had committed himself 'heart and soul' to the Uitlanders. The game was the 'great game for mastery in South Africa'. He intended to win.[23]

His plan was to annex the Transvaal. He would rule it as a Crown Colony, much as his old chief, Cromer, ruled Egypt. It was all part of the larger game of federating the white Empire. He would achieve 'a place in history as big as the man who made the American Constitution, or the authors of the United Germany'.[24] These were the dreams of Milner's life and he saw no reason to abandon them now because of one obstinate (and obsolete) old man in South Africa. But how to prevent Chamberlain 'wobbling' and ruining everything by compromise? A delicate tactical plan, whose object had to be kept as secret from Chamberlain as from Kruger, was taking shape in Milner's mind.

Chamberlain wanted a 'climb-down' by Kruger leading to a settlement. Milner wanted a war leading to annexation. But these opposite strategies could be served by the same tactics. Chamberlain would agree to Milner turning the screw progressively tighter until Kruger climbed down. Milner would argue that to get a peaceful settlement they must first send out enough troops to frighten Kruger. Together the two screws – increased political demands and increased British garrisons – would precipitate the war. This was, in essence, the scenario that Milner had designed.[25]

Hence the Bloemfontein conference was not, as many people later came to believe, staged by Milner as a piece of political theatre, a sham conference he intended should fail. On the contrary, it was Milner's first step, according to his agreement with Chamberlain, in 'screwing' (Milner's phrase) Kruger.[26] At this stage, Milner would pitch his demands low enough – he would be 'studiously moderate', as he had promised Chamberlain. But once he had Kruger publicly seeking a settlement, the screw would tighten till it became unbearable.

Such were Milner's ideas. It was a trap for old Kruger out of which there was no escape, except to precipitate a hopeless war – unless, horrible thought, Kruger picked up the offer of the five-year franchise and accepted a settlement there and then.

The special train had by now left De Aar Junction far behind and was toiling upwards to Naauwpoort, astride the main watershed of the northern Cape, nearly five thousand feet above sea-level. The last time he had come that way – on a trip to Basutoland – he had found the Great Karoo green with rain.[27] But now look at the veld! The grass was burnt grey by sun and frost; there would be no forage for the burghers' horses till September. Well, no doubt that was all to the good. No forage meant no war – no invasion by the Boers, at any rate.

From Colesberg, it was downhill all the way to the Orange River and the frontier. The train steamed into Bloemfontein at five o'clock, true to the minute. President Steyn welcomed them much as he had welcomed President Kruger seven hours earlier: with a twenty-one-gun salute of detonators under the rails, and 'God Save the Queen'. Milner sprang down from the train, a clean-shaven, debonair figure in a morning suit and a grey topper. South Africa seemed to be at his feet. Here was the man, said the Boer newspapers, who would go down into history as one of 'the greatest of Englishmen'. He could bring 'peace with honour' to South Africa.[28]

Bloemfontein ('Flowers-in-the-Springs') was then a delightful place, with jacarandas lining the main street and a picturesque old British fort built on a commanding kopje. Its wealth was based on the single-track railway from the Cape to the Rand completed in 1892.[29] Appropriately, the conference was to be held beside the railway station – in the only room with a round table large enough for the dozen men of the two delegations.[30]

When proceedings opened on Wednesday 31 May the omens seemed encouraging. President Steyn made a joke, perhaps not intentionally. He introduced the two men with 'this, Sir Alfred, is Mr Kruger, of whom you have probably read in the newspapers....' Kruger did what was expected of him, playing the fool and digging Milner in the ribs, according to the papers, 'with many hoarse salutes of affection and respect'.[31]

But despite Steyn's goodwill, Kruger's good humour and Milner's good manners, there was to be no meeting of minds at Bloemfontein.

The conference, according to Milner's Military Secretary, was like a 'palaver with a refractory Chief'.[32] That was hardly the way Milner would have described it. Whatever miscalculations he had made, he prided himself on not having underrated the old man at the other side of the round table. Kruger was an anachronism – and a giant. Yet Milner planned to undermine the giant with the franchise. He would force Kruger to disgorge a 'substantial and immediate' instalment of political power to the Uitlanders. Then, and only for a short respite, would the old beast be allowed to regain his feet.

Throughout the first day of the conference, Milner played his part admirably. He had no wish to 'apportion blame', he said, in this 'deplorable situation' in which both countries found themselves. But it was his 'personal opinion' that the increasing tension between the governments was caused by the Transvaal's policy towards the Uitlanders. Clear this out of the way; then other outstanding questions could be settled amicably. He put his hand on his heart. Britain had no designs on the independence of the Transvaal. Far from it. If only the Transvaal would treat the Uitlanders better, the Uitlanders would cease to call for Britain to intervene. This would 'strengthen the independence of the Republic', as well as re-establishing the 'cordial relations which we desire'.[33]

Kruger, promising to be brief, took most of Wednesday afternoon to reply. (Milner to Chamberlain that night: the old gentleman 'rambled fearfully'.)[34] The nub of Kruger's case was that the political demands of the Uitlanders conflicted with the national rights of the Transvaal. In other countries there was no threat of new burghers out-voting old burghers. Given the same franchise policy in the Transvaal, 'in a very short time those who are brought in can turn the laws topsy turvy, and do as they like and, with that, my independence would fall'. So he must let the newcomers in gradually: 'If we give them the franchise tomorrow we may as well give up the Republic.' Milner was left once again protesting his sincerity. He was not threatening the Transvaal's independence. 'I do not want to swamp the old population,' he declared in a phrase that his enemies would recall later; *all* he asked was an 'immediate voice' for the Uitlanders.[35]

Thursday, the second day, followed the same pattern: Milner, polite and generous to a fault, protesting his sincerity, and Kruger yielding nothing, and gaining nothing. True, Kruger scored a debating point when someone mentioned military preparations. Who could blame the burghers for arming themselves after the Jameson Raid? His Excellency, said Kruger, could 'follow their spoor' since the Great Trek. They had never been attackers, always defenders. They followed the words of the Lord: 'Accursed be he who removeth his neighbour's landmark.'[36] (Major Hanbury Williams to Intelligence Department: 'How the old man wept crocodile tears about the Raid!')[37]

But Milner soon brought the discussion back to the franchise, and now put his first trump on the table. He asked Kruger to go the whole hog: give the Uitlanders back the five-year franchise, and make it retrospective. Any man who had settled in the Transvaal before 1894, and had enough property to qualify – sixty thousand to seventy thousand men, according to Kruger – would thus have the vote for the asking. Back from Kruger came the dogged refrain: no chance of a five-year franchise at all; it would be political suicide for the volk.[38]

On Friday, the third day, the President stopped stone-walling, and negotiations seemed about to begin. He sprang a surprise. He wanted to meet Milner as far as possible on the franchise, and he laid on the table a 'complete Reform Bill, worked out in clauses and sub-clauses' (as Milner reported back to London) that he must have had 'in his pocket all the time'.[39] In return, he wanted Milner to meet him on three outstanding questions: the Raid indemnity, the Boers' control of Swaziland and, most important, arbitration on rival interpretations of the London Convention of 1884. He added, not without pathos, that he had to think of his burghers: 'If I have to go back and convince them on matters, I must tell them something has been given in to me, if I give in to something.'[40]

If Milner had wished to do business with Kruger, here was the golden opportunity. He had been given a remarkably free hand by Chamberlain. He could certainly have offered Kruger something to show his burghers. Chamberlain had agreed in principle that the Chartered Company must pay substantial damages for the Raid. It remained for the sum to be fixed; the Transvaal was claiming £1,677,938 3s. 3d. including £1 million for 'moral and intellectual damages'.[41] (In fact, Beit and Rhodes would have to fork out from their own pockets, as the Chartered Company was too near bankruptcy since the Matabele and Mashona revolts.)[42] Both the Swaziland and the arbitration questions were more complicated. But here again, Milner could certainly have helped Kruger's difficulties with his burghers. Indeed, Chamberlain specifically empowered Milner to humour Kruger about arbitration.[43]

In return, Milner was being offered a deal on the franchise which he admitted in private was a 'great advance' on the existing position.[44] Kruger was prepared to slash the residence qualification from fourteen to seven years. True, Milner had all sorts of objections to the way the proposal would work. It would not give, as he had stated it must, 'substantial and immediate' representation to the Uitlanders. For it was to be only partially retrospective, and the length of delay would vary according to a sliding scale. And Kruger was only offering a total of five out of twenty-eight seats in the Raad for the gold-mining districts, compared to Milner's proposal for these districts to have a minimum of seven seats.[45]

Yet, despite everything, could it not have been bridged, that gap which now divided the two men: five years for the franchise against seven: seven seats for the Raad against five? So it would, without a doubt, if Milner had aimed to negotiate, and not to 'screw' Kruger.[46]

Milner brushed aside Kruger's Reform Bill. It was a 'Kaffir-bargain'. He made a counter-offer that could only infuriate the old man: what about some form of self-government for the Rand?[47] Kruger knew enough about English politics to see the irony in this. Chamberlain had broken with the Liberals because he refused, on principle, to accept Home Rule for Ireland; here he was trying to impose Home Rule on the Rand. Inevitably, the offer was rebuffed by Kruger, who said the Uitlanders were 'like naughty children'. 'If you give them a finger they will want the whole hand, then an arm, then a head, and then they want the whole body bit by bit.'[48]

It was now Saturday, the fourth day of the conference, and the stalemate was unbroken. Milner had sat up half the night preparing an endless list of objections to Kruger's Reform Bill. He plumped it on to the table and the conference

adjourned till Monday. The same afternoon he cabled to London: 'It seems that
the conference will fail.... I have been studiously conciliatory....'[49]

Next day Milner and his staff, in plain dress, attended a service in the Anglican
Cathedral, and heard the Dean's sermon, 'Blessed are the Peacemakers'. To the
Boer public at large the conference still appeared a triumphant success. 'Peace
Assured – Sir A. Milner's Statesmanship', ran the headlines of *The Standard and
Diggers' News*. 'Forebodings dispelled.'[50] In fact, Milner himself was exhausted
by the strain of the last few days. He had failed to 'screw' Kruger, but he had not
been outmanoeuvred himself. Next day he would have to break off the conference, unless Kruger suddenly caved in. For there was always the danger that
Kruger might offer other illusory concessions. 'If we went on and on,' he later
confessed to Chamberlain, 'we might get a little more and a little more,
each concession being *made to appear very big,* and finally feel unable, after
so many concessions, to break off, and yet find we had a perfectly hollow
scheme.'[51]

Milner's cabled warning that he might have to break off the conference did
not reach Chamberlain till Sunday. Chamberlain immediately replied: 'I hope
you will not break off hastily. Boers do not understand quick decisions.... I am
by no means convinced that the President has made his last offer, and you should
be very patient and admit a good deal of haggling before you finally abandon the
game.[52]

But before this cable reached Milner, the curtain had already fallen at Bloemfontein. Kruger, his eyes watering, had stood there for the last time, repeating,
'It is our country you want.'[53] Milner had closed the proceedings with the
chilling words: 'This conference is absolutely at an end, and there is no obliga-
tion on either side arising from it.'[54]

What lesson did the antagonists take away with them from the conference, as
their two specials steamed back the way they had come?

In Milner's eyes, the moral was obvious. He had failed to trap Kruger because
he had failed to frighten him sufficiently. Now they must turn the 'war-screw'.[55]
Before the conference he had warned Selborne privately that they might have to:

> If I fail, it will then be your *turn* ... assume at once the diplomatic offensive and back it
> with a strong show of [military] force.... All the Afrikaners and all the mugwumps will
> howl at us.... I don't care. My view is that (1) absolute downright determination plus a
> large temporary increase of force will ensure a climb down. It is 20 to 1. And (2) that, if it
> didn't, and there was a fight, it would be better to fight now than 5 or 10 years hence when
> the Transvaal, unless the Uitlanders can be taken in, in considerable numbers, will be
> stronger and more hostile than ever. Bold words these, you will say. But remember I
> myself am risking a lot – indeed everything.[56]

Specifically, Milner wanted the War Office to replace General Butler as
Commander-in-Chief. He also wanted some competent officers sent out to
organize the Cape border towns, like Mafeking and Kimberley. He also wanted
an *overwhelming* force – the exact number was for military experts to decide, but
he thought it might be as high as ten thousand men – pushed up into the

dangerous northern triangle of Natal, where General Colley had come to grief at Majuba, both to frustrate a Boer attack and to prove 'irresistible' as a political lever. Unless they took the right military precautions '*before* the crash', they might find themselves involved in 'not only a biggish war, but much civil dissension afterwards'. However, he maintained 'in spite of all those alarms and excursions, that if we are perfectly determined we shall win without a war or with a mere apology for one.'[57]

In short, Milner's advice to London boiled down to detailed advice on three crucial military questions. First, how many soldiers to send out to guard the Cape and Natal. Second, whom to appoint to organize and lead them. Third, how far forward to station them. If his advice was taken, he assured the Cabinet – disingenuously – there would be no war.[58]

Kruger was, predictably, less reassured. His suspicions of Chamberlain were confirmed by what he had seen at Bloemfontein. Fortunately, his war preparations were nearly complete – apart from an important consignment of seventy-two field-guns from Creusot which Joubert did not agree to order until July (when it was in fact too late for them to be delivered).[59] He knew he could have an overwhelming advantage if he chose to strike the first blow. However, the strategic key remained the Free State. Like the Cape Afrikaners, Steyn had pressed Kruger to be generous to the Uitlanders. Still, Kruger did not doubt that, if war came, the Free State would fight shoulder to shoulder with the Transvaal. As a little encouragement, he now sent the Free Staters half a million Mauser cartridges.[60] Yet, though more certain than ever that a collision with England was inevitable, Kruger did not stand in the way of Smuts, who took a different view.

Characteristically, his experiences at Bloemfontein had made Smuts oscillate still more violently between his hopes for peace and his instinct for war.

The politician in him declared that war could still be avoided. 'Britain will never go to war after she knows what the true opinion of the Colonial Afrikaners is,' he told Hofmeyr. By a display of Afrikaner solidarity – discreet enough, at the same time, not to attract 'well-founded' charges of disloyalty – they could force the British government to give up its aggressive designs on the Transvaal. For a war could only be launched from the Cape, and if the Cape government and the majority of its people were hostile, then war was clearly impossible. Moreover, Smuts had high hopes of persuading Kruger to improve on the franchise reforms he had put on the table at Bloemfontein. This would cut the ground once and for all from under the feet of the English war-mongers.[61]

Yet, even while he penned these cool, diplomatic sentences to his friends at the Cape, the passionate side of Smuts's nature asserted itself. 'Milner is as sweet as honey,' he scribbled in a note to 'Lappie' (the pet name for his wife) during the conference, 'but there is something in his very intelligent eyes that tells me he is very dangerous.'[62]

Later, when the conference was over, the pieces of the puzzle began to fit into place. It was Milner who was the clue – Milner, who had contemptuously broken off the conference, Milner who was 'much more dangerous than

Rhodes'. Was he playing this part under Chamberlain's orders, or was *he* the driving force? Smuts confessed he did not know.[63] But he saw ominous parallels between the current situation and the situation on the eve of Britain's first annexation of the Transvaal in 1877: the same 'lying petitions' for imperial intervention, the same outside forces working for war to 'defeat the work of time'. It filled him with indignation to think that this 'academic nobody', this man who fancied himself 'a great imperial statesman', was trying to destroy in a moment everything they had tried to create.[64]

Well, in due course, Milner must pay the price. He had insulted the 'spirit of Afrikanerdom'. Smuts did not conceal the personal satisfaction it would give him to force Chamberlain to have Milner recalled in disgrace, like that other great English proconsul, Sir Bartle Frere.[65]

CHAPTER 7

Milner's Three Questions

Pall Mall, London,
8 June – 19 July 1899

'It is perhaps not altogether remarkable under the
circumstances described [the war inside the British War
Office] that no plan of campaign ever existed for
operations in South Africa.'

Report of the Royal Commission
on the South African War (1903)

The breakdown at Bloemfontein had increased the risk of war. No one, not even
Lord Lansdowne, the Secretary of State for War, could deny that. And for the
first time he and his advisers at the War Office had to consider those three crucial
military questions posed by Milner, questions that were to echo and re-echo in
successive disasters later that year.

Milner's own proposals, we saw, were to send at once an *overwhelming* force'
– 'it may be perhaps 10,000 men;' to replace General Sir William Butler, the
C-in-C in South Africa, with a British general politically and militarily capable
of doing the job; to push most of the reinforcements forward into the frontier-
land of northern Natal.[1] At the War Office, the Commander-in-Chief of the
British army, Field Marshal Lord Wolseley, took an even stronger line than
Milner. On 8 June he proposed that they should mobilize the whole of General
Sir Redvers Buller's 1st Army Corps and a cavalry division (about thirty-five
thousand) and make a 'demonstration' to overawe Kruger from Salisbury Plain.
Wolseley's belligerent minutes, scrawled on the green War Office files, passed to
the desk of the Secretary of State.[2]

The desk was neat and business-like – so it seems, in contemporary photographs.[3] What a contrast to the War Office in which it stood! A century earlier,
this old War Office in Pall Mall had been a row of houses, including the strange
'Temple of Health and Hymen' where Emma Hart (later Emma Hamilton)
was installed as a 'Goddess'. Then, in the fever of army reform that swept
England after the reverses in the Crimea, the War Office had swallowed the row
of houses. Few were demolished; cheaper to botch the buildings together, to
knock holes in the walls and connect up the buildings without even changing the
floor levels. The result was a labyrinth. It was all stairs and passages and
landings, like some rambling old country house left behind in central London.
There was the whiff of colza-oil lamps and leather fire-buckets: an office where

private documents and public men could be lost without trace for weeks at a time.[4]

It was this antiquated and laborious machine, patched and repatched over two centuries, that was supposed to control and direct Britain's new imperial army of 340,000 regulars and reservists.[5] And at its hub, as smooth and flawless as a pillar of black and white marble and utterly out of sympathy with Wolseley's soldiers around him, sat the Secretary of State for War, Henry Charles Keith ('Clan') Petty-Fitzmaurice, fifth Marquess of Lansdowne.

To say that Lansdowne came from one of the great patrician families of England would be to understate his blessings. On his father's side, he was both English and Irish; on his mother's, both Scottish and French. His swarthy good looks were attributed to his French grandfather, Bonaparte's ADC, General Comte de Flahault, supposed to be an illegitimate son of Talleyrand. From his other ancestors, estates had showered on him in a golden rain. Lansdowne House in Piccadilly, Bowood in Wiltshire, Meikleour in Perthshire, Dereen in County Kerry – they straddled half the British Isles. Yet there was nothing vulgar or sensual in the way he disposed of his vast income. You could hardly imagine him romping with Emma Hamilton in the 'Temple of Health and Hymen' like his randy Whig ancestors. From childhood he had been taught the Victorian ideals of service. Dr Jowett had taken him firmly in hand as one of his first pupils at Balliol.[6] Soon it was observed that 'Clan' was a kind of phenomenon.

His abilities were modest. He had flunked his First in Greats, despite all Jowett's coaching. But he had not failed again. At twenty-four, he was chosen by Gladstone for the Liberal front bench. At thirty, he had crossed the floor – understandably disturbed, as an Irish landlord, by Gladstone's first Irish Land Act. At thirty-eight, he had been sent to Canada as Governor-General; at forty-three, to India as Viceroy. Everywhere he had proved himself supremely conscientious. What a credit to Dr Jowett he had turned out after all! He was stylish and patrician and courteous, especially to Indian Maharajahs. He displayed no flaw in his character, unlike men of later vintages from Balliol.[7] He did not drink like Asquith, or put on airs like Grey, or fancy himself a genius like Curzon. In short, Lansdowne was an epitome of the mid-Victorian virtues – the victory of education over breeding, and of character over both (of priggery, so to speak, over Whiggery). He had triumphed over all his advantages.

Yet there was, people had to admit, something missing in 'Clan' Lansdowne. He was too conscientious. If only he had sometimes forgotten his duty. If only he had had something to repress. And in 1895 when he had been brought back from India to be Minister of War, there was little enthusiasm for the appointment. Had people guessed that in 1899 the War Office would suffer its greatest ordeal since the Crimea, how they would have protested! In this crisis, the army needed fire and steel in the man at its head. Lansdowne, pillar of state that he was, had neither – nor the faintest spark of imagination.[8]

It was now mid-June and Lansdowne had to answer that belligerent minute of Wolseley's in the green file – the one calling for the mobilization of thirty-five thousand troops, in response to Milner's request for a twist of the war screw.

In the black months later that year, people were to blame Lansdowne, understandably, for the blunders of the War Office. But there were two things that paralysed Lansdowne's war preparations, apart from his own character.

First, his own Cabinet colleagues regarded the War Office with a kind of amused contempt, as though war was not a serious subject – or could safely be left to the generals to quarrel over. In 1896 Lansdowne had nervously agreed to propose to the Cabinet that they might raise soldiers' pay a few pence in order to get a better class of recruit.[9] (After deductions, Tommy Atkins then received less than the famous shilling-a-day fixed after the Mutiny of the Nore in 1797.)[10] The same year, and again in 1898, Lansdowne agreed to ask the Cabinet for a small increase in the size of the regular army. Grudgingly they accepted these proposals. But their lack of confidence in the War Office was made abundantly clear. Sir Michael Hicks Beach, the Chancellor, publicly denounced the idea of increased army spending. Chamberlain scoffed at the 'rickety and useless' War Office system. Salisbury, the Prime Minister, hinted that he might not be able to support Lansdowne in the Army Debates in the Lords. He relented, but warned Lansdowne: 'I need not say that in respect to these military arrangements ... I shall assent to anything which commends itself to you. But my advice will be, not to pay much attention to your military advisers.' Lansdowne felt he had been 'outrageously' treated – especially by Hicks Beach – and he threatened to resign.[11]

Then in 1898 came Kitchener's twin victories: by moral force at Fashoda, by brute force at Omdurman. Lansdowne's stock with his colleagues rose accordingly. But he was still kept on a tight rein financially: there was only £20·6 million for the army budget. The British army remained frail by international standards: a nominal total of 340,000 (actually 316,000) regulars and reservists, compared with three million in Germany, ten million in Russia, and four million in France.[12] (The navy was, of course, the bulwark of home defence, and traditionally got most of the defence budget.) Unlike its foreign counterparts, the British army had to be ready to fight in every corner of the globe. And after deducting men for permanent garrisons at home, in India, in Egypt and in the colonies, there were only two army corps and a cavalry division – about seventy thousand men – available to send on overseas 'demonstrations'.[13] In short, the British army was an army supposed only to be ready for small wars. But was this small-war army in a fit state for war of any kind? It was seriously below strength, especially in artillery and cavalry and short of essential supplies of every type, according to its Commander-in-Chief, Lord Wolseley.[14]

The second reason for Lansdowne's inertia that year was his distaste for Wolseley and his Ring. What victories they would have won, Lansdowne's generals, if they could have fought an enemy with the vigour they showed in fighting each other! But the senior generals were split into two 'Rings' – Field-Marshal Lord Wolseley's 'Africans', Field-Marshal Lord Roberts's

'Indians' – and the issue was still unresolved. The struggle left Lansdowne alienated from Wolseley and most of the War Office.[15] He himself favoured Roberts and his 'Indians'. Their diplomatic collaboration in India – Roberts as Indian C-in-C, Lansdowne as Viceroy – had made the two men mutual admirers. Unfortunately for both, when Roberts returned to England after forty-one years' service in India, Lansdowne had failed to make him British C-in-C at the Horse Guards. The Cabinet had selected Roberts's rival, Wolseley. Roberts was fobbed off with the job of C-in-C in Ireland.[16] But the battle of the Rings went on. It was no Wagnerian struggle; there was a pettiness about both men as well as a touch of greatness. In 1900 Wolseley was due to retire. Already sixty-seven, Roberts was a year older than Wolseley, yet he was still burning to snatch back the Horse Guards from the 'Africans'. Their second-in-command, and heir-apparent, blocked his way: Sir Redvers Buller, now commander of the 1st Army Corps at Aldershot.[17] So Roberts and the 'Indians' waited their chance, and the closer they drew to Lansdowne the worse for Wolseley, Buller and the efficiency of the Horse Guards.

Lansdowne's reply to Wolseley's belligerent minute of mid-June was characteristically negative. He evaded Milner's three questions. Instead he agreed that they should send a 'hint' to General Butler about the need to be 'on the look-out'. But it was too soon for 'open preparations for a row'.[18] He turned down flat the expensive proposal of Wolseley's to mobilize an army corps of thirty-five thousand men. Lansdowne was unperturbed by the fact that the total of British troops in South Africa was only ten thousand, compared to the Boers' estimated potential forces of 53,700. Why should the Boers invade? What was needed was to make sure the ten thousand men of the British garrison were in a 'thoroughly efficient state'. They would need some ammunition and new boots – a hundred rounds and one pair of boots per man – and extra transport and ten good British officers to put some stuffing into them.[19] That was the Secretary of State's decision of 21 June, conveyed by cable to General Butler. Butler was also reminded that he had never answered an important War Office question of the previous December: what was his plan for defending the colonies in the unlikely event of Boer invasion? Finally, after receiving Butler's cabled reply, Lansdowne sent him a courtly rebuke: 'You cannot understand too clearly that it is your duty to be guided on all questions of policy by the H C [Milner] . . . whom you will of course loyally support.'[20]

In fact, Butler's cabled replies were astonishing. He offered no plan of defence. No suggestions about how many reinforcements were needed. Nor where they were to be positioned. The only question that, by implication, he answered was this. He confirmed the wisdom of Milner's suggestion that Butler himself should be replaced. What Butler had written touched at the very heart of Milner's war-mongering with the capitalists of the Rand (though Butler remained oblivious that it was Wernher and Beit, not Rhodes, who were Milner's partners). He cabled: 'Situation is not understood in England. In the event of crisis arising situation will be more of a civil war than regular military operations. . . . Persistent efforts of a party to produce war form . . . gravest

element in situation here. Believe war between white races coming as sequel to
the Jameson Raid ... would be greatest calamity that ever occurred.'[21]

It was now early July, and the turn of Wolseley and his 'Africans' to attempt a
counter-attack.

If Lansdowne found Wolseley rather trying, Wolseley's own feelings for
Lansdowne were a good deal more passionate. 'Little Lansdowne ... is an
obstinate little fellow, very conceited, and his obstinacy is born of ignorance' – 'I
spend my day struggling with my little gentleman.... Such a small mind it
would be difficult to imagine. I am sure some little Jew must have "overtaken"
his mother before he was conceived.'[22] So Wolseley poured out his feelings to
his wife. In truth, Lansdowne was more than a personal enemy for him, and his
Ring. He seemed to epitomize the worst defects of the British military system,
defects persisting despite the reforms he and his Ring had helped create: defects
like the reckless cost-cutting in the army budget; the pettifogging regulations
and red tape; the muddle and confusion in the War Office; above all, the
encroachment of a civilian War Minister and his officials in a field that should, by
rights, have been the preserve of himself and his Ring.[23]

Wolseley was not, of course, a mere theorist, an armchair army reformer. He
had been a famous fighting general. An early struggle against great handicaps
(his father was an impoverished Anglo-Irish major who had died when he was
seven); outstanding gallantry in the face of the enemy (he had been severely
wounded in the thigh in Burma, and permanently lost the use of his right eye
after being struck by a bursting shell in the Crimea); the *enfant terrible* of his
profession (he was awarded a brevet lieutenant-colonelcy before he was
twenty-seven): this was the stuff that military heroes were made of. Add to that
certain qualities of mind that would have been exceptional in any profession: an
ice-clear brain, combined with a demonic fund of energy, what he called a 'mad
and manly' fury to succeed. Add to that, in turn, an unbroken run of successes as
a military commander in the Ashanti, Zulu and Egyptian campaigns. No
wonder Wolseley's name had become a by-word for military efficiency – 'all Sir
Garnet', as the cockneys put it. By the 1880s, he was 'our only general'. (Roberts
was 'our only other general'.)[24]

However, Wolseley was now sixty-six. There was little trace of the rakish
young Wolseley, the original of W. S. Gilbert's 'Modern Major-General'. His
hair was milk-white. He had had some sort of illness two years earlier (Roberts
claimed it was a stroke) and his memory was now painfully erratic. He was an
'extinct volcano', he confessed to his wife. It was to her that he poured out his
heart in these bitter and hollow years as Commander-in-Chief. 'Dearest Snipe,'
he began these letters, almost gaily, and then the venom would flow. The British
army was doomed in its present form. The C-in-C was a mere figurehead. The
army was controlled by an ignorant and conceited civilian, who had not the
courage to admit to his fellow-ministers the army's deficiencies. 'I believe that
war would be the best thing at the moment for us,' he had noted recently. 'We
should get rid of an impossible army system....'[25]

Meanwhile, Wolseley was tormented by the idea that he ought to resign. Two thoughts held him back. First, his successor would be Roberts – 'little Roberts', the head of the 'Indians'. Roberts might know a great deal about India. He knew nothing about England. And if he took over the army at home, everything would 'go to the devil'.[26] At the same time, Wolseley had himself to confess to a hopeless longing to serve as Commander-in-Chief of an army in the field. It would make a fine, Tennysonian ending. One big command, and perhaps death in harness, rather than in his bed 'like an old woman'.[27] But what chance was there of leading the Ring into battle now? If an expedition were sent to South Africa, its leader would be not Wolseley but his ex-protegé, Sir Redvers Buller. Buller was six years his junior, and Buller's years as Adjutant-General had given him a reputation for reform as brilliant as Wolseley's own. No wonder Wolseley was jealous. In fact, the magic had gone from the Ring. Wolseley could not forgive Buller for having accepted the reversion of the C-in-C's post in 1895, offered by the Liberals before the Tories came to power and appointed Wolseley instead.[28]

Wolseley's July counter-attack on Lansdowne took the form of a triple salvo of minutes proposing a 'forward' policy. He repeated his earlier plan: call out Buller's 1st Army Corps on Salisbury Plain – say, thirty-five thousand men – and terrify Kruger; buy their transport for South Africa (eleven thousand mules, costing nearly £500,000), in case he refused to be terrified. Wolseley added a second proposal: send out to South Africa a first instalment of ten thousand men, as Milner had suggested.

This brought Lansdowne squarely back to the first of the three crucial questions: how many troops would make the two colonies safe from invasion? Ten thousand, according to Wolseley. Lansdowne scoffed at this extravagant idea.[29] And he mobilized the other generals, especially one of the 'Indians', against Wolseley and Buller.

In July, he had appointed Major-General Sir Penn Symons, a brigadier from India, to be GOC in Natal, the more vulnerable of the two colonies. Symons could hardly have been a more unsuitable choice for the job. He knew next to nothing about South Africa, and he was a fire-eater. Only a few days after his arrival Lansdowne cabled to ask his views about the first crucial question. His reply: a mere two thousand extra troops would make Natal safe right up to its northern apex (hemmed in though it was by the two republics).[30]

In the absence of any support from Butler – and Butler recommended no reinforcements at all – Wolseley turned to his old 'African' colleague, Major-General Sir John Ardagh, Director of the Intelligence Department at the War Office. It was Ardagh's responsibility to forecast the enemy's capacity for war. But Ardagh was a shy, cautious man, known for his alarming silences. Moreover, Ardagh had been given only a shoestring budget for the Intelligence Department – £20,000 to cover the whole world.[31] He had no professional intelligence agents in either the Free State or the Transvaal. So his forecasts were hesitant and conflicting. Where they were to prove accurate – and to favour Wolseley – it was easy for Lansdowne to brush them aside.[32]

The underlying strategic question was simple. On paper, the two republics could commandeer citizen armies totalling fifty-four thousand men. Britain had as yet a garrison totalling ten thousand men in South Africa. Would the republican armies be powerful and efficient enough to drive deep into the two colonies in strength? Or could they only adopt a raiding strategy – that is, only push a few thousand men beyond the border areas?

Ardagh was inclined to believe that the Boers would only adopt a raiding strategy. His department's latest intelligence forecast was printed in an eighty-nine page booklet, *Military Notes on the Dutch Republics*, marked 'secret', and largely unpublished even today. He predicted – correctly – that the Free State would throw in its lot with the Transvaal. Together, they would have a potential invasion force of 34,000 men, (including 4,000 Afrikaners from the colonies), leaving the balance of 20,000 to keep an eye on Kaffirs and Uitlanders at home. They would be armed with the latest guns and rifles.[33] (Though the Intelligence Department had underestimated the Transvaal's Mausers by ten thousand and inflated the number of Creusot 'Long Toms' from four to sixteen, these errors more or less cancelled out.)[34] There was a footnote about the possibility of a plan to attack Ladysmith, well inside Natal, from the Free State.[35] But the general impression given in *Military Notes,* and in other ID forecasts, was that the problem of defending the colonies was of checking 'raids' by two thousand to three thousand Boers.[36]

How did Ardagh and his department come to this conclusion, that would seem so astounding in the light of events? *Military Notes* gives the answer: the Boers were not regarded as a serious military adversary. As fighting men, they were expected to be inferior to the Boers who had beaten Colley's small force at Majuba. Boer generals, used to fighting Kaffirs, knew nothing of handling large bodies of men; not even Joubert had commanded more than three thousand. Nor would the officers be able to cope with the problems of transport and supply. Indiscipline would compound the difficulties. When it came to a 'row', they would find their own new artillery – the Krupp and Creusot field-guns bought after the Raid – inferior to the British Armstrongs. And the guns would hamper them if they tried to adopt their old guerrilla tactics. Moreover, they had always had a 'dread' of English cavalry; and they had yet to taste the effect of modern artillery shrapnel. In short, far from the Boers being able to invade successfully, an 'adequate' force of British infantry, supported by cavalry and artillery, would have no difficulty in invading the republics. They would easily beat the Boers in the open plains of the Free State or the Transvaal (though they might have trouble in the broken country of the Natal frontier). *Military Notes* concluded majestically: 'It appears certain that, after [one] serious defeat, they would be too deficient in discipline and organization to make any further real stand.'[37]

Apart from Ardagh, the most important remaining member of Wolseley's Ring was Sir Redvers Buller. Till now Lansdowne had only allowed Buller one interview. But on 18 July Buller was summoned from Aldershot to the War Office, and it turned out that he was even more alarmed than Wolseley about the defenceless state of both colonies.[38] As the designated leader of the main expeditionary force, Buller was the man who would have to pay for those blunders with his own reputation – perhaps even with his life.

In mid-July, however, Lansdowne still dithered, waiting for a lead from Chamberlain and his Cabinet colleagues. He still evaded Milner's three questions. Then, suddenly and dramatically, the confused political situation seemed to clear.

On 19 July Wolseley read in the papers that Kruger had made substantial political concessions, including a seven-year franchise, to be fully retrospective. *The Times* announced that the crisis was over.[39] Wolseley wrote gloomily to his wife: 'The papers look like peace.' Still, the crisis had already achieved something for the army – £100,000 or so already agreed to be spent on boots, mules, and so on. And Wolseley was convinced that Kruger was irredeemable. So war would come in due course.[40]

That afternoon Wolseley left London and took a train to Amesbury, to review the army manoeuvres on Salisbury Plain. It was a job he could take pride in. The manoeuvres were his personal creation. Two years before he had persuaded Lansdowne to buy the land for the army, and the practice of full-scale battle training had thus been revived after a lapse of a quarter of a century. Wolseley revelled in it all; he could still sit a gallop on a fresh horse, despite his age and infirmities. And what a relief to be out of London, that 'horrid Babylon of noise and dirt', as he called it. He hated the crowds, almost as much as he hated the loneliness. Dining alone at his club, the Athenaeum, and reading the *St James's Gazette* over his meal, he felt utterly abandoned. Still, even the Athenaeum was better than that hateful War Office.[41]

As for its chief, Wolseley declared that he was 'worn out by the flabbiness' of the 'obstinate little fellow'.[42] But he was sorry that war had been postponed. A war would be the making of the British army. It would also be the making of the English upper class, that 'vulgar, snobbish' and ignorant class which still infused the army with the redcoat spirit a decade after it had changed its uniform to khaki. Best of all, a big war would 'be the end' of little Lansdowne.[43]

Three weeks before Kruger's 'climb-down' was reported to the Colonial Office, Chamberlain had delivered his first major speech on South Africa. It was at his party's annual meeting – in Birmingham Town Hall on 26 June. The speech ('we have put our hands to the plough') was hailed by *The Times* as a triumph of firmness and moderation. About Milner, Chamberlain was more complimentary than ever before. 'Who is Sir Alfred Milner?' he asked himself rhetorically in that vast gathering, as though Milner was his own personal invention. Then, letting his eye-glass fall, and looking the crowd full in the face, with that all-steel, made-in-Birmingham look that never failed, Chamberlain answered his own question. 'Sir Alfred Milner was chosen because of his great ability, his cool judgement, his unfailing tact, his impartial mind.'[44]

Heavens, the irony of that phrase of Chamberlain's. He himself had at last begun to see the real drift of Milner's policy: to provoke a war and so annex the

Transvaal for the Empire. Chamberlain's own policy, by contrast, was to accept a settlement over the franchise, if sincerely offered, and a new convention guaranteeing the Transvaal's internal independence. The gap between these two policies had been widening ever since May. Chamberlain and the CO (the Colonial Office) were displeased by the abrupt way Milner had broken off the talks at Bloemfontein.[45] Chamberlain and his staff were still more displeased when they read Milner's despatches of May and June. The CO's aim was to publish Milner's despatches in order to educate the British public about the iniquities of Kruger's government, and show the 'studious moderation' of the British proposals. There was nothing moderate about Milner's later despatches. The 'Helot Despatch', intended by Milner to 'break the crockery', certainly rattled the cups and saucers in the CO. What made Milner imagine that this was the language of diplomacy? In the event, the CO published the 'Helot Despatch' in a muted form.[46] Milner's other outbursts, like the 'Nightmare Despatch' (one taunting Chamberlain for his complicity in the Raid), were considered too stiff even to show the Cabinet.[47] And Chamberlain found it 'really rather trying' that, to cap it all, Milner was proposing that the War Office should sack Butler, the general at the Cape. In vain, Chamberlain attempted to laugh off their troubles to Selborne (actually a staunch Milnerite). Milner was 'overstrained. I wish he would remember the advice to the lady whose clothes caught fire, "to keep as cool as possible".'[48]

The climax of this trying period was reached when Milner, intent on getting those ten thousand British troops sent to Natal, admitted that there *was* a case for a war – it was the only way of getting annexation. Milner cabled that if they sent troops 'the most probable result . . . would be a complete climb-down . . . and, if not that, a war which, however deplorable in itself, would at least enable us to put things on a sound basis . . . better than even the best devised Convention can'.[49]

At this, Fred Graham, the Assistant Under-Secretary at the CO, exploded:

To speak frankly, I think there is some danger of our being 'rushed' by the party in So. Africa which, while its sympathy with the Uitlanders is genuine, has for its chief aim the wiping out of Majuba and the speedy annexation of the Transvaal. We are trusting, and rightly trusting to a High Commissioner of singular ability; but I begin to think that there is something excitable in the So. African air which prevents men taking a cool and dispassionate view, and that possibly Sir A. Milner is being carried as rapidly away in one direction as Sir Wm. Butler is in the other. . . .

Chamberlain nodded. He rebuked Milner for suggesting that *any* concessions from Kruger were bound to be a sham. He told him, 'If these appear to be substantial it is our policy to accept them as such and not to minimize them.'[51] But the danger of losing control of the situation alarmed him. By his opportunism at the time of the Raid, Chamberlain had put himself at the mercy of Rhodes. Now, as the minister responsible, he had put himself at the mercy of Milner and the jingos in South Africa.

For, as a result of the activities of Milner – and his capitalist allies (though

Chamberlain cannot have known this) – the tension had risen throughout South
Africa. In the Transvaal, the Uitlanders, who had in early June declared themselves in support of the Bloemfontein minimum, now stiffened their terms.
They had formed an 'Uitlander Council' at Johannesburg – a kind of Uitlander
Parliament – dominated by old members of the Reform Movement. Already
the Council had made demands of the most provocative kind: Kruger must dis-
mantle the forts and disarm his people. Now, five days after the Birmingham
speech, they launched a manifesto demanding immediate and radical reform of
the franchise and redistribution of seats in the Raad: in effect, a political take-
over.[52] This new belligerence was echoed at public meetings up and down the
length of British South Africa: five thousand men at Cape Town on 28 June, and
thousands more at Port Elizabeth and Grahamstown. The local British Press
took up the war-cry. *The Cape Times*, edited by Milner's close friend, Edmund
Garrett, warned that 'the gun must be loaded . . . [the Afrikaners] must be made
to believe it is loaded even by its discharge, if no other way succeeds'.[53] In Natal,
mass meetings were held at Durban and Maritzburg, and these were followed by
petitions, supporting a tough line with Kruger, signed by over half the white
men in the Colony. The Natal Press was as jingoistic as the British Press at the
Cape. The mood of belligerence spread in due course to the colonial government of Natal whose elected members had till now chosen to take a cool line
towards Milner, partly for fear of offending their powerful neighbour, the
Transvaal.[54]

Then in mid-July came at long last the details of Kruger's latest offer: a
retrospective seven-year franchise. It turned out that Kruger had been talked
into the scheme by Abraham Fischer, State Secretary of the Free State, and it had
as much the blessing of Afrikaners all over the Cape – including the Cape
government's – as the Uitlander Council's manifesto had the blessing of the
British party.[55]

After the news of this 'climb-down' of Kruger's on 18 July, Chamberlain told
The Times lobby correspondent that the crisis was over, so Chamberlain
believed and, as we have seen, *The Times* then said the crisis was over.[56] (This
crisis included the crisis of confidence in Milner, of which the public were of
course unaware.) They seemed to have obtained a reasonable settlement. At any
rate, they must not snub the Boers or minimize their concessions, however
violent Milner's reaction. Already the congratulations were beginning to flow
into the Colonial Office. On 19 July Lord Salisbury wrote to congratulate
Chamberlain on his 'great diplomatic success'.[57] The letter crossed one of
Chamberlain's, modestly expressing the same view. It was a 'triumph for moral
pressure – accompanied by 9 special service officers and 3 batteries of artillery'.[58]
(In fact, there were ten of the former, and the latter had not yet been
despatched.)[59]

But it was not in Chamberlain's (or, indeed, Salisbury's) nature to slacken
their hold on their adversary at the very moment they saw him weakening.
There was still the possibility that Milner was right: Kruger's new offer might

be a mere sham to 'bamboozle' the British public. So it was agreed between Chamberlain and Salisbury that the diplomatic screw must be kept tight on Kruger until the details of the settlement were finally arranged. What precisely were to be the effects of the new seven-year franchise? How many of the Uitlanders would immediately be offered the vote? How many would take it? How would the new voting power be distributed in the Raad? These were the great imponderables. And Chamberlain insisted that a joint enquiry must be held to establish whether the new franchise would meet the principle of giving the Uitlanders 'immediate and substantial' representation.[60]

It was a cool, rational way to end a century of wrangling between Britain and the Transvaal, and if Kruger had trusted Chamberlain it might easily have succeeded. In fact 'Oom Paul' was as suspicious of 'Pushful Joe' as 'Pushful Joe' was of 'Oom Paul'. Despite the pleading of Hofmeyr and the Cape Afrikaners, Kruger gave no reply to Chamberlain's proposal for an enquiry. In fact he had rejected it, claiming that it threatened his country's independence.[61] And as July passed into August, the air of uncertainty and deadlock drifted back into Downing Street, intensified by a summer heatwave.

Meanwhile, for the first and last time that session, the House of Commons debated South Africa. It had always been an axiom of Chamberlain's (and Salisbury's) South African policy that it must be bipartisan. Although the coalition of Conservatives and Liberal Unionists could always count on a massive parliamentary majority, Chamberlain wanted the support, or at least the acquiescence, of enough of the centre and right-wing Liberals to avoid a division in the House. It was on these terms that the previous year's Fashoda crisis had been handled. Parliament had presented a united front against French encroachment in the Upper Nile, and the French, with no army behind them, had backed down. Despite the renewed uncertainties about Kruger's intentions, Chamberlain was still hoping that he could repeat the triumph of Fashoda on a larger scale in the Transvaal.[62]

Hence in his speech to the Commons on 28 July, Chamberlain had a delicate task. He must rouse his own imperialist supporters, of course; and continue to keep up the pressure on Kruger. Yet he must also reassure the centre Liberals, led by Campbell-Bannerman. This was one of the chief reasons why the Cabinet had set its face against sending reinforcements to South Africa. For in early July, those fiery minutes of Wolseley's – call out the 1st Army Corps and send out a first instalment of ten thousand men – had been circulated by Lansdowne among the Cabinet. Chamberlain himself was attracted to the idea of sending the ten thousand but the rest of the Cabinet, including Lansdowne, had rejected it. Whatever military weakness this policy entailed, it certainly gave Chamberlain the whip hand in the Commons. His speech was a triumph. He castigated Kruger for his 'retrograde' policy, for breaking the spirit, if not the letter, of the London Convention. He detailed once again the Uitlanders' grievances. He warned the House that Britain had proved impotent in the past to secure redress for British subjects – as even the natives were aware. If this situation were allowed to continue it might cause 'in the future many wars and be the prelude to something like national disaster'. Yet he insisted that his own aim was a peaceful settlement. He announced his new proposal for the joint enquiry. It was Kruger's chance for peace with honour. Chamberlain begged Parliament to give him their support and convince Kruger that he must yield before it was too late. And Salisbury stood shoulder to shoulder with Chamberlain, echoing the solemn words: they had set 'hands to the plough'. In reply, Campbell-Bannerman made no attempt to deny them Chamberlain's case for the Uitlanders, and was not prepared to rule out war as a means of achieving redress. Thus opposition gave qualified support to Chamberlain's policy. The debate ended without a division and the House broke up for its five-month holiday.[63]

With Parliament out of the way, the Cabinet felt it could reconsider once again that tiresome business of military reinforcements for South Africa. Wolseley was still calling for ten thousand men, and Symons, the Natal commander, had raised his own estimate from two thousand to five thousand.[64] On 2 August Lansdowne recommended a token reinforcement after all: a battalion of about a thousand men could be sent to South Africa from England or the Mediterranean; add three batteries of artillery already under orders to go to Natal as a relief, and shift five hundred men from the Cape, and the total of Natal reinforcements would then be two thousand troops. Wolseley naturally protested that a relief was not a reinforcement; they would have no horses, and, anyway, the numbers were ridiculously small to protect the whole colony of Natal. The Cabinet took no notice of Wolseley.[65] The Cabinet was less happy with their Minister of War, however, when Lansdowne revealed a few days later that the War Office had at length worked out the contingency plan for putting the 1st Army Corps (that is, the British invasion force) on the Transvaal frontier. It would take four months, as matters stood – or three months, provided a million pounds' worth of mules, carts, clothing and so on were ordered immediately.[66] Lansdowne's forecast of a four-month delay, when they would be on the defensive, left members of the Cabinet aghast. George Goschen wrote to say that the delay was 'preposterous'. Fortunately, the Boers had not read Lansdowne's 'sickening' document, or they might 'make a dash at Natal'.

How *could* Lansdowne have made such a hash of things?[67] Salisbury, however, took the news more calmly. He had never doubted the 'futility' of the War Office. But, of course, it would be 'uncivil' to criticize them at the moment. The question was: should they *now* spend the extra million in order to cut the delay from four to three months? And Salisbury replied with his splendid sense of detachment,

> I think the wiser plan is not to incur any extra serious expenditure until it is quite clear that we *are* going to war. It may add slightly to the initial delay in the operations: but as I have said I do not think that slight addition will increase materially the scandal which will certainly be created by the conditions of our military preparations.[68]

A few hours after Salisbury had written these lines, extraordinary news reached him from Chamberlain. There was 'another climb-down on the part of Kruger'. And this time it seemed to be 'really complete'.[69] And so indeed it appeared. After a further battering from his Afrikaner friends in the Cape, Kruger had made an offer that went, on the face of it, beyond the Bloemfontein minimum: a five-year franchise, with other complicated concessions thrown in.[70]

In the light of the 'scandal' of Lansdowne's war preparations, this news was even more welcome to the Cabinet than it would have been otherwise. Salisbury had by now retired to his official country residence, Walmer Castle, for the summer. He sent Chamberlain renewed congratulations about Kruger's climb-down. And he added a sideways thrust at Milner, who was, predictably, trying to frustrate the new offer. Milner, said Salisbury, seemed to have been 'spoiling for the fight with some glee, and does not like putting his clothes on again'.[71]

Peace descended on the great departments of state in Whitehall, and the heatwave continued. Balfour left for Scotland, to play golf and ride his bicycle;[72] Lansdowne had already withdrawn to the estate he loved best, Dereen in Kerry; even there, in Ireland, the sun shone and the grey sand sparkled under the blue waters of the Kenmare River.[73] Chamberlain retired to Highbury, where he could tend his beloved orchids. The nights were warm, and he and his young wife strolled in the garden, enchanted by the curious lines of the flowers in the light of the moon.[74]

Peace flooded England at the end of August, in that last golden summer of the century. While in the South African winter, six thousand miles away, Milner saw hope at last – and the hope was war.

CHAPTER 8

Preparing for a Small War
Cape Town, London and Natal,
20 July – 7 October 1899

'My own opinion is, as it has always been, that both
Milner and the military authorities greatly exaggerate the
risks of this campaign.'

Joseph Chamberlain, the Colonial
Secretary, to Sir Michael Hicks Beach,
the Chancellor of the Exchequer,
7 October 1899

The 'crisis may be regarded as ended'. Those were the appalling words Milner
read in *The Cape Times* on 20 July, cabled from *The Times* in London and
inspired by Chamberlain himself. A month of desperate wrangling followed.
Then, on 19 August, the crisis seemed 'ended' once again; this time, Kruger, by
seizing on the Bloemfontein minimum, the five-year franchise, really did seem
to have made his peace with Chamberlain. The thought left Milner gasping.
'Things seem to have been going badly in England during the last few days,' he
noted in his diary, 'and the Raad is making further concessions at a very alarming
rate.'[1] What could be more alarming than the prospect of Kruger's concessions
leading to a settlement that he and every British South African were certain
would prove to be a sham? 'Very great feeling of depression,' he wrote on 23
July, 'as I can see no good is coming of the long struggle against S.A.R.
misgovernment. British public opinion is going to be befooled and that is the
long and short of it.'[2]

And although Milner's advice had at last been taken, and General Butler was
to be sent home, there were no positive answers to his three military questions.
No reinforcements had yet landed, not a soldier – except those ten special service
officers.[3]

Milner's fears that he was going to be sacrificed by Chamberlain were scarcely
relieved by a long and highly confidential letter he received in mid-July from
Fleetwood Wilson, Lansdowne's second most senior civil servant at the War
Office. Fleetwood Wilson was a crony of his from Whitehall days, and shared his
own view, so he said, about taking a firm line with Kruger. But he warned
Milner not to rely on anyone in England for active support. England was
'gorged' by its overseas conquests, and there was 'icy indifference' to the
Transvaal question. The City 'only cares to make money and is anxious to patch

[things] up'. Even if the City had backed him, it would prove a dangerous ally. The public at large felt a strong feeling of resentment towards 'the Beits, Barnatos, [J. B.] Robinsons' and other South African millionaires.

Fleetwood Wilson added the cheery news that two 'bigwigs' (presumably one was Lansdowne) described Milner as 'panicky' after they had seen one of his recent telegrams. There was little hope of his getting 'one single drummer' sent out as a military reinforcement, for Chamberlain was 'freely credited with an absolute resolve not to fight', and Hicks Beach 'curses if one extra penny is to be found'. Hence the advice that Fleetwood Wilson gave Milner was this: 'Make up your own mind ... and then stick to your design like grim death.'[4]

This was already Milner's policy. How to pursue it, that was the question. Chamberlain and the Cabinet had allowed the raging crisis to continue ever since Bloemfontein, and absolutely refused to follow his advice about the next step: to turn the military screw and send out the troops. While British ministers thus dragged their feet at home, at the Cape the ministers of the Crown appeared to have sided with the enemy.

For Milner's long wrangle with Schreiner and the Cape Afrikaners had now reached an acutely painful stage.[5] Schreiner's ministry at the Cape was, as we have seen, a child of the Raid: the result of Rhodes's downfall, the humiliation of his Progressive Party, and the polarization of Cape politics along the lines of the two communities, Afrikaner and British. In fact, Schreiner himself belonged to neither community; his father had been a German immigrant. But he had married into the heart of Afrikanerdom, as his wife was a sister of Francis Reitz, the ex-President of the Free State now serving as the State Secretary of the Transvaal. It was Schreiner's wife whom Milner now believed to be the main obstacle to converting Schreiner to his own way of thinking. 'I have wrestled with the Devil,' he was later to tell his friend Garrett, 'for the soul of that man [Schreiner]. ... But in the end I am only left with two-thirds of it (the Soul I mean), his Afrikander wife, Reitz's sister retaining the other third.'[6]

Milner was trying to squeeze support out of Schreiner for the diplomatic campaign against Kruger – suitably negative support – to help prove that Kruger was irredeemable. In short, the Cape Afrikaners' mediation could only succeed, from Milner's point of view, by failing. And so far they had been alarmingly successful in getting plausible-looking concessions from Kruger. Hence that 'very great feeling of depression'.[7]

On the military front he required positive help from Schreiner. Instead, he had found his attempts to reinforce the frontier areas of the Cape actively obstructed by the Cape government. Milner's military advisers had given him a warning (absurdly optimistic, it would prove in a few months) that to defend Kimberley – Rhodes's diamond capital on the borders of the Cape and the Free State – would need a garrison of a thousand men.[8] In early August, after the Cape Parliament had resumed its sitting, Milner summoned Schreiner to Government House, explaining that the Free State forces and their Transvaal allies might be tempted to 'raid' Kimberley. Could Schreiner sanction the reinforcements? 'It was a very unpleasant interview,' Milner noted. Schreiner refused point-blank.

Kimberley would be safer unarmed. Sending colonial (Cape government) troops to the frontier could only raise the political temperature and threaten the Transvaal negotiations then in progress. The sight of British troops might unsettle the natives. In fact, Schreiner had correctly guessed one of Milner's motives in trying to push troops to the frontier: they *could* be used by Milner for invading the Boer republics.[9]

For the moment, Milner had to bite his lip and accept the rebuff. The arms affair then took a new twist with the revelation that the Free State was importing quantities of ammunition by way of Cape Colony, its chief trading partner: nearly 1½ million rounds of Mauser ammunition had passed up the railway line since the beginning of July. Milner was furious with his Afrikaner ministers. How characteristic of them to leave the colony defenceless, while giving every assistance to the enemy over the border! Schreiner pronounced in Parliament: It is the duty of everyone . . . to maintain this colony at any rate as a place of peace – a little port, perhaps, in South Africa that is not to be riddled and rent by storm and thunder.' To Milner the idea of the Cape's neutrality was preposterous. It was little short of a declaration of independence.[10]

The crisis with Schreiner in August coincided with the appalling news on 19 August that, for the second time, the crisis with Kruger was over. He was conceding a five-year franchise, and ten seats (a quarter of the Raad) for the gold-fields: the same franchise as, and three more seats than, Milner himself had demanded at Bloemfontein.[11]

How could Milner now avert the settlement that fell so far short of his own monumental plan for 'bursting the mould' – annexing the Transvaal and then recasting it from its foundations? He had always recognized one fatal flaw in his Bloemfontein terms. Kruger might actually accept them. In that case the crisis would be over, and with it the hope of taking over Kruger's republic – during his own term of office, at any rate. For the Cabinet would never reject an unequivocal offer of a settlement.[12]

All he could do was to use the same blocking tactics as he had used ever since Bloemfontein. He sent a snubbing cable to Conyngham Greene, the British Agent in Pretoria, who had personally negotiated the new offer with Smuts.[13] He warned Chamberlain that the new offer was, like its predecessors, full of traps and pitfalls. He arranged – though it is possible that this was an accident – that Greene's despatch, commending the offer to Chamberlain, went off to London by sea mail, arriving too late to influence Chamberlain.[14]

A week later Milner learnt Chamberlain's response. His warnings had been believed. At any rate, he had gained a respite.[15] Now for a twist of the military screw, which he knew in his heart – contrary to everything he told Chamberlain – would precipitate war.[16]

When Fleetwood Wilson had written that cheery letter telling Milner he should not count on *any* support at home, Milner perhaps smiled wryly to himself. Did old Fleetwood Wilson really imagine he would leave the key to the success of his South African policy – political support at home – in the lap of the gods? What of those Balliol friends at 'Headquarters', Dr Jowett's young men and their wives (he called them his First and Second Elevens),[17] who trusted him and supported him uncritically? In fact, their work at 'Headquarters' was beginning to take effect.

Without Willie Selborne's help at the Colonial Office, Milner would have achieved nothing. Selborne had backed him at every twist and turn of the crisis. He had also sent Milner a stream of private letters – navigation reports, so to speak, to help him steer clear of rocks and sands in the CO and the Cabinet, especially that unpredictable rock, Chamberlain. 'There was a movement,' Selborne had written à propos Chamberlain's eagerness to accept Kruger's offer of the seven-year franchise on 19 July, 'in a certain impulsive quarter to assume, even to pretend, that we had now secured all we wanted. We got over that and back on the old right tack in 24 hours. . . .'

Back on the old right tack. How that phrase must have been music in Milner's ears! Selborne had gone on to report his other triumphs at 'Headquarters', like the faithful lieutenant that he was. He had had 'periodical' chats with 'A.J.B.' (Balfour, the Deputy Prime Minister) to keep him 'sound', and he had 'had it all out' with the Prime Minister (his father-in-law) at Walmer. The results were 'wholly pleasing'.[18]

It was the same with George Wyndham, stuck in what he called 'the morass' of the War Office, as Lansdowne's Parliamentary Under-Secretary. His reports to Milner would have astonished his chief, as much as Selborne's reports would have astonished his. So far, of course, Wyndham had failed to persuade Lansdowne to send out those ten thousand men as reinforcements. But he was ready with a block of influential Tory MPs who could help swing Parliament behind Milner's policy. Wyndham was ex-chairman of the South African Association – the principal jingo pressure group in England – and continued (privately) to manipulate this lobby according to Milner's instructions. 'The Press are ready and under complete control. I can switch on an agitation at your direction. The French and German shareholders of the [gold-mining companies] are in line . . . [we] are in your hands and we shall wait and be patient, or charge home, just as you decide.'[19]

As regards Milner's network of Liberal admirers, they had helped keep the House of Commons from a division in late July, when the Commons had debated Chamberlain's South African policy. It was essential for Milner to have the Liberal imperialists personally committed to the urgency of ending the stale-mate. And that he was assured of. 'You do not need to be told,' Henry Asquith scribbled, somewhat pompously, 'that you have the sympathy and good wishes of your old friends in your difficult task.' Asquith had been shown Milner's letter by Grey – it was a long, eloquent letter, disclaiming any warlike intentions – and it impressed him.[20] (Asquith had also, of course, an eloquent, not-so-little voice at his side to champion Milner – Margot's.)[21]

The second skein of Milner's invisible network was provided by the English (and British South African) Press. After going down from Balliol, he had himself worked for a short time as a journalist on *The Pall Mall Gazette* in its heyday. W. T. Stead was then editor, and in those days Stead had set everyone's blood racing with the passion of his imperialist convictions. Stead had later fallen from grace – a Lucifer from the imperialist heaven. His *Review of Reviews* now adopted an eccentrically pro-Boer line. But Milner's other cronies from his *Pall Mall* days were now in a position to show their loyalty, and show it they did. E. T. Cook ran the Liberal imperialist *Daily News*, which had hammered home, day after day, the need for the 'amicable compromise' which Milner purported to believe possible. J. A. Spender edited *The Westminster Gazette*, the paper of the centre Liberals; he backed Milner's 'irreducible minimum', the five-year franchise. In Cape Town *The Cape Times* was edited by Edmund Garrett, Milner's closest confidant, whose inflammatory editorials made Milner's despatches seem conciliatory indeed.[22]

All these newspapers had taught British public opinion in the last few weeks of the dangers of delay, and of being fobbed off without a settlement on the franchise. It was *The Morning Post* and *The Times*, both staunchly pro-government, that banged the jingo drum loudest. *The Morning Post* (whose leader-writer was Spenser Wilkinson, another crony of Milner's) warned the nation that delay was now dangerous, and could be 'disastrous' for the Uitlanders.[23] Next day *The Times* (whose editor, Buckle, was also an admirer) warned the government that 'it is time to say distinctly and emphatically that there must quickly be an end to all this delay and prevarication'. And two days later *The Times* taunted Chamberlain with weakness, as Milner could never have dared: 'Johannesburg cannot live for ever on statesmen who put their hands on ploughs and stand resolutely still.'[24]

Such was Milner's invisible nexus of loyalty, the old friends on whom he could rely to keep Chamberlain 'on the right tack'. In addition, and still more active on his behalf, were his secret allies, the London 'gold-bugs' – especially the financiers of the largest of all the Rand mining houses, Wernher-Beit.

Alfred Beit was the giant – a giant who bestrode the world's gold market like a gnome. He was short, plump and bald, with large, pale, luminous eyes and a nervous way of tugging at his grey moustache. Publicity, always meat and drink for his old partner of the Raid, Rhodes, was sheer poison for Beit. He had looked half-dead after his ordeal of appearing before the London enquiry into the Raid (where he admitted financing the venture to the tune of £200,000). Since then he had lived almost like a recluse in his palatial home in Park Lane, among his six dazzling Murillos of the Prodigal Son. When he gave to charities – and he gave lavishly – he did it by stealth.[25] Occasionally he would throw a small lunch party for an especially good cause, as when, that summer, he introduced Dr Jameson and Sir John Willoughby to the editors of *The Daily News* and *The Westminster Gazette* – Milner's friends, Cook and Spender.[26] But Beit, like Rhodes, was in poor health. He entrusted most of his political business to his partner, Wernher, and young Percy Fitzpatrick, brought over to London to put the Uitlander case to the British public.[27] Fitzpatrick's book, *The Transvaal from Within* (published at Milner's suggestion), was to be the best-seller of the season.[28] No doubt the line at Beit's Press luncheons was much the same as in Fitzpatrick's book. The go-it-alone days of the Raid were over. The Prodigal Son had returned.

The Uitlanders were now solidly behind Britain, her Empire and Sir Alfred Milner.

But one thing was certainly not known to the public – nor, indeed, to the Press (though one of their most brilliant contributors, J. A. Hobson, guessed it).[29] Milner's capitalist associates – Beit, Wernher and Fitzpatrick – were encouraging his belligerence. Wernher, the most cautious of the three, had originally hoped that war could be avoided.[30] But the months of crisis and the uncertainties for the gold industry had made him lose patience. In July he had a two-hour interview with Philip Gell (acting as Milner's intermediary). Wernher said the financiers were now 'quite prepared for war', and that they insisted that 'the situation must be terminated *now*'.[31] Six weeks later, he wrote to Georges Rouliot, the director of his firm's South African subsidiary, apologizing for the 'great hardship' which the delays in sending troops had caused; he explained that it had been impossible to act earlier because 'knowledge in the [British] public was absent'. However, finally 'matters are understood – *all* admit something must be done'. He added, in his strange, clumsy English (like Alfred Beit, Julius Wernher was a German who had adopted British citizenship and British imperialism), that Britain's military unpreparedness was 'incredibable [sic] ... for an Empire holding half the world ... but this is a cause why delay takes place'.[32]

Fitzpatrick's own letter from London to the firm in South Africa during this crisis was discreetly destroyed by them as being too 'damaging to Joe Chamberlain'.[33] However, in a letter he wrote to Eckstein a few weeks later, he showed he was enthusiastically backing Milner's plan to annex the Transvaal by means of a war, and impatient for results:

This is not a strong Govt ... it is a wobbly, nervous, cumbersome & unmanageable one. However one can buck them up, & stick pins in their bottoms when they want to sit down; so I wired you that you might communicate it to H.E. [Milner]. My judgment is that he is master of the position – absolutely – because this government dared not let him go if he gave them an ultimatum. They would be out of office in no time.[34]

The gold-bugs, contrary to the accepted view of later historians, were thus active partners with Milner in the making of the war.[35] Of course, they gave no hint of this to Chamberlain. What made them such wonderful allies was that they repeated over and over again the dictum that there would be *no* war – that is, if Britain called Kruger's bluff and sent out troops. Fitzpatrick, acting on Milner's instructions, had told this story to Selborne at the Colonial Office on 3 July.[36] He repeated it to the War Office.[37] Cecil Rhodes had told it to Balfour in July[38] and repeated it at mixed dinner parties. (Margot Asquith saw him there sitting at the centre of a circle of female worshippers 'like a great bronze gong'.)[39] After Rhodes's arrival in Cape Town, he cabled Alfred Beit (it was 23 August): 'President Kruger will give anything demanded he will bluff up to the last moment.'[40] Lord Rothschild passed on Rhodes's message to Balfour.[41] Possibly Rhodes believed his own forecasts.[42] But Beit, Wernher and Fitzpatrick knew the Boers. The despatch of British troops would precipitate war.[43]

*   *   *   *   *   *

With the help of these new allies and old friends, Milner had thus been able to cultivate the ground at 'Headquarters', where he had 'sown the seed' himself earlier that year. Had the time now come for putting this groundwork to the test? Had the moment come for forcing Joe's hand? As Milner shrank from this irrevocable step, a new, passionate friendship propelled him forward.

Among the ten special service officers who had arrived at the Cape from England in late July was Colonel Robert Baden-Powell, and his second-in-command, Major Lord Edward Cecil, both destined to organize the force at Mafeking.[44] Lord Edward was a tall, drooping, rather melancholy young officer, one of the Prime Minister's less successful younger sons. He had been accompanied by his wife, Lady Edward, who was neither shy nor melancholy at all. Milner had, of course, met her before.[45] Who had not? She was a friend of Margot's; Margot especially commended her to Milner. She had all Margot's 'love for life and love'.[46] She was also the sister of the editor of The National Review, Leo Maxse, and she was the Prime Minister's daughter-in-law.

After months of spiritual isolation, of crushing anxiety alternating with crushing boredom, how Milner revelled in Lady Edward's company. Together they sent arrows quivering into the target on the lawns of Government House; they galloped down to Green Point, where the surf thundered; and they rode – rode perhaps on bicycles – up the road towards the heights of Groote Schuur, under the great head of Table Mountain. And then, 'much to my regret', as his diary primly recorded, Lady Edward left for Mafeking with her husband.[47]

Her return to Government House coincided with the new peak of his personal crisis after Kruger's offer of the five-year franchise. Lady Edward – Violet now – was unaccompanied by her husband. It was she (the 'Godsend' he called her) who gave Milner the courage for the impassioned appeal to Chamberlain which he delivered on 30 August.[48]

He quoted Rhodes's famous dictum that Kruger would 'bluff up to the cannon's mouth'. He begged for the long overdue 'big expedition' to be sent out; this would bring Kruger 'to his knees'. And he solemnly warned Chamberlain that there would be a 'break away of our people' – meaning the Uitlanders and Wernher-Beit – unless the troops were sent.[49]

If he gave it to Chamberlain straight from the shoulder, he gave it to Selborne straight from the heart. 'Please realize the strain here is really near breaking point all round. This is not screaming.... But really, really, oh! excellent friend and staunch supporter, we have now had nearly three months of raging crisis, and it is not too much to ask that things should now be brought to a head.'[50]

From a very private channel of his own – no less than a cable from Alfred Beit in London, 'portending a warlike turn of affairs' – Milner learnt on 5 September that his cri de coeur was at last to be answered.[51]

The pace of events had indeed suddenly accelerated in England, and Chamberlain had swung 'back on the old right tack' with a vengeance. The course had been set by Milner, and his friends and allies. The hand on the helm was

Preceding page President Kruger and his advisers.
Above The 'gold-bugs': Cecil Rhodes (left) and Alfred Beit.
Below Sir Alfred Milner, his staff and his 'godsend', Violet Cecil (standing) at Government House, Cape Town.

Lord Lansdowne.

Piet Joubert.

Lord Wolseley.

Jan Smuts.

Sir George White.

Louis Botha.

British reinforcements prepare for kit inspection at Cape Town.

Chamberlain's. The day that he put the helm hard over, so to speak, was Thursday 24 August.

The Cabinet was on holiday. Chamberlain himself was at his beloved Highbury, planning a formal 'pleasaunce' and a wild garden beyond. That Saturday there was to be a political garden party in the grounds.[52]

It was an incongruous moment, one might have thought, for the turning-point in the struggle. Only five days before, the Boers had made that astonishing new offer: the five-year franchise, and a quarter of the seats in the Raad for the Uitlanders. Yet that day, quite suddenly, Chamberlain's patience began to fail.

Why that day of all days? It was more than a mere impulse, certainly. Chamberlain had just received a long, eloquent letter from Milner pleading for the extra garrison of ten thousand troops, which would probably force Kruger to climb down without a shot being fired.[53] He had also received Milner's latest cables pointing out that the new offer was qualified by impossible conditions: that Britain would abandon her claim to suzerainty, and would promise not to intervene in future on behalf of British subjects in the Transvaal. Milner demanded stiffer terms on their part.[54] Moreover, Chamberlain had just seen an alarming new memo of Wolseley's, repeating his plea to send out the ten thousand men.[55]

Words failed him when he thought of the 'hopeless' state of the War Office. If there was war, their preparations were bound to end in 'catastrophe'.[56] At the same time he accepted Milner's repeated claim that there would be no war, if they showed firmness by sending out troops. It was Milner's eloquence, and the impatience of the British Press, that probably decided Chamberlain. Together they had finally shaken his confidence in negotiations with Kruger. He would give Kruger a few more days. Then they must impose their own terms – at the point of a gun.

That Thursday Chamberlain wrote to Lansdowne enclosing Milner's letter, insisting on the despatch of the ten thousand, a copy of which he had sent to the Prime Minister. He told Lansdowne that although the new 'proposals *seem* to give us what we want', he was not certain whether this was a mere manoeuvre. They should now give the Boers a 'week or ten days' to clarify the new offer and withdraw the unacceptable conditions about suzerainty and intervention. If there was no settlement within this time, they must assume that the Boers did not 'want peace'. In that case they must immediately send out the extra instalment of ten thousand troops that Wolseley and Milner were asking for.[57]

On Saturday 26 August Chamberlain made his promised speech, *urbi et orbi*, from a commanding spot on the lawn at Highbury. It was what his biographer was to call a 'short clanging speech'.[58] Certainly, Chamberlain showed ominous signs of strain. It was that morning that he had been taunted by *The Times* for putting his hand to the plough and doing nothing.[59] In his speech he said that Kruger 'procrastinates in his replies. He dribbles out reforms like water from a squeezed sponge.... The sands are running down in the glass.' This was not the urbane Chamberlain that people knew. He seemed frankly exasperated.[60]

For the last time, at any rate, he had tried the policy of bluff – of threatening Kruger without any means of enforcing his threats. A further few days passed and the deadlock with Kruger intensified. On 28 August Chamberlain sent a threatening despatch to Kruger. In reply, Kruger withdrew the five-year franchise offer, and replaced it with an ambiguous new offer – a seven-year franchise, possibly with a joint enquiry.[81] On 2 September – keeping precisely to his new time-table – Chamberlain wrote to Salisbury to call for a Cabinet meeting.[82] The sands were reaching the end of the glass.

In South Africa, Milner and Lady Edward galloped beside the breakers at Green Point. In the Foreign Office in Whitehall, the Cabinet assembled at 12.30 p.m. on 8 September in the room of Lady Edward's father-in-law, Lord Salisbury, Prime Minister and Foreign Secretary. He was more than a figurehead, 'Old Sarum', the leader of the coalition. He was half-crippled by private grief; his wife lay dying of cancer at Walmer Castle. Yet he could still exert himself, on occasion, with something of the old fire, whether thwarted by Hicks Beach, the penny-pinching Chancellor, or hustled by 'Pushful Joe'. He liked to go his own pace, and he usually got his way.

The Cabinet assembled round the horseshoe table overlooking St James's Park. On Salisbury's left was Balfour, in sporting gear (blue serge suit and yellow shoes) and visibly sun-tanned after weeks of golf on the Edinburgh links. Next came Chamberlain, orchid in button-hole.[63] Opposite them sprawled the Duke of Devonshire (usually half-asleep),[64] and there were fifteen other Cabinet members, including Hicks Beach, back from his estate in Gloucestershire, and Lansdowne, fresh from the delights of Dereen in County Kerry.[65]

The political case for sending out the ten thousand troops (and in due course sending an ultimatum after them) was presented to the Cabinet in the form of a memorandum by Chamberlain. His case was, at heart, simple – and how well he knew it, after all those months of Milner's hammering it out. An honourable settlement had to reconcile the political rights of the Uitlanders with the Transvaal's qualified independence and Britain's rights under the two Conventions. Kruger was not prepared to make a settlement of that sort. He had proved this by numerous actions in the twenty years since Majuba and the four years since the Raid: especially his provocative actions in the Edgar Case, and his shilly-shallying in the months since Bloemfontein. He was merely manoeuvring – playing for time. The final proof of this came from his latest offer. To couple the offer of a five-year franchise with two conditions he *knew* to be unacceptable – on suzerainty and non-interference on behalf of British subjects – this conclusively proved that he did not 'want peace'. The only way to make him disgorge the franchise was to put a pistol to his head.

The Uitlanders were treated like 'an inferior race, little better than Kaffirs or Indians whose oppression has formed the subject of many complaints'. But the issue now went further than the grievances of Uitlanders, or natives. What was now at stake was no less than 'the position of Great Britain in South Africa – and with it the estimate formed of our power and influence in our colonies and throughout the world'. Such were Chamberlain's formal arguments to the Cabinet.[66] We do not know all he said, as no Cabinet minutes were taken at this period. Perhaps he also proposed an ultimatum. Certainly he pressed the Cabinet, as Milner had pressed him, to stiffen the terms now demanded of Kruger. Once the troops were sent, the principle of the Sibylline Books must apply: the longer Kruger delayed, the higher the price he must pay for a settlement.[67]

To crown all Chamberlain's arguments for sending the troops was the central paradox: that they would not precipitate war. It had been formulated by Selborne, confirmed by Milner, and echoed by Rhodes, Beit, Fitzpatrick and all the other Uitlanders in London. The best way 'to avoid war was to make preparations for it'; Kruger would 'bluff up to the cannon's mouth'.[68]

How Lord Salisbury replied to Chamberlain is not clear. But we know that he gave support to Chamberlain's views – grudging support. Like his nephew, Balfour, he disapproved of Joe's political style. As Balfour had put it, comparing Kruger to a 'squeezed sponge' was hardly the language of diplomacy. On the other hand, he agreed with Chamberlain that Kruger had proved impossible to negotiate with, and that they now had no choice but to take a firm hand in South Africa. So he agreed with the political case for sending out the ten thousand troops to Natal.[69] The military arguments were also strong. Milner had pressed them since May, Wolseley since June, and that week General Sir Redvers Buller had sent a *cri de coeur*, urging the despatch of the troops, writing direct to the Prime Minister's office to bypass the wretched War Minister.[70]

By contrast Lansdowne was still sceptical of the need for such a large defensive force. He was a friend of General Sir Penn Symons, the GOC in Natal who had recommended first two thousand, now five thousand. He was himself 'profoundly incredulous' at Wolseley's idea of a Boer force of ten thousand invading Natal. He cordially disliked Buller – indeed, he suspected him of pro-Boer sympathies.[71] Still, he was prepared to defer to the Prime Minister's judgement.

It was ironic that the only man in the Cabinet who shared Lansdowne's feelings was his bitter enemy, Hicks Beach. But then Beach opposed Chamberlain for quite different reasons. He was deeply suspicious of the political case for intervention. He disapproved of the provocative way Chamberlain handled the crisis – especially the way he sent his last brusque despatch to the Boers without consulting the Cabinet. He was appalled at the cost: at least £350,000 if they sent only the first instalment of ten thousand men, and over £5 million for the second instalment, the invasion force under Buller.[72] And an alarming sense of *déjà vu* had recently seized hold of him. Twenty years before, he had been a member of the Cabinet which annexed the Transvaal. 'Does not this remind you of all that happened with Bartle Frere,' he said bitterly to Lord Salisbury.[73]

One other man in the Cabinet had serious reservations about Chamberlain's policy: Arthur Balfour. As Salisbury's nephew and deputy, he was, one might have thought, a power to be reckoned with. Four months earlier he had circulated the Cabinet with a brilliant piece of devil's advocacy challenging Chamberlain's case for intervention, with arguments Chamberlain himself had used in 1896. The Transvaal, said Balfour, was a foreign state and Britain had abdicated her right to intervene in internal affairs.[74] Yet Balfour was not the man to press home an attack. The 'divine Arthur', as his friends called him, was too much the philosopher; he saw every side of the case and chose none.[75] In the case of Chamberlain's South African policy he was no more of an obstacle than a beam of sunlight. Besides, Balfour had been persuaded, like most of the Cabinet, that Kruger would surrender rather than fight, once the troops went out. The Cabinet therefore agreed, despite Lansdowne's fussing and Hicks Beach's protests, with Chamberlain's plan. The first instalment of troops would be ordered to leave for Natal as soon as possible.[76]

Should they also send an ultimatum? The Cabinet dug in their heels. On his part, Salisbury was determined not to be rushed. British public opinion was not yet ready for this. Perhaps it was the Boers who could be manoeuvred into issuing the ultimatum. Besides, there was a crucial military argument for postponing hasty diplomatic action. The ten thousand troops they had now agreed to send would not be in position on the Natal borders till the first week of October. It was essential not to break the peace till then.[77]

It was left to Old Sarum himself to predict the real implications of the decision.

Before the Cabinet broke up, Salisbury uttered a solemn warning to its members. He did not share Chamberlain's and Balfour's optimism that Kruger would surrender rather than fight. When the British troops arrived at the front he expected war to begin – or perhaps the Boers would rush Natal when they heard they were being sent. He was afraid that the war would be the greatest war Britain had faced since the Crimea.[78] And perhaps he hinted to his colleagues what he had revealed to Lansdowne a week before: his own bitter reservations about the business. They could not flinch from war. Their only alternative was to resign all pretensions to supremacy in South Africa, the strategic key to the imperial route to India. Yet it was cruel, none the less, to be forced into a war for such a negative object: 'all for people whom we despise and for territory which will bring no power to England'.

He wrote a short comment on Milner's letter to Chamberlain that showed he had, too late, realized how Milner and the Uitlanders and Wernher, Beit and Co had outmanoeuvred Chamberlain and the Cabinet. 'His [Milner's] view is too heated. . . . But it recks little to think of that now. What he has done cannot be effaced. We have to act upon a moral field prepared for us by him and his jingo supporters.'[79]

The Cabinet meeting, which had lasted half an hour longer than usual, broke up at ten to three. A holiday crowd had collected on the sunny pavement outside the Foreign Office, and people noticed how the ministers, who had arrived with such solemn faces, were chattering and laughing as they left. Did that mean peace or war? One well-informed foreign correspondent summed up the situa-

tion: 'The Government is going through with the matter to the bitter end, but
... believe that President Kruger will climb down.'[80]

Lansdowne returned to the generals waiting on tenterhooks in the War Office
in Pall Mall. Soon the morse operator in the cable room began to tap out the
messages drafted by the Commander-in-Chief to the GOCs in India and South
Africa.[81]

Wolseley was almost cheerful. Unlike most of the Cabinet, he believed the
Boers would stand and fight. He expected a small war in Natal before Buller's
Army Corps landed; after that a walk-over; perhaps even Pretoria by Christ-
mas.[82]

Two days earlier, he had taken the chair at the Army Board meeting held in his
room. He had then been plunged in gloom and the weather that afternoon suited
his mood: thunder and lightning and a sky so black that the generals could not
see each other's faces as they sat around his mahogany table, and candles had to
be lit. Now the storm had washed London clean, and Lansdowne and the
Cabinet had caved in at last. Wolseley savoured his triumph. Lansdowne looked
'more like a little Jew today than ever', he told his wife. 'I can now assert from
four years constant work with him that his mind is smaller than his body.'[83]

But where were the ten thousand men to defend Natal actually to be found?
As the yellow cablegrams began to accumulate on Wolseley's desk, and the
green-backed files marked 079 (for South Africa) shuttled backwards and forwards down the twisting corridors, the War Office atmosphere was far from
happy. Lansdowne had already asked the Indian authorities if they could provide
the bulk of the reinforcements. They offered 5,500 soldiers.[84] Wolseley did not
like the sound of this at all. He distrusted the Indian army. It was Roberts's
army. And wasn't it the British regiments from India – the 60th Rifles and the
92nd (Gordons) – who had lost Majuba? Wolseley wanted to send a brigade of
Guards, under a general he could trust – one of the 'Africans'. But he was
overruled by Lansdowne.[85]

Within ten days, the War Office cables were tapping out the news of the
smooth embarkation of seasoned British regiments from Bombay and Calcutta:
the 2nd Kings Royal Rifles, the 1st Gloucesters, the 1st Devonshires and so on,
all seasoned white troops, rich in stores and ammunition, with eighteen field-
guns, three field hospitals, and over a thousand Indian bearers. What of the other
reinforcements? Wolseley managed to scrape together a further three battalions:
the 1st Royal Irish from Alexandria, the 1st Border Regiment from Malta and
the 2nd Rifle Brigade from the British garrison on Crete.[86] The new reinforcements for Natal totalled just ten thousand, including the two battalions sent in
late August. It was the best the Empire could do in the circumstances: the Amir
of Afghanistan was in poor health, and so India's north-west frontier was in
danger. The total force in Natal would come to fifteen thousand by mid-
October, when all the ten thousand reinforcements had landed at Durban. The
total number of troops the Boers could raise in both republics were estimated at
fifty-four thousand. But Symons claimed he only needed five thousand to
defend the whole of Natal. Wolseley reckoned that these fifteen thousand men

would be enough to guard Natal 'as to everything south of the Biggarsberg [range]' – which included the main British military depot, the camp at Lady-smith. Wolseley would 'stake his reputation on it'.[87]

The War Office, it would soon be proved, had disastrously miscalculated in answering the first of Milner's crucial three questions: how many troops were needed to defend Natal? Equally disastrous was their answer to the second: who was to lead and organize the defence?

Even in September, after agreeing to the despatch of the reinforcements, Lansdowne saw no reason to send out anyone to command them. Butler had been sacked, but only a stand-in, a charming nonentity called Forestier-Walker, had been appointed for the Cape. Symons remained GOC in Natal. Well, Symons could hold the fort until Buller arrived. Wolseley pressed Lansdowne. A compromise was reached.[88] The current Quartermaster-General at the War Office was another of Roberts's Ring, Lieutenant-General Sir George White, a sixty-four-year-old general, four and a half years older than Buller. Lansdowne was naturally keen on White, ('not one of the "old gang"', he told Chamberlain) but Chamberlain thought White, still limping after a riding accident, was too old and doddery for the job. Chamberlain had proposed ever since June – very sensibly – that Buller should go himself.[89] But White was appointed GOC in Natal, and he chose for his staff Roberts's two keenest partisans, Colonels Ian Hamilton and Sir Henry Rawlinson. Wolseley gave him, as his intelligence expert, Major Altham, the short-sighted, elderly major who had written that Intelligence Department booklet, *Military Notes*, which predicted that the Boers would only make 'raids' with two thousand to three thousand men, and that 'after one serious defeat' they would throw in the sponge. On 16 September, the day before the first of the Indian contingent embarked at Bombay, Sir George White, Hamilton and Rawlinson sailed for Durban via Cape Town on the *Tantallon Castle*, after a brave display of solidarity by White's War Office colleagues on the platform at Waterloo.[90]

Three days before, Lansdowne had himself sailed for Ireland to resume his interrupted holiday at Dereen, after politely refusing any further concessions. Wolseley and the Army Board wanted to start buying mules, wagons, and so on, for Buller's Army Corps, so that it could be mobilized, if needed, as quickly as possible. Lansdowne replied soothingly to Wolseley. The fifteen thousand men would protect Natal from Boer invasion. What did it matter if their own invasion plans were delayed by the need to economize? All in good time.[91] They would 'press the button' (George Wyndham's phrase to describe the order to buy the mules)[92] as soon as it was clear Kruger wasn't bluffing.

By contrast with Wolseley, Buller remained bitter and frustrated. It was an ironic twist to the story of the Rings that Buller, cold-shouldered by Lansdowne as Wolseley's trusted lieutenant, was now coolly regarded by Wolseley himself. At any rate, on 8 September, the day of the Cabinet's decision to send the Natal reinforcements, Buller had left his base at Aldershot and come up to have it out with Lansdowne at Pall Mall. It proved a stormy interview. Lansdowne reproached him with 'going behind his back' to send that *cri de coeur* to the Prime

Minister. In fact, the two men were hardly on speaking terms. Their natures grated on each other even more badly than Lansdowne's grated on Wolseley's. Buller towered over Lansdowne, and was as blunt and tactless as only shy people can be. Lansdowne told him to his face that he found him 'hard to work with', and in private admitted he thought him a pro-Boer. It was an impossible partnership. Lansdowne did not show Buller the political telegrams. He did not allow him to choose any of the staff of the Army Corps, except for one or two men on his personal staff. How different it was for Wolseley, Buller bitterly recalled, when Wolseley was chosen to command the Egyptian expedition in 1882: he was allowed to organize the whole business. And here he was, himself, stuck at Aldershot, kept in the dark about everything. The transport for his Army Corps was still not sanctioned, and – most disastrous – no defence strategy had been agreed with White or Symons.[93]

It was true. The atmosphere at the War Office, and his own moral isolation, prevented Buller from even discussing the situation with White.

After his return to Aldershot, Buller sent Lansdowne a private letter of the highest importance, which has never been published. It shows that Buller – unlike Wolseley or any other general – had come near to grasping the scale of the danger in which Chamberlain's policy of 'bluff' had put them. Buller knew the Boers better than any other English general. He had himself raised Boers for his Light Horse in the Kaffir War, and he had personal friends among them.[94] (This was probably the reason, as well as Buller's links with the Liberals, for Lansdowne's sneer that Buller 'talked Boer'.) Now he begged Lansdowne to send 'a further force at once' to Natal – in addition to the ten thousand. . 'We have let things drift until we are in a very uncomfortable military position – if the Boers are bold ... they have now the chance of inflicting a serious reverse upon us in Natal – should they do that every day saved in the sending of reinforcements would be worth its weight in gold. ...'[95] Buller moreover made it clear (though not in this letter) that it was essential that White should not push his force too far forward when he arrived in Natal. He must stay on the defensive behind the strong line of the Tugela River. To go nearer the Biggarsberg and garrison Ladysmith – as planned at present – would be to invite disaster.[96]

Lansdowne brushed aside Buller's appeals. They must wait to see if Kruger was bluffing. Anyway, had not Wolseley said that he 'staked his reputation' that they would be 'safe as to everything south of Biggarsberg' when the eight thousand men arrived?[97] Buller remained grimly at Aldershot. When Wolseley had first taken him into his office and shown him the rough list of the regiments in the Army Corps, the flower of the British army and fifty thousand strong, Buller had exclaimed, 'Well, if I can't win with these, I ought to be kicked.'[98] Now his mind was filled with forebodings. He wished to God that Wolseley had himself been chosen to lead the expedition.[99]

While Buller's troops were making dummy night attacks at Aldershot,[100] the *Tantallon Castle*, bearing Sir George White and his staff, was cutting a phosphorescent wake through the waters of the South Atlantic. White was glad to be out of the War Office. He found the battle between 'Africans' and 'Indians' 'disagreeable'. The soldiers were not sufficiently in control and were not either 'united or strong'.[101]

After a few days at sea, White's spirits lightened. He felt younger and brisker already, despite his gammy leg, though it was no fun climbing down the companion-way from his state cabin on the upper deck to queue up for a bath. White was a tall, lean, Anglo-Indian general, whose skin burnt easily in the sun, a country gentleman from the north of Ireland who had worked his way labor-iously up the Indian military ladder. He was conscientious rather than clever. His distinction was that he had won the VC as a young man in Upper Burma. His handicap, apart from his leg, was that he had served only in India and knew nothing about war in South Africa – or, indeed, about any war against white opponents. He spent most of the voyage in a deck-chair, mugging up the subject as best he could. He took a look at Butler's *Life of Colley* (Colley was the British Commander killed at Majuba. Butler was *the* General Butler, the one sacked in August and sent back from the Cape). The voyage was tedious enough. Then, at long last, on 3 October the *Tantallon Castle* steamed into Cape Town harbour, just before dawn lit up the smooth grey flanks of Table Mountain.[102]

White found Milner 'nervous and ... overdone', and he was disturbed by Milner's news.[103] For three weeks he himself had been effectively cut off from the world; there had been no cables waiting at Madeira. When he left Lans-downe, Lansdowne was full of talk of Kruger's 'bluffing'. White himself told a friend the day before sailing, 'Personally, I don't believe there will be fighting of a serious kind. The great financiers who keep their fingers close to the pulse of such affairs are not disturbed.'[104] On board ship he had met the young Dutch-born secretary of the Transvaal State Secretary, Sandberg, who assured him Kruger would not fight. He was inclined to agree. He told his staff, including Ian Hamilton (who had distinguished himself at Majuba, before joining Roberts's 'Indians'), that it was not their task to avenge Majuba and invade the Transvaal. They must defend Natal until the arrival of the Army Corps. He was merely 'St John the Baptist preparing the way.... Redvers Buller is the Messiah.' His plan was to put the bulk of his forces 'just in front of Ladysmith', on the slopes of the Biggarsberg range. He rejected the appeals of some fire-eaters to push up to Laing's Nek – that is, as Colley had done, pushing up into the northern apex of Natal, dominated by Majuba itself.[106]

On the other hand, he had dismissed Buller's warning to avoid the northern triangle altogether and dig in behind the Tugela. He considered Buller was an alarmist.

Now Milner told White that the Boer armies had turned out in very large numbers on the frontiers of both Cape Colony and Natal. An ultimatum was expected. The first shot might be fired 'that day or the next'. The Afrikaners in the Cape were 'ripe for revolt'. At the same time, White learnt that on 25 September General Symons, the fire-eater, had decided on his own authority to push a brigade to Dundee, seventy miles north of Ladysmith, thus dangerously dividing the British forces.[107]

In these alarming circumstances White decided that afternoon that he must short-cut his journey to Natal, by taking the train cross-country to East London and then catching a boat direct to Durban. His baggage was rushed to the station and with hardly a minute to spare he and his staff caught the evening mail by the single-track line to East London.[108] The three-day journey across the Great Karoo was a revelation to White. Despite those instructive books he had read on board ship, he had had no idea of the desert-like character of the South African veld. It reminded him of one of the poorest parts of India, like Baluchistan. He was also surprised (and disturbed) at the sight of the Afrikaners who gathered at the wayside stations – men with slouch hats, beards and rifles, who represented the great majority of the population. They seemed at 'daggers drawn' with the local British, and only too keen to help their countrymen across the borders. From time to time the train halted to allow special trains, crowded with Uitlanders, to pass in the opposite direction. They were refugees from Johannesburg and White was told that they had been beaten up by the Boers. Many were women and children.

At East London, White's party were hurried on board the Union Line's steamer *Scot* – the same ship that had carried Milner to England a year before. He was surprised to find one of the passengers was Colonel Frank Rhodes, Cecil's brother and one of the leaders of the old Reform Movement. Rhodes was now engaged on some mysterious mission in Natal, accompanied by young Lord Ava, eldest son of the ex-Viceroy of India. (Rhodes was also 'playing the old, old game', White noted disapprovingly, with a girl on the boat.)[109]

An hour later the *Scot* sailed for Durban and suddenly White's mind was seized with the same sense of foreboding that Buller had felt for months. What he had seen and heard in the Karoo had shaken him badly. Even when the reinforcements of eight thousand men had all arrived, the Boers would remain superior both in 'strength and position'.

Belatedly, White had begun to grasp the answers to Milner's crucial three questions: he was the wrong choice as commander; Symons had pushed the troops too far forward; the reinforcements were wholly inadequate.

He wrote to his wife despondently, 'Goodbye dear old lady ... we should have 20,000 more troops in South Africa than we have ... the Cabinet have only themselves to thank if they have to reconquer South Africa from the sea.'[110]

CHAPTER 9

The Ultimatum
Pretoria and the Transvaal,
1–12 October 1899

'South Africa stands on the eve of a frightful blood-bath
out of which our volk shall come ... either as ... hewers
of wood and drawers of water for a hated race, or as
victors, founders of a United South Africa, of one of the
great empires [*rijken*] of the world ... an Afrikaner
republic in South Africa stretching from Table Bay to the
Zambezi.'

Jan Smuts's secret memorandum
for the Transvaal Executive,
4 September 1899

By the first week of October, Pretoria was already half deserted. Most of the
burghers had gone to the Natal front. Even the station, awash with cheering
crowds (and stray groups of British refugees) only a week before, was now
empty except for a few stragglers.[1] On the *stoep* (veranda) of his small,
whitewashed house in Church Street, the old President waited in silence, as he
had waited on the night of the Raid, sitting there in the twilight, puffing at his
pipe, while his wife milked the cow in the yard, as though they were a couple of
Boers from the backveld. Outwardly, the old President seemed as immovable as
ever. That week *The Times*'s reporter, Leo Amery, had interviewed Kruger at
his office before he himself went down to the Natal frontier, and asked if there
was any prospect for peace. 'Nee,' roared the old man, 'unless Camberlen
changes his tune.'[2] Yet, till the final month of the crisis, Kruger had in fact
struggled for a settlement. It was his own tragedy that Kruger understood
'Camberlen' as little as 'Camberlen' understood Kruger.

The gap which remained to be bridged at the end of August was actually small
enough. Chamberlain's terms dating from Bloemfontein were still on the table.
If Kruger gave an unconditional five-year franchise to the Uitlanders, Chamberlain had promised to call it a day. Or Chamberlain was prepared to accept a
seven-year franchise, coupled with a joint enquiry to guarantee its good faith.
By the end of August, the pressures on Kruger to make one or other of these
concessions had reached a climax. Smuts's patron in the Cape, Jan Hofmeyr,
strongly criticized the conditional five-year offer they had finally made: 'You
gave too much and you asked too much.' To have offered concessions in 'bits and

pieces', and to have given the impression they were 'extorted' had ruined their effect on British public opinion.[3] From the government of the Free State came similar appeals. Fischer, the State Secretary and the right-hand man of President Steyn, went on a last-ditch mission to Pretoria on 1 September to try to get Kruger to change his mind.[4]

Such was the advice of Kruger's political allies. Their judgement, it seems today, was absolutely correct. If Kruger had accepted it, a settlement would surely have followed. Lord Salisbury, Hicks Beach and Balfour would have seized on the compromise. Chamberlain would have agreed (as Selborne ruefully admitted to Milner).[5] No one – not even Milner – could have prevented it.

Here lay the underlying tragedy of the war; the narrowness of the margin by which the peace was lost.

But on the following day, 2 September, Kruger, like Chamberlain at the same time, had reached breaking-point. Despite his brother Afrikaners in the Cape, and brother Boers in the Free State, he had decided to make no further concessions. For three weeks more he and Chamberlain were still to exchange messages, but these were only manoeuvres to gain the good opinion of their friends and allies. The real negotiations had ended that day.[6]

Why did Kruger, who had, as it seems to us today, so much more than Chamberlain to lose by war, reject the last chance of peace? Certainly not because he was driven to it by the force of Boer public opinion. True, a spasm of war fever – the Boer counterpart of jingoism – had begun to grip the country by the end of August. The Boer Press was virulently anti-British; a noisy war party had emerged in the Raad; many of the younger Boers were spoiling for a fight; it was time, as Ben Viljoen, the member for Johannesburg, declared, to put trust in 'God and the Mauser'.[7]

Yet Kruger, with all his defects, was a statesman. If he had chosen, he could have stood up to his war party, as he had stood up to the burghers whom he had found at the time of the Raid preparing to hang Jameson from the beam brought from Slachter's Nek. Was it, then, that Kruger believed he had a good chance of winning a war against Britain and her Empire? It is true that many Boers honestly believed they could sweep the British into the sea, and create an Afrikaner republic from Table Bay to the Zambezi.[8] Even Smuts, usually so level-headed, thought he smelt military victory.[9] Kruger put his trust in God; that goes without saying. He put less trust in the Mauser. He viewed the prospect of war with the deepest foreboding. If Britain won, then 'the price would stagger humanity' – that was what he told the Press at this time.[10] It was hardly the voice of a man who saw much hope of victory; more like the death-cry of Samson before he pulled down the pillars of the Temple.

The simple fact is that Kruger rejected the chance of compromise because he did not realize it existed. He refused to make further concessions because he thought they would have been futile. Chamberlain, he thought, had set a trap – a trap to humiliate the volk, before he destroyed them. 'We have honestly done our best and can do no more,' Fischer had cabled back to Hofmeyr, after Kruger had convinced him that negotiations were hopeless; 'if we are to lose our independence ... leave us at least the consolation that we did not sacrifice it dishonourably.'[11] Kruger himself cabled, 'With God before our eyes we feel that we cannot go further without endangering our independence.'[12]

This belief that nothing would satisfy Chamberlain except total surrender went back in turn to the cycle of mutual suspicion dating from the Raid. It was this that was the most disastrous result of the Raid. Since then, each man had groped for a settlement in a fog of mistrust: Kruger convinced that Chamberlain, twice frustrated, would try for a third time to steal the Transvaal's independence; Chamberlain believing that any concessions from Kruger would be illusory. Each saw the other's proffered hand as a trap.

The one man who could have enlightened them had set his heart on war.

Ironically, it was Kruger's and Smuts's correct reading of Milner that had led, above all, to their misreading of Chamberlain, and the collapse of negotiations. When Smuts looked into Milner's eyes at Bloemfontein – those 'very intelligent', dangerous, grey eyes – he had perceived only too clearly the threat Milner represented: 'more dangerous than Rhodes ... a second Bartle Frere'.[13] Where Kruger and Smuts were misled was in confusing Milner's aims with Chamberlain's. Had they realized Chamberlain's capacity for compromise – and, still more, the British government's – they would have heeded the advice of their Afrikaner and Boer allies. But all they saw was the Joe of the cartoonists, 'Pushful Joe', and the only voice they heard was Joe's public voice, the voice that made short, clanging speeches about sands-in-the-glass and compared Kruger to a squeezed sponge; and that hardly seemed the voice of compromise. They knew only the political masks of the opponent. They had never once met face to face.

By 2 September, Kruger, like Chamberlain, had decided war was inevitable. Smuts said, 'Humanly speaking a war between the Republics and England is certain.'[14] He then launched into a feverish plan for a military offensive. Its keynote was a blitzkrieg against Natal before any reinforcements could arrive. The numerical advantage would then lie in their favour by nearly three to one – that is, forty thousand Boers against fifteen thousand British troops. By throwing all their troops against Natal, they could capture Durban before the first ships brought British reinforcements. In this way they would capture artillery and stores 'in enormous quantities'. They would also encourage the Cape Afrikaners in the interior to 'form themselves into a third great republic'. The international repercussions, Smuts continued, would be dramatic. It would cause 'an immediate shaking of the British Empire in a very important part of it'. Britain's enemies – France, Russia and Germany – would hasten to exploit Britain's collapse.[15]

The chief obstacle to Smuts's offensive plan, however, had proved to be President Steyn. On 9 September the crucial news had reached South Africa: the British Cabinet had pressed the first war-button and decided to send out eight thousand troops to Natal.[16] This gave the combined armies of the Transvaal and the Free State barely a month to launch their offensive before they lost the advantage of their four-to-one numerical superiority. Yet President Steyn was still not convinced war was inevitable. On 22 September, the British Cabinet pressed their second war-button, and a newspaper report was cabled to South Africa: they had decided to send the Army Corps.[17] On 25 September a spy at Ladysmith cabled to Pretoria that the British were moving north to Dundee.[18] Still Steyn hung back. As the British troop-ships steamed ever nearer Durban, Kruger cabled desperately, 'You still seem to think of peace but that seems to be impossible.... You think Chamberlain is leading us into a trap, but if we wait longer the position may become hopeless and that would be our trap.'[19]

Without waiting for their allies, the Transvaal at last mobilized on 28 September. The plan was accepted with acclamation in the Raad, though six of the members, political associates of Commandant-General Joubert's, were reported opposed. The next step was to send Britain an ultimatum. Steyn was still the stumbling-block. He insisted that the ultimatum should accuse Britain of breaking the London Convention, and the ultimatum had to be redrafted accordingly. By the end of September it was ready to be delivered to the British Agent (all ready 'to tip Greene the black spot', as Frank Reitz, a keen admirer of *Treasure Island,* revealed to Leo Amery). Then, at long last, Steyn's doubts were resolved: Chamberlain was bent on war, and the two republics must strike first.[20]

What decided him is not clear: probably it was a threatened revolt among his own burghers, led by a certain Christiaan de Wet, which tipped the balance.[21] At any rate, the Free State mobilized its forces on 2 October.[22] A further week was lost while the burghers moved up to the frontiers. Finally, at 5 p.m. on 9 October, Reitz called round to Greene and delivered the ultimatum.[23] By the same day the majority of the British troop-ships had docked at Durban. Steyn's search for peace had cost the two republics the whole of their crucial four weeks' advantage.[24]

When Greene opened the packet containing the 'black spot' he must have gasped. He himself had struggled hard for a settlement and been rebuked by Milner in consequence. He had always believed that Smuts was prepared to compromise. The terms of the ultimatum, drafted, it seems, by Smuts, were absolutely uncompromising. It accused Britain of breaking the London Convention of 1884 by interfering in the internal affairs of the Transvaal (that is, by taking up the Uitlanders' case) and by massing troops. It demanded that Britain should give the Transvaal immediate assurances on four crucial points. First, to agree to arbitration on 'all points of mutual difference'; second, that the British troops 'on the borders of this Republic shall be instantly withdrawn'; third, that all British reinforcements that had arrived after 1 June should be withdrawn from South Africa; fourth, that 'Her Majesty's troops which are now on the high seas shall not be landed in any port of South Africa'. And unless HMG complied within forty-eight hours, the government of the South African Republic (Transvaal) would 'with great regret be compelled to regard the action as a formal declaration of war'.[25]

No wonder Greene was astounded. This was not the voice of Kruger, of the exhausted old man who had said at Bloemfontein, 'It is our country you want.' This was something much more virile and dangerous. It was the voice of David as he took his sling to smite Goliath.

The rains had come early to the southern Transvaal that spring, dappling the veld green and scattering stripes of daisies beside the railway line at Sandspruit.[26] It was here, at the station, twelve miles from the frontier, that Joubert and the Transvaal burghers had been waiting impatiently for Kruger's ultimatum. For the last week the Pretoria troop-trains had emptied their loads there: a dozen trains every twenty-four hours, monstrous, slow centipedes of trains; carriages full of men and boys, carrying their Mausers slung over their Sunday clothes; cattle trucks loaded with Creusot artillery, hugger-mugger with ox-wagons and oxen, wives and African servants.[27]

To English witnesses it all looked absurdly unmilitary. And this was how it was described by Leo Amery of *The Times*, who had followed the burghers from Pretoria to the front. There were no straight lines in the Boer army. For miles the sandy plain was dotted with ponies and oxen and covered wagons; all the paraphernalia of the Great Trek. At night the camp-fires glowed like the lights of a city, and bearded old men sat round the fires singing Dutch psalms with their wives and children. Side by side with these trekboers from the backveld were the burghers from Pretoria and the Rand. They were clean-shaven; many talked English, as they were colonial-born or British-born; they sounded almost like regular soldiers as they sang ribald songs round the camp-fire.

In the artillery laager at the centre of the plain, a large white marquee served as the HQ of Joubert, the Commandant-General. In Amery's eyes he seemed a splendidly confident figure: flashing dark eyes, a flowing beard, and a welcome (surprisingly) for the correspondent of a jingo newspaper.[28] In fact, Joubert was anxious, as usual. He was grateful for the rains; though down here, on the Natal border, the veld was only starting to flush green.[29] Everything else had gone wrong during the last fortnight. The arrangements with the Free State, hold-ups on the railway, the ox-wagons – everything.[30] All the time the thought haunted Joubert: was the war necessary at all?

As the leader of the Progressive bloc in the Raad and Kruger's principal political opponent, Joubert had always asserted that a deal could be made with the Uitlanders. Only restore the original five-year franchise, he claimed, and there would be no danger to the republic. Kruger had stubbornly found no alternative to war. And now war was inevitable, Joubert was frustrated by the delays. 'I have never been ... in such a corner in all my life,' he cabled back to Pretoria '... know nothing of the Free State.'[31]

If Joubert blamed Kruger for breaking off negotiations, he could only blame himself for the near-collapse of the arrangements for mobilization. Many of the men had no tents or even macintoshes to protect them against the rain; the mules supplied by dishonest contractors could hardly stand up; the wheels of the wagons were already falling to pieces.[32] It was left to the fifteen thousand Transvaal burghers on the roll – of whom only about nine thousand had yet turned up – to improvise as best they could.[33]

One responsibility, at any rate, Joubert was spared: that of disciplining the burghers. Apart from the eight-hundred-strong grey-uniformed artillery corps, they were a people's army – commandeered willy nilly. As a professional soldier, the Commandant-General was supposed to supply them with the material of war – Creusot and Krupp artillery, Mausers, ammunition, tents, food and so on – and to co-ordinate strategy. Their elected civilian leaders were made commandants – appointed, that is, to lead the five hundred to two thousand burghers of each commando in battle. In this commando system, it was no one's job to train the burghers. Apart from the annual *wappenschauw* (or shooting practice), the men were left to fight as they had always fought – with the tactics of the mounted frontiersmen. If the enemy were superior in numbers, they would provoke the enemy's attack, dismount, take cover and shoot, remount and ride away. In European military manuals it was a formula known as 'strategic offensive, tactical defensive'. The Boers had never seen the manuals. But the tactics had served them well in countless wars against natives – and in 1881 at Laing's Nek against the British. They had not lost a battle since Boomplatz in 1848, when Sir Harry Smith had thrashed General Pretorius.[34]

By 10 October the Boer army had shaken down into some sort of order, and Joubert decided on an unusual ceremony: a military parade. It was Kruger's birthday. The burghers mounted their ponies, and formed up in sections. To one of the Pretoria Commando – Deneys Reitz, the seventeen-year-old son of Kruger's State Secretary – the spectacle was 'magnificent'.[35] In fact, Joubert, sitting there on his horse, commanded an army that was probably the largest body of mounted riflemen ever assembled in Africa.[36]

Beyond the broad valley of Sandspruit was the town of Volksrust ('People's Rest'), a simple place of tin roofs and blue gum-trees, like so many other towns of the veld. A few miles beyond Volksrust were the misty hills of Natal: Laing's Nek and Majuba. How well Joubert knew all that country! He had led the Transvaal forces here, eighteen years before, in attacking General Colley. His victory against four hundred redcoats had echoed round the world.[37] Could he achieve the same today against an army forty times as strong?

The strategic plan that Kruger had concerted with Steyn and ordered Joubert to carry out was a diluted version of Smuts's plan. It also bore the clear stamp of Kruger's character; it was crude, but it was daring.

In early September, when Smuts had proposed the blitzkrieg, there had been only three small contingents of the British army close to the republics: five hundred men of Colonel Baden-Powell's irregulars at Mafeking in northwestern Cape Colony, five hundred regulars at Kimberley, and the two thousand men of the garrisons under General Sir Penn Symons at Ladysmith and Dundee, in the northern prong of Natal.

There were now roughly thirteen thousand British troops close to the frontiers. Nevertheless, Kruger and Steyn had decided to strike with two-thirds of all the troops so far mobilized – twenty-one thousand out of thirty-five thousand – at these three points. (*See maps on pages 6–7 and 127.*)

The two Presidents had sent roughly twenty-one thousand men to Natal – fifteen thousand Transvaalers and six thousand Free Staters, divided into four groups and arranged in a crescent formation. On the south-west were six thousand Free Staters. The Johannesburg and German commandos, led by General Johannes Kock, formed the western horn in the Drakensberg Mountains. The eleven thousand men of the Pretoria and other commandos were with Joubert in the centre. The two thousand men of the Wakkerstroom and other commandos, led by General Lucas Meyer (a Progressive Party ally of Joubert's), were at Vryheid, to the east. This crescent formation was designed to trap the forward British positions at Ladysmith and Dundee – unless they retreated in time.

Co-operation with the fifteen thousand men of the Free State was essential to both Kruger's offensives. Commandos from the Free State must seal off Mafeking (and later Kimberley) from the south, just as the six thousand from the Drakensberg must join hands with Kock's forces forming the western horn of Joubert's attack on Natal.[38]

This was Kruger's daring plan. The Natal part of the plan had not reassured Joubert. He knew that Symons's forces at Ladysmith and Dundee had grown from two thousand to twelve thousand in the last month. At first he had been afraid that the British might invade the Transvaal before his own commandos were in position. Symons was reported to have prepared an armoured train to raid deep into the Transvaal.[39] Then Joubert thought that Laing's Nek railway tunnel might be full of explosive. How could he be sure that Symons was not lurking somewhere in ambush? But September had safely passed. Even Joubert felt it was time to advance.[40]

It was now 3 p.m. on 10 October, the day of the military parade in honour of Kruger's birthday. Commando after commando filed past the Commandant-General: ranchers from the bushveld down at Middelburg; clerks and solicitors from Pretoria; a thousand Dutch and German Uitlanders from the Rand; a hundred Irish Uitlanders, whose second-in-command was a certain Major John MacBride, a name which would be famous one day in Ireland. All the burghers were mounted, though a few (notably the Irish miners) looked as though they would hardly stay mounted for long. As each man passed Joubert, he waved his hat or his rifle, according to his idea of a salute. The commandos then formed into a mass, and galloped cheering up the dry, grassy slope where Joubert sat his horse under an embroidered banner. He rose in his stirrups to address them, but his words were lost in the crowd.[41] Perhaps he pointed across the valley at Majuba. There lay Natal – Natal stolen from the voortrekkers, Natal the Promised Land, that was theirs for the taking.[42]

While he was speaking, the news that Kruger had at last delivered the ultimatum reached Sandspruit. Deneys Reitz saw the quiver in the ranks as the word was passed from man to man. The excitement was immense. People stood in their stirrups and shouted themselves hoarse. Joubert and his retinue had to fight their way back through the crowd. There was singing and shouting from the laagers until dawn.[43]

On 12 October, in the small hours, the Boers struck camp and Joubert's columns began to move forward – 'a weird opening scene to the great drama', as Leo Amery described it, 'an endless procession of silent misty figures, horsemen, artillery, and wagons, filing past in the dark, cold night along the winding road that led to where the black shoulder of Majuba stood up against the greyer sky.'[44]

Meanwhile, on the other side of the Natal frontier, the British general, Sir George White, viewed his own military preparations with even more misgiving than Joubert.[45]

White had landed at Durban on 7 October a fortnight after Symons had rashly divided the Natal field force and pushed forward a brigade from Ladysmith to Dundee. This dangerously weakened the position of White's ten thousand men, already outnumbered two to one by the combined Free State and Transvaal armies.

For two days White was preoccupied with the disembarkation at Durban of the last of the reinforcements. Unlike Joubert's chaotic mobilization, the British disembarkation ran as smoothly as a machine. Down the gang-planks poured a stream of bronzed veterans from India, who were then despatched, five trains for each regiment, up the twisting railway line to Ladysmith.[46] On 9 October White was ready to deal with Symons, who had come down the line to meet him.

Strategically, one crucial question remained (it was Milner's third question). How far north to station the British forces? In the rugged northern triangle at Dundee and Ladysmith? Or south of the triangle, at Estcourt, in the smooth plains beyond the Tugela River? White knew of Buller's warnings. Nothing north of the Tugela.

One of White's ablest staff officers, Colonel Rawlinson, echoed the warning:

> The Boers are thought to have some 15,000 to 20,000 men on the frontier all told. We have not more than 10,000 at present [2,000 were still on the high seas]. Yet they are split up half at Glencoe [Dundee] and half at Ladysmith *both* of which are too far forward to secure the defence of the colony. [The] only thing is to hold the line of the Tugela River and withdraw from Glencoe and Ladysmith. The situation ... which we are going to take up is one which from a military point of view is absolutely false and ... courts disaster for it has no flanks whatever and the Boers can pass and avoid either place or if they choose surround or annihilate either place in detail. If I were in Sir George White's place I would insist on withdrawing to the Tugela or on throwing up the command ... but, and this is the main point, I am not in command.[47]

Nothing north of the Tugela. Symons saw no cause for alarm. 'Symons is brimful of confidence,' Rawlinson added. 'They talk as if the war were over, now a brigade is coming from India, and speak of a British brigade being able to take on five times in Boers, which is silly rot.'[48]

Next day, 10 October, White went to see the Governor of Natal in Maritz-burg, and was shocked to find that he agreed with Symons, for strictly political reasons.

Sir Walter Hely-Hutchinson, the Governor, claimed that a retreat from Dundee would 'disgust' the loyalists in Natal. The most belligerent of these were not Natalians but Uitlander refugees from Johannesburg.[49] At Milner's suggestion, they had been formed into two mounted corps of their own – fifteen hundred strong: the Imperial Light Horse and (at Cape Town) the South African Light Horse. Outwardly, these were similar to other irregular corps being formed in South Africa at this time. Actually, they were a fully fledged Uitlan-der army, eventually twenty thousand strong, largely financed by Wernher-Beit, and led by precisely the same men – Woolls-Sampson, 'Karri' Davies and others – who had been the political leaders of the Rand ever since the Raid.[50] They had their own ideas on strategy, as well as diplomacy, and Hely-Hutchinson was not the man to stand in their way. Second, Hely-Hutchinson was afraid that a retreat from Dundee might precipitate an Afrikaner rising in Natal. Much of that northern triangle of Natal was occupied by descendants of the voortrekkers. Third, he warned White that a retreat from Dundee might stir up the 750,000 Zulus in north-east Natal.[51]

To Sir George, trained like Symons in the Indian army, where political considerations always weighed so high in the balance, this talk of the native peril proved decisive. He could imagine that wave of Zulus sweeping down on the white population. No, better even to risk defeat by the Boers. That evening he agreed to let Symons keep the camp at Dundee, against all his own military instincts[52] – and common sense. A defeat at Dundee would have still worse political repercussions than a retreat.

At Dundee itself, the morale of the small garrison was excellent. Whatever his defects as a strategist, Sir Penn was a popular commander.[53] In private, he admitted being disappointed by three of the infantry battalions the War Office had sent him: they were a 'dull and backward' lot; they seemed not to have been made 'to do any work properly for years'. He was depressed too by the mountain battery: the Cape Coloured drivers could not compare with 'our Punjabi drivers'.[54]

But now he had licked his force into shape. Drill for the men, polo for the officers, field-days for everyone. Some of the officers were astonished at Symons's old-fashioned reliance on close order. Symons did not worry. First, the field artillery. They galloped up, unlimbered and fired off a dozen blank cartridges, filling the air with black smoke. Then the attack. ('In four waves, heaped together à la Gravelotte,' wrote one of Symons' mounted infantrymen. 'He must be mad.') The infantry swept forward, firing volleys by numbers, halting each time the whistle blew. Finally, the Hussars. They charged up to where the referee stood with his red flag, cutting the air with their swords.[55]

On Wednesday 11 October, the Dundee garrison learnt that Kruger's ultimatum had expired, and there were rumours in the town of Dundee that the first shots of the war had been fired. But in Penn Symons's camp, a few hundred yards to the west of the town, under the great shoulder of Mount Impati, the order was 'business as usual'. Apart from a thunderstorm that threatened to wash away the picket lines, life in the camp continued undisturbed.[56] The senior officers' ladies remained at their husbands' sides;[57] there were guest nights in the regimental mess, as if they were still in India; Sir Penn was the life and soul of the garrison. Had they heard the story of the young lady who had been to see Kruger in September? 'Well, Mr President,' she had asked, 'is there going to be war or not?' 'Madame, I will tell you. The Transvaal is a very pretty girl. England is her lover. The lover has been refused several times; now he is going to kill her.'[58]

In the mess of the 60th Rifles, the officers wore their dress uniforms: scarlet and green. Despite the thunderstorm, Dundee's water supply was running short. Yet, as young Lieutenant Charles Trench wrote in his diary that night: There was no shortage of 'soda water and whisky'.[59] It was a convivial evening. People talked of dining in Pretoria that Christmas.[60] 'It will be another Omdurman picnic with halts at Bloemfontein and Johannesburg', wrote Lieutenant Maurice Crum on the day after the ultimatum was issued.[61]

Outside the mess tent, at sunset, the great peaks of the Drakensberg glowed like the peaks of the Himalayas seen from Simla. How well Symons knew that Indian hill country! Here in Natal, he had only one anxiety: that he might miss the 'row'. His Intelligence Officer reported Joubert's army at Sandspruit to consist of ten thousand men, with twenty-four guns.[62] Yet Symons still thought Dundee was too far south for striking at the Boers. Laing's Nek and Majuba would have made a better place. 'I wish every commando in the Transvaal was there in a bunch,' he had told one of White's staff, 'so that I could make one sweep of the lot of them.'[63]

The text of the ultimatum had been received in London on Tuesday 10 October with derision, delight, dismay – and indifference.

Derision was the keynote of the editorials in Wednesday's newspapers. 'Preposterous', 'Mountebank', 'Extravagant farce', 'One is in doubt whether to laugh or to weep,' proclaimed The Daily Telegraph. The Times called the ultimatum an 'infatuated step' by this 'petty republic'. The Globe denounced this 'trumpery little State' and its 'impudent burghers'. Most editorials followed the same line as The Telegraph: 'Of course there can only be one answer to this grotesque challenge ... Mr Kruger has asked for war, and war he must have.' (Privately, Moberly Bell, Manager of The Times, was slapping his sides with laughter. 'The ultimatum was excellent in every way. An official document is seldom both eminently amusing and useful but this was both.')[64]

The first rumours of the ultimatum had reached the public in London late on Tuesday afternoon. By and large, the British public displayed little emotion – or even tension – at the news. Wednesday's Times said that Britain would be at war with the republics 'at tea-time'. People took up the phrase: this was to be the tea-time war. It was Newmarket week, and the Cesarewitch happened to coincide with the moment – 3.10 p.m., Greenwich Mean Time – when the ultimatum expired on Thursday. No one could have guessed this from the behaviour of the crowds, including the Prince of Wales and the Dukes of Cambridge and Devonshire; they saw *Scintillant* win by a short lead from *Ercildoune*. The weather was still perfect. October had brought an Indian summer. On Saturday, working people flocked out to see Aston Villa play Tottenham Hotspur in the first round of the FA cup. In the streets of London – both in Mayfair and Whitehall – crowds were conspicuously absent. Fashionable London was in the country, Parliament still on holiday. The smooth surface of late Victorian life was not to be ruffled by war – not, at any rate, by a war at tea-time, a war in a tea-cup.[65]

It was inside the twisting corridors of Pall Mall that the ultimatum caused the keenest stir on Tuesday, and the sensations it excited were of astonishment – and delight. 'Accept my felicitations,' scribbled Lansdowne to Chamberlain. 'I don't think Kruger could have played your cards better than he has.'[66]

In September the overwhelming fear in the War Office had been that the Boers might try to rush Natal before the Indian contingent was in position to defend it. By early October most of the 'Indians' had arrived. Immediately the anxieties of the War Office had reversed themselves. What if Kruger now tried to cheat them of military victory by further diplomatic manoeuvres? And what if the Free State preserved its neutrality? It was on the ability of Buller's invasion force to choose the easy line of advance – by way of the plains of the Free State rather than through the mountains of Natal – that the strategy of invasion depended. Yet there was no way of forcing the Free State (as opposed to the Transvaal) into war against England. Balfour had admitted privately in early October that he was afraid the neutrality of the Free State would prove the 'Achilles heel' of the whole expedition.[67]

But now the Transvaal ultimatum, amounting to a joint declaration of war from both republics, resolved this problem at a stroke. No wonder that Lansdowne told Chamberlain that morning, 'My soldiers are in ecstasies.'[68]

In Wolseley's case, the ecstasy was somewhat muted. He was still licking his wounds after the three months' struggle to persuade little Lansdowne to send the Natal reinforcements and the Army Corps. He bitterly regretted the extra month's delay in ordering the transport. The price of decades of penny-pinching was also stamped on all their military preparations. They were short of vital armaments – especially heavy guns – and short of mounted troops of all kinds. But Wolseley had to admit that the actual mobilization was going like clockwork.[69]

It was a triumph for the system for which Wolseley had worked all his life. How people like Roberts had scoffed at the short service army, the linked territorial battalions and the army reserve! Yet when the call had come, the twenty-five thousand reservists of the 1st Army Corps had responded manfully. In some battalions ninety-seven per cent. had reported at the depots – ship-workers from Tyneside, screw-makers from Birmingham, farm-workers from Essex. On Saturday the advance guard of this Army Corps were to set sail: Sir Redvers Buller was going out in the *Dunottar Castle*. The main body of the forty-seven thousand men would follow in a fleet of civilian liners chartered by the Admiralty.[70] Wolseley expected only a small war. Yet the army Britain was already committed to sending was the biggest expeditionary force for nearly a century – bigger than Roberts's Afghan expedition of 1878 (the last occasion when the reserves had been mobilized) or Wolseley's Egyptian expedition of 1882, bigger even than Raglan's expedition to the Crimea in 1854.

At Princes Gardens, Chamberlain's comfortable London house, the Master had been the first to receive the news. He was usually late to bed and late to rise. That Tuesday morning he had been woken at a quarter past six by a messenger from the CO. He read the long code cable and then sat up amazed, so his biographer records. 'They have done it!' he exclaimed. Not only had Kruger's impertinent ultimatum resolved the strategic problems. All the interlocking political problems seemed to fall into place.[71]

Kruger's ultimatum pulled the carpet from under the feet of the anti-imperialist Liberals, led by Sir William Harcourt. The terms of the ultimatum were in effect a declaration of independence, and an abrogation of the Conventions by which Gladstone had tried to arrange a settlement after Majuba. In public, Harcourt, Leonard Courtney and their radical friends continued to accuse Chamberlain of provoking the war. Privately, they were aghast at the news. 'What a moment to make a speech,' wrote Courtney's wife after a wretched journey to his constituency at Liskeard. His plea for the Boers was greeted by a 'howl of indignation at Boer insolence'.[72]

Chamberlain had never worried himself too much about Courtney and those other ghosts from his Gladstonian past. It was the centre Liberals, led by Sir Henry Campbell-Bannerman, who were crucial to his chance of keeping the consensus: that is, by avoiding an actual division in the House. The previous week Campbell-Bannerman had told some Liberals at Maidstone that no one could answer the question, 'What is it that we are going to war about?'[73] It was 'a mean speech by a mean man', Chamberlain commented, adding that the Liberals were much divided, but 'the country is clearly on our side'.[74] Yet up to the last moment, Chamberlain had doubted his capacity to carry the country united into the battle.

Chamberlain's main political difficulty before Kruger delivered his ultimatum had been this: to send out the Army Corps, the Cabinet had to ask Parliament for an extra £10 million. So Parliament had been summoned for 17 October. Chamberlain had to be ready then with a politically convincing answer to Campbell-Bannerman's overwhelming question: why was Britain going to war?

Was it to re-establish British supremacy by confirming Britain's status as the paramount power in South Africa? Unfortunately, to many Liberals, including centre Liberals, talking of British supremacy was too easy a cloak for what they regarded as aggressive imperialism –[75] and, from his own side, Balfour had reminded Chamberlain of the danger of appearing to pick a quarrel with the Boers.[76] Was it then to re-establish equal rights for all white men in the Transvaal (and even win a few basic rights for some black men)? Unfortunately, the Uitlanders were far from popular in Britain – despite all that Fitzpatrick, Wernher and Beit had done to improve their image. As Chamberlain himself admitted, there was 'too much of "money-bags" about the whole business'.[77] Lord Salisbury had reminded him that very week that the only chink in their political armour was that they were 'doing work for the capitalists'.[78] Hence Salisbury himself had hoped to play down the franchise issue and 'make the break' with the Transvaal over their refusal to accept a modified Convention.[79] Each *casus belli* had serious political drawbacks, and yet they would have had to incorporate them in any British ultimatum, and debate them in Parliament.

It was the thought of the odium that would be attached to his own ultimatum that had haunted Chamberlain throughout that week.[80] The date had actually been fixed for the following day, 11 October, and the terms – very stiff terms – finally agreed by the Cabinet. Chamberlain assumed that the Boers would reject it. Its intended result was merely to justify the war to the British and to the world. Britain's basic demand remained: concede full equality to the Uitlanders. But now they were to have a one-year franchise and proportionate representation in the Raad. It would be 'full equality' with a vengeance. For if the British Uitlander voters were in the majority, as everyone assumed, they would swiftly take political control of the Transvaal. There was also to be a new 'Great Deal' for the capitalists. And Britain demanded a new agreement to secure her own status as paramount power, and insisted that the Transvaal reduce its armaments. Finally, there was to be 'most favoured nation treatment' – an end to police persecution, at any rate – for the Cape Coloureds, Indians, Africans from the colonies, and other coloured British subjects.

Granted these concessions, the British government was generously prepared to guarantee the republic's independence and security from attack 'from within any part of the British Dominions or from the territory of any other state'.[81]

Having drafted this trenchant ultimatum, Chamberlain had still racked his brains to find a way to avoid sending it. Why not provoke the Boers to strike the first blow by pushing General Symons' force up to the Natal border at Majuba and Laing's Nek? Chamberlain put up this scheme to the War Office in September and early October.[82] It was opposed not only by Wolseley and Buller but (surprisingly) by Milner.[83]

It seemed strange to Chamberlain that Milner should plead caution in view of his earlier impetuosity, and of his conviction, expressed throughout that summer, that Kruger would 'bluff up to the cannon's mouth'. In fact, Milner had reversed his line of argument the moment he had seen the British Cabinet committed to sending out the army. Chamberlain remained true to Milner's earlier opinion that the Boers were no real threat to the British army. 'I am afraid he [Milner] has got scared,' he told Hicks Beach. All this talk of the Boers' military strength was the alarmism of Milner, Wolseley and Buller.[84]

'They have done it!' Chamberlain had exclaimed that Tuesday morning. Kruger had sent his reckless ultimatum, and all these anxieties were forgotten.

His own ultimatum would remain locked away in the files of the CO. How the Lord had delivered the Boers into his hands! For the British government would be free, when peace came, to impose even stiffer terms, if they wished. Above all, Kruger had given him the thing he most desired, the perfect motive for war: to repel an enemy's invasion.[85]

On Saturday 14 October, a huge, cheerful, patriotic crowd gathered at South-ampton Docks to bid General Sir Redvers Buller Godspeed on his passage to South Africa. People had perched on the roofs of railway carriages, others had settled, like a flock of birds, in the lattice-work of a dockside crane; the scene was recorded by the cinema-camera of the Biograph Company. All day, impressive-looking passengers and their equally impressive luggage accumu-lated on board: brass-hats and war correspondents (like young Winston Churchill, son of the unfortunate Lord Randolph); black tin trunks and leather sword scabbards; the General's two war-horses (*Ironmonger* and *Biffin*); polo sticks; even a bicycle. Then, punctually at 4 p.m., the General's special train steamed up to the quayside. A moment later the General himself, wearing a long dark overcoat and a felt hat, strode briskly up the gang-plank of the *Dunottar Castle*.

Buller was not a folk-hero like Wolseley or Roberts – not yet, at any rate. Earlier that day, the crowd at Waterloo Station had not even recognized the tall, burly figure in mufti, the red face with the bulldog jowl, and the sprig of Devonshire violets in his button-hole. Here at Southampton people greeted him as though they had known him all his life. It was, as one of the papers reported, like the home-coming of a victorious General. Buller made a gruff speech of thanks at the head of the gang-plank. He hoped he would 'not be away long'. That was all he had to say. The crowd began to sing 'Rule, Britannia' and then struck up 'For He's a Jolly Good Fellow'.[86]

How many of them could have guessed Buller's feelings at that moment? It was not, as Lord Lansdowne had claimed, that he was a second Sir William Butler – a Boer sympathizer. He had now come to accept the war as inevitable. He blamed the war-mongering of the Hollander (recent Dutch immigrant) clique.[87]

That morning, when Buller had been seen off by the War Office staff at Waterloo Station, towering head and shoulders over both Lansdowne and Wolseley, he was overwhelmed, it seems, by his forebodings. He knew what it felt like to be a Cassandra. All through July and August he had warned the War Office, 'Do not go north of the Tugela, do not go north of the Tugela.'[88] As usual, Lansdowne had ignored his advice. Now he had seen the latest War Office cables from South Africa. The cables left him aghast. White reported that he was allowing Symons to keep the garrison at Dundee. Once again, Lansdowne had upheld White and Symons in the teeth of the protests of Buller – the man who was going to pay the price if the expedition ran into disaster.[89]

In public, Buller gave no hint of these bitter feelings, as he stood leaning lightly on the rail of the bridge of the *Dunottar Castle*. He was fifty-nine, yet he looked fit enough to be fifty, bronzed, heavily moustached, the very archetype of the British warrior. The ship's fog-horn sounded. It was echoed by a hurricane of cheers from the quayside. Somebody (Lady Audrey, Buller's wife, according to *The Times*) began to sing 'God Save the Queen'. Part of the crowd took up the solemn anthem. Others shouted cheerful slogans like 'Give it to the Boers!', 'Bring back a piece of Kruger's whiskers!', 'Remember Majuba!'

Sir Redvers stood on the navigation bridge, waving his felt hat as the *Dunottar Castle* steamed slowly out into the fog. One thing gave him an air of supreme self-confidence. He did not try to hide his own emotion.[90]

The following Tuesday, the House of Commons, recalled prematurely from the grouse moors, voted to pay the £10 million needed for Buller's Army Corps. Chamberlain defended his South African policy from A to Z – or rather, from the Raid to the Ultimatum. He spoke for three hours. His basic theme was this: aggressive republicanism had made war inevitable. Apart from the men of the Irish Party, only a handful of members voted against the government. South Africa would be the political graveyard for Chamberlain – so it had once appeared. Now it seemed to have given him the greatest triumph of his career.[91]

CHAPTER 10

Bursting the Mould

Cape Town and Ladysmith,
14–20 October 1899

'I precipitated the crisis, which was inevitable, before it
was too late. It is not a very agreeable, and in many eyes,
not very creditable piece of business to have been largely
instrumental in bringing about a big war.'

Sir Alfred Milner to Lord Roberts,
6 June 1900

In Cape Town, there were colonial cheers for imperial troops. On Saturday 14
October, the day that Buller and the vanguard of his armada set sail from
Southampton, the rear-guard of the Indian reinforcements steamed into Table
Bay. As the small body of khaki-helmeted troops tramped through Adderley
Street to the barracks – they were four hundred men of the Yorkshire Light
Infantry, rushed from Mauritius in HMS *Powerful* – people gave them a heroes'
welcome. The same war-cries were heard as in England: 'Pull old Kroojer's
whiskers!', 'Remember Majuba!'[1]

The ultimatum itself had caused little public excitement, but this was not for
the same reason as in England. On the contrary, for weeks now the war had
seemed a foregone conclusion to most people in the colony, on whichever side
of the fence they took their stand, British or Boer. Already war cast a long
shadow southwards across the Cape. Ever since August British refugees had
been flooding out of the Rand, as though there had been a breach in one of the
immense, muddy dams built to supply the gold-fields. The first wave brought
the managers and the professional men: men in Homburg hats, wearing gold
watches, with African servants to help with the children and wives who could
afford to dress in the latest Paris fashion; financiers like Friedrich Eckstein (the
South African director of Wernher-Beit's subsidiary) and others of the
Hohenheim set. The second wave brought the shopkeepers and the better-off
working men: people like Tom Edgar's mates, from Florrie's Chambers and
Tarry's ironworks; Cornish miners and Lancashire boiler-men – the 'white
Kaffirs', as they sometimes called themselves. These were the British Uitlanders
who had stood straw-hatted in Market Square, nine months before, as Dodd
read out the text of the Edgar Petition, the solemn appeal to Caesar. Now Caesar
was on the march, and they were refugees till Caesar restored them: pouring

down the railway line, dragging away all they possessed in bundles and boxes in a Great Trek to freedom, British-style.[2]

The exodus from the Rand reached its climax on the Monday before the ultimatum. By now the Uitlander Council had arranged to pay the fares of the poorest class of Uitlander; and there was a rumour (accurate enough) that the Boers planned to expel British subjects. Lights began to go out all over the Rand. The Ferreira, the Jumper, the Bonanza, the Robinson Deep: at all the great mines, the boilers were let out and the huge steel crushing stamps hung up – at all except for a few mines commandeered by the Boers for the duration. The golden streams flowing to the cyanide vats had now been succeeded by a stream of panic-stricken refugees heading for Johannesburg Station. There they were, packed – seventy, even a hundred at a time – into 'Kaffir-trucks' (or coal trucks or cattle trucks, it was all the same).

Three days later they would arrive at Cape Town; and then they really did look like Kaffirs, after those days and nights in the open trucks, exposed to the spring rains, and covered in mud and coal dust. Thirty thousand people, it was said, travelled like this to the Cape and Natal in the space of those few weeks. After the great Johannesburg dam had finally emptied itself, the total number of refugees was thought to be at least sixty thousand.[3] When the spokes of the mine-wheels ceased to turn, when the sky was finally blue above the mine-chimneys, the Boers had become once again the majority in their own country.

Milner himself watched the death struggles of the Rand with apparent composure. He saw the Cape Town refugees on one of his morning rides down to the sands.[4] In one sense he was glad. Milner had never visited the Rand. Now the Rand had come to Cape Town. The Mountain had come to Milner.

Of course, he was sorry for the men who had lost everything – and for the destitute women and children. Luckily, Lady Edward Cecil had proved a tower of strength on the Ladies Relief Committee. The ladies had to go at all hours of the day and night to meet the refugee trains at the station.[5] Milner himself arranged with Eckstein and his associates that he should launch a refugee fund in Britain; it would be a Mansion House disaster fund on the scale of the funds launched for famines in India; Beit and Wernher, and J. B. Robinson, the three biggest London gold-bugs, would contribute £10,000 between them, which would do wonders for their reputation with the British public. (Rhodes was too mean, or too broke, to give more than £700.)[6]

Outwardly, Milner remained calm and restrained. This was the peak of the crisis – 'the most critical point in the long game', he called it – and somehow he must soldier on.[7] 'More tired today,' he wrote in his diary on Saturday, 'than I have been yet during this business ... all the time such a head-ache that I can hardly see to write.'[8] But he had one great comfort. Between drafting cables to London and wrangling with Schreiner about colonial troops to defend the Cape, he would snatch a moment to walk side by side with Lady Edward in the gardens of Government House. Without Violet the strain would have been unendurable, he was the first to admit. Then, after the ominous lull in the week before the ultimatum, the storm had burst on Monday 9 October.[9]

It was nearly midnight. To get a respite, Milner played two games of billiards with Hanbury, and then returned to his room to continue working. He was interrupted by his secretary Ozzy. Ozzy brought the cable from Greene with the text of the ultimatum.[10]

It was, it seemed, the moment of triumph for Milner. To induce Kruger to send an ultimatum, and invade the colonies – that was the key to political success, both with the 'wobbly Liberals' at home and the 'mugwumps' like Schreiner at the Cape. He had taken the last trick by a finesse, so to speak. He had forced Kruger to play a card that could only lose him the game.

In that moment the overwhelming weight of anxiety he had carried so long began to slip from Milner's shoulders. He was still worried about the military situation. He did not doubt that the Transvaal was a real adversary, a real *military* power; he believed in the Boers' capacity for war more than any British politician or soldier – except Sir Redvers Buller. But he had had to conceal this belief from his political associates, especially Chamberlain. Rhodes insisted that Kruger would never fight. If Kruger did, the Boers' military strength was the 'greatest unpricked bubble in existence'. Well, Milner was the first to admit Rhodes was a 'very great man in many ways, but judgement was hardly his strong point'.[11] Milner himself had not made the mistake of underrating the Boers. Nor the mistake of being too frank about it with Joe and the British Cabinet before they committed the country to war.

It was now a relief to be able to admit his fears to Chamberlain. He was anxious about Natal. He was also anxious about the strategic border towns in Cape Colony north of the Orange River: Kimberley, Rhodes's diamond capital, west of Bloemfontein; Mafeking, the Raiders' old base, due west of Johannesburg. He had done his level best to see both towns defended. He had encouraged Baden-Powell to abandon an idiotic plan to invade the Transvaal from Rhodesia; Baden-Powell was now dug in at Mafeking with six hundred Rhodesian troopers.[12] On 7 October he had finally persuaded Schreiner to allow colonial troops to be used to defend Kimberley. Most of the imperial troops – there were five infantry battalions in the Cape now that the reinforcements had arrived – were to be deployed holding Orange River railway bridge and the three railway junctions south of the Orange: Stormberg, De Aar and Naauwpoort.[13] These were the keys to the way to Bloemfontein. They would be needed by Buller and his Army Corps, when this was ready in two months' time to roll north like a great steam-roller. Meanwhile, Milner was 'uneasy'; that was the word he used in his diary. But in the 'wild, rushy days' that followed the ultimatum, nothing occurred especially to alarm him.

On Thursday, the telegraph line to Mafeking went dead, and the Boers were said to have crossed the frontier and torn up the rails. On Friday, there was some sort of incident involving Mafeking's armoured train. On Saturday, the line to Kimberley went dead. By Sunday evening, they had lost touch with all the country down to the Orange River. It was also clear from Hely-Hutchinson's

cables that Joubert was taking the offensive in Natal. But Milner found the
details of these skirmishes 'satisfactory'. Hardly a shot had been fired, hardly a
life lost. There were 'panicky telegrams' on Sunday, it was true, from Kimberley. Milner kept his uneasy calm.[14]

With regard to the two strategic border towns, Kimberley and Mafeking (in
fact both under siege since 14 October), Milner's private feelings were unusually
delicate. Milner had not opposed Baden-Powell's decision to hold Mafeking.
Yet he knew it would be besieged, and now he even feared that it might be
forced to surrender. Why, then, take the risk of garrisoning it?

Part of the answer was the pressure of public opinion in the Cape. To abandon
Mafeking would have outraged the loyalists.[15] But there was probably another
rather more subtle reason. Milner had set his heart on the Boers' invading the
territory of the colony. Stationing Rhodesian troops at Mafeking, the Raiders'
old base, made it an excellent bait. Kimberley, too, made a meaty piece of bait.
Kimberley was the town which had been grabbed from the Free State when it
was found to contain the largest diamond pipe in the world. And on the very day
before the ultimatum had expired, who should appear at Kimberley but the *bête
noire* of the Transvaal, Cecil Rhodes himself.[16] Of course, the garrisons might
have to be sacrificed. But, as Selborne put it (in a very private letter), better to
lose Mafeking than lose the chance of a war.[17]

There was, in addition, an even more delicate issue involving Mafeking.
Major Lord Edward Cecil – the Prime Minister's son and Violet's husband – was
Baden-Powell's second-in-command. His marriage was, to tell the truth, a most
unhappy one. Lord Edward had volunteered to go on this dangerous mission –
had sent himself, almost as the biblical Uriah was sent to the front of the
host. Death and glory. The Last Stand. It would make a fine ending for poor
Lord Edward, who had long wished, as he later told Violet, that he were
dead.[18]

As Milner waited for the news of the first battles of the war, a great hymn of
congratulation began to reach him from England. Joe Chamberlain and the
Tories, Edward Grey, Richard Haldane and the Liberals – now at long last they
all agreed with him. He had *proved* it. War with Kruger had always been
inevitable.[19]

Inevitable? It would have been easy, Milner later confessed to his intimates, to
patch things up with Kruger, and settle those difficulties with the Uitlanders in a
Greal Deal that could have lasted five, ten or fifteen years. He had resisted the
temptation, and 'precipitated' a war before it was too late.[20] The truth was that
Milner believed in 'the clean slate',[21] and the 'Big Things in Life'.[22] He had long
been determined to 'burst the mould' of Kruger's Transvaal. War was the only
means. Britain would annex both republics for the Empire. That would finally
'knock the bottom out of "the great Afrikander nation" for ever and ever
Amen'.[23] He would rule South Africa as Cromer ruled Egypt.

Already he had begun to outline his vision of the great Union of South Africa
which he would create. 'The *ultimate* end,' he confided to his ally Percy Fitzpatrick, 'is a self-governing White Community, supported by well-treated and

justly governed black labour from Cape Town to the Zambesi.'[24] He would rebuilt the stricken Rand from its foundations and on the Rand he would build South Africa. Dams, schools, agricultural colleges – all the unglamorous but essential prerequisites of civilization – would overwhelm the veld. British settlers would pour into South Africa. This was the imperial mission. This was the great exercise in remoulding a nation and a landscape, the grand design that would follow the war – *his* war, as he boasted in private,[25] and the Pax Milneria that would be his monument.

Despite his utter exhaustion, and despite his anxieties about the border towns, Milner could feel a kind of exultation when he contemplated what he had done for the Empire. 'It is a great thing,' he had told his old friend Jim Rendel at the darkest hour of the crisis, when he thought Chamberlain might throw him over, as Bartle Frere had been thrown over before him, 'It is a great thing to be, even for a few brief days and weeks, *the leader of a people.*'[26] How much more exultant he could feel now that his leadership was permanently assured!

Milner's achievements were indeed extraordinary. It was almost exactly a year since he had sailed to England, determined to reverse Chamberlain's 'no-war policy'. Despite Chamberlain's discouragement, he had decided to take things 'forrarder by his own efforts'. He had decided to play the Uitlander card, to put that fool Jameson back on to his horse. And so he had done – in a manner of speaking.

It was true that Jameson himself, like the rest of Rhodes's men, had proved somewhat difficult to control. Jameson had in fact just gone to Ladysmith, with his fellow ex-Raider, Sir John Willoughby. No doubt Rhodes and Jameson and Willoughby all intended to be up with the field, when the time came to invade the Transvaal.[27] But the point was not what had happened to Rhodes and Jameson: they were a spent force, and their antics were largely irrelevant. The point was what had happened to the ex-Reformers, led by Alfred Beit.

Wernher and Beit had proved Milner's chief support at every stage in the game: in the Great Deal, at Bloemfontein, and in the final crisis. They had now agreed, so to speak, to pick up the bill for the war. At any rate, they had accepted without flinching the enormous losses to the gold industry (over £4m losses – in the short term – as it turned out) that the war would entail.[28] Without Wernher and Beit, Milner would have had to throw in his hand.

In a sense, Beit, the paymaster of Raiders and Reformers, had been persuaded to change clothes with Joe Chamberlain. At the time of the Raid, it was Chamberlain who stood in the shadows, waiting to exploit the situation if Rhodes and Beit succeeded. Now it was Beit who stood in the shadows, waiting to exploit the successes of the imperial troops. Beit's men – the Johannesburg Reformers – were now the 'Imperial' Light Horse. ('Beit's Horse' would have been a better name. Or, best of all, the 'Trojan Horse'.)

If Milner exulted in this private alliance with Wernher-Beit and the Uitlanders, he had also to admit to one striking omission. He had not yet stirred a finger to help African and Coloured British subjects in the Transvaal. 'You have only to sacrifice "the nigger" absolutely,' he had told Asquith in 1897, 'and the game is easy.'[29] For the last two years, that was certainly the game he had played. Milner claimed he had two great principles in his work in South Africa. The first was to 'secure for the Natives ... protection against oppression and wrong'. The second was to secure the loyalty of the very men – the Uitlanders – who were determined to keep the natives oppressed. And this second principle, of course, took priority for the time being, even if the ultimate solution was to see the natives 'justly governed'.[30]

The conflict of principle had in fact been exemplified that week in the most cruel way. In terms of human misery, the chief sufferers from the decline and fall of the Rand were not the Uitlanders, but the African mine-workers from Natal and the Cape, and the Cape Coloured population. They were the 'mine-boys' and the artisans. Now their employment had gone. They had little money saved, and the Boers were quite prepared to let them starve on the veld.[31] Should Milner intervene? It was a question that he could not flinch from. Milner was one of the founders of Toynbee Hall and he had shared his friend Toynbee's philanthropic zeal. In a fortnight he had raised £83,000 for the Uitlanders. Could nothing be spared for the tens of thousands of other British subjects, those who were coloured, coffee and black? What about the proud claim in Chamberlain's ultimatum to give coloured British subjects 'most favoured nation status'?[32]

By 6 October Milner had learnt of the plight of seven thousand African mine-workers from Natal, and of other Africans from British territory. It was a British official who cabled the news, a man called Marwick who worked for the Natal Native Affairs Department on the Rand. He reported that the Zulus and other Africans for whom he was responsible had lost their jobs. 'If left to find their own way back to Natal, [they] would starve on the veld.' Despite discouragement from the Natal Ministry, Marwick decided to try to bring the Natal refugees out by himself. The authorities refused to provide room on the railway. There was only one solution, Marwick cabled again to Natal. 'So that my proposed action may not embarrass you, please suspend me from office. If I get natives through without loss of life, you could please yourself about re-instating me.' His offer was accepted. He was proposing to walk with the three thousand Zulus and four thousand other Africans all the way to Natal.[33]

There had been strange scenes in the great exodus from the Rand, but none stranger, perhaps, than the scene that followed. At the head of the Marwick's procession of Africans were a couple of drunken Boer policemen. Behind them, marching thirty abreast, were a group of musicians, playing concertinas. They played popular African tunes. Behind the musicians marched an immense body of men, Zulus in African or European dress, all the tribes of Natal. To Marwick they displayed a touching respect: 'Child of the Englishmen,' they saluted him, 'but for whose presence no one might brave the Boers. ... Gather the orphans of the Zulu.' At the rear of the procession came the stragglers, many of whom were sick men, women and children. Marwick did his best for them. He had brought a pony for himself; the pony was given to a sick African to ride; other Africans were put on a kind of trolley that could be pushed along the road. On the 7th they reached Heidelberg; on the 10th Waterval, over a hundred miles south-east of Johannesburg; by the 13th they had marched the 170 miles to Joubert's camp at Volkrust on the Natal frontier.

By now the ultimatum had expired and Natal was at war with the Transvaal. Many of the natives were starving, as few of the shopkeepers on the road had been able or willing to sell them food; indeed, some Boers had fled from natives in terror. Each day the great procession lengthened as the stragglers fell further behind. Marwick brought up the rear, doing his best to encourage the old and the sick as they limped along the dusty track. On the Natal side of the frontier the procession was stopped by some burghers of Joubert's army. Despite the fact that Marwick had obtained safe conduct papers for his flock, papers personally authorized by Kruger, the State Artillery Commandant refused to let the procession past. It was a bad moment for Marwick. As he later put it, 'With 7,000 natives on the verge of starvation treading on the heels of three thousand armed Boers there were the elements of a great massacre of defenceless people.' Then the Commandant relented.

Four hundred of the Africans were temporarily commandeered. They dragged Joubert's siege guns up to the summit facing Majuba. At dawn next day, the whole procession passed through the Boer lines. On the 15th they staggered down to Hatting Spruit, close to Symons's camp at Dundee – 240 miles from the Rand and almost in sight of home.

Marwick's epic march had saved seven thousand Natal Africans from starvation. Milner read the cables and no doubt approved.[34] But for the thousands of African refugees from the Cape Colony and Basutoland – the people for whom Milner, as High Commissioner, was directly responsible – Milner did nothing.[35] He had to play the game. And the game, easy or not, was to 'sacrifice "the nigger" absolutely'.

'Boot and Saddle!' Dust swirled across the Ladysmith parade ground as it had swirled across the parade grounds made by Dr Jameson at Pitsani and Mafeking, three and a half years before. 'Dress by the left! Bugler!' The words of command floated across the Klip River. Slouch hats, Lee Metfords, brown gaiters and green-khaki uniforms: the six hundred men of the Imperial Light Horse – 'Beit's Horse' – looked uncannily like the men who had ridden with Jameson. In fact, Jameson was himself there at Ladysmith that morning, and perhaps he and Frank Rhodes and Johnny Willoughby came to see the ILH leaders, Woolls-Sampson and Karri Davies; they had also, of course, been fellow-inmates of Johannesburg prison, though the Raid had led to an estrangement between Rhodes' men and the rest.

On their part, Beit's men were already thinking, like Milner, of the new Transvaal they would build after the war. Kruger must go. That was the first principle: 'Insist on Kruger, and all his crowd, being sent out of South Africa,' as one of the officers put it. The Boers were 'like a pack of sheep'. Take away 'their biblical shepherd' and they were 'mere animals to be driven'. Second, there must be a clean sweep of the Transvaal ministries – those Augean Stables. Bring in Englishmen. Get rid of that clique of Hollanders and Germans. That was the plan. Of course, the heads of the departments would have to be Uitlanders. Already jobs were being canvassed: Woolls-Sampson, Wybergh, Dodd, Mullins and so on were the leading candidates.[38] The capital of the new colony would be Johannesburg. 'Joe burg' – it was appropriate enough as a name. Although, as one of the Uitlander leaders put it, 'Milnerton' would be the best name of all, for 'H.E. has indeed been our champion.'[39]

As for the next moves, the Uitlanders' plans coincided almost exactly with Milner's, though they lacked the fine moral polish that Milner added to imperial ideas. Swamp the Boers, kill off pan-Afrikaner nationalism, then 'thoroughly anglicize the country'. Otherwise, as Wybergh bluntly remarked, 'the war is wasted'.[40] Above all, the 'unctuous rectitude' (quoting Rhodes's famous sneer) of the British public must not be allowed to ruin the settlement. No votes for the coloured people in the Transvaal at all costs. There was only one set of laws in the Transvaal that the Uitlanders considered really 'excellent': the laws 'to keep the niggers in their place'. They were glad to think that this was a subject on which they believed that H.E. was as 'healthy' as on the rest of the points.[41]

The bugle sounded the advance. Across the Klip River, under their new imperial flag, rode the six hundred.

It was 20 October – the tenth day of the war – and still hardly a shot had been fired. Yet Milner was not reassured by the stream of code cables sent from Natal to Cape Town. 'Lulled one ethnology cheatingly' the cables would begin. Decoded by Ozzy, that became 'with regard to your message of . . .' The latest military news would follow. At 3 a.m. on the 18th, White cabled to say he was pulling Symons back to Ladysmith. At 5 a.m. he changed his mind. He agreed to let Symons stay at Dundee. It was all very disquieting. Milner himself felt sure that Symons would be cut off if he stayed where he was.[42]

Early that morning Milner went for a ride with Hanbury. At times of greatest strain, he would often ride his horse up to the great Lion of Table Mountain, the crag from which one could see half the Empire. When he returned Ozzy had the cable ready. Its message was clear enough, even without decoding. 'Lulled one ethnology cheatingly,' it began as usual, and continued, 'Bookoath shelling camp.'[43]

Symons was under attack. The war – Milner's War – had definitely begun.

PART II

Buller's Reverse

Redvers Buller has gone away
In charge of a job to Table Bay;
In what direction Redvers goes
Is a matter that only Buller knows....
If he's right, he'll pull us through.
If he wrong, he's better than you.

Black and White Budget, 30 December 1899

SIR PAUL KRUGER

CHAPTER 11

'Taking Tea with the Boers'

Dundee, North Natal,
20 October 1899

'I don't think the Boers will have a chance, although I
expect there will be one or two stiff little shows here and
there.... I think they are awful idiots to fight although we
are of course very keen that they should....'

Lieutenant Reggie Kentish, Royal Irish
Fusiliers, to his parents, 30 September
and 12 October 1899

'I hope to hear this evening or tomorrow morning that
Symons has taken tea with the Boers [at Dundee].'

Sir Walter Hely-Hutchinson,
Governor of Natal, to Sir Alfred
Milner, 20 October 1899

Five a.m. on Friday 20 October, and a damp kind of dawn – real Scottish
weather, one of the English soldiers said. There was a curtain of mist hanging
low on the shoulders of Mount Impati, to the north of the town of Dundee.[1] It
was from the north that Joubert's main army were known to be advancing. In
the valley below, General Symons's garrison of four thousand men was already
on parade in full battle gear, a sombrely warlike spectacle: the 2nd Dublin
Fusiliers, the 1st Royal Irish Fusiliers, the 60th Rifles and the 1st Leicesters,[2]
arranged in a chequerboard of anonymous khaki; brown paint over buckles and
sword hilts and bayonet scabbards, with only the small coloured badges on the
khaki helmets to tell the four battalions apart. The officers carried swords,
knives, revolvers, field-glasses and whistles. They looked as drab as the men.[3]

At 5.20 a.m. the men were told to fall out, and one of Symons's staff came
round with the day's orders: prepare for infantry training. Some officers of the
18th Hussars – the cavalry regiment sent to Dundee along with the four infantry
battalions – were strolling across to the mess tent for a cup of tea. A sudden
shout: 'There they are!' Everyone laughed. For days people had talked of little
else but the coming scrap ('If only the Boers would buck up and do something,'

one had just written home),[4] but the idea of a couple of thousand Boers attacking an entire British brigade seemed comic. Anyway, the expected threat was from Impati, and the north. The men were wearing black macintoshes. Perhaps they were the town guard.[5]

From inside his tent, Lieutenant Maurice Crum, the senior subaltern of the 60th Rifles, heard the shouts and the laughter. He had spent four months in Natal training for this battle, four months of the warscare alternating with depressing rumours of peace, and was desperate not to miss the 'scrap'. But today he was lying on his blanket with a mild dose of fever.[6]

'What's them 'ere blokes on that bloomin' hill?' he heard a man shout. Crum crawled from his tent. Out came the binoculars. The whole camp was now staring across the valley at the steep ridge, two miles east of the town above Piet Smit's Farm: Talana Hill, as the Zulus called it. Intermittently, in the mist, Crum saw groups of figures notching the smooth line of the pale eastern sky, crowds of riflemen with three field-guns. Lucas Meyer's commando. Boers. The officers were still staring in astonishment a quarter of an hour later when the first Creusot 75-mm shell swept with a whirr and a scream high across the valley.[7] The second shell, better aimed, splashed into the wet earth behind the rear file of the Dublin Fusiliers.[8]

Down in the artillery lines, Gunner Netley, No. 5 of No. 1 gun in the 13th Battery, noted the exact time – 5.40 a.m. by the barrack-room clock – and the exact place where the next Creusot shell landed. It struck the wooden peg a few yards behind him; and to the peg he had tethered his pony. Fortunately the shell was a dud.[9] 'Of corse [sic] you can bet that everyone was a bit surprised,' Netley later scrawled in the diary he kept in his haversack, 'and men were running about in all directions, but only for a minute or two. When we were ourselves again the Battery was brought into action and commenced firing at the Bores long ranged gun.... The Bore firing was very erratic.'[10]

All three batteries – six guns to a battery, making a total of eighteen guns – were ordered to open fire. About 6.00 a.m. small white stars of shrapnel smoke spangled the skyline, as the 67th Battery began to thunder away from its position in the gun park.[11] The 69th and the 13th Batteries were slower off the mark; the drivers had just been sent down to water their horses, along with the other transport animals. Gunner Netley was sent off on his pony to tell them to return immediately.[12]

'Battery Column. Sections Left wheel. Action Front.'

The batteries hooked in the horses, limbered up, and jingled off in pairs through the town, then bumped across the railway line, metal against metal, and unlimbered two miles from the enemy's position.[13]

'Battery fire 15 seconds. Fuse 35.' At 6.20 a.m. the 69th opened up. At 6.30 a.m. the 13th joined them, the guns lined up as neatly as on a field day, the gunners counting out loud after each shot to give the regulation interval of fifteen seconds between the firing of each gun.[14]

General Symons himself had been about to have his breakfast when the first Creusot shell landed. The CO of the Hussars, Lieutenant-Colonel B. D. Möller,

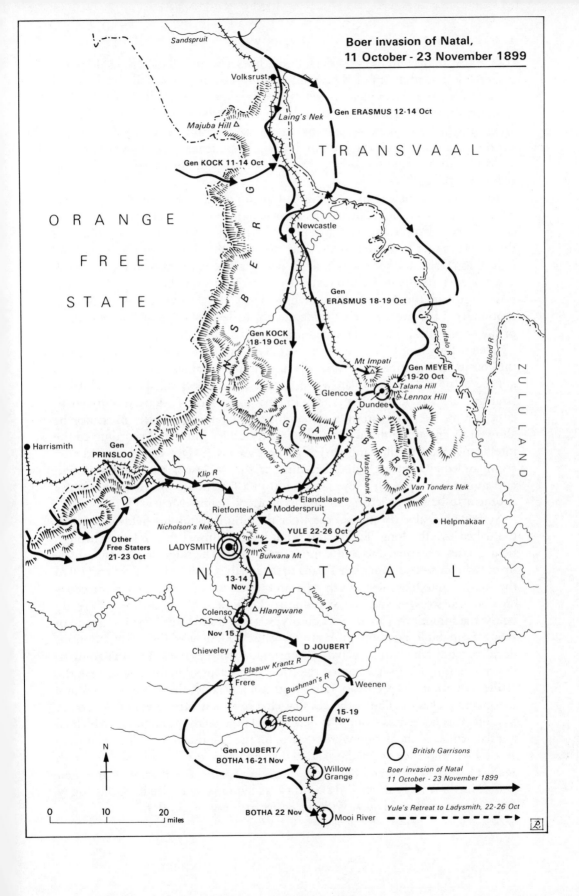

**Boer invasion of Natal,
11 October - 23 November 1899**

Sandspruit

Volksrust

Gen ERASMUS 12-14 Oct

Laing's Nek

Majuba Hill △

Gen KOCK 11-14 Oct

T R A N S V A A L

O R A N G E

F R E E

S T A T E

Newcastle

Gen
ERASMUS 18-19 Oct

Gen KOCK
18-19 Oct

Buffalo R

Blood R

Mt Impati

Gen MEYER
19-20 Oct

△*Talana Hill*
△*Lennox Hill*

Glencoe

Dundee

Z U L U L A N D

Harrismith

Gen
PRINSLOO

Klip R

Sunday's R

Waschbank R

Van Tonders Nek

Helpmakaar

Rietfontein

Elandslaagte
Modderspruit

Nicholson's Nek →

Other
Free Staters
21-23 Oct

LADYSMITH

YULE 22-26 Oct

Bulwana Mt

N A T A L

13-14
Nov

Tugela R

Colenso

△*Hlangwane*

Nov 15

D JOUBERT

Chieveley

Blaauw Krantz R

Frere

Bushman's R

Weenen

15-19
Nov

N

Estcourt

Gen JOUBERT/
BOTHA 16-21 Nov

Willow
Grange

BOTHA 22 Nov   Mooi River

0   10   20
⌐————⌐————⌐ miles

◯ *British Garrisons*

*Boer invasion of Natal
11 October - 23 November 1899*
━━━▶ ━ ━ ▶

Yule's Retreat to Ladysmith, 22-26 Oct
┅┅┅▶

rode across to his tent to get orders. Loose horses were still galloping along the picket lines, sending mud flying. Men were cowering behind the walls of canvas. Orderlies struggled to get the officers' horses saddled and bridled. Symons's tent was unmistakable: outside, on a high mast, flew a huge Union Jack; inside, the General was smoking a cigarette and issuing orders. Shells continued to splash into the ground nearby. 'Impudence' was the word he used to Möller to describe the Boers' attack. Damned impudence to start shelling before breakfast.[15]

By 6.40 a.m., the enemy shelling had begun to slacken. The Boer guns had never had much chance. Three guns against eighteen. Not that Brother Boer, as the officers called the enemy,[16] had proved himself much of a gunner. Many of the Boers' shots had gone wide, and of those that hit the mark, most had percussion fuses, and the shells had failed to explode in the rain-sodden ground. There were virtually no British casualties, apart from poor Trumpeter Horn, the boy bugler of the 69th Battery, whose head was blown off by a Maxim 1-pounder,[17] and the grey mare ridden by the orderly of Colonel Gunning (CO of the 60th Rifles), on which a 75-mm scored a direct hit.[18]

Even before the artillery duel was over, Symons had issued his battle orders to the commanding officers. Despite his interrupted breakfast, he was anxious to get the battle started. His plan was a simple one, in keeping with his ideas on strategy. To attack the enemy, the enemy must have first been allowed to concentrate. Yet the eastern commandos, led by Lucas Meyer, must not be allowed to link up with the main Boer army under Joubert. According to the intelligence reports, the vanguard of Joubert's army (in fact, two thousand men commanded by General Daniel Erasmus) was now close behind Mount Impati and might link up with Meyer's column in a few hours. So there was not a moment to be lost in letting loose the infantry against Meyer.[19]

Symons had already studied the Boer position through his field-glasses. To the naked eye the long hog's-back ridge looked almost featureless. Through field-glasses it seemed, tactically, more promising. The ridge was, in fact, made up of twin hills – 600-foot high Talana to the north, 550-foot high Lennox Hill to the south – and, like most South African kopjes, the hillsides were terraced by erosion and strewn with red volcanic rock, aloes and acacia-thorn. Directly below the summit of Talana was a eucalyptus wood and Smit's Farm: a group of white farm buildings and pink stone walls.[20] Here was the place, Symons decided, from which to launch a concentrated infantry attack. He was going to use conventional field-day tactics, the Aldershot set-piece in three acts. First, the artillery duel and the preparation of the ground. Second, the infantry attack and the infantry charge. Third, the cavalry charge to cut off the enemy's retreat. Symons was no genius – nor was he a fool. These were the tactics in which all regular armies of the period were trained, on the Continent as well as in Britain and India. And they were the tactics that had served Germany well enough against France in 1870, and Britain well enough against the ill-armed tribesmen of the North-West Frontier.[21] By contrast, as Symons reminded himself, Colley had been trapped at Majuba without either artillery or cavalry.[22]

A few of the more intelligent officers, it must be repeated had been alarmed by one feature of Symons's tactics during the field days in Natal. They believed that exceptionally open order was the tactic to use against Boers armed with magazine rifles. Symons believed in the well tried virtues of close order and concentration.[23] He had decided to leave his artillery to cope with the southern part of the ridge, Lennox Hill. He would concentrate his forces in the few hundred yards covered by the stone walls and the wood directly below Talana, and then storm it in overwhelming strength. He wanted to deal a knock-out blow and there was no time for manoeuvring, so he believed, if he was to crush Meyer before Meyer could join hands with Joubert.[24]

By contrast to his belief in the traditional virtues of concentration and close order for infantry, Symons had unconventional (if not reckless) ideas on the handling of cavalry. He told Colonel Möller not to wait for the infantry but to act on his own if he saw the chance. Hence, about 7.00 a.m., Möller took his small group of cavalry and MI (Mounted Infantry) and rode around to the back of Talana to cut off the enemy's line of retreat.[25] Symons had found this tactic effective on the North-West Frontier, although, against the disciplined forces of cavalry textbooks, it would have invited disaster.

It was now 7.30 a.m. and the artillery duel was well finished. Time for the second act of the Aldershot set-piece – the infantry attack.[26]

As the infantry lined up in the sandy bed of a river to the east of Dundee, a war correspondent, Monypenny of *The Times*, late Editor of *The Star*, Johannesburg (where he had, by joint arrangement with Beit and Milner, kept the Uitlanders 'pegging away'), hurried to the front.[27] In the bed of the stream, the men waited for orders. Symons, conspicuous by the scarlet pennant carried by his ADC, rode across to study the position. It was a calculated risk to throw almost everything he had into the battle – three battalions of infantry, two batteries of artillery and all the cavalry and MI. This left only the Leicesters and the 67th Battery to defend the camp if Joubert launched a flank attack, which Symons was well aware might happen. (In fact, the Boers were poised to strike from Impati.)[28] But it seemed to him the only chance of giving it to the Boers straight on the jaw.

'Dublins first line. Rifles second. Fusiliers third.' It was a nervous moment. As the men had marched through the town there had been scenes of hysteria: some of the townspeople were laughing, others crying, and a woman rushed forward to kiss one of the NCOs of the Rifles, shouting, 'God bless you, lad!' The men blustered and joked, but many looked pale enough, swallowing hard and trying not to show it.[29] After all, few of these short-service soldiers had ever seen action. And of those that had not a single one had ever experienced either shell fire or modern rifle fire. In the whole of Europe there was no body of soldiers that had ever seen the concentrated fire of the magazine rifle, with the muzzle end facing them. The people who knew this end of the rifle best from personal experience were the Dervishes of Omdurman – those that survived.

A sudden hush fell on the ranks of the 60th Rifles.[30] This was the regiment whose 3rd Battalion had been almost annihilated at Majuba, and the men

regarded the present war as a personal duel to settle that debt of honour. The
Colonel, Bobby Gunning, called the NCOs together. 'Now quietly, lads.
Remember Majuba, God, and our country.' Then the order was taken up along
the line. 'Forward, men.' And over the top they went.[31]

A few unlucky men dropped, hit by the invisible riflemen firing down from
the misty hilltop. The casualties were scooped up by the Indian stretcher-bearers
of Major Donegan's field hospital, and carried back in green 'doolies' (four in
each doolie) to the dressing-station by the post office.[32] Most of the infantry
reached the wood. Here the panting men found shelter in the ditches and behind
the walls of Smit's Farm. They were now less than a mile from the crest of
Talana, and above their heads the eucalyptus leaves fell in swathes, cut by
Mauser bullets.

But how to advance beyond the wood? On the farther side was a stone wall, a
small gap and then a quick-set hedge covered in brambles. Beyond that was
open ground.[33] Major Bird and most of the Dublins worked their way out of the
wood and crawled up a ditch, but were soon pinned down and unable to make
progress.[34] Lieutenant-Colonel R. F. C. Carleton sent his Fusiliers to line the
stone wall on the left. Others remained jumbled together in the wood, now
heavy with cordite fumes and the smell of crushed eucalyptus. For an hour, the
unfortunate commander of the infantry brigade, Brigadier-General James Yule,
tried to organize the assault. The men were unwilling to brave the invisible
curtain of bullets beyond.[35]

Shortly after nine, they saw the General's red pennant approaching through
the drizzle, and Symons rode up to the wood. He had already sent two of his staff
officers to order the assault. What had caused the delay? Yule explained that
there was still a tremendous fire coming from Talana, despite the pounding they
had received from the shrapnel of the eighteen British field-guns. No doubt
Yule then suggested – it was the view of at least one of his officers and the
obvious point to make – that it would be sensible to postpone the infantry attack
until the artillery had finished its job. Symons refused. His strategic anxieties
were too great. No more delay. Everything depended on attacking Meyer
before Joubert joined him. Despite the protests of his staff, Symons rode
through the wood, dismounted and strode to the gap in the stone wall, his ADC
carrying the scarlet pennant beside him.[36]

There were times in the wars of the nineteenth and earlier centuries when a
general had to sacrifice his life to rally his men. It was the counterpart picture to
the Last Stand: the Death of the General at the Moment of Victory. Perhaps
Symons saw himself in this noble tradition. At any rate, he now had to pay with
his life the price demanded. After a few moments, he returned through the gap in
the stone wall and stiffly remounted, with the help of his ADC. The scarlet
pennant retired slowly from the hill.[37] When Symons was out of sight of the
troops, he let himself be taken by the Indian stretcher-bearers to the dressing-
station. Major Kerin, Commanding Officer of the 20th Field Hospital, found
him there in excruciating pain. He was mortally wounded in the stomach. 'Tell
me, have they got the hill?' was all he could say.[38]

In fact, without the encouragement offered by Symons, some other men had already begun to push forward on the west side of the wood. Despite that deafening tempest of rifle fire – the drumming, roaring, hammering, grinding sound of hundreds of Mausers fired simultaneously, and of bullets ricocheting off the red rocks, and splashing into the ground like a storm of rain on a lake – the infantry began to make some ground. Casualties they suffered in plenty. By 9.30 they had reached the main terrace below the crest line, a terrace bounded and protected by a second stone wall, running parallel to the hillside. By 10.00 a.m. swarms of men from all three battalions could be seen firing from behind this second stone wall, and their presence gave the rest of the infantry new heart to leave the wood.[39]

Down in the valley, the two batteries of artillery had been having the best of the battle. The townspeople treated the gunners to a late breakfast of bread and butter, tea and coffee. ('Here goes to finish this little snack – in case I loose it' [sic] was Gunner Netley's jaunty comment. 'The Mausers are singing . . . they must be crack shots for they only hit one man in the battery.')[40] In the 69th Battery, Lieutenant Trench received the orders to close up to fourteen hundred yards. As the twelve guns opened up on the hill, the shrapnel bursting in balloons of white smoke and red dust, Netley saw the infantry fix bayonets and charge.

But at that moment a new misfortune occurred. Netley and the gunners of the 13th Battery could see the British bayonets clearly – 'like minute flashes of lightning'. Some of the men with Trench and the 69th Battery could not.[41] What happened next was described to *The Times* by Captain Nugent of the 60th:

The ground in front of me was literally rising in dust from the bullets, and the din echoing between the hill and the wood below and among the rocks from the incessant fire of the Mausers seemed to blend with every other sound into a long drawn-out hideous roar. Half way over the terrace I looked round over my shoulder and I confess I was rather horrified at what I saw. S— was close beside me, and a few men here and there, but the whole ground we had already covered was strewn with bodies, and no more men were coming from over the wall. At that moment I was hit the first time. . . . I was hit through the knee. The actual shock was as if someone had hit me with their whole strength with a club. I spun round and fell, my pistol flying one way and helmet another. . . . [Then] I began to pull myself up by holding on to the rocks and bushes and long grass . . . I was hit a second time by a shot from above; the bullet hit me on the back above my right hip and came out in front of my thigh.[42]

Despite a third wound, where a bullet had struck his spine, Nugent crawled to the crest of the hill, which he found deserted by the Boers. His account continued:

I was just beginning to bandage my leg, when a shrapnel shell burst overhead. We both, W[ortley] and I, stared in astonishment. We could see our artillery on the plain below us 1500 yards off. . . . It seemed impossible that they should not have seen our advance from the wall . . . presently I saw another flash from a gun and then with a scream and a crash a shrapnel shell burst just behind us. . . . I felt rather beat then. . . . It seemed so hard, after escaping the Boers to be killed by our own people. W[ortley] and I lay as close as we could under the rock, and below me on the terrace I watched the wretched fellows who were wounded trying to drag themselves to the wall for shelter. Presently a shrapnel burst right over our heads, and the bullets struck the ground all round us.[43]

At last the artillery stopped. And fortunately for Yule's men, the Boers did not attempt to exploit the artillery's error. They crept away down the reverse side of the hill, where their ponies were tethered, and rode away.[44]

The hill had been won. But what a sight greeted the victors. Colonel Gunning of the 60th lay there, shot through the heart; he had stood up close to the crest, shouting 'Stop that firing!' to the British artillery. Colonel Sherston, Yule's Brigade Major, was kicking and groaning on the ground. Captain Connor, the giant of the Fusiliers, was mortally wounded in the stomach. Lieutenant Hambro had lost both legs, smashed by the British shrapnel.[45] Each battalion had lost half a dozen officers killed and wounded; the total loss to the British amounted to 51 dead or dying, 203 wounded.[46] And if the hill had been won, what else had been won with it?

Beyond the ridge, the men of Lucas Meyer's commando were streaming across the veld towards the Buffalo River. It was the moment for Act Three of the Aldershot set-piece: the rout of the enemy. But Möller and the British cavalry had taken Symons at his word and vanished behind Impati – mysteriously vanished – hours earlier. (In fact the disastrous news of their surrender was not to reach Yule for a couple of days.)[47] Still, the enemy were well within artillery range. After some hesitation, the gunners were ordered up the road between the crests of Talana and Lennox Hill. Here the twelve gun crews of the two batteries unlimbered – and waited. Later, people said that the artillery commander, Colonel Pickwoad, had seen a white flag raised by the Boers.[48] There was another reason for inaction: in the mist and drizzle they mistook the fleeing Boers, dressed in capes, for the 18th Hussars. In the 13th Battery, Gunner Netley could see they were the Boers, and cursed the stupidity of their commander.[49] At any rate, both batteries were ordered not to fire. And in a matter of minutes, General Meyer and his commando of three thousand rode swiftly out of sight beyond the curtain of rain.[50]

CHAPTER 12

White Flag, *Arme Blanche*

Elandslaagte, near Ladysmith, Natal,
21 October 1899

'We ... finished just as darkness fell over the field, & then
the reactions came, I calmed down, I felt sick at the sight
of the dead and dying, horrible sight, awful in their
gastleness [sic], blood to meet the eyes, groans to meet
the ears, and among this we had to sleep ... but strange as
it may seem I am eager to be in battle again now ...'

Private Prosper Paris, 1st Manchester
Regiment, in a letter to Gerty,
24 October 1899

'Get dressed quick, C Company. We have to be out in the veld in an hour's time.
The enemy are there.' The Gordon Highlanders were off duty at Ladysmith
camp, forty miles south of Dundee, as Captain Buchanan ran down the lines of
the white bell-tents shouting these strange words of command.[1] It was just
before one o'clock on the day after the action at Talana – thundery, but not too
hot, so it seemed to troops recently arrived from India. These Jocks, off duty,
were busy enough.[2] There were kilts to be patched and mended, khaki covers to
be sewn over the hairy black and white sporrans, and the usual mixture of brown
paint and cow-dung to be painted over the white webbing.[3]

After the Captain had gone, the Jocks burst out laughing. They had just heard
of the victory the previous day at Talana. How could the enemy now be close to
Ladysmith? And the idea of going into action within an hour. It seemed like a
leg-pull.[4]

Yet, an hour later, the battalion was marching, with swinging kilts, down to
Ladysmith station. They were five companies strong: 20 officers and 483 men,
led by their Commanding Officer, Lieutenant-Colonel William Dick-
Cunyngham, the officers inconspicuous except for their claymores, and the
drum-major carrying a rifle instead of a drum. At the station they piled into a
train, their Highland dress half-hidden by all that battle equipment: twin cartridge pouches on the chest, balancing, under the criss-crossed webbing, the
neatly rolled greatcoat, and the water-bottle; Lee Metford rifle; bulging haversack, a hundred extra rounds, field dressings and the rest.[5]

In a few minutes they were off, riding in open cattle trucks, drawn by
two engines, as they had come up from Durban. Ahead of them were seven

companies of the 1st Devons, riding in another train; and also ahead of them had gone, earlier that day, some of the Natal Mounted Rifles and Natal Artillery and four companies of the 1st Manchesters, led by the armoured train. The mounted troops – a squadron each of the 5th Lancers and the 5th Dragoon Guards, and five squadrons of the Imperial Light Horse – rode along to keep pace with the train. Two batteries of field artillery – twelve of the usual 15-pounders – had been galloped out from Ladysmith with double teams of horses.[6] Battle or no battle, it was an inspiring sight; engines steaming into war like battle-cruisers, led by the armoured train, its slate-coloured funnel and boiler encased in half-inch steel plates, like the funnel of a dreadnought.

Just beyond Modderspruit, twelve miles north of Ladysmith on the line to Dundee, the procession clanked to a halt and the order was given to detrain.[7] Beside the track were two red-tabbed generals and a major of the ILH. They stood, booted and spurred, discussing tactics.

The shorter of the two Generals was not a man you could mistake. With his heavy-jowled face, bow legs and bull neck, he looked every inch the cavalry man. At forty-seven, Major-General John French was the white hope of the British cavalry. If this military arm were to prove itself in South Africa – the traditional *arme blanche* of the sword and the lance against modern magazine rifles – it was up to French. Despite his cavalry swagger, French was clever.[8] Cleverer still, people said, was his chief staff officer, Major Douglas Haig. The two men had been rushed out to Natal a week after Sir George White, and had arrived hot-foot from Durban the previous morning.[9]

The second general was tall and somewhat effete – Ian Hamilton, the chief member of Roberts's Ring, sent out with White. Still only officially a colonel by rank (though he had distinguished himself as acting brigadier in the Tirah campaign on the North-West Frontier of India), Hamilton had been given the command of the infantry brigade by White. This was an emotional moment for Hamilton. His own regiment was the 2nd Battalion of the Gordons (that is, the old 92nd), which had been, with the 60th Rifles, one of the chief victims of the First Boer War. Hamilton himself had been captured and seriously wounded at Majuba – hence his crippled left wrist. Today the Gordons were one of the three battalions in his brigade.[10]

The major of the ILH, Aubrey Woolls-Sampson, had the sun-dried looks and the steel and whipcord manner of the colonial, in contrast to Hamilton's. Yet he, too, had been wounded in the First Boer War; there was a scar the size of a shilling that covered his jugular vein. He also bore the psychological scars, like most of the ILH, of the fiasco of the Raid.[11] Ahead of him was the commando that the Uitlanders regarded as their personal enemies: the Johannesburg Commando, led by Commandant Ben Viljoen. Now was the moment to avenge both those two white flags: at Majuba and Doornkop.

The previous evening White had learnt of Symons's tactical victory at Talana, end of part of its heavy cost: Symons's mortal wound. (The British had yet to learn of the surrender of Möller's cavalry.) He was still understandably alarmed by the strategic threat of superior numbers against his divided forces. That morning he had sent out French to make a cavalry reconnaissance before dawn. French was told: proceed to Elandslaagte, where the enemy are reported to have cut the railway and telegraph lines leading to Dundee; cover the engineers who will restore these communications. French had discovered that the enemy had occupied the station at Elandslaagte in strength of a sort. It turned out that this was the Johannesburg Commando, under the overall command of General Kock, with the addition of two hundred German and Hollander volunteers. They had bypassed Symons's garrison at Dundee and ridden boldly down over the Biggarsberg towards Ladysmith (ignoring Joubert's careful plans) with about a thousand men.[12] Hence there was a heaven-sent opportunity for French to destroy this weak commando while it was on its own. There was also the need to restore the links with Dundee. Consequently, French had despatched a sudden telephone message to White, asking for substantial reinforcements of infantry. This was the message that sent the Gordons and the Devons scrambling into their battle kit and steaming down the line.[13]

From the point where the men detrained, the railway line continued more or less level two miles farther to the station at Elandslaagte. On the left of the line was the colliery, marked by black smoke and pit mouths. On the right of the line rose a stony, biscuit-coloured ridge. This looped round in a second ridge to form a horseshoe, and beyond the farther and steeper ridge, about a mile south-east of the station, half hidden among four kopjes, could be seen the white tents and wagons of Commandant Kock's laager. How to attack this natural strongpoint: that was the tactical problem. The hill was only three hundred feet high, half the height of Lucas Meyer's position on the crest of Talana. Yet here there was no wood, there were no walls; in fact, there was no cover except the stones and ant-hills strewn across the rolling veld.[14] And here at Elandslaagte, just as at Talana, the Boers had three 75-mm field-guns, whose shells, with their longer burning fuses, enabled them to outrange the British 15-pounders by a thousand yards.[15]

In numbers of men and guns, however, French vastly outnumbered Kock, owing to Kock's folly in advancing prematurely: he had 1,630 infantry, 1,314 cavalry and 552 gunners with 18 guns, to Kock's 1,000 men and 3 guns.[16] And by now French had hammered out a plan of attack with Hamilton. It was to be, like Talana, the conventional Aldershot set-piece. Yet there were important differences between French's and Hamilton's tactics and those of the unfortunate Symons. French believed in the cavalry textbook. He had no intention of letting loose the cavalry till after the infantry had succeeded. By contrast, Hamilton had his doubts about conventional infantry tactics for use against the magazine rifle. He had noticed the success in North-West India of a few Afridi tribesmen, armed with stolen British rifles, against British troops in the conventional shoulder-to-shoulder formation. He now told his infantry colonels: keep exceptionally open order. The Devons were to have a front of a thousand yards, three yards for each man; their seven companies were to be deployed at such broad intervals that the distance from front to rear would be nearly a mile.[17]

By three o'clock the horses of French's cavalry, who had been out since early morning, had been watered, and the last of the four trains had spilt their loads on to the veld beside the railway line. Hamilton explained his plan. The Devons were to have the honour of making the frontal attack, directly across the inside of the horseshoe. The other two infantry battalions – the Gordons and the Manchesters – with the ILH (dismounted), were to work round by the toe of the horseshoe, and take the enemy's left flank. Men from each regiment cheered and waved their helmets. 'We'll do it! We'll do it, Sir!' At 3.30 p.m. the long, regular lines of khaki began to inscribe themselves on the blank surface of the veld. Beyond them, a melodramatic back-drop, the great anvil-shaped cloud of an approaching thunderstorm.[18]

Among the anxious watchers who stood there on the first ridge were the Press corps from four London newspapers, which Monypenny had scooped when he set off for Talana. This distinguished band had ridden out from Ladysmith that morning, on ponies and in Cape carts. Henry Nevinson, of *The Chronicle* was a critic and a socialist, a champion of women's emancipation as well as a part-time soldier. Steevens of *The Mail* and Bennet Burleigh of *The Telegraph* were the leading war correspondents of their day. Melton Prior of *The Illustrated London News* was the leading war artist. It was men like these who had made the small wars of the late Victorian era familiar to their generation. With pen and brush, they had brought battle into every Victorian drawing-room: Gordon's Last Stand; Gordon's Avenging; and all those countless other battles in outlandish parts of the world which were thought to have added lustre to the Empire. Not that any of these war correspondents were the crude kind of jingo. Each had drawn war as he saw it: a matter-of-fact business, in Prior's and Burleigh's eyes; a battle poem in Steevens's.[19] But all these men (except perhaps Nevinson) had made the vicarious war a familiar and acceptable part of the Victorian experience.

First to go over the ridge were the Devons – nine hundred anonymous brown dots merging into the veld. Except for the extended order, it was exactly like a field-day: company commanders blowing whistles, the men firing together in volleys. They rested, they doubled forward in regular lines, they fired again, all at regular intervals of time and space.[20] As a soldier himself, Nevinson admired the performance: better than they go 'in the bottoms of the Old Fox Hill at Aldershot', he remarked.

Through his high-powered field-glasses, Nevinson could also see the Devons' opponents a mile and a half from where he was standing. 'One man in black,' he later wrote, 'I watched for what seemed a very long time. He was standing right against the skyline, sometimes waving his arms apparently to give directions. Shells burst over his head, and bullets must have been thick about him. Once or twice he fell, as though slipping on the rocks, till at last shrapnel exploded right in his face, and he sank altogether like a rag doll.'[21]

But down in the valley, now concealed from Nevinson, the Devons, too, were wilting under the storm of magazine rifle fire. As the range reduced, the acting CO, Major Park, gave new orders: independent fire. He told the company commanders that Hamilton had instructed him not to press home the frontal attack until the Manchesters, the Gordons and the ILH had worked round the flank. Thankfully, the leading three companies of Devons threw themselves down behind the stones and ant heaps about nine hundred yards from the enemy's position facing them: a small kopje shaped like a sugar-loaf.[22] It was a surprise to the men that they had had so few casualties: 'only Hant heaps to cover us,' as Drummer Boulden of D Company later wrote home, 'and then we had to lay down flat and the Bullits came round us quite thick and we hadvanced in such a splendid order they said they were sirprised to see it and said we hadvanced just like a stone wall, and so we did....'[23]

Meanwhile, the main battle was raging to the right of the Devons, where the Manchesters had run up against the forward position of Kock's mounted riflemen. The Manchesters were in three lines at the time, and the Colonel gave the order: lie down, and commence volley firing. The invisible Boers responded with a perfect storm of Mauser fire.[24] Captain Newbigging, the Adjutant, could find absolutely no cover on the grassy slope. He lay flat, like his men, as the bullets slapped into the veld, kicking earth over him. On his right, a man was hit in the stomach and began to make the most pitiful noises. At long last the front line of Boers, hidden in the rocks ahead of them, withdrew to the main position on the hog's-back ridge to the right of the sugar-loaf. Newbigging ran forward to tell the firing line to advance. And so the Manchesters pushed round the corner of the horseshoe, with the Gordons and the ILH wheeling round to the right of them. As the companies doubled forward, Newbigging looked at his watch. It was 3.47 p.m. So far the battle had only lasted seventeen minutes.[25]

It was now the turn of the Gordons, the old 92nd. As the Colonel, Dick-Cunyngham, led his men forward in a kind of zig-zag formation, Sir George White cantered past on his charger. The General had just arrived from Lady-smith – not to take over the tactical command from French, but simply to be present as a spectator.[26] (The convention was accepted in small wars of the period.) Sir George waved to some of the officers he knew. 'Look at my boys.... I was in that regiment once.'[27] He had last seen the 92nd in action when he commanded it in the Afghan War. He looked pleased – pleased and proud.

But the gallant old 92nd was soon in still worse trouble than either the Devons or the Manchesters. Despite those attempts to camouflage themselves with khaki and cow-dung, the Highlanders were natural targets. Their dark green kilts stood out against the grey-brown veld; and the bull's eye, so to speak, was the place where the black and white sporran hung below the Highlander's belt. As soon as the men reached the skyline at the southern end of the horseshoe, they were caught by a monsoon rain of rifle fire. To add to their difficulties, a barbed wire fence happened to run along the crest of the main ridge they had to cross. By various means they cut gaps in the wire. One of the officers, Lord George Murray, had a pair of pliers. A private snapped a piece of the wire by sheer strength. Mauser bullets completed the work. But the battalion was now losing officers fast. Dick-Cunyngham was hit a hundred yards beyond the fence; his arm was broken. He rose and ran a few paces, shouting, 'On men, I'm coming!'

Then he fainted. Men pushed forward in rushes, firing independently. 'Advance – cease-fire – advance!' The whistles blew. The bullets splashed round them. Men groped and stumbled over their fallen comrades. At long last, the front companies of the Gordons found themselves in the lee of a stony hollow below the hog's-back ridge.[28]

It was at this moment – about 4.30 p.m. – that Steevens and the other war correspondents saw the sky darken, and a full-blooded African thunderstorm swept across the veld. At first, the enemy's position on the skyline was illuminated in eerie detail, each balloon of white shrapnel brilliant against the black sky. Then the air was filled with a hissing sound. Horses trembled and turned their backs to the storm. The dusty veld turned to mud. The battlefield vanished behind a curtain of swooping water.[29]

For the British infantry waiting below the hog's-back ridge, the storm was the moment. The Gordons slowly began to climb the steep hillside, covered in broken stones. On their left, the Manchesters were going at the hill in great style; the men had their blood up.[30] On their right, the Imperial Light Horse had left their horses in shelter and were strung out across the hillside, led by Colonel John Scott Chisholme, waving a Lancer's red scarf (his old regiment's) tied to a walking-stick.[31]

Even now the attack might have faltered, had not the Brigadier, Ian Hamilton, ridden up and pushed his way forwards to the firing-line. He gave the order: 'Fix bayonets. Charge!' Drum-Major Lawrence of the Gordons rushed into the open to play the call. The men gave a tremendous cheer. It was answered by the sound of the Devons' bugler floating up from the valley below. The Devons had resumed their frontal attack.[32]

As Hamilton groped his way upwards behind the ILH he could see Colonel Chisholme's red silk scarf leading the race for the summit. It was a splendid sight, he later wrote, to see Jabber Chisholme's 'little red rag going on and on'.[33] At last the inevitable happened: poor Chisholme fell, shot through legs, lung and head. Woolls-Sampson, the second-in-command, was shot in the thigh. Half the ILH was down. But the swirling, panting, stumbling line of infantry pressed on, fixing their bayonets as they ran.[34]

The first of the attackers to breast the ridge was the Adjutant of the Manchesters, Captain Newbigging. He jumped over a roughly built stone wall, used as a defence line. The Boers had not waited for the bayonets but were firing from a new position two hundred yards away. At first Newbigging's men lay down themselves. 'Our men were so pumped,' he said later, 'they had to return their fire for a few minutes. Then we charged again and they again hooked it and took up another position, which we cleared them out of.' Newbigging now saw one of the Boers' field-guns straight ahead of him, lying abandoned. 'I went for the gun, as hard as ever I could split, and had a great race with a sergeant-drummer of the Gordons, whom I beat by a short head. I then sat on the gun and waited for some of our men to come and take possession.'[35]

It was 5.55 p.m. and victory was assured – so it appeared. Down below the hog's-back of Kock's laager in the gathering twilight, Boers could be seen saddling their ponies and galloping off. Somebody had hoisted a white flag. Hamilton, who had now joined Newbigging on the crest of the ridge, gave the order, 'Cease fire, and let the cavalry in!' Already, true to the field-day principle of stopping when the objective was gained, the troops had grounded their rifles.[36]

But the white flag suddenly vanished. A Boer counter-attack from the rocks below (actually led by General Kock himself) sent the British reeling back forty yards. Newbigging himself had stepped forward to take a prisoner, and had his back to the Boer camp when the storm of firing burst out. He was knocked ten yards by the blast, and lay on the ground with a great gash in his back.[37] Beside him, Lieutenant Danks was mortally wounded. The Gordons and ILH suffered as heavily. The small group of Boers, led by Kock, in a frock-coat and a black top-hat, emptied their magazines into them at fifty yards' range. At Hamilton's side, Major Denne was shot dead. In the confusion, the British line began to recoil from the top of the hill, the soldiers from different units all mixed up. And some Boer gunners emerged again from the rocks to fire a wild round or two.[38]

But the confusion was only momentary. Staff officers ran up, waving their swords. Imploring and cursing, they shoved the men back into the line. Hamilton himself was conspicuous in the front. The pipes began to skirl. Drummer May of the Gordons sounded the advance. And in a moment the heaving mass of kilts poured back across the crest line. The Boers' firing stopped abruptly. The whole affair had only lasted a few minutes. At the same time, the front companies of the Devons had at last cleared the crest of the position by the sugar-loaf.[39] One of the war correspondents who had come up to the firing-line saw the moment of triumph: 'Then wildly cheering, raising their helmets on their bayonets, while line after line of khaki figures, like hounds through a gap, came pouring into position, shouting fiercely: "Majuba, Majuba".'[40]

The infantry had triumphed. Now for the cavalry charge.

In recent years the *arme blanche* of the British army had been something of a disappointment on the battlefield. In the broken country of India's North-West Frontier, regular cavalry were almost useless in attack. At Omdurman the 9th Lancers had made their famous charge – and paid dearly for it. At Talana Möller's cavalry had ridden away – into the arms of the enemy.[41] But here on the veld, as flat as Salisbury Plain, facing a defeated army, here was the chance for cavalry to show what they were made of.

This final act in the battle did not receive the full attention of the war correspondents. They had a long ride back to Ladysmith to cable home their stories. 'Triumph for British arms. . . . Majuba in Reverse.'[42] And anyway, there were certain pungent features of the cavalry charge which were decidedly unacceptable in the Victorian drawing-room. Steevens wrote a brief peroration: 'There also – thank Heaven, thank Heaven! – were squadrons of Lancers and Dragoon Guards storming in among them, shouting, spearing, stamping them into the ground. Cease fire.'[43] Only Nevinson gave any hint of the reality of the charge, which now turned the veld into half a mile of butcher's shop.[44]

The charge of four hundred horsemen galloping across a plain is designed to be an irresistible force. It does not stop simply because the enemy would like to surrender. 'Draw sabres – lances!' In neat lines, the Dragoons and Lancers began to thunder across the plain. It was now six o'clock and twilight was turning fast to darkness. Half a mile away, the Boers, unaware of their danger, had saddled up their ponies and begun to jog back the way they had come. The charging line of horsemen caught them broadside, like the steel prow of a destroyer smashing into the side of a wooden boat. People heard the crunch of the impact – steel against leather and bone and muscle – and saw the flash of the officers' revolvers, and heard the screams of the Boers trying to give themselves up. The Lancers and Dragoons swept on, leaving dozens of Boers, and some of their African retainers, spiked and slashed on the ground. Back came the cavalry for a second charge.[45] ('Most excellent pig-sticking ... for about ten minutes, the bag being about sixty,' said one of the officers later.)[46] Again the shouts and the screams. The Boers fell off their horses and rolled among the rocks, calling for mercy – calling to be shot, anything to escape the stab of the lances. But a story had got round that the Boers had abused a flag of truce and, anyway, the order was: no prisoners.[47]

A third charge, but this time the charge lacked the original demonic momentum. Even the most eager troopers found the fight had lost some of its exhilaration. One of them later wrote, 'We went along sticking our lances through them – it was a terrible thing, but you have to do it. ... '[48] Nevinson himself talked to a corporal of the Dragoons, who told him, 'We just gave them a good dig as they lay.' And most of the lances were bloody after the battle.[49]

By now it was 6.30 and night had fallen, a swift African night, accompanied by a Scotch drizzle. The Indian stretcher-bearers tramped backwards and forwards collecting up the wounded in doolies. The unwounded British soldiers took refuge from the rain in the station at Elandslaagte. General Hamilton himself had to climb under a wagon to find shelter.[50] There were no proper lights. Somebody found a lantern and candles. The Tommies began to boast about their experiences. For one of the officers this was the worst part of the whole battle.[51]

Out on the rocky hillside, the wounded of both nationalities lay in the mud and the cold. Sir George White had sent out only one doctor from Ladysmith. Many of the wounded had to lie there on the hillside all night.[52] Woolls-Sampson was helpless, with his broken thigh; he marked the position of the gallant charge of the ILH.[53] Despite the wound, Woolls-Sampson was content enough. The Boers had lost even more men than the British. Commandant Viljoen had fled. Dr Coster (the ex-State Attorney), Van Leggelo (the State Prosecutor) and about sixty others were dead. General Kock was dying, shot in the side. His nephew, Philip Kock, was wounded. It was his son, the twenty-six-year-old judge, who had driven the Uitlanders to a frenzy by his verdict in the Edgar case.[54]

Next day the survivors of Kock's commandos were marched through the streets of Ladysmith past crowds of Africans, many of whom were ex-miners from the Rand. *'Upi pass, upi pass?'* ('Where's your pass, where's your pass?') the Africans shouted derisively.

To Woolls-Sampson and the ILH it was a victory of a still more personal sort. The slate had been wiped clean at last. The Johannesburg Commando had been annihilated. There would be no more talk of those two white flags.

CHAPTER 13

The Knock-down Blow

Dundee and Ladysmith,
22 October – 2 November 1899

'Long before this reaches you most important events will
have taken place and I shall be either a man or a mouse.'

Lieutenant-General Sir George White
to his brother, 27 October 1899

'In the dead of night we are on the move,' wrote Gunner Netley in the diary he
kept in his haversack. 'Strict orders against striking matches, and no talking
aloud. I would not have minded the talking part of the business being stopped,
but to have to go without a smoke puts my pipe properly out. Of course it
was the correct thing to do as a light would have shown the Bores what we are
up to.'[1]

What we are up to. What indeed? It was a question to which Netley's own
officers, and Major-General James Yule himself, Symons's replacement as
commander of the Dundee garrison, would have dearly liked an answer. It was
Sunday night, the third night after the victory at Talana, and Yule's four infantry
battalions looked anything but victors. There they lay, not even daring to light a
fire; no tents, not even blankets or groundsheets for some, on the stony hillside,
south of the town of Dundee. Officers as well as men, were huddled up in
greatcoats against the freezing rain.[2] And invisible above them in the mist of
Mount Impati, commanding every movement they made on their own side of
the valley, tossing a 6-inch shell from time to time across the intervening four
miles of space, was a thirty-foot long steel prodigy, one of Joubert's new
Creusot siege guns, a Long Tom.'[3]

A few people tried to see the humour in their predicament. Netley wrote, 'We
have not got wonderful mutch ammunition to waste at preasant.' He added,
cheerfully, that they were now cut off and short of food as well as ammunition.[4]
Netley actually possessed many of the admirable qualities that the British public
expected of British privates. He was a farm-worker's son from Pulborough,
Sussex. He and his four brothers had joined the colours after being sacked by the
local farmer ('that fellow,' he would tell his mates, 'he was the best recruiting
sergeant the British army ever had'), and in due course he had found life as a
soldier on a shilling a day preferable to life on sixpence a day as a shepherd. If any
British war correspondents had seen him, Netley would have seemed the very
incarnation of Tommy Atkins. He had that 'unmistakable' imperturbability

that was considered the hallmark of the common soldier. Yet, as he later admitted, these days trapped at Dundee were some of the worst of his life.[5]

Netley's mates – in fact, most of the Dundee garrison – did not look, or even try to look, imperturbable. They had been bowled over by the rush of events. Two days before, they had won a drill-book victory at Talana. Lucas Meyer's commando had been driven back across the Transvaal frontier. But Joubert refused to play by the rules and acknowledge his defeat. His forces had now occupied Mount Impati in overwhelming strength. On Saturday, the day after Talana, they began to shell the Dundee camp with the first of their Long Toms, the Krupp 40-pounder that far outranged the British 15-pounders.[6] According to the book of rules (including the War Office's own secret handbook, *Military Notes on the Dutch Republics*), it should have been out of the question to remove a Long Tom from the forts at Pretoria and take it into the field, let alone install it on the top of a mountain.[7]

As the first of the 5-inch shells began to plump into the valley, killing an officer (he was a young subaltern of the Leicesters, called Hanna, who had volunteered to come out 'for the fun of it'), a state bordering on panic began to seize the British garrison.[8] The world of the field-day – the cosy Aldershot world of umpires and flags and whistles and drill-books – had collapsed into nightmare. That was the message of Joubert's great gun, as it tolled like a bell, in the mist above their heads.

Despite the twelve-foot-high Red Cross flag – the internationally accepted flag of the newly signed Geneva Convention – shells crashed into the field hospitals beside the military camp. A stampede ensued. Major Kerin, the CO of the 26th Field Hospital, found it a 'cruel sight' to see heavily bandaged men crawling out of the hospital tents, some dragging broken legs, to try to escape the shelling. Major Donegan, who commanded the 18th Field Hospital, found most of his medical staff, including one of the army doctors who had been drunk and incapable throughout Friday's battle, had abandoned their posts and fled to the town.[9]

Yule's fighting men did not show such indiscipline; they were not exposed to such danger as the wounded or medical staff. Yule's men had moved to a new camp under the lee of a kopje. Yet that second night after the battle seemed an 'awful night' to Lieutenant Trench, of the 69th Battery. 'Everyone seemed very jumpy and frightened,' he wrote in his diary, 'being under the impression that we were surrounded by the enemy. The batteries formed three sides of a square, and were prepared for case [shot], on the chance of their trying a night rush. We stood to till 2 a.m. in pouring rain.... Every now and then some infantry sentry got the jim-jams and fired off his gun into the dark at nothing.... People became very despondent now as General Yule seemed unable to issue any orders.'[10]

It was not only the sentries who had got the jim-jams. Symons's wild optimism had placed Yule in a predicament that would have tested the most talented and experienced general. Poor Yule was neither. He was an elderly regimental officer, the Devonshires' old CO from India, suddenly promoted by events to the rank of major-general. Already his health was giving way.[11] The strains of victory at Talana seem to have unnerved him and that victory had been marred by the disappearance of Colonel Möller and half his cavalry, whose capture had just been confirmed. Now, with the prospect of his own capture, Yule had become prey to a sort of reckless inertia.

On Saturday – that is, the morning of the Battle of Elandslaagte – Yule signalled to General White begging for reinforcements. White's Chief Staff Officer replied that none could be spared.[12] On Sunday morning, Yule's men heard a burst of cheering from the signallers who had caught the flash of White's heliograph: White had won the Battle of Elandslaagte, and the Boers were believed to be in full retreat. This news was confirmed by a wire from White to Yule, sent by way of Helpmakaar, along a telegraph line the Boers had left uncut. Momentarily Yule recovered his nerve. He ordered the Dundee garrison to march westwards along the valley towards the main road at Glencoe, where it was reported they might be able to intercept the Boers fleeing northwards. But after a day's marching and counter-marching, and the mysterious loss of still more of Yule's few remaining cavalry, it became clear that, like other reports of the elusive Boers, these intelligence reports were fables. Joubert's men, hovering round them in the mist, had sealed off the valley on at least three sides.[13]

On Sunday afternoon Yule still dithered. White would not help him. Well, he would dig in on the top of Talana Hill and try to sit things out. At this point several of his senior officers explained the realities: they were surrounded by ten thousand men, they were short of artillery ammunition, their guns were out-ranged, and they had no defensible water supply. Their only hope was to try and break out of the valley by the Helpmakaar road. Yule gloomily agreed.[14] An hour or so later a wire arrived from Sir George White endorsing Yule's decision. 'I cannot reinforce you without sacrificing Ladysmith and the Colony behind – You must try and fall back on Ladysmith.'[15] If Yule was relieved at White's taking the responsibility, the decision to retreat was still intensely humiliating. Since the days of the Peninsular War, there was hardly a precedent for this. Moreover, only a fortnight before, White had decided that the political risks of peacefully withdrawing Symons's force from Dundee were too great to balance the military advantages. Now, throwing those political arguments to the wind, White was ordering Yule to leave to the enemy not only the town of Dundee, but the garrison's two months' supply of food and stores, and also to abandon their own wounded officers and men, including Symons.[16]

The rain had hardly ceased all day. Indeed, but for the rain and the mist, the garrison would have suffered more from the attentions of the Creusot Long Tom. The night was intensely dark, but fortunately the rain ceased as the column laboriously formed up by sections, the men groping and stumbling over the rocks. Only the officers knew that a retreat had been ordered. The men still believed they were going to encamp on Talana and the townspeople of Dundee were equally left in ignorance.[17] At about 10 p.m. the column moved off. The men marched, as Gunner Netley noted, with no lights, and no talking. Each man took only what he could carry. The officers had to abandon their kits, including the coloured jackets they wore in the mess, and the bandsmen their drums and trumpets. As it was, the column, including the artillery wagons drawn by spans of mules and oxen, uncoiled over four miles, and the men were dog-tired before they began. It was past midnight before the tail of the shuffling, stumbling procession finally cleared the town, passing within less than a mile of the enemy's position, and guided by officers who had tied white handkerchiefs round their waists. Dawn found them astride the south-east shoulder of the Biggarsberg. Soon after, the column was ordered to rest. They had covered twelve miles from the town, fourteen from their camp. No one could doubt they were retreating now. Officers and men threw themselves down beside the road, sleeping in the mud, just as they were.[18]

The Biggarsberg is a carpet of downland, smooth and green at this time of year: more like hills than mountains, despite the romantic names, Dundee and Glencoe, given them by the early Scottish settlers. But there was one six-mile-long pass called Van Tonders Nek, on this south-easterly road from Dundee. It was a rugged, narrow defile. Given a determined leader, it was the place where a few men could lay ambush to an army. Hence Yule's anxieties as the column approached Van Tonders Nek. By ten o'clock on Monday they had resumed the march, led by the Royal Irish Fusiliers. Yule changed his mind after a couple of hours. The men found the sun, blazing down on the treeless downs, almost as trying as the rain of the previous days. Better to halt until darkness. There were also intelligence reports that the Boers lay in wait ahead of them.[19]

At about 11.00 p.m., the march was resumed. The moon rose as they approached Van Tonders. The column must have sounded like a funeral procession, with the silence magnifying the rumble of the wagons, the clank of metal horseshoes on stone, and the jingle of the gun-carriages. It was the music of defeat. Yet, when dawn came on Tuesday morning, the column had emerged from the pass. They were safe. Ahead the dusty road ran down to the Waschbank River and the plains by Elandslaagte. As the column rested by the track, a visible change came over the soldiers. No more jim-jams. Baked by the sun, drenched by the rain, puttees encasing their legs like tubes of clay, hollow-eyed after four nights without sleep, hollow-bellied after four days on bully beef and biscuits. Yet somebody sat on a rock and began to sing a music-hall song. Someone else began to kick a football around. And soon afterwards, to welcome the 'imperturbable' Tommy Atkins, who never lost his British phlegm, the first war correspondent rode out from Ladysmith and hailed the column.[20]

In fact, the column had never been in any real danger. After it had left Dundee the Boer generals – with characteristic caution – had decided to content themselves with capturing the town and camp from the medical officers and wounded men whom Yule had abandoned there. There was no opposition, although the pack store sergeant in Major Kerin's hospital dramatically enquired if he was to call out the Hospital Guard to repel the enemy's attack. The Hospital Guard consisted of a lance-corporal and three men, and the sergeant was told not to be such a fool.[21] They had problems enough. The two senior RAMC officers – Majors Kerin and Donegan – had only learnt late the previous night that they and their hospitals were to be abandoned. Yule had sent a staff officer with the astonishing message: the retreat had been ordered by Sir George White, and Kerin and Donegan must make the best arrangements they could with the enemy. After spending a hard night supervising the removal of stores from the military camp (the hospitals themselves had been left without even a water cart), the two majors waited for capture.

However, despite the Red Cross flag, at 10.30 a.m. shells once again plumped into the hospital tents from the Long Tom on Mount Impati, and caused panic among both the staff and the patients. The stampede only halted when Donegan threatened to shoot the next man who left his tent.[22] It was now apparent to Donegan and Kerin that they must surrender Dundee in the interests of their patients, even if the surrender would reveal the secret of Yule's escape to the Boers. Accordingly, a white flag was hoisted over the hospitals, and an RAMC captain rode up the stony track to the Boers' camp, carrying a second white flag. A long, anxious silence. Then, about half past twelve, two Boers, field cornets in ordinary civilian clothes, rode down the track to Dundee.

They asked Donegan and Kerin this question: was it true that British soldiers had tied wounded Boer prisoners to their gun-carriages and dragged them round the field after the battle?[23] Having received a formal denial of these atrocities and an agreement by the British to hand over all their arms, the Boers accepted the surrender of the town and camp. Donegan's sword, revolver, field-glasses and horse were taken from him; otherwise, he was treated civilly by Boer officers.[24] Yet the scenes that followed were painful enough to British officers, brought up in a military tradition in which surrender was supposed to be a fate worse than death.

Thousands of Boers rode down into the camp, where they found the tents laid out in neat lines, just as they had been left by the British battalions the previous morning. After taking whatever they chose, they reached the hospitals. By this time, some of them had begun to celebrate their victory. A drunken soldier with a loaded rifle lurched into the tent where Major Kerin stood, and kept repeating, 'I want to shoot the British officers.' He then struck one of the Boer field cornets, hitting him in the mouth with the butt end of his rifle. The field cornet took to his heels. There seemed to be no discipline of any sort among them. Over in Donegan's hospital, two other drunken Boers with rifles appeared at the tent door and Donegan found it understandably trying to have them chasing each other backwards and forwards, trying to shoot each other, through the tents full of wounded men. Later in the evening, the hospital staff heard the Boers who had looted the town of Dundee riding past their tents, singing and shouting from exhilaration and drink. Apart from the vast quantity of stores they had looted – forty days' supplies for five thousand men – they carried off as trophies the regimental candlesticks, the brass trumpets of the bands and the elaborate coloured uniforms that officers wore in the mess. They also discovered something else of value: Symons's code-books and his other papers, including his copy of the War Office's secret handbook, *Military Notes*.[25]

If the senior British army officers, Kerin and Donegan, could do nothing to restrain the victors' exuberance, they tried at least to keep their own men from misbehaving. That afternoon, after the two drunken Boers had left Donegan's hospital, a formal little ceremony took place there. Four of the Indian medical orderlies had been found to have left the tents without permission and were accused of looting stuff from the Boers. Donegan sentenced one of them to death (it was later commuted) and had the other three publicly flogged. The public flogging, he found, had an 'excellent moral effect' on the rest of the natives. It was a relief for Donegan, among all those bewildering scenes, to be able to keep up British standards in such exemplary fashion.[26]

That same Monday afternoon, while the Boers looted the tents around him, General Sir Penn Symons finally expired. Despite morphia injections, he had suffered a good deal of pain from the bullet wound in his stomach. He was sick frequently. Added to this was the anguish of hearing that Yule had decided to abandon him to the enemy. He was conscious, but very weak when Kerin came to visit him just before he died. The pain had lessened. He kept saying, 'Tell everyone I died facing the enemy, tell everyone I died facing the enemy,' and he left Kerin in no doubt that he regarded Yule's retreat as a betrayal. 'I would never have done it.'[27]

Next morning the camp was calm. General Erasmus, the Boer commander, visited the hospital to express his condolences on Symons's death. Would it be too presumptuous, he said, if he asked to see the face of the dead General? He had always heard he was so brave. Kerin took him to the general's tent and raised the sheet. 'It is a pity – this war,' said Erasmus with his blunt sincerity. The body was sewn into a Union Jack and taken in procession to the Church of England cemetery. All the hospital staff stood to attention, and so did the wounded, those who could stand. The Boers raised their hats as the cortège passed, and many of them attended the funeral. The cemetery was on the east side of the town, below the splintered eucalyptus wood and the shell-shattered hill of Talana where Symons had won his hollow victory.[28]

Less edifying was the ceremony to dispose of the mangled or bullet-riddled bodies of seven officers and twenty-eight NCOs and men, the victims of Friday's battle. In the haste of his departure, Yule had forgotten to give orders for their burial. Six Kohar hospital sweepers, Donegan's men from India, now carried the bodies, much decomposed, to be identified. It was barely possible to distinguish the officers from the men, but two RAMC captains did their best. The bodies were buried in four graves, according to estimated rank. A few days later, Kerin and thirty slightly wounded men were sent north as prisoners to Pretoria, while Donegan and the more seriously wounded were sent back towards the British lines – back to their comrades at Ladysmith, but not to safety.[29]

* * * * * *

Meanwhile, Yule and the Dundee column had themselves joined hands with White's scouts and marched, or rather staggered, into Ladysmith. That Wednesday's and Thursday's march, during the night of 25–26 October, was described in his characteristically jaunty style by Gunner Netley:

The General came in with an escort of lancers and told us that his force was ... 8 miles further ahead, and of course that bucked us up a bit. He left orders for us to join him, so we moved off amid a drenching rain, and we had not got far before the column was reported broken (in two), which ment another hower's waiting in the Natal April shower. It is also very dark, and what with the roads being about 6 inches deep in mud, it is beautiful. We can't move along sharp because the waggons, which would if not taken in hand properly, probably fall into a donga [ravine] and then something would happen you could bet. At 12 midnight that April shower is still showering and the drenched column is sticking it like Britons, and at 4 am we passed the other column in camp, thank God. It would have done your eye good to see the difference in Tommy that morning, and see the same man at home. ... Worn out, wet through, covered in mud from head to foot. ... A Kodak would have been useful on the scene then especially when the drying clothes business came off. Fancy taking off everything and while it is drying to keep yourself to yourself by running around like a Kaffir. When the clothes were on again, we proceeded again with the column towards Ladysmith and reached it all correct, properly worn out ... the march was a verry long one. Indeed some think it beats Roberts' [march to Kandahar].[30]

Whatever the achievements of Yule and his men – and the chief credit for their escape must go to Joubert, who had decided against pursuit – the Dundee column found the Ladysmith garrison too preoccupied to give them much of a welcome. True, the Dublins were given a special dinner by the Devonshires. But it was no time for celebrations, and anyway, the men of the Dundee column fell asleep as they ate; a man, his chin covered with a week's growth of beard, would take his canteen and be sound asleep before he could put bread and cheese to his lips. When the Dublins' acting CO, Major Bird, rode into the town to report personally to White's headquarters, it was noticed that he was fast asleep in the saddle.[31]

Sir George White had set up his headquarters in the local convent, a pleasant, tin-roofed, red-brick bungalow built on a wooded terrace about a hundred feet above the town. From below, the dust rose in clouds. Ladysmith was the third largest town in the colony and an unpretentious place, as it remains today – a town of two parallel streets, lined with tin-roofed houses and mud-and-wattle shanties for the Africans. If there is a public monument, it is the Town Hall, crowned with a baroque clock tower. If it has a heart, it lies in the wooden-canopied railway station. It was the railway junction that gave life to Ladysmith.[32] Into this dusty outpost of the Empire, White had then crammed thirteen thousand troops, with all the sinews of war. Everywhere there were bell-tents, literally thousands of them, pitched wherever there was a flat piece of ground. Every hour trains steamed into the station carrying new stores: crates of ammunition, boxes of beef, sacks of flour, blankets, tents and medical supplies; bales of compressed forage for the three thousand horses, mealies for the African drivers and grooms. All these stores had to be trundled through the streets on mule-carts or sixteen-span teams of ox wagons. Churches and schools were requisitioned as supply dumps. Here the crates were unloaded – enough to supply the whole Natal army for a siege of three months.[33]

Yet to allow himself to be besieged at Ladysmith was the very last thing White had in mind, that Thursday, 26 October, as the Dundee column staggered into the town. He had only to look out of the windows of the convent to see that Ladysmith was a most unsuitable town, set in a most unsuitable piece of country, in which to let his thirteen thousand men be locked up. Ladysmith straddled the north-west edge of a sandy plain. It was a hot, dusty, disease-ridden, claustrophobic town, walled in on every side by a circle of ridges and hills.[34]

British soldiers had given several of these hills the familiar names of the country around Aldershot: the wooded table-land to the south-west was dubbed 'Wagon Hill' and 'Caesar's camp'. They were not ill-chosen names. Since 1897, Ladysmith had been made into the principal British supply base and training ground in the colony. It was the 'Aldershot of Natal'.[35] There was no question of it being a suitable place for fortification and garrisoning in the time of war. Dominated by those hills, it would have been an absurdity. What British general, retreating before French or German invaders, would have dreamt of trying to take shelter within the walls of Aldershot?

Moreover, the terrain around Ladysmith compounded the disadvantages of choosing it as a place to defend. If White's army was besieged there, a second force would have to be sent to relieve it. The relief force would have to march through that tangle of kopjes and ravines that White had seen from the train: the tangle that made the north bank of the Tugela a natural fortress for the besiegers. Yet only fifteen miles south of Ladysmith, at Colenso on the south bank of the Tugela, one returned to the veld, the familiar landscape of South Africa. It was to these smooth plains, watered by a series of rivers flowing down from the Drakensberg, that White could now retreat in safety. If the enemy proved too strong, he could then retreat, by stages, farther down the railway line.[36] At all costs, as Buller had repeated over and over again, he must not let himself be besieged. 'Do not go north of the Tugela.'[37] Once locked up in Ladysmith, he would become a strategic liability. He had been given two strategic objectives as the commander of the Natal Field Force: to defend Natal, and to prepare the way for Buller's invasion force. If he lost the initiative, he would sabotage Buller's whole plan of campaign. He would also endanger the lives of his own men if he let them be shut up in a garrison town best known for its typhoid.[38]

Such was the case, both tactical and strategic, against acquiescing in a siege. White not only acknowledged this line of reasoning; he accepted that it was on balance overwhelmingly strong. The case against garrisoning Ladysmith was basically the case against garrisoning Dundee: it was the forward strategy that had proved so disastrous.[39] Those political counter-arguments pressed by the Governor of Natal had already been proved to be exaggerated. Symons's garrison had been sent packing from Dundee without precipitating a rising of either Afrikaners or Zulus. The military arguments for occupying Dundee had been buried with Symons in the graveyard below Talana. His death had proved the correctness of the conventional strategic textbooks: if a field force is to remain a field force and not become a helpless garrison, it must either destroy its opponents, or at least be able to keep open its lines of communication. If neither is possible, it must retreat.[40] White knew that his force at Ladysmith, like Symons's at Dundee, was stretched too thin to defend the railway line to the south. Why, then, not retreat, at least south of the Tugela? Those trains carrying mountains of beef and flour and ammunition into Ladysmith – why were they not now steaming back down the railway line towards Colenso?

Moreover, the political arguments that had tipped the balance, in White's mind, in favour of the forward policy had now been transferred to the other end of the scales. Hely-Hutchinson, the Governor of Natal, had suddenly become extremely alarmed for the safety of Maritzburg, the capital. By concentrating his forces at Ladysmith, White had reduced the Maritzburg garrison to a handful of volunteers. 'We are practically defenceless here and in Durban', cabled the Governor, begging for reinforcements. There were unconfirmed reports that Joubert was planning to bypass Ladysmith, push through Zululand and strike for the coast.[41] The Governor's *cri de coeur* made one thing obvious. He would not have objected if White left Ladysmith. So why ever did White stay?

The answer was simple. White hoped there would be no question of a siege. He gambled on being strong enough, though outnumbered, to destroy Joubert by a 'knock-down blow'.[42]

It may seem odd that White, of all men, was prepared to risk everything on this bold gamble. From the first, as we saw, he had felt demoralized. His fears for Dundee – momentarily allayed by the victories at Talana and Elandslaagte, then confirmed by Yule's retreat – left him sleepless and mentally exhausted.[43] In fact, the most sanguine commander would have felt anxious about the position of the Natal Field Force. Throughout that week, evidence of its weakness had accumulated. The intelligence officers reported that there were 24,800 Boers with forty guns (actually an overestimate) opposed to his own force of thirteen thousand and fifty odd guns. The Boer guns included the devastating Long Toms. True, the British had won their two victories. But these had only restored the strategic *status quo;* they merely redeemed the strategic errors of Symons. Moreover, neither was an unqualified tactical success. Talana had been marred by five hundred casualties, including the loss of Möller's cavalry. A numerically superior British force had won the battle, but had suffered twice as many casualties as the enemy. At Elandslaagte, too, the British forces had had the advantage of numbers. What if General Kock had fought General French on equal terms, or just suppose the numbers had been reversed?[44]

To underline this weakness, it emerged on that Tuesday, 24 October, that four of White's battalions of infantry, supported by artillery and mounted troops, could not make much headway against a party of Boers dug into some hills at Rietfontein, eight miles north of Ladysmith. White had sent the brigade there to prevent the Free State Boers joining hands with the Transvaal Boers, and so cutting the line of Yule's retreat. He had achieved this limited object, but the Boers held their ridge of hills and suffered little. The British on the contrary, lost 114 killed and wounded, including the CO of the Gloucesters, Colonel Wilford, who inexplicably broke cover at the height of the action and led forward to destruction one company and the battalion Maxim gun.[45] Wilford was the third CO to die since the war had begun and the Natal Field Force had now lost seventy-three officers – proportionately twice as many as the men – a token of what *The Times* called 'personal leadership at all risk'.[46]

Such was the accumulated evidence of the first fortnight's fighting. It only confirmed Buller's original advice not to advance beyond the Tugela. Yet White still clung to the hope of dealing that knock-down blow. It was an error of judgement that was to have the most fatal consequences: the greatest strategic mistake of the entire war. Why, then, did White make it?

To some extent, he was merely expressing the conventional British general's ignorance of the realities of large-scale war. For half a century Britain had fought small wars against the disunited and ill-armed tribesmen of India and Africa. Often these wars had begun with shattering reverses; small bodies of men, surrounded by savages who gave no quarter, had fought to the last cartridge. In due course, the main British army would come on the scene and inflict a crushing and permanent defeat on the enemy. There was little strategic, or even tactical, manoeuvring, by European standards. To transport and supply his men in desert or jungle – that was the chief problem of the British general. The actual fighting was usually simple by comparison. So it had been for Roberts in Afghanistan, Wolseley in Egypt and Kitchener at Omdurman. The campaign might take months, but the decisive battle could be fought in a matter of hours. War was a one-day event, as practised on Salisbury Plain. Hence it was as natural for White to try to deal a knock-down blow to Joubert, as for Symons to try to deal one against Lucas Meyer.[47]

But there was more to White's error than inexperience of war. He was also a weak man. He knew that his force was inferior in many ways to Joubert's. He believed that if he failed to beat Joubert in the field and he was locked up in Ladysmith, nothing could save Natal. Yet he lacked the moral strength to follow the logic of this and make a fighting retreat. Weak and vacillating and dominated by a fear of appearing so, he was now to stake everything on a single reckless throw.[48]

On Thursday 26 October, White was still looking for a chance to strike out. The enemy was everywhere – and nowhere. The Africans reported them 'like locusts on the land'. He realized he had failed to prevent the Free State forces joining those of the Transvaal. On Friday White learnt that the vanguard of the main Boer army had reached a position about four miles east of Ladysmith. He sent out French to reconnoitre, but recalled him when other Boer commandos, approaching from the north, seemed likely to outflank him.[49] Meanwhile, Ian Hamilton's scouts had reported that the enemy's main laager was almost undefended. He asked for permission to launch a night attack on it with four battalions: the Royal Irish Fusiliers and his own battalion, the Gordons, to lead the attack, which was to begin at 1.00 a.m. White gave permission. Then his nerve failed him. Only two hours before the attack was to begin, Hamilton was informed, to his own bitter disappointment, that White had cancelled the operation because of the risks.[50]

On Saturday, White's forces lay low in Ladysmith, except for part of French's cavalry, who made a desultory reconnaissance. On Sunday, White's spirits recovered again – so it seemed. He cabled to Hely-Hutchinson, 'Hope I have located a sufficiently strong force of the enemy with guns to make a good objective. Move out tonight with a view to attacking early tomorrow.'[51] In fact, White's new plan was of so wild a nature that almost all his staff – including Ian Hamilton – opposed it. 'Let us wait until the enemy is nearer,' they told him, 'and then let us strike.' But White was afraid this might be their last chance of striking out. Already the Boers had cut off the Ladysmith water supply. He insisted on fighting.[52]

The Boers were reported to be holding a position centred on Pepworth Hill, the large conical hill on the Ladysmith side of Rietfontein, about four miles north-east of the town. That day, Sunday, the Boers could be seen building a gun platform there, presumably for one of the Long Toms. White accepted the challenge. He proposed to send his two infantry brigades to storm Pepworth. Now that Yule had reported sick, Colonel Geoffrey Grimwood, the senior colonel, was to take the first brigade, consisting of the men who had marched back to Ladysmith with Yule – that is, the Leicesters, the Dublins, and the 1st Battalion of the 60th – plus the 2nd 60th and the Liverpools. Hamilton was to take the second brigade, consisting of the three battalions he had led to victory at Elandslaagte – the Devons, the Manchesters and the Gordons. Each brigade was to be supported by cavalry and artillery. The plan of attack was based on the success at Elandslaagte: first there would be an artillery barrage to soften the ground; then a flank attack would be launched on Pepworth by way of the hill to the east, capturing the enemy's guns; finally, the cavalry would roll up the fleeing Boers, pursuing them over the plain to the north.[53]

This was the basic plan – a rigid example of the old field-day formula. Its basic weakness was that, as White himself had put it, he '*hoped* he had located a sufficiently strong force of the enemy with guns to make a good objective'.[54] What if the Boers, all mounted and hence exceptionally mobile, decided not to provide the objective in the place he hoped? His plan did not allow any flexibility. It was like a series of chess moves devised without any regard for the moves of an opponent. And if the plan failed them, two British brigades would be forced to improvise one. They would be thrown back on to their own resources – a situation for which neither officers nor men had yet shown any great aptitude.

Yet this was not the feature of White's plan that alarmed his staff officers most. What gave it an air of absolute recklessness was that White proposed to send a second column on a night march through the enemy lines and station it at Nicholson's Nek, four miles to the rear of Pepworth. In some respects, the scheme was like Symons's reckless handling of his cavalry. Symons had merely given Möller and the 18th Hussars the *option* to act independently in the rear, and at least Möller's force was a mobile one. Lieutenant-Colonel Carleton, the CO of the Royal Irish Fusiliers, selected by White to lead the expedition to Nicholson's Nek, had been given no mounted troops of any sort. He had two battalions of infantry and the smallest of guns – a battery of mountain guns carried on mules. What Carleton was supposed to do was not entirely clear, certainly not to Carleton.[55] But White himself had two broad objectives in mind. First, Carleton was to protect the west flank of the infantry brigades as they stormed Pepworth. Second, he was to block the enemy's line of retreat as the cavalry pursued them across the plain.[56] The man who had actually proposed the scheme was one of White's Intelligence Officers, Major Adye. White had been greatly impressed. He was a 'capital officer', Major Adye, who knew 'every inch of the ground'. He assured White that he could seize the position if they made a night march, and, despite the weakness of the column, they could hold it for two days at all events.[57]

. At 11 o'clock on Sunday night, Carleton's column marched off on the track that led northwards to Nicholson's Nek, silent except for the thud-thud of boots and the rattle of the two hundred pack mules that carried the mountain guns and the ammunition. Soon after midnight, like an endless roll of drums, Grimwood's brigade, six miles of men and horses and guns and carts, trundled off along the Helpmakaar road to the east. Grimwood's brigade was followed by Hamilton's, led by Sir George White himself.[58] He had been woken at 3.00 a.m. and rode out to command the force in person. He would be leading his own regiment, the 'dear old 92nd'. As his staff officer, Colonel Rawlinson, passed the railway level-crossing, the first ominous reports reached them. Rawlinson met a 'scared-looking soldier belonging to the Gloucester Regiment'. It turned out that Carleton's column had already suffered a mishap; some pack mules had stampeded and vanished, carrying off the guns and spare ammunition.

White made no change in his plans. Just as dawn broke, he and his staff reached 'Limit Hill', a low ridge facing Pepworth.[59] In a few moments Grimwood's guns would open up from the folds of ground on their right, already silhouetted against the delicate tints of the eastern sky. It was going to be a perfect spring day.

Now for the knock-down blow.

A beaten army is not a pretty sight, except to the victors. There were no Boers to enjoy the sight of the British army in full retreat that morning. The Boers were still hidden beyond the hills. The witnesses were the British war correspondents. 'What shame!' wrote Steevens in a kind of paroxysm. 'What bitter shame for all the camp. All ashamed for England! Not of her – never that! – but for her. Once more she was a source of laughter to her enemies.'[60] The other war correspondents did not elaborate, except for Nevinson. He, too, was overwhelmed by the sight. 'Imperturbable Tommy Atkins': it was hardly the phrase that morning. Yet Nevinson had the courage to record what he saw: 'They came back slowly, tired and disheartened and sick with useless losses . . . as soon as they were out of range the men wandered away in groups to the town, sick and angry but longing above all things for water and sleep.'[61]

It was not only the fact of the retreat but the way that it was conducted that alarmed onlookers. The men's nerve had broken. That was the plain truth of it. The iron bonds of regimental tradition – the acts of self-sacrifice over the years – had snapped after four hours' shelling. Someone had blundered. The men knew that. And they did not do or die. They wandered back to the town.[62]

Understandably, the regiments who had suffered most in the earlier actions were the first to crack. The Leicesters and the 60th, the men who four days before had staggered back down the road from Dundee with Yule's column – now they were just parties of mud-stained men looking for water. The Gordons, the heroes of Elandslaagte, were a 'rabble' in kilts – so the officers said. There was only one bright spot to relieve this Battle of Ladysmith, alias 'Mournful Monday', the day a historian later called 'one of the gloomiest days in the history of the British Army'.[63] The British artillery, although outgunned by their Boer counterparts, covered the retreat. For a quarter of an hour one battery (the 13th – that is, Gunner Netley's battery) received the weight of the Boer attack. ('We are serving them up like Nelson did,' wrote Gunner Netley afterwards, 'only instead of hot potatoes it is "cough-no-more" remedies.')[64] The army gunners were joined by naval gunners using 12-pounders on improvised gun-carriages. These were men of a naval brigade landed from HMS *Powerful,* who had only reached Ladysmith on the morning of the battle. But nothing could redeem the abject state of the infantry. Even French's cavalry came back in disorder. 'A seething mass of clubbed and broken cavalry,' according to one account, 'streamed southwards into the open plain.'[65]

Among the civilians in Ladysmith the army's retreat created consternation. All the morning they had watched the large yellow wagons, blazoned with a Red Cross, unload their gruesome loads at the Town Hall. 'Number, rank, name and corps,' the medical sergeant would call out, as the covers were lifted from the wagons. Sometimes there was no reply; the men had died of their wounds. About midday, when the army had begun to stream back into the town, the enemy's shelling grew hotter. As 94-pounder shells, fired from the Creusot Long Tom on Pepworth, thumped into the town, consternation turned to panic. There was a stampede at the railway station.[66]

In his headquarters on Convent Hill Sir George White waited as the reports came in. He had ridden back ahead of the main body, leaving two of his staff – Major-General Hunter and Colonel Rawlinson – to extricate the stragglers. He was shattered by what he had seen. Nothing had gone right for him. The main attack by Grimwood's brigade had spent itself against air. The Boers had changed their positions during the night and worked round Grimwood's flank.[67] He had planned to roll up the Boers from the right. Instead, he had himself been rolled back into Ladysmith. The humiliation seemed total. It was the first time in the war that two large bodies of troops had met on apparently equal terms. Man for man, general for general, the British were no match for the Boers.

Even now, White had not heard the worst. After Colonel Rawlinson had returned from bringing in the stragglers, he rode out again to see Colonel William Knox, left in charge of the reserve. Knox told him that earlier that day he had heard the sound of rifle fire in the direction of Nicholson's Nek. At about 2.00 p.m. the heavy firing ceased, and Knox thought he heard the sound of a bugle call. With a sinking heart, Rawlinson rode back to report to his chief.[68]

Later that evening, a Boer came in under flag of truce with a personal message from Joubert to White. After a brisk fight, Carleton's column had hoisted the white flag. Both regiments and the gunners of the battery – 954 officers and men – had surrendered. This brought the casualties that day to a total of 1,272.[69] It was the most humiliating day in British military history since Majuba.

The 'knock-down blow' had fallen – on White himself, as he put it. He sent a brief cable to the War Office: 'It was my plan and I take full responsibility.'[70] Then he wrote a long, abject letter to his wife. At sixty-four he was too old for soldiering. His troops had lost confidence in him. He would be superseded – and rightly.[71]

By Tuesday, Ladysmith was still not cut off. Yet White was so broken by the disaster that he would not consider the next strategic step: whether to abandon the town, burn the surplus stores and make a fighting retreat south of the Tugela. Probably it was now too late.[72] The troops might have refused to obey orders.

Two days later, the Boers cut the railway line to the south, and at 2.30 p.m. the telegraph line went dead. The siege had begun.[73]

CHAPTER 14

The Whale and the Fish

SS *Dunottar Castle* and the Cape,
14 October – 26 November 1899

'My dear, the crisis – it's almost too much to be borne –
how that marvellous Milner bears up I can't imagine, but
he does and keeps his sense of humour that is much
needed just now, until the troops come . . .'

Lady Edward (Violet) Cecil to Lady
Cranborne from Cape Town,
autumn 1899

The voyage proved as monotonous as everyone had expected.[1] The *Dunottar Castle* had sailed from Southampton on the Saturday (14 October) after Kruger's reckless ultimatum, amid those wild scenes of rejoicing and wild rumours of battles.[2] Now here the passengers sat in basket chairs on the promenade deck, cut off from the world, the very picture of frustration. The special artist of *The Illustrated London News* sketched the scene: the General, Buller, his massive head under a yachting cap, talking to his ADC, Algy Trotter, who wore a striped blazer; behind them, also in a yachting cap, the boyish war correspondent of *The Morning Post*, trying to pick the brains of Buller's staff.[3] He was young Winston Churchill, and Churchill was finding the voyage 'odious'. 'Fourteen days is a long time in war,' he wrote to his mother, 'especially at the beginning.'[4] Suppose the *Dunottar Castle* arrived at Cape Town to find the fighting over, as many soldiers feared.[5]

This was not actually Churchill's own forecast. He did not think the Boers would cave in after the first defeat. He believed (and he had heard it 'on the best possible authority') that Buller's Army Corps would not begin the campaign till Christmas Day, and not reach Pretoria, by way of Bloemfontein, before the end of February. So he did not himself expect to be back home before the spring. Still, he should be in good time for the Derby![6]

At Madeira the *Dunottar Castle* – like her sister ship, the *Tantallon Castle*, on which Sir George White had sailed three weeks earlier – stopped to take on coal and land passengers. There were also war cables from England: the Boers had launched an invasion of both colonies. In Natal they had driven south towards Dundee. In the Cape Colony they had cut off Cecil Rhodes at Kimberley. The news was not unexpected. Buller himself seemed calm and detached.[7]

To Tory politicians, accredited war correspondents and even Buller's own headquarters staff on the ship – the so-called 'brains of the army' – the General's aloofness seemed almost like arrogance.[8] It was a flaw in his character – though common enough as a form of shyness – and a flaw that tended to make him enemies in high places. Perhaps what especially irritated such people was that towards strangers, and especially to ordinary working folk, he showed no such reserve. 'You can catch me if you can, but I won't pose for you,' he playfully told the man with the 'mutograph' (a prototype of ciné-camera), sent to cover the expedition for the new Biograph film company. Then he let the man 'catch' him several times over: strolling across the deck in his bow-tie and straw hat on the way to the barber's shop, and cheerfully shoving the white-whiskered captain of the ship, Captain Rigby, into the path of the camera so that he too, could have his turn. 'The General is a gentleman, sir,' the barber told the cameraman afterwards. 'Just think how easily he talked to me, yes, he did all the time he was having his hair cut, and when a man came in for a pipe, and I told him to come later, the General up and said, "Why, give him his pipe, I am in no hurry." '[9]

So the voyage passed, in the 'heavy silence' of the sea, as Churchill called it.[10] There were the usual ship's games. And for those who could (literally) stomach them, there were typhoid inoculations dispensed by Captain Hughes, Buller's doctor. Apart from these diversions, and the sight of a whale pursued by small fish[11] – a disturbing omen for the Army Corps – the voyage was notable for only one incident.

On Sunday 29 October, two days before they were due to dock, they saw a small tramp steamer, which turned out to be the *Australasian*, heading away from the Cape. She altered course to pass close to the *Dunottar Castle*. She must have left Cape Town three days earlier, and must have news. A rush for the rail followed. Buller himself emerged from his private saloon on the lower deck and the Biograph made its third capture as he raised his field-glasses. A storm of excitement. What was it to be: war, a truce, a Boer surrender?[12]

As the *Australasian* foamed past, without slackening speed, people saw a huge, long blackboard hung on her rat lines. Chalked out on this were the words: 'BOERS DEFEATED – THREE BATTLES – PENN SYMONS KILLED.' There were no shouts in reply, just a shocked silence.[13] For both pieces of news were bad: the death of the General, and the likelihood that, by the time they arrived, the war would be over.[14]

On this latter score anxiety was soon removed. At 9.15 on Monday evening, in pouring rain, the *Dunottar Castle* steamed into Cape Town harbour. As Churchill and the other war correspondents struggled to find a Cape newspaper, the secret war cables were read out to some of Buller's staff in the half-darkness of the deck. They included White's reports. The fiasco of the Battle of Ladysmith and the crushing disaster at Nicholson's Nek had occurred a few hours earlier.[15]

Soon after 9 o'clock next morning, Buller disembarked and drove in procession to Government House to see Sir Alfred Milner. The news of the disasters in Natal had not yet been published and the streets of Cape Town, like those of Southampton sixteen days earlier, were lined with Union Jacks and bunting.

Once again it was as though this were the homecoming of a victorious general. Buller played the part expected of him. He drove in an open landau – General Sir Redvers Buller, VC, medal ribbons a chequerboard on his chest, John Bull personified. General Bulldog. Cape Town gave him a Roman triumph.[16] Then the play was over. At ten, the procession reached Government House and Buller was shown into the small, austere, book-lined study where Sir Alfred, his face the colour of ivory, was awaiting him. Buller was handed the decoded cables from White with fuller details of the Natal disasters.[17]

When Buller sat down to write his first private letter to Lansdowne after landing, he said, 'The general fear seems to be that we are in measurable distance of a Dutch rising [in Cape Colony]. In our unprotected state that would mean almost a walk-over, I fear. I hope and believe we shall tide over that danger.'[18]

Was Buller exaggerating the perils of the situation? Was he a prey to a despondency more disastrous than the supposed dangers themselves? So it was to appear to many people, especially Milner's admirers, in the years ahead.[19] Yet, from unpublished documents two things emerge. First, the dangers were real enough. Second, it was not Buller who showed weakness and despondency at the news. Buller was the man who breathed new life into the quaking garrison at Cape Town.[20] It was Milner who was in a state of despondency bordering on panic. 'Things going from bad to worse,' he wrote in his diary; 'matters look extremely black ... the blackest of black days ... everything going wrong. ...'[21] To Chamberlain: 'I write this quaking, for one fears every hour for Kimberley.'[22]

It may seem odd that Milner, the firebrand, should quail at the first sight of the flames he had lit. But then Milner's morale, always delicately balanced, had suffered the sort of shock he found hardest to bear: humiliation. He had been proved wrong, absolutely wrong, in his forecasts.[23] By every mail-boat Milner was receiving those letters of congratulation from his imperialist disciples. The war would be the making of the British Empire. It would be the 'crucible', the great steel smelter into which those four weak ingots of British metal in South Africa – Cape loyalists, Natal loyalists, Uitlanders from Johannesburg and Rhodesians – would be cast into imperial steel, fusing with the stronger metals from the mother country.[24] But Milner's political chemistry left little margin for error. To succeed, the casting process must be short and sharp.[25] Now Milner saw nothing but months of disaster ahead.

He was terrified by the thought that White's garrison, locked up at Ladysmith, might be forced to surrender. Even if they held out, there was every likelihood, he thought, of the Boers getting to Durban. Either event would be a blow to British prestige that would send a shock-wave throughout the world. Yet Milner was now still more alarmed by the dangers facing Cape Colony. The day that he called 'the blackest of black days' was 4 November. It was then that he heard that the Boers had decided not to be content with laying siege to border towns: to Mafeking, in the far north, and to Kimberley. They had crossed the Orange River and driven into the heartland of rural Cape Colony.[26]

Why did the invasion of the Cape alarm Milner more than the threat to Natal's capital, Durban, and the possibility that the Boers should capture all the colony down to the sea? A successful invasion of the Cape might prove a political disaster that was irreversible. Nine-tenths of the Natal settlers were British; *their* loyalty could not be conquered, even if the Boers occupied their country. In the Cape, on the other hand, loyalties were a great deal more complicated. Two-thirds of its white population were Afrikaners, whom Milner believed would side with the Boer invaders, given the opportunity. The other third was British, but not true-blue British, like most of the men of Natal. In the days before the Raid, when Cecil Rhodes had been Prime Minister, they had displayed almost as equivocal an attitude to Britain as the Afrikaners. The Raid had changed all that, of course. And Milner had since made an unspoken personal compact with the Cape loyalists: they must put themselves in his hands, commit themselves to him body and soul, and in return he would defend them with the 'whole force of the Empire'.

The 'whole force of the Empire'. It was actully a phrase Milner had coined to describe the reinforcements to be sent out to Natal, General White's force of ten thousand men.[27] But what had he done for the Cape? The total number of imperial troops in the Cape at the outbreak of war was about seven thousand.[28] And now Boer commandos had hemmed in the two chief towns, Mafeking and Kimberley, and were threatening the scattered British communities right across the east of the Colony.[29] Milner's feelings can be imagined. At the centre of his nightmare was the word the first British settlers in the Transvaal had used after the Majuba settlement in 1881: betrayal.

To add to Milner's misery, there was the problem of Rhodes. The Boer invasion had made Kimberley the symbol of imperial resistance in the Cape. Kimberley was Rhodes's diamond capital and Rhodes had rushed out there hell-bent, it seemed, on ruining everything. It was characteristic of the man that when he saw the stage set for a siege, he should make a dash for that stage; that, in his new role as the arch-imperialist, he should wrap himself in the flag, so to speak, and that, when the moment came, he should betray the flag.

This was the truth, and Milner found it most distressing.[30] A stream of cables had come from Kimberley since the siege had begun. 'My opinion,' cabled Rhodes on 5 November, 'is that if you do not advance at once from Orange River you will lose Kimberley.' 'Urgent relief necessary,' cabled the Mayor the same day. 'If lives of inhabitants are to be spared help must come immediately.' 'Town guard,' cabled one of the financiers, 'cannot last much longer ... already some have died ... very great excitement among natives.' 'You must admit that the fall of Kimberley would be most disastrous on account of politics,' cabled Rhodes on the 7th.[31]

In his replies to Rhodes, Milner tried to calm him with the sort of language British officers were supposed to use to their troops – 'You absolutely must hang on a little longer. It is beastly being shelled. But ... I hope you will keep up courage of inhabitants, and not let a few croakers demoralize the rest. Relief of Kimberley is going to be turning point of the whole business.'[32] But the drift of Rhodes's blackmail was clear enough, as Milner pointed out to Buller. They must send a relief expedition immediately, or Rhodes would surrender Kimberley to the Boers.

The strategic situation, as Milner saw it, was thus dominated by three things: the danger of Kimberley's surrender, of the Boers sweeping down on the British communities of the north-eastern Cape, and of a general Afrikaner rising all over the colony. He begged Buller to keep his Army Corps in the Cape: that is, to keep all three infantry divisions and the cavalry division, and so on, totalling forty-seven thousand men, to defend the Cape and rescue Cecil Rhodes. In fact, as we saw, the War Office plan when Buller left London was that the Army Corps should be landed at the Cape ports and then roll forward irresistibly across the veld towards Bloemfontein and Pretoria. So Milner was able to say to Buller: stick to your original plan, but, at first, instead of launching an invasion, let the Army Corps repel one.[33]

Yet implicit in these plausible-looking arguments of Milner's was a proposal of a perfectly abject kind: in effect, a plan to sacrifice the Ladysmith garrison and all Natal except Durban. For if the Army Corps were kept together in the Cape, there would be no spare reinforcements for Natal. Even if a successful advance on Bloemfontein brought in due course relief for the garrisons in Natal, it was barely conceivable that Buller could reach Bloemfontein before January; probably he would take longer. Ladysmith had only supplies to last sixty days – to the end of December. And the Boer commandos might at any moment sweep down on south Natal, which was defended by only two battalions.[34] To this Milner's reply was: 'I think the time has come to be ruthless [in Natal] and sacrifice everything to military necessity.' In fact, he meant the opposite. He was proposing to sacrifice twelve thousand imperial troops – the British regulars of White's garrison – to the political necessity of defending the Cape loyalists, and above all of extricating Cecil Rhodes and his fellow-financiers from their theatricals at Kimberley.[35]

What was Buller to make of Milner's extraordinary proposal? Behind that square jaw and the iron-grey moustache, Buller was an intensely emotional man, as passionate as Milner. In a letter to his younger brother Tremayne, written soon after his first interview at Government House, he burst out, 'I am in the tightest place I have ever been in, and the worst of it is I think none of my creating.'[36] What was he to do now? To strike for Bloemfontein, as originally planned? To take all his army to Natal? Or to compromise, to break up the Army Corps, and spread its battalions wherever the need was greatest?

By 4 November, Buller had made his decision: to break up the Army Corps. It was an excruciating decision – and surely the correct one. Buller could not abandon Ladysmith and Natal to their fate and the two battalions in south Natal could not save the colony.[37] By now Buller had had confirmation in a final cable from White that White was unable to break out of Ladysmith and retreat behind the Tugela. White's cable contained appeal – not a howl like Rhodes's, but still an appeal – for rescue.[38] A few days later Buller received fuller details of the sorry state of Ladysmith, brought in person by General French and Colonel (as he now was) Douglas Haig. At Buller's request, they had taken one of the last trains to leave the beleaguered town, and had nearly been shot in the process. Supplies of food and fodder, they reported, were sufficient for two months, but the garrison was short of ammunition for the naval guns – the only guns capable of matching the Boers' Long Toms. Worse, morale among the troops was undependable, after the defeats at the Battle of Ladysmith and Nicholson's Nek, now christened Mournful Monday. Haig also listed in painful detail White's mixture of weakness and rashness.[39]

Meanwhile, the authorities in London had tumbled to White's appalling strategic blunder in allowing himself to be north of the Tugela at all. Wolseley told Lansdowne that White must be sacked and Lansdowne had cabled to Buller on 1 and 3 November to ask him whether he would oppose this decision.[40] In his reply to the first cable, Buller hesitated: 'I am not in a better position to decide than you, indeed worse, as I have not seen the Natal reports.'[41] It was not until 8 November that Buller learnt the full truth about White's blunders and cabled to Lansdowne that day: 'French is here, conversation confirms doubts I have of White's ability. Besides evident want of military precautions, White seems to have been weak and vacillating and much influenced by [Ian] Hamilton, a dangerous adviser.'[42] In a private letter in reply to this, Lansdowne confirmed that he now agreed with Wolseley: White must go.[43] But meanwhile, of course, the siege of Ladysmith had begun. So White must first be rescued, before he could be sacked.

How soon could rescue come to Natal? That depended on the Army Corps, and not a ship of the great fleet carrying it to South Africa had yet docked in South Africa, except the *Dunottar Castle*. The planning of this splendid expeditionary force, it will be recalled, had been the subject of endless wrangling between Lansdowne and Wolseley, and of scathing comments from Lansdowne's own Cabinet colleagues. The 'scandal', as the Prime Minister had called it, was the expected delay of four months between 'pressing the button' and the moment when the Army Corps would be ready in position to invade the Boer republics. An extra six weeks' delay had been caused by the need to order £645,000-worth of mules and oxen from all parts of the world.[44] The button had not been pressed until 22 September. So, if the War Office arithmetic was correct, the Army Corps would not be ready to move till 22 December.[45] However, nearly half the troops were now on the high seas, and, whether mobile or not, they would be in Cape Town before the end of the month. In fact, the first two troop transports, the *Roslin Castle* and the *Moor*, were due to dock at Cape Town on 8 and 9 November.[46] The leading brigade of the Army Corps would reach Durban by the 15th. They would be followed by the rest of the 2nd Infantry Division, led by Lieutenant-General Sir Francis Clery. This was the time-table, as Buller described it to Milner on 5 November, and he added ruefully, '10 days seems to be a long time to wait in a crisis like this, is it not? It seems to me a lifetime.'[47]

If Milner was still quaking about Kimberley and only half-convinced by Buller's plan to go himself with the twelve thousand men to save Natal, relations between the two men were surprisingly cordial. War makes strange bedfellows.

It would be hard to imagine two men more strongly contrasted in appearance and manner – The General, red-faced, stolid, bluff, inspiring confidence with every heavy stride; Milner, austere, donnish, his ivory skin strained taut by the pull of events. Moreover, Milner had received that week a private warning to beware of Buller. His crony at the War Office, Fleetwood Wilson, had written that General Buller was 'alarmingly influenced by [General] Butler. Verb sap'.[48] Yet, it turned out that Milner and Buller had important qualities in common – patriotism and ambition – hidden under their different uniforms. And when it came to the point, Buller could hardly have behaved less like Butler. Butler had frustrated every scheme of defence and sided with the Bond ministry, led by Schreiner, in blocking Milner's efforts to arm the Cape. Buller flung himself heart and soul into his job, so much so that Milner became alarmed that Buller's forthrightness might provoke a political crisis to add to the military disasters.[49]

The problem of defending the Cape, in Milner's eyes, was bedevilled by two related facts. First, Schreiner's ministry were neutral, at best, towards the war; second, outside the coastal towns, most of the population were Afrikaners who would be only too keen to rise and join the Boers, once they invaded. In this delicate situation, Milner found himself dancing what he called 'a most peculiar egg-dance'. He depended on Schreiner's ministry to restrain the would-be rebels. He depended on the Cape loyalists to hold the fort until the imperial troops were in position. Hence, he must arm the latter without alienating the former. In practice, this meant calling out the colonial volunteers in only a few areas – those where it would be certain that the arms would not get into the wrong hands – and not even allowing the imperial troops into those districts where the Afrikaners were most likely to rise.[50] But the daily 'egg-dance' with Schreiner was almost more than Milner could bear. In his heart, he longed to provoke a crisis and force Schreiner's resignation. But he knew – and this was agreed with Chamberlain – that he could not afford to do that for the time being.[51]

In the event, Buller and Milner hammered out an agreed policy on most of their common problems. The worst wrangles with Schreiner concerned colonial volunteers, martial law, and natives – above all, the natives of the Territories and Griqualand East (today the Transkei). Both Milner and Buller wanted to arm these tribesmen for their own good; already Boers had raided the native districts of Zululand and parts of Bechuanaland, taking cattle and other loot. But Schreiner insisted on the principle that this was to be exclusively a 'white man's war'.[52] As Milner bitterly told Chamberlain, 'I believe he would rather see the whole country overrun than see the natives protect themselves against white men.'[53] Eventually, Schreiner agreed to let these native territories be placed under the overall command of Buller, and Buller arranged for native levies to be raised accordingly. Schreiner was also persuaded, for what it was worth, to agree to the proclamation of martial law in districts that had actually gone over to the enemy.[54]

With other delicate political questions Buller had less success. He wanted the

British navy to be ordered to impose a complete embargo – on the import of food as well as arms into the Boer republics – at the Portuguese port of Delagoa Bay. Milner backed him. But the British Cabinet would only agree on an arms embargo, and this seemed easy to evade. Buller was also anxious to impose news censorship in the colonies; this was blocked by Schreiner.[55] In desperation, Buller devised a scheme for arresting the most notorious Afrikaner agents at the Cape and shipping them off to Durban, after giving the captain orders to take a month, instead of the usual three days, for the voyage. But after the agents had been loaded on board, and the ship had steam up, Milner's nerve failed him. The men were released and went back to their spying.[56]

It was now 8 November, and when Milner went for his afternoon outing, he heard a rumour that the *Roslin Castle* had already anchored in Table Bay. In fact, he could see no sign of it, and he spent a wretched night ('anxiety of all sorts beginning to tell more than it has done yet,' he wrote in his diary). Next day he took his horse out for a ride.[57] Probably he rode up to the flanks of the Lion, the gigantic scarp of rock below the plateau of Table Mountain. Below him was the great sweep of Table Bay and beyond Table Mountain, behind his back the veld, running five hundred miles north-east to the Orange River. The door was wide open from the river to the sea. Wide open to the Boers. This was the nightmare that had sat on Milner's chest throughout these harrowing days. But that day, like a castaway whose heart leaps at the sight of the sail on the horizon, Milner looked down on the red funnels of the *Roslin Castle*, carrying the No. 3 Field Hospital and No. 4 Bearer Company, anchored below him in Table Bay.[58] Table Bay.[58]

The *Roslin Castle* was the first of the armada, whose funnels and masts and rigging soon crowded Table Bay like a forest. South Africa had never seen so many liners, nor so many troops. Nor had the British navy, which had organized the armada, had such a task since they sent sailing ships to carry Lord Raglan and his thirty thousand men to Scutari in 1854. Each day, when Milner took his ride, he could count the new arrivals. There were the transports bringing the 2nd Infantry Division, commanded by Sir Francis Clery and destined for Natal; there were the *Moor*, the *Yorkshire*, the *Lismore Castle*, the *Harlech Castle*, the *Manila*, the *Gurkha*, and so on. What a Homeric catalogue of ships! By 16 November, they had all been sent steaming off to Durban.[59] Still more heart-warming, from Milner's point of view, was the sight of Lieutenant-General Lord Methuen's 1st Infantry Division, Lieutenant-General Sir William Gatacre's 3rd Infantry Division, and a cavalry division – all destined to reinforce the Cape.[60]

On 13 November a south-easterly gale had blown up ('almost a hurricane', it seemed to Milner) and he was intensely anxious for the transports caught out at sea or lumbering in the harbour. The gale lasted four days, but no ships were wrecked.[61] By 18 November – nine days after the *Roslin Castle*'s arrival – more than a third of the forty-seven thousand men of the Army Corps had disembarked at Cape Town, or been sent on to Durban. That day Buller decided he

was strong enough to push Sir William Gatacre's 3rd Infantry Division forward
to Naauwpoort, in the north-eastern part of the Colony, from where they had
earlier been withdrawn.[62] Milner wrote the first cheerful entry in his diary since
October: 'Rather an exciting day, General determined to race back to Naauw-
port which was successfully accomplished late at night.'[63] Milner could give
thanks to the High Gods. In the Cape Colony, if not yet in Natal, the Army
Corps had begun to stem the tide of invasion.

In the meantime, Buller had been performing prodigies down in his headquarters, a small, unpretentious house he had rented in Grave Street.[64] To improvise
half a dozen separate commands out of the four divisions – that was the
beginning of the problem. Major-General French's cavalry division was left in
the Cape more or less intact. However, in the infantry divisions Buller had to
reallocate not only the brigades, but even the battalions within the brigades,
according to the dates of their arrival and according to his assessment of the
strategic threats in each area. His army's deficiencies, Buller found, came from
that jigsaw planning of Wolseley's. And jigsaw it was: an Army Corps that had
never seen a day's parade, but existed only on paper.[65] How different it would
have been, if Buller had been allowed to go to South Africa earlier that year and
prepare the ground.

There was one overwhelming – and, indeed, unique – feature of a war against
the Boers. The Boers were virtually all mounted infantry. The War Office had
made almost no concessions to this fact. Against fifty thousand Mausers, in the
hands of Boer irregulars, they had planned to match roughly fifty thousand Lee
Metfords in the hands of British regulars. That, and the weight of British
artillery, was the thinking behind the War Office 'steam-roller'. But the arithmetic looked very different if one counted feet, not rifles. The Boers had six feet
– two for a man, four for a horse – behind every Mauser. Only an eighth of the
British force was mounted.[66] Hence it would be mobile war, but of a strange,
unequal sort: the war of a whale, like the one they had seen from the deck of the
Dunottar Castle, and the small fish that pursued it.

Buller, in his own fashion, recognized this. In fact, his plan, when he reached
Cape Town at the end of the previous month, had been to put flesh on the War
Office's paper army and give the Army Corps an entirely new mobility. He had
intended to raise large numbers of irregular colonial troops – men who could
ride and shoot exactly like the Boers – and retrain his Army Corps in the novel
principles of war in the veld. Meanwhile the ox and mule transport had still to
arrive (and in fact this would not all arrive until January). Then came disaster:
Rhodes stranded at Kimberley, White at Ladysmith. Buller had to drop everything and speed away – the whale to the rescue.[67]

'Ever since we have been here we have been like a man,' he told one of his staff
before he left for Natal on 22 November, 'who, with a long day's work before
him, overslept himself and so was late for everything all day.'[68] It was true
enough. There was no time to do anything well. Everything had to be improvised: guns, transport, supplies, and, above all, staff. Buller's own headquarters
staff had vanished to the winds, like the Army Corps itself. Lieutenant-Colonel

Charles à Court, who, as Charles Repington, would later be famous as a military historian, was sent off to recruit the new mounted corps – the South African Light Horse – drawn from Uitlander refugees at the Cape.[69] At this he distinguished himself, though Buller was upset to find he had appointed as colonel a man called Villiers, who had ridden with Jameson in the Raid. Colonel Herbert Miles, the Assistant Adjutant-General, took command of the vital railway junction at De Aar, from where Lord Methuen's relief expedition was being mounted. Major Julian Byng, the future Lord Byng of Vimy, was sent to raise more mounted corps.[70] So, when Buller left for Natal on the 22nd, he had only his personal staff – his ADCs and his Military Secretary – for what he recognized would be the greatest struggle of his career. Indeed, it would be almost a 'forlorn hope' to rescue White, Buller thought, with the limited troops and time available.[71]

After Buller's departure Milner relapsed into gloom. Buller had 'done wonders' in the three weeks he had been at the Cape. Milner himself was the first to admit this to Chamberlain. He accepted, if reluctantly, Buller's decision to divert a third of the Army Corps to Natal. But he wished Buller had not decided to lead the Natal relief force in person. It needed a soldier of Buller's stature to keep a grip on affairs at the Cape and Buller had 'grasp'. When he was gone, they would be back to the old state of 'drift'.[72]

Actually, Buller's departure coincided with the improvement in imperial fortunes in South Africa that he had hopefully forecast. The race to stem the tide of invasion seemed to have been virtually won. In Natal, two of the three brigades of Clery's 2nd division – about eight thousand men – were already at Estcourt and Mooi River. They should be able to shield Maritzburg from the Boers' drive south. On the western borders of Cape Colony, Lord Methuen had set off on 20 November from his base at De Aar. He had now crossed the Orange River, taking rations for five days, and it was hoped he would be at Kimberley within a week. In the Midland and Eastern districts of the colony, it was true, the Boers were still advancing. But here, too, the imperial shield had been slipped into position in the nick of time. Gatacre's 3rd 'division' – not yet a brigade, in fact – was holding Queenstown without difficulty. The cavalry division, led by French, now back in the saddle, was holding the line at Colesberg. The Boers might slip through the gaps; that was Milner's new source of anxiety. But only a pessimist would deny that the strategic situation had taken a dramatic turn for the better.[73]

Milner remained a pessimist.[74] His temper was not improved by a number of trivial, but irritating, events that occurred at this time to cast a pall over his personal life.

One of his most intimate friends, Mrs Richard Chamberlain, freshly widowed, had come out to Cape Town. That, one might have thought, would have delighted him. Mrs Chamberlain was high-spirited, with just that touch of wildness he found so attractive in women. She was also a passionate imperialist (she had haunted Dr Jameson's trial in London) and – still more important – she was the Colonial Secretary's sister-in-law. She had helped Milner in a variety of

ways. She would come to see him in London, and spend half the night gossiping
tête-à-tête in his chambers in Duke Street.[75] But since she had been widowed,
the strength of her feelings had become intensely embarrassing to Milner. His
other friends, especially Margot, disapproved of Mrs Chamberlain. 'Please,
please don't marry that woman – promise me that,' Margot wrote.[76] Milner told
people he had no intention of marrying, which was true enough. The news that
she had pursued him to Cape Town especially alarmed him because she was
suspected in the Chamberlain family of having been unfaithful to her husband.
Milner sent a private cypher cable to explain his predicament to Joe. He had not
in any way 'countenanced' her visit; he disapproved of it.[77]

At the same time, Violet Cecil, the 'godsend', as Milner called her, had
deserted Government House. In October she had moved to Groote Schuur,
where Cecil Rhodes kept open house for influential British visitors. Since
Rhodes's enforced absence at Kimberley, she had been acting as his hostess, but
Milner saw her nearly every day. She would arrive after tea and they would go
for long walks. Perhaps they played tennis; for Milner, dissatisfied with his
success at archery, had just taken up the game. Certainly Violet and he went
riding together on the Cape Flats.[78] But something was lacking from their
relationship. Part of the trouble was that Violet, nearly twenty years younger
than Milner and extremely pretty, resented the stiffness of diplomatic life. There
had been a ghastly evening with Milner and the foreign military attachés. They
had all been kept standing for hours. Eventually, she had made a rude face at
Alfred, who had taken the hint. She made no secret that diplomatic life was not
the life for her.[79]

In fact, she had just revealed another annoying facet of her nature – a talent for
gossip quite as dazzling as Margot's. When Buller left for Natal, it had apparently been agreed with Milner that, for security reasons, his destination should
be known to as few people as possible. Hence Milner's astonishment when
Violet rushed round to Government House the evening of Buller's departure to
tell Milner the exciting news. 'You are mistaken,' was his first comment. Then
she told him her source; a young staff officer. 'Well, say nothing about it,' he
replied bluntly.[80] How characteristic of Violet to have wormed out the most
closely guarded secret of the war!

A few days earlier, Milner had heard a depressing item of news from Natal
concerning one of the young men whom he was anxious to help make his way in
the world: Winston Churchill. Milner had received two eloquent letters about
Churchill – one from Chamberlain ('He has the reputation of being bumptious.
Put him on the right lines . . .')[81] the other from George Wyndham, the Under-
Secretary of State for War. Wyndham wrote, 'He is a very clever fellow & is
bringing out an unprejudiced mind.'[82] And there was nothing, no doubt, that
would have pleased Milner more than to tell young Churchill about that little
corner of the imperial chessboard where they both found themselves, though it
might have been Churchill who would have done most of the talking. In the
event, Churchill had not lost a day in Cape Town. He had rushed off to Natal,
hoping to reach Ladysmith before the siege began. And he had now been carried

off as prisoner of war to Pretoria, after some inconceivably stupid incident involving an armoured train.[83] So, for the time being, Churchill's budding career as a war correspondent seemed to have ended in disaster; while Milner had lost the chance of explaining to that 'unprejudiced mind' the background to the 'great Afrikaner conspiracy' to take over all South Africa, a conspiracy whose reality the Boers' invasion now seemed to confirm.[84]

CHAPTER 15

Botha's Raid

South Natal,
9–30 November 1899

'Joubert stopped me from coming to Durban in 1899 to
eat bananas.'

Louis Botha at a banquet in Durban, 1908

Meanwhile, the Boers were poised to strike deeper into British territory. But their aims were more limited than Milner – obsessed with the threat, both military and ideological, which the Boers posed – could ever have grasped. Had Milner had a spy in the laager of Joubert, the Commandant-General, in those first ten days of November, it would have done wonders for his morale.

Poor Joubert was crushed under the weight of his own victories: an old man, tired and ill, beset by problems on every side. No shoes for the horses, no proper supplies, half the burghers ready to ride off to raid Durban, the other half to abandon the struggle and go home.[1] This was hardly an exaggeration. And from Kruger and the Executive Council there was little help or encouragement on the overwhelming strategic problem: how to exploit their victories, the better to defend their own borders.[2]

Younger burghers, like Deneys Reitz, the son of Kruger's State Secretary, rightly regarded Joubert as 'weak and hesitant', because he shrank from attacking the enemy.[3] But it is a moot point whether a young and brilliant general like Louis Botha, who had emerged as Joubert's right-hand man, could now have adopted a very different strategy from Joubert's, given the decisions of the Boer politicians and the practical military difficulties. For what Reitz (and, indeed, Milner, Amery and subsequent British historians)[4] failed to understand was that, despite the urging of enthusiasts like Smuts, the agreed strategy of the two republican governments was defensive. Kruger's main political objective was a new settlement, with Britain giving the Transvaal unqualified independence. A new military victory in Natal – a second Majuba – could achieve this, but the first priority was now, as it had been in 1881, to defend the land and the volk. Hence the crucial fact that the forty-five thousand men of the Boer forces in the field had been disposed at the outbreak of war merely to *block* the enemy's attacks.[5]

True, Kruger's plan was daring. He and Steyn had chosen attack as the best form of defence. But none of their pre-emptive blows was planned, as real offensive strategy demanded, to fall where the enemy was weakest. On the contrary, the aim was to find the strongest points in the enemy's attacking force and then smash them. In fact, their 'defensive-offensive' strategy involved invasion of colonial territory for two reasons. First, they had to block the immediate military threat. This they had now achieved in both Natal and Cape Colony. They had bottled up White and his twelve thousand in Ladysmith; they had put the stopper, so to speak, on Baden-Powell at Mafeking and Rhodes in Kimberley. Second, they had to seize the best strategic positions for blocking the expected British counter-attack, which would probably take the form of at least two relief expeditions, as well as a British invasion of the Free State by the obvious route from the south. It was part of this second task that now faced Joubert and Botha in Natal: how best to trap the expedition hurrying to rescue White?[6]

On the afternoon of 9 November the commandants of the Transvaal army held a council of war in the shade of Joubert's tents at Modderspruit, a few miles east of Ladysmith. It was a moment to take stock. They had been at war for a month, and from some points of view their success had been dazzling. That wild mass of irregulars who had galloped up to Joubert's tent at Volksrust on President Kruger's birthday, cheering and shouting themselves hoarse at the news of the ultimatum – these men had now beaten, in open warfare, the cream of the British army. No doubt they still shouted and cheered Joubert when he made his rounds to inspect the twenty-odd camps of burghers stretched in a great circle around Ladysmith. The reverses at Talana and Elandslaagte had hardly affected morale, for the simple reason that they had involved such a small number of burghers.[7]

Yet Joubert had every reason to regard these first actions of the war as disasters, reckoning up what they had cost him both in men and in opportunities lost. At Dundee, General Lucas Meyer had bungled the first great opportunity of the war: to trap Symons. Had Meyer waited one day before occupying Talana Hill, he could have joined forces with General Erasmus's commandos, whom Joubert had sent forward to Mount Impati, and how could Symons's four battalions have coped with an attack from both directions?[8] The strategic error had been compounded by General Kock at Elandslaagte. Joubert had ordered Kock to lie in wait for Symons's force on the Biggarsberg. Instead, Kock had pushed on to Elandslaagte, where he had recklessly exposed himself to White's attack.[9] Hence Joubert's inability – even supposing he had had the self-confidence to attempt it – to trap Symons' force while it was retreating under Yule's command, a victory that would have put Majuba into the shade. And hence the exceptionally heavy cost, from Joubert's point of view, of these early actions: 607 burghers killed, wounded and captured. These casualties (over half of them the result of Kock's folly[10]) represented, according to Joubert's official report to Kruger, 'a total defeat as great as has ever yet befallen the Afrikaner volk'.[11]

Still, war is, in the last resort, a contest in blunders, and it was thanks to Sir George White, more than to Joubert's own generals, that *all* these British troops were now trapped at Ladysmith. The question was how to frustrate the expected counter-attack. At the council of war on 9 November, Joubert put the three main options to his commandants. They could try and take the town by storm before relief arrived. They could divide their own forces, and dig in along the line of the Tugela. They could drive deep into Natal to reconnoitre defensive positions nearer Durban. It was to the third option that Joubert himself inclined.[12]

This might seem surprising. Joubert was still intensely anxious about the possibility of White's breaking out of the trap. On the second night after the Battle of Ladysmith (or Modderspruit, as the Boers called their victory on 30 October), there had been a somewhat ludicrous moment when Joubert, unable to grasp how shattered was the morale of White's troops, had ordered his officers 'to be on their toes' to expect a night attack; and he had emerged from his tent at 12.30 a.m. 'to put everything in order for the struggle'.[13] Since then, the strength of his own troops had dwindled as burghers took French leave and returned home. Joubert cabled in desperation to Pretoria: '*Als die HEd. Regeering mij nu geen steun kan geven, dan moet de zaak op nul uitlopen....*'

Unless the government can give me their backing, then the whole thing is hopeless. The men come to me in streams asking for permission to go home. Although I refuse them permission every time, the number of burghers is melting away. The officers themselves ... set the example in going off home. Every morning I receive such serious complaints about the melting away of the burghers and disobeying my orders, that I shudder at our situation. Unless the government publishes an order to send back the absent burghers immediately, I shall shortly have no commandos at all.[14]

Pretoria took action immediately. The burghers were ordered back to the front, and the railway authorities were forbidden to accept passengers travelling home without leave passes. But Joubert continued to be troubled by homesick burghers, and the unpredictable fluctuations in his army's size continued to be one of its chief sources of weakness.[15]

If he faced such difficulties, why did Joubert propose such a daring move as the strike at south Natal? He certainly thought it less dangerous than the first option: to try to storm Ladysmith, which would be 'a very risky business with a very doubtful outcome'.[16] In fact, earlier that very day, there had been an abortive attempt to attack the British lines, which had proved that the burghers had neither the organization nor the heart for such a business.

Still, there proved to be numerous obstacles to the plan to go south of the Tugela. First, the horses of the commandos had not yet recovered from the strain of the fighting. Second, the Free State commandants had flatly refused to go south of the Tugela because of the risks involved. They had held their own council of war, independent of the Transvaal's, and Marthinus Prinsloo, their Commandant-General, informed Joubert of this on 11 November. Third, it was reported (quite correctly) that the British were exploiting the ten days' delay since the Battle of Ladysmith to pour reinforcements into Natal.[17]

But Joubert for once was firm and resolute. With fifteen hundred Transvaalers

Boers in laager.

Preceding page 'Mournful Monday': 30 October 1899. White's troops driven back into Ladysmith.
Above 'Horrors of War.' British gunner smashed by Boer shell at Ladysmith.
Opposite above Sir Redvers Buller pacing the deck of the *Dunottar Castle* with his ADC. *Below* Buller's triumphant reception at Cape Town, 31 October 1899.
Following page Cronje's 'Long Tom' preparing to bombard Mafeking.

@TOM
MAFEKING 1899

Above Inside Mafeking, Baden-Powell's officers sentence to death a starving African (extreme left) for stealing a goat.
Below Inside Kimberley, Cecil Rhodes (left centre) dispenses 'siege soup' — price 3d a pint.

– all that could be raked together without dangerously weakening the force guarding Ladysmith – and five hundred Free Staters who had tagged along, despite Prinsloo's decision, he reached the great gorge of the Tugela on Monday 13 November, and next day crossed the river. Then, having laid dynamite under the bridge at Colenso, in case it would be needed in future, Joubert and his cavalcade rode on across the smooth veld beside the railway line leading to Maritzburg and Durban.[18]

At Joubert's side rode Louis Botha, and it was Botha, without a doubt, who was the driving force behind this raid on south Natal. Of all the Boer leaders who were to emerge in the war, thirty-seven-year-old Louis Botha was the prodigy. On his mother's side he came from the voortrekker aristocracy; his grandfather, Gerrit van Rooyen, had been one of Andries Pretorius's lieutenants. His father had been a cattle-rancher at Vrede, in the north-east of the Free State. He himself was a highly successful farmer and a crack horseman. But he had little education and limited experience of public life. As a junior member of the Raad, he had supported Joubert and the Progressives in trying to force Kruger to be more conciliatory in handling Britain and the Uitlanders. Botha is supposed to have been one of the members who voted against Kruger's proposal to precipitate the war. But it was his own natural gift for war that had brought Botha's name leaping to the front. He had distinguished himself as one of Lucas Meyer's commandants at Talana. After the Battle of Ladysmith, Meyer had been invalided home, and replaced by Botha. Now Botha, a stripling among the patriarchs, with his violet eyes and boyish laugh, was the senior combat general (specially appointed general) with Joubert.[19]

By the evening of the 14th, the cavalcade had reached the outskirts of Chieveley, about twenty miles north of Estcourt. It was reported to Joubert that Estcourt was garrisoned by a force of three thousand British troops, supported by two large field-guns and four or five smaller ones. This was less than Joubert had feared.[20] (In fact, most of the reinforcements that Buller was rushing out to Natal were still on the high seas. In early November, the total British forces between Ladysmith and the coast numbered two thousand three hundred men, of whom the bulk were concentrated at Estcourt.)[21] Yet, with a raiding force of about the same number, with fewer field-guns, it was not Joubert's, or Botha's, plan to attack Estcourt. Their primary job was to reconnoitre the country. Of course, if any plums fell into their lap, that was all to the good. And next morning, a large plum, in the shape of an armoured train, whose passengers included young Winston Churchill, did fall straight into their lap.

'Inconceivable stupidity' was Buller's comment when he heard the news of this disaster.[22] It would indeed be hard to imagine a more fatuous proceeding than that adopted by the commander of the Estcourt garrison, Colonel Charles Long. On 3 November the British garrison, sent to guard the all-important bridge over the Tugela at Colenso, had scuttled back to the safety of Estcourt.[23] Since then, Colonel Long had been sending men to patrol the line as far as Colenso. The patrols were made by armoured train, unaccompanied by mounted troops. It was a parody of modern mobile war: an innovation that was already obsolete. Imprisoned on its vulnerable railway line, the armoured train was as helpless against field-guns in the veld as a naval dreadnought sent into battle with its rudder jammed.

Botha, who was leading the column, must have rubbed his eyes. Soon after dawn on 15 November he saw the train – 150 men in three armoured trucks on either side of the armoured engine, with a 7-pounder ship's gun visible in one of the loop-holes – steaming northwards towards Chieveley. The trap was soon sprung. Chieveley was ten miles north of a village called Frere. After three miles, just beyond a bridge across the Blaauw Kranz River, the line swung to the right and climbed a rise. It was here that Botha's party of about five hundred men, drawn from the Wakkerstroom and Krugersdorp Commandos, watched (and were actually seen by the British as the train steamed past. Then they scattered rocks on the line, and waited.[24]

The veld in this part of Natal is a rolling downland, normally silent, and the steam-trains that still carry their loads along this line (now mainly Africans bound for the mines of the Rand) are a delight to the ear. A plume of brown smoke, a distant musical honk and then the panting breath of the train itself, intermittently muffled as the train vanishes into a cutting. That morning, 15 November 1899, there was a thick mist, but Botha must have heard the sweet sound of the armoured train soon after eight o'clock, as it steamed back southwards from Chieveley. He waited till it approached the bend close to the Blaauw Kranz River. Then his gunners loosed off a couple of shells at the armoured trucks. As expected, the engine-driver put on steam. The train swept round the corner and crashed headlong into the rocks blocking the track. The armoured engine half remained on the rails. But all three trucks were derailed: the front truck, which held some unfortunate railway workers, was hurled right off the line.[25]

The fight that followed was exactly to Botha's taste. From nearly a mile away, his men poured shells and Mauser bullets into the stranded steel whale. They soon silenced the 7-pounder ship's gun. The upturned trucks gave little cover to the British. Some of the soldiers scattered across the veld. They were hunted down, and captured hiding in the railway cutting and the river-bed. Only the armoured engine battered its way out of the trap, after some men had struggled heroically for half an hour to free the line. The engine carried fifty survivors (mostly wounded) and the tale of disaster back to Frere.[26]

After the fight, Botha cabled jubilantly back to Pretoria: 'Our guns were ready and quickly punctured the armoured trucks. The engine broke loose and returned badly damaged. Loss of the enemy 4 dead, 14 wounded and 58 taken prisoner, also a mountain gun (the ship's cannon).... Our loss 4 slightly wounded.... Blood visible everywhere. Much rain. Am in good health. Publish. Greetings.'[27]

Neither he nor Joubert mentioned what would become much the most famous feature of the fight: that Winston Churchill was one of the victims. Later Churchill came to believe that he had been captured by Botha in person. Although this cannot have been literally true – the man who captured him seems to have been a field cornet called Oosthuizen, known as the 'Red Bull of Krugersdorp'[28] – Churchill was soon to be grateful to Botha for having given him a chance to make his name. And perhaps Botha should have been grateful to Churchill. For it was Churchill's burning desire to see a battle, it appears, that helped persuade the officer commanding the armoured train, Churchill's unfortunate friend, Captain Aylmer Haldane, not to turn back when they first saw the signs of Botha's trap on their journey northwards.[29]

Botha and Joubert, at any rate, continued their drive southwards, taking a wide detour to avoid the three thousand men reported to have garrisoned Estcourt. Had they known how precarious was the morale of Colonel Long's troops there, they might have been more aggressive. For the same thick mist swirled round both sides' intelligence: a mist that never lifted, whatever the weather. In the eyes of British soldiers – and of subsequent British historians – Joubert's two thousand men with two guns had become magnified to an expedition of seven thousand men with numerous guns, threatening Durban itself.[30] Long had actually packed up his tents on 14 November and loaded his guns into railway wagons in preparation for a hasty retreat.[31] As it was, Joubert had cautiously decided to split his forces into two columns: fifteen hundred men, led by himself and Botha; six hundred men under his nephew, David. Both columns would converge on the railway line south of Estcourt, cutting off the garrison from its base. They would try to deal with it like Ladysmith.[32]

That day, 16 November, it rained incessantly, and it was cold and wretched. Joubert rode in a light covered wagon – a 'spider' – and, what with the rain and the mud, he considered calling off the whole expedition. But he had no way of communicating with his nephew David's column, and could not leave him in the lurch. So he rode gloomily on. The 19th was a Sunday, and the Boer soldiers spent much of it in church. The men of the Heidelberg Commando, for example, attended four church services. On Tuesday 21 November, Joubert's column at last saw ahead the thin line of telegraph posts striding across the veld. They had reached the railway. After breaking up the line, they pitched their forward tents on a kopje commanding the line close to Willow Grange, a small village a few miles south of Estcourt. At the same time, Joubert was glad to be able to join hands with his nephew's column.[33]

Joubert was still intensely anxious, and he had every reason to be. He had inadvertently slipped his small raiding party, two thousand men, with two guns and two Maxims, between two British brigades, led by Major-Generals Hildyard and Barton, totalling nine thousand, seven hundred men, with twenty-four field-guns.[34] And this was only the vanguard of Buller's Army Corps. On 12 November the *Roslin Castle* had docked at Durban. Ever since that day imperial troops had been pouring down the gang-planks to be packed into cattle trucks and sent up the railway line to the front in an unbroken stream.[35]

Clearly the danger now was that the two British brigades would combine and crush Joubert and Botha. But Barton and Hildyard, whose brigades were about twenty miles apart, found communication impossible while the Boers sat astride the railway line.[36] So the British attack, that took place on the night of 22

November, fizzled out like a fire in the rain. It was actually the night of a ferocious thunderstorm, with lightning and hail more lethal than British bullets. The storm killed one Boer and six horses, more than were killed by Lee Metfords.[37]

On their part, Hildyard's force had suffered eighty-six casualties at Willow Grange (including Percy Fitzpatrick's brother, George, who was killed serving in the Imperial Light Horse). The Boers, by their gift for mobility and better use of the ground, had won a tactical victory.[38] The strategic question was what to do next? It appears that Botha, flushed with victory, proposed striking out for Durban ('to come and eat bananas,' he told a Durban audience nine years later).[39] Next day, before a council of war could take place, an accident occurred, an accident with the most important consequences. Joubert's horse threw him. He suffered internal injuries from which he was never fully to recover.[40]

The situation was now changed utterly. Joubert's morale finally snapped. He proposed immediate retreat. Otherwise they would be 'totally overwhelmed'.[41] He did more. He sent an extraordinary, despairing cable to Kruger: 'They must now try to make peace with the enemy in one way or the other.'[42] Peace with the enemy. The idea was, of course, unthinkable to Kruger, and he promptly cabled back that they must stick to their guns, 'dead or alive'.[43] But when the council of war was held on 25 November, its decision was a foregone conclusion. Joubert must be escorted home, and they must all retreat to the line of the Tugela.[44]

By Sunday 26 November, the cavalcade, swollen by nearly two thousand horses and cattle looted from the rich grazing grounds of Natal, had reached Weenen ('Weeping'), the settlement where the Zulus had massacred some of the voortrekkers in the days of the Trek. Many of the burghers attended the local church.[45] It was a solemn moment. The raid on south Natal had been a dazzling success, viewed as a series of tactical operations. But it had added nothing to the defensive strength of the Boers' strategic position. For this they must now look, as Prinsloo and the Free State commandos had urged all along, to the extraordinary natural strength of the Tugela. Its north bank rose in tier after tier of stony, red ramparts. It was here that the hare could lie in wait for the tortoise; or, to put it Kruger's way, once again they would wait till the tortoise had put out its head and then chop it off.

While Joubert was escorted back to Volksrust, broken in body and spirit, Botha took complete command of the army on the Tugela. If ever a kingdom was saved by a horse, it was Kruger's! For, after losing their sixty-eight-year-old Commandant-General, weak and demoralized at the best of times, the Boers had now entrusted their most critical operations to the youngest and most energetic of all their generals, who had shown himself, by his raid on south Natal, to be the most brilliant tactician of the war.[46]

Botha threw himself into the task of fortifying the line of the Tugela. It was an immense undertaking, even for an army, like the Boers', that could draw on an inexhaustible supply of forced black labour.[47] Fifteen miles of riflepits and gun pits, protected by dummy trenches and false gun emplacements, had to be hacked out of those red, boulder-strewn terraces. Though Vauban and the great military engineers of Europe would have turned in their graves at Botha's lack of science, the Tugela line, when Botha had finished, was a work of art. Five thousand riflemen, supported by ten field-guns, would man the trenches. And the British would be within rifle-shot before they realized a single burgher was there.[48]

It was the end of November. The manoeuvrings of the last month had brought the most dramatic change to the war map of South Africa. As an offensive force, the Boers had shot their bolt. It was now the turn of the various detachments of the Army Corps to try their hand at attack. Already, on the western front, Lord Methuen had set out for Kimberley with six thousand infantry, a thousand mounted men and twelve guns. Meanwhile, inside Kimberley, Cecil Rhodes, the Lion of the Empire, was braying like an ass.

CHAPTER 16

The Lights of Kimberley

The Western Frontier, Cape Colony, 20–28 November 1899

'To the indomitable will of the Chairman of this Company [Cecil Rhodes], whose pent up energies found vent in devising ways ... of providing hungry women and children with food ... did Kimberley owe its preservation.'

12th Annual Report of the De Beers, December 1900

Lieutenant-General Lord Methuen looked like a man in his element. He was wearing a 'Boer hat' – a bush hat he had picked up on his travels – khaki trousers and slippers, and was in shirt-sleeves: quite 'the most disreputable man in camp', he claimed in a letter home.[1]

It was 20 November. He was sitting at the desk in his HQ tent near Orange River bridge writing interminable reports and telegrams, and interviewing officers on every subject under the sun. Mule wagons for food and ammunition, 190 of them; horses for war correspondents, four for eight correspondents; goats for the staff mess, six. The telegrams flew as thick as the flies buzzing round the tent.[2]

The pleasure he took in this job was genuine enough. Buller, dear Buller, had given him not only the 1st Division, but a field force, 'Methuen's Force' it was now called. It was years since a British general had had such a beautiful command. He had eight thousand soldiers – the Guards Brigade and the 9th Brigade – here at Orange River. The Highland Brigade had been left to guard his lines of communication. He had to march the main column seventy-four miles across the sandy veld. It was all 'intensely interesting'. They would set out before dawn next morning. It would probably take six days, and at least one battle. He added, with a most uncharacteristic piece of swagger, 'I shall breakfast in Kimberley on Monday.'[3]

Beyond the headquarters tents, and the endless lines of regimental bell-tents, there was white sand, soft and deep, into which you could sink at every step; beyond that the brilliant blue-green of the willows, marking the Orange River itself. Everything else was as khaki as Methuen's trousers: khaki from its coating of dust. The stone huts of the railway workers, the sage bushes and acacia thorns dotted across the veld, the lizards, the ants, the black faces of the African mule-drivers – everything was thick in dust. Even in spring, the veld here on the western front was not green like the veld of Natal, green and glowing with daisies. It was a wilderness.[4] Methuen himself knew it well from his previous campaign here in 1885–6, when he had raised a troop of Light Horse to fight with General Warren in Bechuanaland.[5] The previous week he had refreshed his memory of the Great Karoo from the train that had brought him from Cape Town: a stony beach four hundred miles broad, strewn with kopjes, round and flat-topped like sand castles. This scene of desolation extended all the way to the Orange River. But that day it had begun to rain 'like a shower-bath': a 'grand' thunderstorm. What a godsend! said Methuen. No more worries, for the moment, about getting water for the men or grazing for the animals.

'For once I think I am excited,' he wrote, as the warm rain splashed against the walls of the tent.[6] Excitement was not an emotion that came easily to Methuen. He was rather a solitary man. He was a great English landowner; he had been brought up at Corsham Court in Wiltshire, amid the glow of Rubens and Reynolds portraits. No one had ever claimed he was a great general. 'Painstaking' was the word his friends used about him.[7] He was tall and big-framed, with a drooping moustache, and he tended to stoop. He was not one of Roberts's 'Indians', nor one of Wolseley's 'Africans' despite his service in Africa; he was too detached – an abstemious, taciturn man. His troops had cheered him to the echo when the *Moor* had docked at Cape Town eleven days before, but it was, he said himself, 'because I had hardly spoken to anyone during the entire voyage'.[8]

He had the advantage of having influential friends, including his close neighbour and fellow-magnate, Lord Lansdowne, the War Minister. But recently Lansdowne had partly lost confidence in him. He had caught him 'talking Boer' on the Irish manoeuvres in August.[9] Like Buller, that other English landowner-general, Methuen had a soft spot for the Boers of the backveld, though he blamed the war on those 'rascals in Pretoria'.[10] Lansdowne found this displeasing. He was also aware of Wolseley's doubts about Methuen. 'Paul Methuen is a great friend of mine,' he told Buller, 'and I have always regarded him as an able ... soldier'. He doubted, however, if he was 'man enough ... to "run the show" in the Cape' during Buller's absence in Natal.[11]

Fortunately for Methuen's morale, he could not know of Wolseley's or Lansdowne's strictures. All he knew was that he had been given three splendid infantry brigades and told to relieve Kimberley. His job was not to garrison it himself. He was merely to throw in a few troops and guns, with full supplies, and take out those of the inhabitants who were reported to be giving trouble: the women and children, ten thousand Africans and one notable Englishman, Cecil Rhodes.[12]

Buller had met Methuen and Clery soon after the *Moor* had docked at Cape Town, and told them how White's blunder in letting himself be locked up in Ladysmith had wrecked all the plans for the advance on Bloemfontein. Methuen was as astonished as anyone. When he sailed from England in October, he said that he felt 'almost sure there will be very little fighting', and laughed at General Gatacre, the energetic commander of the 3rd Division, for pounding away on

his typewriter, composing memos for his staff. 'You would imagine,' said
Methuen, 'that we are in for a second Peninsular War.'[13] Then he arrived at the
Cape and heard of White's disaster. 'Everyone was very low,' Methuen reported
to his wife, 'at the state of affairs, but Redvers was perfect. He told Clery and
myself in ½ hour how things are: White frightened to death, Ian Hamilton mad,
and French all right.' The same story had been repeated to him, suitably
modestly, by French himself.[14]

The central problem now facing Methuen at Orange River, as, indeed, it had
faced White in Natal, and was to dominate the war, was intelligence: where and
how strong was the enemy? How strong was the invisible fence of steel,
blocking the path between Kimberley and the Orange River?

Spanning the Orange River – two hundred feet wide in the rainy season, but
now only a third of that and as muddy as the Thames at Windsor – was the
Orange River railway bridge. It was a clumsy affair of wooden planks and
freshly painted red steel lattice-work. It carried the single-track railway line, the
life-line of western Cape Colony, to Kimberley, Mafeking and on to Rhodesia.
Somehow this vital Orange bridge had remained intact in the first month of the
war, guarded by a handful of imperial troops. Nothing showed more clearly
how limited was the Boers' offensive strategy than this: the Free State commandos had never been sent to seize the bridge.[15] Now it was safe, shored up by the
full weight of Methuen's field force. But the Free State commandos remained,
lurking in the heat haze among those blue-grey hills beyond the river. Where
were they now?

The first skirmish of the war, on Methuen's front, had taken place here a couple
of days before Methuen had arrived. Julian Ralph, the *Daily Mail* correspondent,
described it graphically. He had hired a buggy and driven gallantly towards the
battle. He found the station, on the south bank of the Orange River, half
deserted: officers' horses tethered to the wooden fence, tents pitched in the front
gardens, beside the old paraffin tins full of flowers (perhaps petunias); in the
middle of the street, some soldiers working a heliograph, with a thing like a
shaving mirror connected to the morse key. Hardly any other soldiers were to be
seen.

What does it mean?
We have heard that the patrol is cut off by a large force of Boers, and every man-jack in
the place – field batteries, infantry and all – has gone to their relief in the train.

People were scanning the red-hot veld, whole families of Africans, standing
outside their huts, holding up the pink palms of their hands to shield their eyes.[16]
Ralph rode a mile and a half through the camp, clattered over the great red
railway bridge, and then climbed a kopje, from which he was told he would see
everything. He saw nothing. Or rather, he saw a Major Hall of the Royal
Munster Fusiliers, who seemed to have arrived at that god-forsaken spot, a
kopje littered with dirty sandbags, direct from a London drawing-room: not a
speck of dust on his creaseless leather puttees, every star and button and buckle

shining like a woman's jewellery. Beside this mysterious apparition stood a dozen soldiers, coated, like the sandbags, in khaki dust. Standing beside them, scanning the plain with the same upright carriage and intense, professional concentration, was a tame ostrich.[17]

The veld, too, had its apparitions. Northwards, it rolled fifty miles, on and on, almost to Kimberley, with here and there strange funnel-shaped clouds of dust, streaming like vapour from the plain, then a galloping grey horse, whose head and tail, intersected by the dark body of the rider, rose and fell like wings. A ghostly train vanished into an invisible fold of ground, as though it had sunk through a hole in the veld.[18]

Of the actual skirmish Ralph saw only these phantoms. Yet Ralph and the other correspondents had seen one thing that was to be the dominant theme of every battle of the war: invisibility. Like their colleagues in Natal, they began to realize that this was in the very nature of the new warfare – the warfare of the new, long-range, smokeless magazine rifle. The range of the rifle had spread the battlefield over five or ten miles. This and the fact that the ammunition was smokeless made conventional reconnaissance impossible. The enemy were an army of ghosts. Yet the five-shot Mauser magazine – and the ten-shot British Lee Metford and Lee Enfield – made the fighting doubly real.[19]

So it had proved that day. When the trains came clattering back across the Orange River bridge, Ralph saw the casualties from Colonel George Gough's reconnaissance patrol being unloaded: Lieutenant-Colonel Falconer, dead with a bullet through the head; Lieutenant Wood dying; two other officers and two privates wounded. It was Ralph's first sight of the colour of war – the dark patch on the khaki suit. It was also notable that, of the six casualties, four were officers. The Boers 'will not play the game fairly', said one of the soldiers. Ralph drew a different lesson. Those gleaming insignia, the stars and buttons and buckles of the professional soldier, were all very well in the drawing-room. In the sunshine of the veld they blazed like a heliograph. Against an invisible enemy, the British officers had been as conspicuous as redcoats.[20]

Such had been the disastrous end to Colonel Gough's reconnaissance of the Boer positions just before Methuen's arrival at the Orange River. Its immediate result had been more 'quakings' by Milner for the safety of the British positions, even as far south as the main railway junction, De Aar.[21] And Buller had told Methuen: for goodness' sake follow Symons's example in Natal and make the officers dress like the men; and take extra care with reconnaissance. Hence the new dust-coloured look of Methuen's officers.[22] As for Colonel Gough, he was soon to be sent back to the Cape in disgrace: the first of a long line of COs to be 'Stellenbosched', in the phrase soon to be coined from the name of the main base camp. (Gough himself took the disgrace hard. He blew his brains out with his pistol.)[23]

Milner's fears proved unfounded. The Free State commandos did not follow up their success. And now that Methuen had arrived, where were the Boers?

The sketchy intelligence reports, and the inadequate maps supplied to him in Cape Town, had led Methuen to believe that there were two likely positions in which the enemy would try to make a stand. First, at some kopjes at Belmont twenty miles ahead, where they had a laager estimated at fifteen hundred to two thousand men. Second, just across the Modder River, at the lines of kopjes at Magersfontein and Spytfontein sixty miles ahead – that is, about ten miles south of Kimberley. The main enemy force was expected to be at this second position. Buller had warned Methuen that nine thousand men were besieging Kimberley, some of whom would clearly move south to block his advance.[24]

After Gough's disaster, Methuen had sent out various patrols. His best scouts were the 'Tigers'. They were part of a unique corps of two hundred colonial guides raised by Major Mike Rimington, one of the special service officers sent out in July. They were nicknamed 'Rimington's Tigers' after the 'tiger-skin' (actually, leopard-skin) puggaree they wore on their Boer hats. There was little else but this leopard-skin to distinguish them from Boers, for they spoke either the taal or 'Kaffir', and some knew this district as well as any trekboer.[25] But the obstacle to all intelligence-gathering remained the long-range Mauser. Conventional scouting was impossible in flat ground, where the best scout in the world could be picked off by the enemy from more than a mile away.[26] So Methuen had only the vaguest estimate of the enemy's position and strength.[27]

His second handicap (and, again, one that was to haunt Buller in Natal) was shortage of animal transport. The railway he had, and on the railway everything depended. Grinding up that rusty single track, five hundred miles long, had come every box and bale of his supplies: everything from the largest field-gun to the smallest secret weapon, the experimental Marconi wireless set. But, to be fully mobile, he needed animals to haul wagons cross-country. He had 190 mule wagons instead of the 367 promised. There were no oxen. It would be nearly Christmas before any oxen reached the front, as it was only three months since the War Office had 'pressed the button'.[28]

Methuen was also desperately short of mounted troops. This, too, was the price to be paid for starting the expedition more than a month earlier than planned. Buller had only been able to rake together less than a thousand mounted troops for Methuen: the 'Tigers', the 9th Lancers and some mounted infantry.[29] There were not many wings for Methuen's so-called 'flying column'.

These were the handicaps – weak intelligence, poor mobility. It was they – and the need to move at once – that shaped Methuen's plan of attack. A wide detour was out of the question without ox transport. Buller had recommended him to stick to the railway as far as the Modder River. Hence Methuen's plan: to go bald-headed for Kimberley along the railway line. The men would carry greatcoats, rifles, food and ammunition. The engineers would repair the line as they went. Then the trains could follow, bringing up heavy supplies and reinforcements, and the food for Kimberley. If they attacked at night they would march by compass bearing.[30] Surprise – the weapon that had won British infantry so many victories in colonial wars – would have to carry them through. Surprise and British pluck.[31]

That evening, Tuesday 21 November, Methuen's column, more than three miles long, clattered across the bridge and camped on the north bank of the river.

It was a clear night, and cold after the thunderstorm. The men lit fires, using the piles of thorn scrub cut and stacked there that afternoon. The blue smoke, full of the sharp, aromatic smell of acacia wood, drifted back across the river, across the pools of muddy water trapped among the sand-banks and the dykes of black rock.[32] Round the fires sat the men, singing the usual British soldiers' choruses, sentimental, bawdy and ironic, choruses like:

> Hiding in the ammunition van
> Midst the shot and shell I've been
> While my comrades fought as comrades ought
> I was nowhere to be seen
> Tarara ....[33]

Lord Methuen lay in his tent. He did not relish the choruses. They kept him awake. Besides, he liked songs to be patriotic, and war to have a high moral tone. In his own tent he was reading Shakespeare's *Henry IV, Part I*. He was approaching Prince Hal's moment of glory: the battle scene.[34]

At 4.00 a.m., just as the sky began to lighten, Methuen's eight thousand, leaving the tents still standing and having piled more acacia branches on the camp-fires to hide their departure, began to tramp northwards through the soft white sand to Kimberley.[35]

The same morning at the same hour, Lieutenant-Colonel Robert Kekewich, commander of the Kimberley garrison, climbed the 155-foot high ladder leading to the top of the 'conning-tower' and scanned with his telescope the hardening lines of the veld to the south. In the five weeks of the siege he had made this pre-dawn ascent his regular practice – except when he had to organize a sortie against the Boer positions.[36] The conning-tower was a tower of scaffolding built on the headgear of Kimberley's main diamond mine, the De Beers Mine, extending upwards from the huge steel wheel of the winding gear. Kekewich frequently slept in a wooden hut, the size of a ship's cabin, which he had ordered to be built at its foot.[37] From the summit he could see beyond the barbed-wire fence that marked the Free State border four miles to the east; to the south, the view towards the Orange River was cut short by the lines of kopjes at Spytfontein and Magersfontein about ten miles along the railway line; directly below were the geometric lines of defences and sandbagged redoubts that comprised the thirteen-and-a-half-mile perimeter of Kimberley's defences. These redoubts were all connected by telephone to the conning-tower. It needed strong nerves to stand there in the crow's-nest. The tower commanded a magnificent view. It also presented a magnificent target to the Boers' 9-pounders. Kekewich had strong nerves.[38]

Kekewich had taken over the garrison almost by accident. He was a mere battalion commander, the CO of the 1st Loyal North Lancashire Regiment; a pleasant, plump, bald, unassuming man of forty-five, who had fought in the small wars of the eighties and nineties without attracting attention. He was, like Methuen, a serious, painstaking soldier, and he had already shown the diplomatic

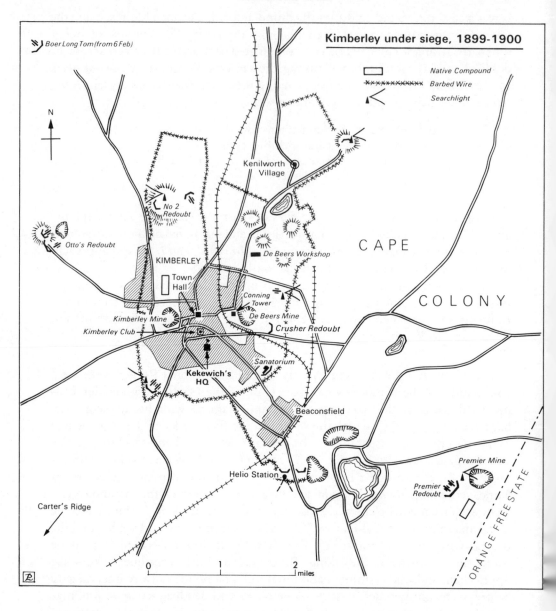

Kimberley under siege, 1899-1900

Boer Long Tom (from 6 Feb)

Native Compound
Barbed Wire
Searchlight

N

Kenilworth
Village

No 2
Redoubt

Otto's Redoubt

CAPE

De Beers Workshop

KIMBERLEY

COLONY

Town
Hall

Conning
Tower

De Beers Mine

Kimberley Mine

Crusher Redoubt

Kimberley Club

Sanatorium

Kekewich's
HQ

Beaconsfield

Premier Mine

Helio Station

Premier
Redoubt

Carter's Ridge

ORANGE FREE STATE

0   1   2
                    miles

gifts that were to be severely tested in the months ahead. He had been sent by
Milner in August to report secretly on the defence of Kimberley; it was the
largest and richest town in the Colony after Cape Town itself, and four miles
from the Free State border.[39] Kekewich telegraphed back: Kimberley was a
sitting duck.[40] So Milner, despite obstruction by Schreiner's ministry, had
arranged for the place to be reinforced by British regulars. Kekewich was given a
half-battalion of his own North Lancashires, and six semi-obsolete 2½-inch
guns.[41] Three weeks later, the war broke out. On the following days, the Free

State commandos poured across the border, cutting both the railway and telegraph lines.[42] By then Kekewich had transformed the place. He was not happy about all aspects – and members – of the garrison. But he was now confident that the battle for Kimberley would not be a walk-over.[43]

It was a claustrophobic place at the best of times. Like many towns which owe their existence purely and simply to the wealth beneath them, it occupied a poor enough situation above ground: no river, no woods, no hills – just a hillock in the sandy landscape to point up the flat lines of the veld. Its climate was severe, even by South African standards: dust-storms in summer, blowing in from the Kalahari Desert to the north-west; icy winds on winter nights that could kill a man caught out on the veld. Here, to this God-forsaken spot, the diggers had come from all over the world, and built South Africa's first boom-town. The diamond rush began in 1870. Twenty-nine years later that hillock was a hole: the biggest man-made hole in the world. Out of Kimberley now came ninety per cent. of the world's supply of diamonds, worth £5 million a year. Even if this was small change compared to the £20 million output of the Rand gold mines, Kimberley was the rock on which the new self-governing Cape Colony was built.[44]

For thirty years Kimberley's diamond crop continued to blossom. The Big Hole got deeper, the mine dumps higher, the citizens more solid and respectable. Kimberley became a place of twenty thousand Europeans and thirty thousand Africans and Coloureds – the prototype of a commercial oasis of the desert, complete with a town hall in the classical taste, and a luxurious hotel-sanatorium.[45] Yet, in a sense, Kimberley was a shadow of what it had been in the days of the diamond rush.

Deeper diggings required more machinery, more capital and more expertise. So individual diggers had sold out to the diamond companies, who came to control both production and marketing. Most of the physical work was now done by African miners imported on contract from all over South Africa. A parallel process, propelled by the technical and financial demands of deep-level gold-mining, had also taken place on the Rand. But Kimberley had taken the process a stage further. Unlike the Rand, controlled by separate groups of foreign companies, Kimberley had passed into the hands of a single corporate giant, De Beers. De Beers thus achieved what the Rand companies longed most of all to achieve: complete control over the pay and conditions of their African contract labour. These Africans were kept confined, almost like slaves, in vast compounds, covered with wire netting. Hence, for both Europeans and Africans, the peculiarly claustrophobic quality of the place. And there were not only the dismal compounds and the mine dumps.[46] There was also the shadow of the Colossus. As managing director of De Beers (though only a minority share-holder), Rhodes behaved as though he had the town in his pocket.

The shadow of Rhodes had haunted Kekewich ever since early September; the man himself, since the day the war began. Rhodes made a few well-publicized expeditions to show the flag; riding out to visit his vegetable garden at Kenilworth; showing off his horses to the cronies he had brought up with him from

Cape Town – Dr Smartt and Mr and the Hon. Mrs Rochfort Maguire – pushing past the street barricade, by the perimeter fence, conspicuous for his white trousers, as though challenging the Boer snipers to pick him off.[47] At first, his relations with Kekewich were not unfriendly. And De Beers provided, apparently with Rhodes's blessing, innumerable services for the garrison.[48]

The town's water-works, at Riverton, were far beyond the defensible perimeter and the Boers soon cut the pipe. De Beers' chief mechanical engineer, a high-spirited American called George Labram, connected the town's supply to the deep springs owned by the company.[49] The town's food supply was estimated to last for seventy days; part of this consisted of food stocks held by De Beers. By now, mid-November, the town's garrison had reached a grand total of 4,606 men. Of these 596 were regulars, 352 were Cape Police, the rest locally raised volunteers[50] for whom De Beers helped Kekewich find horses and mules. The De Beers mines themselves dominated the defences. It was Labram who had constructed the conning-tower on top of the headgear of the De Beers Mine; and the man-made topography of the mine dumps served as fortifications, kept illuminated by arc-lights. In addition, De Beers produced, slightly sheepishly perhaps, some useful little mementos of the Raid: 422 rifles, 6 machine-guns and 700,000 rounds of ammunition sent to Kimberley in 1895 to be ready for the rising at Johannesburg.[51]

In the first three weeks of the siege all had gone as smoothly as Kekewich could hope. The Boers lay low in their laagers; so did Rhodes in his own private laager, the luxurious sanatorium. Kekewich gave the command of the mounted troops to Lieutenant-Colonel Scott-Turner, one of the three special service officers sent to the town in July. Scott-Turner made a few sorties. The armoured train steamed up and down a short length of railway line. The Boers issued a proclamation annexing Kimberley to the Free State. Kekewich issued a counter-proclamation.[52] The town was filled with civilian refugees from the neighbourhood, and with detachments of Cape Police withdrawn from isolated posts. But the siege itself started as a light-hearted affair.[53] There were no casualties except for Captain Scott, the serious-minded commander of the police garrison which had surrendered at Vryburg. Scott had blown out his brains at the sight of the white flag.[54]

On 6 November the Boers began a desultory bombardment with their 9-pounders. The occasion was the rejection of the Boer commandant's ultimatum for Kimberley to surrender; alternatively, for women and children to be removed to a safe distance from the town, a proposal that proved impractical to carry out.[55] The shelling at first caused alarm among the civilians, and the weird triple blast on the mine's steam hooters started a panic. But at this stage many of the shells were duds, and the mine dumps effectively smothered most of the others. The population soon began to take the bombardment in their stride. Some people dug shelters in their gardens. Others relied on the noise of the shell to give them time to take cover. 'You heard the gun boom,' wrote the local doctor, Dr Ashe, in his diary, 'and a few seconds after the "whiz" of the shell came, and you ducked close under a wall or earthbank ... then the shell burst; immediately everyone in the neighbourhood tore frantically towards it to pick up the pieces, for which there was a ready sale, and good pieces ... would fetch from one to two pounds.' At this stage there were only minor casualties – apart from an African woman, whose head was blown off on the 11th, as she walked past Kimberley Club.[56]

At dawn on the day after the beginning of the bombardment, there was a more alarming incident. Kekewich had climbed the conning-tower as usual, and saw in the half-light a 'living mass' of men approaching the 'Crusher Redoubt' on the north-east side of the perimeter. The British field-guns opened up at point-blank range. As the light improved, Kekewich suddenly realized that the men were unarmed African 'mine boys'. He telephoned the cease-fire. It turned out that the men were three thousand Basutos released by De Beers from the mine compounds, without a word to the military authorities. Since the siege had closed the Kimberley mines, Rhodes had become restive about the ten thousand Africans locked up in the compounds. He claimed that this 'hoard of savages' threatened the lives of the Europeans. At any rate, they were using up the De Beers rations. So he had tried to pack them off home to Basutoland. But immediately after their release, the Boers had driven them back to the British lines.[57] (Eventually, Rhodes hit on a less violent solution – to employ the Africans in relief work – and they began to build a great avenue of vines, a mile long, that was to serve as a monument to the siege.[58])

Two days later, Kekewich received a direct hit on his headquarters – in the form of a telegram from the C-in-C, Sir Redvers Buller. It was about midnight on the 9th when a knock was heard on the door of the hut below the conning-tower. Kekewich was dozing. The door was opened by an NCO. He brought in an African runner who had eluded the Boer patrols in the darkness. The telegram was blunt: 'Civilians in Kimberley representing situation there as serious. Have heard nothing about this from you. Send appreciation of the situation immediately.'[59]

Kekewich was flabbergasted. Who were these 'civilians'? What had they told Buller? He himself had been sending out reports by African runner ever since mid-October. He had reported all well. He realized that Rhodes had been sending out alarmist messages behind his back.[60] He could only bite his lip and try to postpone the inevitable showdown with Rhodes. He sent an African runner back the same night with a cautious reply for Buller: the situation was certainly *not* critical, although it might become so if the enemy brought up heavy guns, or if the defenders ran out of ammunition for their $2\frac{1}{2}$-inch guns.[61]

The next ten days brought mixed blessings from both Rhodes and De Beers. The ammunition problem was miraculously solved. Labram was in the habit of climbing the conning-tower to relieve the monotony of Kekewich's long vigils in that eyrie. Kekewich told him that he was running out of shells for his guns. Labram agreed to try and cast shells in the De Beers workshops and succeeded brilliantly.[62] On his part, Rhodes acted with his usual disregard for consistency. Only a week after he had cabled the news of the impending fall of Kimberley to

Milner, he announced to Kekewich that the garrison was quite strong enough to spare mounted troops – about eight hundred of them – to march 220 miles north to help Baden-Powell in the defence of their sister-garrison at Mafeking. Kekewich tried to explain the realities. First, they were needed here. Second, they would be cut off by much larger Boer forces armed with artillery. He did not add (a fair comment) that it would all end in another Battle of Doornkop. As it was, Rhodes was abusive and lost his temper. 'You are afraid of a mere handful of farmers,' he shouted in his curious falsetto voice. 'You call yourselves soldiers of an Empire-making nation. I do believe you will next take fright at a pair of broomsticks dressed up in trousers. Give it up. Give it up.'[63]

A few days passed, and once more Rhodes came to see Kekewich. The see-saw had gone back with a bump. Rhodes was seriously alarmed by the *absence* of mounted troops in the garrison. Why not raise two thousand extra troops in Cape Colony and let them be 'thrown into Kimberley'? He would pay the whole cost himself; he could well afford it. Kekewich told him the scheme would take time, and it would not be fair for him to recommend it to Buller. Rhodes must send the proposal direct to Cape Town himself. Buller would be fully in touch with the whole military situation. 'Military situation,' shouted Rhodes, on one of these occasions. 'You damned soldiers are so loyal to one another that I verily believe if God Almighty even was in a fix you would refuse to get him out of it should [this] interfere with your damned military situation.'[64]

On 21 November, the day that Methuen began his march, Kekewich was still in the dark about Buller's plans to relieve him and take Rhodes off his hands.[65] Two days later, the long-awaited code telegram arrived by runner: 'Greenish manures hydrometer avec swarm gabbler,' it began; '... General leaves here with strong force on November 21st, and will arrive Kimberley on 26th, unless delayed at Modder River. Look for signals by searchlight....'[66] Already this news seemed to be confirmed by a stir in the enemy's laagers. From the conning-tower, large bodies of men had been seen trekking southwards towards the Modder. Kekewich decided to do everything to assist the relief column. But what could he do?[67] He had pitifully small numbers of mounted troops at his disposal – twenty regulars, and about eight hundred police and volunteers – against a force of mounted Boers believed to total eight thousand men between Kimberley and the Modder River; and there were rumours that General Piet Cronje was giving up the siege of Mafeking to come south and attack Kimberley. Kekewich had not the faintest idea of the size of the relief column, nor even of the name of its commander, though he had sent intelligence reports to Orange River pointing out the dangers of taking the direct route up the railway line north of the Modder; the Boers might dig in on the Magersfontein or Spytfontein ridges. So Kekewich naturally decided it would be reckless to try to join hands with the relief column – the policy that Rhodes was now quick to advocate, goading him on with gibes about the cowardice of the English soldier. Kekewich listened with his usual politeness, and as usual paid no attention. He decided on a diversionary tactic: a sortie in strength by Scott-Turner's mounted troops against 'Carter's Ridge', the strong-point where the Boers had installed some of their 9-pounders.[68]

The first attack was a qualified success. It was on the 25th. For once, Kekewich was not up the conning-tower to watch the dawn. He was installed on the 'Reservoir Redoubt', looking across to Carter's Ridge. Under cover of darkness, Scott-Turner's men crept forward. As the sky paled they stormed the ridge, killing and wounding twenty-eight Boers and capturing thirty-two prisoners at a cost to themselves of seven killed and twenty-five wounded.[69] Scott-Turner was cheered by the townspeople back to the Kimberley Club. Next day, a Boer medical officer rode into the town asking permission to buy drugs. Kekewich gallantly arranged this, and the officer confirmed that his side had suffered heavily. Scott-Turner did not, however, capture any of the 9-pounders. The bombardment from Carter's Ridge began again on the 27th.[70]

The second attack, launched next morning, was an unqualified disaster. It was now Wednesday, two days after the relief column had been expected to arrive. The column had made progress of a sort – progress that was visible. The previous evening a searchlight beam appeared in the sky, directed upwards from somewhere close to Modder River railway station. Slowly the wavering beam spelt out the vital message. 'Lord Methuen thanks the merchants of Kimberley for their kind present of cigars. He is a non-smoker. He has given them to his soldiers.'[71] All that the unfortunate Kekewich could gather was that the relief column had been checked. He decided to fling a third of his garrison into the field, to try to detain as many Boers as possible north of the river. Perhaps he had been goaded into this risky enterprise by the gibes of Rhodes. Yet he drew Scott-Turner aside before he left for the attack and gave him a final word of warning: 'My dear chap, remember I do not want you to make an assault on Carter's Ridge ... unless it is unoccupied by the Boers, or so slightly occupied that there is every prospect of an attempt against it succeeding.'[72]

A few hours later Scott-Turner lay dead on Carter's Ridge. The position *had* been heavily defended. Scott-Turner stormed it with reckless daring. Twenty-three others of the garrison died with him, and thirty-two were wounded. When the search parties came for the dead bodies they were so mangled that it was claimed that the Boers had finished off the wounded who had fallen there. There was an ugly mood among the townspeople. Early optimism had given way to mutterings of defeat.[73]

Rhodes did not mutter. He rose to the occasion – as only the colossus could. With breath-taking inconsistency, he accused Kekewich of recklessness – of throwing away the lives of the volunteers. 'Remember,' he sneered, 'you are not in command of a lot of "Tommies" now.' Kekewich did not reply. He felt it would be disloyal to Scott-Turner to expose him as the cause of the disaster. He returned to his gloomy vigil on the conning-tower, where a light had been rigged up, ready to flash a signal to the relief expedition.[74]

The solitary searchlight beam to the south of Modder River flickered on the clouds. What had happened to Methuen?

*   *   *   *   *   *

To say that Methuen was shattered by his victories hardly put it too strongly. After his army had marched from Orange River, he had won two minor victories – at Belmont on the 23rd, at Graspan on the 25th. The high cost sickened him. He 'detested war', he told his wife. 'People congratulate me; the men seem to look on me as their father, but I detest war the more I see of it.' He had written those words on the night of the victory at Belmont. It had been a 'sad day'. They had already buried two officers and thirteen men. Outside his tent he could now hear a 'poor fellow groaning and dying, shot through the chest; he is at last silent, so perhaps God has released him'.[75]

Methuen's officers, too, were shocked by the realities of battle. This was old-fashioned war in all its ugliness. 'I won't inflict you with details of a battle-field,' wrote Captain Gerald Trotter of the Grenadiers to his mother. 'It is too horrible. As I marched back to camp with all the various regiments of the Brigade mixed up it reminded me of Lady Butler's picture, "After Inkerman" ... the hospital was also a gruesome sight.'[76] Trotter's regiment, the Grenadiers, lost thirty-six killed or mortally wounded, and a total of 137 casualties, the highest of any unit engaged.[77]

To add to the bitter aftermath of victory, there were claims – as there were to be throughout the war – of Boer atrocities. People said the Boers had deliberately misused the white flag.[78] 'We had a hot job,' said Trotter, 'with some fellows who showed the white flag, and shot two of the Yorkshire ... and a correspondent [Knight of *The Morning Post*] very badly, so we plugged away till one of them walked out. I believe they hung him at Belmont before we marched away.' There were also stories that the enemy had shot twelve men with dum-dum bullets.[79] In reply, a number of Boers were given no quarter.[80]

Methuen's column had lost 297 men killed,[81] wounded and missing, compared with the Free State Boers' loss of under 150.[82] What had gone wrong?

These first British victories on the western front had proved as expensive as the first British victories in Natal. And most of the tactical errors could be traced to the same basic handicaps: weak intelligence and poor mobility. Methuen had marched his eight thousand troops forward from Orange River and found the Boers at Belmont in a position of their own choosing. He could not bypass them. He had to clear the enemy from his line of communication, the railway. Yet he had no means of satisfactorily reconnoitring the enemy position at Belmont. His official intelligence maps marked no contours and were of little use. Methuen had to base a complex plan on a rough sketch of the Boers' position made the day before the battle – a dangerous proceeding. So it proved.[83]

The Free State Boers were few in number, but their position was strong. They held a mass of broken ground and three strong-points astride kopjes. Methuen's plan was for his two infantry brigades to attack the first two kopjes simultaneously from the west flank, approaching under the cover of darkness, then to work round to the third kopje.[84] But the sketch-map was defective. Methuen saw to his horror that the two brigades had diverged, and the Guards were heading straight for the foot of a jagged kopje. 'An awful moment,' he said later, 'no retreat available, and a brave enemy ready to destroy us. I did not lose my head. I saw I was committed to a frontal attack, and I sent one ADC to get the Guards straight, and another to [tell the] 9th Brigade to stick to the Guards; all was right in 10 minutes, and there came grand work for the Guards, the guns covered the tops with shrapnel, the men went up precipice after precipice. . . .'[85]

The Battle of Belmont was in fact remarkably like the Battle of Talana: a short, crude, bloody affair, a so-called 'soldier's battle' in which all the refinements of tactics were submerged in the simple, overwhelming urge to seize a hill and exterminate the enemy. They seized the hills – three in turn. Then Methuen saw what the victorious British troops had seen at Talana: hundreds of Boers trotting away across the veld, untouched by artillery or cavalry.[86]

The Battle of Graspan two days later had repeated the pattern on a smaller scale. Methuen drove the enemy from the next line of ridges at heavy cost to his men. The enemies' losses were about a hundred. Once again, Methuen had the chagrin of watching the majority of the Boers trotting away across the veld, unhindered by the exhausted 9th Lancers or his own field-guns.[87]

Two more days had passed, and it was now the night of 27 November, the night when Kekewich had seen that wavering searchlight beam signal Methuen's thanks for the cigars. Methuen's army had by now covered fifty of the seventy-four miles to Kimberley and was only a few miles south of the Modder River. His plan was to begin a flank march next morning. Despite the jolt he had received at Belmont and Graspan, his self-confidence had begun to return. He told one of his officers that he intended to 'put the fear of God into the Boers'. He thought the Boers had withdrawn to the Spytfontein kopjes: back across the river and astride the road and railway to Kimberley. His plan was to turn the enemy's left flank by leaving the railway and marching twenty-five miles in a broad arc to the east.[88]

During that night, Rimington's Tigers and the Lancers brought him news that made him cancel the plan for the flank march. Some of the enemy were digging in along the banks of the Modder and Riet Rivers either side of the railway bridge which they had just dynamited. The stationmaster, a loyalist, reported that they were burrowing 'like rabbits'. Major Little of the Lancers put the enemy's numbers as high as four thousand. Methuen doubted this. But he decided it would be dangerous to leave this force at the Modder River – small as it was – astride the line of communication. He would postpone the flank march till he had seized this position.[89]

Methuen began to feel almost jaunty. He was confident that Major Little had greatly exaggerated the numbers of the Boers dug into the river bank. Probably there were only six hundred there.[90] The great majority of the eight thousand were back at Spytfontein. He would strike before they expected him. A frontal attack in overwhelming strength.[91] 'So far as I can judge,' he wrote to Buller,

We are getting to the bottom of the Boers. It is a mere question of pluck. We are terribly handicapped and I quite understand this country has been the graveyard of many a soldier's reputation. The maps are of little value, the information obtained still less, as the open country plus Mauser rifles render reconnaissance impossible. People talk of making a detour, or sending a Brigade round a flank, there is no use talking that way with 8,000 horsemen in front of you, a river, and a position not to be turned. The job has got to be done. . . .[92]

'A mere question of pluck.' Pluck and surprise. Methuen certainly possessed courage. It was the Boers who had mastered surprise.

Early next morning, the men of the two infantry brigades began to tramp down across the open veld towards the clumps of trees marking the line of the Modder River. The men were told they would breakfast at the Modder River.

Silence, except for the swish of the boots in the short, bristly grass, and the 'hui, hui' of the thickhead birds.[93]

'They are not here,' said Methuen to Major-General Sir Henry Colvile, pointing out the tall poplars on the river bank less than a mile ahead.

'They are sitting uncommonly tight if they are, Sir,' replied Colvile.[94]

Ahead, in a natural earthworks along the Modder, hidden in every hole and crevice along four miles of the winding river banks, three thousand Boer riflemen prepared to deliver the most concentrated rifle-barrage yet fired in the war.[95]

CHAPTER 17

Breakfast at the Island

Modder and Riet Rivers, Cape Colony,
28 November – 10 December 1899

> '[The hotel] lay now calm and innocent, with its open
> windows looking out upon a smiling garden; but death
> lurked at the windows and death in the garden, and the
> little dark man who stood by the door, peering through
> his glass at the approaching column, was the minister of
> death, the dangerous Cronje.'
>
> Conan Doyle, *The Great Boer War*

A couple of hours earlier the same morning, 28 November, the Boer generals
had taken their own breakfast of coffee and *boerebeskuit* (rusks) at their headquarters close to that clump of tall poplars Methuen had pointed out to Colvile.[1]

It was a charming spot, this 'island', or 'Mesopotamia', at the meeting of the
Modder (Muddy) River and Riet River. There was a delightfully English look,
to homesick colonials, about the stumpy willows on the banks, the emerald-
tufted mallard and the rowing-boats moored by the dam at Rosmead, a mile
downstream. In fact, this was the Henley of Kimberley, a place for weekend
excursions – for wives and children to picnic by the dam, and for the husbands,
Rhodes's men, to play gin rummy on the veranda of the Island Hotel.[2] Now the
party was over, and the stakes were different. It was this hotel that Piet Cronje
and Koos De la Rey – De la Rey, the most austere of the Boer generals – had
made their headquarters for battle.

Among all the Boer leaders of this period, with the exception of President
Steyn, De la Rey stands out as morally the most powerful and the most
unyielding. It was he who was to keep alight, in its purest form, the fierce flame
of Afrikaner nationalism. The grandson of an immigrant from Holland, he and
his family had settled at Lichtenburg in the dry, empty plains of the Western
Transvaal. De la Rey seemed to epitomize the best side of the Boer character.
'Oom Koos' ('Uncle Koos'), as people called him, was deeply religious; a small
pocket Bible was rarely out of his hand. He was a man of formidable looks. The
long, neatly trimmed brown beard, the large, aquiline nose and high forehead,
the deep-set, glowing eyes gave him, at fifty-two, a prematurely patriarchal
appearance.[3] And he was a man of formidable silences. When he did speak, rising
to his feet in the Raad, people remembered his words. No words of his were to
be better remembered than his speech condemning Kruger's war policy.

Like President Steyn, De la Rey had believed up till the last moment – correctly – that war was not inevitable. In the final debate in the Raad that September, De la Rey had aligned himself with Joubert and the Progressives. They should continue negotiations, he said; above all, they should not put themselves in the wrong by invading the colonies. If there was to be war, it should be war on their own territory. 'The Afrikaners have been chased from one land to another, but in all those lands graves were dug for British soldiers. As England's case is unjust, time will bring her to a fall. Before that happens we have land enough to go on burying British soldiers. But ... is it not better to make more concessions as long as ... independence remains?' Kruger taunted him with a charge of cowardice. 'I shall do my duty as the Raad decides,' retorted De la Rey. Looking Kruger straight in the eyes, he ended: 'And you, you will see me in the field fighting for our independence long after you and your party who make war with your mouths have fled the country.'[4]

Despite the unprecedented bitterness of this exchange in the Volksraad, Kruger had been too shrewd to dispense with the services of De la Rey once war had broken out. Instead he had appointed him combat general to assist General Piet Cronje, the leader of the Transvaal commandos on the western front, and someone with whom Kruger saw eye to eye. Cronje shared Kruger's rough peasant ways and his raw courage, but lacked Kruger's talents. He was short and black-bearded, a buccaneer of a fellow, with a reputation for ruthlessness as native commissioner (an official commission had found him guilty of torturing natives). Not that this had decreased his popularity with the volk. After all, Cronje was one of the heroes of the First War of Independence, and the general who had rounded up Jameson at Doornkop.[5]

Relations between De la Rey and Cronje soon became strained. De la Rey had helped strike the first blows of the war, cutting off Kimberley and Mafeking. But he disapproved of both Kruger's offensive strategy, and the half-hearted way it was conducted; and events seemed to prove him right. Kruger's offensive strategy was crumbling. Methuen had brushed aside Prinsloo and the Free State commandos at their first encounter, Belmont, and at their second, Graspan, by which time De la Rey and seven hundred Transvaalers had joined Prinsloo's force. Now there was only the line of the Riet and Modder, and a double row of hills between Methuen and Kimberley: the hills at Magersfontein and Spytfontein. No wonder Prinsloo's Free Staters fled in confusion after the battle. Even De la Rey's heart faltered. His own men had had the heart so knocked out of them that they were 'streaming off to their homes'.[6]

Characteristically, the two Presidents – Steyn and Kruger – had risen to the occasion. Cronje was told to withdraw most of his burghers from the siege of Mafeking and ride for his life towards the south. Kruger, old warrior that he was, believed there was only one chance of stopping Methuen from reaching Kimberley: all three groups of commandos – Prinsloo's, Cronje's and De la Rey's – *must* join hands before Methuen was ready to cross the Riet and Modder.[7]

Now the three commanders were gathered at the delightful Island Hotel between the two rivers. Yet the danger was still acute. Taking into account their losses at Belmont and Graspan, their combined force only totalled just over three thousand riflemen, almost all mounted, and supported by only six or seven Krupp field-guns and three or four 1-pounder Maxims. What could they hope to achieve against Methuen's eight thousand, and that battering-ram of sixteen guns?[8]

The two rivers, Modder and Riet, together formed a natural line of defence of remarkable strength. There were the river banks; the rivers had gouged out of the plain a broad shelter trench, with banks up to thirty feet deep. There were also the rivers themselves – deep and muddy. Now that the burghers had dynamited the railway bridge, the only crossing-place at the centre was the old drift (ford) beside it. There were only two other areas where the attackers could cross: by a pair of drifts at Bosman's Drift, four miles to the east; or by the drift beside the dam at Rosmead to the west, two miles below the meeting of the rivers.

In fact none of these simple geographical facts had been discovered by the British.[9] Unknown to Methuen, a deep moat lay between him and Kimberley. To De la Rey it had suggested a defensive tactic as revolutionary as Louis Botha's yet unrealized plan, over in Natal, for repelling the British by making a vast moat out of the Tugela River.

De la Rey had naturally never seen a modern battle before the Battle of Graspan. It had proved a revelation. He was appalled by the commandos' losses – small as they were compared with Methuen's – at Graspan and Belmont. He must have known that, if Methuen had had horse artillery and a cavalry brigade to unleash after the battle, these defeats could have become disasters. He thought he knew why they had been defeated. Their basic mistake was in their choice of defensive positions. At both Belmont and Graspan (as in Natal at both Talana and Elandslaagte) the burghers had made a stand on hilltops. In the face of modern field-guns firing shrapnel, the hilltop could become a death-trap.

So De la Rey's plan was this. Give up the kopjes, the traditional eyries of the Boer fighter. Dig into the mud of the Riet and Modder, and make this the grave to bury Methuen and his army. It was the best position for the burghers. It was also the last place in which Methuen would expect to find them.[10]

At five-thirty that morning De la Rey stood waiting in his trench opposite the 'island' and close to the broken railway bridge. He must have seen the tell-tale signs: the smoke of a train steaming north, the frightened coveys of thickhead birds, perhaps some spring buck – and the first lines of mounted khaki figures breasting the purple line of veld a mile beyond the river.[11] He himself and most of his eight hundred Transvaalers – his own neighbours from Lichtenburg, Bloemhof and Wolmaranstad – had dug themselves in on the south bank of the Riet. Beside him were his two eldest sons, Adriaan, just turned nineteen, and young Koos, who was sixteen. The General wore civilian clothes like everyone else: the tweed jacket and floppy-brimmed hat that he used to wear on the farm. He carried no arms. Just the two symbols of authority, divine and human: the

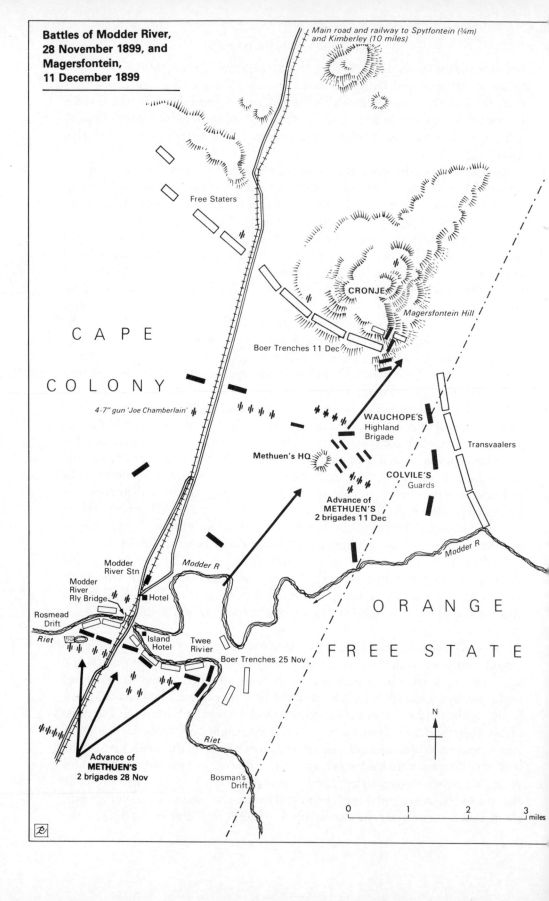

**Battles of Modder River,
28 November 1899, and
Magersfontein,
11 December 1899**

Main road and railway to Spytfontein (¾m)
and Kimberley (10 miles)

Free Staters

C A P E

C O L O N Y

CRONJE

Magersfontein Hill

Boer Trenches 11 Dec

4·7" gun 'Joe Chamberlain'

WAUCHOPE'S
Highland
Brigade

Transvaalers

Methuen's HQ

COLVILE'S
Guards

Advance of
METHUEN'S
2 brigades 11 Dec

Modder R

Modder
River Stn

Modder R

O R A N G E

Modder
River
Rly Bridge

Hotel

Rosmead
Drift

Riet

Island
Hotel

Twee
Rivier

Boer Trenches 25 Nov

F R E E   S T A T E

Riet

N

Advance of
METHUEN'S
2 brigades 28 Nov

Bosman's
Drift

0   1   2   3 miles

well-thumbed pocket Bible, and the small *sjambok* (leather whip) he took everywhere with him.[12]

On his left, straddling two miles of the same side of the Riet River, east from the junction point with the Modder, lay Cronje and most of the other Transvaalers. They had their own slit-trenches. Behind them their horses were tethered under the shelter of the banks of the Riet. Beyond them, in the 'island' between the meanderings of the two rivers, other burghers were concealed in the undergrowth, in case the British tried to turn the Boers' east flank at Bosman's Drift. Dug in beyond De la Rey to the west, and extended as far as Rosmead Drift, were Prinsloo and the Free Staters. They had still not recovered from the mauling they had received from Methuen's troops at Belmont and Graspan.[13]

Whether De la Rey had agreed to the disposition of the artillery is not known. Cronje had concentrated most of his field-guns on the north bank of the Riet River, covering De la Rey's trenches; that is, four of his Krupp 75-mm field-guns were close to the railway line, commanding the central drift. The other two field-guns, and all three of the 1-pounder Maxims, were scattered along the 'island', including one field-gun opposite Bosman's Drift at the extreme east. Not one gun of either sort was backing Prinsloo in his efforts to defend Rosmead Drift on the west.[14] It was a mistake on Cronje's part that was soon to have disastrous results.

Already, after the first few moments of the British infantry's advance, it was clear to De la Rey that a second mistake, equally serious, had been committed by Cronje's men along the banks of the Riet River to the east. Their orders were to hold their fire as long as possible. The farther the infantry advanced towards the two rivers, the more crushing would be the effect of the Boers' fusillade, and the harder it would be for Methuen to extricate his men. But restraint of this kind is notoriously difficult for untrained troops. The nearest lines of 'Khakis' to the angle of the Riet River – actually, the 1st Scots Guards, who were marching forward towards that clump of tall poplars – were at least a thousand yards, and probably nearer twelve hundred yards, from the Boer trenches, when Cronje's men's nerve faltered and they opened fire. Naturally the Khakis flung themselves flat. In that wretched fusillade the burghers had lost all chance of a decisive victory.[15] Now it was to be an affair of blow and counter-blow: an endless struggle between gladiators, differently armed yet more or less evenly matched – the spitting, drumming hailstorm of Mauser fire against the thunderstorm of 15-pounders.

How can we describe from the soldiers' angle of vision that ten-hour duel?

From the British side, there is no lack of material to reconstruct the scene. To his wife, Methuen wrote, 'I thought the enemy had cleared off, as did everyone else, whereas Kronje, De La Ray [sic] and 9,000 men were waiting for me in an awful position. I never saw a Boer, but even at 2,000 yards when I rode a horse I had a hail of bullets round me. It seems like Dante's Inferno out of which we hope some day to emerge.'[16]

Methuen himself, like Symons at Talana, put himself at the head of some Highlanders, and led a charge down towards the river. Unlike Symons, he

emerged from this daring act unscathed. The charge achieved nothing.[17] Both
his brigades – on the east of the railway, the Guards Brigade led by Major-
General Colvile; on the west, the 9th Brigade, led by Major-General Reggie
Pole-Carew – both were nailed down in the veld by the fire of invisible Mausers
and some Martini-Henrys.[18] 'If one asked a comrade for a drink of water,' wrote
Ralph, 'he saw the bottle, or the hand that was passing it, pierced by a dum-
dum.... Or if he raised his head to writhe in his pain he felt his helmet shot
away.'[19] For ten hours soldiers lay flat on their faces, hungry and thirsty, nibbled
by ants, in a temperature that rose to 90°F in the shade (and a sun that blistered
the backs of the legs of the kilted Highlanders). So strong was the craving for
water that, despite the orders to hold fast, men tried to crawl back to the water
carts, and several were killed in the attempt. From sheer exhaustion – and
boredom – others fell asleep where they lay.[20]

Such was the battle, seen from the British side: a ten-hour fusillade in their
faces from an enemy they never saw. 'Pom-pom-pom-pom', went the Boers'
spiteful little 1-pounder Maxim, squirting across the sand like a fire-hose. The
name stuck.[21] As for the sound of several thousand Mausers firing simultaneously, it was like 'the perpetual frying of fat', said Julian Ralph, 'like the ripping
of air, like the tearing of some part of nature ... hell's vomit'.[22]

What of the 'ripping of air' on De la Rey's side? One of Cronje's English-
speaking burghers, stationed four miles up river from De la Rey, later wrote in
his diary,

> The shout went up 'daar kom de Britische' ('there come the British') ... when boom,
> boom went two shells, bursting about 40 yards above us on the bank. I said to myself, Oh
> God, I am in it for now.... Now the cry is to get into some sort of cover, but there is not
> much of that, everyone looking for himself, no order or discipline.... The Maxims kept
> us here [so] that we cannot move, and along the river, down to the station, the fire is
> incessant. Artillery and small arms, from both sides. It is simply 'Hell let loose'. I could
> never have realized, nor can one who is not here, what it is like.... For two hours I lie on
> my stomach making myself as small as possible....[23]

De la Rey himself did not use such graphic language in letters or reports. It
was not in his nature. Yet there were colours enough in the war, seen from his
side of the firing-line; horrors, too. De la Rey came within one footstep of death,
and suffered, as we shall see, a crippling loss.

Despite the initial blunder, made by Cronje's men, of firing prematurely, the
advantage in the battle seemed at first tilted towards De la Rey's side. Through
field-glasses, the Boers could see disaster overwhelm the two leading companies
of the Scots Guards: their solitary machine-gun smashed by the Pom-Pom.[24] An
anxious time followed, and De la Rey blamed Cronje for doing so little to cope
with the threat. The Coldstreams worked their way under fire along the bushy
banks of the Riet to the east. A few waded across to the island, but this was not a
proper ford (they had no map to show them Bosman's Drift). Colvile ordered
them back.[25] After that the Guards gave the Boers little to worry about. It was
the British artillery who took up the cudgels: the twelve 15-pounders of the
18th and 75th Batteries, firing from only just over the heads of the prostrate

Guardsmen; and, escorted to the battlefield by an armoured train, the four 12-pounders of the Naval Brigade. 'Battery column sections, left wheel! Action front!' The shrill commands of the British gunners were not audible to De la Rey, but he must have seen the effects: first, the twelve field-guns wheeling and swooping in that strange, Aldershot set-piece, then the regular pattern of flashes, up to four a minute, as the smokeless shells left the muzzles, and the regular pattern of dust kicked up by the muzzle blast.[26]

In reply, the Boer artillery performed prodigies of improvisation. The day before the battle, it was said, the Boers had calculated the range, for the sake of their own riflemen and artillery, by planting white markers at measured intervals alongside the railway line.[27] The Free State artillery commander, a Prussian ex-NCO called Major Albrecht, had dug a series of unconventional gun emplacements. Outnumbered three to one, Major Albrecht's Krupp field-guns dodged back and forth all day between emplacements. His artillery horses suffered heavily. But the British could not knock out a single one of his guns. Firing from concealed positions, Albrecht's gunners wrought havoc on their British counterparts, standing out there in the veld without sandbags or rocks to protect them.[28]

Meanwhile, alarming reports had reached De la Rey from the men on his right – from Prinsloo and the Free State commandos, who had dug themselves into the riverside village of Rosmead, a mile to the west of the railway line. Cronje had failed to put enough men there to guard Rosmead Drift, to protect it with guns, or to reinforce the place later. Now the price was paid. Opposite the drift was part of the 9th Brigade, Pole-Carew's. For about three hours they, like the Guards, were nailed down in the veld. Soon after eleven they could be seen creeping forward in rushes. Prinsloo's men could not hold them. A fold in the veld gave the attackers better protection at this point. Some of the defenders had occupied a farmhouse which made a perfect target for the field-guns; and they were Free Staters, their morale dented by the reverses at Belmont and Graspan. By midday, these wretched Free Staters, as De la Rey saw, had fled back to the north bank. Using the captured farm as a strong-point to protect their advance, the British followed them.[29]

They were actually Kekewich's men, the half-battalion of North Lancashires that he had left behind at Cape Town when he had taken the other half with him to Kimberley. Now they seized the honour of being first across the drift, slipping and struggling over the slimy stones and floundering waist-deep in the pools. Other men of various units – Argyll and Sutherland Highlanders, and so on – followed on their heels. Some soldiers managed to scramble in single file across the wall of the dam, just above the drift.[30] By one o'clock, the British had dug themselves into the north bank and driven the Free Staters out of Rosmead. They were soon covered by four guns of the 62nd Battery, whose gunners had only left Orange River the previous day, and ridden hell for leather since dawn. (Six dead horses had to be cut out of the traces.) With Pole-Carew at their head, the British now began to push through the hedges of prickly pear towards a second resort hotel behind the Boers' central position.[31]

What did Cronje do to cope with this alarming threat? He did nothing, said De la Rey bitterly.[32] It was De la Rey who organized the counter-attack. Having recrossed the river, he sent the men of the Lichtenburg Commando, left in reserve on the north bank, westwards to block Pole-Carew's advance. They gave covering fire to Major Albrecht's hard-pressed gunners working the Krupp field-guns. They pinned down the leading men of the North Lancashires and Argylls who were crawling forwards through the reeds and bushes along the river bank. They drove Pole-Carew's men back into Rosmead. Assisted by a deluge of British shrapnel bullets fired in error at Pole-Carew's men from the field-guns across the river, De la Rey's burghers then held on to their trenches until darkness put an end to the fighting.[33]

It was just before this that De la Rey's eldest son, Adriaan, was dangerously wounded. He had been at his father's side all day, as De la Rey strode up and down the scattered trenches, exhorting, cursing, lashing the burghers with his small *sjambok*. De la Rey himself had been slightly wounded in the right shoulder by a shell fragment. Adriaan had escaped without a scratch. Then, in the last hour of the battle, a shell splashed on the trench a few yards behind where De la Rey was standing. When the dust cleared, De la Rey saw that Adriaan was wounded in the stomach. He was forced to leave him in a safe place, till an ambulance could be found. There was no ambulance. In the darkness, De la Rey's staff wrapped Adriaan in a blanket and they set out to carry him the nine miles to Jacobsdal, the Boers' base hospital.[34] About eight o'clock they were walking along the road when they met Cronje, whose men were in full retreat. De la Rey later recorded the bitter exchange:

Cronje: 'How did the battle go?'
De la Rey: 'Why did you leave us in the lurch? We saw nothing of you all day.'[35]

De la Rey's party reached Jacobsdal just after dawn. An hour later Adriaan died in his father's arms.[36]

Meanwhile, De la Rey had reached a decision almost as painful as this bereavement. How could they keep their grip on the line of the Riet and Modder? Cronje, Prinsloo and the Free Staters had betrayed them. Had the Free Staters on the west flank stayed firm, he believed Methuen would have been forced to fall back all the way to Orange River; there was hardly sufficient water in the sandy veld between. But the Free Staters had fled. Now Methuen would have no difficulty in reinforcing Pole-Carew's bridgehead on the north bank. So De la Rey had to accept that his own men, too, had to abandon the Riet and Modder.[37]

The moon rose about ten, and the night was clear and cold. Along both sides of the river bank, torches moved in strange, halting patterns, as men collected up the dead and wounded: 460 casualties on the part of the British, about 80 on that of the Boers. Opposite Rosmead, British reinforcements lined up in the darkness and splashed across to join Pole-Carew. They were followed by the first of the Guards.[38]

Methuen's chief staff officer, a personal friend, lay mortally wounded in the field hospital. Methuen lay near him. A bullet had pierced the fleshy part of his thigh, a couple of hours before the end of the action; the wound was slight but painful. It was decided that both his brigades would renew the attack as soon as it was light. All night Methuen tossed and turned in the hospital.[39]

At dawn, the naval guns reopened the bombardment. There was no reply. When the British infantry reached De la Rey's position, they found it deserted. There were traces of a meal eaten in the hotel and a few gin bottles. Outside, the trenches were knee-deep in spent cartridge cases, and there were dead bodies floating in the river (perhaps those of onlookers caught in the bombardment). The Boers themselves had withdrawn to the north and east. Now there was only the Spytfontein ridge, ten miles to the north, violet against the sky – the last natural defensive position this side of Kimberley.[40]

The death of De la Rey's son had one immediate result. De la Rey stayed at Jacobsdal to bury him, and missed the *krijgsraad* (council of war) on the day after the battle.[41] He strenuously objected when he heard the decision of Cronje and Prinsloo. In his absence they had decided to withdraw the burghers ten miles back to Spytfontein, instead of digging in at Magersfontein, six miles back. How to reverse this decision? De la Rey telegraphed to President Steyn over Cronje's head, and Steyn passed on the message to Kruger, who asked Steyn to go to the front line in person to set matters straight.[42]

In fact, both Presidents were already deeply disturbed by complaints about the behaviour of the Free State burghers at the Battles of Graspan and Modder River. Prinsloo, their own commander, complained, 'I was convinced that victory was ours . . . but after their flight there was nothing we could do.'[43] In his reply, Kruger did not mince words. Cowardice was the cause of the flight. Officers and men must both learn to do their duty. He urged Steyn to go to the front line himself, 'because this is the final moment of decision whether we are to surrender the country'. He added, 'Brother, my age does not allow me and my eyes are too painful, or I would be there myself.'[44]

Steyn drove from Bloemfontein in haste, and reached the front six days after the Battle of Modder River (the Battle of Twee Rivier – Two Rivers – the Boers called it, taking the name from the farm on the island). Kruger had given him a long telegram addressed to the burghers. Steyn drove round to each laager, a tall, bald red-bearded figure, and read aloud to them the old President's homely lines:

De Heer heeft gestooned dat Hij met ons is. . . . The Lord has shown that He is with us because the enemy has lost hundreds and we only a few men. . . . This now remains to be decided: are we to surrender the country? If we give in, what might then become of our brother Afrikaners in Natal and Cape Colony, who have attached themselves to us? No, no, even though we must lose almost half of our men, we must still fight to the death, in the name of the Lord.[45]

Steyn reported back next day to Kruger that the burghers were full of heart. Then he summoned the generals to a second *krijgsraad*. Here De la Rey put the case against fortifying Spytfontein. They must try more daring tactics. And he persuaded them all to adopt his own plan.[46]

Everything that had happened at Twee Rivier seemed to confirm his earlier ideas on tactics. The place to lie in wait for a force of British infantry was the plain, not the hill – the plain at the edge of the first line of kopjes between the Modder and Kimberley. These were the kopjes dominated by Magersfontein, not the second line which culminated, to the east, in Spytfontein. Most of the arguments for digging in at the Modder applied equally well to digging in below Magersfontein. They would be safer from artillery. They would catch the British by surprise. If the worst happened, they would still have a second line of defence – Spytfontein – before abandoning the siege of Kimberley.[47]

But how could they avoid further débâcles like the flight of the Free Staters? Many of these burghers were now unmounted. Then put them in the centre of the defences. They would fight better, De la Rey concluded grimly, if they had no obvious mean of escape. Concentrate the mounted burghers where mobility was essential – on the flanks.[48]

The combined Boer armies had now been further reinforced by the main part of Cronje's force which had arrived from Mafeking. There were perhaps eight thousand, two hundred burghers in all, of whom six thousand were mounted.[49] There were the camp-followers and commandeered African labourers. These Africans were set to work digging a twelve-mile-long defence line under the shadow of the Magersfontein ridge. It was a back-breaking job. Beside the Modder the soil was as soft and black as chocolate cake; here it was red and stony. Gradually the fortifications took shape; and no one had seen anything like them. Most of the defences consisted of broken lines of breastworks, built of stone or earth. The main trench itself ran for about a thousand yards along the foot of the Magersfontein ridge. It was three to five feet deep, and only three feet wide, giving much better protection than any equivalent British shelter trenches of the period.[50]

The boldness of De la Rey's plan lay not only in the scale and originality of these home-made defence works. Like Botha's line in Natal, they were camouflaged with the skill of a man who digs a trap for an elephant. All along the line, De la Rey had arranged for grass and acacia scrub to be laid in front of the trenches. In six days the job was done. Methuen's scouts rode within a mile of the trench before they were driven away by Mauser fire. They scanned the plain through their field-glasses without an inkling that the trap had been set.[51]

CHAPTER 18

Marching up in Column

Magersfontein,
9–12 December 1899

Such was the day for our regiment
  Dread the revenge we will take.
Dearly we paid for the blunder –
  A drawing-room General's mistake

Why weren't we told of the trenches?
  Why weren't we told of the wire?
Why were we marched up in column
  May Tommy Atkins enquire ...

'The Battle of Magersfontein',
verse by Pte Smith of Black Watch
December 1899

On Saturday 9 December, eleven days after the Battle of Modder River, Major-General Andrew Wauchope, the commander of the Highland Brigade, rode up to Methuen's HQ on the north bank. He was tall, and clean-shaven, and eager; he had come for his battle orders. Methuen was preparing for a night march that Sunday. The HQ was the Crown and Anchor Hotel, across the river from the hotel where Cronje and De la Rey had installed themselves less than a fortnight earlier.[1] Now the Crown and Anchor was awash with British orderlies and staff officers. A crate of champagne (a present to Lord Methuen from Lord Rothschild) had replaced the empty gin bottles left behind by the Boers.[2]

Wauchope emerged after his interview with Methuen, and paused at the door. 'I do not like the idea of this night march,' he said to Colonel Douglas, the new chief staff officer.[3] Wauchope was not a man to be rattled easily. He was said to have been wounded in every action he had fought.[4] Douglas now urged him to return to Methuen again and explain his doubts. For some reason, Wauchope did not return. He rode gloomily back along the river bank to the brigade camp where the Highlanders were assembled, fixing aprons over their kilts, painting out their buttons and buckles in preparation for battle.[5]

The plan for a night march – followed by a dawn attack – was certainly risky, but less risky than the alternatives. This was Methuen's view, and he had had nearly a fortnight, since the Battle of Modder River, to turn things over in his mind. As a soldier schooled in the short, sharp wars of Africa, it was Methuen's natural inclination to strike at the Boer positions immediately after the latest battle – before they could reorganize themselves. But he had decided to contain his impatience.[6] His own flesh wound had taken a week to heal; his men needed a respite after their three battles; new staff officers had to be brought up to the front; and the last of his reinforcements – including Wauchope's Highland Brigade, an extra cavalry regiment, more field-guns, howitzers, and a 4·7-inch naval gun – would not reach Modder River till next day, 10 December.[7] Finally, he thought it would be folly to advance before repairing the dynamited Modder River railway bridge. Here was a gash in the life-line of his own army. Here was also a broken rung in the rescue ladder essential for the job Buller had given him: to resupply Kekewich at Kimberley and remove those of the garrison who were proving a liability – the women and children, the ten thousand African mine-workers and their employer, Cecil Rhodes.

How long could Kekewich hold out? Methuen had been relieved to receive a code signal from Kekewich on the 4th, in answer to his own searchlight signals: the garrison, said the Kimberley searchlight, still had food enough for forty days.[8] By the 8th the railway bridge had at last been repaired – or, rather, the engineers had rigged up a temporary affair of timber and piles beside the twisted steel girders.[9] On the night of the 10th the Highland Brigade would march off to the attack.

'The job has got to be done,' Methuen had answered Buller.[10] He proposed to use the same tools as before. As usual, his scouts could give him only a sketchy idea of the enemy's defence line. It appeared they had adopted the same kind of position as at Belmont: a line of kopjes. Well, it was Belmont tactics he would use against them. The key to the enemy's position was, he believed, the Magers-fontein Kopje.[11] From his camp at Modder River, it looked like the prow of a battleship.[12] On closer inspection, it was the usual South African kopje, decor-ated with greyish-brown rocks and dusty grey-green *vaalbush*. It was six-and-a-half miles from the camp, though it looked ten at midday, floating in the heat haze, and barely a mile away when the sun first rose.[13] The job of the Highlanders was to storm this strong-point with the bayonet at first light, to deal the same short, sharp thrust at Cronje here that the Grenadiers had dealt Prinsloo on Gun Hill, above Belmont.

About three o'clock on Sunday afternoon, the five artillery batteries trundled off across the plain. The Highlanders tramped along behind: three thousand five hundred men in khaki;[14] khaki aprons to hide the front of the kilts, and no sporrans, claymores or gleaming coat buttons. Yet, viewed from behind, they were still unmistakably Scottish: dark green tartan kilts for the leading three battalions, the Black Watch, Seaforths and Argylls; khaki trousers for the reserve battalion, the Highland Light Infantry.[15] Sleety rain began to fall, and the men had no greatcoats, only a blanket and groundsheet, one for each pair of men, strapped to their backs.[16]

About three miles from the kopje they halted. This was the evening's bivouac: the bare veld, with neither food nor shelter; but the men were cheerful.[17] Wauchope rode back to consult Methuen and Colvile, the commander of the Guards Brigade. There was a final briefing, directed by Methuen, resting his injured leg on the box-seat of a wagon. The Guards and the 9th Brigade were to be held in reserve. Wauchope seemed satisfied with his orders – so Methuen said later.[18] But, as the meeting broke up, Wauchope remarked to Colvile, 'Things don't always go as they are expected. You may not be in reserve for long.'[19]

Meanwhile, the Boers were receiving their dose of British shells, delivered by twenty-four field-guns, four howitzers, and the British answer to Long Tom – 'Joe Chamberlain' himself, the 4·7-inch naval gun. The bombardment, one of the biggest since Sebastopol, seemed to the war correspondents awe-inspiring. To the usual grey puff-balls of shrapnel were now added huge water-spouts of red earth and rocks hurled skywards by a high explosive called 'lyddite'. Onlookers were told by the naval gunners that Old Joey would kill every man within 150 yards of where his shells struck.[20] This assumed, of course, that the enemy was on the hill being bombarded by Old Joey. Of this there was no actual evidence. Later Methuen, who in this respect had only followed Buller's orders, made the admission: the artillery 'preparation' did nothing except prepare the Boers for the British attack.[21]

It was now dark, and the fireworks faded out on the distant ridge. The wind rose and the icy rain continued. The orders were: no fires, no smoking. In the Highlanders' bivouac, spirits waned. Wauchope ate a beef sandwich, then lay down in his sleeping-bag. He was upset by the loss of a knife and compass given him by his wife. He decided he would take his old claymore, despite Methuen's orders.[22]

Wauchope's staff woke him about midnight. It was a night of Shakespearean tempest: moonless, with a furious wind from the north-west, and the distant rumble and flash of an African thunderstorm. 'Quarter column!' The four battalions lined up in the most compact formation in the drill-book: 3,500 men, 30 companies, 90 files, all compressed into a column 45 yards wide and about 160 yards long. Even so, it was almost impossible for the files to keep in touch. The Black Watch and the Argylls used long ropes, knotted every ten feet, held by the left-hand man of every file; the Seaforths and the HLI groped their way along as best they could. At the left-hand of the leading file of A company, Black Watch – that is, at the front left-hand corner of the great stumbling, heaving mass – marched Wauchope with his claymore. Beside him were his ADC and Major Benson, a staff officer carrying a compass in each hand.[23]

A night march by compass bearing is a delicate and dangerous manoeuvre. It is one thing in Egypt, marching over a carpet of sand under a starlit sky – as Wauchope had marched, the night before the Battle of Omdurman. How different in this plain under the shadow of Magersfontein, strewn with rock holes and ant-heaps and thorn-bushes, on the night of a tempest! Yet despite everything, despite the lightning that flashed blue on the rocks and the rain that deluged the compass, Major Benson kept his head. He tacked and veered, but he led the brigade to very nearly the spot Methuen had indicated. As the sky began to lighten, the brigade found itself about a thousand yards from the ridge.[24] The storm had blown itself out, and on the papery sky ahead was printed the prow-shaped silhouette of Magersfontein Kopje.

There were many reasons for the disaster that now loomed over the British infantry. Dominating everything was Methuen's ignorance of the enemy's position. For this Methuen cannot be altogether exonerated. One more day at Modder River, and he could have arranged an aerial reconnaissance – launched the war balloon Buller had sent up the railway on the eve of the battle, and tried to spy out the enemy's line of trenches.[25] As it was, he had ordered the Highland Brigade blithely into the trap De la Rey had set up at Magersfontein, just as he had sent his army into the trap set for them on the Modder. But Wauchope, too, displayed a recklessness that was to compound Methuen's mistakes. His brigade was now within a thousand yards of the kopje he thought the enemy held – nine hundred yards from the line of trenches that was their actual position. Benson halted and turned to Wauchope.

'This is as far as it is safe to go, Sir, in mass.'
'I'm afraid my men will lose direction. I think we will go a little further,' Wauchope replied.[26]

What Wauchope meant by 'losing direction' is impossible to guess. The sky was lightening. Because of the storm, they were already late – as much as an hour later than planned. To extend the ninety lines of men, marching shoulder to shoulder, to three lines of men extended at five yards would take at least ten minutes. Now was the time: when the men could already see well enough to carry out the manoeuvre, and *before* the enemy could see well enough to open fire. This was not only Benson's view, but that of at least two of the battalion commanders. The column marched on in mass, Wauchope and his ADC alone at its head.[27]

The Boers waited in their hidden trench line till the leading files – A and B companies of the Black Watch – were about four hundred yards away. Perhaps they heard the belated command: 'Open order, march!' Perhaps they saw the flicker of the bayonets. A single shot from the kopje.[28] Then a river of flame from the trenches, that made one sergeant of the Argylls later say it was as though 'someone had pressed a button and turned on a million electric lights'. And there was a 'great roaring in the ears', as though a dam had burst its walls.[29]

Even now, the battle was not lost for Methuen. The war correspondents, still asleep in their camp when the battle opened,[30] or waking to hear the fusillade in the half-light of dawn, as faint as the noise of rain drumming on a window-pane, wrote later of the battle being lost in the first wild moments of that fusillade.[31]

But it was not like that. Most of the Boers' first shots went high. In the British column there was a moment of paralysis – of nightmare, prolonged, people thought, for minutes, though actually lasting only a few seconds. Then a babel of orders: advance, retire, left, right – anything: and some joined a stampede to the rear.[32] After this spasm, discipline reasserted itself. Wauchope stood, calmly saying to his ADC, his cousin, Lieutenant A. G. Wauchope, 'This *is* fighting, A.G.' He told the Black Watch to extend to the right. Their colonel fell, shot dead. But most of A, B and C companies began to crawl forward; then scraped themselves some cover behind rocks and ant-hills. The Argylls also lost their colonel, but they, too, managed to deploy. The Seaforths were hopelessly confused with the Argylls, but they had few casualties at this stage. The CO of the Highland Light Infantry was trampled in the stampede, but his battalion regrouped.[33]

What followed for the next nine hours was a duel on the same pattern as the preceding battle. Methuen had tried to play Belmont tactics on Cronje and De la Rey; they had succeeded in playing Modder tactics on him. The sun rose to find the Highlanders pegged down here on the plain, just as the Guards had been pegged down in front of the Riet River.[34]

A movement of a hand, the flash of a canteen tin, even the twitch of an ankle attacked by ants – the price was paid in Mauser bullets.[35] Once again, it was the British artillery that saved the British infantry. The gunners brought their field-guns well within rifle range – within 1,400 yards – of the enemy. That morning they met no opposition from the Boers' own guns, except for three pom-poms.[36] Blessed by their absence, and the calm sunny weather, Methuen launched his aerial reconnaissance force: the captive balloons, manned by Captain Jones and some engineers, and connected to Methuen's field HQ by cable and telephone. In fact, Cronje had somehow left a gap about 1,500 yards wide in the eastern part of the Boers' line – that is, between the end of the great trench at the foot of Magersfontein Kopje and the beginning of the defences on the ridges running down to the river.[37]

People have argued that, even now, Methuen and his army could have blundered into victory. Almost anything is possible in the war of might-have-beens. Methuen should have rushed his reserves into the gap; in other words, the Guards should have punched a hole in the Boers' left, just as Pole-Carew's brigade had broken their right at Modder River. So runs the scenario of the sand-tables.[38] But Methuen had to fight a real battle. He could not have known the size of the gap. And at Magersfontein he had many handicaps. First, Prinsloo was no longer commanding the Free Staters, and they held their ground. Second, the Transvaalers had mustered over six thousand riflemen – not two thousand, as at the Modder.[39] Finally, though Methuen now had three brigades instead of two, he felt that the third must be held ready to parry a blow against his camp. This left only the Gordons and the Guards Brigade free to try to slip through the gap. And, if Methuen failed to seize the chance, the balloon confirmed that the chance was short-lived. Before many of the Guards could have been thrown forward, Captain Jones spotted some Boers (who had arrived there by accident) galloping across to seal off the gap.[40]

As it was, Methuen remained almost like a spectator of the day's humiliations. He sat on a cart in the shadow of the balloon on Headquarter Hill. He had never envisaged what he would do if the Highlanders' attack failed. To prevent them being driven back – that was now his only concern. In this he very nearly succeeded. He sent some Gordons forwards to reinforce the centre;[41] the Guards were used to block the Boers on the east. Casualties they had, but less than twenty were killed. Lieutenant-Colonel Alfred Codrington, CO of the Coldstream Guards, was hit in the right ankle; he called, 'Outer, right low.'[42]

Britain's premier Marquis, Major Lord Winchester, was shot dead; it was said he had turned his back on the enemy to watch the captive balloon.[43] But Cronje, like Methuen, was cautious about seizing his opportunities.[44] The shadows shortened.[45] Disaster passed into stalemate. Men fell asleep over their rifles. Terror gave way once more to boredom.[46]

And then, like a frayed steel cable, the nerve of the Highlanders suddenly failed.

Up to this moment, most of them had withstood their ordeal with stoicism. About two hundred men of the Black Watch and the Seaforths had even reached the east face of the Magersfontein Kopje, where they had been captured or shot, or killed by their own artillery. (By chance, some parties had trickled through the actual gap in the Boer line, when they stumbled on seven Boers, led by Cronje himself, who had lost his way in the storm. 'Skiet, kerels, skiet hulle!' – 'Shoot, fellows, shoot them!' – roared Cronje, and the Highlanders were rounded up.)[47] Now, after nine hours of terror and boredom, nine hours without water in that scorching sun, the Highlanders could take no more.

About one o'clock Lieutenant-Colonel James Hughes-Hallett, the Seaforths' CO, found some Boers working round his right flank, and ordered two companies to trickle back a few hundred yards.[48] Lieutenant-Colonel George Downman, the Gordons' CO, gave similar orders.[49] But the trickle became a flood, and the flood an avalanche. One of the officers described it: 'I saw a sight I hope I may never see again: men of the Highland Brigade running for all they were worth, others cowering under bushes, behind the guns, some lying under their blankets, officers running about with revolvers in their hands threatening to shoot them, urging on some, kicking on others; staff officers galloping about giving incoherent and impracticable orders.'[50]

The pipes skirled, the officers cursed. The men, obedient to their instincts, melted away into the veld. When the ambulance men went out next day to collect the dead and wounded – 902 on the British side, 236 on the Boer side – they found Wauchope dead, within two hundred yards of Cronje's trenches.[51] But most of his brigade died with their backs to the enemy.

From Headquarter Hill, Methuen impassively watched the destruction of the Highlanders. Perhaps his own dreams of military glory died with Wauchope. He was bitter, yet stoical. Only bad luck, he believed – and Wauchope – had cost him the victory. Now 'there must be a scapegoat,' he wrote, 'so I must bear my fate like a man, holding my tongue'.[52]

Even now there was a sliver of hope: the Boers might retreat during the night, as they had retreated after the Modder.

Soon after dawn next day, the balloon rose, its huge membrane flushing pink and gold as it climbed out of the line of shadow. Captain Jones's telephoned report dispelled Methuen's last illusions. The Boers, masters of the new warfare of the western front, were holding fast in their trenches.[53]

CHAPTER 19

'Where are the Boers?'

Tugela River, near Ladysmith, Natal,
11–15 December 1899

'I think with luck that we shall give the Boers a good
hiding this side as we have a strong force in all arms . . .'

Lt Algy Trotter, Buller's ADC, to his
mother, Frere, 11 December 1899

'*God zal voor u strijden . . . En als kop behouden blijft, dood of
levend, dan behoudt gij alles.*'
('God shall thus fight for you . . . If you hold the hill, dead
or alive, you hold everything.')

President Kruger to Botha,
13 December 1899, telegram no. 39

'Now where are the Boers?' asked the distinguished-looking staff officer on the kopje at Frere. It was 11 December. Still unaware of Methuen's repulse, the other half of Buller's army, under his own personal command, were facing Colenso, twelve miles to the north.[1] In the extraordinarily clear light you could not miss the Colenso position, where Botha, the opposing general, apparently had his laager. There were tier on tier of rust-coloured kopjes, sweeping up from the tree-lined bed of the Tugela River to culminate in the peak of Bulwana. Beyond Bulwana was Ladysmith.[2] Its heliograph flashed occasionally, plaintive, inscrutable.[3] But where were the Boers?

'I'll show you, sir,' said the captain of the picket. Sitting beside them were the usual mixed bag of Boer-watchers: a naval officer off-duty; some war correspondents (including John Atkins, of *The Manchester Guardian*, who recorded the scene). There was also a team of heliographists with a tripod. The Boer-watchers picked up their field-glasses, like race-goers studying a distant fence.[4]

'The biggest camp is under Grobler's Kloof among those trees.' 'I don't see it.'

'They're pretty well hidden, sir; they're devils for hiding themselves.'

'You see this kraal?'

'The far one?' 'No, just below this hill.' 'Yes.'

'Very well. Look over that, and you see a white road winding up to the left. Got that, sir?'

'Yes.' 'Well, look over the left tree, and you'll see a reddish low hill.' 'Yes.' 'Well, there's the camp to the left of it. Quite plain. I can see with the naked eye now.'

There was an embarrassed silence, as it became clear that the staff officer was looking in the wrong direction. Not that the right direction held much more to see.

'I believe they've bolted,' said the staff officer after a pause. Under his breath one of the privates added, 'I ain't seen nothing. 'Ope they 'aven't gone. We'll 'ammer you, Kroojer, my son.'[5]

The scene that John Atkins saw from the kopje above Frere had one feature in common with the scene Julian Ralph had witnessed a month earlier at the kopje by Orange River. They were fighting shadows. How many Boers were lying in wait beyond the tree-lined banks of the Tugela? Five thousand? Ten thousand? Or had they melted away at the heavy tread of Buller's army? The Field Intelligence Department (FID) put the enemy's numbers on the Tugela at about seven thousand.[6] It was anybody's guess. And how were they disposed? Reconnoitring the enemy's position here at the Tugela was just as difficult as at the Modder. Neither proper reconnaissance nor an accurate survey of the terrain was possible, though later Buller was to be severely blamed for his ignorance of the enemy's position.[7]

All that week, while the Boer-watchers scanned the scene through their field-glasses, Major Elliot and an armed party of gunners, twenty-five strong, had tried to make a trigonometric survey of the line of the Tugela, and the Boers had hunted them like game.[8] Hence Buller had to rely on the FID survey of the area prepared in Maritzburg. This was an inch-to-the-mile map reproduced as a blueprint, and based on railway and farm surveys, and on a micro-filmed map sent by carrier-pigeon from Ladysmith. Like an explorer's map, the blueprint bore the bold legend: 'Vacant spaces indicate that data . . . is wanting rather than that the ground is flat.'[9] With the FID map, as with choice of generals, the lack of mounted troops and the strategy of the campaign itself, Buller had to make the best of a bad job.[10]

Now he had decided to try to force the passage of the Tugela at Potgieters Drift, a ford fifteen miles higher upriver. The Boer-watchers still thronged the kopje at Frere, as the heliographists beside them began to work the morse key, attached to the mirror on the tripod. 'Clear line. No 72. Cipher 11th December . . . I propose to march with three brigades, two regiments of cavalry, 1,000 volunteers, five batteries of field artillery, and six naval guns to Springfield on the 13th . . . I may be disappointed. . . .'[11]

Poor Buller. It was to be the understatement of the war.

In the last fortnight, Frere had presented an extraordinary spectacle. It was hardly a village, just a station-master's house, a hotel and three other buildings on the railway line from Durban to Ladysmith and beyond. Southwards, lay the meandering wagon road that led to Estcourt, and the crisp arc of the railway line; to the north, the ramparts of kopjes along the Tugela; far to the north-west, the jagged mountain walls of the Drakensberg, over eleven thousand feet at the peak, flushing gold at dawn and wrapped in the smoke of grass fires at sunset, like the bloom on a black grape. Otherwise, Frere had been a speck of corrugated iron in an ocean of sunburnt grass.[12]

That was the old Frere, the Frere that the colonists had named in honour of Sir Bartle and his forward policy. Now it was a speck of corrugated iron in a city of white tents. Four infantry brigades (sixteen battalions), with two regiments of cavalry and other mounted troops – about nineteen thousand men – had tramped its dusty main street since Buller's Army Corps had come steaming up from Durban. The trains still kept coming: a seven-car hospital train, with a distinguished doctor in charge, Dr Treves, the Queen's personal surgeon;[13] a train-load of sailors, with a naval searchlight which could flash a message in morse code sixty miles by way of the clouds;[14] trains full of terrified horses, half dead after the journey up from the coast; trains full of strange-looking bales and crates, spare parts for the 4·7-inch naval guns, sections of pontoon bridges, drums of telephone cable.[15]

To the roar and whistle of the trains, and the calls of the camp bugles, were added other more exotic sounds. Down in the bed of the Blaauw Krantz River lay the iron structure of the railway bridge, twisted and slashed like a jungle creeper. Botha's men had sliced it up with dynamite during their retreat from their raid on south Natal. Now you could hear the chant of the African labourers building the 'deviation' – a temporary railway line laid across wooden trestles. Then there were the yells of the African drivers of the trek oxen – hoarse cries, like parrot calls.[16] 'Ai, Ai, beauty!' cried the drivers in Zulu, flicking their bamboo whips over the animals' backs with a double crack like a Mauser shot. Then the sixteen-span ox wagons would grind forward again, like some monstrous insect, over the desert of rutted tracks and dried-up watercourses.[17]

To the ordinary British privates, the halt at Frere provided a welcome relief. They were dazed by the heat. (At 102°F in the shade, it seemed hot even to some of the colonists.)[18] They were dazed by their surroundings. They had been travelling ever since the Army Corps had been mobilized in October: two months in which they had been shipped out in overcrowded troop ships,[19] packed into cattle trucks and pitched out in the heat of an African midsummer. Few, if any, could be said to be in fighting trim, as there had been no room on the boat for proper exercise. About half were reservists, white-faced men who had come straight from jobs in offices or (like the miners of the Durham Light Infantry) from jobs underground.[20] Yet morale was high enough, and rose higher when Buller himself reached Frere on 6 December. 'Buller's arrival was almost everything,' wrote John Atkins, a veteran of the Spanish-American War. 'I have never seen troops re-tempered like this by one man since I saw the extraordinary change which came over the American army on the sudden arrival of General Miles before Santiago.'[21] Probably few of the English privates could have explained what they felt about Buller. But he was their General, and they believed in him. To beat 'Mr Kroojer' should be easy enough for a great man like Buller.[22]

It was not only what they had heard about him and the war. Before the ships had sailed, many of the Tommies must have seen the popular papers, like *The Daily Mail*, which predicted an easy victory.[23] But the man himself had an extraordinary magnetism. It was partly that splendid Devonshire name, which rolled off the lips like a roll of drums. It was more the result of what he did for his men: the trouble he took to get them their canteens before he started his own dinner, the way he would move heaven and earth to see they could get their letters from home. In a curious way, they could identify with him. He had the massive frame and the red face of a Devonshire farmer. He could be blunt and bloody-minded, and he could make blunders like the best of them. But he was as brave as a lion, and when the lion had ceased roaring there was usually a twinkle in his eye.[24]

He was none of your red-tape generals. He had none of them airs and graces. A real *man* was old Buller.[25]

Their confidence in Buller did not, of course, prevent the men from grousing. Grousing, like swearing, was the background music of the barrack room.[26] And at Frere, despite all Buller's efforts, there was no shortage of things to grouse about. The men were unshaven, and their belts, boots and faces were all one colour: khaki.[27] The flies were everywhere, and so was the dust. Water was short (as this unusual heat-wave had succeeded the spring rains); the Blaauw Krantz River was a series of muddy pools – good enough for washing khaki clothes, but strong drink. The food was the usual soldiers' grub: bread and beef.[28] No wonder some of the soldiers looted and stole; and a crowd of Durham miners, a tough crowd by any standard, were put on a charge by the Provost-Marshal. Major-General Neville Lyttelton, their brigade commander, became worried at the effect on the town.[29] But the looting was fairly good-humoured. Anyway, the victims were mainly Afrikaners, absent fighting with the Boers.

The Uitlanders and colonial volunteers excelled everyone as looters. The 'Imperial Light Looters' and 'Bethune's Buccaneers' they were dubbed.[30] This was in a sense a reprisal for what their own people had suffered. All over this district, British-owned farms had been looted and stripped by Botha's raiders. When the tide of raiders first receded, the station-master's house here at Frere had been left with two or three red geraniums blooming outside in the dirt. Inside, the place was a surrealist wreck of burnt photographs and clocks stuffed down into flower-pots. Since then, the station-master's house had been patched up. There was a Union Jack on a pole outside. It was clean and neat and bare. It was Buller's headquarters.[31]

Buller had arrived at Frere in the small hours of 6 December, alone except for his Military Secretary, Colonel Fred Stopford.[32] Stories were later circulated about Buller's addiction to champagne – stories that he perhaps encouraged, to confirm the reassuring picture of himself coolly emptying his glass within sound of the enemy's guns. But there is no reason to think that Buller actually lived a less modest life than a conventional British commander-in-chief on a major campaign. He did not have a French chef like Clery, his own divisional general, nor was he to make a fool of himself with a court of dukes' sons, like Lord Roberts. He had three ADCs and a Military Secretary, whom he worked off their feet. He spent most of his own day at his makeshift desk in the station-master's house, or riding round the camp on Biffin or Ironmonger.[33]

His feelings when he arrived at Frere were a characteristic mixture of cautious hopes and profound anxieties. He did not, by any means, expect a walk-over. His spirits, always volatile, had been cheered by the dramatic improvement in the situation since he had left Cape Town on 22 November. 'It has been an uphill journey ... but I do believe we are pulling through. . . . I am happier than I was but I cannot say I feel out of the wood.'[34] That was what he told Lansdowne in a private letter on 4 December, and it coincides with the general impression he conveyed in his cypher telegrams and despatches and his personal letters to his wife.[35] Milner, he said, was still 'very nervous' about the chance of an uprising in the Cape. He himself did not think there was much risk; the further he got from Milner, the less impressed he was by these dangers. Gatacre could hold his own in the north-east Cape. Methuen's success at Kimberley, he told Lansdowne, was 'assured'. He personally regretted the long halt Methuen had made at Modder River. 'However it is the sort of delay that only the man on the spot can deal with, so I say nothing.'[36] To his wife he added the admission that he was puzzled by the tactics Methuen had adopted at Modder River: the frontal assault – why not a flank attack? 'I daresay it will be explained later.'[37]

The only problem that Buller faced with a sinking heart was the one that he had set himself: to get White out of the unholy mess he had got into at Ladysmith. He had told the War Minister,

I am in great doubt how to attack Ladysmith. The main road through Colenso goes through a ghastly country exactly the sort made for the Boer tactics and they have strongly fortified it. I can turn it by going across the Tugela at Potgieters Drift some 15 miles up the River, and should have better ground to advance over but I should not be in so good a tactical position to help White, as I should be if I came up the main road from Colenso. I must leave it till I get up to Frere. I don't know that I ever had a problem which has bothered me more.[38]

That was his view the day before he reached Frere. Six days later – that is, on 11 December – he had decided to make the flank march by Potgieters. A flank march from Colenso – but a frontal attack, it must be noted, not a flank attack, on Potgieters.[39] 'The whole Tugela River is a strong position,' Buller explained later. 'There is no question of turning it, the only open question is whether one part of it is easier to get through than another.'[40]

He had chosen Potgieters because it did look easier – or, rather, less ghastly – country to get through. This was the view of the Natal colonists, who should know: Laing (the Lang of Laing's Nek),[41] and T. K. Murray, the member of the Natal Parliament who had lived there all his life and was organizing Buller's corps of African guides.[42] It was also the impression conveyed by the inch-to-the-mile blueprint map, prepared by Captain Herbert at the Field Intelligence Department, and the reconnaissance sketch, on a marginally larger scale, made by Major Elliot's gunners.[43]

Tactically, there seemed to be distinct reasons for preferring Potgieters. Buller had personally inspected the Colenso position by telescope and decided that to force it would be 'too costly'. The approach from the south was dead flat, without any cover, and the north bank was commanded by a line of kopjes systematically fortified by the enemy. There was also a prospect of nine miles of subsequent fighting in the gorges to the north. At Potgieters, the actual crossing might be easier, as the ramparts of hills were set back farther from the Tugela and were only two miles in depth. After that, it would be downhill all the way to Ladysmith.[44] However, Potgieters itself would be a tough nut to crack. Buller's scouts reported the enemy were already beginning to fortify it as they had fortified Colenso, and White heliographed from Ladysmith to say that his war balloon confirmed this.[45]

There were, however, two other tactical arguments against a flank march by Potgieters. First, the practical difficulties and dangers of such a march. Owing to those wretched delays in the War Office arrangements for animal transport, Buller would have an appalling task to assemble the minimum number of oxen and ox wagons: four hundred teams with a thousand African drivers. He had no divisional field hospital, and bearer companies would have to be organized to carry the wounded twenty-five miles back to the railway line. He would have to leave one brigade at Chieveley to hold this line; so he would have three, not four, brigades for the attack at Potgieters.[46] There was a chance that his whole force, if defeated at Potgieters, might lose their line of communications and be beleaguered in turn.[47]

Second, White had heliographed to say that he could send a flying column as far as Onderbrook – that is, about ten miles north of Colenso.[48] There was no doubt that one of the keys to victory was to co-operate with White, and especially with his cavalry, the four precious cavalry regiments that, despite Buller's appeal, White had insisted on keeping with him when the siege began. Buller had convinced himself, perhaps mistakenly, that White would not lift a finger to help him if he attacked Potgieters.[49]

How difficult it was, in every sense, for the two Generals to communicate. Apart from the rugged country – bridged by the flickering searchlight beam, the fitful heliograph and the wayward carrier-pigeons – there was a mountain of resentment between them. Again and again Buller heard his own prophetic voice at the War Office that July and August: 'Do not go north of the Tugela, do not go north of the Tugela.' Penn Symons, White and Lansdowne had wrecked everything.

Buller blamed them all, of course. He also blamed himself. So he said later, when he made a 'clean breast' of everything to his old comrade-in-arms, Sir Arthur Bigge ('You may show any of it to the Queen,' he added rather touchingly). He blamed himself for not 'having insisted on choosing my own generals when in London'. He had not been 'hard enough then'. Apart from the choice of Major-General French, all his proposals had been rejected.[50] He had been too weak – or too much of a gentleman – to throw his weight about and have a showndown with Lansdowne.

This was Buller's outburst of self-criticism in the following March, after much muddy water had flowed under the broken bridges of the Tugela. He was surely right. But what did he feel on 11 December, as he planned the attack on Potgieters? His bitterness towards White is clear. What about his other generals, on his own side of the Tugela? There were two whom he might have chosen himself: Major-General Neville Lyttelton, commander of the 4th Brigade, who had worked under him at the War Office,[51] and Major-General Henry Hildyard, commander of the English (2nd) Brigade, who had made a name for himself as the head of the Staff College, and had trained the 2nd Brigade under Buller's eye at Aldershot.[52]

The other generals inspired less confidence in Buller. There was the divisional commander, Lieutenant-General Sir Francis Clery, the nominal commander of the army at Frere. If Clery had wished, he could have retained full control of this Natal expedition, and Buller would have stayed, as Milner had begged him, to keep a grip on things in the Cape. Clery had insisted that Buller came too. Clery's performance during Botha's raid into South Natal confirmed Buller's own misgivings. He had got in a frightful 'funk', and retreated quite unnecessarily to Estcourt.[53] The same could be said about Major-General Geoffrey Barton, commander of the Fusilier (6th) Brigade.[54] And the cavalry commander, Lieutenant-Colonel John Burn-Murdoch, had made a poor showing in the Sudan.[55] On the other hand, the commander of the Irish (5th) Brigade, Major-General Fitzroy Hart, was brimming with a self-confidence which was almost more alarming than Clery's and Barton's funk. He was a man of the Penn Symons school, a fiery Irishman, beautifully dressed, a master of field-day tactics, who believed in the traditional virtues of close order and dash.[56] Finally, there was the artillery commander, Colonel Charles Long, an intrepid gunner, who believed in taking his 15-pounders up under the noses of the enemy's guns. He had done well as Kitchener's chief artilleryman at Omdurman; but then, at Omdurman there were no guns on the enemy's side. His action in sending forward the armoured train from Frere the previous month had been labelled by Buller as 'inconceivable stupidity'.[57] This disaster does not seem to have knocked the stuffing out of Long. On the contrary, he was keen to redeem himself by some spectacular feat of arms.

These were the commanding officers – some timid, others headstrong, all inexperienced in Boer tactics – that Buller had to make the driving force behind his 'fighting machine', as he hopefully called it.[58] He blamed himself for not choosing better ones.[59] He could not blame himself, except indirectly, for the collapse of the staff arrangements.

It was one of the most extraordinary features of Buller's expedition that he had arrived at Frere with only his personal staff – that is, with Colonel Fred Stopford (his Military Secretary) and the ADCs. As we saw (in Chapter 14), other twenty-odd headquarters staff, provided in the War Office scheme for the Army Corps, had all vanished: locked up in Ladysmith (like Major-General Hunter, his Chief of Staff, and the Intelligence Officer, Major Altham); sent off to help Methuen (like Colonels Miles and Douglas); left behind at the Cape to hold the fort (like Colonel Wynne and Colonel à Court). This was inevitable, given White's blunder, and the need to break up the Army Corps. But the price was to be paid at the Tugela. Buller had to take over Clery's staff and issue his orders through them.[60] This was bound to end in confusion – and was one of the causes of the disasters ahead.[61] There were also embarrassing personal problems concerning two young men attached to Clery's staff.

The first was Prince Christian Victor, a favourite grandson of the Queen's. It was one of Buller's sources of strength that he was an old friend of Sir Arthur Bigge, the Queen's Private Secretary, and hence in touch with the Queen herself. The previous month, Bigge had cabled to ask why Major Prince Christian Victor, who was under Clery's command, had been sent back to base at Durban; what was going on?[62] Now the Prince was a poor fish, and no real use to anyone. But the reason for sending him to base was in fact Clery's 'funk'. He was terrified the Boers might capture him. Buller had then decided to transfer the Prince to Hildyard's staff, and sent him up to the front at Frere to take his chance like the rest of them.[63] Still, it must have been an anxiety for Buller to have a royal hostage-to-fortune so close at hand. Buller remembered the ghastly business of the Prince Imperial, Napoleon III's heir, killed by the Zulus in 1879 while serving in the British flying column of which Buller was one of the leaders.[64]

The other young staff officer was Lieutenant Frederick Roberts, the only son of the Field-Marshal. As one of Roberts's Ring, Sir George White had agreed to take him on his own staff. But the siege had begun before young Roberts could reach Ladysmith. He had joined Clery's staff as a galloper – and so, in effect, Buller's staff. Freddy Roberts was a delightful fellow; but not very bright, unfortunately; that summer he had failed the Staff College entrance examination by a record margin. No doubt Buller, as one of the Wolseley Ring, had heard the embarrassing story. The Field-Marshal had had to go on his knees to his bitter personal rival, Wolseley, to beg him to admit his son on his special recommendation as Commander-in-Chief. Wolseley had refused – but left the door ajar. It was up to Lieutenant Roberts to show by some feat of gallantry that he deserved to be admitted.[65]

Alas, poor Freddy was to win his recommendation – but not in the way that anyone, least of all Buller, would have wanted.

On 11 December Buller sent that heliograph message to White to say that he proposed to march on Potgieters.[66] Next day he moved Barton's brigade up to Chieveley, within five miles of the Tugela, and prepared to send the other three brigades off on their fifty-mile flank march. But that day he received a string of telegrams from the Cape that led him to abandon this plan immediately, and decide that the balance of risk, strategic and tactical, had shifted. After all, he must 'make a run' for Colenso.[67]

The decision was later to bring down a storm of criticism on his head. Buller's reasons were as follows.

The news from the Cape was bad, shatteringly bad. On the 11th he had heard of 548 men missing and captured (actually 696, as it proved), lost by Lieutenant-General Gatacre at the Battle of Stormberg.[68] It was to emerge that Gatacre, although instructed to take no risks until reinforced, had hazarded his small force in a night march to recapture a strategic railway junction. The column had lost its way through the mistake of a guide. Gatacre had pressed on, and at dawn found himself at the mercy of the enemy.[69] Buller did not reproach Gatacre. Accidents were bound to happen when the men and the generals were strange to the country. He sent Gatacre a reassuring telegram: 'Am sorry to hear your bad luck; you are right to concentrate; will reinforce you as soon as possible.'[70]

On the 12th Buller heard of Methuen's crushing reverse at Magersfontein, which Methuen reported with the conclusion: 'Our loss is great. Possibility that further advance is questionable, but shall endeavour to hold my own and keep my communications secure.'[71] Buller telegraphed, 'Fight or fall back.' Methuen dithered – or so it seemed to Buller. 'He was all to pieces,' he said later, 'and could do neither.'[72]

From Buller's point of view, this was the last straw. Ever since he had reached South Africa, six weeks before, Milner had been in 'an unholy terror' of a Cape rebellion. Buller had taken the moral burden of rejecting Milner's advice and striking out against the Boers. Now both the mobile armies in the Cape – Gatacre's and Methuen's – were themselves at risk; Methuen was sending 'lachrymose' messages, begging for reinforcements; clearly he and Gatacre might both be cut off. Milner was 'in agony' about the Cape, and Milner might be right.

In this frightening new twist of the strategic situation, Buller decided he could not hazard the only other mobile force – his own Natal Field Force – in a fifty-mile march away from the railway line. Not only would he himself be unable to communicate with Cape Town in case of emergency. His whole force, if defeated at Potgieters, could be left as helpless as White at Ladysmith.[73] As he later explained, in the light of events, *both* plans of attack, at Potgieters and Colenso, were 'forlorn hopes'. In the case of the latter, 'Colenso was in front of me. I could attack that and control the result. But Potgieters ... I could not pretend I could control that. I might easily have lost my whole force.'[74]

This was Buller's strategic justification for his own change of plans. Given the 'unholy terror' of the High Commissioner, and Methuen's fear that he might have to retreat all the way to Orange River,[75] it cannot be dismissed out of hand. There was also the tactical advantage that at Colenso he 'was closer to the point' where he could join hands with White. Amery later castigated Buller, both for the decision to abandon what Amery called the 'safer and better plan' to go to Potgieters, and for the method Buller chose to attack Colenso.[76] However, it must be said, on Amery's side, that he had to write this volume of his history while the war was still in progress, and before Buller was able to give his own version of events.[77]

Buller, at any rate, was ready to move on Thursday 14 December. He had already heliographed to Sir George White, 'I have been forced to change my plans. Am coming through via Colenso and Onderbrook Spruit.'[8.] He posted a long, anxious despatch to Lansdowne and the War Office, explaining some of the reasons for the change of plan, notably the danger of his own force being cut off, though he tactfully avoided mention of Milner. 'From my point of view,' he said, 'it will be better to lose Ladysmith altogether than to throw open Natal to the enemy.'[79] In a cable to Lansdowne, he struck a slightly more confident note: 'Today I am advancing to the attack and trying to force the direct road. I fully expect to be successful but probably at heavy cost.'[80] He then called his commanding officers to the headquarters tent and briefed them, that Thursday evening, for the attack next day. No doubt they had all climbed the kopje and seen the enemy's position through their glasses and telescopes. They had also the two maps at their disposal: Captain Herbert's blueprint map, and Major Elliot's sketch-map. Buller explained the plan to storm the river, and establish a 'lodgement' – we would say 'bridgehead' – where Botha's men were at present dug in, to the river bank.[81]

Despite Buller's ignorance of certain details, one of which (as we shall see) was to play some part in his misfortunes, he knew the basic facts of the topography of Colenso, and the broad lines of Botha's defence. This is shown not only by his own private and public letters and despatches, but by reference to the two maps themselves, both of which I have succeeded in tracing.[82] In essence, Botha held a triangle of predominantly flat ground across the river, north of the village and railway station of Colenso. The triangle was formed on the south and east sides by the Tugela, which swung through ninety degrees after forming a quarter-circle north of the village; the hypotenuse was formed by the first tier of hills to the north-west, the whole triangle comprising about eight square miles. It was in this spot, relatively safe from artillery fire, that Buller hoped to make his lodgement.[83] (*See map on page* 226.)

But how could they cross the Tugela? The blueprint map showed three drifts (fords) facing the triangle of plain that Botha occupied. The first (the Old Wagon Drift, marked '1' on the map) was close beside the wagon bridge. The second (marked '2' and called Punt Drift) was inside a long, thin loop of the river, cutting obliquely into the plain; the third, (Bridle Drift, marked '3' and on the course of a track) was about a mile to the west of the western end of the loop. There were also two bridges: the railway bridge (now dynamited) and the wagon bridge (called the Iron Bridge on the sketch-map – still intact, but probably laid with charges). Hence Buller believed – reasonably enough – that the best chance of crossing was to ford the river by the two southernmost (and hence safest) drifts shown on the maps upstream of the bridge: drifts 1 and 3.[84] But this two-pronged attack presented grave difficulties.

First, no one could say for certain that the river *was* fordable at these two drifts. The Tugela was not a gentle, muddy river like the Orange or the Modder. It came roaring down from the Drakensberg, a creature of sudden storms high in the mountains. Even during the present heat-wave, it might be just too deep for the soldiers to wade through.[85] And though Buller had a string of pontoons ready to bridge the river, these could not be erected under fire. Second, it was obvious to Buller where Botha would put his strongest defence line: opposite the drifts. This was what made a river crossing such an agonizing undertaking: one's inability to choose one's own points of attack.[86] Third, there was a chain of low kopjes immediately north of the dynamited railway bridge. These commanded much of the plain, though barely within rifle range of the two crossings. If his lodgement were to be successful, the kopjes would have to be stormed at heavy cost.[87]

Such were the difficulties. Though Buller had greatly underestimated the skill with which Botha had dug his trenches, his general appreciation of the tactical problems does not seem too wide of the mark.

But *was* there really no way round? With hindsight, people later were to point out a weak link in Botha's chain of defences: a hill called Hlangwane, a hill on the *south* side of the Tugela, from which Botha's position could be enfiladed by artillery. Why was Buller such a fool as to miss this chance of avoiding a frontal assault? Buller did not miss the tactical importance of Hlangwane. Nor did he – rightly – expect Botha to have missed it. He assumed that Botha would have extended his line of defences across the Tugela, to include Hlangwane. To seize it would thus be a difficult and complicated business. For Hlangwane was not an isolated hill. It was itself commanded by ridges of scrub-covered hills extending over six miles.[88]

Why not then make the capture of Hlangwane the sole objective of the first day's battle? Buller was, in fact, tempted. But he decided that the 'bush-fighting' it would involve – fighting in thick scrub – would be too difficult for his raw troops. Instead, he would seize Hlangwane *after* his lodgement was made. Botha would then be forced to evacuate it. For the present, he must trust to luck at Colenso – luck and the overwhelming weight of his fourteen thousand infantry, his two thousand, seven hundred mounted men and the weight of his forty-four guns.[89]

In the headquarters tent Buller read out his orders to his commanding officers and explained the positions allotted to each unit. Burn-Murdoch, with the two regular cavalry regiments, was to protect the left flank of the infantry; Colonel Lord Dundonald with the mounted infantry and mounted irregulars, the right flank, as far as Hlangwane. Hildyard and his brigade would launch the main attack, storming the Old Wagon drift half a mile above the road bridge. Hart and the Irish Brigade would storm the smaller Bridle Drift three and a half miles higher up the river. The two other infantry brigades would be held in reserve: Lyttelton's between the Irish Brigade and Hildyard's; Barton's between Hildyard's and Dundonald's mounted men. The artillery would, of course, begin the battle.[90] Buller went up to Colonel Long – so he later gave evidence – and put his finger on the precise place on the blueprint map where he wanted Long to come into action. He was to take twelve field-guns and eight naval guns and prepare the ground for Hildyard's attack. The rest of the artillery was divided: Lieutenant-Colonel L. W. Parsons was to prepare the ground for Hart's brigade; the longer-range naval guns were to bombard the position from the rear.[91]

Did these officers question these orders? There is a story that one was heard to murmur, 'And may the Lord have mercy on our souls.'[92] But no evidence exists, as far as I know, to corroborate this. On the contrary, as Lyttelton put it, 'with anything like equality of numbers, we can drive them out of any position, however strong.'[93] Buller's generals accepted Buller's line of reasoning. Colenso would be a hard nut to crack. But crack it they must, if they wanted to join hands with White and help him to extricate himself from Ladysmith.

It was about 4.00 a.m. on Friday 15 December. John Atkins, the *Manchester Guardian* correspondent, woke to the sound of men and horses tramping and the cries of the African drivers to their mules. A cool, windless night, the prelude to a scorching day. Outside his tent, still not a spark of light. Atkins heard, rather than saw, Dundonald's mounted column wind past his tent, the men chaffing each other about how they would like the 'fun' ahead, the horses throwing down their heads and coughing. There was 'a steady, continuous, sweeping noise which resembled silence'.[94] In other words, the hum of Buller's war machine.

At about 4.30 a.m. the sky paled. Atkins saw the field moving before his eyes: massed columns of infantry, still too vague for recognition, coiling and uncoiling until they found their places. The dust from their feet floated up 'like an ethereal powder', through which the column waded, the men waist-deep, the horses up to their bellies in this 'white level tide'.[95] Atkins was a poet of war, and ahead of his time. War, in his eyes, was more full of ironies than of heroes.

One little incident struck him with especial force at this solemn moment. A Zulu driver in the column lashed out at his mule train with his right hand and his left hand dropped the concertina that he, like many Africans, carried on the march. The Zulu gave a sort of cry of despair, but he could not stop to retrieve it. A shout from the mounted infantry company behind: 'Mind that concertina! Pass the word!' The line of mounted infantry swerved. The next company followed suit: 'Look out, mind the concertina! Mind the wind-jammer!' The dancing sea of legs and hooves divided as each came to the precious object. The whole brigade passed, 'hurrying on to use all the latest and most civilized means for killing men and destroying property', tenderly leaving the concertina – an African's concertina – unscratched on the veld.[96]

On the hill beside the pair of 4·7-inch naval guns, Buller and Clery and their staffs were ready for the bombardment to begin another kind of music. No one had had much sleep that night. The formal battle orders, drafted by Buller and signed by Clery, had not been ready to distribute till 10 p.m.[97] At 2.00 a.m. they had struck camp; a cup of tea and a hunk of bread, then they had ridden up to Naval Gun Hill, as the low rise was now christened.[98] Behind them the oxen with the heavy baggage-tents, and the pontoon sections, ready to move forward when the lodgement was made. Buller, wearing a peaked cap and riding breeches, presented a striking and dominant figure. Four-square, a man in whom everybody, from private to brigadier, could trust almost blindly.[99] He kept his misgivings even from his staff. Only to his wife did he reveal in a farewell letter – for bullets could carry a long way in a modern battle – his own wretched conclusion that to take a run at Colenso, the best chance they had, was itself a 'forlorn hope'.[100]

At 5.30 a.m. the 4·7-inch naval guns opened the bombardment. For more than an hour the guns raged across the kopjes beyond the broken railway bridge,

sending red-brown columns of soil spurting high in the air. The lighter 12-
pounders joined in. No reply from the Boers. Had they bolted?

Then, about 6.30 a.m., the Irish Brigade, led by General Hart in close column,
like troops on a field-day, tramped off towards the Bridle Drift, and the men
heard for the first time a new sound, like the sound of rain beating on a tin roof,
the sound Methuen had heard at Magersfontein: a tremendous roar of Mauser
fire.[101]

The 'fun' had started.

Meanwhile, Louis Botha, wearing a small Transvaal cockade on his bush hat and
a bandolier slung over his jacket, stood watching Buller's majestic advance. At
thirty-seven, Botha looked ridiculously young to command a whole Boer
army, a stripling among the grey-bearded generals. He stood there calmly
beside the 5-inch Krupp howitzer. He had spent the night there on the ridge,
250 feet above the plain, and two miles back from the Tugela, snatching a few
hours' sleep on the sandbags of the gun emplacement. Then, about one
o'clock, they had woken him. There were lights moving to and fro in the camp
far to the south: the Khakis; the British attack at last. The news spread rapidly
along the Boers' line, a thin line of slit-trenches and gun emplacements
zig-zagging across hill and plain. Botha gave his final orders. They must hold
their fire till the enemy reached the river bank. He would give the signal with a
shot from the great howitzer.[102]

About 4.30 a.m. the sky paled beyond Hlangwane; the darkness drained off
the valley below. From the ridge they could see that ghostly dust cloud at
Chieveley which John Atkins had seen from his tent door. And out of the dust
came Buller's army. One of Botha's companions trained his telescope and saw 'a
long, wide, brown strip', marching towards the river, as though marching on a
parade ground.[103] It was a sight that would have struck any professional soldier
in the world with awe: sixteen battalions of infantry, supported by cavalry and
heavy guns – the biggest British army to march into battle since the Battle of
Alma, half a century earlier. Botha did not flinch. With the help of God, and the
Tugela, they would smite the British. David in a bush hat against Goliath in
khaki. Not that Botha would have compared himself to a biblical hero. He was a
modest man.

What a contrast between the styles of the two Commanders-in-Chief. A
British C-in-C was a *grand seigneur,* withdrawn behind a ring of ADCs, isolated
even from his brigadiers. Botha's tent was open to the humblest burgher. It was
an ordinary bell-tent, captured from Symons's camp at Dundee and furnished
with a packing-case and a stretcher chair.[104] When an elderly burgher entered,
Botha would give up the chair to him and sit on the ground. There he sat, as a
procession of visitors tramped through the tent. He ate, drank, slept and wrote
his official despatches under their gaze. It won everybody's heart. Botha valued
his privacy, but valued the confidence of his burghers still more. He took trouble
with everything and everybody. He trusted in God – which of the Boers did not?
– but left nothing to chance.[105]

It was God, ably assisted by President Kruger, who had already helped Botha to emerge victorious from a serious crisis that week. In late November, as we saw earlier, he and Joubert and their three thousand burghers had retreated to the Tugela. Botha had then proposed at a council of war that they should fortify the line of the river itself. Other officers wanted to fall back to what seemed a stronger position four miles behind the river – the line of hills from Rooikop to Pieter's Hill.[106] The fact was that, as Buller had spotted (and contrary to the writings of many British journalists and historians in later years), the Tugela crossing at Colenso did not represent an impregnable position. Not by nature at any rate. Its main strength was the strength of the river.

There were three weaknesses. First, there was the great length of the line that would have to be held at Colenso, owing to the series of drifts, at roughly two-mile intervals, by which the river could be forded. Second, there were the meanderings of the river southwards into the plain at this point; the southern part – in fact, the place where Buller intended to push his main attack – was barely within rifle range of the Colenso kopjes. Third, and most crucial, the eastern end of the Boer line would have to be extended across the river in order to retain control of Hlangwane.[107]

So there was a case for retreating to a more conventional position on the hills farther back. It was much the same argument that De la Rey had found at Modder River and Magersfontein. Botha had dealt with it in the same way. The Boers had a secret weapon: the spade. Dig trenches in the tall grass along the river banks. Camouflage the trenches with stones. Scatter the soil behind, where it would be invisible. Dig dummy trenches on the skyline, where the British would expect them. Arm them with dummy guns, made of tree-trunks and corrugated iron. Dig away the stones in the river to destroy (or conceal) the drifts. This was the way to deal with the *rooineks* (red-necks) and their great General.

Dig a trap for General Rooibull, 'Red Heifer'. Bait it with a bridge – the iron road bridge that had been left intact, after the demolition of the railway bridge. This was the plan proposed by Botha, seconded by Joubert (before he had been forced by ill-health to retire to Volksrust) and patiently carried out by the burghers, the last fortnight, with the help of fifteen hundred reinforcements from Ladysmith, and a second army of commandeered African labourers.[108]

Then, on Wednesday 13th, two days before the actual British attack, the blow had fallen on Botha. Buller's troops marched forward to Chieveley and his naval guns began their artillery 'preparation'. Botha would have welcomed this: the shells screamed harmlessly overhead, proof of Buller's ignorance of their actual defence lines and a useful warning of the impending attack. But the mere noise of the bombardment, and the mere sight of so many British troops, sent a shock wave through the burghers. Botha had despatched two commandos, eight hundred men, to defend Hlangwane (Bosch Kop – 'Bush Hill' – as the Boers called it). On Wednesday afternoon, most of these men – all the Zoutpansberg including their commandant, and part of the Boksburg Commando – rode back across the iron wagon bridge over the river and announced that the kop was untenable. Hlangwane, tactical key to the Boers' defence, was now itself virtually defenceless.[109]

It was a crisis like this that displayed both the weakness and the strength of the Boers' citizen army. Military indiscipline of this sort – desertion by officers and men in the face of the enemy – was inconceivable in the British army. So was the telegraphic remedy. Botha at once despatched two telegrams: the first to the Boer lines outside Ladysmith, appealing for the help of the acting Commandant-General, Schalk Burger; the second to President Kruger at Pretoria. Burger was, like Joubert, somewhat ineffective. He sent Botha a cautious message of agreement. He could not come himself, as things were 'also very dangerous' at Ladysmith, and he sent Botha an ex-commandant, called Christian Fourie, to be his right-hand man. Fourie proved nothing but a handicap. It was Kruger, of course, who rose to the occasion. 'God will fight for you,' he reassured Botha. 'So give up position under no circumstances. . . . You will keep all if you keep hold of kop, dead or alive. Kop can be almost strongest of all positions.'[110]

Armed with these telegrams, Botha called a council of war that Wednesday evening. The position demanded both tact and subtlety. Many of the officers were openly in favour of abandoning the entire river line. Botha believed that the commandant of the part of the Boksburg Commando still left on Hlangwane could not be trusted. So he agreed on a temporary compromise: the Boksburgers should abandon Hlangwane, but the Tugela should be held. Meanwhile, the telegraph lines to Pretoria, that two-hundred-mile-long thread on which everything depended, hummed far into the night.[111]

Next morning, a second thunderbolt arrived from Oom Paul:

Gentlemen, I have received report that you gave up position. Understand please, if you give up position there, you give up the whole land to the enemy. Please stand fast, dead or alive, each man at his place, and fight in the name of the Lord. The Kop on the other side of the river must not be given up because then is all hope gone with it. . . . And fear not the enemy but fear God. . . . If you give up position, and surrender country to England, where will you go then?[112]

What an opportunity now existed for Buller, had his scouts realized that Hlangwane had been evacuated; or if, by luck, he had timed his attack to follow one day's bombardment instead of two. As it was, Botha called a second council of war on Thursday, while the shells from the second day's bombardment threw up red and grey plumes of earth from the empty kopjes above his trench lines. Botha read out Kruger's telegram to the officers. 'Fear God not the enemy.'[113] And not only fear God – fear Oom Paul. 'Where will you go then?' This was the *cri de coeur* of the volk, the voice of the trekkers echoing across the century. It was the philosophy of the Last Stand, Afrikaner-style, the ultimate appeal to put their backs to the wall, even if the wall was actually a hill more than a hundred miles inside British territory.

The council of war reversed its decision. The commandants drew lots. After sunset eight hundred men of the Wakkerstroom and Standerton Commandos were sent across the wagon bridge to reoccupy the kop.[114]

Although exhausted by thirty-eight hours without sleep ('half dead with my troubles,' he said himself), Botha found time to send an exultant telegram to Kruger. It was written in the style Kruger expected: 'The hand of the Lord,' said Botha, 'has protected us.'

The British guns were trying to draw their fire in order to locate their positions. He had ordered their own guns not to fire until the enemy came within easy rifle range. He believed he knew where the main attack would be made: on the wagon bridge. 'With all their wagons and cannons they cannot come anywhere but over the bridge'.[115]

In general, Botha's plan of defence was a rough-and-ready affair (like Buller's plan of attack). He had had to extend his four thousand, five hundred men to cover all the main crossing points: a third of them – the Free Staters, and the Middelburg and Johannesburg Commandos – on the edge of the plain opposite Robinson's Drift, a fourth drift eight miles upstream from Colenso; the Ermelo Commando in flat ground opposite the Bridle Drift (this was, in fact, to be Buller's second point of attack); the Zoutpansberg and Swaziland Commandos to cover the Punt Drift at the end of the great western loop; the Heidelberg, Vryheid and Krugersdorp Commandos in the kopjes and along the river bank covering the central loop, the one to the north of Colenso itself; and the Wakkerstroom and Standerton Commandos completing the line on the bushy slopes of Hlangwane, four and a half miles east of Colenso. It was an excellent plan of defence, given Botha's great inferiority in numbers of men and artillery, though Botha was especially weak at the old Wagon Drift (the one which Buller was, in fact, making the first point of attack). No doubt Botha was relying on the trouble his men had taken to destroy or, at any rate, conceal the drifts.[116]

However, the plan was not, as it appeared, merely a plan of defence. One of the reasons for putting fifteen hundred men at Robinson's Drift was to enable them to counter-attack by crossing the river. In fact, Botha's overall plan was exceptionally daring. He was not content to let the Khakis knock their heads against a wall of Mausers, as Cronje had been content at Magersfontein. He hoped to lure the leading battalions across the river at the wagon bridge. Then his two wings – his right at Robinson's Drift and his left on Hlangwane – would counter-attack, and the trap would snap shut.[117]

It was about 5.20 a.m. on Friday when the British naval guns began their bombardment. For the third day in succession, Botha watched the shells searching the kopjes above his trench lines. Originally, he had put one of his 3-inch Krupp field-guns on the kopje nearest the river – at Fort Wylie. But after the previous days' bombardment of that kopje, and because of a report that one of the men there had defected to the British, he moved the field-gun down from the top of this kopje, and the Krugersdorpers to a trench line in front. Now the British shells broke over the hill in cascades of red rock and earth, far away from the nearest burgher.[118] Meanwhile, Botha's telegraph director kept Pretoria informed with a blow-by-blow account of events: '5.20 a.m. *De vyand hebben een paar schoten met kanon geschieten....* The enemy has fired a few shots with cannons.... 6.00 a.m. Heavy cannon fire now takes place. Our cannon still keeps dead silent.'[119]

But just then something occurred that no one – least of all Botha – had expected. And Botha realized that the moment for silence had passed. The long, wide brown strip of attackers had divided into three columns. The central column – actually Hildyard's brigade – began to march forwards in the direction of the wagon bridge. But it was not the infantry who led it. Riding out at least a mile ahead of them were the gunners of Buller's artillery: twelve field-guns in front and six naval guns behind.

Botha stared in amazement. He did not know much about conventional warfare. But he knew that artillery was designed to support the forward line of infantry from the rear, not the other way round. The twelve field-guns halted about a thousand yards from the Tugela, facing the trenches where the Krugersdorp Commando were hidden in the river bank below Fort Wylie. Botha weighed the chances. Once his men showed themselves, goodbye to the hope of luring the infantry across the wagon bridge. But if the British field-guns opened fire at such close range, they could smash his thin defence lines. The burghers begged Botha to give the signal. Surely the Khakis were close enough now.[120]

A moment later, the British gunners – they were the batteries commanded by that fire-eater, Colonel Long – unhooked the leading twelve guns from the limbers. A final arabesque, as the drivers, in parallel arcs, took the limbers to the rear. 'Battery fire 15 seconds ... fuse 20!' The orders floated quietly across the plain towards the river, as though the batteries were on field-day by the Thames.

It was enough for Botha. The great Krupp howitzer boomed out high on the ridge, and an answering wave of Mauser fire – the most violent fire-storm of the war, even more violent than at the Modder and Magersfontein – swept over Long and his doomed gunners.[121]

CHAPTER 20

'A Devil of a Mess'

Colenso, Natal,
15 December 1899

'My own plan is that about the 15th December we shall
have in South Africa a nice little Army & all the materials
for a respectable war except the enemy.'

Moberly Bell, manager of *The Times*,
to L. S. Amery, 13 October 1899

In the great camp at Frere, ten miles to the south, there was hardly a soldier left,
except the staff of the field hospitals. They, too, were now leaving for the front,
glad to see the last of sweltering Frere. Gone were the squares and boulevards of
white tents. In their place, printed on the bald earth, like a photographic
negative, were the tent lines, dotted with empty bully-beef and biscuit tins.

In No. 4 Field Hospital the staff were in especially good humour. Today was
the day. They were going up to the front line at last. Their orders were to pitch
camp at Colenso, on the banks of the Tugela. Already they could hear the
rumble of Buller's naval guns, the prelude to the advance – the 'walk-over', as
everyone spoke of it. The men began to pack the medical equipment into sacks,
boxes and panniers.[1]

Dr Treves, the Queen's surgeon, suddenly transported from Harley Street to
the front line, was the doctor in charge of No. 4 Field Hospital. Treves watched a
fatigue party of grave-diggers, the symbols of death, march jauntily past the
door of his tent. It struck him that this devil-may-care attitude was characteristic
of the private soldiers' attitude to death. They had learnt now to hide their
feelings behind the screen of tobacco smoke and the gallows humour. Treves
was a gentle and percipient man. He recognized that the cheerfulness of No. 4
Field Hospital was not all that it seemed either. With the red cross on their
arm-bands, they, too, carried the symbols of death.[2]

Ahead of the field hospitals marched a strange procession, two thousand
volunteer stretcher-bearers, who were also political symbols. Buller had raked
them up from any source at hand. The War Office ambulances were notoriously
unsuited to the stony veld, so Buller had cut through the red tape, and recruited
these 'body-snatchers'. The majority were Uitlander refugees from Johannesburg, who had failed to find places in any of the various irregular corps but still
wished to do their bit. About eight hundred were members of Natal's Indian
community, led by a twenty-eight-year-old barrister, whose name would one

day be known to more men than either Kruger's or Chamberlain's: his name was Mohandas Gandhi. Gandhi had announced in Durban that the Indian community wished to give active expression to their loyalty to the Empire; unable to fight, they would serve as stretcher-bearers.[3] Years later, men might wonder why Mahatma Gandhi, the anti-imperialist and the arch-pacifist, had served as a non-combatant in an imperial war. At the time, it seemed natural enough to the British. Here was one of the 'subject peoples' showing the solidarity of the coloured races in the 'white man's war'.

Dr Treves's hospital staff had embarked on the train that was supposed to bring them to Colenso. They had already heard rumours that the Boers had fled, and that 'no living thing was to be seen on the heights beyond the river'. But Treves was puzzled by the sounds of battle, as they steamed towards Colenso, past the wrecked armoured train, and up the incline to Chieveley. All that artillery and rifle fire, and the barking of the pom-pom: was it really a walk-over?

Outside Chieveley station, the train was met by a galloper with orders for Dr Treves to go at once to Naval Gun Hill. Things were not going too well.[4] There was trouble with Long's guns. And, over on the left, the Irish Brigade had got itself into a devil of a mess.

It was still dark when the Irish Brigade had paraded under their commander, Major-General Hart. Hart had excelled himself that morning. First, he gave the brigade half-an-hour's drill, as though it were an ordinary parade on the barrack square at Aldershot. Then he marched off the battalions in close order, as though they were on Salisbury Plain. He himself rode ahead, accompanied by an African and a Natal colonist, to help him find the ford described in their orders as 'the Bridle Drift'. Next came the 2nd Dublin Fusiliers, advancing in fours by the right. The three other battalions – 1st Inniskillings, 1st Connaught Rangers and Border Regiment – marched in mass of quarter-columns. It was a drill-block advance and, like Wauchope's advance at Magersfontein, it seemed to several of Hart's officers to be asking for trouble. Colonel C. D. Cooper, the Dublins' CO, tried to open out the battalion to twice the parade-ground interval: about twenty yards. Hart countermanded the order. He liked to keep the men 'well in hand' – that is, in the old Balaclava-style formations – and saw no reason for funk. Indeed, as the brigade marched along over the flat veld, everything seemed extraordinarily peaceful.[5]

It was a beautiful morning, like a June morning in England. The men marched at ease. They carried little, apart from rifles and ammunition pouches, as they had left their greatcoats and canteens on the wagons. There was the usual bantering in the ranks: Where was Johnny Boer? Where was old Kroojer?

Across the river, the sun threw into relief tier after tier of kopjes, culminating in the bulk of Grobelaar's Kloof, about a thousand feet above the river. Nothing stirred over there, except a few black specks. Boer scouts, no doubt. At about 5.30 a.m. the British naval guns began the preliminary bombardment. Still no reply from the Boers, although by now one of the Inniskilling officers had

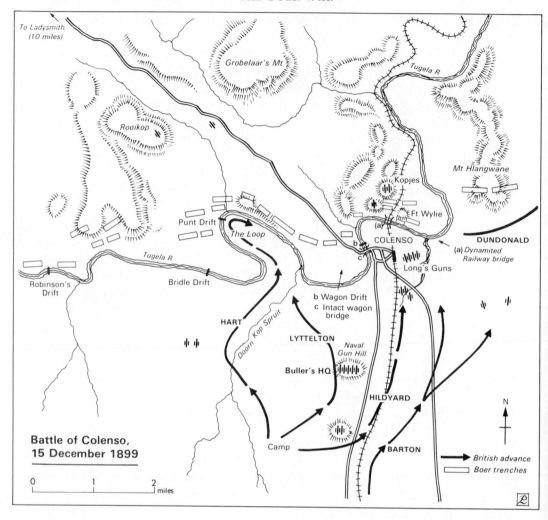

**Battle of Colenso,
15 December 1899**

pointed out a Boer field gun half-hidden in an emplacement high on a kopje.
Hart rode on, and behind him the men tramped through the long grass, wet with
dew. Overhead, the 4·7-inch shells boomed like Big Ben, and continued to
splosh into the apparently deserted ridges north of the long, sprawling loop of
the river on their right.[6]

By this time, patrols of the cavalry regiment sent by Buller to protect Hart's
left flank – the Royal Dragoons, under Colonel Burn-Murdoch – had already
ridden down to the river bank. They were told by an African they met there that
the Boers were dug into trenches and 'sangars' (walls of stones thrown up to
protect riflemen); the African had himself crossed the river that morning after
supplying the Boers with milk. By now the cavalry could actually see large
bodies of Boers moving across the river ahead of Hart's column and to the left.
They sent three gallopers in succession to warn Hart of the danger. Hart replied
that he did not intend to take any notice of the Boers unless they attacked him in

force. The Royals must protect his left flank. He intended to cross, as ordered, by the Bridle Drift ahead.[7]

About 6.15 a.m. Hart reached a patch of mealie plough about 300 yards from the beginning of the loop. He could see the river clearly now. The red, crumbling banks were about 360 feet apart, 15 to 20 feet deep, and lined with dusty green bushes. Between them, swollen with Wednesday's rain, ran the Tugela: brown, and unruffled by shallows. Where was the ford?

At this moment the African guide did something that caused Hart intense disquiet and annoyance. The official Field Intelligence Department blueprint map and the gunners' sketch-map both put the Bridle Drift well to the west of the beginning of the loop – about a mile to Hart's left along the track to the left that Hart was following. The African guide pointed into the loop itself, a mile ahead and to the right. It was up there, the drift, the interpreter explained, and it was the *only* drift.[8]

Now Hart knew enough about war to know that there are few more dangerous places to send men on a battlefield than into a salient – the open end of a loop. To march into a well-defended salient is like putting your head into a noose. There were many other choices open to him. The best, in the light of events, would have been to push forward patrols to try *both* crossing points, meanwhile halting the column, and sending a galloper to tell Buller of his problem. But Hart was not the man to halt, nor to share his problems with Buller. In fact, the maps were correct: the Bridle Drift was a mile to the west. He got it into his head that both his official orders, and the two maps prepared by teams of intelligence staff and gunners, had misplaced the Bridle Drift by several miles. There was no evidence for this, except the word of the African guide, who spoke no English.

Hart did not hesitate. He put himself in the hands of the African guide, and put his head in the noose.[9]

For at this moment, Botha, three miles farther east, had just given the signal from the great Krupp howitzer. The first Creusot shell pitched into the ground ahead of the Dublins; the second shell passed over the whole brigade; the third fell just ahead of the Connaught Rangers; the fourth splashed into the centre of the Connaughts. They were followed by a storm of Mauser fire from somewhere beyond the river bank.[10]

Even now, Hart could have avoided disaster to his brigade. His men, once they deployed, would not have suffered too heavy casualties – although pinned down by an invisible enemy, like Methuen's brigades at Modder River. Some of the Dublins in fact lay down and began to return the enemy's fire. Hart ordered them forwards. The African guide had vanished at the first burst of firing. Hart could see that there was an African kraal at the end of the loop about a mile ahead. He gathered from the interpreter that this was the place where the Africans' ford lay. And on he led his men into the loop, commanded on three sides by an invisible enemy, firing into his men at a range of a few hundred yards.[11]

The advance that followed did not conform to any of the neat manoeuvres so dear to Hart. Apart from the extremely close order – Hart was trying to crowd

the whole brigade of four thousand men into a loop only a thousand yards wide
– there was nothing to recall the parade ground. The Dublins were told to
advance, with the Border Regiment on their right, and the other two battalions
on their left. Of course, the battalions became mixed at once, and so did the
companies. 'Come on, the Irish Brigade!' shouted the officers, and that was
about as far as the orders went. There was no control, no cohesion, no system by
which groups could alternately advance and provide covering fire for their
neighbours. Small bodies of men, led by officers, would jump up, dash forward
fifty or a hundred yards and then fling themselves flat again.[12] One of the
Inniskillings described the advance somewhat poetically as 'like the waves of the
sea without anyone guiding it'.[13] Captain Romer, of the 1st Dublins, put it more
bluntly: 'Nobody knew where the drift was. Nobody had a clear idea of what
was happening. All pushed forward blindly, animated by the sole idea of
reaching the river bank.'[14]

Hart himself acted with great, if not reckless, personal courage. Disdaining to
take cover, he walked calmly about among the flying bullets and shrapnel,
shouting and cheering his men on. The advance was too slow for his liking, and
many men simply refused to budge. They were shaken by the Boers' rifle fire,
whose sudden onset gave it almost the force of an ambush. And the Creusot
shells, though not very effective, made an appalling din as they exploded,
sending columns of dust and stones high in the air. There was no panic. The men
simply lay flat and seemed deaf to the words of command.

'If I give you a lead, if your General gives you a lead – will you come
on?'

'We will, sir,' came the reply, in the thick Irish brogues.

Up they jumped, more or less cheerfully, and followed their General.[15]

A little earlier, Hart had observed, to his great annoyance, the behaviour of the
COs of the two battalions on the left of his line. Lieutenant-Colonel Thomas
Thackeray, the CO of the Inniskillings, had led the men to form a single rank
parallel to the river, instead of remaining, as Hart intended, in two ranks. They
had also worked their way to the left of the loop. In fact, they were now close to
the Bridle Drift, and it is possible that, even now, they might have found that
way across the river. Although Botha's men had apparently dug away part of the
Bridle Drift, it was still probably fordable there; and the high banks of the river
would have given some cover to the Inniskillings, who outnumbered the
defenders and could themselves have been swiftly reinforced. Hart ordered back
the Inniskillings into the loop.[16] It was his final error, and now the repulse of the
brigade was becoming a defeat and the defeat a disaster.

In his official orders, Buller had announced that he would be found during the
battle on Naval Gun Hill, and there he had stood, as the sun rose, impassively
watching the effects of the great bombardment through his telescope. The
mushrooms of shrapnel and the spouts of red earth straddled the kopjes where
Buller – with reason – had assumed the Boers would put their field-guns and
many of their burghers. In both respects, however, the bombardment had

proved ineffective, as Buller realized.[17] When the Krupp howitzer had at last replied to the British gunfire, followed by a number of Creusot field-guns, it was the job of the much more numerous British artillery to seek out and destroy these adversaries. This was the first basic tactical principle of late nineteenth-century warfare – British, French or German. It was assumed that the field-guns would fight it out in the open. But Botha's field-guns were not only concealed behind emplacements like regular siege-guns; they fired the new smokeless powder, only invented in the late eighties. Buller's naval guns were quite unable to locate and hence silence them. By the same token, that storm of Mauser fire came from riflemen firing smokeless cartridges from invisible trenches. Buller believed they must have suffered heavily from the bombardment with the new lyddite high explosive; yet there was no sign of the Mausers being silenced by the heavy guns. (In fact lyddite shells proved almost useless against dispersed troops, even when accurate, as the blast was too concentrated.)[18]

Now invisibility, of course, was the characteristic of the new smokeless war, as Methuen and White had discovered to their cost, though it was the first time that Buller had had a personal taste of this. The failure of the lyddite-firing long-range naval guns threw a larger burden on the shrapnel-firing medium-range field artillery. With this, Buller realized at the very beginning of the battle, things were going seriously wrong.

Through his telescope, he had seen Hart's column march off towards the Bridle Drift, and then suddenly blunder off to the right. The advance was premature, as there had been no preparation from the field-guns. It was also in the wrong direction. Buller sent a galloper to warn Hart to keep out of the loop.[19] Meanwhile, the storm of rifle fire, sounding from Buller's position like a distant drumming noise, greeted Hart's impetuous advance. Buller had told Colonel Parsons, in command of the twelve guns on the left – six 15-pounders in either battery – to prepare the ground for the passage of the Bridle Drift a mile to the left of the loop. Parsons now did his best to help Hart in his new position, but there were no proper targets to aim at beyond the loop, any more for the guns than for the infantry; and some of his shells fell among Hart's leading troops. Buller watched the confusion from Naval Gun Hill with increasing disquiet. He sent off a second galloper, his ADC, Captain Algy Trotter.[20]

Meanwhile, still more ominous things were happening three miles away at the centre of the plain, close to the village of Colenso. From Naval Gun Hill, Buller had watched Colonel Long ride off across the veld at the head of his impressive procession of field-guns: twelve 15-pounders and six naval 12-pounders. His instructions to Long the night before were, as we have seen, to come into action well out of rifle range from the Colenso kopjes – that is, at least two and a half miles back from the quarter-circle that the Tugela transcribes around Colenso. Buller remembered his actual words to Long, as he put his finger on the FID blueprint map to show him the position he had chosen. 'It looks ... too far for the 15-pounders, but I shall be quite satisfied if the naval 12-pounders [the greater length of whose barrels gave them greater range] only come into action.' These were Long's orders. Imagine, then, Buller's astonishment about 7.00 a.m. when he heard Long's batteries suddenly burst into life, apparently close to the river.[21]

'See what those guns are doing,' he shouted to a staff officer. 'They seem to me to be much too close. If they are under any fire causing severe loss, tell them to withdraw at once. There is not the least reason yet for their being in action.' The staff officer returned soon afterwards.
'They're all right.'
'Surely they must be under rifle fire.'
'They are a little, but they seem quite comfortable.'[22]

Soon afterwards Buller's Military Secretary, Colonel Stopford, the only experienced staff officer he had with him, rode up and told Buller that Long's guns were badly out of position. Buller said he knew that already. As soon as Trotter returned with the news that Hart's brigade had been extricated from the loop, Buller intended to go and look at Long's position for himself. Just then there was an ominous silence. Long's batteries had ceased fire. Buller, more certain than ever that disaster had overtaken them, mounted his bay horse, Biffin. He sent a third emissary – Stopford – to order Hart to withdraw to safety. He himself rode off to see what he could do to rescue Long from his folly.[23]

The advance of Long's twelve field-guns and six naval guns, which had so astounded Louis Botha half an hour earlier that morning, seen from the other side of the Tugela, indeed followed one of the great traditions of the British army: courage matched only by stupidity.[24] To see those eighteen gun teams, riding out far ahead of the infantry battalions supposed to screen them, was to return to some scene from Balaclava; Long, like Hart, believed in the old virtues of close order and 'keeping the men in hand'. Despite the protests of Lieutenant Ogilvy, the CO of the 12-pounder naval guns, Long, as we have seen, had brought the 15-pounders to within a thousand yards of the river bank before he allowed a halt. Fortunately for Ogilvy and his men, they had lagged nearly six hundred yards behind the 15-pounders, and when Botha had given the signal for that fusillade of shrapnel and Mauser fire, the naval guns were still comparatively safe. True, the African drivers, who drove the improvised naval gun teams, immediately bolted, like Hart's African guide over in the loop. But it was possible to cut the oxen free from the naval guns, and bring all six guns into action against the kopjes a mile away across the river, from which most of the rifle fire appeared to be coming.[25]

A mile was extreme range for effective rifle fire. Botha's single pom-pom and the field-gun and howitzer hidden farther back on the ridge were noisy enough, but too few and too dispersed to be dangerous. The naval gun detachment suffered next to no casualties. By contrast, the two 15-pounder batteries found themselves in the centre of something to which military textbooks had yet to give a name: in this zone of fire, the air crackled like fat in a frying-pan. There was no question of the Boers being brilliant marksmen. Indeed, one of the things

that struck some survivors most forcibly was how poor was Boer marksmanship, supposed to be one of their great points of superiority to the British. It was
the sheer volume of rifle fire – the emptying of a thousand Mauser magazines –
that had the force of machine-guns and gave the British the impression that they
were facing twenty thousand Boers.[26]

One of the first to be knocked down was Long himself, critically wounded in
the liver; Lieutenant-Colonel Hunt, the second-in-command, was also
wounded, as were officers from both batteries, including Captain Elton, who
had helped make the gunners' sketch-map. The 15-pounders continued firing –
slowly and methodically, the gunners counting out the intervals between shots,
as they had been taught. The second line of ammunition wagons was brought
up, and the first line of empty wagons calmly removed.[27] The story was to be
told of how the gunners now fought on till the last round of ammunition. In fact,
the gunners were brave, but human. When a third of their number had been
killed or wounded, flesh and blood could stand no more. The acting commander
ordered the men to take shelter in a small donga – a stony hollow nearby. The
second-line ammunition wagons, nearly full, were left with the twelve guns,
abandoned in the open plain. Two of the officers then rode back out of the
drumming Mauser fire to try to get help.[28]

It was these two officers, Captains Fitzgerald and Herbert, who met Buller as he
rode down towards the firing-line. One pictures the meeting: Buller, four-
square on his bay charger; the two gunners, dazed and almost incoherent. They
blurt out the news: their own guns out of action; need for the reserve ammunition column. They add (what was, in fact, quite untrue) that the gunners have
fought almost to the last round, and are all killed and wounded; also that all six
naval guns, as well as the twelve field-guns, are out of action.

Buller rode on to meet Hildyard, who was still waiting for the moment to
deliver the main attack: the attack on the wagon bridge and the two fords either
side of the bridge at Colenso. 'I'm afraid Long's guns have got into a terrible
mess. I doubt whether we shall be able to attack Colenso today.' This was the
gist of what Buller told Hildyard. It was eight o'clock, and only one of the four
infantry brigades had come into action. Buller had decided to call off the whole
operation.[29]

Was Buller right to do so? Or had his nerve failed, as some of his critics later
suggested – those who did not, like Leo Amery, pillory the whole plan of attack
itself? Had the disaster to Long's guns shaken Buller's volatile morale?[30] Now
Buller was certainly an emotional man, but the emotion evoked by the news of
Long's guns, and of Hart's fiasco on the left, was suppressed rage, not despair.[31]
And Buller now calculated the risks coolly enough. He decided he must call off
the main attack – postpone it, at any rate, until he had pulled Long's chestnuts
out of the firing-line.

He had a number of reasons. The plan for the main attack on Colenso
depended on Hildyard being supported from one or more sides: on the left, by
Hart forcing his way across the Bridle Drift and moving his brigade down the

left bank of the river; on the right, by Dundonald seizing enough of Hlangwane to install there a battery of field-guns which could enfilade the Colenso kopjes; overhead, by the eighteen guns commanded by Long and supposed to soften up the ground beyond the bridge; from behind, by the two reserve brigades, Lyttelton's and Barton's. As far as Buller knew, Hildyard's attack, if it proceeded as planned, would have support from not one of these four sources. Dundonald had made no progress. Indeed, he, too, seemed to be in trouble. Far from supporting Hildyard's attack, Hart, Long and Dundonald all required help themselves, which meant drawing on both the reserve brigades. So Buller decided that to attack Colenso now would be utter recklessness. Even if, at the cost of most of his brigade, Hildyard established a bridgehead across the river, the victory might prove Pyrrhic. For the worst fighting would be ahead: in those ten miles of hill country across the river. On the other hand, the price of failure was out of all proportion to the value of success. If Buller broke the weapons in his hand, smashed and demoralized his own army, he could lose not only Ladysmith, but, what would be still worse, the whole of south Natal.

These were the reasons that made Buller decide to call off Hildyard's attack on Colenso before Hildyard had fired a shot. They do not seem, in the light of events, unduly alarmist. As it was, Buller had his work cut out in the attempt to rescue Hart and Long. With his personal doctor at his side, Buller rode on towards the small donga where Long's men were sheltering.[32]

'Hart has got into a devil of a mess down there. Get him out of it as best you can.' Buller used almost the same language to Lyttelton about Hart as he had used to Hildyard about Long. Lyttelton pushed forward four companies of the Rifle Brigade and prepared to give supporting fire. At first, it appeared that the loop had swallowed up Hart's brigade. Then hundreds of stragglers and wounded came stumbling back out of the loop, followed by Hart himself and many of his men, falling back in confusion. 'The men have all fallen back. We'll form up in the rear,' Hart told Lyttelton. Hart was wrong. Lyttelton could see the plain ahead dotted with figures. Some were wounded; others, it turned out, had simply collapsed from the heat or were lying flat to avoid the enemy's fire. After Hart had gone, Lyttelton saw seventy of the brigade rise up suddenly out of the long grass. They were as suddenly shot down. Lyttelton doubted if twenty got safely back. Lyttelton's men could not themselves fire a shot to help them, as the stragglers blocked their field of fire. At the same time, Parsons's two batteries, which had found it impossible to give proper support to Hart, now opened up inadvertently on Lyttelton. Lyttelton was sheltering from the Mauser fire at the time, behind the wall of a sheep fold, when he was perplexed to find the wall was under fire from both directions. Fortunately, the British gunners' fire was, as usual, ineffective.[33]

The predicament of the men of the brigade at the end of the loop was now serious, marooned in the open within a few hundred yards of the enemy's trenches, which enfiladed them on three sides, and within easy range of two

Creusot 75-mm field-guns concealed on the kopjes below Grobelaar's Kloof. Their ordeal was not unlike that of the Highland Brigade at Magersfontein, with the extra spice of Botha's field-guns. 'We caught pepper,' was how Lyttelton described the fusillade he witnessed from the Rifle Brigade's firing-line, a full mile in the rear. The air was a good deal spicier where Colonel Thackeray lay beside the African kraal near the end of the loop. It was here, apparently, that Hart's African guide lived, and to the ford here that he had been conducting the brigade with such disastrous results. To cross the muddy, swirling water, at least breast-high, under such rifle fire, was out of the question. Thackeray's men took cover behind the stone walls of the huts. Others used the twenty-foot-deep banks of the river as shelter, and engaged in a furious duel across the water with the still invisible Boers. Behind them, the rest of their own brigade was equally invisible, owing to a rise in the ground.[34]

Meanwhile, Buller's orders to evacuate the loop, relayed by Hart, and by a brave young lieutenant of the Connaughts who volunteered to go forwards, had at length reached the rest of the brigade. Slowly the firing diminished. Most of the Border Regiment and the Connaughts marched back to their camp in tolerable order, though the Connaughts continued to suffer casualties from shell fire while holding the line of the Doornkop Spruit in the rear of the loop. At the camp, the men pitched tents again – everything had been packed up ready to take across the river – and drank gallons of water. Then they flung themselves down, dead beat after the ten-hour ordeal. They had suffered as much from old 'McCormick' (Tommies' slang for the sun) as from old Kroojer. It was all over at last.[35]

Thackeray's ordeal continued. About three o'clock a party of Boers splashed across the river and sealed off the loop. This was not, in fact, the great counter-attack, by way of Robinson's Drift, that Botha had proposed for Fourie and the fifteen hundred men on Botha's west flank. Those men had failed to seize their opportunity, and perhaps it was as well for them; Lyttelton had two battalions eager to parry this thrust. The Boers who cut off Thackeray's retreat were merely a small party, who had crossed when they saw the British ambulance men go forward into the loop under shelter of the Red Cross flag. In the confusion, Thackeray saved himself with a flash of Irish wit. Called upon to surrender, he accused the Boers of sneaking up behind the Red Cross flag. It would be unsporting of the Boers to capture him. 'If you don't like it,' he added, 'go back to where you came from and we'll begin the battle over again.' The victors saw the comic side of this suggestion. 'Well, I won't look at you while you take your men away,' came the Boers' reply.

So the story was told, at any rate, in the regimental mess that night, after Thackeray and some of his men staggered back to camp. When the roll-call was taken that night it was found that the Irish Brigade had lost heavily enough.[36]

In the meantime, Buller had ridden down to the firing-line and started his attempts to rescue Long and his twelve guns. About half a mile to the west of the guns was Colenso station and the railway line, running north and south. Beyond these were about a dozen brick-and-tin houses of Colenso village and the road leading down to the wagon bridge. This was the only available cover from Botha's trenches to the north, apart from the two shallow dongas Long's men had taken refuge in: the front donga about a thousand yards from the river; the rear donga roughly a mile away. The trouble was that the smaller loop of the Tugela enclosed Colenso village on two sides. So both the village and the stranded guns were enfiladed from the Boer rifle pits on the river bank to the west. Buller gave part of Hildyard's brigade the job of neutralizing these latter positions. His orders were on 'no account to commit his men to an engagement' – to extricate the guns with the least casualties to his own brigade. Hildyard had trained his brigade at Aldershot that summer under Buller's eye, and there was mutual confidence between the two men.

Hildyard now lined out his men in half-companies, with six to eight yards between each man, and fifty to eighty yards between each half-company. In this exceptionally open order, the Queen's Regiment and the Devons successfully weathered the storm of rifle fire. By nine o'clock the forward companies had reached Colenso village. Intelligently handled, by contrast to the Irish Brigade, Hildyard's men had suffered few casualties. Now the Queen's cheerfully dug themselves in behind the stone walls and gardens of Colenso. On their right were some of the Devons, led by Lieutenant-Colonel G. M. Bullock. All these men were under cover – sheltered in the eye of the hurricane.[37]

But how to cross that last eight hundred yards of open plain to the guns themselves? About 8.30 a.m. Buller himself had ridden up to the large donga eight hundred yards in the rear. He was pleased to find Ogilvy's naval guns were still in action, though immobilized by the stampede of all but two of the ox teams. He arranged for artillery horses to drag those naval guns back to a safe position. He then rode back along the firing line to get further support. There was no lack of infantry. He had two of Lyttelton's battalions, one of Barton's, as well as the two rear battalions of Hildyard's brigade: a total of about five thousand extra men behind the firing line at Colenso. The problem was how to get them far enough forward to extricate Long.[38]

As Buller and his staff rode along the firing-line, his progress was marked by the kind of incident that wins a general a place in the hearts of his men. '"Advance" was the order,' said a private of Barton's brigade later. 'We did; a riderless horse galloped through us. . . . We got up again unhurt, and as we went, whizz-whizz-whizz, came the bullets, over went a couple of our fellows, and a shell came in front and blinded us. I was spitting out dust for the next few minutes, and it was almost like groping in the dark, but we heard a voice behind us: "Steady, men. Don't lose your heads." It was Buller's. We did not lose them after that, but gripped our rifles and made straight through the smoke.'[39]

Buller himself, attended by his staff and body-guard, was an obvious target to the enemy's riflemen. He 'stood watching the artillery fire while the bullets dropped all about him,' said another private, 'and when he was hit in the side with one, the doctor, Captain Hughes . . . rode up to him and asked him if he

Above Colenso: Botha's Creusot 75-mm commanding the loop where Hart came to grief.
Below Colenso: British side, watching the battle.

Above Battle of Colenso, seen from two miles south of Botha's trenches.
Below After the battle, Colonel Long's field-guns being sent to Pretoria.

Following page: Above Major McGrigor, 1st Scots Guards, taking his bath.
Below Writing home. The army Post Office handled 190,000 letters a week.

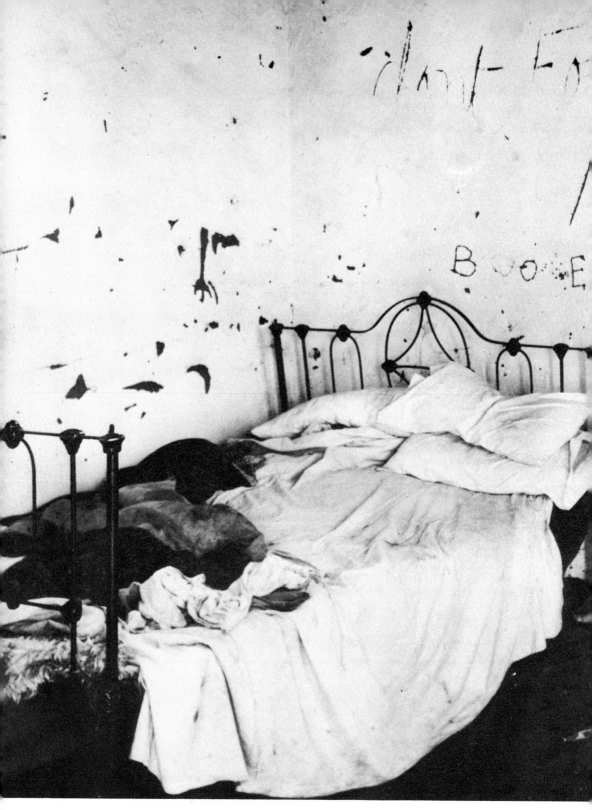

Preceding page: Above Officers' mess, 3rd Grenadier Guards, at Modder River.
Below 'Joe Chamberlain', Methuen's 4.7-inch converted naval gun firing at Magersfontein.

Above (Boers:) 'don't Forget Majuba, Boys.' (British:) 'NO FEAR, BOOJERS, NO FEAR.'
Graffiti on house re-captured by British at the Modder.

Left Helping the wounded at
Driefontein (reconstruction by
photographer after battle).
Below Field dressing station at the
Modder River (real).

could do anything for him. He calmly replied that it had only just taken his wind a bit ... He is as brave as a lion.' In fact, Buller had been severely bruised in the ribs by a shell fragment, but did not admit this till later.[40]

Behind the mask, Buller's spirit was on fire. Rage and frustration with Long's blunder ('I was sold by a d——d gunner, he later told Bigge)[41] vied with the exhilaration, the physical thrill of danger. It was fourteen years since he had last been in battle: Colonel Buller, VC, the dare-devil of the Egyptian and Zulu wars. He now found he had not lost his taste for it. 'I wickedly confess I liked it very much,' he wrote of his personal appearances in the firing-line that day. Still, there were aspects that greatly distressed him. Soon after Buller had been hit in the ribs by the spent shell fragments, Captain Hughes, Buller's own doctor and one of his favourites among the staff, fell mortally wounded in the lungs.[42]

Buller now rode back a second time to the large donga. Out on the plain Long's twelve field-guns still lay abandoned, alone except for a circle of panic-stricken horses, tied by the traces to their dead team mates. By the donga, bullets drummed on the ground, making the drivers duck back under shelter. Buller stood out in the open and shouted, 'Now, my lads, this is your last chance to save the guns; will any of you volunteer to fetch them?'[43]

After a minute, one of the corporals got up, and six men joined him. To make up two teams needed more volunteers. Buller turned to his own staff and Clery's which included Prince Christian Victor. 'Some of you go and help.' Three officers stepped forward: Captain H. N. Schofield, one of the ADCs; Captain Walter Congreve, the Press Censor; and Lieutenant Freddy Roberts.

Congreve was never to forget that ride. He was a personal friend of Freddy's – they had served as brother officers in the Rifle Brigade in India. Congreve mounted a troop horse, as his own pony had vanished in the mêlée. First, they had to hook the two teams into the limbers. Freddy Roberts held the head of Corporal Nurse's horse, while the corporal hooked in. They set off at a canter towards the guns, half a mile away. Congreve watched Freddy Roberts 'laughing, talking and slapping his leg with his stick as though we were on the Mall at Peshawar again'.[44] Then the ride, for both of them, ended:

All we could see were little tufts of dust all over the ground – a whistling noise k'phut where they hit and an increasing rattle of musketry somewhere in front. My first bullet went through my left sleeve and just made the point of my elbow bleed. Next a clod of earth caught me no end of a smack on the other arm, then my horse got one and then my right leg, my horse another, and that settled the question. He plunged and I fell off about a hundred yards from the guns we were going to.[45]

Freddy had vanished. But somehow the two teams with the limbers reached the guns. After a struggle, Schofield and the corporal hooked in, and away they galloped back to safety, with two 15-pounders.[46]

By now Botha's men beyond the river – who could see Long's guns clearly, despite the heat haze – had redoubled their fire. The next team with a limber sent

forward by Buller was brought to a standstill. Further volunteers rode out. It
was hopeless. A final attempt was made by Captain H. L. Reed of the 7th
Battery, the one sent to support Dundonald's mounted brigade. He hooked in
three teams and they rode forward. Twelve of the horses were shot, one man
killed, five wounded. No one reached the guns. Buller now refused to sanction
any further rescue attempts. He then gave the order: retire. The men, who had
been half-dazed by their experiences, leapt to their feet. 'We were off like March
hares,' said one of the gunners.[47]

Was there still no hope of saving the ten lost guns after dark?

Of all the accusations that were later to break over Buller's head, it was this
taunt, perhaps, that would cut him most deeply: that he had needlessly abandoned Long's guns. Indeed, two of the battalion commanders – including the
CO of the 2nd Queen's – later volunteered to try and dig into their positions in
Colenso until dark, and then send out parties to bring in the guns.[48] By then,
Buller had already discussed the idea with Clery, and their surviving staff
officers, and rejected it. To try and extricate the guns, whole battalions would
have to be left in the firing-line till nightfall, eighteen hours without water. As
Buller rode round the men, whose officers cheerfully offered them up as a
sacrifice, he found the men already on the verge of collapse.[49] This was the bond
that held him closest to his army; he knew when flesh and blood could stand no
more. He saw it now as he rode round the firing-line. The extraordinary heat,
the rawness of the reservists, the absolute novelty of being under fire, the
eeriness of fighting an invisible enemy: all had a paralysing effect on them. As he
later cabled to London, in strictest confidence, 'I am frightened by the utter
collapse of my infantry on Friday; on my left I lost nearly 300 missing, and on
my right should have lost as many more but I and my staff rode down into the
dongas and forced the men to get up and go home.'[50] In short, there was a serious
risk, if he left infantry at Colenso, that he would add to the loss of the ten guns a
further loss that would be both more irreplaceable and more humiliating: that of
the British infantry, who would have had to surrender wholesale.[51]

There was a second reason for rejecting such a venture. Dundonald's brigade
had not only failed to establish themselves on Hlangwane. They had been driven
back after suffering heavy losses. With difficulty, they were now extricating
themselves from the valley, and retiring south.[52] When they had gone, and taken
their field-guns with them, the way would be open for the Boers' flanks to snap
shut on Colenso.

One by one, Buller's infantry companies marched back out of danger. Despite
the pain of his wound, Buller stayed in the saddle till he had seen the last of the
infantry safely home. By three o'clock, the last of the mounted brigade had
ridden back exhausted to camp. All firing ebbed away. The sounds natural to the
Tugela slowly returned: the murmur of the water, of the pigeons in the trees on
the river. Out in the shimmering plain, the guns lay abandoned, encircled by the
dead horses. And in the small donga, thirty yards behind, Colonel Long,
wounded gunners, staff, and some infantrymen still lay under the midsummer
sun.[53]

'No water, not a breath of air, and not a particle of shade and a sun which I have never felt hotter even in India.' So Congreve later described the experiences of that interminable day, 'the most beastly day I ever spent'. He had been wounded in the leg. Then he had found Freddy Roberts. He was lying out on the veld, shot in the stomach and two other places. When the fire slackened, Congreve dragged him under shelter. He was unconscious, and there seemed little hope for him from the first. They shaded his head with a coat, and waited.[54]

About 4.30 p.m. some Boers crossed the river, and rode over to the donga. One of them called on the British to surrender. The senior British officer was Colonel Bullock, the CO of the 2nd Devons, who had pushed forward to the east of the railway line, and then taken refuge in this small donga with about twenty unwounded men of his battalion. Bullock refused to surrender. The Boers retreated, then exchanged shots with Bullock at a range of about fifty yards. Two of the Boers dropped – apparently shot. The Boers reappeared with a white flag. They pointed out that the donga was full of wounded, who would unavoidably be shot, if Bullock insisted on fighting. They chivalrously offered to let the wounded be removed, before going on with the fight.

Meanwhile, less chivalrously, about a hundred Boers had crept round the side of the donga, and emerged holding their rifles pointed at the heads of the Devons. Perhaps Bullock would have chosen death and glory. He had no choice. One of the Boers hit him in the face with a rifle butt, knocking out some of his front teeth. Bullock and the rest of the Devons, and the unwounded gunners, were bundled off as prisoners. Congreve, Freddy Roberts, Long and the other wounded were sent back in the care of the 'bodysnatchers', the Indian and British ambulance men, who now reached the donga.[55]

The battle was over – if such an abortive affair could be called a battle at all. The struggle for the lives of the wounded was only beginning. Dr Treves, the Queen's surgeon, watched the lines of ambulance wagons rocking and groaning over the uneven veld like staggering men. Would that dismal procession never end? Treves could hardly believe that it was only a few hours before that the men had marched out to battle in the dew of the morning. Now they were 'burnt a brown red by the sun, their faces were covered with dust and sweat, and were in many cases blistered by the heat ... the blue army shirts were stiff with blood. Some had helmets and some were bare-headed. All seemed dazed, weary and depressed.'[56]

It was here, in the small circle of field hospitals, that the horrors of the whole battlefield now seemed to be concentrated. Treves, an experienced surgeon, felt his stomach turn at some of the sights. Everywhere lay the khaki helmets, crushed, blood-stained and riddled with holes. Some of the men were delirious. They rolled off the stretchers and kicked about on the ground. One man, paralysed below the waist by a bullet in the spine, kept raising his head, staring with wonder at the limbs he could neither move nor feel. The earth seemed to be covered with groaning men. In the evening, it began to rain, and the men on stretchers were covered up with tarpaulins. Somehow this made the scene still more macabre: the shrouded figures, glistening with rain, some motionless, others stirring fitfully. Outside the operation-tent, men waited patiently for their turn. 'Keep yer chivey up, Joe.' 'Good luck to yer, old cock, you won't feel nothing.' Orderlies took the stretchers in through the open flap, as the endless work went on: chloroforming, examining, amputating. Legs rattled in the bucket, or dropped on to the blood-stained grass.

Treves kept thinking of the jolly phrase the soldiers had used when leaving England. They were determined to reach the Cape 'in time for the fun'. Well, they *were* in time. And *this* was the fun.[57]

Buller's struggles, too, were far from over for the day. He had to cable to London about the battle. The Press were howling for permission to use the cable facilities, and the official reports must go first. Yet he was in no mood for sending cables after so many hours in the saddle under that burning sun. When John Atkins watched him climb down limply and wearily from his horse, he looked like an old, old man. No one yet knew about the blow to his ribs. Atkins only guessed of the blow to his pride.[58]

In his cable for public consumption, Buller presented his usual air of calm. 'I regret to report serious reverse,' he began, and then described the outlines of the plan, and its failure. He was generous to Hart. 'Early in the day I saw that General Hart would not be able to force a passage and directed him to withdraw. He had, however, attacked with great gallantry. . . .' He described the heroism of the attempts to save the guns. He gave no hint of the collapse of his infantry. 'The day was intensely hot and most trying to the troops whose conduct was excellent.' Only in his reference to Colonel Long did he give any real explanation for the reverse: 'It appears that Colonel Long in his desire to be within effective range, advanced without any scouts or effective Infantry supports close to the river.' (This sentence was, however, to be censored by the War Office before the cable was released to the Press.)[59]

Had Buller left the matter there, the history of the war might have followed a different course. Certainly Buller would have been spared deep humiliation. But by midnight, his emotions had finally got the better of him. The intense isolation of his position, the frustration of his long struggle with Lansdowne, the bitterness of his feelings towards Hart and Long, the fourteen hours in the saddle under that burning sun, the pain of his wound: they were all written between the lines of a midnight cypher cable to Lansdowne. There was also one other element, a crucial misunderstanding, that explained the outburst.[60]

The day before, he had received a cable from Lansdowne telling him to sack both Gatacre and Methuen. Lieutenant-General Sir Charles Warren, the commander of reinforcements he had long awaited – the 5th Division – was to take over Methuen's force at Modder River. Buller assumed from this that Lansdowne had diverted Warren and his new division to the Kimberley front, overriding his own judgement at the behest of both Milner and the capitalists. In fact, Lansdowne's order applied only to Warren himself, not to his division, which was still at Buller's disposal.[61]

Hence the mood of rebellious rage – what he himself called 'envy, hatred and malice for everyone.'[62] Buller now cabled to Lansdowne: 'No. 87 Cipher. 15 December. 11.15 p.m. My failure today raises a serious question. I do not think I am now [that is, since the apparent diversion of the 5th Division] strong enough to relieve White. Colenso is a fortress, which I think, if not taken on a rush, could only be taken by a siege. . . . I do not think either a Boer or a gun was seen by us all day. . . . My view is that I ought to let Ladysmith go, and occupy good positions for the defence of South Natal, and let time help us. . . .'[63]

Was Buller really proposing to abandon Ladysmith? By 'let go' he did not mean 'let fall', he claimed afterwards, and one can believe him.[64] What he did mean was made clear – though it was some months before the War Office in London came to know of this second, still more ill-advised outburst – in the message he sent early next day by heliograph to Ladysmith.

It was White's blunder in letting himself be locked up at Ladysmith that had wrecked the whole strategy of the war. That was Buller's view, and there was a good deal of truth in it. Now Buller lashed out at White: 'No. 88 Cipher, 16th December. I tried Colenso yesterday, but failed. The enemy is too strong for my force, except with siege operations, which will take one full month to prepare. Can you last so long? Stop. If not, how many days can you give me to take up defensive position, after which I suggest your firing away as much ammunition as you can, and making the best terms you can. Stop. I can remain here if you have alternative suggestions, but unaided I cannot break in. . . .'[65]

This message, on Buller's orders, was clumsily amended a few hours later, and three lines were added (presumably in reference to Yule's reckless abandonment of Symons's code books, and the possibility of White's cutting his way out of Ladysmith): 'Whatever happens recollect to burn your cipher and decipher and code books and any deciphered messages.'[66]

If only Buller could have expressed himself more plainly, and less bluntly. Then there would have been nothing extraordinary about either of his cables. The proposal he had made to Lansdowne was essentially the same proposal that he had made – and then rejected – a few hours after he had stepped off the ship at Cape Town, and the same cry that echoed from Milner. Let Ladysmith look after itself for the time being. Send the bulk of the army to the western front. Advance over the flat veld into the Free State. So, indirectly, relieve Ladysmith.[67] Put like that, the proposal sounded statesmanlike, though probably it was the wrong strategy. But Buller did not put it like that at all. He managed to sound both pessimistic and rebellious. His cable was a protest, and a challenge. Had the Secretary of State for War any better ideas? As a challenge, it was easy enough to answer. It was a gift to Buller's enemies.[68]

Buller's message to White was still more bluntly expressed. White had told him at the end of November that he had food to last seventy days. He had fodder for a mere thirty-five days 'at reduced ration', and he was running short of heavy gun ammunition. The main question, then, in mid-December was, how long could he hold out? The other question was, could he cut his way out? Talk of surrender was premature as well as tactless. For this error, too, Buller was to pay the price, though the cable was to have absolutely no effect on the campaign.[69]

Buller's army marched back the seven miles to Frere, the nearest point to the Tugela with a water supply. Even so, part of the water had to be brought by train from Estcourt. The Boers made absolutely no attempt to attack. The losses of the British, when finally totted up, came to 1,138: 143 killed; 755 wounded; 240 missing, mostly captured unarmed. This was about five per cent of the total force engaged; few of the wounded were serious cases, and after several weeks the losses were probably reduced by a half.[70] By military standards the battle was not a disaster. To call it a 'serious reverse', as Buller had, was putting it correctly. The enemy did not win a yard of ground. The British only lost a small fraction of their men, and ten of their field-guns. In short, Buller had lost little that could not be soon replaced. The men's morale, the key to ultimate victory, had miraculously revived.[71]

Part of the reason was Buller's behaviour the day after the battle. Methuen had raised a storm of protest by dressing down the Highland Brigade the day after Magersfontein: 'There are three things I want you to remember; your Queen, your Country and your regiment.'[72] Buller was as tactful in handling his troops as he was clumsy in handling 'Clan' Lansdowne and George White. He went to the survivors of the abandoned batteries, the 14th and the 66th, and personally thanked them for their gallantry. He breathed calm and stolid self-confidence.[73] John Atkins, perhaps reflecting many men's feelings, wrote about the with-drawal from Colenso: Buller 'gained laurels from his defeat that are not always won by victorious generals. . . . A weaker man, a less correct soldier, would have carried the position with an appalling loss of life. Buller's decision to retire was a proof of his bravery and good generalship.'[74] Churchill later wrote, 'If Sir Redvers Buller cannot relieve Ladysmith with his present force, we do not know of any other officer in the British Service who would be likely to succeed.'[75]

The men at Frere returned to what was the normal routine of army life: drill and parades, regimental cricket matches, a point-to-point for the officers – the 'Colenso Plate' and the 'Tugela Handicap'.[76]

In fact, Buller's own morale, too, was back to normal. After getting those cables off his chest, he felt more philosophical. He began to plan a new flank march to relieve Ladysmith. He wrote to his wife to reassure her. He was, he claimed, 'lucky' not to succeed:

I had to have a play at Colenso, but I did not think I could get in. I had my try on the 15th and did not get in, but I am all the better for it. One knows the worst at any rate – I think quite between you and me that I was lucky in not getting in as if I had I should not have known what next to do [because the worst fighting was still ahead]. But I was much disappointed, and the more so that had I been well served I ought I think to have got in. Kismet. Better luck next time.[77]

While he was writing this letter, the blow fell that Buller had half-expected – indeed, almost courted. A cypher telegram arrived from London: he was superseded as GOC in South Africa, and relegated to the command in Natal.[78] The man appointed over his head was not, however, the man whom Buller had expected would be the government's choice, Buller's own patron, Lord Wolseley, the Commander-in-Chief of the British army.[79] Instead, Lansdowne had appointed his own personal friend from Indian days, Lord Roberts.

The news was painful to Buller, though he accepted that the show 'was too big for one man'.[80] Roberts was the leader of the rival Ring to Wolseley's. There was no love lost there. And Roberts was absolutely out of sympathy with Buller. An added twist to their tense relationship was given by the tragic news that Buller had learnt only the previous day. He had himself just drafted the cable – blunt, yet not without emotion: 'Your gallant son died today. Condolences. Buller.'[81]

CHAPTER 21
Black Week, Silver Lining

British Isles,
16 December 1899 – 1 February 1900

'I'm coming, Oom Paul Kruger,
  To have a talk with you;

A word into your ear, old man –
  I am the kangaroo

The emu, and the 'possum,
  And the eucalyptus tree –

In other words Australia;
  And this I say to thee –

Now Mister Oom Paul Kruger,
  Just let my father be.'

Sydney Bulletin, December 1899

The first cabled report of Buller's reverse at Colenso, printed in the later editions of the morning papers, reached Lord Roberts at Kilmainham Hospital, the ramshackle seventeenth-century HQ of the British army in Ireland, at breakfast time on Saturday. There were, as yet, no casualty lists.[1] Roberts must have been apprehensive about his son, like thousands of other British parents who read their papers that morning. But his overwhelming fears – and hopes – lay in British strategy. Now he must seize his chance with both hands.

It was the chance of a lifetime. 'For years,' as he put it, 'I have [been] waiting for this day.'[2] He scribbled a long, outspoken cable to Lansdowne, and rode off to the cypher office at Viceroy's Lodge, on the other side of Phoenix Park. The cable was for Lansdowne's eyes, and for no one else's at the War Office, least of all Wolseley's. It warned the government that unless a 'radical change' in both strategy and tactics was made 'we shall have to make an ignominious peace'.[3]

How to effect the radical change? Appoint himself C-in-C in South Africa.

'He says his prayers every night, and leaves the rest to God.' So Lady Roberts described her husband.[4] They were odd words to choose, but Nora Roberts, the daughter of an Orcadian squire living in County Waterford, was known for her odd remarks. Her husband's friends found Bobs left remarkably little to God – except in the sense that he believed God helps those who help themselves.

He was the epitome of the 'political' general. In his forty-one years in India he had dominated the great sub-continent. From his father, also a political general, he had inherited power – transmitted through the nexus of British families who controlled the Indian army and civil service. He was a born diplomat. He had a way with viceroys like Lansdowne.[5] He had a way with the men – so Kipling had told the world in his ballads. 'Little Bobs, Bobs, Bobs.... Pocket-Wellin'ton,' went the jingle.[6] Other people called him a 'pusher' and a 'self-advertiser'. Even his staff laughed at the lengths to which he went to advance his career: inspiring articles about himself in the Press, cultivating the female relations of British politicians when they came to India.[7] The one thing he could do nothing about was his size. Though broad-shouldered, he was absurdly short: about five foot two. Now sixty-seven, he was a lithe, grey terrier of a man. But every inch a pro. No one would say he was too much of a gentleman – like Buller – to push his claims with Lansdowne.[8] He knew where the most decisive battles are won: in the War Office and the Cabinet room. He knew that politics, for a general, is war by other means.

His cypher cable to Lansdowne was the climax of a four-year siege of Lansdowne and the War Office. In 1893 he had returned from India, a national hero whose laurels had lost their freshness. It was thirty-five years since he had won his VC in the Indian Mutiny, thirteen years since his famous march to Kandahar. The supreme prize – to be Commander-in-Chief in England – was snatched from him by Wolseley, one year his junior. Buller got Aldershot. Bobs was fobbed off with a barony and a field-marshal's baton, and put out to grass at Kilmainham.[9] He wrote soon after, 'I have never had occasion to ask for an appointment, and would not for the world do anything myself, or ask my friends to do anything to help me in the future.'[10] Then he proceeded to do exactly that. He wrote to both Lansdowne and Chamberlain, proposing himself as the Commander of the expedition to South Africa that was mooted in 1896. After this he kept up a stream of helpful letters to Lansdowne; to help him see how Wolseley's system at the War Office was bound to end in disaster.[11]

When the war broke out he became still more pressing. On 8 December – a week before Colenso – he wrote to Lansdowne suggesting they superseded Buller and installed himself instead. He had been reading Buller's telegrams, he said, and it was clear, before he had ever fought a battle, that Buller had lost his nerve. Roberts begged Lansdowne to keep the letter secret from Wolseley and his Ring, who 'would prefer running very great risks rather than see me in command'.[12] On 10 December he slipped over to the War Office for a secret, one-day visit to see Lansdowne and his friend Sir Henry Brackenbury, the Director-General of the Ordnance.[13] Brackenbury told him of the desperate shortage of heavy guns, and other material, which confirmed his opinion of Wolseley.[14] He also received a reply from Lansdowne to his letter proposing himself as replacement for Buller. They could not sack a general 'merely on account of the gloominess of his views'. But he would show Roberts's letter to Salisbury. The proposal would be 'constantly in his thoughts'.[15]

In fact, on Friday evening, Lansdowne had already moved, with uncharacteristic swiftness, from thoughts to deeds. The moment he received Buller's first

cable – the self-confident public one, sent immediately after the battle, regretting
'to report a serious reverse' – Lansdowne decided that Buller must go. But there
were two solid obstacles: Wolseley himself and the Queen, both of whom, for
different reasons, could be relied on to fight to save Buller. How to outwit them?
Plotting was not quite Lansdowne's style. He appealed to his friend, Arthur
Balfour, deputy Prime Minister, and the master of the Whitehall backstairs.[16]

That Friday evening, Balfour was dining at the house of St Loe Strachey, the
editor of the *Spectator*. He was there to meet young Percy Fitzpatrick, the agent
of Wernher-Beit, who, by arrangement with his employers and Milner, had
remained in London to keep the government up to scratch in the post-war
settlement. Balfour himself was waiting on tenterhooks for the news of what
had happened that day at Colenso, and after dinner he was summoned to the
War Office. He returned with the astonishing news: failure. Fitzpatrick later
described Balfour's reaction: 'The serene unshakable faith in the people, the lofty
inspiring calm of a leader, the firmness, the nerve, the finest-tempered courage.'[17] Doubtless Balfour needed all these qualities in the resolve he now made.
He and Lansdowne would sack Buller, without informing either Wolseley or
the Queen.

Buller now played straight into his hands. Early next day, Saturday, Roberts
was told to make himself ready to go out to South Africa; the message crossed
with Roberts's own cypher cable to Lansdowne. Later, Buller's second cable
arrived, the one he had written just before midnight in a mood of black rage and
resentment: 'My view is that I ought to let Ladysmith go.'[18] A copy was sent to
the Queen at Windsor. Preposterous, said that smooth courtier, Lord Esher. The
cable was the main exhibit when the Defence Committee of the Cabinet met that
evening. Buller had lost his nerve and proposed to leave Ladysmith to its fate.
The Cabinet agreed to send Buller a telegram to bring home the enormity of this
proposal: 'The abandonment of White's force and its consequent surrender is
regarded as a national disaster of the greatest magnitude.' The Cabinet also
agreed to replace Buller as C-in-C by sending out Roberts; Buller would remain
in charge of the Natal army.[19] At Salisbury's insistence, Lord Kitchener, the
Sirdar of Egypt and the gallant young hero of Omdurman (he was nearly
eighteen years younger than Roberts), was to join Roberts as Chief of Staff. Yes,
said Lansdowne, the public would like it.[20]

That Buller's despondent 'let-Ladysmith-go' telegram served as a pretext for
sacking him, in Lansdowne's mind at any rate, is made clear by one simple fact.
The 'radical change' telegram sent by Roberts from Dublin, the morning after
Colenso, was in some respects more despondent, and 'preposterous', than
Buller's. The text of this astonishing cable has never before been published. It
read:

Methuen cannot apparently force his way to Kimberley. He should therefore be
ordered to withdraw to the Orange River without delay. Otherwise his line of communications will be cut and as he cannot have any large amount of supplies and ammunition he
would have to surrender. Kimberley and Mafeking ought not to have been held after the
Orange Free State declared against us, and though their being left to their fate now would

be deeply regretted it seems unavoidable. Ladysmith also ought not to have been retained but as White's force especially the Artillery and Cavalry portion would not easily be replaced it should be relieved and to do this effectually Warren should be sent round with every available man. Meanwhile Buller should be ordered to act strictly on the defensive....[21]

Order Buller to act 'strictly on the defensive' until Warren's 5th Division could be brought up. This was precisely what Buller had himself proposed in the 'let-Ladysmith-go' telegram. But to leave both Kimberley and Mafeking 'to their fates' was to out-Buller Buller.

What did Salisbury and the Cabinet make of this 'surrender' telegram of Roberts? There is no reason to believe that *they* ever saw it.[22] The strategic situation improved; and Roberts, like Buller, recovered his nerve. Before he left England a compromise strategy was agreed by Roberts, Balfour and Lansdowne. Buller was to relieve White, extricate the garrison, and then abandon Ladysmith itself to the Boers. By the same token, Methuen was to relieve Kekewich, extricate Rhodes and the rest, and then abandon Kimberley, diamonds and all. It would be humiliating, and, of course, Milner would shriek, but the government now recognized that this was the strategy that should have been followed all along. Military necessity must finally take precedence over political considerations. The alternative was the 'ignominious peace', and that, of course, no one was contemplating.[23]

Having squared Salisbury and the Cabinet, Lansdowne and Balfour had the delicate task of tackling Wolseley and the Queen. Wolseley was 'dumbfounded', he said. He warned Lansdowne that Buller would resign rather than suffer this humiliation, and said that, even if Buller had made mistakes, he was a better man than Roberts. The Queen expressed her astonishment through the medium of her Private Secretary, Sir Arthur Bigge, Buller's most intimate friend. Her Majesty, said Bigge, was deeply aggrieved at the Cabinet's behaviour on numerous grounds: for not telling her of the decision to appoint Roberts, not seeking her advice, not consulting her before cabling Buller, and failing to consult Wolseley.[24]

However, Balfour went down to Windsor to see the Queen, and found 'no great difficulty in smoothing things down'. The Queen, he told his uncle Robert (the Prime Minister), was taking the disappointments of the war with 'wonderful good humour'. She was now in her eighty-second year. She said herself at this time, 'We are not interested in the possibilities of defeat.' But she was appalled by the losses of men (and horses, too). 'No news today,' she wrote in her Journal, 'only lists of casualties.'[25]

The most painful part of the business, it now emerged, involved Lord Roberts. When the cheerful plan to sack Buller had first been mooted, no one – neither Lansdowne nor Balfour – had dreamt of the personal tragedy overshadowing Roberts's appointment. In succession, the cables reached London: Lieutenant Roberts gravely wounded, Lieutenant Roberts dead. Roberts had meanwhile taken the boat from Ireland, and in the afternoon went to Lansdowne House to receive confirmation of his appointment. Lansdowne had to break the news of Freddy's death. He said later, 'The blow was almost more than he could bear, and for a moment I thought he would break down, but he pulled himself together. I shall never forget the courage which he showed....'[26]

A week later, Lansdowne and many others went down to Southampton to wish Roberts Godspeed on the journey to South Africa. It was two days before Christmas – a raw and cheerless day, fit for the occasion. The ship was the same one, the *Dunottar Castle*, on which they had wished Buller Godspeed to South Africa two and a half months before. The same scenes repeated themselves – respectful crowds, the patriotic songs, the jolly ship's captain with the white whiskers, Captain Rigby. But Roberts and his party made up a sombre group at the quayside; Lansdowne and the others wore black in deference to Roberts.

Roberts silently paced the deck. To his wife he wrote later that the 'rent in my heart seems to stifle all feelings.... I could not help thinking how different it would have been if our dear boy had been with me. Honours, rewards and congratulations have no value to me....'[27]

Balfour – 'divine Arthur', as his friends called him – was deputy Prime Minister, and on his shoulders, elegant, but hardly broad, rested the main burden of directing war policy. Lansdowne, of course, worked industriously away at the War Office. But in Cabinet Balfour seems to have been the leading spirit. It was no great distinction. On the day before Colenso, Selborne wrote to complain to Balfour about the lack of a proper Cabinet committee to handle the war: Chamberlain was away in Birmingham half the time, Salisbury down at Hatfield; and there was no one to take the responsibility of answering urgent cables from Buller and Milner.[28]

There was, indeed, a lifelessness about Salisbury's government which the reverses of the war seemed only to intensify. Part of the reason was that in November Lord Salisbury too had been prostrated by grief. His wife, the prop of his political life for half a century, had finally succumbed to cancer. By now, he himself was slowly recovering. But managing a war was hardly his style. His interests centred on diplomacy, not on the results of its failure. Having been outwitted, on his own admission, by 'Milner and his jingo supporters', he regarded the war with a kind of sardonic detachment. If he intervened at all in military affairs (except on the subject of Kitchener's appointment as Chief of Staff), his intervention seems to have been negative.[29] 'By eliminating your most interesting paragraphs,' he had once written to George Curzon, when editing Curzon's *Persia*, 'I shall always feel that I have had a negative share in a great work.'[30] He might now have said the same, with even greater *Schadenfreude*, about the cuts in Wolseley's army.

For now Britain's modern army – the brainchild of Edward Cardwell (Gladstone's War Minister), Wolseley and Buller, starved by Lansdowne, cabinet and country – this 'small-war' army had a big war on its hands. Somehow or other, it must be inflated to a size even Wolseley had never envisaged. This was the obvious lesson of 'Black Week', as the dismal week of Stormberg, Magersfontein and Colenso came to be called. The problem was how.

To expand the British army in South Africa was not merely a question of recruiting the troops, hiring the ships, and sending them steaming off to South Africa. It was complicated by two political pressure waves, freak storms of public opinion, now making the windows rattle in Whitehall. The first was to prove, for the government, a blessing in disguise: an emotional spasm – astonishment, frustration, humiliation – that shook the British at home and in the Empire when they read the Black Week cables. The second was ominous for the whole world: a shock-wave of anglophobia vibrating across the Continent, precipitated by the war, and prolonged by Britain's failure to win it.

First, the spasm of emotion in Britain. 'Picture the newsboys at the corners,' wrote an Englishwoman in early November, 'shouting "Terrible Reverse of British Troops – Loss of 2,000". Imagine the rush for papers as we all stood about the streets – regardless of all appearances. . . . People walked along speaking in whispers and muttering, while ever echoed round the shrill and awful cry of "Terrible Reverse of British Troops". . . . The War Office is besieged – no one goes to the theatres – concert rooms are empty – new books fall flat – nothing is spoken of save the War. . . .'[31] Another contemporary wrote, 'The dark days of November and December . . . who will ever forget them? And who does not remember with pride the great outburst of patriotism which, like a volcanic eruption, swept every obstacle before it? . . .'[32] Looking back on it from the perspective of the thirties, J. L. Garvin commented, 'Our national life and thought never were the same again.'[33] What was happening? Had the Victorian public lost their heads at the first whiff of grapeshot?

In fact, the public soon saw that Black Week was *not* the 'darkest hour' of the war – as Chamberlain called it. It was the culmination of tactical reverses. But the tide of war had actually turned in mid-November, driving the Boers back in both Natal and the Cape. After Black Week it seemed possible that, despite their inferiority in numbers, the Boers might return to the offensive. This did not happen. The British garrisons of Ladysmith, Kimberley and Mafeking remained in danger. But, taking the war as a whole, it was the Boers, not the British, who now had their backs to the wall.[34]

So there was no sense of national emergency in the days that followed. It was a black Christmas for the restaurant trade: nothing to celebrate; this was the gut reaction in the West End. Publishers complained that no one read any books except war books. The key to the public's mood was disappointment that victory was so long postponed.[35]

The people of Britain had had war on the cheap for half a century. Small wars against savages: the big-game rifle against the spear and the raw-hide shield. Small casualties – for the British. To lose more than a hundred British soldiers killed in battle was a disaster suffered only twice since the Mutiny. Now, in 1899, they had sent out the biggest overseas expedition in British history to subdue one of the world's smallest nations. It would have been odd if the public had not shared the government's confidence in a walk-over. The resulting casualties were thought shattering: seven hundred killed in action or dead of wounds, three thousand wounded since October.[36] Still more shattering was the list of those who had not been either killed or wounded – and had surrendered. There was no precedent in British military history for this kind of battle honour. To the white flags of Majuba and Doornkop had now been added an endless line: the flags of Möller's cavalry at Talana, White's infantry at Nicholson's Nek, Gatacre's infantry at Stormberg; there were more than two thousand of these heroes now in Pretoria.[37] This was at the root of the public's humiliation. Then the spasm of bitterness passed.

It was the Opposition leaders – Asquith and Campbell-Bannerman – who adopted the most statesmanlike tone in the aftermath of Black Week. Not that the government had any objection to their speeches. Asquith himself had inspired the phrase 'Black Week'. But he warned people that it would be 'grotesque' to get these reverses out of proportion. He compared the present 'humiliations and mortifications' with periods of real national crisis during the Napoleonic War or the Indian Mutiny. How would Marlborough, Wellington or Havelock have survived this ordeal by telegraph – every blow they struck and every blow they received made subject to hourly scrutiny by the public? His conclusion might have been drafted by Milner himself. The struggle now went much deeper than a mere question of 'asserting and maintaining our position in South Africa. It is our title to be known as a world power which is now upon trial.'[38]

Campbell-Bannerman's adoption of the same broadly pro-government stance was still more significant. He had long been hostile to Chamberlain, and was beginning to suspect Milner's part in making the war. But, as the new Leader of the Opposition, he had a hard row to hoe. He must rally support in the country, and also try to hold the party together. The lessons of Black Week – that the war was to be long and arduous, and that Britain needed a bigger army – made this job almost impossible. For the country's new instinct was to close ranks, while the Liberal Party seemed keener than ever to smash itself into fragments. So C-B had no choice but to avoid controversy about the government's bungling of the war,[39] insisting that the government should set up an enquiry into the war when it was over.

Four days after Colenso, C-B addressed the electors of Aberdeen with these reassuring words: 'The end cannot be doubted [cheers]. We have in the field the largest army that ever left these shores. It can readily be reinforced. We have a united people in the country and in every part of the Empire [cheers] and with these forces on our side – moral and material – success is certain.'[40]

All this support was heartening, and, if any man needed it, the man was Chamberlain. His own reaction to Black Week was characteristically emotional. He was afraid that the government might fall – an extraordinarily unlikely possibility, given the mood of the country and the ineptness of the Liberals.[41]

What lay behind Chamberlain's fit of gloom? It was partly the personal eclipse he had suffered as a result of the war. Chamberlain was a light-demanding plant; he needed the political sunshine. It must have seemed like being in a morgue, those days spent inside the lead-carpeted corridors of the Colonial Office. The war in South Africa had decreased, not increased, his own ministerial duties. The military work was handled by the War Office. The day-to-day political work was handled by Milner – still 'quaking' about the precarious situation of the Cape.

Chamberlain's relations with Milner were strained once more. It was Milner's predictions that there would be no war – or only an 'apology for a war' – that had given Chamberlain his original over-confidence. Now it was Milner's gloom that rubbed off on to his chief. Encouraged by the Boer successes, the Afrikaners in the Cape were reported to be on the verge of rebellion. Milner said that any moment he might have to turn out Schreiner's ministry and rule the Cape directly as a Crown Colony. Chamberlain forbade it.[42]

Still, there was one result of Black Week in which Chamberlain, the champion of imperial unity, could only take pride. A wave of colonial patriotism, much more astonishing than the home variety, had been set in motion among British people all over the globe.

Why did the governments of the white dominions, with the single exception of Cape Colony, unanimously take sides with Britain and her subjects in the Transvaal? Certainly, blood was thicker than water – the intervening water of the Pacific and the Atlantic. British Canadians, Australians and New Zealanders felt a natural solidarity with the mother country. They could also identify with the Uitlanders to a degree that the public at home could not. They were of the same class. They had shared experiences: cattle-ranching, gold-mining, making fortunes and losing them again. And many of the Uitlanders actually were colonials.[43]

Hence Chamberlain's own task in rallying support in the self-governing white colonies was a light enough burden. The problem had been how to restrain the colonies' enthusiasm. Characteristically, the War Office had done its best to confuse the situation. That autumn they had given Chamberlain the text of the telegram to send to each colony, describing the type of soldier required: 'Infantry most, cavalry least serviceable'.[44] What the War Office meant to convey with this cryptic message was that they intended to make MI (mounted infantry) out of the colonial contingent. In fact, the confusion made little difference to the type of soldiers sent: the colonies despatched both MI *and* cavalry. But the story spread in England, politically damaging for Chamberlain as well as Lansdowne, that offers of mounted men had been refused. At any rate, the first contingents had sailed that autumn, and were already playing some part in the war. These contingents were only token forces – 1,019 from Canada, 875 from Australia and 203 from New Zealand. But no one could now write off the self-governing Empire as an anachronism. That 'slender thread' holding it together, in Chamberlain's famous phrase, now carried more than the force of sentiment. Soon it was to bring twenty-nine thousand white colonial troops to South Africa.[45]

A united country, a united Empire – at any rate *more* united than ever before. Chamberlain's gloom that January might seem hard to understand. But there was a good reason: that shock-wave of anglophobia on the Continent, and especially in Germany. Two months of war had revealed to Britain that there was another side to the 'splendid' isolation (not an adjective used by Lord Salisbury, though it aptly described his policy). If Britain's Continental rivals chose this moment to intervene, amicably or not so amicably, Britain would be in a splendid mess. In fact, intervention, though discussed by the other Great Powers in Europe – Germany, France and Russia – was not to prove a practical possibility. But in the autumn of 1899, the German government had come to a momentous decision: to double the size of the German navy by pushing a great Navy Bill through the Reichstag. It was a new phase in the European arms race.

In the meantime, a violent propaganda war had broken out on the Continent. Kruger's envoy in Brussels, Dr Leyds, fanned the fervour of the anglophobes. The Press of all the major European powers was rabidly anti-British. The public believed, or appeared to believe, the most absurd atrocity stories (the British tortured and murdered prisoners); and the best that was said about the British was that they were the dupes of Jewish financiers.[46]

Unlike Chamberlain, Wolseley was finding the war a great relief to his feelings. He grumbled, as usual, at 'little Lansdowne's utter small-mindedness'.[47] But everything in the War Office seemed to be going Wolseley's way. Treasury Bills were flowing like water. Till September, the Cabinet had gibbed at a mere £645,000 for the most essential war preparations, like making transport wagons serviceable. Now the Treasury was planning for a war costing nearly £10 million.[48]

The latest reverses of the war caught Wolseley, like many soldiers, in a strange conflict of emotions. He was insular and patriotic, and proud of his army's reputation. He regarded the surrender of White's infantry on Mournful Monday as the most humiliating disaster for half a century: 'As a soldier I blush to think that two of our brave Battns should have to surrender in open fight to such canaille as the boers [sic] 40 officers taken prisoners. . . . I know who is to blame for it, my blood boils with indignation.' He reproached himself for one thing: 'For it was I who selected White – faute de mieux . . . he was always crammed down my throat as a great general.'[49] But he principally blamed Lansdowne – and the 'Indians'.

The bitter and sometimes childish feud between Lansdowne and Wolseley – and between 'Indians' and 'Africans' – was the root cause of so many of the disasters in South Africa. As we saw earlier, the fundamental strategic mistake of the war consisted in sending out too few troops in September, led by the wrong commander and pushed too far forward into Natal. Both Lansdowne and Wolseley had to share the blame for this triple blunder. On the other hand, it was Lansdowne's caution that was the main cause of the four-month delay in the arrival of the Army Corps. If Wolseley was a 'fifth wheel' on the War Office coach, as he bitterly complained to Lord Salisbury, then Lansdowne was the brake. Quite apart from the direct effect of this – time lost, battles lost – there was the indirect effect of his negative influence, discouraging and dampening all initiative within the War Office labyrinth.[50]

A dramatic, almost farcical illustration of this was provided on 15 December, to add to the news of Colenso. Brackenbury, the Director-General of Ordnance, had made a detailed investigation of reserves: clothing, stores, guns, ammunition and so on. He was appalled at what he had discovered. He told Lansdowne: either the system was changed, or he would resign.[51]

Brackenbury's report showed that the War Office had not even succeeded in their limited aim of having an army of about a hundred thousand equipped for overseas service. In the first two months' fighting, less than fifty thousand men had gone to the front. To keep this small force in action for only two months had strained War Office reserves to breaking-point.[52] It had simply never occurred to anyone there that a war might mean more than a one-day event, that a field-force would need more than a field-day. In a few weeks the reserves were exhausted. Indeed, it was worse than that. The War Office had first proposed to send out Buller's Army Corps in lightweight khaki drill, then decided (the rainy season began in October) to send them in khaki serge. So there was, for a time, no cloth at all.[53] It was the same with the ·303 magazine rifles. The army had just decided to change its standard rifle from Lee Metford to Lee Enfield. The two weapons were the same, except for the rifling, but no one had noticed that this changed the sighting. Consternation in the War Office that December. Twenty-five thousand reservists had gone out with rifles that fired eighteen inches to the right (at 500 yards). All these rifles had now to be resighted.[54]

With the ammunition itself, there were other embarrassments. That summer there had taken place at The Hague the famous convention on war methods. Among other things, this convention outlawed expanding rifle bullets, such as were used at Omdurman to give better stopping power: 'dum-dum' they were called, after the name of the British arms factory in India. Britain did not sign the convention, but accepted that, at least for a 'white man's war', it had a certain moral force. Hence the decision not to use the reserve supply of ·303 ammunition in store, politely called MK IV and MK V, and meaning 'dum-dum'. Unfortunately, some found its way to South Africa, and had to be recalled in a hurry. (Other ammunition, labelled 'Dum-Dum', was captured by the Boers and caused an international furore; it was actually innocent enough, simply made at Dum-Dum.)[55]

These were some of the War Office problems in resupplying the first fifty thousand men at the front. When it tried to equip a second army corps, the cupboard was bare. To find the minimum of three million rounds of ·303 ammunition a week required was impossible for the civilian suppliers.[56] Brackenbury had to go to the highways and byways to scrounge equipment. The lack of heavy guns and their ammunition was most serious of all. On 15 December, Brackenbury was trying to replace three howitzers; two had to come from the fortress armaments in England. Later, Britain had to buy heavy guns abroad. Ammunition had to be borrowed from the navy and from India; but still Brackenbury could not meet Buller's needs.[57]

Brackenbury's astonishing report – DGO's 'cry of distress', Lansdowne called it – naturally strengthened Wolseley's hand. So did the three battles of

Black Week. The day before Colenso, Wolseley had insisted that they must now flood South Africa with reinforcements. 'We are face to face with a serious national crisis,' he told Lansdowne on 14 December, 'and unless we meet it boldly . . . [it will] lead to dangerous complications with Foreign Powers.'[58] His proposals were far-reaching. They included plans to mobilize the 7th Division (to complete a second army corps) and the 8th Division (the last organized division of regulars in the home army), and to accept civilian volunteers. Together, the reinforcements would total about forty-five thousand, almost doubling the fighting force in South Africa.[59]

On 16 and 18 December the Army Board met, and the War Office generals endorsed Wolseley's scheme. On the 20th, Wolseley was astonished to hear that Lansdowne agreed – or rather, that he had accepted a scheme for raising civilian volunteers of a much more sensational kind than Wolseley's.[60]

The origin of the scheme actually lay in a cypher telegram from Buller sent on the day after Colenso. 'Would it be possible for you to raise eight thousand irregulars in England,' Buller cabled. 'They should be equipped as mounted infantry, be able to shoot as well as possible and ride decently. I would amalgamate them with colonials.'[61] This telegram marked Buller's own final recognition that the War Office had sent out the wrong sort of army to South Africa.

George Wyndham, Lansdowne's junior minister and leader of the Milnerites in the House of Commons, grasped Buller's point at once. He told his chief next day that, whether or not they relieved the besieged garrisons or 'abandoned them to their fate', British mobility must match Boer mobility. At present, their own infantry, even if superior in numbers, could hardly move more than eight miles from a railway line. He agreed that seven thousand volunteers should be sent to help regular MI units. In addition, he suggested raising, as 'a matter of immediate urgency and permanent importance', a total of twenty thousand irregular MI: mainly in South Africa and other colonies, but at least five thousand in Britain.

What especially attracted Wyndham to this idea was the 'singular oportunity' to make a 'revolution' in the existing Yeomanry at home. The best men at present regarded their service as a 'farce' and a 'sham'. The Yeomanry were 'still too largely a theatrical reminiscence of the Cavalry which fought in the Crimea and the Peninsular'. But the material was excellent – better than the men recruited for the regular army. He advised Lansdowne to be guided by some friends of his: 'They are men of affairs, and as masters of fox-hounds, they are in touch with the young riding farmers and horse-masters of this country.'[62]

Three days later, the newspapers carried the announcement of the birth of the 'Imperial Yeomanry'. It was Wyndham's 'hunting and shooting' yeomanry in all its magnificent amateurishness. The regular army would have almost no control over its formation. A committee of fox-hunting gentlemen was to organize it; two rich peers offered to pay part of the cost. A much larger sum – £50,000 – was subscribed by Wernher-Beit, presumably at Percy Fitzpatrick's suggestion.[63] Fitzpatrick wrote to Balfour, explaining how the loyal Imperial Yeoman of today would be the loyal South African settler of tomorrow.[64]

Perhaps Fitzpatrick, who knew Wyndham, had, for political reasons, inspired the scheme all along.

As for Wolseley, he was furious to find his own scheme so dramatically trumped. He protested officially that to go 'into the highways and byways' and pick up civilians, 'quite regardless of whether they have learnt the rudiments of discipline', was a 'dangerous experiment'. The eight thousand Yeomanry would be 'very little use in field'. Lansdowne's comment was: 'The Boers are not, I suppose, very highly drilled or disciplined.'[65]

December 1899 passed into January 1900, January into February, sleet and fog into drizzle. From high summer in South Africa came a cloud of telegrams: 'Lord Bobs' preparing a great flank march; Sir Reverse Buller suffering fresh disasters;[66] Milner 'croaking', as he called it, about the Cape rebellion. In London, the first Parliament of the 1900s emerged – as bland and lifeless as the last one of the 1890s. No effective voice was raised in opposition to the government's handling of the war.[67] Asquith danced a graceful *pas de deux* with Balfour in the debate.

Amid all the self-congratulation, no one noticed one dismal blunder of the Cabinet's. In December, they had conceded a request from Milner for the navy to search foreign ships believed to be carrying war material for the Transvaal or Free State. In succession, three German passenger ships, the *Bundesrath*, the *Herzog* and the *General*, were stopped and forced into port, and then suffered the humiliation of being searched. The search was negative in all three cases, and this only fed the flames of anglophobia in Germany. How dare the British navy stop our mail steamers, cried the German Press.[68] And how convenient it all was for the German government, whose great Navy Bill steamed majestically through the Reichstag. However, this did not worry the British, whose fleet remained more than double the size of her enemies' fleets, as the German Ambassador to Britain noted grimly.[69] Who could have guessed that these earth tremors of 1900 were to lead to the earthquake of 1914?

At the time, the most striking fact about Black Week was that it seemed to have, for everyone except the Boers, a silver lining. The government found that the new Imperial Yeomanry caught the imagination of Press and public. In sporting circles, there was a rush to abandon the fox and pursue the Boer; large crowds formed outside the recruiting office in London;[70] the City of London itself offered and paid for one thousand volunteers.[71] Thirty-four MPs and peers rallied to join the new Yeomanry. People began to talk of the war as a 'national' war, and the several thousand 'gentlemen-rankers' – stockbrokers, journalists, dons and even one MP serving in the *ranks* – brought a new whiff of democracy to the barrack room and the camp-fire on the veld.[72]

CHAPTER 22

Christmas at Pretoria

Pretoria,
12 December 1899 – 1 January 1900

'We hope to be lunching at the White Hart, Pretoria, in
about a month's time....'

> Lieutenant Reggie Kentish to his
> mother, near Ladysmith,
> 12 October 1899

'Lunch is at one o'clock & consists of Bread & Bully beef
... vegetables, cheese, fresh meat ... & the towns people
parade in front of our cage eyeing us up and down as
though we were some weird objects....'

> Lieutenant Kentish to his mother,
> Model Schools (Prisoner of War
> Camp), Pretoria, 9 November 1899

'De God onzer voorvaden heeft ons heden een schitterende overwinning gegeven....'
'The God of our forefathers had given us a dazzling victory....'[1] 'Yesterday was
not only a dazzling victory for our burghers but a new spirit is born....'[2] As the
battle telegrams – and nine hundred British prisoners of war – converged on
Pretoria, confirming that the enemy had been thrown back at Colenso, Magersfontein and Stormberg, men of other nations might have allowed themselves a
day's public rejoicing. Kruger's people were not like that: too modest, perhaps,
or too God-fearing.

Up at the war fronts, it is true, there were celebrations – impromptu sports,
ironic renderings of 'Soldiers of the Queen' sung by the burghers, and 'Maggie
Murphy's Home' played by the Zarp Police Band.[3] The Boer heliograph at the
Tugela teased the British with 'How is Mr Buller today? What has Mr Buller
done that Roberts is coming out?'[4]

But in the capital, always solemn and God-fearing, the church bells rang only
for the dead. On Tuesday, the day after Magersfontein, there was a State funeral.
Shops were closed; the *vierkleurs* hung at half-mast on Government Buildings;
and a special train steamed into Pretoria with the coffins of burghers killed in
battle. A cortège of 120 carriages, including the State Secretary's, clattered down
to Church Square. Five thousand people lined the streets, mainly women and

their African servants; most of the Boer menfolk were away at the front. Military victory brings everyone mixed feelings. To the volk it brought a double shock: relief and delight at their achievements, bitterness at the cost.[5]

Four coffins led the cortège – Pretoria's own share of the hundred-odd Boers and foreign volunteers who had so far given their lives for the two republics. Only four coffins (and one of the dead burghers was a Jewish-American Uitlander from Ohio),[6] but it was almost more than Pretoria could bear. 'Notwithstanding yesterday's victories,' one of the papers said, 'the feeling of sorrow and gloom over the sad losses ... is more intense than ever.'[7] In fact, the price of victory had been heavier for the volk, proportionate to their numbers, than the price of defeat for the British.[8] Besides, in the eyes of the volk, surrounded by black enemies, no white man's death, even a white enemy's, was much cause for rejoicing.

In addressing his people, on the day after Colenso, Kruger had no need to refer to the British dead. It was Dingaan's Day, the Day of the Covenant, the day when the Lord had shown, by the destruction of Dingaan and the Zulus at Blood River, that he had made a covenant with the voortrekkers. For the sixty-first time, Kruger celebrated the great anniversary. In the small Dopper (Baptist) church, packed with women, he shuffled to the rostrum, eyes blinking painfully, black suit hanging in folds, voice hoarse and frail; yet in spirit the epitome of strength and defiance. Perhaps he took his text, as did a speaker elsewhere that day, from Exodus 15:10. 'The enemy said: "I will pursue. I will overtake. I will divide the spoil. My lust will be satisfied upon them. . . ." They sank as lead in the mighty waters.'[9] To Kruger, there was indeed a marvellous symmetry about the pattern of his long life. Blood River, Majuba – now Colenso. Three times in the green hills of Natal, the Lord had delivered them from their enemies. Hence the overpowering simplicity of his call to the volk: put your trust in the Lord; He will protect His people as He protected your forefathers from Dingaan.[10]

Simplicity, of course, was not a characteristic of Kruger's mind. Nor was Dingaan's fate directly relevant to the fate of the British. With the British Empire, Kruger wanted agreement: the final settlement, giving unqualified independence to the Transvaal, which had been the goal of all Kruger's manoeuvring. As he struggled away hour after hour in his small office in Government Buildings, from eight in the morning, when he read the first telegrams from the war fronts, till eleven at night,[11] he had to face a strategic dilemma of extraordinary difficulty. How could he turn tactical successes into real strategic victories, and both, in turn, into a winning seat at the conference table?

Could he, on the one hand, make Colenso into a second and better Majuba? Or must this be a war of attrition against the British, a Fabian war, in which conventional military objectives are hardly pursued at all, and everything subordinated to the supreme (and negative) aim of preserving unbroken the spirit of the volk, both in military victory and the reverse?

The first alternative, a new Majuba, might have seemed a tempting option. The parallels between the events of 1881 and 1899 were uncanny. In both wars

Joubert had crushed a British general – Colley in 1881, now Penn Symons – trapped in the northern prong of Natal. After that, the war had turned on the fate of the British garrisons – then within the Transvaal, now on its borders – trapped by Boer forces. The British public's response to the disasters in 1881 and now was much the same: a spasm of humiliation and patriotism; the call for a military hero to go to the rescue – in both cases, General Roberts – and the sending of a large relief expedition. Here the parallels diverged. In 1881, Gladstone's Liberals had just taken office, pledged to cancel the Tories' annexation of the Transvaal four years before. In 1899, there was a Conservative government, pledged to consolidate the Empire. In 1881, it was questionable whether Majuba itself had helped or hindered Gladstone in making the settlement that followed.[12] In 1899, it was certain that Boer military successes had done wonders for the cause of the jingoes in Britain, and further reduced the slender minority who believed in a negotiated peace.[13]

Kruger may not have grasped all the niceties of British politics, but the Boer newspapers printed plenty of British political news, and Kruger understood these sad truths well enough.[14] The spirit of John Bright was dead, one of his officials had said when war broke out.[15] It was true. Even Henry Labouchère, the most outspoken member of the Gladstonian wing of the British Liberal Party, had now declared his belief in the doctrine of 'my country right or wrong'. The danger of Britain's being humiliated in front of the other Great Powers, he said, outweighed the moral disadvantages.[16]

There was, of course, one way that Britain might be forced to the conference table, other than by the pressure of British public opinion: by public opinion in other countries – in other words, by intervention of one sort or another. But, here again, Kruger was not so simple as to think this a likely possibility, nor did he choose to raise false hopes, just at the moment, by pretending that it was.

Dr Leyds, the Transvaal Ambassador in Brussels, had struggled for the last few months to persuade Britain's rivals – France, Germany and Russia – to make common cause against Britain. That autumn he told a French newspaper, in an interview reprinted in Johannesburg, that 'we have the sympathy of all Europe. I know it and see it. But Europe will not intervene in our favour; at least not at the present moment.'[17] In fact, all Dr Leyds achieved was to inspire a couple of hundred foreign volunteers to fight on the side of the burghers, and to channel public sympathy in a number of countries into providing small ambulance teams for the war fronts. Both of these moves provided practical help, and they were still more useful as tokens of moral support, like the small contingents already sent by Britain's white colonies.[18] But Holland, the country which, for obvious reasons, felt most identified with the Boer cause, was no military power. France and Russia, which were, had to keep a weather eye on the British navy. They did actually offer to intervene – amicably – if Germany would join in. Germany would not.[19]

For both these reasons – lack of moral support in Britain, and of military support on the Continent – there was no chance of Colenso or the other victories turning, of themselves, into new Majubas. Could the Boers, then, follow up their successes and strike offensive blows against the British in Natal and the Cape while the British were still off balance? Many historians have said yes, and criticize the Boers for not having adopted this strategic policy.[20] In principle, Kruger favoured this option, and so did Steyn; still more so, the younger generation of Boers, Smuts's friends, Fischer and Grobler.

But was it practicable? General Cronje, the commander at Magersfontein, was asked to block Methuen's lines of communication. Seize Belmont again, said Steyn, make it a strong-point, and prevent any supplies or reinforcements reaching Methuen.[21] Take fifteen hundred of your best men, said Kruger, with a good field-piece, 'shoot to pieces' the English armoured train, and break up the railway line behind the British.[22] Impossible, said Cronje. The terrain was too flat for offensive action; there was no water there; the commandos were exhausted and so were their horses. Then what about a *direct* attack on Methuen, said Kruger; it was 'not an order', he said, 'but only a suggestion'. To this, Cronje, outnumbered by nearly five to one, gave an understandably flat refusal. Kruger could only reply 'something must be done' or the English would hold Cronje at Magersfontein, and send other troops to outflank him.[23] But neither Kruger nor Steyn felt sufficient confidence in the possibility of real offensive strategy to replace Cronje with one of the two Generals, De la Rey or De Wet, who might have adopted it.

It was certainly an error, as events would soon show, to leave a man like Cronje in such a position of importance; though whether De Wet or De la Rey would have succeeded in cutting off Methuen for long is another question. What evidence there is on the Natal side suggests that the Boer governments, like their British counterpart, had failed to recognize how the new conditions of war – this war of smokeless, long-range magazine rifles, used by infantry concealed in slit-trenches – had dramatically tipped the tactical balance in favour of the defence. Hence, in turn, they underrated the difficulties of offensive strategy.[24] On 15 December Kruger had received Botha's stirring telegram about Colenso: 'The God of our forefathers has given us a dazzling victory.' Excellent, said Kruger.[25] Why not then smite the enemy 'while the terror is still so great' in their hearts? Impossible, replied Botha, just as Cronje had: 'There are no hills [around Buller's camp at Frere] nor the least cover between us and the enemy and I am afraid to undertake something which, if it goes wrong, will hearten the enemy.' More relevant, the burghers' morale, always volatile, might collapse completely, if they were sent on such a risky venture.[26]

If Botha, both the boldest and the most level-headed general of the Boer armies, thought Buller too strong to attack, who is to say that Cronje was wrong to adopt the same view towards Methuen – and the Boer governments wrong not to insist on a counter-offensive? By default, at any rate, Kruger had now chosen the second of the two strategic options: to fight a war of attrition against the British. The two republics' military objectives were now limited to trying to block the progress of the two relief columns, and, meanwhile, to squeeze the three beleaguered garrisons – Ladysmith, Kimberley and Mafeking. It was not a strategy that could win them a seat at the conference table – not directly, at any rate. To capture all three garrisons – White's, Kekewich's and Baden-Powell's, totalling nearly thirteen thousand British regulars – would deal an intensely humiliating blow to the British.[27] In strictly military terms, however, it would leave the task of Buller and Roberts somewhat easier. Relieved of these entanglements, they could make straight for Bloemfontein across the open plains of the Free State.

Kruger regretted Botha's and Cronje's inability to smite the enemy, yet he was soon reconciled. It was, after all, a war of attrition that came naturally to the Boers, not only among the commandos in the field, but among the people as a whole. Kruger himself had fought an eighteen-year diplomatic war of attrition against the British; he had tried to wear down the stronger adversary, as he had worn down those lions he had hunted as a young man. The Transvaal was now prepared for a war that would 'stagger humanity'. Its strength lay, above all, in its self-sufficiency, which no strategic blockade of imports via Mozambique, no blockade, imposed by the British navy, could injure.[28]

There were three civilian cornerstones to Kruger's state, viewed as a military power. The first was the pro-Boer Uitlanders, an important minority of the men who had come to seek their fortunes in this industrial state, with the richest gold-mines in the world. The expulsion of the pro-British Uitlanders, essential on military grounds, had certainly weakened industrial efficiency. But the Netherlands Railways still ran – manned by Hollanders. They were the strategic key to all communications; and in their railway workshops the Boers' field-guns were ably serviced and repaired (including a Creusot Long Tom damaged, as we shall see, on 8 December at Ladysmith).[29] The Transvaal dynamite industry also flourished. This had been organized by the French and German businessmen who had secured the monopoly. Now it proved a godsend, improvising Mauser bullets and Krupp and Creusot shells alike. And the mines could be brought back into production, even if at a reduced level. The coal-mines were needed to supply the motive power on which the railways and all industry depended. The eight gold-mines, restarted by the government, would pay the entire cost of the war – about £100,000 a month.[30]

But who was to work the mines? There was a second, and less visible, cornerstone: quarried from the vast black reserve of African labour. When the young Welsh MP, David Lloyd George, talked of Britain fighting two nations whose population totalled less than that of Flintshire and Denbighshire he forgot the invisible majority: the Africans. In 1899 there were thought to be 754,000 Africans living in the Transvaal, and a further 130,000 in the Free State.[31] Some, it is true, had been expelled, with the pro-British Uitlanders, in the great exodus from the Rand; these were Africans from Basutoland, Natal and the Cape. But over ten thousand 'mine boys' remained – more than enough to work the coal-mines and gold-mines at a reduced level.[32] Everything in the Transvaal depended, ultimately, on the gold-mines. And all the gold-mines depended, in turn, on a supply of cheap African labour.

There was a fundamental irony about the war which would not have amused the British financiers, Beit and Wernher. Their strongest single motive for making that secret alliance with Milner, which had set Britain and the Transvaal on a collision course, was to reduce the cost of African labour on the Rand.[33] They were outraged by having to pay fifty to sixty shillings a month to African miners (though this was, of course, far less than white South African miners received, or those of the rival mines of Australia and California). They blamed the 'outrageous' wages of Africans in the Rand on the incompetence and corruption of Kruger's government.[34] But wartime regulations had transformed the mining industry of the Rand. At a stroke, African wages had been cut to a maximum of one pound a month. Africans, found living illegally in the locations, were commandeered, like the mines themselves, and forced to work.[35] It was a drastic solution – slave labour of a sort – and one which many British mine owners had long tried to persuade the Boers to adopt. Today the roles were reversed with a vengeance. The Boers taunted the British mine owners with having been ridiculously soft. They themselves knew how to use a 'firm hand'. *The Standard and Diggers' News*, which spoke for the pro-Boer Uitlanders, crowed loudest: 'The very people who were never credited with any governing capacity or industrial acumen – that is to say, the Boers – solve the whole problem in an afternoon, put the Kaffir in his proper place ... and establish a new sound and healthy order of things from one end of the Rand to another.'[36]

The great majority of the 700,000-odd Africans, of course, did not live in locations and work in the mines. They lived in the kraals dotted the length and breadth of the country, and supplied the Boers with all the menial labour for cattle ranches and other farms. It was in these farms that the third cornerstone of Kruger's state was pre-eminently found: the indomitable *vrouw*, the Boer housewife. If the Boer commandos had a secret weapon in the shape of the spade, the nation as a whole had a secret weapon in the shape of the cradle. Demographers rubbed their eyes when they tried to measure the Transvaal birth rate. That tidal wave of Uitlanders, the gold rush itself, had failed to offset the simple, dogged, philoprogenitive persistence of the backveld Boer.[37] No one knew even roughly how the score stood. The number of potential voters among the Uitlanders must have outnumbered the Boer menfolk before the exodus in 1899. Without a doubt, the volk were now in the majority. The dedication of the Boer *vrouw* was epitomized by Kruger's own family. In 1900 he had one hundred and fifty-six surviving children, grandchildren, and great-grand-children.[38]

Of course, the *vrouw* did more than rock the cradle. She ran the house, she worked on the farm; Kruger's wife still milked the cows in the farmyard behind the President's house in Pretoria.[39] Already the stress of wartime had entrusted to the Boer wives a mass of tasks previously done by men. They were overseeing the farms, bossing the African labourers as they sowed the millet that spring, and herded the cattle.[40] They supplied regular food hampers for their sons and husbands fighting at the front. Pretoria was full of women that Christmas: lining the streets at the State funeral and crowding the covered wagons into Church Square for the Nachtmaal (communion) celebrations.[41]

CHAPTER 23

'Are We Rotters or Heroes?'

Ladysmith,
2 November 1899 – 6 January 1900

'When I come home I shall want to sleep in my clothes
out on a path in the garden in a blanket. If it isn't raining I
should like someone to pour a watering pot over me
every now and then. And the gardener [to] come out and
shoot every hour or so in the night....'

> Major Robert Bowen, 60th Rifles, to
> his wife, shortly before he was killed
> on 6 January 1900

Six weeks earlier, Gunner Netley, of the 13th Battery, began his diary of the siege of Ladysmith, jauntily written in violet pencil in the leaves of the exercise book he kept in his haversack:

Thur 2nd Nov:... the siege has started. The Boers opened fire with their artillery into the town, but luckily they did no harm....

Sat Nov 4th: Enemy reported marching towards the town, and the troops go to meet them and we can hear firing towards Action [Acton] Holmes. The 69th Battery fired into the Boer camp, while they were in at Breakfast, and of corse they received a little more of our cough medicine....

Sun Nov 5th: All is quiet around but we are keeping a keen eye on anything moving.

Thur Nov 9th: Stood to arms till daybreak, at 5.20 am the Boers opened fire on us from heavy artillery all around us, shelling the camp and Town, firing verry fast all the while. At 7.30 am the Boers attacked King's hill in force; but met with a warm reception, being repulsed three times with loss, then they attacked Ceazers [Caesar's] Hill and met with the same result.... The Naval Brigade fired a Royal salute [for the Prince of Wales' Birthday] with live shell.... Boers losses are estimated at 850 killed and wounded ... our losses are 6 horses and one mule, after having 300 Boers shell fired at you....

Sat Nov 11th: A fiew rounds from long Tom which was responded to by our boys in blue [the Naval Brigade], and they soon quietened them.

Sun Nov 12th: Stoot [sic] to arms, and church parade.

Mon Nov 13th: Boers bid us good morning with long Tom....

Tues Nov 14th: As usual at daybreak the enemy opened a slow artillery fire ... this continued until night when they fired off all their guns, as a transformation scene or grand Finale. Expecting reinforcements from Colenso.

Wed Nov 15th: A fiew shells this morning but it is raining, and so there is 'not mutch ado about Nothing,' as Shakespeare says; no news of reinforcements yet arrives. . . .

Sat Nov 18th: Stood to arms as usual till daybreak Johny Dutchman is still wasting his ammunition.

Sun Nov 19th: Stood to arms but all was quiet ... church parade. . . .

Mon Nov 20th [Boers'] capture of an armoured train [at Frere] ... with an escort of mounted Infantry who made good their escape. . . .

Tues Nov 21st: They are firing an odd shot or two from Gun Hill at us, but we want an extra strong pair of glasses to find out what damage they are doing. . . .

Nov 22nd: A thunderstorm broke out during the morning and the enemy kept it company by putting a few shell down at us. . . .

Nov 23rd: Two privates of the Gloucesters died of enteric, were buried today. . . .

Nov 24th: One shell dropped clean in the midst of D Coy of the Liverpools killing one man and wounding 9 others. . . .

Nov 25th: Up and about early building a shelter from old railway sleepers and stones. . . .

Nov 28th: All verry quiet at daybreak relief column reported from P[ieter] M[aritz] Berg have met a strong force of the enemy and repulsed them. . . .

Nov 29th:. . . the Boers Artillery are verry quiet this morning so we are doing ditto. . . . Another big fight reported near Colenso. Boers were again driven back. Losses of the Boers were estimated at 1400 killed and wounded and 300 prisoners. . . .

Dec. 1st: The Boers bid us good morning as usual, with a few shots, but nothing out of the ordinary occured. . . .

Dec 2nd: At it again with old Long Tom.

Sun Dec 3rd: All quiet – church parade. Cricket match.

Mon Dec 4th: Our old friend Long Tom saluted us as usual. . . . News reached us about Gen. Gatacre defeating the Boers three times. About 8,000 strong the enemy were. Our own relief column drove the enemy north of the Tugela. . . .

Thur Dec 7th: Long Tom spoke to us again whith the same old Talk. . . .

Sun Dec 10th: Boers opened fire with long Tom number 2 from Umbulwana, Church parade as usual. . . .

Sat Dec 16th: Reported that a big fight occured yesterday between Ladysmith and Colensoe. Usual Boer Long Tom fired but damage was nil. Gen. Gatacre had a complete victory with yesterday's fight ... [the disaster at Stormberg].

Sun Dec 17th: All quiet Church parade.

Mon Dec 18th: Stood to arms at 2.30 am till 7.30 am and are ready for an attack but no such luck.[1]

'No such luck.' Gunner Netley talked as though a second attack by the enemy would have been welcomed by the garrison as a diversion from the monotony of the siege. In fact, that first attack – on 9 November, when they stormed King's Post to the north, and Caesar's Camp to the south – had been beaten off with ease, though not without losses.

He was an extraordinary fellow, Gunner Netley. His boots were worn out, his clothes in tatters; he had been living for six weeks in a hole in the ground. He had to confess, years later, that the siege of Ladysmith was actually the worst ordeal of his life.[2] Yet he wrote in his diary of church parades, cricket matches, and his old friend Long Tom, making it all sound so homely and civilized. The truth was a great deal more complicated – and demoralizing.

Disappointment and humiliation. If Black Week sent a shudder through most patriotic Englishmen in England, how much sharper the pain for the garrison of 13,745 white soldiers and 5,400 civilians (including 2,400 African servants and Indian camp-followers)[3] who had spent the last six weeks waiting for Buller to unlock the door of their prison.

The shattering blow, which Gunner Netley did not even refer to in passing, was the news that the relief was postponed. For six weeks the soldiers had expected relief as soon as the Army Corps arrived.[4] Now, on 17 December, a small, bleak Natal Field Force order was posted up on battalion notice-boards. Buller had 'failed in his first attempt at Colenso'.[5] Relief was postponed for weeks – until after Christmas, at least.

For three days, the garrison had heard Buller blazing away at Colenso, the rumble of his guns echoing across the yellow, thorn-covered rim of hills that cut short the view from Ladysmith southwards to the Tugela. From the sound, Buller seemed to be doing great things. All through that boiling hot Friday, the day of the battle, people sat in their dugouts and dogholes, carved out of the sticky black clay of the town gardens or straddling the red rocks of the fourteen-mile perimeter. There was nothing to do but wait for the news.[6]

On Saturday evening, it had come: the story that Buller had won a great victory. 'Killed and wounded three thousand Boers.'[7] Now, with the Sunday lunch of 'T.O.' (trek-ox) and hard biscuits, the hard truth. The Ladysmith Press Corps – nearly a dozen war correspondents from British and colonial papers – were given the unusual privilege of a Press briefing from White's Intelligence Officer, Major Altham. He showed them the Natal Field Force order. The General 'regretted' Buller's reverse, and expected the garrison would continue to display the 'Ladysmith spirit' as before. Further details were refused the Press Corps. They were allowed to send thirty-word censored heliograms to the outside world. They were also told it was their duty to 'keep the town cheerful'.[8] It was a duty they had done their best to perform, in the last six weeks of the siege, by producing a siege newspaper, the *Ladysmith Lyre* ('Liar'), lampooning both Oom Paul and White's HQ staff.[9]

The HQ staff actually knew little more of Buller's situation than they told the Press Corps. Communication was fitful. There were Africans brave enough to risk being shot by running the gauntlet of the Boer lines; the heliograph at

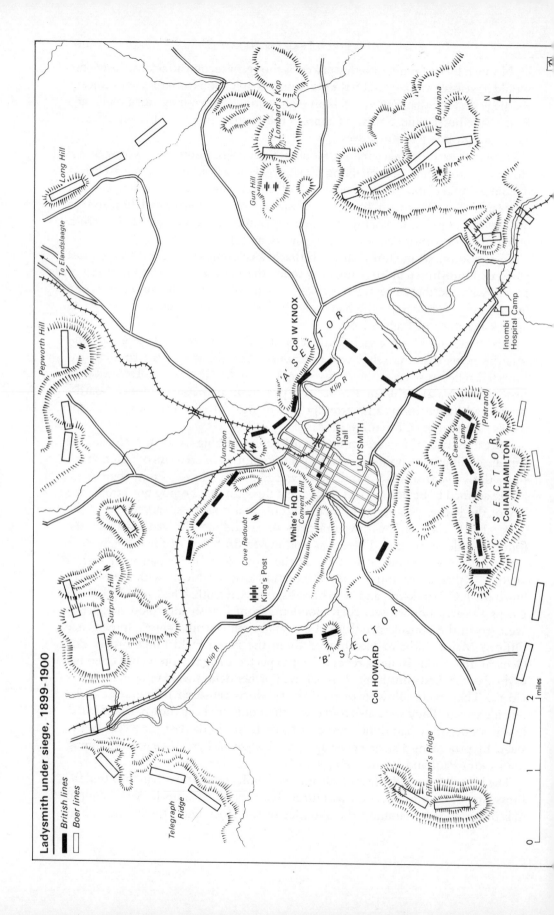

Ladysmith under siege, 1899-1900

British lines
Boer lines

N

To Elandslaagte

Long Hill

Lombard's Kop

Mt Bulwana

Gun Hill

Pepworth Hill

Intombi Hospital Camp

'A' SECTOR Col W KNOX

Klip R

Junction Hill

Surprise Hill

Caesar's Camp (Platrand)

White's HQ
Convent Hill

Town Hall

LADYSMITH

'C' SECTOR Col IAN HAMILTON

Cove Redoubt

Wagon Hill

King's Post

Klip R

'B' SECTOR

Col HOWARD

Telegraph Ridge

Rifleman's Ridge

0   1   2 miles

Weenen flashed when the sun shone; when it was dark, the searchlights at Frere wrote ghostly messages on the clouds. Yet three days after Colenso, the HQ staff still had no idea of the seriousness of Buller's casualties at the battle.[10] They received Buller's gloomy telegrams on the 16th and 17th without realizing the reason for his gloom. Hence, an outburst from even a most level-headed man like Colonel Rawlinson, the Assistant Adjutant-General. The staff mistakenly thought Buller had funked the attempt to break through at Colenso, and was urging them to surrender, in order to avoid having to fight himself.[11]

One can understand their feelings. At the root of their bitterness towards Buller was an overwhelming sense of humiliation. Goodness knows, as Rawlinson put it, they had done little enough to help themselves. The most humiliating fact was this, kept secret by the HQ staff: with the departure of Botha's force, the Boers at Ladysmith were actually outnumbered by the men they besieged – perhaps by more than two to one.[12]

Among the ordinary regimental officers, the news of Buller's reverse set the upper lips quivering. 'Everybody down. ... Everybody's spirits at zero,' said Captain Steavenson, the Adjutant of the Liverpools.[13] 'Buller's got the knock,' wrote Captain John Gough, of the Rifle Brigade. 'It is too awful for words. ... 12 guns lost ... how it happened we have no idea.' There was bitterness, but directed more at the HQ staff than at Buller. 'What annoys me most of all,' said Gough, 'is to see the staff officers come up most beautifully dressed, polished boots, white collars etc and then to hear them buck at their hardships.'[14] 'We on our side,' said Surgeon-Captain Holt, 'are stuffed full of red-tabbed staff officers and the Boers are just ordinary dirty-looking farmers ... and yet they can match us. ... Everybody abuses the staff from top to bottom.'[15]

As Christmas approached – plum pudding in the trenches for regimental officers wearing muddy boots and drinking muddy water; a six-course meal for the gilded staff at Convent Ridge[16] – the 'Ladysmith spirit' was wearing dangerously thin.

They had been forced in on themselves, these British officers, just as they had been forced inwards to the auburn rock and clay of Ladysmith. It was a 'civilized war': a war of the Red Cross and the other chivalries of the Geneva Convention. And it was proving a great education. 'The longer the siege goes on,' wrote John Gough, 'the more I wonder where is the fun and glory of soldiering.'[17] Of course, he was not joking. There *had* been fun and glory for British officers in those 'savage wars'. Now they had to look their profession in the face, and they did not like what they saw.

A siege is a war in microcosm, expressed in heightened, theatrical form. Boredom, discomfort, anxiety, funk, bravery, hope, humiliation – above all, discomfort and boredom. These were the fluctuating rhythms of the siege of Ladysmith – as they are, of course, of most real wars. The town itself was encircled by Boer artillery. Here they were squeezed between the 'iron fingers' of Joubert's army, said George Steevens, jauntiest of the war correspondents.[18] And the defenders had not only to keep control of the town. They had to fight a war of attrition, supported by little polo, cricket or champagne, against their own emotions.

From the first day of the siege, humiliation had proved the moral keynote. 'Rotten show . . . the whole thing is a disgrace,' said Surgeon-Captain Holt after Mournful Monday. 'Awful show . . . too awful for words, a disgrace which it will take some time to get over,' said Captain Gough.[19] Boredom was equally corrosive. 'Weary, stale, flat, unprofitable, the whole thing,' wrote George Steevens in a despatch for *The Daily Mail*. 'At first, to be besieged and bombarded was a thrill; then it was a joke; now it is nothing but a weary, weary, weary bore. We do nothing but eat and drink and sleep – just exist dismally.' 'During morning, languid shelling. Afternoon raining – Ladysmith wallowing deeper than ever. . . . Relieve us, in Heaven's name, good countrymen, or we die of dullness!'

Most of the war correspondents were billeted in pleasant brick houses on the outskirts of the town, and suffered no casualties in the bombardment. Though poor Steevens did not die of dullness. He died, soon after Christmas, of typhoid.[20] To the soldiers who lived in dog-holes along the perimeter, or camped in the open plain, the shelling was 'awfully trying'.[21] No doubt it gave the ordinary soldiers some amusement to watch the officers throw themselves flat on their faces when shelling began.

In exposed sectors, a look-out was posted to give warning. Everyone came to know the routine. A cloud of white smoke from 'Bulwana Tom' or 'Puffing Billy'; they fired black powder, as opposed to the smokeless shells of the howitzers, 'Silent Susan' and 'Weary Willy'. The look-out blows his bugle or bangs his gong.[22]

Thirty seconds to take cover. Up on Cove Redoubt the 'Lady Anne' – the 4·7-inch gun of the Naval Brigade and one of the only two guns with the range to answer the Boers – fires a round back at 'Bulwana Tom'. Twenty seconds to take cover. Terrified Africans running across the open veld. Now the plain is deserted. The civilians cling to their own bomb shelters. Five seconds more. The return shot from Lady Anne, fired with higher velocity, sends up a plume of débris close to Bulwana Tom's huge sandbagged emplacement five miles away. Then, with a scream and a crash, Tom arrives. The 94-pound shell bursts in a shower of steel shell fragments that hum through the air, like birds, for seconds after the explosion.[23] How absurd! No casualties. Or perhaps it is not so absurd, and somebody is lying dead, with his head blown off or his legs smashed.[24]

The garrison were disconcerted to find that the Boers refused to conform in their gunnery, as in so many military matters, to any recognizable rules. At first, there was an understanding that the Sabbath would be a day of rest for both sides: church parades and bathing parades for the British, hymn-singing for the Boers.[25] But at dawn on Sunday, 12 November, the Boers started their bombardment, and henceforth there was no time of day or night when the garrison could feel safe.[26] Even on Christmas Day, Long Tom gave a display of mixed feelings. He fired numerous shells, one of which, when dug up unexploded, proved to contain a Christmas pudding wrapped in a Union Jack, and a note:

'The compliments of the season.'[27] It was this uncertainty how to react to the shelling – whether to treat it seriously or take it as a joke – that added to the strain and humiliation of the experience.

There were days, like 24 November, when Long Tom did not play the fool by any means. That evening, shortly after 6.00 p.m., two shells plumped into D Company of the Liverpools. The men were as 'thick as peas' on the hill, said Captain Steavenson. Everyone had thought the day's bombardment over. But shrapnel rattled down on the tin roof of the officers' mess and, when it was over, nine men, of whom five were dead or mortally wounded, lay smashed on the hillside.[28]

Friday, 22 December, was a still blacker day for the Gloucesters. They had failed to appoint a look-out, and about seven in the morning Long Tom, who had been bombarding the town, turned his attention to the stone shelters of F Company. Lieutenant Hickie saw the explosion and ran forward. He was met by a fearful sight: 'Outside the shelter lay a heap of our men dead or dying – a mangled mass.' One single shell, exploding in that cramped space, had killed eight men and wounded a further nine. After that, the Gloucesters, too, appointed a man with a telescope to watch Long Tom.[29] Most demoralizing of all, there was a direct hit on the Town Hall on 30 November, and ten patients and doctors in the 18th Field Hospital, which was quartered there, were killed or wounded.[30]

At other times, Long Tom proved a real cricket-playing gentleman. On the day of the great match referred to by Netley (it was between the Devons and some gunners), everyone was very jumpy: they expected the Boers to spot the players through their telescopes. Sure enough, a salvo was signalled. The batsman ran forward, as though to play the shell. It dropped, spinning into the earth, a few feet ahead of his bat, but did not explode.[31]

In general, these Boer 6-inch guns did not prove very effective as military weapons: that is, if their direct job was to kill and destroy. At the long range required – six thousand to twelve thousand yards – they could not fire time-fused shrapnel, the kind of shells needed if they were to cause heavy casualties. They had to fire percussion shells, which did not in fact burst if they hit soft ground; so (statistically) it took several hundred shells to kill each British soldier.[32] On the other hand, by pinning down the garrison, they transformed the siege. Without the two Long Toms, there would have been cricket and polo every day; soldiers could have camped in the healthiest parts of the plain, instead of being stuck in insanitary dugouts for half the day; and with better food supplies – much of it was cattle on the hoof – they would not have starved so soon.[33] In short, morale would have been transformed. Fortunately, there was an antidote to the psychological effects of the Long Toms, in the shape of Lady Anne and her twin sister, the other naval 4·7-inch gun, 'Princess Victoria'. They could not prevent the Long Toms from firing – let alone kill any Boers; and by Christmas they were down to their last couple of hundred rounds. But it made a reassuring noise when the jolly bluejackets banged away at Cove Redoubt and Junction Hill. At least the garrison was not *completely* helpless.[34]

It was the inertia and apathy of the defenders, coupled with the increasing toll of disease, that most worried the more intelligent officers.[35] This was at the root of their bitter feelings towards Sir George and his staff. Why, oh why, asked Captain Gough, are we not allowed to raid the enemy's lines? 'God knows we need a success.'[36] It was a question that was echoed by many of the Natal refugees inside Ladysmith. They had embarked on the siege, it must be said, feeling bitter resentment towards the imperial authorities; Milner's splendid promise to defend Natal – 'with the whole might of the Empire' – contrasted with the absurdly small number of troops sent by Joseph Chamberlain to Natal on the outbreak of war. The *Ladysmith Bombshell,* the *Lyre's* twin sister, which reflected colonial opinion, exploded in these lines:

> The hard times we have had to bear
>   We'll slate Great Britain right and left
> We'll curse the British Parliament
>   Of friends and property bereft
> We'll show to all the world we meant
>   To demonstrate the sad delay
> That's caused our misery today.
>   Confound J-C[37]

One of these Natal refugees, a farmer called Willis, was the man who owned the land at Bulwana on which the Boers had installed Bulwana Tom. Willis had made dugouts for his large family in the bank of Klip River, and there he stayed, like many other civilians, during most of the daylight hours. On 6 December, his wife was delivered of a strapping boy, loyally christened Harry Buller Siege Willis. But, towards Sir George White, Willis felt less loyal. 'I could forgive many mistakes,' he wrote later, 'but one ... in allowing the Boers to occupy and mount big siege guns on Umbolwan [Bulwana] Hill. It was a grievous military blunder fruitful in damage, loss of life, and property, and accountable for most of the sickness and distress which followed.' In early December, Willis pressed the authorities to try a raid on Bulwana to silence the guns. A few days later a poster, fiercely worded, appeared in the town, denouncing White's pusillanimity.[38]

In a way, the attitude of the civilians trapped in Ladysmith was the reverse of those trapped inside Kimberley. At Kimberley, Cecil Rhodes and his cronies had threatened to surrender the town unless relief came. Here at Ladysmith, it was the civilians who were most eager for an active defence. One reason, no doubt, was the presence of that contingent of Imperial Light Horse – the Uitlander volunteers from Johannesburg. On the other hand, there were also three notable (if not notorious) civilians in Ladysmith who seemed to have played a most feeble part in the siege: Dr Jameson, Sir John Willoughby, and Cecil Rhodes's brother, Frank. As we saw, these three heroes of the Raid had pushed their way into Ladysmith in order to be first with the Uitlander flag in the triumphant march to Pretoria. Now they were condemned, once more, to be prisoners. Frankie Rhodes, it must be said, did occasionally make himself useful. He supplied strategic war materials, like champagne, to a select group of officers, including Colonel Ian Hamilton. But the realities of war were too much for Dr Jim. His health broke down as it had broken down after Doornkop. He took to his bed, stricken with typhoid.[39]

When civilians like Willis, or regimental officers like Gough, denounced the cowardice of Sir George White's strategy, they may not have guessed how warmly their feelings were shared by the two ablest men on White's staff, Major-General Sir Archibald Hunter and Colonel Sir Henry Rawlinson, later to be famous as 'Rawly', Chief of the Imperial General Staff.

But neither of these was a typical member of White's team. Most of the red-tabbed officers were red-tape men of the old school, obsessed with peacetime rules and regulations. The cavalry brigadier, Brocklehurst (known ironically as 'Pogglehurst'), had neither 'the dash nor the brains' to command cavalry. So said Rawlinson.[40] No one could get on with the CRE (commander of the sappers); he was too obstinate. He refused to allow mine-fields to be laid in front of the British perimeter; it was not in the book of rules.[41] He also refused permission for the corrugated iron huts, used in the peacetime Ladysmith camp, to be dismantled and their pieces reused to reinforce the bomb shelters.[42] The CRA (commander of the gunners) had bungled all the 'unparalleled opportunities' presented him by the Boers; it was his failure to give continuous covering fire to the Gordons at Elandslaagte that had cost them such losses in the charge.[43] Finally, the Principal Medical Officer, Lieutenant-Colonel Richard Exham, on whom the health of the sick and wounded depended, was 'not able to rise to the occasion', to put it mildly.[44] It was Exham's insistence on keeping the wounded in the Town Hall, supposedly protected by a small Red Cross flag, that had led to the disaster of the 18th Field Hospital.[45]

All these criticisms were Rawlinson's own, written confidentially for the eyes of his powerful patrons, Lord Roberts and Lord Kitchener. On Sir George White's strategy, Rawlinson's strictures were still more damning. They had food to last them till January, perhaps early February. And yet, putting it as tactfully as possible, 'we might have done more than we have'.[46] '... Sir George does not intend to stir out until we know that a relieving column is at hand,' he wrote in the fourth week of the siege.

> It is not pleasant neither is it good for the morale of the troops which has to some extent been shaken. We want some small success just to put new life into them. . . . I would have bothered the Boers constantly by night with small parties of say $\frac{1}{2}$ companies or sections – they could have stalked the Boer pickets which are at no great distance . . . anyway they would have given the Boer no peace – then I should have allowed officers to go out and endeavour to destroy some of the guns which might be done at night without much difficulty for they are very slackly guarded – I volunteered myself to try and get at one of the big guns and many others have done the same but not once have we in any way bothered the investing force but allowed them to go on pounding us daily . . .[47]

Such were Rawlinson's damning criticisms. What he did not mention, and perhaps personal loyalty precluded it, was the slack and apathetic way in

which the British had fortified their own defence lines. To make Ladysmith a
'Plevna' (the Turkish fortress which held out against the Russians for months in
1877), that was the declared aim. But only on the northern side of the perimeter
was this seriously attempted. Here, at 'A' sector, in a naturally weak part of the
line, deep trenches and large forts had been constructed. The commander,
Colonel William Knox, had himself studied the Plevna defences.[48] At 'C' sector,
an even weaker part of the line was undefended except by only a few small forts
and sangars (stone shelters). This was the Caesar's Camp-Wagon Hill ridge
('Platrand', to the Boers), the recognized key to the whole southern defences of
Ladysmith. The officer in charge was Colonel Ian Hamilton, Lord Roberts's
speech-writer and protegé, White's friend, the veteran of Majuba, the victor of
Elandslaagte. Hamilton was a poet and wit, debonair, excitable and brilliant, if
somewhat effete. No doubt he found the job of digging trenches a dull one. He
was rarely to be seen in 'C' sector; he messed in the comfortable house in the
town where Colonel Rhodes dispensed champagne.[49] Perhaps he, too, echoed
that phrase used by Gunner Netley – 'No such luck' – and wished the Boers
would try again to attack Caesar's Camp.[50]

Meanwhile, in the week before Colenso, Rawlinson's campaign to prod his
chief into action was at last successful.

White's own moods changed frequently, but were never cheerful. Fortunately, perhaps, for the garrison, he rarely showed his face outside his HQ. He
sat in his small room, hour after hour, the picture of despondency. 'One can
understand', one of the others commented, 'what General Gordon must have
gone through, with no one to talk to. . . .'[51] The shame of Mournful Monday had
burnt into his soul: those white flags. Well, he had expected to be relieved – that
is, to be relieved of his command. And he believed he deserved it. Instead, the
siege had saved him for a more refined kind of torture. Now his mind oscillated
between the various contingency plans of Rawlinson's and the staff's: to break
out to the south; to break out to the north; to attack the Long Toms. With Buller
expected within ten days, he was finally persuaded to authorize an attack on the
guns.[52]

In the small hours of 8 December, after a peaceful day watching Botha's
wagons on the Tugela by telescope, Rawlinson walked up to the Convent Ridge
and took his stand facing the dim silhouette of Lombard's Kop, four miles away
to the east. It was a dry, moonless night, ideal for attack. Six hundred men of the
garrison – appropriately, the Uitlanders of the Imperial Light Horse and the
colonials of the Natal Carbineers, led by imperial officers – had been sent out to
raid the two Boer guns on Gun Hill, the forward slope of Lombard's Kop. For
some time, Rawlinson could see Boer lights moving about on the slopes of the
mountain. Then, at 3.17 a.m., came the rumble of three explosions.[53]

All had gone exactly as Rawlinson had planned. There were two big guns on
the lower slope – a 4·5-inch howitzer and one of the Creusot Long Toms,
protected by a 31-foot-thick emplacement of sandbags. The British had left their
horses and crept forward, led by General Hunter and African guides.
They found the hill almost unguarded. One Boer picket challenged them.

Major Karri Davies, the commander of the detachment, bellowed out: 'Fix bayonets and charge the [bugger]s!' In fact, the ILH, mounted or dismounted, never used bayonets. But it was enough for the Boers. They bolted. The raiding party were back inside the lines by dawn, after disabling both guns with a pair of gun-cotton charges for each barrel. They brought back as trophies the breech blocks of both guns, the sponges, and the Long Tom's gun-sight, set for up to eight miles.[54] Only one thing marred this triumph. The same morning White sent out the cavalry brigade on patrol towards Nicholson's Nek, and old Pogglehurst, by some characteristic piece of bungling, lost twenty-four men.[55]

A triumph for Hunter and the Uitlanders of the ILH. Three nights later, it was the turn of the regulars to raid the Boer guns. The target was the 4·5-inch howitzer on Surprise Hill, and the raiders were five companies of the Rifle Brigade, including Captain John Gough's. Rawlinson went up King's Post, on the northern line of the perimeter, to watch the show. The Boers had installed a searchlight close to this point; its beam searched the hillside, but did not detect the raiding party. The howitzer was duly blown up. However, the gun-cotton misfired the first time. Meanwhile, a party of Boers blocked the raiders' retreat, and they had to cut their way out with the bayonet, killing at least thirty Boers (they believed) and themselves losing nine killed and fifty-two wounded.[56] Gough, who lost twenty-four men from his own company, described the action: 'Colonel shouted out "Fix swords and charge" and in we went. . . . When gun blown up we retired from the left . . . the enemy had got right up all round us, never was in such a hot place in my life. . . . I am so glad that the R.B. have had a chance at last.'[57]

Rawlinson, too, was satisfied. Their own losses were heavy, but the moral effect 'would not be lost on the Boers'.[58]

A further week passed, full of conflicting plans for offensives. Poor White could still not reach any firm conclusion how best to help Buller. 'All this ought to have been settled days ago,' wrote Rawlinson wearily on 15 December.[59] It was then the day of Colenso. Came the news of Buller's reverse, with its shattering moral effect on the Ladysmith garrison. The garrison relapsed into apparent helplessness.[60] Above all, there were the nagging fears of what the British public thought of them. As Lieutenant 'Dodo' Jelf, of the 60th, wrote home, 'Are we rotters or heroes?'[61]

One of the uncertainties, at least, was settled on Saturday 6 January. It was once again a moonless night – the night the Boer leaders had agreed with Kruger to make that decisive stroke against the Platrand.

Something was up. So Rawlinson had decided the evening before. An eerie silence prevailed in the Boer lines.[62] About midnight, some of the outposts on Wagon Hill heard the sound of hymns float up from the bush below. Strange: hymns at midnight. Rawlinson himself believed that all the Boers, except the gunners and the pickets, might have trekked off south. If so, they must have gone to help Botha block Buller's second attempt to force his way across the

Tugela, shortly to be launched. Rawlinson begged White to send out cavalry patrols. Hamilton begged White to let him occupy a farmhouse in the valley beyond Caesar's Camp. White refused both requests.[63] He still could not make up his mind how or when to help Buller. But he had decided to relocate two 12-pounder naval guns and the 4·7-inch Lady Anne on Wagon Hill, ready in case he should summon up courage for the long-delayed plan to break out to the south.[64]

At 2.40 a.m., on that cool, star-studded night, a party of thirteen naval gunners, assisted by twenty-five sappers, with an escort of seventy Gordons, were in the act of lowering Lady Anne's wooden gun platform into the stone emplacement at Wagon Point, the extreme south-west point of Wagon Hill. Lady Anne herself was still lying in the ox wagon at the bottom of the hill, while two other wagons, with the great platform beams and the sappers' tools, had been dragged up to the summit.[65]

In the chiaroscuro cast by the sappers' lanterns came the usual cheery sounds that accompanied Lady Anne on her progress: the grating of the wagons, the similar eloquence of the British NCOs, the grousing of the men, Africans calling their oxen 'damned Dutchmen'. Suddenly, a new sound. Flip, flop, flip, flop: the sound of rifle bullets splashing on the stones around them.[66] One of the sappers later described it. 'What the hell? A report of rifles. We kicked the lamps out and dashed for our rifles. Into the sangar we went. Some poor devils panicked – they couldn't find their rifles and began to run. Young Digby Jones jumped on to a rock . . . drew his revolver and said [to the stampeding sappers] "The first man that passes me I'll shoot him dead." '[67]

Wagon Hill was now a confused mass of shouting men, and criss-crossed by rifle bullets, striking sparks as they bounced off the rocks. The pickets supposed to protect this vital crest line were less than a hundred men of the Imperial Light Horse. They wore the same slouch hats as the Boers, which added to the confusion. Against the glare of a Boer searchlight, somehow brought into action, several hundred Free Staters poured on to the ridge, beating down the pickets. Fortunately for the garrison, the ILH had built one small 'fort': a loop-holed ring of stones, about twenty feet around.[68] This was the sangar into which rushed Lieutenant Digby-Jones and some of the sappers. Others took refuge in the gun emplacement prepared for one of the 12-pounders. Here the naval gunner, Gunner Sims, added to the incongruity of the scene by numbering the men as though on parade. Perhaps it steadied them.

One, twa, three, vower, voive, [he shouted, in his best fo'c'stle bellow]. 'Nos. 1 to 8 will be the right half-section; Nos. 9 to 15 will be the left half section. . . . Now then, men, are you ready? Right half-section, ready, present fire!

The bullets flew, men groaned and screamed, and, final incongruity, the teams of oxen, abandoned by their drivers, stood on the flat hilltop, patiently munching the dewy grass.[69]

Meanwhile, two and a half miles away, at the extreme eastern edge of the same double ridge, other wild scenes were taking place. Here, at Caesar's Camp, the picket lines had a quarter of an hour's warning before a force of Transvaalers stormed over the ridge. But, owing to the extreme feebleness of Hamilton's defences at 'C' sector, there was no real obstacle here to the Boers' seizing the vital crest line. In fact, Hamilton had based his plan on a line of stone 'forts' set back on the inner side of the plateau. There were no accompanying trenches. There were no forts commanding the eastern face of the hill. Above all, Hamilton had failed to insist on the removal of the scrub that gave perfect cover to the attackers. Hence, the Transvaalers not only established a foothold on the crest. They also took the picket line of the Manchesters in the rear, and cut them down in swathes.[70]

When dawn came up, Colonel Royston's colonial troops in the valley to the east could see the whole hillside swarming with Boers, from the crest line to the river-bed.[71]

Two miles away to the north, at Convent Ridge, Rawlinson and Hunter, the Chief of Staff, were woken by the sound of firing. The HQ was connected to each section of the defences by the telephone on the veranda of the house. Before long, astonishing messages reached them. Discarding conventional Boer tactics, the Boers were storming all sides of the perimeter, under the cover of a bombardment from every gun they had.[72] The men in Colonel Knox's miniature Plevna at 'A' section were in no danger. There was a more determined attack on Colonel Francis Howard's 'B' section at Observation Hill. But this, too, was beaten off almost without loss to the defenders, though the Boers left twenty bodies on the hillside. It was the situation at Wagon Hill and Caesar's Camp that was critical. And that morning poor White was hardly able to stir from his house. He was weak with fever. Hunter deputed a party of Natal Police to try to cut a way out of the town for him, if the main garrison was forced to surrender.[73] It was on Hunter's shoulders, and Rawlinson's, that the main burden of saving Ladysmith depended that day.

The first step was to send field-guns to attack from below what a properly sited fort would have prevented the Boers ever establishing: a position on the scrubby, rock-covered south-east slopes of Caesar's Camp. In the early morning sunshine, the six gun teams of Major Abdy's battery, the 53rd, trotted out towards Intombi Camp (the hospital camp beyond the defence lines) and then unlimbered in the unaccustomed shelter of some scrub. A plume of smoke and a rumble from Bulwana Tom. Some 94-pound shells straddled the battery. Princess Victoria, in her turn, tossed some of her precious 4·7-inch shells at Bulwana Tom, and Abdy's six field-guns began to splash the south-east slopes of Caesar's Camp with shrapnel, each gun firing over twenty rounds in rapid succession. Soon after 6.00 a.m., these slopes were cleared of the enemy, except for dead and wounded.[74] But the field-guns could not reach the southern crest line, nor the slopes beyond. To drive the enemy back from these positions, infantry was needed. About 8.00 a.m., six companies of the Rifle Brigade reached the scene, more than doubling the strength of the garrison there, composed of Manchesters and Gordons. One of the company commanders was Captain Gough.[75] He wrote later in his diary:

When we got there, we could not find anyone in command and no one knew in the least what was going on. . . . Sydney Mills was first shoved forward to re-inforce no 5 Piquet. He did not know where it was and no one could tell us whether the Boers were on the ridge or not. . . . Sydney was knocked over and a good many men. . . . D Coy came up on the left and all three officers were knocked over at once. . . . B Coy then came up on their left and worked round the flank, Stephens getting knocked over, George Thesiger in trying to get up to this Coy got shot through the neck. . . . After Thesiger was hit I found myself the senior RB officer under fire, and I could get no orders as to what the authorities were doing on our right, a very nasty position. . . .[76]

The man responsible for this confusion, for the crippling losses of the Rifle Brigade, and, indeed, for the whole débâcle, was Ian Hamilton. He had galloped off to Wagon Hill as soon as he was woken by the firing, leaving no one in command at Caesar's Camp. However, he now did his best to redeem himself by personal gallantry. The situation at Wagon Hill was equally confused, but much more critical, as the 'forts' were still flimsier here, and no help could be given by field-guns firing from the flank. Soon after dawn, the first reinforcements reached the hilltop. The remainder of the ILH, who galloped up, dismounted and flung themselves down in the firing-line. At the same moment, two reserve companies of Gordons, under Major Miller-Wallnut, marched round from their camping ground a mile to the north. At seven o'clock, eight companies of the 1st and 2nd 60th, led by Major Campbell, joined them. There were now two thousand men lying flat in the firing-line – 250 Free Staters, invisible between rocks on the south-western edge of the hill, and eight times that number of British infantry. In places, the combatants were separated by only a few yards of grassy hillside. And never was the fire power of the new magazine rifle – and the inability of British officers to recognize it – better displayed. Three times a small party of men, led by an officer, charged across towards the hidden enemy, and each time they were annihilated (the gallant officers included Major Robert Bowen, of the 60th). At last, Hamilton ordered these suicidal counter-attacks to be stopped. Brother Boer could be dealt with in due course. And, miraculously, the firing melted away as the Boers vanished into dead ground. By 11.00 a.m., Hamilton felt confident enough to order some men to return down the hill. It was fiercely hot, and it was time for lunch.[77]

It was about one o'clock when, for the second time on this astonishing day, the Boers broke all the rules of Boer tactics. Lieutenant Digby-Jones and Major Miller-Wallnut were sitting under an awning close to Lady Anne's gun emplacement at Wagon Point; Ian Hamilton had just joined them. Unseen by them, a party of Boers (led, as it proved, by two gallant Free State field cornets, De Villiers and De Jagers) stormed over the crest line, sending the British line streaming back in a panic. The first that Hamilton knew of this was when one of the sappers in the gun emplacement fell dead beside him, shot from a rifle thrust over the sandbags. Digby-Jones sprang up and shot De Villiers with his revolver. Someone else shot De Jagers from inside the emplacement.[78] Lower down the slope, Gunner Sims heard the shots and the yelling, as the mass of men rushed helter-skelter towards him. 'Naval Brigade,' he roared, 'extend in skirmishing order ... forward-d-d!' Once again, it was Gunner Sims and Digby-Jones who saved the day. The thirteen gunners charged back with the bayonet. On the top of the crest they found Ian Hamilton, pointing his revolver at a grey-bearded Boer. 'Come back, men!' he shouted. 'It's all right. Send up the reserves.' The panic subsided, and the handful of Boers who had followed the heroic field cornets were shot down or driven off, although both the brave Digby-Jones and Miller-Wallnut lost their lives in the mêlée.[79]

All this time, the news of the fighting in 'C' sector had been continuously reported to the HQ by telephone. They were nerve-racking hours for everyone. Sir George White sent a half-despairing telegram to Buller, begging him to create a diversion at Colenso.[80] Virtually all the reserves had been committed. Hunter and Rawlinson kept calm.

At 2.00 p.m., after De Villiers's and De Jagers's attack on Wagon Point had been beaten off, Rawlinson himself wrote in his diary: 'Position much the same.... Boers in large numbers ... advancing down the spruit.... I fancy the Flagstone spruit lot are trying to cut our communications with Wagon Hill which lie across the open plain....'[81] An hour or so later, he received from Ian Hamilton a gallant little note in pencil:

My dear Rawley. Wot [sic] a day we are having.... Probably the first time on record the Boers have been outBoered in this way.... I hope you are all fit and cheery.... Thine Ian H.[82]

By 4.00 p.m., it was obvious to Hamilton that both Boer attacks had failed. He believed that the Boers clinging to their toeholds on the crest line were only waiting for darkness to make their getaway. And for once, Hamilton was absolutely correct. At this moment, however, Sir George White intervened, overreacting violently, as only weak men can. The Boers must be driven off the crest line *before* darkness. That was his decision. The final reserves of the infantry, three companies of Devons, must drive them off with the bayonet. Hamilton told the CO of the Devons, Lieutenant-Colonel Park, the cheerful news. Could he storm the crest line? 'We will try,' Park replied laconically.[83]

All day, the Natal sun had burnished the hilltop, grilling the stones, where both sides sheltered. But now – just as at Elandslaagte, when the Gordons made their charge – the sky turned indigo and a furious thunderstorm burst over the ground.[84] At the HQ, Hunter and Rawlinson were deafened by the storm and had to cut off all the telephones for fear of being electrocuted.[85] Thirty miles away, Buller's signallers watched the flash of heliograph fade in the blackness: 'Attack renewed, very hard pressed....' So the message ended, leaving Buller (and the British public) in suspense for more than a day.[86]

At Wagon Hill, the storm was already passing, when Colonel Park gave the word to the bugler. 'Advance!' The rattle of three lines of bayonets, and a wild cheer. Then across that 130-yard-wide strip of grass, which had already been wet and slippery before the rain came. An answering crash of Mausers from the crest line. Three of the officers were down already. The Devons hardly faltered. They reached the crest line. But there was no chance to use the bayonets after all.

The Boers had merely taken a new position among some rocks, and fired back from below the crest line. So the fight went on till darkness, as confused and bloody as it had begun.[87]

Next morning, there was an armistice to collect up the dead and wounded. The search proved unusually macabre. The Boer dead on the south-east of Caesar's Camp were so mangled by shrapnel that many had to be buried there and then. On the flat top of the hill, Captain Gough counted fifty-two dead Boers.[88] His Regimental Sergeant-Major laid them out, bearded old men in rough clothes, arranged at last in the parade ground order the RSM could understand: heads and feet in parallel lines. The total number of Boer dead was believed to be a good deal higher.[89]

On the British side, the losses were known precisely: 424. Seventeen officers were dead or dying, 28 were wounded; 158 men had been killed (more than at Colenso); 221 were wounded. The brunt was borne by the Manchesters, the ILH and the Devons, whose gallant charge had lost them every officer except for the Colonel.[90] Rawlinson, who went up to have a look at the hillside next day, came back aghast. He had been with Kitchener at Omdurman, where fifteen thousand Dervishes lay dead in the sand after the battle, but somehow this was different. 'White corpses are ... far more repulsive than black,' he noted.[91] Captain Steavenson looked at the horrors and wrote in his diary, 'Civilized war is awful.'[92]

CHAPTER 24

The Tugela Line

Natal,
6–24 January 1900

'It is now the 23rd [January], we have been fighting for
twelve hours a day for four days and are no forwarder, I
really cannot say how it will end.... We don't ... gain
ground as I should like, all the rot they have been writing
in the papers about frontal attacks and now half our
officers have an idea that you can take a position without
fighting....'

General Sir Redvers Buller to his wife,
from Mount Alice, 23 January 1900

The pickets at Chieveley were just standing to arms on 6 January when they
heard a single distant cannon-shot come thundering through the still air to the
north. It was an hour before dawn. Lieutenant Maurice Grant, an excitable
young officer serving with the 2nd Devonshires, whose first battalion was
trapped at Ladysmith, recorded the eerie sounds: 'A pause, then another dull
boom, then a dozen together, far away, muffled and ominous.' As soon as it was
light, there appeared puffs of white smoke 'bellying from the great, dim summit
of Bulwana', and between the rumble of artillery the 'low and continuous growl
of musketry'.[1]

'Boom. Thud, thud. Boom. Boom.' Young Winston Churchill, *The Morning
Post* correspondent, back at the front after a daring escape from Pretoria gaol,
was woken in his tent by these 'queer moaning vibrations'. He lay and listened.
What was happening eighteen miles away over the hills? Another bayonet attack
by the garrison? Or perhaps a general sortie? Or perhaps (though, if this were
true, it would be the end of one more cherished illusion about them) the Boers
themselves were attacking. An officer came to Churchill's tent and asked him
what he thought was going on. 'Something big happening at Ladysmith – hell of
a cannonade – never heard anything like it.' For once, Churchill was without an
opinion.[2]

The first heliogram from White did not reach Buller's HQ at Frere, five miles
farther south, till eleven o'clock. 'Enemy attacked Caesar's Camp at 2.45 a.m.
this morning in considerable force. Enemy everywhere repulsed, but fighting
continues.'[3] Buller immediately signalled to General Clery, commanding the
forward base at Chieveley, to advance on Colenso as a 'demonstration', and

himself sent up the line all troops available.[4] At four o'clock came a more reassuring message from White: 'At present I have beaten off enemy, but great numbers are still around me especially to the south, and it appears very probable they will renew the attack.'[5] Then the sun, the only medium of communication, was swallowed by a storm-cloud – the storm in which the Devons were preparing to make their gallant charge at Wagon Hill. There were no more heliograms that day.[6]

At Colenso, Clery's naval guns were answered only by the roar of thunder; as usual, Brother Boer lay low. But a serious attack on Colenso was out of the question. For one thing, the Tugela was high: for another, Buller believed (and events were to prove him right) that only a few hundred Boers had trekked north to help storm Ladysmith; the rest still manned the trenches.[7] Yet it was galling for the officers, standing outside their tents with field-glasses and telescopes, anxiously watching and listening, and especially for the people whose twin battalions were besieged. 'In Heaven's name are we to do nothing?' Lieutenant Maurice Grant was to write, recalling the agonizing moment. 'Where was the general? *Was* he a general? If Ladysmith has fallen this day he must be so no longer!' And Grant told of 'something like a groan' that ran through the 'idle mob on the Knolls' as the *cri de coeur* from White – 'very hard pressed' – came over the heliograph.[8]

In fact, this was one of Grant's more imaginative pieces of writing. White's message did not reach Chieveley till next day, by which time Chieveley knew of White's victory[9] (though Grant's articles on the war, written anonymously, won him a huge public, and helped get him the post as co-author of the *Official History*).[10] At the time, no one south of the Tugela knew how great was the danger to Ladysmith. Hence the war correspondents, who rode out to watch Clery's naval guns firing, took the situation calmly. Atkins, *The Manchester Guardian* correspondent, was sharing a tent with Churchill. Both men were greatly impressed by the Boers' self-discipline in not replying to Clery's 'demonstration'. Atkins marvelled at the 'wonderful intelligence in the individual' Boer that 'plays the part of a cultivated discipline'.[11] Churchill remarked dryly, 'It needs a patient man to beat a Dutchman at waiting. So about seven o'clock we gave up trying.'[12] Churchill's own mood, since his return from Pretoria, was a strangely vulnerable one. He blurted out to Major-General Hildyard a damning account of the armoured train disaster, which has the ring of truth and differs from later accounts Churchill gave. 'They ran confidently on to within range of the Boers, being unaware they had guns with them, and hoping to give them a lesson.'[13] He blurted out to Atkins how the Boers had rounded up British soldiers – 'like cattle! The greatest indignity of my life!' He had heard a sound after the armoured train disaster which was worse, even, than the sound of shells: the sound of Boers singing psalms. 'It struck the fear of God into me. What sort of men are we fighting? They have the better cause – and the cause is everything – at least, I mean to them it is the better cause.'[14]

Buller remained at Chieveley, as solid and reassuring as a heavy gun or a deep entrenchment.[15] In fact, he himself had never doubted the danger of the Boers attacking Ladysmith. Now their near-success made it all the more urgent for him to resume operations. Besides, Lord Roberts was expected at Cape Town on 11 January.[16] Despite a cable from Roberts, urging caution,[17] Buller had no wish to stay on the defensive a day longer than necessary. Warren's division, the 5th, was now at Estcourt. In a couple of days the extra horse artillery would have arrived. On the 10th, the day before Roberts superseded him as GOC, South Africa, the army at Frere would leave the railway and set off on a flank march to Ladysmith by way of Springfield, twenty-five miles to the west.[18]

'Was there no way round?' the American attaché had asked at Colenso.[19] Well, Buller now believed he had found a way round. Despite all his handicaps – the drought and the floods, the men who could not learn how to defend themselves, the generals who knew only how to attack each other – he hoped it would carry him across those 'beastly mountains' to Ladysmith.

At Frere, that week, the long drought had broken, and broken with a vengeance. 'Day after day,' wrote John Atkins,

a storm, with the blackness of night in its eye, swept across the camp and blotted it out. You could see it coming like a high, forbidding wall, and when it arrived you could not see from one tent to another. It tore and scoured through the camp; cattle and horses turned their backs to it and dropped their heads, or else drifted abjectly before it. . . . But when the rain came it performed a miracle; it simply washed away the old, dry, withered, khaki-coloured face of the country, as though it had swept it out with a stroke of a clean, wet brush.[20]

John Atkins was a newspaperman and a poet. His namesake, Tommy Atkins, took a more prosaic view, as the 5th Division splashed into Frere on 10 January, sliding, sucking, pumping and gurgling through the mud.[21] The Blaauw Kranz River was in spate. Only a few days before, it had been perilously low; the shortage of drinking water had bid fair to force a retreat.[22] Now the river seemed to bar all progress, engulfing the fifteen-mile-long centipede of mule carts and ox wagons.[23] Fortunately, one of Buller's technical innovations, the steam traction engine, came to the rescue, plucking out of the river a great string of broken-down ox wagons. But the cold rain continued, turning all the roads to rivers.[24]

Even to winter-hardened British soldiers (and Warren's division were fresh from an English November), those two nights' march were an ordeal. 'We all dropped down in the road, water and mud and all it made no difference,' wrote Lance-Corporal Bradley of the 1st South Lancashires, 'we were done up and wet through so down we got, slept just as comfortable as if we were in feather beds until the early morning.'[25] 'We had to bivouac,' said Arthur Galley, an NCO in the Army Service Corps, 'that meant lie down on the wet ground with your wet clothing on and to add to our comfort we had a good old thunderstorm so you may guess the happy plight we were in, it was without doubt the roughest time I've ever experienced.'[26] Next morning, the troops had to make do with a breakfast of bully beef and biscuits, Bradley recorded, and the 'sun poured down his glorious rays upon us, but the heat was so terrible, after us being wet through for almost two days and nights, that it nearly flattened us out, as we could not get any water'.[27]

So the men wrote about the flank march in their diaries and letters to England, no doubt trying to put a brave face on the ordeal, for the sake of their families at home. Morale remained relatively high. And in Buller – 'old Buller', as they called him, the man who seemed to epitomize their own best qualities, especially endurance – in Buller *they* still had a faith that was to astonish everyone.[28]

If only the same could have been said about Buller's generals. It was Major-General Neville Lyttelton who was beginning to emerge as the leader of a whispering campaign against his Commander-in-Chief. He told his wife that Buller's 'lack of enterprise' since Colenso was 'deplorable'.[29] He took under his wing the young, impressionable correspondent of *The Times*, Bron Herbert, and told him, off the record, of course, that Buller had lost his nerve.[30] Not that Lyttelton had many good words to say about anybody or anything in Natal. He was sick of the place, sick of the 'beastly Tugela', sick of the fighting in these 'beastly' mountains.[31] How he must have yearned for the clean, clear-cut battle in the desert, where he had led that brigade to victory at Omdurman. His fellow brigade commanders now filled him with despondency. Barton, Coke, Wood-gate – he found them as 'incapable' as the senior generals like Clery; Lord Dundonald was 'Lord Dundoodle'.[32] As for Major-General Hart ('Coeur-de-Lion', the officers called him ironically), Lyttelton thought he should have been sent straight back to base after his performance leading the Irish Brigade at Colenso. 'I am beginning to think Hart is mad,' he wrote home to his wife.[33] Major-General Hildyard expressed the same view less charitably.[34]

But how to cross the Tugela? Later, the impression would be given by Buller's critics that every man in the British army, except its Commander-in-Chief, knew exactly how to relieve Ladysmith. Actually, Lyttelton, one of Buller's more intelligent critics, confessed himself baffled by the 'knotty problem'.[35] It was 'ten thousand pities' that White had not stayed behind the Tugela, instead of entombing himself at Ladysmith.[36] Of course, they were tantalizingly close. They could see the actual shells fired from the Ladysmith garrison (shells that had crossed the path of their own shells, the 'messengers of hope', fired in the opposite direction). White's shells seemed to Lyttelton like 'signals of distress'. But the endless rain only added to the difficulties of crossing the Tugela. 'Our prospects here do not mend,' wrote Lyttelton before leaving Frere on the great flank march, 'rain is still falling and I don't see how we are to force the Tugela. However we must do our best, but you need not be surprised if Ladysmith falls. I don't like croaking and whatever you do don't quote me, but I am bound to say that I think it will.'[37]

'What are we waiting 'ere for? Why don't we go on.'
'Don't yer know?'
'No.'
'To give the Boers time to build up their trenches and fetch up their guns. Fair – ain't it?'

The scene was Mount Alice, overlooking the Tugela at Potgieters Drift, nearly nine days after the troops had set off from Frere in that torrential downpour. The speakers were two British privates, overheard by John Atkins.[38] To Buller, too, the delay was the source of intense frustration.[39] It was all the more galling because everything, at first, had gone better than Buller had dared hope.

They had crossed the Tugela. This was the exhilarating news on 16 January. Paradoxically, thunderstorms had made the crossing easier. On the 11th, the advance guard of Buller's army, Dundonald's mounted brigade, had found that the enemy, apparently afraid of being cut off by the rain, had evacuated the south bank, and six of Dundonald's men stripped and swam across and seized Potgieters ferry on the north bank.[40] Five days later, when the river had fallen, Lyttelton's brigade attempted the crossing at Potgieters Drift. There, at the foot of Mount Alice, was the familiar khaki centipede of troops, its head crawling forwards onto the north bank, while the tail withdrew from the south; the watchers, including John Atkins, waited breathless for a second Colenso – and none came. The men waded across, holding onto each other's rifles, up to their necks in the turbulent river. That night there were British camp-fires on both sides of the river, as Buller's men dried out their clothes and celebrated the first victory they had won, a victory without a shot.[41]

Still, Buller had only flung one arm, so to speak, across the Tugela. He was now convinced that to attack Potgieters directly would indeed invite another Colenso. He must throw a second, and stronger, arm across at Trichardt's Drift, five miles higher up river,[42] west of a strange, hog-backed hill that would soon be famous in a sombre fashion. This was 'Look-out Hill', the place from which voortrekkers had first looked out on the promised land of North Natal. In Dutch, Spion Kop. (*See map on page 289.*)

The plan that Buller had in mind when he left Frere was in essence a return to the original plan for a flank march, discarded in favour of the attempt to storm the river at Colenso. The pros and cons of such a direct strike had been, as we saw earlier, finely balanced with those of the flank march. What had, in December, tilted the balance in favour of the Colenso action were the strategic risks of making the flank march, in the light of Methuen's precarious position at the Modder, and Milner's unholy terror of a Cape rising; and, a tactical attraction, Colenso was within a few miles of the place where White had offered to join hands with the relief column.[43] Of course, none of these three arguments now applied. On 10 January, a day earlier than expected, Lord Roberts had sailed into Cape Town and taken over as GOC.[44] And there was one crucial result of the Boers' near-success in storming Ladysmith on 6 January. This was a heliograph message from White to say that his force was now too weakened by casualties to be able to offer any co-operation with Buller in future.[45]

There were two main advantages, as Buller had known all along, in the Potgieters route. The river crossing itself was at the apex of a great south-facing loop of the river: a safe re-entrant to Buller, a dangerous salient to the Boers. Hence the relative ease with which Lyttelton's brigade had established a foothold on the north bank. Second, instead of ten miles of tangled gorges that separated the Tugela at Colenso from Ladysmith, there were twelve miles of grassy plain, running downhill to Ladysmith, once he was across the river and astride a single chain of jagged hills that lay two to three miles beyond. However, it was in this chain of jagged hills that lay the overwhelming difficulty.[46]

Hence the need for two bridgeheads. At Potgieters, the enemy had been digging themselves into these hills since December, and their positions on the Brakfontein-Vaal Krantz ridge completely blocked the farther side of the south-facing loop. At Trikhardts, by contrast, the Intelligence Department reported fewer Boers, and weaker trenches: only six hundred Boers out of the seven thousand reported to be holding the whole line of the river. So Buller's modified plan was this. He had decided to send to Trikhardts roughly two-thirds of his army. The job of this independent force was to form the second bridge-head there, and then break through the chain of hills three miles to the north, just to the west of Spion Kop. The moment they were on the plain, threatening to outflank Potgieters – that would be the moment for he himself to attack Potgieters with the remainder of the army. Once both forces were across the hills, they could join hands again, and march together across the plain to Ladysmith.[47]

It was a bold, two-pronged plan, demanding a high degree of co-ordination between two separate commands, attacking in sequence. The most risky feature was undoubtedly its complexity. That two-pronged attack at Colenso had represented two *simultaneous* attempts to jump the river, of which Buller had hoped at least one would achieve success. It had been a crude enough plan, but at least it had the merit of keeping both attacking brigades more or less under the eye of their master; when things went wrong, as of course they did at Colenso, Buller could intervene immediately and take command himself. In this intricate new plan, the scale of time, distance and numbers was dramatically larger. For several days, and probably several battles, the two forces would be isolated, at the mercy of the heliograph and the signal lamp. For Buller to keep in contact with the two forces, about seven miles apart, would be hard enough. To retain control of them both at the same time would, he believed, be impossible. Hence he had decided to give his senior subordinate, the commander of the newly arrived 5th Division, Lieutenant-General Sir Charles Warren, an independent command. Warren was to take 10,600 infantry, 2,200 mounted troops and 36 guns, and try to breach the Boers' line west of Spion Kop. Buller himself would follow with 7,200 infantry, 400 mounted troops, and 22 guns, when it was time to try to storm the hills beyond Potgieters.[48]

Why give Warren – a general who was quite untried in the conditions of the new warfare, and a man with whom Buller found personal relations so painful – why give him the bigger army and the bulk of the work? It was a question that Buller never publicly answered, nor have historians offered an explanation. In fact, Buller had an answer, such as it was; he gave it to a friend several years later. 'Warren had an easy task, merely to shoulder the Boers off his left; but I reserved to myself the difficult task, viz·that of thrusting in my best [Lyttelton's] Brigade when Warren's operations had caused a gap in the enemy's line.'[49] An easy task? At any rate, not impossible, as Buller believed (and most historians have agreed), provided always that Warren attacked the enemy's line with speed and decisiveness. But it was precisely in these qualities that Warren now seemed to Buller – and seems to us in retrospect – most dismally lacking.[50]

From the crest of Mount Alice, the view across the Tugela is one of the most theatrical in the whole of Northern Natal. At dawn, it is like the scene from John Martin's *Fields of Paradise*. Range after range of oyster-coloured hills, framed on the left by the pink battlements of the Drakensberg; the swirling silver loops of the Tugela at Potgieters, six hundred feet below; and, on Mount Alice itself, in the jungle of mimosa thorn and aloes and cassia, the murmur of doves, and the whirr of partridges, as though this were an English woodland.[51]

Up here, to see the sights, and a sight themselves, puffing and blowing, came the war correspondents: Bennet Burleigh, complaining bitterly of the Press censorship; Dickson, dragging his enormous ciné-camera;[52] Churchill, now wearing the Boer hat and the 'cockyolibird' feather of the South African Light Horse (Buller had allowed him to enrol as a nominal member of this Uitlander regiment);[53] Atkins, overwhelmed by the vast scale of this landscape, which could swallow up thirty or forty thousand men and make nothing of them. Here at Mount Alice, thought Atkins, was a hill 'fit for Xerxes to watch from'.[54] One of the gunners said, 'We ought to have the Queen up here, in her little donkey carriage.' 'Ah, we'd do it all right then,' replied his mate. No, said Churchill to himself, not the Queen. He could not help thinking of the scenes of horror he expected soon to burst upon those peaceful hills beyond the river.[55]

Strange to say, there is one hill that makes little impression on the eye, seen from Mount Alice across the five-mile-wide gorge of the Tugela, and this is Spion Kop. At 1,470 feet above the river, its summit crowns the ridge, and its sheer, south-facing slopes are scarred with rocks and rock falls; but the long range of hills seems to assimilate it so easily that it half loses its identity among its neighbours, the Rangeworthy Hills (Tabanyama), the Twin Peaks, Brakfontein and Vaal Krantz to the right.[56]

The topography of the impending battle was certainly more complicated than it looked. Yet to Buller, equipped with the blue one-inch map prepared by his Field Intelligence Department, the salient features were clear enough. Warren's job was to break a hole in the Rangeworthy line and strike for the plain at Clydesdale Farm.[57] The question was not where to attack. It was: where's Warren?

Ever since 15 January, when he had given Warren secret instructions to cross at Trikhardts Drift and swing round the hub of Spion Kop from the left, Buller had watched Warren's ponderous movement with mounting alarm. It took Warren two days to cover the ten miles from Spearman's Camp to Trikhardts and to cross by pontoon bridge. It took him two more days to bring over his baggage wagons and establish a bridgehead in the foothills across the river. Instead of striking straight ahead, he spent two more days in indecisive movements on the left; meanwhile, Dundonald's brigade began to roll up the Boer outposts on the extreme left, but were then ordered by Warren to halt. On the 20th, Warren launched the first infantry assault on his real target: Rangeworthy Hills, to the west of Spion Kop. The attack was successful, as far as it went. The eight infantry battalions – Hildyard's 'English' brigade (the 2nd) and Hart's Irish Brigade (the 5th) – forced their way on to the southern crest line of the western plateau. Warren was assisted by a 'demonstration' (a feint) at Potgieters. Casualties in both sectors were reasonably light: one officer and thirty other ranks killed, twenty officers and 280 other ranks wounded, out of both divisions. But after the 20th, Warren's advance petered out. He said he needed heavier artillery than his thirty-six field-guns. Buller agreed to send him four howitzers; he was keeping the ten long-range naval guns for his own advance. Warren crawled. When he had crossed at Trikhardts Drift on the 17th, the enemy had numbered only six hundred men, according to Buller's intelligence. Now there were reportedly (actually an exaggeration) seven thousand west of Spion Kop, out of fifteen thousand guarding the line of the Tugela.[58]

By the 23rd, Buller could bear it no longer. He would later – rightly – reproach himself for his own weakness: he should have been man enough to take command of Warren's flank attack on the 19th. But just as Warren flinched from attacking Rangeworthy Hills, Buller flinched from sacking Warren. Who was to be in charge of the attack on the horseshoe north of Potgieters? And how could he avoid discrediting Warren in front of the troops: Warren, whom the War Office had sent out with secret instructions to succeed Buller if Buller was shot? So Buller, against his own better judgement, left Warren his independent – or, at least, semi-independent – command. He rode over to Warren on the 23rd and put the position with characteristic bluntness.[59] Either Warren must attack or he would withdraw Warren's force. For four days now, Warren had his men 'continuously exposed to shell and rifle fire', perched on the edge of the plateau; the supporting troops were massed in 'indefensible formations', and a panic or sudden charge 'might send the whole lot down the hill at any moment'. His own advice, Buller reiterated, was to swing round to the left of Spion Kop, and try to break through the Rangeworthy Hills. At which Warren explained that, despite his howitzers, he could still not establish an artillery position and so make progress on this western side. Warren had now decided that there was only one practicable place to attack: Spion Kop, the hub and natural strong-point of the whole range.[60]

Warren's plan to try to crack the nut at the hardest point was perhaps perverse, but not stupid. Spion Kop was so precipitous that it was the last place the Boers would expect the British to attack. It commanded the wagon road which Warren needed to use if he was to march north with his supply wagons. If it could be seized, if it could be held, if heavy guns could be installed there – all three very big 'ifs' – it would send the Boers scurrying back to the plain.[61]

There are few excitements like a night attack.

Lieutenant-Colonel Charles à Court, Buller's staff officer attached to Major-General Woodgate's column – young, brilliant, erratic Charles à Court –

had had the good luck to serve with Kitchener in the night attack on Mahmud and his Dervishes. The Atbara, Good Friday 1898, the night after the full moon; sixteen thousand British and Egyptian infantry marching in mass of brigade squares across the vast, crunchy desert, guided by the Dervish watch-fires; a scene from Verdi; dawn, and they were facing the parapets of the great *dem* near the Atbara, six hundred yards away from the enemy; still not a sound from the Dervishes; then Charles Long – the same dare-devil Colonel Long who had lost Buller's batteries at Colenso – had ridden out with his guns in front of Kitchener's army, and the massacre had begun. Total victory in twenty-eight minutes. The enemy 'squashed as flat', said à Court, 'as though a gigantic roller had been dragged over his trenches.'[62]

No chance of getting that steam-roller up Spion Kop tonight. À Court's thoughts went back gloomily to another, still more famous, night attack: the night in South Africa, eighteen years before, when General Colley had tried to outflank the enemy by seizing Majuba Hill. À Court spoke of his premonition to Lieutenant-Colonel Arthur Sandbach, Buller's Intelligence Officer: they were going to attack Spion Kop; it was another Majuba; they must do their best to avoid repeating Colley's mistakes.[63] But what could one of Buller's staff officers do to improve a plan about which their own chief himself had such doubts? À Court made an arrangement with the gunners' commander, Colonel Parsons, to give supporting fire to the column as soon as they signalled that they had gained the summit. The signal would be a burst of British cheering.[64] Woodgate would lead the column of two thousand men – men from three battalions of his own Lancashire Brigade, plus two hundred of Thorneycroft's Mounted Infantry, and half a company of engineers. There would be a few mules, carrying oilskin sheets full of water, and boxes of spare ammunition. But they would not be accompanied by the mountain battery (which was supposed to follow in the morning), and there were no arrangements for heavier guns, although to dig in such guns on the peak was the best argument for seizing Spion Kop. There were no orders to General Clery to make anything more than a 'demonstration' on the left during the next day, when (or rather if) they had succeeded in taking Spion Kop. And there were only twenty picks and twenty shovels, carried up in stretchers, to dig the trenches for two thousand men.[65]

By 8.30 p.m. the troops had gathered at the rendezvous, a gully below Three Tree Hill, about six miles to the south-west of Spion Kop. Nightfall comes swiftly in Natal, and that night it came early, too, as a leaden, sodden evening melted into blackness. Colonel à Court could not see his hand held up to his face. There was the usual orderly confusion: nailed boots and iron-shod hooves grinding on the rocks, sharp African voices and broad Lancashire brogues, laughter and swearing as the men checked over their kit (water-bottle and one day's field rations, rifle, and 150 rounds). Then the order: no smoking, no talking. General Woodgate led the way, lame enough[66] (despite Buller's comment that he had two good legs, and no head)[67] to need a helping hand over the rocks. They marched in fours, and Woodgate carried a rifle, like his men, to avoid being conspicuous to Boer marksmen. He was proud of these Lancashire lads – proud to have been colonel of one of the regiments, the 2nd Lancasters, the old 'King's Own', a few years earlier. But the place of honour in front of the column he gave to the two hundred colonials and Uitlanders, Thorneycroft's men.

After a few minutes, the men changed to marching in file, and Thorneycroft led the column.[68] He had already made quite a name for himself. One of those ten special service officers sent out by Wolseley in the July before the outbreak of war, Lieutenant-Colonel Alec Thorneycroft had raised a MI regiment of five hundred irregulars, mainly Uitlander refugees, in Natal, where they had done good work as scouts, accompanied by a group of Zulu guides, paid for out of Thorneycroft's own pocket.[69] In daylight, he looked like a *Punch* cartoon of a MFH, a great, red-faced barrel of a man: twenty stone, he said proudly, including map and wire-clippers; yet he had energy to match.[70] Now he groped his way forward over the rocks, having earlier imprinted on his mind each of the landmarks up the long spur from the south-west: the kraal of African huts, the ledge of steep rocks, the clump of yellow mimosa bushes just below the summit.[71]

The great danger of a night attack is that the guides lose their way, or the attack is so delayed (as at Magersfontein) that it is the enemy who surprise the attackers. Here, at Spion Kop, progress was alarmingly slow. The Lancashire men were already done-up before they started, after seven days' fighting in Major-General Talbot Coke's brigade. The head of the column kept losing touch with the double companies behind; the men would flop down on the wet grass and fall asleep whenever they halted. It was not till nearly midnight that they began the ascent itself. Occasionally, there were glimpses of stars through gaps in the clouds; and the glimmer of fires down in the valley. There was a moment's alarm when Thorneycroft thought he saw a Boer picket ahead. He threw himself flat. It was only some rocks. The men tramped on in silence. A second alarm when – ultimate incongruity – a large white spaniel, apparently the lost mascot of some regiment, loomed up ahead of Thorneycroft. One yelp would give everyone away. There seemed to be nothing for it except to strangle the wretched animal. But then someone made a lead out of a rifle's pull-through, and a boy bugler took the white spaniel safely back down the hill.[72]

About three o'clock, after passing the final landmark, the mimosa bushes, they found the going easier, and Thorneycroft told his men to line out over the hillside. They had to wait for the rest of the column; these took an age to come up. By then, the darkness was leaving them, but fortunately a dense mist covered the hilltop. The column reached the crest line in safety.[73]

'*Werda?*' ('Who goes there?' in German.)

Suddenly out of the mist the challenge. 'Waterloo,' shouted one of the officers. Then everyone flung themselves flat. A zig-zag line of rifles' flashes. Thorneycroft waited till the rattle of bolts showed that the Mauser magazines were empty, then gave the order: fix bayonets and charge. With a hoarse yell of 'Majuba!', Thorneycroft's men charged into the mist and vanished. When the staff officers came up, they found the remains of the small Boer picket: one man, some said an African, bayoneted by an officer of the Fusiliers, and the boots of the Boers and German volunteers who had fled. At a cost of ten men wounded, the hill was theirs.[74]

It was just after 4.00 a.m. Major Massey, one of the sappers, began methodically to tape out a curved, three-hundred-yard line of trenches on what seemed, in the mist, to be the forward crest of the summit. There was the ring of pick-axe and spade striking the hard rock just below the surface, and perhaps the men talked, as they munched their biscuits and drank from the small spring of drinking water someone had found in the hollow on the south side. Some of the officers fell asleep. Woodgate had set up his HQ at the highest point of the hill, by some rocks behind the main trench line. A Court handed round boxes of extra ammunition to distribute in the trenches, and had a cup of tea with Woodgate.

The mist had given the column three hours' grace to establish themselves. After the tensions of the night, Woodgate seemed relaxed. The sappers began to cut a ramp in the hillside up which to move heavy guns. Everything had gone according to plan, despite the delays – except that the army gunners were dubious about being able to bring up any of their 15-pounders. Well, the blue jackets, the naval gunners, would go anywhere. It was too misty to heliograph. Woodgate decided to send à Court back down the hill to ask for naval guns, and to brief Warren and Buller.[75] He pencilled a curt note for Warren: 'Dear Sir Charles, We got up about four o'clock, and rushed the position. ... We have entrenched. ... and are, I hope, secure; but fog is too thick to see. ... Thorneycroft's men attacked in fine style. I had a noise made later to let you know that we had got in.'[76]

Already that noise, the three cheers, had reached the watchers more than one thousand feet below, and the word had gone out, signalled by a star-shell to Warren's HQ at Three Tree Hill, and to Buller at Mount Alice, and heliographed to White at Ladysmith, and then telegraphed, in ever-widening circles, to the Press at Maritzburg, to Roberts at Cape Town, to Lansdowne in Pall Mall, to Queen Victoria at Windsor.[77] Spion Kop, the key to Ladysmith, was ready to turn in the lock.

CHAPTER 25

Acre of Massacre

Spion Kop, Natal,
24–5 January 1900

'We waded through the Tugela, up to our breasts like, to
get across, and we climbed up this 'ere hill – cor, God it
was a climb – you climbed up so far and you came to a
big flat rock and you had to go all the way round ... cor
it was stinkin' 'ot it was ... and we laid out there firing at
one another, us and the Boers – the Boers was up *above*
us, see – they'd got us in a trap like ... I couldn't see all
round but I could 'ear blokes shoutin' you know, blokes
that was getting 'it and all that ...'

Pte Joe Packer, 2nd Middlesex,
describing the Battle of Spion Kop to
the author in June 1970

The Boer picket – about a dozen men from the Vryheid Commando – had fled
helter-skelter down the other side of the hill, and some of them reached Botha's
tent, a mile and a quarter to the north, before it was fully light. They were out of
breath and confused – and they had lost their boots. Botha sat calmly in his tent,
with a candle burning. He did not flinch at the news. The Khakis had taken the
Kop. Well, the burghers must take the Kop back. He made it sound as simple as
that.[1]

Meanwhile, other fugitives from the Vryheid Commando, and some German
volunteers, had reached the laager of General Schalk Burger, roughly two miles
away, behind the twin eastern summits of Spion Kop.[2] Schalk Burger was
nominally Botha's superior, and Joubert's second-in-command; in effect, Botha
and he jointly commanded this sector of the line; and Botha, much the stronger
character, called the tune. Together, they now fixed the plans for the counter-
attack. Its essence was speed.

Provided that the British could not drag heavy guns up to the main peak, the
situation was dangerous, but not desperate. The fire of their own heavy guns
could be brought to converge on the hub of the hilltop like the spokes of a wheel:
from their right, on the north side of the Tabanyama plateau – that is, from the
heavy guns facing Warren's line on the south side of the same ridge; from
Botha's HQ on a knoll at the centre; from the twin eastern peaks of Spion Kop
on their left. None of these gun positions was more than two miles away, and
though, at best, several hundred feet lower than the main peak of Spion Kop, the

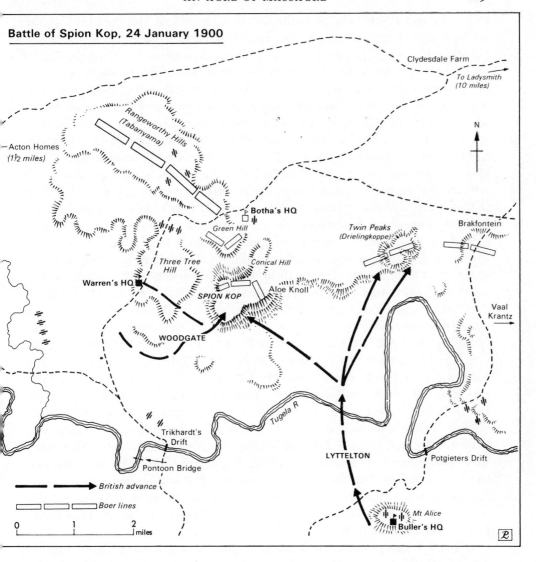

Battle of Spion Kop, 24 January 1900

field-guns' trajectory gave them effective command of it. Closer in, along the same spokes of the wheel, were perfect positions for riflemen: at Green Hill, the knucklebone of Tabanyama, a mile from the west face of Spion Kop across the great gorge holding the main road from Trichardt's Drift to Ladysmith. And on Spion Kop itself there were three excellent positions still unoccupied by the British: at Conical Hill, eight hundred yards north of the British position, and only a hundred feet lower; at the aloe-covered knoll, four hundred yards to the east; and on the nearer of the twin eastern peaks – a mile beyond, but still within long-range rifle fire. Such were the opportunities, if the burghers, scattered over ten miles of the Tugela ramparts, could only seize them in time.[3]

Botha sent orderlies to gallop off to his artillery commanders and order them to bring three Krupp field-guns and two pom-poms into action at close range from

left, right and centre. He also directed the gunners of two Creusots at the
north-west of Warren's line, guarding the Acton Homes road, to give supporting
fire at about three miles' range. But there was no question of knocking the British
off the hill, from a safe distance, simply by the weight of five field-guns and two
pom-poms. If only they had had, like the British, fifty-eight heavy guns. Or,
indeed, if only Joubert had not failed to get the extra guns from Creusot before the
war. To drive the British off the Kop meant that the burghers would have to
storm it.[4] And that, in turn, demanded the kind of heroism shown by the men who
had stormed the Platrand (Wagon Hill and Caesar's Camp) three weeks before.
How many of the burghers had that kind of courage to spare? Botha had watched
with overwhelming bitterness that heroic band at the Platrand; of the four
thousand men ordered to storm the hill, only a few hundred had obeyed.[5] Would
it be the same now at Spion Kop: shirkers crowding the safety of the rocks well
behind the firing-line, leaving their comrades to their fate?

One Boer leader, at any rate, thirty-eight-year-old Henrik Prinsloo, Commandant of the Carolina Commando, rose immediately to the occasion. His
men's laager was only a couple of miles to the east. Before the mist had cleared,
the Carolina men rode up to Botha's side of the hill. 'Burghers,' said Prinsloo,
calling them around him, 'we're now going in to attack the enemy and we shan't
all be coming back. Do your duty and trust in the Lord.'[6] Then the Carolina
men, barely ninety strong, began to climb up the hill through the mist, fanning
out towards the two kopjes – Conical Hill and Aloe Knoll – like hunters stalking
their prey.[7] Botha had called up all the reinforcements he could spare from the
rest of the line: some of the Pretoria men and the Krugersdorpers who were
holding Tabanyama shut tight against Warren, some of the Standerton and
Ermelo men, and Johannesburgers holding the Brakfontein-Vaal Kranz ridge
shut against Lyttelton and Buller. In all, Botha had ordered up less than one
thousand men out of his force of four thousand.[8] But would they respond to his
call? And, meanwhile, could the Carolina Commando hold out alone? If the
British struck vigorously at Conical Hill and Aloe Knoll, the whole of Spion
Kop would soon be theirs.

Botha's private feelings at this moment can well be imagined. Outwardly, he
was like Buller, quite unflustered in battle: an imposing figure, too, with his
neatly clipped beard and moustache, his brown suit and shiny riding-boots; his
rifle, embossed with the motto of the republic, slung over the shoulder of his
African servant.[9] But the last six weeks had been intensely depressing for Botha.
He believed passionately that the republic must adopt an offensive strategy
against the British. For nearly a month – from the battle of Colenso to the attack
on the Platrand – he had had to watch his men idling away the hours beside the
Tugela (bathing in the river, fishing for trout, attacking the flies that settled on
everything),[10] but otherwise leaving the war to Buller. Botha had then set his
heart on the attempt to capture Ladysmith by way of the Platrand, though he
was not himself allowed to take part. Its failure, due to the mismanagement of
Joubert and Schalk Burger, put paid to all his hopes of wresting back the
initiative from Buller. Since then, with Roberts and Kitchener already at Cape

Town, and Buller reinforced with Warren's division, he had been forced back to
the blocking strategy he despised.[11] To cap it all, there was talk of his having to
hand back his command to General Lucas Meyer.[12]

Botha had kept his command, but the last ten days had been a far more severe
ordeal than Colenso. He had to anticipate and parry Buller's second attack. A
new assault on Colenso, this time by night? A wide flanking movement by way
of Acton Homes? An assault by one or more of the dozen drifts along the
twenty-five miles of river between? Buller's movements, that seemed so ponderous to his critics south of the river, so childishly obvious in their intentions,
were not by any means obvious to Botha, the most brilliant of the Boer
commanders. Hence it was true that, as Buller believed, if Warren had carried
out the plan to strike hard and swiftly, he might have cut his way through
Tabanyama (Rangeworthy Hills) on 17 January. As it was, Botha and his staff
had worn themselves out in repeated manoeuvring: galloping backwards and
forwards to plug gaps in the line, dragging heavy guns onto hilltops and down
again, exhorting the men, telegraphing to Pretoria, and again exhorting the
men. Botha was so physically exhausted that he fell asleep while he dictated his
despatches.[13]

Yet now, at the supreme moment, Botha found new reserves of moral and
physical strength. He saw his chance and seized it.

About eight o'clock on 24 January the mist cleared from the peaks; it was the
forerunner of a cloudless, hot morning. Botha himself left only a dry account of
the battle.[14] It was seventeen-year-old Deneys Reitz, fighting with the Pretoria
Commando, who described, almost too graphically, that terrible day.

Reitz had returned, two days before, from a trip to Pretoria. His father,
ex-President of the Free State and now Transvaal State Secretary, had told him
to take the train immediately back to Natal, as Buller's new attack was expected
hourly. So back came young Reitz after only a day's leave. He had reached
Ladysmith on the 22nd, and was enrolled among fifty men of the Pretoria
Commando who volunteered to help Botha's men down at the Tugela.[15] All
that day, he watched Warren's bombardment of the Tabanyama ridge to the
west of Spion Kop. He could see the flashes from the British guns on the wooded
slopes across the river, and the puff-balls of shrapnel hanging in the air. This
shelling was a new ordeal for the commandos, dispersed as they were. There had
been no time to fortify the line properly by building the deep, shell-proof
dugouts that had made Colenso an almost bloodless victory. The men hastily
dug their own trenches, or took cover behind rocks. Reitz himself saw several
men fearfully mutilated, including a father and son of the Frankfort Commando
torn to pieces by a howitzer shell, and their rifles sent spinning down the slope
behind them. Apart from the shelling, and the horrible casualties it caused, there
was the continuous strain of waiting for the British infantry to attack on
Tabanyama. The men were short of ammunition and hopelessly outnumbered.
It was assumed that the bombardment was a prelude to Warren's supreme effort
in this direction.[16]

During the night, Reitz was woken by the sputter of gunfire on Spion Kop, but could not make out what was happening. At daybreak, the British began to pound the Tabanyama ridge once more, and Reitz sipped his coffee, sheltering from spent bullets in the lee of the wagon. Then someone galloped up with orders: Khakis on Spion Kop. They must take it back. Now. Their African drivers saddled up the horses, as Reitz and his friends filled up their bandoliers from a box on the wagon. Shells arched overhead, as they galloped off, reaching the northern foot of Spion Kop in less than fifteen minutes. Hundreds of saddled horses stood there in long rows. And above them was an arresting sight, one of the most arresting of the entire war.[17]

Botha's counter-attack had begun. Three or four hundred men – mainly from the Carolina and Pretoria Commandos – were clambering up the grassy slope. Spion Kop, though steep, is much lower on this northern side, and the ascent itself was not difficult for men carrying only rifles and bandoliers. But the British manned the crest line. Many burghers dropped, shot by invisible marksmen. Others reached the crest line, and Reitz saw the British soldiers suddenly rise up from behind the rocks to meet the rush. There was a moment or two of confusion. Then the struggling figures surged over the rim of the plateau and were lost to view. Reitz dismounted, tied up his horse with the rest, and started to clamber up the slope in search of his comrades.[18]

He found them all along the way up the hill: John Malherbe, with a bullet between his eyes; his own tent mate, Robert Reinecke, shot through the head; De Villiers dead – he was another member of the original corporalship, as was Tottie Krige, Jan Smuts's brother-in-law, shot through both lungs, but still alive; and Walter de Vos, another tent mate, hit in the chest, but somehow smiling bravely.[19] The counter-attack had been led by the Carolina Commando, and the rocks on the crest line were strewn with their dead. Reitz found that the burghers had succeeded in seizing this northern edge of the summit, supported by Mauser fire from Conical Hill behind them, and from Green Hill, across the gorge on the right. It was marvellous how far they had got in the frontal assault on such a strong position. The main British line was that long, shallow, crescent-shaped trench dug in the misty morning. The main Boer line was the rocky rim of the plateau one to two hundred yards behind.[20]

Some of the Pretoria men had been ordered to work their way round the left flank of the trench. They took up a position four hundred yards beyond it at Aloe Knoll. Reitz tried to follow, and was met by volleys of Lee Metford fire. Ahead of him, he saw the body of Charles Jeppe, the last of his tent mates, huddled out there in the open. He dived behind the rocks, and crawled back to the main firing-line. By nine o'clock, the enemy's rifle fire began to slacken, as the Krupp and Creusot shrapnel shells started to crash into the tableland ahead. But the sun was growing hotter, and the burghers had neither food nor water. Have we killed many of the enemy? Reitz wondered. Nothing could be seen of them. The British trench was screened by a breastwork of rocks, and by the spouts of earth thrown up by the shells. Their own casualties lay there, hideously evident: stiffening corpses covered with flies, the men who had drunk coffee with him beside the wagon only an hour before.[21]

As the sun rose higher, the few hundred burghers on the crest line became increasingly demoralized. Events were taking the same form as at the Platrand. At a terrible cost, their attack had only half succeeded. Large bodies of horsemen could now be seen collected in the plain below them. They shirked the battle. The leaders – Opperman, the Pretoria Commandant, and Prinsloo, the Carolina Commandant – tried promises, tried threats. On the crest line a sense of betrayal, anger and hopelessness began to sweep over the burghers. Hunger and thirst and indiscipline did their work – and a belief that the British were easily holding their own. By midday, the burghers were beginning to melt away like the mist of that morning, stealthily abandoning the crest line they had seized with such heroism such a short while before.[22]

How different that long, shallow, crescent-shaped trench appeared from the other side of the hill, twenty yards away: the British side. Facing the Boers, a blank wall, impervious, unshakeable, the stiff upper lip embodied in a line of stone. Facing the British, a scene from a butcher's shop.

In two senses, Spion Kop was a gruesome anachronism: a relic from the past, a portent for the future. The new-style war – an invisible enemy firing from a distant hilltop, death signified only by the small blue hole in the forehead or the dark patch on the khaki uniform – had seemed like a gentleman's war. It was the fulfilment of every officer's dream: to die in battle as one would die on the hunting-field, with the bugle in one's ears, after a victorious run. And so it had seemed, no doubt, to some of the officers who had died gallantly on the hillsides of Elandslaagte and Talana. It was only in the hospitals and dressing-stations that war had re-emerged in its old brutality.[23] But here at Spion Kop, concentrated into an acre of trampled grass, was the old-style 'soldier's battle' of pulped faces, of headless trunks, of men fighting like animals.[24] It was the precursor, too, of course, this Armageddon in the trenches under the African sun, of a greater one, fifteen years later, in the mud of Flanders.

Woodgate was dead, so it seemed; actually, he was mortally wounded, by a shell splinter. Soon after 8.30 a.m., when the mist had finally cleared, Colonel Blomfield, CO of the Lancashire Fusiliers, had pointed out to him some Boers creeping up the path towards Aloe Knoll. Woodgate went to have a look, and a splinter struck his head above the right eye. He was carried back to a dressing-station.[25] Soon after, Blomfield himself fell, severely injured, and was pulled back under cover; Major Massey, the sappers' commanding officer, the man who had taped out the trenches, fell dead, and so did Captain Vertue, Woodgate's Brigade Major.[26] With their deaths, the column suddenly lost its leaders, such as they were.

The next senior officer was now Colonel Malby Crofton, CO of the Royal Lancasters. He was appalled by the situation. Woodgate had made a series of blunders in preparing the summit as a strong-point. In fact, it was not altogether Woodgate's fault: the mist, Warren's failure to brief him carefully, the inadequacy of Herbert's inch-to-the-mile blueprint map – all these played their part in Woodgate's disastrous ignorance of the ground. But the fact was that the defensive perimeter was too small, and the trenches were in the wrong place and too shallow.[27]

To seize Conical Hill, eight hundred yards ahead, and hold that position, would have been difficult; but, if held, it would have been a master-stroke. To seize Aloe Knoll, four hundred yards away on the right, was absolutely essential and would have been perfectly easy, had Woodgate realized its importance before the mist cleared. As it was, the main British trench should have been two hundred yards farther forwards, on the tactical crest line that commanded the valley below. In the mist, Major Massey had taped out the trench on a false crest line. When the mist began to clear, the sappers tried to dig a new trench on the right place. But by then it was too late. After the Boers had seized Conical Hill and Aloe Knoll, they were able to enfilade the east side of the main trench. Moreover, the trench itself was too shallow to shield the head from rifle fire properly, let alone to protect the body from shrapnel and pom-pom shells. It had been dug by that half-company of sappers, using the twenty picks and shovels, while over a thousand soldiers lay idle, sleeping or smoking or collecting up the enemy's boots as trophies.[28] Officers and men, the British had still not understood the power of the Boers' secret weapon, the spade. This was the new rule of war – dig your own trench now, or they'll dig you a grave later.[29]

Lieutenant Lionel Charlton, in the Lancashire Fusiliers on the right, had been half-asleep when he heard Colonel Blomfield's sharp voice ordering forward the company next in line. He looked up numbly. The air was full of those whip-like cracks and that shrill, hissing noise.[30] He flattened himself on the ground. His company commander scurried forwards to get his orders. It was now his own company's turn. How was he to launch himself into that stream of sleeting bullets? For a moment, Charlton's heart failed him, then he saw the eyes of the men were on him. He sprang up. He forgot the weight of his equipment: rifle in hand, water-bottle, haversack swinging from the leather straps. He plunged forwards, half-crouching, looking neither to left nor right, and flung himself down behind the boulders close to the crest line. Then, beyond all that storm of bullets, far away across the distant plain, he saw a sight like an oasis in a dream: a mass of tall trees and greenery; it was Ladysmith.[31]

To Corporal Will McCarthy, the battle was more like nightmare. 'I got into the Trenches,' he later told one of his pals, 'and laid down at the side of Bodies with heads, legs, or Arms, it was terrible I can tell you and it was enough to completley [sic] unnerve the bravest of men. But we had to stick it. I had been laying there I think about half an hour when Bang went a shell at my back wounding me.... I thought my back was blown in....'[32]

For the first time in this war, the Boers' gunners had a nice, old-fashioned target, like the British gunners in Kitchener's war on the Nile: the enemy in massed ranks. And, like the Dervishes then, the British could not reply to the guns. 'The most awful scene of carnage,' wrote one of Thorneycroft's Uitlanders. '*We had no guns*, and the enemy's Long Toms swept the Hill. Shells rained in among us. The most hideous sights were exhibited. Men blown to atoms, joints torn asunder. Headless bodies, trunks of bodies. Awful. Awful. You dared not lift your head above the Rock or you were shot dead at once. Everything was confusion, officers were killed or mixed up in other regiments, the men had no one to rally them and became demoralized. . . .'[33]

Demoralization and confusion: above all, confusion. Already, by nine o'clock, Colonel Crofton had decided, understandably, that they needed reinforcements. But where to dispose them? And how to co-ordinate with the British gunners below? Accurate information of the situation on the summit, and of the location of the Boers, was absolutely essential. Crofton, however, was an ordinary, unimaginative regimental officer. He could not find the heliographists. He should have written a proper report to be taken by hand to Warren's HQ, only an hour away for an orderly with a horse. Instead, he merely dictated a brief SOS to an officer, who was signalling with a flag. Crofton then himself retired from the scene.[34]

It was Colonel Thorneycroft, huge, red-faced, bull-headed Thorneycroft, who did most to rally the men. By ten o'clock, the battle, ebbing and flowing between the main trench and the forward trench on the crest line, had reached a crisis. One of his young officers, Lieutenant Sargeant, dashed out with twenty men towards some rocks on the right front. A private pushed his rifle over a boulder, felt something soft, and inadvertently pulled the trigger. It was the waistcoat of a Boer, who was thus shot dead just before he could fire his rifle. But Sargeant's party was soon beaten back to the main trench, losing half their men.[35]

Then Thorneycroft himself led a charge of forty men, half his own, half the Fusiliers. He found three officers, Captain Knox-Gore, Lieutenant Ellis and Lieutenant Newnham, surrounded by the bodies of their men – wounded, dying, dead. Newnham himself was bleeding to death from two wounds; he had propped himself up against a rock, and was still firing; a third bullet killed him. Knox-Gore stood up and shouted something to Thorneycroft; he pointed to the right; his shouts were lost in the uproar; he fell dead. Ellis died too. Thorneycroft himself was only saved by the fact that he tripped and crashed down on the ground. Almost all the forty men were shot down. Three officers of the Royal Lancasters tried to lead further charges, and were felled too: Lieutenant Wade, Lieutenant Nixon, Major Ross, the latter so ill with dysentery that he had been left behind the night before, but had somehow struggled to the firing line that morning.[36]

Thorneycroft lay on the stony ground, under the grid-mesh of bullets. His own injury was nothing worse than a twisted ankle. How long would it take Warren to send reinforcements, he wondered? And how long would it be before his own men, exposed to this inferno, would stick it no longer, and run?[37]

At his HQ, three miles away at Three Tree Hill, just before 9.50 a.m., Warren received a message that struck him as very strange. Warren, the man who 'knew the Boer', had been absolutely unprepared for the speed and ferocity of Botha's counter-attack. Now this message came from Crofton: 'Reinforce at once or all is lost. General dead.' He forwarded copies to Buller and Lyttelton, then replied brusquely to Crofton: 'I am sending two battalions, and the Imperial Light Infantry are on their way up. You must hold on to the last. No surrender.'[38]

In fact, Warren had already concluded, from the distant rumble of the guns, that the column needed reinforcements, and had told General Coke to take up there the Imperial Light Infantry (the infantry counterpart of the ILH), the 2nd Middlesex and the 2nd Dorsets. But he simply could not understand this panicky message of Crofton's. Colonel à Court had just ridden up with Woodgate's note, written only two hours earlier: the note that said, 'We have entrenched . . . and are, I hope, secure.' Warren, however, now bestirred himself to send some of the vital equipment Woodgate had left behind; some missing sandbags were brought up by the Middlesex and Dorsets. And he agreed with à Court: it was vital to get heavy guns on the summit as soon as possible.[39] He also sent an officer to find out what had become of the small guns of the mountain battery (they had been delayed at Frere through a mistake by one of Buller's staff). What about a diversion at Tabanyama on the left? General Hart and many officers of his Irish Brigade were keener than ever to launch this long-delayed attack, now it was evident that the burghers had thinned down this section of their line in order to reinforce Spion Kop. Warren remained unshakeable. His tactic remained to force the enemy to attack *them* at Spion Kop, to make the Boer break his head on that steel wedge hammered into his stone wall.[40]

One new idea did occur to Warren, however, which was to have a dramatic effect on events, though not in the way he anticipated. At 9.53 a.m., immediately after receiving Crofton's despairing note, he heliographed to Lyttelton, whose brigade was dug in north of the river at Potgieters, five miles to the east. 'Give every assistance you can on your side; this side is clear, but the enemy are too strong on your side, and Crofton telegraphs that if assistance is not given at once all is lost.'[41]

'This side is clear.' It was a strange way to describe the state of the beleaguered garrison on Spion Kop. The fact was that, though the mist had now cleared completely, Warren had only the haziest idea of what was going on. The grassy slope between Conical Hill and the main summit of Spion Kop he could see clearly, and Parsons' gunners plastered it with shrapnel. But Botha's gun positions were all masked by the wooded flanks of Tabanyama. So was the northern crest line, where Prinsloo and Opperman's men had made their heroic charge. And, most important of all, so was Aloe Knoll. The result was a confused optimism in Warren's own mind about the extent and strength of the British position. He sent off his weakest brigade commander, poor, lame Coke, to lead the reinforcements. Still more disastrous, he stopped Lyttelton's long-range guns, which had begun to shell Aloe Knoll from the east, for Warren apparently thought Aloe Knoll was part of the British position.[42]

At Mount Alice, on the forward ledge of Buller's camp at Spearman's, it was impossible to have the illusion that the battle was going well.

Here, beside the two 4·7-inch guns, the HQ staff and the war correspondents took turns to look through the naval telescopes. The ridge opposite, three miles away over the shadowy gorge of the Tugela, quivered in the glare of the sun. John Atkins wrote:

I shall always have it in my memory – that acre of massacre, that complete shambles, at the top of a rich green gully with cool granite walls (a way fit to lead to heaven) which reached up the western flank of the mountain. To me it seemed that our men were all in a small square patch; there were brown men and browner trenches, the whole like an over-ripe barley-field.... I saw three shells strike a certain trench within a minute; each struck it full in the face, and the brown dust rose and drifted away with the white smoke. The trench was toothed against the sky like a saw – made, I supposed, of sharp rocks built into a rampart. Another shell struck it, and then – heavens! – the trench rose up and moved forward. The trench was men; the teeth against the sky were men. They ran forward bending their bodies into a curve – they looked like a cornfield with a heavy wind sweeping over it from behind.[43]

Buller stood watching the scene, as impassive-looking as Xerxes on the hill above Salamis. In fact, he was burning with resentment. If the Boers, unknown to him, were reminded of their disastrous attack on the Platrand, Buller himself was reminded of Colenso. Once again, he thought, trying to suppress his rage at Warren, a good plan had been thrown away by subordinates. He had been sold by 'a damned gunner' at Colenso. Now he had been sold by a damned sapper. Warren had failed to strike at Tabanyama on the 17th, when it was almost undefended. Warren had funked attacking it on the 21st, when to attack needed courage, yet was practicable.[44] Today, Warren's obstinacy had wrecked Buller's own two-pronged plan of attack.

The point was, a point that cannot be overemphasized, that Buller had not only authorized Warren to attack Spion Kop. The plan was that the moment Warren made the break-through there, Buller would himself launch the right-flank attack, north of Potgieters. And now this right-flank attack was in jeopardy, if not impossible.[45] For, as we saw, before ten o'clock that morning Warren had heliographed to Lyttelton to send reinforcements, instead of drawing on the eleven battalions – nearly ten thousand infantry – he had on his left flank. Without consulting Buller, Lyttelton had responded by sending two infantry battalions, and most of his scanty mounted troops.[46] When Buller discovered this, the men had already left for Spion Kop, and it was too late either to recall them, or to divert men from the left flank.[47]

When Buller had learnt of Hart's and Long's blunders at Colenso, he had immediately decided that the whole operation had to be called off. Now, on the Upper Tugela, the frustration of his plans only stiffened his determination to press on. He had already heard from à Court, who had galloped off to his HQ after reporting to Warren some of the deficiencies of Woodgate's defences: above all, the need to get naval guns onto the main summit. Buller arranged for two naval guns to be sent up at once. Equally vital, he sent up his own Intelligence Officer, Colonel Sandbach, to report back to him personally on the situation on the summit.[48] How he would later reproach himself for not taking back the three brigades from Warren. Weakly, he still shrank from this step, afraid to humiliate Warren in front of the army.[49] And perhaps he still hoped to launch the attack beyond Potgieters when Lyttelton's troops returned.

That morning, he only made one further intervention, though it was to be of crucial importance. Crofton appeared to have lost his head. Well, he had heard from à Court that Thorneycroft had been the life and soul of the column during the night march.[50] And he could now see Thorneycroft, literally a tower of strength among the brown figures in that acre of massacre visible through the telescope. At 11.40 a.m. he sent a wire to Warren: 'Unless you put some really good hard fighting man in command on the top you will lose the hill. I suggest Thorneycroft.' Warren agreed. Ten minutes later, the heliographists on the south-west lip of Spion Kop, crouching in the storm of Mauser fire and shrapnel, received a curt message. Thorneycroft had superseded Crofton in command.[51]

It was well after midday before Thorneycroft himself heard of his promotion. He was in the main trench, where he had been dragged back under cover, after the failure of his gallant attempt to recapture the crest line. Someone ran up with the message and, before he could speak, collapsed across Thorneycroft, shot in the head. Later, a lieutenant crawled forward and shouted the news above the uproar: 'You are a general!'

The situation was more critical than ever. Apart from his left, where some of the men were still holding out among the rocks, somewhat protected by a fold in the ground, the main trench was now the forward line. Thorneycroft himself was the only officer in this part of the firing-line. Unknown to his men, the reinforcements sent by Warren and led by General Coke – the Middlesex and the Imperial Light Infantry – were now hurrying up the hill, a string of brown figures, bayonets flashing like diamonds, mixed with the dark blobs of the ammunition mules. But in the firing-line, five hours without food and water had brought the men to the limit of endurance – and beyond.

Soon after one o'clock, Thorneycroft heard a commotion in the main trench on his right. Some men, chiefly Lancashire Fusiliers, dropped their rifles and put up their hands. Three or four Boers came out and signalled to their comrades to come forward. They were greeted by a burst of ineffective fire – in the confusion – and then by a line of handkerchiefs fluttering above the trench.[52]

'Majuba!' the British had shouted exultantly when they had seized Spion Kop in the mist of dawn. Indeed, they seemed to have a Majuba now. De Kock, one of the Transvaalers, described the next moment: 'The English were about to surrender, and we were all coming up, when a great big, angry, red-faced soldier ran out of the trench on our right and shouted, "I'm the Commandant here; take your men back to hell, sir! I allow no surrenders." '[53]

The great, big, angry, red-faced soldier was, of course, Thorneycroft, hobbling forward with the help of a stick. He shouted to his men to follow him to a line of rocks behind the trench, from which they opened fire at De Kock and the others. Some of the Boers flung themselves flat, others managed to hustle back the prisoners they had already seized (nearly 170 Khakis, according to their accounts).[54] There was deafening fire at a range of a few yards.

At this desperate moment, Thorneycroft looked back across the rocks and saw, at long last, the reinforcements. A company of the Middlesex was advancing with fixed bayonets. Thorneycroft ordered them to charge. The sudden reversal knocked the Boers off balance. They fled back to the crest line, dragging their exhausted prisoners with them. Thorneycroft's men reoccupied the main trench, and pushed forward once more to within yards of the crest. The Boers' artillery began to pound the hill again, but in the next hour fresh British troops continued to stream on to the summit. Thorneycroft reinforced the battered Royal Lancasters on the left with those new Uitlander volunteers, the Imperial Light Infantry; the remnants of his own Uitlanders still held the forward line; on the right, he pushed the Middlesex forward, despite heavy casualties, to plug the gaps left by the Fusiliers. He then crawled back to the rocks at the highest point of the plateau, and scribbled a note, which he gave to a newly arrived staff officer, Colonel Sandbach, to take down to Warren. The mirrors of the heliograph had long since been smashed by a shell.[55]

It was 2.30 p.m. For the first time since dawn, Thorneycroft had a respite, of a sort, from that inferno in the trenches. The note read:

Hung on till last extremity with old force. Some of the Middlesex here now, and I hear Dorsets coming up, but force really inadequate to hold such a large perimeter.... What reinforcements can you send to hold the hill tonight? We are badly in need of water. There are many killed and wounded.

                                                                    Alex Thorneycroft.

[PS] If you wish to make a certainty of hill for night, you must send more Infantry and attack enemy's guns.[56]

The confusion in Warren's own mind about the situation on Spion Kop was not dispelled by this brief, somewhat desperate note of Thorneycroft's, which reached him at about four o'clock. Perhaps he imagined that Thorneycroft, like Crofton before him, was losing his head. Warren was only partly to blame for the optimism he felt. Soon after Thorneycroft had written the note, it had passed through the hands of Major-General Coke, his immediate superior. Now it was Coke's job to take overall charge of the defence of the summit: to reassure Thorneycroft and relieve him, if necessary, of the crushing strain, physical and mental, of command. Warren was not to know that Coke had not even reached the plateau, but contented himself with reassuring Warren about the situation from the safety of the track below. He endorsed Thorneycroft's message with this addition: 'Spion Kop – 3 p.m. – I have seen the above, and have ordered the Scottish Rifles and King's Royal Rifles to reinforce.... We appear to be holding our own.'[57] The sun was hot. According to one report, General Coke then took a nap in the shade of the mimosa-trees.[58]

Warren himself was by no means asleep, even if his preparations, as usual, appeared to critical observers to be somewhat ponderous. One thing *was* clear.

To protect Thorneycroft's men, Spion Kop must be made secure against artillery. They must drag up the mountain guns and naval guns to the summit. They must deepen and improve the British trenches.[59] Why did he not go there himself? Warren was a man who liked to work with his hands – a sapper general, an expert on trenches, military and archaeological; he had involved himself so closely in laying pontoons for his men to cross the river that they had taken him for a junior officer.[60] The foot of Spion Kop was less than an hour's ride from his HQ at Three Tree Hill. Why did he not take his horse and go?

Unknown to Warren, Major-General Lyttelton had meanwhile taken a decisive step to relieve the pressure on Thorneycroft's force, and was in the process of succeeding, better than Lyttelton had ever thought possible.

There are times in a battle when to send direct reinforcements is much less effective than to make a diversion elsewhere. Arguably, Warren's overriding error that day was his failure to make a diversion to the west. He could have sent Hart's, Hildyard's or Dundonald's brigade to strike at Tabanyama. His failure to do so will remain one of the great might-have-beens of the battle. What is certain is that where Lyttelton did make a diversion – to the east – it had the most dramatic effect on the minds of the Boers and their commander.[61]

The eastern ridge of Spion Kop is marked by twin, crinkly peaks, two thousand yards and three thousand yards respectively from the main summit and tableland to the west. From Mount Alice, these Twin Peaks give the illusion of being higher than the main summit, though actually lower by a couple of hundred feet.[62] It is, at any rate, a formidable defensive position; the approach from the south, across the Tugela and then up the sheer, rocky face of the mountain, is more arduous than the approach by the track to the main summit. Still more formidable would it be as an offensive position for the British. Once they were firmly astride this eastern ridge, they would have the Ladysmith plain at their feet. They would command not only Aloe Knoll, but the two Boer gun positions – the pom-poms and the Krupps – and the white tents of General Schalk Burger and the Carolina Commando, immediately beyond.

Imagine, then, the feelings of Schalk Burger when it was reported late that day that the Khakis were storming the 'Drielingkoppe' ('Triplets'), as the Twin Peaks were called by the Boers. In fact, Lyttelton's reinforcements had been visible since midday: the long, khaki snake winding across Kaffir Drift, a small intermediate drift between Trikhardt's and Potgieters, and twisting up the hillside. The snake had then divided: the head (actually the Scottish Rifles) trailing away to the west, to reinforce Thorneycroft's men directly; the tail (the 60th Rifles) striking due north, up towards the peaks. To the watching Boers, the sight must have seemed as arresting as their own men's ascent of Spion Kop that morning had seemed to Deneys Reitz. There were hardly more than seven hundred men, split into two groups, each group tackling one of the peaks. Yet so thin was the burghers' line stretched – most of the Carolina Commando were, of course, fighting for their lives more than a mile away on Spion Kop itself – that the burghers could not hold back the Khakis. Casualties they inflicted in plenty. They were firing downwards at the British, who were clambering up on hands and knees over the rocks and scree. By 5.00 p.m. they had been forced to evacuate their hastily dug trenches.[63] About sunset, Schalk Burger must have heard the grim news. The Khakis were astride – precariously, perhaps, yet astride – the Drielingkoppe. It was too late to affect the battle for the main summit that day. But next morning the burghers would have a simple choice. Either to storm the Drielingkoppe, or to gallop back to Ladysmith.[64]

Schalk Burger was, like Joubert, first and foremost a politician – not a particularly successful politician at that.[65] He was now utterly demoralized.[66]

The situation on the burghers' side of the main summit was in fact desperate. At seven, darkness came at last: the crash of the heavy guns, beating like surf on the stones and rocks of the summit, the boiling, grinding waves of sound had faded into silence. There were odd bursts of rifle fire. Otherwise, the sounds of the night were the ghastly sounds of Elandslaagte, where so many burghers had died: the scuffling and moaning of the wounded, delirious men crying out in the dark, as though the sun still shone and the battle still raged.[67]

Deneys Reitz found himself with hardly two dozen men left to defend the crest line. By ten o'clock, even his own leader, Commandant Opperman, had to admit defeat – at least, he decided they must abandon the position for the time being. They scrambled down to the foot of the hill, where they found the long lines of horses tethered there earlier had gone, apart from their own; there were mealies, sacks of coffee and boxes of ammunition strewn everywhere in the circles of light around the camp-fires.

Just as the first wagons were leaving, someone galloped up and shouted to the burghers to halt. Reitz could not see the man's face in the shadows, but people said it was Botha. Addressing them from the saddle, he told them to think of the shame of deserting their posts in the hour of danger. Some, at any rate, answered his appeal, and returned to their positions east and west of Spion Kop. But no one returned to the abandoned positions on the main summit.[68]

If ever Botha's extraordinary optimism was needed, it was at this moment. The main summit abandoned, a second gap – at the Drielingkoppe – knocked in the line. What hope now of avoiding utter rout? Yet Botha sent reassuring reports to Kruger and Joubert. 'The bravery and courage of our burghers I cannot praise too highly.... The artillery has worked beautifully and if the enemy does not retreat during the night, the fight will be continued tomorrow. The enemy's force is so great and if we look at the small number of [our] men... we cannot be sufficiently thankful to the merciful Father for vouchsafing us protection in this grievous struggle....'[69] So wrote Botha, in the special biblical style of telegram that he knew Kruger expected. To his colleague and senior general, Schalk Burger, he wrote more bluntly and desperately: 'Let us struggle and die together. But, brother, let us not give way an inch more to the English.' He promised to send reinforcements as soon as the moon rose. Meanwhile, Burger must take one hundred Free Staters from his own left wing to reinforce the line behind the Drielingkoppe. Botha added that he knew the English. They were so '*kopschuw*' (bone-headed) 'that if we only have faith and confidence and do not retreat, the enemy will give in'.[70]

Botha's appeal fell on deaf ears. About midnight, his messenger reached the site of Burger's camp behind the Drielingkoppe, and found the tents had vanished. In a panic, Burger had taken part of the Carolina and Lydenburg Commandos, complete with their Krupp field-gun and pom-pom, and fled northwards to Ladysmith.[71]

The sky paled, and the dew settled on the trampled grass beside the handful of burghers who remained – brave men like Opperman, gallant boys like Deneys Reitz. They looked up at the skyline, waiting and watching for the inevitable. Nothing, and no one – so it seemed – could now prevent the British from streaming through the two breaches in their position, and rolling up the whole of their line along the Tugela.[72]

But one man had this power, the power to snatch defeat from the jaws of victory, and that was poor, plodding General Warren.

Napoleon once said that victory goes to the general who makes fewest mistakes: in other words, that war is, at bottom, a contest in blunders. The saying has never been illustrated in a more stylized way than in the Battle of Spion Kop. Here was a battlefield hardly bigger than the floor of a large theatre. Here were two armies, separated by a gap across which you could have thrown a biscuit as easily as you could have thrown it across a stage. And all the protagonists – all except Botha – stumbled about the stage as though they were blindfold.

It was inevitable that the British should know almost nothing of what was happening on the other side of the hill: it was a central paradox of the new, smokeless warfare that ignorance hung over the battlefield, ignorance deeper than any battle smoke; and now that darkness itself had followed, who can blame Thorneycroft for not recognizing his unseen victory? But why on earth was Thorneycroft equally ignorant of Warren's own plans? It was this ignorance, for which only Warren can be blamed, which lay at the root of the extraordinary blunder which now brought tragedy to the verge of farce.

All around Spion Kop, the work of preparing to exploit the advantage they had gained was, at long last, being taken in hand by the British.

On the face of it, it must be said, Lyttelton had taken a step that might appear to have the opposite effect. At 2.30 p.m. he had received a message from one of his staff, who was on the main summit of Spion Kop: 'Do not think that the King's Royal Rifles [the 3rd/60th] can get up on right; it is held by Boers. We are only holding up to your left of saddle.'[73] Lyttelton immediately ordered the recall of this battalion, the one then storming the Twin Peaks; he had misgivings that there was a dangerous gap between their position and the main summit.[74] Fortunately, however, for the British, a series of urgent messages from Lyttelton, sent at 3.00 p.m., 3.30 p.m., and 4.50 p.m., produced no effect: apparently the CO of the 60th, Lieutenant-Colonel Riddell, turned a Nelson eye to these orders recalling him. Hence the successful capture of the Twin Peaks. Despite the death of the Colonel, who fell dead with the crumpled orders still in his pocket – and despite the battalion's loss of one hundred men – it was a brilliant tactical feat, the only brilliant feat of the day.[75] After 7.00 p.m., Lyttelton's orders were finally obeyed, and the battalion withdrew under cover of darkness. But they had achieved, as we have seen, far more than Lyttelton could have guessed, even if he had known they had reached the summit. Indeed, the fact that they had withdrawn from the Twin Peaks made little difference to events. The thought of them being there was enough to send Schalk Burger scurrying back across the plain to Ladysmith, leaving that second great breach in the Boers' line wide open for Buller and Lyttelton to exploit next day.[76]

Meanwhile, Warren was hastening slowly – very slowly – to send relief to Thorneycroft. One thing must be said in Warren's defence. Even more than Buller's own force, Warren's force was handicapped by the defects in the War Office's preparations. He was short of properly qualified staff officers; he needed batteries of long-range guns; flimsy heliographs and oil-lamps were no substitute for proper field telegraph lines, designed to be run up close to the firing-line.[77]

Yet what were Warren's handicaps compared to Botha's? Where was the 'mad and manly fury', the quality that had carried British generals in the past to victory in the teeth of every obstacle? Warren's ponderous time-table, that appalled Buller, cannot seriously be defended. It was not until 9.00 p.m. – two hours after darkness – that he even ordered Lieutenant-Colonel Sim, the sappers' commander, to proceed to Spion Kop with a fatigue party of fourteen hundred men. These were to help dig the huge (twenty-three-foot diameter) emplacements for the two long-range naval guns, and the smaller emplacements for the mountain battery, as well as perform the all-important job of digging proper trenches for Thorneycroft and his men.[78] Nor did the rest of Warren's preparations reflect any greater sense of urgency. Stretcher-bearers, water, ammunition, fresh troops, above all, heavy guns – these were the crucial deficiencies that had racked Thorneycroft's brain. Now it had been dark for five hours, and they were still missing.[79]

Still, perhaps it was not Warren's failure to remedy these deficiencies that proved his worst error. It was his failure to tell Thorneycroft of his plans to do so. Astonishing as it may seem, he had sent no direct instructions to Thorneycroft since the heliogram apppointing him a general at midday. He had left it to Coke to reassure Thorneycroft, although (by another astonishing blunder) Warren had never actually told Coke that he had put Thorneycroft in charge. Then, to compound all these blunders, at 9.00 p.m. Warren had ordered Coke to return to the HQ for consultation, leaving Thorneycroft alone among the horrors on the summit.[80]

Midnight. The scales still quivered in the balance, each army weighed down with the sense of disaster. There are battles enough in history after which both sides have claimed victory. Here both commanders (though not Botha) claimed defeat.

Then, out of the darkness and confusion, appeared one man, one self-appointed messenger who might have turned the balance in favour of the

British. It was young Winston Churchill, not content with his double job as *Morning Post* correspondent and lieutenant in the South African Light Horse, instinctively taking over the role of general.[81]

Churchill's troop of the SALH, in keeping with Warren's distrust of his cavalry, had been confined that day to camp. It drove them all mad. They had to stand idly by as the Boer shells plumped, seven to a minute, into the summit of Spion Kop; to hear the pom-poms lacerating the hillsides with chains of smoke and dust; to see the village of ambulances accumulate at the foot of the mountain. At four o'clock, Churchill could bear it no more. Without permission, he and a companion rode off the few miles to Spion Kop to see for himself, left his horse by the village of ambulances, and began to climb the narrow track to the summit.[82] 'Streams of wounded met us and obstructed our path,' he wrote later.

Men were staggering along alone, or supported by comrades, or crawling on hands and knees, or carried on stretchers. Corpses lay here and there. . . . The splinters and fragments of shell had torn and mutilated in the most ghastly manner. I passed about two hundred while I was climbing up. There was, moreover, a small but steady leakage of unwounded men of all corps. Some of these cursed and swore. Others were utterly exhausted and fell on the hillside in stupor. Others again seemed drunk, though they had had no liquor. Scores were sleeping heavily. Fighting was still proceeding. . . .[83]

Churchill had seen fighting in Tirah and at Omdurman, but what he saw here, well behind the firing-line, profoundly shocked him. He went no further to the summit. He rode back to Warren's HQ and told him what he had seen. The General listened to Churchill's story 'with great patience and attention', according to Churchill. (Warren's ADC later gave a different version.) At any rate, the crucial debate was still in progress: how to drag the heavy naval guns to the summit. When this had finally been settled, darkness had fallen. Churchill volunteered to take a note to Thorneycroft and to take him the news – that the guns and the fourteen hundred men of the working party were on their way.

Churchill's second visit to Spion Kop was, if less macabre, more unnerving than before. The stony track was still crowded with ambulances, stragglers and wounded. The darkness, which hid the horrors, had also doubled the confusion. Only one solid battalion now remained, the Dorsets, the one that Coke had kept in reserve. The others were all intermingled: the remnants of the seventeen hundred – that is, Thorneycroft's MI, the three Lancashire battalions, and what was left of the two thousand-odd men sent to reinforce them, the Imperial Light Infantry, the Middlesex and (sent by Lyttelton) the 2nd Scottish Rifles. As regiments they had ceased to exist. In their place were isolated groups of men, clustered around individual officers, cool and cheerful; some of the men were even eager to fight. 'But the darkness and the broken ground,' Churchill said, 'paralysed everyone.'[84]

On the summit he found Thorneycroft sitting on the ground, surrounded by the remnants of the regiment he had raised. Churchill gave him Warren's note and told him the good news. The navy was coming – so were the sappers. Thorneycroft was in a state of shock, of complete physical and moral break-down. Twelve hours in the firing-line had finished him. No messages from the

General, no time to write any himself, he mumbled. Fighting too hot, too close to attend to anything else. Must retire. Had already decided it. 'Better six good battalions safely down the hill than a bloody mop-up in the morning.'[85]

Even now, withdrawal – and disaster – were not inevitable. Thorneycroft had called a brief council of war, before making his decision. Two of the COs agreed, somewhat hesitantly. But Lieutenant-Colonel Hill, the CO of the Middlesex, had insisted he was senior to Thorneycroft; he refused to believe Thorneycroft's story that he was now a brigadier, and Coke (not having been told by Warren) upheld Hill's claim to be senior. This farcical, Gilbertian argument was now renewed. Hill appeared out of the darkness, and challenged Thornycroft's right to order the withdrawal. No one listened to Hill.[86]

As Thorneycroft led the rear-guard down the track, leaving the dead, and many seriously wounded, alone on the summit, they were met by another obstacle. When he had been recalled to see Warren, earlier that evening, Coke had left his staff officer, Captain Phillips, at his HQ on the shelf half-way up the hillside. Phillips was woken by the sound of tramping feet. He woke too late to challenge Thorneycroft. But he wrote a formal memorandum – a remarkable feat, considering the darkness and confusion – addressed to all commanding officers. 'This withdrawal is absolutely without the authority of either Major-General Coke or Sir Charles Warren. . . . Were the General here he would order an instant reoccupation of the heights.'[87]

If only Phillips could have signalled to Warren's HQ. But, of course, there was no oil in the signalling lamp. The battle was lost for want of a pennyworth of oil. No one listened to Phillips. The withdrawal continued. Churchill advised Thorneycroft to do what he thought best.[88]

Near the foot of the hill, Thorneycroft met his final obstacle: Colonel Sim and the rescue party, the van of the company of sappers, gunners and the fourteen hundred infantry. Sim gave Thorneycroft Warren's second note, urging him to hold the hill at all costs. It was too late. 'I have done all I can,' said Thorneycroft, 'and I am not going back.' Sim and the gunners retired somewhat sheepishly, like the principal actors of a play whose arrival on the stage has been delayed till the end of the final act.[89]

Spion Kop was left to the dead and the dying of both armies: on the British side, 243 had died; bodies were piled three-deep in the scanty shelter of the main trench. The moon rose.[90]

It was 2.00 a.m. before Lieutenant Churchill reported back to Warren's tent at Three Tree Hill. The General was asleep. Churchill put his hand on his shoulder. 'Colonel Thorneycroft is here, sir.' Warren took it all very calmly, according to Churchill. What a charming old gentleman. Churchill felt genuinely sorry for him. He also felt sorry for Warren's army.[91]

Soon after dawn, the small party of burghers with Reitz and Opperman looked up at Spion Kop and saw an amazing, unbelievable sight. Two figures stood on the summit, triumphantly waving their rifles and their bush hats.

Burghers. The hill was theirs. The Khakis were *kopschuw*. Botha's extraordinary optimism had been proved correct.[92]

Buller was woken by the news, sent by telegraph, and rode immediately to Three Tree Hill, arriving soon after dawn. He was spared the knowledge of the ultimate irony: that Schalk Burger and his Boers had, for seven hours, abandoned their positions. As it was, the news proved a bitter disappointment, yet not, after all, a surprise. He did not blame Thorneycroft, who had exercised 'a wise discretion'. He blamed Warren. 'If at sundown the defence of the summit had been taken regularly in hand, entrenchments laid out, gun emplacements prepared, the dead removed, the wounded collected, and in fact the whole place brought under regular military command . . . the hills would have been held I am sure.'[93]

Buller also blamed himself. He should have obeyed his instincts and superseded Warren six days earlier.[94] Both Buller's verdicts on the disaster – especially his verdict on Buller – were to be echoed by Roberts. And they can hardly be challenged.[95]

Belatedly, Buller was now again the commander of his own army. High on the summit, Botha exchanged condolences with the British medical officers, and that fatally shallow main trench was made deep enough to serve as a satisfactory grave. The burial parties could see the army had begun their retreat across the river below. But the Boers had lost 335 men in the fighting. Though their line was now reinforced, they were too exhausted to follow up their success.[96]

All that day and the next, the immense coil of wagons, stores on mule wagons, the thirty-six heavy guns in ox wagons, over one thousand wounded in the ambulance wagons and on stretchers, wound its way across the pontoon bridge at Trichardt's. Buller took charge in person, calm, stolid, inscrutable as ever, Buller riding hither and thither with an exhausted staff and a huge notebook, Buller at last 'gripping the whole business', as Churchill wrote with relief, 'in his strong hands'.[97]

That night, the majestic retreat continued: back to the white tents and the relative comforts of Buller's camp behind the flanks of Mount Alice. It was an appalling night – pitch-dark, with driving rain – a worse experience even than the night march of a fortnight before. But the retreat was accomplished without the loss of a man or a pound of stores. As the engineers pulled up the last of the pontoons, a single shell – a parting gift from Botha – sploshed into the Tugela behind them.[98]

They had lost fifteen hundred men killed, wounded or captured, and after ten days were back where they started.[99]

Had they also lost confidence in Buller? It would have been odd if there had not been recriminations. Sacrifices and hardships they had been led to expect. But humiliation was still a novelty. And, anyway, what had gone wrong? No one knew about the failure of the signal lamp. They wondered why Buller had ever given Warren command of his army? Why had they retreated? Officers were baffled – as well they might be.[100] Among the more senior generals, that whispering campaign against Buller, led by Lyttelton, gathered momentum. People began to talk of 'Sir Reverse' Buller, and 'The Ferryman of the Tugela'.[101] *The Times* correspondent, Buller's cousin, wrote home, 'The worst of it all is that everyone is beginning to lose confidence in Redvers.'[102] Even the NCOs, who had previously shown blind faith in old Buller, began to grumble about their great General. 'Everyone is very downhearted,' wrote Sergeant-Major Galley of the Army Service Corps, 'they can't understand why they have to take these places at such great cost only to vacate them afterwards, I think it's a laundery Gen. Buller should be manager of and let Mrs Buller come out here and see what she can do. . . .'[103]

On the south bank of the Tugela, Buller himself addressed his army, praising their courage, and thanking them 'from the bottom of his heart' for their great sacrifices. There was something about the way he did it – the ill-suppressed emotion – that disarmed most opposition.[104] Buller told the men that they had given him 'the key to Ladysmith', and promised them that they would be there within a week.[105]

Buller's superiors did not, however, share his optimism. The news of the abandonment of Spion Kop caused more heart-searching even than the news of Colenso. Roberts, at Cape Town, reacted by proposing that Buller should temporarily abandon Ladysmith by acting, for the time being, on the defensive.[106] Wolseley and the War Office went much further. They actually suggested – a suggestion later sheepishly withdrawn – that Buller should permanently abandon Ladysmith. White and the fittest of the garrison might be ordered to cut their way out. The rest would have to blow up their stores and surrender.[107]

Both suggestions surprised Buller. Strange to say, there was no return, after Spion Kop, to the black mood of rage and resentment Buller had felt after Colenso. He did not tell White of Wolseley's surrender telegram.[108]

'We were fighting all last week,' he wrote to his wife cheerfully, 'but old Warren is a duffer and lost me a good chance. However, if I have the least luck I think I have at last found out how to get through these beastly mountains.'[109] He had 'the key'.

Poor Buller, he was doomed, ten days after he had written this, to be retreating yet again across the river: the Ferryman of the Tugela, General Charon, with a new load of dead and dying, 333 casualties suffered at the Battle of Vaal Krantz.[110] Yet, in a sense, as he said, Spion Kop had given him the key to Ladysmith. Victory was not to be only a question of geography: a suitable drift, a commanding hill, the right position for the guns. It was a question of method. From their mistakes, humiliating as they were, Buller's nineteenth-century army – GOC, generals, officers and men – were all learning how to fight a twentieth-century war.[111]

PART III

Roberts's Advance

What 'e does not know o' war,
    Gen'ral Bobs,
You can arst the shop next door –
    can't they, Bobs?
Oh 'e's little but 'e's wise,
'E's a terror for 'is size,
An' – 'e – does – not – advertise
    Do yer, Bobs?

Rudyard Kipling, 'Bobs', 1898

"WHO SAID 'BOBS'?"

CHAPTER 26

The Steam-Roller

The Western Front,
11–15 February 1900

'It was the worst run war ever – no transport, no grub,
nothing . . .'

One of Roberts's old soldiers
describing Roberts's great flank march
to the author in June 1970

Rimington's Guides – the van of Roberts's great army of forty thousand –
clattered into Ramdam about ten o'clock on the morning of Sunday 11 February. They were about one hundred strong. Behind them, they left a trail of dust
hanging in the fiery blue sky. When they rode on, they left their name, 'Tigers',
scrawled in letters of chalk over the farmhouse doorway. They met no opposition.[1]

It had never been much of a place, Ramdam: one square, whitewashed,
tin-roofed farmhouse astride a low ridge in the almost featureless veld; a few
weeping willows; across the farmyard, some outhouses for the plough oxen, the
donkeys and the Africans; and below the ridge, key to the whole place, the dam,
or glorified horse-pond, fed by the summer rains.[2]

This was Ramdam, one among a hundred other Dutch homesteads in the
endless plains to the south of the Modder and the Riet Rivers. It was still less of a
place after Rimington's Tigers had made their bivouac there. You would not
have needed their signature to tell you they had passed that way. The square
whitewashed hall, the four smaller rooms, the Africans' quarters – all smashed
and stripped and gutted as efficiently as those British settlers' homes had been
smashed and stripped and gutted in Natal. The Tigers were Uitlanders and
colonials. Judged as scouts and fighting men, they were the élite of the army, but
'not [the] men I should invite to bivouac on my estate', as one of Roberts's
generals dryly observed.[3] They did not talk rhetoric about wiping something off
a slate. They looted as quietly and thoroughly as they fought and scouted.[4]

For this was enemy country. Ramdam was the first halting-place within the
borders of the Free State. The counter invasion had begun.

Roberts's advance on Bloemfontein, launched that day, had some of the
majestic momentum of Kitchener's march to Omdurman eighteen months
before. Here at long last was the imperial steam-roller: a whole army corps in
motion across the sand, under the canopies of dust and amid the yells of the

African drivers, the wheep of the long whips, the squealing of the mules.[5] Here, too, was the Sirdar in person, for Kitchener was the Chief of Staff to the Field-Marshal, Lord Roberts. There might be less glamour about this great army than its predecessors in imperial history. There were no flags or drums as the men pushed their way through the strands of barbed wire that marked the Free State frontier. True to the new style of warfare, the officers carried rifles instead of swords, and Kitchener himself had not even a medal ribbon on his broad chest.

It was the sheer scale of this army that took away one's breath. Roberts and Kitchener had five divisions – about forty thousand men, with one hundred guns, including a whole division of cavalry commanded by Lieutenant-General John French.[6]

It was French's cavalry that, on the heels of the Tigers, led the army into Ramdam. For the first time in the war, a real flying column was available – five thousand cavalry and MI, horsemen enough to out-Boer the Boers. Before they left their base camp at Modder River, Kitchener summoned French and his staff officer, young Douglas Haig. It was their job to relieve Kimberley. They must outflank Cronje's line at Magersfontein. Everything depended on 'surprise'. Kitchener added, somewhat ominously, 'If it fails neither I nor the Field Marshal can tell what the result on the Empire may be.' He stressed that word 'Empire'.[7]

No doubt French understood the nuances. Cecil Rhodes, the man who was in a sense the Empire made flesh, was locked up in Kimberley; and the flesh was weak. There was food enough in Kimberley, yet Rhodes had given Roberts a characteristically reckless ultimatum: make the relief of this town your first priority or I shall surrender it to the Boers.[8]

So this was the cavalry's task: to ride like the wind to Kimberley, to save the town from the Boers and Rhodes from his own worst enemy, himself.

What did General French make of the task? He knew that transport would be the key to success in this war. And he had serious misgivings about Roberts's and Kitchener's transport arrangements. Since Bobs and K had arrived at the Cape they had turned on its head the regimental system of transport and supply by taking it under their own central control. Perhaps they would be proved right by events. French did not think so. He had dug in his heels and kept his own cavalry division's transport safe from Kitchener's grasp.[9]

Now Rhodes's SOS had made a difficult situation worse. To ride like the wind to Kimberley would exact a heavy price from the cavalry: half-rations for the men, horses dropping dead with hunger, heat and exhaustion. This would be the case assuming that the cavalry were ready for the campaign. But his six regular cavalry regiments were not ready. Some of the horses were green after a long voyage from abroad. All of them had suffered a gruelling train journey from Colesberg (where French had been based since November) or from the ports.[10] The state of the irregular horse was still more alarming. Some British regulars had been turned by Roberts into makeshift MI, and they would have been excellent, if only they had had time to learn to ride. The new colonial corps raised at the Cape by Bobs and K was a 'Scallywag Corps', a lot of ruffians. (This did not include Rimington's Tigers, who had been raised much earlier.)

'They disappear the moment a shot is fired or there is a prospect of a fight.' So
Major Haig confided to his sister.[11] And, assuming they arrived in time to save
Kimberley, what would be the price of success? Would that solitary searchlight
beam flashing its SOS from the beleaguered town have wrecked the new phase
of the campaign that had just opened, the long-delayed march to Bloemfontein?

Yet failure to break through the enemy's line was hardly possible. French was
part of an army that outnumbered the Boers by four to one. Methuen had
attacked the line at Magersfontein and nearly broken through. Methuen had had
three brigades; Roberts had five divisions.

The steam-roller rolled into Ramdam–thirty-four thousand white troops
supported by four thousand African drivers – and out across the veld. After
French's cavalry plodded Major-General Charles Tucker's 7th Infantry
Division. Next came Lieutenant-General Thomas Kelly-Kenny's 6th Division.
These were the two new infantry divisions ordered out to the Cape as a result of
Black Week. Finally, there was a newly constituted 9th Division, commanded
by Major-General Sir Henry Colvile. It consisted of the newly landed 19th
Brigade, led by a young brigadier called Smith-Dorrien, and of the original
Highland Brigade that had 'caught pepper' at Magersfontein. (The balance of
Roberts's forty thousand was left to guard the rear including the Guards stuck
with Methuen at the Modder.)[12]

Of all the cheerful men in Roberts's army, the Highlanders were probably the
cheeriest. They had had enough of the Modder. Nine weeks of flies and dust and
muddy water; too hot in the day, too cold at night; and always Magersfontein
Kopje, there across the plain. They had had their fill of Methuen, too. After
Wauchope's death, Major-General Hector MacDonald ('Fighting Mac') had
taken over the brigade. He reported to Roberts the extraordinary, burning
hatred for Methuen. Methuen did not need to be told. He wrote to his wife,
'They will never agree to serve under me again.'[13]

Leaving the leading infantry – Tucker's division – snoring around their
camp-fires at Ramdam, French's cavalry division trotted out towards Kimberley at two o'clock on Monday morning. There was a waning moon. Ahead of
them lay the only two obstacles in the veld: the two rivers themselves, the Riet
and the Modder. Cronje had a force at Magersfontein estimated to be larger than
their own. But the two infantry brigades left behind with Methuen had been
ordered to engage Cronje's attention by launching an artillery barrage. Speed
should carry French's cavalry division safely through. They were taking a wide
détour to the east, tracing an arc about eighty miles long. And they were, after
all, the cream of England's cavalry regiments, with two mounted infantry corps
and seven batteries of horse artillery to complete the flying column.[14]

It was not Cronje that proved the main obstacle to rapid progress, nor the Riet
nor the Modder. The obstacle was the transport arrangements of the infantry –
or their absence. On Monday, the cavalry halted at the Riet, after fording the
river at three places almost without opposition. Their column of baggage mules
then became trapped behind the slower-moving line of Tucker's column of
bullock transport. Roberts had failed to give orders for priority for the cavalry's

baggage, so it did not leave Ramdam till 5.00 p.m. At the Riet, the cavalry's baggage again became hopelessly entangled with Tucker's. On Tuesday, the cavalry could not leave the Riet till ten o'clock in the morning, the worst time of the day for men and horses. Soon, the cavalry was separated from its baggage again. The whole of Wednesday was spent waiting for it on the north bank of the Modder. By Thursday morning, Kelly-Kenny's infantry had caught them up. Finally, at 9.30 a.m., French was free to go. His scouts reported that two parties of Boers, together perhaps one to two thousand men, were holding two ridges at Abon's Dam, about four miles north of the Modder. There were only a few Boers at the end of the rise. French gave the order to charge through the gap.[15]

Sabres and lances sparkled in the sun. For the first and last time in the war, the *arme blanche* of military textbooks flashed like King Arthur's sword. Then French and his cavalry division rode forward at a fast gallop and vanished into a great fog of dust, veiling the distant chimneys and mine wheels of Kimberley.[16]

The same morning found the Field-Marshal twenty miles to the south, in his field HQ, a wagon marked by a red flag, at Waterval Drift, a notch in the deep, broken banks of the Riet River. He was modest-looking, Lord Roberts; when he went out for a ride, people did not at first recognize the little, white-moustached man in anonymous khaki, with a forage cap, and a black band on his arm. Then the red-tabbed staff officers would come up. There would be a mutter of 'Bobs' and someone would call for a cheer.[17] His field HQ was modest, too; just a covered wagon, with a canvas awning attached to one side.[18] Here he sat for hour after hour, writing reports and receiving or despatching telegrams by way of the mobile telegraph line unrolled behind a special cart. Its Morse key was one of the keys to the whole campaign; day or night, it gave him the ear of Lord Lansdowne in London, as its Boer counterpart gave General Cronje the ear of Presidents Kruger and Steyn.

That morning, the line to London was busy and the news was good. How well Roberts played the part that the public expected of him: little Bobs, the pocket Wellington, the magician who had only to wave his field-marshal's baton and victory was assured, and all those humiliations, earned by boobies like Methuen and Gatacre and Buller, would vanish with the dust.[19] In fact, Roberts was both confident and anxious. The invasion of the Free State had been greatly complicated by the need to advance by way of Kimberley. The great flank march to bypass Cronje's trenches at Magersfontein seemed to be working. Apart from a few isolated Boer raiding parties, Cronje's army was reported to be still pinned down by one British brigade, left behind with Methuen at Modder River Station.

The flank march was not, however, working smoothly. Roberts had anticipated that transport and supply would be the main difficulty, and arrangements were indeed chaotic.[20] Besides, Roberts was upset by the news from Natal. Buller's third attempt to relieve White – an attack on Vaal Krantz, a ridge five miles to the east, ten days after the attack on Spion Kop – had ended in a third reverse.[21] Roberts had now ordered him to act 'strictly on the defensive', even if this meant abandoning Ladysmith to its fate, until the results of his own flank march to Bloemfontein led to the withdrawal of the Free State forces in Natal.[22]

There were also serious anxieties for Cape Colony. The Boers had taken advantage of the way he had had to weaken the garrison at Colesberg, in the midlands, in order to strengthen his invasion force. They were now attacking again on that sector, and Milner, as usual, expected the worst.[23]

Still, to say that Roberts was overwhelmed by worries would be to exaggerate. He was usually a level-headed man. 'He knows what he wants to do, and he does it,' said Captain Lord Kerry, whom Roberts had taken the precaution of securing as an extra ADC[24] (it was an extra way of getting the ear of Kerry's father, Lord Lansdowne). He seemed unemotional – or, at any rate, he showed little difficulty in suppressing his emotions at moments of stress. Only once had he collapsed, almost in public – under the weight of grief at poor Freddy's death. It was soon after his ship docked at Cape Town. He found himself talking to Captain Congreve, Freddy's former comrade-in-arms from the Rifle Brigade, the man who had ridden beside him in that heroic attempt to save Colonel Long's guns at Colenso. 'Tell me what happened,' he said to Congreve, and then, to Congreve's horror, the Field-Marshal broke down and wept.[25]

How unthinkable that Kitchener would ever have allowed himself even that moment of weakness. It was the great fascination of Kitchener that he liked to behave as though he had no human emotions to suppress. The face like a bronze idol's, painted with impossibly blue eyes, the moustache like a palm tree. Here was a prodigy that had put his stamp on the new imperialism, as surely as if his figure was stamped on the penny instead of Britannia's; here was an allegorical figure of the imperial virtues – energy, will, virility – sprung to life in super-human form. Of course, this was only the hero's iron mask. But what was behind the mask: more iron? No one could imagine Kitchener, like Wellington, sickened by the sufferings of his own soldiers. He preferred to be thought a monster than to be thought sentimental. He flaunted his indifference to pain: he allowed oriental punishments, like the lopping of hands and legs for trivial offences, to be continued after his conquest of the Sudan, gloated in the desecration of the Mahdi's tomb, ordered the Mahdi's bones to be cast into the Nile; he himself toyed with the skull, and said it might be fun to make it into an inkstand or drinking cup.

At this point, the Mahdi had almost won his revenge. The affair of the Mahdi's skull caused a hullabaloo in England. The row fizzled out, but many people were left with an unpleasant taste in their mouths.[26] There was something altogether too oriental, and too unBritish, about Kitchener. 'Not a very likeable fellow,' said Cromer to Salisbury, with masterly understatement. Could he not be made C-in-C in India or somewhere?

Even Kitchener's intimate friends – and he did have a small circle of men (his 'band of boys') with whom he could relax – were appalled by the callous way he talked. They were also aware of other flaws in his character. In private, he would occasionally give way to outbursts of self-destructive rage.

Throughout his career he suffered agonies of frustration. Strange to say, for someone endowed with such marvellous talents of organization, Kitchener also found it impossible to delegate. He was a maze of contradictions. In his personal habits he was fastidiously clean, his uniform spotless, his moustache oiled and clipped. But his office looked as though it had not been tidied for years. Papers littered every chair and window-sill, and woe betide anyone who tried to tidy the Sirdar's desk; by some magic, the Sirdar knew where everything was kept.[27]

This was the extraordinary man – K of K, a forty-nine-year-old *enfant terrible* – whom Roberts had chosen as his Chief of Staff in South Africa. Politically, it made sense, and political considerations were always uppermost in Roberts's mind. It represented the merger of the 'Indians' with the 'Egyptians', a tactical alliance that would snatch control of the British army and the War Office from Wolseley and his 'Africans'. But what military role was Kitchener to perform? Not that of Chief of Staff, as normally understood: the subordinate who administers the plans and interprets the orders of the C-in-C.[28] Kitchener was hardly someone who could play second fiddle easily. Kitchener would be the right-hand man, and partner. He was to be trouble-shooter, cutting the Gordian knots in the War Office red tape, in his well-known fashion; his demonic energy in organization, coupled with Roberts's nimble strategy, would sweep them both to victory.

Such were the ideas shaping themselves in Roberts's mind, in the harrowing days he had spent in London in December, and in the fortnight on the boat going out to the Cape.[29] The reality had proved somewhat different. History sometimes repeats itself in terms of farce, more often in terms of irony. The irony of Roberts's position was that he had more than once denounced Buller for weakness in abandoning his own strategic plans, feeling the squeeze of circumstances. Now he found himself acting in much the same way when feeling the same squeeze.

The main pressure came, as we have seen, from Rhodes. The strategy on which Roberts had set his heart was to postpone the relief of Kimberley until after the capture of Bloemfontein. He had been determined to break out of the treadmill set by White's blunder in letting himself be locked up at Ladysmith, and Rhodes's folly in getting himself locked up at Kimberley. Roberts wanted to recapture the strategic initiative – strike out at the Free State – as originally planned before the war. By itself, this should relieve the pressure on both Kimberley and Ladysmith, as well as on the frontier areas of Cape Colony, south of the Orange River, threatened by Boer invasion.[30]

He had worked out the details with the foremost British military thinker of the day, Colonel George Henderson, the author of the recent best-seller, *Stonewall Jackson*. Henderson had begged for a job, and Roberts had taken him from his desk at the Staff College and made him Director of Intelligence.

The line of attack was to be a most daring one, worthy of the Confederates' march on Washington. Instead of allowing the lines of railways to dictate strategy – like his plodding predecessors, Methuen and Buller – he had gathered together enough bullock wagons and mule carts to make his whole force independent of the railway for several weeks. His armada would mass at a railhead somewhere on the western railway, north of Orange River Bridge. This was the only bridge across the Orange River that had remained in British hands (as we saw, it had somehow survived the Boer invasions of the previous autumn, and provided the vital link for Methuen's line of railway to the south). From this point, the armada of oxen and mules would launch themselves boldly into the veld. They would strike the midland railway at Springfontein, one hundred miles south of Bloemfontein.[31] It would be a *coup* worthy of Stonewall Jackson himself: to take the Free State capital virtually by surprise, to trap the Boer raiding parties south of the Orange River (after cutting off their main line of supply), as well as helping to relieve Kimberley and Ladysmith.

Surprise was to have been the keynote of this plan. Henderson had achieved prodigies constructing a *ruse de guerre*; he was ably assisted by an intelligence officer, Captain Willy Robertson (later to be the first Englishman ever to rise from the ranks to become field-marshal). The ruse was to persuade the Boers that the point of attack was to be Norval's Pont, the bridge over the Orange River held by the Boers and facing the British garrison at Colesberg. There was a complete security blanket cast over the operations. Only a handful of officers were told the real route of the invasion force: by way of the flank march from the western railway. Bogus telegrams 'in clear' were sent to field commanders and then cancelled in cypher. Rumours were concocted and spread among the camps. Off-the-record briefings were given to a war correspondent who could be relied on to publish confidential information.[32]

Fortunately for Roberts, these ingenious games were largely unsuccessful in drawing the stolid Boers south to defend Norval's Pont. For between 26 and 27 January, Roberts had decided to cancel this daring scheme, and it might have been distinctly awkward to have several thousand extra Boers threatening his line of communications at Colesberg.

The new plan was, in fact, to be what the Boers had expected all along: that Roberts would march to Bloemfontein by way of Kimberley. For a whole series of reasons, Roberts had weakened in his resolve. What weighed most in his mind was Rhodes's begging and bullying. And what tipped the balance was the news of Buller's reverse at Spion Kop, which had reached him on 26 January. In addition, Milner was quaking about a Cape rising. He himself was anxious about his lines of communication, while Cronje remained at Magersfontein. And could they rely on getting water while on a flank march across the open veld?[33] How the pattern had repeated itself! These were the same reasons (apart from the events in Natal) that had decided Buller to abandon his own flank march to Potgieters in December.

It was in his decision not to reinforce Buller in Natal that Roberts took the greatest risk. It was a striking paradox that, of all the reinforcements pouring into South Africa since Warren's 5th Division had joined Buller in early January,

none had gone to Buller, except the drafts to replace casualties. Buller had
double the number of Boers to cope with: twenty-five thousand estimated to be
around Ladysmith, compared with ten thousand around Kimberley – twenty-
five thousand dug in to a series of natural fortresses. Yet Roberts had given
himself a fighting force not only much more mobile than Buller's, but larger by
one quarter: forty thousand compared with thirty thousand.[34] It was the arithmetic of a walk-over – for Roberts's 'grand army'.

Buller protested too late – on 9 February, after his reverse at Vaal Krantz. Not
that protests would have helped, one suspects: Roberts was a ruthless and
formidable man – even to his friends. Buller claimed that he could not relieve
Ladysmith with thirty thousand men. Then he must stay on the defensive, was
Roberts's curt reply.[35] And, *pour encourager les autres*, Roberts proceeded to sack,
or demote, a number of generals: Brabazon, the cavalry commander ('said to be
too old for real work. The fact is he is too fond of comfort'); Babington, one of
French's brigadiers ('so "sticky" that the regiments have lost all their go');[36] his
personal friend, Methuen ('I am resolved that he shall not be entrusted with any
independent command').[37] His choice of the first two victims seems to have
been arbitrary enough; in Babington's case it was said he had been punished
simply as he was a friend of Buller's, and the policy of summary punishment
tended to make commanders more, rather than less, 'sticky'.[38]

Arguably, Roberts kept too many troops for himself and starved Buller and
the army of Natal, who were faced with the harder task. Arguably, Roberts was
hasty in the way he sacked his subordinates. But, in one respect, there can be no
argument about his shortcomings as a general, shortcomings due to impatience.
His sweeping changes in the system of transport and supply were to prove one
of the great blunders of the war.

Strange to say, for the two most famous British soldiers of the period, neither
he nor Kitchener knew much about the working of the British army. They were
both, in a way, outsiders. Bobs, the 'sepoy general', had lived all his army life in
India. Kitchener, the Sirdar, had served so long, in both senses, in the wilderness.
As a result, they did not understand the War Office system of transport and
supply adopted in South Africa: the so-called 'regimental', or decentralized,
system.[39]

The key to this system was that each battalion CO was made responsible
for their day-to-day food supplies, each battalion had a transport officer, and
the system was integrated into the normal army organization. Roberts and
Kitchener shared two crucial misconceptions about the system. They believed
that to allow each battalion its own carts must be extremely wasteful in transport, not realizing that the system had proved quite flexible enough for battalion
transport to be recalled at any time by the superior officer who had overall
charge of transport. Nor had they grasped the existence of the non-regimental
transport, the brigade's supply columns. Apart from the 'first-line' regimental
transport (with ammunition and fighting material), they decided to sweep away
the system completely. Instead, they created a 'general transport' system, an
extraordinary makeshift in which largely untrained transport officers, hustled

into mule-cart and ox-wagon transport companies, were to supply all the different needs of the army.[40]

When a highly technical part of the army system, evolved and refined over a long period, is suddenly replaced in the middle of a war, there is bound to be trouble. And trouble there was. Kitchener, K of K, became known as 'K of Chaos'.[41] The professional transport officers prophesied disaster. They did not have to wait long.

Meanwhile, Roberts was all set to move up to the front. On 6 February the official train, luxuriously equipped as a mobile HQ, was sent ahead to De Aar with the HQ staff but without the Chief or the Sirdar on board. There was fear that there might be an attempt to sabotage the train. Roberts himself seemed calm and self-possessed. 'Preparations well advanced,' he cabled Lansdowne that day. 'First move will probably be made on the 10th. All well and very confident. Inform my wife. Roberts.' He recommended that Kitchener, though junior in the Army List to many of the generals in South Africa, should succeed him as C-in-C if anything happened to him. ('It is unfortunate that there are no men of military genius amongst the senior officers, but I believe this has always been the case. Napoleon experienced this; and Wellington always said that he had not a single General he could trust to act alone.') Then, travelling incognito, the modern Wellington drove to a small station outside Cape Town and took the ordinary mail-train to the north.[42]

He made only one change of policy after reaching the Modder. Originally, he had decided to conceal from Rhodes the news of the march. Kekewich cabled him on 9 February: 'I fear it will be very difficult to resist pressure of large section of public many more days.' This so disturbed Roberts that he decided the same day to allow Rhodes to be told the news that he was marching directly to relieve Kimberley. This should reassure Rhodes and the other faint hearts. He also ordered Kekewich to warn Rhodes of the 'disastrous and humiliating effect of surrendering after so prolonged and glorious a defence'. Later the same day, he told Kekewich that he had full permission to arrest 'any individual, no matter what may be his position', who threatened 'national interests'. In short, his advice was this: if Rhodes tries to put up the white flag, put him in gaol.[43]

By the 15th, Roberts was installed at his field HQ at Waterval Drift on the Riet River, waiting on tenterhooks for the news of French's dash to Kimberley. Early that morning, he rode along with Colvile's (9th) division north-westwards to a second ford, Wegdraai Drift, a few miles downstream. Delays in crossing at Waterval Drift had been so appalling, owing to the steep, broken river banks and the soft, sticky mud, that the supply convoy of two hundred ox wagons, acting as the mobile supply park for the divisions, was left behind on the north bank of the Riet at Waterval Drift for the three thousand oxen to graze and recuperate.[44] About 9.00 a.m., a few hours after he had reached the second ford, Roberts was handed an alarming field telegram; the news threatened the whole future of his expedition.

It was not about French, who had yet to launch his cavalry charge. It was about the ox wagon convoy at Waterval Drift. A Boer raiding party (it was actually led by De Wet, the man who was to prove the outstanding guerrilla leader of the war) had ambushed the convoy and stampeded most of the three thousand oxen. Now the two hundred wagons, nearly a third of the entire transport available to Roberts for the advance to Bloemfontein, were stranded with their African drivers beside the Riet. Their precious loads – biscuits and bully beef, medicines and bandages, without which the army could not fight – were at the mercy of De Wet. To save time, Roberts abandoned the wagons.[45] And what had he gained in return? As we shall see, that one day saved was worth little to Roberts; on the contrary, to delay De Wet for some days at Waterval Drift would have saved him a great deal of anguish. Moreover, Roberts did not, as his admirers later claimed, react to the disaster with the unflinching spirit of a great general.

According to evidence later supplied to the Royal Commission on the war, and not denied (though the witness was not a friendly one, it must be said, for it was Buller), Roberts lost his head momentarily when he heard of the disaster to the convoy. He proposed to abandon the advance, to throw away the chance of catching Cronje and beat a retreat to the railway line.[46] Fortunately, he had a supply officer who saw there was a way out. French had managed to keep his transport safe from Kitchener; it was 'regimental' transport, organized on the old lines. French's divisional supply park could come to the rescue. And so it turned out. French's mule carts made up for part of the lost ox wagons, and other wagons (without animals) were captured from the Boers.[47]

Perhaps this humiliation at Waterval Drift gave Roberts some insight into the difficulties of the new-style war, and softened his attitude to Buller. For after Buller's latest reverse – at Vaal Krantz the previous week – Lansdowne had cabled to Roberts giving him full power to sack Buller if Roberts saw fit.[48] Roberts did not see fit.

And fortune smiled on him once again. A few hours after the news of the disaster to the convoys came the word that French was sweeping towards Kimberley like a torpedo across the veld.

CHAPTER 27

The Siege within the Siege

Kimberley,
9–17 February 1900

'You low, damned, mean cur, Kekewich, you deny me at
your peril.'

Cecil Rhodes to Colonel Kekewich,
10 February 1900

Events had moved swiftly inside as well as outside the gates of Kimberley. That
desperate telegram from Kekewich, suggesting that Rhodes was threatening to
surrender the town, was the climax of the siege within the siege, the four-month
struggle for power between Kekewich and the Colossus.

'Was ever another British commander in a more trying position?' asked Major
O'Meara, the garrison Intelligence Officer.[1] Kekewich's predicament was certainly odd. All very well for Roberts to tell him to take Rhodes and clap him in
irons if he defied him. Who was to enforce this order? As Kekewich replied,
somewhat lamely, in a note to Roberts, 'The key to the military situation here in
one sense is Rhodes, for a large majority of the Town Guardsmen, Kimberley
Light Horse and Volunteers [the improvised colonial garrison] are De Beers
employees.'[2] In short, Rhodes was De Beers and De Beers was Kimberley – or at
any rate, the English-speaking part of Kimberley. How could a handful of
imperial troops arrest half a town? It was the classic problem of the new
imperialism – how to impose the imperial will on a self-governing white colony
– a dilemma reduced by Rhodes's colossal ego to the level of cheap melodrama.

Kekewich found it no laughing matter. True, he thought Rhodes was
bluffing. And here he was surely correct. Bluff was the tactic that had been
Rhodes's making and his undoing; it had launched Jameson on the Raid and led
Chamberlain down the path to war. It was also true that Rhodes, despite his
general recklessness, had been careful never to make the threat to surrender
explicit.

What had happened was this. That Friday, 9 February, the Mayor had called at
Kekewich's HQ near the Kimberley Club and warned him that Rhodes was
planning to hold a public meeting to protest against the delays in relieving the
town. Kekewich warned the Mayor in turn that it would be a suicidal proceeding. There was the actual danger of shellfire. There were also a dangerously large
number of Afrikaners among the population – perhaps ten thousand out of the
twenty thousand white people – and it was reported that some of these had

started a movement to stampede the town into surrender. What could be more calculated to play into the enemy's hands than Rhodes's public meeting?[3]

Rhodes himself called at Kekewich's HQ later that morning. He was in an ugly mood. He told Kekewich that the purpose of the meeting would be to forward the townspeople's views to Lord Roberts. Kekewich told him (as was true enough) that he had already most strongly impressed their views on Lord Roberts, and he officially banned the meeting. Rhodes became violent, and threatened to hold the meeting despite the ban, unless Kekewich revealed within forty-eight hours 'full and definite' information about Lord Roberts's plans. 'Before Kimberley surrenders,' he shouted, 'I will take good care that the English people shall know what I think of all this.' He rushed from the office.[4]

Next day he returned to the attack. A long, bombastic editorial landed on Kekewich's desk; it was in *The Diamond Fields Advertiser*, the local newspaper, owned by Cecil Rhodes. 'Why Kimberley cannot wait', was the impetuous headline. 'How utterly the public and military authorities,' the leader-writer thundered, 'have failed to grasp the claim which Kimberley, by the heroic exertions of its citizens, has established upon the British Empire.... We have stood a siege that is rapidly approaching the duration of the siege of Paris.... Is it unreasonable, when our women and children are being slaughtered, and our buildings fired, to expect something better than that a large British army should remain inactive in the presence of eight or ten thousand peasants?'[5]

It was a characteristic literary production of Rhodes's, crude, egocentric. It was also a flagrant breach of the military censorship. Kekewich ordered the editor to be arrested, only to be told Rhodes had hidden him down one of the mines. Instead, Rhodes himself stormed the HQ and taunted the unfortunate Kekewich with the news: 'You forbade a public meeting, but I have held the meeting all the same; it was attended by the twelve leading citizens of Kimberley.' Rhodes was then shown Roberts's latest tactful messages for him, but still insisted on a long petition, drawn up by the twelve good men, to be sent to Roberts. Kekewich undertook to send a précis of this. At this, Rhodes lost his temper completely. He accused Kekewich of keeping him in the dark about the relief, repeated his now familiar insults against the British army, and finally, clenching his fist, made a rush at Kekewich, shouting in his falsetto voice, 'I know what damned rot your signallers are wasting their time in signalling. You low, damned, mean cur, Kekewich, you deny me at your peril.' Rhodes was a big man, and his clenched fist shot over the shoulders of the Mayor and a staff officer who happened to be standing in front of Kekewich's desk. Kekewich rose to his feet – his face ashen, according to a witness, and his eyes ablaze. Perhaps he would have knocked Rhodes down. But Rhodes suddenly turned tail and made for the door, hastily followed by the Mayor.[6]

At any other time, this would all have been ludicrous. Now it only confirmed Kekewich's feeling that Rhodes had put the whole town in peril. Characteristically, Rhodes took the top-secret news that Roberts was marching directly to Kimberley – handed him in a cable marked 'secret' – and read it aloud to the passers-by from the steps of the Kimberley Club.[7]

There was a real reason for a collapse of the townspeople's morale, which partly explained Rhodes's antics, and the way the reported news of the postponement of the relief had caused such despondency. (And the overwhelming irony of the situation was that Rhodes, who had actually succeeded in diverting Roberts from his plan for first striking at Bloemfontein, had been so long unaware of his own success.) At 11.00 a.m. on Wednesday 7 February, a sinister new sound was heard in all quarters of the town. It was the day when Roberts was stuck in the mail-train from Cape Town, grinding along that narrow-gauge, single-track railway running for six hundred miles through the wilderness of the Great Karoo.

In Kimberley, people had got used to the sound of ordinary shelling. Over seven thousand shells had thumped into its broad, dusty streets from the Boers' gun positions on the slate-green slag-heaps beside Kamfersdam Mine, Carter's Ridge and half a dozen other places. The shells, fired from 9-pounders and 15-pounders, did little or no damage. Either they did not burst, or were smothered by the slag-heaps forming part of the British perimeter. The main result was a cheerful trade in old shell-cases collected by curio hunters. True, it was depressing to be fired at without being able to fire back. The garrison's own artillery had been completely out-ranged. They were 7-pounders, what Rhodes indignantly called 'pop-guns'. Then George Labram, De Beers' enthusiastic American engineer, had succeeded in improvising a 4-inch gun, building it to his own design from a piece of steel shafting in the De Beers workshops. On 19 January, 'Long Cecil', as the gun was christened, first opened his mouth, and out came a 28-pound shell that flew, accurately enough, five miles through the air, smack into the Boer laager by the intermediate pumping station.[8]

Now, that Wednesday, came the Boers' reply to Long Cecil, spoken by their own Creusot 6-inch gun, Long Tom. At eleven o'clock, the officer on watch on the conning-tower saw a puff of smoke by the winding-gear at Kamfersdam Mine, and 90-pound shells began to smash into the town. It was actually Ladysmith's old friend, the Long Tom from Gun Hill, the gun that had been stuffed full of cotton on the night of 8 December by General Hunter and his raiding party, and then apparently blown to smithereens. But he had returned from the dead, his barrel several inches shorter, after extensive repairs in the railway workshops in Pretoria, and a long, roundabout journey to Kimberley.[9] The effect was almost all the Boers could have hoped. There was panic in Kekewich's HQ: the telephone operators, mainly civilians, took to their heels. Several buildings were set on fire. The noise of the explosions deafened Kekewich, and they were followed by an eerie, wailing diminuendo, as the twisted fragments of shell casing cut arcs through the air. Like some of his counterparts at Ladysmith, Kekewich acted at once to take precautions against the blitz. A signaller, posted on the conning tower, waved a flag when he saw the smoke of each shell, and buglers, suitably posted, sounded 'G' ('take cover') on their bugles. People then had fifteen seconds to find shelter in trenches or dugouts, in the slag-heaps or railway cuttings. But Long Tom achieved more in three days than the other six guns had in four months. On Wednesday, there were twenty-two Long Tom shells, and a coloured child was mortally wounded, a civilian wounded; on Thursday, thirty Long Tom shells, and another man dead, with four people and a child injured; on Friday, seventy-four Long Tom shells, and four died, including George Labram, the father of Long Cecil.[10]

Labram had been the life and soul of the siege. His amazing inventions had kept up everyone's spirits: the 155-foot-high conning-tower, the 1400-cubic-foot cold meat plant, the water supply from Wesselton Mine, the home-made shells for the 7-pounders, the charges made from blasting powder, and, finally, Long Cecil – everything was owed to George Labram. He could hardly have been more of a contrast to Rhodes: modest, good-humoured (he would climb the conning-tower most mornings to brighten Kekewich's dreary vigil) – above all, discreet. He had, however, scorned to take shelter. He was killed on Friday evening while dressing for dinner in his room at the Grand Hotel. They pulled him from the wreckage beside the wash-basin; half his head had been blown away, and his chest and thighs were smashed. Hundreds of people turned up at his funeral, held at night to avoid the bombardment. But still the Long Tom shells crashed down, hitting, indiscriminately, private houses, the railway and the hospital.[11]

For many people, it was this night blitz that proved the last straw. In the day, you could at least see where the shells landed. After dark, all the terrifying sounds were magnified: the bugler's alarm call, the boom of the explosion, the wail of the shell splinters. Dr Ashe, the town's Chief Medical Officer, had to leave his shelter and visit some patients. He cowered by a galvanized iron fence as earth and stones rattled all round him, but left him untouched. At the hospital, terrified patients watched a piece of shrapnel smash through one of the outlying wards.[12]

The cumulative strain of the siege had been severe, even though (or even because) so little had occurred during its course. The lack of news, especially news about plans for the relief, intensified the nagging sense, expressed in *The Advertiser*'s hysterical editorial, that their efforts were not appreciated by the outside world. No one is recorded to have signalled 'Are-we-rotters-or-heroes?' like the defenders of Ladysmith, but perhaps the thought was the same.

As at Ladysmith, the most destructive weapons used by the Boers were the classic weapons of a siege: starvation and disease. Soon after Christmas, Kimberley began to 'feel the nip', as Dr Ashe put it. 'At last,' he wrote in his diary on 10 January:

—we have begun to feel the siege a little more acutely. On Monday the people who went for meat were told that they could only take half their allowance in beef; the other half must be taken in horseflesh or else gone without. Lots of people went without.... I brought my chunk of horse home, and that night we had it for dinner. If I had not known what it was, I am sure I should not have known it from beef. It was tender and good for anything, but all the same it took some pushing down.... I guess I am not hungry enough yet.[13]

As a visiting doctor, Ashe had had the foresight (and the money) to stock up his larder in the first weeks of the siege. He still had several months' supply of flour; he sowed seeds of beetroot and sweet corn in his garden, and soon had plenty of vegetables.[14] But for most of the townspeople the siege diet was increasingly poor and monotonous. After Christmas, Kekewich had ordered all the stocks of beef, flour, sugar and so on to be commandeered by the military. Ration cards were issued, meat, bread and vegetables were sold at a fixed rate to long queues of white civilians at the market. (Africans had to queue elsewhere.) Luxuries – like milk, butter, stout, cheese – were only to be issued on production of medical certificates. Predictably, the scale of rations was highest for the garrison and lowest for the blacks: a pound of bread per day, and half a pound of meat, for soldiers; twelve ounces and four ounces respectively for white civilians; barely a pound of mealies for Africans. The white civilians soon lost their sense of delicacy about eating the horses that made up more than a third of the available meat supplies (164,183 pounds of horsemeat, 269,455 pounds of ox meat, and 45,653 pounds of mutton were eaten in the two months after January, according to Kekewich's tally). The siege pinched the Africans worst, as they were not allowed to buy meat or vegetables, even if they could afford to.[15] Infant mortality, fifty per cent among the white population, was catastrophic among the black and brown populations. In the four months between October and mid-February coloured children died at a rate of 93·5 per cent, according to official statistics.[16] Infant mortality was (and is) an accepted part of life in Africa. What gave the siege a more unusual flavour was the deaths by scurvy among the 'mine boys', the ten thousand Africans confined, under a roof of wire-netting, in the Kimberley compounds.

To say that Rhodes deliberately starved his African workers to death would be absurd. That would have been worse than a crime, in Rhodes's eyes; it would have been bad for business. For the mine boys were De Beers' most important asset, apart from the diamonds themselves; without such a vast pool of cheap and regulated black labour, no diamond mine could be worked.

Still, the business-like principles that governed the running of the Kimberley compounds did not allow much room for sentiment. The fact was that the Africans – Zulus, Basutos, Fingos and so on – were starving. They had been recruited for the diamond mines; now they were temporarily redundant. Only a few of them managed to escape, and the only food that the rest were allowed by their employers was a few ounces of mealies. Vegetables grow rapidly in South Africa. The Wesselton mine could supply 250,000 gallons of water a day, and that mile-long avenue of vines planted at Kenilworth, Rhodes's model village, had ripened by early February.[17] Men carried the brimming baskets to the Sanatorium Hotel: grapes, nectarines, peaches for Mr Cecil, a tribute to the great man's ingenuity and unconquerable spirit. Down in the compounds, there were fifteen hundred cases of scurvy, of which a third proved fatal. Starving people lay about under the wire netting, with bloated stomachs – hearing the muted boom of the shells, waiting to die.[18]

There was one thing that the townsfolk had to say for the Boers: here at

Kimberley (though not at Ladysmith) the pious burghers had never believed in fighting on Sunday. Punctually at 11.15 p.m. (11.55 p.m. Transvaal time) came Saturday's final shell. Then Long Tom rested for the sabbath. The townsfolk did not rest. In peacetime, the town had always been such a dreary place on Sunday, for the days of the diamond rush were long over, and Kimberley was highly respectable. That Sunday, 11 February, there was a frantic effort to complete building shell-proof shelters before the shelling began again on Monday. White people found themselves doing heavy labouring work for the first time in their lives, as there were not enough African 'boys' to go round.[19]

Dr Ashe rattled through the town in a Scotch cart, wearing dirty grey flannels and a big Boer hat and sitting on a pile of dirty sacks. He found his fort very 'jolly': a sandbagged shelter, reinforced with huge mine props; seven feet square and seven feet high; furnished with beds, a mirror, a clock and some books; the walls lined with sheets, and decorated with a photograph of Kitchener, pinned to the wall with a big diamond brooch. That was, as he wrote in his diary, a Sunday he would not forget in a hurry: 'Everywhere you went, forts were being built, and the clang of sheet steel, railway rails, and iron railway sleepers etc. was heard all over the place.' People stuffed their sandbags with the first materials that came to hand – coarse kitchen salt for a grocer's fort, flour for a baker's – and an ingenious coolie in the Malay location evicted a dog from a kennel and squatted there, Ashe recorded, 'like a little King in that yard'.[20]

Meanwhile, the other more famous King of Kimberley had not been idle. It was obvious that the two great diamond mines, deep enough to supply the whole world with diamonds, could also provide Kimberley with shelter against Long Tom. Although the mines were not in use, there was still enough coal for the steam-engines that worked the mine lifts and drove the electric dynamos; and as De Beers had not paid too much attention to the order commandeering food supplies, the mines were well supplied with corned beef and condensed milk. That afternoon, notices were posted up in prominent parts of the town, and a cart toured the streets displaying the same text:

SUNDAY.I RECOMMEND.WOMEN AND CHILDREN.

WHO.DESIRE.COMPLETE.SHELTER.TO.PROCEED

TO.KIMBERLEY.AND.DE BEERS SHAFTS.THEY

WILL.BE.LOWERED AT ONCE IN THE MINES

FROM 8 O'CLOCK.THROUGHOUT.THE.NIGHT.

LAMPS.AND GUIDES.WILL.BE PROVIDED.

C. J. RHODES[21]

It was a typical *coup de théâtre* by the great man: spiriting people away to safety in the treasure chests of De Beers. And respond the people did, with only too much alacrity. There had been rumours about the new bombardment to come: two new Long Toms; twenty new Long Toms; anyway, Monday would be a black day. Now it was assumed that Rhodes had had definite information, and a regular panic ensued. Of course, if Rhodes had told Kekewich of his scheme, the panic could have been avoided – and proper sanitary facilities in the mines could have been arranged. As it was, people fled for refuge to the mine heads as though their last hour had come, dragging their children and bundles of bedding. All that evening, from 5.30 till after midnight, the great mine wheels rotated and counter-rotated on the headgear, as the lifts ascended and descended. Down the mine-shafts, the scenes beggared description: two and a half thousand women and children and babies huddled together in the mine galleries, packed so tight, twelve hundred feet below the surface, that it reminded Dr Ashe of a colony of sea-gulls he knew in Lincolnshire; you could not put a foot down there without treading on a young bird.[22]

Up at the Sanatorium Hotel, Rhodes savoured his triumph. True, Monday and Tuesday brought anti-climax in the shape of a very half-hearted bombardment. But Rhodes was now setting the stage for the final scene in the great drama of the siege: the relief. It was to be a transformation scene. Rhodes, whose threats to surrender Kimberley continued to distort the whole strategy of the war, naturally cast himself as hero. Champagne, peaches, and grapes were prepared for a victory banquet in honour of General French and the cavalry division – and, more important still, the war correspondents. Rhodes had always excelled at handling Press men, even when he did not own their newspapers. As for Kekewich, that low, mean cur, Kekewich – Rhodes had not yet finished with him, though it was not to be many weeks before he was saying, 'Kekewich? Who's he? You don't remember the man who cleans your boots.'[23]

The great cavalry charge at Abon Dam that same Thursday, 15 February, had swept across the veld like a torpedo across the sea. It was brilliant; the German military attachés, who later wrote the German official history of the war, hailed it as a master-stroke[24]. But was it not almost too brilliant? To explode, a torpedo must actually hit something; otherwise, it expends itself in vain. French's cavalry galloped on through that immense dust-cloud, spearing a handful of Boers on the way (and losing a handful of their own men); otherwise they did no damage to Cronje's marching troops. Of course, to damage the enemy had not been Roberts's first aim. French's instructions were simply to ride like the wind to save Kimberley. How different the instructions would have been if it had not been for Rhodes. French's five thousand men were Britain's only large mobile force in South Africa, a unique instrument for hunting down a mobile enemy and their not-so-mobile siege guns. Instead, the five thousand had to expend themselves in a magnificent, but quite unnecessary dash to self-destruction across the veld.[25]

The extraordinary fact was that the mere effort of galloping a few miles had been the death of so many British cavalry horses. Their bloated bodies marked the route of French's triumphant swoop: cutting the Boer line at 'Susanna', the Boer redoubt facing Premier Mine, through the barbed-wire fence, and so back into Cape Colony and on towards Kimberley. It was not only that many cavalry horses were still unacclimatized; their masters, too, had yet to learn that they could not gallop across the veld as though hunting with the Quorn; and trained cavalry horses were impossible to replace.[26] So heavy was the toll in dead or exhausted horses, that the cavalry division was virtually destroyed as an effective fighting force.

Meanwhile, Kimberley waited agog for the end of the 124-day ordeal. About lunch time, Long Tom fired his last shell. At 3.30 p.m. a man told Dr Ashe that the cavalry division could be seen from the Beaconsfield slag-heaps. Dr Ashe could not believe it. They confirmed it at the club. Ashe went straight away and bought the largest Union Jack he could get hold of, and hung it out, at the end of a long pole, from the veranda on the second storey. When the vanguard of the relief column finally appeared – the Tigers, and some Scots Greys – there were uninhibited scenes: the ladies almost pulled the first man off his horse – respectable ladies hugging a dust-covered soldier. At the club, people took their freedom more calmly. 'Everybody was far too deeply moved,' said Ashe, 'to be noisy.'[27]

Rhodes, too, was deeply moved – and rather noisier. He held his own private party at the Sanatorium. While Kekewich was arranging for a mounted force to try to capture Long Tom, Rhodes had captured a much more important prize: the ear of General French. Whatever his other defects, Rhodes certainly had a marvellous gift for words. French was a hard-headed soldier, and he must have been told by Roberts that Rhodes's antics had jeopardized the whole strategy of the war. Yet half an hour at Rhodes's party in the hotel was enough to swing French head over heels to Rhodes's side. When Kekewich finally tracked down French at the Sanatorium Hotel, he found a strange scene. One of his staff officers later wrote, 'As we approached the building we heard sounds of merriment and many voices in the hall. . . . Tables were laid in the hall, laden with all manner of luxuries, champagne was flowing freely, and to us, who had seen nothing but the meagre rations . . . for many weeks past, this display of dainties came as a great surprise.'[28]

There were to be more surprises. Kekewich sent a message to say that he wished to report himself officially to French, to ask for instructions. Rhodes happened to be in the hall and pushed forward, shouting, 'You shan't see French; this is my house, get out of it.' (Actually, it was not Rhodes's house but De Beers', like most things in Kimberley.) Kekewich took no notice, went upstairs and saw French alone in a private room. Exactly what took place is not clear. But it was an icy interview. Kekewich was not an articulate man; no doubt he got the worst of it. He was accused of being overbearing and tyrannical towards Rhodes.[29]

Two days later, the seal was set on Rhodes's triumph. When Kekewich arrived at his office at the HQ in Lennox Street, he found his desk occupied. Colonel Porter, the CO of the 1st Cavalry Brigade, had been appointed in his place as garrison commander. Without informing Kekewich of this fact – in effect, that he had sacked Kekewich – French had galloped away on urgent orders from Roberts.[30]

With the raising of the siege, French had redeemed Milner's and Rhodes's original strategic blunder of garrisoning Kimberley. The price to the garrison had not been heavy – apart from the death-rate among young white children and Africans of all ages. The military price of victory had been paid by the relief expeditions: first Methuen's losses, now the destruction of the cavalry division as an effective force. 'A week ago I commanded the best mounted regiment in the British Army,' wrote a cavalry colonel that week, 'and now it is absolutely ruined.'[31] It was the same with other regiments. Throughout the division, the horses were in a pitiful state. The last straw had been French's totally ineffective attempt, on the 16th, to capture the Long Tom.[32]

Still, if ever the truth of Napoleon's dictum, that victory goes to the side that makes the fewer blunders, was confirmed, it was on the following day, 17 February. For the Boers now made a blunder that eclipsed all those on the British side, the fiasco of Lord Roberts's transport arrangements, the loss of the convoy and the ruin of French's cavalry division included.

Kimberley was relieved, De Beers 'indomitable' chairman was happy giving champagne to the Press; and the curtain rose on an utterly changed strategic situation. The advantage implicit in the ever-increasing British superiority in numbers, since the Boers' advance had been checked in mid-November, had at long last been realized. Three months of stone-walling were finished; and over the Free State borders hung those vast dust-clouds, obscuring the sun and the moon, dust-clouds raised by Lord Roberts's invading army.

The overwhelming question that Cronje had to answer was this: where would Roberts strike? And not merely: in what direction? Would Roberts only try to seize enemy territory, or would he try to seize the enemy himself?

Cronje's own strategic role, now that the static blocking campaign had failed, was hazardous, yet full of opportunities. Since the collapse of the British cavalry, he could safely withdraw to the north along the railway towards Mafeking. Alternatively, he could lie in wait for Roberts's ponderous bullock columns, and wage guerrilla war against his communications. Or, third, he could retreat eastwards across the open veld to help block the expected advance on Bloemfontein.[33] But whatever he did, there was one iron law of strategy imprinted on the mind of the Boers, like a law of the wild: the answer to superior numbers is superior mobility; in other words, fight to the last ditch, but, when facing defeat, pick up the ditch and run. And it was this military instinct, making the Boers such a formidable military nation, that Piet Cronje, the fox, paradoxically forgot.

Cronje, at any rate, chose the third, and more risky, strategic option. On the night of 15 February, while Rhodes was giving his great party in Kimberley, and Roberts was making his disastrous decision to abandon the convoy at Waterval Drift, Cronje began his retreat. About five thousand Transvaalers and Free Staters at last uprooted themselves from their earthwork guarding Magersfontein, their home for the previous two and a half months. Both of Cronje's ablest commanders – Generals J. S. Ferreira and De Wet – had objected in principle to the line of retreat Cronje had chosen: eastwards along the wooded banks of the Modder River towards Bloemfontein. De Wet had, of course, already embarked on his guerrilla campaign. Ferreira now rode north across the veld beyond Kimberley, and then hovered there, understandably anxious to see how Cronje fared.[34]

Luck at first remained faithful to Cronje. On the 15th, in brilliant moonlight, his five-mile-long train of bullock wagons passed a few miles to the north of General Kelly-Kenny's 6th Division, encamped on the Modder River at Klip Drift. Incredibly, no one in the 6th Division saw the bullock train.[35] Apart from abandoning some seventy-eight loaded supply wagons (this was a prize for Roberts's half-starved troops), Cronje had stubbornly kept his whole laager with him, and this restricted the pace of his retreat to the pace of the bullock: about ten miles a day.[36] On the 16th Kelly-Kenny's infantry caught up with Cronje's rearguard. However, that night Cronje shook them off, and the ponderous bullock train was alone again in the veld. On the 17th, French's surviving cavalry – the fifteen hundred out of the original five thousand who were still fit for duty –[37] at last intervened. Alerted by Captain Chester Master of The Tigers, they caught up with the van of his column near Paardeberg Drift, about twenty miles north-east of Ramdam.[38]

Cronje was still not in any great danger, provided he kept moving. He could have brushed aside French's pitifully small force – though he was probably unaware that they were a mere fifteen hundred. He could have cut loose from his heavy baggage (and the womenfolk who haunted every laager) and struck northwards to link up with Ferreira. He could have joined hands with De Wet. He did none of these. In a mood of self-destructive inertia, worthy of Sir George White, he halted – as though determined to let Roberts's thirty thousand infantry catch up. Two nights after leaving the great rabbit-warren of trenches at Magersfontein, Cronje's men were once again burrowing into the earth – digging trenches for horses, bullocks, women and all, down in the thirty-foot-deep white sandy banks of the river at Paardeberg.[39]

But the old fox had not found a new earth. He had found a steel noose and put his head in it.

CHAPTER 28

Gone to Earth

Paardeberg,
17–27 February 1900

'We then had a regular fusillade all day and were doing splendidly when Lord K. getting impatient ordered ½ the Cornwalls ... over the river to charge with the Canadians. I was horrified when I saw them moving forward to charge about 3.30 pm as I could see they had not a ghost of a chance ...'

Major-General Horace
Smith-Dorrien's diary
18 February 1900

At midnight on Saturday 17 February, the moon rose, and already De Wet had decided to leave his hiding-place at Koffyfontein. They must do what they could to rescue Cronje and the main force of Boers. The Modder was thirty miles away to the north: nearly a day's ride. The word passed round: up-saddle.[1]

A Boer commando travelled light, light and fast. De Wet's commando moved like a hunting cat on the veld. One minute the men lay there: formless, huddled around the small fires of cow-dung, sipping coffee, or trying to sleep, wrapped up against the cold in their blankets; behind them squatted the African servants of the better-off burghers; ponies picked at the bare veld, hobbled by foreleg and halter. The next minute the raiding party was on the move, bobbing heads under slouch hats, Mausers erect, bandoliers swathed across the men's shoulders, strips of biltong (dried meat) and pouches of flour tied to the saddle-bow. De Wet's commando was not a majestic fighting machine, like a British column. It was a fighting animal, all muscle and bone: in one sense, the most professional combatant of the war.[2]

To look at, *Vecht-Generaal* (Combat-General) Christiaan De Wet was curiously unimpressive and unassuming. He was forty-five, and might have been a country lawyer or a small businessman. There was little to suggest the steel of his character: no vast, black, patriarchal beard like De la Rey's, no chest like a mountain-side. He was short, stocky and wore his beard neatly clipped; a gold watch-chain cut an arc across his tweed waistcoat; he carried a brief-case to hold the heliograms and other military papers. This and his field-glasses were his only concession to a general's uniform. His eyes were his one remarkable feature: brown and very bright – a hunter's eyes.[3]

In fact, De Wet had travelled far and learnt fast in the previous four months. He himself had missed most of the great set-piece battles of the war, as he had been recalled from Natal to reinforce the Free Staters on the western front in early December, and had spent the great days of Black Week cooped up in a railway carriage. But he had seen enough to realize that, quite apart from the blunders of Boer generals like Cronje, the overwhelming numerical superiority of the British now demanded new strategy from the Boers. Indeed, the commando system was best suited not to large-scale, set-piece battles, but to smaller-scale, guerrilla strikes. A smaller group could make better use of their best asset, mobility; and their worst defect, indiscipline, would prove less of a handicap.[4]

De Wet's views, reflecting those of many of the more intelligent younger Boers, had certainly paid off in practice. His hunting bag since Roberts had begun his advance was prodigious. He had half-crippled Roberts by capturing the two hundred wagons at Waterval Drift (and what trophies this raid had produced – 140,000 rations of biscuits, jam, milk, sardines, salmon, corned beef and so on, to be sent on in triumph, together with twenty white prisoners and thirty-six Africans, out of the convoy's four hundred African drivers, to Bloemfontein). He had also captured a second group of Khakis, fifty-eight mounted men.[5] But how could he gather strength enough to help Cronje? He had been joined by only one hundred and fifty extra men at Koffyfontein, Philip Botha's party sent on President Steyn's orders. And he had had to detach a hundred of his own men to escort the captured convoy. So his commando totalled three hundred, a mere pebble in the way of the British steam-roller.

An hour after dawn on Sunday 18 February, they heard the rumble of heavy guns, 'an indescribable thunder', it seemed to De Wet, though they were still fifteen miles away to the south. The worst had happened – or was about to happen. De Wet gave his men and horses only the briefest pause for food.[6] Then they saddled up once again and rode on with the sun on their right cheeks. The heat came early that Sunday; it was the kind of Sunday morning when farmers would sit on the *stoep* reading their Bibles and mopping their brows with their handkerchiefs. The commando rode on. The echo of the guns grew louder and harsher, and the hot dust caked on their lips.

The Modder River, seen from the veld to the south, first appears as a long, meandering line of willows and tamarisks, dark against the sandy plain.[7] At 4.30 p.m., De Wet's commando caught their first sight of the river. They were now about six miles to the east of Paardeberg: 'Horse-Hill', the kopje that had given its name to the ford above Klip Drift. De Wet lifted his field-glasses. He later described the scene:

Immediately in front of us were the buildings and Kraals and there on the opposite bank of the river stood Paardeberg. To the left and right of it were khaki-coloured groups dotted everywhere about.... What a spectacle we saw! All round the laager were the guns of the English, belching forth death and destruction, while from within it at every moment, as each successive shell tore up the ground, there rose a cloud – a dark-red cloud of dust.

It was necessary to act – but how? We decided to make an immediate attack on the nearest of Lord Roberts's troops ... and to seize some ridges which lay about two and a half miles south-east of the laager.

So, while Cronje's circle of covered wagons was attacked on every side, hemmed in by the British just as the voortrekkers had been hemmed in by Dingaan, De Wet's gallant little band rode off to storm the kopje south of the river: three hundred against Kitchener's fifteen thousand.[8]

Eleven hours earlier, Kitchener, too, had gazed out across the river at Cronje's laager. Kitchener had reached a kopje, two miles to the west, a little after dawn.[9] Beside him stood the tall, grey figure of Lieutenant-General Thomas Kelly-Kenny, the commander of the 6th Division.

How peculiarly ill-matched were these two British officers, on whose co-operation a British victory depended. Both were bachelors and both Irish-born – though Kitchener's Irish birth was due merely to the unwelcome accident that his parents had been living in Kerry. Kelly-Kenny was, by contrast, a Catholic, an Irish nationalist of a sort and a Wolseleyite – like his intimate friend, Sir William Butler, the man deposed by Milner for his sympathy with the Boers. Kelly-Kenny did not sympathize with the Boers.[10] Nor did he sympathize with Kitchener. In fact, he found his 'fussiness and interference' intensely irritating. For the last four days, ever since the 6th Division reached the Riet River, Kitchener had been breathing down his neck. 'Who is in command?' asked Kelly-Kenny on Wednesday. 'You,' said Kitchener, and proceeded to infuriate Kelly-Kenny by pressing him to storm some hills without sending scouts ahead.[11] On Saturday, a private message arrived from Roberts to say that Kelly-Kenny was to take anything Kitchener told him 'as an order from Roberts'. Kelly-Kenny found this most humiliating. As a lieutenant-general, he was a step above Kitchener, at least by South African rank, and to the public would still appear to exercise an independent command. But at least this new arrangement cleared up his own doubts as to who was in actual command at Paardeberg. It was Kitchener.[12]

The new arrangement was the result of Roberts himself being detained at Jacobsdal, twenty-five miles downstream. Roberts was laid up with a chill. What was even more humiliating to Kelly-Kenny was the realization that Roberts did not trust him. Clearly Kitchener had been sent along to hustle him. The Commander-in-Chief and his Chief of Staff apparently thought him too slow and cautious. Well, they would see. His own view was that Kitchener was recklessly impatient.[13]

In fact, Kelly-Kenny was no genius, but he had a sensible plan for dealing with Cronje that, if Kitchener had not interfered, would probably have succeeded at very small cost.

His own scheme was to extend a ring around Cronje's laager in order to seal him off from outside help: especially from the commandos known to be hurrying to his rescue, Ferreira's and De Wet's. His own division had marched all night in order to catch up with Cronje, and the men were exhausted.[14] They were also quite unused to the new style of warfare. Except for a few odd skirmishes, they had no first-hand experience of the power of magazine rifles in the hands of entrenched opponents. Moreover, the terrain did not favour an infantry attack. Cronje had let himself be cornered. He was now squeezed between the upper millstone of French's surviving cavalry at Koodoosrand, and the nether millstone of two infantry divisions at Paardeberg. But he had turned his laager on the north bank of the river into a natural fortress. The white, sandy banks of the Modder River up here made just as effective trenches as they had against Methuen at Modder River Station, thirty miles downstream. Cronje's four thousand men had fortified them with their usual ingenuity. They had dug a network of rifle pits for two miles below the circle of wagons and for a mile above it; these connected with flanking trenches constructed from the numerous dry dongas that joined the river at right-angles.[15]

It is not clear how far Kelly-Kenny was aware of these elaborate earthworks. At any rate, his instinct was sound: use the infantry to seal off Cronje; rely on the artillery, for which the terrain was ideal, to bombard Cronje into surrender. He had already begun to extend his force for this purpose, when Kitchener brusquely countermanded the plan. The infantry must storm the laager immediately.[16]

Kitchener's plan, like his attitude to tactics in general, was aggressive and brutally simple. Strike at the heart. That was his instinctive reaction, and he had no second thoughts. He decided to throw all his infantry into the battle before Cronje could bolt – or help could reach him. Kelly-Kenny and most of the 6th Division must launch a frontal attack from the south bank. Meanwhile, Colvile would divide the two brigades of his 9th Division. MacDonald's Highland Brigade would attack upstream from the south bank; Smith-Dorrien's 19th Brigade would ford the Modder at Paardeberg Drift and attack upstream from the north bank, Cronje's side of the river.[17] And to complete the encircling movement, a small force would attack downstream along the north bank. This was to be Hannay's MI (part of the 6th Division), supported by the other two battalions of Stephenson's 18th Brigade, the 1st Welsh and the 1st Essex.[18]

Hold the Boers down with a frontal attack from the plain to the south. Then simultaneously fling a right hook from upstream and a left hook from downstream. This was Kitchener's simple tactical plan. And simply disastrous it was to prove.

To understand both the causes of its failure and the enormity of Kitchener's blunder, one must turn back to the other two major battles of the war involving a river crossing: Methuen's costly success at Modder River in November, and Buller's humiliating reverse at Colenso. In each case, the Generals had tried to force a river crossing in the teeth of an entrenched enemy – and had paid the price. In the new-style war pioneered by the Boers – long-range, smokeless, rapid-firing rifles plus trenches – the balance of advantage, as we have seen, had tilted dramatically to the side of the defenders. New, more subtle methods of attack were needed, as well as greater numerical superiority. It was true that Kitchener could deploy twice as many men and heavy guns against Cronje here as Methuen had had available at Modder River in November. But why attack at all? Cronje showed no sign of budging. De Wet's and Cronje's expected reinforcements comprised only a mere sixteen hundred men, one-twentieth of Kitchener's own three divisions.[19] Unlike Kitchener, Methuen and Buller had not had the good fortune to be able to choose whether to attack or merely invest the enemy. Mistakes they had certainly made in plenty. But both Generals had had exceptionally difficult problems to contend with, and no chance to profit by learning from the mistakes of others. Kitchener displayed no interest in learning from the mistakes of Buller and Methuen. He probably attributed their own failures, as Roberts did, to their own personal defects, especially, in Buller's case, to his own supposed lack of self-confidence.[20] Of the revolution in tactics – of the new, invisible war of the rifle-plus-trench – he showed himself supremely unaware.

Kitchener looked at his watch and turned to his staff officer. 'It is now seven o'clock. We shall be in the laager by half past ten.'[21] He might have been taking a train to Birmingham.

But the days of such short cuts to victory were over, days when a whole war could be won by willpower and rifle power in the space of a few hours. Something more was needed: insight and patience. The same Kitchener who had helped Roberts sweep away Wolseley's transport system when he reached South Africa, now recklessly swept away Kelly-Kenny's tactical plan. To compound his error, Kitchener showed himself quite unable to delegate authority or even to issue coherent written orders. It was one of the oddest traits in the Sirdar's extraordinary character that he abhorred having to write things down.[22] No doubt he was reluctant, like Cecil Rhodes, to let anything – even a letter – come between his subordinates and his own supremely personal authority. At any rate, the battle that now ensued was made especially disastrous by the fog of conflicting orders emanating from Kitchener's HQ.

To some extent, the blame must be shared by Roberts, who had put Kitchener in the embarrassing position of trying to fight a battle without a proper staff to transmit his orders.[23] But Kitchener was not the man to use a staff properly even when he had one. 'No written orders of any sort. Kitchener only sends verbal messages – takes my Staff and my troops on no order or system.'[24] These were Kelly-Kenny's unpublished comments written that black Sunday, and they were to be confirmed, hardly more politely, by General Maurice, the official historian. The study of this battle, Maurice wrote, was 'exceptionally valuable from the obvious results which followed from the very chaos'.[25] In short, Kitchener had well earned his nickname, 'K. of Chaos'.[26] Paardeberg was a study in how not to fight a battle.

At eight o'clock, Kitchener sent a brief, confident cable to Roberts: 'We have stopped the enemy's convoy on the river here. General Kelly-Kenny's Division is holding them to the south, enemy lining the bank of Modder, convoy stationary in our immediate front.' After detailing his plan of attack, he predicted, 'I think it must be a case of complete surrender.'[27]

Already, from Kitchener's viewpoint on the kopje west of the laager,

Kelly-Kenny's frontal attack could be seen to be developing: brown dots, strung out across two miles of absolutely exposed plain, approaching the enemy, invisible in the trees and scrub across the river. Ahead of them the shells of twenty heavy guns – naval 12-pounders, two batteries of field artillery and a howitzer battery – threw up spouts of earth in the laager itself. Soon the covered wagons began to catch fire, and yellow smoke and flames began to rise from exploding ammunition carts.[28]

Down in the plain, Kelly-Kenny's infantry, too, caught sight of Cronje's circle of wagons, and the effect on the troops was electric. It was a week since they had left the railway line, perhaps the longest week in their lives. Half rations (that is, mainly dry biscuits, and sometimes not even that, for days on end); no blankets at night, when the transport broke down, and everyone was soaked to the skin by a thunderstorm. Now they had been marching ever since five o'clock the previous afternoon, marching grimly on without a chance to fill their water bottles, nor any means of knowing where they were going. Then, quite suddenly, as they came over a rise, they saw, only four thousand yards away, that great circle of covered wagons, glinting in the sun. Old Cronje. Cornered. A shiver of excitement passed through the exhausted columns. And the men themselves seemed as keen as Kitchener.[29]

First into the attack were the 1st Welsh and the 1st Essex, sent forward to support the right hook from Colonel O. C. Hannay and the MI upstream of the laager. Both units suffered heavy casualties, pinned down in the plain, with only occasional glimpses of the enemy. Behind these battalions came four more from Kelly-Kenny's 6th Division, charging straight across the plain from the south-west towards the line of trees marking the Modder. The Yorkshire Regiment, advancing by rushes of alternate sections, got within two hundred yards of the river bank, but lost their CO, Lieutenant-Colonel Bowles, and many others in the process. A party of this battalion then tried to ford the river, but found it in flood, and were driven back by a storm of bullets. To their left, two other battalions fared a little better. The West Riding were more extended and found some cover in broken ground. With the Oxfordshire Light Infantry, they succeeded in charging up to the Modder itself, where they captured some outlying trenches held by the Boers on the southern bank. But the commander of the brigade (the 13th), Major-General Charles Knox, was himself wounded. And shortly before noon a message came from Kelly-Kenny himself: on no account attempt to cross the river and storm the laager.[30]

Meanwhile, four battalions of the 9th Division – the Highland Brigade – closed up with the left of the 6th Division. No one was more surprised to see their advance than the 9th Division's commander, General Colvile. His own instinct had been to concentrate both his brigades on Cronje's side of the river and then attack upstream from the west. But Kitchener had ordered off the Highland Brigade for some purpose of his own. Colvile watched them moving across the plain. Then one of his staff pointed out that they had wheeled and were making a frontal attack. Colvile was astonished. But it was too late to recall them. Anyway, it was out of his hands. Presumably Kitchener had ordered this reckless attack. 'One can hardly say,' wrote Colvile, 'the ground was worse for advancing over under fire than that which the Guards had to deal with at the Modder River fight' (Methuen's November battle) 'for that would be imposs-ible to find; but it was certainly as bad, and I never hope to see or read of anything grander than the advance of that thin line across the coverless plain, under a hail of lead from their invisible enemy in the river-banks.'[31]

It was, indeed, the story of Methuen's Battle of the Modder over again: caught by surprise; the endless duel with snipers, flat on the face behind an ant heap, where the flash of a canteen on the hip, or a hand stretched out to scratch an ant bite, could bring instant retribution; all this under an African sun that, as usual, burnt the backs of the Highlanders' legs as raw as meat; and the men lying, tortured with thirst, nailed down a hundred yards behind the cool, dark waters of the Modder.[32]

The Highlanders, who had survived the Battle of Magersfontein, did not this time lose their heads. But that thin line grew 'thinner and thinner,' as Colvile put it, 'and thicker and thicker the brown patches on the grass behind it. What men are able to do, the Highlanders did. . . .'[33] By midday, the attack had petered out. Apart from a few companies of the Seaforths and Black Watch, who had forded the river, MacDonald's brigade was nailed down along the south bank below Knox's brigade; and MacDonald, like Knox, had been taken off wounded to the field hospital.[34]

At one o'clock, Kitchener left the kopje, where he had stood all that morning, and rode over to Colvile's HQ at Signal Hill, about half a mile to the west. What about Colvile's men, Kitchener asked, making a 'more determined assault?' Colvile replied that he had only a handful of fresh troops: the half-battalion of the Cornwall Light Infantry who had been guarding the baggage. The Corn-walls must go at once, said Kitchener. They must ford the river and rush the position with the other brigade of the 9th Division – the 19th Brigade, led by Smith-Dorrien. This was the long-delayed left hook. After Kitchener had ridden off, Colvile told the Cornwalls' CO, Lieutenant-Colonel W. Aldworth, the cheerful news. Aldworth explained that the exhausted men were just about to have their dinners. Postpone the attack till afterwards, said Colvile. At least the poor devils would not have to attack on an empty stomach.[35]

An hour or so later, Kitchener returned to tell Kelly-Kenny that the 6th Division must renew the attack. Relations between the two men had reached a nadir. Kelly-Kenny wrote tersely in his diary:

I was terribly strained . . . the battle lasted all day. Kitchener kept pressing me to press flanks. I did so at great loss. He took away ½ . . . Battn. from Cope [kopje] on my R. flank to support Stevenson [sic], said I could hold it [kopje] . . . . I resisted assault in front, as troops were exhausted and I could not get the Brigade together.[36]

It is clear that Kelly-Kenny successfully resisted Kitchener's attempt to renew the frontal attack. Where he failed was to prevent Kitchener continuing the flank attack – the long-delayed right hook. He had also failed to prevent Kitchener making a new blunder by weakening the British hold on the kopje on his right flank (soon ironically called 'Kitchener's Kopje'). It was this kopje, near Stinkfontein Farm, that was later recognized as the tactical key to the whole position, and Kitchener had offered it to the enemy on a plate.[37]

After Kitchener had gone, Kelly-Kenny rode gloomily down towards the field hospital where both the Brigadiers lay wounded. He was an old man, the oldest man in the army after Roberts himself, and the strain of keeping his temper with Kitchener, coupled with an attack of dysentery (the 'Modders', it was called), had left him in a state of collapse. When he was near the river, one of the Boer pom-poms got the range, and sent a string of 1-pound shells drumming through the white hospital tents. There was a scene of panic: wounded men tried to crawl out of the tents. Kelly-Kenny himself did not visit the hospital that day, perhaps because the sights so appalled him. 'Awfully sad. Poor fellows' legs being amputated,' he wrote in his diary, 'it sickens one with war.'[38]

Meanwhile, Kitchener drafted a note to Colonel Hannay ordering him to launch the right hook at once: 'The time has come for a final effort. All troops have been warned that the laager must be rushed at all costs. Try and carry Stephenson's brigade on with you. But if they cannot go the mounted infantry should do it. Gallop up if necessary and fire into the laager.'[39]

It would be hard to beat this extraordinary note of Kitchener's either for its callous tone or for its reckless misstatement of facts. Kelly-Kenny had, of course, refused to renew the attack. Nor had any of the Brigadiers – Stephenson, MacDonald, Knox, Smith-Dorrien, or their replacements – been 'warned that the laager must be rushed at all costs'. In the event, the note read like the orders of a madman, and it was in this spirit that Colonel Hannay received it. He assumed that he had not time to co-ordinate with General Stephenson, whom he knew to be two miles away. He sent away his staff on various pretexts; then gathered a handful of men – perhaps fifty at most – and they mounted the horses of the MI in the firing-line ahead. 'We are going to charge the laager,' he said quite simply. Then he mounted and galloped forward. For some time he survived the storm of Mauser fire, though many of his men were struck down behind him. His horse fell. Somehow he staggered on, till he, too, fell at last, far out ahead of the firing line, two hundred yards short of the Boer trenches. The left hook had failed, and Hannay had died just as he intended: as a supreme act of protest against the way Kitchener sacrificed his army.[40]

Three miles away, on the north-west side of the laager, Smith-Dorrien, the commander of the 19th Brigade, heard the drumming beat of Mauser fire, in which Hannay cast away his life. It was just before 3.30 p.m. Ever since early that morning, when his brigade had waded waist-high across the Modder at Paardeberg, Smith-Dorrien had been waiting for orders from Kitchener or his staff. No orders came. 'I was in a complete fog as to what was happening,' he later wrote, 'and knew nothing of the situation, either of our own troops or of the Boers, beyond what I could see and infer myself.' Apart from the half-battalion of Cornwalls, under Lieutenant-Colonel Aldworth, left behind to guard the baggage on the south bank of the river, his 19th Brigade had been extended along the north bank as far as a kopje, christened Gun Hill, commanding the laager. From this kopje, the 82nd Field Battery had a perfect field of fire into the lines of wagons and trenches a mile and a half away. Smith-Dorrien found it a 'thrilling sight'. No matter that the brigade was hungry, dirty and unshaven after the ordeal of the last few days, and the Modder was in flood, so that they could get no food or supplies across the river. He made a solemn vow, and the men were told: the General wouldn't shave his beard until they had captured the laager.[41]

At 5.15 p.m. Smith-Dorrien was amazed to see the troops on the right of his line rise up and charge forward, with a ringing cheer, towards the Boer trenches. He knew nothing at the time of Kitchener's orders to Colvile to send the half-battalion of Cornwalls across the river. All he could see was that his battalion of the 1st Royal Canadians had suddenly advanced without his orders. He had not time to try to recall them – nor to co-ordinate the attack with the Shropshires (another of his battalions) and the 82nd Battery at Gun Hill. The wave of attackers rolled forward. Then, like all the attacks all day, the line wavered, paused and vanished. Colonel Aldworth was killed. The gallant charge was gallantly led, Smith-Dorrien noted, but its futility was clear: the right hook had failed, without anyone getting within three hundred yards of the Boer trenches.[42]

It was now an hour from sunset, and even to Kitchener the battle seemed to be over. It was the most severe reverse, judged by the British losses, of any day in the entire war. Casualties totalled 1,270: 24 officers and 279 men killed, 59 officers and 847 men wounded, and 2 officers and 59 men missing.[43] Characteristically, Kitchener reported the reverse to Roberts as though it was a minor victory. 'We did not succeed in getting into the enemy's convoy, though we drove the Boers back a considerable distance along the river bed. The troops are maintaining their position and I hope tomorrow we shall be able to do something more definite. ...'[44]

But was the battle over? Among the bitter wrangles between Kitchener and Kelly-Kenny was the matter of how to defend the kopje immediately south of the Modder – 'Kitchener's Kopje'. It was to this vital kopje, stripped of troops by Kitchener's own orders, that De Wet, with an uncanny instinct for an enemy's weakness, launched his own attack shortly after five o'clock. The timing proved perfect. Kitchener's own attention was concentrated on trying – and failing – to co-ordinate the left hook and the right hook. A handful of irregulars, about one hundred Uitlanders of Kitchener's horse, were holding both the kopje and the farm buildings nearby. They were quite unprepared for an attack. Their horses were stampeded. They themselves surrendered to De Wet with hardly any opposition.[45]

Before dusk, De Wet had completed his extraordinary mission. With only three hundred of his own men, and Commandant Steyn's even smaller detachment, he had snatched the whole south-east ridge line from under the noses of a

British force totalling about fifteen thousand. The kopje itself was the tactical key to Paardeberg. Not only could it make the British position on the south of the river untenable. It could also provide a rescue ladder for Cronje. Try as he would, with artillery and infantry, Kitchener could not force De Wet to release his grip on the kopje.[46]

Darkness came, and with it a scene of utter exhaustion and confusion on the British side. Kitchener decided that the men should entrench where they were. Few units received these orders, and, anyway, the men were desperate after twenty-four hours without food or water. They trickled back to camp.[47] Kelly-Kenny watched the ineffective attempt to recapture Kitchener's Kopje. He had told Kitchener not to remove that half-battalion. This was the result. In the confusion, Kelly-Kenny could not find his own camp, and spent hours wandering on the veld. It was, as he said, an 'awful night', and the worst of it was that it was now open to Cronje to escape.[48]

The night was even more awful for Cronje and his men. Of the four thousand who had taken shelter there in the river bed, comparatively few had been killed or injured by the waves of attacking infantry or the day-long artillery bombardment: the official casualty figures for this whole period were only 100 killed and 250 wounded, although these figures may be too low.[49] The great majority of Cronje's men had been protected by the canyon walls of the Modder, into which they had dug a honeycomb of trenches. Still, the moral destruction was devastating. To stand all day in a fox-hole, while the air screamed and the earth shook with lyddite shells: this was no new experience for them. They had withstood Methuen's bombardment two months before at the Modder and at Magersfontein, like their comrades who had faced Buller at Colenso. But the ordeal had proved far worse at Paardeberg. They had been retreating for three days, hunted down and encircled by a vastly superior force. They were exhausted and demoralized before the battle began. The bombardment had now smashed and burnt their covered wagons – and with them all that many burghers possessed. Worst of all, Kitchener's guns had cut the life-line on which the Boers' fighting strength depended: their horses. Paardeberg, 'Horse Hill' (alias Stinkfontein), had proved the graveyard for most of Cronje's horses, as the river bed, deep as it was, had proved too small to give many of them shelter.[50]

Perhaps it was the sight of the horses, the symbol of their mobility, lying bloated and putrefying on the veld beside the burnt-out wreckage of the wagons, that filled many burghers with despair. Or perhaps they were numbed by the sight of the women – about fifty or so of the Boer *vrouws*, including Cronje's wife, had followed their menfolk on the retreat, but could clearly go no further.

The supreme irony was that, for the menfolk at any rate, De Wet had now restored their life-line. That Sunday night, his guns on Kitchener's Kopje flashed out a message of hope. Here was the escape ladder, a miraculous hand held out by De Wet to Cronje; fresh horses to enable them to ride away and vanish once again into the veld.

But all that Sunday night, and all Monday, De Wet's guns flashed and De Wet's heliograph winked from Kitchener's Kopje, and less than a hundred burghers seized the chance of safety.[51] The rest of the four thousand stayed with Cronje amid the stench of the battlefield. Cronje asked the British for a truce to bury the dead. It was refused. Cronje sent a final message of defiance: 'If you are so uncharitable as to refuse me a truce as requested, then you may do as you please. I shall not surrender alive. Therefore bombard as you please.'[52]

The resoluteness and moral strength of Lord Roberts have been contrasted, countless admirers of his, writing in the last seventy years, with the weakness and vacillation of Sir Redvers Buller.[53] The characters of the two generals were indeed very different. Yet in the agony of the moment, Roberts, too, could give way to impulses he was later to regret. The cock was to crow for him after Paardeberg, as it had crowed for Buller after Colenso.

After resting at Jacobsdal, he reached the scene of the battlefield at ten o'clock on the morning of Monday 19 February. His first impulse was to renew Kitchener's infantry attack.[54] Fortunately for the British, Cronje's request for an armistice intervened; Roberts refused it because Cronje insisted that Roberts lend him British doctors, as he had none to tend his own wounded; the exchange of messages took most of that day.[55] On Tuesday, Roberts decided to renew the attack, as Kitchener demanded. But the other generals, though taunted by Kitchener, were firmly opposed. After inspecting the position himself, Roberts cancelled the plan of attack.[56]

Roberts then swung to the opposite extreme. Perhaps he was shaken by the sight of the British wounded. It was they who had to pay the price of Roberts's and Kitchener's new transport system. Before leaving Cape Town, he had cut the number of regimental ambulance wagons by three-quarters, in order to save transport. So the eight hundred-odd wounded had to be sent from Paardeberg to the railway line in ordinary bullock carts, an agonizing experience.[57] No doubt he was also (like Buller after Colenso) alarmed by the general strategic situation; Milner was crying woe, as usual, about the dangers of a Cape rising. In fact, a small rising had taken place at Prieska.[58] There were also certain cumulative problems – the bad water, the chaos of the transport, the disorganized state of the army – that now seemed to Roberts quite overwhelming. And, of course, there was the shadow cast over everything by Kitchener's Kopje: De Wet's Kopje, as it had in fact become. At any rate, Roberts's nerve failed him.

On Wednesday, he had a confidential talk with Kelly-Kenny and (as Kelly-Kenny wrote in his diary) Roberts 'strongly urged' retirement to Klip Kraal Drift. Kelly-Kenny opposed retirement. But Roberts told him he was to command the rearguard, and he actually went to inspect the positions.[59]

To beat a retreat at that moment, and to let Cronje escape: it would have been one of the great blunders of the war. Fortunately for Roberts, he was saved (as in the similar crisis when he had heard the news of the disaster to the convoy at Waterval Drift) by a sudden twist of events. He was also fortunate in having colleagues loyal enough never to reveal the existence of the plan to retreat, which has not, in fact, been published up till now.[60]

This time it was Cronje and De Wet who saved Roberts. For three days, Cronje's men had stubbornly rejected the ladder outstretched to rescue them. And, for three days, Kitchener had tried to sweep De Wet off that ridge. By Wednesday, De Wet's men could stand no more. Had De Wet guessed at Roberts's loss of nerve, had he had a spy in the British HQ, how different would have been the course of the struggle! But even De Wet's insights had their limits. An hour or two before Roberts was to abandon the hunt, De Wet himself abandoned the kopje.[61] The British army breathed again. All talk of retirement was over.[62]

The following Tuesday, on the nineteenth anniversary of Majuba, General Piet Cronje, with 4,069 Transvaalers and Free Staters (including 150 wounded and 50 women), surrendered to Roberts's overwhelmingly strong army and was led away to captivity.[63] Cronje's blunders had outmatched Kitchener's and Roberts's after all. It was the first great British victory of the war.

CHAPTER 29

The Key Turns

The Tugela Line and Ladysmith,
12–28 February 1900

There once was a general who said:
'If to Ladysmith you would be led
The key's in my pocket
The door I'll unlock it.'
– But he went back to Chieveley instead.

From the diary of Lieutenant Alford,
February 1900

Buller's army had recrossed the Tugela. They were back to Chieveley, back to
Frere – wretched, sweltering Frere. The city of tents sprang up again beside the
khaki water of the Blaauw Krantz River and the wreck of the armoured train,
now grown rusty in the summer rains.[1]

Camp life had its compensations after a fortnight of hard tack and bully beef,
and of sleeping on bare ground. There had been no tents, even for the generals;
and for the men not even a change of underclothes or a chance to take off their
boots.[2] Now there were real army rations, and Zulus did some of the fatigues,
singing the slow chant, 'oom-bang-way' ('too much "oom-bloody-way" about
those fellows,' said a sergeant) as they heaved logs out of ox wagons.[3] Some
sailors of the Naval Brigade, with time on their hands, had decorated the new
armoured train, hiding it in a veil of woolly ropes from the top of the funnel to
the rims of its wheels; it was christened the 'Russian poodle' by the officers,
'Hairy Mary' by the men. But that Monday, 12 February, such jokes tended to
fall rather flat. Two months' bloody fighting. And they were back at the
beginning, back to square one – or worse.[4]

At sunset, three days earlier, a wild-looking procession had stumbled into
Frere. They were nearly two thousand strong, dressed in tattered khaki tunics,
and a strange assortment of hats: helmets, bowlers and tam-o'shanters. They
were the 'body-snatchers': Uitlander refugees and Gandhi's Indians, recruited as
stretcher-bearers. They brought in the last of the wounded: 150 bad cases,
covered in brown blankets, with their special belongings, boots, haversack and
perhaps a pot of jam and a lump of tinned meat, carried in the hood of the
stretchers. Most of the wounded were too shocked, or deeply encased in
bandages, to speak. But sometimes a head would peer out of the hood to look at
its neighbour. 'Fancy *you* here, Tom?' 'Thought you were stiff.' Many men were
delirious. One shouted that he was going to 'chuck it', and promptly rolled off

the stretcher. Another was babbling about the harvest and the great time he was having at home.[5]

These were the latest instalment of the 3,400 casualties the South Natal Field Force had suffered in the last three months.[6] Buller had told his troops after Spion Kop that they had given him 'the key to Ladysmith'. But where had the door led? On 5 February Buller had launched an attack on Vaal Krantz, a ridge of kopjes across the Tugela a few miles east of Spion Kop. The ridge had proved a blind alley; there was no room to drag up artillery to the crest. On the third day of the battle, Buller called a council of war. All his generals agreed that there was nothing for it except to try a new attempt elsewhere. Then Buller, 'the Ferryman', piloted his army for the third time back across the Tugela.[7]

Buller's men would not have been human if their General had not come in for some bitter jokes as they tramped back across the worn wooden chesses of the pontoon bridge. Even at the best of times, an army cherishes its freedom to belly-ache – an army marches, so to speak, on its belly-aches. Now everyone was demoralized.[8] People felt that all those sacrifices had been wasted. But losing faith in Buller did not mean losing appetite for fighting. On 12 February, Buller gave the orders to launch the fourth – and presumably final – attempt to relieve Ladysmith. The men did not need to be urged; they were still 'romping, raving mad to finish this wretched business', in Sergeant Galley's words. As for Buller and the key to Ladysmith, 'I sincerely hope he'll find the door and use it and stop trying to get over the wall.'[9]

The strange bond that Buller, the Devonshire aristocrat, had built up between himself and the common soldiers may have been frayed by mishaps – and mistakes. But when the strain came, the bond still held. They were sorry for themselves; they were also sorry for him. At heart, they believed that Buller had been given a near-impossible task. 'Buller didn't have the men to do the job. ... Lord Roberts took all the men over to the Orange River side.'[10] So the tape-recorded voices of Boer War veterans, anxious to record their loyalty to Buller more than half a century after his death. And Winston Churchill gave his sincere opinion at the time (though he changed it later): 'A great deal is incomprehensible, but it may be safely said that if Sir Redvers cannot relieve Ladysmith with his present force we do not know of any other officer in the British service who would be likely to succeed.'[11]

Among the officers themselves, many disagreed. Already, after Spion Kop, Bron Herbert, *The Times* correspondent, had written home to his father, Buller's cousin, to say that people were losing confidence in Redvers. 'He's splendidly brave and doesn't shrink from accepting the full responsibility for his disasters when as at Colenso they were greatly due to other people. But even General Lyttelton who is looked upon as the soundest brigadier here said to me after Spion Kop: "My faith in Buller is shattered." Don't tell anyone this.'[12]

Herbert had failed to get a single proper interview with Buller and had been taken under the wing of Lyttelton, charming, ambitious, and Buller's leading detractor. Still, Herbert believed that the task given to Buller was impossible.[13] And even Lyttelton agreed that Buller would have needed twice as many troops to have a real chance.[14] Lyttelton's Brigade Major, Henry Wilson (later the famous Field-Marshal), put it this way in his diary after the retreat from Vaal Krantz: 'Poor Sir R.B., it must be bitter work for him, and they won't like it at home, but Buller is right. I am certain in my own mind that if we pushed on here we would probably have to lay down our arms. It's quite impossible with 15,000 men to turn 8, 10 or 12,000 men out of lines and lines of entrenchments. We should have at least 50,000.'[15]

Unfortunately for Buller's reputation, modern writers have dismissed this view of his difficulties, and the fact that, of any British general in the war, it was he who had the hardest task. Modern writers follow the lead of Leo Amery's *The Times History of the War*, weighty, brilliant, but partisan. Amery was an army reformer, a propagandist by his own admission, who had chosen Buller to serve in his narrative as the symbol of all that was most absurd in the unreformed Victorian army. He wrote of Buller's difficulties at the Tugela, 'Almost any reasonably planned attack anywhere along the Tugela would have succeeded if pushed with the least promptitude and resolution' – a breathtaking judgement from a twenty-eight-year-old reporter, who never even witnessed one of Buller's battles, let alone had to take any responsibility in war.[16]

There are few short cuts in war. What was needed now by the British on the Tugela was an answer to the novel and complicated problems posed by Botha's brilliant defensive tactics and strategy. And Buller, grope and fumble as he did, was beginning to find the answer.

Buller was quite cheerful that day, 12 February, as he installed himself again in the station-master's house at Frere, now surrounded by sandbags and equipped with steel plates to screen the windows and *stoep*.[17] His emotions after Vaal Krantz, like his emotions after Colenso, had swiftly run their course. He had cabled Roberts, as we saw, to ask for reinforcements.[18] Roberts had rebuffed him: 'I must therefore request that while maintaining a bold front you will act strictly on the defensive. ... The repeated loss of men on the Tugela river without satisfactory result is that which our small army cannot aim at.'[19] Perhaps the rebuff served as a tonic. At any rate, Buller believed – with reason – that to 'act strictly on the defensive' could be fatal for the Ladysmith garrison. He decided to press on with his fourth attempt by way of Hlangwane, the Boer-held ridge commanding Colenso from the British side of the river.

The new plan sounded simple enough.[20] In fact, it represented a venture, both in terms of geography and tactics, into largely unmapped territory.

The true key to Ladysmith was a new system of offensive warfare: the offensive counterpart to Boer defensive tactics. Buller realized that the old three-act, one-day battle of the past had been killed stone-dead by the combination of the trench and the magazine rifle. To win a modern battle, troops would have to endure a series of interlocking engagements, spread not only over a great number of miles, but over a great number of days, even weeks. New infantry tactics had begun to emerge: better use of ground, more individual initiative, much more skill in taking cover. The artillery's role was being revolutionized;

instead of merely supplying the first act in the three-act drama, the gunners would be in demand, day after day, throwing a creeping barrage ahead of the advancing infantry. Buller was not alone in recognizing the significance of these dramatic innovations in offensive tactics. Hildyard (the Staff College expert), Warren (the sapper), and, above all, the younger artillery commanders like Colonel Parsons, shared Buller's views; indeed, they complained of Buller's caution in putting them into practice. What they all agreed was that the real 'key' to Ladysmith was the tenacity of the British infantry.[21]

In the simple geographical sense, there was not so much a 'key' as a double combination lock, whose first sequence of positions centred on a hill nicknamed 'Monte Cristo', a hill on the British side of the Tugela.

The fact that the river cut a six-mile-long gorge through the hills to the east of Colenso, and so isolated the Boers' left flank on the south bank of the river, had long seemed to offer tempting possibilities. Hlangwane, the first hill south of this gorge, had been attacked, somewhat feebly, by Dundonald's mounted brigade at the Battle of Colenso. Buller had originally rejected the idea of making a serious attack on Hlangwane for two main reasons. First, the country here to the east was quite unlike the open hills to the west: Hlangwane was pitted with ravines and hidden in a maze of mimosa thorns. Second, it was only five hundred feet high, and was itself commanded by a series of tangled, wooded ridges to the east, culminating in the thousand-foot ridge at Monte Cristo.[22]

Then why not attack these eastern ridges in turn?

With hindsight, people later claimed that this had always been the obvious course. The fact was that no one – not even clever young men like Winston Churchill, nor Bron Herbert, nor experienced generals like Lyttelton – pinned much hope on the possibility at the time. It was known that, since the Battle of Colenso, the Boers had greatly strengthened and extended their trench lines here on the east. Lyttelton wrote pessimistically to his wife on the 9th, 'What will be done next? . . . Probably an attack from Chieveley on Hlangwane which will be carried but will lead to nothing.'[23]

Buller's answer was: what other choice was left? They had tried the frontal attack at Colenso. They had tried two flank marches to the west. A flank attack from the east was the final 'forlorn hope', if they were to arrive at Ladysmith before it fell.

They must trust to their immense superiority in heavy guns, and to the new tactical skills of both gunners and infantry, hammering and squeezing out the Boers, step by step, hill by hill; crumpling their line from Hussar Hill to Cingolo, from Cingolo to Monte Cristo, from Monte Cristo to Hlangwane.

It was a ponderous style of fighting – to be made more ponderous by mistakes in the way the plan was executed. But the style itself was indisputably correct: the painful prototype of modern warfare.[24]

Hussar Hill was a brown, grassy wave in the veld, about four miles north of Chieveley; it was named after some of the 13th Hussars who had been surprised there six weeks before, and had lost two men killed.[25] The first step now was an armed reconnaissance. Despite the great improvement in his field intelligence, supplied by Lieutenant-Colonel Arthur Sandbach ('Sandbags') and forty well-paid African agents, Buller was hesitant about the best line of advance.[26] At eight o'clock on Monday 12 February, he sent a group of Dundonald's irregulars, including Lieutenant-Colonel Julian Byng's South African Light Horse, to seize Hussar Hill. He followed himself at midday, stolidly surveyed the country through his telescope, then ordered the whole force back to Chieveley.[27]

These Cape Town volunteers (the Cockyolibirds, alias 'Bingo's Own') included that intrepid young soldier-cum-reporter, Lieutenant Winston Churchill. He rode back in the rearguard with the Colonel, the ground behind them alive with jumping dust; the Mauser bullets fell short. Then Winston saw that the handful of casualties included his own younger brother, Lieutenant John Churchill, who, in a flush of patriotism, had taken ship to South Africa and arrived at the front that morning.[28] ('It seemed as though he had paid his brother's debts,' was John Atkins' comment.[29]) Fortunately, Jack had suffered only a slight wound in the foot. Relieved to have him safely out of harm's way, Winston had him packed off down the line to Durban, where their mother, Lady Randolph had just sailed into the harbour, opportunely enough, in her American-sponsored hospital ship, *Maine*.[30]

During the next seven days, the advance resumed, faltered, resumed. The men gave a ringing cheer at the news, announced on the 16th, that French had relieved Kimberley.[31] The delays were mainly caused by the lack of water and the exceptional heat – 100° in the shade.[32] The men grumbled about the heat, the officers about the delays. Buller, as usual, seemed deaf to his critics: he was going to go at his own pace.[33] On Wednesday 14 February, Hussar Hill was reoccupied after a race to the summit by Dundonald's men. On Thursday, Buller threw his right: pushing up Lyttelton's division crabwise into 'Green Hill', the ridge linking Hussar Hill and Cingolo. Heavy guns were dragged on to Hussar Hill, and soon the white globes of smoke marked the infantry's way forwards, probing the scrub and thorns. There were thirty-four guns on that one small hill, including two new 5-inch Royal Garrison Artillery guns rushed out from England. In all, Buller had fifty heavy guns and field-guns concentrated at the Tugela, compared to the Boers' eight.[34] To give the Boers a sporting chance, one British gunner officer, Major Callwell, took up his seat in a deck-chair beside one of the 5-inch guns.[35] General Warren took a bath out in the open during a Boer bombardment; he emerged, with a towel round his waist, to receive a visit from Buller.[36] The men must have enjoyed seeing these antics. At any rate, by Saturday, the original fingerhold on Hussar Hill had become a firm grip on four miles of tangled ridges east of Colenso: 'a gigantic right arm', in Churchill's phrase, 'its elbow on Hussar Hill, its hand on Cingolo, its fingers, the Irregular Cavalry Brigade, actually behind Cingolo'.[37] Now to grasp Monte Cristo.

Success is comparatively dull, Atkins observed. The struggle for Monte Cristo, on Sunday the 18th, displayed none of the impotent heroism of Colenso or Spion Kop (nor, indeed, of the suicidal attack at Paardeberg that Kitchener was launching the same day, three hundred miles away to the west). Atkins

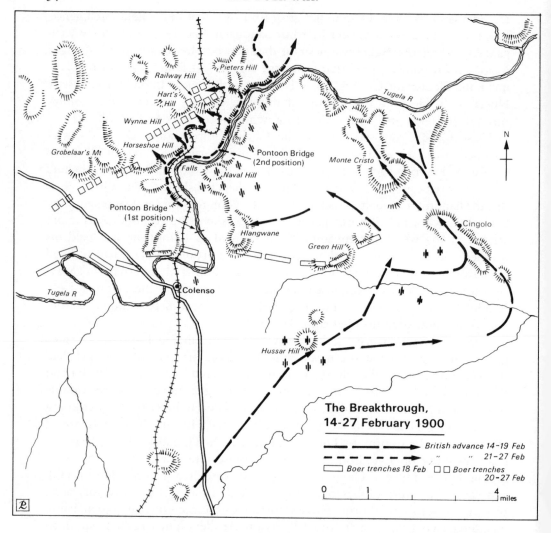

Railway Hill
Pieters Hill
Hart's Hill
Tugela R
Wynne Hill
Horseshoe Hill
Grobelaar's Mt
Pontoon Bridge (2nd position)
Monte Cristo
Falls
Naval Hill
Pontoon Bridge (1st position)
Cingolo
Hlangwane
Green Hill
Tugela R
Colenso
N
Hussar Hill

The Breakthrough,
14-27 February 1900

British advance 14-19 Feb
" 21-27 Feb
Boer trenches 18 Feb Boer trenches 20-27 Feb

0   1   4
                                       miles

observed the battle from the rear. He heard the hated pom-pom. He saw the
'sky-line thickly toothed' with men. It was Hildyard's 2nd Brigade – the West
Yorks, the East Surrey and the Queen's. On the opposite ridge, Green Hill,
Barton's (6th) Fusilier Brigade picked their way over the scarred and pock-
marked ground, to the skirl of the pipes of the Scots Fusiliers. There was a thin
cheer, answered by the men on Monte Cristo. The hill was theirs.[38]

On Monte Cristo itself, success was more eventful. Lieutenant Crossman, in
command of H Company of the leading battalion, the West Yorks, had celebrated his twenty-third birthday that day:

The hill was awfully steep and the top at the centre for about 40 or 50 yards was sheer
cliff. When we were nearing the foot of the hill, Kitchener [the Sirdar's young brother,
now commanding the 5th Brigade in Natal] caught me and said: There are two
of our companies almost at the top. You have got to *catch them* up ... or the Boers will
knock 'em off. ... It was an awful climb. Huge boulders all the way & phit! phit!

of bullets & whizzz-bang-burr as a shell would go over you & down would go a man,
till at last thank God we neared the top. Just as I got up there poor old Berney was shot
clean through the head, & Porch was hit in the head. There we lay for some time blazing
away at the Boers footing it in the distance. . . . Then I moved on to the spot where I got
Gretton & bound him up. . . . The shell that scratched his beak knocked us both head
over heels as I was shaking his paw & congratulating him on getting safe to the top. Poor
old Snakeface! He was wild at being hit and used the most appalling language. . . .
On the way down I stopped to see the last of poor old Berney as they put him in his
grave.[39]

Two days later, Buller himself stood on the summit of that hill, stolidly
surveying tier on tier of hills through his telescope. The capture of these ridges,
culminating in Monte Cristo, had made him master of the south bank of the
Tugela, giving him the whole six-mile arc of ground east of Colenso. Overnight, the Boers had fled across the river, leaving lock, stock and barrel behind
them: pom-pom shells, sacks of flour, Dutch Bibles. The capture of Monte
Cristo on the 18th had turned the trench lines at Hlangwane; the capture of
Hlangwane, on the 19th, and the installation of heavy guns on its summit,
opened the way to Colenso. It was a sound tactical victory – even if Buller,
perhaps mistakenly, did not risk sending his forward troops to cut off the fleeing
Boers.[40] Morale soared. Churchill cabled *The Morning Post* that 'now at last
success was a distinct possibility'.[41] Buller heliographed White. Fifteen battalions of infantry, covered in dirt, their khaki in tatters, loaded with kettles and
firewood for their bivouacs, surged forward, insect-like, over the maze of hills
and valleys that had baffled them so long. It was like a dream.[42] The first part of
that combination lock had sprung open with a clang.

The problem was how to open the second part of the combination lock –
between the Tugela and Ladysmith. On Monday morning 19 February, two
infantry companies marched into Colenso village unopposed, and next day
Thorneycroft's Uitlanders splashed across the Tugela and occupied the kopjes at
Fort Wylie. That evening, the station at Colenso was puffing with trains again.[43]
It was nine weeks since the day of the battle there. The skeletons of Colonel
Long's artillery horses, harnessed together in a *danse macabre*, lay eight hundred
yards from the river-bank. People pointed out the shallow donga, marked by the
thorn-tree, where Freddy Roberts had been dragged, mortally wounded.[44] Of
the Boers there was now no sign, except for the occasional ineffective outburst
of shelling. But if they intended to block further advance, both roads from
Colenso to Ladysmith – the new road to the north-west, the old road to the
north-east alongside the railway line – were heaven-made for the job. They were
dominated by high hills which presented tier on tier of natural defence lines. It
was for this reason that Buller had blurted out to his wife after the Battle of
Colenso, 'I think quite between you and me that I was lucky in not getting in, as
if I had, I would not have known what next to do.'[45]

Why then double back to Colenso, to enter what John Atkins called a
'shell-trap'?[46] Buller's plan, when he left Chieveley on the 14th, was to try
to bypass Colenso.[47] From the summit of Monte Cristo, five miles to the

north-east, he could, at long last, see Ladysmith beckoning to him: it was the patch of gum-trees and tin roofs just to the left of Bulwana.[48] Colonel à Court, one of his staff officers, urged Buller to press on northwards: either by swinging round to the north-east of Monte Cristo or by cutting a way through the great gorge to the north-west.[49] No one could have been more eager to follow one or other of these routes than Buller. But Colonel Sandbach, Buller's Intelligence Officer, and an engineer by training, reconnoitred them and reported both of them to be out of the question.[50] Buller saw no choice but to double back to Colenso.

On the 21st, the sappers floated out the pontoon bridge – the same wood-and-canvas bridge that had already carried the army four times across the river – and anchored it across the swift current where the Tugela turned north to avoid Hlangwane. On the 22nd, the advance resumed. Major-General Arthur Wynne was ordered to take the Lancashire (11th) Brigade and seize the kopjes three miles north of Colenso, and a mile above the falls. The main Boer position was reported by White to be at Pieters Hill, two miles farther north, and beyond Pieters it was downhill all the way to Ladysmith.[51]

Colonel à Court remained unconvinced. 'Three days' more bloody fighting in a hole,' he told Sandbach's subordinate. To Winston Churchill, hunting for a story for *The Morning Post*, he confided the cheerful news: 'It will be like being in the Coliseum and shot at by every row of seats.'[52]

But most people believed that Buller, assisted by Roberts's sweeping success in the Free State, had at last got Botha on the run. Roberts himself cabled to say that 'lots of special trains' were taking the burghers from Natal to the Free State and other parts of the western front.[53] White's staff claimed that *all* the Free State burghers had now left. Hence Sandbach's confident prediction on the 22nd: 'Many men have left the besieging force around Ladysmith; & the Boers have consequently been forced to draw in . . . we shall have one more big battle before we get to Ladysmith.'[54]

One more big battle. Even that had seemed too pessimistic to Buller, as he heliographed cheerfully to White the previous day: 'I am now engaged in pushing my way through by Pieters. I think there is only a rearguard in front of me. The large Boer laager under Bulwana was removed last night. I hope to be with you tomorrow night.'[55]

Relief by tomorrow night. It seemed an impossible dream to the men of the Ladysmith garrison. Despite the series of encouraging heliograms which had reached them from both fronts since mid-February – including copies of Roberts's reports that he had relieved Kimberley and had hemmed in Cronje – there was a stagnant, exhausted air about the garrison. At its heart lay the low spirits of the GOC, Sir George White – 'invisible White', he had been nick-named, because he kept himself hidden away at Convent Ridge.[56]

'The siege has now lasted longer than the siege of Paris . . . fast approaching Troy,' wrote one of the officers. A fortnight earlier, they had celebrated the siege's hundredth day. Next day a Boer heliographer, clearly a cricket fan, signalled from Bulwana: '101 not out.' And back came the signaller of the Manchesters, 'Ladysmith still batting,' quick as the flash of the heliograph.[57]

But most jokes had worn thin, like the garrison itself; the emotions had been rubbed as raw as the backs of the starved horses and mules. For four months they had lived a 'pendulum existence' (to borrow a phrase used by Violet Cecil),[58] swinging from hope to disappointment and back again during each of Buller's attempts to rescue them. 'Buller is a myth,' wrote one man in his diary.[59] 'If he doesn't come soon, there'll be no one to relieve,' wrote several others. Gone were the days when people found the men writing jaunty letters home. 'We have had a very hard time of it,' were the blunt words of Private Steinberg of the 60th, 'very near starving. . . . And hardly any boots or clothes on and what we had was lousy.'[60] Gunner Netley had ceased to fill his notebook with stories about his 'old friend Long Tom'. His diary was now as drab as the life: 'day passed without events' . . . 'stood to arms at 3.30 a.m. . . . all well'.[61] Few of the other men could rise to that. 'The troops are not so cheerful,' said Colonel Rawlinson on 8 February, 'it gives me pain to see their woe-begone faces pinched by want of food. . . .'[62]

The officers, many of whom could afford to supplement the meat and bread ration with expensive luxuries like eggs and potatoes, had only recently begun to feel the pangs of hunger. But they had long felt the pangs of humiliation. Towards Buller, and Buller's army, there was a corresponding bitterness that ebbed and flowed with each of his reverses. 'Most foul news,' wrote Captain Gough of the Rifle Brigade after Spion Kop, 'how on earth men who call themselves Englishmen could allow themselves to be turned off a hill by a pack of Dutch peasants.'[63] 'It is just too absolutely sickening to think of,' said 'Dodo' Jelf of the 60th, 'that all that loss of life and splendid work should have been absolutely chucked away simply because some filthy funking Regt. get the blue panic and runs away. I should think by now their CO has probably been court-martialled and I hope shot for cowardice. . . .'[64]

It was Buller's battle for Spion Kop that had set the pendulum of hope and despair swinging most violently.[65] The chief vantage points of the town – Convent Ridge, Observation Hill, Wagon Hill – commanded a tantalizing view over the shoulders of the surrounding hills, rather like the oblique view from the wings of a stage. The actors at the front of the stage, Buller and his army, were audible but invisible. 'Hear fighting going on,' Gunner Netley wrote on 17 January. 'I suppose it is our relief column fighting its way through.'[66] 'Buller ought to have done great things,' said Captain Steavenson two days later, 'by the noise he has been making with his guns day and night.'[67] On the 23rd, Gunner Netley wrote, 'In the evening we saw our relief column's searchlight about 25 miles away – am every moment expecting relief.'[68] Buller's balloon, circling up from behind Zwart Kop, looked 'hardly bigger than a vulture', according to Nevinson, watching it against the pale blue of the Drakensberg precipices. On the 24th, Nevinson and other correspondents climbed Observation Hill, for the umpteenth time that week, to watch the bombardment of Spion Kop and the ridges on either side. They could see shells bursting among Boer tents at the foot of the hill – not only brown spouts of earth from long-range naval guns, but white puff-balls of shrapnel fire, clearly from British field-guns close behind the ridge. In the afternoon, Nevinson, who had moved to Wagon Hill, saw what he realized were British soldiers – 'a series of black points' in extended formation, creeping up to the summit of Spion Kop.[69] Other correspondents saw still more heart-warming sights: Boers fleeing for their lives, wagon-loads of fugitives, and ambulances loaded with Boer wounded.[70]

Next day there was a strange calm on Spion Kop. It was misty at first; then the sun broke through, but there was no reassuring flash of the heliograph. Through telescopes, people saw those black points again, and this time they seemed to be digging trenches, unopposed. 'We hardly know what to think,' wrote Nevinson. By afternoon the pessimists began to gain strength. And, next day, no one could deny what it all meant. The Boers' white tents were back on Spion Kop.[71]

Buller's reverses at Spion Kop and Vaal Krantz, and White's own pessimism, did, however, have one unexpectedly good result. White decided to abandon the pretence that Ladysmith was a 'field force' – a mobile striking force – and accept that it was a beleaguered garrison. It may seem odd that after a hundred days of siege, White had not accepted this somewhat obvious fact before. But sieges – and defeats – can have an odd effect on people's psychology. White had clung to the idea that he could redeem the disasters of Mournful Monday by some great feat of arms. Hence all the underlying mistakes of the siege such as the failure to extend the perimeter to include Bulwana, and the failure to send away the cavalry. Hence, too, the blunders during the siege: above all, the extraordinary decision to go on feeding cavalry horses with mealies, that could be the largest single source of foodstuff for the garrison.[72]

Rawlinson himself was relieved to learn of this change of heart in his chief on 30 January, psychologically and strategically the turning-point of the whole siege. Rawlinson and General Hunter had always believed that to abandon their sick and wounded and try to cut their way out of Ladysmith would be a reckless and futile act. The chief drew Rawly aside after Buller's third reverse and told him:

He had decided to stop the issue of mealie meal to all horses and to reserve it for the men, that he had settled in his own mind that the next attempt of Buller's at Bulwana [the fourth attempt to relieve Ladysmith] could not be successful and that we should have to stick it out here as long as our provisions lasted – He has given up the idea of the flying column and the mobile artillery – I am very glad he has at last come to the conclusion which to my mind has been palpable from the beginning that Ladysmith must depend on her food and her defences that her garrison must stick to their sick and wounded and that to march out before our guns and Buller's can cross their fires is courting disaster.[73]

White's new policy had two immediate and dramatic effects on the garrison's own food supply. The remaining stock of mealies – the balance of the one million pounds in stock in November – could be used for the men's rations. And most of the horses themselves could be turned into men's rations.[74] Of course, the cavalry brigade set up an outcry: not so much at having to eat their horses as at having to fight on a level with the infantry. But who could deny the compelling arithmetic of these new arrangements? Keep the cavalry brigade, and the garrison would have had to surrender by mid-February. Dismount it, and they could hang on till at least mid-March, perhaps even April.[75]

The garrison munched their tough new rations with enthusiasm. 'We get a capital horse steak every day,' wrote Captain Gough in his diary, 'which I tuck into like the deuce. Have not tasted vegetables of any kind for about two months.'[76] Captain Steavenson actually preferred the new steaks to the previous meat ration: 'Nothing can be as tough as old T.O.' (trek ox).[77] There was not only horse meat on the menu. In the railway workshops, Lieutenant McNalty, Army Service Corps, set up an ingenious factory for making an equestrian version of Bovril, called 'Superior Ladysmith Chevril'. There was a picture of a train with the text 'Iron Horse' on the label, with the still more ominous word, 'Resurgam'. But, pungent as it was, most people managed to keep it down.[78] The mealie bread was no worse than the cast-iron biscuits that were the staple bread-stuff of the siege.

Unfortunately for the garrison, White had decided not only to sacrifice the horses and make mealies available for the men, but to cut the men's rations. By doing so, he could spin out food supplies right into April. The new basic ration consisted of one pound of horse meat, but only half a pound of biscuits or mealie-bread, one ounce of sugar, and $\frac{1}{16}$ ounce of tea.[79] This cast a gloom on everyone. 'They are making preparations,' said Captain Steavenson on 30 January, 'for the food to last 42 days more. This sounds hopeless.'[80]

Morale reached bottom ten days later, when White reduced the ration still further, after Buller's failure at Vaal Krantz. 'We expect to be here for another three weeks,' wrote Steavenson on 10 February, 'then Buller or starvation.'[81] But, of course, there were other cheerful prospects as well as starvation: above all, death by disease.

Typhoid and dysentery, and the other traditional diseases of poor diet and worse hygiene, now did the Boers' work for them. Every week since November, the death-toll from disease had risen, till by January it had reached the rate of ten to twenty a day at Intombi, the British-run hospital camp in no-man's-land beyond D Section of the perimeter. Every day, the hospital trains, carrying white flags, steamed out there with new carriage-loads of victims; and the trains steamed back again empty. Civilians told alarming rumours about Intombi, rumours that it was hard to confirm or deny, as, by the original agreement with Joubert, no civilian was to return once he had left for Intombi. 'I hear that men sleep on sacks placed on the ground. What horrors must be out there!' wrote Gilbert, a local schoolmaster. 'People say there's a big trench and as fast as a person dies he is put in with a little sand sprinkled over him.'[82] A Natal volunteer who had actually returned from Intombi was hardly more reassuring. 'They sent me into a tent in the field hospital where there were forty soldiers and nearly killed me outright. The hospital had been intended for three hundred at first and there were fourteen hundred in it when I was there and fifteen nurses to look after them. Food and medicine were both very short and the sun came through the tent like a ball of fire. The place was a perfect hell on earth. ... What it must be now [15 January] with two thousand out there I dread to think.'[83]

How bad, in fact, were the medical arrangements during the siege? There were three field hospitals, the 11th, 18th and 24th, inside the town of Ladysmith, in addition to the large hospital out at Intombi. The statistics, if nothing else, were excellently looked after. Together, these hospitals handled a total of 10,688 cases – out of 13,500 soldiers – during the four months between November and the end of February; 551 people died of disease in that period.[84] During these latter two months, when the typhoid epidemic raged, conditions were bound to be bad. They also proved much worse than they need have been. Intombi was deliberately starved of medicines and medical comforts. All typhoid patients were supposed to go there. No wonder any sick man who could manage it elected to stay in one of the hospitals in Ladysmith. And, to prevent the Press seeing too much for themselves, it was decided that when a journalist was struck down by fever (as Nevinson was struck down in early February), he should be allowed to stay in the town.[85]

Even in the hospitals *inside* Ladysmith, conditions were needlessly bad. At the centre of this scandal was the man in overall charge of the garrison's health, Colonel Exham, the Principal Medical Officer. There is a very detailed account of the siege, kept by Major Donegan, in charge of the 18th Field Hospital, which fully documents the case against Exham. In January, he had verbally instructed Donegan to cut off *all* medical comforts to the sick men in the 18th Field Hospital: that is, to stop even the pitifully small allowances of sago and arrow-root and brandy that he had been allowed to distribute. Donegan, of course, protested. The order was fantastic. Could he have it in writing? 'You will be removed from charge of your hospital if you ask for orders again,' was Exham's reply. Donegan believed Exham's motives for deliberately starving the men were as follows: 'All he cares about is to have some medicines and medical comforts when the relief column comes in & then pretend he made a most splendid [defence] whereas in reality he is leaving the men [to] starve at present & does not care. As can be seen ... all the P.M.O. cares about is looks and appearances.'[86]

This was one of Exham's odder motives: to be able to display a neat list of stores on hand when the siege ended. At the same time, by cutting off supplies to the soldiers, Exham was able to divert them to his cronies among the civilians, journalists and the more influential officers. Donegan was forced by Exham to 'indent' for pounds of sago and numerous bottles of brandy which were then collected by civilians, although it appeared from the official records that they had actually been used by the 18th Field Hospital.[87]

On 28 January, Donegan had a characteristic exchange with Exham, which he recorded in order to make a formal complaint to a senior officer:

PMO: I have been around your hospital three or four times myself and the place does not look tidy.

Donegan: It's always clean when I go round.

PMO: It's not tidy.

Donegan: You can't expect the place with 40 dysentery cases to be always like a new pin.

PMO: The men's clothes were not in bundles neatly under their beds & their boots anyhow.

Donegan: You really can't expect otherwise.

PMO: Gen. Buller will be here in a day or two & he will look into all these things.

Donegan: He is more likely to ask the men if they get enough to eat.

PMO: They do.

Donegan: You forget, sir, that you ordered me to issue no medical comforts to patients in hospital but to give them to civilians on your chit.[88]

'God almighty!' said Donegan, after one of these interviews. 'We have four doctors for 120 patients scattered over three churches and thirty-six tents, and the PMO only worries whether the men's clothes are neatly folded, or if their boots are in line. Why can't the HQ staff intervene?'[89]

But Sir George White did not even visit the hospitals. Instead, he blamed Hunter, the Chief of Staff, if he tried to make these inspections; he called it trying to usurp his authority. 'Hunter has I am glad to say gone round hospitals this morning,' wrote Rawlinson on 11 February, 'but the chief gets so jealous of him that he hardly dare do much in this way.'[90] Like the PMO, White had retreated into a world of his own during the siege, and that world grew ever more distant from reality. He was still talking of the flying column, although it was now over a month since he had agreed that the horses should be eaten. The men could barely march five miles. No matter. They would march out at the end, with flags flying. If he died, his death would help redeem the humiliations of the siege. He would never be taken prisoner.[91]

Each day that last week of February, Buller's guns sounded closer. Each evening, he heliographed to confirm that, though it was slow going, he was making progress. One by one, the pessimists in the Ladysmith garrison allowed themselves to be convinced – or half-convinced – of the possibility of relief. Among the ordinary soldiers, there was a dramatic change of morale on 22 February, when White restored full rations of bread: one pound of mealie bread or biscuit.[92] As the pendulum swung back for the fourth time, the woe-begone, helpless look that Rawlinson had seen in the soldiers' eyes, began to give way to the wan smile. 'We just lie here,' said one of the starving typhoid patients at Intombi, 'and think of all the good tuck ahead.'[93]

White remained deeply pessimistic, and continued to talk of his flying column. On 27 February – actually the day of Buller's culminating battle – he ordered the men to be put on half-rations once again.[94] He was girding on his sword. the General Gordon of Ladysmith, for the Last Stand.

CHAPTER 30
The Handshake

Across the Tugela,
27 February–15 March 1900

'However even sinners are allowed their relaxation, and I
must confess I did enjoy the getting in here [after] 15 days
fighting with only one check, and 72 hours without a
break was indeed excitement for a combative man, and
the beauty of it was that I felt all through I had got them
this time and was going to win . . .'

Sir Redvers Buller to Sir Arthur
Bigge, 15 March 1900

It was 27 February – Majuba Day. A triumphant clear-the-line telegram from
Roberts to Buller, announcing Cronje's capture.[1] Now for the double.

But how wretchedly slow was Buller's advance. It was already five days since
his brigades had tramped across the pontoon bridge east of Colenso, and begun
to batter their way north-eastwards along the railway corridor between Botha's
ramparts and the Tugela. By the night of the 22nd, Wynne's Lancashire Brigade
had cut out a solid hand-hold on the first pair of green hills, now called
'Horse-Shoe Hill' and 'Wynne's Hill'. Next day, Hart's Irish Brigade had
established a precarious foothold at 'Hart's Hill' in the part of the corridor a mile
farther along. The Boers clung to their line of ramparts. Beyond Hart's Hill, the
last two miles of the corridor to the great Ladysmith plain were barred. It
seemed only too reminiscent of Spion Kop and Vaal Krantz: days of hard
pounding and a position, dearly bought, astride the apparent crest line; then, out
of the mind-battering noise and confusion, one solid, irrefutable fact: the real
crest line was, as usual, still in the hands of the Boers. And somehow there was
never enough elbow-room to exploit the two great British advantages: their
four-to-one superiority in numbers, and their ten-to-one superiority in artillery.[2]

Hart's Hill had given the bloodiest lesson of this sort. The attack was from
across the river, supported by long-range guns, but they were too distant to be
effective. About an hour before dusk on the 23rd, John Atkins saw the thin
brown line of Hart's Irish battalions clambering up, terrace by terrace, rock by
rock, to storm the ridge. Every tooth in the jagged stone trenches on the summit
showed up hard and black in the garish evening light, and from behind the teeth
emerged the enemy. 'And now followed the most frantic battle-piece that I have
ever seen. Night soon snatched it away, but for the time it lasted it was a frenzy, a

nightmare. Boer heads and elbows shot up and down; the defenders were aiming, firing, ducking; and all the trenches danced madly against the sky....'[3]

Atkins, watching through field-glasses from nearly two miles away, could only imagine the frenzy and the nightmare. Lieutenant Henry Jourdain, leading D Company of the Connaught Rangers, was in the thick of it. His account fits into what else we know of the battle. Hart's failure was not only due to the usual basic cause – topography that was unequivocally pro-Boer, and so frustrated the use of British artillery – but also to the usual unfortunate delays, and to Hart's still more characteristic impatience.

'Hart is a dangerous lunatic,' wrote Lyttelton;[4] it was perhaps less of an exaggeration than most of Lyttelton's comments. Hart had continued to play up to his nickname of 'General No-Bobs', refusing to duck his head when shells came over, and deliberately exposing himself to rifle fire as he rode along on his charger. Perhaps this impressed his men. What did not impress them was that, just as at Colenso, they had to march in Aldershot order – in columns of fours – in full view of the enemy's firing-line on the hills. A single shell crashed down on sixteen men of E Company, spraying Jourdain, whose company was just behind, with mud and stones. 'Steady, Rangers, you'll get used to it.' Hart ordered the men to march on with eyes front, leaving seven men smashed and dying at either side of the track.[5]

Jourdain's battalion, the Connaughts, tramped on doggedly behind the Inniskillings along the shot-spattered corridor that led towards Hart's Hill. He was suffering from dysentery, like many of the men, and had had no sleep for two nights; the sun beat down; there were endless hold-ups. The least dangerous course seemed to be to follow a winding path alongside the Tugela, although the water hissed and bubbled with long-range Mauser fire. They passed one spot by the river in which there were six dead Inniskillings, and you had to trudge knee deep in mud with the white faces of these men staring up at you, while the bullets whistled overhead.[6]

A few yards beyond, they had to cross a swollen stream by way of a sixty-foot-long railway bridge. The Boers had got the range exactly. There was a string of pom-pom shells, and Mauser bullets rattled against the iron lattice-work like the hammering of a team of riveters. Eventually, Jourdain's company reached a sheltered hollow below Hart's Hill itself, where they found an abandoned Boer laager. The air was rank with the smell of dead horses and mules, killed by British shell fire, and of two railway trucks loaded with food and (incongruously) fresh trousers for the burghers – tweed trousers made in Britain. But there was no time for food or looting. The Connaughts were late already. Ahead, the helmets of the Inniskillings flickered and vanished as the men clambered up through the slimy red rocks and jungle growth of aloe and mimosa towards the skyline.[7]

Hart had been unable to control his impatience. Those wretched delays, beyond his control, had hamstrung his brigade. The shadows lengthened before the Inniskillings, the first of the six battalions Buller had given him, reached the hollow below the hill. The next two battalions – Connaughts and Dublins –

were still strung out along the valley. The last two, sent along from the 4th Brigade, were hours behind. At the very least, he should have waited for his first three battalions. Hart did not hesitate. He sent up the Inniskillings. After that, he flung the men, company after company, into the firing line, just as they arrived. The result was, of course, a weak attack on a narrow front, and it was now too late for proper artillery support. Instead, Hart offered his own cheerful brand of encouragement, the same kind as at Colenso.[8]

He stood up on one of the hummocks at the foot of the hill, shouting and waving at the battalions. The buglers sounded 'Advance!' – not once, but again and again. To some of the Inniskillings, winded after the stiff climb, it seemed he was taunting them. Then over the skyline they charged. They were four companies. The Boers stood up and fired. They were standing in trenches on the real crestline, 250 yards away across an open grassy plateau, as flat and storm-swept as the summit of Spion Kop.[9]

Jourdain's company reached the skyline just as darkness fell. The second charge was over. Hart apparently insisted that the Inniskillings, with two companies of Connaughts and two companies of Dublins, should try again. It was all the same. The attackers strewed the summit, several hundred dead and wounded in the space of a couple of tennis courts. Jourdain wrote,

> We lay down about 5 yards from the crest [the false crest] but few slept. They were parched with thirst, they had no water and no food ... the bullets kept splashing on the stones around, and exploding in the darkness with small sparks like fireworks. The wounded men in front of the plateau were left to their fate, and many a man got wounded even as much as 6 times during the night. There was a major and a subaltern and two men of the 27th [Inniskillings] in front of me who were badly wounded but we were powerless to give them water, or to take them away, so badly were they wounded. The shrieks of the wounded during the night were awful.... To add to this a Zulu, who had been wounded early in the afternoon, kept up a yell all the night....

Almost more macabre, other people heard Dutch hymns floating across no-man's-land. Once again, the burghers were celebrating their deliverance.[10]

Next morning, the Irish Brigade drifted back to the valley, dazed and humiliated. Some of the men had fled, abandoning their officers. All the wounded were left to their fate on the plateau. The battle had cost them mainly five hundred casualties in less than twenty-four hours; the colonels of both the Dublins and the Inniskillings were dead. In all, the Inniskillings had lost seventy-two per cent of their officers and twenty-seven per cent of their men: the highest proportion of any regiment in the war so far.[11] 'My brave Irish,' said Queen Victoria when she read the war telegrams.[12] And when the telegrams reached London, the wounded still lay, untended, out on the hillside.

Tactically, however, Hart's Hill did not prove a dead-end like Spion Kop. Hart's two missing battalions – the Durham Light Infantry and the Rifle Brigade – turned up in the morning, just in time to prevent a rout. The fresh battalions dug in along the lower ridges.[13] Perhaps Hart's Brigade were only holding on by their eyelids, as à Court said.[14] But they were holding on.

Hart's aim was, predictably, to keep battering on down the corridor. Buller and Warren were convinced there must be a way round. Colonel 'Sandbags', Buller's Chief Intelligence Officer, was sent to take a second look at the beginning of the gorge of the Tugela a mile downstream from the Falls, where 'crossing-point' was marked on the FID blueprint map. Sandbach returned with the advice that he thought the pontoon bridge could be relayed there and a track for the guns hacked out along the line of a narrow African path. At last, the topography had turned pro-British. The shelter of the deep gorge could be used to push up new brigades to the end of the corridor, without running the gauntlet of the Boers' camp located on their ramparts.[15]

By the 27th, Buller's arrangements were complete. The plan was an ingenious, two-handed manoeuvre. (Botha, at any rate, had no inkling at all of what was intended.) The left hand, Lyttelton's division, would maintain its grip on the hills at the lower part of the corridor, pinning the main part of Botha's men to their trenches along this line. The right hand, Warren's division of three brigades, under Barton, would make a three-pronged attack on the upper part of the corridor, protected by the resited artillery. The three hills commanding the upper part of the corridor – Hart's Hill, Railway Hill, and Pieters Hill – were now to be attacked in reverse order, and from the east, thus outflanking the Boer line.[16]

Meanwhile, on Sunday 25th, a six-hour armistice had at last put an end to the nightmare of the wounded British soldiers trapped in no-man's-land on the flat plateaux above the corridor. On Wynne's Hill they had been lying there for three nights and two days without food or water; on Hart's Hill, for two nights and a day. On Saturday, it rained and perhaps it was as well it did. But when the sun came out again, it was British artillery searching for Boers, not British stretcher-bearers searching for wounded, that had combed the brown hillsides. When help came, many were beyond it.[17]

From his eyrie by Naval Hill, John Atkins had watched some of the luckier ones: men who had fallen on the nearer hillsides. He wondered which of those limp, yellow heaps were dead men and which alive. Then one of the heaps began to crawl, urging itself on its back with hands and feet, towards the valley below. It took the man from morning to night to do it.[18] Winston Churchill, nearby with the SALH, saw similar scenes. They reminded him of the wounded after Kitchener's triumph at Omdurman, when thousands of Sudanese had been left untended, wriggling and kicking in the sand.[19]

To abandon white men to such a fate went against the grain for both Boers and British. On the night of the 24th, Buller had first learnt of the men's plight, and had arranged an armistice with Botha.[20] Up there on Wynne's Hill and Hart's Hill, a strange silence prevailed, the first kind of peace for five days and nights. Then, about eleven o'clock, the white flags rose shakily above both lines of trenches, and an eerie day of fraternization began.

No one could remember anything like it. Nearly half a century of 'uncivilized wars' (Omdurman and all its bitter little colonial predecessors) had intervened since a British army, at the Crimea, had last enjoyed such civilities, reaching out into no-man's-land to shake the enemy's hand. And this time, the experience had an extra depth. Who *were* these men who had beaten back the cream of the British infantry? For four months, the British had been fighting an enemy so invisible that many had never yet seen a Boer, alive or dead.

Lieutenant-Colonel E. O. F. Hamilton, CO of the Queen's, now led the procession from the British side, halting in the precise centre of no-man's-land under his white flag. The officers of the Queen's and Devonshires behind him tried to look nonchalant. (Lieutenant Grant wrote later, 'From the airy and easy demeanour that dreadful plateau might have been a London club.'[21]) The privates stood awkwardly in a neat row, folding their arms across their chests and staring across the grassy plateau, dominated by the great whale-back of Grobelaar's Kloof. The dead stared back: uncouth, angular, bloated, tumbled about the rocks, bodies twisted, faces blackened by sun and rain.

Johnny Boer at last – Brother Boer. Out of the shell-torn earth the burghers came, straightening their backs (Grant: 'Like a gamekeeper straightening his back from the cramp of setting his traps in a weasel run') and glancing warily from side to side.[22] To Lieutenant Claud Lafone, they looked a 'rum-looking lot'. There were old men with flowing, tobacco-stained beards, middle-aged men with beards burnt black by sun and sweat, clean-shaven young men with homely Dutch features, the broad nose and the strong chin. Their clothes, too, comprised the homely muddle of a peasant's wardrobe – tweeds of all sizes and colours, homespun and 'shoddy'. By contrast, their leader (it was actually Commandant Trichardt) dressed like a dandy and talked like a gentleman. He wore a kind of uniform – a khaki suit, studded with silver buttons and silver stars – and bewailed, with comic exaggeration, the loss of his boots and hairbrushes when the British had overrun Monte Cristo.[23]

The other Boers at first maintained a sullen reserve. Then Grant managed to strike up a conversation with one old oak-tree of a man:

Grant: Good morning!
Oak-tree: Gumorghen.
Grant (after a pause): Surely we can be friends for five minutes?
Oak-tree (with sudden beaming smile): *Why* not indeed! *Why* not, officer! Have you any tobacco?

It was Grant's magic pouch of Goldflake – for the Boers a shortage of tobacco was a kind of famine – that loosened the Boers' tongues. They crowded round Grant, as he distributed a fill for half-a-dozen pipes. Soon the scene became animated. Characteristically, the British officers felt it was natural for them to play the part of hosts. Lafone took out his camera, and four of the Boers self-consciously posed for a snapshot. A young Boer insisted on shaking hands, although he spoke no English. Grant at length popped the overwhelming question: 'Aren't you fellows sick of this?' Bluntly came the reply: 'Of course, we don't like it any more than you do, but three years, yes! three years we will stay out and fight!'[24]

Meanwhile, the mutilated bodies of about eighty dead, and three survivors, were carried off on stretchers. Also the tall figure of Lyttelton, the divisional general in command of this sector, had appeared on the hillside. It was a Boer who put to Lyttelton the same question that Grant had asked.

Boer: How long do you think the war will last?
Lyttelton: That depends on you. We'll go on for as long as you like. In fact, I think it'll be a long business. (Jokingly) I'm sending for my wife and children.
Boer (gloomily – he did not realize Lyttelton was joking): I thought it was nearly over.
Lyttelton: It's only just beginning. We don't care how long it goes on. Fighting is our business. We've nothing else to do. But it's rather rough on you.
Boer (with feeling): Yes, it's rather rough on us.[25]

Tobacco exchanged. A handshake across the gulf. But no meeting of minds.

The armistice ended at sunset. At first, each side felt an instinctive diffidence about resuming hostilities. There were no shots till about 10.00 p.m. Then, as Lafone put it, 'we were blazing away at each other like fun' – fun that was to last until Majuba Day.[26]

Majuba Day, and the supreme effort. Victory. It was hard to believe – not least for Buller. 'My dearest,' Buller wrote four days later to his wife,

It has all seemed to me like a dream. Every day some new complications to meet and every day the same roar of guns and rattle of musketry, with alas, every day the long list of killed and wounded, which is what I cannot bear. However I thought that if I got in it would cost me 3000 men, and I hope I have done it under 2000 which is something. . . . I must say the men were grand, they meant to do it and it was a real pleasure to command them. . . . I wish you could have seen my fight of the 27th. It was intensely interesting and it is only a country like this that you can stand 3000 yds off & see a whole battle. There was a moment that I thought it was touch and go, but it was only a moment.
Dearest from your rather pleased R.[27]

Buller's uneasy moment must have been about 2 p.m. on the 27th when Barton's Fusilier Brigade – the first of the three brigades ordered to attack in turn from east to west – seemed to falter astride the spiky walls of the Pieters plateau. Earlier, he had watched them tramp off across the pontoon bridge and vanish down the great gorge to the right, among the jungle growth of aloes and the towering red cliffs and the splintered boulders jostling in the Tugela. Soon after midday, they reappeared as black dots two miles away on the first kopje of the Pieters plateau.[28]

As at Cingolo and Monte Cristo, he had outmanoeuvred Botha, who had left his flank at Pieters hardly defended, apparently because he thought the country was too rugged for Buller to attempt to cross the Tugela and turn his flank.[29] Moreover, from a long, high, bony platform across the river, Buller's artillery could cover the attack with converging fire. For the first time, Colonel Parsons's gunners could fully exploit Buller's revolutionary new tactic for co-ordinating artillery and infantry: to send, skimming over the heads of the creeping infantry, a creeping curtain of shell fire. Only a hundred yards ahead of them, the hillside foamed and thundered with rocks and earth and flying steel. While, on their side of the curtain, the sun still shone and the butterflies glittered on the rocks.[30]

But once Barton's brigade were actually astride Pieters plateau, Parsons's gunners were too far away and too low to cover them. The Boers began to recover themselves. Botha, recognizing the danger to the whole line if the British turned his flank at Pieters, had in fact desperately thrown reinforcements into the breach.[31] At 2.30 p.m., Barton sent forward a company of Scots Fusiliers and part of his reserve battalion – two companies of the Dublins – to storm the Boer strong-point on the northern kopje of Pieters. They were beaten back into the rocks, with severe casualties. Meanwhile, the Boers on the next hill, a mile away to the west – Railway Hill, the third hill along the railway corridor – poured a violent cross-fire into them with impunity.[32]

But not for long. At about three o'clock, small brown dots began to emerge on the rocks and scree of Railway Hill. It was Walter Kitchener's brigade – and the turning-point. Four days earlier, when Hart's brigade had tried to storm Hart's Hill from the west, Railway Hill had proved impregnable. Now Walter Kitchener's men, the West Yorkshires and South Lancashires (previously commanded by General Wynne), attacking from the Pieters side, gradually squirmed and wriggled their way up the series of terraces. To John Atkins, watching from below, it seemed the critical moment. How were they to cross that ghastly open hillside? 'And then came the most extraordinary revolution, sudden, astounding, brilliant, almost incomprehensible. Across the railway the South Lancashires suddenly rose up out of the ground, stones rose up too, and turned out to be infantrymen ... and all began to run, not in stiff lines, but with the graceful spreading of a bird's wings straight up the hill.... I watched, stricken with admiration and suspense.'[33]

Closer to, it was a stabbing, jabbing, flailing bayonet charge that won the nek of ground between Railway Hill and Hart's Hill to the west.[34] It also made the novel acquisition of some Boer prisoners: forty men, the first real bag of enemy prisoners since Elandslaagte four months earlier. Some had been wounded by bayonet thrusts. They came tumbling out of their trenches, waving white flags, anything – a shirt or a towel. Atkins met one of the captors, who answered, when asked if he had hurt the man, 'Oh, no. I bayoneted him as gently as I could. And I gave him water, too; he had more than I did. Ah, I told him he was a lucky man to fall across *me*.'[35]

Winston Churchill, with the SALH, was waiting impatiently for the order for the mounted troops to charge. He saw the glorious moment when Kitchener's three infantry battalions – West Yorkshires, Royal Lancasters and so on – spilt over the whole grassy summit with cheer after cheer. Then he saw the prisoners come past. 'Only forty-eight, sir,' said a private soldier, 'and there wouldn't have been so many if the officers hadn't stopped us from giving them the bayonet. I never saw such cowards in my life; shoot at you till you come up to them, and then beg for mercy. I'd teach 'em.' But the Tommy, having got this off his chest, felt generous. He fed his prisoners with bully beef, and took his own water-bottle to give them all a good drink.

Churchill was puzzled by the contrast between the violent words and the generous acts. Then he himself looked at the prisoners: forty-eight – about the same number as the British prisoners at the time of the armoured train disaster – and such ordinary men. What a puzzling contrast between these men, chattering and grinning like loafers outside a public house, and the terrible foe they had represented in the trenches an hour or two before.[36]

Meanwhile, Norcott's 4th Brigade had fanned out in the third and final phase of the attack. The eastern positions in the Boer line – the trenches in the front of Pieters and Railway Hills – had fallen in turn like skittles. Now for the storming of Hart's Hill. From their grandstand seats across the river, the HQ staff and correspondents saw the last gallant moments of Botha's four-month-long defence of his trench lines. The 4·7-inch naval guns had redoubled their efforts.[37] 'The shell bursts seemed almost continuous,' wrote Captain Limpus, of HMS *Terrible*, 'lyddite and shrapnel throwing up earth and stones at each trench. The bombardment was now terrible, especially at a little mischievous entrenched kopje near the top of the nek; several times the Boers had to be brought back by a determined man who seemed to be in charge, until at last he himself disappeared in a great Lyddite shell-burst – and that trench was silenced.'[38]

Other parties of Boers were deliberately spared by the British guns – but not for long. Major Weldon, Wolseley's ADC, who had somehow wangled his way out to South Africa, described the scene in a letter to Wolseley's daughter:

The enemy made a most gallant 'Last Stand'. A large number had gone into a deep trench running right across this valley & had lined a big stone wall which they had erected & which ran over the sharp summit of the hill. They could not well get·out of these trenches without exposing themselves to a merciless fire from our guns – so our gunners left them alone till our attack was beginning to develop in order to get as many as possible into the 'hot corner' (as a keeper drives his pheasants up to the edge of a wood before flushing them). . . . Our men . . . were near enough to advance by rushes & then the real grim fighting began . . . the Lyddite played on the doomed trenches with *fearful* effect – No one could live under such a fire but still some of the enemy kept on firing. At last a tremendous cheer rose up as our men ran forward with bayonets at the charge. . . .[39]

As the Boers melted away, British cheers echoed backwards and forwards across the canyon walls of the Tugela. The key had found the lock at last. Pieters Hill (enough of it, at any rate) – Railway Hill – Hart's Hill. The three last notches of the combination lock had dropped into place. Something extraordinary had happened – something 'better than feast or couch', Churchill romantically called it, 'for which we had hungered and longed through many weary weeks, which had been thrice forbidden us, and which was all the more splendid since it had been so long delayed – victory'.[40] The wave of cheering lapped against Buller's staff, who took off their helmets and cheered and shook each other's hands, as merry as schoolboys. They had done it at last.[41]

Buller stood there, paradise regained. 'It has all seemed like a dream.'[42]

* * * * * *

In Ladysmith, the pendulum swung across with a dazzling suddenness, and people were dazed by the shock of relief.[43]

The 28th dawned cloudy and empty. There was no rumble of guns and no heliograph from Buller. It was the kind of day when the boredom lay like lead on everyone's backs. No one dreamt that this, the 118th day of the siege, was to be the last. Gunner Netley's battery stood to arms as usual. Colonel Rawlinson was glad not to have to go to Caesar's Camp to see if there was any sign of Buller; his eyes were hurting after days of futile peering through the telescope.[44]

Before midday, the sun emerged, a garish sun, advancing the claustrophobic rim of hills even closer to the edge of the town. Donald MacDonald, *The Argus* correspondent, glanced out of the window to the east and half-curiously picked up the binoculars to study the green hills in the direction of Zululand. There was something odd about the view that morning. 'Look there! What do you make of it?' 'It's a trek ... a great trek. They're retreating at last.'

Through the binoculars it was plainly visible: a long silver snake of retreating wagons, white canvas covers flashing in the sun, strangely uniform in colour and build for anything belonging to the Boers, yet unquestionably Boer. MacDonald climbed Maiden Castle to see the view to the west. His hand trembled and he could not hold the binoculars steady. But there was no doubt. It *was* the great trek – a five-mile train of wagons. And not wagons only, but riders – 'galloping black-coated horsemen moving forward in groups of twenty, fifty, a hundred, a continuous living stream ... coming into view round the corner of End Hill, sweeping away in a long curve, and disappearing northward behind Telegraph Hill' towards the railway station. 'They went their way and they went fast.' MacDonald was a colonial, an Australian, and he admired the Boers' undisciplined speed. 'In any other army it would have been evidence not merely of defeat but demoralization. But we knew the Boer way ... [to go] rapidly and effectively; that is why pursuit is such a hopeless thing. ... Their retreat was as masterly a thing as their desperate clinging to the hills of the Tugela ... The one thing, the great thing, was that they were going.'[45]

Of course, it was frustrating to see the Boers go free – under the noses of Ladysmith guns. 'Look yonder,' said one of the Gordons at Maiden Castle, 'look yonder, mon; ain't they rinnin'! Aye, it's a pity we canna get at them.' If only the field artillery gun teams, or the cavalry, could have galloped out to try to stop them. But most of the cavalry horses had been eaten, and the men would have fallen down after a few miles from sheer exhaustion. The 12-pounder naval guns did their best, and their best only hammered the veld hundreds of yards short of the target.[46]

At Sir George White's HQ in the convent, the news of the sudden stream of fleeing Boers was greeted with the same mixture of nervous enthusiasm and frustration. At 1.00 p.m. they received a triumphant telegram from Buller: 'I beat the enemy thoroughly yesterday and am sending my cavalry ... to ascertain where they have gone to. I believe the enemy to be in full retreat.' If only they could have joined in themselves.[47]

Even Bulwana Tom had taken his final bow before his admirers in Ladysmith.

'The naval boys,' wrote Gunner Netley cheerfully (though envious of their longer-range guns), 'gave Long Tom a warm time of it as the Boers were trying to remove him.'[48] A wooden derrick, shaped like a giant letter A, loomed up in Tom's sand-bagged gun emplacement. The moment had come for which the gunners from the *Powerful* had hoarded the last of their 4·7-inch ammunition. Lady Anne let fly from Caesar's Camp (she had been moved there, once again, in the hopes of covering Buller's advance). Bloody Mary thundered from Cove Redoubt. The giant letter A vanished in a curtain of smoke. But no one could say if Tom himself had been hit. Then there appeared one of those operatic African thunderstorms, which always seemed to coincide with Ladysmith's climactic days, and the whole of Bulwana vanished behind the curtain.[49]

It was soon after the rain had stopped that the relief column itself came in sight. Rawlinson spotted it first about five o'clock: two squadrons of mounted infantry, totalling about 120 men, plodding along on tired horses, winding over the low ridge to the east of Bulwana and down and into the plain by Intombi. Colonel Royston's Natal Volunteers were sent out to meet them, and Sir George White prepared himself for the ordeal of the relief.[50]

Meanwhile, the incredible news was spreading, carried by a thin ripple of cheering from the direction of Intombi. People began to run down through the streets of the town, shouting and pushing, black men, brown men, white men, forgetting caste and colour. MacDonald was sitting at dinner, about to eat horse stew. He heard the rush of feet, then one sentence clearly above the uproar: 'Buller's cavalry are in sight; they are coming across the flats.' He dashed into the street. The last of the evening sun caught the little column of khaki as the horses jogged along towards the Klip River bridge at the edge of the town. The horses were fat and well, and so were the riders. They *were* Buller's men.[51]

Nevinson, still groggy after a fortnight's fever, had driven up to King's Post to see the tail-end of the great trek. On his way back, he found that Ladysmith had gone wild. All the world was running. He followed as best he could. Already the pavements were lined with soldiers off duty, officers, townsfolk, Zulus and doolie-bearers – all yelling and cheering like lunatics. The two strange-looking squadrons clattered up the street, and paused opposite the gaol (where the few unfortunate Boer prisoners had been kept). Sir George White and his staff appeared.[52] Then the junction of the two armies was sealed in a handshake: Ladysmith's pale, thin hand reaching out to grasp the bronzed and battle-hardened hand of the rescuer.

The most famous eye-witness descriptions of this meeting, the most dramatic moment, perhaps, from a British point of view, of the whole war, come from the pen of Winston Churchill: 'It was not until evening', he wrote in *My Early Life*:

that two squadrons of the SALH [actually ILH and Carbineers] were allowed to brush through the crumbling rear-guard, and ride into Ladysmith. I rode with these two squadrons, and galloped across the scrub-dotted plain, fired at only by a couple of Boer guns. Suddenly from the brushwood up rose gaunt figures waving hands of welcome. On we pressed, and at the head of a battered street of tin-roofed houses met Sir George

White on horse-back, faultlessly attired. Then we all rode together into the long
beleaguered, almost starved-out, Ladysmith. It was a thrilling moment.

I dined with the Headquarters that night. . . .[53]

In fact, despite the eye-witness description, Lieutenant Winston Churchill
was not there to witness the meeting of Sir George White and his rescuers, who
were led by Lieutenant-Colonel Gough. It was just about six o'clock and there
was still some daylight. Mr Churchill, *The Morning Post*'s special correspondent,
might be inside Ladysmith. Lieutenant Churchill, of the SALH, was still miles
away – galloping across the veld, miles in the rear, with the commander of the
2nd Mounted Brigade, Lord Dundonald, Major William Birdwood and the
orderlies. They did not arrive till all was darkness, and the public celebrations
were over – not till eight o'clock, according to Gough.[54]

The real meeting between Gough's column and White had a quality of pathos
that is missing from Churchill's imaginative account. 'Poor old man,' said
Rawlinson about the Chief, 'he has quite broken down.'[55] Other people had
noticed the way White now looked ten years older than the trim, taut soldier
of his official photograph; a stooped, patient, almost pathetic figure, walking,
cane in hand, through the streets of Ladysmith. He had known that many of
the garrison mocked him and protested at his own inertia and feebleness.
Now, when the cheers echoed round him, his emotions were too much to
bear.

His voice broke as he tried to thank the cheering, yelling mob. He began
almost inaudibly, then, in firmer tones: 'Thank God we kept the flag flying.' He
faltered again: 'It cut me to the heart . . . to reduce your rations as I did.' Another
long, agonizing silence, and it looked as though White would break down
completely. He squeezed out a wan smile. 'I promise you, though, that I'll never
do it again.' Everyone laughed and cheered. Relief was, in every sense, the word.
The crowd melted away into the night. But the flag, that White had kept flying –
the Union Jack on the tall pole outside his HQ – the flag flew no longer. The
emotions of the relief had proved stronger than the cotton it was made of.
Forgetting themselves completely, some officers had gathered round the pole,
pulled down the flag, and ripped it into shreds, each shred a curio for the
button-hole.[56]

Nevinson watched the wild scenes, still only half able to comprehend that the
118-day siege was over. The new arrivals had found billets in the other ILH's
squadron's camp – alas, empty enough because of their exceptionally heavy
casualties. 'To right and left the squadrons wheeled, amid greetings and laughter
and endless delight. By eight o'clock the street was almost clear, and there was
nothing to show how great a change had befallen us.'[57]

The ordeal of the relief was still not complete. Three days later, it was arranged
that Buller should lead a ceremonial march-past through the town, and his two
divisions accordingly tramped through the streets from 11.30 a.m. to 1.45 p.m..
Rawlinson was immensely impressed by the sight of Buller's strange, tatter-
demalion army:

I never heard the troops cheer like they did when they passed Sir George White today – they waved their helmets in the air and simply yelled, such magnificent men, too, full of reservists of course, making our poor garrison look mere boys – their clothes are tattered and torn of course, for it is now 18 days since they changed them – their khaki is split and torn to pieces, some of them hardly decent – many of them have got hold of Boer trousers of various shades of blue and brown to protect their nether ends – they carry no cooking pots but are all cooking in their mess tins ... most of the men carried a little bundle of dry sticks to cook their dinner with when they reach camp....[58]

Rawlinson was the man who had actually first proposed the march-past; White took up the idea; Buller agreed, though reluctantly.[59] Perhaps he had sensed the curiously mixed reactions to the first meeting.[60] Some of White's force did not conceal their resentment at the slowness of the relief. 'The garrison,' wrote Lieutenant Alford, 'seemed half inclined to be angry with us for taking so long....'[61] John Atkins, too, received that impression, and was struck by the coolness displayed by the garrison towards their rescuers. It seemed as though, after the sudden frenzy of delight, when Gough's two squadrons had ridden in, that Ladysmith had relapsed into a kind of emotional exhaustion. Atkins overheard the greeting of one general to another. 'Well, how have you been getting on?' 'All right, thanks.' A long silence, that Atkins found reassuringly British.[62]

Some of the relief column, too, regarded the victory parade as a cheap stunt, and an insult to both relieved and relievers. Lieutenant Grant found it 'un-British and undignified': it was 'infamous stage management'.[63] Colonel Sim called it 'one of the most mournful pageants that could have been devised by idiotic Generals'.[64] Warren himself wrote years later, 'I cannot even now bear to think of it, the march of 20,000 healthy men triumphant and victorious, through the ranks of the weary and emaciated garrison, who were expected to cheer us and who actually tried to do so – it was an ordeal for me and many others.'[65]

Paradoxically, other officers in the relief column were surprised – and even resentful – of how *fit* the garrison looked. Fleet-Surgeon Lilly, of HMS *Terrible*, fresh from meeting the long-lost men from HMS *Powerful*, said, 'We all thought the garrison looked more robust than we had expected.'[66] Major (later Field-Marshal) Henry Wilson, who had reached the town on 1 March, wrote, 'The relief is an accomplished fact. It all seems so curious. I was struck by how well most of the men looked. Rawly told me they could have held out for another month. It appears they were practically not under rifle fire, and only under big gun fire which did little damage....'[67]

To suggest that Ladysmith was not, after all, at its last gasp – this was hardly tactful to the garrison, true though it was. And it was on this issue and others that, as soon as the victory pageant was over, all the submerged mutual resentment between White and Buller finally broke surface.

Buller had himself ridden into Ladysmith on 1 March, the morning after Gough's squadrons had made their dramatic entry. White met him in the street, a moment of history that passed quite unnoticed, and conducted him back to the HQ at Convent Ridge.[68] There followed a small banquet: champagne, and trek ox, no doubt, hoarded for a special occasion. Unfortunately, Buller made some kind of tactless remark about the abundance of the food – or so White believed. One of White's staff reported a few days later: 'Buller himself arrived and made himself as unpleasant as he could. We had saved up a few stores . . . and used up everything giving him a good lunch. The ungrateful ruffian now goes about saying that the Ladysmith garrison lived like fighting cocks and that stories of hardships are all nonsense.'

White's bitterness towards Buller, and the furious resentment of White's confidant, Ian Hamilton, were fanned by the wave of anti-Buller stories that now reached them from Buller's own army. Lyttelton, whom Buller himself trusted, arrived at White's HQ on 6 March 'full of abuse of Buller', according to Rawlinson. And it was not only Lyttelton who abused the C-in-C. One of Buller's own staff – presumably Colonel à Court, whose feelings had clearly been wounded by Buller's bluntness in rejecting his advice after Monte Cristo – launched into a tirade against Buller's errors as a field commander. 'He [Buller] seems to work everything off his own bat,' wrote Rawlinson after one of these tirades, 'never even telling his staff what he is going to do, hence there is often chaos in his staff. . . .' Still, Rawlinson had to be fair to Buller. He was not the only man to have enemies. 'The Divl. leaders [Lyttelton, Warren, and Clery] all crab each other and they say that in the whole force they have not a brigadier worth a damn – the fact is that they are all at loggerheads.'[69]

Generals, like poets, are an angry race. And here in Natal, the moment the enemy was beaten, the real battle began: among Buller's generals. Buller, himself, was partly to blame. His *grand seigneurial* manner, his brusqueness, his habit of not explaining himself to the outer circle of his staff: these were all dangerous flaws in a commander-in-chief – even though their source, in Buller's case, was a kind of shyness. Those he knew well (his personal staff, his ADCs, and Colonel Stopford, the Military Secretary) were all devoted to him.[70] Colonel Sandbach, his Intelligence Officer, wrote of him in March, 'Whatever may be said as to the gallant defence of Ladysmith . . . it will be Buller who will stand out before Europe as the man who . . . [saved] the honour of England from the disgrace of a surrender of 10,000 men to the Boers.'[71] Regimental officers echoed the tribute.[72]

And the ordinary rank and file of his army also revelled in old Buller's success. 'General Buller has had a hard task,' wrote Corporal Hurley, of the 3rd 60th, to his sister at home, three days after the victory parade, 'the hardest of any, and if people at home find any fault with him it is because they are ignorant of the country, the enemy and their positions. All the men under Buller's command . . . would go through fire and water for him.'[73]

As for Buller himself, it was his poor bloody infantry's moment of triumph, and he delighted in it. To his wife he wrote on the day of the victory parade, 'I am filled with admiration for the British soldier, really the manner in which the men have worked, fought and endured has been something more than human. . . .'[74] To the men themselves he paid the compliment of a Special Army Order, beginning, 'Soldiers of Natal! The relief of Ladysmith unites two forces, both of which have, during the last few months, striven with conspicuous gallantry and splendid determination to maintain the honour of their Queen and Country.'[75] Queen and country echoed the congratulations. A shower of telegrams poured into his HQ: from the Queen, from Lansdowne, from Roberts, from friends and enemies alike. It was indeed like a dream. And with what depth of feeling Buller looked back on his ordeal: 'However it is all over and well over thank God.'[76]

For the moment, it seemed that Buller was right. The squabbles among his own generals seemed to have fizzled out. The Roberts faction among the Ladysmith garrison – Ian Hamilton, Rawlinson, and so on – were called away by Roberts to serve with him on the western front.[77] White went down with fever, a few days after the relief.[78] The two Natal armies soon looked hardly recognizable: after the Ladysmith garrison had had a fortnight's bread and potatoes, and the relief column had been given new seats to their trousers.[79]

Meanwhile, Botha's and Joubert's armies had dug in along the line of the Biggarsberg range, sixty miles to the north, between Dundee and Ladysmith. Buller was anxious to press on. On 7 March he cabled to Roberts that he believed he could turn the Biggarsberg line by attacking the Drakensberg passes on the Free State frontier to the west. In three weeks, the Ladysmith garrison would be fit. Could he have permission to continue the advance?[80]

Poor Buller, the most humiliating defeat of his life was still ahead of him. The Boers were no longer to give him great trouble. On the contrary, an unbroken record of successes in the field against the Boers stretched ahead. But, against Buller himself, the campaign was only beginning.

The vanguard was led by Ian Hamilton: brilliant, excitable, vindictive, burning from his own humiliations in Ladysmith (it was Hamilton's rashness that was partly responsible for White letting himself be locked up there; it was Hamilton's failure to fortify Caesar's Camp and Wagon Hill that had nearly led to disaster). He told Roberts, writing from Maritzburg, on his way to join his old chief, 'Buller was very rude to Sir George and spoke to him in the vilest way of you and Kitchener, whom he appears to dislike and to attribute dishonest motives to, almost as much as he does you....'[81]

He denounced Buller to Spenser Wilkinson, the military correspondent of *The Morning Post*, and a leading imperialist writer on military questions. (Significantly, Wilkinson was on intimate terms with Milner and Roberts, and no doubt shared their fundamental distrust of Buller as supposedly 'pro-Boer'.)[82] What Hamilton wrote to Wilkinson was almost ludicrously violent in tone; in fact, Hamilton had fever at the time. He gave a grossly distorted text of the telegram White had received from Buller after Colenso: 'After the battle he wired us that we had better fire off our ammo and make the best terms we could. We thought at first our cypher and helio must have fallen into the hands of the Boers, it seemed so incredible the Great Buller of all men could be giving such unworthy advice.'[83] In fact, of course, the real text of Buller's 'surrender' telegram to White was that it would take him a month to relieve them, and *if* he could not hold out a month, then White would have to make terms *or* cut his way out.[84]

Ian Hamilton's tirade contained another remarkable passage:

I want you to know sharp, *Buller is no use*. He is indeed far, *far* worse than useless, and I write to beg you to use all your influence to get the man recalled before he does more mischief . . . generally officers and men have lost all confidence in Sir Reverse as they call him. I should think 100 of his army have been in to see me since I have been ill and from General to Subaltern they agree that he is as unsatisfactory as a general could be . . . except in the case of the Colenso fight, everyone is confident that the Battalions could in every case have fought their way through all right had they been given their heads. . . .[85]

A fortnight later, Hamilton reached Cape Town where doubtless he met Leo Amery, *The Times* chief correspondent, and talked to him in the same wild, vindictive spirit. It was heaven-sent ammunition enough for the generation of young imperialists who yearned to find one simple explanation for Britain's humiliations '*Buller is no use*'. 'Buller ordered Ladysmith to surrender.' A whispering campaign was launched in the imperialist Press, brilliantly orchestrated by Leo Amery, and tacitly encouraged by Roberts and Lansdowne.[86] This Press campaign was to culminate in Buller's dismissal from the army, a year after his return to England. And the idea that Buller was the main cause of defeat has passed into permanent currency through the medium of *The Times History of the War*, edited by Amery.[87]

All this lay in the future. At the time, it was Sir George White whose reputation seemed to have found the proverbial graveyard in South Africa. Roberts, a personal friend of White's from Indian days, refused to employ White in any responsible position because of his original strategic blunder. Buller offered him a division in Natal, a sad come-down for the man who had commanded a field force. White's illness came as a relief to everyone. He went down to Durban with Rawlinson, and was invalided home.[88]

As the two men took the train down the line to Durban, past all the battlefields where Buller's men lay buried – past Hart's Hill, where the Irish Brigade had lost five hundred men; past Colenso, where the skeletons of Long's battery horses lay bleached in the sun – a sudden, astonishing change of heart occurred in Rawlinson. A week before, he had remarked, at the sight of Buller's men at the victory parade, 'After seeing them it is to me astounding that they did not get through before.'[89] Now he saw, from an open railway truck, some of the physical difficulties Buller had to contend with: the boulders and the precipices, the thorn-covered mountain-sides, everything that went to make up the extraordinary natural strength of Botha's line on the north side of the Tugela.

Rawlinson was at heart a fair-minded man, as well as one of the most able of all Roberts's admirers. Perhaps he was ashamed at the way Buller was being made the scapegoat for the set-backs. At any rate, he wrote in his diary that night, '*Most* interesting – it was marvellous they got through at all . . .'[90]

CHAPTER 31

The Plague of Bloemfontein

The Orange Free State,
13–28 March 1900

Who recalls the noontide and the funerals through the
    market,
    (Blanket-hidden bodies, flagless, followed by the flies?)
And the footsore firing-party, and the dust and stench and
    staleness,
    And the faces of the Sisters and the glory in their eyes?

Rudyard Kipling *Dirge of Dead Sisters*

'Far more people have been killed by negligence in our
hospitals than by Boer bullets ... Men are dying by
hundreds who could easily be saved ...'

Lady Edward (Violet) Cecil to the
Prime Minister 30 May 1900

'Bloemfontein is a pretty little place,' wrote one of Rimington's Tigers, 'but it takes you by surprise.'[1] And its fall, too, took everyone – not least Lord Roberts – by surprise.

The place, a capital city of four thousand souls (including African souls), emerged more or less out of nowhere. Coming from Kimberley, you could follow the victors' trail, blazed by great, empty biscuit tins, letters from home, and dead or dying horses,[2] across a hundred miles of brown, grassy, undulating void. Nothing else but the odd whitewashed farmhouse, with its muddy dam, and two or three Lombardy poplars like tall, lonely chimneys. Then, all of a sudden, below some flat-roofed kopjes, a crowd of red-brick, tin-topped, colonial-style bungalows, with white chrysanthemums, tended by African servants – so many black and white stripes across the front gardens. There was a duty market square; the Flemish gables of a British insurance office and the Indian-looking balconies of the English Club; and the tall, cool, Ionic columns of the Raadzaal (Parliament Building) and the Railway Bureau. Without warning, you had ridden into the heart of the enemy's capital.[3]

The fall of Bloemfontein occurred equally without warning on the morning of 13 March. Where were the Boer armies? They had fled, vanished like a mirage in the veld. Those men who fought so stubbornly to hold their trenches in British territory around Kimberley, abandoned the trenches around their own capital without even an apology for a fight. The result was something of an anticlimax. Roberts did not complain.

The previous evening, President Steyn had fled northwards by one of the last trains to get away before the British blew up the line. At midnight, Roberts heard that French and the cavalry division had seized the flat-topped kopjes south of the African location, and the tactical key to the town. At eight o'clock, Roberts and his staff breakfasted at the country estate belonging to Steyn's brother, whose wife served them with fresh milk and butter to supplement the good things on the HQ mess cart. One of the Press Corps then rode up with some news. In reply to a threat by Roberts to bombard the city, the Mayor, the *Landrost* (magistrate) and other worthies – including Mr Gordon Fraser, the English-speaking South African who had stood against Steyn at the last election – had already surrendered.[4] They were now on their way to present the Field-Marshal with the keys to the public offices: keys to empty buildings, since the state archives had been evacuated a few days earlier. Wire-cutters would have been more suitable tokens of surrender, said one of the Press, in view of the barbed wire that swathed the veld.[5]

It was appropriate that the Press, rather than the army, should be first in to Bloemfontein. Roberts had always believed in the pen as a weapon of war, and had always given good relations with the Press a high priority. Now three of their more enterprising members – H. A. Gwynne of Reuters, Percival Landon of *The Times*, and 'Banjo' Paterson of *The Sydney Morning Herald* – had galloped into the city, to find Boers leaping off their bicycles, and throwing up their hands in token of surrender, as though their lives depended on it. (A rival claim to have captured Bloemfontein was later lodged by some telegraph men of an RE company. They had been told to follow on and take the telegraph line into the town, and plodded along, unrolling the great wooden drum down the road, without realizing they were ahead of the army.)[6]

In due course, the Field-Marshal arrived and the Flag followed the Press into the town. As a triumphal procession, this column of battle-stained khaki presented an austere, almost drab, impression, though it did have its moments.

Bloemfontein, the home of the Free State's small Uitlander community, had always looked incongruously colonial, a country cousin of Johannesburg's. It looked especially English now that the Boers had taken to their heels. People were waving Union Jacks, and handing out sandwiches, as though it was the relief, and not the capture, of Bloemfontein. Of course, it was, for some, a relief. Forty-six years earlier, the British had handed back the country, and its African majority, to the voortrekkers. Today, the Africans celebrated. 'Thank you, thank you, thank you,' cried a burly African over and over again. Other Africans looted the Boer artillery barracks, to celebrate the new freedom of the Free State under the Empire.[7]

Roberts's arrival was graphically described by Lord Kerry, the War Minister's eldest son and one of the nobility with whom Roberts chose to decorate the HQ staff, 'Entered in procession,' wrote Lord Kerry, 'about 12 o'clock.'

> 1st Chief riding alone, then 4 ADCs, then rest of HQ s[taff] in fours, mil. attachés kept in order by [Lord] Downe, escort of a cavalry regt., as no infantry up. Received with much enthusiasm by few remaining inhabitants, chiefly English women, who *all* insisted on shaking hands with Chief . . . ex-government official [the Landrost] in shooting suit and knickerbockers acted as guide . . . men decorated with red, white and blue rosettes, walked alongside singing 'Soldiers of the Queen' 'Tommy Atkins' and other popular airs (some had drink taken) passed south fort built by us about 1850 'staats artillerie', and barracks which Kaffirs busy looting, drove them off and put guard on, rode through town and market square to . . . statue of late President Brand [the President who had kept the Free State neutral in the war of 1880–1] which Chief inspected. Thence to [Steyn's] Presidency crowd sung national anthem, as we entered gate . . . hoisted small union jack worked by Lady Roberts, on extemporised flag staff in garden, good house . . . marble Hall, Tottenham Court Road furniture . . . all in good order, lunch and dinner in club. Chief's health proposed by Gen. French, capital speech in reply: 'good work of Cavalry', 'endurance of all ranks. . . .'[8]

It must have seemed a convivial evening, that first banquet in the enemy's capital. In the main square, by the wooden veranda of the English Club, the band of the Highland Brigade entertained the Boers. Outside Steyn's Presidency, the small, silk, imperial flag, sent out by Nora Roberts (as the wife of an Irishman, she had worked a discreet Irish shamrock into the design) fluttered like washing on a washing-line.[9] Inside, in the reassuringly English bad taste of the President's marble hall (Maples had supplied the furniture from their Tottenham Court Road emporium), the victors drank each other's health out of the President's glasses, and goggled at an incongruously nude statue of a lady.[10]

But behind the cigar smoke and the clubland toasts – 'good work of the cavalry' – there were growing tensions and ironies. Success, like defeat, magnifies the inner strains of a campaign. Roberts and his generals were no different in kind from Buller and his generals. Roberts blamed French and Kelly-Kenny for losing him one of the great opportunities of the war, at Poplar Grove, a week earlier. French and Kelly-Kenny agreed – only they blamed Roberts for the failures.[11]

It was Roberts's miscalculations, they claimed – his reckless re-arrangement of the transport – that had crippled his own army, especially the cavalry and artillery, by starving men and horses. 'Endurance of all ranks.' It was Roberts's blunders they all had to endure.

Who was, in fact, to blame? The Battle of Poplar Grove on 7 March shares one feature with many battles that disappointed the British. It is easy to say what went wrong, hard to apportion responsibility. Certainly there was a chance that morning of making a most sensational bag, one that would have far over-shadowed the capture of Cronje and his four thousand. Among the six thousand burghers on the battlefield (though Roberts did not hear of this till next morning) was Oom Paul himself, who had come to help the Almighty put new heart into His people.[12]

The Boers' hastily improvised trench lines at Poplar Grove had straddled a line of kopjes, on a ten-mile-wide front at either side of the Modder River, about thirty miles upstream (east) from Kimberley. It seemed to be the last natural line of defence before Bloemfontein. Roberts's plan of attack was based, understandably, on taking to heart the lessons of Paardeberg. He had told French to go with the cavalry division, some MI units and horse artillery, and make a seventeen-mile détour around the Boers' east flank. He was to make a wide enough sweep to avoid the Boers' lines, and then to attack the laagers in the rear, and cut off the Boers' escape route to Bloemfontein.[13] After the cavalry had passed round, the three infantry divisions were to attack from the right, supported by an artillery barrage: Kelly-Kenny's (6th) Division, the Guards Brigade and Tucker's (7th) Division against the main position on the south bank of the river; Colvile's (9th) Division, and some MI on the north bank.[14] This was the plan: an improved version of Paardeberg tactics – that is, a plan to get the greatest possible bag with the fewest possible losses; at all events, to avoid the reckless losses incurred by Kitchener three weeks before. In a sense, it was a plan for some rough shooting. Take some guns and go round to the back of the hill, said Roberts to the beaters (French and the cavalry division). When you're in position, the main line of guns (Kelly-Kenny and the infantry divisions) will walk up the birds.

The trouble was the Boers did not behave like well-bred pheasants. They ran. Roberts had assumed the Boers would sit tight, as Cronje had sat in the riverbed of the Modder, then fly at the approach of the guns. Instead, the Boers started to run, *ventre à terre*, the moment they saw the cavalry coming to outflank them.[15] In itself, this might not have seemed fatal to Roberts's scheme. For what was the actual purpose of the cold steel of the cavalry – the famous *arme blanche*, in which the hunting gentlemen who made up the cavalry so passionately put their trust? Was it not to hunt down a panic-stricken enemy? Then here was the place and the moment: six thousand Boers, led by President Kruger in his top-hat, fleeing across the veld, as smooth and flat and grassy as Salisbury Plain, while the cavalry division, with forty-two mobile guns, thundered after them.[16] View halloo! A sight to dream of! But it was not what Roberts saw through his binoculars.

To Roberts's disgust, French never gave chase at all. Instead of hacking and skewering the fleeing enemy, the cavalry advanced at a walk. Indeed, they fought dismounted, several thousand cavalry checked by groups of absurdly few riflemen (in fact, a masterly rearguard action organized by De Wet). Roberts held French principally to blame for this fiasco: 'We should have had a good chance of making the two Presidents prisoner if French had carried out my orders of making straight for the Modder River, instead of wasting valuable time going after small parties of the enemy.'[17]

Roberts also accused French of wretched horse-mastership. If the cavalry had treated their horses better, they would not have broken down.[18] French bitterly resented this charge. The cavalry blamed Roberts's hopeless transport arrangements for the breakdown of the division. 'I have never seen horses so beat as ours that day,' wrote Douglas Haig, his Chief of Staff. 'They have been having only 8 lbs of oats a day and practically starving since ... February 11th. So many Colonial Skallywag Corps have been raised that the horses of the whole force could not have a full ration.'[19] As these colonial corps were quite useless, according to Haig ('good only for looting ... disappear the moment a shot is fired'), he ridiculed Roberts's expedient of reducing the regular cavalry's ration in order to feed 'these ruffians'. Presumably Haig was right, and Roberts had partly himself to blame if the 'pick-up' of Boers after the shoot (in Haig's sporting phrase) was so wretched.[20] But the basic fact was that the day of cavalry charges was over. The Mauser had made conventional cavalry tactics obsolete. The 'white arm' had become a white elephant.[21]

Roberts also blamed Kelly-Kenny for being slow and cautious in attacking the Boers' trenches. Kelly-Kenny admitted that he would have attacked earlier if he had known the Boers were so demoralized.[22] But he blamed Roberts for the collapse of his own men and horses. The 6th Division had been 'starving' ever since De Wet had captured the food convoy at Waterval Drift, and there was only one water-cart for each battalion, barely enough for half a water-bottle for each man.[23]

Whoever was to blame, the effects of the Battle of Poplar Grove were disastrous and long-lasting for the British.

Not only did Roberts fail to catch Kruger and the rest. He also made the crucial deduction from the panic-stricken way the Boers had fled – only De Wet saved them from losing all their guns and wagons[24] – that the Boers' morale was broken, and the war nearly over.[25] This, apparently confirmed by an action at Driefontein on 10 March,[26] and by their abandoning Bloemfontein on 13 March without a shot, was to be the greatest strategic miscalculation of his career, though Milner, as we shall see, shared the responsibility.[27]

Bloemfontein (rechristened 'Bobsfontein') was certainly a pretty place, and so were many of its female inhabitants. The mutual recriminations among the invading force were, for the moment, submerged in a whirl of unaccustomed entertainment.[28] To fraternize with the enemy was an essential part of Roberts's and Milner's short-term plans for the Free State. The take-over, for both military and political reasons, must be accomplished as smoothly and painlessly as possible. Many Boer officials were therefore left undisturbed at their posts. At the same time, every encouragement was given to English-speaking burghers, like Mr Gordon Fraser, to fill the gaps left by Steyn and the burghers in arms.[29] To the Boer population in general, the message was friendship: trust the army to behave like gentlemen; trust the Empire to welcome the newcomers. Hence the parties and banquets, to which Boers were invited, and the band of the Highland Brigade that played every evening in Market Square. And hence a new bilingual daily newspaper, with the heart-warming title of The Friend, started by Roberts, only two days after his triumphal entry, by closing down the anti-British Express.[30]

The Friend used the presses of The Express, and was run by British war correspondents in their spare time. The idea was both Milner's and Roberts's.

They had roped in a dazzling team of patriotic pen-men, including the unofficial laureate of the Empire, Rudyard Kipling. Kipling, an old admirer of Roberts's since India days, arrived at the war front just after St Patrick's Day. He wrote a stirring poem about the Irish regiments being ordered to wear shamrocks:

> From Bobsfontein to Ballyhack,
>   'Tis ordered by the Queen
> We've won our right in open fight,
>   The wearing of the Green.[31]

In general, Kipling did not add much lustre to his literary reputation. But *The Friend*, whimsical and heavy-handed as it was, gave a boost to the army's morale. The Boers, on their part, could only be reassured by its message. The new regime would continue the 'civilizing' work of the old. All Africans must carry passes. Twenty-seven African 'boys' were found without passes after nine o'clock and were each given five lashes by the Boers' Native Police, who were complimented by the British for 'their good work'.[32]

As well as giving his army a new voice, Roberts gave them, or began to give them, what they needed even more urgently: new boots and new uniforms.[33] They had marched into Bloemfontein half-naked, with their feet showing through the sides of their boots. The Commander of the 9th Division, Sir Henry Colvile, drily observed, 'Some of the men's nakedness would have been less striking if they had taken off their rags altogether.'[34] Step by step, garment by garment, the army returned to decency. And to meet women and girls again seemed almost like a dream. 'I shall never forget the extraordinary impression,' wrote Lieutenant Rankin, of Rimington's Tigers, 'after weeks spent in exclusively male society, and amid all the horrors and blasphemies and filthiness of constant fighting, by the sight of three pretty little girls in sun-bonnets and spotless muslin frocks giving cigarettes to the soldiers.'[35] Still more delightful was the young, flirtatious Lady Edward Cecil, invited by Roberts to visit the front at the end of March, when she inspected the Guards. What 'great big men', she commented.[36]

Apart from such heady thrills, the ordinary soldiers took time off to write letters back to England in reply to those thousands of letters from home that littered the veld at every camp site.[37] It was the first dramatic test of the new mass literacy, this orgy of letter-writing by the working class. The men whose grandfathers in the Crimea, and great-great-grandfathers in the Peninsula, had relied on the officers and war correspondents to keep the world informed, now had the means to give their own versions of their experiences. 'Thank God I am still in the land of the living but I have been very very lucky, my word.' 'I write these few lines to you hoping to find you at home and in good Health and enjoying yourself. . . .' 'If you see anyone that knows me, please give them my kind regards. . . .' 'I am afraid there will be another fight . . . but buck up we will pull through allright . . .' 'Dear old chum . . . remember me to your Mam and Dad and Bert and Wal, I beg to close hoping it will find you quite well, believe me to remain your Old Friend. . . .'[38] The soldiers' mail poured out a stream of

reassurance. On the realities of war – the horrors, the blasphemies, the filthiness
– these letters were silent.[39]

Roberts, too, sent a reassuring and somewhat stilted letter back home – to the
Queen. It was weeks since he had had the opportunity.[40] How dramatically the
pattern of the war had changed since then! The relief of Kimberley, the capture
of Cronje, the relief of Ladysmith, the capture of Bloemfontein – all accomplished within a month. No wonder Roberts enjoyed the respite at Bloemfontein, though impatient to resupply the army and be off. The South African
autumn he found 'perfection':[41] in those shady gardens, the sun became a friend
once more. Every morning 'the little man',[42] as people called the Chief, attended
a service in the Anglican Cathedral, the red-brick, neo-Gothic pile in which
Milner had heard that sermon, the previous June, 'Blessed are the Peacemakers'.
Now the cathedral was full of burly, young, khaki-clad soldiers, their faces
burnt raw by the sun, and the cheerful red and blue uniforms of the nursing
sisters. The Chief sat in the front pew, below the pulpit, a frail, white-haired
figure, with the black arm-band, alone.[43]

To Queen Victoria, Roberts first expressed his gratitude for her congratulations: 'It is a great satisfaction to me ... to learn that the operations in which we
have been engaged have met with the approval of your Majesty. ...' He
continued: 'It is impossible for me to describe to your Majesty how admirably
the troops have behaved ... want of transport prevented tents being carried ...
officers and men had frequently to bivouac under a drenching rain, and more
than once they had to be satisfied with half rations. ... But nothing damped their
spirits. ... Your Majesty's soldiers are indeed grand fellows.'[44]

Roberts was not given to boasting. He prided himself on the level-headed way
he looked fortune in the face. But now, with the astonishingly sudden collapse of
the Boer armies, and the singing of 'Soldiers of the Queen' in Bloemfontein, he
made the great miscalculation:

The Orange Free State south of this [he forecast to the Queen] is rapidly settling down.
The proclamations [of an amnesty] I have issued are having the desired effect, and men are
daily laying down their arms and returning to their usual occupations. It seems unlikely
that this State will give much more trouble. The Transvaalers will probably hold out, but
their numbers must be greatly reduced, and I trust it will not be very long before the war
will have been brought to a satisfactory conclusion.

We are obliged to rest here for a short time to let men and animals recover, and provide
the former with new boots and clothes.[45]

'Not very long' till the end of the war. To rest 'for a short time'. Together,
both these crucial strategic estimates – of Boer weakness and British strength –
were to prove disastrously optimistic. The first was based on a fundamental
misconception about the Boers; the second compounded the error. Roberts was
no fool – and no genius. He was a highly successful imperial general, with the
tactical and diplomatic skill, and the limitations, born of forty years' peace and
war in India. He had no insight into South Africa, knew nothing of the complex-

ity of colonialism, nothing of the tenacity of Afrikaner nationalism, and the extraordinary resilience of the Boer – hunter and hunted, fighting animal and political animal.[46]

Significantly, it was Buller, who had served side by side with Boers in the final Zulu War, who accurately predicted the peculiar difficulty of a war against them. It would be a 'civilized' war, meaning a war according to the rules of the Geneva Convention; but in an 'uncivilized country', meaning a country with few railways and other man-made assets, which themselves could easily be laid waste. It would also be a 'national war' – that is, a trial of strength not merely between governments, but between peoples and nations. It would be war against a young nation composed of communities scattered across an enormous territory.

In this type of pioneering, colonial society, there was no highly organized machinery of administration, and the central government carried little influence or authority. 'Time has not yet glorified the seat of Government with a halo of sentiment,' wrote Buller. 'To every man his own home is the capital. Hence there is no commanding centre by the occupation of which the whole country or even a whole district can be brought into subjection; no vital spot at which a single blow can be struck that will paralyse every member of the body. There are living organisms which can be divided into a multitude of fragments without destroying the individual life of each fragment.'[47]

These were the lessons that Buller drew both from history and his personal insights. He predicted that the set-piece war would change into a fragmentary war. He believed that military strategy based on the conventional idea of the 'single blow' would not bring much closer the conquest of the Boers. He compared the present task with the one set Generals Howe, Clinton and Cornwallis in the American War of Independence. It was no good capturing capitals, as they had captured New York, Philadelphia and Charlestown, unless they could subdue the territory between. As soon as the enemy re-emerged, the population would revert to its earlier allegiance – understandably, unless they could be protected against intimidation. The real task was to beat 'every armed man in the field'. Otherwise, to march through an enemy's country would be like trying to arrest the flow of a river by walking through it. 'Such a man may indeed stem its force where he stands, but let him move where he will, the waters always close before and behind and around him.'[48]

Buller, of course, had played Cassandra before: in September 1899. Now he forecast a guerrilla war.[49] His advice to Roberts was this. No good to march on Pretoria before he had thoroughly crushed the Free State armies. Otherwise, across the Vaal, those waters would close around him.

Roberts, by contrast, stuck to the conventional idea of surrender. Capture the capital and you have cut off the head of the enemy. Their spirit must die, too. And he had long intended to use political means – the kind that was often used in Indian frontier wars – to smooth his march to Pretoria. On 15 March he offered an amnesty for every Free State burgher except the leaders. All they need do was to return home, take the oath of allegiance and surrender their arms.[50]

The complete contrast between these two strategic options can never have been more apparent than in the fortnight after the fall of Bloemfontein. The Boer forces in the field, according to Roberts's Intelligence Department, had been reduced to a total of about thirty-seven thousand in mid-March. (The actual numbers were probably still smaller.)

The largest single concentration was still believed to be the Boer invasion force in Natal: thirteen thousand, most of whom were now dug into the line of the Biggarsberg, forty miles north of Ladysmith.[51] In Cape Colony, a raiding party of about one thousand burghers, led by General Steenkamp, had set alight a local Afrikaner rebellion in the scattered settlements around Prieska, in the north-west Karoo.[52]

The other Boer forces had, by 17 March, abandoned their posts south of the Orange River, after blowing up both the strategic railway bridges that linked Bloemfontein with the Cape Ports – Norvals Pont on the Cape Town and Port Elizabeth lines, Bethulie on the East London line. The total of Boer forces still occupying British territory was thus estimated at 15,500, including General Snyman's band of 1,500, still ineffectually besieging Baden-Powell at Mafeking. 21,500 other burghers were believed to be scattered about the Free State. There were thought to be 5,000 to 6,000, led by De Wet and De La Rey, who had abandoned their trenches and fled north from Bloemfontein. There was a large force under General Du Toit to the north of Kimberley. And 4,000 men under General Olivier were known to have abandoned Colesberg at the end of February and to have retreated somewhere to the north-east.[53]

It was these commandos of Olivier's, above all, that would have been a prime target for offensive strategy, if Roberts's priority had been to crush the Boer armies in the Free State. For Olivier was trapped a hundred miles behind the main British lines. But Roberts had decided to consolidate his position by halting at Bloemfontein until he could build up a still larger army ready for the next great 'tiger-spring', in The Times's phrase[54] – the march on Pretoria. His strategy was for the moment defensive: to protect Bloemfontein from a raid by De Wet from the north, to reopen the town's water-works twenty miles to the east, and to reopen the railway line to the south. (The first train to Cape Town actually rumbled across temporary rails laid on the road bridge at Bethulie on 19 March.')[55] He ordered Buller to remain on the defensive in Natal, too: Buller protested violently.[56] Where Roberts did take the initiative his aims were political. He sent out small parties of troops into the country to distribute the proclamations of amnesty and to collect surrendered arms.[57]

On 15 March he heard important intelligence: General Olivier and a column, said to consist of six to seven thousand Boers from both Colesberg and Stormberg, were advancing north up the road that passes about forty miles east of Bloemfontein close to the frontier with Basutoland. Further reports amplified this intelligence during the next few days. Still, Roberts issued no instructions for any of his main Free State army, consisting of over 34,000 men, to try to block Olivier's column of 6,000. He waited till 20 March before he told French to take one cavalry brigade, a few guns, and some MI to go to Thabanchu, astride Olivier's route. To send so small a force so late was hardly more than a gesture. Olivier side-stepped French. After an epic march of three weeks, Olivier's ponderous wagon train, twenty-four miles long, passed safely behind the British lines, their morale as intact as their ox wagons.[58]

Some people have argued that it was beyond the power of Roberts's large army even to attempt to attack so small and cumbersome a Boer force. Significantly, The Times History's school of historians, so quick to blame Buller for failing to send his 2,500 mounted men to pursue Botha's and Joubert's 15,000-strong army the day of the relief of Ladysmith, reversed their arithmetic when facing critics of Lord Roberts. It would have been a 'very grave risk', we are told by Amery, to send 20,000 in pursuit, leaving only 15,000 'exhausted men' to guard Bloemfontein. (In fact, there was not the least danger to Bloemfontein.) Yet even Roberts's keenest admirers admitted that the main reason why he did not try to crush Olivier was that he thought the Free State burghers would, if simply left to themselves, accept the amnesty, take the oath of allegiance, and disperse to their homes. It was this preconceived belief, that the fall of Bloemfontein would knock all the fight out of the Free State, which was to be his fundamental miscalculation.[59]

His second miscalculation was that his own army would be ready to move forward 'in a short time'. It is also significant that the same critics, led by The Times, should have treated the breakdown of Roberts's army at Bloemfontein as a mere act of God, a misfortune that could happen to the best of commanders.[60] For breakdown it was to be. By the end of March, when this first golden fortnight of peace in the Free State was to come to a sudden end, Roberts's force was not to be much nearer being ready to move.

The underlying reason was that, by temperament and background, Roberts was not interested in the dull grind of military administration. The Army Service Corps – Buller's great innovation at the War Office – he dismissed, as we have seen, calling it one of the aberrations of the 'Wolseley ring'.[61] But he had failed to create a competent HQ staff to whom he could delegate.[62] His friend from India, Major-General William Nicholson, newly created Director of Transport, could not abide Kitchener; anyway, Kitchener was far too self-willed to act as anyone's Chief of Staff.[63] The result was chaos in the marble hall of the Presidency, as there had been chaos on the banks of the Modder. In the hall (the 'Hall of Idlers', as someone called it) sat that dazzling collection of red-tabbed princes, dukes and other nobility, fingering their medal ribbons (DSO was said to mean 'Duke's son only') and enquiring about the supply of 'medicines' that had come up the railway line. 'Medicine' or 'cod-liver oil' was the code name for champagne.[64]

Meanwhile, the problem that bedevilled everything remained that triple-headed monster, transport: trains, horses, oxen.

A glance at the map showed the peculiar and dangerous isolation of a British garrison in the Free State; kept alive by the single-track, narrow-gauge railway that ran due south for the first hundred miles before diverging at Springfontein towards the three Cape ports. When Buller had suggested in December that a special military railway line might be built to extend the Cape railway by a new westerly route towards Bloemfontein, Roberts had ridiculed the idea.[65] Yet it was predictably in this hundred miles nearest Bloemfontein that railway conges-tion was now proving most acute, after the 'reopening' of the line. Moreover, Roberts had wasted months before ordering extra rolling stock from outside South Africa. On 20 March, he found himself cabling to England for twenty-five engines and three hundred wagons as a matter of the highest urgency.[66] It would be months before they arrived. Meanwhile, all supplies – every boot and blanket, every round of ·303 and every 6-inch shell, every biscuit and every bandage and bottle of medicine – had to run the gauntlet of that wretched single-track railway line.[67] As we shall see, one of the direct results of the defects in railway transport was a loss in men's lives that made Spion Kop relatively cheap.

Horses, too, horses by the thousand, Indian horses, Burmese horses, Argen-tinan horses, had to come up the same railway line, battered and bruised after travelling half-way across the world. Roberts's grand army swallowed horses as a modern army swallows petrol. French's cavalry division alone had lost fifteen hundred killed, died or missing during the relief of Kimberley. On a single day – the Battle of Poplar Grove on 7 March – the division reported a further 213 casualties.[68] If this was the wastage of one division on one day, what would it cost to make a really mobile *army*? For it was Roberts's plan to mount fifteen thousand men as MI.[69] Where were the horses to come from? Ever since February, there had been a series of plaintive exchanges between Roberts's Field HQ and Pall Mall on this subject.[70] But, whatever Pall Mall's failures, it is clear that Roberts had grossly underestimated the scale and complexity of the prob-lem. The vital position of Director of Remounts at Stellenbosch had been given to an officer considered totally unfit (he was a manic-depressive) for any other duty. Eventually he shot himself.[71]

The third kind of transport was conducted by Africans: eleven thousand mules led by about two thousand African drivers. There was a simple reply to the claim that the arrival of Roberts's army in Bloemfontein in a state of total exhaustion was one of those unavoidable misfortunes of war. The breakdown of men and horses was, in fact, due to their being put on half-rations, largely because of the loss of the virtually unguarded convoy at Waterval Drift, itself the result of Roberts's abolition of 'regimental' transport.[72] Ironically, Roberts had now been forced by events to restore the 'regimental' system in all but name.[73] Never had an attempt to economize on transport proved more of a false economy. A little less impatience, and the thirty thousand men that Roberts had marched into Bloemfontein might have been in no worse condition than the twenty thousand that Buller marched into Ladysmith.

The most dramatic and painful symptom of the defects in Roberts's military system was the death-rate from typhoid. Summer was the season for typhoid in all the large South African towns. The disease feeds on poor hygiene and overcrowding, the natural state of the African kraal. It was, in a sense, Dingaan's revenge on his conquerors. But by the end of the nineteenth century, the disease was largely tamed.[74] To prevent typhoid, you needed careful sanitation; to treat it, you needed careful nursing and a careful diet. During the siege of Ladysmith, this, as we saw, had not been achieved. Hence that death-rate of 563 out of the garrison, of whom 393 were typhoid victims. Bloemfontein soon began to outstrip Ladysmith's grim record of ten deaths a day. The Raadzaal was taken over as a hospital. There were funeral processions every afternoon along those dusty streets where the triumphal troops had marched: a few soldiers, stumbling along with arms reversed, gaunt mules dragging a buck wagon, and on the buck wagon, sewn into a blanket, a human bale. There was no solemn music here, and rarely a flag as a last tribute. The dead were as commonplace as any other burden the mules carried. Marching feet, the creak of wheels, the jingle of harness, the cries of the African drivers: this was reveille and Last Post together.[75]

Why was there a typhoid epidemic at Bloemfontein? The basic source was obvious enough – it was endemic. And men, unsatisfied by Roberts's ration of half a water-bottle a day, had drunk water wherever they found it, including the water of the Modder River at Paardeberg, polluted by Cronje's camp. But why had typhoid *spread* so rapidly, weeks after Cronje's surrender? Negligence, was the simple answer. Neglect of elementary sanitary precautions in the army camps, as Bloemfontein's population soared from four thousand to forty thousand in a month; neglect of the patients in hospitals that turned a crisis into a disaster. This was the view of a crusading British Unionist MP – William Burdett-Coutts, husband of the philanthropist – who came out on Roberts's invitation and returned to denounce the scandal of Roberts's hospitals in both Parliament and the columns of *The Times*.

Burdett-Coutts described in *The Times* what he saw at Bloemfontein on 28 April, using language reminiscent of Sidney Herbert's famous despatches from Scutari:

> ... hundreds of men to my knowledge were lying in the worst stages of typhoid, with only a blanket and a thin waterproof sheet (not even the latter for many of them) between their aching bodies and the hard ground, with no milk and hardly any medicines, without beds, stretchers or mattresses, without linen of any kind, without a single nurse amongst them, with only a few ordinary private soldiers to act as 'orderlies' ... and with only three doctors to attend on 350 patients. ... In many of these tents there were ten typhoid cases lying closely packed together, the dying with the convalescent, the man in his 'crisis' pressed against the man hastening to it. There was no room to step between them. ...[76]

There is no reason to think Burdett-Coutts exaggerated what he saw, nor that what he saw was not typical of the field hospitals around Bloemfontein.[77] Of course, part of the reason for these appalling conditions was, like so much else at Bloemfontein, the failure of one single-track railway line, short of rolling stock, to supply all the needs of the army. But there were volunteer hospitals at Bloemfontein, staffed by civilian doctors, including Dr Conan Doyle. There was also a Boer government hospital, the Volks Hospital, doing excellent service for the British.[78] These hospitals, too, were dependent on that single-track umbilical cord. And *they* had beds and doctors and medicines and nurses for their patients; so much so that Conan Doyle found several hours a day, at the height of the typhoid epidemic, to write his *Great Boer War*.[79]

The army hospitals were bad because they were run by the army. They represented all that was most inflexible about the British army: the endless form-filling, and obsession with rules and regulations, that made red tape and red cross almost synonymous. The ideas of Colonel Exham – White's fearsome PMO, with whose triplicate forms Major Donegan had wrestled during the siege of Ladysmith and whom Buller had sent packing after the siege – dominated Bloemfontein.[80] It was the spirit of Scutari reborn. Where were the ladies with the lamps? Roberts himself had recognized as early as February that there was a serious outbreak of typhoid in the hospitals on the Modder, and that orderlies and nurses were even then unable to cope. However, he had asked for a mere twenty extra nurses from England. Later he raised the figure to forty, then to fifty, for the whole of South Africa. The reason: he found his own PMO, Surgeon-General Wilson, 'not very responsive or sympathetic' to the idea of lady nurses.[81]

There was an astonishing difference in Roberts's attitude to field generals and surgeon-generals. Field generals – sometimes good field generals – were sacked wholesale by Roberts. But where it was only a matter of health and hygiene, Roberts was prepared to leave in charge a general in whom he had absolutely no confidence. He had personally visited the army hospitals at De Aar and Orange River Station on 9 February, on his way to the north; Wilson had called them 'as good as could be expected'; Roberts found them as bad as he feared. He then told Lansdowne, 'The fact is he [Wilson] is a poor creature and does not seem to have any idea of what is required.'[82] But Wilson – and Colonel Exham himself – were left for weeks almost unchecked in control of the hospitals at Bloemfontein. It was not until late April that an SOS was sent to England asking for three hundred extra orderlies and thirty doctors. Why did not Roberts intervene weeks earlier? Because it was not Roberts's style to concern himself overmuch with the life (or death) of Tommy Atkins. Perhaps it was his long years in India, commanding an army largely consisting of natives, that had dulled his interest in these questions. At any rate, there is a note of breath-taking complacency about his letter to the Queen in mid-April, the week before the SOS for extra orderlies and doctors: 'The health of the men, too, is very good. There are some 2,000 in hospital [at Bloemfontein] but this is only at the rate of 4 per cent, a very small proportion during a campaign. ... The climate now is quite perfect, and I hope that Lady Roberts and my daughters will be able to come here ere long. They will find it an agreeable change after Cape Town.'[83]

Meanwhile, a great change had come over the Free State. One of their leaders, exploiting Roberts's naïve belief that the struggle was nearly over, now re-kindled the Boers' determination to fight, and thus changed the whole course of the war.

A week before this new phase opened, a tall, stiff, careworn figure slipped inside the marble hall of Roberts's HQ at the Presidency.[84] The High Commissioner,

Sir Alfred Milner, had come up to the front for a first glimpse of his shy young
bride, 'Miss Bloemfontein', as *The Friend* called her.[85] He had also serious
political matters to concert with Roberts. The generous terms of Roberts's
proclamation of 15 March, offering amnesty to all except leaders, were originally inspired by Milner. In January, he had modified the draft of the amnesty to
include combatants as well as civilians. He now stood firmly behind Roberts, as
Roberts held out the olive branch.[86]

It might seem out of character that Milner, the man who had precipitated the
war, was now prepared to gamble on this short cut to peace. After all, *he* had
never underrated the tenacity and resilience of Afrikaner nationalism, any more
than Buller. And the political task he had set himself was no less than to crush the
'Afrikaner idea' once and for all. 'An irreconcilable enemy has tried to extinguish
us,' he wrote from Bloemfontein that very week. 'We must extinguish him.'[87]
Why not then let the war go on?

One can guess the working of Milner's mind, reading between the lines of his
letters to London. He was much more aware of the risks than Roberts, yet he
was prepared to take these risks for two tactical reasons. First, he was intensely
impatient to get on with the peace. Although he shared the current hero-
worship for Old Bobs ('a wonderful old creature with a heart of gold'), the
continuation of the war left him bitter and frustrated. 'The more I see of the
army,' he wrote to Lady Edward Cecil, after this visit to Bloemfontein, 'the
more unhappy I feel about it.'[88] It was the endless blunders of Roberts's military
administration – the hopeless muddle of the transport system, the appalling
redtape of the hospitals – that drove him near despair.[89] The dream of his life – to
forge the weakest link into the strongest in the imperial chain – could not even
begin with this blundering army in occupation. Meanwhile, it was the enemy
who were forging a new nationalism in the crucible of the war.

There was a second reason why Milner wanted a quick end to the war, and it
was equally fundamental. The secret alliance he had made with those two
Empire-minded millionaires – Alfred Beit and Julius Wernher – depended on the
profitability of the gold-mines. Now he had recently had word from Eckstein,
the local manager of Wernher-Beit's and the leading representative of all the
gold bugs, that the Boer authorities planned a scorched-earth policy against the
Rand mines: to mine them with a vengeance, by blowing them up with dynamite. The shafts were already drilled for the purpose.[90] Clearly, the damage
could run to millions of pounds. Hence Milner was prepared to lean over
backwards to be conciliatory to the Boers – at least, until the British army had
seized hold of the Rand.

Milner kept these anxieties to himself. He accepted only one important public
engagement on his flying visit to Bloemfontein. On 28 March he was guest at
the banquet in the Railway Bureau given for Lord Roberts by four members of
the staff of *The Friend*.[91] It was an irresistible imperial occasion: sword and pen,
they were fighting the same battle: Bobs, the hammer of the Boers; Kipling, the
Orpheus of the Empire. Kipling proposed the toast; a short, sturdy figure, with
pale features behind the black moustache and the spectacles. He raised his glass.

To Kruger, the man to whom they owed everything – 'who has taught the British Empire its responsibilities, and the rest of the world its power, who has filled the seas with the transports and the earth with the tramp of armed men. ...'[92]

Milner, who might fairly have claimed that particular toast for himself, was his usual modest and self-deprecating self. He must have remembered, with mixed feelings, when he had last saluted Kruger. It was here, at this actual table, in Bloemfontein's Railway Bureau, at the conference in June of the previous year. Milner proposed a toast and raised his glass: to Roberts, 'the military magician'.[93]

This was, indeed, the honeymoon after the shot-gun marriage with Miss Bloemfontein. Roberts's praises were on every lip. 'This wonderful little man, it was said [wrote Winston Churchill] had suddenly appeared on the scene; and, as if by enchantment, the clouds had rolled away and the sun shone once again brightly on the British armies. ...'[94]

But the weather in South Africa runs to extremes, and the storm-clouds were gathering fast.

CHAPTER 32

'Keeping De Wet from Defeat'

Northern and Eastern Free State,
17 March–April 1900

Question: Why do the Boojers go to bed with their boots
on?

Answer: To keep De Wet from defeat.

Story told to the author by one of
Roberts's veterans in 1970

Four days after the fall of Bloemfontein, on St Patrick's Day 1900, the Free State
and Transvaal leaders had held a *krijgsraad* at Kroonstad. The atmosphere was
cordial; Francis Reitz, Kruger's State Secretary, composed a humorous poem in
English, mocking Kipling's poem in *The Friend* about the Irish regiments and
their St Patrick's Day shamrock.[1] But the problems facing the *krijgsraad* were
nothing to joke about – no less than how to find a new way of pursuing the war.

Kroonstad, 130 miles north of Bloemfontein, across the rolling, brown void –
a void bisected by the single railway line, and intersected by an occasional
railway bridge – was a typical Free State town. Now declared the official capital
of the state, it possessed no real public building. When the two Presidents –
Steyn and Kruger – addressed a large rally in the Market Square, they braved the
rain standing on a butcher's stall.[2]

The sight of Kruger's top-hatted figure in the sister republic had a quality of
pathos and desperation that no one could miss. Despite his failing eye-sight, the
old President had been persuaded to make the two-day train journey to Natal in
early March to rally the burghers sent reeling by Buller's advance. Then, hardly
pausing at Pretoria, Kruger had taken the train down to Bloemfontein, to rally
the burghers on the western front. He had arrived at De Wet's HQ near Poplar
Grove on 7 March, at the actual moment the battle began. De Wet bundled him
back into his carriage, and off the tired mules trotted with their precious
burden;[3] one shell, from French's horse artillery, fell just behind the carriage;
Kruger turned disdainfully to look at the thing, according to a famous story –
'So that,' he remarked, 'is one of the Queen's pills.'[4] But even Kruger's wit failed
him after so many burghers had fled in panic from Poplar Grove, and the
defection of one commando had caused Bloemfontein to be abandoned without
a shot. At the *krijgsraad*, both deputations decided to prosecute the war 'more
energetically than ever'.[5] But were these just brave words? What could a war

council achieve if the volk in the Free State decided to take Lord Roberts at his word, go home and call it a day?

The man who claimed to have the answer to this overwhelming question was Christiaan De Wet. He had been appointed the Commandant-General of the Free State army, after General Ferreira had been accidentally shot dead by one of his own sentries. De Wet's response to the débâcle at Bloemfontein was nothing if not original. His commandos were exhausted after six months away from home. Well, let them go home. But they must return to their posts by 25 March. De Wet's ideas brought him into conflict with General Piet Joubert. Joubert, though an invalid and soon to succumb to his final illness, still nominally controlled the Transvaal army, and had come to the Free State for the *krijgsraad*. 'Do you mean to tell me,' the old warrior enquired, 'that you are going to give the English a free hand, whilst your men take their holidays?' 'I cannot catch a hare, General, with unwilling dogs.'[6]

De Wet was well aware that some of those dogs would not return to hunt the Khaki hare. But the best would return – their spirits restored after a ten-day furlough. Better ten men who really wanted to fight than a hundred men who shirked their duties. Already the basic principles for the new phase of the war were taking shape in De Wet's mind: guerrilla principles. First, to weed out the men whose unreliability endangered everyone's life; and so to make his own commandos into an élite striking force. Second, to increase their mobility, by abolishing the great wagon trains that made every Boer expedition into a Great Trek, and had proved Cronje's undoing (and would have proved General Olivier's, if Roberts had chosen to attack him in strength). Third, to tilt their defensive strategy progressively away from the conventional method of trying to block or delay an invasion by fighting at the front. The enormous numerical superiority of the British made such direct strategy a forlorn hope. Instead, they should develop the raiding strategy, behind the enemy lines, the strategy which had proved so successful against the 180 wagons at Waterval Drift. Apart from the military value of raiding the enemy's lines of communication – and De Wet recognized that the success of Roberts's advance hung by a thread, that single-track railway to the ports – there was also the all-important question of the burghers' morale. Give me one day's 'good work', said De Wet. And he'd have the burghers flocking back to join the commandos – even the burghers who were now taking the benefit of Roberts's amnesty.[7]

In principle, the *krijgsraad* accepted De Wet's ideas, which coincided with those of the most successful Transvaal general on the western front, General De La Rey. It was to be many months before the ideas were fully developed; and, meanwhile, the overall fortunes of the Boers were to fall to their nadir. But the credit for avoiding a national collapse that month, March 1900, must go primarily to De Wet. He was now to give, less than three weeks after the fall of Bloemfontein, a sensational demonstration of what these ideas meant, by taking a mere fifteen hundred men to operate on the flank of the British army of thirty thousand.

The two Presidents themselves agreed to De Wet's plan, although they did not abandon conventional defensive strategy. They also decided to use political methods to stiffen the burghers' shattered morale, and prevent the Free State men from abandoning their comrades in the Transvaal and accepting Roberts's amnesty. Already they had made one or two important manoeuvres in the propaganda war. On 5 March, they addressed a joint appeal to Lord Salisbury, repudiating the claim that they had gone to war with aggressive intentions. The war, on their part, was 'only commenced as a measure of defence ... and was only continued in order to ensure the indisputable independence of both Republics as Sovereign International States' and to protect Afrikaners, from the Cape and Natal, who had joined them.[8] Of course, this was not an olive branch offered to Lord Salisbury. It was a challenge to Britain to state its own intentions, to expose Britain as an aggressor both in the eyes of the world and of their own burghers. It was a counter-ploy to offset the blandishments of Lord Roberts, by proving the humbug of Lord Salisbury's speech the previous autumn: 'We want no gold, we want no territory.'[9] Well, did that stand today? Or was Britain now proposing to annex both republics? When Salisbury replied on 11 March, the reply was, as expected, quite uncompromising. There was no argument now about the oppressed Uitlanders, or the rights of the suzerain power. Salisbury simply stated that Britain was 'not prepared to acknowledge the independence' of either republic.[10] Moreover, Kruger made great play with that copy of the secret Intelligence Department pamphlet, *Military Notes on the Dutch Republics*, captured with Symons's baggage at Dundee on 23 October. It proved that the British aim, all along, was to annex the two republics.[11]

Surrender would thus entail the destruction of the volk as a political nation. This was the first point the two Presidents wished to demonstrate: to play on the fears of losing their political manhood that had always been central to the very existence of the voortrekkers. Fear, and shame (the 'blood of their fellow-citizens' would be on their heads), were indeed powerful moral propellants. But something more was needed to add to the mixture: hope.

Characteristically, the two Presidents offered very different brands of that precious commodity. Steyn had told the *krijgsraad* that there was 'reliable news' of a Russian 'plan' to occupy Herat and threaten India; if the republics could hold out another six to eight weeks, Britain would have to come to terms.[12] In a public manifesto, Steyn also spoke of 'favourable news' from Europe and Cape Colony. In fact, Steyn knew, by then, that the rebellion at Prieska in the Cape was crumbling. And though it was true that there was much evidence of moral support for the cause of the two republics among people in Holland, France, Germany, Russia, and their kith and kin in the United States of America, support of any other sort was, Steyn well knew, a forlorn hope. The Russian 'plan' to occupy Herat had been reported to Reitz by Leyds on 10 February: 'From very good authority I gather that the Russians will be in Herat in May. I send the news for what it is – a probability, but not a certainty.'[13] But even if this story were true (it rapidly proved false), Herat was close to the Russian border in the extreme north-west of Afghanistan. It was a long step from being a serious threat to Britain's grip on India.

More to the point was Steyn's plan to send a Boer diplomatic mission permanently abroad, which would offer a continuous source of vague hope to the burghers, without risk of disappointment. It was agreed to send abroad some Boer politicians who could be spared. In early March, these fortunate men – including Smuts's friend, Abraham Fischer, of the Free State – took the train down to Lourenço Marques, and from there embarked on a conveniently slow boat for Europe.[14]

Kruger had endorsed this scheme, and publicly acknowledged the various ways in which foreign sympathizers continued to aid the twin republics. Russia, Holland, France and other countries had sent Red Cross teams; 'the whole world is on our side in this struggle for right and liberty'. At the *krijgsraad*, Kruger also agreed to promote to the rank of general the most distinguished of the various foreign freebooters serving in the commandos: a Frenchman, Colonel the Comte de Villebois-Mareuil. (He did not survive the honour long. He was killed, after a quixotic Last Stand, on 5 April.[15]) But Kruger did not, like Steyn, believe in stressing the hope of foreign military intervention, or even hope of diplomatic mediation, by one or more of the Powers. The volk must trust in themselves, and trust in the Lord. That remained Kruger's simple text. The calamities that had befallen them, the death of their friends, were a sign of God's will; His people needed to be tried and purified by suffering. But they must not doubt the Lord's purpose. 'How did it go with Ahab? The mighty enemy came before the walls of the city, and the people had lost courage. Then came the prophet of God, and said "Fear not". Then God arose, and in that God we must place our trust. ... It is still the same God Who led Israel from the wilderness and hardened Pharaoh's heart to the end, until at last all the first-born of the Egyptians died [a reference to the typhoid epidemic at Bloemfontein] where-upon Pharaoh allowed the Israelites to depart.'[16]

It was as broad as it was narrow, Kruger's appeal to the volk. They must remember that *they* were the chosen people; remember, too, that victory over the Beast was a victory for all Christianity. 'See the three youths in the fiery furnace. Did they rejoice alone? No, but God's people over the whole earth. Was it only for Daniel, what happened in the lion's den?' To this theme of the holy war Kruger was to return again and again. And, predictably, he denounced the British for the most emotive of all atrocities: the employment of black Africans to fight the Boers.[17] As we shall see, the claim that Baden-Powell had enrolled black troops at Mafeking was correct, though the charge of atrocities – atrocities *against* blacks – was one that would principally be laid at the door of the Boers. Still, the image of Dingaan's successors fighting for Lord Salisbury struck at the very heart of the volk; it was one more apocalyptic sign that Lord Salisbury's side was the side of the Beast; and that the Lord God of Hosts would work miracles for His people.

Probably Kruger, the prophet, stirred more hearts than Steyn, the statesman. The geography of the Bible was more familiar to the volk than the geography of Russia and the Great Game. At any rate, Boer spirits, always mercurial, rebounded. De Wet wrote that 'there was only one word on every tongue:

"FORWARD!"'[18] And if the Lord was to work miracles, it was De Wet, above all, who saw himself as the chosen instrument.

For the new-style war, De Wet and De la Rey had proposed, and the *krijgsraad* unanimously agreed, that the commandos would be divided into flying columns. A large column, led by De la Rey and Philip Botha, would drive southwards in the direction of Bloemfontein, 'to entice the enemy out of it'. Meanwhile, De Wet's Free Staters would swoop down to the south-east, join hands with General Olivier's six thousand men who were withdrawing from the Orange River, and together attack the British lines of communications.[19]

By the end of March, De Wet was ready to strike. Roberts had taken the bait offered by De la Rey, and moved troops north. To screen the capital, and repair the railway to the north, Roberts had stationed part of French's cavalry at Glen, sixteen miles to the north, where the Free State railway intersected the arc of the Modder River at the end of the first stage of its meandering, 150-mile journey towards Kimberley. So De Wet decided that his first target would be the Bloemfontein water-works at Sannah's Post on the Modder, twenty-three miles to the east, and the source of all drinking water for the capital. He gathered that this pumping station at Sannah's Post was only defended by a couple of hundred men. With two thousand burghers, he should not have much difficulty in turning off that strategic water tap. The main danger was the close proximity of Roberts's enormous army. De Wet expected to be able to strike fast – and run fast – now that he had got rid of the wagon columns. He relied on speed and its counterpart, secrecy. He also hoped to make a tactical ally of the Modder, the river whose crumbling, white banks had played such a decisive part, for better or worse, in all the great battles of the Free State.[20]

To trap those two hundred men between two parts of his raiding force of fifteen hundred. That was the plan; and it sounded simple enough. De Wet, its author, was the most aggressive and confident of all the Boer commanders. Yet even De Wet was overwhelmed by the sight of the great fish that he was now to find flapping in his nets beside the Modder.

Nothing concentrates the military mind so much as the discovery that you have walked into an ambush. Brigadier-General Robert Broadwood was confronted with this disagreeable news soon after dawn on 31 March.

Broadwood was the man with whom Roberts had replaced the unfortunate Major-General Babington as commander of the 2nd Cavalry Brigade. It may not have been true, as Methuen said, that Babington had been sacked simply because he was a friend of Buller's. But it was true that Broadwood had got the place because he was a favourite of Roberts's and Kitchener's. He had what those generals admired in a cavalry leader: 'dash'; he was also, like them, somewhat impatient; and the lapse that sent him straight into De Wet's arms suggests that he was no military genius.

He had failed to send out scouts at the head of his column.[21]

The trap was sprung as Broadwood was withdrawing back to his base at Bloemfontein from a 'bill-posting' expedition in the district of Thabanchu close

to the Basuto frontier. This was the 'kill-Boer-rule-with-kindness' expedition
that had originated in Roberts's half-hearted attempt to block Olivier. After this
military failure, the cavalry had been given sheaves of Proclamation forms to
distribute. French and Haig had then retired, leaving Broadwood in charge –
both grumbling (reasonably enough) at the use of the precious cavalry on this
political mission. As Haig said, 'many poor creatures brought in their guns and
swore on oath not to fight against us again. Then we withdraw our troops and
the Transvaalers burn all the farms!! Such conduct merely brings us into contempt.'[22]

It was to bring worse than contempt. After a few days, Broadwood had been
forced by Olivier's commander to retire from Thabanchu. On 30 March, he
wired to Roberts's HQ in Bloemfontein that he was retiring to the safety of the
water-works. He had a relatively small force of 1,700 men: some of the 'Tigers',
two cavalry regiments (or, rather, the skeleton of two regiments, for they had
only 332 horses between them), U and Q Batteries of horse artillery and
Lieutenant-Colonel Edwin Alderson's brigade of 830 MI. He also had a convoy
of 92 wagons, many of which belonged to civilian refugees, seeking the protection of Roberts's great army.[23]

The pumping station at Sannah's Post comprised a collection of buildings
astride the western bank of the Modder. Here was the ford where the main
Bloemfontein-Thabanchu wagon road crossed the river. There was a second
ford, two and a half miles to the west, where the road crossed the tributary, the
Korn Spruit, which joined the main river a couple of miles below. The road itself
thus formed the south side of a small triangle of land whose east and west sides
were formed by the Modder and Korn Spruit respectively. For twenty miles
beyond the Korn Spruit, right up to the outskirts of Bloemfontein, the veld was
almost featureless – apart from a boulder-strewn kopje, Bushman's Kop, south
of the road, about five miles to the west of Korn Spruit.[24]

It was midnight before the first of Broadwood's straggling column splashed
across the Modder drift and reached the pumping station. This was the convoy
of ninety-two wagons, and their African drivers, the civilian refugees and an
escort of MI. Broadwood and the rest did not turn up till 3.30 a.m., about an
and a half before dawn. Everyone was exhausted after the long slog along the
muddy road from Thabanchu, and a running fight with Olivier's commandos
the previous day. The men threw themselves down beside the wagons and were
soon asleep. No special orders were given by Broadwood to guard the bivouac.
He assumed that the only danger came from Olivier, and Olivier was far behind.
He knew nothing of De Wet's two forces. He consulted the commander of the
water-works garrison, Major Amphlett, and was reassured. Four men had
already gone out to patrol the road westwards as far as Bushman's Kop, as they
did every night. Before dawn, patrols would be sent out to scout the country
across the Modder to the north and east.[25]

Soon after dawn, these patrols returned. They were followed, to everyone's
astonishment, by rifle fire and shelling from some kopjes on the far bank of the
Modder. Broadwood then made his fatal lapse. He decided to withdraw his

whole force to Bushman's Kop. But no scouts were sent ahead. The convoy of wagons rumbled off, followed by some dismounted men, and U and Q Batteries of horse artillery, and fell straight into De Wet's lap at Korn Spruit.[26] 'Hands up!' shouted the burghers, concealed in the river banks. A forest of hands went up. In a few minutes, De Wet's men had captured two hundred soldiers and were all set to capture twelve pieces of artillery, a bigger *coup* than the capture of Long's ten guns at Colenso.

Broadwood – two miles to the rear at Sannah's Post pumping station – at last realized his predicament. He was trapped between two forces, with a third, General Olivier's, somewhere to the east. An officer of the 10th Hussars was sent to ride like the wind to Bloemfontein. They were in a devil of a mess.[27] The 'little man' must get them out of it again.

The little man was not one of those people who look best in a crisis. It was partly that, as a flyweight, Roberts could not, like Buller, hope to reassure people simply by the jut of his jaw and the thrust of his massive shoulders. Partly, too, that Roberts, unlike Buller, tended to over-react, unable for once to control the nervous and impatient side of his character.[28]

Sannah's Post was a mere twenty miles from Roberts's HQ, a couple of hours' ride on a good horse, not twice the length of one of the battlefields of the Tugela or the Modder. Roberts's new staff officer, Colonel Sir Henry Rawlinson (brought over from Ladysmith at Roberts's special request), actually heard the distant rumble of Broadwood's guns as he rode out of Bloemfontein before breakfast. Rawlinson returned and told Roberts: an ominous noise indeed, so close to the capital. Roberts did nothing. Two hours later, Broadwood's first SOS message, relayed from the post at Bushman's Kop, reached the HQ. It was followed, about half an hour later, by the breathless report of the officer of the 10th Hussars.[29]

The way to respond to this SOS seems, with hindsight, somewhat obvious. Send a flying column down the road to Bushman's Kop. Make it a communications centre (the rocky hilltop overlooked the whole meandering line of the Modder and comprised both a telegraph and heliograph station). Reach out a controlling hand to co-ordinate the vast numbers of men that could be sent to overwhelm De Wet. After all, Broadwood's difficulty was also Roberts's opportunity. Ever since Poplar Grove, the problem of fighting Boers had been to find them. Here was De Wet's forward line – less than five hundred men – isolated between Broadwood and Bloemfontein. Roberts had thirty thousand men within twenty miles. And if Roberts were to seize this opportunity, to catch De Wet in his own trap, why not go in person to establish a forward HQ nearer the action? It was a fair criticism of Buller (Buller had made it himself) that he did not do one thing that the complexities of modern warfare made it essential for the GOC to do – to assert himself during a battle and not delegate the chief command. Why did Roberts not now ride out the fifteen miles to Bushman's Kop and take a grip on affairs?

It is easy to say this, in the clear light of future events: it was hard, in the fog of the present, to achieve. As it turned out, Roberts had swung from over-confidence to near-panic. What was the strength of De Wet's raiding force? Somehow he got it into his head that Bloemfontein itself was in danger. The best mobile force – what was left of French's cavalry division – was not despatched at once to help Broadwood, and give chase to De Wet. French wasted the whole morning and afternoon hunting for Boers around Bloemfontein. An infantry division was sent, led by Colvile.[30] In the meantime, Broadwood was left to cut his way out as best he could.[31]

If the root cause of the disaster went deeper than Broadwood's blunder, the reason why the disaster was not still more serious can largely be ascribed to the behaviour of one man.

In that shot-spattered triangle of wet grass between the Korn Spruit and the Modder, the battle had now resolved itself, like the second phase of the Battle of Colenso, into a struggle to save – or to capture – the twelve British guns. The man in charge of the six guns of Q Battery of the Royal Horse Artillery was Major Edward Phipps-Hornby. He had stumbled into his bivouac beside the water-works at 4 a.m. At 5.30 a.m., he was woken by someone shouting, 'Major, there's a lot of rifle fire going on! Hadn't we better harness up?' There was no sign of the enemy. (Generals Froneman's, Wessels's, and Piet De Wet's 1,150 men were dug into the kopje on the far bank of the Modder.) After a minute, shells began to go shrieking overhead or crashing into the rain-sodden ground among the horses and wagons. The two British batteries found that the Boer guns outranged them by nearly a thousand yards. Broadwood ordered a retirement: Major Taylor, of U Battery, to lead, followed by Q Battery. Ahead of both of them, as the shells smacked down, the wagons of the convoy, and the refugees, galloped pell-mell towards the Korn Spruit.[32]

Now a battery of the RHA, however choreographic their manoeuvres on the parade ground, was by nature a cumbersome force. Each of the six guns had its individual ammunition limber; there were the wagons, with reserve ammunition; a total of fifty officers and men rode astride or beside the guns.[33] When the two batteries had retired about a mile from the bivouac, Taylor's battery was ordered to cross the Korn Spruit and occupy the ridge beside a farmhouse on the far side.[34] Phipps-Hornby and Q Battery followed quietly. He watched the confused mass of convoy halt and spread out along the deep, crumbling banks of the Korn Spruit. He thought the convoy had halted to let Taylor's battery pass; Taylor's battery did, in fact, ride up on their right, and they, too, halted at the ford. Suddenly a gunner ran up: 'We are all prisoners! The Boers are *there*.' (He pointed to the river-bank.) 'They are in among the convoy and among the guns.'[35]

Phipps-Hornby was now only three hundred yards from the ford. He could see a cluster of Boers standing up on the top of the river bank, and thought they must be unarmed. He did not believe the gunner. However, he realized there was some kind of ambush. He ordered Q Battery to get into line. Then he gave the order: wheel to the left, back the way they had come. As the leading horses wheeled, an invisible wave of bullets splashed the ground all around. Three horses and a wagon team were down. Then the gunner in front of Phipps-Hornby was hit in the back. He pitched forward; another bullet caught him in the head. Now there were riderless horses galloping past – belonging to the men of Roberts's horse whom Broadwood had failed to send ahead as scouts. One of the guns was upset and had to be abandoned. But somehow Phipps-Hornby got the other five guns back to a firing line on a ridge 1,150 yards from the ford. Soon they were in action, blasting away at those black dots on the river bank, Boer heads that ducked at each flash of the guns.[36]

At Colenso, Long's two field-gun batteries had tried to reply at much the same range to Botha's riflemen concealed in trenches on the other bank, a dialogue that did not last long. Perhaps here, at the Modder, Phipps-Hornby had no choice, because of the broken ground, between taking up a firing position that was too close or not taking one at all. In the event, Q Battery was soon silenced, and, of the original fifty officers and men, only one officer (Phipps-Hornby), one sergeant, one corporal and eight men were still in action. Broadwood's ADC then appeared. The General ordered them to retire with the guns. The question was how?[37]

About seventy yards behind the firing line were a stone parapet and some station buildings, part of a new branch line to Thabanchu in course of construction. Phipps-Hornby found some of his missing gunners, and a crowd of infantry, cringing among the horses against the lee side of the station. 'I called them cowards,' he said later, 'and gave them the rough edge of my tongue, and said I would shoot any man who didn't go out. . . . I said "Go out and fight – or come and help me." They went somewhere but I never saw them again.'[38]

Meanwhile, the ten NCOs and men and some of the Essex had begun to bring in the five guns and gun limbers. The guns had to be brought in by hand, as it was impossible to hook in the limbers under that blizzard of Mauser and Martini-Henry fire. Some of the limbers, too, had to be manhandled part of the way. Each time the men went back into the blizzard, Phipps-Hornby noticed how they jammed their helmets on their heads and leant forward as though meeting a wind. One of the gunners, called Humphreys, lost his stick, swept out of his hand by a bullet, but calmly bent down and picked it up again. Eventually, all except one gun and one limber were safely brought under cover; these had to be abandoned, like the gun lost earlier. Then the surviving men – four of whom were to be awarded VCs – galloped the four guns back across the Korn Spruit by a new ford higher up river, which the Tigers had discovered, and joined the rest of Broadwood's column.

So there were no more captures for De Wet. Phipps-Hornby, splashed all over with blood, but unscathed, rode back to Bloemfontein with the débris of the battery. He had three whiskies and sodas, and some sausages and bacon. He was the hero of the hour. Everyone complimented him for his gallantry. He broke down and wept.[39]

De Wet's nimble column of fifteen hundred easily eluded the bear-hug of Roberts's ten thousand – Colvile's lumbering infantry division and French's shattered cavalry division, belatedly sent in pursuit. Colvile was later blamed for the fiasco. Broadwood was privately censured, officially exonerated. The seven captured guns (five of U Battery's and the two of Q Battery that Phipps-Hornby had been forced to abandon), 117 wagons and 428 prisoners were sent back northwards.[40] Meanwhile, De Wet's column continued their raiding expedition to the south. De Wet himself went ahead to reconnoitre, and managed to persuade some local farmers, who had given up their arms in Bloemfontein, to rejoin the army. His force only totalled eight hundred, some of whom were not properly armed, when he attacked a British garrison of about six hundred men of the Royal Irish Rifles near Reddersberg on 3 April. De Wet had three field-guns and the British had none. After a twenty-four-hour fight, the entire garrison surrendered, losing 45 officers and men killed and wounded, and 546 taken prisoner.[41] Next, De Wet attacked and laid siege to nineteen hundred men of Brabant's Horse at Wepener. These were mostly Afrikaners from Cape Colony, and the thought that they had volunteered to serve the Crown (and earn five shillings a day in the process) whetted the appetites of De Wet's men. However, the Wepener garrison dug themselves in with skill; they had their backs to Basutoland (and an open telegraph wire throughout the siege). Meanwhile, Roberts's infantry divisions were plodding along to the rescue. After sixteen days, De Wet let go of Wepener, and swooped back to his eyrie in the north. When the British arrived, the eagle had flown.[42]

What De Wet would have achieved, if Steyn and Kruger had wholeheartedly supported his brilliant raiding strategy, one can only guess. He had had to rely on an active force of a mere fifteen hundred, supported by local burghers, who were distrustful of the sincerity of the Proclamation offering amnesty. Many claimed to have been put under arrest, despite its terms. With this handful of men, he had opened a new front. He had done more; he had opened a new dimension in the war. He had failed, however, to cut the railway line. To achieve that all-important strategic task, he would have needed a much bigger share of the Boer armies. And Steyn and Kruger and the rest were not yet convinced of the need for such a revolution in their strategy. They still clung to the hope of somehow halting Roberts's combined force of fifty thousand men as they plodded north alongside the railway line to the Transvaal.[43]

From Roberts's point of view, De Wet's raid thus postponed, but did not prevent, the advance of his grand army. And, on 3 May, he was finally ready for a double 'tiger-spring': the advance on Pretoria with his main army, while Colonel Bryan Mahon's flying column struck out far to the north-west to relieve Baden-Powell at Mafeking.

CHAPTER 33

'The White Man's War'

Mafeking (Cape Colony Border),
30 April–May 1900

'It is understood that you have armed Bastards, Fingos
and Baralongs against us – in this you have committed an
enormous act of wickedness . . . reconsider the matter,
even if it cost you the loss of Mafeking . . . disarm your
blacks and thereby act the part of a white man in a white
man's war.'

General Cronje's message to Colonel
Baden-Powell, 29 October 1899

On the last day of April, a patrol from Mafeking, plodding through the sandy
veld of no-man's-land, came across a curious letter addressed to Baden-Powell
and attached to the abandoned railway line.

To Colonel Baden-Powell. I see in *The Bulawayo Chronicle* that your men in Mafeking
play cricket on Sundays and give concerts and balls on Sunday evenings.
In case you would allow my men to join in the same it would be very agreeable to me as
here outside Mafeking there are seldom any of the fair sex and there can be no merriment
without their being present. . . .
Wishing you a pleasant day,
I remain your obliging friend
S. Eloff. Commandant of Johannesburg Commando.[1]

The letter was brought to Baden-Powell's sandbagged, two-storey HQ in a
lawyer's office in Market Square, from which he spent hours scanning the
empty veld. He read the letter, his biographers record, with a sardonic smile.[2]
One can well believe it. Baden-Powell may have had his shortcomings, but he
did not lack a sense of the absurd. A cricket match with the Boers, a *Sunday*
cricket match with the Boers, whose senior commander had earlier denounced
the British for desecrating the Sabbath with sports. This was just B-P's form
(even if 'merriment with the fair sex' was not). B-P knew Eloff by reputation.
He had lately arrived from Johannesburg, determined to win his spurs. He was
cocky, people said, and ambitious, one of Kruger's immense brood of grand-
sons, but surprisingly anglicized, none the less.[3] B-P sent Eloff a jaunty reply,
under the white flag, that was both a challenge and a rebuff:

Sir, I beg to thank you for your letter of yesterday. . . . I should like nothing better –
after the match in which we are at present engaged is over. But just now we are having

our innings and have so far scored 200 days, not out, against the bowling of Cronje, Snijman, Botha ... and we are having a very enjoyable game.

I remain, yours truly

R. S. S. Baden-Powell[4]

Two hundred days not out: a fine innings, a double century. And so it must have felt in the other sense: two centuries spent in Mafeking. Colonel Robert Stephenson Smyth Baden-Powell would not have been human if he had survived the six and a half months locked up at Mafeking without feeling the strain. He showed no outward sign of it, except by that odd habit he had taught himself of whistling when he was frustrated.[5]

Baden-Powell ('B-P' for short; appropriately, these initials coincided with the current slang for the 'British Public') was a most unusual kind of British colonel. He was neat and dapper and bald; his favourite coat, a coat of many colours. He was a man of parts: the conventional pig-sticking colonel (he had commanded the 5th Dragoons in India); the exhibitionist (he revelled, wearing a wig and a girl's dress, in amateur theatricals); the military eccentric (he had ideas about the importance of scouting that most officers would have considered laughable). He had a boyish enthusiasm for hard work and new knowledge. Ingenuity was, in a sense, his second name – the 'Stephenson' stood for the one who had designed the 'Rocket', for he had been his godfather.[6] B-P would have made an ideal headmaster in a Victorian adventure story. A ripper when the going was good, but an alarming man to have as your enemy.

In his messages from Mafeking to the outside world, B-P played the stereotype of the stiff-upper-lip Englishman to perfection. 'All well. Four hours bombardment. One dog killed.' So he had reported the first day's shelling to Lieutenant-Colonel Herbert Plumer,[7] the commander of the nearest British military force, a Rhodesian MI regiment at Tuli, and it was exactly what the other B-P, the British Public, wanted to hear. For six and a half months of the siege he remained (in contrast to poor, demoralized Sir George White) the life and soul of his own garrison. 'Col. Baden-Powell is one of the best fellows going,' wrote Trooper Alfred Spurling, B Squadron Protectorate Regiment; 'he sings comic songs, and had a lot of sketches at an Exhibition which was held the other day.'[8] His versatility astonished even his admirers. 'He was able to assume very various roles with "Fregoli-like" rapidity,' wrote a lady of the garrison, describing one Sunday concert. 'Suddenly there was an alarm of a night attack. ... In an instant the man who had been masquerading as a buffoon was again the commanding officer, stern and alert.'[9]

The siege itself had been no picnic. There was the cumulative strain of its length, now nearly double the length of the sieges of Kimberley and Ladysmith. There were proportionately much heavier casualties, both from enemy shelling and from raids on the enemy lines. There was, above all, the utter isolation. Mafeking ('The Place of the Stones', the Africans called it)[10] was on the borders of nowhere: a railway siding, 250 miles north of Kimberley on the line to Rhodesia, an oasis of tin roofs and mud walls in the sandy wastes where Cape

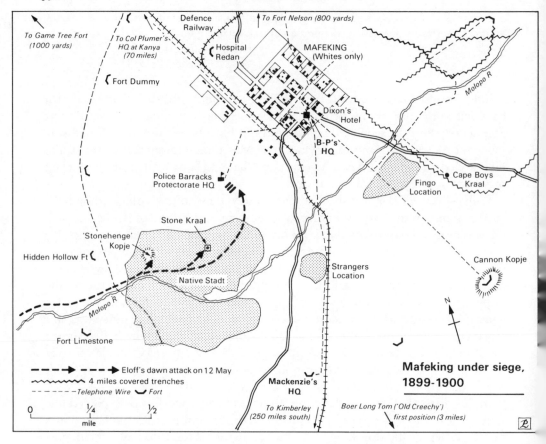

To Game Tree Fort
(1000 yards)

To Col Plumer's
HQ at Kanya
(70 miles)

To Fort Nelson (800 yards)

Defence
Railway

Hospital
Redan

MAFEKING
(Whites only)

Molopo R

Fort Dummy

Dixon's
Hotel

B-P's
HQ

Police Barracks
Protectorate HQ

Cape Boys
Kraal

Fingo
Location

Stone Kraal

'Stonehenge'
Kopje

Cannon Kopje

Hidden Hollow Ft

Strangers
Location

Native Stadt

Molopo R

N

Fort Limestone

Eloff's dawn attack on 12 May

4 miles covered trenches

Telephone Wire   Fort

Mackenzie's
HQ

**Mafeking under siege,
1899-1900**

0   ¼   ½
mile

To Kimberley
(250 miles south)

Boer Long Tom ('Old Creechy')
first position (3 miles)

Colony, the Bechuanaland Protectorate and the Transvaal all touched fingers on
the flank of the Kalahari Desert.

For months, the garrison had felt utterly abandoned. The same awful thought
that haunted the Ladysmith garrison obsessed B-P: 'Are we fools or heroes?' To
that, at least, there came splendid reassurance.[11] In February, a native runner
brought him the congratulations of Lord Roberts.[12] In April, a runner brought
him a letter from his sister, Agnes: 'Everybody is talking of you. You are the
hero of the day. All the papers describe your many-sided talents. . . . Your photo
is in all the shops now.'[13] A few days later, the Queen's own accolade: 'I continue
watching with confidence and admiration the patient and resolute defence . . .
under your ever resourceful command. VRI.'[14] He was *the* hero of the war.

It is easy to underrate today a man whose contemporary reputation was so
over-sold. What is forgotten is that it was B-P's *job* to play the fool – not merely
to keep up the spirits of the garrison at Sunday sports days, but to act out the
strategic role designed for him, the previous summer, by the Cabinet. B-P had
been Lansdowne's and Chamberlain's secret weapon in that wild mood of
optimism in early July. They had hoped to force Kruger to a 'climb-down'
simply by the 'moral effect' of B-P and a thousand men threatening the northern
borders of the Transvaal.[15] Failing the climb-down, B-P's secret instructions

(and, strange to say, these have never been published before) were to *raid* the Transvaal the moment that war broke out.[16]

Looking back on it now, the idea seems almost incredible: a plan to attack the Transvaal 'à la Jameson', as B-P rightly described it.[17] Two regiments of colonial irregulars ('loafers' he called them) to be raised, like Jameson's men, in Bulawayo and other colonial towns, and then sent galloping into the Transvaal.[18] But those were B-P's orders. 'In the event of hostilities with the Transvaal, you should endeavour to demonstrate with the largest force at your disposal, in a southerly direction from Tuli, as if making towards Pretoria.' Demonstration was a polite word. In effect, B-P and his 'loafers' were to play the fool in the northern Transvaal. The object, however, was of great strategic importance: to draw off large numbers of Transvaal burghers and so protect the vulnerable parts of Cape Colony and Natal in the first weeks of the war before reinforcements arrived.[19]

In the event, circumstances decided that the raiding strategy must be abandoned. B-P had successfully raised two regiments of slouch-hatted MI: a Rhodesian corps at Bulawayo, a Bechuanaland Protectorate corps at Ramathlabama, just across the border from Mafeking. But, by September, Milner had proposed that B-P's Mafeking force was needed as a garrison to protect that northern outpost from a Boer attack across the frontier.[20] B-P acquiesced in this, failing proper artillery and other reinforcements being sent to Mafeking. He put the Rhodesian force at Tuli under Colonel Plumer, and took personal command of the Bechuanaland force at Mafeking. His new plan was to provoke the Boers, without exposing himself to the risks of a raid. Mafeking itself would be the bait. It was not only the most vulnerable town in Cape Colony. It was also the exposed nerve of the Boers' political consciousness.[21] For it was from Mafeking, and nearby Pitsani, that Dr Jameson and his grey-shirted, slouch-hatted Raiders had set off four years before.[22]

The Boers swallowed the bait whole – that is, with B-P inside. During the first agonizing month of the war, the whole of Cape Colony south of Kimberley had been guarded by less than seven thousand regulars; the whole of Natal south of Ladysmith, by a mere three thousand.[23] Here was the Boers' greatest strategic opportunity of the war. It was largely thanks to B-P that they had not taken it. His two regiments of loafers, with a dozen imperial officers, had actually drawn off General Cronje and 7,700 Boers to the northern and north-western borders: nearly a fifth of the two Boer armies.[24] Recently, it has become fashionable for historians (unaware of B-P's secret War Office instructions) to deride his claims to have played a crucial part in the strategy of the first phase of the war.[25] The figures – a dozen imperial officers and the loafers enticing away nearly eight thousand Boers – speak for themselves. Arguably, B-P's antics saved South Africa for the British.

Of course, that heady phase of the war only lasted a month. Once the Army Corps arrived in mid-November, once Buller reached the Tugela and Methuen crossed the Orange River, Mafeking became, in conventional strategic terms, a side-show. Cronje left for the south, to block Methuen's advance towards

Kimberley, on the road that was to lead him to the Modder River, Magersfontein, and eventually to Paardeberg. The siege of Mafeking was left to an even more stolid general, Snyman, and a much smaller force: fifteen hundred burghers.[26] Hence the second, and most depressing, phase of the siege. For many dismal months, holding on to Mafeking meant little more than denying it as a base for the Boers; and what had Mafeking got – apart from eighteen railway engines –[27] that would prove of practical use to the Boers? Arguably, if Mafeking had surrendered in December 1899, as the other smaller garrison towns along the railway line to Rhodesia had surrendered, it would have made no direct difference to the war.[28]

That Mafeking had not surrendered was largely due to B-P's remarkable professionalism – the will to win, hidden behind the mask of good clean fun. He was a junior member of Wolseley's magic circle, one of the élite of British officers thrown up by those endless little frontier wars of the new imperialism. He served as Chief of Staff in Rhodesia in 1896.[29] The War Office Intelligence Department recommended him as a man who could be trusted to succeed in an independent command.[30] He paddled his own canoe. Indeed, he had paddled it on the Limpopo almost too single-mindedly during the Matabele War (though this incident had been hushed up). He had been accused by the Colonial Office of murdering an African chief, Uwini, whom he had taken prisoner. He admitted killing him, but claimed that the man deserved what he got. The case had been referred to Lansdowne, but Lansdowne had backed B-P, and it fizzled out.[31]

There was, it must be said, one rather chilling facet to B-P's character: he played to *win*, and he made his own rules as he went along. But the charge of murdering an African chief had lost him no friends among white Rhodesians.[32] In fact, he was something of a hero to them – and this was one of the reasons why the War Office had chosen him for his present command. He had also published a popular book on the Matabele campaign that showed that he could out-Boer the Boers, both in his skill at scouting and in what he called the 'sport' of 'nigger-hunts'.[33]

Still, whatever B-P's methods, his success in defending Mafeking cannot be questioned. From the beginning of the siege, he displayed the right mixture of 'audacity and wariness' (i.e., bluff) recommended by the War Office for the raid from Tuli.[34]

The basic problems were simply stated. There was the all-pervading question of arithmetic. To hold a perimeter of twelve to fifteen miles at Ladysmith, Sir George White had had twelve thousand regulars and 55 guns. To defend a perimeter of ten miles at Kimberley, Kekewich had had six hundred regular troops and 14 light guns; to these he had added over two thousand colonial irregulars, police and town guards.[35] Now take a circle round Mafeking wide enough to keep a proper field of fire: say, five to six miles. How were twenty imperial officers, and the 680 men of the newly raised Protectorate Regiment, and police, to defend this against Piet Cronje and six thousand Boers? Add another three hundred white men – every able-bodied man in the town – and the garrison were still at a disadvantage of one to six. Add the Mafeking field-guns – an *opera bouffe* collection, the best of which were two muzzle-loading 7-pounders sent up from Cape Town by mistake for two howitzers – and set them against Cronje's nine modern field-guns and a 94-pounder Creusot Long Tom (alias 'Gretchen' or 'Old Creechy').[36] There was no avoiding the conclusion. The Mafeking garrison was a paper tiger.

B-P had survived the first two months – the Cronje phase – partly owing to his own audacity, partly owing to the good fortune of having Cronje for an enemy. There can be no doubt that if any Boer commander worth his salt had commanded the six thousand besiegers, B-P's men would now have been enjoying a quiet game of cricket in the prisoner-of-war camp at Pretoria. (Still, by the same token, if Sir George White had commanded the Mafeking garrison, even Cronje would surely have captured it.) B-P, at any rate, bluffed Cronje into believing that the tiger had sharp claws. On seven different occasions in October and November, he sent out raiding parties to make what he called 'kicks' at the Boers. These were expensive in casualties; about a sixth, 163 of the garrison (ten times the casualty rate at Ladysmith) were killed, wounded, or missing during this period.[37] At the same time, he improvised dummy forts, guns and armoured trains to draw the enemy fire. This kind of military prank were good for British morale, as well as producing a regular crop of spent shells, cheerfully collected up by the African 'boys' to be sold as curios to the white population. The shells from the Boers' 7-pounders were particularly to be prized. For these two guns, now turned against Dr Jameson's old base, were the two 7-pounders captured from Dr Jameson at the Battle of Doornkop.[38]

On their own part, the garrison, like the Kimberley garrison, improvised heavy artillery from unlikely materials. The Mafeking counterpart of 'Long Cecil' was the 'Wolf' (a name that B-P was pleased to claim as tribute from the Matabele; *impeesa*, the 'wolf-that-never-sleeps'). The gun had started life as a piece of 4-inch steel pipe. Add a threshing-machine, as a chassis; cast a breech in the railway foundry: with a roar of smoke and flame, the Wolf could throw an 18-pound shell four thousand yards across the veld.[39] Still more heart-warming was the way that a gun called 'Lord Nelson' rose to the occasion. One day, Major Godley of the Protectorate Regiment had found this interesting antique, a ship's cannon, made of brass and dated 1770, employed as a gate-post on a local farm. It turned out that, years before, the local Baralong tribe had bought it from some German traders as a protection against Boer raiders. By one of those odd chances of war, the initials 'B.P. & Co.' were found to be engraved on the barrel. B-P modestly disclaimed it as a family heirloom – in fact, the initials stood for Bailey, Pegg, ironfounders – and had it rechristened 'Lord Nelson'. And in one of his official reports to Lord Roberts, B-P spoke most highly of the effects of its 10-pound solid cannon-ball. ('It bumped down the road,' said Major Godley later, 'exactly like a cricket ball ... and one old Boer tried to field it with disastrous results to himself.')[40]

Other terrifying 'specialities' of the garrison included dynamite bombs made up in potted meat tins. They were thrown by Sergeant Page, the champion bait thrower of Port Elizabeth, 'with accuracy over ... 100 yards'. There was also a miniature railway, constructed within the precincts of the town. A patent fuel, cow dung and coal dust, mixed in equal parts, helped mitigate the coal shortage. (Firewood was also commandeered in vast quantities from the roofs of the wretched Africans' huts in the 'Stadt', as their shanty town was called.[41]) Finally, there were some expedients, of laughably little practical value, but designed to be just that: laughable. B-P had some Mafeking stamps printed, and his own head replaced the Queen's; the lese-majesty was actually the idea of his staff, but B-P, as 'a sort of tyrant or president', was delighted. '*My* head on it,' he told his mother. 'That, I think, is proof of our being an independent republic in Mafeking!'[42]

It was in his policy towards the Africans that B-P showed himself most masterful in his flair for improvisation – and in his ability to bend the rules. It had been an axiom of the war so far for both British and Boers that it was to be a 'white man's war'.[43] In practice, this had meant that fighting was limited to white men, with the exception of Colonel Holdsworth's raid on Derdepoort on 26 November, but that each army had enrolled thousands of brown men and black men as unarmed scouts, grooms, drivers, and (principally on the Boer side) the all-important diggers of trenches.[44] B-P took a daring step towards making it a black man's war.

Beyond the neat, colonial lines of tin-roofed bungalows, a thousand yards square, lay the other Mafeking: a picturesque native town of gaudy mud huts, sycamore trees, and huge elephant-grey stones, sprawling along the greasy banks of the Molopo River. Within this black Mafeking, known as the native Stadt, were concentrated seven to eight thousand Africans: five thousand of these were the regular inhabitants, Baralongs, ruled by a Chief and a Queen Mother; the rest comprised various African refugees, Fingoes driven into the town when their villages were burnt by the Boers, and unfortunate Shangan 'mine boys', expelled from the gold-mines of the Rand, and robbed of their savings by the Boer authorities.[45]

Now B-P, like the Rhodesian settlers he admired, knew how to handle Kaffirs. You had to be fair but firm. He sacked Wessels, the Baralong Chief, for 'want of energy'.[46] He executed by firing squad some starving Africans caught stealing food. He had 115 others flogged.[47] With these little encouragements, he persuaded the Africans to play the important part he had designed for them in the siege. Gangs of Shangan mine boys were set to work digging the maze of trenches, four miles of covered ways,[48] that were quite as intricate as any that the Boers designed. Other Africans were roped in, as at Ladysmith and Kimberley, to serve as scouts, spies, runners, and cattle herds. Where B-P departed completely from precedent was that he *armed* three hundred Africans with rifles. Christened the 'Black Watch', they were set to guard part of the perimeter. This remarkable step B-P took for two different reasons. There was the simple arithmetic: he had added a third to the size of his garrison. And, after all, the native Stadt comprised a tempting part of the perimeter; if the Boers attacked the Stadt, the natives must pull their weight in repelling them.[49]

Such were the broad lines of B-P's policy for the siege: professional, practical, ruthless even, behind the practical jokes. What about the men (and women) of the garrison?

During the first phase of the siege, morale was generally high. The twenty imperial officers at Mafeking had one great advantage, apart from having such a resourceful commander. They were supposed to be an élite, chosen either by the War Office or by B-P for the difficult and dangerous operation of his raid. There were relatively few civilians to make trouble[50] – nothing, at any rate, to compare with the colossal nuisance of Cecil Rhodes. B-P's right-hand man in the siege was the Adjutant of the Protectorate Regiment, Major Alick Godley, a jolly, polo-playing, pig-sticking, bush-whacking Anglo-Irishman on loan from the Dublin Fusiliers.[51] Another Irishman in whom B-P had every confidence was 'Fitz', Captain FitzClarence, in charge of B Squadron of the Protectorate Regiment, and B-P recommended him for a VC for his part in the attacks and counter-attacks along the perimeter.[52]

By contrast, B-P found two of his most senior officers – Lieutenant-Colonel C. O. Hore, the CO of the Protectorate Regiment, and Major Lord Edward Cecil, his Chief of Staff – a considerable strain. Why he did not hit it off with Hore is not clear. But in the case of poor Lord Edward Cecil, it was all too easy to understand. His natural diffidence had been intensified by the unfortunate marriage with Violet and – since the siege had begun – by the news of the death of his mother, Lady Salisbury, the woman who had dominated his life. Now his mood amounted to a kind of moral surrender. Fortunately, B-P was able to give him a task in which he could do no great harm – looking after an improvised cadet corps (ironically, the most famous product of the siege; it was the prototype of the Boy Scout movement).[53] Cecil never got over Mafeking. 'I dread anything that reminds me of that ghastly time, I really dread it,' he said years afterwards when he heard B-P might be coming to live near his house in Sussex.[54]

There were also some civilians with whom B-P found himself at loggerheads. The leading local doctor, Dr Hayes, had been made PMO, but was 'in continual hot water'; B-P told him to resign 'before I have to order you out'.[55] The Press Corps was at first a thorn in B-P's side: 'more of the reporter than the correspondent, all with very incorrect views of the situation – some alarmist, others incautious'. In November, some of them had thought they could make good their escape, and asked B-P permission to leave. He forbade it. 'I consider it,' he noted, 'best that they should not thus evade Censorship by a staff officer, and spread all the gossip of the place in "interviews" on reaching Cape Town.'[56] Later, their mutual relations mellowed – though not before the melodramatic evening when *The Daily Chronicle* correspondent, Parslow, was shot dead by a half-pay, half-mad artillery officer called Murchison. (Murchison was sentenced to death by B-P, but later released because of gallant services in the siege.[57])

For the first couple of months, B-P coped well enough with the civilians' tensions. The second part of the siege saw morale fluctuating dangerously

'Heard from three sources,' B-P wrote in his diary on 18 March, 'that the townspeople are expressing themselves tired of the siege and of me etc. They say ... that I am asking for reinforcements not to be sent in order that I may gain Kudos afterwards....'[58]

There was little physical danger from 'Old Creechy', the Long Tom. Sometimes he threw seventy shells into the town during one day.[59] But the town was so open, and the white inhabitants were so few and so dispersed, that the shelling killed, B-P was relieved to find, few except natives. From the beginning, B-P realized that the most serious threat from shell fire was the threat to morale, and took counter-measures.[60]

Through binoculars, you could see the precise direction in which Creechy's barrel was pointing. An alarm would be telephoned to the threatened target. People ran to the deep shelters, excavated beside all the main buildings, chattering and giggling with nervous excitement. (In fact, the shelters were deliciously cool, after the burning heat above ground.) Then the heads bobbed up again, like rabbits' heads after the hunter has passed, to see what damage old Creechy had done. And damage he certainly did.[61] The convalescent home run by some Catholic missionaries, the only two-storeyed building in the town, received at least a dozen direct hits. 'How near that sounds!' remarked one of the visitors, Lady Sarah Wilson, hearing the report of the gun one evening. The next moment, she and the Resident Commissioner, who had dropped in for an evening game of cards, vanished under a wave of gravel and tomato-coloured brick-dust. When the wave passed, it was found no one had been injured. Yet the 94-pounder shell had exploded four feet from where the two were sitting, and two tons of masonry descended on the card table between them. There were other equally strange escapes – a shell carried a canary out of the window, intact in its cage; and a large African wedding party, the bridegroom complete with top-hat, morning coat and a rifle over his shoulders, passed unscathed through a downpour of Mauser bullets as they paraded along the street.[62]

It was Lady Sarah Wilson whose high spirits added something to the siege that even B-P, with all his ingenuity and hard work, could not offer the men of the garrison. She was a duke's daughter, sister of Lord Randolph Churchill, aunt of the dashing young Winston Churchill, young and extremely pretty. She had come out to Rhodesia with her husband, a cavalry officer, to escape the monotony of the English season – and found herself, after being exchanged with a Boer cattle thief, sent in as a prisoner to Mafeking. How the staff officers snatched at an invitation to Christmas lunch in her 'bomb-proof': an elegant, white-panelled hole carved out of the red soil of Mafeking, the walls decorated with African spears from the Matabele War and an immense Union Jack, the roof made of wooden beams with small port-holes. It reminded you of the picture of the cockpit of HMS *Victory*, one of her guests remarked cheerfully, 'as Nelson lay a-dying'.[63]

Still, even the glamour of Lady Sarah could not altogether dispel the agonizing boredom that covered Mafeking like the dust from the Kalahari. It was the need to cope with boredom that led B-P to make his only serious tactical error of the siege.

The day after that convivial Christmas lunch in the dugout – 'Black Boxing Day', as it became known – B-P decided to try to capture Game Tree Fort. This was a Boer strong-point three thousand yards north of the town. There was nothing greatly to be gained by the attack, apart from extending the area for cattle to graze and giving the Boers a 'kick' to show them the garrison was still alive. But B-P believed that the Boers were in the process of strengthening the fort and was keen to have a go at them before it was too late.[64] It *was* already too late. At 4.30 a.m. the townspeople were awoken by loud firing: the puny roar of the muzzle-loaders, the snarl of Lord Nelson, the answering jingle of Mausers. The firing continued for several hours. It was a beautiful, clear, sunny day, but no one in the town could see what was happening. Major Godley, Adjutant of the Protectorate Regiment, went out in the armoured train and reported the grim news back to B-P. Since the last reconnaissance, the Boers had roofed in the strong-point; it was a real block-house – impregnable, unless the attacking force had proper artillery support. With the gallantry of regulars, C and D Squadrons of the Protectorate Regiment had thrown themselves against the sandbagged parapet and been shot down at point-blank range. When the armoured train, flying the white flag, returned for the casualties, the ground was heaped with bodies.[65] The death-toll of twenty-four (including three officers) brought the total of deaths in action to nearly fifty, and the total casualties comprised ninety-six, almost exactly a tenth of the white garrison.[66]

Then Angus Hamilton, *The Times* correspondent, who had been all in favour of the garrison having a go at Game Tree Fort, was allowed to go and look himself, under the flag of truce. It was a sobering sight, this first view of the invisible enemy, and the last view of their victims, some of whom were Hamilton's personal friends.

The heavy vapour from the shells still impregnated the air, and hanging loosely over the veldt were masses of grey-black and brown-yellow smoke clouds. Boers on horse-back and on foot were moving quickly in all directions. . . . The scene here was immensely pathetic, and everywhere there were dead or dying men. . . . The attitude of the Boers around us was one of stolid composure, not altogether unmixed with sympathy . . . big and burly, broad in their shoulders, ponderous in their gait, and uncouth in their appearance, combining a somewhat soiled and tattered appearance with an air of triumph. . . . Here and there they made some attempt to rob the wounded and despoil the dead. . . .[67]

Later that afternoon, the dead were buried, and the Last Post sounded over their mass grave. B-P took the disaster with his usual air of mastery. He praised the men's heroism in General Orders. And with perhaps unconscious irony, he wrote to Roberts that it would be a lesson to the enemy not to make frontal attacks.[68]

January was a bad month for the garrison. Food was at last running short. B-P's calculation before the start of the siege was that he had food enough for the white garrison to last four months – that is, till the end of February. Supplies for the Africans, meaning their staple diet of mealies, were not expected to last beyond December.[69] The chief reason why the white garrison was relatively well off was the lucky chance that recently the firm of Weil had stock-piled thousands of tons of flour, meal, grain, and other supplies at Mafeking, to take advantage of a change in the custom duties for exports to Rhodesia. B-P had snapped up Weil's stock-pile; and, when the Cape authorities had refused to authorize the deal, Lord Edward Cecil (encouraged by Milner) had given his personal IOU for a cool half a million pounds.[70] Still, even this stock-pile was near exhaustion in January. How, then, was the garrison still fat and well – at least, the white part of the garrison – as *April* drew to its close? How was the conjuring trick performed – B-P's version of the miracle of the loaves and fishes?

There have been numerous accounts of the siege of Mafeking, and numerous biographies of its hero, B-P, and none of them explains this extraordinary feat. The answer has been hidden for seventy-eight years in B-P's confidential staff diary of the siege. In a word, the white garrison took part of the rations of the black garrison. And part of the black garrison was accordingly given the choice of starving to death in the town or running the gauntlet of the Boers.

That this *was* B-P's policy is made clear in the chilling, mouthful-by-mouthful details of B-P's confidential diary:

> Nov 14: The census shows our numbers to be as follows:
>   Whites: men 1,074, women 229, children 405
>   Natives: 7,500 all told
>   Supplies: Meat plentiful live and tinned 180,000 lb
>   Meal and flour 188,100 lb
>   Kaffir corn and mealies 109,100 lb
>   White rations required daily 1,340
>   Native   ,,   ,,   ,,   7,000
>   Thus we have 134 days for whites
>   ,,   ,,   ,,   15 days for natives.[71]

This was the first stock-taking and very serious it seemed. All the meal and flour supplies in the town – whether belonging to merchants, individual Africans, the railway authorities, or the army itself – were therefore to be rationed. And B-P forbade Africans to buy bread. He was determined not to allow the 'white' rations, meaning flour or meal considered edible by white people, to be used to eke out the proportionately far smaller supplies labelled as 'black' rations.[72] How could he then prevent the Africans from starving?

By feeding them part of the 362,000 lb of *horses'* rations of grain and oats, not included in the original tally. That was B-P's first answer to the dilemma. This levelled up the 'white' and the 'black' rations exactly. 'Dec 30: Food reinspected: of meat and groceries there are plenty ... and on going into meal I found that there is 60 days for both white and natives if my present system of rations for all is strictly adhered to.' [73]

At the beginning of January, B-P decided on a second economy. He would slightly reduce the horses' rations of grain (though horses were still to receive ten times the men's ration). 'Jan 1: By reducing the grain supply to 4lbs daily + 6 or 8 of oathay or hay, we could then ensure a month's extra meal for whites, or nearly 4 weeks for natives.'[74]

By now, B-P was beginning to put the rationing of the Africans on a regular basis. And it was here that a new source of economy presented itself. The members of the white garrison, who could not afford to buy rations out of their own pockets, were provided with rations anyway, either on credit, or by drawing on a fund set up by the special authorities. The Africans were all made to pay, and pay handsomely, for their food, including food commandeered from their own stocks. In fact, there was a total of 2,470 natives registered on B-P's books (most of them representing families), and only 428 received food as part of their wages, while a further 240-odd were employed on defence works; many of the others obviously could not afford to buy their rations. B-P, however, believed that there was large-scale hoarding of grain by natives.

Dec 31: In coming through the stadt we saw some very thin Matabele stripping inner bark from fresh cut wood to make into food.

Jan 1: Believe that 'large stores of grain hiden away' in the stadt. Closed shop [ie refused rations to all Africans] 'to see if there is any real want'.

Jan 7: Baralong natives in stadt are getting a little suspicious of us. They want to know... why we are trying to take all the grain from them.[75]

By early the following month, B-P made the astonishing decision that he could stretch the 'white' rations, after all, right up to the third week of May – that is, a hundred and five days from 8 February. The 'black' rations, on the other hand, would only last thirty-four days.[76] What ever had happened now?

It turned out that it was not the wretched Africans in the Stadt who were the hoarders of grain. It was the white merchants and their cronies who had been distinguishing themselves in this exercise. Weil, the main army supplier, proved to have deliberately understated his supplies in the hope of raising his prices ('his duplicity,' wrote B-P, 'has been a constant source of annoyance if not danger'[77]). And the Army Service Corps sergeant-major in charge of rations was found to be running his own black market in food for whites who could pay the army bakers.[78] However, as well as discovering that there was more food than had at first appeared, B-P had also discovered that 'some of the mealie meal set aside for natives will be available for bread-making for whites'. The reason was that an ingenious baker had found how to grind the horses' oats to make flour.[79] As a result, B-P came to a very remarkable decision: to expel part of the garrison. In his own words:

Feb 8th: I propose therefore to try to get all the refugee and foreign natives to leave the place by laying down stock [of food] through Col. Plumer at Kanya [the British force now seventy miles away in Bechuanaland]: and stopping the sale in the town. The amount thereby saved, eked out with occasional issues of meat, should keep the local Baralongs and defence natives; the others could break out on stormy nights and make their way to Kanya.[80]

In effect, B-P's ingenious solution to the problem of conserving food supplies in a beleaguered town was to say to the part of the garrison that was militarily (and politically) expendable: leave here or starve here. There was to be no other choice. Using one method or the other, he would reduce the garrison by a quarter. The two thousand 'refugee and foreign natives' were, in fact, mainly Baralongs who had taken refuge in the town after their kraals had been looted and burnt by the Boers, and the Shangan mine boys from the Rand who had now completed digging B-P's defence works for him. B-P closed the grain store to these two thousand outsiders and banned all employment for them. They were to have no food at all. Some were still being smuggled into working parties, he was sorry to hear. He lectured the other Baralongs on such misplaced humanity. These local Baralongs he was prepared to allow to continue buying rations (from their own food stocks), though much smaller rations than allowed the whites. In the stock-taking of 4 March, it was decided that 113,930 lb of the horses' oats and 279,000 lb of meat would be needed for the 1,500 whites and the 400 native combatants, which left a balance of 227,000 lb and virtually no meat (only 23,000 lb) and no vegetables for the five thousand local Baralongs and so on.[81]

By April, B-P discovered yet another economy which released still more oatmeal flour for white use. It was possible to use oat husks, left over after grinding the meal, to make a kind of porridge called 'sowen'. Oat bran and mealies could also be mixed with horse-meat stew to eke out rations for the Africans fortunate enough to be allowed them.[82]

The leave-here-or-starve-here policy towards the Africans was not, in general, unpopular with the whites. True, the sufferings of the Africans did not pass entirely unnoticed. Two of the Press Corps, who had already fallen foul of B-P for 'grousing', said that this was not cricket, B-P's drastic ration policy. Angus Hamilton of The Times thundered (though The Times was not to print this): 'There can be no doubt that the drastic principles of economy which Colonel Baden-Powell has been practising in these later days are opposed to . . . the dignity and liberalism which we profess, and which enter so much into the settlement of native questions in South Africa.'[83] The most graphic description of the plight of the African garrison was given by Emerson Neilly of The Pall Mall Gazette, and Neilly was apparently writing of the five thousand Africans fortunate enough to be allowed rations by B-P:

I saw them fall down on the veldt and lie where they had fallen, too weak to go on their way. The sufferers were mostly little boys – mere infants ranging from four or five upwards. . . . Hunger had them in its grip, and many of them were black spectres and living skeletons . . . their ribs literally breaking their shrivelled skin – men, women and children. . . . Probably hundreds died from starvation or the diseases that always accompany famine. Certain it is that many were found dead on the veldt . . . words could not portray the scene of misery; five or six hundred human frameworks of both sexes and all ages . . . dressed in . . . tattered rags, standing in lines, each holding an old blackened can or beef tin, awaiting turn to crawl painfully up to the soup kitchen where the food was distributed.[84]

The other two thousand Africans, outcasts, hunted for bones on rubbish heaps, and dug up the corpses of dogs buried outside the town.[85]

How many of these wretched black 'Uitlanders' (the real helots of the Rand), expelled from Johannesburg, or of the neighbouring Baralongs expelled from their villages in Bechuanaland, died of starvation in Mafeking? How many died in attempting to break through the Boer lines and reach Colonel Plumer's food-depot seventy miles away at Kanya? The figures will never be known. B-P's own diary reveals that, in a census completed by 30 March, the number of natives in the garrison had been reduced by about five hundred – that is, to a total of 7,019 – and of these the Mafeking Baralongs in the Stadt, and the coloured 'defence natives' in the location, were receiving a pint of sowen; the others – 1,042 unlicensed natives – received no ration. The diary also records other not unconnected facts. Ninety-four unlicensed dogs had been killed during the last month; and natives were permitted to eat them. Twenty-one other natives were found dead; they had no relations to attend to them, and were buried by the authorities.[86]

Early in April, B-P adopted the final and most drastic solution for survival. He decided to cut by half the number of natives employed digging trenches for the defence works; by thus reducing it to 122, he achieved an economy in garrison food, and also in garrison funds (always an important aim for such a careful housekeeper as B-P). He decided to try to reduce the native garrison by a further two thousand souls, by forcing the Mafeking Baralongs to abandon their homes and go to Kanya.[87]

The reason for this drastic new twist of policy was that, at the beginning of April, B-P had received bad news from his subordinate and would-be rescuer, Plumer. B-P himself had doubted the ability of Plumer's Rhodesian Regiment – less than seven hundred strong, and with no proper guns – to cut its way into Mafeking. On 31 March (the same day, incidentally, as Broadwood's disaster at Sannah's Post), Plumer had made his run for it. He came within five miles of Mafeking. Then he was driven back. The disappointment was heavy – and so were Plumer's losses.[88]

What made this especially shattering for B-P was that Plumer's column included the élite of the young men B-P himself had raised at Bulawayo the previous year, and one of them was a handsome young captain, B-P's lifelong friend, 'The Boy' McLaren. At first, the Boers said McLaren was one of the dead. Then it turned out he was alive and wounded, a prisoner in Snyman's camp. Apart from writing daily letters to McLaren, telling him to keep his chin up, B-P was now, for many weeks more, doomed to sit tight. He had already warned Lord Roberts that if he heard no news of Plumer's success by mid-April, they must send a larger relief column of their own. There was nothing for it but to wait for this column. And on 20 April, B-P heard mixed news from Bloem-fontein, brought by native runners. His brother, Major Baden B-P, was helping to organize the relief. But owing to 'unexpected difficulties' (De Wet's victory at Sannah's Post), it might not arrive till the end of May – that is, *after* the last date to which B-P had originally told Roberts he could hold out, although, in fact, 12 June was the new limit.[89]

Meanwhile, B-P's attempts to run more food into Mafeking and run more Africans out of Mafeking had both run into trouble. Two large parties of native 'cattle-thieves' (B-P's phrase) had been sent out. A party of forty Baralongs had tried to bring in a hundred cattle on the hoof; these cattle had been sent down by Plumer, but all were captured (even at night, it was rarely dark enough to elude the Boers and their own armed Africans), and two of the Baralongs were shot. Other Africans – some of them Fingoes, some of them men of McKenzie's 'Black Watch' – were caught trying to drive some of the Boer cattle into Mafeking. Snyman's burghers shot thirty-two out of thirty-three. They had been betrayed, and were found huddled in some reeds. Mausers and a maxim gun were turned on them. Snyman sent a letter, protesting against the use of natives in the war. B-P tried to put a brave face on it: 'I know nothing of the 32 men, they were certainly not under my orders, or as far as I was aware of my officers.' Of course, B-P had organized the system of cattle-raiding, and McKenzie had even been accused (justly, it seems) of flogging the 'Black Watch' if they did *not* go out and fight the Boers.[90]

The most savage incident, however involved the Baralong women. On the night of 7 April, seven hundred of them were persuaded to try to attempt a mass exodus. Only ten got away; the rest returned. Many had been stripped naked and flogged by the Boers. On the night of 13 April, two hundred got away undetected. Then, on the 15th, a party of thirteen women was caught and nine were shot and killed. Only four returned, two of them wounded. They claimed that the Boers had deliberately finished off the rest of the wounded women. It was now B-P's turn to protest to the Boers, and he was no doubt genuinely shocked. However, B-P's tactic of expelling the surplus native garrison had certainly succeeded in its aim. In all, 1,210 natives reached Plumer. By the end of April, there were only sixteen hundred pints of sowen a day 'needed' for the Baralongs (compared to four thousand pints for the whites and the 'defence natives'), and B-P's diary recorded that he hoped to be able to *increase* white rations again.

Ap 20: Meat and meal stocks at present will last to June 12. But by forcing natives away from Mafeking we can get their share of horseflesh for whites and their sowen which would improve the [white] ration in size.[91]

It was, indeed, a 'white man's war', as both British and Boers were so fond of saying.

Twelve days after Field Cornet Eloff had invited himself to a Sunday 'merriment' at Mafeking, the game took place, and not even B-P himself could have dared hope for a more sporting expedition, nor a more dashing and melodramatic finale to the siege.

It began just before four o'clock on the morning of 12 May, in the brittle, starry darkness between moonset and sunrise. Eloff, the leader, in fact already knew that Colonel Mahon and the two thousand horsemen of his relief column, sent from Kimberley by Lord Roberts, had reached Vryburg two days earlier, and were sweeping rapidly across the veld. Vryburg was only five or six days' ride away to the south, so it was now or never. The plan of attack proposed by Eloff was so daring that his superior officer, General Snyman, was only half-convinced that it was worth attempting. As soon as the moon had set, the burghers would make a feint against the eastern lines of trenches, Fitzclarence's forts, and the redoubts of Lord Nelson, the Wolf and the other British artillery, such as it was. Meanwhile, Eloff would break into the native Stadt with seven hundred men. The burghers would be led by some fire-eating French and German volunteers, newly arrived from Beira, and guided by friendly Kaffirs and a British trooper called Hay, who had recently gone over to the enemy.[92]

It was really excellent, Eloff's plan. For the Stadt, the other Mafeking, was, in military as well as human terms, B-P's blind spot. There was a tempting gap between two small forts called Hidden Hollow and Limestone Fort.[93] Beyond these, and hidden from view in the bed of the steep and greasy banks of the Molopo River, dotted with red and yellow thatched huts and the elephant-grey stones, led a path straight to the Stadt. Once inside this, there were no defence lines, only one small, ancient, mud-caked police barracks, between the attackers and B-P's HQ. Of course, the plan also had its weaknesses. When a small attacking party tries to surprise one part of a siege line under cover of darkness, and break into a town, its success in actually capturing the town will probably depend on its ability to receive reinforcements after daylight has come. And for this dangerous task, Eloff relied absolutely on a man, Snyman, who had shown himself the most stolid and supine of all the Boer generals in the war.

Sarel Eloff was, however, an enthusiast: one of the daring young Transvaalers whose patriotic ardours, the counterpart of British jingoism, had brought them into conflict not only with the Uitlanders but with the Boer traditionalists. Eloff had won notoriety with both groups by making an insulting comment on Queen Victoria. He had thus got into hot water with his grandfather, President Kruger. However, the President had now given him a chance to redeem himself by capturing Mafeking. And capture it he meant to, whatever the odds. With characteristic swagger, he posted up a notice in the laager that Friday evening: 'We leave for Mafeking tonight: we will breakfast at Dixon's Hotel tomorrow morning.' But few burghers took up his invitation. When he counted his party, Eloff found it was only 240 men – not 700, as proposed.[94]

Still, the first phase of the attack succeeded brilliantly. Snyman's large force launched the feint as soon as the moon had set. Eloff's small force, assisted by Trooper Hay, slipped unobserved past the two forts, up the Molopo and into the Stadt. It was here they made what was probably a tactical error. To signal to Snyman, and also to strike terror into the Baralongs, Eloff's men set fire to the densely packed huts. The flames, catching at the wood-and-mud door frames, and the piles of firewood on the flat mud roofs, soared up impressively into the darkness and sent a useful screen of smoke, sparks, and a mob of panic-stricken Baralongs flying far ahead of them.[95] However, the fire was also an alarm-signal to B-P.

Before Eloff had got far, the garrison awoke. There were frantic bugle calls, and the bell on the Catholic church, beyond Dixon's, sounded the general alert.[96] Even so, Eloff's men rushed on, without opposition, beyond the Stadt. Mistaken, in the smoky half-light of dawn, for British troops, they surrounded the Protectorate HQ staff in the old BSA (Chartered Company) barracks. And, with hardly a shot (one shot, in fact, for an officer's soldier servant, called Maltuschek, who stubbornly refused to put up his hands, and paid with his life), they captured the other twenty-nine occupants, including Colonel Hore, the second-in-command after B-P and commander of the Protectorate Regiment. It was about 5.25 a.m. The sun, lemon-coloured, filtered through the eucalyptus trees by the market gardens, while in the west the Baralongs' huts still burned fiercely, throwing up streamers of golden sparks.[97] Eloff was understandably pleased. Someone picked up the telephone connecting the fort with the HQ at Dixon's. It was still working. With a final piece of swagger, Eloff informed B-P that Hore and his fort were theirs; and they were only eight hundred yards from his HQ.[98]

The news can have been no great surprise to B-P. He had never had much confidence in Hore and he was already aware that the position was critical. He had been woken about four o'clock by a bullet hitting the veranda below his bed. Was the attack a feint or the real thing? B-P had taken no chances. The church bells sounded the general alarm.[99] In the town, there were incongruous scenes: volunteers (including war correspondents) rushed to their posts, dressed in underclothes or pyjamas; Ben Weil handed out shot-guns from the boxes in his store; Lady Sarah Wilson climbed through the window into the locked hotel dining-room, to snatch a cup of coffee; guns were given to the prisoners in the town gaol (including Murchison, the half-mad artillery major who had murdered Parslow, and Sergeant-Major Losey, who had stolen those army rations).[100]

Up on his look-out post, B-P soon identified the shape of Eloff's attack. The most successful of all B-P's 'specialities' – the web of telephones connecting forts and outposts with HQ – did sterling work that morning. 'A force of about three hundred Boers are advancing up the Molopo valley.... They are in the Stadt.' The telephone message was confirmed, soon after, by the line of flames sweeping towards the town. B-P reacted calmly and quickly. He sent the reserve squadron of the Protectorate Regiment, under Captain FitzClarence, a party of armed railway-men, and some people from the hospital redan. This reinforcement for Godley only amounted to a couple of hundred men. He could not risk further laying bare the eastern defence lines, which might be the target of a large-scale attack by Snyman at any moment. To deal with Eloff, the main responsibility rested with Godley himself. B-P telephoned to him after 5.30. Things were 'rather serious'. He must do his best with A and B Squadrons – and perhaps he added, 'the niggers' – to round up Brother Boer.

B-P resisted the temptation personally to supervise the rounding-up; it was his job to co-ordinate things at the centre of his web of telephones. But he did yield to one impulse that was later to cause raised eyebrows. He sent a reassuring note, under flag of truce, to 'The Boy' McLaren, a prisoner in Snyman's camp: 'Dear Boy, I hope you were not too disturbed by heavy firing in the night, but the Boers made an attack on us and we have scuppered the lot. Let me know if you want any clean pyjamas. . . .' This note, according to his official biographer, was part of a plan to bluff the Boers; for Eloff was by no means 'scuppered' at this moment.[101]

Meanwhile, Major Godley, his two squadrons, and his natives, had all risen to the occasion. In fact, it was the Africans, most of all, who bore the brunt of the fighting and saved the day. When Eloff's fire-raisers stormed through the Stadt, scattering the women and children, the 109 armed Baralongs did not try to bar their progress. They stood aside, as if a pride of lions was rampaging through a cattle kraal. Then, once the lions were in the kraal, the Baralongs re-formed, waving their blunderbusses and shouting war cries. It was the turning-point, the time when the burning Stadt beckoned to Snyman. Now was the moment to pour in a stream of reinforcements. But the Baralongs barred the way – and cut off Eloff's line of retreat.[102]

When FitzClarence rode up with D Squadron, the worst was already over. Godley could be seen galloping along the south side of the Stadt, a tall, thin figure on his pony, rallying his two squadrons, after strengthening the men in the outposts. Eloff's men were taken piecemeal: a party huddled behind the stone kraal six hundred yards beyond the police barracks; another on a kopje covered with that Stonehenge of limestone boulders; the third with Eloff in the barracks itself. The stone kraal was dealt with first. After a wave of bullets from two squadrons broke over the stone walls, a white flag was seen fluttering about the place. Then the Baralongs rushed forward, eager to pay off old scores. If Captain Marsh, of B Squadron, had not raced them to the kraal, there would not have been many Boers left to surrender. Later, the second group of Boers – holed up in the Stonehenge – were driven off by the same squadrons, assisted by B-P's ancient muzzle-loader. B-P himself directed the attack by telephone, and, for some reason, let most of this party make their escape.[103]

In the old police barracks Eloff's fiery dream was now fast turning to ashes. *The Times* correspondent, Angus Hamilton, witnessed the scene, and got the scoop of his career. Hamilton had been captured when he wandered along to the barracks, not realizing it was at the centre of the battle. ('That is the worst of being educated under black powder,' said Major Baillie of *The Morning Post*, who narrowly missed the same fate, and the scoop.) As Eloff's prisoner, Hamilton spent the day with Colonel Hore and the rest of his men. Eloff treated them chivalrously; one of the officers was allowed to go out in a lull and bring in a young orderly called Hazelrigg, bleeding to death from a wound in the groin; the Boers made no attempt to stop Hore's troopers looting (with scant regard for their Colonel's orders) their own regimental stores, still surprisingly abundant; crates of whisky, Beaune, and so on had been kept in reserve in the barracks, along with a huge box of tinned fruit, peas, and parsnips. But there were unpleasant moments. Trooper Hay, the deserter who had led the Boers into the town, swaggered around with Hore's sword and his gold watch tied to his belt. Hay suggested that the prisoners should either be put out on the veranda as a way of keeping down the garrison's fire, or else be asked to join in defending the barracks. Hamilton explained he was a war correspondent. 'You be damned!' said one of the Boers pleasantly in English. 'We'll put you on the roof.' Eloff then put the thirty-two prisoners, for their own safety, in the store-house, where the whisky had been kept; it was a fetid little place, made worse by the fact that one of the prisoners was suffering acutely from dysentery; but it protected them from the Boers and from British bullets.[104]

From time to time, Eloff visited his prisoners to chat about the battle. 'He sat within the door upon a case of Burgundy, his legs dangling, his accoutrements jingling,' said Hamilton later, 'and the rowels of his spurs echoing the tick-tacking of the Mauser rifles.' No young British officer, surrounded by Dervishes, could have kept a stiffer upper lip. 'He seemed to possess the complete mastery of the situation, his buoyant face was impressed with the confidence of youth, reflecting the happiness he felt . . . that his ambition seemed about to be realized.' As the shadows lengthened, so did the odds against him, and even Eloff began to recognize it. 'At times he lost control of himself and complained querulously in Dutch about the non-appearance of his reinforcements; at other moments he regaled the prisoners with scraps of information [actually quite untrue] . . . that Limestone Fort had fallen, and that the [British] trench beneath the railway bridge had surrendered.' After dark, Hamilton and the other prisoners became extremely demoralized. Outside, there were deafening sounds; British bullets smashed through the wall, the roof, and the door of their prison; through the grating of the window they caught glimpses of the Boers, huddled at their posts. The darkness inside the room was lit up by rifle flashes. The door flew open, and three wounded men fell forward into the room. The strain became almost unendurable. Hamilton, no coward, was convinced that they were about to be led out to execution.

Just then Eloff reappeared in the doorway. To the prisoners' amazement, Eloff offered to surrender, if Hore could arrange a cease-fire. By this time, the telephone had ceased working; and waving the white flag in the dark had had no effect on the town guard. So Hore bellowed out, 'Cease-fire, cease-fire!' His voice was recognized and the captors surrendered to their prisoners.[105]

Next morning, Eloff, accompanied by a French and a German officer, was sitting down to the delayed breakfast at Dixon's Hotel. B-P played host, and Lady Sarah Wilson sat on his right.

Despite these mutual acts of gallantry, the battle had been costly enough for both sides. Eloff had lost about 60 killed and wounded, as well as 108 prisoners. B-P had lost 12 dead and 8 wounded; most of them were Africans.[106]

The relief itself, accomplished the following Wednesday (with three weeks' breadstuffs for the white garrison still in stock),[107] seemed almost an anticlimax after the melodrama of Saturday's battle.

Early on Wednesday, the feeling pervaded the town that at long last, after 217 days, rescue was at hand. The two relief columns – Plumer's from the north,

Mahon's from the south – had already joined forces. People climbed on to the roofs to look for signs. There were trails of dust; Boers', it turned out. Then an hour's distant rumble of artillery about seven miles away to the north-west, then silence. Interest in the relief ebbed away again. People returned to a more pressing pursuit – the final of the siege billiards tournament, in progress at the club. Others carried on with the prosaic job of food-gathering; somebody was shooting sparrows for the pots; natives were cutting up a horse for the soup kitchens.[108]

At seven o'clock, in bright moonlight, a major and eight troopers, with ostrich plumes in their hats, clattered into the market square. The major said they were the advance guard of the relief. 'Oh yes, I heard you were knocking about,' was all he got from a passer-by, who then went off to draw his rations, or do some other task, as though the relief was no business of his.

At first, the fact that Mafeking was relieved was too big for many to grasp. But the news spread, gathering momentum. The nine mysterious horsemen were helped from their horses, clapped on the back, hands pumped, friends recognized by friends. It turned out the major was 'Karri' Davies, the Johannesburg Reformer, and second-in-command of the Uitlanders' regiment, the Imperial Light Horse. He seemed as surprised as anyone to be there in Mafeking, and, of course, delighted. For him, as for many of the Reformers, the war had the quality of a personal vendetta with the Boers. He and his men had been first to ride into Ladysmith, along with Major Gough. Now they had pulled off a double. There were ragged cheers, and the crowd took up 'Rule, Britannia' and 'Red, White and Blue', before the exhausted troopers flung themselves on the ground, and slept by their horses. The moon had set before the main column, including a convoy of food wagons and horse artillery, rumbled after them into Mafeking, unseen by the men they had come to rescue.[109]

Mahon's flying column had, by contemporary standards, certainly flown. They had left Barkly West, on the Vaal, 240 miles to the south, only twelve days earlier, and marched as fast as a stony desert road and near-empty waterholes would allow. Drought and dust and sickness, not Boers, had proved their most dangerous enemies, though the advance of this weak, western column would have been impossible if Roberts's main army had not also begun, at long last, its great advance at the same time. For most of the time Mahon's column nimbly side-stepped any Boers who shadowed it.[110] On 11 May, Mahon sent a cryptic message by runner to warn Plumer and B-P of his own relative weakness. The code was a special old-school-tie code invented for the occasion: 'Our numbers are Naval and Military Club multiplied by ten [94 Piccadilly × 10 = 940]; our guns the number of sons in the Ward family [The Earl of Dudley and 5 brothers = a battery of six]; our supplies the O.C. 9th Lancers [Lt-Col Little = few].'[111]

In fact, the column totalled 1,149, and largely consisted not of British troops, but of rough-and-ready South African mounted irregulars. The great majority were Uitlanders, the men of the 'Imperial' (i.e., ex-Johannesburg) Light Horse – both the squadrons who had, with Woolls-Sampson, been locked up in

Ladysmith, and the one that had, with Karri Davies, triumphantly unlocked them; they amounted to 814 officers and men. There were also 122 colonials from Rhodes' diamond city, the Kimberley Mounted Corps. The truly *imperial* troops were the hundred men of the Royal Horse Artillery. In addition, it had been decided, after consultation with Milner, to send exactly a hundred British infantry: twenty-five from each of the four regions, England, Scotland, Wales, Ireland.[112] This was, of course, a mere token, a flutter of the Union Jack, but there was no missing the political message: that the Imperial factor in South Africa had come to stay. Otherwise, there would have been an extraordinary sense of *déja vu* about Mahon's relief column. Apart from Mahon himself, the column was dominated by those would-be revolutionaries of the Rand, the Reformers. There was not only Karri Davies. Colonel Frank Rhodes, Cecil's brother – sentenced to death in 1896 by Kruger and released from gaol in Pretoria, only to be locked up for those 120 days with White at Ladysmith – Rhodes was Mahon's Intelligence Officer, and the man who had, in effect, planned the expedition. The Raiders, too, had somehow pushed their way to the front of the stage. Colonel Sir John Willoughby, Jameson's Number Two during the Raid, sentenced at Bow Street to ten months' imprisonment and dismissed from the British army, had re-emerged as (acting) Major Sir John Willoughby, Mahon's DAAG. Lieutenant-Colonel Bobby White, Jameson's Number Three, was attached to Plumer's relief column.[113] It was as though the main actors of that tragi-comedy (apart from Jameson) had decided on a repeat performance, but flying the imperial flag: the play to be acted in reverse. For in 1895 the Raiders had ridden from Mafeking to Johannesburg; and now Johannesburg had ridden to Mafeking. And it was in this sense – an inverted victory, rather than the conventional kind – that the news of the relief of Mafeking was received with hysterical acclaim all over the British world.

The hysteria may look ludicrous in retrospect. 'They are behaving as though they had beaten Napoleon,' said Wilfred Blunt.[114] Yet the instinct of the public was also correct, for there was much, in the short term, to celebrate. The relief of Mafeking proved to be only the first of a new run of victories for the British. In the fortnight since Mahon's column had clattered across the Vaal, a great change had come over the war map of South Africa. Roberts's grand army had made its second, and by far its most successful, 'tiger-spring'. Already the golden mine dumps of the Rand glittered on the horizon. By early June, that small, silk Union Jack, worked by Nora Roberts, would be floating over Pretoria, and the seat of Kruger's government would be a Netherlands Railway coach, fleeing northwards.[115]

And Mafeking was not only a new English word (*OED*: 'maffick'). It was taken as a symbol of the new imperial unity forged by the war. B-P's garrison had been raised in the Cape; Plumer's column in Rhodesia (and Plumer could not have succeeded without his Canadian guns and Australian infantry); and where would the garrison have been if the Rand had not come riding to the rescue?

In Britain, Mafeking meant, in every sense, relief: hysterical, euphoric relief.

Relief from that 'nightmare' (as Balfour, the deputy Prime Minister, had called it)[116] of national humiliation. A clear-cut, happy ending, so it seemed, to the series of confused disasters that had characterized the first part of the war. The strange kind of victory – the avoidance of defeat – in which people could take unqualified pride. Not a blood-bath like Waterloo, or a massacre like Omdurman, but something reassuringly closer to a game of cricket. It was a story that the sporting British public could take immediately to their hearts (where it was to remain for two generations). How one man and some loafers, with little help from the War Office, had fought against fearful odds and had, by English pluck and ingenuity, turned a forlorn hope into a triumph.

In short, Colonel B-P had given back the other BP, the British Public, its faith in itself. 'It is good to be an Englishman,' said Major Baillie, the war correspondent, and he would have been echoed by English people of every social class. 'These foreigners start too quick and finish quicker. They are good men but we are better, and have proved so for several hundred years.'[117]

Was it in fact a triumph? Of course, in direct military terms it was no such thing, once the 'Cronje phase' of the siege was over. But wars, except wars of extermination, are not about troops and guns and positions on the map (a lesson that was to prove a bitter one for the British all through the following year). Wars are ultimately about morale. And B-P had not only given back Britain its self-confidence, but dealt the Boers a crushing psychological blow by denying them Mafeking, the symbolic birth-place of the Raid. No other British commander in the war had done so much with so little.

By contrast, the celebrations, and the mood, of the garrison in Mafeking were modest enough. There was a ceremonial march-past of the relief column, just as there had been in Ladysmith. B-P took the salute. It happened to be the Queen's birthday, and bunting decorated the shattered buildings. The Queen's Christmas chocolate was distributed, five months late, but no less appropriate. People sent the chocolate home as a curio, and with it the other valuable trophies of the siege: 'Lord Nelson' depicted on the bank-notes, B-P's head on the stamps, already £19 for each set. There were fireworks that evening, just as there were in half the towns in the Empire, but people decorously sang 'God Save the Queen' before retiring early to bed under the stars.[118]

At the march-past, B-P had been, uncharacteristically, unable to control his emotions. Perhaps it was the natural reaction to the end of that ordeal, or the moral burden he had carried for so long in his lonely vigil on his watch-tower. Perhaps the sight of his friend, 'The Boy' McLaren, back at his side was too much for him to bear. Or perhaps it was just the grousing he could not take; bitter things were already being said about him by the men of Plumer's column, cheated of the glory of the relief by Mahon.[119] B-P a hero? 'To me the whole affair of the siege ... was an enigma,' wrote one of Plumer's captains. 'What in the world was the use of defending this wretched railway-siding and these tin-shanties? To burrow underground on the very first shot being fired ... seemed to me the strangest role ever played by a cavalry leader ...'[120]

Already myth and counter-myth were beginning to overlay the history of the siege, as the sand from the Kalahari began to drift over the graves of the 354 Africans officially recorded as having died of shell and shot, and of countless others who died of hunger or disease.[121]

In one respect, B-P *did* behave entirely in character. Apart from a brisk mention of some of the Baralongs in despatches, no thanks were given to the majority of the garrison – the Africans. A relief fund – £29,000 – was generously raised in England to put Mafeking back on its feet. None of this went to the thousands of Africans whose farms had been looted, towns burnt, and families expelled or died of starvation. The Stadt, the other Mafeking, represented the plight of all black South Africa in microcosm. This was 'white man's country'. The Africans were there to be useful to white men. When no longer useful, they must go back to where they belonged, wherever that might be. So, in the 'white man's war', they had to pay, like the animals, a terrible price.

After B-P had left Mafeking to found the Boy Scout movement and become one of the most famous Englishmen alive, and after 'Lord Nelson' was put, appropriately, in a museum, people erected an official war memorial to the Mafeking dead. A small plaque was, strange to say, added; recording the services of the 'Black Watch'.[122]

Better still would have been to quote that lapidary phrase of Milner's: 'You have only to sacrifice "the nigger" absolutely, and the game is easy.'[123]

CHAPTER 34

Across the Vaal

The Orange River Colony
and the Transvaal,
31 May–June 1900

Cook's son – Duke's son – son of a belted Earl –
Son of a Lambeth publican – it's all the same today!

Rudyard Kipling,
'The Absent-Minded Beggar'

'The long-looked to, long-waited for moment has come at last,' said the newly promoted young officer of the Tigers, Lieutenant March Phillipps.[1] He felt pleased with himself, and with good reason. They had ridden 260 miles in twenty-six days. He was the front pair of legs of a triumphant, undulating centipede – of 860 centipedes, in fact, the forty-three thousand men of Roberts's 'Grand Army'.[2] It was 31 May, and victory now seemed as close to the touch, in the champagne-clear light of the high veld, as the golden mine dumps of the Rand. Over there was British Johannesburg, only ten miles down that avenue of iron mine chimneys and spidery winding gear. And beyond the Golden City, awaiting relief, there was Kruger's Pretoria, awaiting her conquerors.

It had been a breathtaking leap, that twenty-six-day march from Bloemfontein to the Rand. No one had expected the Boers to give much of a 'show'. But the speed and the momentum had surprised even Roberts, who had planned the march, and was never one to doubt his own success.[3] Here at last, it seemed, those war dreams of the previous year had come to reality, if not in time for Christmas, at least before the Derby: the 'walk-over', the 'apology for a fight' (Milner's phrase to Chamberlain),[4] the 'irresistible force' meeting some highly movable objects and scattering them like dust beneath the wagon wheels.

Exit the old Orange Free State; thus Roberts's official proclamation on 28 May.* Enter the new 'Orange River Colony'.[5]

The pattern of the advance rarely faltered. The enemy was the veld, not the Boers: a sun to fry you, and a frost to freeze you (for winter had come, encrusting the men's blankets with hoar-frost as they slept), too little trek ox to eat, too few biscuits – when there were rations at all. Each morning, under the stars, the cry is raised, 'Saddle up!' and the Tigers curse as they lie there, huddled in greatcoats, their saddles as pillows. Then the great column, which has curled itself up for the night like a caterpillar, begins slowly to stretch itself and crawl, wagon after wagon, horse after horse, kicking up dust from the road.[6] And soon

---

* Standard history books give the wrong date for the annexation. It was formally proclaimed on 28 May – not 26 May (as in Lord Roberts's official despatch), nor 24 May, when it was issued in Army Orders.

the infantry column is off 'on the tramp':[7] an army of sixty thousand boots, marching to Pretoria under the eye of a war balloon. Winston Churchill, who had now turned his attention to the western front, compared this war balloon to the 'pillar of cloud that led the hosts of Israel'.[8]

To the young officer of the Tigers, the march seemed less biblical: 'The Huns or the Goths, in one of their vast tribal invasions, may have looked like this.' That day, 31 May, the whole of the double column of Roberts's invasion force converged on Vredefort, astride the central railway. For a few hours, the right flank could see the main column and grasp the immensity of it all: 'Endless battalions of infantry, very dusty and grimy ... guns, bearer-companies, Colonial Horse, generals and their staffs go plodding and jingling by ... long convoys of the different units ... groaning and creaking along, the oxen sweating, the dust whirling, the naked Kaffirs yelling, and the long whips going like pistol-shots. The whole thing suggests more a national migration than the march of an enemy.'[9] So it was in a sense: Britain's great trek.

How did it look to the British trekkers – including that new-fangled recruit to the British army, the gentleman-trooper?[10] Kipling was right.[11] Never had war looked so democratic. Over half of the ten thousand rank and file of the Imperial Yeomanry and City Imperial Volunteers, raised in that whirlwind of patriotism that followed Black Week – over half of these troopers were from the middle class.[12] About four thousand of these recruits were now marching with Roberts to Pretoria.[13] But raising these volunteers was not just an imperialist stunt. The recruits included many competent amateur soldiers. They believed – and soon they would have their chance to prove it – that a British soldier, like his Boer counterpart, could make up with common sense what he lacked in military training. Already, these gentlemen-rankers, like Trooper 8008 and Driver Erskine Childers (alias the Hon. Sidney Peel, barrister-at-law, and Mr Childers, Clerk of the House of Commons), had made important discoveries about the facts of war. The 'big things' were not the battles, let alone the rights and wrongs of the war.[14] They were the personal things: how to get wood for the fire, how to steal a duck from a farm without being caught, how to make their biscuits last tomorrow's march.[15] And, above all, the boots:

> Don't-don't-don't-look at what's in front of you.
> (Boots-boots-boots-boots movin' up an' down again).[16]

The Field-Marshal rode in his covered wagon – the mobile HQ – and his anxieties were of a more elevated sort. There was one thing about this war he could not explain, not even to himself. His own army had marched at prodigious speed – having covered that distance at a speed never equalled by his hero, Wellington. How had the Boers marched faster? Theirs was a retreat, chaotic and demoralized, he thought, yet never, for one moment, a rout. At each of the natural defence lines – five broad, muddy, brown rivers that intersected railway and road; the Vet, the Zand, the Vaalsch, the Rhenoster, and the great Vaal itself – at each of them the Boers had dug trenches, as though determined to defend them as they had defended the Modder. Roberts, with ten times the mounted

troops that either Buller or Methuen had had, sent his men to outflank the
trenches. The Boers had fled. The main column had hardly a skirmish.[17] All that
Roberts and his staff, standing on a kopje, ever saw of the enemy was more like a
mirage than a battle: a train steaming away into the distance, a shadowy group of
horsemen, the pillar of black smoke as the bridges and railway culverts were
dynamited by the Boers own 'Irish Brigade' ('Wreckers Corps') led by Major
John McBride. Somehow the cavalry never 'got into' the Boers, as the phrase
went. Why couldn't the fellows stand and fight like gentlemen? 'They slip away
in the most extraordinary manner,' explained Roberts to Lansdowne.[18] Somehow there was always a rearguard strong enough to hold off French's cavalry
and horse artillery. Somehow the Boers always saved even their wagons and
heavy guns without paying the price in casualties.[19] Botha's army was in full
flight – yet they marched like victors.

So the great question still remained open, as the army approached the Rand at
the end of May. Roberts could save the gold-mines, perhaps. He could rescue the
three thousand British prisoners held at Pretoria, probably. He could capture
Pretoria, certainly, and proclaim the Transvaal, like the Free State, a British
colony. But would this end the war?

There was an intelligence report supplied by the Director of Military Intelligence, Colonel McKenzie, who forecast that Kruger would retreat north to
Lydenburg, and only defend Pretoria lightly. The war would go on. This view
was echoed by Colonel Rawlinson, at the heart of Roberts's inner circle. 'It looks
to me,' Rawlinson wrote on 13 May, 'as though the war could last for a good
many months more. The enemy will, as I have always said, break up into small
parties and take to guerrilla war, which will entail much time and blood to
conquer.' Ian Hamilton, however, Roberts's confidant and closest protegé, took
his usual optimistic view,[20] and Roberts now agreed with Hamilton.

Roberts pinned his faith on the psychological effect of a blow to the heart –
striking at Pretoria. He rejected the alternative: to deal with De Wet and Steyn
first. Not that he ignored the fact, when he had set out from Bloemfontein, that
about seven thousand of Christiaan De Wet's Free State burghers would be left
behind his own lines. On the contrary, he had detached nearly half the force,
designed to invade the Transvaal, to protect the Free State and the all-important
railway to the Cape ports from raids by De Wet. The job of these twenty
thousand men was to disarm the Boer population (and unhorse them, too), so as
to deny any further support to De Wet.[21] At the same time, Roberts was most
anxious to be lenient to any Boers who were prepared to co-operate. Thus,
looting was strictly forbidden in Army Orders, except where farms had been
used as bases for attacking the British (a practice which was fortunately widespread, according to the looters).[22] But Roberts had set his face against trying to
crush De Wet *before* marching out of the Free State. He was impatient to end the
war, anxious to keep his losses down, as demanded by the British public. The
risk of De Wet's and President Steyn's re-emergence as the centre of Boer
resistance was a 'risk he had to run', so he told Lansdowne. He did not expect it.[23]

Thus on 3 May, he had started the push northwards, preceded by General

Hunter's column (and its offshoot, Colonel Bryan Mahon's flying column) fifty miles to the west, swooping along the banks of the Lower Vaal. His own double column stayed within reach of the main railway line – Tucker's and Pole-Carew's divisions (the 7th and 11th) under his own eye, and a new division, specially created for his favourite, Ian Hamilton, marching ten to twenty miles away to the east.[24] On 10 May, Buller had at last agreed to bestir himself with the two remaining Natal divisions, from his bases south of the Biggarsberg.[25] So, on this broad front of 330 miles, Roberts still retained crushing superiority of numbers, despite the twenty thousand troops he had left in the Free State: eight thousand with Hunter along the Vaal; thirty thousand with himself and Hamilton in the centre; twenty thousand with Buller in Natal.[26]

At first, Roberts assumed that he could find some way to entrap the Boers, as Cronje had been trapped. 'All is going well but it is a pity we shan't have a fight at the Zand,' wrote Rawlinson in his diary on 8 May. 'No bag again. ...'[27] A couple of days earlier, Roberts himself had told Hamilton to make a 'supreme effort to run the Boers down between this and Kroonstad'. Roberts soon had to reconcile himself to his failure to make any 'bag'. After driving the Boers out of Kroonstad, he halted ten days (to Rawlinson's disgust), in order to allow the railway to be repaired behind him.[28] His mobility was bedevilled, like Buller's in Natal, by the problem of transport and supply. Despite the improvement made by largely restoring the old transport system, the troops still went hungry when they stepped far from the railway; and the repairs to the railway could not even keep up with the pace of the ox. The Boers' own 'Irish Brigade' had blown up every culvert and bridge from Bloemfontein to the Vaal, and each mine left a tangle of steel rails knotted to the permanent way. The man who straightened out these knots – in effect, the chief hero of the advance – was the Director of Railways, a thirty-three-year-old engineer called Lieutenant-Colonel Percy Girouard, whose promotion so young was one of Kitchener's few really success-ful ideas; Girouard was one of K of K's band of 'boys' from the Sudan. But even Girouard, and thousands of black railway navvies, could not bridge the Vet and the Zand and the Vaal in a day. Meanwhile, the British went hungry, or lived on emergency rations of meat paste, and the Boers had leisure to consolidate their flight.[29]

The most costly aspect of these interruptions to the railway was not the few days they held up Roberts's advance, or the meals they lost his troops, but the way they exacerbated the crisis of the field hospitals. Nothing better illustrates Roberts's limitations as a military commander than the fact, as it emerged at Kroonstad, that his field medical services were in as scandalous a state as the fixed hospitals at Bloemfontein. Typhoid, Dingaan's revenge, assiduous camp-follower of the victors ever since Paardeberg, caused more British casualties that month than all the battles of Black Week. Belatedly, Roberts was coming to recognize the disaster and its causes – although he did not admit it in his letters to Lansdowne.[30] He told the Surgeon-General, Wilson, to find a new sanitary officer instead of the notorious Colonel Exham, the PMO from Ladysmith transferred to Bloemfontein.[31] He gave Wilson himself a stiff reprimand for failing to send doctors and nurses to keep up with the army. 'Hospital arrangements,' he wrote from Kroonstad on the 21st, 'are most unsatisfactory, and I trust you to come here and superintend them ... some hundred mattresses are urgently needed. ... The requirements for Kroonstad should have been foreseen and spare surgeons should have been on the spot. ...'[32]

Perhaps one should not blame Roberts for what he styled 'unfortunate incidents' in the hospitals of the Free State, any more severely than one should blame Buller for the reverses in Natal. Both Generals made errors of judgement, and their men paid the price. In lives, Roberts's errors to date were the more expensive of the two.[33]

Indeed, a new contrast was emerging between the two rivals: Roberts and Buller. Since the great advance had begun in May, they had both been fighting on roughly comparable terms against relatively weak and demoralized Boer forces. Both were triumphant. But the reverses that blighted the triumphs changed the whole character of the war and, above all, trebled its length. These reverses, as we shall soon see, were all on Roberts's side.

Twenty miles east of Kroonstad, Ian Hamilton was in his element. He had two infantry brigades, including the 1st Battalion of his own regiment, the Gordon Highlanders.[34] Beside him rode a dashing new ADC, the Duke of Marlborough, transferred from Roberts's staff, and beside Marlborough rode his first cousin, *The Morning Post* correspondent, Winston Churchill; Hamilton had persuaded Winston to come along and see 'the show'. As they rode into Lindley, Hamilton's shattered wrist flapped at the saddle: a 'glorious' deformity, as Churchill tactfully said. It was a reminder of a personal account with the Boers still not paid off in full; for this was the wrist smashed when he had served with the Gordons at Majuba.[35]

One can guess why everyone (except Buller and the remnants of the Wolseley Ring) found Hamilton so attractive, why Bobs himself praised him as he praised none of his other field commanders. Hamilton's character supplied what Roberts pre-eminently lacked: style. Hamilton was gallant and boyish, the *beau idéal* of the warrior, whether seen through the eyes of Sargent, and painted in full-dress uniform, or of Winston Churchill, as the hero of his forthcoming 'Ian Hamilton's March'. And how Hamilton loved to be loved. In the Army List he was a mere colonel still. Now the little man had made him acting *Lieutenant-General*, with a force of fifteen thousand men and thirty-eight guns. What a contrast to those dismal days locked up with poor old White at Ladysmith! He had now been given the right flank of Roberts's double column: that is, two mounted brigades (Broadwood's cavalry and Ridley's MI) and two infantry brigades (Major-General Horace Smith-Dorrien's 19th and Major-General Bruce Hamilton's 21st). His job was to smooth the path of the main column, and smooth it he would.[36]

To say that Ian Hamilton's column had thus seen some brisk fighting was not to say much. There had been a stiff action at Houtnek on 7 May; and, in turning the flank of the Boers at Zand River on 10 May, he had suffered rather less than a hundred casualties. But the pattern of Hamilton's advance was hardly less monotonous than Bobs's. It was a lumbering leap towards the Rand: days of plodding along dusty tracks east of the railway; a moment's skirmish with the Boers' rearguard; then back to the other adversaries: hunger, thirst, frost, sun, disease.[37]

It was 18 May when the column approached Lindley, which had been proclaimed the new provisional capital of the Free State after the fall of Kroonstad. It had already been abandoned by Steyn and his government when Hamilton's vanguard rumbled into the town. Lindley struck people as a depressing place. It was one of those strange, bare little towns, whose presence on the veld was so inexplicable: no visible roads led to it; no fertile fields, let alone trees or gardens, surrounded it; it was just a cluster of tin roofs and a bleak, tall church. The veld carried Lindley on its lap as casually as the sea carries a ship.[38] And a kind of ship Lindley was soon to be: the flagship of De Wet and his raiders.

Hamilton himself found the omens understandably difficult to read. The inhabitants were unwelcoming, except for the British settlers who owned the two shops; their loyalty was embarrassing. (Churchill warned one of them to haul down the Union Jack; this column was not a garrison.)[39] On the other hand, an encouraging message reached Broadwood, the cavalry commander, from Christiaan De Wet's brother, Piet: he was contemplating surrender, and he would bring in a thousand burghers, too; could Broadwood guarantee he would not be sent as a prisoner to Cape Town? Broadwood guaranteed it. Hamilton (incidentally, Churchill, too) agreed that it would be wise to offer the most generous terms. Then a telegram arrived from HQ: Roberts told Broadwood he had no authority to make these terms; so the offer of surrender lapsed.

The column lumbered out of Lindley, with Piet De Wet's men snapping at their heels. There was an unfortunate incident when Hamilton lost fifty-nine of his rearguard. This was partly offset by a minor *coup* of Broadwood's: he captured fifteen Boer wagons. Lindley sailed off into the heat-haze. General Colvile and the Highland Brigade, whose job was to sweep up behind Hamilton, would be able to deal with De Wet in a few days. After that, the Union Jacks could be run up and could stay up. So it was fondly imagined.[40]

Hamilton crossed the Vaal, the Boers' Rubicon, on 26 May. By this time, Roberts had switched Hamilton's army from the east flank to the west of the railway line. Roberts's plan for taking Johannesburg, forty miles beyond the Vaal, was straightforward enough. The two most mobile columns – twenty thousand men, led by French and Hamilton – were to swing round to the west of the city, and cut the main road leading from the townships along the Rand: Krugersdorp, Florida and so on. Meanwhile, the main force, of about the same size, would go straight up the railway line to the east and so outflank Johannesburg from the other side. These were the tactics that had worked time and again all the way north from Bloemfontein, the tactics of the walk-over.[41] But for once Hamilton saw his way to the honours of a real battle. The Boers were entrenched at Doornkop, beside a small white farmhouse, on a high ridge in sight of the mine chimneys of Krugersdorp. Here, perhaps for the last time, was a chance to wipe that 'something' off the slate. For this was *the* Doornkop, the actual kopje, beside the farmhouse, where Jameson had raised the white flag, five years before.[42]

There seemed a special appropriateness about both the setting and the actors in this final scene of the struggle for the gold-mines. The four infantry battalions in Bruce Hamilton's 21st Brigade included not only the Gordons – the Majuba regiment – but also the Lord Mayor of London's much-publicized gift to the nation, the City Imperial Volunteers. Hamilton gave the CIV a place of honour in the front of the battle line. The City now had its turn to redeem the Raid by storming the Rand.[43]

Ian Hamilton agreed with French that French should take the mounted troops, including Hamilton's own two brigades, and outflank Doornkop from the west. Then, to the surprise of one of the brigadiers (Major-General Edward Hutton) and of one of the correspondents (Churchill), Hamilton launched his two infantry brigades in a four-mile-wide frontal attack on the ridge.[44]

The charge that followed – the CIV and the Gordon Highlanders charging up a hillside, without cover from fire or proper support from artillery – was to provide one of the last set-piece battles of the war. It was, in a way, magnificent. Lieutenant March Phillipps, who had fought at Graspan, Magersfontein and the other big battles on the western front, wrote about the Gordons' charge: 'This was, I think, the finest performance I have seen in the whole campaign.' The Gordons marched up, with the swing of their kilts and a swagger that only Highland regiments had, and then lay down quickly, beside Hamilton's staff officers, on the crest line facing the Boer position. 'Advance!' The front line got up, and walked slowly forwards down the slope. 'Advance!' and another kilted line rose and followed them; and then another. The lines were widely separated and there were gaps of about fifteen yards between each man; otherwise, the advance was conducted with the same drill-book tactics as Hamilton had used at Elandslaagte (and, indeed, Raglan at Balaclava).[45]

Before the front line had reached the floor of the valley, Hamilton and the watchers could hear the dull, vicious 'crick-crack' of the Mausers. (In fact, the Boers were a few hundred Johannesburgers, led by Viljoen, and the Lichtenburgers, led by De la Rey.) Soon there were puffs of dust among the lines of men. Farther on, where the hill sloped up to the stony kopjes held by the Boers, the grass was burnt black and bare, and the bullets cut through the cinders, throwing up dust, white against black. Still, the lines advanced. Here and there, visible through binoculars, men staggered and fell; but no one knew if they were hit or had thrown themselves down to take aim. The shooting became fast and furious. The British guns thundered; smoke from the burning grass drifted across the view. Then, there was a gasp and murmur among the watchers. Against the backdrop of burnt veld, sparkling in the sun, the ripple of steel. Fixed bayonets! The figures gained the skyline, a few at first, then more. There was a sharp, rapid exchange of shots, then the firing flickered and died away. The Gordons had the hill. They had lost a hundred men in ten minutes, but they had done the trick.[46]

It was now dusk, and Ian Hamilton galloped forward and, in the glare of the grass fires, addressed the victors. 'Men of the Gordons, officers of the Gordons, I want to tell you how proud I am of you; of my father's old regiment, and of the regiment I was born in. You have done splendidly.'[47]

Next day, Churchill, whose own feelings about war were more complicated, visited the spot where the worst slaughter had taken place. It was the grassy hollow between two crest lines – the false and the true crest lines. Churchill interviewed one of the Gordons, a kind-faced man with the Indian Frontier ribbon on his tunic.

'Well, you see, sir . . . we was regularly tricked. We began to lose men so soon as we got on the burnt grass. Then we made our charge up to this first line of little rocks, thinking the Boers were there. Of course they weren't here at all, but back over there, where you see those big rocks. . . .

We knew we was for it then; it didn't look like getting on, and we couldn't get back – never a man would ha' lived to cross the black ground again with the fire where it was. . . .'

'What was done? What did you do?'

'Why, go on, sir, and take that other line – the big rocks – soon as we'd got our breath. It had to be done.'

Faced with the melancholy sight of the grey-stockinged feet of eighteen dead Highlanders waiting for burial, Churchill found himself seized by a strange burst of anger. It was illogical, he thought; for, like almost all patriotic Englishmen, Churchill refused to believe that this was a war fought to win control of the gold-mines. Yet, faced with the dead men, lying there only a few miles from the great gold reef, Churchill found himself, he wrote later, 'scowling at the tall chimneys of the Rand'.[48]

There was another question that Churchill did *not* ask himself. 'It had to be done,' said the Highlander. But did it have to be done in that particular fashion?

As it happened, the battalion leading the attack on the western end of the Boer-held ridge had employed less spectacular, but rather more up-to-date tactics. The CIV, being an amateur battalion, had little of the Balaclava mentality to unlearn. They had made their charge in short rushes (one group giving covering fire to another), and they took care to offer as little of a target as possible. They, too, took the hill. But they suffered few casualties, compared to the Gordon's seventeen killed and eighty wounded.[49]

Yet, despite the relative success of the CIV's new tactics (roughly the same as had been painfully hammered out by Buller and his men in Natal), there remains the question: was any charge necessary at all? Hamilton later gave three reasons for risking a frontal attack: first, that he thought that the enemy's line was weak because it was so extended; second, that the men, short of rations for days, must march by the direct road to Florida; third, that he was afraid of dividing, by too wide a gap, his main force from the men guarding the hills behind him. None of these explanations is very convincing. The battle lasted till dusk, so the men did not reach Florida (and its meagre food supplies) till next afternoon. And there *was* a way round: through the gap opened up by French and the seven thousand

South African Light Horse marching through Cape Town, early 1900.
Inset Lord Roberts, the new C-in-C.
Following page Spion Kop: the morning after.

Opposite above Dickson's newsreel of Buller's troops retreating from Spion Kop.
Below Roberts, in the Free State, plans the advance.
Above The relief of Kimberley: the first train-load of refugees.

Cronje surrenders to Roberts at Paardeberg.

Above De Wet and other Boer generals at a council of war outside Bloemfontein, early March 1900.
Below Cronje's men after the surrender at Paardeberg.
Following page Roberts occupies Johannesburg, 31 May 1900.

mounted men, a four-mile detour west of Doornkop. It is hard to believe that the infantry could not have shouldered through that way, too. Of course, Hamilton had little experience of the new twentieth-century-style warfare. After Elandslaagte, he had spent most of the war locked up in Ladysmith. He knew nothing of those creeping artillery barrages, evolved to support the infantry attacks in Natal. His handling of his artillery at Doornkop proved lamentable, considering he had fourteen guns, including two 5-inch 'cow-guns' – heavy guns drawn, like the Boers' Long Toms, by bullocks.[50]

A more convincing explanation for Hamilton's decision to fight the battle of Doornkop, rather than go round, was that Hamilton wanted to fight it. He could not resist the challenge to redeem the two white flags.

He received nothing but praise from Roberts and Roberts's admirers. Leo Amery wrote in *The Times History* a eulogy that already – that is, before Ypres, Mons and the Somme – had a ghastly, anachronistic ring. Even if the attack had not been necessary, wrote Amery, 'it would not have been wasted, for the steady enduring discipline of the men under fire, *their absolute indifference to losses*, contributed to carry on the glorious traditions of the British infantry'.[51]

Meanwhile, Roberts's central column – Colonel Henry's MI, Tucker's 7th Division and Pole-Carew's 11th Division – had plodded on to Elandsfontein, the strategic railway junction eight miles up the valley to the east of Johannesburg.[52]

Prevost Battersby, another of *The Morning Post*'s intrepid men-at-the-front, watched the incongruous scenes at the railway station on the 29th. Coming from the empty veld, it was odd to find this valley full of mining machinery, bristling with chimneys, winding gear, and blue-grey spoil heaps. Odder still, to see that some of the mines were still working. 'Trains were shunting in and out of the station, smoke from the pumping engines rose from some of the chimneys, and save for an occasional distant thud there was no suggestion of war.'[53]

Battersby rode up to the great muddy dam built to provide water for the Simmer and Jack mine. Suddenly Henry's MI were pinned down by some Boers firing from behind the spoil heaps, five hundred yards away. The troopers lost a third of their number; the rest took cover behind some prospecting trenches. The firing stopped; the trains continued shunting. Over by the station, passers-by thought the battle was over, and gathered on the pavement. The battle was by no means over. Skirts fluttered, women screamed, bullets pattered on the tin-roofed houses 'like the first heavy stones of a hailstorm'. In the station, people crouched under the platform, or huddled against the brick wall; others crawled between the wheels of railway trucks. Bullets hissed and shrieked as they smashed through the corrugated iron and bounced off down the street.

It was all very quaint [wrote Battersby later], and much more like melodrama than an event of life and death; but that is the charm of street fighting – its extraordinary air of unreality. The reality was there. A man lay on the platform pushed up against the wall, with a great patch of cloth blown out of his thigh, where some foul bullet had passed out through his leg; and a Boer was lying back against the white slope of cyanide ash [cyanide is used in refining gold ore] with his throat visible through the gap which had held his eye. And below were the women, peering and screaming, and starting hysterically at each fresh phase of the fight.[54]

Apart from this small affair ('a piece of interesting colour, the only piece of the kind, so far, in the campaign'),[55] there was nothing further to check the army here, and they pushed on a few miles before dark; then their bivouac fires glowed among the gum-trees, grown for pit-props, filling the valley. Next evening, two bicyclists came pedalling down the road from the west, carrying official despatches from Hamilton, modestly describing his triumph at Doorn-kop. The two daredevils on bicycles had ridden through Johannesburg itself. They were shown into the local *landrost's* house, which Roberts had made his HQ, and one was taken in to see the Chief. One of them was bumptious young Winston Churchill. If he had not captured Johannesburg single-handed, he had done the next best thing.

Churchill later reported how the Field-Marshal's eyes 'twinkled' when he reported his adventures. The Chief was in high spirits.[56] There was unpleasant news from Colvile and the Highland Brigade; they had got themselves into a 'tight corner' somewhere north of Lindley, in the Free State. Otherwise, the news seemed, in every sense, golden. Commandant Krause, the Boer official now in charge of Johannesburg, had promised that the mines of the Rand would all be left intact. Johannesburg would be surrendered next morning, at eleven o'clock. There was one vital condition imposed by the Boers. Roberts must give them twenty-four hours to withdraw their army from the town. And to this kind of armistice Roberts had been perfectly willing to agree.[57] He halted his two divisions at Germiston and allowed the Boers to withdraw their army intact, instead of continuing the advance and trying to crush them.

It was probably the most serious strategic mistake of his career – as we shall see. But there is no mystery about Roberts's reason. It was in keeping with the 'velvet-glove' strategy of trying to bring the war to a speedy and humane conclusion, and of giving priority to saving the gold-mines. Go for the Boer capitals. Offer the Boers individually (but not as a government) the most lenient terms. These were Roberts's two guiding principles. Now the gold-mines were virtually safe, and with them Wernher-Beit's millions,[58] and, indeed, the whole idea of a Federation of British South Africa.

The war was nearly over, so Roberts believed. So why waste British lives by attacking the Boers now? It seemed a sensible and humane short-cut. In fact, it was only by the narrowest of margins that the policy was to fail, and lead to disaster: to extend the fighting by nearly two years of dismal guerrilla warfare.

All that day, Wednesday, Louis Botha's army trundled northwards to Pretoria in a vast cloud of dust and scenes of utter confusion. All the heavy guns, all the strategic supplies – including the last boxes of gold mined on the Rand – were dragged safely out of Johannesburg.[59] Next day, the conquerors marched in from the opposite direction. The scene was as incongruous as the one on 13 March, when the Grand Army had marched into Bloemfontein. Lord Kerry,

Roberts's ADC, later described the imperial moment of glory to his father, Lord Lansdowne:

Formal surrender of town brought in early, so started off at 10-o'clk riding right along Rand ridge with 11th, and 7th Divisions following, met Dr Krause, who accompanied the procession outside Jeppestown then all down Commissioner Street to the Law Courts; a good many people all along the road chiefly niggers and Jews, and a big crowd waiting outside law courts, unattractive looking people speaking with tongues, mostly friendly and wearing red white and blue badges but an occasional groan could be heard.

Arrived at Law Courts, Chief dismounted and went into a room where members of municipality etc assembled; these introduced to Chief, who afterwards came outside for the ceremony. Drums of the Guards Brigade marched into the square followed by about two companies of Essex regt, the leading one of 18th Brigade; there was not room for more. The vierkleur flying on flag staff in the square was then pulled down and Union Jack hoisted in its stead, Royal Salute, God Save the Queen, and three cheers for the Queen called for by Chief. . . . Dr Krause sat on his horse next to the Chief and apparently thought the whole show was partly in his honour, as he as well as Lord R. took all salutes. Some of Tuckers (VII Div.) . . . started cheering as they past [sic] the saluting base and this was taken up by the remainder, the men taking off their hats and getting wildly excited, to the great horror of experts in drill and Queen's regulations who were present. About 4 o'clock got away and went to lunch, a good one, more especially as no member of the establishment was perfectly sober.[60]

After these brief antics, the humdrum life of the big city began to return to Johannesburg, especially the life of the Africans. There were fourteen thousand mine boys still employed on the Rand;[61] they were the worker bees of the golden hive; they had kept the gold vats full in enough of the commandeered gold-mines to pay for the whole Boer war effort, with a balance of £1,294,000 still on hand.[62]

Now the Africans found that their celebrations of Roberts's victory, celebrations which included widespread burning of 'passes', had been premature. Indeed, when Lord Kerry saw those 'niggers' cheering the Chief from the pavements during the march-past, he had probably not fully grasped the incongruity of the occasion. Pavements were forbidden by Transvaal law to all Africans and coloured people. So the first step of Roberts's military government in Johannesburg was to get them off the pavements and back into their locations. This was one set of Transvaal laws that the conquerors had no intention of changing: the laws affecting the natives. Indeed, it was ironical that the laws that made Africans into the helots were now to be applied with an efficiency that the Boers had never been able to muster.[63]

What of Chamberlain's brave words in the draft of the British ultimatum of October 1899, of 'most favoured nation status' for coloured British subjects in the Transvaal? Fortunately for the British, this ultimatum was still collecting dust in the Colonial Office files. At any rate, the men who were now to administer British Johannesburg were not interested in this particular type of reform. They were Uitlanders. Their aim was to take political control of the country in which they had such vast wealth at risk. One reform, they had always said, made sense for African labour – indeed, it was absolutely vital: to cut mining costs by cutting the absurdly high level of African wages.[64]

It was no coincidence that the two principal civilian Commissioners whom Roberts appointed to administer the Rand, under the military governor, were not only both Uitlanders, but also employees of the mining firms. Wybergh, the mining engineer sacked by Rhodes's firm when he led the League agitation, now re-emerged as Commissioner for Mines. And Sam Evans, Wernher-Beit's man in Johannesburg, was made Commissioner for Finance. In due course, Milner, who had sent them, by agreement with their employers, would follow them north, to begin that Herculean task of clearing out the 'Augean stables' at Pretoria.[65]

The Augean stables. For once, Milner's colourful phrase did not seem so out of place, that Saturday, 2 June, as Botha's burghers streamed back from the line of the Rand and vanished into Pretoria as if into a quagmire. The mess, the confusion, the shame, the humiliation – they beggared description. Jan Smuts, the State Attorney, was to remember 'that awful moment' all his life. 'It was not Lord Roberts that they feared; it was the utter collapse of the Boer rank and file which staggered the great officers.' Smuts, Botha, De la Rey, Viljoen – all the stoutest hearts and strongest wills in the Transvaal army – had become convinced of the 'utter hopelessness' of continuing the struggle.[66] If ever Lord Roberts had victory there for the asking, it was during the three awful days – 30 May to 1 June – of the retreat to Pretoria.

Kruger himself – the unflinching, unyielding old President, whose iron will had sustained the volk, like Abraham, lifting his arms in the long hours of battle – Kruger had given way to despair. On the day of the Battle of Doornkop, he had been smuggled out of Pretoria, after a last farewell to his invalid wife in the little house in Church Street (they were never to meet again). Then he had taken the train eastwards to Machadodorp, 140 miles down the line towards the Portuguese frontier.[67]

With Kruger went most of the Transvaal government, including Frank Reitz, the State Secretary. The occasion for the hasty retreat was a report that a British flying column was to cut the railway east of Pretoria. In fact, Roberts cast away this opportunity, as he cast away so many opportunities that week, by sending French's cavalry division to the *west* instead of to the east of Pretoria. The actual 'flying column' sent consisted of a small dynamite party, led by Majors Hunter Weston and Fred Burnham, the daredevil American scout. They were themselves demolished.[68]

Although Kruger's flight passed unnoticed in the general confusion, other strategic decisions could not be hidden. When it became known that the last guns were being removed from the four elephantine forts built after Jameson's defeat – Schanzkop, Klapperkop, Dasspoort and Wonderboom – a spasm of utter misery seized the volk. Pretoria was the holy of holies, the Boer Jerusalem; to Pretoria they had been drawn like a magnet throughout that awful, endless retreat; here was the 'great Armageddon', Smuts called it, when the Boer forces, drawn from all points of the compass, could deliver 'that final united blow' that might send the British reeling back to the coast. And now the forts at Pretoria were to be abandoned without firing a shot. With a cry of '*Huis-toe!*' ('Off home!') the burghers began to pour out of Pretoria, after looting anything they could find. Others, including the Chief Justice, formed a committee of 'peace and order' (Smuts called it the 'surrender committee'), prepared to go out and hand over the town to Roberts.[69]

The nadir was reached on 1 June, when a *krijgsraad* was held at the telegraph office in which the senior officers, led by Botha and Smuts, drafted a telegram to Kruger suggesting immediate surrender.[70] Kruger replied with an equally despairing telegram to Steyn. Could arms be laid down in protest (at British aggression)? How many men were willing to continue the struggle – a handful?[71]

One of the handful was certainly Deneys Reitz. In April, Reitz and his three brothers, with Charley (their African 'boy') had, like Botha, the Boer forces in Natal to switch to the western front. They had then fought with Botha against Roberts's huge columns as they trundled north from Bloemfontein. They had watched the great pillars of dust, day after day, as the British outflanked them. Gradually the commandos had disintegrated. By 1 June, all resistance seemed to have ended. They reached the main road to Pretoria, where horsemen, wagons, and herds of cattle were all mixed up in 'dreadful confusion'. They met a British column which made no attempt to stop them. (Said Charley, the African servant: 'Baas, those English people don't know the way to Pretoria so they are coming along with us to make sure.') Reitz was sure that the Boers would have made no resistance if the British had ridden in among them, as both sides believed that the Boer army was disbanded and the war was at an end.[72]

At length, Reitz and his party reached their homes in Pretoria, to find them bolted and barred. They banged on the doors with their rifle butts. Neighbours told them that the President and their father had 'run away', and that Pretoria was to be surrendered in the morning. The city was in confusion; looting was in full swing. Reitz and his friends filled their own saddle-bags, abandoned Charley, the faithful servant, and then rode out of the town to the east. This was the direction in which most of the fugitives had gone. Next day, 5 June, they met their father's friend, Jan Smuts, off-saddled under a tree. Smuts told them that the war was by no means over; indeed, a new phase was just beginning in both republics. De Wet and Steyn were on the warpath. Louis Botha, acting Commandant-General since Joubert's death, was starting to gather together the nucleus of a new Transvaal army. This was better news than Reitz had heard for a long time; and already he could see, from the way the burghers were talking and laughing round the camp-fires, that a new spirit was stirring.[73]

That spasm of despair had, in fact, passed from the leaders as rapidly as it had come. And now Botha and Smuts (and Kruger, from the railway saloon at Machadodorp) had begun to infuse the rank and file with a new spirit of hope. How had this miracle been achieved?

The first vital breathing space had been provided by the Johannesburg armistice of 30 May, the work of the gallant Dr Krause.[74] It was this which was to prove Roberts's supreme blunder. For it allowed Botha to extricate his best men and all his heavy guns from the Rand, and preserved Pretoria from the British long enough for Smuts to remove and load on to railway wagons all essential war materials: the reserve ammunition from the Magazine, and all the gold and coin, totalling £400,000–£500,000, from the Mint and the Standard Bank. (The Boer bank officials challenged Smuts's authority to do so, and the job was performed at gun-point.[75])

Krause had won the first breathing-space from Roberts by sheer bluff. The implicit threat was that the gold-mines would be blown up unless the Boer armies were allowed to withdraw. In fact, the Boer leaders – Botha in consulta-tion with Kruger – had already decided that to blow up the mines would antagonize foreign opinion (about a fifth of the shareholders of the Rand companies were French, German, and American). Dr Krause then had had to block an extremist attempt to blow up the mines. On 27 May Judge Kock, the reckless young judge whose behaviour in the Edgar Case had helped to precipi-tate the war, had arrived at Krause's office at the head of a hundred foreign adventurers. He told Krause he had come to fire the dynamite charges. (As earlier reported to Milner, charges had in fact, been laid ready to blow up the principal mines.) After a scuffle, Kock was forcibly restrained – and the Rand saved for the capitalists.[76]

So Krause had won them the breathing-space. But the man who had inspired Botha and Smuts was Steyn. The Free State President had seen his own capital subjected to the same humiliations two months before, and had realized that it was not a city, but the illimitable veld, that was the true symbol of the volk. When Kruger's despairing telegram reached him on 1 June in his hide-out near Lindley (by an oversight, Roberts had left the telegraph lines to the north-eastern Free State intact),[77] Steyn's reply was characteristically blunt. *We* shall never surrender.[78] Smuts, who was one of the first to see a copy of Steyn's telegram, said later that Steyn 'practically accused the Transvaalers of cowar-dice'. After they had involved the Free State and colonial rebels in ruin, Steyn said, they were now ready, as the war reached their own borders, to conclude a selfish and disgraceful peace.[79]

Steyn's reply was the most important telegram of the war.

It came like a slap in the face to the wavering generals at a *krijgsraad* on 2 June. The younger officers, like Captain Danie Theron, the leader of the Scouts' corps, had never suffered the same shattering loss of faith in themselves as their elders. Now Theron made a violent speech against 'traitors' and condemned Kruger for abandoning the capital. Botha and Smuts decided that the honour of the volk, as well as their personal honours, demanded a fight to the death. Talk of surrender was forgotten. The *krijgsraad* settled for a fighting retreat.[80] Even to retreat successfully needed a few precious days to restore the morale of the burghers. Negotiations were begun to dispose of Pretoria, and peace-feelers were put out to Roberts. But this was a mere stratagem, similar to Dr Krause's work of the previous week. The idea of capturing the capital intact would delay Lord

Roberts as effectively as if the great guns in the forts had still been manned. Pretoria would serve, like Johannesburg, to keep the wolf from the fold, and win a second, all-important breathing-space. At the same time, among the Boer leaders, all eyes looked to Steyn and De Wet to give them what they hungered for after so many weeks of humiliation: a taste of success.[81]

Roberts, meanwhile, received a visit from Botha's secretary, proposing peace talks, and took the bait as Botha had expected. Roberts was hardly to guess that, once again, he had snatched a tactical reverse from the jaws of victory. All he knew was that Pretoria was his. How could it not be the end of the war?[82] He savoured the moment – the climax of his career. The triumphal entry into Pretoria took place at two o'clock on 5 June, by arrangement with the Boers. There were the usual cheering crowds of 'niggers' on the pavements (before being sent back where they belonged); down came the vierkleur, up went Nora Roberts's little silken flag, a crashing salute, and a solemn 'God Save the Queen'.[83]

To some of the British war correspondents, this was the climax of anti-climaxes. Three times already the army had won these petty triumphs: at Bloemfontein, Kroonstad, and Johannesburg. And, like the Boer rank and file, the British Press felt cheated of their Armageddon. 'Here in the rock-bound rolls of its mountains, where forts were bound defiant like crowns of red gold about the brows of its hills; here where for years it had prepared to meet us, we should see the last great fight of a free people brought to bay.' Instead, they witnessed a dull march-past, battalion after battalion tramping through choking dust, as though Pretoria had merely exchanged one mayor for another. This was the view of Battersby, *The Morning Post*'s correspondent, who had served on the western front since the start of the war. He had, no doubt, become somewhat blasé at triumphal entries by now. Yet there was substance in his criticism of Roberts. These triumphs were all lacking in the authentic signs of victory: 'no ruin of streets, no cringing people, no débris of an army, none of the very needful adjuncts of success'. The mistake was to talk, as Roberts did, of civilized warfare. 'There is nothing civilized in warfare, and never can be; it is a barbarian's game.'[84]

Roberts, however, remained confident that this was a gentleman's war, and he had won it. He sent an advance guard of Pole-Carew and the Guards into Pretoria, to make arrangements for the march-past at two o'clock. He had not arranged to capture any Boers – or even to rescue the large number of British prisoners-of-war locked up in Pretoria. Winston Churchill, *The Morning Post*'s other correspondent, witnessed that morning the extraordinary spectacle of a Boer troop-train gliding unopposed out of the main railway station. The train was crammed with Boers, whose rifles bristled from every window; to Churchill's unfeigned relief (though it was sad not to bag the train), not a shot was fired.[85]

There followed Churchill's moment of glory. It was six months since he had made good his escape, in a brown civilian suit, out of Pretoria Model Schools, then the officers' prisoner-of-war camp. He now cantered off to find the new POW 'cage', to which he was directed by a friendly Boer. He saw a long tin building, surrounded by barbed wire. He raised his hat and cheered. There came an answering cheer from inside the cage. The next scene seemed to Churchill like the end of an Adelphi melodrama.

Enter Churchill and his cousin, the Duke of Marlborough. 'Surrender!' cries the Duke to the camp commandant. Out rush the prisoners, hatless and coatless, in a frenzy of excitement. The sentries throw down their rifles; the prisoners seize them. Someone produces a Union Jack (a piece of vierkleur cut up and rearranged). Wild cheers as the flag goes up, the first British flag over Pretoria since 1881. Time: 8.47 a.m. Tableau![86]

Throughout the next week, Roberts waited confidently for the surrender of Botha's army. It was not until 10 June that he discovered his mistake, and sent his army back into battle.[87] By this time, his own fighting force at the front had been reduced to sixteen thousand. Botha, on the other hand, had succeeded in scraping together five thousand Transvaal burghers. The battle that followed (called 'Diamond Hill' by the British, 'Donkerhoek' by the Boers) was another resounding anticlimax. Roberts achieved his aim, modest enough: to drive Botha away from his own east flank. (He lost 180 men in the battle, including Lieutenant-Colonel the Earl of Airlie, CO of the 12th Lancers.)[88] Unfortunately for Roberts, Botha achieved his own aim, too; it was, in the circumstances, ambitious. Thanks to those two heaven-sent breathing-spaces, Botha had restored to the volk the gift of hope. They had fought with a spirit they had not felt since the balmy days of Magersfontein. They fled from the battlefield, but it was *'vlug in vol moed'* ('flight in good spirits'). This defeat, Smuts remarked, had 'an inspiriting effect which could scarcely have been improved by a real victory'.[89]

Meanwhile, a kind of sea-change had come over the war in the veld; something extraordinary had happened in the Free State which explained both the relative weakness of Roberts's men at Diamond Hill, and the new self-confidence of Botha. Christiaan and Piet De Wet, masters of guerrilla strategy, had lashed out with both fists against the lines of communication in the south.

The entire Free State forces had now been reduced to a mere eight thousand men by the combined effect of Cronje's surrender and the partial success of Roberts's velvet-glove policy. Of these eight thousand, Christiaan De Wet had only a tenth – eight hundred men with three guns, by his own account – under his direct control. They were deficient in most essentials: Mauser ammunition, boots, blankets for winter nights – above all, morale. De Wet's own morale had sunk low since his *coups* at Sannah's Post and Reddersburg two months earlier. That endless, dispiriting retreat through the northern Free State had eroded his own self-respect. 'To flee – what could be more bitter than that?' he said as he poured out his soul later. 'Ah! many a time when I was forced to yield to the enemy, I felt so degraded that I could scarcely look a child in the face! Did I call myself a man, I asked myself, and if so, why did I run away? No one can guess the horror which overcame me when I had to retreat. . . .' But how could they make a stand, outnumbered by twelve to one?[90]

On 27 May, Roberts had crossed the Vaal; on 28 May he proclaimed the annexation of the Free State. Already, a new defensive plan had been agreed between the two Boer governments. Their two armies should now separate. De Wet was thus free to resume guerrilla strategy, the policy he had always recommended in preference to set-piece battles. On 3 June, he received a letter from Louis Botha, confirming the details. 'What I desire from your Honour,' wrote Botha, 'now that the great force of the enemy is here, is to get behind him and break or interrupt his communications. We have already delayed too long in destroying the railway behind him.' The very next day, De Wet ambushed a convoy carrying supplies from the railway to General Colvile and the Highland Brigade at Heilbron; the telegraph wires had first been cut, so the officer in charge did not receive Colvile's warning against sending the convoy without a decent escort. The convoy was duly snapped up by De Wet, without firing a shot; this supplied him with fifty-six food wagons and 160 prisoners, mainly Highlanders.[91]

De Wet, however, was after bigger game. At Roodewal railway station, roughly half-way between Kroonstad and the Vaal, was a mountain of ammunition, mail-bags, and other supplies, dumped beside the line, pending the restoration of the nearby bridge over the Rhenoster. It was a part of the country that De Wet, above all, knew well; four miles off across this flat, dusty plain was his own farm. On 6 June, he sent off his eight hundred men, divided into three raiding parties: Steenekamp to take three hundred men, with one Krupp field-gun, and attack Vredefort road station, about fifteen miles up the line; Froneman to take three hundred men, with two Krupp guns and a quick-firer, and attack a camp at Rhenoster railway bridge, four miles up the line; he himself, with a mere eighty men and one gun, would strike at Roodewal station and the mountain of supplies.[92]

De Wet's plan, based on careful reconnaissance by scouts, was deficient in only one respect. He had been told that Roodewal was lightly guarded; in fact, a whole British infantry battalion, the 4th Derbyshires, had been sent up the line on 5 June, as a result of the attack on the convoy; and there were other small reinforcements. However, from De Wet's point of view, all turned out for the best. The Derbyshires, a raw battalion of militia, dumped down beside the railway bridge at dusk on 5 June, were in no tactical position to defend themselves effectively against Froneman's attack. After several hours' fighting from behind the embankment (they had no field-guns), they put up the white flag. Froneman then joined in a combined attack with De Wet on Roodewal station. Here the post-office workers, a railway pioneer corps company, and some Anglo-Indian volunteers struggled heroically to build breastworks of mail-bags and bully beef tins. Then at noon they, too, were forced to put up a white flag. De Wet's combined bag of prisoners in this triple raid was 486 officers and men; 38 British soldiers were killed, and 104 wounded; his own losses were negligible.[93] His only regret was that he could carry off only a small part of the booty.

He seized all the ·303 ammunition he needed (his men were now beginning to use captured Lee Metford and Lee Enfield rifles) and buried several spare wagon-loads in a sandy river bank beside his farm. Then he put a torch to the rest: half a million pounds' worth of plum-puddings, bully beef, blankets, cordite, and 5-inch cow-gun shells.

It was dark before De Wet rode out of Roodewal; the burghers were so burdened with loot that they had to use their horses as pack animals; the captured Tommies had also been allowed to rip open some of the two thousand mail-bags and bring any loot they could carry. When they were a mile from the station, the shells began to catch fire, and everyone in the strange caravan turned round to look at the 'most beautiful' display of fireworks De Wet had ever seen.[94]

A still more humiliating *coup* (inflicted by De Wet's brother, Piet) was the capture of 13th Battalion of the Imperial Yeomanry at Lindley on 31 May. To British eyes, this mounted battalion was the social and political show-piece of the new volunteer army: a company of Irish MFHs, known as the Irish Hunt Contingent, including the Earl of Longford and Viscount Ennismore; two companies of Ulster Protestant Unionists, including the Earl of Leitrim, a whisky baronet (Sir John Power) and the future Lord Craigavon; and a company of English and Irish men-about-town, raised by Lord Donoughmore, who had insisted on paying their own passage to South Africa.[95] This patriotic band was commanded by a British regular, Lieutenant-Colonel Basil Spragge; and Spragge proved himself a regular ass. They were supposed to join General Colvile, who was desperately short of mounted men. When they arrived at Lindley on 27 May, they found Lindley had somehow slipped back under the control of the Boers.[96] Instead of making a fighting retreat towards Kroonstad, as he acknowledged was perfectly possible ('I can get out but shall lose in doing so'),[97] Spragge sent an SOS to Colvile. Then he and his men sat down astride some kopjes outside Lindley and waited to be rescued. Unfortunately, Colvile, who had been ordered to be at Heilbron by 29 May, and was not fully aware of Spragge's dangerous situation, decided not to delay his brigade by returning to rescue the mounted troops; he marched on to Heilbron, leaving them to their own devices.[98] On 1 June, when the rescue column – three yeomanry battalions led by Lord Methuen (down-graded by Roberts) – reached Lindley and stormed the kopjes, they found the hills already strewn with dead: Spragge's dead.[99] The rest of Spragge's yeomen had surrendered to Piet De Wet on the previous day, when De Wet brought up field-guns.[100]

The surrender of Spragge's Irish yeomanry was to cause a ripple of mirth in nationalist circles in Ireland.[101] In fact, there was a gallant Last Stand, made by the Irish Hunt Company. Lord Longford, blood streaming from wounds in the neck, face and wrist, ordered his men to fight to the end. 'I knew it to be madness,' said one of the gentlemen-troopers (son of the Irish Lord Chancellor), 'and so did everyone else, I think, but not a man refused.'[102] In general, raw Irish yeomen fought no worse than British regulars had fought in similar situations.

A respectable total of eighty were killed or wounded before the white flags went up.

Piet De Wet's bag totalled about 530, including Spragge, Lord Longford (seriously wounded), Lords Ennismore, Leitrim and Donoughmore (and the future Lord Craigavon) all captured, and the whisky baronet killed. The wounded were left at Lindley; the other prisoners were marched away northwards to the eastern Transvaal; their captors evaded the net of twenty thousand British troops trying to rescue them.[103]

The Lindley raid brought the total of the De Wet brothers' captures, within one week, to over a thousand. How ironic that these victories should occur in the same week that had seen the release of three thousand British prisoners-of-war from the camps at Pretoria.[104] Moreover, De Wet's attacks on the main railway between Kroonstad and the Vaal caused panic along the line of Roberts's communications. For a few days it was believed in Roberts's HQ at Pretoria that Christiaan De Wet was in possession of Kroonstad itself. De Wet's own men actually let slip through their hands a capture of the most sensational interest. They ambushed a British train; in the confusion, a single horseman galloped out of one of the horse wagons, and away into the night to safety. The horseman was Kitchener.[105]

By mid-June, De Wet had vanished again in the direction of Lindley. Roberts had counter-attacked by sending back across the Vaal Ian Hamilton's column.[106] But the war would never be the same again. De Wet had now amply demonstrated that the guerrilla tactics he had so long urged on the Boer government could achieve strategic successes impossible in conventional warfare.

The ball was in Roberts's court. The future of the main advance had now become of secondary importance to the task of hunting down the twin leaders and symbols of the Boer resistance, Steyn and De Wet.

CHAPTER 35
'Practically Over'

The Ex-republics,
8 July – September 1900

'We sat down and had a nice song round the piano. Then
we just piled up the furniture and set fire to the farm. All
columns were doing it . . . The idea was to starve the
Boojers out.'

Pte Bowers, tape recorded by the
author in 1970, describing Roberts's
farm burning in October 1900

On 8 July, General Hunter's two-thousand-strong column plodded into Bethlehem, in the east of the new-born 'Orange River Colony', hard against
the Basuto frontier. Apart from a handful of Rimington's Tigers, they were
Scottish, like their general – the Black Watch, the Seaforth, the Highland
Light Infantry, veteran battalions of the Highland Brigade led by Hector
MacDonald, and the Lovat Scouts, two squadrons of Highland Yeomanry; and
they had been tramping across the veld for weeks past. Now they saw something which made them rub their eyes, like sailors who sight land after weeks at
sea.[1]

Mountains. The horizon was purple with them. Some were smooth and
round and Scottish-looking enough to make the Highlanders and the Lovats feel
homesick (the Lovat Scouts had been raised by Captain Lord Lovat from among
the ghillies and stalkers on his Beaufort estate). The main ranges of mountains
were unmistakably alien, the Wittebergen and the Roodebergen ('White Mountains' and 'Red Mountains'): gaunt, bony terraces of red rock, streaked with
fresh snow, even where they faced north to meet the slanting winter sun; a line of
red and white battlements thirty miles wide. And who was to know what lay
beyond them in that tangled void of purple gorges and black ravines, half-
obscured by grass fires?[2]

Fine scenery, said an officer; bad business for Hunter's column. Within this
mountain fastness – down there, in the green basin of the Brandwater River –
was De Wet's latest refuge. What better country for Boer tactics? 'We always
serve out extra ammunition,' explained the young officer of the Tigers, 'when
we come to a pretty bit of scenery.'[3]

Lieutenant-General Sir Archibald Hunter was overall commander of all five
columns converging on De Wet, and he, too, was anxious about the tactical

difficulties of launching his columns at what looked to him like an almost impregnable mountain range. But he was still more anxious about the danger of *not* fighting there. The strategic task the Chief had given him was to bring De Wet to action and so force him to surrender. The method proposed was to corner him and the other eight thousand survivors of the Free State army within the Brandwater Basin – that is, to use this horseshoe of mountains (Roodebergen on the east, Wittebergen on the west) to pin De Wet against the Basuto frontier.[4] It was like a chess move, forcing the king into a corner. Of course, De Wet might break the rules and cross into Basutoland. The frontier was the Caledon River, easy enough for horsemen to ford during the winter (though not for wagon columns). But Jonathan, the Basuto ruler, had been forbidden by the British Resident to give the Boers safe passage through their country; not that the Basutos had any wish to help their traditional enemies.[5]

The main problem for Hunter was to keep his own converging columns all in step, so to speak; the main anxiety, that De Wet's columns would break back through the mountains and creep through the meshes of the net.

It was Hunter who had been the main prop of Ladysmith's defence during the siege, a heart and a nerve that had never faltered, despite White's feebleness. Since he had left Natal (he had taken the 10th Division off to the western front in April), he had proved himself one of Roberts's few really able senior generals. His fine advance across the Vaal had made possible the relief of Mafeking. Then, after Diamond Hill, when Ian Hamilton had broken his collar-bone, he had been given Roberts's main mobile force of three divisions to hunt out De Wet.[6] The total seemed large: Lieutenant-General Sir Leslie Rundle's 8th and Colonial divisions; four more infantry brigades – that is MacDonald's Highland Brigade, Major-General R.A.P. Clements's (12th), Major-General Arthur Paget's (20th) and Bruce Hamilton's (21st); and two mounted brigades, that is Broadwood's (2nd) cavalry and Ridley's MI. But many detachments had to be left behind to guard the convoy route. So he was aware that even this force was not large enough to do all that was required: 'I am not strong enough,' he telegraphed to Roberts, 'to close Naauwpoort, [the pass at the north-east of the Roodebergen] 'and to be in sufficient strength at essential points to prevent enemy breaking through, as well as attack and force passes....'[7]

Already, to Hunter's chagrin, about a third of the enemy had escaped. On the night of 15 July, while he was still stuck at Bethlehem, waiting for ox convoys, one of the Boer columns had slipped through the central pass, Slabbert's Nek. Broadwood's and Ridley's mounted brigades were sent hot-foot in pursuit; the Boers had swung round Bethlehem and doubled back north towards Lindley, threatening Hunter's own ox convoys. Hunter reported the bad news to Roberts by telegraph; no doubt Roberts would take up the chase. But Hunter blamed himself. If only he could have set up a proper system of field intelligence; he could get nothing out of the Boer farmers in this country. And if only his own cavalry had been as mobile as the Boers. The Boers who had escaped were hampered by a great train of ox wagons; yet Broadwood's cavalry could not keep up.[8]

Hunter might have blamed himself still more if he knew who were the leaders of the Boers who had escaped.

Despite this set-back, and his dry, Scottish manner, Hunter remained immensely popular with his men. He had that rare gift – Buller's gift – of making ordinary people feel that he cared. 'He has a way of looking at you,' said one of the Tigers, 'no matter who you are, Tommy or officer or what not, with a wonderfully kind expression, as if he felt the most friendly interest in you. And so he does; it is not a bit put on.'[9]

In one respect, Hunter's goodness of heart was not unlimited – not towards the Boers, at any rate. Perhaps he was irritated by their refusal to give him information. Anyway, there had been official changes in Roberts's 'kid-glove' policy. Nothing was yet said publicly, neither in orders to the men nor in a new proclamation to the Boers. But as Roberts himself explained privately, 'More stringent measures than hitherto are being taken as punishment for wrecking trains, destroying telegraph lines,' etc.[10] For long there had been little effective check on the natural tendency of an army to loot and destroy 'enemy' property. Now there came advice to the generals to burn certain selected farms. So, as Hunter's columns had tramped on towards the Roodebergen, they left a new kind of signature in the sky behind them, a pillar of black smoke to add to the cloud of reddish dust that marked their progress.[11]

The burning of Boer farms, as a collective punishment, may not have worried a professional soldier like Hunter. It certainly shocked a sensitive young amateur like Lieutenant Phillipps, of the Tigers.

The worst moment is when you first come to the house. The people thought we had called for refreshments, and one of the women went to get milk. Then we had to tell them that we had to burn the place down. I simply didn't know which way to look....

I gave the inmates, three women and some children, ten minutes to clear their clothes and things out of the house, and my men then fetched bundles of straw and we proceeded to burn it down. The old grandmother was very angry.... Most of them, however, were too miserable to curse. The women cried and the children stood by holding on to them looking with large frightened eyes at the burning house. They won't forget that sight, I'll bet a sovereign, not even when they grow up. We rode away and left them, a forlorn little group, standing among their household goods – beds, furniture, and gimcracks strewn about the veldt; the crackling of fire in their ears, and smoke and flames streaming overhead.[12]

The aim of farm burning was strictly military: to make an example of certain families, and so deter the others from aiding De Wet and the guerrillas. But was it practicable, even in military terms? Hunter's column met many Boer women out in the veld, and good-naturedly helped remove their furniture, before burning their homes. The women's ideas about the war seemed peculiar, for they believed the war was going well enough for them. 'Of course we shall go on fighting,' they said, surprised to be asked. 'How long?' 'Oh, as long as may be necessary. Till you go away.' It struck the British as odd that the women and children should be so unanimous in their determination to fight on. Husbands and sons in the hills fighting. Homes in the valley blazing. And the women sitting there watching, with the same patience, the same absolute confidence in ultimate victory, as the guerrillas. Some of the more intelligent British officers were disturbed – and impressed. They had never seen anything before quite like this 'big, primitive' kind of patriotism.[13] But most British officers were all for farm burning. They thought that Sister Boer was as stubborn and stupid, to put it no worse, as Brother Boer himself.[14]

After sending his two mounted brigades back northwards in pursuit of the escaped Boers, Hunter decided to halt a further week at Bethlehem before striking out for the mountains. Clements's brigade, delayed by their supply convoy, could not be ready before the 20th. Hunter's own supply convoy, the usual lumbering affair of ox wagons, did not reach him till the 19th, and the oxen were dead-beat after the sixty-mile journey from the railhead of Kroonstad; they would not be able to start again before the 21st.[15]

Meanwhile, he had at last begun to gather some idea of what was going on behind the screen of mountains. He had received daily reports from two British agents in Basutoland relayed to him by native runners;[16] and he had imagined that the Boers were preparing to break out of the Brandwater Basin by Ficks-burg and the road to the west. On the 19th, two of the Lovat Scouts had managed to slip across by Retief's Nek and reported the grass burnt for miles, and no sign of Boers. Then, the same day, other Scouts reported that the eastern pass, Naauwpoort, was still held in force. Excellent news. The enemy were still intent on barricading themselves inside the basin. Their HQ was apparently Fouriesburg, the small town at the green heart of the valley where Steyn had set up his latest provisional government.[17]

So the plan of attack was finally settled. There were six wagon roads into and out of the mountains. Rundle and four battalions, with ten guns and sixteen hundred mounted troops, would block the two most westerly passes: Commando Nek and Witnek. Clements's and Paget's brigades would attack Slabbert's Nek in the centre, while Hunter's own force, three battalions of Highlanders, simultaneously attacked Retief's Nek. Bruce Hamilton would take a battalion of Cameronians and five hundred MI and make for Naauwpoort. This left no troops to block the most easterly pass – Golden Gate – until reinforcements could be sent.[18] But there it was. Hunter had a hunch, presumably based on the reports from Basutoland, that the enemy were not trying to break out to the east. And the hunch was right.

The concerted attacks on the two northern passes were launched a few hours after dawn on 23 July. On the summit of Slabbert's Nek, the wagon road passed close to an African kraal, and among the huts the Boers had dug a well concealed series of rifle pits. But the pits were empty.[19] As the first lines of scouts advanced (some raw Imperial Yeomanry, commanded by Captain Bromley-Davenport, MP), the Boers raced for cover, and so did the yeomanry. The yeomanry got there first. 'The position is enormously strong,' said the Captain later, 'and against any troops in the world *except Boers* we should have had hardly any chance of taking it.' After a couple of hours, two infantry companies – they were the Royal Irish – joined the yeomanry. They were ordered to advance with the bayonet. 'Why not?' said the fellow lying next to the Captain. He got up, and walked calmly forward. Within fifty yards, the Royal Irish had lost four killed and twelve wounded. But the two companies had carried an almost impregnable position.[20]

At Retief's Nek, the Boers had more fight in them, and there was a battle of a sort. It had been a cold and miserable night for the Lovat Scouts: icy rain in the valley; snow on the mountains – Scottish weather, indeed. The scouts found dense masses of cloud blocking the passes, but there was no sign of the enemy. A few of the Tigers were sent forward into the foothills to poke them out (it reminded Lieutenant March Phillipps of tufting for deer on Exmoor). Then the overture of the battle began: scattered Mauser notes to left and right, dull and muffled in the swirling mist. Next moment, Captain Damant and the Tigers stumbled on the Boers' main position in a rocky hollow, where green tufts of grass poked through the snow. It was lucky they first heard the challenge, '*Wie gaat daar?*' and caught an alarming glimpse of the heads and shoulders, cuddling down behind the rocks. There they were; no mistake. The Tigers rode for their lives, as the bullets crackled and whistled about them. One of the ponies went broadside into a barbed-wire fence, and was caught there, struggling like a fly in a web: horse and rider a mark for every rifle; the rider sitting on the horse's tail, bush-hat in his hand, both stirrups dangling, as the bullets splashed round. Then the man (it was March Phillipps) somehow wrenched the pony free. And in a few seconds he was away over the hill and out of shot.[21]

That dangerous little hollow, high up under the precipitous, bald buttresses of the nek itself, kept the whole of Hunter's column occupied for the next day and a half. Two battalions – Black Watch and Seaforths – lost eighty-six men, despite their overwhelming superiority in artillery. Then the Boers melted away into the mist. Once across Retief's Nek, Hunter's column joined hands with Clements's and Paget's brigades, who had crossed by Slabbert's Nek. Hunter sent the Highland Brigade marching off ahead, with two 5-inch guns, to back up Bruce Hamilton in blocking the eastern exits: Naauwpoort Nek and the Golden Gate. The main body halted to wait for Rundle, then plodded on down the valley, giving time for the trap to be closed.[22]

They marched slowly, sauntering, so to speak, down to Fouriesburg. Everyone was on tenterhooks, laying bets on the amount of the catch. But were the eels still in the eel-trap? Had Bruce Hamilton succeeded? It seemed too good to be true, to catch most of the Free State army in this miraculous fashion. Roberts had failed so often in the last year to inflict a really decisive defeat on the enemy. Now, after only a few skirmishes, the enemy lay at their feet, cornered between the mountains and the Caledon River. Or were they?

By dawn on the morning of 29 July, Hunter's vanguard had pushed the Boers to Slaap Kranz, midway between Fouriesburg and the Golden Gate. About seven, they heard a sound that was music to their ears: the deep baying of a very heavy gun in the distance. That was one of Bruce Hamilton's 5-inch 'cow-guns'. The way was blocked. In terms of the chess-board, mate next move.[23]

*   *   *   *   *   *

The main body of some five thousand Free Staters prepared to meet their fate with an odd sense of resignation. For a whole week they had dithered: ever since the boom of Hunter's 5-inch guns had first echoed down the valley towards Fouriesburg. The wagon road by way of Golden Gate had remained open till the 28th. Even now, if they were prepared to abandon their covered wagons, and set out on horseback across the numerous Kaffir tracks over the mountains, they could have made good their escape. But what then? They could make their way to Harrismith, on the borders of Natal; but Natal was now a British stronghold. They had been hunted and harried long enough. A sense of hopelessness came over them when they contemplated the prospects of an extended guerrilla war. *'Huis toe'* had been intermittently heard ever since the capture of Bloemfontein. Now it became the *cri de coeur* of the volk. All they wanted was to be allowed to take their wagons and go home.[24]

There were only two men big-hearted enough to prevent a moral collapse of this sort: Christiaan De Wet and President Steyn. Neither was now present in the Brandwater Basin. It was their column of eighteen hundred men that had slipped through the British net on the night of 15 July, while Hunter was stuck at Bethlehem. Their escape had proved a great triumph for the cause. But it also led naturally to one of the great disasters. Once the two men had gone – the embodiments, military and political, of the Boers' will to resist – the morale of the volk evaporated.

The original agreement with President Steyn was this: the Brandwater Basin was not to be defended and the army would split into four divisions. The first, led by De Wet, would escort Steyn to safety on the night of 15 July; the next two, led by Generals Roux and Crowther, would follow; General Marthinus Prinsloo and the fourth division would stay behind to guard the cattle in the mountains.[25] This agreement was forgotten the moment that Steyn and De Wet turned their backs. Instead of escaping, the burghers made, as we have seen, half-hearted attempts to defend Slabbert's Nek and Retief's Nek. It was as though they had only been waiting for a pretext to surrender. On the morning of 29 July, as soon as Golden Gate was finally sealed off, General Prinsloo sent a message under a white flag in the area to General Hunter. As the commander-in-chief he was prepared to surrender the whole force, on condition that all except leaders would be free to go home.[26]

But was Prinsloo in fact Commander-in-Chief? General Roux claimed that *he* was in overall command. However, Roux was too cautious a man (despite the extra moral authority he had by virtue of being a Minister of the Church) to force a showdown with Prinsloo; anyway, his laager was some way off in the direction of Golden Gate. By the time he reached Hunter's field HQ near Fouriesburg to declare Prinsloo's surrender invalid, he had to acquiesce in his own surrender.[27]

The terms offered by Hunter were stiff, but not, in the circumstances, too stiff. It was fortunate, perhaps, for the British that the cable cart connecting with the telegraph line to Roberts's HQ in Pretoria worked badly that day. Roberts, at Milner's insistence, demanded unconditional surrender. Hunter, off his own bat, offered to allow the burghers a concession: 'I have promised not to confiscate private property or personal effects of the burghers.' In practice, this meant that, although Hunter refused Prinsloo's principal demand – not to treat the burghers as POWs, but to let them go home – he was prepared to let them keep their carts and covered wagons. There were sensible reasons for this concession (apart from Hunter's goodness of heart). Hunter was in a hurry to leave the mountains. The pursuit of De Wet was now in full swing; Pretoria was crying out for Hunter's divisions to go north. And the long, red line of his ox convoys, leading into the Brandwater Basin, was stretched dangerously thin.[28]

The actual surrender took days to accomplish and presented one of the great spectacles of the war. The covered wagon had always been the symbol of the Boer frontiersman, as it had been the symbol of his American counterpart: the wheel-going home of the trekboer, which, together with his herds of cattle, his horses and his rifle, was his main possession. Now the valley was full of trekking wagons. They poured into Fouriesburg, and for each Boer the brief ritual of surrender was accomplished: Mausers taken, barrels opened to remove the ammunition, then thrown on to the fire, an immense victory bonfire that burnt night and day.[29]

The yeomanry helped gather up the spoils, still astonished at the ease and cheapness of their triumph. Their prisoners they regarded with mixed feelings, just as the British had regarded the prisoners taken with Cronje five months earlier: 'We had many days of receiving prisoners,' wrote Captain Bromley-Davenport.

> They came in about 300 to 500 at a time, threw down their arms and ammunition and were then marched away south. They are all allowed to ride, a privilege *never* awarded to any prisoners whom they took, and even to keep their cape carts and wagons – altogether they were treated with great leniency. They struck me as a good-natured lot and entirely destitute of pride or shame. They did not appear to mind being beaten – all that they were concerned about was the safety of any property.... I had a long talk with Roux, the fighting parson of Senekal, a very dangerous fanatic.... I am glad we have got him. But I could not help liking him. He appeared to be honest, & all the Boers say that he at least is full of personal courage.[30]

By 10 August, Hunter had passed through Bethlehem again, on his way north to Lindley. The total of surrenders had already reached 4,314 men – including three generals and half-a-dozen commandants. Two British field-guns had been recaptured: they were Broadwood's guns, lost by U Battery at Sannah's Post. In the end, only one important Boer leader, Olivier, refused to recognize the validity of Prinsloo's surrender. Olivier left by the Golden Gate just in time, taking several commandants and fifteen hundred men with him. Hunter regarded this as a breach of faith, but he could hardly complain. He had made the greatest haul of prisoners in the war, at astonishingly little cost: a total of 33 dead and 242 wounded throughout the fortnight's campaign in some of the wildest terrain in South Africa.[31] In scale and cheapness, Hunter's victory put all others, including Paardeberg, far into the shade.

Yet decisive victory still eluded the British. The ugly fact was that the surrender of one lot of Boers only seemed to encourage the others to fight. De Wet was now roaming the veld, unhampered by Prinsloo and his faint-hearts, eager to get a grip, once again, on the jugular of Roberts's main army.

The news of Prinsloo's surrender reached De Wet three days later in his laager south of the Vaal, jubilantly relayed by Major-General Charles Knox, commander of one of the British columns surrounding him. Next day, it was confirmed by Prinsloo's secretary – a young man called Kotze, who had been sent post-haste by Hunter. Steyn and De Wet rode out into no-man's-land beyond the laager to meet Kotze. He brought the brief, sad message from Prinsloo: 'Sir, I have been obliged, owing to the overwhelming forces of the enemy, to surrender unconditionally with all the Orange Free State laagers here. I have the honour to be, Sir, your obedient servant – M. Prinsloo Commander-in-Chief.' '*Commander-in-Chief*,' replied De Wet, icily. 'By what right do you usurp that title?' He was actually thunderstruck by the news. 'It was nothing short of an act of murder,' he admitted later. 'One could gnash one's teeth to think that a nation should so readily rush to its own ruin!'[32]

Possibly De Wet's anger had been sharpened by the thought that he himself was not entirely blameless. After all, he had failed to stay and supervise the evacuation of the Brandwater Basin, though he must have known that the burghers were near the end of their tether; and he had taken both the special corps of scouts to make good his own escape. According to his later published version of events, he did not blame himself.[33] It was not his style, reproaching himself when he blundered. And, it must be said, he rarely had occasion for it.

In the eyes of the British public, De Wet's exploits – dazzling, infuriating, baffling – had by now earned him the reputation of a magician.[34] Who was this extraordinary man, who could lead Roberts and his generals such a dance, swooping down on Broadwood at Sannah's Post, cutting up the Royal Irish at Reddersburg, pouncing on the Derbyshires at Rhenoster River, and always vanishing as swiftly as he had come? In the eyes of his own men, and of the British prisoners he captured from time to time, there was little mystery about him. On the contrary, he seemed intensely painstaking, one of the few really professional commanders on either side.[35]

Professionalism, in Boer eyes, meant common sense raised to the highest level. In De Wet's case it was a kind of genius. He had none of the charisma of Louis Botha: the personal magic that cast a spell on the volk (and was later to make Botha a hero even in the eyes of British imperialists). De Wet was blunt, charmless, even brutal.

One British officer, Captain Molyneux Seele, acting staff officer to Colonel Ridley's MI, spent an enforced holiday as De Wet's guest in the laager that July and was greatly impressed. How he envied the Boers their commander, Captain Seele admitted ruefully. His own capture had been partly the fault of the Intelligence Department, who had reported no Boers for miles; and De Wet's laager proved to be just over the hill. That 'ass' of a CO, Ridley, had failed to send out scouts. So Seele found himself one morning running unarmed across the veld, with fourteen mounted Boers firing from the saddle at him; 'not the ideal conditions in which to meet Brother Boer'. The burghers who caught him apparently regarded the whole thing as a 'huge joke'.[36]

In due course, he was brought to De Wet's laager; it was Sunday morning and the burghers were singing hymns, 'yelled out in a nasal drawl'. He was searched, and his field-glasses were confiscated (but his greatcoat and other possessions were handed back). Then he met De Wet's other 'guests', a few prisoners sitting round a 'big pot of Kaffir corn boiled and smeared with grease ... an awful compound they pronounced excellent'. De Wet himself spoke no English, but his hand was everywhere. 'He rules his mob by the strength of his right arm and character. About 5 foot nine with broad chest and a very upright seat on his grey horse, he was continually conspicuous.' Superficially all was confusion in the laager, but there was 'order in disorder'. No tent lines, no dressing by the left or right, and no noise, but every wagon, cart and tent was laid out in the same relative position, wherever they laagered. Hence the extraordinary speed with which De Wet could strike camp. A mounted Boer would give the signal; then 'the whole conglomeration of tents, wagons, capecarts, horses and oxen, white men & Kaffirs' were on the move in ten minutes. But this feat would have been impossible if the Africans had been left to inspan the animals unassisted, as they were left in the British army (twelve mules or sixteen great, dour trek oxen to harness to each wagon). In De Wet's camp, everyone was a countryman and lent a hand with the transport, as they had been trained since boyhood. Discipline was severe. Sentries who slept on duty were punished by being put on ant heaps and shot if they moved.[37]

As regards De Wet's fighting methods, Seele was immensely impressed, though he did not suggest such techniques would have been desirable in the British army. 'His method of fighting, say, a rearguard action is as follows. He gets his wagons under way then places his fighting men in position then hands over to his second in command. After this he gallops, usually alone, to the head of the wagons and drives back any skulker by fierce invective &, if that fails, with his *sjambok* into the fighting line. Once there he resumes command. . . . De Wet is a wonderful man.'[38]

Such was the flattering view of an English staff officer. In fact, De Wet's strong right arm was hardly tested after the news of Prinsloo's surrender. 'It was impossible to think of fighting,' De Wet wrote, 'the enemy's numbers were far too great – our only safety lay in flight.' And flee they did. In early August, he estimated that there were five or six generals and forty thousand men pursuing them. Their own column was a mere 2,500, including Steyn, his entourage, and four hundred wagons and carts. How De Wet hated those wagons! Against his orders, the burghers clung to those wretched possessions, and even De Wet was powerless to make them give them up, though their part in precipitating Prinsloo's surrender was obvious enough. This handicap meant that De Wet could only flee at the pace of an ox; and even De Wet's oxen could barely do thirty miles a day.[39] How, then, could he elude the forty thousand men (actually twenty thousand) converging on his lair at Reitzburg?

The secret lay in De Wet's professional scouts. Significantly, De Wet had not, like the British, left this vital part of field intelligence work to ordinary mounted troops. He had trained up two special corps – under Captains Danie Theron and Gideon Scheepers (and, oddly enough, foreigners, too, were recruited into these élites). It was through these scouts that De Wet now discovered that, though the cordon was pulled tight behind him, frustrating all means of escape inside the Free State, Roberts had failed to block one drift across into the Transvaal. He crossed the Vaal on 6 August by the regular crossing at Schoeman's Drift. His situation was still critical. He had lost the advantage of campaigning in the home ground of the Free State, where his men knew every kopje and every farmhouse and every hidden source of food, where they were conscious of fighting for their own country. Moreover, the mountainous country ahead suited his pursuers better than the open plains of the Free State. His route lay across the western flank of the Rand, well to the west of the line of Roberts's advance two months earlier. Beyond the Rand lay a higher chain – the Magaliesberg – that dominated the fertile river valley to the west of Pretoria. To shake off his pursuers, he must cross the Magaliesberg. But where? All the mountain passes were likely to be blocked by the English.

'"Inspan!" No man uttered a word of complaint'; (so went De Wet's own somewhat rose-coloured account of this ordeal), 'each man did his work so quickly that one could hardly believe that a laager could be put on the move in so short a time.' Behind them they left the veld black and smoking. It was De Wet's form of scorched-earth policy. This dry grass – the winter grazing – burnt like tinder. They reached the tall poplars of the Magalies valley on the morning of 14 August, and set off uphill towards a rocky pass called Olifant's Nek: the main south-western pass over the Magaliesberg.[40] It had been occupied by Lord Methuen's column a few days earlier. De Wet's men had marched two hundred miles in the last month to reach the Magaliesberg, only to be trapped, it would seem, more completely than Prinsloo in the Roodebergen.

Two days earlier, Roberts had sent a jaunty cable to Lansdowne, predicting the imminent doom of Steyn and De Wet. The pack was in full cry: three columns – about twelve thousand men, led by Kitchener, Methuen, and Smith-Dorrien – baying at his heels; Ian Hamilton, and a further eight thousand, hurrying across to block Olifant's Nek. 'I shall be greatly disappointed if De Wet and Steyn manage to escape,' cabled Roberts.[41] To the Queen, he wrote a long letter, conveying the same sentiments in more courtly terms. Hunter's successes in the Brandwater Basin, and the flight of Steyn and De Wet over the Vaal, 'practically closes the war so far as the Orange River Colony is concerned'. He was now hoping to corner De Wet and Steyn, 'an intensely interesting and exciting operation, rendered more so by the great size of the country and the extra-ordinary mobility of the Boers, who manage to slip away in the most marvellous manner'.[42]

Roberts wrote effusively every few weeks to the Queen, sending her copies of some of his victory cables. But Roberts was aware he was not one of her favourites; at any rate, he had had his knuckles rapped at various times. For example, after capturing Pretoria, he had cabled to ask about the huge bronze statue of Kruger that was to have been erected. The massive pedestal was already in place in Church Square. Would Her Majesty like to be put up there instead? The Queen was not amused at the thought of stepping into Kruger's shoes.[43] Most distressing to Roberts were the Queen's hints about his own wife. The Queen disapproved of camp-followers; indeed, she felt so strongly about ladies going to the front that an official announcement had been made, quoting her disapproval.[44] Roberts had insisted on bringing Nora Roberts and his two daughters up to Bloemfontein. In early July, Nora steamed on to Pretoria, in a special armoured train, guarded with pom-poms and maxims.[45] He claimed that his wife was needed for hospital work. As the echoes of the great hospital scandal were now reverberating around Britain, including Balmoral, this was not a safe line of defence.[46] In and out of the hospitals, so the gossip went, Nora Roberts's interference was a menace. People spoke of 'petticoat government'; as though the Field Marshal's baton was in Nora's large knapsack (and large she was, towering over the little man). Was there any truth in these stories? Lord Kerry, Bobs's ADC, was asked this precise question by his mother, wife of the War Minister. He defended the Chief, while admitting that Bobs's recent conversion to a tougher line against Boer women and children was probably due to Lady Roberts's violent hostility to them.[47]

The stories of petticoat government did perhaps signify something: a certain arbitrariness – pettiness, even – about the way the Field-Marshal ruled his army. He had decided to sack two of his senior divisional generals – Gatacre and Colvile – after the 'unfortunate affairs' at Sannah's Post, Reddersburg and Lindley.[48] Yet the way he had singled them out for humiliation – simply because they were not part of the Roberts's charmed circle, people said – did not encourage the other generals. They blamed Roberts's and Kitchener's own staff work. And they began to shrink from taking risks.[49] Not that Roberts's drastic sackings had achieved his object. There had been a spate of new 'unfortunate affairs' in July: the most recent, disaster to the Scots Greys and Lincolns at Zilikat's Nek on 11th July; 189 had surrendered to De la Rey, when he struck out from his lair north of the Magaliesberg. In due course, Roberts, too, struck out, sacking the COs of the Scots Greys and the Lincolns.[50]

Still, despite these set-backs – bad omens for an early end to the war – and despite the formidable presence of Nora Roberts at the Pretoria HQ, the staff officers led a cheerful enough existence. There was a regular paper-chase; Lord Kerry played polo most days. It was almost like Simla, sitting out in the cool evenings at Mimosa Cottage, where Kerry had his billet. Of course, there were fewer coronets now among the red-tabs: 'Sunny' Marlborough had sailed off home, and so had his cousin Winston (eager to try his luck again at Oldham in the next election); the poor old Duke of Norfolk had fallen into an ant hole and broken his thigh. To fill the gap, the little man had made a new raid on the nobility. Prince Christian Victor, Queen Victoria's favourite grandson, had had an undistinguished enough war so far, stuck with Buller in Natal. He was now made an extra ADC to the Chief. It was a compliment to the Queen, though the sequel was to be melancholy indeed.[51]

Roberts himself was little in evidence. He was writing, endlessly writing, at his desk. What could he make of this strange new twist of fortune? Six weeks ago, he had been convinced that the war was virtually over. Now he was not so sure. Once again, there were two basic choices. Give priority to rounding up the guerrilla leaders: that is, crush De Wet, and De la Rey, who had now emerged as the leader of 'unrest' (Roberts's euphemism for guerrilla strikes) west of Pretoria? Or press on with regular warfare: that is, march against the last real Boer army in the field, Botha's army, now at Machadodorp, and push on eastwards along the railway towards Mozambique?[52]

Linked with these strategic questions was the overwhelming political one: what terms to offer the Boers. The senior general, on whose judgement Roberts relied most of all (and whom he had recommended should take over as GOC in South Africa on his own departure) was Ian Hamilton.[53] Hamilton had strong views against imposing terms of unconditional surrender on the Boer governments. He had also protested against the Proclamation of 31 May, which, while offering amnesty to the rank-and-file on certain terms, made it clear that the leaders would be deported if they surrendered. 'If I had my way,' Hamilton told his wife (and the Chief knew), 'every single big man who had surrendered up to date should be living in his own house in receipt of a handsome allowance.... But of course if Chamberlain, Milner & Lord Bobs are going to grind them down utterly, then they must be prepared to spend a great many millions of pounds and many hundreds of lives before they bend desperate men to the breaking-point.'[54] In fact, Milner had changed his 'velvet-glove' strategy, now that the Rand mines had been saved intact. They must stick to unconditional surrender for the governments, and change the terms of the Proclamation for individuals, so that all the rank-and-file, as well as the leaders, would be made prisoners-of-war, and not be allowed merely to take the oath of allegiance and hand in their arms.[55]

In the event, Roberts had compromised on both these interlocking issues, strategic and political. He had decided to attempt both a round-up of De Wet *and* try to push on to the Portuguese border. He resisted Milner's attempts to revise the official Proclamation, although privately the generals were ordered, as Hunter had been, to extend the practice of burning farms.

Perhaps, as Kerry thought, Lady Roberts's arrival in Pretoria had something to do with this hardening of policy towards civilians. Certainly, Roberts reacted with a new severity that month. There had been a half-baked conspiracy in Pretoria to kidnap him. A German Uitlander, Lieutenant Hans Cordua, led the plot, and was led on in turn by a British *agent provocateur*. Roberts, much to the surprise of Kerry and the other ADCs, had Cordua court-martialled and shot.[56] At the same time, Roberts expelled from Pretoria several hundred Boer women and children, sending them by railway in open trucks to Botha's laager near

Machadodorp. He warned Botha that he refused to feed and house Boer dependants as long as the Boers were raiding the railway. Botha protested that it was
inhuman. (In fact, many refugees seemed glad to be off; they sang the 'Volkslied'
defiantly at the station. And Roberts took care not to expel Botha's own wife,
still less the wives of Steyn and Kruger, who were treated as show-pieces of
imperial generosity.[57])

After a fortnight's rest in his lair near Reitzburg, De Wet had finally broken
cover on 6 August, slipped across the Vaal, and the hunt was on. How could
20,000 men fail to hunt down a mere 2,500? The hunters had command of the
railway and of the telegraph system, and the terrain itself was all on their side.[58]
But fail they did, and in a way that was peculiarly humiliating for the two
generals Roberts believed were the brightest stars in his army.

The first failure was Kitchener's, as the co-ordinator of the four columns near
the Vaal. 'K of Chaos' he had been called because of the disaster to the convoy at
Waterval Drift in February; and for several of the later disasters, like the loss of
the Derbyshires at Rhenoster River, Kitchener's chaotic staff work had been
equally to blame.[59] In early August, he was supposed to have boxed De Wet in at
Reitzburg. To the south were his own column – Broadwood's and Little's
cavalry brigades – and Charles Knox's mixed force. Just across the Vaal, which
was only fordable at a few places, was Methuen's column, mainly yeomanry.
Standing back on the Klerksdorp-Krugersdorp railway (a kind of long-stop)
were Smith-Dorrien and his brigade.[60]

All that was needed to crush De Wet was for one of these four columns to
delay him sufficiently long – say, in a one-day action – for the other columns to
lumber up and overwhelm him. So when De Wet had crossed the Vaal at the
main crossing-point at Schoeman's Drift on 6 August, it was Kitchener's chance
to close in for the kill. But first, Kitchener had mistakenly told Methuen to move
to a ford farther downstream, allowing De Wet to slip through the gap. Then,
equally mistakenly, Kitchener had sent his cavalry on a detour upstream, leaving
Methuen to take up the pursuit almost unaided. Methuen redeemed his earlier
failures by his skill in this campaign. He and his yeomanry dogged De Wet so
closely that De Wet was forced to abandon a field-gun and all his prisoners. On
the night of 10 August, De Wet swung westwards across the Krugersdorp
railway line and side-stepped Smith-Dorrien. Now the main mountain range
west of Pretoria – the Magaliesberg – loomed ahead, and Ian Hamilton joined
the chase, only to prove still more incompetent than Kitchener.[61]

Ian Hamilton had 7,600 men. On 11 August he was ordered by telegraph to
block Olifant's Nek, to prevent Steyn's and De Wet's escape. Hamilton knew
the crucial importance of this. Yet somehow his military instinct – the quality,
above all, which Roberts prized in his generals – now deserted him. He telegraphed back to Roberts that he would try to intercept the Boers on the Rand
before they reached Olifant's Nek. He then took a detour along the Rand,
instead of striking out directly to the nek. And his men dawdled. In the two final
days of the hunt – the 12th and 13th – Hamilton's men covered barely thirty

miles, compared with De Wet's forty-five miles. So the hopes of ending the war at a stroke had vanished, as they had begun, in a great cloud of red dust, the only trace that remained of De Wet's ox wagons.[62]

The results of the nine-day chase were especially ill-received by Kitchener. He sent a private telegram of protest to Roberts's HQ. 'We ran him hard into a corner and fully relied on your closing the door at Olifants Nek how was this missed.'[63] (Rawlinson's comment was that this telegram of K's was the 'cry of the hound when the fox gets away into an earth that has not been stopped'.)[64] Roberts's own reaction was tight-lipped. His official despatches – so vocal on the failures of men like Buller, Warren, Colvile – preserved a deafening silence on the question of Hamilton's blunder. Even in his letters to Lansdowne, Roberts did not give the game away.[65] But the same day, Rawlinson, who was at Roberts's elbow, put the blunt truth in his diary: 'We ordered Johnny [Ian Hamilton] to go to Olifants Nek but he did not go there and in consequence De Wet has eluded us. This will prolong the war considerably I fear, and we are all down in our luck....'[66]

Having lost one dazzling opportunity, Roberts now turned to grasp the other: to beat Botha in regular warfare and disperse or destroy the last of the Transvaal army.

And here, despite himself, he was soon to be grateful for Buller.

Buller's 4th Infantry Division joined up with Roberts's 4th Cavalry Brigade on 20 August, when the cavalry reached Twyfelaar, south of Belfast, and there was some sly self-congratulation among Buller's men. Buller's infantry were a strange sight: many officers bearded to keep out the cold, khaki in tatters and burnt black by the ash from the grass fires; but they noted that Roberts's men seemed half-starved, as well as in rags. It was reported that the brigade major of the 4th Cavalry 'burst into tears' at the sight of a pat of butter, and a bottle of beer 'brought on a fit'.[67]

As the divisional commander, Lieutenant-General Neville Lyttelton declared himself shocked by the ill feeling that had grown up between the two British armies ('war lets loose a flood of envy, hatred, malice ...'[68]), but he welcomed friendly competition. Next day, his division was to have its chance. The combined armies were to advance against the Boers' strong-point west of Machadodorp, where Botha was reported to have seven thousand men and fifteen guns.[69] Lyttelton did not expect much of a 'show': worse luck, for nothing would have suited him better than to have a chance of finishing the enemy off. He was afraid they would keep up their new sort of war – 'hovering about, sniping at very long range, & occasionally making a pounce on our communications' – for weeks, even months.[70]

This final phase of the advance of the Natal army had begun on 7 August, when Buller pushed up twelve thousand men – Lyttelton's infantry and Dundonald's mounted brigade, with forty guns – leaving the rest of his force as a garrison in the rear. Buller had chosen Lyttelton's division as a compliment partly to its commander, partly to the men themselves, who were, with the exception of the Inniskillings, all from the battalions who had survived the siege of Ladysmith. It seemed appropriate that the battalions who had had the misfortune to initiate the war should be given a chance of concluding it.

Lyttelton himself reciprocated the compliment; he had mellowed a good deal in his feelings towards Buller. 'Buller has learnt much and we have every confidence in him,' he wrote on 8 August, and though his views about 'Sitting Bull' (the new nickname) fluctuated, as they did about Lord Bobs and Kitchener, he was, in a fashion, loyal to his own chief.[71] True, he did not think Buller's recent victories – victories, as we shall see, on the advance into the Transvaal – had been especially testing ; and he flattered himself in private that he had taught Buller a few lessons, and generally kept him up to scratch. On the other hand, the blunders over on the western side – the endless 'unfortunate incidents' reported in Roberts's despatches – these blunders had taught Lyttelton much about Buller. There was something to be said for Buller's slow-but-sure strategy after all. The shortcomings of Roberts's 'sudden rapid pounces' (the tiger-spring strategy) were now clear to Lyttelton. As he said, 'It makes it very difficult to safeguard his communications or to make proper arrangements for his hospitals, & it also usually involves prolonged halts to make good these shortcomings, during which the enemy has time to pull himself together. It is a question whether a slower but continuous advance is not sometimes better.'[72] He had warmed to Buller's point of view, when considering that the advance in Natal had been delayed weeks by the blunders in the Free State.

He also blamed Roberts for his failure to evacuate his typhoid patients promptly by train to the base hospitals, using supply trains going back empty. He had no doubt that the failure of Roberts's cavalry was partly Kitchener's fault. 'I hear that both horses and men are in a most dilapidated state . . . they all combine in cursing Kitchener. . . .'[73]

Praise from Lyttelton, even if only the product of his disenchantment with Roberts and Kitchener, was praise indeed; for Lyttelton was a military member of the new imperialist élite, in whose eyes Buller was profoundly suspect.[74] By contrast, Lord Dundonald, an old friend of Buller's, took personal pride in the change that had come over the fortunes of his chief. He contrasted the unbroken run of success of the Natal army – not a gun, not a wagon captured in their two-hundred-mile advance from Ladysmith – with the tales of disaster from Roberts's side. He also contrasted their own self-restraint with the practice of collective punishment by looting and farm-burning now officially sanctioned by Roberts. Buller refused to sanction either, and woe betide the marauder who fell into the hands of the Chief! Dundonald agreed that collective punishments were neither fair nor politic. Attacks on the railway were not the work of locals; 'and when once these farms were burnt the country round became a desert and their owners inveterate haters of the British'.[75]

Buller himself did not spell out his reasons for opposing farm burning. One can guess them. Twenty years before, he had raised a troop of Light Horse among the Boers of this part of the Transvaal. There was hardly a man in the Wakkerstroom district who did not have a relation who had fought with Buller against the Zulus.[76] And he had not only a personal and humanitarian objection. Buller, as we saw, differed radically from Roberts on the question of the strategy to pursue after the capture of Bloemfontein and the relief of Ladysmith. Buller believed the priority was to destroy the armies of the enemy in the field, not occupy their towns, and burn their farms. Hence he had wanted to push on and attack Botha's army in north Natal immediately after the relief of Ladysmith, while he had Botha on the run. And hence his belief, expressed in aggrieved tones to Wolseley in early April: 'If I had been allowed to go on I feel certain that I should have been at Harrismith [the railway terminus on the Natal-Free State border] with the railway behind me and Natal clear south of Ingagane by [April] the 11th.'[77]

Instead, Roberts, as we saw, had set his heart on the psychological effects of capturing Pretoria. So he postponed both Buller's objectives – clearing Natal and crushing De Wet and the Free Staters. He ordered Hunter's division to join him, and so reduced Buller's mobile force to three infantry divisions and two cavalry brigades. And he had told Buller in March and April to stay 'strictly on the defensive'. (It must be said that Buller interpreted these orders more strictly than Roberts intended.) The wrangle between the two men continued throughout April and early May. Roberts proposed that Buller send another division north-west across the Drakensberg, and that he should then join him on the Vaal for a converging thrust on Pretoria. Buller insisted on the need to cross the Biggarsberg and clear the main railway northwards. Eventually Buller had got his own way. Roberts's five divisions made their tiger-spring on to Pretoria, unassisted. Buller took his three divisions scrambling over the Natal passes, under the shadow of Majuba, and so into the dusty plains of the Transvaal and up to Standerton.[78]

Buller found his own success understandably exhilarating. He showed no great tact (or tactics) in the wrangles with Roberts ('I cannot help thinking the little man is not well-disposed to me,' he naïvely confessed to his wife, 'and will do me an ill-turn if he can.')[79] What he enjoyed was success in the field. Between 10–15 May he outflanked an estimated seven thousand Boers dug into the Biggarsberg. 'We have had an almost perfect little expedition,' he wrote on 15 May from Symons's old camp at Dundee. 'I have surprised and outmanoeuvred the Boers and have got a very considerable force out of an enormously strong position, with very small, and indeed infinitesimally small loss, only five wounded.'[80] It was, indeed, one of the neatest tactical feats of the war, the proof that for Buller, too, the war could become a walk-over, given sufficient troops.

On 6–12 June, he repeated the trick, in the spectacularly difficult country around Majuba. The Boers, led by Louis Botha's brother, Christian, and estimated at ten thousand, had built miles of intricate entrenchments to guard the main passes, including Laing's Nek. Buller left Clery's division to mark them. Meanwhile, Hildyard's division pushed through a minor pass over the Drakensberg to the west, fought a brief battle at Alleman's Nek, and so outflanked the Boers at Laing's Nek without more ado.[81]

To take such a famous strong-point – the Gibraltar of Natal – without a shot delighted Buller. It had been 'a sort of fetish with them', he gathered from the prisoners. 'To have been kicked out of it . . . after all their preparations' seemed to him 'the hardest knock the Boers have had in this war'. And what pleased him most, so he told his wife, was the telegram that arrived from Roberts four hours after Buller had captured the nek. Roberts told him 'the Boers were at least 4500 strong on Laings Nek with 14 guns and were determined to fight and that I was not to try and turn them out as it was too great a risk of heavy loss – and I had already turned them out. That was rather pleasant.'[82]

The Natal army had spent the next six weeks by turns advancing then consolidating their hold on the south-east of the Transvaal. There was much to be done: the first task, strategically, was to open the second railway line from the sea to Pretoria, the Natal line down which Joubert had poured his troops before the outbreak of war. The railway tunnel at Laing's Nek, dynamited by the Boers, was brought back into service by Girouard's railway gangs. A prize of eighteen engines, intact except for their connecting rods (some Africans found them buried), was captured at Standerton. On 4 July, units of the two armies – Buller's and Roberts's – first met. The linking of the Natal railway with Pretoria, accomplished a few days later, transformed the supply situation from Roberts's point of view. Prinsloo's surrender, at the end of the month, averted the main threat to Buller's lines of communication posed by the commandos in the Free State. So, by early August, the way was at last clear for the combined armies – Roberts's from the west, Buller's from the south – to strike at Botha.[83]

Meanwhile, as significant as the meeting of the two armies was the meeting of the two commanders. Nothing is so striking in the story of the feud between Buller and Roberts, that had bedevilled each stage of the war, than the simple fact that the two men had never met in their lives. Roberts was the leader of the 'Indians'; Buller the second-in-command of the 'Africans'. That was enough to cripple their co-operation. Then, on 7 July in Pretoria, they first met face to face. But if this first meeting in Pretoria was somewhat chilly (Roberts was haunted by the thought of who had issued those orders that had killed Freddy at Colenso), both men did their best to bury the hatchet – for the time being.[84]

Their second meeting took place at Belfast on 25 August, as soon as Roberts arrived to direct the combined attack on Botha's army. Buller was impatient at Roberts's slowness. Privately, he grumbled at the splendid chances Roberts had made him lose. He had arrived at Carolina, thirty miles to the south, on the 14th, and there he was told to halt till the 22nd – 'a pity, as during this week Kruger with us so near will certainly move back from Machadodorp, while if I had forced right forward from Carolina or Machadodorp I should certainly have caught some of his staff, and I was quite strong enough to do so. . . . It is an unfortunate delay, at an unfortunate moment. . . .'[85]

The tactical problem that now presented itself was troublesome to Roberts – more troublesome, because of the terrain, than the similar problem at Diamond Hill in early June. Botha's army – estimated at seven thousand men, with twenty guns, including several Long Toms – straddled the main watershed that carried the railway between Belfast and Kruger's HQ farther east. As usual, Botha's men were virtually all mounted. So they had been able to extend their front to twenty miles. And the appalling country either side of the railway – deep ravines to the north, streams and bogs to the south – made their flanks still more impregnable. As usual, the British had the overwhelming advantage of numbers – nineteen thousand men, with eighty-two guns – but less than five thousand of these men were mounted.[86] At first, Roberts planned to outflank Botha on the east, where the bogs were. Fortunately for his reputation (Roberts's cavalry might well have got into a worse mess than at Diamond Hill), he was dissuaded. Buller's own plan was adopted: Lyttelton's two infantry brigades to attack near the centre of the line, supported by a converging artillery barrage; French's cavalry to push round by the Lydenburg road to the north. Roberts accepted this plan, perhaps reluctantly. For his own infantry, the Guards Brigade, under his favourite, 'Polly' Carew, were left without a role.[87]

The Battle of Belfast (alias Bergendal), the last set-piece battle of any size in the war, began on 27 August with a cavalry strike and then the usual artillery barrage. Buller had spotted the tactical key to Botha's position.[88] It was a big red kopje near a farm called Bergendal, a jumble of fantastic boulders, spread across three acres, whose own great natural strength belied its fatal weakness in relation to Botha's defence line. Like a miniature Spion Kop, it jutted out in a salient from the centre of Botha's twenty-mile front. Unlike Spion Kop, it could not be supported from sides or rear, owing to the ground that screened Botha's view but gave Buller's massed artillery a field-day. So Botha had entrusted the crucial kopje to sixty men of his élite: the Zarps, alias the Johannesburg Police. They were given a pom-pom and ordered to hold it to the end.

The Zarps did exactly that. Their Last Stand out-rednecked the rednecks. How ironic that the notorious Zarps, the 'bully-boys' of Johannesburg, the epitome of the brutal Boer, who had helped precipitate the war by shooting Tom Edgar – how ironic that it should be these men who now came to be regarded by the British as heroes cast in their own mould. Down crashed the thunderstorm of lyddite on that single, isolated red nob of boulders: a three-hour broadside of naval guns, howitzers and field-guns – forty guns, grinding and hammering that strong-point to powder. And the Zarps took it on the jaw like Tommies. 'No ordinary Dutchman would have held on like that,' said Lyttelton admiringly. It must be a 'perfect inferno'.[89]

About 2.30 p.m., Buller gave the nod to Lyttelton, and Lyttelton let loose four battalions of infantry: Lieutenant-Colonel Metcalfe, with Lyttelton's own regiment, the Rifle Brigade, converging from the left, supported by the Devonshires; the weaker Inniskillings (after their disastrous losses on the Tugela they were mainly raw militia) and the Gordons behind them. By now, Lyttelton thought that the Zarps' resistance had been crushed. Yet, though the artillery still hammered the kopje ahead of the advancing infantry, the surviving Zarps had only held their fire. As the infantry went over the skyline, Lyttelton saw his riflemen 'falling pretty thick, but there was little flinching'. The Inniskillings, by contrast, 'came under pom-pom fire & forthwith ran away but were rallied and came on again'. Both battalions, still under the screen of artillery, converged for the final charge on the kopje. Their own losses were severe, especially in officers: Metcalfe and six other officers wounded, three dead (all of the Rifle Brigade); a hundred men wounded or missing, and twelve dead. But when they captured the smoking remains of the kopje, they found that, for once, the enemy had suffered severely, too: fourteen dead bodies (including a police lieutenant's) lay there beside their post; nineteen prisoners were taken (of whom eight, including the commander, were wounded); other wounded had been removed by the Boers. As a force, the Zarps had been annihilated.[90]

The storming of the kopje achieved much more. Buller had smashed open the weak joint in Botha's armour. At once, the Boer lines caved in along the whole front (pursued, with the usual lack of success, by the over-weighted and under-armed British cavalry).[91] But it was a crushing victory, and Roberts was most impressed by Lyttelton. 'The best of it,' wrote Lyttelton, 'was that it was done under Bobs's own eye, & he was delighted with the manner in which the Natal Army fought. He told Buller that he did not think the Koppie [sic] could be carried.'[92] Buller was understandably delighted too. 'Here I am, as happy as a pig,' he wrote to his wife, Lady Audrey, three days after the battle.

We had a very pretty little fight on Monday, with [the] Field Marshal and the whole Guards Brigade looking on, so we had plenty of swagger. Certainly it went off very well and exactly as I could have wished. I got on to Machadodorp the next day, then up the Berg and the following day executed a manoeuvre which I think procured the release of all the [2000 British] prisoners at [the POW camp at] Nooitgedacht. Tomorrow I am off to Lydenburg having just missed catching Kruger. I hope to catch him next time. The end cannot be far off now I do believe, but between you and me I wish the Field Marshal would move a bit quicker. He lets so many chances slip....

Today I have a very nice telegram from the Queen, and I hope the fight has been thought something of in England. It was a very difficult job and came off well so I was really pleased, and it was not the least pleasure that I defeated the army and opened the road to Machadodorp, while Lord Roberts' army, which had got there before me, had missed the chance and had to sit looking on. What a beast I am! I don't mean that. But the men liked it.[93]

In September and October, Buller's two divisions plodded northwards among the misty gorges and precipices of the Mauchberg – Spitzkop, Hell's Gate – that culminate in the great eastern escarpment of the Transvaal. It was God-given country for Boer tactics. Buller's veterans manoeuvred the commandos out of a series of Spion Kops with less than a hundred casualties. Botha's northern army, now only 2,500 strong, concentrated on flight.[94] At the end of October, Buller took the train for Durban and sailed for Southampton. By British crowds, he was to be given a hero's welcome.[95] (Buller behaves 'as if he was Napoleon after Austerlitz', grumbled one of Kitchener's friends.)[96] The British government's welcome was to be less rapturous. Despite eight months of unbroken success in an independent command, at the head of a third of the British fighting force, Buller was to be given no official honour of any kind – though Roberts gloomily predicted Buller would be given a peerage. Roberts himself was to be given an earldom and £100,000, and was to be appointed to succeed Wolseley as C-in-C in December 1900, as soon as he returned.[97] Buller was packed off to his pre-war job, training the Army Corps at Aldershot.

It was a quiet ending to the long feud between 'Africans' and 'Indians'. So it seemed. Even Ian Hamilton, the most partisan of the 'Indians', conceded that in the last phase of the campaign Buller had 'handled his troops very well indeed'. He said that Buller 'certainly *was* generous' in his acknowledgements to him. On his own part, Hamilton confessed he no longer felt that 'strong dislike of him amounting to hatred' he had felt hitherto.[98]

But a different future lay ahead. In January 1901 – in the first month of the new century, and the last of the old Queen's reign – Roberts and the 'Indians' returned to claim their kingdom at the Horse Guards from Wolseley. The old wounds reopened; the feud between Buller and Roberts was resumed. St John Brodrick, the new War Minister, compared their feuding to the wrangles between Lucan and Cardigan. He did his best, he claimed, to keep the peace; but Buller was 'impracticable'.[99] In October 1901, Roberts and Brodrick concerted a plan for a '*coup*' (Roberts's phrase) against Buller.[100] Roberts's clever young protegé, Leo Amery, wrote an anonymous letter to *The Times*, taunting Buller with the so-called 'surrender telegram', in which Buller was supposed to have ordered General White to surrender Ladysmith; the government had refused Buller permission to publish the true text. Buller then blurted it out at an official lunch at which Amery was present.[101] Roberts threatened to resign if the Cabinet would not allow him to have Buller sacked for indiscipline.[102] Roberts was given Buller's head on a plate.

Buller's sacking set the seal on Roberts's victory in the war between 'Africans' and 'Indians' that had bedevilled the war against the Boers. In succeeding years, most historians have sided with Roberts, beguiled by Leo Amery's masterly polemic, in *The Times History of the War in South Africa*. I have tried to restore a balance in our judgement of Buller. It is my view that Amery and his school have used a double standard, over-generous to Roberts, over-harsh to Buller.[103] Neither Buller nor Roberts can be rated as *great* generals, judged on their performance in South Africa. The great generals of this war were to prove exclusively Boer: Botha, Christiaan De Wet, De la Rey, perhaps Smuts. On the other hand, Buller's achievements have been obscured by his mistakes. In 1909, a French military critic, General Langlois, pointed out that it was Buller, not Roberts, who had had the toughest job in the war – and it was Buller who was the innovator in countering Boer tactics. The proper use of cover, of infantry advancing in rushes, co-ordinated in turn with creeping barrages of artillery: these were the tactics of truly modern war, first evolved by Buller in Natal. And, as General Langlois said, 'he is entitled to a share of the glory which in England appears to have gone almost exclusively to Lord Roberts'.[104]

Buller's most obvious limitation, that emerges from a study of his hitherto unpublished papers, was not, as his enemies claimed, any lack of self-confidence. On the contrary, he was too self-contained – and isolated from his colleagues. Later, he blamed himself for not having insisted that he be allowed to choose his own generals and staff for the South Africa expedition. He blamed himself for his outburst to Lansdowne and White after Colenso. In this self-appraisal he was surely correct. But these were not the errors of a weak, vacillating man. And they were partly the result of a situation that was not of Buller's making and would have proved intensely frustrating to anyone – the feud between 'Indians' and 'Africans'.

By contrast, Roberts's principal defect as a commander was impatience. It was this that had landed him in a series of administrative blunders that marred all his successes: the immobility of his cavalry, the break-down of his transport, leading in turn to the break-down of his hospital service, and his crowning error – to imagine in the autumn of 1900 that he had as good as won the war.

The war was 'practically' over. That was what Roberts told an audience in Durban at the beginning of December.[105] President Kruger, after weeks as a fugitive in a railway carriage, had finally crossed over the border of Mozambique on 11 September and taken ship for Europe. (The *Gelderland*, a Dutch cruiser, was sent to fetch him.) Routed at the Battle of Belfast, Botha's army split into fragments. They were pursued by three British armies: Buller's in the north; French's at the centre; while Pole-Carew and Ian Hamilton plodded east, sweeping three thousand Boers before them down the railway line to Komati Poort and the Mozambique frontier. The British inflicted few casualties. About two thousand Boers and foreign volunteers surrendered to the Portuguese colonial authorities after making a spectacular bonfire of fifteen hundred railway trucks and their contents – and abandoning their last Long Tom and the last British 12-pounders captured at Sannah's Post. Most of these Boers were later returned to the Transvaal after taking the oath of allegiance; five hundred foreign volunteers, including a hundred of MacBride's 'Irish Brigade', were repatriated to Europe and America.[106] On 25 October – six weeks after publishing it in Army Orders – Roberts jauntily proclaimed the annexation of the Transvaal. He proposed to hand over the command to Kitchener early in November, and return to England by way of Durban after a sombre visit to Natal to see poor Freddy's grave near Colenso.[107]

What of the thirty thousand Boers still at large in the Free State and the Western Transvaal, including De Wet, Botha and De la Rey? Characteristically, Roberts gave the public the impression that he opposed harsh measures to stamp out the embers of the war. In fact, he ordered his generals like Hunter, to continue to extend the use of farm burning as a means of denying food to the guerrillas and punishing their civilian supporters. According to official records, October brought a bumper crop of burnt farms. All over the Free State that spring, the blue sky was tainted with the black smoke of burning homesteads.[108] To one of his admirers, Roberts confessed that he had perhaps erred on the side of weakness in the past. He would 'starve into submission' the last of these 'banditti', as though he were leading a punitive expedition on the Indian frontier.[109] He would be home for Christmas.

Painful events, as it turned out, delayed his departure for England. The Queen's soldier grandson, Prince Christian Victor, died of typhoid in Pretoria;

perhaps his death hastened the Queen's own end. And Roberts's daughter, Aileen, nearly died of typhoid, too. So he did not reach England till January 1901.[110]

By then, the whole strategic map had changed once again. Roberts was right when he told his audience in Durban that the war was 'practically over'. So it was: the war of set-piece battles. But a new war – just as costly in time and money and human lives, and far more bitter, because it directly involved civilians – had only just begun.

PART IV

Kitchener's Peace

'I do not want any incentive to do what is possible to finish.... I think I hate the country, the people, the whole thing more every day.'

Lord Kitchener to St John Brodrick,
the new War Minister, 1901

SENDING THE INNOCENTS TO HEAVEN.

CHAPTER 36
A Muddy Election
London, Autumn 1900

'You see, I had read a book,' the Knight went on in a
dreamy far-away tone, 'written by someone to prove that
warfare under modern conditions was impossible. You
may imagine how disturbing that was to a man of my
profession. Many men would have thrown the whole
thing up and gone home. But I grappled with the
situation. You will never guess what I did.'
Alice pondered. 'You went to war, of course –'

'Yes, *but not under modern conditions.*'

> The White Knight (Lord Lansdowne)
> explaining the Cabinet's war policy in
> Saki's satire *Alice in Westminster*,
> autumn 1900

The news that the war was 'practically' over came as no surprise to the government; a well deserved victory, if somewhat belated. Lansdowne's own feelings of disappointment at the unexpected stubbornness of the Boer governments had kept pace with Roberts's; his ear was equally well tuned to British public opinion. The public had become restive. Small wonder the war had dragged on three months since the triumphant entry into Pretoria.[1]

In August, *The Times* had grumbled that this state of affairs could go on 'indefinitely', unless Roberts took sterner measures against the Boers. 'As in other matters, we have pushed leniency to weakness,' was the Thunderer's verdict in mid-August. These guerrillas must be treated as 'simple bandits'. The civilian population must be taught a lesson by 'retaliatory measures'.[2] Lansdowne had sent a soothing message to Roberts to say he was glad he had discarded the 'kid glove' policy, and started farm-burning.[3] But, of course, all this was academic, now that the war was nearly over.

Nearly, but not quite. And was it not the moment, with victory in sight, to spring a trap on the Opposition, by calling a general election? It was a paradox that a government whose talent for governing was generally reckoned so low, should now be expected to win an overwhelming majority at the polls. All the more so because their preparations for war, the conduct of the war itself, and the debates in Parliament on these subjects – especially on the hospital scandals – had confirmed their reputation for incompetence.[4] But the war, which had damaged the government, had left the Liberals flat on their backs, divided into three warring parts – radicals, moderates, imperialists – with Campbell-Bannerman quite unable to unite them.[5] Hence the need, from the government's point of view, to spring an election *before* the war was over – the war in South Africa, and the war among the Opposition.

For weeks, arguments for an early election had been anxiously debated by the government and whispered by the Press. Chamberlain, with characteristic impatience, originally plumped for June, a post-Mafeking election. Salisbury, as usual, refused to be hustled.[6] Then the telegrams from South Africa had turned sour for a time. There was the Boxer Rebellion in China. After that, golf courses, grouse moors and foreign watering-places beckoned. An arid Parliamentary session expired with the rumours of dissolution still unanswered. In September, Lord Salisbury returned from his summer holiday in the Vosges, read the telegrams from South Africa, and agreed. This was the moment. They could go for a double mandate: to confirm that the war could not be ended by a compromise, this time, over Boer independence (not 'a shred of independence' were Salisbury's words), and to confirm that the immediate future of the newly annexed states was for them to be governed as Crown Colonies. The opposition would be trapped. They would have to take their medicine in the election by swallowing both these distasteful propositions. Even so, they could be labelled 'pro-Boer', and anti-British. This was the plan agreed by the government parties.[7] On 18 September, *The London Gazette* revealed that the Queen, at Balmoral, had duly dissolved Parliament (it was to be the last complete Parliament of her sixty-four-year-long reign) on the previous day. Polling for the election – the 'Khaki election', as people called it, alias the 'patriotic election' – would start in a fortnight.[8]

This sudden declaration of war caught Campbell-Bannerman majestically returning from the spa at Marienbad, where he had gone, as usual, for his summer holidays. His party remained in total disarray.[9] 'The political position is just maddening,' wrote Herbert Gladstone, the Chief Whip, 'with CB away. The whole party waits for the smallest scrap of inspiration, but it is all smothered in Marienbad mud. The situation is grotesque. . . . Our efforts to find a leader are about as successful as Tommy Atkins's efforts to shoot a Boer.'[10] CB reached England on the 22nd, unruffled as usual. He had published a kind of manifesto in June, around which he hoped to unite the party. The theme was reconciliation: between Britons and Boers, and thus among the Liberals, too. He hoped for an honourable defeat in the election. But the best anyone could expect was that the government might come back for a new seven-year lease of life, without an even bigger majority; they had had a 130-seat majority at the dissolution. No one imagined that the Liberals, whose wounds still gaped so wide, could actually win.[11]

'The war, more than any other in modern times, was and is a popular war.' So *The Times* declared on 18 September, speaking with the self-satisfaction of one of its principal promoters.[12] In fact, it was hard to say how much part 'Khaki' played – directly – in the election. Of course, the war was popular in a negative sense. There was no outburst of pacifism. On the other hand, there was no evidence of war-fever; no jingo mobs – now – to break up the meetings of the 'pro-Boers', as David Lloyd George's had been broken up in March at Glasgow, and in April at Caernarvon. 'Good-humoured indifference' was the way one paper described the public's attitude to Leonard Courtney, one of the few MPs who actively opposed the war. Probably it was true. John Bull had run the gamut of emotions in the last few months. The decisive election issue was not particularly emotive. It was, simply, how could a divided Opposition govern?[13]

How different it had been only a few months earlier! Between Black Week and Mafeking night (between mid-December 1899 and May 1900), the war had been *the* burning topic – a 'nightmare', indeed, as Balfour said, when it looked as though White and his twelve thousand troops at Ladysmith might be forced to surrender.[14] Hence the hysterical jingoism of that period, and the popular fury directed at the so-called 'pro-Boers'. The word was merely a gibe, when applied to British MPs. CB had successfully persuaded most of the radicals, including John Morley, Sir William Harcourt, and even young David Lloyd George, not to imperil their own and their party's electoral chances by supporting anti-war resolutions in Parliament. By contrast, John Redmond's Irish nationalists took an unashamed delight – patriotism, Irish-style – in British humiliations; and *they* did vote for the Boers. In February they supported an amendment: 'The war . . . should be brought to a close on the basis of recognizing the independence of the Transvaal and the Orange Free State.' Only a couple of dissident Liberals supported this resolution.[15] Morley and the rest contented themselves with attacking the government where most Liberals could find most common ground: in bungled war preparations, and a bungled war itself. In June, CB made them swallow the pill: accept the *fait accompli*, annexation of the republics.[16]

It was the end of a long struggle for CB's own survival as a credible party leader. His differences with the Liberal imperialists had become increasingly public. Rosebery still played Achilles, sulking in his splendid tent. Grey and Haldane hoped to oust CB and restore Rosebery. Asquith was less hostile to CB, but thought he would resign.[17] This was wishful thinking by Margot Asquith, Milner's go-between. She confessed to Milner on 9 July, 'I feel *strongly* tho. entre nous that CB is *not* the man to lead us.'[18] Actually CB, exasperated as he was, had no intention of resigning. And he had a strong suspicion who was the man who kept the Liberal imperialists so alienated: 'One of the main influences causing the determined support given by them to the Govt. SA policy has been Milner-worship.'[19]

In the event, the election restored CB's morale, although not the party's fortunes. The Tories' tactics were obvious enough: to impale the Opposition on the issue which above all divided them – South Africa; and to tar all Liberals, except the Liberal imperialists, with the 'pro-Boer' brush. The methods they used recoiled on them – at any rate, on Chamberlain.

It was Chamberlain who was thought to have taken to extreme the use of 'pro-Boer' taunts. He chose as a kind of slogan the remark said to have been made by Whiteley, the loyalist Mayor of Mafeking (actually troublesome enough to B-P during the siege). The remark was: 'Every seat lost to the government was a seat gained by the Boers,' and it proved an explosive bullet indeed when Chamberlain's speech was telegraphed to Lancashire with 'gained' accidentally transcribed as 'sold'.[20] In fact, other Conservatives and Unionists chose weapons equally remote from the unofficial Hague Convention usually observed at elections. A political cartoon, showing Liberals cheerfully support-ing the Boers in the firing-line, was issued by party headquarters. Gerald Balfour, brother of Arthur and Chief Secretary for Ireland, used a stirring poster depicting K of K and Bobs alongside the patriotic text: 'Our Brave Soldiers In South Africa Expect That Every Voter This Day Will Do His Duty.... Remember! To Vote For A Liberal Is A Vote To The Boer.' And there was an uncharacteristic crudity about young Winston Churchill's poster at Oldham: 'Be it known that every vote given to the radicals means 2 pats on the back for Kruger and 2 smacks in the face for our country.'[21]

The response was equally obvious, equally crude: to 'go for Joe' (CB's phrase) and make Joe the Aunt Sally of the election.[22] Dislike of Chamberlain was one of the few things that Liberals did not have to pretend to have in common: it came naturally. And it certainly suited CB to call this 'Chamberlain's election', just as they talked of the war as 'Chamberlain's war'. There stood Joe, the Brummagem Goliath, challenging all comers. How CB was sickened by his vulgarity! The Liberals had been trapped: unable to broaden the election to include bread-and-butter issues, on which they could win seats and unite the party. So why not narrow the issue down to 'Pushful Joe'?

And this time, Goliath seemed to have met his David – David Lloyd George. 'Unionists very glum,' wrote CB on 30 September, after a barn-storming tour of Scotland. 'Joe has overshot the mark, and three things damage him – the election trick, the publication of private letters, and the shares in contracting companies.... Then AJB is drivelling – and the others nowhere.'[23]

The last of the 'three things' had been most skilfully exploited (venomously, some said) by Lloyd George, the pushing young Liberal member for Caernar-von. Lloyd George's charge was quite simply that Joe was a war-profiteer, exploiting the war to swell the profits of his family's armaments firms, including Kynoch's and a naval contractor's called Hoskins.[24] Kynoch's was the principal private firm supplying the army with small-arms ammunition, and Joe's brother, Arthur, who had taken over Joe's business interests, had recently become chairman and a substantial shareholder.[25] An irony probably not known to Chamberlain's enemies was that the firm was actually in very bad odour with the War Office, because of late delivery and poor quality. In January, General Brackenbury had protested to Lansdowne (adding pointedly, 'You can show the letter to Chamberlain') that nearly half of Kynoch's ·303 ammunition – 1,749,000 out of 4,035,116 ball cartridges sent that week – had been rejected as below standard.[26]

Most of Lloyd George's political ammunition was also below standard. The charge of Joe's war-profiteering because of his links with Kynoch's, was just rhetoric. Joe and Arthur Chamberlain were two very different people, as Joe

Chamberlain duly pointed out. Joe had sold all his shares in the family firms when he took office – at a loss, so he said. And, anyway, Kynoch's was losing money. He answered these 'abominable' charges with the same maddening, all-steel, hand-on-the-heart manner that he had used to answer the charges of complicity in the Raid. (An extra irony was that Arthur Chamberlain was actually an old-fashioned Liberal who deplored Joe's conversion to Unionism; Joe's 'wrong-doing' and 'reaction', he told his own children, had brought 'shame' on the family.[27])

Lloyd George was unrepentant, and, on the charge that Joe's family had profited from the naval contractors, Hoskins, he turned out to have a point – a debating point. Austen, Joe's elder son, and a junior member of Salisbury's government, had a small holding in Hoskins. Although, in fact, defence contracts were only a small part of Hoskins's business,[28] it was enough to poison the election from Chamberlain's point of view. His frustrated anger, his sense of outrage at Lloyd George's tactics ('an avalanche of mud' assailed him, wrote his shocked biographer),[29] surprised even Tories like Balfour, who knew him well.[30]

One sort of mud, however, was notable for its absence in the election campaign. The Liberals made almost no references to the drastic methods which Roberts had begun to adopt in an effort to end the war. Perhaps they were still unaware of the realities of war; even *The Guardian*'s war correspondent was slow to recognize the implication of Roberts's farm burning, just as he had been slow to spot the scandal of Roberts's hospital arrangements.[31] On the other hand, they were acutely aware of the political danger, in a Khaki election, of attacking the gentlemen in khaki. Yet it is odd, considering the political storm that would soon burst over the government's head because of farm burning, how meekly the Liberals accepted the policy at the time.

Muddy or not, the 'Khaki election' certainly looked conclusive in its results. To say that it was a 'drawn contest', as *The Daily Chronicle* claimed, seemed an odd way of representing the polling. As predicted by Chamberlain, the government gained an even more copper-bottomed majority: 134 seats more than the Liberals and the Irish Nationalists combined. In votes, however, the country was more evenly divided: 2·4 million for the government, against 2 million for the Liberals, without counting the Irish votes. (So if every vote for a Liberal *had* been a vote for the Boers, as the Tories claimed, the Boers had won two million.)

Naturally, these results raised the government's spirits. Another six-year lease of life for a government that not even its best friends claimed was popular: this was a bonus that no one could have dared predict a year earlier. Despite the 'abominable flood of slanders ... on my unfortunate head', Chamberlain was satisfied. He was delighted to hear of the victory of young Winston Churchill, for whom he had gone down to Oldham to speak (he owed it to Lord Randolph's memory). He thought it curious that there were so few other changes on either side.

That autumn, the weather was again glorious, and he found solace in reshaping his beloved garden at Highbury. 'We are hard at work on the changes in the garden,' he wrote on 12 October. 'Austen has been indefatigable ... in pruning trees and there has been a great deal of lopping of the old oaks.' A fortnight later he was off on holiday to Gibraltar, sailing (to *Punch*'s mirth) aboard a warship called HMS *Caesar*.[32]

The same glorious autumn weather found Salisbury at Hatfield, reshaping his Cabinet. He did not prune many of these trees or lop many of these old oaks. In fact, the changes, though small, certainly justified the gibes about Salisbury's running the government like a family business, the 'Hotel Cecil' (himself, the two Balfours and Selborne). Goschen, First Lord of the Admiralty, was dropped overboard. Salisbury's son-in-law, Selborne, came up into the Cabinet to replace Goschen. One old oak did receive some lopping: himself. He could no longer carry the double burden as Foreign Secretary and Prime Minister, so he gave Lansdowne the Foreign Office and Lansdowne handed over the War Office to St John Brodrick. New blood in the government included his own eldest son, Cranborne, as Lansdowne's Under-Secretary.[33] The 'Hotel Cecil' had increased its accommodation to five.

Despite the massive majority against them, the Liberals drew comfort from the results of the election. There was a feeling that the government had played a fast one on the electorate, and they would not be forgiven.[34]

CB himself was hopeful: 'In the circs, we have not done badly.' The results in Scotland had been 'horrid'; his own majority had been cut to 630, as the Catholics voted for a Liberal Unionist. (The victory of Lloyd George at Caernarvon he no doubt regarded with mixed feelings.) CB was sure that 'we shall never have so many adverse conditions again'. The natural divisions in the party, he believed, were not as great as people imagined, though there were extremists. The Roseberyites he regarded as 'more insidious and deadly'. Indeed, it was on them that he largely blamed the fiasco of the last five years in opposition. 'As long as he hangs on our flank we are paralysed.'[35]

Another five years in the wilderness; it was, indeed, to be the fate of the party. Yet that paralysis was soon to be relieved by exciting events in the quarter least expected: in South Africa.

The newly installed War Minister, St John Brodrick, had still hardly found his feet in the labyrinths of Pall Mall when he received a long, emotional, and disheartening letter from Milner. Brodrick was one of the few people to whom Milner could speak absolutely frankly. Brodrick was one of the 'Souls'; his sister had married Philip Gell; Milner was one of her trustees. The letter, written in early November, predicted disaster in South Africa unless they adopted a more systematic military strategy. The men at the front were 'all tired'. But the war was not, as Roberts still claimed, 'practically over'. It had burst out in October in a more virulent form: guerrilla war. Milner put the blame fairly and squarely on Roberts. His arguments were of the same sort, though more violently put, than some of the ones Buller had expressed earlier:

The fatal error is not to hold district A & make sure of it before you go on to district B – I mean the fatal error latterly, not at first when you had to rush. The consequence is we have a big army campaigning away in the front & the enemy swarming in the country behind it. . . . But it is no earthly use dashing about any more when there is nothing to get at the end of the dash, & you only wear out your footmen [sic] and kill your horses. The time for over-running is over . . . stage 2 is a gradual subjugation, district by district, leaving small entrenched & well-supplied garrisons behind your columns as they sweep the country & mounted police to patrol between these posts.[36]

Milner regretted that Roberts had stayed so long; but he had little more confidence in Kitchener, who was shortly to replace him. 'Kitchener, a man of great power, is stale. Worse than that, he is *in a hurry*. Now the essence of the business in its present form is that it must be done gradually.' Milner boasted to Brodrick that he could do better than the generals. 'What classical character does A. Milner most resemble?' wrote Milner. 'The answer is Cleon. Yes Cleon. He was, as you remember, a loud-mouthed, pushing demagogue (parallel perhaps not quite perfect [Milner's own comment] at this point). But the great feature of his history was that he appealed to the Athenians against the military.'[37]

What was Broderick to make of this extraordinary outburst? An increasingly bitter guerrilla war, an increasingly bitter rift between Milner and Kitchener: these were indeed serious matters. And Brodrick's instructions from Salisbury and the Cabinet were based on Roberts's opposite advice: that the war was 'practically' over. There were plans for bringing back various regular battalions. Already it had been agreed that the Canadian contingents should sail for Canada. The Imperial Yeomanry were leaving, too. The CIV had marched back into London at the end of October, their procession from the docks a kind of victory parade.[38]

Was Milner exaggerating the dangers? The War Office, in December 1900, gave Brodrick little help. Wolseley's twenty years of power were over. But Roberts himself was not due at the Horse Guards till early January.[39]

Understandably, perhaps, Brodrick did not raise the alarm after receiving Milner's private letter. At any rate, he took no steps to halt the planned reduction of the army in South Africa.[40] That question would have to await the arrival of the new C-in-C at the War Office. Meanwhile, he reassured the Cabinet and hoped for the best.

CHAPTER 37

The Worm Turns

South Africa,
30 October – 16 December 1900

'Low types of animal organism will survive injuries
which would kill organisms of a higher type outright.
They die, too ... but it takes time. For the moment the
severed pieces wriggle very vigorously ...'

Alfred Milner to Richard Haldane
21 January 1901

Milner was not exaggerating. Indeed, it is Roberts's optimism that now seems
so astonishing, considering the set-backs the British had suffered in the weeks
before Milner wrote that letter. Spring had come, breathing new life into the
veld, and into the commandos scattered over it. With spring came an intoxicat-
ing belief, fed by small successes in the field – a belief that the war was only just
beginning. Valley after valley of the rugged south-western Transvaal had slipped back under the control of De la Rey's guerrillas. In the great open plains
either side of the Vaal, De Wet was back in his hunting-ground, snapping up
convoys, swallowing prisoners; a small, swirling cloud on the horizon, the size
of a dynamited train.[1]

At the epicentre of this miniature cyclone, for a few days at the end of
October, was a Transvaal farm called Cypherfontein, belonging to one of the
Grobler family. It was in the Zwartruggen Hills, about seventy-five miles west
of Pretoria. From this ridge, you could see for miles: to the south, the western
Witwatersrand, grassy downs along whose crest Dr Jameson had ridden on his
way from Mafeking to Doornkop; to the north, a chain of fertile valleys,
watered by the rivers that flow down from the Witwatersrand – the Marico, the
Elands, the Kosters and the Selous; to the east, the jagged grey crescent of the
Magaliesberg, a safety curtain between these wooded valleys and Pretoria.

It was a delightful place to camp in spring, Cypherfontein; so the State
Attorney, Jan Smuts, now De la Rey's second-in-command, later described it.
'Our tents were hidden by the sweet-smelling mimosa now in full blossom, the
grass was excellent for the animals, all around lay a district rich in forage for the
horses, and oranges and *nartjes* [tangerines].' In fact, the farm was strategically
placed at the head of the Kosters River valley, near enough for attacking the lines
of communication between Rustenburg and Zeerust, yet secluded enough to be
safe from British farm-burning expeditions. Apart from the attractions of being,

literally, a land of milk and honey, it had other amenities. There was a helio-graphist to exchange on-the-spot reports with the local commandos; the command of such a wide sweep of country made it an ideal helio-station. There was also a telegraph line a mile beyond the farm to give up-to-the-minute reports on their enemies. Incredibly, it had never dawned on Roberts's Field Intelligence Department that their military telegraph line – the main line connecting Pretoria with Rustenburg and Zeerust – could be tapped by the Boer telegraph operator at this aptly christened farm of Cypherfontein.[2]

At this magical lair, for a few days in late October, there gathered, snatched from the ether, so to speak, the leaders of both governments: General Louis Botha and President Steyn. Both men had trekked hundreds of miles, cutting a great arc through the northern bush veld, to avoid the British columns. De la Rey and Smuts played host. The absent guest was General De Wet. He was expected shortly. The newcomers must have enjoyed the respite. Each day they bathed in the pool close to the farm, and after a breakfast of fresh oranges and *nartjes* they would discuss plans.[3] But their task was a heavy one. Roberts's policy of large-scale farm burning had changed the war utterly: to the eyes of the guerrillas, it was both a curse and a blessing. They must now hammer out a joint offensive strategy to counter it. A strategy *agreed* by the allies; that was the key to success. How could they achieve it?

From the beginning of the war – indeed, shortly before its outbreak – relations between the two allies had been dangerously variable. In September 1899, the Transvaalers had been eager to rush Natal before White's reinforcements arrived from India. The Free State had dragged its feet. But since then, the Free State had been setting the pace, and had virtually accused the Transvaal of cowardice. The two republics were, of course, fundamentally opposite kinds of state: a sheep-and-cow-republic compared with a gold-republic. Hence the divergent attitudes to war and peace. There was also the cleft of personalities, the clash of Steyn with Botha.

It was Steyn who had taken over from Kruger the role of the iron-willed prophet of the volk; and a prophet he looked – with his glittering dome of a head, flaming red beard and whiskers, and stern, upright carriage. How well the President suited the bleached red plains of the Free State![4] There were no mixed blessings there, no gold in those hills (this was half a century before the discovery that the Free State, too, had its own Rand near Kroonstad), no diamonds to muddy the veld with their slag-heaps, and so few Uitlanders that they were welcome. The wealth of their neighbours had imperceptibly and painlessly rubbed off on these sheep-farmers and cattle-ranchers; the railway profits paid more than half their taxes, and bought their guns and rifles.[5] Unlike the volk of the other three states, they remained an unchallenged majority of the white population. Hence the purity of Steyn's Afrikaner nationalism. Despite the wholesale surrenders of the burghers ever since the fall of Bloemfontein, Steyn and De Wet had never wavered in their denunciation of peace talks. *They* would fight to the bitter end to preserve their independence.[6] They would keep their part of the map from being coloured red. It was a recipe for national suicide,

an Afrikaner equivalent of 'better-dead-than-red'. Yet, given that the Free State
had virtually no economic attractions for new immigrants, Steyn had no potential political rivals to challenge his leadership of the volk to a glorious death.

How different, of course, was the position of all the Transvaal leaders. In a
mixed white community – part-Boer, part-British, part-Jewish and cosmopolitan
– politics led inevitably to compromise. Hence an extra dimension to that spasm of
despair just before the fall of Pretoria, felt by even the most resolute Transvaalers:
Kruger, Botha, De la Rey, and Smuts. What was the point of going on fighting, if
their efforts were certain to come to an inglorious end, if there was no hope of any
success in the field, and if the country would be devastated from end to end in the
process? This was the *cri de coeur* of the Transvaal at the end of May. Botha had
repeated it again in September, demoralized after the collapse of his army following Buller's victories in August. Behind it was more than simply a difference of
character (and Louis Botha was, by contrast to Steyn, a delightfully warm-hearted
person). There was also a simple political calculation. Death and glory had less
attraction for the volk in the Transvaal, when a hundred thousand Uitlanders were
waiting to pick up the pieces.

The Transvaalers had now largely recovered their morale. Indeed, Smuts later
claimed that they had all been converted unequivocally to Steyn's way of
thinking, by Steyn's threat to go-it-alone. Botha, however, seems to have
continued to oscillate between the emotional attractions of fighting on regardless, and the duty to save the volk from further sacrifices. No minutes of the
conference at Cypherfontein have been preserved, but we can guess the main
lines of discussion.[7]

The case for continuing the struggle rested on the proposition that guerrilla
war was – at present – practicable. From the end of March, De Wet had proved
this in the Free State: snatching up Broadwood's guns at Sannah's Post from
under Roberts's nose, snapping up the Irish Rifles at Reddersburg. From July,
De la Rey had proved it in the Western Free State by his daring ambush of the
Scots Greys at Zilikat's Nek. Since then, the techniques of guerrilla war, and the
areas that the guerrillas controlled, had been dramatically extended. But, however practicable, was a guerrilla war a 'civilized war'? This was the question that
obviously troubled the consciences of the Transvaal leaders, especially Botha,
and explains why they clung so long to the strategy of regular warfare on the
eastern front. Botha must have read enough military history – Smuts certainly
had – to know what a guerrilla war inevitably entails for civilians. Sherman's
march through Georgia, the Prussian treatment of the French *franc-tireurs*; they
cast ugly shadows on the veld, these international precedents. And a guerrilla
war in South Africa, however gentlemanly the main combatants professed to be,
threatened to have elements of savagery absent from warfare in more civilized
states.[8] Already the Derdeport 'massacre' – actually only two white civilians had
been killed by Holdsworth's and Linchwe's Africans – had woken the spectre of
a black peril, which, however exaggerated in Boer propaganda,[9] was real
enough at the back of every Boer's mind: the 'black care', that rode with every
commando.

In short, here was a daunting moral problem. Was it fair to the volk (women and children, as well as the menfolk) to involve them in such a savage kind of war? For the women and children it would be like a return to the dark pages of voortrekker history, when their grandparents had struggled against the Kaffirs: women and children pressed into service, each farm a commissary and an arsenal; their homes looted and burnt; then forced to choose between going as refugees to the cities, or following the laagers into battle.

This brutal pattern, inevitable in guerrilla war, had already begun to emerge on the western front. Whole areas had been ravaged; Linchwe's Africans were said to be on the warpath once again. The veld was reverting to desert, the western border to anarchy.[10]

There were also doubts about the practical sides of the problem. How long would guerrilla war be possible, assuming that Roberts continued to ravage the countryside? Farm burning, as practised by Roberts, was a blessing of a sort, but only in the short term. To get the burghers back into the field, it had perhaps been essential. How else to persuade the law-abiding burgher that he was absolved from his oath of neutrality? How better to illustrate the point, than with a burnt and looted farmhouse, that this was the way Roberts honoured his side of the bargain, kept his promise to protect (or at least pay compensation for) the property of all burghers who surrendered? Drastic as the fiery medicine was, it did wonders for the morale of the burghers. But what of the long term?[11] Farm burning was designed to make guerrilla war impossible, and in certain areas it had already begun to achieve this. The Magalies valley was becoming a blackened desert, useless as a base for De la Rey's guerrillas, so efficient were Clements's columns at burning grain, seizing stock and trampling crops. Hence the retreat to the Kosters River valley. But where to next, when this retreat was denied them? In such an arid country as South Africa, once the commandos let themselves be squeezed off the farm land they would wither away.

So it was vital from both points of view – humanitarian and military – to find an answer to farm-burning. And the answer both republican governments gave was simple: invade Cape Colony and Natal, British territories where farm-burning would be politically impossible.[12]

This was the policy agreed by Botha and Steyn at Cypherfontein during the conference. Had it been carried into effect as a joint offensive, it might possibly have changed the whole course of the war. But the divisions between the two allies ran too deep – and, anyway, luck was against them. After a few days, the telegraph wire behind the farm began to vibrate with secret British plans for raiding the Kosters valley. Forewarned, the various commandos – Botha, Steyn, De la Rey, Smuts and all – dispersed. De Wet thus never reached them; instead, Steyn joined him before he reached Cypherfontein, and they both recrossed the Vaal and rejoined De Wet's men at Bothaville, on the Valsch River. All thought of concerted strategy was abandoned – indeed, Steyn and De Wet suffered a near-fatal disaster.

Their departure put paid to hopes of carrying out, first, another dramatic joint offensive: attacking the gold-mines of the Rand. The plan, proposed by Smuts, was a *volte-face*, perhaps as a reprisal for farm burning. Smuts, like Botha, had repudiated the idea of attacking the mines in May, before the British had seized Johannesburg. Now that the mines were politically controlled by Britain, Smuts thought it fair to try to destroy them. He also recognized that at the root of the war were the mine-owners: Beit, Wernher and the others. Threaten their money-bags, and they would lose their appetite for war.[13] For Smuts, it was a curiously naïve plan, even if De Wet and Steyn had been prepared to help.

Meanwhile, Smuts and De la Rey lay low beyond the Magaliesberg, carrying out the main task of a guerrilla movement: to survive. Their time would come.

The near-fatal disaster to Steyn's and De Wet's Free State Commando at Bothaville on the Valsch River happened soon after dawn on 6 November. What it proved was that even De Wet could be caught napping. Only the speed of their own flight, the heroism of their rearguard, and the slowness of the main British column, commanded by Major-General Charles Knox, saved both De Wet and Steyn from death or capture. As it was, De Wet lost his entire artillery: his four last Krupp field-guns, a pom-pom, and trophies from both Colenso and Sannah's Post (a 15-pounder from Colonel Long's 14th Battery and a 12-pounder from Broadwood's Q Battery). Still worse, the Khakis trapped the rearguard: 155 men, 25 of whom were killed and 30 wounded. And of those who escaped, others, too, were wounded. It was the most shattering defeat De Wet had yet suffered himself. What made it doubly humiliating was that the British had exchanged roles with the Boers. The men of De Wet's main outpost had simply gone to sleep (despite those threats of the ant-heap punishment), and then the small British advance guard – only six hundred, compared to De Wet's eight hundred – routed the burghers.

It was the totally unexpected appearance of the British, in full daylight, that precipitated the disaster. De Wet himself had that moment received a report from a corporal sent to watch the British camp. 'Yes,' said the corporal, 'we saw the smoke rising from General Knox's camp-fires on the other bank of the Valsch.' This was about seven miles off. A moment later, De Wet heard rifle fire. Was someone shooting cattle for food? But it was the Khakis, on a hill three hundred yards away. 'The scene which ensued,' De Wet confessed later, 'was unlike anything I had ever witnessed before.' Many burghers were lying asleep, for it was only twenty minutes after dawn, rolled up in their blankets. Now there was pandemonium. Some people threw their saddles on to their horses and galloped away, leaving everything; others did not even try to up-saddle, but galloped away bare-back. 'Don't run away! Come back and storm the position!' roared De Wet. No use. He galloped after them (using his *sjambok* freely, no doubt). Still no use. As De Wet grabbed one group of terrified burghers, another group slipped through his hands. And so it went on, De Wet dodging from group to group, as they fled in a wild, panic-stricken rout that only ended when the burghers were out of range of the guns.[14] The one great blessing was the safety of the most precious thing entrusted to the Commando: the life of President Steyn. Steyn's Adjutant, Du Preez, had kept his horse, Scot, ready saddled and tied to a food wagon. Steyn galloped off, leaving Du Preez to give covering fire. Steyn lost nothing except his cuff-links.[15]

Meanwhile, a small rearguard – burghers who could not find their horses – began to return the enemy's fire from some white farm buildings across the road from the laager, not only to help De Wet's retreat but to save the Krupp field-guns parked in a kraal. In turn, the British advance guard (actually, Lieutenant-Colonel P. W. J. Le Gallais, with the 5th and 8th MI) galloped forward and seized a red farmhouse, only about two hundred yards away. A four-hour duel followed, a duel between about 150 men on either side, firing field-guns at a range almost close enough to throw a stone. The heroism displayed on both sides made it one of the most ferocious and gruesome little actions of the war.

No eye-witness accounts survive from the Boer side, but one can picture the scene: Lee ·303 bullets hammering on the stone walls of the garden, where the burghers were huddled in the early morning sunshine; three snipers hiding in the pig-sty out in the open (for hours they led a charmed life, then they were spotted, and vanished in a cloud of red dust and shrapnel); four more took refuge in a white farmhouse, where there were some women and children; all four men were killed by a shell, but the women and children were miraculously spared.[16]

From the British side there is one vibrant description of that terrifying ordeal. Major William Hickie, staff officer to Le Gallais, had been sent back to heliograph for reinforcements. It was not till eight o'clock that General Knox finally appeared on the scene. 'The General is an old woman,' said Hickie bitterly, 'and now he had better go home. . . . If Knox had had the same dash as Le Gallais we should have taken the whole lot, bagged the whole crowd.' As it was, Le Gallais was left beleaguered for hours in the red farmhouse, and Hickie himself had to set off to organize reinforcements as best he could. He then plunged back into the whirlpool of bullets, losing his horse, shot in five places.

He found the red farmhouse had become a butcher's shop. Through the open doorway, the Boers had picked off the officers: the chief himself, Le Gallais, with a ghastly wound in the body; Lieutenant-Colonel Wally Ross, the CO of the 8th MI, with the lower part of his jaw shot away; Major Williams, Ross's staff officer, with six bullets in him – altogether, eight men, with ghastly wounds.

Hickie took charge, but for the next two hours he lay there, unable to stir. 'It was a *terrible* two hours,' he confessed later. The British 12-pounders were bursting case and shrapnel on the kraal only forty yards away; and the Boers were using explosive (that is, hollow-nosed or soft-nosed) bullets which smashed to pieces the walls of the farmhouse above his head. Eventually, Knox's main force began to arrive; so Major Hickie and Major Lean, who had forty men of the 5th MI, gave the orders to their men: fix bayonets and charge. The Boers were too quick for them. At the white farmhouse, up went the white flag, and out came the Boers with their hands up.[17]

After such an ordeal the British soldiers were in no mood for gallantry. In

Hickie's words: 'Our men were all wild as nearly all our casualties were from explosive bullets. . . .' (contrary to the unsigned Hague convention). 'I had all the prisoners searched for explosive bullets and found 2 with them in their pockets. These I ordered to be shot in half an hour. Unfortunately I met the general [Knox] & told him – he said "All right, I leave it to you." Ten minutes afterwards he sent to me that he would have them tried first. Result that now we have cooled down, we won't shoot a man in cold blood.' But the incident only increased his men's bitterness towards that 'old woman' the General and his 'brilliant' staff of red-tabbed officers, whose *only* interest in the battle seemed to concern the equitable disposal of De Wet's laager. (Official orders: 'The wagons on the left hand side of the Road are for De Lisle's force to loot, and those on the right for Le Gallais.') Hickie was too busy to loot. There were dead comrades everywhere; dying men to attend to; Le Gallais himself, perhaps the most gallant leader of mounted men in the whole British army, died the same evening.[18]

Characteristically, General Knox made little attempt to follow up Le Gallais's victory, and De Wet's men recovered their self-confidence. Within a few days, De Wet was back to his old form, plundering and burning garrisons with apparent impunity. On 23 November he captured De Wetsdorp (the small town named after his father).

The golden chance, for which Generals Smuts and De la Rey had been waiting so long, presented itself a fortnight before Christmas in the great gorge at Nooitgedacht.

For three months, ever since General Clements had first stormed up the Moot (the nickname for this once fertile valley of the Magalies), breathing smoke and flames, the burghers had been forced on to the defensive. Smuts himself bore the brunt of the campaign, wearing both his official hats: member of Kruger's old government (he was still, technically, the State Attorney) and newly created Assistant Commandant-General, making him De la Rey's right-hand man. The double task had proved mainly concerned with administration, political as well as military, but was anything but dull. Smuts had to regroup and revitalize the commandos of the Western Transvaal. This meant appointing new leaders, expelling the burghers whose loyalty was suspect (almost as brutal a business as Clements's rampage up the Moot), even condemning and executing those found guilty of treason. For political commissar's work of this kind, Smuts's legal training and cool brain admirably suited him. To the tactical demands of the guerrilla war, an endless series of humiliating retreats, he was less well suited. Hence his delight in early December, when the British, grown careless after weeks when the guerrillas had lain low, gave Smuts and De la Rey their first small chance to seize the initiative.[19]

It was 2 December, when Smuts heard from the special corps of scouts which he had organized that a large, ill-defended British ox-wagon convoy was heading westwards for Rustenburg along the road that runs north of the Moot. Here was the chance of getting their hands on the supplies urgently needed by Broadwood and his column at Rustenburg. Next morning at dawn, Smuts and De la Rey pounced on the convoy as it passed some kopjes at Buffelshoek. Though only partially successful (and a bullet aimed at Smuts at twenty-five yards' range killed his companion), the guerrillas got a fine haul of Christmas presents: 118 wagons and fifty-four prisoners. The British lost sixty-four other casualties. Smuts released the prisoners, kept fifteen wagons that had boots and clothing; then made a bonfire of the rest.[20] Broadwood would have no champagne for Christmas.

The success of this ambush naturally whetted Smuts's and De la Rey's appetite for bigger game. A week later they found it: General Clements, Broadwood's collaborator and the destroyer of the Moot, a bull-necked Englishman caught by the horns, so to speak, in the gorge at Nooitgedacht ('Never Expected') inside the Moot. 'I do not think,' Smuts wrote later, 'it was possible to have selected a more fatal spot for a camp and one which gave better scope for Boer dash and ingenuity in storming the position.' The sheer walls of the Magaliesberg, a thousand feet high at this point, dominated the camp from the north – indeed, commanded the whole valley. In fact, Clements had had two reasons for choosing this site, and neither had anything to do with defence. He had put a signalling station here on the crest of the mountain to keep in touch with Broadwood, whose heliograph flashed out at Rustenburg, twenty miles away in the shimmering plain to the north-west. He had also acquired a rare prize, a supply of pure mountain water. For Nooitgedacht was the place where a romantic stream, plunging down in a series of waterfalls, had cut a twisted cleft out of the side of the gorge. No doubt Smuts and De la Rey guessed Clements's motives. They had three days to spy out the land. It was obvious that Clements's intelligence service was so poor that he had no notion that they were intending to attack him, and attack him with superior numbers. For while Clements's men were quietly bathing at Nooitgedacht, General Christiaan C. J. Beyers, with fifteen hundred more burghers, was hurrying to join hands with Smuts and De la Rey. The three men jointly reconnoitred the camp on the 12th. It was agreed that half of Beyers's men would wait behind, to mark Broadwood in case he tried to come to the rescue. The others – about fifteen hundred, against Clements's twelve hundred – would storm the camp next day at dawn.

For an offensive plan as bold as this there was no recent parallel on the Boer side; nothing since the January day, nearly a year before, when Joubert's men stormed Caesar's camp and Wagon Hill at Ladysmith. Still, that opportunity had been a forlorn hope, given the small number of the attackers, and the size of the garrison. The position was very different now. The fatal defect of Clements's camp site was that the mountain commanded it, and the mountain was only held by a weak line of pickets. Hence the plan of attack: General Beyers's fifteen hundred men to roll up these pickets along the mountain; Commandant Badenhorst, detached from De la Rey's force, to attack the camp from the west. Smuts and De la Rey were to seize the kopjes in the Moot to the south, and so block the only route to escape.[21]

A dawn attack means, almost inevitably, a night march, and night is a notoriously fickle ally. So Wauchope had discovered at Magersfontein, trapped in close order in front of De la Rey's trenches, and so had Woodgate, caught in Botha's frying-pan at Spion Kop. Tonight, the Boers stumbled and blundered, but there was no disaster – for the attackers. Their guides, who knew every fold of the Moot and every gully on the mountain, and carried lanterns, lost their bearings. It was so dark just before dawn that Smuts, marching up the Moot from the west, could not even make out the shadowy profiles of the kopjes. On the mountain walls, north-west of Clements's camp, Commandant Badenhorst and his men stumbled straight into the British picket lines. There was a brief explosion of firing: bang and flash in the blackness; a sudden storm in the night (like the struggle for the naval gun on Wagon Hill at Ladysmith) which killed the local British commander, Lieutenant-Colonel Legge, and others, Boers included; but Badenhorst was driven back. Down in the Moot, Smuts heard rifle fire, followed by gunfire, rolling off the mountains. Then there was silence. Beyers made no answering move, and doubtless Smuts cursed the wretched Badenhorst, whose blunders had forewarned the British.[22]

However, to be forewarned was not enough, not in the few minutes available. The British pickets on the mountain were three hundred men of the Northumberland Fusiliers, under Captain Yatman. He had no extra ammunition beyond the spare rounds kept in the men's pouches. And the sun, when it rose, was too hazy to flash the vital SOS message to Broadwood. Already, as soon as it was daylight, the storm had broken. Beyers's men charged like veteran British infantry against the sangars of the twin lines of pickets, each section hidden from the others as well as from the camp itself. Yatman's men fought doggedly for a while, losing over a hundred casualties. Then, just before seven o'clock, Yatman could bear it no more, and hoisted the white flag, surrendering with all the surviving men. Soon after, what was described as a 'warm, plunging fire' (a fusillade fired downwards on the camp) announced to the astonished Clements that the key to his camp was in enemy hands.[23]

Clements seems to have been an odd mixture of folly and flair. He had lost half his force, and all chance of signalling to Broadwood. The camp was doomed. By all the rules, a general who had been fool enough to get his men into such a mess should have found it hopeless to try to extricate them. Clements, however, not only spotted the one theoretical chance that remained, but acted with dash and resolution into the bargain. He had always been famous as a horseman. Now he had somehow to pull his broken force together, calm the stampeding oxen and mules, and organize the retreat. Before the camp itself was overrun, they must get back to a hill, Yeomanry Hill, in the Moot below. That was the only chance. Somehow the impossible was achieved: 350 riflemen, horse-guns, and all, crawling back to Yeomanry Hill, a small enough perimeter for the survivors to hold, and out of range of Beyers's riflemen on the mountain. Only the largest gun was left behind in the general retreat, the six-ton 4·7-inch naval gun, waiting in an emplacement on the hillside above the camp and pointing (futilely) down into the valley below.

Strange to say, the fact that the 4·7, the symbol of Clements's strength, pointed the wrong way, pointed to its salvation. Earlier, Clements, never dreaming that the enemy would attack from the overhanging cliffs, had given no orders to the artillerymen to clear a field of fire for the 4·7 on this side. Thus, the gun's gallant commander, Major Inglefield, was hidden by brushwood as he crawled back to try to rescue his tame juggernaut. Somehow he roped up nine out of the sixteen-span team of oxen which had stampeded earlier in the day. But it was impossible to drive the oxen back uphill to fetch the gun. The gun must come down itself. And it came. Out of the disaster emerged a kind of comic miracle: Inglefield's gun-crew heaved the great gun bodily round in its emplacement; it shook itself free, rose like a great elephant from the mimosa scrub, rolled down the hill, gathering speed, every Mauser levelled at it; now it was travelling fast; it thundered through the camp; and at length Inglefield, the triumphant mahout, roped it up and conducted it safely onwards to Yeomanry Hill.[24]

Meanwhile, no doubt unaware of this triumph, Smuts and De la Rey were still trying to storm Yeomanry Hill (or Green Hill, as they called it). In timing their triple plan of attack, they had assumed that De la Rey could seize this hill at the same time as Beyers crushed the picket lines. In fact, Smuts and De la Rey had overrun all the kopjes in the Moot except Yeomanry Hill. The reason was, paradoxically, Beyers's own speedy success, and the speedy retreat it precipitated. As the tide of defenders rolled down on Yeomanry Hill, De la Rey saw the chance of his own success slip away. Perhaps Badenhorst's premature attack had something to do with it; when Smuts's men attacked the outlying kopjes in the first glimmer of daylight at 4.30 a.m., they could see that the Khakis, already forewarned, were streaming out to man the forts. At any rate, to subdue these kopjes had taken an hour too long. Smuts's men had only a foothold on Yeomanry Hill itself, when, at about eight o'clock, Clements swept them off again. The way that Clements concentrated on Yeomanry Hill aroused even Smuts's admiration: it was a proof of Clements's 'insight and soldierly qualities'; his retreat was 'stubborn and skilful', and he did everything possible to redeem the 'hopelessly wrong choice of a site'.[25]

But was Clements still doomed? That depended on the insight and soldierly qualities of Smuts, De la Rey and Beyers. Clements was surrounded. Up and down the Moot, he had rampaged for three months. Now he was trapped there. There was no prospect of either Broadwood or Paget (the nearest commander on the east side) arriving before next day, at the earliest. There was no proper water supply on Yeomanry Hill. There was little cover, and no time to dig trenches. All the Boers had to do was bombard the place for all they were worth, killing the transport animals. Even if Clements did manage to cut his way out, most of his equipment, including the guns, would be captured. But the chances were that the whole of Clements's force would be forced to surrender: the greatest blow to British prestige, measured in prisoners, of the whole war. And after Clements was in the bag, Broadwood might follow. Such was the likely result if the Boers, who had planned and executed a tactical plan with such mastery, could follow it up with a united attack on Yeomanry Hill. Instead,

Smuts watched wretchedly as Clements's survivors rode off at four o'clock that afternoon, almost unopposed, back on the road towards Pretoria.

Why did the victors flinch? In his memoirs of the war, Smuts said that he could always count on the British generals, during their offensives, flinching at the last moment from the final move, from 'that last desperate resolve which would clinch the whole matter, and reap the fruit of all the deep-laid planning'.[26] The same retort could have been made that day by Clements. There were, in fact, a number of bread-and-butter reasons why Smuts was forced to acquiesce in the burghers flinching from that desperate resolve that would reap victory.

Everyone was exhausted, having had nothing to eat or drink since the previous evening. The burghers took one glance at the loot in Clements's camp, and nothing would get them back into battle. Anyway, what was the practical advantage to be gained by risking their lives in renewing the attack on Clements? Apart from capturing Clements's field-guns, of which they were admittedly in the greatest need, they would merely take a lot more Khakis prisoner. And taking prisoners had lost its appeal, since they would have to be released again within a few hours; for the guerrillas had no secure base to which to send them back. More fundamental, Smuts and Beyers were out of sympathy with each other; that odd mixture of 'praying and pillage', for which Beyers was famous, grated on Smuts, as did Beyers's habit of flogging his men into battle; indeed, it was something of a miracle that the two Boer columns had linked hands for a few hours so effectively.[27]

The truth was that the loosely organized Boer armies, as ill disciplined in the ranks as they were ill co-ordinated at the higher level, had always been unsuited to large-scale offensive strategy. The fragmented character of guerrilla warfare only intensified this, making each group of commandos more or less independent. Without a telegraph system, communications from the government could take weeks rather than minutes. Anyway, there was no one capable of imposing his will on the volk, now that Oom Paul's gigantic shadow had faded from the scene. A major offensive, involving grand strategy and a cumulative series of operations: that would have been the next step, in theory, if Clements could have been crushed at Nooitgedacht. Broadwood could have been dealt with next. Then they could have launched a combined offensive to blow up the cursed mines of the Rand. This was part of the grand strategy that Smuts had advocated at Cypherfontein, and still passionately believed in.[28] But was it, given the nature of the Boer armies, like crying for the moon?

The answer, revealed to Smuts that very evening, brought him back to earth with a bump. At sunset, he rode back up the hill, dispirited after the feeble pursuit of the Khakis. He found that Beyers's victory (like De Wet's near-fatal defeat at Bothaville a month earlier) had created pandemonium in the camp. After any victory there were the accepted incongruities: jokes and laughter and comic songs a few yards away from the blanched faces and bloody uniforms of the dead. But that night the burghers had excelled themselves. 'What a sight met my eyes,' he wrote later.

An indescribable pandemonium in which psalm-singing, looting and general hilarity mingled with explosions of bullets and bombs. ... Kemp had unwisely set most of the wagons on fire, and as many of them contained ammunition cases the camp resembled more the rattling fire of an action. ... All round the camp groups of our horses were tethered together having a good time from Clements' ample commissariat. Here parties were wandering about the tents looking for rare objects in the officers' kits; there another group were discussing over a bottle of rum, with tears of enjoyment in their eyes, the incidents of the day; here some zealous young fellows were poring over the papers of General Clements for valuable information. ... On the other side of this wagon the veteran Rev. A. P. Kriel was eloquently expressing the feelings of joy and thanks of his large audience, into which a broadside or volley would from time to time be poured from the fateful ammunition wagon. ...

And there, sitting on some officer's stool, hawk eyes taking in everything, was Smuts's chief, De la Rey, usually so solemn and austere, shaking with silent laughter.[29]

Three days later, the Boers celebrated the Day of the Covenant, Dingaan's Day, at Naauwpoort, on the farm of Commandant Steenkamp. It was only forty miles from Pretoria. Yet how remote in time the last celebration of that anniversary, when President Kruger had addressed the congregation from the pulpit of the church and described with his usual gusto how, as a boy of nine, he had seen the Zulus storm the laager of wagons and how the Boer women had cut off their hands with axes. That anniversary was 16 December 1899, the day after Colenso, a victory celebration indeed. Now, despite the *coup* against Clements at Nooitgedacht, what was there to celebrate? Kruger had been forced into exile. About three thousand burghers had been killed or crippled. Fifteen thousand others were languishing in prisoner-of-war camps at home or in Ceylon or in St Helena. Both the capitals, all the main towns, and all the main railway lines of both republics were in British hands.[30]

Despite the dangers, thousands of burghers – women and children, too – now trekked out to Naauwpoort to attend the celebration. Almost all had relatives to mourn, killed in the war. They were addressed by the three Generals with the expected words of comfort and consolation. It was through suffering and defeat, said De la Rey, that the Lord strengthened His people and prepared them for ultimate triumph. Beyers probed into the reasons for their past defeats: the flaws in national character (presumably the capacity for compromise) that threatened the continuation of resistance. Then it was Smuts's turn. He reminded the men how it was the Boer *vrouw* to whose heroism they owed so much. The women had insisted that the men should trek out of Natal, although they could have stayed there in peace and plenty; they preferred to go barefoot over the Drakensberg and endure nameless sufferings among the Kaffirs, rather than submit to the British flag. This must remain the inspiration of the men, the refusal of these heroines ever to submit. He did not explain how the victory was to be won.[31]

In private, Smuts still clung to the hope of returning to the offensive. But he pinned his faith in the immediate future on the results of the war *outside* the

CHAPTER 38
Disregarding the Screamers
Cape Town and Beyond,
17 December 1900 – 28 May 1901

'If we are to build up anything in South Africa, we *must
disregard* and absolutely disregard the screamers.'

Alfred Milner to Richard Haldane,
7 June 1901

It was four nights after Clements's disaster at Nooitgedacht, and a Cape south-easter had begun to play the devil with the garden at Government House, Cape Town, bullying the palm-trees, spitting dust and pebbles on to the tennis lawn, and drumming its fingers on the *stoep* where the High Commissioner liked to sleep out in summer. Tonight, Sir Alfred was still hard at work, although it was midnight; there he sat, an angular shadow against the cold, grey, gaslit book-shelves of his study, hard at work on the scarlet boxes embossed with the Queen's golden monogram, undisturbed by the raging storm.[1]

He might have been a medieval monk reading his breviary or a medieval knight at his prie-dieu. Milner was not in the mood for such Gothic imagery. At times like these, he preferred the language of the stiff upper lip. The 'everlasting see-saw' was the way he described this phase of the struggle to Chamberlain.[2] 'Fearfully grey ... as grey as badger,' was how he described himself ruefully to a woman friend.[3] How 'pumped' he felt. He was dog-tired, and no wonder, after this dog's life, chained to the desk in his study, month after month, ten, twelve, fourteen hours a day, with none of his 'chums' to help him. Worse than the physical strain was the moral exhaustion. He had used the word 'stale' to describe his soldiers, especially Roberts and Kitchener, in that *cri de coeur* to St John Brodrick, the new War Minister. To even more intimate friends, like Violet Cecil, or dear old Gell, St John's brother-in-law, he confessed it was true of himself.

There were times when his vision of the 'big things' (and the 'Greater Britain Idea' was the biggest thing in his life, a shining sword, Excalibur, held out in a mystic white hand to his Knights of the Round Table), there were times when these Arthurian colours faded and the imperial vision blurred. Then he would tell his most intimate friends, playing Jonah, half seriously, in his letters that this endless grind could not continue. 'I am naturally lazy.'[4] Sometimes, during these black moods, he yearned to return to a life of 'contemplative obscurity';[5] then he half-decided he would give up trying to make history and make millions instead.

He actually wrote, that month, to warn Clinton Dawkins, now working for J. P. Morgan, the American financier, hinting that he might after all be available soon to join him in the City.[6] He would throw up this whole Herculean labour in South Africa. Not that Hercules ever had this kind of bungling soldier, like General Clements, to deal with. He felt more like Sisyphus, fighting a war, *his* war, which kept rolling back on its author like a gigantic stone.[7]

Of course, these black moods soon blew themselves out, like the odious Cape south-easters. But he needed a break, a run home to England, he knew that. He would go in May if the war could spare him. Not that it would be much of a rest. Three years before, when there had been a lull in the diplomatic struggle with Kruger, he had taken a 'holiday' in England; and, delightful as it had been, it was a 'rushy' time (apart from the stolen five days on a bicycle with Cécile), so busy was he 'sowing the seeds', interviewing everyone who was anyone, 'without seeming to run after them', and stamping on 'rose-coloured illusions'.[8] He would have plenty of stamping to do on this coming visit. Besides, he had an exciting task: to recruit imperially minded young men (Cromer had set the style in modern Egypt), his own 'Kindergarten' they would be called, for the much bigger task of nation-building in modern South Africa.[9] Thus, the visit to England would mark the beginning of peaceful exploitation of the war – provided always that K of K and his blundering generals allowed the process to begin.

K of K! What a chaos of emotions the initials aroused in Milner's mind. There were few, if any, great men (apart from Rhodes) whom Milner so admired, and so fundamentally distrusted. With Buller, there was now no ambivalence on Milner's part. Buller he accused of being 'pro-Boer', presumably meaning that Buller, as an old-fashioned Liberal, did not share Milner's zeal for imperial expansion and believed that conciliation was the way to the hearts of the Afrikaners in the Cape. Kitchener could hardly have been accused of such sentimentality! Yet Milner, while recognizing K's titanic qualities (since Roberts's departure there was 'a remarkable increase of energy, and more sense in the military management all round'), resented his tactless and autocratic way of handling things. He had blurted out to Violet Cecil, even before K had succeeded Bobs:

> Kitchener! It is fortunate that I admire him in many ways so much, and admiring, that I am prepared to stand a lot and never take offence. . . . I am determined to get on with him, and I think he likes me and has some respect for me, if he has for anybody. But shall I be able to manage this strong, self-willed man 'in a hurry' . . . and to turn his enormous power into the right channel? At present he is wasting himself utterly . . . as he frankly confesses, he has no plan, is puzzled. *I have a plan*, but as yet he is unconvinced. . . .[10]

Now that K was in the saddle, would he be more susceptible to Milner's whispered advice? It was hardly in character. Milner was now, in theory, civilian administrator of the Transvaal and the Orange River Colony, but was pointedly kept ignorant about plans for the war.

Kitchener is absolutely autocratic. . . . But I don't mind that, *if he will only end the war*. I am quite willing to lie low, and let my administratorship be a farce, until the country is pacified, if there is only progress in that direction. And I know that he wants to go as soon as he can – therefore I shall just possess my soul in patience, till he has finished his rough work in his own strong way and not interfere with him. My only fear is that he may make promises to people, to get them to surrender, which will be embarrassing afterwards to fulfill. . . .[11]

'Progress in the right direction.' There was irony enough in the phrase. Ever since the capture of Pretoria, they had, Milner felt, been slipping slowly back-wards. The month since K had taken over from Roberts had proved a month of rapid progress in the wrong direction.

Lord Bobs himself had been given a triumphant send-off from Cape Town on 10 December. No one could have felt warmer feelings towards the 'little man' than Milner, or felt a deeper sense of relief that he was going. It was not only that Roberts seemed 'stale' and played out. By his misplaced optimism, by claiming the war was practically over, Milner believed – and events were to prove him right – that Roberts had done great damage both at home and in South Africa. Hence Milner's mixed feelings, expressed to Violet Cecil, about the great ovation for Bobs when he finally set sail. 'We have all shouted ourselves hoarse over him and I am glad for his sake. . . . But I must own that, apart from him, there is something ill-omened, and bizarre and almost repulsive in all this triumphing and congratulations – *in the middle of war*.' However, Milner could not help enjoying one part of the celebrations. There had recently been a ferocious attack on him, as a war-monger, in the local newspapers. Now, when Milner's health was proposed at the banquet, a tremendous roar of applause broke out among the loyalists present, 'which I was amused to see altogether bewildered Lord Bobs's staff'.[12] Milner had always prided himself on not caring a hoot about personal honours. When they came, he felt all the more surprised and touched.

The news of Clements's disaster had followed in the week after Bobs's triumph, and tonight, 17 December, the news was worse.

The telegrams reported the invasion of Cape Colony by three thousand Boers (actually two thousand) led by General P. H. Kritzinger and Judge Barry Hertzog. Although De Wet had been foiled in his own attempt to lead them across the Orange River, Kitchener in his turn had been foiled in his attempt to trap De Wet in the south of the old Free State, between the Orange and the Caledon Rivers. So it was still on the cards that De Wet would break loose again, follow Kritzinger, and raise the Cape.[13]

The fact that these Boers from the Free State could slip through the hands of the enormous number of troops guarding the frontier, and spill out again, nearly a year after the collapse of their first invasion, into the great empty plains of the Cape, was naturally most depressing to Milner. The political consequences of the invasion were what terrified him most. Milner shared with Smuts (though neither could yet have known it) the heady belief that a general Afrikaner rising in Cape Colony was to be expected, once given the lead. Milner believed that, despite their firm measures to stamp out the Prieska revolt six months before – the arrest of Afrikaner rebels, the collection of arms and ammunition, and the gathering up of food and horses that could be used by the enemy – the whole of Cape Colony, outside the main towns, where the British were in the majority, was still tinder-dry for revolution. He attributed this almost entirely to the effective propaganda of the Afrikaners, who were, of course, the white majority in Cape Colony. It was partly the 'saturnalia' of violence in the Cape Assembly, during the three-month session that had ended in October; open defiance of the government and 'outspoken treason' by members of the Afrikaner Bond, encouraged in its turn by the absurdly 'meek and apologetic' attitude of the loyalists in the coalition government, led by Rhodes's nominee, Gordon Sprigg. It was also due to the 'unbridled influence' of Press and pulpit. Parsons of the Dutch Reformed Church, as leaders of the local farming communities, were reported to be preaching a crusade against the Empire. Together, these 'rebels' had seized on certain 'acts of harshness' by British troops in the last few embittered months of guerrilla war and distorted them to create an atmosphere of 'national hysteria'.

How was he to cope with this doubly alarming situation: the guerrilla war in the ex-republics, which was spreading down into the colony; and the enemy within, the Afrikaner 'traitors' who were egging on the Boers to invade? Milner had absolutely no doubt what should be done. First, if he was not allowed to suspend the self-governing constitution of Cape Colony (*'the system is an impossible one'*), at least the loyalists should be armed in their own defence, and martial law proclaimed to help deal with the traitors.[14] Second, in the two new colonies, Kitchener should adopt his – that is, Milner's – military plan.

In fact, the invasion of the Cape by Kritzinger and Hertzog, painful though Milner found it, provided him in the next fortnight with exactly the opportunity he needed to achieve the first of these aims. Every mile that Kritzinger's commandos rode southwards brought martial law nearer. By the end of December, Kritzinger was riding (literally) down to Bangor, and Milner was writing, exhausted but triumphant, in his diary: 'Dec 31: I managed by a gigantic effort to galvanise people into activity today. Prolonged interviews with Sprigg, the General, and Rose Innes [Attorney-General], finally resulted in a "call to arms" of all loyal inhabitants issued by the military. I am also pressing for Martial Law.'[15]

By 17 January, Sprigg had grasped the nettle in both hands: martial law for virtually all the colony, except the native districts and the Cape ports; the creation of a loyalist militia that was soon to comprise ten thousand men. And, as if by magic, Kritzinger's invasion began to fizzle out.[16]

If only, thought Milner, he had had the same help from the Boers in dealing with Kitchener, and so pacifying the Transvaal and the Free State. Indeed, the precise opposite was to be the case. Milner soon found himself paying the political price for Kitchener's military blunders at an exorbitant rate of interest.

The military plan that Milner had proposed first to Roberts, then to

Kitchener, could hardly have been more different from the one actually adopted. It was a plan for progressive reconquest of the two new colonies by 'gradual securing of each district before tackling the next, and slowly occupying the country, bit by bit, rather than rapidly and repeatedly scouring it'. Milner believed (and, as we have seen, Buller shared this view) that Roberts's fatal mistake, the result of his misplaced optimism, had been his failure to garrison and police each district before marching on to the next one. 'What the bulk of the people [in the new Orange River Colony] require is protection not punishment,' he told Kitchener in October. 'I do not mean to say that they do not all hate us. They do. But they love their property more than they hate the British and ... would be glad to see the back of the Guerrillas.'

As well as being the most efficient way of ending the war, this system would have two other vital advantages. First, it would avoid the need further to devastate the country, with all the legacy of bitterness that would create. Second, the key to the Transvaal was, of course, to get the wheels of the gold-mines turning. And the moment Johannesburg was made a protected area, the mines could begin to reopen and the Uitlanders, howling in the refugee camps of the Cape, could be allowed back up the railway to their homes in the Rand.[17]

Instead, repeated Milner in early January, it was a 'farce' to talk of himself as administrator of the new colonies, as the government was only holding the lines of the railway and a few big towns and 'confining our operations in the rest of the country to chasing commandos whom we never catch'.[18] Of course, he did not doubt that, with such overwhelming military superiority, they would wear down the guerrillas in the end, *whatever* policy they adopted. 'But I fear that on present lines we shall be at it for another 12 months, and that the amount of destruction [and, he might have added, political damage] will be enormous.' It was this unnecessary devastation, the burning of crops, the burning of houses (as opposed to Milner's plan simply to remove *horses*), the sieving, scrubbing, scouring of the whole countryside, that sickened Milner.[19] 'I believe if we were to devastate the whole of South Africa,' he had forecast '– an impossibility anyway – we should only find that we had a greater number of roving black-guards to deal with.' He added (and it was a prophetic phrase, though he scratched it out with his pen) 'besides tens of thousands of homeless women and children to keep and feed – Heaven knows how or where'.[20]

This was Milner's bitter forecast to which he still held fast in February. Now, however, his thoughts turned to a prospect that he regarded with still more horror than that of a protracted and destructive war: the prospect, offered by a plan for Kitchener to parley with Botha at Middelburg, of an immediate negotiated peace. This was the short-cut he dreaded: some kind of botched-up settlement, a 'Kaffir bargain', he called it. It would not only save the faces of the Boer leaders, but preserve the separate identity of the volk as a political force after the war. Anything rather than accept that: even the risk of a 'smash-up', meaning his own resignation.[21]

Privately, he felt 'totally opposed' to any peace terms for these 'banditti'. 'It is a question of staying power pure and simple,' he wrote to a trusted New College friend. 'The future is all right here, if we can bring the war to a clean finish. Otherwise we had better clear out bag and baggage at once. There is no room for compromise in South Africa.'[22] He repeated the same message – the *arcana imperii* – to the Liberal imperialist he trusted most, Haldane. They must shut their ears to the 'pro-Boers' and 'screamers'. They must get the job 'cleanly done', finished once and for all. They must be 'victors, out and out, and past a doubt'.[23] That was his aim: *total* victory, 'to knock the bottom', he revealed in a phrase his biographer excised later, 'out of the "great Afrikander nation" for ever and ever Amen'.[24]

Milner was certainly correct about one thing: that Kitchener, confident as he was of victory, was baffled in his search for the means needed to achieve it.

Ironically, these peace talks with Botha, now planned to take place at Middelburg in the eastern Transvaal at the end of February, were indirectly the result of one of Milner's own 'thoughts' expressed to Kitchener – to send delegates of prominent Boers to persuade the others to come in from the cold. Kitchener had taken up the idea, but with disappointing results. Piet De Wet, Christiaan's brother, who had surrendered in July, was sent down to Cape Town as a prize exhibit of a tame guerrilla. But these ex-heroes were cold-shouldered by the Afrikaner Bond Party and the Dutch Reformed Church in the Cape.[25] When these surrendered Boers tried to explain to their brothers in the field that the game was up, they found, on the contrary, that it was their own lives which were forfeit. With uncharacteristic ruthlessness – as we have seen, Smuts was one of the men who carried on this policy – the Boers court-martialled and sentenced as traitors men who had collaborated with the British. Morgendal, an emissary to De Wet's laager, was first flogged and then shot by General Froneman in a paroxysm of rage. Meyer de Kock, the Secretary of the 'Burgher Peace Committee' (formed soon after Christmas), was sentenced and executed.[26] So the Burgher Peace Committee did not long survive the season of goodwill.

How, then, Kitchener asked himself, to approach Botha with the news that, on very reasonable terms, peace was there for the asking? There were some intermediaries old enough or frail enough to be in no danger of being shot. In November, Mrs Joubert, the general's widow, had been persuaded to take an appeal to Louis Botha, urging him to accept the inevitable; the appeal, reflecting the views of twenty-four leading citizens of Pretoria, was written by Sammy Marks, Kruger's famous protegé, the Jewish millionaire who had built up his business empire in the Transvaal, after acquiring the lucrative whisky concession. Marks begged Botha to tell Reitz and Steyn of his intervention quite openly ('I should not like anybody to say or think old Marks is going to make a lot of money out of the British Government and that is why he is writing to the General'). He estimated that there were only ten thousand burghers still under arms in the field. How could this pygmy army hope to prevail against the mighty British Empire? 'Ours is not the first country that has fought and lost, nor will it be the last. Bigger and greater nations than ours have had to acknowledge themselves beaten. ...' He reminded Botha of his resolution on the previous 5 June – this was the day when there had been a great council of war in Marks's office at Hatherley, near Pretoria – a resolution, apparently, to continue with regular war but not to fight as guerrillas. And he warned Botha that the price of the war would be paid by the women and children: the widows and orphans, and the families who would lose everything as the country was progressively destroyed. 'Do you not think that, as a man, a general, a husband and a father, you should determine to make the best of things and prevail upon others to do the same?' Another appeal to Botha was written by a prominent Boer called Junius, who had opposed Kruger's hard-line policy before the war: 'Our cause is hopeless; if we were not convinced of this we would, with thousands of others, still be with you this day. However, Paul Kruger has brought us so far, and now left us in our misery. . . . You and other Progressive Raad members did try your best to avoid this unfortunate war, but Kruger *could* not and would otherwise. . . . The Afrikander looks upon you as the only strong man who could make an end to the war.'[27]

The replies to these appeals were somewhat puzzling. Botha accused the intermediaries of being traitors. So did A. H. Malan, one of Botha's aides, writing to Sammy Marks. The twenty-four leading burghers of Pretoria who were pressing for peace talks included many who had been most active in instigating the war: 'Those who brought it about or gave cause to our real enemies to jump upon us have long ago left the field, and in a great many instances never did anything. It would be a blessing to the country were they all expelled from it and sent to Ceylon. . . .' Malan stressed the paradox that 'most of my brother officers still in the field and most of the burghers still defending their rights belong to the party that opposed the war most strenuously and also everything that could lead to it'. However, what was promising about Malan's reply was that he said that if the British wanted peace it was they who must make the first move. 'If we are to lose our independence, which is still a matter of doubt, yet we are not prepared to sacrifice our honour as well by coming as dogs to sue for peace . . . let him [Roberts] then as the stronger offer such to the weaker direct.'[28]

So, in January, Kitchener renewed his efforts to get the talks started. He called up from retirement – indeed, it seemed almost from the grave – eighty-one-year-old Marthinus Pretorius, whose father had given his name to the capital of the Transvaal, and who had himself, in the years before Kruger's ascendancy, served as President of each republic in turn. However, Pretorius returned at the end of January from his hazardous mission with the gloomy report that Botha and Schalk Burger, the acting President, 'would not discuss any question of peace, stating only that they were fighting for their independence, and meant to do so to the bitter end'.[29]

The break-through came in late February after Botha's own wife, who had helped arrange the talks the previous June (the abortive talks before Diamond Hill) had been asked to try her luck as mediator once again. Kitchener had assured her that, provided the Boers understood that the annexation of the twin republics was not negotiable, he would discuss anything else. In fact, he had already informed London of the main points which he anticipated discussing at the peace talks. First, he wanted to confirm the legal position of (and, of course, discrimination against) the native majority. Kitchener recommended extending the native laws of the Free State over both republics. 'I believe these laws were very good.' Second, he wanted to compensate the Boers for war damage. 'I have little doubt that this could be arranged by making the mines pay for it; a million would go a long way to putting matters right and when the Rand is working they turn out 2 millions a week.' Third, he would like to reassure the Boer politicians that they would not be ruled by the capitalists and would have a voice in their own affairs, 'They are I believe absurdly afraid of getting into the hands of certain Jews [Wernher and Beit] *who no doubt wield great influence in the country*.' Finally – and here Kitchener was asking for the biggest concession – he wished to offer an amnesty not only to the Boers of the republics, but to the colonial rebels – that is, to the Afrikaners from Cape Colony and Natal who had taken up arms on the side of the volk and against the British flag.[30]

On Mrs Botha's return, Kitchener cabled to London again recommending 'conciliatory attitude' on all these points; it might end the war there and then. He added, somewhat plaintively, 'I should like to know how far I may have a free hand in discussing such points. ...'[31]

His doubts were justified. The conference duly took place on the last day of February at Middelburg, and Botha's principal points were exactly on the lines that Kitchener had forecast.[32] But Kitchener did not get his 'free hand' to deal with them in a conciliatory manner. If he had thought the war was nearly over, he had not reckoned with Milner. The High Commissioner insisted on meeting him at Bloemfontein to vet the proposed peace terms before Kitchener cabled them to London for the Cabinet's approval.

The two men met in the railway station at Bloemfontein, where Milner had been welcomed by the Boers before his celebrated, abortive meeting with Kruger in June 1899. From Milner's point of view, the wrangle with Kitchener that followed was not dissimilar. Although the two men *openly* disagreed on only one major point – the question of amnesty for colonial rebels – Milner disapproved of the peace talks in principle, and was prepared to seize on any pretext to make them fail. However, Kitchener, not to be outflanked, adopted an argument calculated to frighten Milner into agreeing to the peace terms. He claimed that 'our soldiers can't be trusted not to surrender on the smallest provocation, and that consequently disaster is not even now impossible if the Boers stick to it'. Was Kitchener simply bluffing? Milner honestly did not know. Nor did he know to what extent Kitchener, the sapper General, had undermined his position at home. Who would the Cabinet side with? And was there evidence that British public opinion was 'wobbling'?

Milner explained his dilemma to Violet Cecil that week: 'Knowing the feeling at home, which is of increasing disgust at this business, and anxiety of Ministers at the increasing cost of it, and the difficulty of keeping the national resolution at the sticking point, I felt I could not afford a rupture with K ... it would not be possible to compel the army to fight on against *the wishes of its own Chief and the whole popular sentiment*, and an attempt to do, which failed, would only encourage the enemy to still further efforts, and demands, and end in a terrible fiasco.' Milner therefore felt himself forced to compromise after all with Kitchener.[33] The cable went off to London with Kitchener's proposed concessions somewhat toned down by Milner, but at any rate endorsed by him, with one important qualification: Milner publicly dissented from the wisdom of giving amnesty to the colonial rebels, even if disfranchised.

Kitchener's original four points had thus become a ten-point peace plan: (1) Amnesty for all bona fide acts of war (with disfranchisement for the colonial rebels). (2) Prisoners of war to be brought home. (3) The two new colonies to be governed at first by a governor and executive (that is, as Crown Colonies) but to be given self-government 'as soon as circumstances permit'. (4) Both the English and Dutch languages to be used in schools and in courts. (5) Property of the Dutch Reformed Church to be respected. (6) Legal debts of the State, even if contracted during the war, to be paid, with a limit of one million pounds. (7) Farmers to be compensated for horses lost during the war. (8) There would be no war indemnity for farmers. (9) Certain burghers to be licensed to keep rifles. (10) 'As regards the extension of the franchise to Kaffirs in the Transvaal and Orange River Colony, it is not the intention of His Majesty's Government to give such a franchise before a representative government is granted to those colonies.'[34]

When the British Cabinet's cabled comments were received a week later, it was clear that two of these points – the first and last – had aroused serious objections in London. Kitchener was rebuffed on the first point – his proposed amnesty for colonial rebels – and Milner's opposition was endorsed. Both Kitchener and Milner were rebuffed on the question of the civil rights of Africans. Chamberlain insisted on tacking on to the clause about the native franchise: 'And if then given it will be so limited as to secure the just predominance of the white races, but the legal position of Kaffirs will be similar to that which they hold in the Cape Colony.'[35] He added, for the benefit of the two proconsuls alone, a sentence that re-echoed his claim in 1899 that one of the war aims was to protect the natives. 'We cannot consent to purchase a *shameful peace* by leaving the coloured population in the position in which they stood before the war, with not even the ordinary civil rights which the Government of the Cape Colony has long conceded to them.'[36]

The revised text of this ten-point plan was duly forwarded to Botha at Middelburg on 7 March. Kitchener had understandable misgivings that Milner, by toning down the concessions, had tilted the balance disastrously against peace. Botha had warned him that he would have difficulty in convincing his fellow-generals. Kitchener hoped for the best, but feared the worst. In the interval – that is, while Botha and the generals were digesting these proposals – he threw himself with his usual demonic energy into prosecuting the war.[37]

There was one aspect of Kitchener's strange character that no one, not even his worst enemies, could question: his passion for work. How unthinkable it would have been for him to say, like Milner, that he enjoyed being lazy! Kitchener loved work as Milner loved Bohemian social life; Kitchener gorged himself on work. No job was too tough or too indigestible for him. He strode into his office at 6 a.m., an awe-inspiring figure, with those porcelain-blue eyes, and the inscrutable glare of an oriental idol. All day, he sat at the desk (apart from a furious gallop across the veld with his staff), devouring files and telegrams, and scattering papers to the winds. And so he went on, day after day, week after week, the very incarnation of superhuman will-power and machine-like energy. Yet, though the pleasure he took in hard work was real enough, what else, what deeper sense of satisfaction, or avenue to promotion, could Kitchener get out of this war? To Brodrick (and even to Milner) he confessed openly his distaste for the business. He was sick of the war, saw no possible credit to be derived from prolonging it, and was consumed by the fear that it might cost him the prize on which he had set his heart: India.[38]

It was the dream of becoming Commander-in-Chief in India that had added bitterness to Kitchener's wrangle with Milner and desperation to his rough, soldierly desire to accommodate Botha and make peace. By the end of February, he had virtually given up hope of displacing General Palmer, the acting Indian C-in-C. Roberts had promised to do everything to help, but there was stiff opposition from both Cabinet and the Palace. The Queen understandably felt that the Sirdar, with all his great qualities, might prove a trifle heavy-handed for her sensitive Indian subjects. Brodrick tried to persuade Kitchener to come back to the War Office instead, to help Roberts sweep the Horse Guards clean. Kitchener was adamant. It was India, or back to the Sudan – or he would leave the army: 'I feel sure I am not the man,' he told Brodrick, 'for the place [the War Office] . . . and that I should be a certain failure.'[39] He spoke still more bluntly to Lady Cranborne, the Prime Minister's daughter-in-law, one of the few people to whom he ever bared his heart. 'I could do no good there, and would sooner sweep a crossing.'[40] At last, Roberts's importunities – and Brodrick was pledged to back Roberts for all he was worth – together with the death of the Queen, removed the final obstacles in Kitchener's path. A week after the Middelburg talks, Brodrick cabled him with the news that, once the war was over, India would be in his grasp.[41]

'I should be a certain failure' might seem an odd phrase for Kitchener to choose to describe himself, if he tried to reorganize the War Office, but it was not false modesty. Kitchener knew his limitations. The paradox of Kitchener, as we saw, was that he had made his name as a brilliant organizer as Sirdar in Egypt, yet his talents did not lie in that direction at all. He had none of the true administrator's qualities: delegation he hated; letter-writing he despised; he used a pen like a broadsword – that is, to cut Gordian knots. His gifts were raw and heroic, and, like Rhodes, he suffered the all-consuming frustrations of a man who fancied himself a colossus, frustrations that sometimes found expression in a child-like petulance. Still, unlike Rhodes, he had no gift for the political arts of persuasion and diplomacy. His real forte was not organization, but leadership, and leadership of a strange, personal kind; a human whirlwind, driving his men to the limits of endurance – and beyond – all in the pursuit of clear-cut military victory.[42]

To end the war quickly was Kitchener's overwhelming objective. But how to end it if the enemy refused to fight a pitched battle? It was the guerrillas' refusal to play the game and fight like men that appalled Kitchener, not his doubts (though doubts he certainly had) about his own troops' ability to fight. Hence the policy that he now proposed to London: a policy for progressively adopting more drastic methods of forcing the enemy either to give battle or throw in the sponge. This was the 'policy of punishment' that Milner so totally opposed; the reverse of Milner's proposal to create protected areas, starting with the Rand and the industrial districts, and to let the war in other areas gradually 'fade away'.

In the three months since he had taken over the supreme command at Pretoria, the honours and dishonours had been fairly evenly distributed, militarily speaking – Smuts and De la Rey had dealt Clements that crushing blow at Nooitgedacht on 13 December; Wiljoen had surprised a garrison at Helvetia in the Eastern Transvaal on 29 December and temporarily captured 235 men and a 4·7-inch gun; there were attacks on other British garrisons nearby on 7 January, all repulsed; meanwhile, Kritzinger and Hertzog had invaded Cape Colony on 16 December. The culmination of the guerrillas' offensive was reached on 8 February, when De Wet, on his second attempt, succeeded in breaking through the cordon guarding the fords over the Orange River and followed Kritzinger into Cape Colony.[43]

However, in all these four cases, the initiative had rapidly passed to the British, as the invaders became fugitives in turn. De Wet's new 'invasion' lasted only a fortnight, and was something of a fiasco from all points of view. On his part, De Wet failed to raise new recruits among the Cape Afrikaners; and lost some of his own commando and his guns. But once again, his pursuers excelled him in blunders – despite the apparently overwhelming odds in their favour: numerical superiority, fresh horses, unlimited supplies and the use of the railway and telegraph lines. Soon the fox was back in his earth to the north of Bloemfontein, and the opportunity to catch him in the open had slipped through Kitchener's hands once more.[44] This set-back was especially disappointing for Kitchener, as the capture of De Wet and Steyn, had it occurred then, would presumably have given Botha decisive help in convincing his fellow-generals to accept the Middelburg peace terms.

In early March, Kitchener decided to break the stalemate by a double sweeping operation: to flush out the guerrillas in a series of systematic 'drives', organized like a sporting shoot, with success defined in a weekly 'bag' of killed, captured and wounded; and to sweep the country bare of everything that could give sustenance to the guerrillas: not only horses, but cattle, sheep, women, and children. But where could the women and children be put, if removed from their homes?

As we shall see, it was the clearance of civilians – uprooting a whole nation – that would come to dominate the last phase of the war. At the time, however, it hardly held much interest for Kitchener's far-ranging but narrow-angled mind. Administrative problems of this kind, involving civilians, always bored him. There was a double need, he thought, for concentrating women and children in protected 'laagers' alongside the railway lines. To prevent the guerrillas being helped by civilians was the first priority. He had also to protect the families of the Boers who were at risk because their menfolk had surrendered: Botha, Smuts, and De la Rey had made it official policy to drive these unfortunates from their homes. Therefore relief camps must be set up in places where it was administratively convenient. The two sorts of 'refugees' (the word 'internees' would have better described the first and much larger category of women and children) could be concentrated in the same huge 'laagers', run on military lines, with reduced-scale army rations. This was the rough idea, and rough it was, for Kitchener wasted no time in complicated preparations. He left the details to the administrators in the two new colonies: Major-General John Maxwell in the Transvaal, Colonel Hamilton Goold Adams in the Orange River Colony. They, in turn, arranged with Milner for the despatch of tents and mattresses, plus a hurriedly selected skeleton staff of civilians to run the camps: roughly, one superintendent, one doctor, and a few nurses for each of twenty-four camps.[45]

Thus, the plan had all the hallmarks of one of Kitchener's famous short cuts. It was big, ambitious, simple, and (what always endeared Kitchener to Whitehall) extremely cheap. There were two ration scales. Meat was at first not included in the rations given the women and children, whose menfolk were still out on commando, which provided both a useful economy and a useful encouragement for the men to come in and surrender. Even after rations were improved, they still remained extremely low. There were no vegetables, nor jam; no fresh milk for babies and children; just a pound of meal and about half a pound of meat a day, with some scrapings of sugar and coffee; much worse than the diet of the barrack room, or the official diet of the troops on campaign; a diet quite poor enough to allow the rapid spread of disease.[46]

Was Kitchener alarmed at the prospect of what might happen in his new 'laagers'? He does not appear to have worried in the least, though in March he decided to make Milner responsible – in theory – for all the camps in the new colonies. At this time, there were the first hints from London that all might not be well with the camp system. Brodrick cabled for full reports.[47] Kitchener replied cheerfully that the inmates were 'happy'; as for the camps, 'though they are not all so good they will be very shortly'.[48] In a letter of explanation, Brodrick added,

One point, however, we shall have trouble about. I wired to you for a full report on the laagers for refugees. Pretty bad reports have been received here of the state of the Bloemfontein laager in Jany – insufficient water, milk rations, typhoid prevalent, children sick, no soap, no forage for cows, insufficient medical attention. . . .

I think I shall have a hot time over these probably in most cases inevitable sufferings or privations – war of course is war. . . . Tell me all that will help the defence.[49]

And Kitchener, of course, blandly replied that there was no defence needed. It was true that recently the military governor of the Transvaal had launched a public appeal for the donation of blankets and clothes for the camps; he himself disapproved of the appeal, as to admit shortages would play into the hands of 'pro-Boers'.[50] The camps were not supposed to be comfortable. They provided a minimum. Everything was under control, and, though he had never visited one, the inmates were 'happy'.

Today, Kitchener is not remembered in South Africa for his military victories. His monument is the camp – 'concentration camp', as it came to be called. The camps have left a gigantic scar across the minds of the Afrikaners: a symbol of deliberate genocide. In fact, Kitchener no more desired the death of women and children in the camps than of the wounded Dervishes after Omdurman, or of his own soldiers in the typhoid-stricken hospitals of Bloemfontein. He was simply not interested. What possessed him was a passion to win the war quickly, and to that he was prepared to sacrifice most things, and most people, other than his own small 'band of boys', to whom he was invariably loyal, whatever their blunders.

War was war. But when would it be over? In February, Kitchener was told by his Field Intelligence that there were about twenty thousand Boers still in arms against him.[51] Hence his scribbled note to Brodrick, just before De Wet's third 'invasion' on 10 February: 'I cannot say how long it will go on. Not counting voluntary surrenders we reduce their forces at the rate of about a 1000 a month [.] That was my bag for Decr, and January may be a little more. It is a most difficult problem, an enemy that always escapes, a country so vast that there is always room to escape, supplies such as they want abundant almost everywhere.'[52] At this rate, the war could drag on for months.

Now, in March, while the result of the peace talks still hung in the balance, Kitchener felt no nearer being able to predict the date of victory. The problem was made more urgent by the Cabinet's pressure on him to economize. Kitchener must have guessed (rightly) that the Cabinet favoured Milner's own plan for protected areas; it might win the war quicker – and would certainly save a great deal of money. The question of economy touched Kitchener on the raw, as he had always prided himself on his gift for cheap victories, measured in British lives and British money. But, as Brodrick had pointed out – in a revealing phrase – until the wheels of the gold-mines began to turn, they could not 'profit by victories'. On the contrary, the civilian administration of the new colonies would go on piling up a thumping deficit, quite apart from the frightening cost of the war: £2½ million a month.[53] To humour Milner and Brodrick, Kitchener had agreed to reopen a handful of gold-mines. At the same time, he had examined the local contracts for supplying meat and transport to the army and found that the firm of Weil (who had supplied B-P in Mafeking) had pulled the wool over Roberts's eyes and had been making enormous profits; he cancelled Weil's and other local contracts and so cut the total cost of the war by about a fifth – that is, by £500,000. He also hustled a number of British officers out of South Africa – 'hangers-on', he called them – in order to encourage the others.[54]

But, much as he would have liked to be able to make other economies in beef, horse-power, ox-power and man-power – the main items on the bill for the war – Kitchener had to agree, after weeks of hedging, that, as regards the two latter, he needed substantial reinforcements. What kind of reinforcements? Native cavalry from India, he told London, and London gasped. Kitchener's enthusiasm for 'native' troops – if politically naïve – is hardly surprising. It was to the vigour of African troops in the Sudan that he principally owed his triumphs as Sirdar, and he found British troops spineless by comparison. 'The men are getting indifferent. The Boers treat them very well as prisoners and I believe they are not always pleased when they are released. . . .' If only they had some proper native troops, real men who would 'forget their stomachs and go for the enemy', how different the war would be.[55] But Brodrick reminded him that this was a white man's war (the 'racial objection was very keenly felt'), and Kitchener had to make do with raw British irregulars of various kinds.[56] After Roberts had reached London, the Cabinet had in fact decided to provide thirty thousand new recruits as reinforcements: partly from Australian and New Zealand contingents (Canada, politically divided, refused further assistance), partly from new recruits to the Imperial Yeomanry, and partly from the ten thousand new South African Constabulary being raised in Britain; B-P was supposed to be organizing this SAC to form both a permanent British garrison and that crucial injection of British settlers (according to Milner's plan to anglicize South Africa). However, B-P had not yet got cracking. Kitchener agreed with Roberts that, as a serious military figure, B-P had been somewhat overrated.

With the first ten thousand, at any rate, expected to embark in early March,[57] Kitchener planned to hustle the enemy more vigorously. He still complained of how few fighting men of any sort he had available for sending out to hunt down and destroy the guerrillas. On paper, Kitchener's superiority was already crushing: he had inherited a sledge-hammer of 200,000 men (including 140,000 regulars) to crack a nut of 20,000 guerrillas. The real contest was much less unequal. In fact, it was the war of the sieve (guerrilla wars often are); and the guerrilla forces, progressively reduced in size, were becoming progressively finer material. Moreover, Kitchener's superiority in numbers was partly offset by the vast distance Cape Colony added to his supply lines and by its political unreliability. As most white South Africans in Cape Colony consisted of Afrikaners, and most Afrikaners appeared to sympathize with the Boers, Kitchener had to station troops to guard the Cape ports, the main towns and the railway lines. Deduct more for the garrisons in the main towns of the Free State and the Transvaal. This left 22,000 (of whom only 13,000 were combatants) for French's eight mobile columns – set to do the actual work of 'sieving' and 'scouring' in the Eastern Transvaal.[58]

Of course, Kitchener tried to choose the best men and best generals for the columns. Divided and redivided for extra mobility, many were now commanded by relatively junior officers. Kitchener, in keeping with his waywardness as an administrator, had a hungry eye for talent, and no scruples about hustling a bright young man to the front, over the heads of his superiors, especially if he was one of his 'band of boys' from the Sudan. Hence the way that he favoured Rawlinson and Broadwood – and, more eccentrically, Captain Frank Maxwell, VC ('The Brat'), the handsome young ADC whom Kitchener allowed to play the fool, teasing the Chief, like a court jester, to the amazement of outsiders.[59] Others whom he selected were chosen for their professionalism. They were the counterpart to the new breed of young Boer generals being gleaned by the guerrilla war – Lieutenant-Colonels Julian Byng and Edmund Allenby, and Colonel Douglas Haig – all future British field-marshals.

It is from Allenby's letters home that one receives the clearest insight into the frustrations of this 'hustling' phase of the war. Allenby was unusually intelligent and sensitive. He noted the novel – indeed, extraordinary – feature of this campaign: the uprooting of thousands of families; women and children given a few minutes to clear their homes, and then driven off in wagons; the making of a new Great Trek and a new mythology of suffering and bitterness. Allenby noted this and found it 'beastly work'. Most other British officers did not even bother to mention this part of 'the show' in their letters home. (Nor, for that matter, did Kitchener mention it in his current public despatches.) Ironically, however, Allenby criticized the unsystematic way the women were cleared from their farms. If the job had to be done, it had better be done properly. And, characteristically, Kitchener was in too much of a hurry to let anything be done properly, being hopelessly out of touch with the realities of war.

When Kitchener interviewed bright young men at GHQ – Herbert Plumer, Edmund Allenby – he impressed on them that they were mere pawns on his chess-board. He was Grand Master. One false move by them, and they would be out of the game.[60] Games-playing also dominated the walls of his intelligence staff: checkerboards of intelligence maps; 'drives' and 'bags' and 'kills'. A war reduced reassuringly to facts and figures, cut and dried formulas for victory.[61]

How different it looked out here on the veld. The struggle, described in Allenby's letters, took shape and dissolved like a fog. There were no lines or fronts, no battles – mere skirmishes with an invisible enemy, whose only aim, apparently, was to run faster than their pursuers.

Allenby, newly promoted Lieutenant-Colonel, had been given a force of fifteen hundred men, with horse-artillery guns, and joined the other seven columns sweeping the Eastern Transvaal, led by General French. Their job was to hustle Boers, clear the country, and stop Botha breaking south towards Natal. They had begun this wearisome trek in late January. Allenby found 'John Boer' a 'slippery customer' – and, indeed, the whole campaign intensely frustrating. He longed to be home with his wife. 'As French says we "hustle" them well,' he told her. 'I'm tired of hustling Boers, though & should like to get back to England and you, Dear Love. We caught one of Botha's staff officers yesterday. He said the war would last another year at *least*!!'[62] Allenby thought the Boers would throw in the sponge before that, though he saw no immediate end to this sickening campaign:

I should rather like some of those fashionable warriors, who went home at 'the End of the War' to come out and see what the war looks like now that it is at an end. It might give them a few new ideas. As far as my experience goes, the '*War*' was the easiest part of the campaign. We've had more fighting since the 'War' ended, more trekking, and much more discomfort. . . . I've lost 32 horses in 9 days, only two of which were lost in action. The rest have died from exhaustion and short food. There is no help for it. Isolated like we are, we must patrol a lot to keep Brother Boer at a distance, as well as collect grub. . . . I must say all the men of my column are splendid; keen as mustard and one never hears a grumble.[63]

The endless rainstorms that lashed Kitchener's columns in the first two weeks of March virtually marooned Allenby's column on the borders of Swaziland. Floods broke the telegraph wire connecting them with French, the ox convoys were unable to ford the Assegai River, and the men had to sleep in a quagmire without shelter of any sort. Fortunately for them, the Swazis were most accommodating, and kept them alive on mealies. Indeed, to show their good will, some assegai-throwing warriors ambushed a Boer commando which had taken shelter in Swaziland and killed fourteen men – more than Allenby's column bagged in any single action. Allenby reproved them, with his tongue in his cheek.[64]

The physical strain of the three-month trek, and the moral strain of making war on women and children, left him exhausted and ill. He returned to GHQ in late May. His own column had made the following bag: 32 Boers killed and wounded, 36 prisoners captured in the field; 154 surrendered; 5 guns taken (including one of Buller's guns from Colenso), as well as 118 wagons, 55 carts, 28,911 rounds of rifle ammunition, 273 rifles, 904 horses, 87 mules, 483 trek oxen, 3,260 other cattle and 12,380 sheep. He also brought in 400 women and children.[65] The relative absence of fighting Boers in this otherwise impressive total naturally disappointed Allenby. He attributed this partly to the slowness of his fellow–commanders, partly to the impatience of GHQ.

It's quite absurd the way we are hurrying through this work [he had written in early May]. There's a good months' police work to be done in these fastnesses. . . . I have to leave heaps of people behind. . . . In cases like that we leave the families enough wagons to live on, burn the rest, drive off the cattle, & wish them good day. Their own people can get them when we have gone away. It's beastly work; but ought to be done thoroughly if done at all. That's what makes me angry; that they won't even give me a chance of finishing up a job; either of fighting or police work. I presume it is to throw dust in the eyes of the British public. I hope I am wrong. . . .[66]

Similar grumbles at the unsystematic strategy pursued by Kitchener were expressed by others of his élite commanders. Smith-Dorrien, who had not forgotten the way Kitchener had treated him at Paardeberg, wrote in his diary: 'I much fear that we are leaving a lot of work unfinished . . . and am sorry the authorities won't listen to my opinions.'[67]

Colonel Douglas Haig, who had three columns under him (more than many generals) complained continually at the lack of co-ordination.[68] And Kitchener himself was not unaware of this failing. When the bag for nearly three months' work of French's eight columns was totted up, it came to the ridiculously small total of 1,332 Boers killed, captured and surrendered (although the numbers of horses, sheep, and cattle taken prisoner – 272,752 head of stock – was immensely impressive).[69]

In fact, by May Kitchener had already settled in his own mind that 'hustling' the enemy was not enough. True, the monthly bag (of killed, captured, and surrendered) for the whole country was rising: 859 in January, 1,772 in February, 1,472 in March, 2,437 in April.[70] But, at this rate, the war could still drag on for months. How to evolve a better system of co-ordinating the 'drives'? How to create some form of net to trap the quarry?

The answer, presenting itself to Kitchener, was to be found in two new weapons: barbed wire and the blockhouse. It might seem odd that these lumpish tin-and-concrete structures – pill-boxes, the symbol of defensive war – should be the key to making Kitchener's mobile columns more effective. But Kitchener, the sapper, had spotted a new possible use for the blockhouses, originally built to defend the railway lines. What about a gigantic grid-mesh of blockhouse lines: barbed wire, alternating with blockhouses, each miniature fort within rifle-range of each other? Wouldn't this create just the steel net into which the columns could drive their quarry? Always assuming that the Boers had no field-guns, and so the blockhouses could be made more or less impregnable.

To have to string barbed wire, and throw up tin-and-concrete forts across half South Africa, was not, of course, an ideal short cut to ending the war. Nor was it going to be cheap. Kitchener saw no alternative – except offering conciliatory terms to Botha. When Rawlinson arrived in Pretoria in March (after escorting Bobs to England, he had been recalled by K), he found Kitchener pacing up and down the garden at Pretoria, and in high spirits. He explained to Rawlinson his plans for the prototype of a new kind of drive. 'He sees that we made a big mistake in talking as if the war was over. He is working out a new system, greatly increasing the number of columns, and fortifying the railway lines with block-houses. The columns will drive from line to line and will find supplies at both ends. This is the right way to deal with guerrillas.'[71]

On 16 March, a week after this cheerful meeting with Rawlinson, Kitchener received the bad news which he had expected. Botha had turned down the terms offered at Middelburg – apparently because of the British Cabinet's refusal to allow an amnesty for the colonial rebels.[72] The news hardened Kitchener's heart. He would press on with his gigantic grid-mesh of blockhouse lines.

He was, in fact, furious with the way Milner had thwarted his plans to end the war by giving Botha generous terms. Perhaps Kitchener was mistaken. There may have been other insurmountable obstacles to peace, as well as Milner; perhaps, even if Kitchener had been given a free hand with Botha, Botha could not have persuaded Steyn and the Free State generals, like Hertzog and De Wet, to abandon their treasured independence. This will always remain one of the great might-have-beens of the war.

Kitchener, however, regarded Milner as the villain of the peace talks.

Outwardly, the relations between the two men were warm enough; and Kitchener envied Milner his diplomatic ways, no doubt. To Brodrick, Kitchener could not resist expressing his own blunt feelings about Milner's policy. A policy of 'extermination', Kitchener called it. And was it not 'absurd and wrong' to make war, costing £2 million a week and thousands of lives, just to put three hundred colonial rebels in prison?

I did all in my power to urge Milner to change his views ... an amnesty or King's pardon for the two or three hundred rebels in question (carrying with it disfranchisement which Botha willingly accepted) would be extremely popular amongst the majority of the British and all the Dutch in South Africa; but there no doubt exists a small section in both Colonies who are opposed to any conciliatory measures being taken to end the war, and I fear their influence is paramount; they want extermination, and I suppose will get it. . . .

Milner's views may be strictly just but they are to my mind vindictive, and I do not know of a case in history when, under similar circumstances, an amnesty has not been granted. . . . I wonder the Chancellor of Exchequer did not have a fit.[73]

Brodrick's soothing reply ('Is it not likely that with one more turn of the military screw, they will be ready for submission?') did not soothe Kitchener.[74] Indeed, it spurred him on to make some provocative new suggestions of his own. If there was talk of turning the screw, what about confiscating all the property of the Boers still out on commando? It was repugnant, 'but in this war we have had to do much that is repugnant'. Or what about mass deportation of all Boers who had fought in the war, together with their families and dependents? They could be sent to the Dutch East Indies, Fiji, or Madagascar. These country Boers could never be an asset to the British; they were 'uncivilized Afrikander savages with a thin white veneer', savages produced by generations of lonely life on the veld. Their expulsion would make room for decent British settlers.

In the intervals between despatching these wild proposals, Kitchener gave the British Cabinet an astonishingly sound piece of political advice. They could prolong the war, if they chose, by agreeing to Milner's 'vindictive' desire to impose unconditional surrender. But in the end, the Boers would still have to be given the same generous terms of peace. This was because South Africa was a 'white man's country' and the British colonials would have to share the country with the Boers, and, in due course, the mother country would have to give back South Africa – white South Africa – the freedom to govern itself, just as they had given it to all the other white nations of the Empire.[75]

A few weeks after the collapse of the Middelburg talks, Milner temporarily handed over the keys of his new kingdom, making Kitchener acting High Commissioner of the two new colonies, and took the train back to the Cape. On 8 May, he boarded the *Saxon* to take his 'holiday' in England. He was exhausted, after weeks of wrangling with Kitchener, but victorious.[76]

To Violet Cecil he did not pretend to shed tears over the collapse of the peace talks. 'I hope we shall take warning and avoid such rotten ground in the future.'[77]

He was content that the war would have no 'definite end' at all, but merely fade away. In the meantime, would Kitchener behave himself? Milner can hardly have forgotten the farcical episode the last time he had taken leave in England, when General Sir William Butler, as acting High Commissioner, had sided with the Boers.

He was not unduly worried now. The secret of Milner's recent triumph over Kitchener was the care he had taken to prepare the ground at 'Headquarters', where his old Balliol chum, St John Brodrick, was War Minister, with a seat in the Cabinet. He had packed off Hanbury Williams, his own Military Secretary, to serve as St John's Private Secretary. It was a wrench to lose Hanbury, but Milner was taking no chances. There must be no 'wobbles' at home – either in the Cabinet, or among his own allies in the Opposition. Hence the need to 'cut sticks', and go back for a spell at Headquarters himself, to prepare for the first moves of the new game: reconstruction under arms.[78]

In the last two months, Milner had begun some of the groundwork in the Transvaal. He had acquired a splendid, red-tiled villa on the hills north of Johannesburg; Milner laughingly compared it to the 'residence of a prosperous tradesman at Hendon or Chislehurst'; it had its back to the mine shafts of the Rand, and commanded 'magnificent rolling country' up to the Magaliesberg. In fact, it was 'Sunnyside' – the suburban HQ belonging to Wernher-Beit, next to Hohenheim where the Raiders had dreamed and plotted. Milner said he liked it because it faced north – towards home.[79] But did it not have somewhat unfortunate associations, this new imperial HQ? If there were protests, Milner allowed himself to ignore them. The economic future of South Africa depended largely on the late owners of Sunnyside. Now the origins of the war were forgotten, and the war itself was fading away, their alliance with the imperial government would become eminently respectable. In fact, Milner had chosen a mine manager, Wybergh, as one of a four-man team running the new Transvaal administration.[80]

Already, behind Sunnyside, the mine chimneys were beginning to smoke and the mine wheels beginning to turn once more. Protesting about the extra transport it cost him, Kitchener had allowed a trickle of both black and white miners back to the Rand. Three hundred and fifty mine stamps were now in operation, and a trickle of gold had begun to flow into the vaults of Wernher-Beit.[81] It might be only a drop in the ocean, compared to what was needed to reshape South Africa. It was a beginning.

On board the *Saxon*, Milner felt 'mentally torpid'. No doubt it was a reaction to the struggle with Kitchener. He played a little whist some days; he chatted to some congenial lady passengers; and, of course, he counted the hours till he would be back at 'Headquarters', back with his friends at Duke Street, St James's.

One of the lady passengers on the *Saxon* whom he did not find so congenial was a dumpy, middle-aged English spinster called Emily Hobhouse. Milner had given her lunch in February (she had letters from influential Liberals), and helped arrange for her to tour the burgher refugee camps. He now regretted his generosity. There had been numerous protests about her trouble-making, especially protests from loyalist ladies. A 'pro-Boer', he realized, and a 'screamer', too. Milner lay in his deck-chair, and dismissed Miss Hobhouse from his mind. At Madeira, he received a ridiculous cable that the Cabinet was going to make him a peer. The cable must be a hoax.

On 24 May, the *Saxon* docked at Southampton. The voyage had been as uneventful as that dreary voyage home on the *Scot* two and a half years before. And there the similarity ended. In 1898, he had slipped into England, almost unknown, a man of the shadows, a death duties expert, sustained by a private dream of 'big things'. Now he belonged to the public; he was the Empire made flesh.

Milner found that most of the government had come to celebrate his apotheosis on the platform at Waterloo: Salisbury, Balfour, Chamberlain, Lansdowne, as well as Lord Roberts. To prove their impatience to honour him, Salisbury and Chamberlain whisked him off immediately in an open landau, and then drove through cheering crowds to be received by the King at Marlborough House. Milner arrived back at his lodgings under the heady name of Baron Milner of St James's (after these lodgings) and Cape Town.

How Milner was later to regret his own fatal blunder at this moment of triumph. He still dismissed Emily Hobhouse as a 'pro-Boer' and a 'screamer'. In fact, the story she told was only too true. Over sixty thousand men, women and children were now stuffed in those 'refugee' camps set up by Kitchener. Their population was rising like the waters in a dam. But where were the doctors, the matrons, the orderlies; the clothes and blankets; the medicines and comforts? It was the twin spirit of neglect and red tape – the Exham spirit – that had haunted the white tents at Bloemfontein a year earlier. And this year the rows of tents were not intended for soldiers used to the ways of the barrack room. They were for women and children, used to the free life of the veld, and (for the richer farmers) ubiquitous African servants. Now they were themselves treated like Africans, herded in, exhausted, destitute, starving, to Kitchener's camps of 'refuge'.[82]

As the telegrams of congratulation flooded into Milner's lodgings in Duke Street, Emily Hobhouse set off on her own self-appointed mission to waken the conscience of England. Epidemics had broken out in the camps and were spreading with terrifying rapidity.

CHAPTER 39

'When is a war not a war?'

London and South Africa, 1901

'*Ons mans, kinders, vaders, broers, susters, huis, alles ja alles moet ons agterlaat, en ons – wat sal van ons word?*'
('We must leave our menfolk, children, fathers, brothers, sisters, house, everything, yes everything, and us – what shall become of us?')

> Maria Fischer's diary for 29 May 1901, the day she was taken off to a British concentration camp

Emily Hobhouse lost no time in telling her story to any politicians who would listen.

She was an odd choice for the leader of a great moral crusade, this dumpy, forty-one-year-old spinster from Cornwall. Passionate in public, yet inwardly reserved and lonely, a refugee from the claustrophobia of Victorian family life, she had spent years in a remote village near Liskeard as companion to her father, an invalid archdeacon. Her first taste of freedom came at thirty-five, when she vanished into the wilds of Minnesota, where she laboured to convert Cornish miners to temperance. Then she went back to England (after being jilted by a fiancé in Mexico), just as the war-clouds gathered.[1] Her political patron was her uncle, Lord Hobhouse, a distinguished Liberal of the old school and a friend of the 'pro-Boers', Harcourt and Courtney.[2] So it was natural she should fling herself, head and heart, into the work of the 'pro-Boers'' relief fund, the South African Women and Children Distress Fund. Humour, tact, organizational power, common prudence: they were not her gifts. (Lord Hobhouse: 'Oh well, we've tried prudence, and we've tried caution. Perhaps a little imprudence may do better.')[3] Emily Hobhouse was no Florence Nightingale. But she was aglow with moral indignation. And she, she alone, had seen the camps.

In the first week of June, St John Brodrick gave her a long hearing at the War Office. He listened to her recommendations politely. In fact, they were reasonable enough – indeed, too reasonable, it would turn out. Brodrick did not commit himself.[4] A week later, she saw Campbell-Bannerman. His reaction was more than polite. He listened aghast. As she poured out her story – 'the wholesale burning of farms ... the deportations ... a burnt-out population brought in by hundreds of convoys ... deprived of clothes ... the semi-starvation in the camps ... the fever-stricken children lying ... upon the bare earth ... the appalling mortality' – CB began to murmur something to himself: 'Methods of barbarism ... methods of barbarism.' It was a phrase that would soon echo round the world.[5]

The story she told was, indeed, shocking to anyone not committed to believe in the inevitability of the war, and of harsh methods to end it. To CB it threatened to precipitate a political, as well as a moral, crisis. Despite his solid, reassuring figure ('well suited to a position of ... a sleeping partner in an inherited business', said Beatrice Webb, the Fabian and imperialist), CB was often depressed these days. 'I agree with all you say,' he told Lord Ripon in January, 'as to the black outlook and the Slough of Despond in which we are wallowing at the Cape.'[6] The slough seemed, if anything, deeper in May. Paradoxically, CB's position as official leader of the Opposition had not been improved by the reaction against the government after the Khaki election, when the public discovered how hollow were those claims that the war was 'practically' over. For the war in South Africa continued to breed war within the Liberal Party: 'pro-Boers' shooting it out with the Liberal imperialists ('Limps'); CB trapped in no-man's-land between them; and all three fair game for Joe and the government. Where was CB to find a common target for his own party? Certainly not in the increasingly bitter debate about the way that the war was being conducted.

Apart from the way it maddened the 'Limps' to criticize the handling of the war they believed was a just war, there was the question of the electorate. 'We must be very careful,' wrote CB, 'not to take any line which might seem to be anti-British, for our countrymen, though sick at heart, are all the more touchy and obstinate....'[7] Hence CB stayed, heavily upright, on the greasy pole between the two Liberal extremes, motionless, apart from occasionally waving his arms to keep his balance.

Since the first South African debate of this year – the debate on the Address in February – this arm-waving had attracted little attention. He concentrated on the two main points on which he believed he could be critical without seeming unpatriotic: on the government's insistence on 'unconditional' surrender, and the policy of farm burning and deliberate devastation. But the first point had become partly academic since the publication of the terms offered to Botha at Middelburg. CB could only criticize the refusal to give the amnesty to colonial rebels. On the second point, the relevant facts were frustratingly obscure. For the government claimed (optimistically, it turned out) that Kitchener had reversed Roberts's policy, and only resorted to farm-burning in exceptional cases. And, as CB himself soon 'cordially' seconded the proposal to grant Roberts £100,000 for his services, his strictures were not calculated to be too wounding.[8]

By contrast, Loyd George, in full cry at the head of the 'pro-Boer' pack, infuriated both the government and the 'Limps'. He exulted in attacking not merely the system, a great deal more vigorously than CB, but (unlike CB) attacked the army itself. He quoted a notice posted up by General Bruce Hamilton, who had burnt the town of Ventersburg and then told the women and children to go and apply to the commandos for food. 'This man is a brute,' said Lloyd George, 'and a disgrace to the uniform he wears.' He quoted a Reuters report, describing (correctly) how there were two scales of rations for the 'refugees' in the burgher camps, the lower scale being for those whose husbands and fathers were on commando. 'It means that unless the fathers come in their children would be half-starved. It means that the remnant of the Boer army who are sacrificing everything for their idea of independence are to be tortured by the spectacle of their starving children into betraying their cause.'[9]

The attack on the camp system had been taken up by two other radical MPs, C. P. Scott and John Ellis. It was these two who first used in March an ominous phrase, 'concentration camps', taking it from the notorious *reconcentrado* camps, set up by the Spanish to deal with Cuban guerrillas.[10]

It was Ellis who sent out his relative, Joshua Rowntree, to report on the camps. When Rowntree was refused entry into the two new colonies by Kitchener, Ellis's instincts were aroused.[11] Brodrick continued to insist that the camps were 'voluntary camps'; the inmates went there, of their own free will, as refugees. Ellis charged – correctly, of course – that most were effectively prisoners. How many lived in them, asked Ellis in March, and, indeed, how many had already died in them?[12] Although he and Lloyd George had little enough information of their own (despite their links with Afrikaners at the Cape), they succeeded in exposing St John Brodrick as apparently having still less.[13] It was not till April that the House was given the first statistics of the numbers in the Transvaal camps (21,105); not till May, those of the ORC – Orange River Colony – and Natal (19,680 and 2,524 respectively).[14] Even then, the facts remained extremely obscure. For example, Brodrick claimed – erroneously – that many of these 'refugees' were coloured people. As for the death-rate in the camps, all he could say was that there had been several hundred deaths in the early months of the year: that is, 284 in the Transvaal and 382 in the ORC.[15] These were high, but not outrageously high death-rates for a period of several months. Less reassuring were the reports of Joshua Rowntree, and of a mission of Cape Afrikaners who arrived in England to lobby the Liberals. But they, of course, had not visited the camps. It was in this that lay the overwhelming importance of Emily Hobhouse and her story.

She did not claim to know the latest statistics. What she said – and she repeated it not only to politicians, like CB, but at public meetings all over the country – was that she had seen the conditions in the camps. They were bad, and they were *deteriorating*.

In brushing off criticism of the camps, Brodrick's original claim was that they were well-run refugee camps, designed to encourage the Boers to come in and surrender. After Lloyd George and Ellis had exposed this as largely humbug, Brodrick developed a new double line of defence. Speaking to the brief supplied by Kitchener, he claimed that the camps were both a military and moral necessity. The country had to be cleared of food, and how could the women and children be left to starve? He also claimed that there had originally been certain discomforts in camp life, but that everything possible was now being done to alleviate these. The fullest exposition of this reassuring line was given by Leo Amery, *The Times* correspondent, in a long cable sent from Bloemfontein on 18 June. Amery stressed that the death-rate was 'rapidly decreasing', and that nothing augured better for the new administration than the 'progress' in the 'refugee camps' like the camp at Bloemfontein.[16]

Now came an eye-witness account from Emily Hobhouse of what progress looked like at Bloemfontein. She first visited Bloemfontein, the largest of the ORC camps (and one where thousands were to die of disease) on 24 January 1901. There were eighteen hundred people then in the camp: a village of white bell-tents, dumped down on the southern slope of a kopje rising from the brown veld.[17] She found the city's military governor, Major-General Pretyman, hospitable and co-operative – indeed, anxious to know what she thought of the place. She was not long in telling him. She had imagined that her mission was to distribute her twelve tons of 'little extras' paid for by the relief fund – comforts, clothes and so on – and she found that the bare necessities were lacking.

The shelter was totally insufficient. When the 8, 10, or 12 persons who occupied a bell-tent were all packed into it, either to escape from the fierceness of the sun or dust or rain storms, there was no room to move, and the atmosphere was indescribable, even with duly lifted flaps. There was *no soap* provided. The water supplied would not go round. No kartels [bedsteads] or mattresses were to be had. Those, and they were the majority, who could not buy these things must go without. Fuel was scanty.... The ration [the punitive double scale was still in force] was sufficiently small, but when ... the actual amount did not come up to the scale, it became a starvation rate.[18]

She applied to a friendly superintendent to supply the most vital deficiencies: soap, forage, more tents, brick boilers for drinking water, a tap water supply. He duly requisitioned for them. After three weeks, back came the official reply: agreed to supply soap (at an ounce a week per head) and to build brick boilers; but forage 'too precious' and tap water impossible as 'the price was prohibitive'. Still more ominous, the camp latrines were quite inadequate, and the authorities negligent in dealing with them. Hour after hour, the unemptied pails stood in the sun, making the tents, downwind of them, unbearable to live in.[19]

In dealing with soldiers – the masters of this man's world – Emily did her best to keep a civil tongue and a stiff upper lip. Her own feelings, feminine and feminist, poured out in letters home: 'The authorities are at their wits' end – and have no more idea how to cope with the ... difficulty of providing clothes for the people than the man in the moon. Crass male ignorance, stupidity, helplessness and muddling. I rub as much salt into the sore places of their minds as I possibly can, because it is good for them; but I can't help melting a little when they are very humble and confess that the whole thing is a grievous mistake and gigantic blunder and presents an almost insoluble problem and they don't know *how* to face it.'[20]

After Bloemfontein, Emily set off by train, with her wagon-load of comforts, to inspect as many of the other camps as Kitchener – and De Wet – would permit. She was able to see half of those administered by the ORC – Norvals Pont, Aliwal North, Springfontein, Kimberley and Orange River. She also saw one – Mafeking – administered from the Transvaal.[21] Her conclusion was that all the camps, in varying degrees, shared the defects of the Bloemfontein camp. Precisely how bad conditions were depended on circumstance: how energetic the superintendent, how near the supply of water and fuel, how distant the base, how helpful the public nearby, and how early the camp was started (for the earliest camps got first pick of supplies).[22]

Meanwhile, as Emily travelled round the hopelessly congested railway lines, Kitchener's columns began a new series of 'drives'. Everywhere along the railway she saw the resulting 'bag': open trucks full of women and children, exposed to the icy rain of the high veld, sometimes left in railway sidings for days at a time, without food or shelter. The sight shocked her even more than the sight of the camps. For the camps bore at least the appearance of order: neat villages of white tents, numbered in military style, so that you could find your way round. In the railway sidings what you could see was war unvarnished: truck-loads of homeless mixed up with the animals of the veld, 'frightened animals bellowing and baaing for food and drink, tangled up with wagons ... and a dense crowd of human beings'. Here was 'war in all its destructiveness, cruelty, stupidity and nakedness'.[23]

On her return in April, for a second look at Bloemfontein camp, she found all the improvements, inadequate as they were, had been swamped by the weight of new arrivals. 'If only the camps had remained the size they were even six weeks ago,' she reported, 'I saw some chance of getting them well in hand, organizing and dealing with the distress. But this sudden influx of hundreds and thousands has upset everything, and reduced us all to a state bordering on despair.'[24] In fact, the numbers at the camp had doubled since her last visit, and more were expected.

More and more are coming in. A new sweeping movement has begun resulting in hundreds and thousands of these unfortunate people either crowding into already crowded camps or else being dumped down to form a new one, where nothing is at hand to shelter them. Colonel [Goold-Adams] says, what can he do? The General wires: 'Expect 500 or 1,000 at such a place.' And he has nothing to send there to provide for them.... No wonder sickness abounds. Since I left here six weeks ago there have been 62 deaths in camp, and the doctor himself is down with enteric [typhoid]. Two of the Boer girls we had trained as nurses and who were doing good work are dead, too....[25]

At first, Emily Hobhouse herself hardly realized what was the most striking single fact about the camps: not the discomforts, nor hardships of life, but the appalling rate at which people were dying. 'I began to compare a parish I had known at home of 2,000 people where a funeral was an event – and usually of an old person. Here some twenty to twenty-five were carried away *daily*.... The full realization of the position dawned upon me – it was a death-rate such as had never been known except in the times of the Great Plagues ... the whole talk was of death – who died yesterday, who lay dying today, who would be dead tomorrow.'[26]

By April, she had seen enough. Those soldiers had been right. The whole system was a gigantic, lethal blunder. She must return to England as fast as possible to state the 'plain facts' to the British public.[27]

Her fifteen-page report to the Committee of the Distress Fund was first circulated to MPs and published in late June. It consisted of some letters home, carefully edited (no mention of 'crass male ignorance, stupidity, helplessness and muddling') and a summary of the camps' chief defects: lack of fuel, bedding, soap, clothes; inadequate diet and water supply; overcrowding; bad sanitation. Her basic conclusion was that the whole system was cruel and should be abolished. All those who had friends or relations able to take them should be allowed to leave the camps. No further people should be brought into them. 'May they stay the order to bring in more and yet more. Since Old Testament days was ever a whole nation carried captive?' (She added to her recommendations one further one, showing how closely she identified herself with the Boer *vrouw*: 'That considering the growing impertinence of the Kaffirs, seeing the white women thus humiliated, every care shall be taken not to put them in places of authority.')[28]

This was the report that, coupled with Emily's personal testimony, sent a shock-wave through the 'pro-Boers'. Lloyd George and Ellis intensified their attack on the government in an adjournment debate on 18 June. Still more important, the shock at last dislodged CB from his place on the tight-rope between the two Liberal factions. Great emotion underlay the bantering tone. He told a Liberal dinner party at the Holborn Restaurant on 14 June that he was sickened by the policy of sweeping the women and children into camps, as the Spaniards had done in Cuba: 'A phrase often used is that "war is war". But when one comes to ask about it, one is told that no war is going on – that it is not war.' (Laughter.) 'When is a war not a war?' (Laughter.) 'When it is carried on by methods of barbarism in South Africa.' (Cheers.)[29]

Three days after CB's outburst at the Holborn Restaurant, Lloyd George pinned down the government to a short adjournment debate on the subject in the Commons. The House, he said, must discuss as a matter of urgency the condition of the concentration camps, and 'the alarming rate of mortality amongst the women and children detained there'. During Question Time earlier that day, Brodrick made two crucial admissions: there were now 63,127 people, white and black, in the camps (a much higher figure than ever previously admitted, though in fact much lower than the real figure); and deaths in the Transvaal camps in May totalled 336 – 39 men, 47 women, 250 children. Mortality figures for the other three colonies were still not available.[30] It was enough for Lloyd George. 'The answer given today proves that, so far from this being the result of temporary conditions, it is growing worse.'

These new figures, extrapolated over a year, gave a death-rate of twelve per cent, compared with the British army's death-rate of five per cent at the height of the Bloemfontein epidemic. He accused the government of pursuing 'a policy of extermination' against the women and children. Not a direct policy of extermination, but a policy that would have that effect. 'I say that this is the result of a deliberate and settled policy. It is not a thing which has been done in twenty-four hours, for it has taken months and months to do it. The military authorities knew perfectly well it was to be done, and they had ample time to provide for it. They started clearing the country about six months ago, and it is disgraceful that 5 or 6 months after that children should be dying at the rate of hundreds per month.'

Why pursue this disgraceful policy, he asked; why make war against women and children? It was the men that were their enemies. 'By every rule of civilized war we were bound to treat the women and children as non-combatants.' The novel method of warfare adopted was all the more disgraceful because it would prolong, not shorten, the war. 'We want to make loyal British subjects of these people. Is this the way to do it? Brave men will forget injuries to themselves much more readily than they will insults, indignities, and wrongs to their women and children.' He concluded, after quoting Emily Hobhouse's report: 'When children are being treated in this way and dying, we are simply ranging the deepest passions of the human heart against British rule in Africa.... It will always be remembered that this is the way British rule started there, and this is the method by which it was brought about.'[31]

Half a dozen other radicals and one Irish nationalist echoed Lloyd George's denunciation; and CB himself reasserted his own new radicalism. 'It is the whole system which they [the Army] have to carry out that I consider, to use a word which I have already applied to it, barbarous.' Why not (as proposed by Emily Hobhouse) release the internees who could fend for themselves? Above all, why not send out from England teams of properly qualified doctors and nurses to deal with the epidemics?[32]

To all such suggestions, well intentioned or not, Brodrick turned a bland face and a deaf ear. He repeated, for the twentieth time, that the policy of sweeping the country had been forced on them by the guerrillas. Some of the women had been assisting the enemy; others had been abandoned by them; none of them could be simply left on the veld to starve. As for the 'alarming mortality figures', he shrugged them off, secure in the knowledge that no one, least of all himself, knew the latest figures and the actual trend: 'It is urged that we have not done sufficient to make these camps sanitary, and to preserve human life. I deny it altogether. It is said that they are going from bad to worse. Those who have been out there ... assured me that things, so far from going from bad to worse, have been steadily ameliorating.'[33]

The concentration camp debate fizzled out, predictably, in cries of 'Divide!' and a downpour of heavy voting for the government: 252 against Lloyd George and his motion, compared with 149 in favour; the 'Limps' abstained.[34] And there the matter rested for the moment, as far as the imperial Parliament was concerned. To make out their case against the government, the radicals needed to know more mortality figures. Kitchener kept the figures discreetly dark. It was not until 17 July that more or less complete returns were at last published, not until 16 August that the published returns confirmed the trend, and proved that Emily Hobhouse's worst fears were true.

There were now 93,940 whites, 24,457 blacks in the so-called 'camps of refuge', and all the improvements had been swamped by the increase of numbers. Every month the deaths rose, relatively as well as absolutely: May, 550; June, 782; July, 1,675. Crisis was becoming catastrophe.[35]

But 16 August was almost the final day of the session for 1901; the next day, the House dispersed for its five-month holiday. No one bothered Brodrick with further questions about the camps. Both political parties were preoccupied, it must be said. Despite tactical losses and gains here and there, the strategic stalemate was unbroken in the war of attrition on the main battle-fronts: the double war of Kitchener against the Boers, and Kitchener against Milner; and, of course, the Liberals against each other.

Among the Liberals, CB's 'methods-of-barbarism' speech in the Holborn Restaurant had set the cups and saucers rattling up and down the country. The jingo newspapers bellowed abuse. *The Manchester Guardian* and *The Westminster Gazette* offered their congratulations. The delight of the pro-Boers was matched by the indignation of the 'Limps'. Rosebery regarded CB's speech as evidence of a deliberate plan to widen the split in the party. The banquet was a 'sinister event' – in effect, a declaration of war by the centre and left on the right of the party. The party crisis that followed was labelled by Henry Lucy as 'war to the knife and fork'. The 'Limps' counter-attacked in a series of furious engagements at dinner.[36]

After suffering for so long the indignities of guerrilla war from the 'Limps', CB found the open war stimulating. It gave him a chance of calling the 'Limps' bluff: did they want him to continue as leader? 'You know me; you know my faults, and my good points if I have any.... It is for you to say whether I enjoy that confidence which my position necessarily requires.' The result was, predictably, that the centre rallied around CB, and the 'Limps' had to put away their cutlery. They were divided from the Liberal Unionists on most domestic issues; they had nowhere to go except to slink back under the shade of CB's umbrella. By early July, the nine days' wonder was over. The 'Limps' over-reaction had confirmed CB's position as leader of the party, for what that was worth. But, as Leader of the Opposition in Parliament, CB was still stalemated by them, paralysed by the loyalty that Asquith, Grey, and Haldane retained for Milner.

Milner had descended on London at the end of May, in time to stop any 'wobbles' by the 'Limps' in the direction of misplaced leniency. He had a similar job to do with regard to the government: to stop their wobbles in the direction of severity.

By persisting so unexpectedly, the war was certainly kind to the Conservatives and Unionists; it kept the inner strains of the alliance more or less under control (despite the squabbling between Hicks Beach and Lansdowne); it united the government as effectively as it divided the Opposition. But it did not give the Cabinet a clear-cut policy to agree on. They remained uncertain *whose* policy to pursue, as they had remained for months: Milner's or Kitchener's; the 'policy of protection' (of gently phasing out the war), or the policy of devastation (of trying to end it by some sudden, violent stroke). So far, the result of this uncertainty, not to say feebleness, was that the Cabinet had pursued a kind of blocking strategy against Kitchener. It was natural that, after meeting Milner in the flesh, the Cabinet should screw up their courage to try his policy.

The detailed course of negotiations between Milner and the cabinet is obscure. What is certain is that the new 'protection policy' (alias 'localizing' the war) hammered out in the Cabinet in late June, was basically the policy proposed all along by Milner.

There were many reasons for the Cabinet's decision. In their hearts, most of them, doubtless, were queasy about Kitchener's rough-and-ready methods of war, which culminated in the concentration camps. This was the irony behind the hullabaloo in the Commons caused by Emily Hobhouse's report. Chamberlain, who remained a personal friend of pro-Boers like Harcourt, had never believed in Kitchener's sweeping-and-scouring system, and no doubt shared Milner's view, expressed the previous autumn, that to make war on women and children was 'barbarous'.[37]

However, politically, the most telling argument against this policy was not a moral one. It was that Kitchener's policy was not working: in short (as Milner could press on the Cabinet), worse than a crime, a blunder.

It says much for the subtlety of Milner's diplomacy that at the time when he was moving heaven and earth to reverse Kitchener's policy, he should be writing affably to the man himself, posing as a kind of honest broker between him and the Cabinet:

I have seen all sorts of people [he wrote to Kitchener in early June], statesmen, journalists, the man in the street. I have been doing nothing else since I came but sucking in opinions. In the clubs and drawing-rooms there is the usual Babel of nonsense. The country is as *sound as a bell*. The pro-Boer ravings produce astonishingly little effect. I don't believe we have ever had a big war in which the Opposition has had less weight. Any Ministry is much more likely to fall for not conducting the war with sufficient vigour, than for persisting in it with the greatest energy at any cost. On the other hand there is a very natural impatience, not at the war not being over – people are prepared to see it drag – but at the want of clearly visible progress. What is wanted, if people are to be kept in good humour with us – not in a rage with the Boers, which they will be anyway – is definite evidence that we are nearer the end by the end of the winter. With the end of winter they will want to see:

More [mine] stamps at work. Some considerable district clear of the enemy. Some reduction of the force in South Africa within sight. If these symptoms that we are progressing, even slowly, are forthcoming, they will stand a lot more. If not, they will not relent towards the enemy, but they will want some of *our heads* on a charger, possibly yours, more likely mine, still more likely the Ministry's....[38]

Clearly visible progress. In other words, let the reconstruction begin. That was what Milner, in early June, said the public wanted. As for heads on the charger, he had his own preferences, and it was not either for his own or for St John Brodrick's. He went to see Roberts in private and begged him: any hope of Kitchener's going straight away to India?

Milner's most telling arguments against Kitchener's policy were financial. The British public might be 'sound as a bell', but how would their pockets feel when the latest bill for the war was presented? Apart from the Napoleonic Wars, it was the most ruinously expensive war in British history. The current bill was too high to pay out of direct taxation, even by raising income tax from [8d] to 1/–, as Hicks Beach had been forced to raise it in 1901. The balance had to be borrowed from home and abroad.

On 2 July, the Cabinet made its wishes clear to Kitchener in a long cable sent through the mouth-piece of Roberts (who, incidentally, disapproved). The cable amounted to an ultimatum, or, at any rate, to a time-table: either Kitchener must end the war by September and the end of the South African winter, or he must adopt Milner's policy:

> We must now face the possibility that your winter campaign, however successful, will not conclude the war. Indeed its very success in reducing the larger commandos to small unorganized guerrilla bands may render some change of method necessary by the end of August ... the winter once over, the Government do not think it either possible or desirable to continue indefinitely to spend £1,250,000 a week, and keep in South Africa 250,000 soldiers to deal with an enemy who cannot be crushed simply because they are too few and too scattered ... estimated not to exceed 18,000 men. The Government also think that the first necessity of the new Colonies is to make a beginning in them of civil and industrial life. ...

The cable spelt out the 'protection policy': protecting the Rand and the other parts of the country that were potentially revenue-producing or populous or otherwise important; and then gradually pushing the lines outwards from these protected areas. This new policy, Kitchener was told, should enable him to reduce his army by 110,000, from 250,000 to 140,000 men on the pay-roll of the imperial government.[39]

First round, victory for Milner.

The reply received from Kitchener was predictably masterful. He neither resigned nor turned the Cabinet's scheme down flat. He stalled. For weeks, he argued about the phased reduction of the army, but gave no signs of being ready to carry it out. And here, it must be said, British successes and British reverses both came conveniently to hand as arguments on Kitchener's side.

The column war – roughly sixty thousand British soldiers in mobile columns pursuing less than a third that number of Boers – was formless by nature. It seemed even more formless when relayed to London in Kitchener's brusque cables. Who was winning? On the credit side, from the British point of view, was the 'bag': the monthly grand total of Boers killed, captured, or voluntarily surrendered. The total continued to be disappointingly small – 2,585 in May, 2,277 in June, 1,820 in July.[40] This was progress, but only if the Boers received no reinforcements from among the Afrikaners of the Cape. Even then, the war could drag on for months, unless there was a sudden collapse of the guerrillas' morale, speeding the rate of surrender and perhaps causing the Boer leaders to throw in the sponge.

This prospect seemed, certainly as regards the Free State, farther off than ever. It was a peculiar irony of this phase of the war that, by a double intelligence *coup*, the British now learnt just how firm was the Free State's will to fight on.

The first opportunity was presented by a peace overture of Botha's, whose gloomy result was known by the end of June: indeed, it helped precipitate the Cabinet's desire to try a new policy.

Botha was allowed by Kitchener to send a cypher cable to Kruger, to consult him about peace terms. The cables were exchanged by way of the Dutch Consul-General in the Transvaal. There followed much the same pattern as at Middelburg: British hopes raised; the Transvaal, as peace-maker, apparently anxious to persuade the Free State to come to terms; then a devil-may-care challenge, signed by the acting Presidents of both so-called governments, that they would accept no terms short of preserving their independence.[41]

In mid-July, British intelligence at the War Office broke the cypher used in the cables to Kruger. The cypher turned out to be in French, based on dictionaries, and was jointly cracked, according to an unpublished account, by a crypto-grapher in Ireland and the assistant librarian at the War Office Intelligence Department.

The cables showed how confident President Steyn felt of his ability to continue the struggle. True, they also confirmed that Botha and the Transvaal were genuinely anxious for peace. But Steyn appeared to be able to paralyse Botha's peace efforts indefinitely.[42] Ironically, Steyn himself had a hair's-breadth escape, in his shirt-sleeves, from his laager at Reitz that same week in July. Brigadier-General Broadwood surrounded it and captured twenty-nine other members of the 'government', £11,500 (including 800 sovereigns) and all the government papers. The papers confirmed that the Transvaal was in dire straits, but also that Steyn was determined to prevent a surrender.[43]

These were the British successes that Kitchener seized on to show the danger of abandoning the sweep-and-scour policy. Why weaken their grip on the enemy just when this strategy was beginning to succeed? He used the opposite argument when pointing to the enemy's own occasional flashes of success.

In general, the commandos in the last few months had dealt only pin-pricks to the elephantine hide of Kitchener's army of 250,000. (A number he disputed, pointing out that his 'effective' army was only 156,000, and the number able to pursue the enemy only half that.)[44] True, the commandos regularly raided the railway lines and blew up trains, causing general irritation, and sometimes even casualties. They even dynamited Modderfontein, one of the Rand mines.[45] But the latter was a unique incident (after this, the mines had to be protected) and attacks on the railway tended to decline as the year wore on. The main guerrilla threat was to the empty veld.

Occasionally, however, the columns hunting a needle in the haystack got their fingers badly cut. On 29 May, Brigadier-General H. G. Dixon, combing the south-west Transvaal alongside General Babington, Colonel Rawlinson and Lord Methuen, was attacked near his camp at Vlakfontein. Dixon had been searching for buried guns. He had been given information which proved false, not so the information which General Kemp and 1,500 Boers had been given about him. Kemp, one of the most daring of the new men whom guerrilla warfare had thrust to the front, snapped up Dixon's rearguard, and captured two guns. The guns were recaptured, but the action cost Dixon 49 men killed and 130 wounded.[46]

The battle was not even a clear tactical victory for Kemp, as he left forty-one men dead on the field and was forced to flee as soon as Dixon's fellow-commanders lumbered up to reinforce him. The direct strategic result of Vlakfontein was nil: the columns continued the combing operation undeterred. Yet the psychological effect – the capacity to prolong the war – of this and similar actions seemed to Kitchener serious enough.

Most serious of all was the effect of Kritzinger's 'invasion' of Cape Colony, which had now been in progress for seven months. In itself, this seemed a small enough affair: a midget army of about two thousand (half of whom were believed to be Cape rebels), without much food or ammunition or the means to concentrate and deal an effective military blow.[47] Provided they were kept hustled, they could be kept weak and dispersed. Yet as a symbol of the unbroken spirit of the two republics, of the idea of militant republicanism mounted, so to speak, on horseback and galloping across British territory, this Lilliputian commando had to be destroyed as a matter of urgency.

Hence Kitchener's second line of argument: to reduce my army is out of the question until I have cleared the Cape.

As soon as Milner had set sail again for South Africa, the full weight of Kitchener's counter-attack on the Cabinet developed. He proposed a new stick-and-carrot policy of his own: mild, one-year sentences for Cape rebels who surrendered voluntarily; otherwise, death sentences for Cape rebels captured in arms; lenient treatment for burghers of the Transvaal and Free State who surrendered voluntarily; otherwise, first fines and then confiscation of their goods, and permanent banishment for the leaders.[48]

The Cabinet were forced back on to the defensive. They blocked Kitchener's wildest ideas – including a plan to deport the women and children from South Africa to join their husbands abroad;[49] and, as the alternative, to pay the entire cost of the concentration camps by selling property belonging to the men out on commando.[50] They also protested at the brutal circumstances in which Kitchener had allowed General French to execute some captured Cape rebels at Dordrecht; the townspeople had been forced to witness these public executions.[51] When Kitchener rounded on Brodrick – let me take a 'strong line' and I'll finish the war quickly – he was quietly reminded that 'severity' had not proved itself a great success so far.[52] On the major issues, the bitter wrangle continued. Kitchener was forced to accept a much-diluted version of a proposed new proclamation, warning the Boers to expect tougher measures after 15 September.[53] The Cabinet had to accept that if the proclamation failed (as it did fail) there would be no troop reductions after all and the government would be heavily out of pocket. They would have to go crawling to Parliament to ask for extra money.[54]

Meanwhile, the Fawcett Commission – that daring experiment, a ladies-only commission to report on the concentration camps – embarked on their work. From August to December, they steamed up and down the veld in their special second-class train.[55] They had one important political qualification, these industrious ladies: they all believed that the war was just, and that this in turn justified certain unpleasant measures directed at the civilian population.

This was the crux of the difference between them and the friends of Emily Hobhouse.[56] Otherwise, they were a diverse band. Mrs Millicent Fawcett, the lady chairman, was both an active Liberal Unionist and an active feminist, the leader of the women's suffrage movement. Lady Knox was the wife of Major-General Sir William Knox, Kitchener's general. The four other ladies included a nurse from Guy's Hospital and two doctors already in South Africa (one of whom married a camp official during the tour).[57]

They presented their official report in December; meanwhile, their comments were constructive and pungent. If Brodrick expected them to add a ladylike coat of whitewash to the camps, Brodrick was in for a surprise. They were not objective (who ever could be in a war?) but they tried to be fair.

By 18 September, the ladies had already surveyed seven of the camps in the ORC, including those visited by Emily Hobhouse. Their impressions were predictably mixed. Sometimes they saw an incongruous game of lawn tennis being played in the camps.[58] Occasionally, when they tramped along the dusty lines of white tents, someone would hurl out abuse at them: 'De British not able to conquer de men, are now making war on de women and children.' (They responded, somewhat tactlessly, by reminding them how the Boers treated the womenfolk of the Zulus and Basutos they had beaten in battle.) But generally they were received as politely as Emily Hobhouse had been received; and they were touched by the way most of the Boer *vrouws* accepted their good intentions.[59]

In their criticisms of the camp system, Mrs Fawcett and her Commission confirmed in all essentials the accuracy of Emily Hobhouse's account, and the long-overdue nature of her proposed reforms. Indeed, their chief recommendations went further:

1. Forty trained nurses to be sent out immediately to South Africa.
2. A 'strong effort' to be made to improve the railway transport allocated to camps.
3. Rations to be raised by $\frac{1}{2}$ lb rice per week.
4. Where no other fuel was available, coal rations to be at least $1\frac{1}{2}$ lb a day.
5. Wood to be provided for bedsteads, so no internees had to sleep on the ground.
6. Every camp to have proper apparatus for sterilizing linen used by typhoid patients.
7. A travelling inspector of camps to be appointed.

To this list they soon added the following:

8. Water boilers to be provided enough to boil all drinking water.

9. Vegetables to be added to the rations.

10. Camp matrons to be appointed as rapidly as possible.

They gave similar recommendations to the Natal and Transvaal administrations. In due course, they visited thirty-three white concentration camps (though a characteristic flaw in their philanthropy was in their failure to help, *or even visit*, a single camp for Africans; there were thirty-one camps for Africans in the ORC alone). They concluded that the whole scale of rations was too low, and advised additions in a long list of items, including bread, sugar, coffee, and milk, as well as fuel and soap.[60]

Such were their general recommendations. On individual camps, their comments were occasionally flattering, often not. They were impressed by Norvals Pont, and recommended energetic young Mr Cole Bowen (just as Emily Hobhouse had recommended him months before) to be made travelling inspector. They were shocked by the state of the hospital at Bloemfontein camp, where there were no arrangements to sterilize linen infected by typhoid patients. They were still more shocked by the camp at Brandfort, where an epidemic killed 337 (nearly a *tenth* of the inmates of the whole camp) in the first three weeks of October. There were three other camps where they blamed grossly incompetent staff, and recommended complete reorganization.[61]

Often, too, they blamed the army. At Heilbron, Kitchener's men sent a new wave of measles-infected internees into the town, which swamped all facilities:

> The death-rate was very heavy, 10 dying on one of the nights of the Commission's visit. Though some of the houses were comfortable, others were miserable sheds or stables, and one hovel was one surely meant for a pig or perhaps some poor native and yet a young girl, dangerously ill, lay in it. . . . There is barely language too strong to express our opinion of the sending of a mass of disease to a healthy camp; but the cemetery at Heilbron tells the price paid in lives for the terrible mistake.[62]

But Mrs Fawcett's most damning criticisms (the old criticisms about failure to follow elementary rules of sanitation) were reserved for Mafeking. Emily Hobhouse had visited Mafeking camp in April and found morale low. On 20 August the special train, bearing Mrs Fawcett and her ladies, steamed into the town. They found the camp exceptionally dirty. Women were washing clothes in water fouled by excrement. Slop water was thrown on to the ground beside the tents. Latrines were not properly disinfected. The Commission warned the superintendent of the dangers of a typhoid epidemic. The superintendent paid no attention, pointing out that only forty deaths had occurred since March. By the time they returned in early November, there were four hundred deaths *a month*, many of them caused by typhoid.

If anything could be missing from a camp, it was missing at Mafeking. Medicines 'deplorably deficient', said the Commission; 'many deaths and no mortuary'; complete break-down in the supply of fresh meat; no rations of vegetables, although they could have been bought in the town; and, behind it all, grossly culpable neglect by the staff.[63]

It was Millicent Fawcett, not Emily Hobhouse, who came closest to playing the role of Florence Nightingale in the terrible crisis that had overwhelmed the camps. There was a touch of steel about Millicent, masculine steel (though she would never have used that adjective as a compliment; men could be such idiots!), and a professionalism that made Kitchener look like a bungling amateur. She did not mince her words when she told Milner the facts of death in the camps.[64] The terrible mortality figures had continued to rise, contrary to Brodrick's assurances, based on Kitchener's ridiculously ill-informed forecasts: August – 1,878 deaths among 105,347 white 'refugees' and 467 among 32,272 coloured ones;[65] September – 2,411 deaths among 109,418 whites, about 600 among 38,549 coloured people;[66] October – 3,156 deaths among 111,619 whites, 698 deaths among 43,780 coloured people. These October statistics were now plague-high, proportionately as well as absolutely: 34·4 per cent., calculated as an annual death-rate for white inmates of all ages; 62·9 per cent. for children in the ORC, 58·5 per cent. for children in the Transvaal.

At individual camps like Mafeking, the October figures represented an annual death-rate of 173 per cent.[67]

Mrs Fawcett spelt out the causes to Milner. The deaths were *not* simply the result of circumstances beyond the control of the British. True, her Commission attributed the epidemics partly to the especially insanitary conditions of wartime South Africa, and to the almost total devastation of the country. They also blamed the unhygienic habits of the Boer women ('even at the best of times, the Boer woman has a horror of ventilation. ... It is not easy to describe the pestilential atmosphere of the tents ... the Saxon word "stinking" is the only one which is appropriate.') But the Fawcett Commission pointed a feminine finger at the military (and, of course, male) red tape in which the camps had been trussed: the spread of the epidemics should have been foreseen; elementary rules of sanitation should not have been forgotten; vegetables should have been provided; doctors and nurses should have been rushed to the scene from England when the epidemics first broke out.[68]

These were the formal conclusions reported by Millicent Fawcett and her ladies in December. Of course, they were of no comfort to the government. But Chamberlain had at long last got the message. And it is clear he recognized the ultimate causes of the catastrophe: Milner was in theory the man responsible for the camps, but the main decisions (or their absence) had been left to the soldiers, to whom the life or death of the 154,000 Boer and African civilians in the camps rated as an abysmally low priority.

In mid-November, Chamberlain cabled to Milner what amounted to a rebuke. He assumed that Milner was now in a position to exercise 'full control of the arrangements for all camps'. In that case, 'it is necessary ... that I should be satisfied that all possible steps are being taken to reduce the rate of mortality, especially among children, and that full and early reports should be sent to me. ...' A few days later, he added, with a blinding glimpse of the obvious, 'If you are in any need of trained men ... you must not fail to ask for such assistance', which could easily be obtained in India.[69]

Milner's reaction verged on panic. The women and children would 'all be dead by the spring of 1903. Only I shall not be there to see as the continuance of the present state of affairs for another two or three months will undoubtedly blow us all out of the water.'[70]

In fact, the terrible mortality figures were at last declining. The common-sense of the Fawcett Commission had a magical effect on the annual death-rate, which was to fall by February to 6·9 per cent. and soon to 2 per cent., less than the average in Glasgow.[71]

Ten months after the subject had first been raised in Parliament, Lloyd George's taunts and CB's harsh words at the Holborn Restaurant had been vindicated. In the interval, at least twenty thousand whites and twelve thousand coloured people had died in the concentration camps, the majority from epidemics of measles and typhoid that could have been avoided.[72]

Meanwhile, things were at last stirring in the long-static guerrilla war. Kitchener's sweep-and-scour policy was beginning to work. And, deprived of their old bases in the ex-republics, the Boers were forced to try the dangerous experiment of raiding the Cape and Natal.

CHAPTER 40

Raiding the Colonies

Cape Colony and Natal,
3 September–December 1901

'Dams everywhere full of rotting animals; water
undrinkable. Veld covered with slaughtered herds of
sheep and goats, cattle and horses. The horror passes
description ... Surely such outrages on man and nature
will lead to certain doom.'

Jan Smuts's diary, 7 Aug 1901, while
he and his 200 men were trekking
through the Free State

Smuts decided to make for Kiba Drift, with his 250 men, the moment that
Commandant Wessels got back from patrol. It was 3 September, and the
light was already failing. Ahead of them lay a long, dark line, the lip of the
great canyon cut by the Orange River as it comes swirling out of the mountains of Basutoland. Wessels had brought a local farmer, a veteran of the Basuto
War, to guide them over the river. For several days, Smuts's men had been
scouring the brown veld to the north, hunting for a suitable drift. The Orange
River was still low – the spring rains had not yet broken – but every sandy
footpath leading down to the river seemed to be blocked by files of white
tents.[1]

Except the bridle path to Kiba Drift, the path to the Native Reserve at
Herschel. It was still open – that night. On his return, Wessels confirmed that
they must go at once. The Khakis were sweeping down from the north, clouds
of them.[2]

'Up saddle.' People recognized the General, 'Oom Jannie' ('Uncle Jannie'), by
his pointed yellow beard, clipped in the French style, the grey riding breeches,
and the cluster of staff, including three heliographers.[3] Most of the other men,
like most of the Boer guerrillas everywhere, were dressed in rags. Deneys Reitz,
the irrepressible eighteen-year-old son of Kruger's State Secretary, belonged to
a group who called themselves, ironically, the Rijk section – the 'Dandy Fifth'.
He had no shirt under his ragged coat, and his raw-hide sandals had been patched
and repatched for eight months.

A few men wore khaki uniforms captured from the British (a dangerous
blessing, it would soon prove).[4] Others carried British Lee Metfords slung over
their backs. Apart from these trophies, the commando was short of nearly
everything: no medical supplies, little Mauser ammunition. They had plenty of

horses – perhaps two apiece, as well as the pack animals. But forage was scarce at that time of the winter.[5]

About three in the morning, the going became rougher as the path began to descend; far below there was a glint of white in the bed of the canyon. By dawn, they were splashing through the turbulent, creamy current in single file. As the sun worked down the walls of the canyon, Smuts's band rode out into Cape Colony, into British territory.[6]

What was this mission of Oom Jannie's? A forlorn hope, a last despairing throw of the dice, or a perfectly feasible strategic stroke that might well change the whole course of the war? Deneys Reitz was himself puzzled about their mission. He had been warned of the dangers. In the last ten months, all the most famous 'invaders' of the colony had been hunted back into the Free State, with heavy losses: De Wet, Hertzog, Kritzinger. The scattered guerrilla bands operating at present in the colony were able to survive only at the cost of their effectiveness as a striking force. Reitz believed that the purpose of their own mission was to take a plunge into the central districts of the Cape, to test the difficulties of launching a large-scale invasion later on, an invasion to relieve the increasing pressure against the main Boer armies to the north. Smuts had welcomed him as a recruit for the commando; Smuts was, of course, an old friend of his father. But he offered no reassurance about success. ('Terrible privations awaited them. ... Their tombs would become a hallowed memory for the generations to come.') As for the precise purpose of the mission, Smuts was distinctly uncommunicative.[7]

In fact, Smuts, the twenty-eight-year-old enthusiast, the ex-admirer of Cecil Rhodes, did not by any means regard his mission as a forlorn hope, though danger heightened its romantic colours.

For eight months, ever since that conference in December at Cypherfontein, he had believed passionately in the need for the third front, for carrying the war into the enemy's country: into the Cape, politically British but morally the Afrikaner heartland where, outside the towns, the volk were still the overwhelming majority. The advantages were, he claimed, obvious: friends in every village, ready to feed, clothe and hide the guerrillas; friends whose farms could not be burnt and their herds destroyed, for the Afrikaner-dominated ministry would never allow it.[8] This had been his argument in December – and he deeply regretted that the opportunity had been let slip meanwhile. How to account, then, for the failure of successive missions by De Wet, Kritzinger and Hertzog? To Smuts these Free State expeditions only proved his point. They were unco-ordinated; there was no joint strategy between them, let alone with the Transvaal. Of course, they were beaten back over the Orange.

In June, Smuts put his own plan again to the war council at Standerton in the Transvaal. This was after the receipt of Kruger's telegram urging them to fight on. Botha, as the Transvaal Commandant-General, had asked what hope of success remained. Botha, in fact, conceded the success of Kitchener's sweep-and-scour strategy. How could the guerrillas operate in the republics when their bases were destroyed, when their men were surrendering at the rate of hundreds a month, there were no new recruits, and the blockhouse lines along the railways were beginning to criss-cross the country? To this, Smuts repeated his plan for a Cape offensive. He would join forces with Assistant Commandant-General Kritzinger, and help him reorganize the surviving Free State bands holed up in the tangled mountains of the Eastern Cape. Then he would cut his way through to the Western Cape, to prepare the ground for a large-scale invasion of Transvaalers led by De la Rey. Even this pilot expedition should have a disproportionate effect in relieving the hard-pressed forces commanded by Botha and De Wet. At best, it would set the whole Cape alight, raise that fire-storm of a great Afrikaner rising that represented the last positive hope of winning the war by force of arms.

Of course, there was a less spectacular alternative, the classic of guerrilla warfare: not to win the war, but to preserve a country's independence by forcing a stalemate on the enemy. Smuts was far too intelligent and politically astute to despise this negative strategy. He had noted with enthusiasm that Chamberlain, according to the Cape papers, was weakening. His old friends and political allies in the Cape, Sauer and Merriman, had been to England and stirred up a great wave of outrage about the concentration camps, a wave that might propel the Liberals back into power. But would they come to power in time? And would they then wish to repeat the conciliatory policy pursued after Majuba? It was here that the Cape invasion, however weak in a military sense, could tip the balance in the political war.[9]

Anyway, whether successful or not, it seemed hard for war to be more wretched in the Cape than the current war in the Free State. Kitchener's attempt to sweep all animals off the Free State farms had been only partially successful; yet Smuts had lost thirty-six men crossing the exposed veld. He was sickened by the destruction he saw everywhere he trekked: every dam on the farms choked with dead cattle and horses; bleating lambs beside their dying mothers; sheep-pens filled with sheep mangled by dynamite. 'Surely such outrages . . . on nature will lead to certain doom,' wrote Smuts grimly in his private diary. Then, to take refuge from these horrors, he turned to his beloved *Anabasis*, Xenophon's account of his own epic march across Asia Minor in the sixth century BC. Smuts carried it, and his copy of Erasmus, in his saddle-bag.[10]

On 4 September, their first day in the Cape, they met danger from a new kind of enemy. The Africans at Herschel, the Native Reserve on the borders of Basutoland, had been told by the British to repel invaders, and repel them they did, attacking some of Smuts's foraging parties, killing three men and wounding seven. However, the Boers' rifles were more than a match for African spears and blunderbusses. Next day, the commando reached the safety of some Afrikaner farms, where for the first time after so many months they saw a people at peace: men working in the fields, women and children standing unafraid beside the doors. They gave the commando food; it was the first slice of bread and butter and the first sip of coffee Deneys Reitz had tasted for a year. They could not spare any clothes, as the British army controlled their distribution, in order to prevent farmers helping the invaders. Still, the coffee put the commando in excellent spirits; they whistled as they rode along.[11]

Two days later, Smuts himself narrowly missed disaster. At a place called Mordenaar's Poort ('Murderer's Gorge'), he took three men and went forward to reconnoitre. The spring rains had begun at last, after so many months of winter sunshine. The men huddled in thin blankets around the fire, waiting for the General's return. He came back at midnight on foot and alone. All three companions had been shot by the Khakis. By a miracle he had escaped down a ditch.[12]

The troubles of the commando were only beginning. The rain increased as they headed south-west towards the Stormberg Mountains, a tempest of wind and icy rain which demoralized men and killed horses. It was clear that the British general (French) was drawing a cordon around them. For three days, from 9 to 13 September, they tried to fight their way out. On the third day, the Khakis surrounded the commando at a wretched little farm on the grassy summit of the Stormberg. The men had been marching for forty hours without sleep. The Khakis blocked every pass. So it seemed. Then a man on crutches hobbled out of the farm – he was a hunchback – and promised to show them a way out. He led them by a squelching path that brought them so close to the British camp that they could hear voices and the champing of bits. It led to the edge of the escarpment.

There followed a miraculous escape in the darkness, as the whole commando of 250 men, and at least 500 horses, went glissading down the south face of the Stormberg. Fortunately, the fall was cushioned with grass, otherwise few would have come down alive. After sliding and slithering into the valley, they crossed the first railway, the line leading to some coal-mines, just as the lights of a train swung into view. Should they put stones on the rails and try to ambush the train? Smuts refused. He had no wish to attack civilians here in the Cape Colony. So the hungry and exhausted men crouched in the darkness as the lighted carriages went thundering by, and Reitz caught a wistful glimpse of British officers, smoking and drinking in the dining-car. (His wistfulness increased, later on, when he heard that this elegant company included French and his staff, in hot pursuit of the commando.)

Although they had missed their dinner, their spirits were raised when they caught an empty goods train soon afterwards. The guard's van contained something almost as precious as a hot meal – a Cape newspaper. Smuts, it declared, had invaded Cape Colony 'with the riff-raff of the Boer armies. There was also a copy of Kitchener's solemn proclamation of 7 August, threatening perpetual banishment for those who did not surrender by 15 September, now two days away. Both items of news were received with ribald laughter.

There was, however, a thin edge to the laughter. By 15 September they were in fact on their last legs: many horses dead, little ammunition, starving.[13]

It was the spring rains, not the British, that had nearly finished them. All that terrible night, while their pursuers apparently retired to their tents, the commando floundered in the mud. The guides lost the path. About midnight, the rain turned to sleet. The grain bag which passed for Reitz's greatcoat froze solid like a coat of mail. The cold was so intense that the ponies, hardy mountain ponies at that, began to die of exposure. Reitz stumbled over their carcasses. Near daybreak, they found a deserted farm, where they came back to life, huddled together, breaking up the chair and tables, floors, and windows, anything that would burn, to dry their clothes and blankets. But fourteen men were found to be missing, and the survivors were too exhausted to send out a search party. Outside the farmhouse, the bodies of the ponies, fifty or sixty of them, lay in heaps where they had fallen.

That ordeal – the 'Night of the Great Rain', as it came to be called – brought Reitz closer to despair than any other experience in the war. The horses were like scarecrows. A quarter of the commando were horseless, carrying their saddles. Bandoliers were almost empty. Worse, the men had begun to lose confidence in Smuts. Where was he leading them? Where were the Afrikaner recruits Smuts had promised them? There was a whispering campaign to have Smuts replaced by his second-in-command, Commandant Van der Venter. Smuts remained uncommunicative. Next night, they were near Tarkastad, and found a farm with unthreshed oats for the horses; they slaughtered sheep for themselves. But the Khaki noose still tightened, slippery with rain. French had sent two columns splashing after them. Ahead of them, every muddy pass in the mountains was blocked, so some cheerful Kaffirs assured them. After floundering for a fortnight, Smuts's 'invasion' seemed to have come to a still more bitter end than Kritzinger's or Hertzog's or De Wet's: the winged feet of the commando stuck fast in the mud of the Bamboo Mountains.[14]

After all the airy talk of prospects in the colony ('only cross the river and the volk will rise in thousands'), Smuts had come squelching back to earth. It was impossible to live off this country. The Khakis had taken the food, the forage, and the horses. It was as simple as that. This was the reason why the volk would not join them. Even if the commando broke through the net, how could they survive without food and horses – and ammunition? There was only one place to reap that harvest: in the Khakis' own laagers.

As it happened, Smuts's commando found a hole in the net *and* a chance of reaping that harvest all in the space of one afternoon.

On the 17th, still heading south, they came to a long gorge leading to the Elands River valley. The leaders had to drag their horses after them. The wounded followed in the rear. But the sun was warm on their backs for the first time since they had crossed the Orange. Smuts sent Reitz and the 'Dandy Fifth' to ride forward and investigate. At the place where the gorge began to widen out, a farmer rushed out of his cottage and shouted, hoarse with excitement. Khakis. Two hundred of them. With mountain guns and Maxims. Laagered on the pass at the end of the gorge, Elands River Poort. Smuts decided to attack at once, and Reitz overheard him say, 'If we don't get those horses and a supply of ammunition, we're done for.' The 'Dandy Fifth' trotted on down the valley, forded a stream, and were brushing through a mimosa wood when they met, less than ten yards from the leaders, fifteen or twenty British troopers, cantering towards them.[15]

The Battle of Elands River, that followed, was brief, bloody, and decisive – as near a massacre as anything that spring. Smuts's men's shooting at Elands River was deadly accurate. They were, after all, De la Rey's veterans, their battle skills honed and polished by two years' grind in the Transvaal. Their sporting opponents, Captain Sandeman and Lord Vivian, with 130 men of the famous 17th Lancers (the 'death and glory boys', with a skull-and-crossbones blazoned on their uniforms), were relative amateurs. Moreover, the weather had suddenly sided with the commando. The morning was foggy, and, at first, the passes to the north were invisible from the British camp. When Reitz's scouts were sighted by a British patrol, they were mistaken for irregulars of Colonel Gorringe's column, that was pursuing them. This was not simply a matter of fog. Many of the Boers were wearing captured khaki. 'Don't fire. We are 17th Lancers!' shouted the officer. 'And we are the Dandy Fifth,' said an answering volley of bullets. Reitz himself used up his last two rounds, then threw away his rifle and grabbed a Lee Metford and bandolier from one of the first British soldiers to fall. He shot two gunners dead, having crawled up to within a few yards of the main British encampment, under the lee of a rocky outcrop.[16]

A desperate duel followed, 'almost at handshake distance', as Reitz put it. One wounded officer (it was Lieutenant Sheridan, a cousin of Churchill's) rose to his feet, his face streaming blood, and was shot through the brain. Reitz shot another man in the heel. The shock made him leap in the air, and Jack Borrius, the Boers' field cornet, brought him down. In all, Reitz's party claimed to have killed twelve or thirteen, without loss to themselves, though, earlier, three of their men were wounded.

Meanwhile, the main commando had worked up to the British camp from the rear. Many Boers here, too, were dressed in captured khaki, and this meant that they were allowed to approach to within a few hundred yards, a crucial advantage. When the confused butchery was over – twenty-nine killed and forty-one wounded on the British side, compared to one dead and six wounded among the Boers – the victors took stock of their captures. And well stocked the camp was, beyond the dreams of hunger. 'We were like giants refreshed,' wrote Reitz later. 'We had ridden into action that morning at our last gasp, and we emerged refitted from head to heel. We all had fresh horses, fresh rifles, clothing, saddlery, boots and more ammunition than we could carry away, as well as supplies for every man.'

Reitz helped himself from Lord Vivian's bivouac tent. He had started the day with two cartridges, a foundered horse, and a grain-bag as an overcoat. Now he had a khaki cavalry tunic, with a skull-and-crossbones and 'or glory' on the badge; a sporting Lee Metford; an Arab polo pony (this was the unfortunate Lieutenant Sheridan's), and an extra mule for trekking.

Smuts told the men to set fire to the surplus, including a field-gun, too immobile to be any use. As the wagons blazed up like torches, Reitz paid a personal visit to see the gunners he had killed, to check his bag, so to speak. He did not hate the British, he said, but he was proud of his share in the day's work. 'A fight is a fight.' Then, leaving the prisoners and their African retinue to shift for themselves, the new race of giants broke out of the Bamboo Mountains and rode in triumph into the open plain, their confidence in Smuts reborn.[17]

Colonel Douglais Haig, the commander directly responsible, under the overall direction of General French, for this section of the cordon, did not regard Smuts or his commando as giants. 'Brutes' and 'ruffians' were the words he used. The news of the smash-up suffered by C Squadron of the 17th Lancers reached him at Tarkastad, fourteen miles from Elands River Poort. It was 4.30 p.m. Haig galloped that fourteen miles in an hour and a quarter, splashing down the water-logged track. He was appalled by what he saw. 'The brutes had used explosive bullets.' Four of the six officers were dead, and Sandeman and Lord Vivian were wounded – Lord Vivian, whose sister Haig was to marry.

Haig, newly appointed CO of the 17th Lancers, as well as director of five different columns, had sent the regiment round the mountains in the train from Stormberg, to head Smuts off. He had sat with Sandeman during a break in the appalling weather of the previous day and picknicked off a hamper of delicacies, sent from England, out on that fatal kopje.[18] He did not blame poor Sandeman for what had happened now. The tactical weakness of C Squadron's camp at Modderfontein was that it was commanded by high ground on the west side of the valley. Smuts's capture of this high ground, combined with his men's use of captured khaki uniforms, had enabled the commando to storm the camp from the rear.[19]

How was Haig to deal with such 'ruffians'? The week before, he had written a jaunty letter home, describing the execution of colonial rebels at Colesberg: 'The authorities are all for blood I hear! This will have a good effect. There were 3 men shot at Colesburg [sic] when I was there. I did not care to go and see the spectacle but all the local Dutch magnates had to attend and a roll was called to see they were present. – I am told the sight was most impressive and everything went off well. – Just think what amusement old Baxter and even Hobday would have if they were now in this country! By the way I wired Gilbey for some more claret and champagne.'[20]

Now that champagne tasted bitter enough, as Haig saw the smashed and mangled bodies of Lieutenant Sheridan and the other young officers of the 17th Lancers. He renewed his orders (they were French's and Kitchener's, too): all Boer prisoners caught wearing British uniforms were to be shot on the spot.[21]

For the next four weeks, the guerrilla war in the mountains of the eastern Cape Colony centred on a personal duel between Haig and Smuts, between two well matched, though differently armed, opponents, each intensely professional, each relentless drivers of men.

From Haig's point of view, the loss of seventy cavalrymen, humiliating as it was, did not alter the main issue: whether he could catch the fox – or at least drive it back over the river out of the Cape farmyards. For this fox-hunt French had given him three packs – that is, three columns totalling roughly two thousand men.[22] The excitement of the chase raised everyone's spirits. 'From my point of view,' Haig said earlier (it was at a time when Kitchener 'used to get a fit of the funks' and think De Wet was going to invade the Colony), 'nothing would have pleased me and my column better than a good hunt after De Wet... the next best fox is Kritzinger.'[23] Now it was Smuts who had slipped over the river on 3 September – unchallenged, owing to K's bungling. Haig and French were exasperated by the way Kitchener interfered in the work of the columns. On the night of the 3rd, Kitchener had excelled himself. He wired to Major-General Fitzroy Hart, the Natal fire-eater, now serving as a humble column commander, telling him to take his men from guarding the ford at Kiba Drift and march them off to attack the Boers a few miles to the north of the Orange. Enter Smuts and his Two Hundred crossing Kiba Drift. (French's furious comment: 'What is the use in us doing our best to clear the Colony, if, the moment we drive Boers out at one corner, Lord K. drives them in another?')[24]

This fiasco was all the more galling, as French's FID (Field Intelligence Department) was now pouring out telegrams full of information, much of which, events would show, was surprisingly accurate. What complicated the hunt for Smuts's commando was that it was the most important, but not the only, needle in the haystack – or (to borrow Milner's phrase) not the only 'severed worm' wriggling about in the veld. The FID identified six smaller enemy fragments in Cape Colony south of the Orange: Commandants Myburg with a hundred, Fouchée with a hundred, Wessels with two hundred, Malan with fifteen, Theron with eighty, and Scheepers with two hundred and fifty. Add General Smuts and his two hundred and fifty and the total, south of the river, was reckoned, rightly, at about a thousand. (Roughly the same number of Boers were reckoned to have invaded the Western Cape Colony, north of the river.)[25] The counter-strategy comprised three basic aims. First, they must prevent these severed fragments from combining; second, 'hustle' them, so that they were unable to recruit followers or effectively raid the countryside; third, wear them out, so that they could eventually be overtaken and hunted down.

The first two of these aims – the negative two – had proved easy enough to accomplish in the Cape, without the drastic sweep-and-scour methods pursued by Kitchener in the conquered republics. It was mainly a question of keeping the commandos on the move, and then denying them fresh horses. How simple an antidote to guerrilla warfare, compared with that immense operation of burning farms and carting off the whole civilian population of the countryside into the camps! Yet Smuts himself (and his official report soon fell into British hands) admitted how his inability to get fresh horses, coupled with difficulty in getting food, had crippled his whole enterprise.[26]

Of course, 'invasions' by a total of two thousand men could hardly be compared to the military threat posed by the main guerrilla armies in the Free State and the Transvaal. But the guerrillas in the Cape had topographical advantages. The Cape was huge, four times the area of the old republics, with desert lairs to the west of the railway lines, mountain lairs in the east and midlands – though lairs, it must be said, made extraordinarily unpleasant by the spring storms.

It was these spring storms that had played a crucial tactical role in French's operations and helped bring to fruition the first real British success in the guerrilla war in the Cape. On the night of 5 September, the night after Smuts slipped across the Orange River at Kiba Drift, Commandant Lotter, with a commando of 130 rebels (Afrikaners from the Cape), was run to earth by Colonel Harry Scobell's column in a gorge near the village of Petersburg.[27] Scobell was perhaps the most dashing of all the column commanders in the Cape, a 'rattling good man' in the eyes of the troopers (he gave a ball at Cradock in May, where champagne flowed like water and some troopers were invited as well as the officers).[28]

Not that there was anything effete about Scobell. On the veld, he lived like his men, and, if they ever got a decent meal, it was off Boer food that they had looted. The speed with which his column travelled put it in a different class from other British columns – in the Boer class. He had hunted Malan and Kritzinger and Scheepers up and down these same mountains ever since May. It was largely Scobell's work (he had caught Kritzinger's commando asleep at a farm on 6 June and killed six and captured twenty-five) that eventually drove Kritzinger back in despair across the Orange River.[29] Since then, Scobell had refined his own counter-commando tactics still further by adopting Boer supply methods. He had discarded his wagons in favour of pack mules, carrying three days' rations for a six-day Boer-hunt. The gain was not only in speed. The column could climb like goats up a mountain-side – so steep that the odd pack mule would lose its footing and come somersaulting down the scree.[30]

On the night of 4–5 September, a storm was raging in the Tandjesberg, the tangle of mountains cutting off Cradock from Graaf Reinet. It was the fifth night of Scobell's six-day trek, and the column was almost dead-beat. Trooper Edingborough, of the Cape Mounted Rifles, who had been trekking for sixteen months, found those five days the stiffest of all. He had lost his boots (stolen by some kind Tommy); he had to make do with canvas shoes; his mare had to be dragged (Scobell's treks would reduce a fat pony to a ghost in a few weeks); he himself had eaten almost nothing. Then Scobell gave the order: a night march. And – because it was Scobell – the men followed almost without a grumble, sliding and slithering up the mountain.[31]

Scobell's plan to nail Lotter was the counterpart of Smuts's successful plan to smash the 17th Lancers. He had far better scouts than Lotter – African Intelligence scouts; and the appalling weather was all on his side. After that, everything depended on dash and courage and extra numbers. With eleven hundred men of the 9th Lancers, the Cape Mounted Rifles, and the yeomen, he outnumbered Lotter's rebel commando by nearly ten to one.[32] Still, Scobell did not expect to have things all his own way. He said himself, 'These rebels ... know they are fighting with a rope round their necks, and it makes them fight very well. ...' Nor did Scobell have it all his own way.[33]

Scobell expected Lotter's commando to have spent the night at a farmhouse in a mountain gorge called Groenkloof. In fact, almost all the commando had taken shelter from the rain in a kraal a few hundred yards away, a stone sheep-house, thirty feet long and fifteen feet wide, roofed with corrugated iron. Before dawn, Scobell disposed the main party along the ridges commanding the farm. Then, as the sky paled, a squadron of the 9th Lancers, led by Lord Douglas Compton, rode down cautiously to the kraal. At the doorway, Compton dropped his revolver and dismounted to retrieve it.[34]

A hundred sleeping Boers, curled up in blankets, like so many exhausted sheep in the kraal – this was, indeed, one of the strangest sights of the war. Lord Douglas did not have long to enjoy it. From sheep into lions. Their rifles were cocked and a fusillade cut down the six behind Lord Douglas. He grabbed his revolver and galloped past the doorway. Other survivors fired and scattered. Meanwhile, a tempest of bullets burst over the kraal. It came from all the surrounding ridges, as well as from point-blank range, smashing and grinding the stones and wood and bone and flesh, as though the bullets were explosive themselves: half an hour of frenzy.[35]

Trooper Edingborough was one of the first to enter the kraal. Seventy years later, he remembered that morning with pride, as though it were a victory described in *The Boy's Own Paper*.[36] At the time, he was appalled, as appalled as Haig at the sight of the Lancers. 'The sight was horrible in the extreme.' Someone had tried to wave a white flag, but, as there was still some resistance, the butchery had continued. Edingborough entered:

8 were lying dead huddled under the wall, men were lying about with half their faces shot away, blood spouting out of their chests, thighs etc in fact the place was like a butchers shop, some men making awful noises groaning clutching the ground and rolling in the dirt in their agony it was awful; we buried the dead [13 Boers, 10 British – mostly Lancers] by the kraal in a donga covering them up with large stones from the wall.[37]

Scobell had well and truly scuppered Lotter's commando. Apart from thirteen dead, there were forty-six wounded and sixty-one other prisoners, including Lotter (he and seven others were in due course executed as Cape rebels). Then, ten days later, Smuts, as we saw, set the score even again by killing and wounding a similar number of the 17th Lancers at Elands River. Not that the score was really even. In losing Lotter, the Boers had lost more than a tenth of the guerrillas in the Colony north of the Orange, and their élite commando at that.[38] Moreover, the British Empire was a bottomless well, when it came to replacing lost troops. The Boer wells were virtually dry.

Meanwhile, dangerous new blobs of red ink had appeared on the battle maps at Kitchener's HQ, and they threatened to transform the whole strategic situation. By the day of Smuts's victory, Botha had reached the Buffalo River, poised to invade Natal.[39]

Botha and his commandos had, in fact, marched south a week earlier, slipping out of their hunting grounds on the remote eastern border of the Transvaal, and skirting the mountains on the Swazi border. Botha's commandos marched as light and fast as Smuts's force. They had hundreds of pack mules and pack horses, instead of the old ox wagons that had been the bane of earlier campaigns; and they had hundreds of Mausers and captured Lee Metfords, without the impediment of a single field-gun (the last of the State Artillery's Creusots had been deliberately left behind in the north). This invasion of Natal was the other half of the grand strategy agreed with Smuts at Standerton: its military aim, to divert pressure from the occupied republics; its political aim, to prove that the war was by no means over. Botha's raid, planned in mid-August, was also a direct answer to Kitchener's proclamation of 7 August: a piece of panache, a challenge accepted.[40]

Yet was the Natal raid practicable, and not a Boer counterpart of Dr Jameson's? What could less than a thousand horsemen achieve, when Kitchener could despatch twenty thousand men by railway to turn them back? Botha remained as uncommunicative as Smuts on these questions. The green hills of Natal haunted Botha – just as his father's vineyards around Malmesbury beckoned to Smuts. This was Botha's home country, the place where he had fought his pre-war campaign (fighting with one Zulu army against another), and this was the land of Colenso and Spion Kop.[40]

Botha's march south took him past Piet Retief, and on across the bleak open veld of the south-east Transvaal, still relatively untouched by the war. The pace was too hot for the British columns to intercept him. The pace was also too hot for his own horses. In good weather, they might have stood it. But the horses were weak after the winter; and spring here in Natal, just as in the Cape, several hundred miles to the south-west, turned cruelly pro-British. Far from giving fresh grass to the horses, the cold rain made the roads into rivers; the horses were left shivering and starving. By 14 September, when Botha had reached a farm near Frischgewaagd, east of Utrecht, the transport problem was critical. Four hundred horses of the Bethel and Middelburg Commandos were so knocked up that he had to halt at the farm for several days to let them recover. And, if the rain also hampered the Khakis, the Buffalo River, which marked the Natal frontier, was now in spate. Could they ford it? Or should they splash on through the mud towards Zululand?

Botha's first target was the British camp at Dundee, ten miles the Natal side of the river. No doubt he planned to get fresh food and horses there, and then to cut the railway at Glencoe, on the main line between Durban and Pretoria, one of the two main arteries of the British army. But the rain ruined everything. He had arranged a dawn attack on the same lines as the attack on Sir Penn Symons's position two years before. Yet his horses were too weak to attempt the night march. So Botha's commando splashed on towards Zululand, hoping to dodge the British patrols and cross the Buffalo River somewhere to the south.[41]

Major Hubert Gough, the nearest British commander, had plenty of 'dash', the quality Kitchener liked to see (and seldom found) in his cavalry COs. K had cabled him the moment the Intelligence at Pretoria got wind of Botha's plan to invade Natal: Gough's Mounted Infantry 'to entrain without delay for the north'. Gough accepted the mission without enthusiasm. He and the 24th MI battalion were exhausted by the strain of twenty months' scouring and sweeping the republics. It was not only the monotony ('There is so much sameness about this trekking that it bores one nearly as much to write about as to carry on'), and the hardship of riding all day in the sun and then bivouacking with ice on the ground. Gough was also disgusted with the 'aimlessness' of K's scouring strategy. He also accused his fellow column-commanders of 'funk'. ('They move about in solemn masses down the main roads, expecting and usually fearing (!!) a *battle*, which the Boers would not and could not fight.') Now the prospect of a wild-goose-chase after Botha through the beastly hills of Natal did not entice Gough. He had just written off to Pretoria (privately, of course, to his friend Major Birdwood): any hope of a 'quiet billet' among the red-tabs up there?[42]

Gough's temper did not improve after his battalion had completed their five-hundred-mile journey in railway trucks to Natal. One Irish company got drunk on beer while entraining at Kroonstad; the other Irish company got drunk on port while detraining at Dundee. What an 'awful pity', he thought, that he could not, like a Boer commandant, order his men to be flogged! He marched them off in pouring rain to De Jager's Drift, a depressing little camp guarding the main crossing-point of the Buffalo River, astride the old Natal–Transvaal frontier; Botha and up to seven hundred men were reported by Natal Intelligence to be threatening an attack.

Gough himself doubted he would have any such luck. He expected the Intelligence were exaggerating; they generally were. Next day, 17 September, he was astonished – and delighted – to find Boers after all.[43] As his three companies splashed forward to reconnoitre the plain on the Transvaal side of the Buffalo, he saw some two to three hundred Boers riding northwards from the stony ridge, called Scheeper's Nek, astride the main road leading to Vryheid.[44] Through his binoculars, Gough watched them off-saddle at a farm close to Blood River Poort, the mouth of the gorge a few miles from the meeting of the Blood River and the Buffalo River. He sent a message the few miles back to Lieutenant-Colonel H. K. Stewart, who was holding 450 MI in reserve: he could 'surprise' the enemy; he would gallop to the laager and give Brother Boer a good 'dusting'. After months and months of trekking, there was, at last, hope of battle.[45]

It was 2.00 p.m. on 17 September. An hour or two earlier, 350 miles away to the south-west, Smuts launched his own desperate charge at Elands River Poort, to break free from the cordon of the 17th Lancers. Now, at Blood River Poort, it was Botha's turn.

He had no field-guns, and only a thousand men. He had set no trap for the Khakis. But he saw his chance. The Khakis were still in the minority; soon the main British army, outnumbering his burghers by ten or fifteen to one, would be brought up by railway against them. He must turn the Khakis' chosen weapon – surprise – back against them. Three hundred of his burghers off-saddled at the farm. Meanwhile, his main force, seven hundred men under his own command, galloped round the right-hand company of Khakis, who were holding a ridge. In twenty minutes, they had cut through them, as neatly as a man rolls up a carpet or a plough peels open a field of stubble.[46]

From the centre of the bare plain, Gough watched, aghast. Botha's men, hundreds of them. Swarming all over the ridge. He rode across to his two field-guns. The gunners were trying to fire case-shot, but could not find a target in the confusion. Some Boers galloped up, pointed their guns at the gunners and shouted, 'Hands up!' Gough put his hand down to his holster; it was empty; his batman had forgotten to put in his revolver that morning. 'Shoot them, shoot them,' Gough shouted, with the impotence of a man in a nightmare. Lieutenant Price-Davies, a subaltern of the 60th, drew his revolver, but was shot in the shoulder at point-blank range. (For this he later earned a VC.) Gough threw himself off his horse and tried to use it as a shield. But Botha's men had overrun them completely.

The nightmare of humiliation passed soon into farce. Gough, stripped of his helmet, field-glasses, coat, riding-boots and gaiters, played hide-and-seek with his captors under cover of darkness. He had grabbed someone else's boots, five sizes too large, and with only a shred of a bootlace. He hid in an ant hole. The Boers ignominiously pulled him out. Later, when it grew inky black, he made good his escape, and groped his way, with blistered feet, to the nearest British patrol.[47]

Next day, up and down South Africa, the telegraph lines were humming with the news of Gough's disaster: Captain Mildmay and 19 men killed, 5 officers and 19 men wounded (including 3 officers mortally wounded), 6 other officers and 235 men taken prisoner.

It was the most humiliating reverse since Clements's smash-up at Nooitgedacht nine months before.[48]

But for Botha, it was less than enough. He had captured 180 Lee Metford rifles, thirty thousand rounds of ammunition, two hundred horses, and two field-guns, as well as the Khakis. What he desperately needed was fresh horses, food and fodder, and a smooth path into Natal. He found the British horses were almost useless – ridden to death by Gough's MI. The field-guns were too cumbersome for raiding warfare. So were the prisoners. They were simply stripped and sent back after Gough to their lines. Botha's own ponies were badly knocked up. The icy spring rains beat down on Natal as they beat down on Cape Colony. To break into Natal, Botha had to ford the Buffalo somewhere and launch his men down the same road over the Biggarsberg towards Ladysmith that he and Joubert and their fifteen thousand men had taken two years before. Now he decided his force was too weak to cross the Buffalo. Three hundred of his sick ponies had to be sent northwards back to Vryheid. The rest continued south-east, inside the old Transvaal frontier, feeling their way for some opening into Natal not blocked by the British.[49] The rain continued, too. The men were cold and wet and hungry, and Botha decided to raid two British camps – 'Fort Itala' and 'Fort Prospect' – astride the Zulu frontier.

It was at this point, on 26 September, that Botha succumbed to a fit of over-confidence quite as serious as Gough's – more fatal, in fact, for the Boers than Blood River Poort for the British. Botha had been told by the local burghers that these two British laagers would be easy meat, because they were not entrenched. Actually, they had not only good trenches, but good men to man them, too. Botha's blunder was the result of poor intelligence, a failure that was usually the prerogative of the Khakis. To cap it all, the burghers threw themselves with British-style recklessness against the trenches at Fort Itala. They lost at least fifty-eight men, killed and wounded. The attack on Fort Prospect was equally brave and equally futile.[50] Botha's demoralized men scampered hastily back into the Transvaal, just as a whole herd of Khakis, fifteen thousand strong, lumbered up to overwhelm them. The invaders were now fugitives once more.

'I must report that it was impossible for our commandos to enter Natal,' said Botha in his official report on the expedition, 'because the enemy were aware of our plans, and he already had laagers [forces] just opposite all the drifts of the Buffalo River. ... We had specially unfavourable weather; for 11 days it rained almost day and night. This weakened the horses very much. ...'[51] The rain certainly added to Botha's problems, as it added to Smuts's. Yet the Natal invasion could never have been more than a forlorn hope. What positive military advantage could one thousand men achieve there, except to buy a little time for the Boers? And the raid itself had cost Botha some of his best men and brought the others into a *cul de sac*. The Zulus stood grimly on this south-east borderland, twelve thousand assegai-waving tribesmen, instructed by the British to repel invasion of their own territory.[52]

The fiasco of the Natal 'invasion' must only have confirmed what Botha, in his heart, had soberly recognized ever since Middelburg. There *were* no other options: only to fight to the end or to accept Kitchener's peace.

Smuts, the enthusiast, had persuaded his colleagues that the raid into Cape Colony might achieve much more than the raid on Natal. It would not merely take the pressure off the main commandos in the republics. It would also bring a dramatic accession of strength to the cause by adding thousands of colonial Afrikaners to their ranks. Now, by the standards he had set himself, Smuts failed more completely than Botha.

In October, he broke south through Haig's cordons in the direction of Port Elizabeth. In November (after a nightmare of hair's-breadth escapes), he found a refuge from his pursuers near Calvinia in the Western Cape.[53] But what military advantage had Smuts achieved by marching two hundred men across the length and breadth of Cape Colony, except in striking a blow to British pride?

Smuts himself put the best gloss, understandably, on his epic march. In his first report to the two governments, he listed his achievements and claimed: 'The feeling of my burghers is strong, although they have perhaps suffered more heavily than any other commando in this war, and they look forward hopefully to the future.'[54] In his secret report, by contrast, he admitted his failure in the main task he had set himself: to pave the way for De la Rey's arrival in the colony with a large Transvaal army, and the official establishment of a Cape Afrikaner government as a third belligerent in the war. The colonial Afrikaners had decided not to join the commandos. This, Smuts claimed, was due to the shortage of horses.[55] The underlying reason, which he did not admit, was that most colonial Afrikaners now believed that the republics were too weak to achieve anything by prolonging the struggle.

In January, Smuts was still writing bravely to De la Rey as though he were master of the whole west and north-west of Cape Colony. Given reinforcements, they could soon invade the rich southern heartland of the Cape, including his own homeland, Malmesbury. And Smuts claimed that he was sure there had been a dramatic change of heart in Britain, where 'not only the English people but also the leading men are getting sick of the endless war'. The Liberals wanted to offer new peace terms which would preserve the republics' independence. The terrible death-rate in the concentration camps, said Smuts, had turned other nations bitterly anti-British, and even influential supporters of Salisbury's government were shocked by this fearful disaster. 'Perhap's God's will,' he told De la Rey, 'is that through our ill-treated women and children a decisive end should be made to this war.'[56]

But in his heart of hearts, Smuts must now have recognized that no diversions outside the two republics (military campaigns in the Cape like his own, or political campaigns by Boer sympathizers inside Britain) could alter the grim logic of Kitchener's 'bag'.[57] In the twelve months since Kitchener had taken over, he had hammered and beaten and ground down the Boer forces to about twenty-five thousand – roughly half their number when Roberts had left.[58] If this process went on, the end would be bitter indeed.

To his brother, Kosie, Smuts sent a sombre letter of farewell: 'I have hardly any hope of seeing you in this life.'[59]

CHAPTER 41
Blockhouse or Blockhead?

The New Colonies,
November 1901 – March 1902

> 'This war is fast degenerating into the same kind of dacoit
> hunt we used to have in Burmah. The Boer is becoming
> just as cold-blooded a ruffian as the dacoit was and his
> wholesale slaughter of Kaffirs ... has I think forfeited his
> right to be considered a belligerent. I found the bodies of
> four Kaffir boys none of them over 12 years of age with
> their heads broken in by the Boers and left in the Kraal of
> their fathers. Strong measures will be required to stop this
> slaughter.'
>
> Colonel Rawlinson to Lord Roberts
> 28 August 1901

'Who would have thought when you left Johannesburg,' wrote Kitchener
ruefully to Roberts at the end of November 1901, 'that I should be *a year* in
command with the war still going on?'[1]

Then, a few days later, Kitchener saw, at long last, light at the end of the
tunnel. The war should be over by April. This was the forecast he made to
Brodrick on 13 December. 'I think we can fairly count on the Boers not keeping
us here after April.' He confided to Roberts by the same post: 'I think about
April we shall have pretty well exhausted the boers [sic], and so enclosed them in
areas that they will find it very hard to keep up much form of resistance. . . . The
blockhouse system is telling very well. . . .'[2] And, by April, the South African
winter would be upon the survivors. Then the drought and the frost would burn
the grass as yellow as a Coloured man's skin, adding the final touch to the havoc
created by Kitchener. No grass, no war – was the equation as simple as this?
Now that the guerrillas were almost completely dependent on grass to feed their
ponies (the hay had vanished in smoke), surely winter must freeze them to
immobility.

For once, Kitchener's forecast was almost correct, though there were to be
other reasons than blockhouses, and no grass, that were to bring the Boers to
their knees. And there were to be dark days in March, when the light in the
tunnel would flicker and fail, before Kitchener finally escaped, sadder and
perhaps even wiser, from the humiliations of victory in South Africa.

The turning-point of the guerrilla war – that is, the beginning of Kitchener's final, successful phase – had begun in late November. It followed a phase of intense frustration, which precipitated one of those extraordinary spasms of near-despair on Kitchener's part, no less alarming to his staff because these volcanic eruptions were so rare.

It was soon after Kitchener read the news of Buller's downfall. Not that this event depressed him. He was in close enough alliance with the Roberts Ring to know how well this *coup* against Buller could serve his own career. He told Roberts, 'However sorry one may be for Buller, the example will have I am sure a most salutary effect throughout an army where ... strict discipline is much wanted.'[3] However, the Press campaign against Buller had whetted the Press's appetites. In early November, Kitchener learnt that an article had appeared in *The Spectator* denouncing him for incompetence, and calling for his removal.

These spiteful attacks in *The Spectator*, perhaps prompted by Milner, a close friend of the editor's, confirmed K's fears that the government had lost patience with him and were preparing to throw him to the wolves. He had, it must be said, more or less invited this fate. Ever since the collapse of the Middelburg peace talks, Kitchener had been conducting the war under protest: against Milner, for 'vindictively' blocking the amnesty for colonial rebels, which Kitchener believed could have ended the war;[4] against Milner, too, for prematurely restarting the gold-mines at the expense of the war effort;[5] against the War Office, for the tens of thousands of sub-standard horses sent out to South Africa; against Chamberlain, for refusing him a free hand to crush the guerrillas by banishment, confiscation, and execution.[6]

There was ill-concealed resentment in every line of Kitchener's reports to Brodrick in mid-October: 'Extermination ... is a long and very tiring business ... they seem as fanatically disposed to continue the war as ever, and I fear it can only end by our catching all or almost all of them. It is hard work for our men... if you think that someone else could do better out here, I hope you will not hesitate to for a moment in replacing me. I try all I can but it is not like the Soudan and disappointments are frequent—'[7]

Indeed, it was not the Sudan. And it was not so much a question of disappointment as of desperation. The Cabinet's overriding priority, to which Kitchener was supposed to be committed, was to cut the cost of the war by cutting the number of troops in South Africa. Kitchener wanted *more* troops. On 1 November, he sent an SOS: 'I now think the remainder of the Boers are so determined to resist to the last that it would be admirable to send any troops you can spare.'[8] A few days later, he cabled Roberts secretly: '... the strong rumours current everywhere that I am to be relieved of my command. ... Perhaps a new commander might be able to do something more than I can do to hasten the end of the war.'[9]

Roberts's swift reassurance ('Believe me we all have absolute confidence in you and are satisfied you have done and are doing all that is possible to hasten end of war') was followed by a list of promised reinforcements: two infantry battalions, three companies of MI and possibly more MI, cavalry and infantry from India. But it soon emerged that all these 'reinforcements', except the three companies of MI, had to be exchanged for troops already in South Africa.[10] And Kitchener was not so foolish as to doubt that the Cabinet was considering whether to sack him. He was cheered to learn that Roberts was sending out his special favourite, Ian Hamilton, to act as Kitchener's Chief of Staff.[11] 'I blame myself,' cabled Roberts, 'for not having tried to provide you with assistance of the valuable nature you so generously afforded me.'[12] But Kitchener must have guessed that part of Hamilton's job was to report back privately a vital question to the Cabinet: was K on the verge of a breakdown?

The last straw that broke Kitchener's self-confidence was the 'smash-up' of Lieutenant-Colonel G. E. Benson and his column at Bakenlaagte, in the Eastern Transvaal, news of which filtered through to Pretoria on 1 November. 'It is the usual story,' K reported to Roberts bitterly. In fact, he had found it much more disheartening than recent disasters, including the cutting-up of Gough's column in Natal, and of Lord Vivian and the 17th Lancers in the Cape. Benson was virtually his best commander, led by the best Intelligence Officer.

The Boers observe the movements of a column from a long way off, only showing very few men, then having chosen some advantage, in this case it was the weather, then charge in with great boldness, and the result is a serious casualty list. Benson's was one of the very best columns, and had an excellent and efficient intelligence run by Woolls Sampson [the Uitlander leader]. He knew every inch of the ground having been constantly in that part of the country and my last telegram from him on the 29th was to the effect that the country was clear . . . if a column like Benson's operating 20 miles outside our lines is not safe it is a very serious matter and will require a large addition to our forces to carry on the war . . . what makes me most anxious is, if they can act in this way with Benson's columns, how far easier it would be for them to catch some of my less efficient columns. . . .'[13]

Fortunately, this spasm of near-despair had passed by the time Ian Hamilton himself arrived in Pretoria. By then, the facts about Benson's death at Bakenlaagte were clearer, and they were not, after all, so discouraging to the British, nor so cheering to the Boers. Benson's rearguard had fought heroically, losing 66 men killed and 165 wounded, and sacrificing themselves to save the main column. On their part, the Boers, led by Louis Botha himself, had suffered a heavy loss in the death of General Opperman.[14]

The grand strategy to which Kitchener had now reluctantly applied himself was, in effect, Milner's strategy: to establish 'protected areas', centred on Bloemfontein, Pretoria, and the Rand, and then progressively work outwards from these areas, clearing the country of all guerrillas and restoring civilian life within them. By the end of October 1901, ten thousand square miles in the Transvaal and Northern Orange River Colony, and 4,200 square miles around Bloemfontein, had been officially declared 'absolutely clear' in this fashion.

This new policy was Milner's, the new weapons were Kitchener's. And no patent weapon could have been simpler than the lines of ordinary barbed-wire fence, guarded at intervals by homespun earth-and-iron blockhouses (costing £16 each), which had sprung up at Kitchener's command. The system had originated in January 1901 as a line of fortified posts protecting the railways.

Then Kitchener had developed the network to provide a fence for the protected inner areas of the country itself. In effect, the fence lines of blockhouse-plus-wire served as a linear garrison, a low wall of high-tensile wire, in which wire and the infantryman, stretched to miraculous thinness, could fence out the mounted enemy (provided always, of course, the enemy had no field-guns – or time to use wire-cutters). Kitchener's latest step was to turn part of the system the other way about. On the periphery, the barriers served as offensive, not defensive, weapons; not as cordons to keep out the enemy, but as cages in which to trap them, a guerrilla-catching net stretched across South Africa. By May 1902, there would be over eight thousand blockhouses, covering 3,700 miles, guarded by at least fifty thousand white troops and sixteen thousand African scouts.[15]

Already, by the end of October 1901, despite Kitchener's black moods, the blockhouse system had dramatically improved the strategic map of the war, looked at from a British point of view. The 'bag' had averaged two thousand a month since March. Natal was clear. In Cape Colony, the two thousand-odd guerrillas had been hustled into the two least important areas: the wastelands of the extreme west and extreme north-west. In the Transvaal and the Orange River Colony, the guerrillas were fragmented and powerless to attack even the most remote railway line. Most of the central parts of both new colonies were clear. The grand total of the enemy was believed to have been reduced to ten thousand, at a 'liberal estimate', in both republics. (The actual number of the enemy, including those lying low in their homes, was actually to prove nearly double this figure.)[16]

There were three main centres of resistance: first, in the north-east corner of the ORC, where Steyn and De Wet had gathered 2,000–2,500 men in the plains between Reitz, Lindley, Bethlehem, and Basutoland; second, the semi-deserts of the Transvaal, west of where De la Rey had 2,200 men beyond the Magaliesberg; third, the plains of the Eastern Transvaal, to which Botha had returned after his abortive raid on Natal.

Obviously, it was to crush these leaders and their men that Kitchener attached the highest priority. They were not only the driving force behind the guerrilla war itself; Steyn and De Wet were believed (with reason) to be the principal obstacle to renegotiating peace on Middelburg principles. Hence the vital importance of extending the blockhouse lines rapidly in both new colonies. Progress was indeed rapid. In November, the cleared areas were more than doubled: rising from 10,000 to 14,450 square miles in the Transvaal, from 4,200 to 17,100 square miles in the ORC. Beyond this cordon, the hunted Boers would have only three choices: to try to break through the blockhouse lines, to break back through the mounted infantry pursuing them – or to give up the hopeless struggle and voluntarily pay toll to the 'bag'.[17]

By its nature, the war of the columns had always been a confused and shapeless kind of war, despite the clusters of neat red flags, moved by Kitchener every morning before breakfast on his war map at GHQ. Sometimes, that alarming enemy concentration depicted there proved to be nothing worse than a herd of *blesbok* (wild deer); at other times, the hunted would become hunters in turn (as Gough and Benson had found to their cost) and then vanish again into the veld. Invariably, great expectations ended in a let-down. Yet, with the extension of the blockhouse lines, the 'bag' was once again on the increase (270, 321, 435, 453 in the four weeks ending 23 December), and Kitchener's pendulum swung up again. 'Progress,' he cabled on 5 January, 'though slow, all points to the inevitable conclusion.'[18]

Frustration, the keynote of most wars, whether regular or irregular, took a thousand forms: from Kitchener's helplessness at being unable to give the *coup de grâce* to the guerrillas, to Tommy Atkins's sense of the excruciating boredom of life in the blockhouse. But boredom was the enemy that the Tommy knew best. The regular soldiers who had served in India were inured to this double frustration: the overpowering heat and claustrophobia of the barrack-room, the equally crushing sense of isolation from home. They made the best of the blockhouses. They planted petunias in bully-beef tins; they chalked up the usual facetious names ('Kruger's Castle', 'Rundle's Starving Eighth', 'Chamberlain's Innocent Victims') and they wrote letters home, tens of thousands of them, stiff-upper-lip letters for the most part, to be collected by the weekly mail wagon. Of course, life remained terribly tedious. There was little to gossip about on the telephone that connected every blockhouse to its neighbours. But there were pets to be looked after: dogs, goats, pigs, even lizards. There were the convoy's visits. And just occasionally, a whirlwind in the night, a summer storm rattling the tin-cans on the trip-wires so that they rang like a xylophone, and, setting off a fusillade of shots into the darkness, there was a visit from a party of guerrillas.[19]

Among Kitchener's scattered mounted columns, the isolation intensified the sense of bitterness against an enemy who would not fight, or broke the rules when he did. The sight of the bodies of British scouts – mainly black or Coloured but occasionally white men – taken prisoner and then shot by the Boers, started a spiral of reprisals. It was an open secret that some of the irregular colonial corps made it a principle not to take prisoners. '"Hold up your hands, men," said Charlie Ross.' Captain Ross was second-in-command of a Canadian corps of Scouts raised by Major 'Gat' Howard. 'We held up our hands. "I want you to take an oath with me not to take another prisoner," said Charlie. We held up our hands.' These Canadians, according to the story of one of the sergeants, had just found the bullet-riddled body of 'Gat' Howard, shot after capture.

The guerrilla war was fast brutalizing both adversaries. The worst scandals on the British side concerned colonial irregulars – Australians, Canadians and South Africans – whose official contingents, ironically, had won a reputation for gallantry in so many set-piece battles. The most notorious case involved a special anti-commando unit, raised by Australians to fight in the wild northern Transvaal, and called the Bush Veldt Carbineers. Six of its officers (five Australians, one Englishman) were court martialled for multiple murder. The facts were admitted: in August 1901, twelve Boers, earlier taken prisoner, had been shot by the Carbineers on the orders of their officers. The Australians'

Left Lord K and 'the Brat', Captain Maxwell. 'K made a vile fuss about my appearance', Maxwell wrote about this photograph.
Below Christiaan De Wet (second from right) and staff.

Above Boer children in a concentration camp. One in five died.
Left Flogging an African tied to a wagon wheel, an everyday occurrence in British and Boer camps.
Right Cape rebels, sentenced to death, sent to Pretoria. Fifty-one were executed.

Kruger's farewell, October 1900.

Milner, the new master of
the Transvaal, October 1900.

defence: as a reprisal, shooting prisoners was now accepted practice. Two of the Australian officers, Lieutenants 'Breaker' Morant and Handcock,* were executed in February 1902, on the orders of Kitchener. The affair caused an outcry in Australia. There arose a misconception (still current) that foreign political pressures had induced Kitchener to make scapegoats of Morant and Handcock. In fact Kitchener's motives were cruder: evidence of his own army's indiscipline drove him wild with frustration.

Kitchener's own sense of isolation at GHQ had reached a climax. Even with his 'band of boys', he found ordinary human contact impossible. Only 'the Brat', Captain Frank Maxwell, VC, his fair-haired young ADC, had found a way to Kitchener's heart, if heart it was. 'He is awfully shy,' the Brat wrote home, describing K. 'He really feels nice things, but to put tongue to them … he would rather die.'[20] Exactly what K felt for the Brat will never be known. There was the odd incident when K, who normally detested being photographed, insisted on being taken sitting docilely beside the Brat. (To the Brat's embarrassment, he made a 'vile fuss about my appearance. "*Good* heavens, your hair's all over the place."'[21] At any rate, the Brat was the apple of K's eye. As a kind of jester at Kitchener's court, he was allowed to take liberties forbidden to senior generals. 'We are now High Commissioner of South Africa,' the Brat wrote home in May, and explained: 'In talking at or to K., we always say "we made a speech", "we drew so much pay", "we are this or that".'[22] Of course, this did not endear the Brat to the rest of the staff ('Poor boy, I fear his brain is not his strong point'),[23] which further appealed to the Chief's oriental sense of humour.

K had also acquired another pet: perversely, he had insisted on rescuing two lost baby starlings that had fallen down the chimney of his bedroom at GHQ. One died. He made the GHQ staff, to their intense disgust, put the other in a cage and look after it. Even the Brat's sense of loyalty was strained by this chore – and by the sight of the Chief fussing about worms all day, and chirping at the starling through the wire, and rolling his porcelain-blue eyes at the little beggar, leaving the war to look after itself. In due course, the bird escaped – while the Chief was on a visit to Pietersburg – to the consternation of everyone at GHQ. The Brat was told to draft the telegram to prepare K for this shock. 'C-in-C's humming bird … broke cover and took to the open. Diligent search instituted; biped still at large. Mily. Secy. desolate; ADC in tears. Army sympathizes.' On his return, K seemed to take the matter stoically. But he rushed through the accumulation of two days' telegrams, then organized a great drive ('a small army of staff officers, menials and orderlies', grumbled the Brat) to hunt down the missing bird. It was found at 7.00 p.m., having taken refuge in a neighbour's chimney – but not before the Chief himself was covered in mud, 'having repeatedly fallen prone in wet flower-beds'. Earlier, K remarked breathlessly, 'I've never been so fond of that bird as since it's been loose.'[24]

Towards De Wet, Botha – and the rest of the Boers still loose on the veld –

---

* In June 1970 I talked to the officer, Lieutenant (later Colonel) Thompson, who had commanded the firing squad. He described Handcock as a 'charming young man'. I was shown the cigarette case he gave Thompson before he was taken out to be shot.

Kitchener gave equally dogged pursuit. In December there was some good news from that front. Colonel Rawlinson, one of the 'band of boys', had been given an 'extra mobile column' of two thousand mounted men, co-ordinated by Major-General Bruce Hamilton. Few of the eighty-odd column commanders had so dominated the columns' score-board as Rawlinson's (apart from the unfortunate Benson), and that month Rawlinson had excelled himself in three dramatic *coups* against Benson's old adversaries in the Eastern Transvaal. Rawlinson's night raiding tactics were a model for the British army – and almost indistinguishable from the tactics now adopted by the Boers. Here was the modern counterpart of the cavalry charge (charging with rifles, instead of the *arme blanche*), combined with the long-term mobility that had always come naturally to the Boer with his rifle, his blanket, his biltong, and his pony. Ever since September, Kitchener had strained every nerve to make his columns as mobile as their opponents. Now Rawlinson, like Scobell in the Cape, had proved it was possible to leave tents and food wagons behind them for up to six days, relying, except for medical supplies, guns, and ammunition, on what his men could carry on their saddles.[25]

March at night, gallop the enemy's laager at dawn. These were the dazzlingly simple new rules of the game. But success demanded not only an extra mobility. The other ingredient, as always, was extra intelligence. In this respect, Kitchener's mobile columns had come to be deeply in debt to Colonel David Henderson's reorganization of the Field Intelligence Department. When Roberts had left South Africa, this department had only numbered thirty officers and 250 white subordinates. Now there were over two thousand white troops serving in the FID (132 officers, and 2,321 white troops, at the end of the war). There were also thousands of Africans employed. The key to the success of the columns was the column's Intelligence Officer, and the key to his success, in turn, was the skill with which he organized his black scouts, guides, and spies.[26]

Rawlinson's new Intelligence Officer was Benson's former one, that eccentric Uitlander, Colonel Aubrey Woolls-Sampson, ex-gold-miner, ex-Reformer, ex-Commander of the ILH, a man better suited to serve as the hero of a novel by Rider Haggard than as an irregular soldier. As commanding officer of the Imperial Light Horse, Woolls-Sampson had proved a severe trial to Kitchener – indeed, his idiosyncrasies had become so alarming that Kitchener had cabled an SOS to London asking for him to be removed. But now, as the leader of a team of specially paid African scouts (specially paid, that is, out of his own pocket), Woolls-Sampson had pulled off successive feats of intelligence. Three times in succession, as Rawlinson reported to Kitchener, Woolls-Sampson had led them at 3.40 a.m. 'bang on top of the laager'. The result: of the total of 756 Boers, the official bag throughout South Africa in the second and third weeks of December, no less than three hundred had fallen to Rawlinson's column, and two other small columns under Bruce Hamilton's overall command, for a loss of only three men wounded in Rawlinson's column.[27]

Rawlinson's account of the night raid made by the column of 2,000 mounted troops, 6 guns, and no less than 450 Africans illustrates the exhilaration of the new-style war, hunting down the Boers like 'game':

Dec 10. Tuesday. Bethel (Transvaal)

We struck the road all right soon after midnight but there was not a sign of a spoor on it so we turned north towards Trichardtsfontein – It was three thirty when the [African] boys that [Woolls] Sampson had sent on returned to say the boers were all there – a tremour [sic] of excitement ran through us all and I got the 2nd MI up quickly on my right whilst I sent [Colonel 'Bimbash'] Stewart off well to the left. It was just light enough to see as we began to trot on, and then just at 3.45 AM, as we came over the rise, the whole of the Boer laager lay at our feet only some 800 yards off. The Mounted Infantry let go a cheer and a whoo-hoop which must have been a rude awakening to the laager – a few odd shots, the whiz of one or two bullets and the whole of our line of over 2000 mounted men set off at a gallop, yelling with delight – we never waited to shoot – The more the Boers shot the more we yelled – My orders were that none of the men were on any account to stop at the laager, there was to be no looting of wagons or waiting to shoot, our objective was to be the mounted boers and the gun we heard was with them –

I don't think I have ever seen a prettier or more exhilarating sight than that was in the grey of dawn – The M.I. all streaming away just like a pack of hounds and giving tongue like Red Indians – we had a good long gallop of nearly 7 miles – The horses did well and we were rewarded by collecting 53 prisoners ... only 6 got away – we killed 4 and had one officer, 8th M.I., slightly wounded in the leg. . . . Having stopped the hunt and collected the 'game' we went back to the laager. . . . There we found some 67 more prisoners about 3000 cattle and some 30 carts and wagons. . . . The Chief will be delighted and W[oolls] Sampson deserves the utmost credit for having led us so well.

Rawlinson added a chilling footnote 'The stand cost the Boers 16 killed for *our men were angry and shot freely* when they got close up.'[28]

By the end of December, Botha's commandos in the Eastern Transvaal had been so crippled by these raids, that Kitchener decided to transfer Rawlinson and Woolls-Sampson to a still more important sector: the north-east corner of the Orange River Colony, where Steyn and De Wet, the twin spirits of Boer resistance, had for months been able to baffle their pursuers. Meanwhile, a new British humiliation had been suffered in that district, demonstrating how De Wet, despite all his handicaps, still had sharp teeth when he found a chance of using them.

De Wet himself has left a lively account of his exploits that summer. The blockhouse system, he claimed, did not worry him. Far from it. He called it the '*blockhead*' system. 'The building of these blockhouses cost many thousand pounds, and still greater were the expenses incurred in providing the soldiers in them with food. . . . And it was all money thrown away! and worse than thrown away ... this wonderful scheme of the English prolonged the war for at least three months.'

It was their excellent African Intelligence and their new raiding tactic, the tiger-spring on the laager at night, that alarmed De Wet. From May 1901 onwards, he knew that British column-commanders had made a whole series of *coups* against the Free State laagers, using this tactic: indeed, it was, directly or indirectly, responsible for much of the 'bag'. (Somewhat ruefully, De Wet had adopted Kitchener's picturesque phrase.) De Wet's reply was to borrow the tiger-spring tactic for his own purposes. He needed what guerrillas traditionally needed: fresh horses, food, and clothing. So the blockhouse system – not so much the blockhouses themselves as their supporting network of ox-wagon convoys and protecting columns – seemed to provide a heaven-sent opportunity.[29]

During November, desultory sweeping movements had been conducted by the British columns, which De Wet found no difficulty in side-stepping. Fourteen columns marched and counter-marched. Hundreds of engineers (and thousands of African labourers) continued to push out the blockhouse lines – bobbing across the veld, like floats supporting a net at sea.[30] De Wet lay low. He had to conserve his men's and his horses' strength.

At the heart of the north-eastern corner of the Free State there is an archipelago of three small towns – Lindley, Bethlehem, and Reitz – grouped in a triangle forty miles across. It was here that, ever since June 1900, De Wet had found the safest base from which to conduct his raids. Little was now left of the towns themselves: in Lindley, for example, every building, including the large church, had been burnt by one side or the other. But the grass of the district, dry and brown, even in early summer, was good enough to support De Wet's threadbare little force, if they dispersed among the neighbouring farms. On 28 November, De Wet called a *krijgsraad* for the leaders: General Michael Prinsloo, with Commandants Olivier and Rautenbach of the Bethlehem Commando; Commandant Van Coller, with the Heilbron Commando; Commandant Hermanus Botha from Vrede, and others. The *krijgsraad* took place at Blijdschap, near Reitz. The leaders decided to seize the first chance to launch a concentrated attack, De Wet's first serious attempt to take the offensive since early in 1901. The strength of his own main force was seven hundred.[31] Pitted against him were at least twenty thousand men, including his own brother, ex-General Piet De Wet, now fighting for the British as one of General Andries Cronje's National Scouts. But the columns were, of course, scattered in fragments all over the North-eastern Free State.[32] De Wet waited and watched for his chance.

The place he found it was near Bethlehem, and the time, grimly apposite, was Christmas Day. Indeed, this opportunity was a Christmas present from the local British commanders. Clearly, the most vulnerable point of the incomplete blockhouse line was the head: that is, the unsupported end on which the engineers were still working. Just before Christmas, General Rundle had half completed the eastern half of the great line, 160 miles long, which was being pushed from the railhead at Harrismith to link up with the line from Kroonstad. The blockhouse head on the eastern side had reached Tweefontein, a farm straddling a series of kopjes about twenty-five miles east of Bethlehem. To cover the engineers, Rundle had been allocated a weak force, mixed in quality as well as type. He had further weakened them by dividing them into four groups: the main force (four hundred yeomanry and two guns, commanded by Major

Williams) encamped at Groenkop, a two hundred-foot knob of a hill commanding the convoy road from the south; Rundle's own force (270 Grenadier Guards,
60 MI, and a gun, plumped down alongside the wagon road); a few more
infantry (150 of the East Yorks) directly guarding the actual head of the blockhouse line; and a regiment of 400 irregulars, the ILH, stationed at Elands River
bridge, thirteen miles to the east.[33]

Any of these three weak detachments, separated by so many miles from the
fourth, would have made a tempting prey for De Wet. But it was the lines of
white tents in the yeomanry camp at Groenkop, the bully beef tins and cases of
rum, that looked especially appetizing to the hungry and thirsty burghers. In
theory, it should have been a natural strong-point, this craggy hill, commanding
such a Claude-like prospect: the wagon road cutting across the raw plain, the
tangled chasms called Tiger Kloof, the blue rim of the Langeberg Mountains to
the south. But it was a lesson to be learnt from all South African kopjes (a lesson
still not learnt, despite Majuba, Spion Kop, and Caesar's Camp) that kopjes were
dangerous allies for the British. Attack the steep side of the kopje, the side where
attack is least expected and the cover, at the same time, is best. This had long
been the Boers' guiding principle. At Groenkop, the craggy west face of the hill
seemed insurmountable, yet, in fact, there was the line of a gully to help the
burghers scramble up to the summit. Negligently, the British had failed to
station pickets below this face.[34] De Wet made this discovery after three days of
carefully reconnoitring his prey. Then, at 2.00 a.m. on the morning of Christmas Day, half-concealed by a hazy moon, the tiger left Tiger Kloof – and sprang.

De Wet described what followed:

When we had gone up about half-way we heard the challenge of a sentry:
'Halt, who goes there?'
My command rang out through the night – 'Burghers, storm.'
The word was taken up by the burghers themselves, and on all sides one heard, 'Storm,
storm.'
It was a never-to-be-forgotten moment. Amidst the bullets which we could hear
whistling above and around us, the burghers advanced to the top calling out, 'Storm,
Storm.'[35]

Never-to-be-forgotten was indeed the word. Sixty-nine years later, Trooper
Bowers, a survivor of the massacre, recalled on tape that same breath-catching
moment, looking from the opposite side:

Well, at 2 o'clock in the morning I was awakened by a shot. . . . The sentry who shouted
'Halt, who goes there', he fired the shot, and I think that woke me up, and immediately
after that there was a fusillade and the bullets were ripping through the tents all the way
down the slope, and I was in the top one.
I think there was about 14 of us in the tents and we had got our breeches on, and I seized
the rifle (the rifles were piled up around the tent pole), I seized the first rifle I could get hold
of a rushed out, and thinking the top of the hill was our strong point I made for the top
of the hill. But of course it was already in the hands of the Boers. And when I got near the
top, I could see by the stars there and the flashes from their rifles, hundreds of them, I was
on the wrong track. Bullets were whistling round me like an overturned bee-hive. Well,
there were some oat-sacks lying about, sacks full of oats (which of course were no

protection whatever) and there was one solitary sack by itself and I plumped down straight on my belly behind this sack, and there was another chap there, and behind this one sack we cuddled ourselves to try to get a bit of shelter.

Well, this chap and I were cuddling one another when a bullet went through his stomach – tore the oat sack and went through his stomach. We were cuddled close together, and he yelled in his agony – and he was very quickly dead.

Well, there were a few more oat sacks . . . and behind them were three men. One was Lt. Watney, a young fellow of 17, a very dandy young fellow whom we used to make fun of; he was in the Middlesex Yeomanry. He died most bravely. When the Boers came shouting and shooting, shouting and shooting as they ran down the slope, young Watney with his revolver in his hand shouted: 'Come on boys, charge!' Well it was of course a very noble thing to say but perfectly ridiculous. And he and his two men ran out, and I ran across to join him. . . . I was only a few yards from him, only a few yards, and the Boers were all round us. And they put in a volley into us. They riddled those 3 poor chaps. . . . Yet not a single bullet touched me. And the next moment (of course it was hardly daylight, hardly daylight) somebody had ripped off my bandolier of cartridges and snatched my rifle out of my hand. And all the time the bullets were coming up from the bottom of the hill, from our fellows. . . . [The Boers] said get in that tent, get in that tent, and don't move (they could all speak English, of course, the Boers) and I got into the tent, and after that other fellows began coming in. . . . And presently a black-bearded chap with a *sjambok* in his hand came and put his head in the tent and said, 'Don't move or we'll shoot you!' And when he'd gone, the sentry said 'Don't you know who that was? . . . That was General Christiaan De Wet.'[36]

By daylight, Trooper Bowers saw the camp, now a terrible sight. The Boers (like the Boers that Hickie fought at Bothaville) had used expanding bullets. Captain Bryce had the bottom of his face shot away. Other men had their stomachs ripped open. Bowers, who helped carry the wounded to a makeshift hospital, was soon caked in blood from head to foot. But for Bowers – at any rate – the horrors dissolved in the morning sun. The British prisoners were struck by the incongruous dress of De Wet's men: they were so short of clothes that many were wearing the poke bonnets and black dresses of the Boer *vrouw*. Bowers himself was stripped of his uniform and sent back to Rundle's camp without a stitch of clothing.[37]

Major Williams's disaster at Tweefontein depressed Kitchener, who was afraid it might give the Boers new heart. The disaster was blamed on Williams's 'carelessness', and no doubt this was the principal cause. If the pickets had been stationed at the bottom of the hill as well as on the top, the camp could never have been surprised. Christmas 'slackness', snorted Kitchener. He told Brodrick, 'It is very sad and depressing that the boers are able to strike such blows, but I fear . . . we shall always be liable to something of the sort from the unchecked rush of desperate men at night.'[38]

Then it became clear that De Wet's *coup*, like Botha's and Smuts's before him, had only marginally impeded progress. Of this the January bag seemed conclusive evidence: below the December average, yet still reasonable, totalling 378, 327, 255, 426 in the four weeks.[39]

Kitchener stuck doggedly to his steam-roller strategy. Indeed, the humiliation at Tweefontein only sharpened his appetite to have the great machine made ready to go. As soon as the blockhouse lines were safely completed, the new experiment in steel and barbed wire – that is, forcing the enemy up against the network of blockhouse lines – could at last begin.

By 5 February, the steam-roller was ready.[40] The Field Intelligence Department reported De Wet and Steyn to be still based at Elandskop, a hill near Reitz which commanded the country for miles in every direction. Elandskop lay to the east of the centre of an open rectangle roughly fifty miles square: the west side formed by the Kroonstad-Wolvehoek line of railway and blockhouses; the south side, by the Kroonstad-Lindley-Bethlehem blockhouse line; the north side, by the Wolvehoek-Heilbron-Frankfort blockhouse line. It was from the open side – from east to west – that the columns would advance, squeezing the enemy against the blockhouse lines, like a gigantic piston bearing down the walls of a cylinder block. Kitchener had welded together his best MI columns and superimposed four élite commanders to forge this piston: Rawlinson and his veterans of night raids in the south-east Transvaal, the 2nd and 8th MI, strengthened by the 12th and 20th MI, and the two regiments of the ILH; Lieutenant-Colonel Byng, with Lieutenant-Colonel F. S. Garratt's New Zealanders and Lieutenant-Colonel J. W. Dunlop's new-fangled Royal Artillery Mounted Rifles (a new expedient for turning gunners into MI); Colonel Rimington, with another corps of RAMR and Major Charles Ross's Canadian Scouts (the men who had sworn to take no prisoners); Major-General E. L. Elliot, with his whole division. None of these extra-mobile units was cavalry; many were colonial irregulars; they were the élite of the army.

On the night of 5 February, these four super-columns, about nine thousand strong, roughly one man for every ten yards, lined out across the fifty-four miles of the open end of the rectangle. Meanwhile, other columns were sent to reinforce the blockhouses on the three other sides, and seven armoured trains, equipped with guns and searchlights, steamed up and down the railway tracks, like ships in line-ahead formation. At dawn on the sixth, the commanders were given Kitchener's sealed orders: march west.[41]

To Kitchener, waiting at Army HQ, the next two days passed in ill-suppressed frustration. When his column commanders were resting on the blockhouse line, he could at least try to communicate; sometimes, he could even converse with Rawlinson over the open line, using the morse of the telegraph like a telephone.[42] Now, the nine thousand men were virtually incommunicado. Meanwhile, the coils of blue telegraph tape accumulated at Pretoria. London had an insatiable appetite for detail, now Parliament had reassembled:

no 885. From the Secretary of State for War to Lord Kitchener. War Office, 7th February 1902. (Telegram No. 11370, Code.) Question in Parliament. Telegraph numbers of each kind – horses and mules purchased in South Africa.

no 886. From the same to the same. Question in Parliament. Can Merriman of Stellenbosch freely send and receive letters to and from friends and legal advisers in South Africa and England?

no 888. From the same to the same. My no. 11352, code. Question in Parliament. Is Mrs C. De Wet in a refugee camp?

no 890. From the same to the same. 8th February, 1902. Your no. 860. Parliamentary question on Monday. In what camp is Mrs C. De Wet? Is she compulsorily detained, and, if so, on what grounds? Please report fully. . . .

London remained unanswered.[43] Kitchener had left Pretoria with the Brat on the 7th to see for himself the climax of his drive, the moment when the piston met the end of the cylinder. His armoured train, microcosm of the new war machine, rolled into Vredefort Road station that afternoon. The results he pronounced 'considerable', if 'disappointing'. The experiment, in fact, proved part success, part anticlimax. By dawn on 8 February, only 285 out of 2,000-odd Boers had been accounted for (including 140 bagged by Rawlinson's columns on the right). Cattle, it is true, were captured in huge numbers. For the first time, large numbers of exhausted saddle-horses were also brought in, proof of the extent to which the Boers had been hustled. But the blockhouse lines had not held firm. And bagging Steyn and De Wet, the aim which now transcended all other objectives in the war, for Kitchener believed it might end the war at a stroke – this great *coup* still eluded K's grasp. It happened just as Kitchener had himself predicted.[44] De Wet sensed where the human meshes of the net were weakest: in the south-west corner, along the Kroonstad-Lindley blockhouse line. And, with the help of an ordinary pair of wire-clippers, De Wet and Steyn broke the line at 1.00 a.m. on 7 February, and trotted out of the trap, losing only three men out of seven hundred.[45]

Kitchener grimly thrust the gears of the war machine into reverse. A few days spent strengthening the south-west corner, then back eastwards along those sandy tracks towards the starting-point, and beyond it, up to the blue mountain walls of the Drakensberg. These were the new battle orders for the four super-columns. Meanwhile, Kitchener himself steamed off to Cape Colony to hustle General French, to put to him the same question that haunted Kitchener, day and night: how on earth, armed with such a sledge-hammer, could he fail to crack the nut?[46]

Was the blockhouse system in fact a 'blockhead system', a gigantic white elephant, as De Wet claimed? It is a question that cannot be finally answered even today. Certainly the new arrangements still left much to be desired: in the tensile strength of the wire fences (soon to be increased); in the distances between blockhouses (progressively being reduced); above all, in Kitchener's failure to trust senior generals sufficiently to create a proper chain of command (there was no one in the field deputed as overall CO of the four super-columns). On the other hand, the blockhouse system was a great improvement on its predecessor, the aimless sweep-and-scour policy. It was a *system*. Outside the blockhouse lines, keen young column commanders like Colonel Allenby continued to be utterly demoralized by Kitchener's failure to co-ordinate the columns. Here, inside the lines, even K of Chaos had had to accept the discipline of a co-ordinated plan of attack. Moreover, the system automatically provided other advantages: lines of blockhouses served as lines of communication and lines of supply, thus adding both to the mobility and the intelligence of the columns.

Yet the blockhouse system was not in itself a short cut to end the war. There were two other innovations adopted by Kitchener, both forced upon him by circumstances, and arguably just as decisive as moral weapons.

The first was the large-scale use of native troops. In all the myths that have accumulated around the war, none has been as misleading as the idea that it was, as both sides claimed, exclusively a 'white man's war'. From the beginning, Africans had played a central role as non-combatants serving both armies. No one will ever know the total number of black 'Boers', or black British, many of whom were forced labourers. At a conservative estimate, there were forty thousand labourers during the war on each side. At any rate, there were never enough to serve either army willingly, just as there were never enough black labourers to serve the Uitlanders in the mines. White South Africa had always valued the strength of the African's arm, and had often been prepared, as it was cheaper than a white arm, to pay for it. Behind every white artisan there had always been a black man, and so now, behind every white man with a rifle was a black man with a spade, hewing out the white man's trenches, driving his ox wagons and mule wagons, guarding his cattle; diggers and drivers and drovers, as ubiquitous and docile as the cattle themselves – and (to most white men) as invisible.[47]

When an African had a gun in his hand, however, he became suddenly very visible indeed. And it was Kitchener, despite his protestations to the contrary, who had armed the Africans with rifles. The total to which he finally confessed in answer to questions in Parliament came to over ten thousand: 4,618 in Natal, the Orange River Colony and the Transvaal; 2,496 in Cape Colony (both these groups referred to armed men employed as 'watchmen' on railways and block-house lines); 2,939 Cape Coloured men who served as 'scouts and police' on the western blockhouse lines; and an unspecified number of armed 'guards' in the native districts of Cape Colony, Swaziland, and Basutoland.[48]

It was claimed by Kitchener – and was, indeed, to be repeated as a confidential circular in April 1902 – that these men were only armed for their own defence, for 'protection of stock and occupied blockhouses', but were not to be used 'as garrison of blockhouse lines instead of troops'. Such was the claim.[49] The intelligence reports in Cape Colony give the reality. The 'watchers' were the key to the blockhouse line; they took an offensive role; and they certainly accounted for more of the bag than white troops in certain areas. (Sometimes they also inadvertently bagged British troops, it must be said.)[50]

In addition to the 'watchers', and not included in Kitchener's totals, were the Africans who were a large minority in every mobile column. How large, is difficult to say. When Rawlinson had commanded the 2nd and 8th MI in December, his column had contained nearly a quarter Africans: 453, to add to the 79 white officers and 1,380 white troops. Lieutenant-Colonel J. S. S. Barker's column in the ORC consisted of 1,000 Africans and 2,500 white men.[51] No doubt the proportion varied, column by column, but the total number of

Africans serving with Kitchener's ninety-odd columns must have been enormous: twenty thousand, perhaps. Some of them served in the exacting and dangerous role of scouts; in fact, it was these Africans who were the main source of each column's intelligence. It was Kitchener's policy to arm these scouts, like other combatants. In the Transvaal, as we shall see, this did more than protect the scouts. It struck terror into the Boers.

Arming the natives came naturally to Kitchener, the Sirdar, whatever the political embarrassment this caused. In his second innovation, political and military interests coincided better. Some time at the end of 1901, Kitchener reversed his concentration camp policy. No doubt the continued 'hullabaloo' at the death-rate in these concentration camps, and Milner's belated agreement to take over their administration, helped change Kitchener's mind.[52] By mid-December at any rate, Kitchener was already circulating all column commanders with instructions *not* to bring in women and children when they cleared the country, but to leave them with the guerrillas.[53]

Viewed as a gesture to the Liberals, on the eve of the new session of Parliament at Westminster, it was a shrewd political move. It also made excellent military sense, as it greatly handicapped the guerrillas, now that the drivers were in full swing. Indeed, this was perhaps the most effective of all anti-guerrilla weapons, as would soon emerge. It was effective precisely because, contrary to the Liberals' convictions, it was less humane than bringing them into the camps, though this was of no great concern to Kitchener.[54]

A week after the nine thousand men of the four super-columns had rolled westwards towards the Wolvehoek-Kroonstad railway line, they began to roll back in the opposite direction. The same grouse-moor tactics were adopted: every day, the men lined out along the veld, like sportsmen walking-up birds on a moor. Every night, they dug themselves 'butts', to prevent the birds breaking back over their heads. The scale of operations was still more ambitious. Strategically, the obvious weakness of the previous drive (on 5–8 February) was that the aims of the hunters were soon made clear to the hunted; only a few strands of wire, and a handful of private soldiers in a blockhouse (and African Scouts outside it) stood between them and freedom. This time, Kitchener had devised a much more complicated drive. By adding extra columns to the four super-columns, he would first flush the birds back into the main cage from north and south; then all columns would converge on the south-east corner of the box, driving the birds into the angle formed by the Bethlehem-Harrismith blockhouse line and the Drakensberg.

It would be tedious to describe the operations of 16–28 February in detail. This drive, like its predecessor, failed in its principal object: once again, that old fox, De Wet, sidled out of the trap. His men were hustled and harried, and abandoned most of their mobile food supplies, their herds of cattle. Otherwise, the bag of this second drive seemed even thinner than usual. With one exception, every organized commando made good its escape.[55] Then, on the last morning of the drive, 27 February (Majuba Day), one column achieved the greatest single *coup*, judged by the number of prisoners taken, since Hunter's capture of Prinsloo in the Brandwater Basin eighteen months earlier.

When Kitchener and the Brat steamed into Harrismith next morning, they found that Rawlinson had surrounded a laager at Lang Riet, only a few miles from that ill-omened kopje at Tweefontein, and captured 650. The commando, Meyer's, was physically intact, but completely demoralized by the drive. It surrendered to Rawlinson, on condition that the burghers could keep their personal property. The total bag for the drive came to 25,000 cattle, 2,000 horses, 200 wagons and 778 prisoners.[56] It was sweet revenge after Tweefontein. And Kitchener's prisoners were prisoners indeed, gloomy, plodding pedestrians bound for the POW camps – not sent back, naked and blushing, to their friends, like British prisoners, with the compliments of De Wet, after being relieved of their rifles, boots, and clothes.

Kitchener's thunderous third drive, on grouse-moor principles, lasted from 4–11 March, and was a thunderous flop. The central 'cage' was driven westwards for the second time. The bag was a mere hundred. De Wet and Steyn flew to safety once again – and worse. They broke clean out of the Orange River Colony (across no less than three blockhouse lines) and by mid-March had forded the Vaal and touched hands with De la Rey in the Western Transvaal.[57]

By then Kitchener's eyes, too, were turned to that wild and inhospitable region.

There was no blockhouse system, no steam-roller there; impractical to build blockhouses where water was so short. Instead, Kitchener had given 'extra mobile' columns to nine separate column commanders, the most important of whom was that veteran Lord Methuen. Their job was to hunt down De la Rey in his lair between the Mafeking railway and the Magaliesburg.

After two months of desultory manoeuvring, the hunters at last came in touch with the hunted – and for the British the results were utterly disastrous. On 24 February, at Yzer Spruit, De la Rey swooped on a wagon convoy belonging to Lieutenant-Colonel S. B. Von Donop. De la Rey killed, wounded, or captured 12 officers and 369 men, at a loss to his own force of 51.[58] Emboldened by this success, De la Rey then attacked Methuen himself, and crushed his force at Tweebosch on 7 March in circumstances that could hardly have been more humiliating. Most of Methuen's 'extra mobile' men were freshly recruited yeomanry and other irregulars. They panicked and fled. Methuen, wounded in the thigh, was forced to surrender, the first and last British general to be captured by the Boers in the campaign.[59]

The news of Methuen's smash-up at Tweebosch was telegraphed to Kitchener next day, and the news knocked him flat. A column of twelve hundred men, with four field-guns, virtually wiped out: it was the biggest disaster for two years. Kitchener's elastic morale, frayed by months of alternating hope and disappointment, finally snapped.

He shut himself up in his bedroom and refused to see anyone – or eat anything – for two days. Then the Brat managed to coax him out of his hole, and sternly told him that if 'we' felt rotten, as Kitchener himself admitted ('My nerves have gone all to pieces,' were K's own words), then this was quite the most natural thing in the world, as 'we' hadn't eaten a thing for two days. K meekly agreed, and ate a hearty breakfast.[60]

However, it turned out that the Boers, as usual, were unable to turn a tactical victory to any strategic account. De la Rey was driven back onto the defensive. A fortnight later, Kitchener heard that a six-man delegation of Boers, led by Schalk Burgher (acting President of the Transvaal since Kruger had sailed for Europe), were taking the train to Pretoria to talk about ending the war.[61]

CHAPTER 42

Peace 'Betrayed'

Pretoria,
11 April – June 1902

Not by lust of praise or show,
 Not by Peace herself betrayed –
Peace herself must they forgo
 Till that peace be fitly made ...

Rudyard Kipling, *The Pro-Consuls*

There was only one satisfactory way to end the war, Milner told his crèche, and that was 'by winning it'.[1] He now waited, heart in mouth, as the special train carrying Botha, Smuts, De Wet, Steyn, and the other leaders, clanked into Pretoria on the evening of 11 April.[2] Was this victory, the clear-cut military victory that Milner had yearned for ever since 1897, the victory that would give him a free hand to 'break the mould' and recast South Africa, as Cromer had recast Egypt (and, indeed, Milner's hero, Bismarck, had recast Germany)? In other words, had the Boers come to discuss the military details of surrender? Or had they, by contrast, come to bargain about peace?

The idea of peace, on political terms negotiated between governments, filled Milner with a kind of disgust. Peace terms meant compromise – and, as he had admitted to his intimates, 'there is no room for compromise in South Africa'.[3] His loathing for British parliamentary democracy ('that mob at Westminster')[4] was all the keener because of his own sense of helplessness at this supreme moment:

I see things as they are, and recognize that it is a fool's trick to waste the energy and devotion of a 1,000 men in trying to do the impossible, and to keep an Empire for people who are dead set on chucking it away. I could wrestle with Boers for ever. But British infatuation is too much for me. What with our sentimentality, our party system, our Government by Committee, our 'Mandarins', our 'Society' and our Generals.... The game is just hopeless. It's rather hard on the nation, a sound nation as ever was, but that's not enough.... Our political organization is thoroughly rotten, almost non-existent.... Never was there such an absurd waste of power, such ridiculous inconsequence of policy – not for want of men, but for want of any effective central authority, or dominant idea, to make them work together. Joe is a strong man. Under other stars he might be as big as Cavour or Bismarck. But all he can do is maintain himself. K is a strong man, but all he is doing is to paralyse me. Rosebery is not a strong man.... Yet his influence has, in the main, been exceedingly mischievous. He has ruined the Liberal Imperialist movement by putting himself at the head of it, I can't say *leading* it, for he is incapable of leading anything.... After all, the only people who know their own minds, and constantly, if with a pathetic feebleness, strive in the same direction, are our poor old South African loyalists....'[5]

No wonder Milner styled himself 'Sisyphus', and was often talking of abandoning his political dreams, and returning to the pleasant obscurity of private life. Yet now, if this was in fact to be the beginning of peace negotiations, everything depended on him. Could he save South Africa – British South Africa – from a disastrous peace? Above all, could he stop Kitchener from throwing away their own trump card, that *they* had no need to end the war?[6]

Milner was not kept long in suspense. The Boers had, in fact, come to bargain for peace, and he himself was not invited to the first meeting. Yet even Kitchener had to admit that the Boers' proposals were somewhat unreal. On 11 April, the Boer delegates produced a plan for a 'perpetual treaty of friendship and peace' which would settle all the points of difference between governments, including the franchise. The proposal explicitly stated that the Boers did not recognize the annexation of the republics. After desultory argument, the terms of the offer were cabled to Brodrick, and were, of course, rejected out of hand.[7]

It was not until 14 April that Milner, now permitted to negotiate jointly alongside Kitchener, first met his adversaries. He shook hands with them all: the ten leaders of the two republics. He found them surprisingly fit (no doubt to his irritation), all except for Steyn. The proceedings he found 'farcical'. Kitchener, to his disgust, was 'extremely adroit in his management of negotiations, but he does not care what he gives away'.[8] Milner cabled his protests to Chamberlain: they must at all costs try to nail down the Boers – and Kitchener – to the terms of the abortive Middelburg peace conference held the previous year. He asked for 'definite instructions' on the most important points. Above all, they must not go beyond what Kitchener had proposed at Middelburg as regards the length of time the ex-republics would be governed directly as Crown Colonies; they must avoid fixing a date for the restoration of self-government.[9]

Two days later, Milner and Kitchener received the Cabinet's instructions, cabled from London. The cable was almost exactly what Milner had asked for: Middelburg was to be the guiding principle of the conference, and only on the subject of amnesty was there to be any substantial concession. This news was given to the Boers on 17 April. They asked for a general armistice and a safe conduct for the deputies in Europe. Kitchener refused both requests, but agreed to give them facilities – a sort of local armistice – to consult their own burghers.[10] For the Boer negotiators had earlier pointed out that they had no right to discuss the surrender of independence without first consulting the volk, meaning the minority of the burghers still out on commando. (Milner had objected that the prisoners of war should be consulted too. He was out-manoeuvred by Steyn, who asked what would happen if the prisoners decided that the war should be continued, and the fighting burghers that it should not. Laughter.[11]) Then the meeting broke up, without commitment on either side – the Boers to ride back into the veld, Milner to take a train for Cape Town. He had long planned – and postponed – discussions about the constitutional crisis in the Cape.[12]

That night, Milner wrote up his diary, usually a bleak, unemotional record of events. Considering how the Cabinet had shown no sign of supporting Kitchener in preference to himself, his mood was now remarkable for its bitterness. The irony, the supreme irony, was this: the blundering British army had at last found out how to beat the Boers – and win the great game for South Africa. So he believed. Yet here was Kitchener, 'dead set on chucking it away'.

April 17. Got up early. Telegrams coming in from home about the negotiations. K. came to see me at 9. We met the Boers at 10, but adjourned immediately in order to consider the last message of H.M's G. . . . The delegates met again at 3 pm and asked for an armistice wh. Lord K. conceded in substance if not in name. . . . I think it a very bad arrangement. Returned to my house, sent telegrams to S. of S. [Secretary of State] & worked till dinner time. . . . Very tired & not a little disgusted to bed.[13]

Was Milner in fact correct in claiming that Britain held the trump card? Was the war 'dying' of itself? Given a few more weeks of Kitchener's new aperient medicine – barbed wire, blockhouses, and élite columns – would the guerrillas be flushed down the drain? The Boers, as we shall see in due course, had their own conflicting answers to these questions. But it must be said that, despite Methuen's disaster at Tweebosch, the civilian side of the see-saw had come down with a bump on the side of the British, since those dark days of the previous November.

Reconstruction, at first a 'farce', was becoming a fact. It was one of the few redeeming features, so Milner thought, of having allowed the Boer leaders to come to Pretoria: they could see for themselves how well their capital was faring without them. 'The Dutch in the town are hot for peace,' Milner told Chamberlain, 'and the spectacle of an established government working on quietly as if the war did not exist, must impress them with the hopelessness of their cause.'[14] Milner's own elite corps had already got their noses to the grindstone. Patrick Duncan, Geoffrey Robinson (later Dawson), John Buchan – these were his 'crèche' (or 'Kindergarten', as Merriman rechristened them, to poke fun at Milner's Germanic earnestness), South Africa's new guardians, intellectual blues recruited by Milner from Balliol, New College, and other parts of 'Headquarters'.[15]

True, little of the crèche's time was spent on building the future, on building dams and railways to develop this 'magnificent estate', as Milner called the new colonies, which had been so 'woefully mismanaged'.[16] One day he would out-Cromer Cromer. At present, his hands were full enough with the task of clearing up the mess left by Kitchener. John Buchan, Milner's personal assistant since November, struggled to deconcentrate the camps, though transport was still critically short.[17] Schools were set up in the camps themselves; in the Orange River Colony, 12,123 children were being educated in November 1901, compared with a peak of 8,910 before the war.[18] Under proper civilian management, which included two experts brought over from India, the flood-tide of deaths in the camps subsided as rapidly as it had come surging in, propelled by Kitchener's heavy hand. The statistics for the twin annual death-rates, white and black, in both colonies combined, astonished everyone: October, the appalling peak, thirty-four per cent death-rate for Europeans in the camps, twenty per cent for Africans; November, thirty-one per cent, twenty-five per cent; December, twenty-six per cent, [twenty-six] per cent; January, sixteen per cent, [twenty-eight] per cent; February, seven per cent, [sixteen] per cent; March [four] per cent, [nine] per cent; April, [three] per cent, [six] per cent.[19]

Of course, this astonishing achievement was not so much to the credit of Milner and his young men, as an indictment of Lord K of Chaos. There was a less dramatic contrast between Milner's achievements in other fields – especially in making the gold-mines hum – and those of his other dominant predecessor, Kruger.

On the credit side, Milner claimed that he had abolished the corrupt administrative practices long denounced by the mine owners. According to Milner's new Mining Commissioner, Wybergh (ex-leader of the Uitlanders), one of the main problems was that Kruger's administrators had been *under*paid; this was the reason for the system of bribery and jobbery.[20] The British diagnosis of the black labour problem was rather different. New 'pass laws', better enforced, had tightened up things. And Milner's new Native Commissioner, Sir Godfrey Lagden, argued unblushingly the case for cutting African wages, and his arguments were published: 'The native races of South Africa are not now taxed in proportion to the benefits conferred upon them. They should in my opinion contribute adequately towards the expense . . . [of] their protection and welfare. At present they are deriving much advantage from labour at disproportionately high rates which I trust may in the public interest soon be reduced.'[21]

Of course, there was nothing unusual about these sentiments; indeed, the view that the Kaffir was underworked and overpaid had long been one of the few things, perhaps the only thing, that united all white South Africa. Hence, Milner's reassuring hints that Downing Street was sound enough on the native question: a message that, as we shall see, was to be confirmed at the forthcoming peace talks.

For the moment, however, competition from the army had pushed up African wages alarmingly: fifty shillings a month for underground workers, compared to thirty shillings before the war. Yet demand still far outstripped supply. To appease their appetite for black labour, the mine owners had, before the war, recruited eighty per cent of such labour from abroad. Now the first train-loads from Mozambique had begun to steam southwards again. Already in November, the black labour force on the Rand had reached sixteen thousand. At the same time, the white miners had flooded back up the railways from Natal and the Cape, despite Kitchener's grudging allocation of railway space, so that, by April, thirty-nine thousand Uitlanders were safely home again.[22]

Hence the encouraging figures for gold output, the counterpart of Kitchener's 'bag':[23]

	No. of mine stamps working (out of 6,000)	Ounces of gold × 1,000 (pre-war monthly peak 300)
May 1901	150	7·4
Nov. 1901	600	32
Dec. 1901	953	53
Jan. 1902	1,075	70
Feb. 1902	1,540	81
Mar. 1902	1,760	104
Apr. 1902	2,095	120

Everything depended on the Rand. This was the rock on which Milner would build the new British South Africa. So it was these gold figures that were, for better or worse, the measure of Milner's achievement in putting the Transvaal back on to its feet. By April, production had still only reached a third of its pre-war level. Yet reverse the golden medal: with only a third of existing mines back in production, the two new colonies were actually self-sufficient in current revenue.[24] Only get Kitchener off the country's back, restore the railways to civilian use, and introduce a flood of African labour (paid at suitably low rates), and this new 'estate' would be magnificent indeed.

Meanwhile, more blue ticker-tape, carrying news from the veld, had been decoded in Kitchener's HQ at Pretoria. There was the whiff of success, if not of the clear-cut military victory everyone longed for; enough success, at any rate, to clean the slate from the humiliation of Methuen's disaster at Tweebosch; enough, perhaps, to tip the balance towards peace.

On 11 April – the very day that De la Rey himself, with Botha and the others, had steamed into Pretoria, looking so sleek and well – Lieutenant-General Ian Hamilton's columns had dealt a stinging blow to De la Rey's veteran commandos at Rooiwal, two hundred miles to the west.

The success was not so much to the credit of Hamilton, the newcomer, as to the officers and men of the thirteen columns who had at long last, by the right mixture of perspiration, inspiration, and sheer luck, forced the enemy to stand and fight. And a fight it was: a real 'soldiers'' battle, fought out on the kind of terms that British generals had despaired of ever seeing again in their lifetime – a final, reassuring echo from the nineteenth century. This was the astonishing news from Rooiwal.[25]

The frustrations of fighting in the Western Transvaal, on the British side, were exceptional, even by the standards of the period. It was partly the terrain. They are half-wilderness, these plains in the huge, diamond-shaped box, enclosed by the lines Lichtenburg-Klerksdorp-Vryburg and the Vaal – two hundred miles of rolling, sandy plains intersected by shallow river valleys, dry (except in the rainy season) and almost as desolate as the Karoo.[26] De la Rey's commandos had dominated this barren ocean like a pirate fleet – or a shoal of sharks. The Boers had always understood the principle that best ensures survival: invisibility. De la Rey had perfected the shark's tactic: to remain submerged until it was the moment to strike.

How were the British to force to the surface this large and well-fed marauder? Three times, De la Rey had emerged recently, only to gorge himself on his pursuers: at Moedwil, on 30 September of the previous year, when he had mauled part of Kekewich's column; at Yzer Spruit, on 24 February of this year, when he had devoured most of Von Donop's wagon convoy, seven hundred men strong, 150 wagons brimming with food and ammunition;[27] and at Tweebosch, when he had swallowed Methuen whole. The last two attacks confirmed De la Rey's position as commander of the largest and fittest concentration of Boer commandos left in the war; out of the twenty thousand 'bitter-enders', about three thousand were De la Rey's. As well as looting British bully beef and ·303 ammunition, he had looted six field-guns, Methuen's 15-pounders taken at Tweebosch.[28] Of course, Kitchener still had overwhelming superiority in manpower and fire-power. Yet De la Rey's men were veterans. Many of the British were callow, half-trained yeomanry, like Methuen's men, who had fled at the first shot.

To crush De la Rey, Kitchener had predictably decided to let loose his ponderous steam-roller again, the same war machine that had flattened the Orange River Colony – and some of its inhabitants – in the new-style drives of February and March. He ordered up Rawlinson, his most successful column commander; he also roped in Woolls-Sampson as Intelligence Officer. Klerksdorp, the western railhead on the Vaal, was now made the base of operations. On this small tin-roofed town converged sixteen thousand mounted troops – that is, thirteen columns arranged in four super-columns, and commanded by Rawlinson, Kekewich, Colonel A. N. Rochfort, and Walter Kitchener. The steam-roller lumbered off for the first drive on 23 March, only a fortnight after the end of the last, disappointing drive in the ORC. The result was equally disappointing here: only 8 Boers killed and 165 captured. However, the bag did include three of Methuen's six field-guns and two of his pom-poms, discarded by De la Rey as obstacles to mobility.[29]

On 26 March, the GOC's armoured train sailed into Klerksdorp. (These armoured trains were treated like ships. They carried guns and searchlights; Kitchener's staff travelled in one called Her Majesty's Train *Cobra*, commanded by an 'admiral'.)[30] Kitchener had come to Klerksdorp to see for himself what had gone wrong. The situation was admittedly intractable. Intelligence, the key to success, was virtually a blank sheet. Even Colonel Woolls-Sampson, whose network of African agents had changed the whole war in the Eastern Transvaal, confessed himself beaten here in the west (De la Rey, it appears, had ruthlessly cleared the whole region of African families to protect himself).[31] Perhaps a more subtle tactician than Kitchener would have used some *ruse de guerre* to flush out the enemy: disguising some of his men, as Colonel Plumer had disguised them the previous year, in the poke bonnets of Boer refugees.[32] Kitchener relied instead on sheer weight and mass, weight of concrete, mass of horseflesh.

Predictably, De la Rey again slipped through the net, after mauling part of Walter Kitchener's force at Boschbult on 31 March. It was Colonel G. A. Cookson's column, Canadians and others, making a reconnaissance, unsupported. Although they fought bravely, and killed some Boers (at a loss to themselves of 178 men killed and wounded), this achieved little else except to confirm a blatant defect in Kitchener's anti-guerrilla system.[33]

To succeed, the steam-roller demanded, above all, that someone should be on the spot to co-ordinate the super-columns: a chief engineer to supervise the day-by-day adjustment of the gigantic machine. Kitchener's temperamental dislike of delegating anything to subordinates had blinded him to this defect, although already implicit in the mixed success of the system in the Orange River Colony. Now it was embarrassingly obvious in this inhospitable region, where the net of blockhouse lines had to be cast so wide (no water, no blockhouses). The crisis prompted the generals to take the liberty of sending a round robin to K: why not appoint Ian Hamilton as the overlord? It was thus that Ian Hamilton, K's Chief of Staff, was appointed overlord to all thirteen columns. With a staff of only one ADC and one Indian servant, Hamilton raced down to Klerksdorp on the afternoon of 6 April, and set the steam-roller in motion again.[34]

The new plan was not particularly subtle, though competent; Hamilton and his commanders had worked it out for themselves. Poor Woolls-Sampson had lost the commandos once again, after sending Rawlinson on a wild-goose-chase in the direction of a dried-up pond called Barber's Pan. Hamilton now planned to march three of the four super-columns for two days south-westwards from the blockhouse line. (Rochfort, with the fourth column, was to guard the line of the Vaal.) Then Hamilton would swing the three super-columns southwards at the point where two small rivers, the Brakspruit and the Little Hart's River, flowed into the main western tributary of the Vaal, the Great Hart's River. It was this relatively fertile valley at the centre of the 'box' formed by the western blockhouse lines that had proved De la Rey's main lair and main hunting-ground. Here was Boschbult, here was Tweebosch. Hamilton assumed that the Boers were still somewhere there, too. Presumably they would expect the British to continue westwards beyond the valley, and would themselves break away to the south. In fact, Hamilton had arranged for the columns to double back instead and squeeze the Boers against the line of the Klerksdorp block-house.[35]

So things looked hopeful. It was about time for a 'scrap', said Rawlinson. De la Rey and Steyn themselves had gone to Klerksdorp for the peace talks. A 'good chance', said Rawlinson, to 'smash up their subordinates'.[36] Hamilton agreed. 'Once more all my fortunes on the die!' he wrote to Winston Churchill with a flourish.[37]

The steam-roller lumbered off on 10 April, Walter Kitchener at 6.00 a.m., Rawlinson at 6.45 a.m.; Kekewich was somewhere ahead. The advantage of having someone actually in charge of the steam-roller was immediately apparent. Hamilton had intended that his three super-columns should dig in for the night of the 10th along the line of the Brakspruit to within about twelve miles of its junction with the Great Hart's River. On the night of the 9th, his intelligence warned him that there were Boers ahead. So he was able to alter his battle plan, to change feet in mid-action. He flashed a signal to Kekewich: push on towards a farm called Rooiwal ('Red Valley'), to close the gap between the current west flank and Great Hart's River. This telegram miscarried, and thus Rawlinson found Kekewich 'comfortably settled bang in the middle of my line'. Kekewich was told by Hamilton, who had been riding at Rawlinson's side: inspan and decamp. By dusk, the British lines thus extended for twenty miles, from close to the Great Hart's River to east of Boschbult: a line of hastily dug trenches, held by groups of 100 to 150 men at intervals of half a mile.[38]

By virtue of being on the spot, Hamilton had been able to prevent a serious blunder; indeed, unknown to anyone, he had achieved a great deal more. The confusion of Kekewich's move westwards, late on the evening of the 10th, served to confuse the enemy better than any *ruse de guerre*. Early next morning, Kekewich closed ranks, and concentrated three thousand men at Rooiwal, to prepare for the drive. So the western part of the British line, which had been the weakest when reconnoitred by the enemy, was now the strongest: a steel hook, hidden, quite by accident, in a tender piece of bait.[39]

It was a cool, sunny morning, about 7.15 a.m., when the 'bait' – an advanced screen of forty MI, commanded by Major Roy – witnessed one of the eeriest sights of the war: a great wave of a thousand, perhaps even fifteen hundred, slouch-hatted figures on horseback, sweeping knee-to-knee up the hillside towards them. Were they Rawlinson's men? Roy passed on the question to Kekewich. The men opened fire from the saddle, and, still firing, cantered up the hillside. Then, led by someone in a blue shirt (it was General Potgieter), the wave of horsemen broke over Major Roy's head, killing and wounding half his small party.[40]

For two and a half years, from Magersfontein to Tweebosch, it had been the Boers' natural gift for tactical surprise that had won them numerous victories, both in defence and attack. Moreover, in the last few months, the Boers had developed a twentieth-century version of the cavalry charge: to gallop the British line, fighting from the saddle – not with that obsolete *arme blanche*, but firing unaimed shots from magazine rifles.[41]

Now they had overreached themselves. To succeed, these revolutionary tactics not only demanded courage, and good luck and bad weather; the terrain, too, must be pro-Boer. Here at Rooiwal, the veld was implacably pro-British. There was no cover or camouflage for the attackers: no trees, no kopjes, no kloofs to hide them. By contrast, the stony hillside of Rooiwal, half a mile to the north, hid Kekewich's two columns like a curtain. The Boers, led by Generals Kemp and Potgieter, galloped on towards destruction, as though possessed by the spirit of Lord Lucan and the Light Brigade.

Actually, in General Potgieter's case, the comparison was not to prove so far-fetched. When they were about a mile and a half from Rooiwal, they breasted the rise, and the curtain rose, revealing the overwhelming odds: their own force numbered seventeen hundred strong in all, without field-guns; opposite them,

in close order, were Kekewich's two columns of nearly three thousand dismounted MI – supported by six guns and two pom-poms. To continue the
charge seemed folly, if not madness. Yet Kemp and Potgieter both accepted the
challenge; in their attempt to out-do De la Rey's achievements, they threw his
tactics to the winds. They cantered on, forming a massed phalanx, two, three,
and four deep. The six British guns began to tear holes in the column. Still they
came on, gambling everything on the chance that the British would turn and
run.[42]

If fortune always favoured the brave, Kemp and Potgieter would have won
the most spectacular victory of the war. As it was, they were assisted by the
shooting of Kekewich's MI, which was dismally wide of the mark. Some of the
raw yeomen turned and fled. Lieutenant Carlos Hickie, Lieutenant-Colonel H.
M. Grenfell's signalling officer, had just gone off to tell the commanding officer
of the convoy to laager it up. Suddenly he saw a mob of panic-stricken yeomen
galloping back. 'I tried to get hold of these faint-hearted ones to line them up on
the flank but nothing would stop them. It takes a strong man to shoot one of his
own men but I thought I should be driven to it that day.... The galloping men
stampeded the convoy.'[43] But no Boers followed. A mile away,
Potgieter lay sprawled thirty yards from the South African Constabulary line,
conspicuous with his neatly trimmed beard and his blue shirt, and there were
three bullets in his head and body. Beside his corpse lay fifty other dead Boers,
and those too seriously wounded for their comrades to carry back on their
horses.[44]

The Boer charge had failed, and now it was Ian Hamilton's turn. If ever there
was a chance to display those dashing qualities which Roberts and Kitchener so
admired in Hamilton, it was surely this moment. There were five thousand
reinforcements under Walter Kitchener away to the east. And here, concentrated
within seven miles, were about seven thousand British mounted troops:
Kekewich's two columns at Rooiwal, Rawlinson's two columns close at hand to
the east. In fact, Hamilton and Rawlinson were actually riding together at
Boschbult, inspecting the battlefield where Cookson had been mauled by De la
Rey on 31 March, when they both heard the sound of heavy firing at Rooiwal. It
was soon after 7.00 a.m. What was 'Keky' up to? The two men cantered off
towards the camp, where they arrived in time to see Potgieter's repulse. View
halloo![45] But it was an hour and a half later, 9.30 a.m., before Hamilton was
prepared to allow Kekewich and Rawlinson to go after the fox, and 11.30 a.m.
before Walter Kitchener, who was twenty miles away to the east, got the signal
to follow. The delay was largely caused by Hamilton's fear of a counter-attack
on Kekewich's convoy.[46] No doubt Hamilton should not be blamed – any more
than Buller for his delays in similar circumstances. Moving men on a battlefield
is not like moving men on a hunting-field. At any rate, the fox went to ground.
All that Hamilton's men captured after a fourteen-mile gallop were fifty
stragglers, the last of Methuen's field-guns, and a pom-pom which De la Rey
had taken at Tweebosch. Rawlinson commented: a good run, 'but hard on the
horses'. Kekewich thought bitterly of the bad shooting of his own MI. With one

good company of infantry, he could have killed three hundred of Potgieter's line.[47]

Meanwhile, at the scene of Potgieter's charge, among all the mangled bodies, there was the usual incongruous aftermath: Africans shouting at their oxen, British soldiers hunting for grub, someone taking snaps of someone else with a Kodak, Tommy Atkins brewing up tea in a captured kettle, as though the battle itself were already an irrelevance. One officer, however, was struck by the unusual sight of so many dead and wounded Boers. 'Although it seems rather brutal to say so,' said Grenfell's signalling officer, 'it made one glad. For so often one had seen the opposite.' At the same time, he suddenly felt a rush of admiration for the enemy. What 'brave fellows' they were 'who charged up in such gallant style'. It was really a 'wonderful sight the way they came on – Potgieter must have been a splendid man'. As he was standing there, one of the other British officers called out for someone to shoot a wounded Boer who was found to be wearing British khaki; according to Kitchener's rules, he could be shot out of hand. The signalling officer protested: he felt 'too much respect for his bravery'. The Boer was spared. Then everyone laid to, collecting up the Boer wounded and carrying them to the ambulance-wagons.[48]

So ended, if not in a blaze of glory, at least with an echo of chivalry, the last formal battle of the war. Ian Hamilton led the columns backwards and forwards for a further four weeks, flattening De la Rey's old hunting-ground, without any great addition to the bag.[49] His opposite number, Bruce Hamilton, played a similar game in Botha's old hunting-ground in the Eastern Transvaal.[50]

But all eyes were now turning to Pretoria, where, on 19 May, De la Rey, Botha, and the others resumed the peace talks with Kitchener. The 'interminable' war was fizzling out at last. So it appeared. A new question, a new battle, not only between Briton and Boer, but between Kitchener and Milner, was to be fought out over the terms of peace.

When Milner complained, 'K is a strong man. But all he can do is paralyse me,' he was not exaggerating. The clash of personality, and of principle, had now reached a climax.

Of course, Milner still held his cards close to his chest. He did not admit to Kitchener, any more than to the Boers, that he hoped to see the peace talks fail. But there was something in Milner's sarcastic manner, in those grey eyes, behind the frock-coat and the eye-glass, that alerted Kitchener and his staff to the danger.

'Now, Heaven forgive me if I am wrong,' [Ian Hamilton had written in March to Winston Churchill, who was told to show the letter discreetly to the Cabinet if he chose] 'but I doubt if Milner himself (consciously or unconsciously) wants peace yet . . . once you accept this idea, you will see it holds water from whatever point you look at it. Just think of the thousands of difficulties we were able to keep off from him by Martial Law with its delightfully simple and summary processes. . . . Therefore if I am right, Lord K. will as likely as not find his chief difficulties are not so much with the Boer Government as with the irreconcilable attitude of some of our own people.'[51]

When the Pretoria conference began, Hamilton found his insights dramatically confirmed. Suddenly the pieces of the jigsaw fell into place. Strange, he thought, to look back on the Bloemfontein conference which had failed three years before. Now he saw why it had failed – because of Milner. The inevitable result, 'under the circumstances', had been 'this bloody war'. In fact, Hamilton believed that the war was 'providential', because of the need to confirm imperial supremacy over all South Africa, 'but the time has now come when we want quite another sort of winding-up to the palaver'.[52]

Rawlinson was equally hostile to Milner's policy, which he rightly suspected was to drag out the war, in order to impose Crown Colony government on the Cape. Yet 'I am inclined to think that we shall not be able to make Milner "King" of S. Africa'.[53] No doubt both Hamilton's and Rawlinson's views reflected, to a great extent, their Chief's. Why was there this deep gulf between their views and Milner's?

For himself, of course, Kitchener was utterly sick of the war, longing to be off to India. He was also alarmed – as indeed was the Cabinet – by the numerous ways in which the continuation of the war was damaging both the army and the nation: the direct cost in money, men, and morale; the indirect cost, which meant postponing army reform, and continuing to advertise to the world that Britain was almost naked of regular troops.[54] At the same time, a subtle change had recently come over Kitchener and his staff in regard to their attitude to the Boers.

It was only a few months since Rawlinson had recommended executing 'cold blooded ruffians' like the Boers out of hand: 'It will be no congenial task to fight white men under those conditions, but I do not see there is any alternative ... it is certainly best for the future peace of the country.'[55] Kitchener himself had had no compunction in executing Cape rebels, like Scheepers and Lotter, as war criminals. His executions now totalled fifty-one.[56] Yet now, when the enemies sat down together round a table, a sense of solidarity immediately sprang up between the soldiers on either side. Perhaps Hamilton, always excitable, exaggerated the feeling. But he had noticed that there had grown up 'a strange sort of mutual liking' between the soldiers in the field. He himself found the Boer leaders the 'best men in South Africa'. On their part, the Boers invited Hamilton to attend a birthday party given for Smuts on 24 May. Hamilton was in ecstasies. He told Churchill, 'I sat between Botha and De la Rey. On Botha's right was De Wet: on De la Rey's left sat Smuts. I had the most enchanting evening, and never wish to eat my dinner in better company. They told me a great many stories about the War which would give me much joy to repeat to you ... of their escapes from myself and others.'[57]

The 'best men' in South Africa? A sneer at the loyalists, it would seem. So it was – especially the non-British variety. Hamilton had not only grasped that Milner was trying to block the peace talks. He realized why: Milner wished to destroy the Boers as a political force and tip the balance in favour of the 'loyalists'. The idea of the war resulting in *their* supremacy filled Hamilton with disgust. He had warned Churchill in January that real loyalists were 'precious scarce' – except in so far as 'loyalty is a South-African political expression, meaning anti-Dutch'.[58] He told him a month later,

> Do let us profit by our experience when we smashed the Zulus for the Boers, and not repeat the mistake by annihilating the Boers for the Jewburghers. You have no idea what arrogant insolent devils you will discover as soon as Mr Boer had lost his mauser. If one could only keep a tame commando in perpetuity within striking distance of the mines, all would go as merry as wedding bells. Otherwise your great Government will find itself rather vulgarly snubbed as soon as you wish to interfere in the smallest degree with the Chamber of Mines pretension to run the whole of Africa for its own particular advantage.[59]

Churchill agreed. He had 'very little admiration' for the Cape loyalists or for the Uitlanders of the Transvaal. The Boers, not they, must be 'the rock' on which the British position must be founded. On their part, it was a 'shrewd' move of the Boers to pre-empt the loyalists.[60]

Meanwhile, a few days before Hamilton's hurried return from Klerksdorp in a coal truck, to be 'at K's elbow during the crisis', Milner had managed to block the first dangerous offers of peace.

By 15 May, the national delegates, elected by the commandos scattered all over the two countries, had safely reached Vereeniging, astride the Vaal, fifty miles south of Pretoria. These sixty delegates duly chose a five-man negotiating team: Generals Botha and De la Rey and State Attorney Smuts for the Transvaal; Judge Hertzog and General De Wet for the Free State. The team had still not been given plenary powers, so the peace terms, if agreed, had to be ratified by the delegates at Vereeniging. By the same token, they had to be ratified by the British Cabinet in London. Negotiations resumed at noon on 19 May.[61]

The new peace offer seemed to Milner as farcical as the old. What about a protectorate, asked the Boers? They offered to surrender independence as regards foreign relations, preserve internal self-government under British supervision, and hand over part of the Rand and Swaziland. In effect, this meant that part of the two countries would be a Crown Colony, part a protectorate. Kitchener agreed that these proposals were unworkable, even in military terms. However, Milner remained intensely suspicious of Kitchener. After several hours' manoeuvring, the Boer team suggested that Smuts had an informal talk with Kitchener and Milner. This gave Milner the chance of a *pis aller*: to restore the talks to the Middelburg line. After lunch, the three men worked out a draft of a preamble to the surrender terms, in which the Boer leaders were recognized to be 'acting as the Government of the South African Republic', and 'acting as the Government of the Orange Free State' (two governments officially abolished by the British nearly two years earlier). In return, they were to agree that the burghers would recognize King Edward VII 'as their lawful sovereign'. It was then proposed that a sub-committee would begin to draw up the details of the agreement to add to this preamble.[62]

At this point, De Wet exploded. It was he and Steyn who had long been recognized as the main obstacles to a peace conference (and thus Milner's principal remaining hope of a breakdown). Steyn was now too ill to come to Pretoria, but clearly De Wet spoke for him.

De Wet: 'I cannot agree. I think it would be dishonourable if I did not say so. I see no chance of putting a body on such a head. Whatever conditions may be added to the preamble, I cannot get over the difficulty of the preamble.'

Milner: 'Very well, then; it is clear that we cannot go further.'

But Kitchener and Smuts were equally intent on keeping the talks going.

Kitchener: 'I think we should draft a document and let General De Wet see it before he expresses an opinion.'

Smuts: 'I am willing to assist in putting the draft into proper form. ....'[63]

All the generals then withdrew, leaving the Boer lawyers, Smuts and Hertzog, to wrestle with Milner and his legal adviser, Sir Richard Solomon, Attorney General at the Cape.[64] Predictably, negotiations ran smoothly once De Wet was out of the room. The draft agreement was duly put to the full committee and, with one long addendum, the text was cabled to London.[65]

Compared with the Middelburg terms, there were only three significant changes – all to the benefit of the Boers. First, the amnesty for colonial rebels, the rock on which Kitchener believed Middelburg had been wrecked a year earlier. As a concession, Milner had now arranged with the Cape government that all Cape rebels, except for leaders, would be exempted from imprisonment, and they would be let off with permanent disfranchisement. Natal rebels, by contrast, would have to take their chance under the ordinary law.[66]

Second, there was the question of native rights in the two new colonies. Would the right to vote depend on education? Would at least the better-off Africans and Coloureds be given the same political rights as they had in Cape Colony? Or would the present colour bar be continued? At Middelburg, it had been proposed to exclude the grant of the franchise to 'Kaffirs' (there was no mention of Indians or Coloureds) *'before'* representative government was granted.[67] Now it was proposed to exclude the consideration of the question of granting the vote to 'natives ... *until after'* its introduction.[68] This subtle change in prepositions meant, in effect, that Milner was proposing that they should make the exclusion permanent. Once self-governing, no Boer state would give the vote to Africans. What about Chamberlain's claim: 'We cannot consent to purchase a shameful peace by leaving the Coloured population in the position in which they stood before the war'?[69]

Third, financial help for the shattered ex-republics. According to the Middelburg terms, Britain was to pay their enemies' pre-war debts up to a figure of £1 million. By the new Clause 11 and its addendum, Britain would agree to increase this figure to £3 million. And, by the new Clause 12, Britain would offer generous loans to burghers, in addition to assisting loyalists.[70]

The increasing chance of agreement naturally increased Milner's sense of frustration. He had sent a last 'over-my-dead-body' cable to Chamberlain on the

21st. Negotiations had 'taken a turn for the worse'. The Boers were making 'preposterous proposals'. He was himself 'in a weak position, as Kitchener does not always support me even in the presence of Boers'. He begged the Cabinet to postpone replying if Kitchener sent them 'strange proposals'; this would give him time to block them. 'My own conviction is that Boers are done for, and that if the assembly at Vereeniging breaks up without peace they will surrender left and right. The men here are either anxious to upset negotiations or bluffing, in reliance on our weakness, probably the latter.'[71]

Still, Milner recognized that he could not hope for much from Chamberlain, given 'public feeling' at home in Britain, and abroad.[72] (The Kaiser had sent a cable to the King *en clair* on 2 May, congratulating him on offering 'most liberal' terms and 'fervently hoping' the Boers would accept them.) Chamberlain had made it clear in January that the Middelburg terms still lay on the table. If there was any hope for Milner's policy of fighting the war to the bitter end, it all depended on Steyn and De Wet.

The proposed terms of peace ('terms of surrender' was the phrase Chamberlain preferred)[73] astonished the frock-coated officials of the Colonial Office when they received the text on 22 May. It did not strike them as 'preposterous' at all.

H. W. Just: 'The document seems on the whole to be very satisfactory. It is practically the same as the terms under the Botha negotiations. ...'

F. Graham: 'To my mind the arrangement is so satisfactory that I suspect a trap; but I fail to find it. .... The native franchise ... is the only point worth hesitating about. As clause 9 stands the native will never have the franchise. No responsible Govt. will give it to him. I should have preferred the words "If the franchise is given it will be so limited as to preserve the just predominance of the white race as in the Cape Colony."'

H. W. Just: 'Yes, it would not be in accordance with the traditions of British policy in South Africa to use words implying a doubt whether any civilized native would ever receive the franchise.'

Sir Montague Ommaney (Permanent Secretary): 'Clause 9 seems to me to want nothing except the omission of the word "after" ...

'Clause 11 does not bear close examination. The proposed Commission will be no real safeguard against wholesale fraud. .... The point is, are we prepared to pay these three millions to secure the termination of the war, knowing that it involves still heavier payments to the loyalists.'

Next day, Chamberlain saw the Permanent Secretary and they discussed what changes in the terms to recommend to the Cabinet. By this time, he had received Milner's private cables denouncing the new terms, especially the 'detestable' Clause 11.[74] To Milner he cabled back, acidly, 'There should be some argument more cogent than the money cost to justify risking failure on this point. Can you supply it, and would you go so far as to wreck agreement at this stage upon this question.'[75]

The Cabinet discussed the new terms on the 23rd, and were pleased with them – especially with the introduction; the terms were an 'improvement' on

Middelburg. Chamberlain raised two main points of objection, following the line of the Colonial Office staff. What about Clause 9 and native political rights? It seemed a bit odd. Why not strike out the crucial word 'after'? Otherwise, the natives would be permanently disfranchised.[76]

Back came Milner's reply: 'Clause 9. Yes. That was the object of the clause. Clause suggested by you would defeat that object. It would be better to leave out clause altogether than propose such a change. While averse in principle to all pledges, there is much to be said for leaving question of political rights of natives to be settled by colonists themselves.'[77] Chamberlain, and the Cabinet, gave way to Milner. The crucial 'after' remained in Clause 9, the word that made mockery of Chamberlain's claim that one of Britain's war aims was to improve the status of Africans.[78]

On Clause 11 and its addendum (£3 million to cover their enemies' war debts), the Cabinet compromised with Milner. The clause was amalgamated with Clause 12 (loans to cover war losses), and so avoided the objection that the £3 million would now be paid as a free gift.[79] Otherwise, Milner failed to change the terms, and Salisbury's Cabinet left Kitchener's new peace terms much as they had found them. On 27 May, the text was cabled back to South Africa, to be put at once before the Boer delegates at Vereeniging. One slim chance of blocking agreement had been gained by Milner. The Cabinet had agreed to allow the Boers only time for a simple 'yes' or 'no'.[80]

Should they say yes, or should they say no, and fight on to the bitter end? It was a question that had echoed and re-echoed around the tents of the burghers ever since Roberts's peace offer of June 1900, nearly two years before. There was not a single leader who had set his face unequivocally against coming to terms with the British. Even the most tenacious champions of independence, Steyn and De Wet, the twin war gods of the Free State, had now agreed that the volk must swallow their pride, surrender territory (including the richest part of the country, the Rand), and accept protectorate status for the rest – terms that were ten times as humiliating as those rejected by Kruger at Bloemfontein three years before.[81] (Indeed, nothing showed more clearly how much enthusiasts like Smuts had over-estimated the Boer military strength in 1899, and 'provoked the war', as Smuts now confessed at Vereeniging.)[82] But Milner and Kitchener on 19 May had, of course, rejected that protectorate plan, even with all the gold of the Rand thrown in. Peace was to cost still more, nothing short of annexation. Could they say 'yes' to this?

What if they said 'no'? The military answers to this question were given in detail at Vereeniging, and broadly confirmed Kitchener's – and Milner's – claims. For months now, Kitchener had pinned his faith on the 'bag'. Despite all his set-backs, he had asserted he was on the verge of victory, and he was right – in the Transvaal, at any rate.

When the sixty delegates had first gathered in the great marquee at Vereeniging on 15 May, each man had been asked to report on his own district. There were recognized to be three main military obstacles to continuing guerrilla war:

shortage of horses, shortage of food, and the miserable condition of the commandos' women and children – those who had *not* been put in concentration camps, but had remained with the commandos in the veld. One by one, the Transvaal delegates confirmed Kitchener's own claims that the burghers were at the end of their tether. Despite their large strength on paper – ten thousand in the Transvaal alone, and as many again in the Free State and Cape, compared to the British estimate of a grand total of twelve thousand – the picture was one of almost unrelieved gloom. One-third of the men had no horses. Food, especially mealie grain, was critically short. Some fourteen Transvaal districts would have to be abandoned to the enemy, who could then concentrate their strength against the rest.[83] On 1 May, the Middelburg delegate, de Clercq, reported his area 'almost hopeless'. There were no slaughter cattle, and enough grain to last only a short time. Out of eight hundred horses, only a hundred remained. The district must be abandoned; yet how could burghers escape anywhere with horses like theirs? The picture was equally dismal in much of eastern and southern Transvaal: no slaughter cattle, horses wretched, impossible to sow mealies, because of the continual hustling between blockhouses. Commandant Schoeman (Lijdenburg) was reported to have said, 'Although but a short time ago there had been eight hundred head of cattle, they had now all been carried off. Grain there was none.' Should fighting be continued, he was at a loss to know how to provide for the women.[84] Landrost Bosman (Wakkerstroom): 'The men in my district told me that if I came back and reported that the war was to be continued, they would be obliged – for the sake of their wives and children – to go straight to the nearest English camp and lay down their arms.'[85]

It was the sufferings of their women and children, above all, that had demoralized the Transvaal commandos. Not, it must be emphasized, the sufferings of the women and children in the concentration camps. On the contrary, it was the plight of those who had been left in the veld and refused, according to Kitchener's latest policy, admittance to these camps. 'The women were in a most pitiable state,' Botha was quoted as saying, 'now that the lines of the blockhouses had been extended in all directions over the country. Sometimes the commandos had to break through the lines and leave the women alone. . . .'[86] The plight of the women was in turn exacerbated by another ominous new development: the African menace, real or imaginary.

Throughout the war, the meekness of the African majority had been one of the most striking features. None of the peoples who had been worsted in recent native wars – Basutos, Zulus, or Magatos – had seized their opportunity to pay off old scores and recover lost territory. With the exception of Linchwe's raid on Derdepoort in November 1899 (and Linchwe was led by a British officer), the Africans had behaved with unexpected restraint. This was all the more surprising, given the way they had been treated by the Boers, who had cheerfully looted their cattle, flogged and murdered those who helped the British, and even massacred the whole civilian population of a Transvaal village, Modderfontein.[87]

However, it was now apparent that the natives were stirring. The worm had turned. At Zoutpansberg in the north, they were 'getting out of hand'. Much the same was said at Bethel and Carolina.[88] And, in May, a most alarming episode occurred at Holkrantz, near Vryheid, in a part of Zululand annexed by the Transvaal.

Dinizulu, the Zulu Chief, had protested repeatedly to the British against cattle raids and murders by Boer commandos. The British had done nothing. Recently, the Boers had taken the cattle, burned the kraals, and driven out the women and children of a Zulu tribe, whose Chief was called Sikobobo. The Boers claimed this was a just punishment for the tribe's helping the British as scouts and guides. Sikobobo claimed that he owed first allegiance to Dinizulu, the paramount Chief, who lived on the Natal side of the border, and had asked for his assistance. Potgieter, the local field cornet, then sent an insulting message to Sikobobo, read out in front of the men of the tribe: 'That Sikobobo and his people were no better than fowl-lice and challenging him to come to Holkrantz and retake his cattle before they were all consumed.' Sikobobo took up the challenge in traditional Zulu fashion.

That night, 6 May, his impis, armed with guns and assegais, attacked Potgieter, killed fifty-six Boers, wounded three more, and recaptured 380 cattle, at a loss to his own force of fifty-two killed and forty-eight wounded. So far, the women and children in this district had not been molested, but the Zulus had been restrained with difficulty.[89]

Thus, the Transvaal was now threatened from two sides: the natives were stirring, and the women and children were correspondingly vulnerable, just when their menfolk were least able to protect them. These commandos – 'bitter-einders' they called themselves – were a dwindling band, facing extinction as a military force. This was how Botha had summed up the situation in the Transvaal in early May; Acting President Burger, and even General De la Rey, agreed. 'Fight to the bitter end?' asked De la Rey. 'Do you say that? But has the bitter end not come?'[90]

In the Free State, no. That was De Wet's blunt answer, and his own report as Commandant-General of 6,120 men was echoed by most of the Free State leaders.[91] Grain was scarce, and so were horses, naturally. But morale was still reasonably good, largely because the commandos' womenfolk were either safely in the concentration camps, or could fend for themselves on the veld; and the Free State Kaffirs were generally prepared to collaborate. General Froneman (Ladybrand) had eighty families in his district; the local Kaffirs were helping the commandos by buying clothes for them in Basutoland. General Badenhorst (Boshof) said he had enough cattle to last years. General Prinsloo (Bethlehem) had enough slaughter cattle and corn to supply other districts. However, the blockhouses were a 'source of constant annoyance'. General Brand (Bethulie) said parts of his division had been entirely laid waste, but he could still hold out for a year.[92]

What of the third front, the 3,300-strong invasion force in the far west and north-west of Cape Colony? Smuts answered equally bluntly that nothing much could be expected from this quarter. The commandos could maintain themselves. But there would be no general Afrikaner rising in the Cape. Too few horses, too little forage, and the colonials were afraid of the penalties for rebellion. Should *all* the Boer forces try to concentrate in the Cape? An attractive idea; but how were they to transport them there? asked Smuts. The Boer cause must stand or fall by virtue of what could be achieved in the republics.[93]

In mid-May it had been the Transvaal government – represented by Acting President Burger and Generals Botha and De la Rey – who had most vehemently argued the case for peace. Now, a fortnight later, eloquently supported by Smuts, the Transvaal generals continued to press their case, and the Free State's counter-arguments began to falter.

The case for ending the war, at its simplest, was that the war was ending anyway. They must now win the peace.

Six months earlier, the tide had set finally against them – their commandos immobilized and starving, beaten at last by blockhouses and food burning; their womenfolk threatened by Kaffirs. And, to set against all these sacrifices, there was no prospect of foreign intervention, or any corresponding gain. Negotiate now, said Botha and De la Rey and Smuts, while we still have control of our destiny, and can keep the volk together as a nation. Fight on, and the volk will die (or suffer a fate worse than death). The threat was not only to the lives of individuals, but to the continued existence of the nation. And, most ominously of all, Botha added, 'There are men of our own kith and kin who are helping to bring us to ruin. If we continue the war, it may be that the Afrikaners against us will outnumber our own men.'[94]

Botha was not exaggerating. There were already 5,464 *handsuppers* (or 'ensoppers' or 'yoiners') – Boers recruited to fight in the British army as National Scouts, guides, transport drivers and so on.[95] De Wet's own brother, Piet De Wet, was leading the 'handsuppers' in the Free State. It was not difficult to imagine the new politics of the Transvaal if the volk were thus left divided. In the next six months, the remnants of the guerrillas could be squeezed out into the deserts and forests, and the Uitlanders would become the political heirs of Milner's clean slate, the de-Afrikanerized Crown Colonies. In short, the Beits and the Wernhers, the Rhodes' and the Fitzpatricks, would have at last worked their will on South Africa – hand in hand with Milner. This was the fate worse than death from which Botha intended to save the volk: the 'Pax Milner'. Instead, they must accept the 'Pax Kitchener'. They could retain their political supremacy, at least in the long term, by reasserting Afrikaner unity, by keeping their political majority intact for the day when, according to the terms now offered, Milner's new Crown Colonies lapsed, and white South Africans were free to govern themselves, as free as Canadians or Australians.

Such was the political thinking (echoing Ian Hamilton's) behind Botha's argument for winning the peace while they could still fight for peace. Let us be warned, Botha might have said, by the way we were outmanoeuvred by Milner, three years ago, at Bloemfontein.

De Wet and his generals clutched at the counter-arguments. They were convinced that military resistance was still possible, though they could not say how. At what cost to the women and children? De Wet: 'Their sufferings are among what we may call the necessary circumstances of the war. ...' So on the struggle must go. But even De Wet was to recognize that the Free State could not – and must not – struggle on without the Transvaal's help.[96]

Probably, before those anguished debates, spread over so many days, the outcome had already been a foregone conclusion, once the meeting at Vereeniging had been arranged. As De Wet's close ally, Judge Hertzog, put it, the strongest *argument* for peace was that 'some of their own people had turned against them, and were fighting in the ranks of the enemy'. Yet if he could have believed that to maintain their independence was practical, he would have disregarded even that argument. What made him see that the collapse of resistance was inevitable was that all the scattered commandos had come together and exchanged information, and heard Botha himself declare the condition of the whole country 'hopeless'.[97]

The vote was taken in the great marquee at Vereeniging, soon after 2.00 p.m. on Saturday 31 May. A motion was drafted, summing up the six main reasons why the governments must accept the British terms: no food for women and children, and no means to continue the war; the concentration camps (this was for propaganda purposes); Botha had actually admitted 'one is only too thankful nowadays to know that our wives are under English protection';[98] the 'unbearable' conditions caused by Kaffirs, especially the Holkrantz 'murders'; Kitchener's proclamation of 7 August, which threatened the confiscation of burghers' land; the impossibility of keeping British prisoners; in short, no hope of success. To avoid a disastrous split, Botha and De la Rey went to De Wet and asked him and the Free State leaders to accept the resolution of the Transvaal. De Wet and most of the others agreed. The delegates voted for Kitchener's peace by an overwhelming majority: fifty-four to six. It was the bitter end, but the alliance stood firm.[99]

Acting President Burger added the solemn words: 'We must be ready to forgive and forget. ...' He referred, significantly, not to the British, nor even to the Uitlanders, but to the volk. 'We may not cast out that portion of our people.'[100]

In the great marquee at Vereeniging, the moral ordeal had stamped its mark on everyone. 'How great was the emotion,' wrote Kestell, the official reporter. 'I saw the lips quiver of men who had never trembled before a foe. I saw tears brimming in eyes that had been dry when they had seen their dearest laid in the grave.' The ordeal continued, as the members of the two governments were rushed back by train to Pretoria, to sign the death-warrants – technically 'terms of surrender' – of the republics. It was now eleven o'clock on Saturday night. They were driven to Kitchener's HQ, where they were met by Kitchener and Milner, the latter looking grey and ill. Burger signed first for the Transvaal, De Wet for the Free State. Kitchener and Milner signed last. It was all over in five minutes; the republics finally dead and buried. There was an embarrassed silence, broken by Kitchener's well-meant 'We are good friends now.'[101] Kitchener's new friends retired, dazed, to their hotels. Kitchener, Ian Hamilton,

and the staff retired to celebrate their forthcoming departure from South Africa
– and the £50,000 victory grant which Parliament was to vote K. (He hastily
cabled for it to be put in South African gold shares.)[102]

Milner did not celebrate. In his heart, he must have known he had lost the
'great game for mastery' in South Africa. When he had decided to try to
precipitate war, three years earlier, he had not been hopeful. Yet to have the
game thrown away by Kitchener, with victory in sight – that was hard to bear.
All that he could say was that he had prevented a disastrous peace being signed.
He had stopped Kitchener from putting a date to the restoration of self-
government. That was the vital thing. He had bought time for himself, and his
crèche. They must now strain every nerve to build up the gold industry, and
thus bring new blood into the Transvaal, settlers for the Rand, settlers for the
farms, united, loyal, imperial-minded British settlers by the thousand, drawing
on loans offered by Wernher-Beit.[103]

Peace. Apart from the Uitlanders (who shared Milner's forebodings), the
hundred-odd British columns in the field took the news with the same mixture
of delight and incredulity with which the army had taken the news of the Boers'
ultimatum in 1899. Peace was the message of the joy-shots crackling along the
three thousand miles of blockhouse lines, and the garrison guns thundering all
over South Africa like a victory peal. 'Peace.' There was just that one surrealist
word on the message carried to the Addo Bush, where Colonel Beauchamp
Doran's column was floundering in a freak snowstorm. ('Don't let's meet a Boer
who hasn't heard,' said young Lieutenant Pym.)[104]

Colonel Rawlinson was at church parade when he was handed the telegram
from the Chief. It gave him a 'thrill . . . the like of which I have never felt before.
So here is the end of all our hardships and labours. I kept the telegram in my hand
until the service was over when I formed up the troops and announced the glad
tidings . . . calling on them not to forget those friends we had lost and finishing
up with three cheers for Lord K.'[105]

A few days later, the trek to the ports began: all but 20,000 of the 250,000
British troops were being sent home or disbanded.

There was a new song as they marched to the docks, about the christening of a
baby called Blogs.

> *Chorus*
> The Baby's name is Kitchener Carrington
> Methuen Kekewich White,
> Cronje Plumer Powell Majuba
> Gatacre Warren Colenso Kruger
> Cape Town Mafeking French
> Kimberley Ladysmith Bobs
> The Union Jack & the Fighting Mac
> Lyddite Pretoria Blogs.
>
> The Parson said these names upon this infant I can't pop
> So my wife she bruised his rolling veld & jumped on his Spion Kop

She kicked his mounted infantry till his Bloemfontein was sore
Then she did a flanking movement & she started out once more.

    Chorus
    The Baby's name, etc[106]

The commandos, too, seemed glad the struggle was over. Twenty-one thousand 'bitter-einders' emerged from their hiding-places (over twice as many as British Intelligence had bargained for). There was the same brief ritual as in previous surrenders: their rifles thrown in heaps (mostly captured British Lee Enfields, by this stage of the war); prayers uttered by the commandants. Then they trekked off to the concentration camps, to look for their families. Their discipline and morale – they held their heads high, like men who have won a moral victory – were conspicuous.[107] Their time would come. Equally conspicuous was the hang-dog look of the '*hensoppers*' and '*yoiners*' (the National Scouts and other collaborators). Politically, they were to be outcasts – skeletons well hidden away in the cupboard. The fact that a fifth of the fighting Afrikaners at the end of the war fought on the side of the British was a secret that has remained hidden till today.

As the British officers marched their men down to the docks, their own mythology was also being born. 'A very pleasant time for a young fellow. . . . A regular sort of picnic. . . . A gentleman's war. . . . The happiest year of my life.'[108] The easy phrases covered the crudities of war, like the sand blowing in over the graves of their comrades. Yet, if we may judge from the talk of ordinary soldiers, this mythology did not extend far into the ranks. 'It was a cruel war, it was. . . . We were half-starved all the time. . . . I never saw the point of it. . . . It was the worst war ever. . . . Johnny Boer, he used to shoot niggers like you'd shoot a dog. . . . It was all for the gold-mines.' So the majority of the veterans whose voices I recorded, seventy years later.[109]

But, whatever it was, and whatever it was for, it was over.

'Winners and Losers'

'They took the hill (Whose hill? What for?)
But what a climb they left to do!
Out of that bungled, unwise war
An alp of unforgiveness grew.'

William Plomer

In money and lives, no British war since 1815 had been so prodigal. That 'tea-time' war, Milner's little 'Armageddon', which was expected to be over by Christmas 1899, had cost the British tax payer more than £200 million.[1] The cost in blood was equally high. The War Office reckoned that 400,346 horses, mules and donkeys were 'expended' in the war.[2] There were over a hundred thousand casualties of all kinds among the 365,693 imperial and 82,742 colonial soldiers who had fought in the war. Twenty-two thousand of them found a grave in South Africa: 5,774 were killed by enemy action (or accident) and shovelled into the veld where they fell; 16,168 died of wounds or were killed by the action of disease (or the inaction of army doctors).[3] Today, their sombre last parades – marked by lines of white crosses – can be seen outside Bloemfontein. Here, the carefully tended dead dominate the landscape like their successors in the fields of Flanders.

On the Boer side, the cost of the war, measured in suffering, was perhaps absolutely as high; relatively, much higher. It was estimated that there were over 7,000 deaths among the 87,365 Boers – including 2,120 foreign volunteers and 13,300 Afrikaners from the Cape and Natal who served in the commandos of the two republics.[4] No one knows how many Boers – men, women and children – died in the concentration camps. Official estimates vary between 18,000 and 28,000.[5] The survivors returned to homesteads devastated almost beyond recognition. Several million cattle, horses and sheep, that had comprised their chief capital, had been killed or looted. In theory, the policy of farm burning had been stopped on the British government's orders in November 1900. But, as Kitchener himself admitted, most farms came to be destroyed one way or the other; doors and windows made valuable firewood in a treeless landscape, and the tin roofs helped build the blockhouses. In due course, the vanquished enemy submitted their claims: 63,000 separate claims for compensation for war losses. The imperial government made free grants of more than the £3 million promised at Vereeniging, but a disproportionate amount went to 'handsuppers'. In addition, the Uitlanders and other loyalists received compensation totalling £2 million.[6]

Most severe were the losses borne by the Africans. The damage to their property may not seem large: yet they filed compensation claims of £661,000 in the Transvaal. But few Africans owned much property in the ex-republics. The British government paid them compensation at the rate of seventeen per cent – a lower rate than the Boers were paid.[7] How many Africans were injured or died as a result of the war? No one bothered to keep full records of the deaths among the 107,000 'black Boers' (as one of them described himself) in the Africans' concentration camps. They were the farm servants and their families – the retainers of the better-off burghers. The incomplete records give their death roll as seven thousand, but the actual total probably exceeded twelve thousand.[8]

How many deaths were there among the Africans who fought on the side of the British – the ten thousand armed Africans who served as scouts, guides and blockhouse guards, and the thirty to forty thousand unarmed Africans who worked as drivers, labourers and so on?[9] The Boers openly admitted killing the armed Africans when they captured them, and there is much unpublished evidence that they killed the unarmed ones too.[10] Canon Farmer, one of the leading British missionaries in the Transvaal, wrote privately in 1901,

Of all who have suffered by the war, those who have endured most & will receive least sympathy, are the Natives in the country places of the Transvaal . . . they have welcomed British columns & when these columns have marched on they have been compelled to flee from the Boers, abandon most of their cattle & stuff & take refuge in the towns or fortified places, or be killed. I have been asking after my people & this is the account I get of them all. . . . For instance, at Modderfontein, one of my strongest centres of Church work in the Transvaal, there was placed a garrison of 200 [white] men. The Natives – all of whom I knew – were there in their village: the Boers under [General Jan] Smuts, captured this post last month & when afterwards a column visited the place they found the bodies of all the Kaffirs murdered and unburied.

I should be sorry to say anything that is unfair about the Boers. They look upon the Kaffirs as dogs & the killing of them as hardly a crime. . . .[11]

If this was how Jan Smuts, as high-minded as any of the commando leaders, treated the hundred-odd Africans of Modderfontein, the fate of others can be imagined.[12]

The fruits of victory tasted sweet and sour to the British army. Of course, the old class-conscious British army was not destroyed, as Wolseley had hoped. On the other hand, the antiquated War Office machine in Pall Mall was given new premises, a new general staff, and a thorough overhaul. Wolseley must have allowed himself a wry smile when the Cabinet decided the partnership with the Commander-in-Chief was impossible, without warning the incumbent, Roberts. Roberts arrived at the Horse Guards one morning in 1904 to find he had officially ceased to exist. ('They stabbed you in the back,' cried Ian Hamilton.)[13] The Cabinet created a Chief of the General Imperial Staff instead. Roberts died in the autumn of 1914, in his eighty-third year, when gamely pushing his way to the BEF front line at St Omer.

Other generals came to grief in bizarre circumstances. As C-in-C in Ceylon, 'Fighting Mac' (General Hector MacDonald), the grizzled general who had risen from the ranks, fell victim to a love affair with a Ceylonese boy of noble birth. He died like a gentleman: to save the army, and his wife, from scandal, he shot himself in the Hotel Regina in Paris.[14] General Colvile, sacked by Roberts, was killed cycling near Bagshot, and it turned out that the car which ran him down was driven by Colonel Rawlinson. General Gatacre ('Backacre'), also sacked by Roberts, got a job with a rubber company, and died of fever, trying to tramp through the jungles of western Abyssinia.[15]

On the Boer side, General Piet Cronje also came to a sad end. He died ostracized by the volk for his bad taste in re-enacting the Last Stand at Paardeberg in the St Louis World Fair of 1904.[16]

By contrast, Buller took his sacking philosophically. He withdrew behind the bluff mask of the West Country landowner. 'It will all be the same in 100 years,' he told his wife.[17] Perhaps he was wrong. But before he died in 1908, his admirers put up a monument to him in the main street of Exeter. It said simply – and perhaps rightly – 'He saved Natal.'

Ian Hamilton, Roberts's chief protégé, rose rapidly to fame and power, but was made a scapegoat for the disaster in the Dardanelles campaign. He died in 1947, excitable and brilliant to the end.

Strange to say, two of Roberts's least favoured senior generals – Methuen and White – later became field-marshals. Methuen returned in 1908 to South Africa as GOC. White, whose weakness in letting himself be trapped at Ladysmith had wrecked the whole strategy of the war, was made Governor of Chelsea Hospital. After his death, to millions of Englishmen who read of the annual celebrations of Ladysmith Day (28 February), Field-Marshal Sir George White, V C, became the symbol of endurance and courage.

Among the younger generation of Roberts's and Kitchener's officers, there were many other future field-marshals: Byng, Robertson (the first to rise from the ranks), Birdwood, Allenby, and the leaders of the BEF in 1914–15, French and Haig.[18] The last two named had learnt something from their days in the veld: above all, the need for a staff system to plan, organize, feed, doctor and co-ordinate the huge, far-flung armies that modern war demanded. They improved the artillery, increasing the calibre of the British field-gun in 1909[19] (though this remained lower than that of the 4·7-inch guns Buller had improvised a decade before). They left the *arme blanche* as it was – a white elephant.

The central tactical lesson of the Boer War eluded them. The reason for those humiliating reverses was not the marksmanship of the Boers, nor their better guns or rifles, nor the crass stupidity of the British generals – all myths which British people found it convenient to believe. It was that the smokeless, long-range, high velocity, small-bore magazine bullet from rifle or machine-gun – plus the trench – had decisively tilted the balance against attack and in favour of defence.[20]

The world learnt this lesson the hard way: in the bloody stalemates of the Dardanelles and Flanders.

In politics, too, the war brought results no one could have predicted. Rhodes had died in 1902. Kruger died in exile in Switzerland in 1904. Meanwhile

Milner's 'crèche', alias Kindergarten, started their race to rebuild the Transvaal and Free State on British lines, before the British Parliament ('that mob at Westminster') handed them back to the volk. The careful work of reconstruction partially redeemed for many Boers the wanton destruction that had made it necessary. Before the war, Chamberlain's budget in the Colonial Office, to cover the whole world, totalled £600,000. Now, such was the fashion for peaceful imperial development that Milner and Chamberlain (and Alfred Lyttelton, after Chamberlain resigned as Colonial Secretary in 1903) arranged for £35 million to be borrowed for investment in South Africa. There was also to be a war contribution of £30 million, guaranteed by Wernher-Beit and others. (They were never called to pay.) Soon a grid-mesh of new railways and irrigation channels began to criss-cross the veld, as impressive as the ones built by Cromer in Egypt and the Sudan.[21]

But Milner's arithmetic in anglicizing the old republics rested on one crucial foundation: the need for new British immigrants. When the first census was taken in 1904, it turned out that potential Boer voters roughly balanced the number of British voters in the Transvaal. Hence Milner's desperate need for British immigrants, which depended, in turn, on the expansion of the Rand. The alliance with Wernher-Beit, indispensable to the making of the war, now proved Milner's undoing. The deep level mines, controlled by Wernher-Beit and other British magnates, were still short of sufficient African miners prepared to work underground at sufficiently low wages. Milner agreed that the best expedient was to import indentured labourers from China. The British Cabinet agreed – subject to regulations that the Chinese were not to be flogged as though they were Africans. But such was the hostility felt by white miners towards Chinese immigration, that Milner lost the support of the mass of the British Uitlanders; their political representatives formed an alliance with the emergent pan-Afrikaner party (Het Volk) of Botha and Smuts. When it was discovered in Britain that Chinese labourers were being flogged after all, a vote of censure was passed on Milner in the British House of Commons. He resigned as Governor in 1905. His fall – and the hullabaloo over 'Chinese slavery' – helped sweep CB and the Liberals to power in 1906.

Milner's political blunder in allowing the flogging of Chinese labourers cut short his experiment in building a Greater Britain on the veld. But the experiment was already doomed, Chinese or no Chinese. The blunt demographical facts undermined all Milner's hopes. There was so little immigration that the Boers remained in the majority. In 1906, CB and the Liberals promoted, according to their understanding of the agreement at Vereeniging, the two Crown Colonies to the status of self-governing colonies. When the votes were counted after the first general elections, Smuts's and Botha's Het Volk had swept the board. It set the seal on the failure of Milnerism.[22] From now on, there would be a series of shifting alliances in power in South Africa. The loyalist party, led by Sir Percy Fitzpatrick (knighted, along with other Randlords or ex-Randlords, George Farrar, Abe Bailey, Julius Wernher, and Alfred Beit's brother, Otto), would have no chance.

On the other hand, the grant of self-government by CB transformed Smuts's and Botha's own attitude to the Empire. While Milner exchanged the public service for international banking (re-emerging only in December 1916, as the man of destiny in Lloyd George's war Cabinet), Botha and Smuts travelled the world as imperial statesmen. In fact, the paradox of the war was that, despite the bitterness that it created among the volk, it gave Britain during the same period an apparently contented addition to its Empire. In two World Wars, South Africa stuck by the side of its mother (and stepmother). The naval base at Simonstown, hinge of Britain's global strategy, remained a British-controlled base until 1955.

True, there was an attempt at a Boer rebellion in 1914, led by De Wet and other irreconcilables, and possibly supported by De la Rey. (He was shot by accident during the rising.) But Botha and Smuts had no difficulty in stamping out the rebellion, without calling on imperial troops. De Wet served a year in prison. He died in 1922, isolated and apparently forgotten.

Then, nearly forty years later, in 1961, the Great Trek happened all over again. Dr Verwoerd led the volk out of the Commonwealth – and took all other South Africans, black, brown and white, with them. He declared the Union a republic fifty-nine years, to the day, after the Peace of Vereeniging. The party founded by Botha and Smuts had been replaced in 1948 by Malan and the Nationalists. The last of the war heroes were then vanishing from the scene: Hertzog in 1942, followed by Smuts in 1950. But the new governments were heirs to the old uncompromising republican tradition of Steyn and De Wet – tempered in the fire of war. Today, the Nationalists rule white South Africa on their own terms, and the memory of the *Tweede Vryheidsoorlog* (the 'Second War of Independence' as they call the Boer War) is kept green.*[23] It is a reminder to English-speaking South Africans that they do not belong to the volk, and must earn their place in the white laager. The war ('that wretched war', as the sons of loyalists call it) helps to weaken white opposition to the Nationalists.

What of the black majority? Perhaps the worst legacy of the war was the political price it exacted from Africans to pay for white unity.

Bringing two new states into the Empire made urgent the need to reconcile the white communities. The war made that process a great deal more difficult. It has taken seventy-six years and is still not fully accomplished. And, in the end, the grand design defeated itself. The two half-reconciled communities left the Empire. And the price of trying to reconcile the whites was paid by the blacks and browns. In fact, the end result of Milner's destruction of the old republics was not only to lose the two old colonies, too, but to cast away that priceless Liberal legacy: the no-colour-bar tradition of the Cape.

The first payment of the price was at Vereeniging. Milner had inserted that subtle preposition 'after' into Article 8 (Clause 9) of the peace terms. There was to be no franchise for the natives until *after* the introduction of self-government, that is, never (or, as people used to say in Ireland, not until Monday-come-

---

* In the official War Museum at Bloemfontein, recently refurbished, there is an exhibition of concentration camp relics, including the ground glass supposed to have been put in the camp food by the British authorities.

never-in-a-wheel-barrow). This led to the second payment in 1906–7, when CB introduced self government to the Transvaal and ORC. Because of Article 8 at Vereeniging – and because of a guilty conscience towards the Afrikaners – the Liberals did not prevent the restoration of the colour-bar in the constitutions of the two ex-republics. The third payment was made when the Union was being negotiated in 1909. Once again, Article 8 was cited to explain why Britain could do nothing to stop the colour-bar poisoning the new Union constitution. There had been no colour-bar (although the coloured seventy-seven per cent had only fifteen per cent of the vote) in the old Cape Parliament. The Liberals mag-nanimously agreed that the new constitution would permanently exclude all potential coloured MPs from the new Union Parliament. The process of pact-making between the whites, at the expense of the blacks and browns, occurred several times more before the Nationalists completed the job. The pact between Hertzog's Nationalists and the Labour Party in 1924 extended the colour-bar to industry; the coalition of Hertzog and Smuts in 1934 involved the removal of the African voters of Cape Province from the common roll; the reunion of National-ist parties in 1948 led to the removal of the Coloured voters of the Cape from the common roll. This was the tortuous path down which Milner's short cut had led South Africa.[24]

Today, the wheel has turned full circle. With the Boer War, the Second War of Independence, finally won, the volk are facing a third. The new adversary, black nationalism, can match Afrikaner nationalism in stamina and perhaps outmatch it in bitterness. Otherwise, there are many parallels between the situation today and in 1899. If an African read Milner's 'Helot Despatch' in the United Nations Assembly, no black man would dispute the force of the rhetoric. 'The case for intervention is overwhelming ... the spectacle of thousands of helots ...' To save white South Africa and its economy from ruin, a chorus of sensible advice is offered by the gold magnates and other well-wishers. And in 1978, as they heard Vorster pleading for time, promising reforms, yet dribbling them out like a squeezed sponge (if at all), it was almost as though Oom Paul was alive and well and living in Pretoria. The enlightened (*verligte*) wing of the Nationalists oscillates today – as Smuts did in 1899 – between hope for compromise and a fear that it is too late. The hard-liners (*verkrampte*) put their faith in their French Mirages as Kruger's war party put their faith in God and the Mauser. 'There is only one way out of the troubles in South Africa: reform or war. And of the two war is more likely.' How grimly prophetic is Milner's phrase today. But, this time, no one expects the war to be over by Christmas.

Milner did not live to see the complete overthrow of all he had tried to accomplish. The Higher Powers had reserved a more ironic fate for him. With Violet, his wife (they married in 1921), he made a trip to South Africa in 1924 to revisit the scene of his labours, was bitten by a tsetse fly, caught sleeping sickness, and died. On Milner, Africa had had its revenge.

Postscript: Wernher's death occurred in 1912, preceded by Beit's in 1906. Their personal estate (Beit – £8 million: Wernher £14 million) made them in turn the

Important Dates Before
and During the Boer War

1652 Dutch East India Company found shipping station at Cape
1795 Dutch lose Cape to British
1803 Dutch (Batavian Republic) resume control
1806 Second British occupation begins
1815 Slachter's Nek Rebellion by Afrikaans-speaking settlers. British rule at Cape confirmed
1820 4,000 British settlers arrive at Cape
1834 Slavery abolished at Cape, following decision of British Parliament
1835–7 The Great Trek. Frontier farmers (Boers) pour across Orange River. But majority of the Afrikaans-speaking settlers (Afrikaners) remain in the Cape
1838 (16 Dec) Pretorius beats Dingaan, Zulu king, at Battle of Blood River
1838–43 Boers concentrate in Natal
1843 British annex Natal as colony
1848 Transorangia annexed as Orange River Sovereignty. Smith defeats Pretorius at Battle of Boomplaatz
1852 Sand River Convention confirms independence of Transvaal Republic
1854 Bloemfontein Convention restores independence of Transorangia as Orange Free State
1868–9 British annex Basutoland as Crown Colony at request of King Mosweshwe
1870–1 Diamond rush to Kimberley
1871 Annexation of Kimberley to Cape Colony, now self-governing. Cecil Rhodes, aged 18, joins diamond rush, followed by Alfred Beit (in 1875)
1877 Proclamation of Transvaal as British Crown Colony. Arrival of Frere
1879 British forces invade and (1887) annex Zululand, soon incorporated in Natal, now self-governing
1880–1 Kruger leads Transvaal rebellion against British rule: First Boer War (alias 'First War of Independence')
1881 Peace talks after Battle of Majuba (27 Feb). Pretoria Convention: Transvaal Republic obtains limited independence

1884   London Convention: Transvaal (South African Republic) obtains greater independence

1886   Gold rush to Witwatersrand begins

1888   Cecil Rhodes obtains British Royal Charter for his British South Africa Co. to exploit Lobengula's territory (Mashonaland and Matabeleland)

1889   Formation of Wernher, Beit & Co, soon to become the principal Rand mining-house

1890   Rhodes's BSA Co. (Chartered Company) sends pioneers to occupy Lobengula's country, renamed Rhodesia

1895 (29 Dec)   Dr Jameson launches Raid into Transvaal with 500 Chartered Company police from Pitsani and Mafeking

1896   Battle of Doornkop. Jameson surrenders. Arrest and trial of Johannesburg Reform Committee. Rhodes resigns as Prime Minister at the Cape. Cape Enquiry into Raid

1897   London Enquiry into Raid. Sir Alfred Milner takes over as British High Commissioner at the Cape

1898   Kruger elected for fourth term as President of Transvaal

1898–9   Milner back in London for 'holiday'

1899

31 May–5 Jun   Bloemfontein Conference

8 Sep   British Cabinet decides to send 10,000 men to defend Natal

26 Sep   Penn Symons pushes up troops to Dundee

27 Sep   Kruger calls up Transvaal burghers, and persuades Steyn to follow suit in Free State

7 Oct   British mobilize 1st Army Corps etc. White lands at Durban

9 Oct   Kruger sends ultimatum

11 Oct   Expiry of ultimatum and outbreak of war

14–16 Oct   Boers begin siege of Kekewich at Kimberley and of Baden-Powell at Mafeking

20 Oct   Penn Symons gives battle at Talana. Möller surrenders

21 Oct   Battle of Elandslaagte

24 Oct   Battle of Rietfontein

30 Oct   'Mournful Monday': Joubert outmanoeuvres White at Battle of Ladysmith (Modderspruit) and Carleton is forced to surrender at Nicholson's Nek

31 Oct   Buller lands at Cape Town

2 Nov   White's 'field force' accepts siege at Ladysmith

15 Nov   Botha wrecks armoured train between Frere and Chieveley

21 Nov   Battle of Willow Grange

23 Nov   End of Botha's and Joubert's raid southwards into Natal. Methuen's first battle: Belmont

25 Nov   Methuen's second battle: Graspan

26 Nov   Holdsworth, with Linchwe's Africans, attacks Boer laager at Derdepoort

28 Nov   Methuen's third battle: Modder River

7 Dec   Hunter's night raid on Long Tom besieging Ladysmith

10 Dec   Gatacre's mishap at Stormberg

11 Dec   Methuen's repulse at Magersfontein

15 Dec   Buller's first reverse: Colenso

18 Dec   Roberts appointed to succeed Buller as C-in-C in South Africa, with Kitchener as Chief of Staff

26 Dec   Baden-Powell's abortive attack on Game Tree Fort

29 Dec   German mail-steamer *Bundesrath* seized by Royal Navy

1900

6 Jan   Boers attack Caesar's Camp and Wagon Hill (Platrand) at Ladysmith

10 Jan   Roberts and Kitchener land at Cape Town

24 Jan   Battle of Spion Kop

5–7 Feb   Vaal Krantz captured, then evacuated

11 Feb   Roberts begins great flank march

14–27 Feb   Buller's fourth attempt to relieve Ladysmith

15 Feb   French relieves Kimberley

18 Feb   Battle of Paardeberg

27 Feb   Surrender of Cronje at Paardeberg

28 Feb   Buller relieves Ladysmith

7 Mar   Battle of Poplar Grove. Kruger escapes

10 Mar   Battle of Driefontein

13 Mar   Capture of Bloemfontein

15 Mar   Roberts's first proclamation: amnesty except for leaders

17 Mar   Boer Council of War at Kroonstad

27 Mar   Death of Joubert

31 Mar   De Wet ambushes Broadwood at Sannah's Post

4 Apr   Surrender of Royal Irish at Reddersburg

3 May   Roberts resumes march to Pretoria

4 May   Mahon's relief column sets out for Mafeking

11 May   Buller resumes advance

12 May   Roberts occupies Kroonstad. B-P beats off Eloff's attack on Mafeking

14 May   Buller outmanoeuvres Boers from Biggarsberg

17 May   Mahon and Plumer relieve Mafeking

28 May   Annexation of Orange Free State proclaimed: renamed Orange River Colony

31 May   Roberts captures Johannesburg
        Piet De Wet captures Spragge and Irish Yeomanry at Lindley

5 Jun   Roberts captures Pretoria. Release of prisoners

7 Jun   Christiaan De Wet's success at Roodewal

11–12 Jun   Battle of Diamond Hill

12 Jun   Buller turns Drakensberg position and occupies Volksrust

11 Jul   Surrender of Scots Greys at Zilikat's Nek

15 Jul   Steyn and De Wet escape from Brandwater Basin

21 Jul   Roberts begins advance towards Komati Poort

31 Jul   Surrender of Prinsloo to Hunter in Brandwater Basin

14 Aug   Ian Hamilton fails to prevent De Wet's escape
27 Aug   Buller defeats Botha at Bergendal (Dalmanutha)
30 Aug   Release of last 2,000 British prisoners at Nooitgedacht
6 Sep   Buller captures Lydenburg
25 Sep   Pole-Carew reaches Komati Poort
19 Oct   Kruger sails for France on board the *Gelderland*
24 Oct   Buller sails for England
25 Oct   Formal proclamation at Pretoria of annexation of Transvaal
6 Nov   De Wet defeated at Bothaville. Le Gallais killed
29 Nov   Kitchener succeeds Roberts as C-in-C in South Africa.
        Roberts to succeed Wolseley as C-in-C at home
13 Dec   De la Rey and Smuts surprise Clements at Nooitgedacht
16 Dec   Kritzinger enters Cape Colony
29 Dec   Helvetia post captured

1901
27 Jan–26 Mar   French's drive in E. Transvaal
31 Jan   Smuts captures Modderfontein. Massacre of Africans
10–28 Feb   De Wet's 'invasion' of Cape Colony
28 Feb   Abortive Middelburg peace talks between Kitchener and Botha
10 Apr   First drive in N. Free State begins
8 May   Milner sails for leave in England
18 Jul   First drive in Cape Colony northwards
7 Aug   Kitchener's proclamation of banishment for Boer leaders captured
        armed after 15 Sep
12 Aug   Kritzinger driven out of Cape Colony
3 Sep   Smuts invasion of Cape Colony via Kiba Drift
5 Sep   Scobell captures Lotter's commando
7 Sep   Smuts cuts up 17th Lancers at Elands River Poort
17 Sep   Botha cuts up Gough's force at Blood River Poort
26 Sep   Botha attacks Forts Itala and Prospect
6 Oct   Botha escapes northward
11 Oct   Execution of Commandant Lotter. Capture of Scheepers
30 Oct   Benson killed at Bakenlaagte
7 Nov   Ian Hamilton appointed Kitchener's Chief of Staff
7 Dec   National Scouts inaugurated
16 Dec   Kritzinger captured
23 Dec   Kroonstad-Lindley blockhouse line completed
25 Dec   De Wet captures Yeomanry at Tweefontein

1902
17 Jan   Scheepers executed
6–8 Feb   New drive in E. Orange River Colony. De Wet breaks out
13–26 Feb   Second drive in E. Orange River Colony.
        Rawlinson's success
7 Mar   De la Rey captures Methuen at Tweebosch
24 Mar   First drive in W. Transvaal

26 Mar   Death of Cecil Rhodes

4 Apr–3 May   Smuts besieges Ookiep

11 Apr   Battle of Rooiwal

12–18 Apr   Boer peace delegates' first meeting at Pretoria

1–10 May   Last drives in N.E. Orange River Colony

6 May   Zulu attack on Holkrantz

11 May   End of Ian Hamilton's last drive in W. Transvaal

15–18 May   First meeting of Boer delegates at Vereeniging

31 May   Final meeting at Vereeniging.

Surrender terms signed at Pretoria

SOURCES

General Abbreviations

B	St John Brodrick
BM	British Museum, Additional MSS
C	Joseph Chamberlain
EGO	From personal observation
K	Lord Kitchener
L	Lord Lansdowne
M	Sir Alfred Milner
NAM	National Army Museum, London
PRO	Public Record Office, London
W	Lord Wolseley

A. *Unpublished Sources and Abbreviations*

Abad	Lt Abadie, Brenthurst Library, Johannesburg
Alf	Lt Henry Alford, University of St Andrews
All	Col E. Allenby, King's College, London
Ard	Maj-Gen. Sir J. Ardagh, PRO 30/40
Asq	H. Asquith, Bodleian Library, Oxford
Bal	A. J. Balfour, BM 49722–49835
Bar	Capt. S. L. Barry, NAM 6807
Beer	De Beers, Kimberley
Bel	Capt. Bellew, NAM 5707/8
Big	Sir A. Bigge
Bird	Maj. Bird
Bobs	F-M Lord Roberts, NAM 7101/23
Brod	St John Brodrick, PRO 30/67
Brom	Capt. W. Bromley Davenport, Rylands Library, Manchester
Bry	J Bryce, Bodleian, Oxford
Bull (PRO)	Gen. Sir R. Buller, PRO 132
Bull (Crediton)	Gen. Sir R. Buller, Downes, Crediton
Cab 37	Cabinet Papers (photocopies), PRO
CB	Sir H. Campbell-Bannerman, BM 41206–41252
Cham	J. Chamberlain, Birmingham University
Ches	Capt. R. Chester Master
CO 179	Colonial Office (Natal), PRO
CO 417	Colonial Office (South Africa), PRO
CO 879	Colonial Office (Confidential Print), PRO
Con	Capt. W. Congreve
Cros	Lt G. L. Crossman, NAM 6305/24/4

Cru	Lt M. Crum, National Library of Scotland
CT	Confidential Telegrams (1899–1902), War Office Library, Whitehall, London
Deev	D. Deeves, Killie Campbell Library, Durban
Dow	Pte A. Down, NAM
Dun	Maj-Gen. Lord Dundonald, Scottish Record Office, GD 233
Eck	H. Eckstein & Co, Barlow-Rand, Johannesburg
Fitz	J. P. Fitzpatrick, Amanzi, Uitenhage, South Africa
Fren	Lt-Gen. J. D. French, Brenthurst Library, Johannesburg
Gell	P. Gell, Hopton Hall, Derbyshire
Gil	W. Gilbert, NAM 6309/114
Gou	Majs H. & J. Gough
Haig	Col D. Haig, Bemersyde
Hal	Capt. A. Haldane, National Library of Scotland, Acc 2070
Ham	Col I. Hamilton, King's College, London
Herb	A. Herbert
Hick	Maj. W. B., Lt C. & Pte M. Hickie, Slevoir, Terryglass, Co. Tipperary
H & O	Home & Overseas Corr of Lord Roberts, War Office Library, London
Holt	Surgeon-Capt. M. Holt, NAM 6309/42
Hut	Maj-Gen. E. Hutton, National Library of Australia
Jelf	Lt R. G. Jelf, NAM 6903/6
Jou	Capt. H. F. Jourdain, NAM 5603/10
Kek	Col R. Kekewich, North Lancs Regiment Museum
Kel	Capt. H. R. Kelham, R H Fusiliers Regiment Museum, Glasgow
Kell	Lt-Col T. Kelly-Kenny
Kent	Lt R. Kentish
Ker	Maj. M. Kerin
KG	Kommandant-generaal MSS, Transvaal Archives, Pretoria
Kit	Lt-Gen. Lord Kitchener, PRO 30/57
Laf	Capt. Lafone, BM 39558
Lan	5th Marquess of Lansdowne, Bowood House, Wilts
Ley	Dr W. Leyds MSS, Transvaal Archives, Pretoria
Lyt	Maj-Gen. N. Lyttelton, Westfield College, London
Man	Manchester Regiment Collection, Manchester Public Library
Maur	Capt. F. Maurice, King's College, London
Meth	Lt-Gen. Lord Methuen, Corsham Court, Wilts
Mil	Sir A. Milner, Bodleian Library, Oxford (deposited by New College)
Pal	Lt O. Palmer, NAM 6503/72
PC	*See below*, Pakenham Collection
Rawl	Lt-Col Sir H. Rawlinson, NAM 5201/33
Rhod	C. J. Rhodes, Rhodes House, Oxford
Roy	Capt. Roy, Sherwood Regiment Museum
Sal (Hat)	3rd Marquis of Salisbury, Hatfield House
Sal	3rd Marquis of Salisbury, Christ Church, Oxford
Sand	Lt-Col A. Sandbach
Scho	Scholtz, Cullen Library, University of Witwatersrand
SD	*Secret* South Africa Despatches, War Office Library, London
Sel	Lord Selborne, Bodleian Library, Oxford
SJ	*Secret* Journal of the Principal Events etc, War Office Library, London
SM	*Secret* Miscellany, War Office Library, London
Smit	Maj-Gen. H. Smith-Dorrien, Sherwood Regiment Collection
SPG	Society for Propagation of the Gospel in Foreign Parts, London
Stea	Capt. Steavenson, Liverpool Museum

Tren	Lt C. Trench
Trot	Capts A., E. and G. Trotter, Charterhall, Duns, Berwickshire
Warr	Lt H. C. Warre, NAM 6508/40
Weil	B. Weil, BM 46848
Whi	Lt-Gen. Sir G. White, India Office Library, Eur F 108
Wilk	S. Wilkinson, Army Museums Ogilby Trust, London
WO 32	War Office Registered Papers, PRO
WO 105	F-M Lord Roberts Papers, PRO
WO 108	Various Boer War Papers, PRO
Wol	F-M Lord Wolseley, Central Library, Hove

In Pakenham Collection

1. Belonging to the author: MSS of Gen. Buller, Col Jones, Maj. Donegan, Capt. 5th Earl of Longford, Capt. E. M. Pakenham, Gunner Netley, Nurse Egan, Lt Chandos-Pole.
2. Tape recordings, made by the author, of war veterans Lang, Thompson, Netley, Bowers, Packer, Parker, Hutton, Whitton, Eade, Edingborough, Pain, Blackmuir, Steevens, Goschen, Hall, Ball, Blunson, Brayne, Higgitt, Stericker, Pym, Stock, etc.
3. Copies of MSS lent to author by war veterans Lang, Eade, Edingborough, Pain.
4. Copies of MSS lent to the author written by Maj. E. Phipps-Hornby, Capt. Molyneux-Seele, Lts Addison, Macpherson, Clive, Sgt Galley, Cpl Hurley, Trooper Gibson, Ptes Gibbons, Key, Pegum, Kennedy, Brymer, Dr Dobbs.

B. *Published Sources*

Breyt	See J. H. Breytenbach *Geskiedenis van die Tweede Vryheidsoorlog*
C, Cd	Papers presented to Parliament by royal command
DNB	*Dictionary of National Biography*
DSAB	*Dictionary of South African Biography*. See W. J. De Kock (ed.)
Hansard	4th Series Parliamentary Debates
MP	*Milner Papers*. See C. Headlam (ed.)
OH	*Official History of the War in South Africa (1899–1902)*. See Sir Frederick Maurice (ed.)
PPW	*Pen Pictures of the War*
PRAI	*Proceedings of the Royal Artillery Institution*, Woolwich
RCSAW	*Royal Commission on the War in South Africa* (vols I–IV–Cd 1789–92)
SP	*Smuts Papers*. See Hancock and Van der Poel (ed.)
TH	*The Times History of the War in South Africa (1899–1902)*. See L. S. Amery (ed.)

Select Bibliography

Note: all books were published in London unless otherwise stated

Abbott, J. H. M. *Tommy Cornstalk* (1902)

Amery, L. S. (ed.) *The Times History of the War in South Africa.* 7 vols (1900–1909)

—— *Days of Fresh Air* (1939)

An Average Observer [Flora Shaw?]. *The Burden of Proof; or England's Debt to Sir Redvers Buller* (1902)

Arthur, G. *Life of Lord Kitchener* 3 vols (1920)

—— (ed.) *The Letters of Lord and Lady Wolseley 1870–1911* (1922)

Ashe, E. Oliver. *Besieged by the Boers* (New York and London 1900)

Atkins, J. B. *The Relief of Ladysmith* (1900)

Baden-Powell, Maj. B. F. S. *War in Practice: Tactical Lessons of the Campaign in South Africa, 1899–1902* (1903)

Baden-Powell, Col R. S. S. *Sketches in Mafeking and East Africa* (1907)

Baillie, Maj. F. D. *Mafeking. A Diary of the Siege* (1900)

Bakkes, C. M. *Die militere situasie aan die benede-Tugela op die vooraand van die Britse deurbraak by Pietershoogte, 26 Februarie 1900* Archives Year Book I (1967)

Barnard, C. J. *Generaal Louis Botha op die Natalse front, 1899–1900* (Cape Town 1970)

Barnes, J. *The Great War Trek. With the British Army on the Veldt* (New York 1901)

Battersby, H. F. P. *In the Web of a War* (1900)

Baynes, Rt. Rev. A. H. *My Diocese during the War* (1900)

Beet, Arthur J. *Kimberley Under Siege* (Kimberley 1950)

Begbie, H. *Story of Baden-Powell* (1900)

Billington, R. C. *A Mule Driver at the Front* (1901)

Birdwood, Lord. *Khaki and Gown: An Autobiography* (1941)

Blake, Col J. Y. F. *A West Pointer with the Boers* (Boston 1903)

Brandt, J. *The Petticoat Commando* (1913)

Breytenbach, J. H. *Die Geskiedenis van die Tweede Vryheidsoorlog in Suid-Afrika, 1899–1902* 4 vols (Pretoria 1969–1977)

Bron, Alice. *Diary of a Nurse in South Africa* (1901)

Brunker, Lt-Col H. M. E. *Boer War, 1899–1900. Organization of the British and Boer Forces* (1900)

Bryce, James. *Impressions of South Africa* (new ed. 1897–1899)

Buchan, John. *Memory Hold the Door* (1940)

—— *The African Colony* (1903)

Burdett-Coutts, W. *The Sick and Wounded in South Africa* (1900)

—— *The Hospitals Commission. Comments on the Report* (1901)

Burleigh, Bennett. *The Natal Campaign* (1900)

Burne, Lt C., RN. *With the Naval Brigade in Natal, 1899–1900* (1902)

Burnett, Maj. C. K. *The 18th Hussars in South Africa* (Winchester 1905)

Burnham, Maj. F. *Scouting on Two Continents* (1926)

Butler, Col Lewis. *Sir Redvers Buller* (1909)

Butler, W. F. *Sir William Francis Butler: An Autobiography* (1911)

Callwell, Maj-Gen. Sir C. E. *Stray Recollections* (1923)

—— *Field-Marshal Sir Henry Wilson* 2 vols (1927)

Cartwright, A. P. *The Corner House. The Early History of Johannesburg* (Cape Town 1965)

—— *The First South African: The Life and Times of Sir Percy Fitzpatrick* (Cape Town 1971)

Charlton, [L. E. O.] *Charlton* (1931)

Childers, Erskine. *In the Ranks of the CIV* (1901)

—— *War and the Arme Blanche* (1910)

Churcher, Maj. D. W. (diary) *With the Irish Fusiliers from Alexandria to Natal 1899–1900* (Reading n.d.)

Churchill, R. S. *Winston S. Churchill* vols 1 & 2 and companion vols 1 & 2 (1966–9)

Churchill, Winston S. *Ian Hamilton's March* (1900)

—— *London to Ladysmith via Pretoria* (1900)

—— *My Early Life: a roving commission* (1943)

Colvile, Maj-Gen. Sir H. E. *The Work of the Ninth Division in South Africa in 1900* (1901)

Colvin, I. *The Life of Jameson* 2 vols (1922–3)

Comaroff, J. L. (ed.) *The Boer War diary of Sol. T. Plaatje; an African at Mafeking* (1973)

Cook, E. T. *Rights and Wrongs of the Transvaal War* (1902)

—— *Edmund Garrett: a memoir* (1909)

Corner, William. *The Story of the 34th Company (Middlesex) Imperial Yeomanry. From the point of view of Private no 6243* (1902)

Craw, B. *A Diary of the Siege of Ladysmith, 27th Oct 1899 – 23 March 1900* (Ladysmith 1970)

Creswicke, Louis. *South Africa and the Transvaal War* 7 vols (1900–2)

Crowe, George. *The Commission of HMS Terrible. . .* (1903)

Crum, Maj. F. M. *With the MI in South Africa, 1899–1902* (Cambridge 1903)

Cunliffe, F. H. E. *The History of the Boer War* 2 vols (1901–4)

Cunliffe, Marcus. *The Royal Irish Fusiliers 1793–1950* (Oxford 1952)

Curtis, L. *With Milner in South Africa* (Oxford 1951)

Cuthbert, Capt. J. H. (ed.) *The 1st Battalion Scots Guards in South Africa 1899–1902* Harrison & Sons (n.d.)

Davis, R. Harding. *With Both Armies in South Africa* (New York 1900)

Davitt, M. *The Boer Fight for Freedom* (New York 1902)

De Kiewiet, C. W. *British Colonial Policy and the South African Republics* (1929)

—— *The Imperial Factor in South Africa: A Study in Politics and Economics* (Cambridge 1937)

De Kock, W. J. and Kruger, D. W. (ed.) *Dictionary of South African Biography* vols I, II & III (Cape Town 1968, 1972, 1976)

De La Warr, The Earl. *Some Reminiscences of the War* (1900)

De Montmorency, H. *Sword and Stirrup: memories* (1936)

Denoon, D. *A Grand Illusion. The Failure of Imperial Policy in the Transvaal Colony during the Period of Reconstruction 1900–1905* (1973)

[D'Etechegoyen] Ex-Lieutenant of General de Villebois-Mareuil. *Ten Months in the Field with the Boers* (1901)

De Villebois-Mareuil, Count G. H. *War Notes. . .* (1901)

De Villiers, O. T. *Met de Wet en Steyn in het Veld. . .* (Amsterdam 1903)

De Wet, C. R. *Three Years' War* (1902)

Dickson, W. K-L. *The Biograph in Battle* (1901)

Dixon, C. M. *The Leaguer of Ladysmith* (1900)

Dooner, Mildred G. *The Last Post* (1903)

Dormer, F. J. *Vengeance as a Policy in Afrikanderland* (1901)

Doyle, A. Conan. *The Great Boer War* (1900–2)

Du Cane, H. *See* Waters, Col W. H. H.

Dugdale, Blanche. *Arthur James Balfour* vol. 1 (1936)

Drus, E. 'The Question of Imperial Complicity in the Jameson Raid' (*Eng. Hist. Rev.*, LXVIII, October 1953)

—— 'A Report on the Papers of Joseph Chamberlain relating to the Jameson Raid and the Inquiry' (*Bulletin of Inst. Hist. Res.*, XXV, 1952)

—— 'Select Documents from the Chamberlain Papers concerning Anglo-Transvaal Relations, 1896–1899' (*Bulletin of Inst. Hist. Res.*, XXVII, 1954)

Dum-dum's der publieke opinie. Een honderdtal caricaturen op den Transvaalsch-Engelschen oorlog (Amsterdam 1900)

Dundonald, Lt-Gen. The Earl of. *My Army Life* (1926)

Dunn-Pattison, R. P. *The History of the 91st Argyllshire Highlanders* (Edinburgh 1910)

Durand, M. *The Life of Field-Marshal Sir George White* 2 vols (1915)

Engelenburg, F. V. *General Louis Botha* (1929)

Esher, Viscount. *Journals & Letters Vol. I* (1914)

Farrelly, M. J. *The Settlement after the War in South Africa* (1900)

Farwell, Byron. *The Great Boer War* (1977)

Ferreira, O. J. O. (ed.) *See* Trichard, S. P. E.

Fisher, J. *That Miss Hobhouse* (1971)

—— *Paul Kruger, His Life and Times* (1974)

Fitzgibbon, Maurice. *Arts under Arms* ... (1901)

Fitzpatrick, J. P. *The Transvaal from Within* (1899)

—— *South African Memories* (1932)

Fort, G. Seymour. *Alfred Beit* (1932)

Fortescue, Sir John. *The Royal Army Service Corps* vol. I (Cambridge 1930)

Fremantle, F. E. *Impressions of a Doctor in Khaki* (1901)

French, Maj. Hon. Gerald. *The Life of Field-Marshal Sir John French, First Earl of Ypres, KP etc.* (1931)

Fry, A. Ruth. *Emily Hobhouse: a memoir* (1929)

Fuller, J. F. C. *The Last of the Gentlemen's Wars* (1937)

Gandhi, M. K. *An Autobiography* Paperback (1966)

Gardiner, A. G. *Life of Sir William Harcourt* 2 vols (1923)

Gardner, Brian. *Mafeking, A Victorian Legend* (1966)

—— *The Lion's Cage* (1969)

Gardyne, Lt-Col A. D. G. *The Life of a Regiment. History of the Gordon Highlanders* vol III, 1898–1914 (1939)

Garrett, F. E. and Edwards, E. J. *The Story of an African Crisis ... The Jameson Raid and Johannesburg Revolt of 1896* (1897)

Garvin, J. L. vols 2 and 3, and Amery, J. vol. 4. *The Life of Joseph Chamberlain* (1934 and 1951)

Gilbert, S. H. *Rhodesia and After. 17th and 18th Battns. I.Y. in South Africa* (1901)

Girouard, Lt-Col Sir Percy. *History of the Railways during the War in South Africa* (Chatham 1904)

Godley, Gen. Sir Alick. *Life of an Irish Soldier* (1939)

Goldmann, C. S. *With General French and the Cavalry in South Africa* (1902)

Gollin, A. M. *Proconsul in Politics: a study of Lord Milner in opposition and in power* (1964)

Gooch, G. P. *Life of Lord Courtney* (1920)

Gordon, C. T. *The Growth of Boer Opposition to Kruger, 1890–1895* (Cape Town 1970)

Gough, Gen. Sir Hubert. *Soldiering On* (1954)

Gore, Lt-Col. St John. *The Green Horse (5th Dgn. Gds) in Ladysmith* (1901)

[Graham, Harry]. *Coldstreamer. Ballads of the Boer War* (1902)

[Grant, M. H.]. Linesman. *Words of an Eye Witness. The Struggle in Natal* (1901)

Grenville, J. A. S. *Lord Salisbury and Foreign Policy: the Close of the Nineteenth Century* (1964; revised 1970)

Griffith, Kenneth. *Thank God We Kept the Flag Flying. The Siege and Relief of Ladysmith 1899–1900* (1974)

Grinnell-Milne, D. W. *Baden-Powell at Mafeking* (1957)

Haldane, Capt. J. A. L. *How we escaped from Pretoria* (1900)

—— General Sir Aylmer. *A Soldier's Saga* (1948)

Hales, A. G. *Campaign Pictures of the War in South Africa, 1899–1900* (1900)

Hall, D. D. 'Guns in South Africa, 1899–1902' *Mil. Hist. Jnl. of South Africa II* (1) (June 1971)

Hall, Col Sir John. *The Coldstream Guards 1885–1914* (Oxford 1929)

Hamer, W. S. *The British Army, Civil-Military Relations 1885–1905* (Oxford 1970)

Hamilton, Gen. Sir Ian. *Listening for the Drums* (1944)

—— *The Commander* (1957)

Hamilton, Ian. *The Happy Warrior: a Life of General Sir Ian Hamilton* (1966)

Hamilton, J. Angus. *The Siege of Mafeking* (1900)

Hammond, J. Hays. *The Autobiography of John Hays Hammond* 2 vols (New York 1935)

Hancock, W. K. *Smuts Vol. I: The Sanguine Years, 1870–1919* (Cambridge 1962)

—— and Van Der Poel, J. (eds.) *Selections from the Smuts Papers* (Cambridge 1966)

Harington, Gen. Sir C. *Plumer of Messines* (1935)

Hart-Synnot, B. M. (ed.) *Letters of Major General FitzRoy Hart-Synnot* (1912)

Hassell, A. R. I. and Hiley, J. A. *The Mobile Boer* (New York 1902)

Hatch, Dr. F. H. and Chalmers, J. A. *The Gold Mines of the Rand* (1895)

Headlam, Cecil (ed.) *The Milner Papers Vol. I: South Africa 1897–1899; Vol. II: South Africa 1899–1905* (1931, 1935)

Headlam, Maj-Gen. Sir John. *The History of the Royal Artillery* vols II & III (1937, 1940)

Henderson, G. F. R. *Science of War* (1905)

Hicks Beach, Lady Victoria. *Life of Sir Michael Hicks Beach* 2 vols (1932)

Hillcourt, W. and Baden-Powell, O. *Baden-Powell: the two lives of a hero* (1964)

Hillegas, H. C. *With the Boer Forces* (1900)

Hippisley, Lt-Col R. L. *History of the Telegraph Operations during the War in South Africa* (War Office 1903)

Hobhouse, Emily. *The Brunt of the War and Where it Fell* (1902)

—— *Report of a Visit to the Camps of Women and Children in the Cape and Orange River Colonies* (1901)

Hobson, J. A. *The War in South Africa; its Causes and Effects* (1900)

Hofmeyr, Adrian. *The Story of my Captivity during the Transvaal War . . .* (1900)

Hofmeyr, J. H. and Reitz, F. W. *The Life of Jan Hendrik Hofmeyr* (Cape Town 1913)

Hofmeyr, N. *Zes Maanden by de Commandos [Six Months with the Commandos]* (The Hague 1903)

Hole, H. M. *The Jameson Raid* (1930)

Holt, E. *The Boer War* (1958)

Hutchinson, G. T. *Frank Rhodes, a Memoir* (privately printed 1908)

Iwan Müller, E. B. *Lord Milner and South Africa* (1902)

Jackson, M. C. *A Soldier's Diary in South Africa 1899–1901* (1913)

Jacson, Col M. *The Record of a Regiment of the Line –1st Bn. Devonshire Regiment – during the Boer War, 1899–1902* (1908)

James, D. *Lord Roberts* (1954)

James, Lionel. *High Pressure* (1929)

[James, Lionel]. *Intelligence Officer. On the Heels of de Wet* (Blackwood 1902)

Jameson's Heroic Charge (Johannesburg 1896)

Jeans, Surgn J. T. (RN). *Naval Brigades in the South African War, 1899–1900* (1901)

Jeppe, Carl. *The Kaleidoscopic Transvaal* (1906)

Jones, R. *A Life in Reuters* (1952)

Jorissen, Dr E. J. P. *Transvaalsche Herinneringen, 1876–1896* (Amsterdam 1897)

Jourdain, Lt-Col H. F. N. *Memories*

—— *The Natal Campaign 1899–1900* (privately printed 1948)

Judd, D. *The Boer War* (1977)

Kearsey, A. H. C. *War Record of the York and Lancaster Regt., 1900–1902* (Bell 1903)

Kestell, J. D. *Through Shot and Flame* (1903)

—— and Van Velden, D. E. *The Peace Negotiations between the Governments of the South African Republic and the Orange Free State* (1912)

Khaki Letters. See *Post Office Telegraphists*

Kimber, Charles Dixon. *Memorials of C. D. Kimber* (1902)

Kinnear, A. *To Modder River with Methuen* (Bristol 1900)

Kipling, R. *Definitive Edition of Rudyard Kipling's Verse* (1973 edition)

Knox, E. Blake. *Buller's Campaign* (R. Brimley Johnson 1902)

Kotzé, J. G. *Biographical Memoirs and Reminiscences* 2 vols (Cape Town 1934, 1947)

Kritzinger, P. H. and McDonald, R. D. *In the Shadow of Death* (1904)

Kruger, D. W. *Paul Kruger* 2 vols (Johannesburg 1961)

Kruger, Rayne. *Goodbye Dolly Gray: the Story of the Boer War* (1959)

Kruger, S. J. P. *The Memoirs of Paul Kruger . . . told by himself* 2 vols (1902)

The Ladysmith Bombshell 8 parts (reprinted Durban 1900)

The Ladysmith Lyre 4 nos (Ladysmith 1899–1900)

Langlois, Gen. *Lessons of Two Recent Wars* (Tr. for HMSO 1909)

Lehmann, J. H. *The First Boer War* (1972)

Le May, G. H. L. *British Supremacy in South Africa 1899–1907* (Oxford 1965)

Leyds, W. J. *Correspondentie, 1899–1902* 9 vols (The Hague 1919–34)

Lloyd, J. Barclay. *One Thousand Miles with the CIV* (1901)

Lockhart, J. G. and Woodhouse, C. M. *Rhodes* (1963)

Longford, Elizabeth. *Victoria RI* (1964; paperback ed. 1966)

Lucas, C. P. *The History of South Africa to the Jameson Raid* (Oxford 1899)

Luther, E. W. *Diary of E. W. Luther of Blake's Brigade* (Pretoria 1900)

Lynch, G. *Impressions of a War Correspondent* (1903)

Lyttelton, Gen. Sir Neville. *Eighty Years* (1927)

Macdonald, Donald. *How we Kept the Flag Flying. The Story of the Siege of Ladysmith* (1900)

McHugh, R. J. *The Siege of Ladysmith* (1900)

Mackern, H. F. *Side-Lights on the March* (1901)

Mackinnon, Maj-Gen. W. H. *Journal of the CIV in South Africa* (1901)

Maclean, A. H. H. *Public Schools and the War in South Africa* (1903)

Macnab, Roy. *The French Colonel. De Villebois-Mareuil and the Boers, 1899–1900* (Oxford 1975)

Macready, Gen. Sir Nevil. *Annals of an Active Life* (1924)

Magnus, P. *Kitchener: Portrait of an Imperialist* (1958)

Mahan, Capt A. T. *The War in South Africa to the Fall of Pretoria* (New York 1901)

Marais, J. S. *The Fall of Kruger's Republic* (Oxford 1961)

Marden, A. W. and Newbigging, W. P. E. *Rough Diary of 1st Bn. Manchester Regt. 1899–1902* (Manchester 1904)

Marling, Col Sir P. *Rifleman and Hussar* (1931)

Marquard, L. (ed.) *Letters from a Boer Parsonage: Letters of Margaret Marquard during the Boer War* (Cape Town 1967)

Martin, Col A. C. *The Concentration Camps 1900–1902: Facts, Figures and Fables* (Cape Town 1957)

Maurice, Maj-Gen. Sir Frederick M. *The Life of General Lord Rawlinson of Trent* (1928)

—— and Arthur, Sir George. *The Life of Lord Wolseley* (1924)

Maurice, Maj-Gen. Sir Frederick and Grant, M. H. *Official History of the War in South Africa, 1899–1902* 4 vols text, 4 vols maps (1906–1910)

Maxwell, Mrs Frank. *Frank Maxwell: a Memoir, and some letters edited by his wife* (1921)

May, Lt-Col E. S. *A Retrospect of the South African War (from the artillery standpoint)* (1901)

May, H. J. *Music of the Guns: based on two journals of the Boer War* (1970)

Meintjes, Johannes. *De la Rey: Lion of the West* (Johannesburg 1966)

—— *General Louis Botha* (1970)

—— *President Steyn* (1969)

—— *President Kruger* (1974)

Melville, C. H. *Life of General the Right Hon. Sir Redvers Buller* 2 vols (1923)

Menpes, M. *War Impressions. A Record in Colour* (1901)

Methuen, A. M. S. *The Tragedy of South Africa* (1905)

Midleton, Earl (St John Brodrick) *Records and Reactions* (1939)

Milne, James. *The Epistles of Atkins from South Africa* (1902)

Milner, Viscountess – formerly Lady Edward (Violet) Cecil *My Picture Gallery 1886–1901* (1951)

Moore, H. *Ladysmith during the Siege, 1899–1900* (1970)

Mouton, J. 'Generaal Piet Joubert en sy aandeel aan die Transvaalse geskiedenis'. *Archives Year Book for South African History* (1957)

Muller, C. F. J. etc. (ed.) *A Select Bibliography of South African History: a Guide for Historical Research* (Pretoria 1966). *A supplement to above* (Pretoria 1974)

Muller, C. H. *Oorlogsherinneringe* (Cape Town 1936)

Musgrave, G. C. *In South Africa with Buller* (1900)

Naudé, J. F. *Vechten en vluchten van Beyers en Kemp 'bokant' de Wet* (Rotterdam 1903)

Neilly, J. E. *Besieged with B-P. Siege of Mafeking* (1900)

Nevinson, H. W. *Ladysmith. The Diary of a Siege* (1900)

Newbigging, W. P. E. *See* Marden, A. W.

Newton, Lord. *Lord Lansdowne – a Biography* (1929)

Nimocks, W. *Milner's Young Men: the 'Kindergarten' in Edwardian Imperial Affairs* (1970)

Oberholster, J. J. *The Historical Monuments of South Africa* (Cape Town 1972)

O'Meara, Lt-Col W. A. J. *Kekewich in Kimberley* (1926)

Pakenham, E. *Jameson's Raid* (1960)

Parritt, B. *The Intelligencers. Intelligence Corps* (privately printed n.d.)

Pearse, H. H. S. *Four Months Besieged. The Story of Ladysmith* (1900)

Peel, Hon. Sidney. *Trooper 8008 I.Y.* (1901)

Pemberton, W. B. *Battles of the Boer War* (1964; paperback edit. 1969)

Pen Pictures of the War. Anon (1900)

Penning, L. *De Oorlog in Zuid-Afrika* (Rotterdam 1899–1903)

Phelan, T. *The Siege of Kimberley, its Humorous and Social Side* (Dublin 1913)

Phillipps, L. March. *With Rimington* (1901)

Phillips, Mrs Lionel. *Some South African Recollections* (1899)

Phillips, Lionel. *Some Reminiscences* (1924)

Piennar, Philip. *With Steyn and De Wet* (1902)

Pilcher, Col T. D. *Some Lessons from the Boer War* (Isbister 1903)

Pirow, O. *James Barry Munnik Hertzog* (Cape Town 1957)

Plaatje, Sol. See Comaroff

Pohl, Victor. *Adventures of a Boer Family* (1944)

Pollock, Maj. A. W. A. *With Seven Generals in the Boer War* (1900)

Post Office Telegraphists. *'Khaki Letters' from my Colleagues in South Africa* (1900–1)

Price, R. *An Imperial War and the British Working-Class: Working-Class Attitudes and Reactions to the Boer War, 1899–1902* (1972)

Pyrah, G. *Imperial Policy and South Africa, 1902–1910* (Oxford 1955)

Ralph, Julian. *Towards Pretoria* (1900)

—— *At Pretoria* (1901)

—— *An American with Lord Roberts* (New York 1901)

—— *War's Brighter Side* (1901)

Ram, Kapt. J. H. *Lesson uit den Zuid-Afrikaanschen Oorlog* (The Hague 1902)

[Rankin, R.]. *A Subaltern's Letters to his Wife* (1901)

Ransford, O. *The Battle of Spion Kop* (1969)

[Reichmann etc.]. *United States Report on Military Operations in South Africa and China* (Washington 1901)

Reitz, D. *Commando: A Boer Journal of the Boer War* (1929)

Reitz, F. W. [actually Jan Smuts]. *A Century of Wrong* (1900)

Repington, Col Charles à Court. *Vestigia* (1919)

Richardson, Sir W. D. *With the Army Service Corps in South Africa* (1903)

Riley, P. (ed.) *The Ladysmith Siege Diary of Dr James Alexander Kay* (1971)

Robertson, Sir William. *From Private to Field-Marshal* (1921)

Robinson, R., Gallagher, J. and Denny A. *Africa and the Victorians: the Official Mind of Imperialism* (1961)

Romer, C. F. and Mainwaring, A. E. *The Second Battalion Royal Dublin Fusiliers in the South African War* (1908)

Rompel, F. *Heroes of the Boer War* (1903)

Rose-Innes, Cosmo. *With Paget's Horse to the Front* (1901)

Rose-Innes, J. *Autobiography* (Cape Town 1949)

Ross, P. T. *A Yeoman's Letters* (1901)

Rosslyn, Earl of. *Twice Captured* (1901)

Royal Inniskilling Fusiliers. *History of the Regiment 1688 to 1914* (1928)

St Alwyn, Countess. *See* Hicks Beach, Lady Victoria.

St Leger, Capt. S. E. *War Sketches in Colour* (1903)

Sampson, V. and Hamilton, I. *Anti-Commando* (1931)

Sandberg, Dr C. G. S. *Twintig Jaren Onder Kruger's Boeren in Voor – en Tegenspoed* (Amsterdam 1943)

Schiel, Adolf. *23 Jahre Sturm und Sonnenschein* (Leipzig 1902)

Schikkerling, R. W. *Commando Courageous (A Boer's diary)* (Johannesburg 1964)

Schreiner, T. L. *The Afrikaner Bond and other Causes of the War* (1901)

—— *The Black Man and the Franchise. Imperial South African Association* (1901)

Seely, J. E. B. *Adventure* (1930)

Smith-Dorrien, Sir Horace. *Memories of Forty-Eight Years' Service* (1925)

South African Native Races Committee (ed.) *The Natives of South Africa* (1901)

Spender, J. A. *The Life of the Right Hon. Sir Henry Campbell-Bannerman* 2 vols (1923)

Spurgin, K. B. *On Active Service with the Northumberland and Durham Yeomen* (1902)

Stead, W. T. *How Britain Goes to War* (1903)

—— *The War in South Africa. Methods of Barbarism* (1901)

—— *Shall I Slay my Brother Boer?* (1899)

Steevens, G. W. *From Cape Town to Ladysmith* (1900)

Sternberg, Count A. *My Experiences of the Boer War*. English translation by G. F. R. Henderson (1901)

Stirling, John. *Our Regiments in South Africa* (1903)

Stuart, John. *Pictures of War* (1901)

[Swinton, Gen.]. *Backsight Forethought. The Defence of Duffer's Drift* (1904)

Sykes, Lady. *Sidelights on the War in South Africa* (1900)

Symons, J. *Buller's Campaign* (1963)

Tatham, G. F. *Diary of the Siege of Ladysmith, 1 Nov 1899–1 March 1900* (Ladysmith 1970)

Taylor, J. B. *A Pioneer Looks Back* (1939)

Thomson, Ada. *Memorials of C. D. Kimber, Lieut IY* (1902)

Thomson, Col S. J. *The Transvaal Burgher Camps, South Africa* (Pioneer Press, Allahabad 1904)

Thornton, A. P. *The Imperial Idea and its Enemies: a Study in British Power* (1959)

Thorold, A. L. *The Life of Henry Labouchère* (1913)

Treves, F. *The Tale of a Field Hospital* (1900)

Trichard, S. P. E. *Geschiedenis Werken en Streven* (ed.) O. J. O. Ferreira (Pretoria 1975)

Tullibardine, Marchioness of. (ed.) *A Military History of Perthshire, 1899–1902* (Perth 1908)

Unger, F. W. *With 'Bobs' and Kruger* (1901; reprinted Johannesburg 1977)

Vallentin, Dr W. *Der Burenkrieg* (Leipzig 1903)

Van Der Poel, J. *The Jameson Raid* (1951)

Van Wyk Smith, M. *Drummer Hodge: The Poetry of the Anglo-Boer War 1899–1902* (Oxford 1978)

Viljoen, B. *My Reminiscences of the Anglo-Boer War* (1902)

Vindex. *Cecil Rhodes: His Political Life and Speeches, 1881–1900* (1900)

Vulliamy, C. E. *Outlanders: a Study of Imperial Expansion in South Africa, 1877–1902* (1938)

Walker, E. A. *W. P. Schreiner: a South African* (1937)

Wallace, Edgar. *Unofficial Despatches on the Boer War* (1901)

Wallis, J. P. R. *Fitz: the Story of Sir Percy Fitzpatrick* (1955)

Warmelo, D. S. Van. *On Commando* (1902)

Warren, T. H. *Prince Christian Victor* (1903)

Warwick, Peter. *Black Industrial Protest on the Witwatersrand 1901–2*. (Centre for South African Studies, York University 1975)

Waters, Col W. H. H. and Du Cane, H. (German official account). *The War in South Africa* vols I & II (translation) (1904, 1906)

Watkins-Pitchford, H. *Besieged in Ladysmith* (Pietermaritzburg 1964)

Wauchope, Capt. A. G. *The Black Watch, 1725–1907* (1908)

Weinthal, L. (ed.) *Memories, Mines and Millions: Being the Life of Sir Joseph B. Robinson* (1929)

Wilde, R. H. 'Joseph Chamberlain and the South African Republics, 1895–1899; a Study in the Formulation of Imperial Policy'. *Archives Year Book of South Africa* 19 I (1956)

Wilkinson, Frank. *Australia at the Front* (1901)

Williams, B. *Cecil Rhodes* (1938)

Williams, Charles. *Hushed Up* (1902)

Williams, W. W. *The Life of General Sir Charles Warren* (Oxford 1941)

Wilson, Capt. C. H. *The Relief of Ladysmith. The Artillery in Natal* (1901)

Wilson, H. W. *With the Flag to Pretoria* 2 vols (1900–2)

—— *After Pretoria: the Guerrilla War* 2 vols (1902)

Wilson, John. CB. *A Life of Sir Henry Campbell-Bannerman* (1973)

Wilson, Monica, and Thompson, Leonard. (eds) *The Oxford History of South Africa*, Vol. I to 1870, vol. 2 1870–1966 (Oxford 1969, 1971)

Wilson, Lady Sarah. *South African Memories* (1909)

Wrench, J. E. *Alfred Lord Milner: the Man of no Illusions, 1854–1925* (1958)

Wyndham, George, *Life and Letters*. ed. J. W. Mackail and Guy Wyndam 2 vols (n.d.)

Yardley, Lt-Col J. Watkins. *With the Inniskilling Dragoons during the Boer War, 1899–1902* (1904)

Young, Filson. *The Relief of Mafeking* (1900)

Younghusband, Capt. F. E. *South Africa of To-Day* (1899)

Parliamentary Papers

C and Cd series. (The fuller unpublished versions of most of these documents are printed in the War Office's Secret Despatches or in CO 879)

Newspapers, Periodicals (including Journals)

BRITISH
Annual Register
Black & White Budget vols 1–3 (1900)
Blackwoods
Contemporary Review
Daily News
Daily Telegraph
Draconian (Oxford)
Graphic
Illustrated London News
Manchester Guardian
Morning Leader
Morning Post
National Review
Nineteenth Century and After
Proceedings of the Royal Artillery Institution
Review of Reviews

Sphere
Statesman's Yearbook
The Times
Westminster Gazette

SOUTH AFRICA
Cape Times (Cape Town)
Diamond Fields Advertiser (Kimberley)
Express (Bloemfontein)
Ladysmith Bombshell (Ladysmith 1900)
Ladysmith Lyre (Ladysmith 1900)
Military History Journal of South Africa
Natal Mercury
Natal Witness
Standard & Diggers' News (Johannesburg)
Star (Johannesburg)
The Friend (Bloemfontein)
Volksstem (Pretoria)

Notes

In the notes, I have given unpublished sources (including the government confidential prints), a two-, three- or four-letter abbreviation. Italics are reserved for published sources. Full stops separate each reference

PROLOGUE: RHODES'S 'BIG IDEA'

1 Tels nos 73, 77, 79, 80, 81, 82, 26–28 Dec 1895, *C 8380/195–8*
2 Jameson's ev, *House Paper 311* nos 4513, 4518, 4594–60. Garrett etc. *African Crisis* 86 (and see 76)
3 Troopers' accounts in *Times* 24, 25 Feb 1896. EGO
4 Phillipps *With Rimington* 2–6
5 Garrett 90. Hole *Jameson Raid* 291. Colvin *Life of Jameson* II, 64
6 Fitzpatrick *Transvaal* 98. Phillips *Some Reminiscences* 141–2
7 Colvin I, 266, 272–82: Rhodes-Beit Aug 1895 (cy) PC
8 Willoughby's official report. Fitzpatrick *Transvaal* 411–21
9 *Standard and Diggers News* 18 Jan 1896 *C 8380/175*, 273
10 Jameson's ev, *House Paper 311* nos 4513 and 4596. Hole *Jameson Raid* 145–7
11 Colvin I, 13–14
12 Taken from Coventry's speech at Mafeking. Jameson's was similar. See *Standard and Diggers News* 4, 11 and 18 Jan 1896
13 *C 8380* (no 61) 191–2. *Times* 1 Jan 1896. Hole 222–3
14 Hole 223–4
15 Willoughby's ev, *House Paper 311* 5512–5548
16 *c 8380/185–8*
17 *C 8380* nos 863–90, 906–26 and app p. 198. Hole 125–6, 137, 151–2
18 Garrett 28–9
19 Jameson's ev, *House Paper 311/4605*
20 See for example Col Sandbach–Gen. Chapman 23 Nov 1899 in Sand
21 Hole 15–16, 79, 45–6
22 Heany's ev, *House Paper 311/5898.* Willoughby's official report loc cit. Hole 154–5
23 Trooper H. Acton-Adams diary, *The Critic* Dec 1933–Jun 1934 (Rhodesia National Archives)
24 Trooper Acton-Adams loc cit.
25 Willoughby's official report loc cit. Hole 172–9

26 Trooper Acton-Adams loc cit. *Standard and Diggers News* 4, 11, 18 Jan 1896
27 Hole 179
28 The scene was particularly well known to Jameson since the death of Wilson on the Shangani Patrol in 1892
29 Willoughby's official report loc cit 418
30 Hole 188. *Standard and Diggers News* 4, 11, 18 Jan 1896
31 *C 8390/170. Standard and Diggers News* 22 Feb 1896
32 *Standard and Diggers News* 18 Jan 1896
33 *Jameson's Heroic Charge* 25. CO 879/501/927. Hole 292

PART I

CHAPTER 1: OUT OF THE ABYSS
Head of chapter John Buchan *Thirty Nine Steps* 62–3 (London 1958)

1 M's diary 16 Nov 1898, Mil (dep 68)
2 M. Murray *Union-Castle Chronicle* (London 1953) 121–4. *Illustrated London News* 27 Jun 1891. M–Fiddes 12 Nov 1898, Mil 8 (SA 45)
3 M–Gell 26 Jun, 7 Jul, 19 Oct 1898, Gell 507, 510, 514
4 O. Walrond–Gell 25 Jun, M–Gell 28 Jun 1897, M–Gell 11 Jan 1898, Gell 360, 361, 501
5 M–Gell 2 Jun, M–E Gell 12 Oct 1897, Gell 359, 363
6 M–Bertha Synge 4 Aug 1898, *MP* I, 286
7 M's diary 1–17 Nov 1898, Mil (dep 68). Cf O. Walrond–Gell 6 May 1897, Gell 358
8 Menpes *War Impressions* 89–100. Cook *Garrett* 151 fn. Cf Buchan *Memory* 97–103. Beatrice Webb quoted Marais 171
9 Gell's note of talk with M 17 Feb 1897, Gell 346. Wrench *Milner* 19–30. Gollin *First Proconsul* 4–8
10 Wrench 30–46
11 See Smuts–wife 1 Jun 1899 *SP* I 242. For 'Bohemian' see M–Ly Ilbert 7 Dec 1897, Mil (kept separately at New College)

12 *Cape Times* 1 Jan 1896 saying he was very nearly chosen by Rosebery's Cabinet instead of Robinson. See also C's speech reported *Times* 27 Jun 1897 p. 10 col 4–6
13 Hicks Beach–M 22 Mar 1897 quoted Wrench 160–1
14 M–Iwan-Müller 9 Feb 1897, Mil 192
15 *Times* 29 Mar 1897
16 M–Gell 20 Apr 1898, Gell 503
17 M–Goschen 14 Jul 1897, Mil
18 C. Lucas *History passim* esp 204–5, 213–14, 222, 336–7
19 De Kiewiet *British Colonial Policy passim.* M. Wilson and L. Thompson *Oxford History of South Africa* I 244
20 M. Wilson and L. Thompson I, 245
21 De Kiewiet loc cit.
22 M. Wilson and L. Thompson I, 245, 292, 355–63, 405–8
23 Lucas 160–2
24 M. Wilson and L. Thompson I, 368, 409–10
25 Ibid I, 369–373
26 Ibid I, 416–24
27 Robinson, Gallagher etc *Africa and the Victorians* 2–16. M. Wilson and L. Thompson II, 11–12
28 Ibid II, 289–298
29 Ibid
30 Ibid II, 298–300
31 Lehmann *The First Boer War* 262–307
32 C. Lucas 300–1, 336–7
33 M–Mrs Montefiore 12 June 1900, *MP* II, 104–5. M–Gell 2 Jun 1897. Gell 359
34 M–Ly Ilbert 12 Dec 1897, Mil New College
35 M's credo *Times* 2 Jul 1925 quoted Marais *Kruger's Republic* 172. See also Gell's note on M in Gell 346
36 M–Parkin 28 Apr 1897, *MP* I, 42
37 M–E Gell 26 Jan 1899, Gell 525
38 M–Dawkins 11 Apr 1904, Mil (S3)
39 See M–Gell 22 May 1899, Gell 521
40 See [Selborne's] memo 26 Mar 1896, Sal
41 Kruger *Memoirs* II, 261–3. Van der Poel *Jameson Raid* 104
42 *Blue Book* 311. Hole 269–71. Van der Poel 166–7
43 *Blue Book* 311, see esp Q 6827–38. Van der Poel 73–4
44 Garrett etc *Crisis* 81. Van der Poel 89–90
45 *C.311* Q 3304–7, 3401–4. Van der Poel 96–7
46 Robinson and Gallagher 430, 433. Van der Poel 260–2
47 B. Williams *Rhodes* 225–92. Lockhart and Woodhouse *Rhodes* 350
48 M–Gell 22 May 1899, Gell 531
49 M–Gell 19 Oct 1898, 3 Mar 1899, Gell 514, 528
50 Ibid
51 M–Gell 3 Jan 1899, Gell 521. See also M–Gell 28 Jul 1898, Gell 510

52 *Standard and Diggers News* 16 Nov 1895
53 See note 51. Gell's notes [nd], Gell 518. M–Gell 30 Jan 1899, Gell 527. M's diary 30 Nov 1899, Mil
54 M–Gell 11 Jan 1898, Gell 501. M–C 23 Feb 1898, *MP* I, 220–1. M–Bertha Synge 26 Apr 1899, Mil 191
55 M–C 23 Feb 1898, *MP* I, 222
56 C–Ellis 14 Oct 1897, Cham JC 10/5/1/62
57 C–M 16 Mar 1898, Garvin *Chamberlain* III, 366
58 M–Fiddes 23 Dec 1898, *MP* I, 299. See also *MP* I, 286–7
59 M's diary 1891–2, Mil 252/161–6. Wrench 111–16, 124–34, 136–54
60 M–Gell 17 Apr 1892, Gell 290
61 For M's success in society see esp M's letters to Mrs Grenfell (copies in PC) and diary esp 30 May–4 Jun 1895, bicycling trip in Normandy ('Lady Alice made little headway against the wind')
62 M's diary 18 Nov 1895, Mil (dep 65)
63 M's diary 22 Nov 1898, Mil (dep 68). M–Fiddes 25 Nov 1898, *MP* I, 299
64 M–C, M–Selborne 23 Feb, 7 Sep 1898, *MP* I, 222, 287

CHAPTER 2: NODS AND WINKS

Head of chapter C, House of Commons 8 May 1896 *Hansard* XL/914–15

1 Garvin *Chamberlain* III, 10–14 quoting Sir H. Wilson and Ly Lugard. Sir R. Furse *Aucuparius* (London 1962) 22–3
2 Garvin III, 11–12
3 *DNB*
4 See esp Balfour–Salisbury 31 Jul 1892, Sal E/Balfour. Garvin II, *passim*
5 Selborne–Salisbury 7 Apr 1895, Sal E/Selborne
6 Garvin III, 4–5
7 Salisbury–Selborne 30 Jun 1895, Sel Box 5/31
8 Garvin (quoting H. Wilson) III, 15. See contemporary photo album of CO in FCO library
9 For Highbury see account in Edward Hamilton's diary 22 Jan 1899, BM 48764
10 See C–Selborne 14 Oct 1896, Sel Box 8
11 *Statesmen's Yearbook* CO figures for 1895–6
12 Garvin III, 19–20 quoting C in *Times* 24 Aug 1895. Cf Lucas *History passim*
13 *Times* 7 Nov 1895
14 *Statesmen's Yearbook* CO figures for 1899
15 C 22 Aug 1895 *Hansard* XXXVI/641–2. Garvin III, 20
16 C–Flora Shaw quoted Garvin III, 82–3
17 Van der Poel 261–2
18 C–Salisbury 13 Nov 1895, Sal E/Chamberlain. Selborne–C 6 Oct, C–Selborne 14 Oct, Sel–C 18 Oct 1896, Sel Box 8/91

etc. C–Harcourt 4 Sep, C–Ellis 14 Oct 1897, Cham JC 5/38/2261 JC 10/5/1/62. See also note 40
19 Wilde *Archives Year Book* I, 1956, 9–18. Drus *Documents* 49
20 Van der Poel *passim* esp 27–30, 34–6, 47–51, 54–6. Wilde 19
21 Garvin III, 88–9
22 C–Salisbury 26 Dec 1895, Sal E/Chamberlain
23 C–Salisbury 29 Dec 1895 ibid
24 Garvin III, 89
25 See note 20
26 Maguire–Rhodes 20 Dec 1895 quoted Van der Poel 66–72. Drus *Report* 49–50
27 *C. 8380* App 168 foll reprinted from *Green Bk no 2* of Transvaal
28 C's memo June 1896, Drus *Report* 47–8
29 Garvin III, 106–8
30 Report of Select Cttee of Commons, House paper *311*
31 E. Longford *Victoria RI* 684 (Pan edit 1976)
32 Van der Poel 259. See Lockhart & Woodhouse 342–4. Note the relative *absence* of material on Raid now in CO 417/152, 160, 177–80 and CO 879/44 etc.
33 Van der Poel 195–6
34 Van der Poel 227, 234, 244–8
35 Fairfield–Bower 31 Oct 1896, Bower–Ommaney 11 May 1906, Bower–Rose Innes 3 Feb 1932 cited Van der Poel 189–95
36 C's ev at Select Cttee Inquiry Q 6223–7 etc.
37 E. Pakenham *Jameson's Raid* 97–101, 64. Garvin III, 92–7
38 For rumours re Rosebery see C–Selborne 30 Dec 1896, Sel Box 8/144
39 Morley's phrase quoted Van der Poel 230
40 C's minute 15 Apr 1896, Drus *Documents* 160–2. E. Pakenham 248–9
41 Shakespeare *Macbeth* Act II scene 3 lines 33–5
42 M's diary 22, 30 Nov 1898, Mil (dep 68)
43 M–Selborne 9 May 1898, *MP* I 232–5. M–Fiddes 3 Jan 1899, Mil 8/28–33
44 C–M 16 Mar 1898; *MP* I 227–9. Cf Selborne–M 23 Mar, *MP* I 229–31
45 See C–Selborne 3 Mar 1897, Sel Box 11/162: will 'end in self-strangulation'
46 M–Selborne 31 Jan 1899, *MP* I, 301–2 (clauses reversed)
47 M–Fiddes 23 Dec 1898, *MP* I, 299–300
48 M's diary 24–6 Nov 1898, Mil (dep 68). W Churchill–Rosebery 13 Aug 1903, Rose. B–Selborne 16 Aug 1898, Sel Box 2
49 M's diary 24–6 Nov 1898, Mil. See other visits to Panshanger 20–22 Apr, 18–21 Nov 1895, Mil 258
50 M's diary Dec 1891, Mil 252/161–6
51 M–Gell 17 Apr 1892, Gell 290
52 *MP* I, 301. M's diary 18 Nov–Jan 27 1898–9, Mil (dep 68)

53 M–Gell 19 Jun 1899, Gell 534
54 See note 52
55 M–Rosebery 12 Dec 1898, Rose 75/160–4. M–Selborne 23 Jan 1899, *MP* I, 301
56 See Margot–M 9 Jul 1900, Mil 29 (SA 32)
57 M's diary 1891–1901. 'CD' lived at Norwood until 1893 then Croydon till 1896 then Brixton. She cost M £392 in 1893, £359 in 1894, £378 in 1895, £354 in 1896. In 1901 she cost £600
58 See M's diary 1891–7, 98–9, Mil (dep 60–69)
59 M's diary 1–2 Dec 1898 (Windsor), 4–5 Dec (Highbury), 5–6 Dec (Hatfield), 6–11 Dec with 'CD', Mil (dep 68)
60 Countess of Jersey *Fifty-one Years of Victorian Life* (London 1923) p. 370
61 M's diary 8 Dec 1898, Mil (dep 68)
62 M's *credo, Times* 27 Jul 1925
63 M's diary 9–10 Dec 1898, Mil (dep 68)
64 M's diary 8 Dec 1898, Mil (dep 68)
65 M's diary 23 Jan 1898, Mil (dep 68)
66 M–Fiddes 3 Jan 1899, Mil 45 (SA 37). M–Gell 27 May 18 Jun 1899, Gell 531, 533

CHAPTER 3: CHAMPAGNE FOR THE VOLK

Head of chapter story told me by Mrs Williams, one of Kruger's great-granddaughters
1 *Standard and Diggers News* (weekly edit) 31 Dec 1898. *Volksstem* 24 Dec 1898
2 Ibid. Kotzé *Memoirs* II, 36. S E Trichard *Geskiedenis* 57–110
3 P. Kruger *Memoirs* I & II *passim*. Fisher *Kruger* 141–52, 240. Meintjes *Kruger passim*. DSAB I, 445 foll
4 See note 1
5 Kotzé *Memoirs* II 216 foll
6 *Volksstem* 29 Dec 1898
7 Kotzé II, 30–31. Marais 6–7
8 Mouton *Archives Year Book* 1–264. DSAB I, 412–17. Gordon *Growth of Opposition* 246–74. Kotzé loc cit
9 See note 1
10 Oberholster *Historical Monuments* 305–6 (inc photos)
11 C's minute 5 Apr 1896 Drus *Documents* 160–2. Casement 30 Apr 1896 (Cy) PC
12 Kotzé loc cit. Marais 9–10
13 W. Monypenny & G. Buckle *Life of Disraeli* (London 1920) VI, 416
14 Jorissen *Transvaalsche Herinneringen* 16–17. Marais 7. Fisher 156. But Kruger had too keen a sense of humour to be a real flat-earther. See chapter head
15 P. Kruger *Memoirs* I, 3–103. DSAB I, 444–7
16 P. Kruger *Memoirs* I, 143–190. DSAB I, 448–9
17 Kotzé loc cit

18 Quoted Marais 10
19 *DSAB* I, 449–451
20 Gordon 207–28
21 Gordon 46–57. Marais 27–45 (esp 31). *Cd 623*. A quarter of the £2m profit went to the state
22 Marais 13–14
23 P. Kruger II, 269–72. Scholtz diary Jan 1896, Scho. Fitzpatrick *Transvaal* 229–30. Van der Poel 143–65. Actually the beam went to the museum
24 Bryce *Impressions of South Africa* 311–18
25 Ibid. See Bryce's footnote 318 added Oct 1899
26 *Standard & Diggers News* (weekly edit) 30 Sep 1898. Terms of pact printed in WO *Military Notes* (cy) PC 90–3
27 *Breyt* I, 406, 564–7. Mouton 225
28 *Breyt* I, 406–11. Mouton 226
29 Ibid
30 SD II, 192. Cf *Military Notes* (cy) PC and *Breyt* I, 276 foll
31 Joubert quoted Mouton 227
32 *RCSAW* I, 193: M–C 7 Feb 1898 quoting public statement by Kruger. Cf *Breyt* I, 274–7, Oberholster loc cit
33 *Star passim* 1899
34 The combined force was nominally 54,000–57,000 acc *Breyt* I, 153, but only 32,000–35,000 actually mobilized at outbreak of war. Cf *OH* I, 458–9 giving figure of over 48,000 commandeered
35 Gordon 184–203
36 Hancock *Smuts* I, 67–9. P. Kruger II, 298–9
37 Hancock I, 3–63, 68
38 Ibid I, 33–53
39 *SP* I, 80–100, 123–6
40 *SP* I, 103–6
41 Hancock *Smuts* I, 58–67
42 Smuts–Merriman 18 Jun 1899 *SP* I, 257–8
43 *Cd 623*. Marais 27–33. Gordon 55–6
44 Hancock *Smuts* I, 86
45 *Standard & Diggers News* (weekly edit) 23 Sep 1898
46 *C 9345/83*, 95–6. Marais 234–7
47 Hancock *Smuts* I, 83
48 *Cape Times* 21 Dec 1898. Sir W. Butler quotes slightly different text in *Autobiograhy* 396–8
49 *SP* I 212–13. Original Dutch notes in indirect speech
50 Smuts–Hofmeyr 10 May 1899 *SP* I 233–5
51 *Standard & Diggers News* (weekly edit) 24 Dec 1899

CHAPTER 4: 'VOETSAK'
Head of chapter G. Rouliot–J. Wernher 21 Jan 1899, Eck HE 175
1 *Cape Times, Star* 21, 23 Dec 1899. *Standard & Diggers News* 24 Dec 1899. Wallis *Fitz passim* esp 78. L. Phillips *Reminiscences* 101

2 Buchan's *African Colony* 77–83. Cartright *Corner House* 39–40, 72–3
3 Bryce 296–308. Buchan op cit 311–13
4 *Star* 21 Dec 1899 (quoting *Mining Journal*). *Standard & Diggers News* 14 Jan 1899 (weekly edit). Bryce 301–2. Younghusband *South Africa of Today* 9–11
5 Selborne's memo for Salisbury 26 Mar 1896
6 Younghusband 3–4, 42–5. Hobson *War in South Africa* 10–14. Cartright *Corner House* 50–1
7 Marais 1, 26–7, 180–1. Hobson 287–8
8 Fitzpatrick *Transvaal* 275–81, *Memories* 159–60. *DSAB* I 292–3
9 Fitzpatrick *Transvaal* 105–6. Hobson 286. Marais 27–33, 228. Info R. Mendelsohn
10 S. Evans–M 12 Jun 1897. Mil 66: Native labour should be halved in cost per ton. *Standard & Diggers News* (weekly edit) 10 Jun 1899. See letter from Uitlander, *Star* 30 Dec 1898. Bryce 303–4. Marais 187–8
11 Fitzpatrick *Transvaal* 96–103, 327. Marais 25–7. *MP* II 308. *C 9345/10*
12 Fitzpatrick *Transvaal* 73–7. Marais 53
13 *C 9345/83* Marais 235–7
14 *SP* I, 213
15 Bessie Edgar ev *C 9345/110–11*, 122–3, 150. See her £4,000 compensation claim 10 Jun 1899, CO 879/59/19
16 A Shepherd, A Sylvester, M McKenzie, *C 9345/118*, 119, 121, 149
17 Bessie Edgar ev *C 9345/122–3*
18 See note 9
19 Bessie Edgar, D. Bowker, J. Friedman, I. Kantorowitz, M. McKenzie, A. Shepherd, A. Sylvester, Constables Muller, Roux, Rood, Dr Lillpop *C 9345/110–53*
20 *Star* 21–22 Dec 1898
21 Marais 238
22 Evans's report and a photo in CO 417/259/456–464. *Cape Times* 28 Dec 1898. Marais 237–8
23 Butler–C 18 Jan, 25 Jan 1899, CO 879/56/3, 7
24 *C 9345/131*, 136–8, 144–7
25 Ibid 159–75. Marais 239–40
26 Greene–M 3 Mar (enc Fitzpatrick 3 Mar), 10, 13, 15, 17, 18, 21 Mar 1899, Mil 13 (SA 27). *MP* I 318–31. Fitzpatrick *Memories* 164–5. Wallis 74. Marais 247–9

CHAPTER 5: 'WORKING UP STEAM'
Head of chapter M–Fiddes 3 Jan 1899, Mil (dep 69)
1 Butler–C 4 Jan 1899, CO 417/259. W. Butler 400–3
2 M–Selborne 31 Jan 1899, *MP* I, 301
3 M–Selborne 23 Jan 1899, *MP* I, 301. M–Fiddes 23 Dec 1898, *MP* I, 299. M–Bertha Synge 11 Feb 1899, *MP* I, 302. M–Iwan-Müller 28 Nov 1898, Mil 192

4 M–Rosebery 12 Dec 1898, Rose Box 75/160–4

5 M's diary 31 Mar 1899, Mil (dep 69). Fitzpatrick–Wernher 6 Apr 1899, Fitz. Menpes 99

6 Fitzpatrick–Greene, M–C 3 Mar 1899, Mil 13 (SA 27). *MP* I, 319–32. See also *MP* I, 329. Fitzpatrick *Memories* 171–4. Marais 248–56

7 M–C 4 Mar 1899, CO 879 (Af 572 11). C's min 8 Mar 1899 etc, CO 417/259/557

8 M–Greene 14 Mar 1899, Mil 13 (SA 27)

9 Fitzpatrick–Greene 3 Mar 1899, MS cit. Copy of Fitzpatrick's speech Mil 13 (SA 27)

10 Selborne's min 9 Mar 1899, CO 417/259/561. Marais 250–1

11 M–C 11 Mar and C's min 14 Mar 1899, CO 417/259. Marais 252–3

12 Greene–M 18 Mar 1899 and typescript copy of speech Mil 13 (SA 27). Marais 253

13 Fitzpatrick–Wernher 6 Apr 1899, Fitz. See M–Fiddes 1 Apr 1899, *MP* I, 331. And see M's earlier comments in M–Selborne 8 Mar 1899, *MP* I, 324–5; and later note M–Selborne 14 Jun 1899, *MP* I, 437

14 Fitzpatrick–Wernher 6 Apr 1899, Fitz

15 Ibid

16 Ibid. Cf M–Fiddes 3 Jan 1899, Mil 45 (SA 37)

17 M–Selborne 5 May 1899, *MP* I, 348

18 M–Greene 3 Apr 1899, *MP* I, 345–6

19 Greene–M 5 May 1898, *C 9345*. Marais 257, 263–4. Fitzpatrick *Transvaal* 360, 364

20 Fitzpatrick–Wernher 1, 8 May 1899, Fitz

21 E. Hamilton diary 1899, BM 48764/99–102

22 M–C 29 Mar 1899, CO 417/260/9383–5, 9398–9

23 M–Hely Hutchinson 8 May 1899, *MP* I, 358: 'before the bomb bursts'

24 M–C CO 417/260/9969

25 M–C 19 Apr 1899, CO 417/260/11467. Wilde 102–3

26 *MP* I, 347–8. Wilde 97–8. Marais 266

27 *C 9345*/209–12 edited version. *MP* I, 349–53 gives full text

28 M–Selborne 5 Apr 1899, *MP* I, 348

29 M–Gell 18 Jun and nd 1899, Gell 533, 534. M–Selborne 24 May 1899, *MP* I, 400

30 O. Walrond–Gell 26 Apr, 7 May 1899, 1 Mar 1898. Gell 502, 529, 530

31 Walrond–M 28 Dec 1898, Mil 31 (SA 25)

32 M's diary 13 Apr 1897, Mil (dep 67). No refs in the diary for 1899

33 M's diary 28 Apr, 1, 2, 5 May 1899, Mil (dep 69)

34 Fitzpatrick–Wernher 6 Apr 1899, Fitz

35 M's diary Apr–May 1891, Mil (dep 59)

36 M's diary 9 May 1899, Mil (dep 69)

37 C–M (tel) 8 May 1899, Mil 14 (SA 28)

38 M–Gell 22 May 1899, Gell

CHAPTER 6: 'IT IS OUR COUNTRY YOU WANT'

Head of chapter Major H. Williams–DMI 31 May 1899, CO 417/275/363

1 *Volksstem* 31 May, *Express* (Bloemfontein) 2 Jun, *Cape Times* (weekly edition) 3 Jun, *Standard & Diggers News* 30 May 1899

2 *Volksstem* 31 May 1899

3 Fisher *Kruger* 218–19 quoting Rompel *Uit den Tweeden Vryheidsoorlog*

4 *Volksstem* 31 May 1899 (indirect speech in original)

5 Smuts–Hofmeyr 10 May 1899, *SP* I, 233–5

6 Ibid

7 Smuts–Leyds 30 Apr 1899, *SP* I, 227–9

8 Schreiner–Smuts 6 May 1899, *SP* I, 229–30

9 Hofmeyr–Smuts 6, 10, 15 May 1899, *SP* I, 230, 236–7

10 Schreiner–Smuts 19 May 1899, *SP* I, 237–9

11 Smuts–Hofmeyr 10 May 1899, *SP* I, 231–5

12 *Volksstem* 31 May 1899

13 *Cape Times* (weekly edit) 3 Jun, *Standard and Diggers News* 30 May 1899

14 See note 1

15 M's diary 30 May 1899, Mil (dep 69). M–C 25 May 1899, Mil 14 (SA 28)

16 C–M 10 May 1899, *C 9345* 226–31

17 For 'screw' see M–C 8 May 1899, CO 417/261 and M–Gell 18 Jun 1899, Gell 533

18 See Marais 1–3, Wilde 112–13. Cf Balfour–C 6 May 1899, Cham 5/5/39

19 Selborne–M 7 Oct 1899, Mil 17 (SA 31)

20 M–Gell 9 Aug 1898, Gell 511

21 M–Dawkins 4 Jan 1902, Mil 28 (SA 46)

22 M–Bertha Synge 19 Dec 1901, Mil 28 (SA 46)

23 M–C 8 Jul 1898, *MP* I, 267

24 M–Dawkins 4 Jan 1902, Mil 28 (SA 32)

25 The evidence that Milner already *wanted* a war is circumstantial. See esp. M–Bertha Synge 20 Apr 1898 Mil 8 (SA 45) 'The Boer Govt is too great a curse to all S. Africa to be allowed to exist, if we were not too busy to afford the considerable war, wh. alone can pull it down.' Cf M–Selborne 17, 24 May 1899, *MP* I, 384–5, 400–3

26 M–Gell 18 Jun, Gell 533

27 M's diary 3 Apr 1898, Mil (dep 68)

28 See M–Selborne 24 May 1899, *MP* I, 400. *Express* (Bloemfontein) 2 Jun 1899

29 *TH* I, 102–3

30 *Express* (Bloemfontein) 2 Jun 1899

31 *Standard and Digger's News* 31 May 1899

32 Maj Hanbury–Williams–WO 31 May 1899, CO 417/275/363

33 *C 9404*/14–15

34 M–C 31 May, CO 417/261/13894

35 *C 9404*/15–19
36 *C 9404*/20–1
37 Maj. Hanbury-Williams–Intell Dept c. 1 Jun 1899, CO 417/275
38 *C 9404*/25–7
39 M quoted *MP* I, 418
40 *C 9404*/34
41 *TH* I, 186–7
42 Selborne confid min 17 Feb 1898, Sel Box 9/8
43 C–M 5 Jun 1899, CO 417/262 (Af 572/84). Chamberlain was annoyed. See Wilde 110–11
44 M–C CO 417/262/14169
45 Ibid
46 See H. W. Just's min of 4 Jul 1899, CO 417/262
47 *C 9404*/38–41
48 *MP* I, 418–19
49 M–C 4 June 1899, CO 417/262
50 *Standard and Diggers News* 3 Jun 1899
51 M–C 14 Jun 1899, *MP* I, 423–4
52 C–M 5 Jun 1899, CO 417/262 (Af South 572/83–4)
53 *MP* I, 407 pres from M's notes of conference. These words are not in *C 9404*
54 *C 9404*/44
55 M–Gell 18 Jun 1899, Gell 533
56 M–Selborne 17 May 1899, *MP* I, 384–5 ('material' mistake for 'military'?)
57 M–Selborne 24 May 1899, *MP* I, 400–2
58 Selborne–M 25 Jun 1899, *MP* I, 445–6
59 DMI report on captured docs re Schneider's orders, CO 417/335/96–113
60 Hofmeyr–Smuts 17 Jun 1899, *SP* I, 254–6. *MP* I, 449, 502
61 Smuts–Hofmeyr 13 Jun 1899, *SP* I, 248–9
62 Smuts–'Lappie' (S.M.) Smuts 1 Jun 1899, *SP* I, 242
63 Smuts–Hofmeyr 13 Jun 1899, *SP* I, 248–50
64 Smuts–Merriman 18 Jun 1899, *SP* I, 257–8 ('nobodies' in orig.)
65 Smuts–Hofmeyr 9 Jul 1899, *SP* I, 264–5

CHAPTER 7: MILNER'S THREE QUESTIONS

Head of chapter *RCSAW* I, 22–3
1 M–Selborne 24 May 1900, *MP* I, 400–3
2 W's min 8 Jun and L's comments and W's calmer reply 16, 17, 18 Jun 1900, WO 32/7846, 7, 9. Note C–M 16 May 1900, CO 879/56
3 H. Wilson *With the Flag* I, 210
4 See WO clerk's account in *Standard & Diggers News* 3 Feb 1900. See also LCC *Survey of London* XXIX, XXX, and H. Gordon *The War Office* (London 1935)
5 *RCSAW* I, 31–4
6 Newton *Lansdowne* 1–9
7 Ibid 9–126. *DNB*
8 For a satirical view of Lansdowne see 'Saki' quoted at the head of Pt IV chap 36

9 Newton 138–9. Maurice etc *Wolseley's Life*, 308–13. For the calibre of recruits see *RCSAW* I, 41–6
10 Sir J. Fortescue memo for B 1902, Brod 9/494–8
11 Newton esp 139. L–Balfour Bal BM
12 B (memo on WO) Bal 49720/221–45. *RCSAW* I, 31–4
13 *RCSAW* I, 34, 217, 249–56
14 B–Brackenbury 15 Dec 1899, Brod. *RCSAW* I, 278–9
15 Brackenbury was, however, an 'Indian', and Lansdowne was described as 'Brackenbury-ridden' by C, C–Balfour Cham 5/5/81
16 See R–Ian Hamilton (then his ghost-writer) 18 May, 2 Jun, 15 Aug 1893, Ham Misc Box/4–6. I. Hamilton *Listening for the Drums* 160–70. James Roberts 238–50. J. Symons *Buller* 3–54
17 For Buller's own difficult position see Buller–CB 18 Jun 1895, 28 Jun 1899, CB 41212/227, 230
18 L–W 29 May, L–C 14, 28 Jun 1900, Lan 5/31, 26–7
19 L's minutes 16, 17 Jun, WO 32/7846–7. For estimate of Boers' force see *Military Notes* (cy) PC 48 (including allies)
20 L–Butler 21, 27 Jun, WO 32/7849 (079/8686)
21 Butler–L 23 Jun 1899 quoted W Butler 440–50 and SM 21/
22 W–wife 6 Sep, 13 Jul, 24 Jun 1899, Wol 28/50, 40, 30
23 W–wife passim esp Arthur etc *Wolseley Letters* 272. W's ev to *RCSAW* II, Q 9080–3, 9035
24 Sir J. Fortescue *Following the Drum* (London 1932) 121–62. *DNB*
25 W–wife 24 Jun etc. 1899, Wol 28/30
26 W's note of 2 Apr 1898, Wol SSL 10/1/230
27 W–wife 4 Jun 1898 and 1894 quoted Arthur *Letters* 362, 316
28 See note 17
29 W's minutes 4–12 Jul 1900 & L's comment, WO 32/7847. See also L–C 21 Aug 1899, Cham JC 5/51/67
30 W. P. Symons's view reported by Gov of Natal 16 Jul 1899, SM 1/2
31 Sir J. Ardagh ev *RCSAW* II, Q 5126
32 See the series of Intelligence reports in 1899, CO 417/275
33 *Military Notes* (cy) PC 19–38, 48, 51. *RCSAW* I, 174–5
34 SM
35 *Military Notes* 52 fn
36 See Prof Oman's comment in *National Review* vol. 37 1901. See also *RCSAW* I, 174–80
37 *Military Notes* 49–52 (cy) PC
38 Buller's ev *RCSAW* III, 169–70. Buller–Bigge 19 Feb–15 Mar 1900, Big.

Buller's aim and statement 6, 18 Jul 1899, *RCSAW* I, 263–4

39 *Times* 19 Jul and W–wife 19 Jul 1899, Wol

40 W–wife 11 Jul 1899, Wol 28/38

41 W–wife 26 Jul, 24 Jun 1899, Wol 28/30

42 W–wife 13 Jul 1899, Wol 28/40

43 W–wife 13 Jul 1899, Wol 28/40. W–wife 10 Sept 1894 quoted Arthur *Wolseley Letters* 321

44 *Times* 27 Jun 1899 p 10 cols 4–6. He sent a summary to M. See CO 879/56/55

45 C–M 5 Jun 1899, CO 879/56. Wilde 110–11

46 C's min 5 May 1899, CO 417/279/12596. *C 9345*

47 Wilde 103

48 C–Selborne 26 Jun 1899, Cham JC/10/4/2/42

49 M–C 23 Jun, CO 879/56/110

50 Graham's min, CO 417/262/16194

51 C–M 6 Jul 1900, CO 417/279/17501

52 *C 9415*/41. *C 9518*/17–21

53 See CO/879/59/251

54 *C 9518, 9521*. Hely-Hutchinson 26 Jul 1899, CO 879/56/150–1. Marais 294–5. *MP* I, 462–4

55 *Times* 18 July 1899. CO 417/263/18070. Wilde 119. Marais 290–2, 295–9

56 Garvin III, 418–19

57 Salisbury–C 19 Jul 1899 Cham JC/5/67/114

58 C–Salisbury 18 Jul 1899, Sal E/154

59 SJ 1 Jul 1899. See L–C 11, 15 Aug 1899, Cham JC/5/51/59, 61

60 C–M 27 Jul 1899, CO 879/59/245–9. Salisbury–C 20 Jul 1899, Sal E/155. Wilde 122–3. Marais 303–4

61 Kruger–Steyn 2 Aug 1899, *MP* I, 483. *Cd 369*/3. J. H. Hofmeyr 546, 548–9. Marais 305–6

62 See Garvin III, 224, 237

63 *Hansard* LXXV 28 Jun–4 Aug 1899

64 Hely-Hutchinson–C 25 Jul 1899, CO 879/59/240. SM 1/2

65 L's min 2 Aug, W's min 3, 18 Aug 1899, *RCSAW* I, 266–7

66 L's min for Cabinet 12 Aug 1899, *RCSAW* III, 507–8

67 Goschen–C 23, 28 Aug 1899, C–Selborne 14 Aug 1899, C–Salisbury 15 Aug 1899, Sal E/156. Garvin III, 454–5.

68 Salisbury–C 16 Aug 1899, Cham JC/5/67/115

69 C–Salisbury 16 Aug 1899, Sal E/157

70 M–C 15 Aug 1899, CO 417/264. Marais 308–12

71 Salisbury–C 17 Aug 1899, Cham JC/5/67/116

72 Dugdale *Balfour* I, 192, 194

73 See Lansdowne papers passim

74 Mrs Chamberlain 25 Aug 1899, Garvin III, 437

CHAPTER 8: PREPARING FOR A SMALL WAR

Head of chapter C–Hicks Beach 7 Oct 1899, Cham JC 10/4/2/53

1 M's diary 18 Jul 1899, Mil (dep 69)

2 M's diary 23 Jul 1899, Mil (dep 69)

3 SJ Jul–Aug 1899. The Manchesters and Munsters did not *sail* till 23 and 24 Aug

4 Fleetwood Wilson–M 22 Jun 1899, Mil 15 (SA 31)

5 Walker *Schreiner* 87–90 (Central News Agency paperback edi nd)

6 M–Garrett 15 Jul 1900, Mil 28 (SA 46)

7 See Marais 295–7

8 Trotter's report 29 Jul 1899, SM 2/1–2. Trotter's ev *RCSAW* III, Q 13873–8

9 M–C 4, 24 Aug 1899, CO 879/56/174, 223. M's diary 7 Aug 1899, Mil (dep 69). Walker *W. P. Schreiner* 88–90. See also *C 9521*/3

10 M–C 30 Aug 1899, *MP* I, 503–4. Walker 92–3

11 M–C 22 Aug 1899, *C 9521*/44–6

12 Selborne–M 7 Oct 1899, Mil 17 (SA 31). See letter to Grey 7 Aug 1899, *MP* I, 476–9

13 M–Greene 17 Aug 1899, *MP* I, 490–1

14 M–C 22, 23 Aug 1899, *C 9521*/46, 60–4. CO 417/264/21624. CO 417/265/22484, 22259, 22260. Wilde 129/136

15 C–M 28 Aug 1899, *C 9521*/49–50

16 See esp M–R 6 Jun 1900, Bobs 45. And see M–Bertha Synge 20 Apr 1898 Mil 8: 'considerable war'

17 M–Ly Ilbert 7 Dec 1897, Mil (kept separately at New College)

18 Selborne–M 27 Jul 1899, *MP* I, 4732

19 Wyndham–M 18 May 1899, Mil 14 (SA 30)

20 M–Grey 7 Aug 1899, *MP* I, 476–9. Asquith–M 17 Jul 1899, Mil 15 (SA 31). Robbins *Grey* 76–7. H. Matthew *Liberal Imperialists* (London 1973) 171–5

21 See Margot Asquith–M 9 Jul 1900, Mil 29 (SA 32) 'I cd have wished that you & you alone in the beginning had had the presentation of the case ...'

22 *MP* I, 13–17. Cook *Rights and Wrongs of the War* passim. Cook *Edmund Garrett* 151–6. And see *Review of Reviews*, *Daily News*, *Westminster Gazette*, *Cape Times* Jul–Aug 1899

23 *Morning Post* 23 Aug 1899. See also 20 Jul and the signed articles in the paper by Wilkinson in July 1899

24 *Times* 24, 26 Aug 1899. Buckle–M 18 Aug 1899, *MP* I, 497

25 House Paper 311. Fort *Alfred Beit* 145–62. The Raid etc cost Beit £300,000 acc Lockhart and Woodhouse *Rhodes* 367

26 H. W. Just (of the CO)–M 6 May 1899, Mil 14 (SA 30)

27 See series of letters in 1898–9 Wernher–

Eckstein, Fitzpatrick–Eckstein and Rouliot–Wernher, Eck HE 167, 116 and 175. See also Rhodes–Beit 23 Aug 1899, Eck 67

28 Fitzpatrick *Memories* 181–7

29 Hobson *War in South Africa* (from articles published in *Manchester Guardian*) 189–240

30 Wernher–Rouliot 6 May, 9, 13 Jun 1899, Eck HE 167

31 Gell–M 2 Jun [1899], Gell 532. Eckstein–Wernher, Beit & Co. 22 Jul 1899; 'apparent weakness of Imperial Government', Eck 121. See also Rouliot–Wernher 7 Aug 1899: 'life is becoming intolerable', Eck HE 175

32 Wernher–Rouliot 15 Sep 1899, Eck HE 167

33 Eckstein–Evans 21 Sep 1899, Eck HE 130

34 Fitzpatrick–Eckstein 24 Nov 1899, Eck HE 116

35 Cf J. Grenville *Lord Salisbury and Foreign Policy* (1970) 267

36 Selborne–C re Fitzpatrick's visit on 3 Jul 1899, Cham JC/10/4/2/43

37 Intell note 28 Jul 1899, CO 417/275/513–21. Fitzpatrick also claimed OFS would be neutral

38 Balfour–[Bryce?] 2 Dec 1899, Bal 49853/138–43

39 Margot Asquith *Autobiography* (London 1962) 227

40 Rhodes–Beit (cy) 23 Aug 1899, Eck 67

41 Rothschild–Balfour 8 Sep 1899, Bal 49746/136

42 M–Dawkins 16 Jan 1902, Mil 28 (SA 32). Cf Cook *Rights* 265

43 See esp Rouliot–Wernher 17 Apr, 17 Aug 1899 and Wernher–Rouliot, Eck HE 175, 167

44 L–Butler 7 Jul 1899, WO 32 (079/8686)

45 M–Ly E. Cecil, *MP* I, 164. Ly Milner *Picture Gallery* 125, 132

46 Margot Asquith–M 9 Jul 1900, Mil 29 (SA 32)

47 M's diary 25, 26, 27 Jul, 3, 5, 6, 7, 14 Aug 1899, Mil (dep 69)

48 M's diary 1 Sep 1899, Mil (dep 69)

49 M–C 30 Aug (letter), 31 Aug 1899 (tel), *MP* I, 499, 500

50 M–Selborne 30 Aug 1899, *MP* I, 498–9

51 M's diary 5 Sep 1899, Mil (dep 69) 'Eckstein came to see me with a private telegram from Beit.'

52 Garvin III, 438, 460. *Times* 25 Aug 1899

53 M–C 2 Aug 1899, *MP* I, 513–14

54 CO 417/264/21624. Wilde 130–2

55 W's memo 18 Aug 1899, SM 1/4 (note 27 copies ptd). L–C 21 Aug 1899, Cham JC/5/51/67

56 C–Selborne 14 Aug 1899, Garvin III, 454–5

57 C–L 24 Aug 1899, Lan X 15–17

58 Garvin III, 438–9

59 *Times* 26 Aug 1899

60 Garvin loc cit

61 C 9521/49. Wilde 134. Marais 312–16

62 C–Salisbury 2 Sep 1899, Sal E/159

63 See Salisbury–C 18 Sep 1899, Cham JC/5/67/122, Selborne–M 11 Aug 1899, *MP* I, 486–7. Askwith *Lord James of Hereford* (London 1930) 255. *Daily News* 9 Sep 1899 etc.

64 L–Balfour 22 Apr 1900: 'Devonshire's yawns', Bal 49727/129–30

65 *Times* 9 Sep 1899

66 C's memo of 6, 7 Sep 1899, Cab 37/50/70–1. Wilde 140–1

67 Ibid. Cf Salisbury's memo on subject 5 Sep 1899. Cab 37/50/64. Garvin III, 441–2

68 See C–L 5 Oct 1899, Cham JC/5/51/87; when C *still* believed Boers would not take offensive

69 Salisbury–C 29 Aug 1899, Cham JC/5/67/116

70 Buller's min 5 Sep 1899 (with C's, L's, W's comments) Cab 37/50/62–8. L's further comments on above to C, L–C 9 Sep 1899, Cham JC/5/51/80

71 L–C 15, 21 Aug 1899, Cham JC/5/51/61–7. L–G Wyndham 15 Aug 1899, Lan VIII 17–20

72 Hicks-Beach–Salisbury 24, 31 Aug 1899, Sal E/

73 Hicks-Beach *Life* 106. A. G. Gardiner *Life of Sir William Harcourt* II, 498

74 Balfour's memo quoted Drus *Documents* 173–5 and Wilde 99–101. Balfour–C 6 May 1899, Bal 49773/162–5

75 Asquith–Bryce 28 Sep 1899, Bry UB 1. Balfour–Bryce 2 Oct 1899, Bal 49853/120–2

76 SM 1/3. SJ 8, 9 Sep 1899. *Times* 9 Sep 1899

77 C 9521/64. Salisbury–C 19 Sep 1899, Cham JC/5/67/122

78 Goschen–Salisbury Sep 1899 Sal E/: 'I agreed with all you said in emphatically warning us of the big character of the job before us.'

79 Salisbury–L 30 Aug 1899, Newton *Lansdowne* 157

80 *Cape Times* 11 Sep (London 9th) 1899

81 SJ 8, 9 Sep 1899

82 See esp W's min 8 Jun 1899, *RCSAW* I, 262: 'Operations should begin in South Africa as soon as possible, so as to be over by next November.'

83 W–wife 6 Sep 1899, Wol 28/50

84 Gen Gaselees' report 28 Aug 1899, SM 3/1–12

85 W–L 24 Aug 1899, *RCSAW* I, 267. W's min 5 Sep 1899, *RCSAW* I, 269. L–C 21, 26 Aug, 1 Sep 1899, Cham JC/5/51/67, 72–3

86 SJ 16–17, 20–8 Sep 1899

87 White–J White 3 Sep 1899, Whi 98B. W

reckoned on only '9,800 bayonets, 1,900 sabres and 42 guns' W's min 3 Oct 1899, *RCSAW* I, 272. L–C 9 Sept 1899, Cham JC 5/51/80. SM 1/3

88 Ibid and W–C 12 Sep 1899, Cham JC/5/51/81

89 C–L 14 Jun, 10 Sep 1899, Lan 5/26–7, 7/8–9

90 SJ 16 Sep. *Times* 17 Sep, Rawlinson diary 19 Sep–6 Oct 1899 Rawl 7–1

91 L–C 9 Sep, Cham JC/5/51/80. L–C 12, 15 Sep 1899, Lan X/18, 26

92 G. Wyndham–Balfour 8 Aug 1899, Bal 49803

93 Buller–brother 3 Nov 1899, Bull (PRO) WO 132/6. Buller–L WO 32/7902/287. Buller's ev *RCSAW* III, 170

94 Buller–A. Herbert 13 Oct 1899 Herb Butler *Buller* 33–8

95 Buller–L 9 Sep 1899, Lan 2/3–4

96 Buller–Bigge 4 Jan 1900, Big

97 L–C (rejecting Buller's proposal) 9 Sep 1899, Cham JC/5/51/80

98 Quoted Symons 91

99 Lyttelton *Eighty Years* 200–1

100 'Pom' MacDonnell–Curzon 29 Aug 1899 (Cy) PC

101 White–brother 3 Sep 1899, Whi 98B/

102 White–brother 19 Sep, 1 Oct, Whi 98B/264–9. White–Ly White 19 Sep, 1 Oct 1899, Whi 101/I. *DNB*

103 White–brother 6 Oct 1899, Whi 98B

104 White–Miss Warrender 15 Sep 1899, Whi 97B

105 White–Ly White 1 Oct 1899, Whi 101/I. Cf Sandberg *Twintig Jaren* 204–9

106 White–brother 1 Oct 1899, Whi 98B. Rawlinson diary 19 Sep–6 Oct, Rawl MS cit

107 White–brother 6 Oct 1899, Whi 98B. SJ 26 Sep 1899. Hely-Hutchinson–C 25 Sep 1899, CO 879/59/598

108 Rawlinson diary 6 Oct 1899, Rawl 7–1

109 White–Ly White 6 Oct 1899, Whi 101/I. Rawlinson diary 7 Oct 1899, Rawl 7–1. I. Hamilton–wife 5 Oct 1899, Ham 25/12/4

110 White–Ly White 6 Oct 1899, Whi 101/I

CHAPTER 9: THE ULTIMATUM
Head of chapter Smuts's plan 4 Sep 1899, *SP* I, 322–9

1 *Standard and Diggers News, Volksstem, Cape Times* 2–4 Oct 1899. Batts *Pretoria From Within* (nd) 27–32

2 Kotzé *Memoirs* II, 239–40. L. Amery *Days of Fresh Air* 129

3 Hofmeyr–Smuts 30 Aug 1899, *SP* I, 307–8

4 Fischer–Smuts 24 Aug, *SP* I, 303–4. Steyn–Kruger 1 Sep, Mil 11/247 (SA 82). Fischer–Steyn 1, 2 Sep 1899, Mil 60/248, 254

5 'If Steyn had got Kruger this week to accept your Bloemfontein terms we could not have rejected them.' Selborne–Milner 7 Oct 1899, Mil 17 (SA 31)

6 See Marais 316. Wilde 133–5. Le May *British Supremacy* 25–6

7 *TH* I, 376. Barnard *Botha* 6–12. Meintjes *De la Rey* 78–82. Viljoen *Reminiscences* 28–9

8 *A Century of Wrong* sponsored by F. Reitz, written by Smuts (see *SP* I, 476)

9 Smuts strategic plan, *SP* I, 322–9

10 *New York World* interview (dated 12 Oct 1899) quoted Cook *Rights* 263

11 Fischer–Hofmeyr 13 Sep 1899, Mil 60/296

12 Kruger–Hofmeyr (via Fischer) 16 Sep 1899, Mil 60/

13 *SP* I, 242, 249

14 *SP* I, 323

15 Ibid 323–9

16 *Volksstem, Cape Times* 9 Sep 1899

17 Ibid 23 Sep 1899

18 De Beer 25 Sep, Kruger–Steyn 26 Sep 1899, Mil 60/360, 377

19 Kruger–Steyn 29 Sep 1899, Mil 60/390

20 P. Kruger *Memoirs* II, 331–6. SJ 27 Sep 1899. L. Amery *Days of Fresh Air*. Breyt I, 132

21 C. De Wet–Steyn 30 Sep 1899, Mil 60/

22 SJ 3 Oct 1899. *Breyt* I, 133

23 *C 9530/65–7*

24 SJ 2, 6, 8, 9 Oct 1899

25 *C 9530/65–7*

26 *Cape Times* 29 Sep, 3 Oct 1899. Burleigh *Natal* 10

27 Totals acc official railway report: 8,369 men, 5,381 horses, 398 wagons, 1,909 oxen, 1,525 tons of stores. *Cd 625/25*

28 L. Amery *Days of Fresh Air* 132–7. *Times* 7 Nov 1899 p. 12. Reitz *Commando* 20

29 Symons–White 17 Oct 1899, Whi 56A

30 Mouton *Joubert* 230–1

31 Mouton 230 quoting Joubert's telegram book in KG 346

32 Ibid

33 Reitz–Leyds 9 Oct 1899 W. Leyds *Correspondentie Tweede Verzameling* I, 42–3. Breyt I, 158–62 quoting KG 353

34 Breyt I, 31–106. Hillegas *With the Boers* passim. *TH* II, 53–97

35 Reitz *Commando* 22–3

36 Ibid

37 Lehmann *First Boer War* 223–305. Col G. F. R. Henderson draft of *OH*, University of Witwatersrand, Cullen Library 99/A320

38 *Breyt* I, 146–62. Cf *OH* I, 48, *TH* II, 121. For origin of plan see Kruger–Steyn 27 Sep 1899, Mil 60/381a

39 Kretschmar diary 16–24 Aug 1899 *Cd 624/36–8*. See also railway report in *Cd 625/25*

40 Joubert's telegram-book KG 346 quoted Mouton 321. *Breyt* I, 166–7. Trichard 114–19
41 Reitz 23
42 *Volksstem* 21 Oct 1899. Mouton 234
43 Reitz 23
44 *TH* II, 142
45 See previous chapter note 110
46 SJ 7–9 Oct 1899. Rawlinson diary 7–11 Oct 1899 Rawl 7–1. Hely-Hutchinson–C 7 Oct 1899, CO 179/206
47 Rawlinson diary loc cit
48 Ibid
49 Note on interview, *Cd 44/26*
50 Maurice's unpub draft chapter for *OH* I, in *PC*
51 *Cd 44/26*
52 White's ev *RCSAW* III, 144
53 Lt Crum memoir 16 Aug 1899, Cru I/11
54 Symons–White 29 Jul 1899, Whi 52
55 Lt Crum memoir 29 Jun, 2, 9 Aug 1899, Cru
56 Lt Max Trench diary 13–19 Oct 1899, Tren
57 Ibid. Cf Maj. G. Bird's diary 15 Oct 1899, Bird
58 Symons–White 2 Sep 1899, Whi 52
59 Lt Trench diary 16 Oct 1899, Tren
60 Lt Kentish 12 Oct 1899, Kent
61 Lt Crum 12 Oct 1899, Cru
62 White–L 10 Oct 1899, Whi 56A
63 V. Sampson and I. Hamilton *Anti-Commando* 94
64 *Times, Daily Telegraph, Globe* 10 Oct 1899. Moberly Bell–L. S. Amery 13 Oct 1899, *Times*
65 *Times* 7, 9–10 Oct 1899
66 L–C 10 Oct 1899, Cham JC/5/51/89
67 Balfour–C 2 Oct 1899, Cham JC/5/5/ Mins of Buller 24, 25, 28 Sep 1899, *RCSAW* I, 270–1
68 See note 66
69 *RCSAW* I, 84–96. And Stopford's ev *RCSAW* II, Q 951
70 *RCSAW* I, 37 note only 20,000 reservists were fit. *Times* 9–14 Oct 1899. *OH* I, 101
71 Garvin III, 471–2
72 Gooch *Courtney* 381–2. Gardiner *Harcourt* II, 508–12
73 J. Wilson *CB* 311
74 C–Hicks-Beach 7 Oct 1899, Cham JC/10/4/2/53
75 See J. Wilson 314
76 Balfour–C 2 Oct 1899, Bal 49773/173–6
77 C–M 6 Dec 1899, Mil 17 (SA 31)
78 Salisbury–C (cypher tel) 9 Oct 1899, Cham JC/5/67/129
79 Salisbury–C 19 Sep 1899, Cham JC/5/67/124
80 C–Balfour 3 Oct 1899, Bal 49773/177–8. C–Hicks Beach 2 Oct 1899 quoted Marais 322
81 Drus *Documents* 182–6. Garvin III, 463–4. Wilde 144–5

82 L–C 15 Sep, C–L 7 Oct 1899, Cham JC/5/51/82, 88
83 *RCSAW* I, 270–5
84 C–Hicks-Beach 7 Oct 1899, Cham JC/10/4/2/53
85 C–Hicks Beach 29 Sep 1899, Drus *Documents* 188
86 *Times, Daily News* 16 Oct 1899
87 Buller–A. Herbert 13 Oct 1899, Herb
88 Buller–Sir A. Bigge 4 Jan 1900, Big
89 Buller's ev *RCSAW* III, 170
90 See note 86
91 *Hansard* 19 Oct 1899 LXXVII cols 254 foll. Garvin III, 481–9

CHAPTER 10: BURSTING THE MOULD
Head of chapter M–R 6 Jun 1900, Bobs 45
1 SJ 14 Oct 1899. *Cape Times* 16 Oct 1899
2 *Standard and Diggers News, Cape Times* 4–9, 11–14 Sep 1899
3 *Standard and Diggers News* 5–9 Sep, *Cape Times* 5, 9 Sep 1899. Ly E. Cecil–'Tim' 8 Oct 1899 Sal (Hat)
4 M's diary 8 Oct 1899, Mil (dep 69)
5 Ly E. Cecil–'Tim' 8, 30 Oct 1899, Sal (Hat). Ly Milner *My Picture Gallery* 137–8
6 M's diary 6, 7 Oct 1899, Mil (dep 69). M–C 10 Oct 1899, CO 879/59/709. *Times* Oct 1899. See also SJ 20 Oct
7 M's diary 24 Sep 1899, Mil (dep 69)
8 M's diary 7 Oct 1899, Mil (dep 69)
9 Ibid 1–7 Oct 1899. See Ly E. Cecil–'Tim' 2, 8 Aug, 2, 20 Sep etc. 1899, Sal (Hat)
10 M's diary 9 Oct 1899, Mil (dep 69)
11 M–Dawkins 16 Jan 1902, Mil 28 (SA 46). Cook *Rights* 265
12 *MP* I, 521. SJ 20 Sep, 1 Oct 1899. BP's ev *RCSAW* III, 423–4
13 *OH* I, 52–3, 455. CT no lc
14 M's diary 9–18 Oct 1899, Mil. SJ 9–18 Oct 1899. M–Selborne 11, 18 Oct 1899, *MP* I 559, II, 378
15 See tel from Mafeking to M SJ 1 Oct 1899. M–C 23 Aug 1899 CO 859/56/262. See M's diary
16 *TH* IV, 436
17 Selborne–M 7 Oct 1899, Mil 17 (SA 31)
18 Lord E. Cecil–Ly E. Cecil Kent Record Office
19 C–M 6 Dec, Wyndham–M 13 Oct, Haldane–M 11 Oct 1899, Mil 17 (SA 31). Grey–M 4 Oct, 1 Nov 1899, *MP* I, 560–1
20 M–Rendel 30 May 1900, Rendel–M 23 Jun 1900, Mil 24, 27. M–R 6 Jun 1900, Bobs 45
21 Fitzpatrick–Balfour 1 Jan 1900, Bal 49853/158
22 M–Edith Gell 26 Jan 1899, Gell 525
23 M–Rendel 25 May 1900, Mil 24 (SA 108)
24 M–Fitzpatrick 28 Nov 1899 *MP* II, 35
25 See quote at head of chapter
26 M–Rendel 21 Jul 1899 *MP* I, 473
27 Cecil Rhodes disapproved of Jameson

going to Ladysmith, acc his letter quoted
Sarah Wilson 190. Cf *Frank Rhodes*
130–1, and Colvin *Jameson* II, 189

28 The actual losses directly caused by the
war were calculated at about £4·2m. See
Wybergh's report 11 Dec 1901, *Cd 903*

29 M–Asquith 18 Nov 1897, Asq

30 Ibid. M–Fitzpatrick 28 Nov 1899, *MP* I,
35–6

31 The Rev J. Darragh–M 17 Oct 1899, Mil
17 (SA 31)

32 See chap 9 note 81

33 Marwick–Hely-Hutchinson 5 Oct 1899,
Cd 43/130–1

34 Marwick–Hely Hutchinson report 19
Oct 1899, *Cd 43*/167–71. M–C 6 Oct 1899
enc cables, CO 879/59/853

35 For African reactions see P. Warwick
Black Industrial Protest 1–2

36 Capt G. Thompson 29 Oct 1899, PC. L.
March Phillipps 165

37 C. L. Anderson–Fitzpatrick 7 Mar 1900,
Fitz

38 S. Evans–Sir E. Vincent 15 Nov, S.
Evans–Fitzpatrick 30 Oct, 3 Nov 1899,
Fitz

39 C. L. Anderson 7 Mar 1900, MS cit.
Evans–Fitzpatrick 22 Nov 1899, Fitz

40 Wybergh–Fitzpatrick 4 Aug 1900, Fitz

41 C. L. Anderson MS cit. S. Evans–
Fitzpatrick 11 Nov, S. Evans–Sir E.
Vincent 14 Nov 1899, Fitz

42 M's diary 18–19 Oct 1899, Mil (dep 69).
M–C 18 Oct 1899, CO 879/207/14

43 H. Hutchinson–C 7.32 a.m. 20 Oct 1899,
CO 179/206/814

PART II

CHAPTER 11: TAKING TEA WITH
THE BOERS

Head of chapter Lt Kentish–parents 30 Sep,
12 Oct 1899, Kent. Hely-Hutchinson–M
20 Oct 1899, Mil 17 (SA 31)

1 Gunner Netley tapes, PC. Monypenny
Times 18 Nov 1899 (report 27 Oct)

2 Sir G. White despatch 2 Nov 1899, SD I,
3–6. *OH* I, 123, 456. *Breyt* I, 215–36. *TH*
II, 141–74. Barnard *Botha* 22–5

3 Lt Kentish letters Oct 1899, Kent. Lt
Crum letters & Memoir, Cru

4 *PPW* 23 quoting letter of 16 Oct 1899

5 Romer & Mainwaring *Dublin Fusiliers* 6.
Lt Stirling *Times* 8 Dec 1899. Lt Crum
MS cit. Maj. Burnett *18th Hussars* 12–13

6 Lt Crum letters & memoir, Cru

7 Lt Trench diary 20 Oct 1899, Tren

8 Maj. Bird diary 20 Oct 1899, Bird

9 Netley tapes and Netley diary 20 Oct
1899, PC

10 Netley diary 20 Oct 1899, PC

11 Lt Trench MS cit. Maj. Kerin diary 25–6,
Ker

12 Netley tapes, PC. Romer & Mainwaring
7

13 Lt Trench MS cit

14 Ibid. Netley tapes, PC

15 Maj. Burnett loc cit

16 See Maj. Marling's diary entry 255, 266
in response, presumably, to W. T. Stead's
best-selling pamphlet, *Shall I slay my
Brother Boer?* published London Sep 1899

17 Netley diary 20 Oct 1899, PC. Netley
tapes and Kerin diary, 26 Ker. Lt Trench
MS cit

18 *PPW* 30 quoting NCO's letter

19 Symons–White 17 Oct, Symons–White
(tel) 18 Oct 1899. Whi 52, 56B. Kerin
diary 23 Ker. Maurice *Rawlinson* (quoting journal) 45

20 *OH* I, 128–9 and Map Vol I. *TH* II, 157.
EGO

21 See note 19

22 Symons–White 29 Jul 1899 Whi 52. For
tactical criticism of Majuba see chap 8 of
G. F. R. Henderson's unpublished draft
of *OH*, loc cit

23 Crum diary 2 Aug 1899 quoted memoir
11, Cru. *TH* II, 157–8

24 Symons's ADC quoted Bishop Baynes
My Diocese 61

25 Col Möller 15 Jun 1900 *RCSAW* III, 402.
Möller was censured by Roberts for
incompetence and later put on half pay.
Marling 254

26 White SD I, 5

27 James *High Pressure* 112–13, 127–8. *Times*
18 Nov 1899. *Times* MS letterbooks
1899

28 Barnard *Botha* 22–3. *Breyt* I, 217

29 *PPW* 31

30 Ibid 31

31 Ibid 31

32 Maj. Kerin 28 Ker. Maj. Donegan diary
entry 20 Oct 1899 PC

33 *TH* II, 159–60

34 Maj. Bird diary 5 Bird. Romer & Mainwaring 7–9

35 *TH* II, 160–1

36 Ibid 161

37 Symons's ADC quoted *PPW* 33

38 Maj. Kerin diary 33 Ker. Cf *PPW* 35

39 Maj. Bird loc cit

40 Netley diary loc cit

41 Ibid. Trench MS cit

42 *TH* II, 164–5. (Capt. Nugent's identity
established by Kerin's diary 48 Stirling's
letter 8 Dec 1899)

43 Ibid 165–6

44 Barnard 23. *Breyt* I, 226–7 quoting
Meyer's official report 21 Oct 1899

45 Lt Stirling *Times* 8 Dec 1899. Lt Kentish
loc cit. Kerin loc cit

46 *OH* I, 462. Cf *Breht* I, 233–6

47 *OH* I, 138–41. *Breyt* I, 224–6

48 White SD I, 6. Conan Doyle *Great Boer
War* 91–2

49 Netley loc cit
50 *Breyt* I, 227–8. *OH* I, 137. Note Barnard 22. Half Meyer's force stayed out of firing-line

CHAPTER 12: WHITE FLAG, 'ARME BLANCHE'

Head of chapter Prosper Paris–Gerty 24 Oct 1899 Man
1 Gordon 10 Nov 1899 quoted in *PPW* 54
2 Ibid 54, 56. White SD I, 6. Macready *Annals* 76. Haldane typescript autobiography I, 133–203 Hal
3 Gardyne *Gordons* III, 15, 457–9
4 *PPW* loc cit
5 Haldane–mother 22 Oct 1899, Hal. Gardyne III, 16, 26
6 White loc cit. *OH* I, 160–1, 464. *TH* II, 178–9. *Breyt* I, 241–2
7 Steevens *Cape Town to Ladysmith* 43–7. White loc cit. *OH* I, 163
8 French *Life* 3, 56. Goldmann *With General French* frontispiece
9 Haig diary 20 Oct 1899, letter to Henrietta 26 Oct 1899, Haig 148, 157
10 Sampson and Hamilton *Anti-Commando* 112
11 Ibid 49, 79–82, 98–9. Steevens 68
12 *Breyt* I, 197–9. Viljoen *Reminiscences* 23. Schiel *23 Jahre* 417–19
13 Haig diary & letter loc cit. *OH* I, 160–1. *TH* II, 177–9
14 *OH* map vol I. *TH* II, 181–2
15 Lt-Col Coxhead *PRAI* XXVII 439, 441–2
16 *OH* I, 464. *Breyt* I, 197
17 *TH* II, 183
18 Ibid II, 182
19 See Nevinson *The Siege of Ladysmith Changes and Chances*. Steevens op cit. Burleigh *Natal*
20 Steevens 47–8. *Times* 11 Nov 1899 (report of 25 Oct). *TH* II, 184
21 Nevinson 36–8
22 Jacson *Record of a Regiment* 14–19. White SD I, 6–7. *OH* I, 164–5
23 Drummer Boulden 24 Mar 1900, Devonshire Regt Museum Exeter
24 Manchester Regt Records Man. *OH* I, 166–7
25 [Newbigging] *Times* 8 Dec 1899. Another Manchester Officer *Times* 18 Nov 1899
26 *OH* I, 164
27 Haldane unpublished autobiography 140 Hal. Gardyne III, 18
28 Haldane diary 21 Oct 1899 Hal. Ibid 18–19. Steevens 51–2. *TH* II, 185–6
29 Steevens 52. (James) *Times* 18 Nov 1899
30 James loc cit
31 Sampson & Hamilton *Anti-Commando* 113–4
32 Gardyne III, 21–2

33 Sampson & Hamilton loc cit
34 Gardyne III, 21–2
35 Newbigging loc cit
36 White loc cit. *OH* I, 169. *TH* II, 187–8
37 Newbigging loc cit
38 *OH* I, 169–70. *TH* II, 188
39 Steevens 54. *OH* I, 167–8
40 Nevinson 38. Steevens 54
41 *OH* I, 138–40
42 Cable in *Natal Mercury* 22–3 Oct 1899. James *High Pressure* 124–6
43 Steevens 55
44 Nevinson 38
45 *OH* I, 169. Gore *Green Horse* 18–24. *PPW* 64–5 quoting ptes in 60th and 5th Lancers. *TH* II, 190–1
46 Officer quoted in *Times* 13 Dec 1899
47 Pte of 5th Lancers *PPW* 65. Nevinson *Ladysmith* 38
48 Trooper in 5th Lancers quoted *PPW* 64–5
49 Nevinson loc cit
50 Steevens 64. *TH* II, 192–3
51 Manchester officer quoted *Times* 18 Nov 1899. See for example Gunner Williams's boasting quoted in *PPW* 66
52 Steevens 56–65. *TH* loc cit
53 Sampson and Hamilton *Anti-Commando* 114–15
54 *Breyt* I, 256–60
55 *TH* II, 188–9

CHAPTER 13: THE KNOCK-DOWN BLOW

Head of chapter White–brother 27 Oct 1899, Whi 98B/183
1 Netley tapes & diary 22–3 Oct 1899, PC
2 Lt Trench 21 Oct 1899 (written 25), Tren. Lt Kentish 21 Oct 1899 Kent. Netley diary, PC. Cpl Hallahan quoted *PPW* 75
3 'Long Tom, as everyone in the forces called the Big Gun on Impati Hill' Lt Trench 21 Oct 1899, Tren. See *Breyt* I, 266. Cf *OH* I, 143, 145. *TH* II, 198–9
4 Netley diary, PC
5 Netley tapes, PC
6 White SD, I, 8 para 28. Note Krupp howitzer was actually short-barrelled
7 *Military Notes* 24–5. See C–Devonshire 5 Nov 1899, Garvin III, 491
8 *OH* I, 143
9 Maj. Donegan 21–2 Oct 1899, PC. Kerin 61, 59, Ker
10 Trench loc cit. Kentish loc cit
11 White–Buller 31 Oct 1899, SD 9. *OH* I, 146
12 *OH* I, 144
13 *OH* I, 145–6. *Breyt* I, 265–8. Trench 22 Oct 1899, Tren
14 Maj. Bird diary 22–3 Oct 1899, Bird. *OH* I, 145–6
15 *OH* I, 146
16 'This must sound like a dreadful reverse

at home' Lt Trench 23 Oct 1899 Tren. Maj. Donegan loc cit

17 Dundee postmaster, H. Paris, quoted *PPW* 77. Maj. Bird loc cit

18 Ibid. Trench loc cit. Netley diary 22–4 Oct, PC. *OH* I, 146–7

19 *OH* I, 147. Bird loc cit

20 Netley diary loc cit. Nevinson *Ladysmith* 49. *OH* I, 148–51

21 Kerin 64, Ker

22 Ibid 61–4. Donegan 22–3 Oct 1899, PC

23 Kerin 64–5, Ker. Donegan 23 Oct 1899, PC

24 Donegan 23 Oct 1899, PC. Kerin 65, Ker

25 SJ 21 Oct 1899. Kerin 65–8, Ker. Donegan 23 Oct 1899, PC. Cf Reitz *Commando* 32–3. Crum Memoir, Cru

26 Donegan 23 Oct 1899, PC

27 Kerin 62, 75–6, Ker. Donegan loc cit

28 Donegan 24 Oct 1899, PC. Cf Kerin 76–7, Ker. *TH* II, 209

29 Donegan 25, 29 Oct, 2 Nov 1899, PC

30 Netley diary & tapes loc cit

31 Bird loc cit. Kentish loc cit. *TH* II, 206–8

32 *OH* I, 44. *TH* II, 212–13

33 *TH* II, 212–13. SJ 29 Oct 1900 '100 days reserve'

34 'Hills & hollows – wind and dust-storms perpetually, hills covered with sharp stones' Capt. Steavenson 20 Aug 1899 Stea., EGO

35 SM 2/1. Butler *Autobiography* 414, 418

36 Butler's plan, he later claimed: *Autobiography* 420–1

37 Buller–Bigge 4 Jan 1900, Big

38 Butler had moved half the garrison *out* because of typhoid. *Autobiography* 416

39 See Rawlinson diary 7–11 Oct 1899, Rawl 5201/33/7–1

40 *TH* II, 260–4

41 Hely-Hutchinson–White Oct 1899, Whi 56A

42 White–brother 17, 23 Oct 1899, Whi 98B/3. White–wife 27 Oct 1899, MS cit

43 White–wife 19 Oct 1899, MS cit. White–brother 27 Oct 1899, MS cit

44 SJ intell letter 6 Dec 1899. The disproportion between British and Boer numbers at both Talana and Elandslaagte was actually much larger than White knew. Breyt I, 215–16, 241 and cf White SD I, 9

45 White SD I, 8, 62–3. *OH* I, 152–6. For vivid account by company COs of Gloucesters see C. J. Hickie diary 24 Oct 1899, Hick

46 *Times* 30 Oct 1899

47 For excellent comparison of old-style and new-style war see *PRAI* XXVIII 351–64

48 See esp White–wife 27, 30 Oct 1899, MS cit and White–brother 27 Oct 1899 quoted at head of chapter

49 White–brother 27 Oct 1899, MS cit. *OH* I, 172–3

50 *TH* II, 214–15. Gardyne III, 30. Sampson & Hamilton *Anti-Commando* 119

51 White–Hely-Hutchinson Oct 1899, Whi 56A

52 White–wife 30 Oct 1899, MS cit. White–WO (tel) 30 Oct 1899 reprinted in *Times* 1 Nov 1899

53 White–L 2 Dec 1899, SD I 63–4

54 White–brothers loc cit

55 Carleton's report *RCSAW* IV, 403. Cf R's memo SM 18/3–5

56 White–L 2 Dec 1899, SD I, 64. White–Buller 31 Oct 1899, SD I, 9

57 White–wife 30 Oct 1899, MS cit.

58 *OH* I, 175–7

59 Rawlinson diary 30 Oct 1899, MS cit. *OH* I, 176–7

60 Steevens 80

61 Nevinson 58

62 White–Buller 31 Oct 1899, MS cit. 'Some of them [our troops] do not fight with the spirit they had at first.'

63 *TH* II, 255–6. Gardyne III, 32

64 Netley diary 30 Oct 1899, PC

65 *TH* II, 235. Capt. Steavenson: 'very nearly a stampede' (30 Oct 1899), Stea

66 Gilbert diary 20 Oct 1899, Gil

67 *OH* I, 174–86. Rawlinson diary 30 Oct 1899, Rawl

68 Ibid

69 *OH* I, 186–95. *PPW* 88–97. Breyt I, 337–8. De Wet *Three Years War* 21–5. Van Dam *PRAI*

70 White–L 30 Oct 1899, Whi 56B

71 White–wife 30 Oct 1899, MS cit

72 SJ intell letter 6 Dec 1899. Buller–L CT no 2

73 J. Wolfe Murray SD I, 16. Haig diary 2 Nov 1899 Haig. SJ 2 Nov 1899

CHAPTER 14: THE WHALE AND THE FISH

1 J. Atkins *Relief of Ladysmith* 28

2 W. Churchill *London to Ladysmith* 3–4. A. Pollock *Seven Generals* 1–2

3 *Illustrated London News* 1899 684–5

4 W. Churchill op cit 2. W. Churchill–mother 25 Oct 1899, quoted R. S. Churchill Companion Volume to *W. S. Churchill* II, 1055–6

5 Repington *Vestigia* 196. W. Churchill *My Early Life* 249

6 W. Churchill–mother 25 Oct 1899, MS cit

7 Dickson *Biograph in Battle* 2–6. W. Churchill *My early Life* 249

8 Repington 201, 208. See J. Symons *Buller in Natal* 133

9 Dickson 10–11, 17 (inc photograph)

10 W. Churchill *Ladysmith* 3

11 Repington 195

12 Dickson 15–16. Atkins 33–5. Pollock 4

13 Dickson 15–16

14 Churchill *My Early Life* 251. Pollock 4
15 Churchill *Ladysmith* 16–19. Repington 196. Pollock 5
16 *Cape Times* 31 Oct, 1 Nov 1899
17 Buller's ev *RCSAW* III, 171. M's diary 31 Oct 1899, Mil (dep 69)
18 Buller–L 7 Nov 1899, Lan IV
19 See *TH* II, 280–1
20 See Buller–L 7, 14 Nov, 4 Dec 1899, Lan IV. Buller–M c. 5, 7 Nov 1899, Mil 12 (SA 92)
21 M's diary Oct–Nov 1899, Mil (dep 69)
22 M–C 9 Nov 1899, *MP* II, 25
23 Ibid
24 Parkin–M 31 Oct 1899, Mil 17 (SA 31). See also Wyndham–M 13, 27 Oct 1899, Mil 17 (SA 31)
25 See Le May *British Supremacy* 36–7
26 M's diary 4 Nov 1899, Mil (dep 69)
27 M–Hely-Hutchinson *Cd 43*. *MP* I, 461–2
28 L's memo 3 Oct 1899 quoted *RCSAW* I, 37
29 SJ 1–6 Nov 1899
30 See re-assurance Buller–M 7 Nov 1899, Mil 12 (SA 92) 'I take heart …' And see Ly E. Cecil–'Tim' 6 Nov 1899 Sal (Hat)
31 Rhodes–M 5, 7 Nov, Mayor–M 5 Nov, Kimberley MLA 7 Nov 1899 CO 879/62/135–40
32 M–Rhodes 7 Nov 1899, CO 879/62/136
33 M–Hely-Hutchinson quoted 1 Nov 1899 SJ. M–C 23 Nov 1899, CO 879/56/437
34 *OH* I, 196–205. *TH* II, 286–8
35 M–Buller [c. 5 Nov 1899], Mil 12 (SA 92)
36 Buller–(brother) Tremayne 3 Nov 1899, WO 132/6/841
37 Buller–L 4 Nov 1899 CT no 8. Buller–L 7, 14 Nov 1899, Lan IV. See Henderson *Science of War* 368
38 White–Buller 1 Nov 1899, Whi 56B
39 See appendix to Duff Cooper *Haig* (London 1935) I, 381–2
40 L–Buller 1, 3 Nov 1899, CT nos 2G and 3C
41 Buller–L 2 Nov 1899, CT no 3A
42 Buller–L 8 Nov 1899, CT no 15B
43 Buller–L 11 Nov 1899, Lan IV/25
44 See chap 8. And see Wolseley's furious letter W–Ardagh 23 Sep 1899, Ard 30/40/3
45 SJ 22 Sep 1899
46 SJ 9 Nov 1899
47 Buller–M 5 (?) Nov 1899, Mil 12 (SA 92)/86
48 Fleetwood Wilson–M 14 Oct 1899, Mil 17 (SA 31)
49 Buller ev *RCSAW* III, 171
50 M–Selborne 18 Oct 1899, *MP* II, 24
51 M–Selborne 26 Oct 1899, *MP* II, 25. M–C 11 Oct 1899, *MP* II, 18
52 M–Buller 6 Nov 1899, *MP* II, 21. For phrase 'white man's war' see *TH* II, 138–40
53 M–C 24 Nov 1899, CO 879/Af 629/46
54 M–Buller 6 Nov 1899, *MP* II, 21
55 Buller ev *RCSAW* III, 171. *MP* II, 33
56 Buller ev *RCSAW* loc cit
57 M's diary 9 Nov 1899, Mil (dep 69)
58 M's official diary 9–14 Nov enc M–C 16 Nov 1899, CO 879/Af 629/136. SJ 9 Nov 1899
59 SJ 9–16 Nov 1899. See list with dates *OH* I, 471–6
60 Ibid
61 M's official diary enc M–C 16 Nov 1899, MS cit
62 *OH* I, 285–7. SJ 18–19 Nov 1899
63 M's diary 18 Nov 1899, Mil (dep 69)
64 Capt. Algy Trotter–mother 8, 15, 21 Nov 1899, Trot
65 Buller's ev *RCSAW* III, 172
66 Buller estimated he had 54,000 'fighting men' including cavalry and gunners. Buller–L 4 Dec 1899, Lan IV. For 'steam-roller' see *TH* II, 289
67 Buller's ev *RCSAW* III, 171–3. Buller–L 14, 21 Nov 1899, SD I, 12–16
68 Buller–Forestier-Walker 20 Nov 1899, quoted *OH* I, 209
69 Repington 198–200
70 Melville *Buller* II, 66. Buller's ev *RCSAW* III, 173
71 Buller–wife 18 Dec 1899, Bull (Crediton)
72 M–C 22 Nov 1899, CO 879/Af 572/437
73 *OH* I, 269–70, 215–16, 285–7. Buller–L 14 Nov 1899, Lan IV/31–6 'matters are going better now'
74 M's diary 22 Nov foll 1899, Mil (dep 69). Cf Buller–L 4 Dec, 1899, Lan IV, and Buller–wife 2 Dec 1899, Bull (Crediton)
75 Possibly she acted as the intermediary with C when M was appointed High Commissioner. M's diary 19 Apr, 25 Nov 1896, 15 Mar 1897 etc, Mil (dep 66, 7)
76 Margot Asquith–M 9 July 1900, Mil 29 (SA 32)
77 Chamberlain family information, PC. M–C cypher nd, Mil
78 M's diary 26, 28 Sep, 2, 3, 6, 7, 8, 11, 13, 17, 19 Oct 1899, Mil
79 Ly Milner 4 Dec 1899, quoted *Picture Gallery* 149
80 Ibid 146–8. See also *MP* II, 27 (inspired by Ly Milner). Ly Milner, I take it, had misunderstood M. That he knew Buller was going is clear from his protests. See also M's diary 23 Nov 1899, Mil (dep 69)
81 C–M 5 Oct 1899, Cham JC/10/9/70
82 Wyndham–M 13 Oct 1899, Mil 17 (SA 31)
83 SJ 15 Nov 1899
84 For the 'conspiracy' see Le May 31–4

CHAPTER 15: BOTHA'S RAID

Head of chapter Botha quoted Barnard 41 (loosely translated)

1 *Breyt* I, 346–7, 362–3
2 See *Breyt* I, 458–62
3 D. Reitz 17, 35–6. Viljoen 71
4 *TH* II, 48. *OH* I, 121
5 *Breyt* I, 153–5. He estimates Boers had only 32,000–35,000 in the field at outbreak of war
6 *Breyt* I, 153, 166 foll. Barnard 32–3
7 Reitz 45–7. See Viljoen 55–6, 67. Their defeat was ascribed to cowardice
8 *Breyt* I, 233–4. Viljoen 57
9 *Breyt* I, 260–3. Viljoen 55
10 SJ 20, 21 Oct 1899. Cf *Breyt* I, 235–6, 259–60. (At Elandslaagte 336 Boer casualties)
11 Joubert–Reitz 22 Oct 1899, quoted *Breyt* I, 465
12 Joubert–Prinsloo 9 Nov 1899, KG 346 (V)/16–17. Engelenburg *Botha* 28. Barnard 33. *Breyt* I, 362
13 Joubert quoted Barnard 32. *Breyt* I, 343
14 Joubert–Reitz 1 Nov 1899, Leyds 710. *Breyt* I, 346–7
15 Ibid
16 Joubert–Prinsloo 9 Nov 1899, KG 346 (V). *Breyt* I, 362
17 *Breyt* I, 362–7
18 *Breyt* I, 367–8. Barnard 33–5. Cf *OH* I, 265
19 Barnard 1–16, 32. Jones *Life* 34–5, 43–7. Rompel *Heroes* 127
20 *Breyt* I, 367
21 Buller 6 Nov 1899, quoted SJ 6 Nov. *OH* I, 264–5. *TH* II, 300–2
22 Buller–L 16 Nov 1899, CT no 25
23 SJ 3 Nov 1899. *OH* I, 263–4
24 Capt. Haldane 3 Jan 1900, SD I, 121–3. Botha–wife 16 Nov 1899, Ley 710 (b). W. Churchill *Ladysmith* 76–93, *My Early Life* 257–8
25 Barnard 35–8. Naude *Vechten en vluchten* 51–6. *OH* I, 267–8. *TH* II, 305–8. *Breyt* I, 368–9. *PPW* 152–6
26 Ibid. Haldane *Soldier's Saga* 139–44. Churchill loc cit
27 Botha–wife 16 Nov 1899, Ley 710 (b)/541
28 Barnard 37–8 quoting tel Theron–Reitz 28 Nov 1899. Cf R. Churchill *Churchill* I, 461–74. W. Churchill *My Early Life* 266–71, *Ladysmith* 96–7
29 See chap 24 note 13. See also Col Long's telegram enc in report Clery–Buller 17 Nov 1899, Bull (Crediton) code tels Box
30 See Buller 2 Dec 1899, SD I, 21. *OH* I, 268–70. *TH* II, 304
31 *TH* II, 304–5. Amery *Days of Fresh Air* 140–1
32 Barnard 38–9. *Breyt* I, 372–3
33 Ibid
34 *OH* I, 269–70, 477
35 For landing dates see SJ 12 Nov 1899, foll *OH* I, 473–6
36 *OH* I, 269–70
37 One other Boer was killed acc Botha, two acc Joubert. Joubert–Reitz (no 10) 25 Nov 1899, Ley 711 (b). *OH* I, 271–2. Hildyard's report 24 Nov 1899, SD I, 22–3. *PPW* 166–7. Barnard 40–1. Viljoen 71
38 Botha–wife no 39 28 Nov 1899, Ley 711 (c). Barnard 41
39 Botha speaking at a Durham banquet in 1908, quoted Barnard 41
40 Joubert–Reitz (no 51) 28 Nov 1899, Ley 711 (c). Barnard 41–2. Davitt *Boer Fight for Freedom* 250
41 Barnard 41
42 Joubert–Reitz (nos 11 etc) 25 Nov 1899, Ley 711 (b)
43 Kruger–Joubert (no 25) 25 Nov 1899, Ley 711 (b)
44 See note 42. Barnard 41. Cf *TH* II, 214
45 Naudé 66–8. Barnard 41
46 Mouton 246–7. Barnard 42–3
47 P. Warwick loc cit. And see missionaries' reports of commandeered natives in SPG
48 Barnard 47

CHAPTER 16: THE LIGHTS OF KIMBERLEY

Head of chapter De Beer's 12th Annual Report, Beer

1 Methuen–wife 19 Nov 1899, Meth
2 Ibid 20 Nov 1899. Battersby *In the Web* 25
3 Methuen–wife 18–21 Nov 1899, Meth. *OH* I, 214
4 Ralph *Towards Pretoria* 94–7, 151–7. Battersby 17–19, 24–5
5 *DNB*
6 Methuen–wife 18–21 Nov 1899, Meth
7 L–Buller 10 Nov 1899, Lan
8 Methuen–wife 12 Nov 1899, Meth
9 See note 7
10 Methuen–wife 20 Nov 1899, Meth
11 See note 7
12 Methuen–wife 21 Nov 1899, Meth. Methuen ev *RCSAW* III, Q 14147
13 Methuen–wife 22 Oct 1899, Meth
14 Methuen–wife 12 Nov 1899, Meth
15 Ralph op cit 139–40. Wilson *With the Flag* I, 150, 130. *Breyt* I
16 Ralph op cit 134–8
17 Ralph op cit 139–45
18 Ralph op cit 146–7
19 Ralph *At Pretoria* 29–34. See also G. Henderson *Science of War* 371–2
20 Ralph *Towards Pretoria* 147–8. SJ 10 Nov 1899. *OH* I, 213. March Phillipps 7
21 M–C 9 Nov 1899, *MP* II, 25. *OH* I, 213–14
22 Buller–wife Nov 1899, Bull (Crediton). SJ 16 Nov 1899
23 R–L 1 Apr 1900 H & O I, 87–8: 'It is a

terribly sad business, but I hear that Gough showed signs of insanity as far back as 1885'

24 Methuen–wife 18 Nov 1899, Meth. Methuen ev *RCSAW* III, Q 14142. SJ 13 Nov 1899

25 Rimington ev *RCSAW* III, 26–7. March Phillipps 4–5. Chester Master MSS, Ches

26 Burnham *Scouting* 290–301

27 Methuen–wife 18–20 Nov 1899, Meth

28 SJ 10 Dec 1899. Methuen ev *RCSAW* III, Q 14147–52

29 Methuen loc cit Q 14159–12. *OH* I, 214

30 Methuen loc cit Q 14142–3. *OH* I, 211–13

31 Methuen–Buller 2 Dec 1899, Bull (PRO) WO 132/15

32 *TH* II, 323–4

33 C. Rose-Innes *With Paget's Horse* 97 foll

34 Methuen–wife 26 Nov, 2 Dec 1899, Meth

35 *TH* II, 323–4. Photos in J. Cuthbert *Scots Guards* 3–5

36 Kekewich diary passim, Kek. O'Meara *Kekewich* 20, 38

37 Ibid 20, 64. Wilson *With the Flag* II, 371

38 Kekewich ev *RCSAW* III, Q 21889 *OH* II, 52

39 *DNB*. O'Meara 13–15. Kekewich ev *RCSAW* III, Q 21853, 56–61.

40 O'Meara 17. Kekewich loc cit Q 21863

41 SD I, 160–1. *OH* II, 47

42 SJ 12–18 Oct 1899

43 Kekewich loc cit Q 21866–70

44 *Diamond Fields Advertiser* 17 July 1971 (Centenary supplement)

45 Lockhart & Woodhouse 46–7, 73–8 etc

46 However Moffat thought compound system preferable to its absence on Rand. See S.A. Native Races Committee (ed)

47 Ashe *Besieged by the Boers* 14–15. Mrs Maguire in *Times* weekly edit Apr 1900. Meintjes *De la Rey* 102

48 O'Meara 58

49 *OH* II, 53

50 Kekewich diary 15 Nov 1899, Kek. SD I, 164–6, 207–10

51 O'Meara 19

52 SD I, 162–3, 173. SJ Oct 1899, passim

53 O'Meara 48–9. SD loc cit

54 SJ 17 Oct 1899. SD I, 162

55 Kekewich diary 5–6 Nov 1899, Kek. O'Meara 51–5. SD I, 163, 171–2

56 Ashe (London edit) 43, 38. SD I, 173

57 O'Meara 55–6. But cf Kekewich diary 7 Nov 1899, Kek

58 P. Jordan *Cecil Rhodes* (London 1911) 119–20. Photo in H Wilson *With the Flag* II, 393

59 O'Meara 58. Kekewich diary 9–10 Nov 1899, Kek

60 O'Meara 59

61 Ibid 59–61. Kekewich diary, MS cit

62 Ibid 62–4. SD I, 169

63 O'Meara 64–6. Kekewich diary, loc cit

64 O'Meara 66–7, 11

65 Kekewich diary 20–22 Nov 1899, Kek

66 O'Meara 68–9 (plate IV)

67 O'Meara 70

68 SD I, 207–8. O'Meara 70–2. Kekewich diary 24–5 Nov 1899, Kek

69 SD I, 180–1, 165. O'Meara 71, 174. Kekewich diary, MS cit

70 O'Meara 71–3

71 Cf SJ 27 Nov 1899. *OH* 11

72 O'Meara 74–5

73 Kekewich diary 27 Nov 1899, Kek. SD I, 181–6. SJ 27 Nov 1899. O'Meara 74–5

74 O'Meara 77–8

75 Methuen–wife 23–6 Nov 1899, Meth

76 Gerald Trotter–mother 26 Nov 1899, Trot

77 *OH* I, 227, 466

78 *PPW* 204–14

79 Gerald Trotter, MS cit

80 See *PPW* 221–5

81 *OH* I, 466

82 *Breyt* II, 53. Cf SD I, 28

83 Methuen ev *RCSAW* III, Q 14147–51, 14376–9, 14453. Colvile *Ninth Division* 2. *OH* I, 216

84 SD I, 26–8. *OH* I, 218–22

85 Methuen–wife 26 Nov 1899, Meth

86 Methuen–wife 23 Nov 1899, Meth. Trotter MS cit. March Phillipps 12–14. Ralph *Towards Pretoria* 165–6. *PPW* 18

87 Methuen–wife 25 Nov 1899, Meth. *OH* I, 229–42. *Breyt* II, 53

88 SD I, 45. *OH* I, 245–6. Pemberton *Battles* 62–5

89 *OH* 246–7. Info from Miss F. Barbour

90 Lt B. Lang–mother 4 Dec 1899, (cy) PC. Lang tape, PC

91 Methuen SD I, 45–6

92 Methuen–Buller 2 Dec 1899, Bull (PRO) WO 132/15

93 Ralph *Towards Pretoria* 179–80

94 Colvile 5–6. *TH* II, 350 (copy at Corsham with 'yes' in margin inscribed by Ld Methuen)

95 *Breyt* II, 57, 61. Info from Miss F. Barbour. Cf *OH* I, 248

CHAPTER 17: BREAKFAST AT THE ISLAND

Head of chapter Conan Doyle *The Great Boer War* (1900 edit) 127

1 Meintjes *De la Rey* 118

2 H. Wilson *With the Flag* (photo) I, 156. Ralph *Towards Pretoria* 255. See photos in Cuthbert *Scots Guards* 9, 12. EGO

3 *DSAB* I 214–15. Meintjes *De la Rey* passim

4 Meintjes *De la Rey* 79–81

5 See damning evidence of law case of Queen of Sekukuni *v* P. A. Cronje and others, C 417/226/363

6 *Breyt* I, 390–402, II, 37–8, 53–5, 466–7

7 *Breyt* II, 56, 61

8 *Breyt* II, 57–8

9 Ibid II, 58–62 (map opp 96). Methuen's despatch SD I, 46. For Maj O'Meara's sketch-map used by Methuen see Meth. See also Cuthbert 9, 12–13

10 *Breyt* II, 58–9. *OH* I, 243–4. Meintjes *De la Rey* 37, 48–52, 112–14

11 Ralph *Towards Pretoria* 180. Account of Boer eye-witness (cy) PC

12 Meintjes *De la Rey* 116–18, 133

13 *Breyt* II, 60–1. Cf *OH* I, 247–8

14 See map *Breyt* II, 96

15 *Breyt* II, 93–5. *OH* I, 248–9. According to one account Cronje had ordered the men not to fire till the British were *100 yards* away but they fired when they were 400 yards off. See *Narrative of a Boer* in *PRAI* XXIX/7

16 Methuen–wife 1 Dec 1899, Meth

17 Dunn-Pattison *Argyll & Sutherland*

18 Colvile 10–11. Hall *Coldstream Guards* 53–8

19 Ralph *Towards Pretoria* 184

20 Colvile 10–11. Kinnear *Methuen* 108–33. *TH,* II, 352. Capt Chandos–Pole diary 28 Nov 1899, PC. Lt Lang–mother Nov 1899, (cy) PC. Capt E. M. Pakenham–Ly Longford 30 Nov 1899, PC. Capt G. Trotter–mother 30 Nov 1899, Trot

21 Colvile 8–10. Methuen–wife 1 Dec 1899, MS cit. Kinnear Methuen 103–33 called it 'plom, plom')

22 Ralph *Towards Pretoria* 182–3

23 Account of Boer eye-witness, (cy) PC. See also *Narrative of a Boer PRAI* loc cit. And see Boer correspondent's report (Laffan's Agency) quoted *Daily Telegraph* Jan 1900

24 Methuen's despatch SD I, 46. Hall *Coldstream* 53–4

25 Colvile 7–8. *OH* I, 249–51

26 *OH* I, 251–2

27 H. R. Kelham's account, Kel

28 *Breyt* II, 61, 74, 78. *OH* I, 251. See interview with Albrecht quoted G. Trotter–mother 4 Mar 1900 Trot 110

29 *Breyt* II, 75–6 inc quotes from van der Heever *Hertzog* 97–9. *OH* I, 252–4. *TH* II, 353

30 Methuen's despatch SD I, 46. Lt Lang–mother Dec 1899 (cy) PC. *OH* I, 254–6. *TH* II, 355–6

31 Ibid

32 De la Rey–Steyn no 22 Nov 29 1899, Ley 711 quoted *Breyt* II, 468–9. De la Rey's memoirs quoted *Breyt* II, 80–2. Meintjes *De la Rey* 120–1. *OH* I, 257

33 Ibid

34 Meintjes loc cit

35 De la Rey's memoirs loc cit

36 Ibid. Meintjes loc cit

37 *Breyt* II, 90

38 *Breyt* II, 87–9

39 Methuen–wife 1 Dec 1900, Meth. Colvile 11–13. *OH* I, 259–60

40 Ralph *Towards Pretoria* 192–3. *TH* II, 358–9

41 De la Rey's memoirs loc cit

42 *Breyt* II, 468–70

43 Prinsloo no 60 29 Nov 1899, quoted above

44 Kruger–Steyn no 1 30 Nov 1899, Ley 711. *Breyt* II, 91

45 Ibid

46 Steyn–Kruger no 7 30 Nov 1899, Ley 711. *Breyt* II, 96

47 De la Rey memoirs loc cit. *Breyt* II, 96–9, 100–2

48 *Breyt* II, 97–8

49 *Breyt* II

50 Info from Miss F. Barbour. For description of the trench in Feb 1900 see G. Trotter–mother 20 Feb 1900, Trot, and Percy Clive diary Feb 1900 (cy) PC. EGO in 1972 and 1977

51 *Breyt* II, 105. *OH* I, 305–8. *TH* II, 384–8

CHAPTER 18: MARCHING UP IN COLUMN

Head of chapter Verse by Pte Smith reprinted *Morning Leader,* 10 Feb 1900

1 Methuen's despatch SD I, 130. *OH* I, 311 and Map Vol I

2 Methuen–wife Nov 1899, Meth. Ralph *Towards Pretoria* 193

3 *OH* I, 311

4 *DNB.* Wilson *With the Flag* I, 178

5 *OH* I, 311. *TH* II, 397

6 Methuen SD I, 130. Methuen–wife 10 Dec 1899, Meth

7 Methuen SD I, 130. SJ 9 Dec 1899. *OH* I, 308

8 Kekewich diary 4 Dec 1899, Kek. *OH* I, 304. SJ 9–10 Dec 1899

9 For railway problems see Sir P. Girouard *Railways.* Lt Lang–mother 4 Dec 1899, (cy) PC

10 Methuen–Buller 2 Dec 1899, Bull (PRO) WO 132/15

11 SD I, 120. *OH* I, 312–15

12 March Phillipps 100

13 EGO

14 SD I, loc cit

15 Info from Miss F. Barbour

16 *OH* loc cit. Lt B Lang–mother 14 Dec 1899, (cy) PC

17 Lang MS cit. Wilson *With the Flag* I, 180

18 Colvile 14. SD I, 132 para 31

19 Colvile 14

20 March Phillipps 30–5. Ralph op cit 210–11

21 Pemberton 85. For his earlier confidence in the 4·7″ see Methuen–wife 10 Dec 1899, Meth

22 *TH* II, 398. Cf *OH* I, 312–15
23 SD I, 130 para 13–17. *OH* I, 316. *TH* II, 397–9
24 Info from Miss F. Barbour
25 See J. H. Cuthbert 17. However, after a helicopter trip over the trench at balloon altitude, Miss F. Barbour is sceptical
26 A. G. Wauchope *Black Watch* 154–6
27 Ibid. Hughes Hallett's report 13 Dec 1899, Bull (PRO) WO 132/14. Gardyne *Gordons* III, 97
28 *OH* I
29 Dunn–Pattison *91st* 272. Pemberton 91–2
30 Lt Lang–mother 2 Feb 1900, (cy) PC
31 Ralph op cit 214–15. Wilson *With the Flag* I, 187–8 Conan Doyle 103
32 *TH* II, 400–1. Wilson op cit 183
33 Wauchope 155–6. Kelham's account, Kel. Dunn-Pattison loc cit. SD I, 131
34 *OH* I, 401–2
35 Gardyne III, 101
36 SD loc cit. *OH* I, 321
37 Info Miss F. Barbour. SD I, 130 para 24. *OH* I, 329
38 *TH* II, 408–10
39 *Breyt* II, 114–15
40 *OH* I, 328–9
41 SD loc cit paras 26–7. Gardyne III, 100–2
42 Methuen–wife 14 Dec 1899, Meth
43 Ibid
44 See Col Crabbe ev *RCSAW* III, Q 19761
45 Lt B. Lang–mother 14 Dec 1899, (cy) PC
46 *TH* II, 410–11
47 *Breyt* II, 139
48 Gardyne III, 103–4, 429–30. Hughes-Hallett's report loc cit. *OH* I, 327
49 Gardyne III, 103–4
50 Roger Poore quoted Pemberton 105
51 Gardyne III. *OH* I, 327–9, 429–30, 469. *Breyt* II, 170–4
52 Methuen–wife 14 Dec, 22 1899, Meth
53 SD loc cit paras 36–8. *OH* I, 329–30

CHAPTER 19: 'WHERE ARE THE BOERS?'

Head of chapter Capt A. Trotter–mother 11 Dec 1899, Trot. Botha–Kruger 13 Dec 1899 tel no 39, Ley
1 J. B. Atkins *The Relief of Ladysmith* 140. Capt A. Trotter–mother 11 Dec 1899, Trot
2 See *OH* map vol I 'Colenso and the Surrounding Country'. See also sketch-map by Capt A. Trotter 7 Dec 1899 Trot from kopje outside Frere
3 Heliographic communication established on 7 Dec 1899. See Buller's ev to *RCSAW* III, 173
4 Atkins 140–1
5 Ibid
6 *OH* I, 334–5
7 *Breyt* II, 328–30. *TH* II, 424
8 Maj Elton, *PRAI* XXVIII 397–8.
9 Maps in Sandbach MSS Sand. Maps in Jones MSS PC. Cf sketch-map in Hart-Synnot *Letters*
10 Buller's ev to *RCSAW* III, passim
11 SD I, 485 (tel no 19)
12 Atkins 129–30. Treves *Tale of a Field Hospital* 3–4. B. Herbert diary 7–13 Dec 1899, Herb
13 Treves 4
14 Lyttelton–wife 1 Dec 1899, Lyt 548. SJ 29 Nov 1899
15 Buller's tel quoted SJ 26 Nov 1899
16 Treves 5. It was open by 6 Dec. See SJ 6 Dec 1899
17 Lt Alford Dec 1899–Jan 1900, Alf
18 *Natal Mercury* 23 Dec 1899
19 See complete list of sailings in *OH* I, 471–6
20 Lyttelton–wife Nov–Dec 1899, Lyt
21 Atkins 128–9
22 See note 5 and soldiers' diaries, (cy) PC
23 *Daily Mail* early Oct 1899 passim
24 Melville II, 293–4, 302–10. Lewis Butler 78–82. Nevinson *Essays in Freedom* 96–9 (London 1911). See testimonials from ordinary soldiers, Bull (Crediton)
25 Tape interviews in 1970 with Ptes Packer and Hall, PC
26 Ibid
27 Treves 6
28 See note 25
29 Lyttelton–wife 1, 20 Nov 1899, Lyt 544, 545
30 Atkins 131
31 Atkins 124–5. Treves 5
32 Capt A. Trotter–mother 7 Dec 1899, Trot
33 Capt A. Trotter passim, Trot. See Melville II, 307–8. There were similar stories about Kitchener's drinking
34 Buller–L 4 Dec 1899 (Pte), Lan
35 See CT and SD I, passim. Cf Buller–wife 2 Dec 1899, Bull (Crediton)
36 See note 34
37 Buller–wife 2 Dec 1899, Bull (Crediton)
38 See note 34
39 Buller–L 8 Dec 1899, CT no 42. Buller–L 12 Dec 1899, SD I, 24. Buller–White 7 Dec 1899, CT no 7, 11 Dec, CT no 19. Buller's ev to *RCSAW* III, 174 17 Feb 1903
40 Buller–R 28 Dec 1899, Bobs R 10/18
41 H. Lang–Buller (enc with Buller–L 12 Dec 1899), SD I, 25
42 Buller's ev to *RCSAW* III, 174
43 See note 9
44 Buller–L 12 Dec 1899, loc cit
45 White–Buller 8 Dec 1899, CT no 14. Buller–White 9 Dec 1899, CT no 16
46 Buller–L 12 Dec 1899, loc cit

47 Buller–L 13 Dec 1899, CT no 50
48 White–Buller 8 Dec 1899, CT no 12, SD I, App 487
49 Buller's ev to *RCSAW* III, 174
50 Buller–Sir A. Bigge 4 Jan, 15 Mar 1900, Big
51 See Lyttelton–wife 1 Nov 1899, Lyt 544. Lyttelton *Eighty Years* 182, 203–4
52 See Buller–L 2 Dec 1899, CT no 7, SD I, 20. Hildyard–wife 22–8 Dec 1899, Hil
53 Buller–L 4 Dec 1899 (Pte) Lan
54 Buller–L 1 Dec 1899, CT no 34C 'Barton I hear is useless'
55 See note 53
56 Lyttelton *Eighty Years* 211. Romer & Mainwaring 36. Hart–Synnot *Letters* passim. *TH* II, 444
57 See Atkins *Incidents and Reflections* 126 (1947). For Buller's later comment see *RCSAW* IV, 409 'ridiculous expedition'
58 Buller–L Nov 1899 (Pte) Lan. Cf *TH* II, 40
59 Buller–Bigge 15 Mar 1900, Big
60 *OH* I, 334. For Douglas see Buller–Bigge 15 Mar 1900, Big
61 Hildyard–brother 22–8 Dec 1899, Hil
62 Bigge–Buller 25 Nov, Buller–Bigge 26 Nov, Bigge–Buller 10 Dec 1899, Bull (PRO) WO 132/7/841. Cf Warren *Christian Victor* 306–9
63 Buller–L 4 Dec 1899 (Pte) Lan
64 Melville I, 128–9
65 Sir E. Wood–R 24 Sep 1899, Bobs R 91/7
66 See note 39
67 Buller–L 13 Dec 1899, CT no 50. Buller–Bigge 15 Mar 1900, Big
68 GOC Cape quoting Gatacre 11 Dec 1899, CT no 49B
69 SJ 10 Dec 1899. Gatacre SD I. *OH* I, 285–303
70 Buller–Gatacre 11 Dec 1899, CT no 49D paraphrase
71 Methuen–L (via Cape) 12 Dec 1899, CT no 49H
72 Buller–Bigge 15 Mar 1900, Big
73 Ibid. Buller–wife 18 Dec 1899, Bull (Crediton) 'forlorn hope'
74 Buller–Bigge 15 Mar 1900, Big
75 Ibid. The 'lachrymose telegram' has not apparently survived. But that Methuen was planning a retreat to Orange River is confirmed by Methuen–wife 14 Dec 1899, Meth
76 *TH* II, 427
77 Vol II was published in 1902. Buller gave his evidence to the *RCSAW* in 1903
78 Buller–White 13 Dec 1899, SD App I, 489
79 Buller–L 13 Dec 1899, SD I, 25
80 Buller–L 13 Dec 1899, CT no 50
81 Buller–L 17 Dec 1899, SD I, 36, 40. Buller's ev *RCSAW* 174. Buller–R 27 Mar 1900, WO 105/25/34. *OH* I, 345–6
82 FID blueprint maps in Sandbach MSS Sand, and Jones MSS PC. Gunners' map in *PRAI* XXVIII 397–8
83 Buller's ev *RCSAW* III, 174
84 *OH* I, 341 (lines 4–9) omits 'punt drift' (2)
85 See Hely-Hutchinson–CO 23 Nov 1899, CT no 32B 'Tugela rose during day, and is now reported to be impassable.' Cf Hildyard ev *RCSAW* III, Q 16154–8
86 Buller's ev *RCSAW* III, 174
87 Buller's orders SD I, 40
88 *OH* Map Vol I. EGO (I got lost there!)
89 Buller's ev *RCSAW* III, 174. *OH* I, 341. Melville II, 100 quoting earlier draft of Buller's ev for *RCSAW*
90 See note 81
91 Buller–R loc cit
92 Pemberton 124
93 See Lyttelton–wife 14 Dec 1899, Lyt 550 Hildyard–Gedge 22–8 Dec 1899, Hil. Capt A. Trotter–mother 11 Dec 1900, Trot
94 Atkins 148 and ('fun') 155
95 Ibid 149
96 Ibid 149–50
97 *OH* I, 346
98 Capt A. Trotter–mother 18 Dec 1899, Trot
99 Biograph photo in Wilson *With the Flag* I, 91. See also Capt A. Trotter–mother 18 Dec 1899, Trot
100 Buller–wife 18 Dec 1899, Bull (Crediton)
101 Atkins 155–8. Bron Herbert diary 10–15 1899 Herb. Capt A. Trotter loc cit. *OH* I, 354–5
102 Barnard 58
103 Hofmeyr *Zes Maanden bij de Commandos* 209
104 W. J. de Kock *J. de V. Roos* 40–2, quoted Barnard 47–8
105 Barnard 48, 57
106 Barnard 46. *Breyt* II, 238–9. Naudé *Vechten en Vluchten* 69
107 *Breyt* II, 244–5. *OH* I, 340–1 & Map Vol I. Cf *TH* II, 427–32
108 Barnard 47–9
109 Barnard 53–4. *Breyt* II, 246–7
110 Kruger–Botha 13 Dec 1899, Ley 713 (d) tel no 39. Gen Burger–Kruger 14 Dec 1899, Ley 713 (b) tel no 14. Barnard 54
111 Barnard 54–5
112 Kruger–Botha 14 Dec 1899, Ley 713 tel no 6. Barnard 55
113 Barnard 55–6. *Breyt* II, 249
114 Barnard 56. *Breyt* II, 249–50
115 Botha–Kruger 14 Dec 1899, Ley 713 (b) tel no 51. Barnard 56–7
116 Barnard 57. *Breyt* II, 250–1
117 Barnard 49–50
118 Barnard 57
119 Ewing–HTD Pretoria Ley 713 (c) tel no 1–2 Dec 15 1899
120 Barnard 58–9

121 Barnard 59. C Burne *Naval Brigade* 15–16

CHAPTER 20: 'A DEVIL OF A MESS'
Head of chapter Moberly Bell–Amery 13 Oct 1899, *Times* MS Letterbooks

1 Treves 9–11
2 Treves 46–7
3 *TH* VI, 517–18, III, 99–100. Treves 74–6. Buller–L 12 Dec 1899, SD I, 107. But see *PPW* 270 for evidence they stole from wounded! See M. K. Gandhi *An Autobiography* (1930) 142–8
4 Treves 11–13
5 Jourdain *Natal* 8. *TH* II, 444. Romer & Mainwaring 34–5. *OH* I, 352–3
6 Romer & Mainwaring 35. *TH* loc cit
7 *OH* I, 354
8 *OH* I, 354. Jourdain 8. *TH* II, 464–5
9 *OH* loc cit. *TH* loc cit
10 Jourdain *Natal* 8 (see also diary and autobiog). *OH* loc cit
11 Romer & Mainwaring loc cit. *OH* loc cit. *TH* II, 445
12 Romer & Mainwaring 36–7. *OH* I, 356–7
13 *Royal Inniskilling Fusiliers* 400
14 Romer & Mainwaring 37
15 Gen Hart 26 Dec foll 1899, Hart–Synnot *Letters* 296–308
16 *Royal Inniskilling Fusiliers* 400–2
17 Buller–L 19 Dec 1899, SD I, 42 (WO 32/7890)
18 See esp Buller–L 16 Dec 1899, CT no 55. Buller–L 19 Dec 1899, SD I, 42. For failure of Lyddite see *PRAI* and Hildyard ev *RCSAW* III, Q 16134–8
19 Buller's draft ev for *RCSAW* quoted Melville II, 108
20 Capt. A. Trotter–mother 18 Dec 1899, Trot. Buller loc cit. *OH* I, 357
21 Buller loc cit 108–9. Buller–R 27 Mar 1900, and Long's own 4-page report, WO 105/25/34
22 Buller's draft ev for *RCSAW* quoted Melville II, 109
23 Ibid
24 Long's action was afterwards severely censured both by R and W. 'Grave error' acc R–L 5 May 1900, 'disastrous' acc Grove–R 11 Oct 1900, WO 105/25/34. See Barton's ev, *RCSAW* III and see Rawlinson diary Dec 1900, Rawl
25 Buller–R 27 Mar 1900 quoting Col Hunt's objections, WO 105/25/34. *OH* I, 358–61. Jeans *Naval Brigades* 246–8 (inc Lt Ogilvy's account)
26 Ibid. And see Herbert–Dods 26 Dec 1899, Herb
27 Burleigh 216–20. *PPW* 289. Wilson I, 91–3
28 Botha–Kruger 15 Dec 1899, Ley 713 no 54. Barnard 67. Cf *OH* I, 360–1, 365 and see note 55 here
29 Buller's draft ev for *RCSAW* quoted

Melville II, 109. Buller–L 17 Dec SD I, 36. Buller's ev *RCSAW* III, Q 15303. quoting Hildyard's report on Colenso. *OH* I, 363–4
30 W. Waters *German Official Account of the War* I, 72–3 Cf *TH* II, 458
31 'Sold by a d–d gunner' Buller–Bigge 15 Mar 1900, Big. Note irony: Bigge was a gunner, too
32 See note 29. Cf *TH* II, 459. Pemberton 136–7
33 Lyttelton–wife 15 Dec 1899, Lyt 550. Lyttelton *Eighty Years* 208–10. *OH* I, 369–70
34 *Royal Inniskilling Fusiliers* loc cit. Lyttelton–wife loc cit
35 Jourdain loc cit. Maj-Gen Hart 26 Dec 1899 Hart–Synnot *Letters* 293–8. *OH* I, 369–70
36 *Royal Inniskilling Fusiliers* 404. *PPW* 312–13
37 See note 29. Also Lt Lafone–mother 18 Dec 1899, Laf 39558/27–30. Lafone was in F Coy of the Devonshires
38 *OH* I, 364–5. Jeans *Naval Brigades* loc cit
39 Anon quoted *PPW* 304. See also Trooper Billings, one of Buller's bodyguard, quoted *PPW* 292
40 Pte Richardson RAMC quoted *PPW* 292–3. *TH* II, 452
41 Buller–Bigge 15 Mar 1900, Big
42 Buller–wife 18 Dec 1899, Bull (Crediton). Capt A. Trotter–mother, Trot
43 Gunner C. H. Young quoted *Morning Leader* 9 Feb 1900
44 Capt Congreve–Henry Wilson 18 Dec 1899, Con Cpl [Nurse] quoted *PPW* 296–7. See letter of Hildyard quoted Warren *Prince Christian Victor* 313–14
45 Capt Congreve – 16 Dec 1899, and diary 15 Dec 1899, Con MSS
46 Corpl [Nurse] loc cit
47 Pte Burnett quoted *PPW* 294. Bombardier Stephenson quoted *PPW* 298–9. *OH* I, 365–6
48 *TH* II, 453–4. Lyttelton *Eighty Years* 210. No doubt Lyttelton was one of Amery's main informants. Cf *OH* I
49 Buller's ev *RCSAW* III, 201–2 Q 15305–7. Buller's draft ev quoted Melville II, 110–11
50 Buller–L 16 Dec 1899, CT no 65
51 Buller's draft ev for *RCSAW* loc cit
52 Dundonald *My Army Life* 104–8. *OH* I, 366–9. Barton's ev *RCSAW* III, 660 in protest against *TH* account. See *TH* II, 447–9
53 *PPW* 135
54 See note 45
55 Col Bullock's ev at inquiry 6 Aug 1900, also Col Hunt's ev on 15 Jun 1900, and Maj Walter 8 Aug 1900, *RCSAW* IV, 411–12. Congreve loc cit

56 Treves 14–15
57 Treves 15–23. See also Atkins 155: 'fun'
58 Buller–Bigge 15 Mar 1900, Big. Atkins 174–5
59 Buller–L 15 Dec 1899 6.20 pm (code 0215), WO 32/7887 Cf published version *Times* etc
60 Buller–Bigge 15 Mar 1900, Big
61 L–Buller 14 Dec 1899, CT no 51
62 Buller's ev *RCSAW* III, 174–5. L's ev *RCSAW* III, 516 (Q 21259)
63 Buller–L 15 Dec 1899, CT no 54
64 Buller's ev *RCSAW* III, 175 and 202–3 esp 15315–8
65 Buller–White 16 Dec 1899 (no 88), SD App I, 490
66 Buller–White 17 Dec 1899 (no 92) ibid
67 Buller–L 1 Nov 1899, CT no 2H 'I shall be sorry if Kimberley and Ladysmith go.'
68 See next chapter
69 Significantly, there is no reference to *this* cable in Rawlinson's diary. The story that White's staff doubted it was genuine appears to have originated with Hamilton after the siege ended. See garbled version in *TH* II, 460 and see Buller's speech (partially misquoted) in II, 461–2
70 Buller–L 17 Dec 1899, SD I, 36–8. Note the footnote in the original MS indicating that 'the original return showed that over 400 men were missing'. The original is in WO 32/7887
71 The idea that Colenso was a 'catastrophe' for Buller's army was simply the rhetoric of Buller's enemies. Of course it *was* catastrophic for certain units.
72 Methuen's speech to the Highland Brigade in Lan MSS. See also Gardyne III, 431
73 Corpl [Nurse] quoted *PPW* 297
74 Atkins 180
75 Churchill *Ladysmith* 366
76 *Black and White Budget*. Hildyard–brother 24–8 Dec 1899, Hil
77 Buller–wife 18 Dec 1899, Bull (Crediton)
78 L–Buller 18 Dec 1899 (two), CT no 62 and 62a (p. 57). Note no 62a was not printed in the *RCSAW* III, App J
79 Buller–Bigge 8 Jan 1900, Big
80 Buller–L 20 Dec 1899 SD I, 43 (no. 15). Buller–Bigge 4 Jan 1900 Big: 'Of course I don't *like* Roberts's appointment, but I don't complain ...'
81 Buller–R 17 Dec 1899 9.10 am, Bobs R 10/17

CHAPTER 21: BLACK WEEK, SILVER LINING

Head of chapter *Sydney Bulletin* quoted *Black & White Budget* 23 Dec 1899
 1 *Times, Irish Times* 16 Dec 1899 etc. Ly (Aileen) Roberts memo Bobs 181
 2 Balfour–Ly Elcho 23 Dec 1899 quoting R on 17 Dec 1899 Bal 49835/16–17 (Dugdale *Balfour* I, 299–300 omits first para)
 3 R–L 16 Dec 1899, Bobs 110–11 (NB mis-dated in R's H & O I, 1)
 4 Garvin III, 526–7. D. James *Roberts* 55–6
 5 *DNB*. Col Repington–Marker 19 Aug 1904, BM 52278. James passim
 6 Kipling *Definitive Edition of Verse* 396
 7 I. Hamilton *Drums* 165
 8 D. James passim. Abbott *Tommy Cornstalk* 193–5. Menpes 69–81
 9 *DNB*
10 R–S Wilkinson quoted Symons 21
11 R–L 1896–9, Bobs 110
12 R–L 8, 11 Dec 1899, Bobs 110
13 Ly (Aileen) Roberts loc cit
14 R–Brackenbury 12 Dec 1899, H & O I, 1
15 L–R 10 Dec 1899, Bobs 181
16 Ly Roberts loc cit. Dugdale *Balfour* I, 295. L–Balfour 12.30 pm 16 Dec 1899, Bal 49727/97. Newton *Lansdowne* 165
17 Fitzpatrick *Memories* 144
18 Balfour–Ly Elcho 23 Dec 1899 loc cit: 'and on Saturday a still worse telegram ... completed the tale of woe'
19 Esher *Journal* I, 251. L–Buller 18 Dec 1899, CT no 62. Note also no 62a that was not later published. G. Buckle *Queen Victoria's Letters* (3rd series) III, 445
20 L–Balfour 17 Dec 1899 saying K had expressed a wish to come out, Bal 49727/98–9. Newton 165. See also Arthur *Kitchener* I, 266 (orders 'not wholly unexpected'). The package had been arranged in advance by Ian Hamilton and Rawlinson. K had also written to the Prime Minister's daughter-in-law, Ly Cranborne, proposing himself: K–Ly Cranborne 20 Sep 1899, Sal (Hat) 'If you see the chance I hope you will put in a word as if the Cape war comes off it will be a big thing and they might give me some billet.'
21 See note 3
22 Most, if not all, important papers presented to the Cabinet at this time have been collected up in Cab 37/51/92–105. The Roberts letter is not included, nor can I find a reference to it in the Balfour, Chamberlain, Selborne or Salisbury papers
23 R–Buller 23 Dec 1899, CT no 75. Balfour–Selborne 22 Dec 1899, Bal 49707/52
24 Balfour–Salisbury 19 Dec 1899, Bal 49691/82–4. Newton 165–6. *Wolseley Letters* 377–8
25 Balfour loc cit. *Queen Victoria's Letters* 3rd series III, 346. Longford *Victoria RI* 695 (paperback edit)

26 Ly Roberts's memo, Bobs 181. L–Ly Roberts May 1921 ibid. Balfour–Ly Elcho 23 Dec 1899 loc cit. Balfour–Salisbury 18 Dec 1899, Bal 49691/2
27 Times 24 Dec 1899. R–Nora 11 Jan 1900, Bobs (misplaced, it escaped destruction!). James 278 and 326 (quoting R–Nora 26 May 1900)
28 Selborne–Balfour 14 Dec 1899, Bal 49707/49–51
29 See Dugdale I 293, 289–90
30 Salisbury–Curzon, Bal 49732
31 Bertha Synge–M 3 Nov 1899, MP II, 44
32 Ross Yeoman VIII. See also Fitzgibbon Arts I, Peel Trooper 8008 I, Seely Adventure 53. Fitzpatrick Memories 124–5
33 Garvin III, 522. See also Bertha Synge–M 3 Nov 1899 quoted MP II, 43
34 C's speech in Dublin on 18 Dec 1899 quoted Garvin III, 526. The Army Corps began to arrive in SA on 8 Nov 1899 and the tide turned a fortnight later
35 See note 32. Balfour–Kinnaird 1 Jan 1900, Bal 49853/9 'more disappointment ... than defeat'. Balfour–Ridgeway 6 Mar 1900, Bal 49812/301–2. Balfour wrote off the possible fall of the Ladysmith garrison as 'a great disaster, but an even greater humiliation'. See also Selborne–M 26 Dec 1899 quoted MP II, 44–5. See also G. Wyndham–mother 16 Dec 1899, Wyndham Life and Letters I, 381
36 OH I, 462–70 casualties for 10 main battles only
37 Ibid
38 Asquith speech 16 Dec reported in Times 18 Dec 1899
39 CB–Birrell 5 Jan 1900 quoted J. Wilson 323. CB 19 Nov 1899 quoted op cit 318
40 CB's speech at Aberdeen 19 Dec Times 20 Dec 1899. See J. Wilson 313–22
41 Garvin III, 522, 539–40
42 Garvin III, 518–19, 538, 572–4. M–C 27 Dec 1899, MP II, 30–1. M–Selborne 30 Nov 1899, MP II, 37–8
43 Garvin III, 527–36. Barbara Penny Australian Debate on the Boer War (Univ of Melbourne) Historical Studies XIV, 526–45
44 RCSAW II, Q 8033–9
45 RCSAW I, 70; II, Q 8343–60, 8686; III, 199–200, 277; IV, Q 20, 807
46 Annual Register 1899. TH III, 48–61
47 W–wife 21 Dec 1899, Wol 28/83
48 W's ev RCSAW II, Q 8191–4
49 W–wife 31 Oct 1899 (two letters), Wol 28/70–1. See W letters passim
50 See W's memo for the Queen RCSAW IV, 283. W's ev RCSAW II, 382–3 (Q 9080–3)
51 Brackenbury–L 17 Dec 1899, Lan IV
52 Brackenbury's minute 15 Dec 1899 ptd RCSAW I, 278–80
53 Ibid 279. Brackenbury's ev RCSAW I,

73–8 esp Q 1599, 1600, 1644
54 Brackenbury op cit Q 1777–9
55 Brackenbury op cit Q 1602. Note MK IV was also defective in heat. See also the Cabinet paper on the subject Cab 37/51/94
56 Brackenbury–Balfour 23 Jan 1900, Bal 49853/13
57 Brackenbury's ev RCSAW II, 73–8 esp Q 1599, 1616
58 W's min 14 Dec 1899, WO 32/7887
59 W's min 13, 14, 15 Dec, WO 32/7887
60 Procs of Army Board 16 Dec 1899, Lan. L's minute 20 Dec 1899, WO 32/7887
61 Buller–L 16 Dec 1899, CT no 56. See also Buller–L 29 Nov 1899, CT no 33: 'I shall mount infantry and let them ride in trousers as the Boers do.'
62 G. Wyndham–father 20 Dec 1899, Wyndham Papers I, 382
63 Times [?] Dec 1899. RCSAW I, 70–2. See also Report on Yeomanry Cd 803. Col Lucas ev RCSAW II, 272–6. Col Sir Howard Vincent ev RCSAW II, 230 (Q 5453). Gen. MacKinnon ev RCSAW II, 315–17.
64 Fitzpatrick–Balfour 1 Jan 1900, Bal 49853/10
65 W's minute 28 Dec and L's reply 30 Dec 1899, WO 32/7866
66 SJ Jan–Feb 1900. TH II
67 Hansard LXXVIII 30 Jan–8 Feb 1900. Cf J. Wilson 325–6. Dugdale I, 307–8.
68 Times. Garvin III, 513–16 quoting Metternich–Bülow 18 Mar 1900.
69 Prince von Bülow Memoirs I (London 1931) 301–3
70 See note 32
71 A. W. Myers Memory's Parade (London 1932) 26–7
72 Blue Book 158 gives a total of 27 MPs and 36 peers who fought in war. Price calculated that roughly half Yeomanry came from the middle class. Price Imperial War 200, 254–8

CHAPTER 22: CHRISTMAS AT PRETORIA

Head of chapter Lt Kentish–mother 12 Oct, 9 Nov 1899, Kent
1 Botha–State Secretary 15 Dec 1899, Ley 713 (no 54)
2 Fichardt–President 12 Dec 1899, Ley 713 (no 11)
3 Standard & Diggers News 12, 28 Dec 1899. Volksstem 28 Dec 1899
4 Symons quoted Breyt III, 7
5 Volksstem 14 Dec (Pretoria 13th) 1899
6 Ibid 13 Dec (Pretoria 12th) 1899
7 Ibid
8 Breyt I, 233–6, 258–60, II, 170–4, 221–2, 320–2. OH I, 462–70
9 Standard & Diggers News 15, 20 Dec 1899

10 See speech 2 Oct 1899 quoted P. Kruger *Memoirs* II, 433–5
11 P. Kruger *Memoirs* II, 347–8
12 Gardiner *Harcourt* I, 379–81. *Annual Register* 1881
13 See CB–Bryce 10 Nov 1899, CB 412 11/61. J. Wilson 314–15
14 See *Volksstem* 1899 passim
15 Hancock, *Smuts* I, 106, 568
16 Thorold *Labouchère* 385–414
17 Dr Leyds quoted *Echo de Paris* re-printed *Standard & Diggers News* 9 Dec 1899
18 The total of foreign volunteers, mainly Uitlanders already in the Transvaal, came to about 2,000. See *Breyt* I, 62–8, 73
19 For prospect of foreign intervention see Sal A/121/40–6
20 *Breyt* II, 359
21 *Breyt* II, 354
22 *Breyt* II, 355
23 *Breyt* II, 355–6
24 Henderson *Science of War* 371–2
25 Kruger–Botha Ley 713 15, 16 Dec 1899 (nos 9 and 59). *Breyt* II, 358
26 Botha–Kruger 17 Dec 1899, no 3 Ley 713. *Breyt* II, 358–9. Kruger–Botha 17 Dec 1899, no 4 Ley 713. *Breyt* II, 359
27 British regulars (including non-combatants) at Mafeking 20, at Kimberley 600, at Ladysmith 12,250. Figures at beginning of sieges. See SD I, 333, *OH* II, 45–6, 601
28 In fact the British Cabinet overruled M and Buller who proposed a blockade of Transvaal's food imports as well as arms imports. See Garvin III, 493–4
29 E. T. Cook *Transvaal* 274–5. *Cd* no 623, 624, 625
30 *Volksstem* 30 Jan 1900. *The Friend* 18 Dec 1899. *Times* (weekly edit) 12 Jan 1900 quoting Laffans Agency (Pretoria) 19 Dec 1899
31 According to the British government's estimates just before the war, these were the totals in the Transvaal: Dutch 108,800, other whites 180,000, natives 754,000. But many of the 180,000 non-Dutch were not British either, and many had now left. SJ 6 Dec 1899. See Marais 1–3
32 *Standard & Diggers News* 9, 14 Dec 1899
33 SA Chamber of Mines *Annual Reports* 1897–9 (Johannesberg)
34 Ibid
35 *Standard & Diggers News* 9 Dec 1899
36 *Standard & Diggers News* 14 Dec 1899
37 See Selons, the explorer, quoted *Standard & Diggers News* 9 Dec 1899
38 Fisher *Kruger* 235
39 Meintjes *Kruger* 125
40 *Standard & Diggers News* 25 Dec 1899
41 *Standard & Diggers News* 14, 25 Dec 1899. *Times* (weekly edit) 12 Jan 1900 quoting Laffans (Pretoria) 19 Dec 1899
42 Botha–Kruger 2 Jan 1900 quoted *Breyt* III, 11–12

CHAPTER 23: 'ARE WE ROTTERS OR HEROES?'

Head of chapter Maj R. Bowen–wife 4 Dec 1899 quoted K. Griffith *Thank God We Kept the Flag Flying* 147
1 Gunner Netley's diary 22 Nov–18 Dec 1899, PC. Cf British soldier's diary described Nevinson 121
2 Netley tapes, PC
3 '21,000 mouths' acc White, SD I, 236. *OH* II, 538,601 (NB 249 sick and wounded not counted among 21,300 'souls')
4 Capt Steavenson diaries Nov–Dec 1899, Stea. Capt J. Gough diaries Nov–Dec 1899, Gou. Nevinson 176. Stuart/140, 221 *Pictures of War*
5 Col Rawlinson diary 17 Dec 1899, Rawl 7/1
6 Steavenson diary 15–17 Dec 1899, Stea
7 Ibid 16 Dec
8 Nevinson 176–7. Pearse 130. MacDonald *How we Kept the Flag Flying* 171. James 139. McHugh *Siege of Ladysmith* 139–40
9 *Ladysmith Lyre*
10 Rawlinson diary 16 Dec 1899, Rawl 7/1
11 Ibid 17 Dec 1899
12 Ibid
13 Steavenson diary 17 Dec 1899, Stea
14 Capt J. Gough diary 19 Dec 1899, Gou
15 Surg-Capt Holt diary Nov 1899, Holt 6309/42
16 Rawlinson diary 25 Dec 1899, Rawl 7/1
17 Capt J. Gough diary Jan 1900, Gou
18 Steevens 133
19 Surg-Capt Holt diary 1 Nov 1899, MS cit. Capt J. Gough diary 30 Oct 1899, Gou
20 Steevens 125, 122–4. James 133–5, 144–7. See McHugh 68–73, Pearse 26–8
21 Lt Jelf 3 Nov 1899, Jelf. For war correspondents see Stuart 104
22 James 134
23 Steevens 93, 103–4. James 134–5. McHugh 98–102
24 McHugh 71 and Nevinson 105–6 describing death of Dr Stark
25 Netley diary Nov 1899, PC. Nevinson 156
26 Surg-Capt Holt 12–13 Nov 1899, MS cit. Steavenson diary 19 Nov–25 Dec 1899, Stea. Cf Nevinson 156
27 MacDonald 156. Cf Jeans 230–1
28 Steavenson diary 24 Nov 1899, Stea
29 Lt C. Hickie diary 22, 23 Dec 1899, Hick. Cf *OH* I, 553 giving 9 dead
30 Maj Donegan 30 Nov 1899, PC ·
31 Rawlinson diary 1–3 Dec 1899, Rawl 7/1. Lt C. Hickie diary 3 Dec 1899, Hick
32 Col Coxhead *PRAI* XXVII 437 foll.

Rawlinson–K & R Rawl 6/. Capt Lambton's ev *RCSAW* III, Q 19102–12

33 Coxhead loc cit
34 Rawlinson–K & R Rawl 6/157–8. Capt Lambton's ev *RCSAW* III, Q 19112–27 quoting others
35 Rawlinson–K & R 25 Nov 1899, Rawl 6/92. Steavenson diary 20 Nov 1899, Stea. Cf Stuart 233, Nevinson 105–6
36 Capt J. Gough diary 30 Nov 1899, Gou
37 *Ladysmith Bombshell*
38 Text of Willis letter kindly supplied by Mr Christopher, of Ladysmith. See also MacDonald 161
39 Hutchinson *Frank Rhodes* 133–5. Colvin *Jameson* II, 191–2. Pearse 42–3. Stuart 221, 290. Rawlinson diary loc cit. Sampson & Hamilton *Anti-Commando* 122–3
40 Rawlinson–K & R 19 Dec 1899, Rawl 6/121
41 Ibid
42 Capt J. Gough diary Nov 1899, Gou
43 Rawlinson–R 19 Dec, 13 Nov 1899, Rawl 6/121, 39
44 Rawlinson–R 19 Dec 1899, Rawl 6/121
45 See note 30
46 Rawlinson–R 25 Nov 1899, Rawl 6/89–90
47 Ibid. See also Gen Hunter's ev *RCSAW* III, Q 14583
48 Ibid Q 14540. Col W. G. Knox diary of siege Nov 1900 Bobs Misc Box
49 Col W. G. Knox diary 6 Jan 1900, Bobs Misc Box. Rawlinson–R 10 Mar 1900, Rawl 6/. Capt J. Gough diary 7 Jan 1900. Cf *OH* II, 534–6, 555–7
50 See note 1
51 Hutchinson *Frank Rhodes* 137. Rawlinson–R 8 Dec 1899 Rawl 6/106–8
52 Rawlinson diary 6–7 Dec 1899, Rawl 7/1
53 Ibid
54 Ibid. Stuart 142–51 (hon member of ILH). Nevinson 143–50 (based on Maj Henderson's account etc). *OH* II, 546–7. Rawlinson–R 11 Dec 1899 loc cit. *Breyt* II, 437–43. MacDonald 118–19. Pearse 103–17. McHugh 109–27. *TH* III, 167–9
55 Rawlinson loc cit. Casualties as given in *OH* II, 548
56 Rawlinson–R loc cit. *OH* II, 548–9. Nevinson 158–64. McHugh 128–38. MacDonald 130–6
57 Capt J. Gough diary 7 Dec 1899, Gou
58 Rawlinson–R 11 Dec 1899, Rawl 6/
59 Rawlinson diary 15 Dec 1899, Rawl 7/1
60 Steavenson 17 Dec 1899, Stea. James 140–1
61 Lt 'Dodo' Jelf–parents 4 Dec 1899, Jelf. For other versions see Lt Harold Fisher 3 Dec 1899 'fools or heroes' (cy) PC. James 140. Pearse 136–7
62 Rawlinson diary 5 Jan 1900, Rawl 7/1
63 *TH* III, 182 (footnote)
64 *OH* II, 558. *TH* III, 181

65 Ibid. Jeans 218–19
66 Jeans 196, 219–20. *TH* III, 183–4
67 Sapper G. Hall quoted K. Griffith 214. Hall tape, PC
68 *OH* II, 558–9. *TH* III, 185
69 Jeans 220. *OH* II, 558–9. *TH* III, 185
70 *OH* II, 559–60. *TH* III, 186–8
71 *TH* III, 189
72 Rawlinson diary 5 Jan 1900, Rawl 7/1. Gen Hunter's ev *RCSAW* III, loc cit. *OH* II, 560–1, 563
73 Hunter loc cit. *OH* II, 562
74 Jeans 222–3. *OH* II, 562–3
75 *OH* II, 565
76 Capt J. Gough diary 5 Jan 1900, Gou
77 *OH* II, 563–4. *TH* III, 185–96. Jeans 223–4. For Bowen see quote at head of chapter
78 Jeans 224
79 Ibid. *OH* II, 565–7. *TH* III, 196–7
80 White–Buller 9.30 am 6 Jan 1900, SD I, 494 (no 45)
81 Rawlinson diary 6 Jan 1900, Rawl 7/1
82 Ibid
83 *TH* III, 197–9. Cf *OH* II, 568
84 Pearse 203. Nevinson 216
85 Rawlinson diary 6 Jan 1900, Rawl 7/1
86 White–Buller 3.15 pm 6 Jan 1900, SD I, 495 (no 47)
87 Col Park diary 6 Jan 1900, Dorset & Devon Regt Museum. *OH* II, 568–9. *TH* III, 197–201
88 H. Gough *Soldiering On* 72
89 Ibid. See *Breyt* III, 57 for other estimates of Boer dead
90 *OH* II, 569–70. *Breyt* III, 57. Col Park diary loc cit
91 Rawlinson diary 7 (?) Jan 1900, Rawl 7/1
92 Steavenson 6–12 Jan 1900, Stea

CHAPTER 24: THE TUGELA LINE

Head of chapter Buller–wife 23 Jan 1900 Bull (Crediton)

1 [Lt Grant] 'Linesman' *Natal* (8th impression) 12
2 W. Churchill *Ladysmith* 236–7. Atkins 196–7
3 White–Buller 6 Jan 1899, cy enc Buller–L 6 Jan 1899, CT no 92B
4 Buller's ev *RCSAW* III, 177 col 2. *OH* II, 336–7
5 White–Buller 6 Jan 1899, SD I, App 494 (no 46). See paraphrase in *OH* II, 337
6 *OH* II, 337. Cf *TH* III, 198
7 Buller's ev *RCSAW* III, 117 col 2. *Breyt* III, 18 puts figure as low as 300
8 [Lt Grant] 'Linesman' *Natal* 13
9 See Buller's cypher index 14, Bull (PRO) 7/841. *OH* II, 337. Cf SD I, 495
10 Grant wrote several chapters of Vol II under Maurice's editorship and himself edited Vol IV
11 Atkins 200

12 W. Churchill *Ladysmith* 243
13 Hildyard–Gedge (22)–27 Dec 1899, Hil
14 Atkins 193–5
15 [Grant] 27. See also 6 and 11
16 Buller's ev *RCSAW* III, 175 col 1
17 R–Buller 27 Dec 1899, CT no 89
18 Buller–L 10 Jan 1900, CT no 98. *OH* II, 340–1. R actually arrived a day earlier than expected
19 Burleigh 235
20 Atkins 186–7
21 Atkins 201
22 Lyttelton–wife 27 Dec 1899, Lyt 551d. Dickson *Biograph* 107
23 Burleigh 240–2, 281. See Warren 6 Aug 1900, SD II, 34
24 Pte Hall tape PC. Dickson 114 (photo). Atkins 192–307. For steam traction see *RCSAW* II, Q 2212–16, and *OH* II, 334
25 L/Cpl Bradley 10 Jan 1900, (cy) PC
26 Sgt Galley 10 Jan 1900, (cy) PC
27 Bradley 11 Jan 1900, (cy) PC
28 Ptes Hall & Packer tapes, PC
29 Lyttelton–wife 2 Jan 1900, Lyt 552a
30 B. Herbert 29 Jan 1900, Herb. Lyttelton–wife 30 Dec 1899, Lyt 551
31 Lyttelton–wife 21 Dec 1899, Lyt 551
32 Lyttelton–wife loc cit. Hildyard loc cit. H. Gough *Soldiering On* 70
33 Lyttelton–wife 28 Dec 1899, Lyt 551c and e
34 Hildyard loc cit
35 Lyttelton–wife 21 Dec 1899 loc cit
36 Lyttelton–wife 28 Dec 1899, Lyt 551d
37 Lyttelton–wife 28 Dec 1899, Lyt 551e
38 Atkins 216–17
39 Buller–wife 18, 23 Jan 1899, Bull (Crediton)
40 Buller–R 11 Jan 1900, CT no 99B. SJ Dundonald 116–17. Churchill *Ladysmith* 264–5
41 Atkins 212–14. SJ 16 Jan 1900
42 Buller's ev *RCSAW* III, 177–8
43 See note 74 chap 19
44 SJ 10 Jan 1900
45 White–Buller 7 Jan 1900 (no 50), *RCSAW* III, 635
46 See note 41 chap 19
47 Buller's ev *RCSAW* III, 177–8. *OH* II, 338–41, 345–9, 623–8
48 Ibid
49 Lewis Butler–Sir John Fortescue quoting Buller after the war, Bull (Crediton)
50 Buller's ev *RCSAW* III, 177–8
51 EGO. Info kindly supplied by Mr and Mrs Fabian
52 Burleigh 277. Dickson 122
53 Churchill *Ladysmith* 240, 264–5
54 Atkins 212–13
55 Churchill *Ladysmith* 266
56 See the sketch from Mt Alice in *OH* Map Vol II
57 Blueprint maps in Sandbach MSS and see

sketch-map in Sal (Hat)
58 Buller's ev *RCSAW* III, 178. *OH* II, 345–9. *Breyt* III, Cf Warren's comments, SD I, 96–7
59 Buller–L (two letters) 30 Jan 1900, SD I, 89, 95–6. Buller's ev *RCSAW* III, 178
60 Ibid. Warren–C in C SD I, 96–7, II, 33–41. *OH* II, 372
61 Warren's ev *RCSAW* III, 650. *OH* II, 372–4. For Boer counter moves see *Breyt* III, esp 184–9
62 Col (À Court) Repington *Vestigia* 116–21. *Annual Register* 1898
63 Ibid 217
64 Ibid 218
65 Warren's orders *OH* II, 635–6
66 Repington 218–19
67 Buller–L 30 Jan 1900, SD I, 95. Warren–M Sec 6 Aug 1900, SD II, 36
68 Repington loc cit. Thorneycroft–Warren 26 Jan 1900, SD I, 100–1
69 Thorneycroft's ev *RCSAW* III, Q 12374 foll esp 12385, 12559, 12605
70 E. Knox *Buller's Campaign* (photo) 78. F. P. Crozier *Impressions and Recollections* (London 1930) 28–30
71 Repington 217–18. Knox *Buller's Campaign* 57–8
72 Repington 218–19. *OH* II, 379–81
73 Thorneycroft–Warren 26 Jan 1900 loc cit. *OH* II, 380–1. Repington 220
74 Ibid
75 Ibid 221–2. *OH* II, 381–2
76 Woodgate–Warren 24 Jan 1900, SD I, 98
77 SJ 24 Jan 1900. *Times* 25–6 Jan 1900

CHAPTER 25: AN ACRE OF MASSACRE

Head of chapter Buller–wife 23 Jan 1900, Bull (Crediton)
 1 Barnard 94–5. Du Cane *War in South Africa* II, 167. Sandberg 257, 266. *Standard & Diggers News* 29 Jan 1900. (Note Botha's words are not recorded)
 2 Ibid 95. Cf *OH* II, 383–4
 3 Barnard 95–6, (map) 88–9. *Breyt* III, 236. *OH* Map Vol II, 20 etc
 4 Interview with Botha *Standard & Diggers News* 3 Mar 1900. Report of Ram & Thomson 703–4 (Leyds 279 III) cited Barnard 183
 5 Ibid 76
 6 Grobler *Die Carolina Commando etc* quoted Barnard 96
 7 Barnard 96
 8 On the hill itself never more than 350 at most acc Botha. See Barnard 97 and 84
 9 See Barnard photos 1, 8
10 Barnard 74–5
11 Ibid 75–6
12 Ibid 77
13 Sandberg 272–3
14 Botha tel 46 25 Jan 1900, Ley 715 (f).

Botha's interview in *Standard & Diggers News* 3 Mar 1900

15 Reitz 69 (date wrongly given as '23rd')
16 Ibid 69–72
17 Ibid 72–3
18 Ibid 73. Sandberg 266
19 Reitz 73–4. See also *SP* IV; 345
20 Reitz 73–4. Barnard 98
21 Reitz 74–5. Cf *TH* II, 263–5
22 Reitz 75–7
23 Treves 15–19
24 See note 33. *PPW* 172, 179, 181, 183 etc
25 Capt Carleton, his ADC, letter–wife 1900, (cy) PC. Blake Knox 67. Cf *OH* II, 384 'shrapnel ball in the head'
26 Knox 67. *TH* III, 257–8
27 *OH* II, 381–3. See blueprint map 'D' in Sand MSS
28 Charlton 110. *OH* II, 381. Cf Repington 220–1
29 See Thorneycroft's ev *RCSAW* III, Q 12441
30 Charlton 110
31 Ibid 110–13
32 Cpl W. Macarthy [1900] enc with letter to Sir R. Buller, Bull (Crediton)
33 TMI man's letter in Leicester Record Office. Cf Lt A. Wood–Sir E. Wood 9 Feb 1900 quoted Sir E. Wood *Winnowed Memories* 298–9
34 Col Crofton–HQ c. 9 am 24 Jan 1900 ptd *OH* II, 639, 384–5
35 Knox 69–70
36 Thorneycroft's report of 26 Jan 1900, SD I, 100. Thorneycroft's note 24 Jan 1900, 2.30 pm, SD I, 98–9. Knox 70–1. *OH* II, 386–7. *TH* III
37 Ibid
38 Warren's report Jan 1900, SD I, 97 para 3. *OH* II, 385
39 Ibid II, 385–6. Repington 223
40 Warren loc cit & Warren's ev *RCSAW* III, 650
41 Cy of tel in SD I, 117. See also Lyttelton's memo 4 Sep 1900, SD II, 43 *OH* II, 385, 639
42 Warren's report Jan 1900, SD I, 97–8
43 Atkins 237–8
44 See Buller's comments on Warren's report 30 Jan 1900, SD I, 89, 95–6 and Buller's ev *RCSAW* III, 178
45 Lewis Butler–Sir John Fortescue loc cit. Buller's ev *RCSAW* III, 178
46 Lyttelton's report 25 Jan 1900 and memo 4 Sep 1900, SD I, 115–18 and II, 43. Lyttelton–wife 25 Jan 1900, Lyt. Cf Warren's letter 6 Aug 1900 and Buller's comments on this 4 Sep 1900, SD II, 37, 42
47 Buller blamed Lyttelton for sending them, hence Lyttelton's bitterness. Lyttelton–wife 1 Feb 1900, Lyt
48 Repington 223. Sandbach–mother 30 Jan 1900, Sand. Warren's letter 6 Aug 1900, SD II, 38 section 11

49 Buller's comment to Sec of State 30 Jan 1900, SD I, 89 esp para 6
50 Repington 223
51 Buller–Sec of State 30 Jan 1900, SD I, 95 section 4. *OH* II, 388–9. Cf Warren's report Jan 1900, SD I, 97 section 4 and his letter of 6 Aug 1900, SD II, 37 section 8
52 Knox 72–9. Thorneycroft's reports 26 Jan, 24 May 1900, SD I, 100, SM 6/2–4. *OH* II, 389–90
53 Ibid 79
54 Ibid 79–80. Botha tel no 46 25 Jan 1900, Ley 715 (f). Barnard 98, 101. *TH* III, 268–9
55 Thorneycroft's reports loc cit. *OH* II, 386–7. *TH* III, 269–71. Knox
56 Thorneycroft's note 24 Jan 1900, SD I, 98–9. Cf diff version in SM 6/2
57 Coke's report 25 Jan 1900, Coke's message enc with Warren's report Jan 1900, SD I, 99, 102. *OH* II, 394–5
58 *TH* III, 271–3. Possibly this is one of the scandalous 'episodes' Buller referred to in his letter to R of 19 Sep 1900, WO/105/24
59 See Col Sim's report 28 Jan 1900, SD I, 104–5. *OH* II, 395–6
60 W. W. Williams *Warren* 276–7
61 Barnard 102. *Breyt* III, 210–12
62 *OH* Map Vol II. EGO. *Breyt* III, 236
63 *TH* III, 276–7. *OH* II, 393–4
64 Barnard 102
65 *DSAB* II, 106–8
66 Barnard 102
67 Reitz 77. Cf Knox 81–2, Treves 81–2. L. Oppenheim *Nineteenth Century* Jan 1901
68 Reitz 77–9. Knox 88–9. Barnard 102–3
69 Botha tel no 46 25 Jan 1900, Ley 715 (f)
70 Botha–Burger quoted Barnard 102 note 111
71 Barnard 102–3. Report of Ram and Thomson quoted *Breyt* III, 228
72 Reitz 79
73 Maj Bayly–Lyttelton (recd 2.30 pm 24 Jan) enc with Lyttelton's report 25 Jan 1900, SD I, 116–17
74 Lyttelton's report 25 Jan 1900 loc cit. Lyttelton–wife 25 Jan 1900, Lyt
75 Lyttelton's report 25 Jan 1900 and encs, DD I, 117–18. *OH* II, 398–9. Cf *TH* III, 276– foll.
76 'It is said that the Boers were preparing to withdraw ... If that is so we have lost the best chance we are likely to have ...' Lyttelton–wife 25 Jan 1900 loc cit
77 Warren's ev *RCSAW* III, 644–54 esp section 19
78 Col Sim's report 28 Jan 1900, SD I, 105. Cf Warren's letter loc cit
79 Thorneycroft's note to Warren (after 6.30 pm) 24 Jan 1900 and his official

report of 26 Jan 1900, SD I, 99, 100–1. *OH* II, 397

80 Coke's report 25 Jan 1900, SD I, 102. *OH* II, 400

81 Churchill *Ladysmith* 307–8, *My Early Life* 326

82 Ibid

83 Churchill *Ladysmith* 308

84 Ibid 309–11

85 Ibid 311–12. For Thorneycroft's state see F. P. Crozier op cit

86 Thorneycroft's report of 26 Jan 1900 loc cit. *OH* II, 397

87 Coke's report 25 Jan 1900 enclosing Phillips's memo, SD I, 103–4

88 Coke's report loc cit

89 Sim's report loc cit

90 Knox 87–94. Reitz 79

91 Churchill *My Early Life* 328–9

92 Reitz 79. Barnard 102–3

93 Buller's comments of 30 Jan 1900, SD I, 95–6

94 Buller's confid letter 30 Jan 1900, SD I, 89. Buller–Mil Sec 4 Sep 1900, SD II, 43

95 NB R's criticism of Buller for not superseding Warren was published in the despatches (*London Gazette* 17 Apr 1900) but Buller's criticism of himself not until 1902 (*Cd 968*). R's exoneration of Thorneycroft has never been published. See WO 105/24. R changed his mind after personally seeing battlefield

96 Barnard 104–6. Cf *Breyt* III, 230–1

97 Churchill *Ladysmith* 342. Buller's report 30 Jan 1900, SD I, 77–8

98 Ibid. [Grant] *Natal* 26. Churchill op cit 343

99 *OH* II, 597 (casualty total for 8 days was 1,733)

100 Churchill op cit 343–4. Birdwood *Khaki and Gown* 102. Callwell *Life of Wilson* I, 32

101 Lyttelton–wife 1 Feb 1900, Lyt

102 B. Herbert–parents 29 Jan 1900, Herb

103 Sgt Galley, (cy) PC

104 Nevinson *Essays in Freedom* (London 1909) 96–9. [Grant] *Natal* 27–8. Lt Crossman diary 29, 30 Jan 1900, Cros 6306/34

105 Lyttelton–wife loc cit

106 R–Buller 27 Jan 1900, *RCSAW* III, 627. See R's despatch that *doesn't* mention Buller's self-criticism

107 W–Buller 26, 27 Jan 1900, *RCSAW* III, 627–8

108 See Buller–White tels in SD I

109 Buller–wife 30 Jan 1900, Bull (Crediton)

110 *OH* II, 403–22, 598

111 Buller's ev *RCSAW* III, 178. For a sympathetic view of Buller's difficulties, see Stopford ev *RCSAW* III, 266, Repington 206–9, Henderson *Science of War* 371–2

PART III

CHAPTER 26: THE STEAM-ROLLER

Head of chapter Tape recording with Pte Bowers, PC

1 Phillipps 59–62. Colvile 24. Rankin *Subaltern's Letters* esp 30–3. Chester–Master MSS Ches. French diary 11 Feb 1900, Fren. Haig–Henrietta 22 Feb, Haig–Lonsdale Hale 2 Mar 1900, Haig. *OH* II, 11–12

2 Colvile 23–4

3 Ibid

4 Chester–Master MSS, Ches

5 Battersby 29–32

6 See table SD I, 124–8. *Total* strength in Cape on 31 Jan 1900 comprised 60,296 men and 150 guns. See also SD I, 53

7 Haig–Lonsdale Hale loc cit. See also R–L 9 Feb 1900, no 132 H & O I, 36

8 Kekewich diary 8–10 Feb 1900, Kek

9 French ev *RCSAW* III, Q 17201–3. Haig–Lonsdale Hale loc cit

10 French ev *RCSAW* III, Q 17178. Capt Bellew diary 30 Jan 1900, Bel

11 French ev *RCSAW* III, 301 col 1. Haig–Henrietta 16 Mar 1900, Haig

12 SD I, 124–8

13 Phillipps 59–62. Methuen–wife 14 Dec 1899 etc Meth. R–L 12 Jan (tel no 8), 30 1900 H & O I, 9, 24

14 Capt Bellew diary 12 Feb 1900, Bel. Haig–Hale loc cit

15 Ibid. Capt Bellew diary 12–15 Feb, Bel. Lt Abadie diary 12–15 Feb Abad. French diary 12–15 Feb 1900, Fren

16 Ibid. *OH* II, 33–6

17 Lt Addison diary 1 Jun 1900, (cy) PC. Photos H. F. Mackern *Sidelights*

18 *Black & White Budget* and H. Wilson *With the Flag*

19 W. Churchill *My Early Life* 342–3

20 R ev *RCSAW* III, 462–3. *OH* II, 15–33

21 Buller ev *RCSAW* III, 179–80

22 R–Buller 10 Feb 1900, CT no 150

23 R ev *RCSAW* loc cit. M–R 4 Feb 1900, *RCSAW* III, 529–30. R–M 5 Feb 1900 ibid 30–1

24 Kerry–L Feb 1900 Lan

25 Capt Congreve–parents Jan 1900, Con

26 Magnus *Kitchener* 115, 133–6

27 Ibid 109–15

28 Robertson *Private to Field-Marshal* 112–13

29 R–Gen Lockhart 26 Dec, R–L 27 Dec, 2 Jan 1900–1, H & O I, 4–7

30 R ev *RCSAW* II, 460–1

31 R–L 27 Dec 1899, 2 Jan 1900, 15–17 Jan 1900 and 22–4 Jan, H & O I, 4, 7, 10 and 17

32 Robertson 103–9. *OH* I, 411–12

33 R–L 27, 29 Jan 1900, H & O I, 20–3. R ev *RCSAW* II, 462. M–R 4 Feb, R–M 6 Feb 1900, *RCSAW* II, 529–31

34 R ev *ORCSAW* III, 461–2. Cf Buller ev *RCSAW* III, 179

35 Buller–R 9 Feb 1900, CT nos 193, 195. R–Buller 10 Feb, CT no 150B
36 R–L 30 Jan 1900, H & O I, 24–5
37 R–L 29 Jan 1900, H & O I, 22
38 Methuen–wife 4 Jan 1900, Meth
39 Sir John Fortescue *History of Army Service Corps* 229–65
40 Col Clayton ev *RCSAW* II, Q 2655–91. Fortescue loc cit. *OH* I, 416–20. Cf R ev *RCSAW* II, Q 10506 and *RCSAW* IV, 234
41 Lyttelton–wife 1900, Lyt 562d
42 R–L 6 Feb 1900 (tel no 112), H & O I, 30. Ld Kerry diary 5–6 Feb 1900, Lan
43 Kekewich–R 9 Feb, R–Kekewich 9 Feb 1900, Bobs 23 Misc IV
44 Colvile 26
45 *OH* II, 74–8. De Wet 47–9
46 Buller ev *RCSAW* III, 218. Cf R ev *RCSAW* II, 463
47 Ibid
48 L–R Feb 1900 (Personal & Pte), Bobs 23/IV and 34

CHAPTER 27: THE SIEGE WITHIN THE SIEGE
Head of chapter C. Rhodes–Kekewich quoted Kekewich's official report to Roberts WO 105/14
1 O'Meara *Kekewich* 120
2 Kekewich–R 11 Feb 1900. See also Kekewich–R 9 Feb 10 am, 4 pm 1900, Bobs 23 (IV) 5 (b). O'Meara 120. R's ev *RCSAW* II, 462
3 O'Meara 109–10. Kekewich diary 9 Feb 1900, Kek
4 O'Meara 111. Kekewich diary, MS cit
5 *Diamond Fields Advertiser* 10 Feb 1900. O'Meara 112–13, 144–6
6 O'Meara 113–15. Kekewich's tel is in R–L 12 Feb 1899, CT no 156E. Kekewich diary 10 Feb 1900, Kek
7 O'Meara 117–18
8 Kekewich diary 19 Jan 1900, Kek. O'Meara 103–4. Ashe 112–14 (with photo)
9 De Villebois-Mareuil *War Notes* 341 foll. O'Meara 107. Macnab *French Colonel* 120–30. Sternberg *Experiences of Boer War* 143–5
10 O'Meara 106–9, 111. Kekewich diary 7 Feb 1900, Kek. Ashe 119–34
11 Ashe 134–42
12 Ashe 140–2
13 Ashe 93–4
14 Ashe 78–92
15 Ashe 83–9, 98–9. O'Meara 100–1
16 Kimberley MO quoted Kekewich ev *RCSAW* III, 560
17 Ashe 91
18 Kimberley MO quoted Kekewich loc cit. Ashe 98–9. H. Wilson *With the Flag* II, 393
19 Ashe 142–7

20 Ashe 147
21 O'Meara 122. Ashe 148
22 Ashe 165–8
23 O'Meara 133. B. Gardner *Lion's Cage* 191
24 Waters *War in South Africa* I, 146–7
25 French diary 9–16 Feb 1900, Fren. Capt Bellew diary 15–17 Feb 1899, Bel. Haig–Lonsdale Hale 2 Mar 1900, Haig 203–4. French blamed bad selection and treatment of remounts. See French–COs 18 May 1900 and French–R 1 Dec 1902 gives losses of horses 11–17 Feb 1900 total 341, Bobs 23 IV. *OH* II, 26–7, 37–8, 92–6
26 See comments of Childers *Arme Blanche* 96–117. Cf Goldmann 95–6
27 Ashe 171–3
28 O'Meara 133–4. Kekewich diary 15 Feb 1900, Kek
30 O'Meara 137. Kekewich diary 16–17 Feb 1900, Kek
31 Capt Bellew loc cit. Maj Allenby–wife Feb 1900, All
32 See note 25
33 *OH* II, 80–1
34 Ibid II, 81–2
35 Ibid II, 81. Kelly–Kenny diary 15 Feb 1900, Kell
36 Ibid II, 87
37 Ibid II, 97. G. French *Life of French* 83–5. Haig–Lonsdale Hale 2 Mar 1900, MS cit
38 Ibid II, 99–100. Haig–Lonsdale Hale 2 Mar 1900, MS cit. Chester–Master MSS Ches
39 *OH* II, 100–9. EGO

CHAPTER 28: GONE TO EARTH
Head of chapter Smith–Dorrien diary 18 Feb 1900, Smit
1 De Wet *Three Years' War* 51, 46
2 De Wet passim. See also Seele-Molyneux's diary (cy) PC
3 *DSAB* I, 233–40. Rosslyn *Twice Captured* 256
4 De Wet 79–80, 85
5 Ibid 47–8. Cf *OH* II, 78–9
6 De Wet 49–55
7 EGO. See *OH* Map Vol II no 23 (a). Sternberg 155. Pte Edwards diary 12 Feb 1900, 'Sun comes up *very* hot,' Edwards MSS in Essex Record Office
8 De Wet 55–6. O. T. De Villiers *Piet de Wet en Steyn in het Veld* 13–16. *OH* II, 135–6 gives De Wet's force as 600
9 Kelly–Kenny diary 18 Feb 1900, Kell. Kelly-Kenny SD I, 185. *OH* II, 106, 116
10 Kelly–Kenny MSS, Kell
11 Kelly–Kenny diary 12–17 Feb 1900, Kell
12 Kelly-Kenny diary 18–19 Feb 1900, Kell. Kelly-Kenny, SD I, 186. *OH* II, 105, 589
13 Kelly-Kenny diary 18–19 Feb 1900, Kell

14 See Smith-Dorrien diary 18 Feb 1900,
   Smit. Smith-Dorrien *Forty-Eight Years*
   149–50
15 *OH* II, 108–10, Map Vol II, 24
16 Kelly-Kenny diary 18–19 Feb 1900, Kell
17 Colvile 35–7. Smith-Dorrien loc cit
18 *OH* II, 110–14
19 De Wet 64
20 See K's defence in letter K–French nd
   quoted Maurice & Arthur *Kitchener* I,
   288–91
21 *TH* III, 423–5
22 I. Hamilton *The Commander* 99–112
23 *OH* II, 105, 112
24 Kelly-Kenny diary 18–19 Feb 1900, Kell
25 *OH* II, 112
26 Lyttelton–wife 1900, Lyt 562d
27 K–R 8am 18 Feb 1900 quoted *OH* II, 123
28 De Wet 55–6
29 *OH* II, 118. Pte Edwards (1st
   Essex)–father 3 Mar 1900, Edwards, MS
   cit
30 Kelly-Kenny SD I, 186. *OH* II, 118–34
31 Colvile 34–7
32 Battersby 39–44
33 Colvile 37
34 Kelly-Kenny diary 18–19 Feb 1900, Kell.
   OH II, 123–6
35 Colvile 39–40
36 Kelly-Kenny diary 18–19 Feb 1900, Kell
37 *OH* II, 136–8
38 Kelly-Kenny diary 18–21 Feb 1900, Kell
39 K's order to Hannay quoted *OH* II, 132
40 *OH* II, 132–3
41 Smith-Dorrien diary 18 Feb 1900, Smit.
   Smith-Dorrien *Forty-Eight Years* 150–4,
   161
42 Ibid
43 *OH* II, 143, 590
44 K–R 18 Feb 1900 quoted *OH* II, 142. See
   also K–French, MS cit
45 *OH* II, 135–8
46 Ibid
47 Pte Edwards 18–19 Feb 1900, MS cit.
   OH II, 142–3
48 Kelly-Kenny diary 18–19 Feb 1900, Kell
49 *OH* II, 604
50 De Wet 57
51 O. T. De Villiers loc cit
52 Cronje–R 2nd message 19 Feb 1900
   quoted *OH* II, 148
53 eg *TH* III, 595–6
54 *OH* II, 148
55 Ibid
56 R–L 20 Feb 1900, H & O I, 47. Cf R–L 21
   Feb 1900, H & O I, 49
57 *OH* II, 153–4. Methuen–wife 3 Apr 1900,
   Meth
58 *OH* II, 152–3
59 Kelly-Kenny diary 19–23 Feb 1900, Kell
60 See C. Williams *Hushed Up* 48–9
61 De Wet 60. *OH* II, 159–60
62 Kelly-Kenny diary 19–23 Feb 1900, Kell
63 R SD I, 219–20. Note 'considerable

number of native refugees' from laager.
Acc O. T. De Villiers (loc cit) 50 women

CHAPTER 29: THE KEY TURNS
Head of chapter Lt Alford 8 Feb 1900, Alf 85
1 Dundonald 138. Treves 92–3. Regt Diary
   2nd Devons 11 Feb 1900 Devon & Dorset
   Regimental Museum. Pte Key Diary 11
   Feb 1900, (cy) PC
2 Hubert Gough diary Jan–Feb 1900, Gou.
   Pte Kennedy diary 10–11 Feb 1900, (cy)
   PC. Pte Pegum diary 10–13 Feb 1900,
   (cy) PC
3 Alford, MS cit 72–3
4 Treves 93. Pte Kennedy diary 8–12 Feb
   1900, (cy) PC. Sgt Galley diary 3–9 Feb
   1900, (cy) PC
5 Treves 77–83
6 *OH* I, 268, 470, II, 597–8
7 Buller SD I, 253. *OH* II, 408–22. Lyttelton–wife 1900, Lyt
8 Churchill *Ladysmith* 362
9 Galley 3, 9 Feb 1900, (cy) PC
10 Tapes, PC
11 Churchill *Ladysmith* 366. Cf *My Early
   Life* 336
12 B. Herbert–Dodds 29 Jan 1900, Herb
13 B. Herbert–Dodds 25 Jan 1900, Herb. See
   also Dundonald 138
14 Lyttelton–wife 9 Feb 1900, Lyt 554d
15 Wilson diary quoted Callwell I, 33–4
16 *TH* III, 301–2, 549–52
17 Treves 43–4
18 Buller–R 9 Feb 1900, *RCSAW* III, 628
19 R–Buller 10 Feb 1900, *RCSAW* III, 629
20 Buller–White 7 Feb 1900, SD I, 505
21 Buller SD I, 253 para 3. Hildyard ev
   RCSAW III, 247. Warren ev *RCSAW*
   III, 223–4. Col Parsons *PRAI* XXVIII
   503–20. For best account of new tactics in
   a 14-day 'battle' see Maj A. Hamilton-
   Gordon *PRAI* XXVII, 347–64
22 Buller ev *RCSAW* III, 174. See also Capt
   H. Wilson 95
23 Lyttelton–wife 9, 13 Feb 1900, Lyt
   554b, d
24 See Gen Langlois *Lessons* HMSO (1909)
25 Churchill *Ladysmith* 371
26 Col Sandbach–mother 3 Mar 1900, Sand
27 Churchill *Ladysmith* 371–2. Dundonald
   139–40. WO Tel SA 3177B quoted SJ 12
   Feb 1900
28 Churchill *Ladysmith* 372–6
29 Atkins 270
30 Churchill *Ladysmith* 376. R Churchill I,
   511. Pte Kennedy Diary 16 Feb 1900, (cy)
   PC
31 Buller SD I, 253–4. *OH* II, 441. SJ 14, 17
   Feb 1900, quoting Natal Army Staff
   diary
32 Lt Alford 13 Feb 1900, Alf
33 But note Lyttelton *asked* for delay as too

hot. Lyttelton–wife 22 Feb 1900, Lyt 555a

34 Buller SD I, 254. SJ 12–19 Feb 1900. *OH* II, 437–46, 429. Treves 92–3. NB also 6 mt guns and 22 machine guns
35 Atkins 272–3
36 Warren's account quoted W. W. Williams 354
37 Churchill *Ladysmith* 383. See also [Birdwood's] account quoted Dundonald 142
38 Atkins 279
39 Lt G. L. Crossman diary 18 Feb 1900, Cros
40 Buller SD I, 253–4. *OH* II, 447–53. Warren's account W. W. Williams 357. Cf Lyttelton–wife 22 Feb 1900 loc cit
41 Churchill *Ladysmith* 396
42 Buller–White 21 Feb 1900, SD I, 508. *OH* II, 453. W. Williams 355 quoting Barton's report
43 Buller–WO tel no 3347D SJ 20 Feb 1900. Dundonald 145. Romer & Mainwaring 59
44 Treves 106, 104 (photo)
45 Buller–wife 18 Dec 1899, Bull (Crediton)
46 J. Atkins 287
47 See note 20
48 Churchill *Ladysmith* 395–6
49 Repington 234–5. Churchill *My Early Life* 337–8
50 Sandbach MSS Sand
51 Buller ev *RCSAW* III, 181. SJ 21 Feb 1900 quoting Buller's tel no 3373. White–Buller 22 Feb 1900, SD I, 509
52 Churchill *My Early Life* 338
53 Buller ev *RCSAW* III, 181
54 Sandbach–mother 22 Feb 1900, Sand
55 Buller–White 21 Feb 1900, SD I, 508
56 C. Hickie diary 19, 21, 22 Feb 1900, Hick. Stuart 194, 247, 233–4. Field Force Orders Jan–Feb 1900, Ham
57 MacDonald 248
58 Ly E. Cecil–Tim 16 Nov 1899, Sal (Hat)
59 Capt J. Gough diary 21 Feb 1900, Gou
60 Pte Steinberg Feb 1900, (cy) PC
61 Netley diary 1–25 Feb 1900, PC
62 Rawlinson 8 Feb 1900, Rawl 7
63 Capt J. Gough diary 30 Jan 1900, Gou
64 Lt Jelf 29 Jan 1900, Jelf
65 Nevinson 1 Feb 1900, *Ladysmith* 255–6, 272–3. MacDonald 227–8. Pearse 214–15
66 Netley diary 17 Jan 1900, PC
67 Steavenson 19 Jan 1900, Stea
68 Netley diary 23 Jan 1900, PC. Nevinson *Ladysmith* 245
69 MacDonald 225. Nevinson *Ladysmith* 255
70 MacDonald 228. Pearse 215
71 Nevinson 257
72 See Stuart 220–2. White–Buller 28 Jan 1900, SD I, 502
73 Rawlinson diary 30 Jan 1900, Rawl 7

74 White SD I, 236. White's letter 3 Feb 1900, Whi
75 Gore 104–7. McHugh 199–200. Gilbert diary 1, 3 Feb 1900, Gil. See illustration in Nevinson 276
76 J. Gough diary 21 Feb 1900, Gou
77 Steavenson diary 29 Jan 1900, Stea
78 Griffith 286. Field Force Orders 30–1 1900, Ham
79 Cf Hickie diary 31 Jan 1900, Hick
80 Steavenson diary 30 Jan 1900, Stea
81 Steavenson diary 10 Feb 1900, Stea
82 White SD I (appendix to despatch). Gilbert diary 17 Jan 1900, Gil
83 H. L. Norton-Smith–cousin 15 Jan 1900, Killie Campbell Library, Durban
84 White SD I, loc cit
85 Nevinson 285–90. Donegan 19 Feb 1900, PC
86 Donegan 20 Feb 1900, PC
87 Ibid
88 Ibid 28 Jan 1900, PC
89 Ibid 22 Jan 1900, PC
90 Rawlinson diary 11 Feb 1900, Rawl
91 Ibid
92 Gilbert diary 14–22 Feb 1900, Gil. Netley, Hickie and Jelf diaries 22 Feb 1900 loc cit
93 Dan Deeves 26 Feb 1900, Deev
94 Field Force Orders 27 Feb 1900, Ham

CHAPTER 30: THE HANDSHAKE

Head of chapter Buller–Bigge 15 Mar 1900, Big
1 R–L WO tel no 3494 SJ 27 Feb 1900. Buller SD I, 256 para 39
2 Atkins 309. Lyttelton–wife 3 Mar 1900, Lyt 556c. Buller SD I, 254–5 paras 21–31. *OH* II, 469–97. Cf *TH* III, 515–31
3 Atkins 295
4 Lyttelton–wife 3 Mar 1900, Lyt 556b. See also Lt Crossman 14 Jan 1900, Cros. Jourdain *Memories* 99–101
5 Jourdain ibid
6 Jourdain diary 23 Feb 1900, Jou. Jourdain *Natal*
7 Ibid
8 Royal Inniskilling Fusiliers 439. *OH* II, 488–9. *TH* III, 523–7
9 Ibid 439–45
10 Jourdain diary 23–24 Feb 1900, Jou
11 *OH* II, 500, 600 (including 24 missing). Cf Spion Kop losses in *OH* II, 597. And see *TH* VI
12 For her view of Irish see Longford *Victoria RI* (paperback edit) 697–8
13 Buller SD I, 255. *OH* II, 495–6
14 Repington 237
15 Buller SD I, 255. Buller ev *RCSAW* III, 182. Sandbach–mother 30 Mar 1900, Sand
16 *OH* II, 497–8
17 Lyttelton–wife 3 Mar 1900, Lyt 556a

18 Atkins 298–9
19 Churchill *Ladysmith* 423–4
20 Buller ev *RCSAW* III, 182 SD I, 255. *OH* II, 501–2
21 [Lt M. Grant] *Natal* 59–61. Lt Lafone 27 Feb 1900, Laf 57–8
22 [Grant] *Natal* 60
23 Lafone loc cit
24 [Grant] *Natal* 61–2
25 Lyttelton–wife loc cit
26 Lafone loc cit
27 Buller–wife 3 Mar 1900 reproduced Lewis Butler 84 (order of one sentence changed)
28 Atkins 304–9. Buller SD I, 255–6
29 *Breyt* III, 526–42. Bakkes *Archives Year Book* 30 (i) 1967
30 Buller SD I, 256–7. *OH* II, 509–13
31 Barnard 141–2. Bakkes loc cit
32 *Breyt* III, 542–6
33 Atkins 309–10
34 L/Cpl Bradley diary 27 Feb 1900, (cy) PC
35 *OH* II, 517. Atkins 311–12. *TH* III, 540
36 Churchill *Ladysmith* 446–7
37 Ibid 443–4
38 Cdr Limpus *Terrible* quoted Jeans 269–70
39 Maj Weldon–F. Wolseley 18 Mar 1900, Wol
40 Churchill 447–8
41 Atkins 312–13
42 See note 31
43 Steavenson diary 28 Feb 1900, Stea
44 Rawlinson diary 26–8 Feb 1900, Rawl 7. Netley diary 28 Feb 1900, PC
45 MacDonald 273–5 (last sentence reversed)
46 Ibid 275. Nevinson 292–3. Stuart 247–8. Pearse 234–5
47 Rawlinson diary 28 Feb 1900, Rawl 7
48 Netley diary 28 Feb 1900, PC
49 Nevinson loc cit
50 Rawlinson diary loc cit
51 MacDonald 278
52 Ibid 278–83. Nevinson 293–5. Stuart 248. Pearse 238
53 Churchill *My Early Life* 340–1
54 Churchill *Ladysmith* 462–6. H. Gough 74–9. And see Gough's notes on Churchill's *My Early Life*, Gou. Cf Birdwood 106–7. Dundonald 151–2
55 Rawlinson diary c 10 Mar 1900, Rawl 7
56 MacDonald 282–6
57 Nevinson 294–5
58 Rawlinson diary 3 Mar 1900, Rawl 7
59 Ibid
60 C. Hickie diary Feb–Mar 1900, Hick
61 Alford 3 Mar 1900, Alf
62 Atkins 314–15
63 [Grant] *Natal* 65
64 Sim's diary quoted Williams 368
65 Warren's account quoted ibid
66 Lilly in Jeans 273. Cf Treves 98
67 Wilson's diary quoted Callwell I, 39
68 Algy Trotter diary 1 Mar 1900, Trot

69 Rawlinson diary 3 Mar 1900, Rawl 7/
70 Col F. Stopford–Ly Buller, PC. Algy Trotter MSS, Trot. Numerous letters in Bull (Crediton)
71 Sandbach–mother 14 Mar 1900, Sand
72 Crossman 14, 30 Jan 1900, Cros
73 Cpl Hurley–sister 6 Mar 1900, (cy) PC
74 Buller–wife 3 Mar 1900 loc cit
75 Natal Army Order, Ham
76 Buller–wife 3 Mar 1900 loc cit
77 Rawlinson diary Mar 1900, Rawl
78 R–L 11 Mar 1900 and L–R 12 Mar 1900, CT no 202A, 202B
79 Lyttelton–wife c. 28 Mar 1900, Lyt 557c
80 Buller–R 7 Mar 1900. Buller ev *RCSAW* III, 183
81 Hamilton–R c 10 Mar 1900, Ham
82 R–Wilkinson 23 Jan 1900, Wilk. M–Wilkinson Nov 1898, 26 Jul 1899, Wilk
83 Hamilton–Wilkinson 8 Mar 1900, Wilk
84 See full text printed in *RCSAW* III, 655 (no 26)
85 Hamilton–Wilkinson loc cit
86 See file of Buller's letters of protest SM 22
87 For a modern example see B. Farwell *Great Boer War* 165 etc
88 R–L Mar 11 (no 277), 16 Mar (letter) 1900, H & O I, 69, 73–4
89 Rawlinson diary 3 Mar 1900, Rawl 7
90 Ibid 3–12 Mar 1900 Rawl 7. See also MacDonald 296–7

CHAPTER 31: THE PLAGUE OF BLOEMFONTEIN

Head of chapter Rudyard Kipling *Verse* 219. Also Ly E. Cecil–Ld Salisbury 30 May 1900, Sal E (Ox)
1 Lt March Phillipps *With Rimington* 92
2 Ralph *At Pretoria* 128–9
3 Phillipps 92–3. *Black & White Budget* 31 Mar 1900 (photos). SD I, 267 para 23
4 SJ 13 Mar 1900. R–L 12, 13 Mar 1900, H & O I, 70 tels no 281, 282, 282A, 283. *OH* II, 233–8
5 Battersby 101. Ralph *At Pretoria* 140–1
6 Ralph loc cit 139–48
7 Battersby 101. Ralph loc cit 138
8 Lord Kerry's diary, Lan XII, f14–15
9 Rawlinson diary 13 Mar 1900, Rawl. *TH* III, 590
10 Rawlinson diary loc cit. Menpes 68–9, 82–3. See Ly E. Cecil [Milner] description *My Picture Gallery* 181
11 Kelly–Kenny diary 7 Mar 1900, Kell. French diary Mar 1900, Fren. Haig
12 De Wet 68–9
13 *OH* II, 190–5 & Map Vol II, 26
14 R SD I, 264–5 paras 7–11. R ev *RCSAW* II, 465
15 *OH* II 196–203. Kelly–Kenny diary 7 Mar 1900, Kell. Haig–Henrietta 16 Mar 1900, Haig. H & O I, 72

16 Childers *Arme Blanche* 133–49
17 R–L 16 Mar 1900, H & O I, 72
18 R's notes for L enc by N. Chamberlain 28 Aug 1900, Bobs 23/IV
19 Haig–Henrietta 16 Mar 1900, Haig
20 Ibid
21 Childers loc cit
22 Kelly–Kenny diary 7 Mar 1900, Kell
23 Ibid 7–9 Mar. 6th Div'n Staff Diary in SJ 14 Mar 1900
24 De Wet 69
25 *OH* II, 213–29. R SD I, 266 paras 18–20
26 Kelly–Kenny diary 10 Mar 1900, Kell. R–L 16 Mar 1900, H & O I, 73–4
27 See note 90
28 Ralph *War's Brighter Side* 182–3
29 R–L 16 Mar 1900 loc cit
30 Ralph *War's Brighter Side* 5–15. [Rankin] *Subaltern's Letters* 168
31 Ralph op cit 117
32 *The Friend* Mar–Apr 1900
33 R–Queen Victoria 15 Mar 1900, H & O I, 71–3
34 Colvile 67
35 [Rankin] *Subaltern's Letters* 174
36 Ly E. Cecil–'Mama' 15 Nov 1899, Sal (Hat). Ly Milner *Picture Gallery* 180
37 For the scale of letter-writing note average number of army letters received at Cape Town each *week* was 190,000. See *OH* IV, 625–8
38 Copies in PC
39 [Rankin] *Subaltern's Letters* 226–7
40 See note 33
41 R–Brackenbury 27 Mar 1900, H & O I, 84
42 See Rawlinson diary passim, Rawl 7
43 [Rankin] *Subaltern's Letters* 174–6
44 See note 33
45 Ibid
46 Nor, it must be said, did his own Intelligence Officers. Col Henderson had been invalided home. See Robertson 117 and R's preface to Henderson's *Science of War* xxvii
47 Buller ev *RCSAW* III, 170–1
48 Ibid
49 Ibid
50 R–L 16 Mar 1900 and tel no 293 of same date, H & O I, 73. *OH* II, 260 gives text of Proclamation of 15 Mar
51 *OH* II, 230–1
52 *OH* II, 189
53 *OH* II, 230–1, 259–60
54 For Amery's eulogy see *TH* III, 594–7
55 *OH* II, 258
56 R–Buller 3 Mar 1900 quoted R *RCSAW* II, 464, Buller *RCSAW* II, 183
57 Haig–Henrietta 22 Mar 1900, Haig. *OH* II, 250–3
58 *OH* II, 263–5
59 *TH* IV, 6–10
60 *TH* IV, 11
61 R–L 15–17 Jan 1900, H & O I, 11

62 Fortescue *Army Service Corps* 229–65.
63 Hamilton memo for Arthur c 1920, Ham
64 Menpes 79–80. Cf *TH* IV
65 Buller ev *RCSAW* III, 176. R–L 27 Dec (ltr) 1900, H & O I, 4
66 R–L 20 Mar 1900, H & O I, 77
67 R–L (tel) 24 Mar 1900, (ltr) 25 Mar, H & O I, 80–1
68 French ev *RCSAW* III, Q 17186 and 17189. *OH* II, 32, 37–8, 203
69 R–L 24 Mar 1900 (tel no 331), H & O I, 80
70 See esp R–L 9 Mar 1900 (tel no 271), H & O I, 68
71 Kelly–Kenny diary 29–30 Mar 1900, Kell. R–L 29 Mar 1900 (tel no 348), 1 Apr (ltr), H & O I, 85, 87–8
72 See note 19
73 See note 62
74 For full report on typhoid see *Report of the Commission on Dysentery* (1903), and see *Cd* 453 (Romer Report)
75 Battersby 125–6
76 Burdett-Coutts quoted *TH* VI, 523–4. See his ev to Romer Commission and comments published separately
77 *BMJ* 2 Feb 1901 quoted above. See Prof Ogston ev *RCSAW* II, 472–85 esp Q 10965
78 *Cd* 453
79 *Life* of Conan Doyle, and see Menpes 152–5. For Exham see *Cd* 453/32
80 For an eye-witness account see diary of Dr Dobbs at Kroonstad (cy) PC
81 R–L 15–17 Jan (ltr), 22 Jan (tel), 22–4 Jan (ltr), 29 Jan (ltr) 1900, H & O I, 11, 15, 17, 21
82 R–L 9 Feb 1900 (ltr), H & O I, 35
83 R–Queen Victoria 15 Apr 1900 (ltr), H & O I, 98
84 Menpes 89–90. Ralph *War's Brighter Side* 203–4
85 *The Friend* 17 Mar 1900 quoted Ralph *At Pretoria* 166
86 M–R 21 Jan 1900, *MP* II, 52–3. M–C CO 879/511. Cf M–R 23 Aug 1900, *MP* II, 85
87 M–Selborne Mar 1900, Mil
88 M–Ly E Cecil 30 Mar 1900, *MP* II, 68
89 See Ly E. Cecil–Salisbury 30 May 1900, Sal E. And see letters *Times* Jul–Aug 1900 passim
90 M–C Mar–Apr 1900, CO 879/63
91 M's diary 27–28 Mar 1900, Mil
92 Ralph *War's Brighter Side* 200–8. See signed menu in Bobs 23/IV/2
93 Ralph loc cit
94 Churchill *My Early Life* 342–3

CHAPTER 32: 'KEEPING DE WET FROM DEFEAT'
Head of chapter Pte Whitton tape recorded by author 1970

1 M. Davitt 34

2 De Wet 77–80. *TH* IV, 26–8. Hales *Campaign Pictures of War* 75–82.

3 Kruger *Memoirs* II, 348–9. De Wet 68–9

4 Hillegas 230. Cf Menpes 66–7

5 De Wet 79. Steyn's proc 17 Mar 1900 quoted *OH* II, 266–7

6 De Wet 78

7 De Wet 81. *OH* II, 265–6

8 Kruger *Memoirs* II, 350. SJ text of appeal to Ld Salisbury and reply

9 *Times* 10 Nov 1899

10 Salisbury's reply 11 Mar 1900, *Cd 261/20–2*. Steyn's comment quoted Kruger *Memoirs* II, 439–40

11 Kruger's 2nd speech to the Raad 7 May 1900 Kruger *Memoirs* II, 451–2

12 *OH* II, 265. Meintjes *Steyn* 115–16

13 Leyds–Reitz 10 Feb 1900, Leyds *Correspondentie Tweede Verzameling* II, 358

14 Kruger's 1st speech to Raad 3 May 1900, Kruger *Memoirs* II, 446–7. *TH* IV, 28

15 R. Macnab *The French Colonel* 154, 204–9. Kruger *Memoirs* II, 349

16 Kruger's 2nd speech 7 May 1900 loc cit 456–7

17 Ibid 453–6

18 De Wet 80

19 Ibid 85. Villebois captured diary 17–20 Mar, WO 105/25

20 De Wet 85–8

21 WO 105/35: Broadwood's 1st des, Alderson's statement and R's comment that Broadwood had been 'injudicious'. Cf R's later comment and his des 19 Jun 1900, SD I, 326–30 and SM 18/3

22 Haig–Henrietta 7 Apr 1900, Haig

23 Broadwood's 1st des 20 Apr 1900 loc cit. *OH* II, 275–6

24 *OH* II, 276–7 Map Vol II, 33. See photos in Goldmann 218–19

25 Broadwood's 1st des loc cit. *OH* II, 276–7

26 *OH* II, 279–80

27 Broadwood 1st des loc cit

28 For his outburst after Driefontein see Kelly-Kenny's diary 11 Mar 1900 'he would not listen to reason'.

29 Rawlinson diary 31 Mar 1900, Rawl 7/2

30 Ibid. Cf *OH* II, 295

31 Haig's comment: 'Broadwood has got off very cheaply' Haig–Henrietta 14 Apr 1900, Haig. See Childers *Arme Blanche* 183 – 'no valid excuse'. Battersby 121

32 Maj Phipps-Hornby's narrative (cy) PC

33 Broadwood's 1st des loc cit

34 Ibid

35 Phipps-Hornby loc cit

36 Ibid. *OH* II, 283–4

37 Phipps-Hornby loc cit

38 Ibid

39 Ibid

40 De Wet 91–2. *OH* II, 298–9, 596 (note total loss of Broadwood's force was 571)

41 De Wet 95–100. *OH* II, 306–11

42 De Wet 103–7. *OH* II, 314–27

43 See Kruger–Steyn tel quoted *OH* II, 314

44 R SD I, 320–2. *OH* III, 40

CHAPTER 33: 'THE WHITE MAN'S WAR'

Head of chapter Cronje's message via Dr Dyer 29 Oct 1899, Weil 46848/659

1 B-P's Staff Diary 30 Apr 1900, B-P. Hillcourt *Baden-Powell* 197 and note 432

2 Hillcourt 197

3 Grinnell–M 181–2. Hillcourt 197

4 Hillcourt 197

5 Begbie *Story of Baden-Powell* (London 1900) 109

6 Hillcourt passim

7 B-P–Plumer, WO 105/15

8 Trooper Spurling 9 Apr 1900 re-ptd *Draconian* Aug 1900 468

9 Ly Sarah Wilson 200

10 Staff Diary Oct–Apr 1900, B-P

11 Sarah Wilson 195–6

12 Staff Diary 28 Feb 1900, B-P. See also SJ 25 Jan 1900

13 Agnes–B-P 25 Nov 1899 quoted Hillcourt 195, 432

14 Queen Victoria 1 Apr 1900 (tel) quoted Ibid 196, 432

15 See chap 8

16 See Gardner *Mafeking* 35–9. *OH* III, 140. B-P SD I, 332. B-P's ev *RCSAW* III, 423–6. B-P *Lessons* 200. Col Everett's memo 1 Jul 1899, WO 32/7852

17 B-P ev *RCSAW* III, 424

18 Ibid 426 Q 19843

19 Sir E. Wood–B-P 7 Jul 1899 079/8697 WO 32/7852. B-P ev *RCSAW* III, Q 19823–5, 19845

20 M–C 12 Sep 1899, *MP* I, 520–1

21 B-P ev *RCSAW* III, Q 19871–2

22 See prologue

23 *OH* I, 455–6. *RCSAW* I, 21

24 *Breyt* I, 153, 386. Cf B-P SD I, 335 and B-P ev *RCSAW* III, 424

25 Gardner *Mafeking* 212–13, 228–9

26 *Breyt* II, 56

27 B-P SD I, 343. B-P ev *RCSAW* III, 424

28 Compare B-P SD I, 333, 335 ev *RCSAW* III, 424, 428 and *Lessons* 200

29 Hillcourt 126–43

30 See note 17

31 Memo for L re B-P Lan VIII. Hillcourt 139–42

32 Hillcourt 32

33 B-P *The Matabele Campaign* (London 1896) 154–5, 475. *Aids to Scouting* (London 1899) 156 'better than any other game is that of man-hunting'.

34 See note 17

35 SD I, 178. *OH* II, 45–52

36 B-P SD I, 333, 334, 339. Staff Diary passim B-P. B-P ev *RCSAW* III, 424, 427

37 B-P SD I, 333
38 Ibid 339
39 Ibid 343. Hillcourt 162, 189. Gardner *Mafeking* 131
40 Godley *Life of an Irish Soldier* 77. Hillcourt 188–9. *OH* III, 163
41 B-P SD I, 343–4
42 Hillcourt 191–3, 432. Godley 79–80
43 *TH* II, 138–40
44 For Holdsworth see CO 417/283/99–105. See P. Warwick loc cit
45 B-P SD I, 342. EGO. Sol Plaatje *Diary*
46 B-P SD I, 342
47 Ibid 346. Staff Diary entries 18 Mar, 2 Apr 1900, B-P. See photo in H. Wilson II, 623 and see Neilly *Besieged with B-P* 229–30
48 B-P–R 26 Feb 1900, Bobs 6
49 B-P SD I, 333. Cf B-P ev *RCSAW* III, Q 19874
50 B-P SD I, 333. B-P ev *RCSAW* III, 424. *OH* III, 142
51 Godley 11, 69–91. B-P *Aids to Scouting* 156
52 Godley 75. Gardner *Mafeking* 73. B-P SD I, 346–8, 354, 356–61
53 Hillcourt 178–9, 192–3, 345. B-P SD I, 352
54 See K. Rose *The Later Cecils* (London 1975) 188–9, 201. B-P SD I, 352
55 Staff Diary 10 Jan, 18 Mar 1900, B-P
56 Ibid 16 Nov 1900
57 Ibid 2–3 Nov 1900. Baillie *Mafeking*/42, 277–8. Hamilton 106–7. Neilly 107
58 Staff Diary 19 Mar 1900 B-P. Ibid 18 Mar 1900
59 Hamilton 67–87. Baillie 156–8, 193–5. Neilly 66–8, 189–91. Gardner *Mafeking* 131–3
60 B-P SD I, 339. B-P ev *RCSAW* III, 424
61 S. Wilson 163–8
62 Ibid 168, 183–7
63 Ibid 57–159
64 B-P SD I, 350. Godley 78
65 Staff Diary 25–6 Dec 1900, B-P. Godley 78. Hamilton 175–182. Neilly 135–9. Baillie 93–8
66 B-P SD I, 350. *OH* III, 549
67 Hamilton 175–6, 182–7
68 Staff Diary 26 Dec 1900, B-P
69 SJ 3 Oct 1899. Staff Diary 14 Nov 1899, B-P
70 Hillcourt 160. Milner *My Picture Gallery* 125–6
71 Staff Diary 14 Nov 1899, B-P
72 Ibid 22 Nov 1899
73 Ibid 30 Dec 1899
74 Ibid 1 Jan 1900
75 Ibid 31 Dec 1900, 1, 7, 10 Jan 1900
76 Ibid 8 Feb 1900
77 Ibid 14 Feb 1900
78 Ibid 12 Feb 1900
79 Ibid Feb 1900
80 Ibid 8 Feb 1900
81 Ibid 14–27 Feb, 4 Mar 1900
82 Ibid 24 Mar, 4 Apr 1900
83 Hamilton 248–50. See also Press enquiry, Staff Diary 19 Apr 1900, B-P
84 Neilly 227–9 (some lines transposed)
85 Neilly 229
86 B-P Staff Diary 27, 30 Mar, 4 Apr 1900, B-P
87 Ibid 4, 7, Apr 1900
88 Ibid 3 Apr 1900. Plumer's report in SJ 31 Mar 1900. *OH* III, 201
89 Staff Diary 2, 3, 13, 20 Apr 1900. Hillcourt 195
90 Staff Diary 5, 6, 8, 14 Apr 1900, B-P
91 Ibid 8, 16, 20 Apr. Cf account from Boer side Scho
92 Ibid. Hamilton 290–1. *OH* III, 176–7
93 See *OH* Map
94 S. Wilson 212–13. Baillie 274–5
95 Hamilton 291–3
96 B-P Staff Diary 12 May 1900. S. Wilson 206
97 Hamilton 292–7. Neilly 256–9
98 Hillcourt 198
99 Hillcourt 198
100 S. Wilson 205–6. Baillie 259
101 Hillcourt 198–9. Godley 81. Staff Diary 12 May 1900, B-P. *OH* III, 177–8
102 *OH* III, 180
103 Baillie 264–5. B-P SD I, 358–9. Gardner *Mafeking* 186–7
104 Hamilton 301–4. Baillie 253
105 Ibid 304–10. S. Wilson 211–13
106 *OH* III, 181. Cf B-P SD I, 351
107 B-P–R 7 May 1900 quoted R-L 15 May 1900, H & O I, 121. But cf B-P ev *RCSAW* III, 424 (10 days' provision left)
108 Hamilton 312–13. Baillie 278. S. Wilson 214
109 Trooper Steevens tape recording PC. Hamilton 313–17. Baillie 278–90. S. Wilson 214–17. Neilly 273–6
110 Col B.Mahon SD I, 381–3. *OH* III, 181–4
111 Harington *Plumer* 35–8 (inc tracing of message). Hutchinson *Rhodes* 143
112 *OH* III, 551
113 Mahon SD I, 383–4
114 Wilfrid Blunt *My Diaries* (1932 edition) 367
115 SJ May–Jun 1900
116 Balfour-Ridgeway 6 Mar 1900, Bal 49812/301–2
117 Baillie 270
118 Trooper Steevens tape, PC. Hamilton 330–2. S. Wilson 219 Hillcourt 191–3, 432
119 Hamilton 331. Neilly 280
120 Montmorency quoted Gardner *Mafeking* 197–8
121 Casualty list B-P SD I, 336. See Hamilton for monthly figures
122 EGO (by generosity of Mrs Minchin)
123 M-Asquith 18 Nov 1897 Asq 9

CHAPTER 34: ACROSS THE VAAL

Head of chapter Kipling *Verse* 460

1 Phillipps 12
2 R SD I, 320–5. *OH* III, 41–2, 536–9
3 R–L 17 May (ltr) 1900, H & O I, 122
4 M–Selborne 24 May 1899, *MP* I, 401
5 SJ 28 May 1900. R dated proc 24 May but it was not formally proclaimed till 28th. See *OH* III, 126 and 559. The wrong date (26th) was given by R in WO 5950 (tel) H & O I, 133
6 Phillipps 147–9. See also R–L 30 May 1900, H & O I, 131
7 Pte Brymer 1900, (cy) PC
8 Churchill *Ian Hamilton* 234
9 Phillipps 119–20 (sentence order reversed)
10 Hon S. Peel *Trooper 8008* 54
11 Kipling *Verse* 459–60
12 Price *Imperial War* 200, 254–8
13 Ibid 178–84. Lloyd *With the CIV* 3–5. *OH* III, 34
14 Lloyd IX–X
15 Peel 58–63. Erskine Childers *CIV* 152–3. Phillipps 90–1, 128–36. Trooper Edingborough (ex-city clerk) tape recording, PC
16 Kipling op cit 473
17 R–L (ltrs) 4, 17, 30 May 1900, H & O I, 112–13, 122–3, 130–2. Rawlinson diary 3–30 May 1900, Rawl
18 R–L (ltr) 29 Apr 1900, H & O I, 107–8
19 See Childers *Arme Blanche* 190–2
20 Rawlinson diary 13 May 1900, Rawl 7/2
21 R–L loc cit
22 See Capt Bromley Davenport May–Jun 1900 Brom. Colvile 28. Phillipps 131–2
23 R–L 4, 17 May, 7 Jun 1900, H & O I, 112–13, 122–3 and II, 3. *OH* III, 104–7
24 R ev *RCSAW* III, 46–9. *OH* III, 40–2
25 For Buller–R wrangle see *OH* III, 249–59, 552 and Buller ev *RCSAW* III, 183
26 *OH* III, 525–39. NB R's figures misleading as they 1) omit static forces in OFS and CC and include them in Natal, 2) omit the IY battns
27 Rawlinson diary 8 May 1900, Rawl 7
28 Ibid May 1900
29 R–L (ltrs) 4, 17, 30 May 1900 loc cit. *OH* III, 42–64
30 R–L 6 Jun 1900, H & O II, 2–3
31 R–Wilson 21 May 1900 no 324 and 327, Bobs III
32 Ibid
33 For 'unfortunate occurrence' see R–L 5 Apr 1900, CT no 244a
34 I. Hamilton–wife 24 May 1900, Ham
35 Churchill *Ian Hamilton* 109, 121. Phillipps 139–40
36 I. Hamilton–wife 24 May 1900, Ham
37 SJ 1, 10 May 1900. *OH* III, 58–9.

Smith-Dorrien 196–205. Churchill *Ian Hamilton* 179
38 Phillipps 116–17. Colvile 173–4. Peel 87
39 Churchill *Ian Hamilton* 199–201. Hamilton–R (tel) 18 May no 185 and R–Hamilton 19 May, WO/105/
40 Hamilton–R (tel) 22 May 1900, WO/105. Hamilton–R 27 Jun 1900, WO 105/8. Churchill loc cit 205–27
41 R ev *RCSAW* III, 49–56. *OH* III, 72–7. Cf Childers *Arme Blanche* 184–95
42 EGO and Oberholster *Historical Monuments* 295–6
43 Lloyd 178–9
44 Hutton May–Jun 1900, Hut. Churchill *Ian Hamilton* 246–7
45 Phillipps 122
46 Ibid 122–30. See also Smith-Dorrien 205–10
47 Phillipps 123
48 Churchill *Ian Hamilton* 247–62
49 *OH* III, 80–6. Lloyd loc cit. Reports of Col Spens and Gen Smith-Dorrien to R, WO 105
50 See Reports of French and Hamilton to R, WO 105. Cf *OH* III, 78–80
51 *TH* IV, 146
52 R ev *RCSAW* III, 56. *OH* III, 86. SJ 29 May 1900
53 Battersby 195–6
54 Ibid 196–9
55 Ibid 199
56 Churchill *Ian Hamilton* 268–83. Diary of Ld Kerry 28–30 May 1900, Lan
57 R ev *RCSAW* III, 56. *OH* III. SJ 30 May 1900
58 R ev *RCSAW* III, 56. *OH* III
59 J. Brandt *Petticoat Commando* 20–3. Viljoen *Reminiscences* 143–4
60 Ld Kerry's diary 31 May 1900, Lan. SJ 31 May 1900
61 Dr Krause–R 30 May 1900 quoted Brandt 29
62 *MP* II, 77–8. This included notes and coin
63 Warwick loc cit
64 SA Chamber of Mines *Annual Reports* 1897–8
65 *MP* 137 and M–C 9 May 1900 quoted *MP* II, 143
66 *SP* I, 539–41
67 Ibid I, 538
68 Burnham *Scouting* 329–37
69 *SP* I, 537–44. Warmelo *On Commando* 37–8
70 *SP* I, 541
71 Quoted Meintjes *Kruger* 243. Cf text quoted SJ 31 May 1900
72 Reitz 94–108
73 Ibid 109–11
74 Botha later told R how he was nearly captured. See R ev *RCSAW* III, 56
75 *SP* I, 539, 544–6
76 SJ 31 May 1900. J. Brandt 15–23. NB Dr Krause's own notes in J. C. Roos MSS

Rhodes House Library Oxford confirm Brandt's account

77 R ev *RCSAW* III, 57
78 See note 76
79 *SP* I, 541–2
80 Ibid I, 543
81 SJ I, 30 Jun 1900 quoting Botha's tels to De Wet. See also *SP* I, 549–53
82 R–L 7 Jun 1900, H & O II, 3
83 SJ 4 Jun 1900. Battersby 222–4. Ralph *At Pretoria* 239
84 Battersby 220–7
85 Churchill *My Early Life* 365. Cf MacKern 228–30
86 Churchill *Ian Hamilton* 293–5
87 See Botha–R exchanges 4–15 Jun 1900 in SM 9/64–70
88 SJ 8–12 Jun 1900. L–R 19 Jun 1900 (ltr), H & O II, 11–13. *OH* III, 204–25
89 *SP* I, 547–61
90 De Wet 118
91 Ibid 129–30. *OH* III, 128 quoting Botha's tel 3 Jun 1900
92 De Wet 130–1
93 SJ 7 Jun 1900. *OH* III, 126–31
94 De Wet 132–6. See *Khaki Letters* 313
95 See *Morning Post* 6 Jun 1900. Fitzgibbon *Arts Under Arms* 3–57
96 Ibid 122–7. *OH* III, 115–16
97 Spragge–Rundle 30 May 1900 quoted *OH* III, 118
98 Fitzgibbon 128–9. *OH* III, 115–17, 120–1, 124. SJ 26, 29 May 1900
99 Peel 78–84
100 SJ 1 Jun 1900
101 Scrapbook in PC including *Daily Nation* and *Irish Daily Independent* 7 Jun 1900 and *Longford Leader*. Cf Lindley surrenders: courts of enquiries' findings published *RCSAW* IV, 416–17
102 Trooper Gibson narrative (cy) PC. See also Trooper M. Hickie 28, 29 May, 8 Jun 1900, Hick
103 *OH* III, 119–25. Cf II, 14–25
104 SJ 8 Jun 1900
105 R–L 12 Jun 1900, H & O II, 7
106 R–L 19 Jun 1900, H & O II, 13. *OH* III, 134–9

CHAPTER 35: 'PRACTICALLY OVER'
Head of chapter Pte Bowers tape recording PC 1970
1 Phillipps 145–7, 152. Childers *CIV* 110–30. Hunter–R 21 Jun 1900, WO 105/17. SJ 3, 7, 8 Jul 1900
2 Hunter–R official report 4 Aug 1900, WO 105/18. Phillipps 151–2
3 Phillipps 152
4 R–L 16 Jul 1900, H & O II, 32. Hunter–R report loc cit
5 Lagden–R Jul 1900, WO 105/18
6 SJ 24–5 Jun 1900

7 Hunter–R (tel) 21 Jul 1900, WO 105/18. *OH* III, 292–4
8 Hunter–R 17 Jul 1900 and his report loc cit. SJ 15 Jul 1900
9 Phillipps 180
10 R–L (tel) 12 Aug 1900, H & O II, 58
11 Hunter–R, WO 105/17. See also R–Hart 29 Jun, R–Hunter 30 Jun, R–K 3 Jul 1900, Bobs. SA Tels 28, 32, 38. Childers *CIV* 122
12 Phillipps 187–8 (paragraph order reversed)
13 Ibid 201–4
14 Capt W. Bromley Davenport May–Jul 1900, Brom 14–20
15 Hunter–R report loc cit. *OH* III, 297–8
16 Lagden–R 11–20 Jul 1900, WO 105/18
17 Hunter–R report loc cit
18 Hunter–R 21 Jul 1900, WO 105/18
19 SJ 23 Jul 1900. *OH* III, 299–301
20 Capt Bromley Davenport 10 Aug 1900, Brom 21
21 Phillipps 155–8
22 Hunter–R report loc cit
23 Ibid. Phillipps 164–9. SJ 27, 29 Jul 1900
24 Corner *34th IY* 234–43. Childers *CIV* 182–4
25 De Wet 161–4
26 Hunter–R report loc cit
27 *DSAB* I, 660–1. *OH* III, 304–5. De Wet 164–6
28 Hunter–R report loc cit. Hunter–R 29 Jul 10.30 am and 4.50 pm, 30 Jul (A 232, 233, 234), WO 105/18. Hunter–R 29, 30, 31 Jul ibid. R–Hunter 29, 30 Jul (C 3121, 3127A, 3136) Bobs SA tels 110–11. SJ 29, 31 Jul 1900
29 Tape recordings with Ptes E. Higgitt & T. Pain, PC. Corner 233
30 Capt Bromley Davenport loc cit
31 Hunter–R report loc cit and tel 10 Aug 1900, WO 105/18. *OH* III, 305–6
32 De Wet 175–6, 166
33 Ibid
34 See Phillipps
35 J. D. Kestell passim. *DSAB* I, 233–40
36 Capt Molyneux-Seele diary 1–27 Jul 1900 1–3, (cy), PC
37 Ibid 7 7
38 Ibid 17–18
39 De Wet 169–77. *OH* III, 341–5
40 De Wet 177–81
41 R–L 8 Aug (ltr) 10 Aug 1900, H & O II, 55–7. *OH* III
42 R–Queen Victoria 8 Aug (ltr), H & O II, 54 43R–L 16 Jun 1900, H & O II, 10
44 R–L 18 Aug 1900, H & O II, 61
45 Kerry–mother Jul 1900, Lan
46 R–Queen Victoria 8, 21 Aug (ltrs) 1900, H & O II, 54, 63
47 Kerry–mother Jul 1900 Lan. See F. Maurice–wife 28 Apr 1900 Maur 30: 'Lady B has appointed herself PMO and

makes all the doctors and nurses hop around.'

48 R–L 28 Jun, 7 Jul, 21 Aug (ltr) 1900, H & O II, 20–1, 27, 65

49 Churchill *Ian Hamilton* 24–8. F. Maurice–wife 17 May 1900, Maur 34

50 SJ 11 Jul 1900. *OH* III, 238–40. L–R 17, 19 Jul 1900, H & O II, 34–5, 37

51 Kerry–mother Jul 1900, Lan. R–Queen Victoria 18 Aug 1900, H & O II, 61. Warren *Prince Christian Victor* 400–1

52 For the dilemma see L–R 18 Aug 1900, H & O II 62

53 Hamilton–wife quoted Hamilton *Happy Warrior* 171–2

54 Hamilton–wife 12 Jul 1900, Ham 25/12/27

55 M–R 23 Aug 1900, *MP* II, 85–6

56 L–R 16 Aug (ltr) 1900, H & O II, 59–60. SJ 10, 23 Aug 1900

57 Kerry–mother Sep 1900 Lan. R–L 2 Sep 1900, H & O II, 74. SJ 2, 6 Sep 1900

58 *OH* III, 335–45

59 See protest re K of K in report 21 Jun 1900, Sherwood Regt MSS Box 17

60 SJ 27, 29, 30 Jul, 3, 5 Aug 1900. *OH* III, 341–4. R–L 31 Jul, 6 Aug 1900

61 *OH* III, 344–51. Rawlinson diary Aug 1900, Rawl 7/3

62 *OH* III, 335–41, 348–9, 351–6

63 K–R quoted Rawlinson diary 12–14 Aug 1900, Rawl 7/3

64 Ibid. Smith-Dorrien *Memories* 233–4. *OH* III, 351–3

65 R–L

66 Rawlinson diary loc cit

67 Lyttelton–wife 19 Aug 1900, Lyt 578a, b

68 Lyttelton–wife 5 Aug 1900, Lyt 576d

69 SJ 19 Aug 1900

70 See note 67

71 Lyttelton–wife 8 Aug 1900, Lyt 577

72 Lyttelton–wife 6 Jul 1900, Lyt

73 See note 67

74 See R–L re Lyttelton's qualifications as C-in-C

75 Dundonald *Army Life* 167

76 Melville I, 88 foll

77 Buller–W Apr 1900, Wol

78 Buller ev *RCSAW* III, 183–5. *OH* III, 249–83. R ev *RCSAW* II, 464, III, 53–55

79 Buller–wife nd [May] 1900, Bull (Crediton)

80 Buller–wife 15 May 1900, Bull (Crediton). Buller ev *RCSAW* III, 185

81 Ibid. SJ 6–12 Jun 1900

82 Buller–wife 9, 18 Jun 1900, Bull (Crediton)

83 SJ Jun–Aug 1900

84 R–wife 11, 26 Jan 1900, Bobs 202. SJ 7 Jul 1900

85 Buller–wife 18 Aug 1900, Bull (Crediton). SJ 14–25 Aug 1900

86 *OH* III, 392

87 Buller–wife 16 Sep 1900, Bull (Crediton)

88 *OH* III, 396. For Buller's eye for ground see Dundonald 175

89 Lyttelton–wife 30 Aug 1900, Lyt 578

90 Ibid. *OH* III, 399–402. Stuart 396–405. Viljoen 183–4

91 *OH* III, 402–3

92 Lyttelton–wife 30 Aug 1900, Lyt 578

93 Buller–wife 30 Aug 1900, Bull (Crediton)

94 Ibid 16 Sep 1900

95 Melville II, 264–5

96 Ralli–K 1 Nov 1900, Kit 17/S8

97 James 342–5

98 Hamilton–wife 12 Sep 1900, Ham 25/12/27

99 B–Balfour 17, 21 Oct 1900, Bal 49720. Midleton *Records* 119–57. SM 22/1–11

100 R–B 11 Oct 1900, Bobs 122. B–R 13 Oct 1900, Bobs 13/113

101 *Times* 11 Oct 1901. *TH* II, 461–2

102 See notes 99 and 100. Cf Kelly-Kenny diary 11–21 Oct 1901, Kell

103 Compare *TH* II, 458–66 with *TH* III, 595–7 and IV, 501–2

104 Gen Langlois *Lessons of Two Recent Wars*

105 Rawlinson diary Nov–Dec 1900, Rawl 7/3

106 SJ Sep–Oct 1900. *OH* III, 406–21

107 Rawlinson diary Oct 1900, Rawl 7/3

108 *Cd 524*. *TH* IV, 492–5

109 R–Spenser Wilkinson 28 Sep 1900, Wilk 79

110 Rawlinson diary 29 Oct–10 Dec 1900, Rawl 7/3. T. H. Warren 350–73. E. Longford 702

PART IV

CHAPTER 36: A MUDDY ELECTION

Head of Part IV K–R draft [Nov 1901], Kit 21
Head of chapter Saki in *Westminster Alice* autumn 1900

1 See L–R 8 Nov 1900, Bobs 34

2 *Times* editorials 10, 11 Aug 1900. See Curtis *With Milner* 185

3 L–R loc cit. Note R's summary R–L 26 Nov 1900, Ct p. 222

4 *Annual Register* 1900. *Times* 8 Aug 1900. Garvin III, 605

5 J. Wilson 332–3

6 Garvin III, 582–5 esp C's diary for 5 Jul 1900

7 *Times* 18 Sep 1900 commenting on C's and Balfour's election addresses

8 *Times* 18 Sep 1900

9 J. Wilson 332–3

10 Herbert Gladstone, H. Gladstone MSS, BM 46020/48–9

11 Wilson 334 quoting Gladstone's speech at Leeds on 18 Sep. *Annual Register* 1900

12 *Times* 18 Sep 1900

13 Spender *Contemporary Review* Dec 1900, 746–60

14 Balfour–Ridgeway 6 Mar 1900, Bal 49812/301–2
15 *Hansard* LXXVIII 7 Feb 1900
16 J. Wilson 327
17 J. Wilson 329–31
18 M. Asquith–M 9 Jul 1900, Mil 29
19 CB–Ripon, Ripon 43517f 157 quoted J. Wilson 336. *Hansard* LXXXVI. J. Wilson 330 quoting Rendel–M, Mil 29 f 369. Harcourt-Spencer quoted J. Wilson 331
20 Garvin III, 600–1
21 *Liberal Magazine* vol 8 Nov 1900 Supp VI
22 *Annual Register* 1900. J. Wilson passim esp 333
23 CB 30 Sep 1900, C–B 41246/73
24 *Hansard* LXXXVII 8 Aug 1900
25 See W. J. Reader *History of ICI* Vol I (London 1970)
26 Brackenbury–Balfour 23 Jan 1900, Bal. 49853/13
27 Arthur Chamberlain–C 29 Mar 1910, PC
28 *Hansard* LXXXVIII 10 Dec 1900. Garvin III, 613–16
29 Garvin III, 593
30 Selborne–Balfour 16 Oct 1900, Bal 49707 f 72–3
31 *Annual Register, Times* and *Manchester Guardian* 1900
32 *Annual Register* 1900. Garvin III, 596, 603–6, 611–12
33 *Annual Register* 1900
34 Spender *Contemporary Review* loc cit
35 J. Wilson 335 quoting CB 41214/85 etc
36 M–B 5 Nov 1900, Brod 30/67/6
37 Ibid
38 R–L (tel) 22 Oct 1900, H & O III, 49. *Times* 24 Oct 1900
39 B–R 21 Nov, B–K 16 Dec 1900, CT nos 379, 397

CHAPTER 37: THE WORM TURNS

Head of chapter M–R Haldane 21 Jan 1901 *MP* II, 206
1 *SP* I, 568–602. *OH* III, 357–79, 497–552
2 *SP* I, 617–20
3 Ibid I, 619–20. Meintjes *Steyn* 127–35
4 Meintjes op cit 16–17
5 See *Cd 903* and 1163
6 Meintjes op cit 134–5
7 *SP* I, 540–3. Meintjes *Botha* 76
8 *SP* I, 621–2. See also Smuts's highly coloured account to Stead, *SP* I, 466–75. Cf letter to Reitz in *SP* I, 346
9 See Col Holdsworth's report 10 Dec 1899, CO 417/283. Cf *Standard and Diggers News* 5 Dec 1899
10 Smuts–Reitz 29 Nov 1900, Smuts–Botha 22 Sep 1900. *SP* I, 342–4, 346–7. See also Junius–Botha 1 Nov 1900, quoted H & O II, 73–4
11 *SP* I, 579–80
12 Ibid I, 621–3
13 Ibid I, 623–7

14 SJ 6 Nov 1900. *OH* III, 486–9. R–B (tel) 8 Nov 1900, H & O II, 71
15 De Wet
16 W. B. Hickie narrative Nov 1900, Hick. *TH* IV, 17–8
17 W. B. Hickie loc cit
18 Ibid. See also R–B 8 Nov 1900 loc cit
19 *SP* I, 627–36
20 Ibid 636–40. *OH* IV, 3–7. EGO
21 *SP* I, 641–3. EGO. See also Barnard, quoting Beyers, *Mil Hist Jnl* vol 2 no 1 151–64
22 *SP* I, 643–40. D. Reitz 132–4. Col Inglefield *PRAI* XXIX, 519–20
23 Clements–K 14 Dec and Capt Yatman's report 16 Dec 1900 SD III, 13–15. *OH* IV, 13–16
24 Inglefield loc cit. *OH* IV, 16–19
25 *SP* I, 644
26 Ibid I, 628
27 Ibid I, 645–6. Barnard loc cit
28 *SP* I, 626
29 Ibid I, 646–7. D. Reitz 137–8
30 SJ 27 Dec 1900 and passim
31 *SP* I, 653
32 Smuts–De la Rey, Smuts–Botha 17, 21 Feb 1901 *SP* I, 378, 382–5
33 *OH* IV, 20–2

CHAPTER 38: DISREGARDING THE SCREAMERS

Head of chapter M–Haldane 7 Jun 1901, *MP* II, 264
1 M diary 17 Dec 1900, Mil (dep 70). Menpes 89–94, 99–100
2 M–C 5 Dec 1900, *MP* II, 171
3 M–Fanny Goschen 3 Jan 1901, Mil 28
4 M–Ly Ilbert 7 Dec 1897 (Milner Papers in New College)
5 M–Mrs Gaskell 15 Aug 1900, *MP* II, 130
6 See Dawkins–M 21 Dec 1901, Mil
7 See Birchenough–M 29 Jan 1901, Mil 47
8 See chap 5 note 3
9 See W. Nimocks *Milner's Young Men* 21–2
10 M–Ly E. Cecil 10 Oct 1900, *MP* II, 166
11 M–Ly E. Cecil 27 Dec 1900, *MP* II, 179
12 M–Ly E. Cecil 10 Dec 1900, *MP* II, 191
13 SJ 16–20 Dec 1900. *OH* IV, 60–70
14 M–C 11 Nov 1900, 5 Dec 1900, 2 Feb 1901. *MP* II, 170–2, 193–202
15 M's diary 31 Dec 1900, Mil (dep 70)
16 SJ 17–30 Dec 1900. *OH* IV, 60–74
17 M–K 31 Oct 1900, Kit 30/57/17
18 M–Pretyman 7 Jan 1901, Mil 47 (SA 59)
19 M–K 31 Oct 1900, Kit 30/57. NB mistranscribed 'houses' instead of 'horses' in copy printed *MP* I, 164
20 M–K 31 Oct 1900 (first draft), Mil 47 f8 (SA 59)
21 M–Ly E. Cecil 3, 8 Mar 1901, *MP* II, 211, 214–15
22 M–Warden Spooner 2 Feb 1901, Mil 47

23 M–Haldane 21 Jan 1901, *MP* II, 206
24 M–Rendel 30 May 1900, Mil 51/34 omitted in *MP* II, 103–4
25 M's CO letter quoted SJ 20 Feb 1901
26 SJ 8, 10 Jan, 13 Feb, 15 Apr 1901. *Cd 547/7–11*
27 S. Marks 31 Oct 1900, SM 51–3
28 A. H. Malan 10 Nov 1900, SM 55–6
29 K–B 30 Jan 1901, CT no 466
30 K–B 25 Jan 1901, Kit 30/57/22/Y18
31 K–B 22 Feb 1901, CT no 479A
32 K–B 1 Mar 1901, CT no 489B. Mrs F. Maxwell *Frank Maxwell* 77–80, *Cd 663*
33 M–Ly E. Cecil 8 Mar 1901, *MP* II, 214–15
34 M–C 3 Mar 1901, CT no 487B
35 C–M 6 Mar 1901, CT no 491A
36 C–M 6 Mar 1901, Mil 43
37 Arthur *Kitchener* II, 26
38 K–B 3 Dec 1900, 15 Mar 1901, Kit MS cit Y/5, 31. M–Ly E. Cecil 29 Oct 1900, *MP* II, 166
39 K–B 3 Dec 1900, Kit MS cit Y/5
40 K–Ly Cranborne nd 1900–1, Sal (Hat)
41 K–B 15 Mar 1901, Kit MS cit Y/31
42 Hamilton *The Commander* 98–114 and see Hamilton's memo for Arthur (c. 1920), Ham
43 SJ 29 Dec 1900, 7 Jan, 8 Feb 1901
44 *OH* IV, 77–91
45 WO 32/8059–64 esp report Maj Goodwin 22 Mar 1901
46 SJ 6 Feb 1900, quoting CO letter. WO 32/8008–10, 8059–61 esp Maj Goodwin's report of 22 Mar 1901. *Cd 819*
47 B–K 18 Mar 1901, CT no 500
48 K–B 7, 22 Mar 1901, Kit MS cit Y/30, 33
49 B–K 12 Apr 1901, Kit MS cit Y/43
50 SJ 12 Mar 1901
51 SJ Feb 1901
52 K–B 1 Feb 1901, Kit MS cit Y/19
53 B–K 24 Nov 1900, Kit MS cit Y/4
54 K–B 20 Dec 1900, Kit MS cit Y/9
55 KB 1, 16 Feb 1901, Kit MS cit Y/19, 23
56 B–K 8 Feb 1901, Kit MS cit Y/21
57 R–K 4 May 1901, Kit 30/57/20/
58 SJ 26 Feb, 13 Apr 1901
59 Mrs F. Maxwell 71–90
60 Plumer 16 Mar 1901, quoted Harington *Plumer* 49
61 Hamilton *The Commander*. For intelligence summaries see Bar
62 Allenby–wife 31 Jan 1901, All
63 Allenby–wife 11 Feb 1901, All
64 Allenby–wife 23 Mar, 6, 30 Apr 1901, All. SJ 3 Apr 1901
65 SJ 13 Apr 1901
66 Allenby–wife 4 May 1901, All
67 Smith-Dorrien *Memories* 29
68 Haig–Henrietta 12, 25 Feb 1901, Haig
69 SJ 13 Apr 1901
70 *OH* IV, 705
71 Rawlinson diary Mar 1901, Rawl 7
72 K–B 16 Mar 1901, CT no 498A

73 K–B 22 Mar 1901, Kit 30/57/22/Y/34
74 B–K 22 Mar 1901, Kit MS cit Y/32
75 K–B, Kit MS cit Y/48, and 21 Jun 1901, quoted Magnus *Kitchener* 185–6
76 M diary 8 May 1901, Mil (dep 71)
77 M–Ly E. Cecil 22 Mar 1901, *MP* II, 215
78 M 8 Feb 1901, Mil 47. *MP* II, 185–6. Hanbury-Williams–M 30 Jan 1901, Mil 39/153
79 M–Mrs Montefiore 17 Oct 1901, Mil 47
80 SJ 18 Mar 1901
81 K–B Apr 1900, Kit MS cit Y/50
82 Fawcett Report *Cd 893*

CHAPTER 39: 'WHEN IS A WAR NOT A WAR?'

Head of chapter M. Fischer *Kampdagboek* (Cape Town 1964) 7
1 A. Fry *Emily Hobhouse* 1–6, 295–306. J. Fisher *That Miss Hobhouse* 11–43
2 L. T. H. Hobhouse etc *Memoir of Lord Hobhouse* (London 1905) 221, 241
3 Fry 297
4 Ibid 308–11
5 J. Wilson 348
6 Ibid 347 and 342 (quoting CB–Ripon 9 Jan 1900)
7 Ibid 342 (quoting CB–Bryce 18 Jan 1900)
8 *Hansard* XCVIII 31 Jul 1901
9 *Hansard* LXXXIX, IX 18 Feb 1901
10 Ibid XC 1 Mar 1901
11 Ibid XCV 17 Jun 1901
12 Ibid XC 1026 8 Mar 1901
13 Ibid XCVI/148 27 Jun 1901
14 Ibid XCII 22 Apr 1901, CXIII 7 May 1901
15 Ibid
16 *Times* 19 Jun 1901
17 Fry 107
18 Hobhouse *Brunt of War* 116–18, *Report* 1
19 Hobhouse *Brunt of War* 118–19
20 Fry 106 quoting E. Hobhouse–Ly Hobhouse
21 Hobhouse *Brunt of War* 119–20
22 Hobhouse *Report* 10
23 Fry 132
24 Fry 134
25 Ibid 135
26 Ibid 121
27 Ibid
28 Hobhouse *Report* 15, *Brunt of War* 127
29 *Times* 15 Jun 1900. J. Wilson 349
30 *Hansard* XCV 573 17 Jun 1901
31 Ibid 573–83
32 Ibid 583–622
33 Ibid 590–7
34 Ibid 622
35 *Cd 608*, 694
36 J. Wilson 352–3
37 M–C 28 Oct 1900, Mil 27 (SA 54)
38 M–K 7 Jun 1901, *MP* II, 258
39 R–K 2 Jul 1901, CT no 571
40 *OH* IV, 705
41 CT nos 563, 570

42 R–K, Bobs 122/289 (no 86)
43 SJ 10–11 Jul 1901 (inc Staff Diary Elliot's Division). SD III, 129 (8 Aug 1901)
44 K–R 6 Jul 1901, CT no 580 (see also CT no 587, 590)
45 K 8 July 1901, SD III, 101
46 SJ 29 May 1901. *OH* IV, 186–8
47 *OH* IV, 179–80
48 K–B 30 Jul, 18 Aug 1901, CT nos 608, 619. K–B 19 Jul, Kit MS cit
49 K–B 38 Jun 1901, Kit MS cit Y/67
50 K–B 30 Aug 1901, Kit MS cit
51 SJ 20 Jul 1901
52 K–B 12 Jul 1901, Kit MS cit Y/71
53 SJ 6, 24 Aug 1901
54 B–K 23 Aug, Kit MS cit Y/8
55 M. Fawcett *What I Remember* (London 1924) 157–8. *Cd 893/1–2*
56 R. Strachey *Millicent Fawcett* (London 1931) 196
57 M. Fawcett 153–8. *DNB*
58 At Norval's Pont. See *Cd 893/50*
59 M. Fawcett 160–2
60 *Cd 893/9–13*
61 Ibid 10, 21, 44–5, 82
62 Ibid 89–93
63 Ibid 170, 174–9
64 M. Fawcett–M 19 Nov 1901 quoted R. Strachey 201
65 *Cd 789*
66 *Cd 793*
67 *Cd 853/130*. E. Fry 144–7
68 *Cd 893* passim
69 C–M 16, 20 Nov 1901, *Cd 819*
70 M–Goold-Adams 4 Dec 1901, Mil (un-numbered Hobhouse box)
71 Appendices to Hobhouse *The Brunt of war* 327–55, relevant *Cd* papers, and Martin 30–3
72 My estimate. See above for incomplete figures

CHAPTER 40: RAIDING THE
COLONIES

Head of chapter Smuts diary 7 Aug 1901 quoted Hancock 137
1 Smuts diary and official report *SP* I, 416, 431. SJ 5 Sep 1901. SD III, 198–9
2 Reitz 202–3
3 Fouché's statement 29 Oct 1901, Bar 187/339–42
4 Reitz 198, 209. See note 21
5 Bar MS cit
6 Reitz 203
7 Ibid 200–1. But see J. A. Mulder's statement below
8 *SP* I, 362–3, 378, 382–5. *OH* IV, 270
9 *SP* I, 396–7. J. A. Mulder's statement 8 Nov 1901, Bar 187/365–9
10 *SP* I, 408–9, 430
11 Reitz 203–210. *SP* I, 416, 431
12 Reitz 210–11. *SP* I, 416, 431–2
13 Reitz 211–22. *SP* I, 416–17, 432

14 Reitz 222–5
15 Reitz 225–6
16 Reitz 226–7. Haig–Henrietta 22 Sep 1901, Haig 250. Intell Summary, Bar 188/29
17 Reitz 227–33. *SP* I, 417, 432–3
18 Haig–Henrietta 22 Sep 1901, Haig 249–50
19 *OH* IV, 275
20 Haig–Henrietta 7 Sep 1901, Haig 248
21 Haig–Henrietta 30 Sep 1901, Haig 251. Bar 188/50
22 SJ 23 Sep 1901. SD III, 199. *OH* IV, 290
23 Haig–Henrietta 9 Sep 1901, Haig 248
24 Haig–Henrietta 14 Sep 1901, Haig 249
25 Intell Summary 28 Sep 1901, Bar MS cit
26 Captured 5 Feb 1902 – see Bar 191. *SP* I, 441–5
27 *OH* IV, 240–1. SJ 5 Sep 1901
28 S. Edingborough 26 Jul 1901, PC
29 *OH* IV, 175–6, 178–80, 225–6. S. Edingborough MS cit
30 S. Edingborough MS cit
31 S. Edingborough 13 Aug, 9 Sep 1901, PC
32 *OH* IV, 244
33 Scobell–McCalmont 9 Sep 1901, Mortimer–McCalmont 9 Sep 1901, NAM 6807/492/4
34 Scobell MS cit. *OH* IV, 240–1
35 S. Edingborough 9 Sep 1901, PC. Scobell MS cit. *OH* IV 241
36 S. Edingborough tape recording Jul 1970, PC
37 S. Edingborough 9 Sep 1901, PC
38 They numbered 600 acc CC intell Summary 8 Sep 1901. Bar 188/11
39 Botha–Emmett 15, 16 Sep 1901, ptd SD III, 288–9. SD III, 188–9. SJ 30 Sep 1901
40 Engelenburg 32
41 Botha–Emmett MS cit. Botha–Reitz 18, 28 Sep 1901, ptd SD III, 289–91
42 H. Gough letters Jul–Sep 1901, Gou
43 H. Gough MS cit
44 *OH* IV, 217. *TH* V, 339–40
45 H. Gough MS cit
46 Botha–Reitz 18 Sep 1901, ptd SD III, 289–90. K's des, SD III, 189–90
47 H. Gough MS cit
48 *OH* IV, 217–18
49 Botha–Reitz 18, 28 Sep 1901, SD III, 289–91
50 Botha–Reitz 28 Sep 1901, SD III, 290–1. SD III, 190. *OH* IV, 219–22. SJ 26 Sep 1901 (reporting Boers lost 550)
51 Botha MS cit
52 SJ 21 Sep 1901
53 *SP* I, 436
54 *SP* I, 430–7
55 *SP* I, 441–5
56 Smuts–De la Rey 26 Jan 1901, *SP* I, 499–503
57 For K's public use of term 'bag' see B–K 11 Sep 1901, Kit s cit Y/94

58 *OH* IV, 705
59 Smuts–Kosie 4 Jan 1901, *SP* I, 507

CHAPTER 41: BLOCKHOUSE OR
BLOCKHEAD?

Head of chapter Rawlinson–R 28 Aug 1901,
Bobs 61/22

1 K–R 24 Nov 1901, Bobs 33/61
2 K–B 13 Dec 1901, Kit 22/Y/111. K–R 13
Dec, Bobs 33/63
3 K–R 25 Oct 1901, Bobs 33/54
4 K–B 15 Oct 1901, CT no 683
5 K–B 27 Dec 1900, 23 Feb 1901, Kit
22/Y/116, 129
6 K–B 15 Nov 1901, Kit 22/Y/102. K–R 4
Oct 1901, Bobs 33/52
7 K–B 11, 15 Oct 1901, Kit 22/Y/94, 95
8 K–B 1 Nov 1901, CT no 704
9 K–R 5 Nov 1901, (Pte) Bobs 123 (note
absence from CT)
10 R–K 8, 15 Nov 1901, Bobs 122, 170, 171
11 K–R 7 Nov 1901, CT no 715
12 See note 10
13 K–B 1 Nov 1901, Kit 22/Y/100
14 SJ 30 Oct 1901. SD III, 254–6. *OH* IV,
306–15
15 RE's history of blockhouses, WO
108/295. *OH* IV, 568–76. SJ 8 Nov 1901
16 K–B 28 Oct, 22 Nov 1901, CT nos 694,
756. Intell Summary Bar 190 Oct–Dec
1901 and maps 194. SD III, 253–61,
349–57. *OH* IV, 705
17 Ibid esp CT no 756
18 K–B 5 Jan 1901, CT no 806. Dec 1901
Intell Summaries, Bar 190. Hamilton *The
Commander* 100–1
19 Tape recorded interviews in 1970 with
Ptes Bowers, Dart, Trooper Edingborough, Major Allott etc, PC
20 F. Maxwell 13 Sep 1901, *Life* 89. Cf
Birdwood 117
21 F. Maxwell 4 Oct 1901, *Life* 90
22 F. Maxwell 3 May 1901, *Life* 85–6
23 H. Hamilton–Marker nd Mark 21
24 F. Maxwell 15, 24 Mar 1901, *Life* 80–2,
86–7
25 Rawlinson–R 25 Nov, 15 Dec 1901, Bobs
61. WO 108/104
26 Col D. Henderson–DMI 13 Jun 1902,
WO 32/8112. Fuller *Gentlemen's Wars* esp
194. Cf B. Parritt *The Intelligencers*
203–15
27 Rawlinson diary 4, 11, 3 Dec 1901,
Rawl. Rawlinson–R 30 Nov–13 Dec
1901
28 Rawlinson diary MS cit 10 Dec 1901.
Rawlinson–R 15 Dec MS cit Bobs 61
29 De Wet 340. De Wet–J. C. Smuts 8 Feb
1902, quoted *OH* IV, 379
30 K's des of 8 Dec 1901, SD III, 353–6
31 De Wet 329–30
32 *OH* IV, 382–92, 405, 572, note blockhouse garrisons at 30 men to mile

33 SJ 25 Dec 1901. *OH* 392–3. *TH* V,
433–43
34 *OH* IV, 393–4
35 De Wet 343
36 Bowers tape recorded May 1970, PC
37 Ibid
38 K–B 27 Dec, 3 Jan 1902, Kit 22/Y/116,
117. K–B 21 Feb 1902, CT no 941
39 Dec 1901 Intell Summaries, Bar 190
40 SJ 5 Feb 1901. Rawlinson diary 5 Feb
1902, Rawl
41 SJ 4–6 Feb 1902. *OH* IV, 400–2
42 K–R 7 Feb 1902, Bobs 33/73
43 CT 384–5
44 K–R 14 Feb 1902, Bobs 33. K–B 14 Feb
1902, Kit 22/Y/126. *OH* IV, 402–4
45 De Wet 350–4
46 K–B 14 Feb 1902, Kit 22/Y/126
47 Pte Bowers tape recordings, PC
48 B–R 5 Mar 1902, CT no 980. K–B 11, 17
Mar 1902, CT nos 1004, 1022
49 Confid circular Apr 1902, WO 108/109.
K–B 15 Aug 1901, CT no 617. K–B 9
Mar 1902, Kit 22/Y/131a
50 Intell Summary passim, Bar 190
51 Rawlinson diary 13 Dec 1901, MS cit.
Rundle staff diary 25 Jan 1902 WO
32/8090
52 See K–B 6 Dec 1901, Kit 22/Y/09
53 Chief of Staff – all column COs 16 Dec
1901, WO 108/99. But see Fuller 245, 262
54 See Gen T. Smuts–Botha 2 Sep 1901, SD
III, 312–13
55 Rawlinson diary 16–28 Feb 1902, Rawl.
De Wet *Three Years' War* (NB Van
Merwe's commando captured) 355–61.
OH IV, 423–8
56 SJ 16–28 Feb 1902. Rawlinson diary MS
cit. *OH* IV, 429
57 Rawlinson diary 4–11 Mar 1902, MS cit.
OH IV, 475/8. SJ 4–11 Mar 1902
58 SJ 25 Feb 1902. *OH* IV, 409–14. *TH* V,
498–9
59 SJ 7 Mar 1902. *OH* IV, 416–20. *TH* V,
503–8
60 Frank Maxwell 16 Mar 1902, *Life* 94–5
61 Frank Maxwell 23 Mar 1902, *Life* 95–6.
SJ 22 Mar 1902

CHAPTER 42: PEACE 'BETRAYED'

Head of chapter Kipling *Verse* 108

1 M–Iwan-Muller 6 Feb 1902, Mil 36 (SA
41)
2 SJ 11 Apr 1902
3 M–Spooner 2 Dec 1901, Mil (Hobhouse
vol)
4 M–Iwan-Muller 4 Jan 1902, Mil 36 (SA
41)
5 M–anon 5 May 1902, *MP* II, 364–5
6 M–Dawkins 16 Jan 1902, Mil (S 3)
7 K–B 12 Apr 1902, CT nos 1075, 1076,
1077. B–K 13 Apr 1902, CT no 1078
8 M diary 14 Apr 1902, Mil (dep 72). M–C

16 Apr 1902, *MP* II, 337

9 M–C 14 Apr 1902, Cab 37/61

10 B–K 16 Apr, K–B 17 Apr 1902, CT nos 1090, 1097

11 SD III, 463. Kestell *Through Shot and Flame* 290

12 M–Dr Jameson 11 Mar 1902, Mil 35/279. M's diary 21 Apr 1902, Mil (dep 72)

13 M's diary 17 Apr 1902, Mil (dep 72)

14 M–C 16 Apr 1902, *MP* II, 337

15 Nimocks *Milner's Young Men* 22–9. M–C 15 Nov 1901, *MP* II, 300 (see also *MP* II, 381–2)

16 M–C 14 Dec 1901, *Cd 903*/171

17 J. Adam Smith *Buchan* (London 1965) 114–17

18 Goold–Adams 3 Jan 1902, *Cd 903*/169 foll

19 E. Hobhouse *Brunt of War* 329, 351–2

20 W. Wybergh report 11 Dec 1901, *Cd 903*

21 Sir G. Lagden, *Cd 903*

22 Ibid. See also Wybergh's report loc cit

23 *Cd 903*

24 *Cd 903, 1163*/112

25 SJ 11 Apr 1902

26 EGO. *OH* (Maps) IV

27 SJ 30 Sep 1901, 24 Feb 1902. *OH* IV, 293–8, 411–14

28 *OH* IV, 417–20

29 Rawlinson's diary 20–26 Mar 1902, Rawl 7. *OH* IV, 492–3

30 W. Congreve Ap 1902, Con

31 I. Hamilton–R 18 May 1902, Ham

32 C. Hickie 1901 Hick

33 SJ 31 Mar 1902. *OH* IV, 494–5

34 Rawlinson's diary 1–6 Apr 1902, Rawl 7. Hamilton–Churchill 5, 18 Apr 1902, Hamilton–brother 6 Apr, 31 May 1902, Ham

35 Ibid. *OH* IV, 498

36 Rawlinson's diary 1–6 Apr, Rawl 7

37 Hamilton–Churchill 5 Apr, 18 Apr 1902, Ham

38 Rawlinson's diary 9–10 Apr 1902, Rawl

39 Ibid. *OH* IV, 499

40 Maj Roy Apr–May 1902, Roy. *OH* IV, 499–500

41 Childers *Arme Blanche* 239–60 of Goldmann 423

42 SJ 11 Apr 1902. *OH* IV, 499–500. *TH* V, 531–3. Tullibardine *Military History of Perthshire*

43 C. Hickie 3 Apr 1902, Hick

44 Ibid. Cf *TH* V, 534

45 Rawlinson's diary 11 Apr 1902, Rawl 7

46 Hamilton–R 18 May 1902 enc in letter to W. S. Churchill, Ham I/15

47 Rawlinson's diary MS cit. *OH* IV, 502–3. Cf *TH* V, 534–5

48 C. Hickie loc cit

49 His 'great drive' brought in 367 see *OH* IV, 505–10

50 *OH* IV, 517–21

51 Hamilton–Churchill 22, 23 Mar 1902, Ham I/15

52 Hamilton–Churchill 24 May 1902, Ham I/15

53 Rawlinson's diary 27–31 Dec, 27 Mar 1901–2, Rawl 7

54 B–K 1901–2 Kit 22. Cf A's memo for Cabinet Jun 1901, Mil 47/77–87

55 Rawlinson–R 28 Aug, 14 Sep 1901, Bobs 61/22, 23

56 See *Cd 981*, 1423

57 Hamilton–Churchill 20 Jan, 31 May, 24 May 1902, Ham I/15

58 Hamilton–Churchill 20 Jan 1902, Ham I/15

59 Hamilton–E. Stanley (copy to WSC), Ham I/15

60 Churchill–Hamilton 25 Jun 1902, Ham I/15

61 SD III, 475. *MP* II, 342–3

62 SD III, 475–81

63 SD III, 482–3

64 Ibid

65 K–B 21 May 1902, CT no 1164

66 See full text in *MP* II, 350–1 (Addendum not in SD)

67 *Cd 663*

68 See note 66

69 See Pt IV chap 3 28–29

70 See note 66

71 M–C 21 May 1902, Pte and Pers Cab 37/61/93

72 M–C 14 Apr 1902, Pte and Pers CO 417/351/744

73 C's phrase in Cabinet draft 27 May 1902, Cab 37/61/104

74 M–C 21 May 1902, Pte and Conf Cab 37/61/94

75 C–M 22 May 1902, Sec and Pers Cab 37/61/95

76 C–M 23 May 1902, Conf Cab 37/61/96

77 M–C 25 May 1902, Cab 37/61/101

78 Compare C's draft for Cabinet of 24 May (Cab 37/61/97) with the text given Cabinet on 27th (Cab 37/61/104)

79 See note 76

80 C–M 27 May 1902, CO 417/351/708

81 Kestell 310–12

82 Ibid

83 De Wet *Three Years' War* 401–35. Kestell 298–312

84 De Wet *Three Years' War* 413

85 Ibid 432–3

86 Ibid 406–7

87 SPG Series E (Ref 47) Pretoria and see lists of atrocities against Africans SD III and WO 32/7886, 8122, 8547

88 De Wet 411, 415, 420–1

89 Col Mills report on Holkrantz in WO Library London. SJ 6 May 1902

90 De Wet 426

91 Ibid 404–435. Kestell 305–12

92 De Wet 408–9

93 Ibid 409–11

94 Ibid 427

95 CO 417/362/8–9
96 De Wet 431, 477–86
97 Ibid 486–90
98 Ibid 491–2
99 Ibid 502–6. Kestell 335–9
100 De Wet 506. Kestell 343
101 Ibid 343–5. *MP* II, 362–3
102 M–Ly E. Cecil 30, 31 May 1902. *MP* II, 364–5. Ld Salisbury was horrified. Dawkins–M 13 Jun 1902: 'K, wahid Turk, has really surpassed hisel in indecencys' [sic] Mil
103 M–Friend 30 May 1902, *MP* II, 364–5
104 Lieut (later Sir Charles) Pym tape recorded 1970
105 Rawlinson diary 1 Jun 1902, Rawl 7
106 Pte Whinnell tape recorded 1970
107 Rawlinson diary loc cit
108 Lieuts Pym, Lang, Stericker, Dr Stock tape recorded 1970
109 Ptes Blunson, Brayne, Bowers, Whitton, Higgitt etc tape recorded 1970

EPILOGUE: WINNERS AND LOSERS
Head of chapter William Plomer (with acknowledgement)
  1 Gross £201m, net £187 m on army votes: *RCSAW* IV, 340. For other payments see *MP* II, 372–3

2 *RCSAW* IV, 258
3 Ibid I, 35
4 Ibid
5 Martin 31
6 *Cd 3028. MP* II, 372–3
7 D. Denoon in B. Ogot *War and Society* (London 1972) 116
8 See chap 39 note 72
9 At war's end there were 23,000 Africans working in Native Labour Dept, 5–6,000 on railway, and thousands of others in SAC. See CO 417
10 *Cd 821*, 822, 888, 981, 1423 etc
11 Canon Farmer 29 Mar 1901, SPG Series E (Ref 47) Pretoria
12 See *TH* V, 513–15
13 I. Hamilton–R 28 Mar 1904, Bobs 36/125
14 *DNB*. Ridgeway–R 20 Apr 1903, Bobs 36/113
15 *DNB*
16 *DSAB* III, 187
17 Buller–wife 1900, Bull (Crediton)
18 *DNB*
19 *TH* VI, 476
20 J. De Bloch *RUSI Journal* Dec 1901
21 *MP* II, 367–402
22 Le May 155–91
23 M. Wilson & L. Thompson Vol II, passim
24 Ibid 335–48

Index

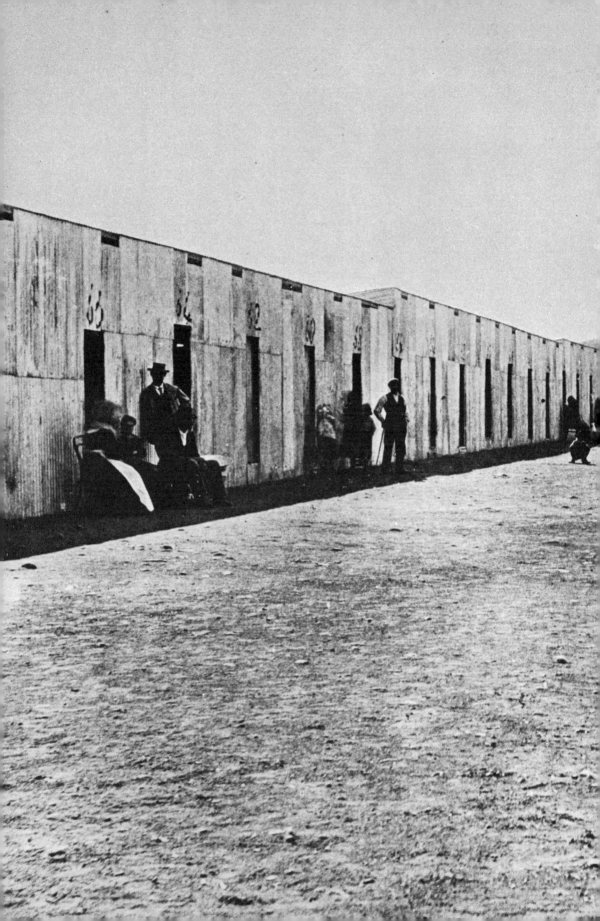